American Corrections

13th Edition

Todd R. CLEAR
Rutgers University

Michael D. REISIG
Arizona State University

CENGAGE

Australia • Brazil • Canada • Mexico • Singapore • United Kingdom • United States

CENGAGE

American Corrections,
Thirteenth Edition
Todd R. Clear and Michael D. Reisig

Senior Vice President, Higher Education & Skills Product: Erin Joyner

Product Director: Matthew Seeley

Product Manager: Michael Worls

Content Manager: Aiyana Moore

Marketing Manager: Mark Linton

Marketing Coordinator: Haley Hulett

Intellectual Property Analyst: Deanna Ettinger

Intellectual Property Project Manager: Kelli Besse

Production Service: MPS Limited

Art Director: Felicia Bennett

Text Designer: Felicia Bennett

Cover Designer: Chris Doughman

Cover Image: iStockPhoto.com/AVNphotolab

For product information and technology assistance, contact us at **Cengage Customer & Sales Support, 1-800-354-9706 or support.cengage.com.**

For permission to use material from this text or product, submit all requests online at **www.cengage.com/permissions.**

Library of Congress Control Number: 2020952226

Student Edition:
ISBN: 978-0-357-45653-8

Loose-leaf Edition:
ISBN: 978-0-357-45659-0

Cengage
200 Pier 4 Boulevard
Boston, MA 02210
USA

Cengage is a leading provider of customized learning solutions with employees residing in nearly 40 different countries and sales in more than 125 countries around the world. Find your local representative at **www.cengage.com.**

To learn more about Cengage platforms and services, register or access your online learning solution, or purchase materials for your course, visit **www.cengage.com.**

Printed in Mexico
Print Number: 03 Print Year: 2022

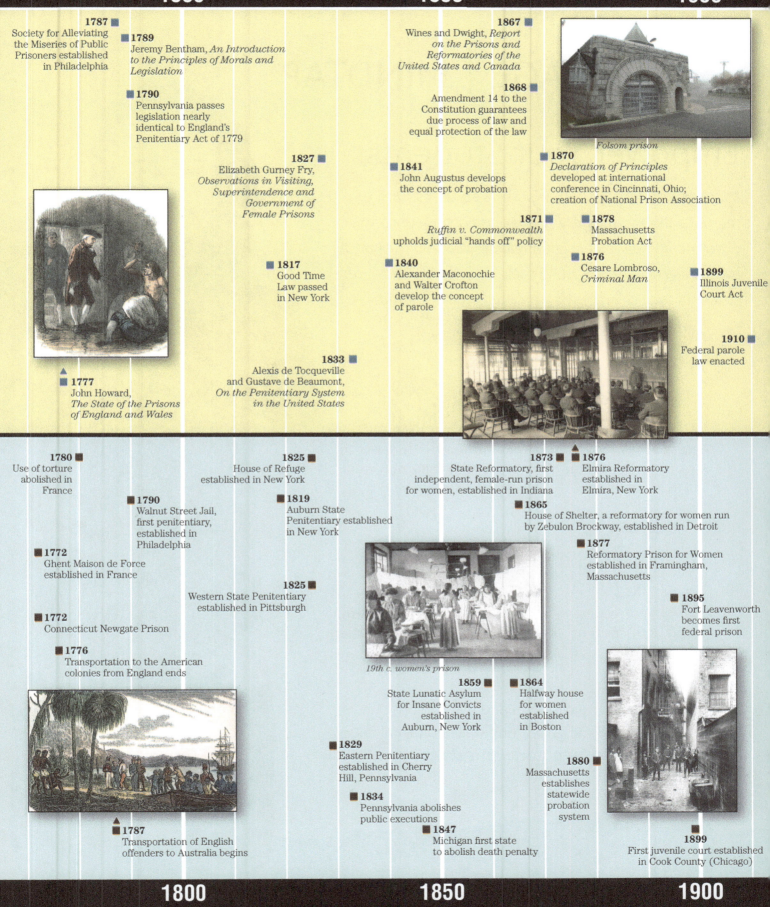

1800 **1850** **1900**

1787 Society for Alleviating the Miseries of Public Prisoners established in Philadelphia

1789 Jeremy Bentham, *An Introduction to the Principles of Morals and Legislation*

1790 Pennsylvania passes legislation nearly identical to England's Penitentiary Act of 1779

1777 John Howard, *The State of the Prisons of England and Wales*

1827 Elizabeth Gurney Fry, *Observations in Visiting, Superintendence and Government of Female Prisons*

1817 Good Time Law passed in New York

1833 Alexis de Tocqueville and Gustave de Beaumont, *On the Penitentiary System in the United States*

1867 Wines and Dwight, *Report on the Prisons and Reformatories of the United States and Canada*

1868 Amendment 14 to the Constitution guarantees due process of law and equal protection of the law

Folsom prison

1841 John Augustus develops the concept of probation

1870 *Declaration of Principles* developed at international conference in Cincinnati, Ohio; creation of National Prison Association

1871 *Ruffin v. Commonwealth* upholds judicial "hands off" policy

1878 Massachusetts Probation Act

1840 Alexander Maconochie and Walter Crofton develop the concept of parole

1876 Cesare Lombroso, *Criminal Man*

1899 Illinois Juvenile Court Act

1910 Federal parole law enacted

1780 Use of torture abolished in France

1790 Walnut Street Jail, first penitentiary, established in Philadelphia

1772 Ghent Maison de Force established in France

1772 Connecticut Newgate Prison

1776 Transportation to the American colonies from England ends

1787 Transportation of English offenders to Australia begins

1825 House of Refuge established in New York

1819 Auburn State Penitentiary established in New York

1825 Western State Penitentiary established in Pittsburgh

1829 Eastern Penitentiary established in Cherry Hill, Pennsylvania

1834 Pennsylvania abolishes public executions

19th c. women's prison

1859 State Lunatic Asylum for Insane Convicts established in Auburn, New York

1847 Michigan first state to abolish death penalty

1873 State Reformatory, first independent, female-run prison for women, established in Indiana

1876 Elmira Reformatory established in Elmira, New York

1865 House of Shelter, a reformatory for women run by Zebulon Brockway, established in Detroit

1877 Reformatory Prison for Women established in Framingham, Massachusetts

1895 Fort Leavenworth becomes first federal prison

1864 Halfway house for women established in Boston

1880 Massachusetts establishes statewide probation system

1899 First juvenile court established in Cook County (Chicago)

1800 **1850** **1900**

(continued inside back cover)

TODD R. CLEAR is University Professor of Criminal Justice at Rutgers University-Newark, where he previously served as Dean of the School of Criminal Justice and Provost of the University. In 1978 he received a Ph.D. in Criminal Justice from the University of New York at Albany. Clear has also held professorships at Ball State University, Florida State University (where he was also Associate Dean of the School of Criminology and Criminal Justice), and John Jay College of Criminal Justice (where he held the rank of Distinguished Professor). He has authored 12 books and more than 100 articles and book chapters. His most recent book is *The Punishment Imperative* (NYU Press, 2014). Clear has served as President of the American Society of Criminology, the Academy of Criminal Justice Sciences, and the Association of Doctoral Programs in Criminology and Criminal Justice. He was the founding editor of the journal *Criminology & Public Policy*, published by the American Society of Criminology.

MICHAEL D. REISIG is Professor of Criminology and Criminal Justice at Arizona State University. He received his Ph.D. from Washington State University in 1996. Previously, he was a faculty member at Michigan State University and Florida State University. His research focuses on institutional corrections and on women who are returning to the community. His studies have appeared in several leading criminology journals, including *Criminology, Crime & Delinquency, Criminology & Public Policy, Justice Quarterly,* and *Punishment & Society*.

BRIEF CONTENTS

PART ONE CORRECTIONAL CONTEXT

PART TWO CORRECTIONAL PRACTICES

PART THREE CORRECTIONAL ISSUES AND PERSPECTIVES

CONTENTS

PART 1 CORRECTIONAL CONTEXT

CHAPTER 1 The Corrections System 4

© John Moore/The Journal News, Rockland/Westchester Journal News via Imagn Content Services, LLC

CHAPTER 2 The Early History of Correctional Thought and Practice 30

Mia2you/Shutterstock.com

CHAPTER 3 The History of Corrections in America 48

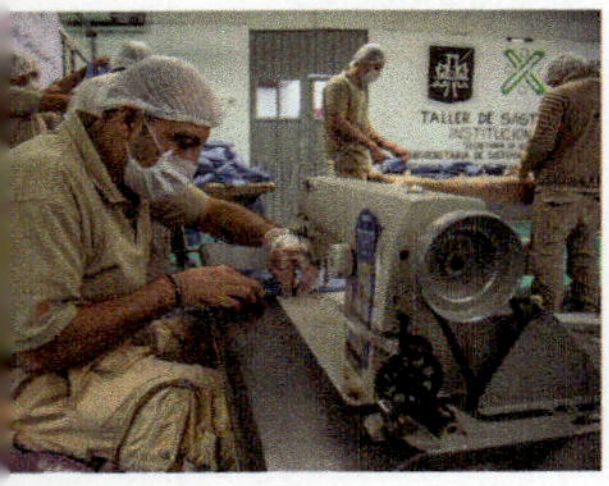
dpa picture alliance/Alamy Stock Photo

Jefferson Siegel/Pool/Sipa USA

CHAPTER 5 The Law of Corrections 102

© Sarah Kloepping/Green Bay Press-Gazette via Imagn Content Services, LLC

CHAPTER 6 The Correctional Client 134

© USA TODAY Network, USA TODAY NETWORK via Imagn Content Services, LLC

© Kelly Wilkinson/IndyStar, Indianapolis Star via Imagn Content Services, LLC

© Mitsu Yasukawa/Northjersey.com via Imagn Content Services, LLC

CHAPTER **9**

© Jon Stinchcomb/News Herald

© Briana Sanchez/Argus Leader

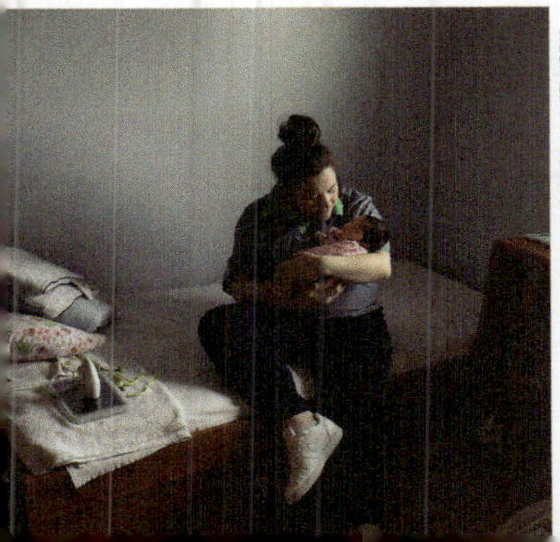

Fred Squillante-USA TODAY NETWORK

© Rick Cruz/PDN via Imagn Content Services, LLC

Carol Rosenberg/Miami Herald/MCT/Sipa USA

Aerial Archives/Alamy Stock Photo

CHAPTER 19

© Danielle Parhizkaran/NorthJersey.com via Imagn Content Services, LLC

CHAPTER 20

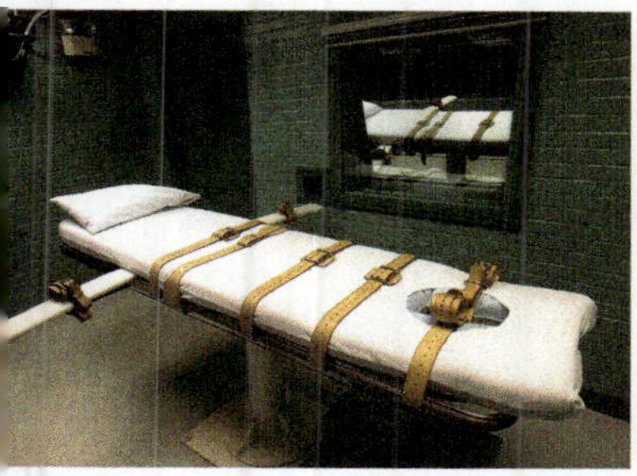

Chuck Berman/Chicago Tribune/TNS/Sipa USA

CHAPTER **21**

Lucy Nicholson/REUTERS

CHAPTER **22**

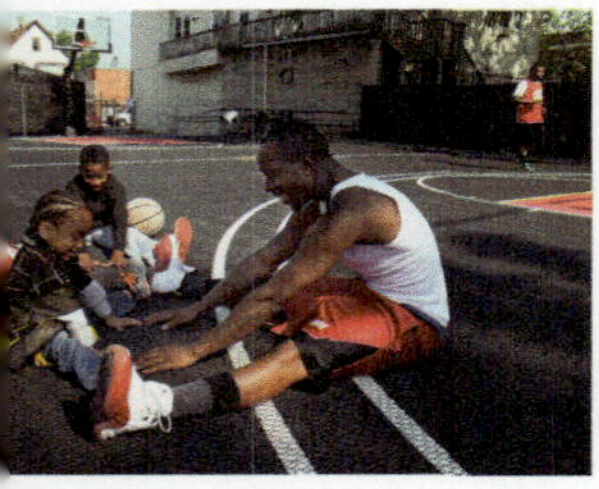
Melanie Stetson Freeman/Christian Science Monitor/The Image Works

Michael Santos

PREFACE

The publication of the thirteenth edition of a textbook is a cause for celebration. This is especially true if the book is *American Corrections*, which has been a leader in the field for more than 30 years and has introduced more than half a million students to this most interesting portion of the U.S. criminal justice system.

The first edition of *American Corrections* was inspired by our shared belief that undergraduate students must be exposed to the dynamics of corrections in a manner that captures their attention and encourages them to enter the field. The thirteenth edition continues this tradition.

We celebrate this milestone, but we also recognize that, as authors, we have a responsibility to provide readers with the most up-to-date factual material, policy trends, and changes in correctional practices.

Since 1986, when *American Corrections* was first published, this dynamic field has undergone many revolutions of both policy and practice. For example, the shift to mass incarceration was already under way then, with state and federal prisons holding 463,000 people—equal to a rate of 188 per 100,000 Americans. At that time, few policy makers would have dreamed that the rate would continue to rise to more than 600 per 100,000 in 2010, until it began to decline as a result of declining crime and changes in correctional policy. We also note the shift away from the goal of rehabilitation, dominant in the 1970s, to the primacy of crime control goals since the 1980s. During the past quarter-century, corrections has also seen the rise and fall of boot camps, the growth of privately owned and operated prisons, interest in community and restorative justice, and the present emphasis on evidence-based decision making. *American Corrections* has kept pace with these and countless other shifts.

Corrections is so rich in history, innovative in practice, and challenged by societal problems that it deserves to be taught in a way that is both interesting and accurate. Fortunately, our teaching and research cover different areas of corrections so that each of us can focus on our strengths while challenging the other to do his best work. We hope that this book reflects our enthusiasm for our field and the satisfaction we have found in it.

The looming economic recession caused by the COVID-19 pandemic has already placed great fiscal burdens on local, state, and federal governments, and their often severe budgetary deficits have greatly affected corrections. As criminal justice students know, corrections has little to no control over the inflow of people to community corrections, jails, and prisons; nonetheless, correctional budgets also often face cuts imposed by fiscally strapped governments. To operate with the resources mandated, some corrections systems have had to release prisoners, cut back rehabilitative programs, expand community supervision caseloads, lay off staff, and take other actions to save money.

To address these problems, correctional professionals and the public are increasingly focusing their attention on research by scholars who have demonstrated the shortcomings of correctional practices and have urged alternatives. In the thirteenth edition, we thus not only examine the history of corrections and the exciting changes that have occurred to make the field what it is today, but we also look to the future of corrections by examining research-based solutions to current problems.

In *American Corrections*, thirteenth edition, we offer an accurate analysis of contemporary corrections based on up-to-date research. By acknowledging the problems with the system, we hope that our exposition will inspire suggestions for change. We believe that when human freedom is at stake, policies must reflect research and be formulated only after their potential effects have been carefully considered. In other words, we hope that any changes we inspire will be good ones. We also hope that a new generation of students will gain a solid understanding of all the aspects of their complex field.

THE APPROACH OF THIS TEXT

In learning about corrections, students gain a unique understanding of how social and political forces affect the way that organizations and institutions respond to a particular segment of the community. They learn that social values come to the fore in the correctional arena because the criminal sanction reflects those values. They also learn that in a democracy, corrections must operate not only within the framework of law but also within the boundaries set by public opinion. Thus, as a public activity, corrections is accountable to elected representatives, but it must also compete politically with other agencies for resources and "turf."

Two key assumptions run throughout the book. One is about the nature of corrections as a discipline; the other concerns the best way to analyze correctional practices:

- **Corrections is interdisciplinary.** The academic fields of criminal justice, sociology, psychology, history, law, and political science contribute to our understanding of corrections. This cross-fertilization is enriching, yet it requires familiarity with a vast literature. We have structured our text with a strong focus on coherence to make this interdisciplinary approach comprehensive yet accessible.

- **Corrections is a system.** In our book the concept of a system serves as a framework for analyzing the relationships among the various parts of corrections and the interactions between correctional professionals and their clients. The main advantage of this perspective is that it allows for dispassionate analysis of correctional practices.

ORGANIZATION

Correctional officials and political leaders are continually asking "Where is corrections headed?" In this thirteenth edition of *American Corrections* we explore the context, practices, and special issues of corrections in three major sections. Each part opens with a guest perspective by a recognized expert who discusses correctional innovations and ideas related to the topics presented in that part. Marc Mauer, Executive Director of the Sentencing Project, opens Part 1: The Correctional Context by assessing criminal justice reform. Mauer notes that we are currently on the cusp of significant changes in corrections, changes that could result in a major policy reformulation for the entire corrections system. Part 2: Correctional Practices opens with a guest perspective by Glenn Martin, founder of JustLeadershipUSA (JLUSA). Among the most respected correctional reformers in the nation, Martin explains why it is crucial to have people who have been affected by the justice system engaged in reform debates. To open Part 3: Correctional Issues and Perspectives, Fatimah Loren Muhammad, Director of the Trauma Advocacy Initiative, Equal Justice USA, describes the importance of understanding how trauma affects both the victims of violent crime and the people who engage in that violence. Each of these guest perspectives lays the groundwork for the chapters that follow.

In Part 1 we describe the historical issues that frame our contemporary experience of corrections. We examine the general social context of the corrections system (Chapter 1) and the early history of correctional thought and practice (Chapter 2). We also focus on the distinctive aspects of correctional history in the United States (Chapter 3), analyze current theory and evidence regarding methods of punishment (Chapter 4), and survey the impact of law on corrections (Chapter 5). In Chapter 6 we portray the correctional client. We consider the correctional client in relation to criminal legislation, criminal justice processing, and larger societal forces that are associated with crime. Part 1 thus presents the foundations of American corrections: context, history, goals, organizations, and correctional clients.

In Part 2 we look at the current state of the major components and practices of the system. The complexity of correctional organization results in fragmentation and ambivalence in correctional services. Jails and other short-term facilities are scrutinized in Chapter 7, probation in the community, by which most correctional clients are handled, in Chapter 8, and the new focus on intermediate sanctions in Chapter 9. Because imprisonment remains the core symbolic and punitive mechanism of corrections, we examine it in detail. We discuss incarceration (Chapter 10), the prison experience (Chapter 11), the incarceration of women (Chapter 12), institutional management (Chapter 13), and educational, industrial, and treatment programs in correctional institutions (Chapter 14). In being both descriptive and critical, we hope to raise questions about current incarceration policies. In Chapters 15 and 16 we examine the process of releasing people from incarceration and the ways that formerly incarcerated people adjust to supervised life in the community. In Chapter 17 we describe the separate system of corrections for juveniles. Thus, in Part 2 we focus on the development, structure, and methods of each area of the existing corrections system, portraying them in light of the continuing issues described in Part 1.

In Part 3 we analyze those current correctional issues and trends that deserve individual attention: incarceration trends (Chapter 18), race, ethnicity, and corrections (Chapter 19), the death penalty (Chapter 20), immigration (Chapter 21), and community justice (Chapter 22). In Chapter 23, "American Corrections: Looking Forward," we take both a retrospective view of American corrections and a view of its future. These chapters are designed to raise questions in the minds of readers so that they can begin to grapple with important issues.

SPECIAL FEATURES

Several features make this book an especially interesting introduction to corrections. Each of these features has been revised for the thirteenth edition.

- **Opening vignettes:** Each chapter opens with a description of a high-profile correctional case. Taken from today's headlines, each vignette dramatizes a real-life situation that draws the student into the chapter's topic. Instructors find these "lecture launchers" an important pedagogical tool to stimulate interest. We have made special efforts to provide new vignettes for this edition. For example, Chapter 17, "Corrections for Juveniles," describes Connecticut's impending changes to its juvenile justice laws. This leads into a discussion of the distinctions applied to the juvenile corrections system.

- **Critical Thinking:** Each chapter includes critical-thinking boxes that pose questions linked to the opening vignette. We believe that this feature will prompt students to reexamine their initial thoughts about the vignette.

- **Focus on . . . :** In this feature the real-world relevance of the issues discussed in the text is made clear by vivid, in-depth accounts by correctional workers, journalists, formerly incarcerated persons, people on parole, and relatives of those who are in the system. In this thirteenth edition we have increased the number and variety of these features, which are placed into three categories: People in Corrections, Correctional Policy, and Correctional Practice. We believe that students will find that the material in each feature enhances their understanding of the chapter topic.

- **Thinking Outside the Box:** Corrections needs new ideas, and some of the most significant new ideas propose major changes to the way that the corrections system does its work. This feature draws attention to today's most innovative evidence-based practices or programs, designed to get students thinking beyond traditional aspects to new possibilities. Examining these new ideas provides fresh insight regarding the future prospects of corrections.

- **Do the Right Thing:** Correctional workers are often confronted with ethical dilemmas. In each of these boxes we present a scenario in which an ethical question arises. We then provide a writing assignment in which students examine the issues and consider how they would act in such a situation.
- **Evidence-based practice:** Correctional professionals are being encouraged to base decisions on research evidence. This is especially true in probation, intermediate sanctions, and parole. Implementation of this approach is presented in the relevant chapters.
- **Myths in Corrections:** Faculty have told us that they spend much of their classroom time debunking popular myths about corrections. In this new edition, most chapters contain a special boxed feature presenting research that challenges correctional myths.
- **Careers in Corrections:** In appropriate chapters throughout the book, students will find one or more boxes in which a particular correctional occupation is described. The material includes the nature of the work, required qualifications, earnings and job outlook, and a source of more information.
- **Glossary:** One goal of an introductory course is to familiarize students with the terminology of the field. We have avoided jargon in the text but include terms that are commonly used. Such indispensable words and phrases are set in bold type, and the term and its definition have been placed in the margin. A full glossary with definitions of all terms is located at the back of the book.
- **Graphics:** We have created tables and figures that clarify and enliven information so that it can be perceived easily and grasped accurately. For this thirteenth edition, tables and figures have been fully updated wherever possible.
- **Photographs:** The thirteenth edition contains an enlarged program of dynamic photographs spread throughout the book. These reveal many aspects of corrections ordinarily concealed from the public eye. The photographs provide students with a real view of correctional policies and practices.
- **Other student aids:** The beginning of each chapter includes an outline of the topics to be covered, followed by a set of learning objectives. These tools are designed to guide students as they progress through the chapter. Many chapters also offer brief biographies of people who have made an impact on the field of corrections. At the end of each chapter, students can find a summary keyed to the learning objectives, a list of any key terms presented in the chapter, discussion questions, and suggestions for further reading.

OTHER CHANGES IN THE THIRTEENTH EDITION

As textbook authors, we have a responsibility to present current data, provide coverage of new issues, and describe innovative policies and programs. Toward this end we have completely updated and rewritten this edition, line by line. We have been assisted by the comments of an exceptionally knowledgeable team of reviewers who pointed out portions of the text that their students found difficult, suggested additional topics, and noted sections that should be dropped. Among the new or expanded topics found in this thirteenth edition are the following:

- **Death penalty:** Public support for the death penalty is declining, partly because the regular exonerations of people on death row erode public confidence in the accuracy of death penalty verdicts. Juries in many states now seem to prefer life imprisonment without the possibility of parole. Still, 2016 saw 20 executions. But many problems with the death penalty remain, including difficulties with lethal injection, effectiveness of counsel, execution of people with mental illnesses and developmental disabilities, execution for crimes not involving murder, and erroneous convictions (issues examined in Chapters 4 and 20). The death penalty continues to provide a major source of debate.

- **Incarceration trends:** After rising almost continuously for the past four decades, incarceration rates have dropped over the last seven years. This seems not to be related to a drop in violent crime—which for many years has been at 1973 levels—but rather because of doubts about the wisdom of mass incarceration and budgetary pressures at all levels of government. In many states, prisons have been closed, and judges are under pressure to incarcerate fewer people convicted of a felony. The potential long-term implications of correctional downsizing are only now starting to be felt.

- **Reentry:** Each year more than 600,000 people are released from prison and returned to their communities. Disturbingly, the largest group of new admissions to prison in some states is made up of recidivists. A concerted effort by both liberal and conservative policy makers is now focused on ways to reduce recidivism. Assisting people convicted of a felony in the reentry process has become a major focus of correctional policy, and a plethora of new programs are being proposed to make reentry more successful. The problems encountered by people on parole as they adjust to the community are dealt with extensively in Chapters 15 and 16.

- **Evidence-based practice:** There has been a growing movement for "evidence-based" practice in dealing with those under community supervision. Probation and parole officers are encouraged to make decisions based on methods that have been shown to be effective by well-designed research methods. Public statements by former U.S. Attorney General Eric Holder and the development of programs within the U.S. Justice Department's Office of Justice Programs have spurred this thrust. The Justice Department maintains a website called "Crime Solutions" that contains information and research on "what works" for all aspects of the criminal justice system.

- **Incarceration of women:** Reflecting important ongoing research on the impact of maternal incarceration on children, correctional administrators have revisited the importance of programs for women. In particular, several states have devised programs to provide opportunities for women to maintain contact with their children. Chapter 12 describes the "Achieving Baby Care Success Program" at the Ohio Reformatory for Women.

- **Privatization:** Since the advent of private prisons in the 1970s, questions have been raised about whether they are more cost-effective than public prisons. Until recently, research on this question has been lacking. As states deal with severe budgetary problems, the future of private prisons remains uncertain. However, the privatization movement has now carried over into nonprison areas, with proposals for private contracts for community-based correctional methods. Chapter 22 discusses the advent of social impact bonds, which attempt to create fiscal incentives for privately funded innovation in corrections.

- **Corrections as a profession:** With all these changes in correctional policy and practice, there is a need for a "new correctional professional." Throughout this book we describe the challenges that the changes in corrections pose for people who work in the field, and we offer new ideas about the skills and knowledge that correctional professionals will have to bring to their work in order to be successful.

- **Immigration justice:** No issue has been more at the forefront than problems related to immigration. The corrections system is called upon to deal with immigration issues, of course, but the response to immigration illustrates the systems aspect of all justice actions—we describe how law enforcement and adjudication interact with corrections to produce an immigration justice system. We also show how evidence bears on policies regarding immigration.
- **Language:** In this thirteenth edition we have made a shift in language. People who have been caught up in the corrections system—people whose voices we repeatedly turn to in this book—tell us that terms such as "inmate" and "offender," even though they are commonly used, promote painful stereotypes and make reintegration to society harder. To the extent we can, we have edited our language in this edition to move away from these labels and refer to those caught up in the justice system as "people."

ANCILLARY MATERIALS

For the Instructor

MindTap for *American Corrections* MindTap from Cengage Learning represents a new approach to a highly personalized online learning platform. A fully online learning solution, MindTap combines all of a student's learning tools—readings, multimedia, activities, and assessments—into a singular Learning Path that guides the student through the curriculum. Instructors personalize the experience by customizing the presentation of these learning tools for their students, allowing instructors to seamlessly introduce their own content into the Learning Path via digital applications that integrate into the MindTap platform. Additionally, MindTap provides interoperability with major learning management systems (LMS) via support for open industry standards, and fosters partnerships with third-party educational application providers to provide a highly collaborative, engaging, and personalized learning experience.

Online Instructor's Resource Manual and Lesson Plans for *American Corrections* Revised to reflect new content in the thirteenth edition, the instructor's manual includes learning objectives, key terms, a detailed chapter outline, a chapter summary, lesson plans, discussion topics, student activities, "what if " scenarios, media tools, and a sample syllabus. The learning objectives are correlated with the discussion topics, student activities, and media tools.

Online Test Bank The expanded test bank includes 30 percent more questions than the prior edition. Each chapter of the test bank contains questions in multiple-choice, true/false, completion, essay, and new critical-thinking formats, with a full answer key. The test bank is coded to the learning objectives that appear in the main text and includes the section in the main text where the answers can be found. Finally, each question in the test bank has been carefully reviewed by experienced criminal justice instructors for quality, accuracy, and content coverage so instructors can be sure they are working with an assessment and grading resource of the highest caliber.

Cengage Learning Testing Powered by Cognero This assessment software is a flexible, online system that allows you to import, edit, and manipulate test-bank content from the *American Corrections* test bank or elsewhere, including your own favorite test questions; create multiple test versions in an instant; and deliver tests from your LMS, your classroom, or wherever you want.

PowerPoint® Lectures for *American Corrections* Helping you make your lectures more engaging while effectively reaching your visually oriented students, these handy Microsoft PowerPoint® slides outline the chapters of the main text in a classroom-ready presentation. The PowerPoint® slides are updated to reflect the content and organization of the new edition of the text, are tagged by a chapter learning objective, and feature additional examples and real-world cases for application and discussion.

For the Student

MindTap for *American Corrections* MindTap from Cengage Learning represents a new approach to a highly personalized online learning platform. A fully online learning solution, MindTap combines all of a student's learning tools—readings, multimedia, activities, and assessments—into a singular Learning Path that guides the student through the curriculum. Instructors personalize the experience by customizing the presentation of these learning tools for their students, allowing instructors to seamlessly introduce their own content into the Learning Path via digital applications that integrate into the MindTap platform. Additionally, MindTap provides interoperability with major learning management systems (LMS) via support for open industry standards, and fosters partnerships with third-party educational application providers to offer a highly collaborative, engaging, and personalized learning experience.

ACKNOWLEDGMENTS

In writing this thirteenth edition of *American Corrections*, we were greatly assisted by people who merit special recognition. Instructors and students who used prior editions were most helpful in pointing out strengths and weaknesses; we took their comments seriously and hope that new readers will find their educational needs met more fully.

We have also been assisted in writing this edition by a diverse group of associates. Chief among them is Michael Worls, Product Manager, who supported our efforts and kept us on course. Aiyana Moore, Content Manager, reviewed our efforts and made important suggestions in keeping with the goals of this revision. Mark Linton, Senior Marketing Director for Criminal Justice, has skillfully guided the presentation of *American Corrections*, thirteenth edition, to faculty and students. The talented Felicia Bennett and Chris Doughman designed the interior and cover of the book, respectively. Many other people worked hard on the production of the thirteenth edition of *American Corrections*, including Production Manager Greg Hubit, Copy Editor Donald Pharr, and Proofreader Debra Nichols. Ultimately, however, the full responsibility for the book is ours alone.

Todd R. Clear
tclear@rutgers.edu

Michael D. Reisig
reisig@asu.edu

PART ONE

Correctional Context

Part I of *American Corrections*—"the Correctional Context"—describes the corrections system, its history, the way people are punished for crimes, the law as it relates to prisons and corrections works, and the clients of corrections. As you study these chapters, consider the approach from Square One, that emphasizes the importance of the social and historical context for a just correctional system. What do you think of this approach to correctional reform? What obstacles must be overcome if it is to work?

GUEST PERSPECTIVE

Square One Thinking

JEREMY TRAVIS
BRUCE WESTERN
KATHARINE HUFFMAN

Katharine Huffman

It is now well-documented that the American penal system is the largest in the world. With more than two million people incarcerated in U.S. prisons and jails, one out of five of all incarcerated people on the planet resides in the United States. Although only a minority of the U.S. population, over half of the incarcerated population is Black or Latino.

Since 2008, the U.S. incarceration rate has fallen slightly, reversing 35 years of uninterrupted increase. The policy conversation has also begun to change. Crime rates have been low by historical standard since the early 2000s, and community representatives and policymakers have begun to look beyond the era of mass incarceration to reimagine a different kind of justice system that does not rely on harsh punishment concentrated in low-income communities of color.

What ideas could guide a different kind of justice system? The past decade has seen a variety of incremental changes that have reduced sentences for drug crime, restricted a system of cash bail that incarcerates poor people, and elected a new slate of prosecutors who are open to criminal justice reform. These are steps in a new and better direction, but to what end?

Despite these advances, recent reforms will not fundamentally change mass incarceration. People convicted of drug crimes account for less than 20 percent of the state prison population. Bail reform mostly reduces the number of very short jail stays, and leaves long prison sentences untouched. Even a new generation of more progressive prosecutors still must operate in a legal context that imposes very long terms of imprisonment.

Some advocates, scholars, and policymakers say it is time to go both deeper and broader—to go to a new square one on justice policy. Going to square one means reimagining the very foundations of the system in an effort to design something that makes a break with our ugly and racist history of overpolicing and overincarceration.

Square one thinking is built on three big ideas as a way of addressing the challenges of crime and violence—individual, state, and structural—that arise in contexts of poverty and deep racial inequality: reckoning with history, empowering communities, and placing the value of human dignity at the center of doing justice.

This undertaking is about much more than how to run a safe prison or supervise people in the community or deal with the challenges of jail administration. Properly understood, "going to square one" requires engagement with fundamental questions of the purposes of the criminal law, the appropriate limits on human liberty, the role of the state in exercising control over the polity, and the potential for human thriving and transformation.

Prisons, jails, police, and courts are powerful institutions, rooted in inertia, and often staffed by those with a strong stake in the status quo. Ultimately the transformation of these institutions will depend in significant part on the leadership of newcomers to the field and the contributions of embedded change-makers who are seeking to make a break with the past and chart a new vision of the future.

People who have leadership positions in the criminal justice system, whether running government agencies or in the private sector, have an opportunity to grapple with the challenge of institutional change. In the larger enterprise of creating a just society, incarceration is intertwined with systems of health, education, housing, and civic life. A new generation of leaders needs a larger vision for justice that encompasses the work being done in these adjacent fields. For those working within existing agencies, each interaction with a person under some form of correctional control presents an opportunity to reinforce human dignity, to demonstrate fairness and respect, and to advance the cause of justice broadly defined.

Being a "reformer from the inside," always risks strengthening the status quo. Professionals in the field have an opportunity—an obligation we would say—to challenge that status quo, and to continually ask hard questions of themselves and all around them. Why do we do things this way? Are we contributing to foundational change, even if in small steps, or are we simply rearranging deck chairs on a titanic system that has become the largest and farthest reaching tool of racial oppression in our society? Do we know the role of police and prisons in a long history of racial oppression? Are we building stronger communities rather than dividing and exploiting them? Are we promoting the dignity and human potential of all, including those who have come into conflict with the law?

The project to reimagine justice from square one requires the creation of a big table with a wide range of perspectives represented in the decision-making process. Beyond traditional stakeholders, this table must be led by those who are under state control, their families, those harmed by crime, those historically marginalized by the operations of the justice system, and the communities that serve as the wellsprings of safety and justice. Doing the hard work of reimagining justice in this inclusive way will not only bring us closer to thriving, equitable communities, but also honor the imperative that our democracy serve as the ultimate guarantor of justice.

CHAPTER 1

The Corrections System

© John Meore/The Journal News, Rockland/Westchester Journal News via Imagn Content Services, LLC

What can be done with a prison that has been closed down? Here, weeds are overtaking Mid-Orange Correctional Facility in Warwick, NY, closed in 2011 because the state's prison population had dropped so much it was no longer needed. Vacant for nearly a decade, it was set up for recreation with a nearby bike path. It finally found an investor to refurbish its old buildings for the state's expanding hemp industry.

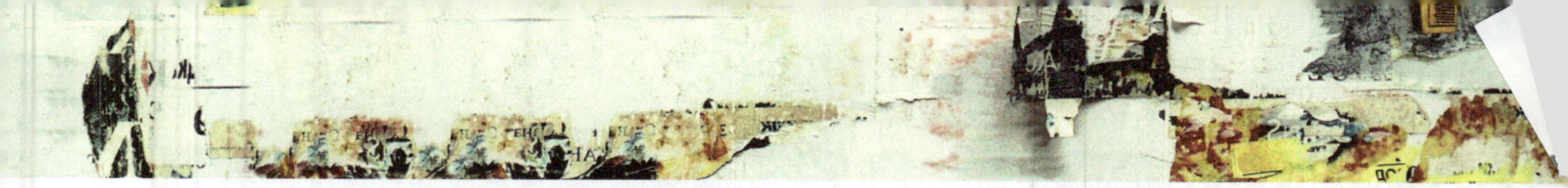

A PROFOUND CHANGE IS HAPPENING TO THE CORRECTIONAL SYSTEM OF THE UNITED STATES. It started at year end of 2008, when, for the first time in nearly 40 years, the total number of people under correctional control—either in prison, in jail, on probation, or on parole—was smaller than the year before. At the time, many thought it was an anomaly. After all, the growth of the corrections system had been continual for over a generation. But what happened in 2008 has now repeated itself every year for a decade. What seemed at the time like a quirk turned out instead to be a true turning point. By the time a decade had passed, the system had declined by about 1 percent, and the total corrections population was down by almost 10 percent. The number of people in prison is down 7 percent.[1]

These changes have come after nearly *four decades* of uninterrupted correctional growth (see "The Great Experiment in Social Control"). The scope of America's long-term commitment to a big corrections system has been described as one of the greatest policy experiments in modern history. In 1973 the prison incarceration rate was 96 per 100,000 Americans. For 38 consecutive years after that, the number of people in prison increased—during periods when crime went up, but also during periods when crime declined; during good economic times and bad; during times of war and times of peace. (See "Myths in Corrections.") By 2010, the U.S. prison incarceration rate had grown to exceed 500 per 100,000 Americans—more than a fivefold increase—and many people thought that this generation-long pattern had become a more or less permanent feature of U.S. penal policy.

LEARNING OBJECTIVES

After reading this chapter, you should be able to . . .

1. Describe the range of purposes served by the corrections system.
2. Define the systems framework and explain why it is useful.
3. Name the various components of the corrections system today and describe their functions.
4. Identify at least five key issues facing corrections today.
5. Discuss what we can learn from the "great experiment in social control."

FOCUS ON

CORRECTIONAL POLICY: The Great Experiment in Social Control

About two-thirds of the members of the current U.S. population, including most of the readers of this book, were born after 1971. For them it has been entirely normal to see yearly increases in the number of Americans in prison, in jail, and under correctional supervision. This group of citizens has seen corrections grow every year—in good economic times and bad, during periods of rising crime and of dropping crime. This growth trend began with the "baby boom" generation: When Americans born in the two decades after World War II hit their twenties and thirties, the peak crime-prone age, they clogged the criminal justice system.

The large and growing correctional populations that seem so normal have not always been so. From 1900 until about 1970, U.S. prison populations were quite stable, hovering between 90 and 120 per 100,000 citizens. After more than 35 years of steady growth, the rate of incarceration is now five times as high as it was in 1973. In 2007 the correctional population reached its highest point in U.S. history—by most accounts the largest correctional population in the world, with the United States putting more people in prison than China, which has four times more citizens.

This period of U.S. history could be called the "great experiment in social control," for it has defined a generation of Americans who have witnessed the greatest expansion in government control ever undertaken by a democratic state. Researchers have tried to explain the sources of this growth. Some of it stems from increases in crime, but most of this crime growth occurred during the first half of the "experiment." Some is because of increased effectiveness at apprehending, arresting, and convicting criminally involved people. But this aspect of the "experiment" is minor compared with changes in punishment policy. In the United States the chances of a person convicted of a felony getting a prison sentence instead of probation have increased steadily for several decades, to the point where the chance of getting a probation sentence is now a fraction of what it used to be. One reason prison sentences became more common is that the drug war increased the number of arrests in defendants' criminal histories, which led judges to impose more severe sanctions.

Therefore, more people are going to prison, and they are serving longer terms as well. Further, the strictness of postrelease supervision has also increased so that more people on probation than before are being sent back to prison because of a failure to abide by strictly enforced rules. This triple whammy—less probation, longer prison terms, and stricter postsentencing supervision—has fueled a continuing increase in correctional populations, especially prison populations, even when crime rates are dropping.

Some scholars have tried to explain the unprecedented punitiveness of the late-twentieth-century U.S. policy (see "For Further Reading"). They discuss the importance of U.S. politics and culture, and they expressly point to the effects of two decades of the "war on drugs." This is certainly a part of the explanation, but nationally less than 15 percent of people in prison are there for a drug crime.[2] Yet *why* this punitiveness occurred is far less interesting than *what* its results have been. Today, researchers, scholars, and intellectuals will begin to try to understand what we have learned from this great experiment.

The effects of this experiment in social control fall into three broad categories: its effects on crime, on society, and on the pursuit of justice. First, and most important, how has the growth of corrections affected rates of crime? Because so many factors affect crime, we cannot easily distinguish the effects of a growing corrections system from those from other factors, such as the economy or times of war. Researchers who have tried to do so have reached divergent conclusions, but even the most conservative scholars of the penal system agree that further growth will have little impact on crime. Others note that because the crime rate today is about the same as it was in the early 1970s, when the penal system began to grow, the corrections system has not likely had a large effect on crime.

Second, there is a growing worry that a large corrections system—especially a large prison system—damages families and communities, and increases racial inequality. For example, as many as six million children have a parent who has been to prison or in jail.[3] How do these experiences affect their chances in life? And what does it mean that more than one in four male African Americans will end up in prison?

Third, how does a large penal system affect the pursuit of justice? Do people feel more confidence in their justice system? Is it right to have people who break the law end up punished the way that America punishes them? In this great experiment in social control, have we become a more just society?

One theme in this book is that things are not as simple as they look. New laws and policies seldom achieve exactly what they were intended to do, and they often have unintended consequences. In this text we explore the most important issues in penology, from the effectiveness of rehabilitation to the impact of the death penalty, with the knowledge that each has more than one side.

We begin with a seemingly simple question: What is the purpose of corrections? In exploring the answer to this question, you will discover a pattern that recurs throughout the book. Any important correctional issue is complicated and controversial. The more you learn about a given issue, the more you will see layers of truth, so your first findings will be bolstered by evidence and then challenged by further investigation and deeper knowledge.

In the end, we think you will see that there are few easy answers but plenty of intense questions. Near the beginning of each chapter we present questions for inquiry that each chapter will explore. We hope that these will help focus your exploration of corrections and serve as a study guide, along with the summary at the end of each chapter.

Sources: Ryan D. King, "Cumulative Impact: Why Sentences Have Increased," *Criminology* 57 (no. 1, 2019): 157–180.

It was not only the prison systems that were growing. Counts of people on probation, parole, or in jail grew at a similar pace. By 2006, one American in every 31 was under some form of correctional control—more than 3 percent of the population.[4]

During this time, correctional budgets grew by over 600 percent. The United States now has almost 3,000 people on death row[5] and another 206,000 serving life sentences, nearly a third of them ineligible for any parole.[6] Counting **prisons** and **jails**, almost 2.2 million citizens are incarcerated, making the adult incarceration rate 860 per 100,000 adult citizens—nearly 1 percent.[7] When all forms of corrections are taken into account—including probation, parole, and community corrections—more than one out of every 40 adults are under some form of correctional control.[8] The extensive growth of the correctional population since 1980 is shown in Figure 1.1 and Figure 1.2.

prison An institution for the incarceration of people convicted of crimes, usually felonies.

jail A facility authorized to hold pretrial detainees and sentenced misdemeanants for periods longer than 48 hours. Most jails are administered by county governments; sometimes they are part of the state government.

Some say that when prison populations grow, crime rates decline because prisons prevent crime. But between 1973 *and* the early 1990s, we saw both imprisonment growth and increases in crime. Most observers concluded that when more people commit crime, more people end up behind bars. This suggests that as crime declines, so will correctional caseloads. But studies show that, aside from the 1970s, there has been little relationship between the nation's crime rate and the size of its prison population. Between 1990 and 2007, for example, the swelling prison population seemed to be entirely caused by tougher criminal justice policies, since crime rates were falling.

But now the long-lasting period of correctional growth has ended, replaced by a decade-long period of declining numbers of people under correctional control. To be sure, the current pace of decline does not come close to matching the pace of growth over the preceding 38 years. But it is clear that we have entered a new era. For the first time in more than a generation, it seems that the long-term pattern of correctional growth may be changing. And by any measure, the U.S. corrections system has seen a sustained period of remarkable, steady growth for more than a generation.

Why is the U.S. correctional system contracting? One answer is that crime has been declining: between 2007 and 2015, violent crime dropped by almost one-fourth. But the drop in crime is not enough of an explanation. Between 1991 and 2007, violent crime

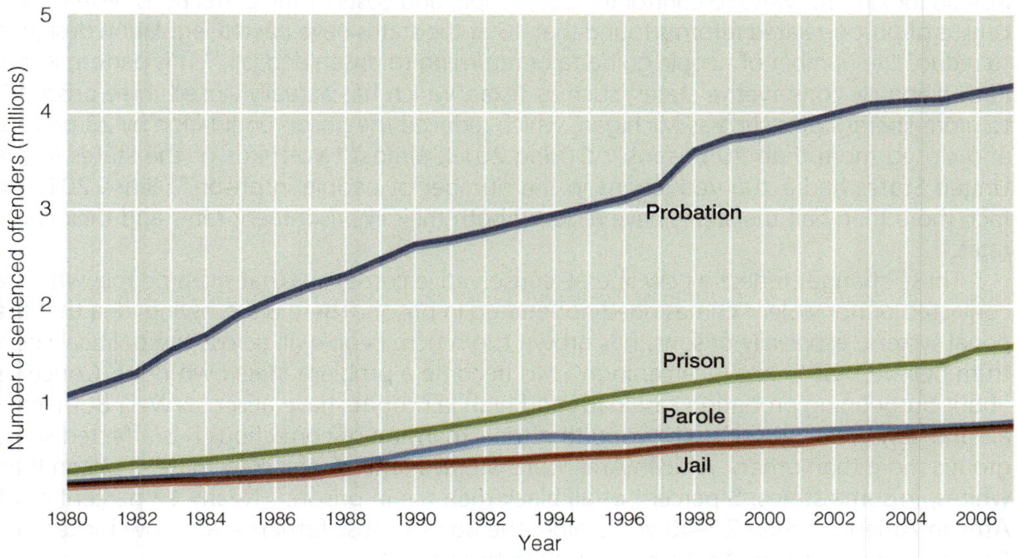

FIGURE 1.1 Correctional Population Growth in the United States, 1980–2007

Although the increase in prison population received the most publicity, a greater proportion of correctional growth occurred in probation and parole.

Sources: Latest data available from the Bureau of Justice Statistics correctional surveys, www.ojp.usdoj.gov: Bureau of Justice Statistics, Annual Probation Survey, Annual Parole Survey, Annual Survey of Jails, Census of Jail Inmates, and National Prisoner Statistics Program, 2000 and 2005–2007.

MYTHS in Corrections

High U.S. Crime Rates

THE MYTH: The United States has such a large prison system, compared with the prison systems of other countries, because it has much more crime.

THE REALITY: Using rates of homicide and rape reported to the police in the United States and in Europe, as the basis of comparison, the United States imprisons its citizens between two and four times higher than any of those countries. While the European nations have somewhat less violent crime, their incarceration rates are much lower than that of the United Sates.

Sources: M. F. Aebi and Tiago MM. *SPACE-2018: Prison Populations* (Strasbourg: Council of Europe, 2019), http://wp.unil.ch/space/files/2019/06/FinalReportSPACEI2018_190611-1.pdf; World Population Review. 2020. *Crime Rate by Country 2020*, http://worldpopulationreview.com/countries/crime-rate-by-country/#dataTable; Jennifer Bronson and E. Ann Carson, *Prisoners in 2019* (Washington, DC: U.S. Department of Justice, 2020).

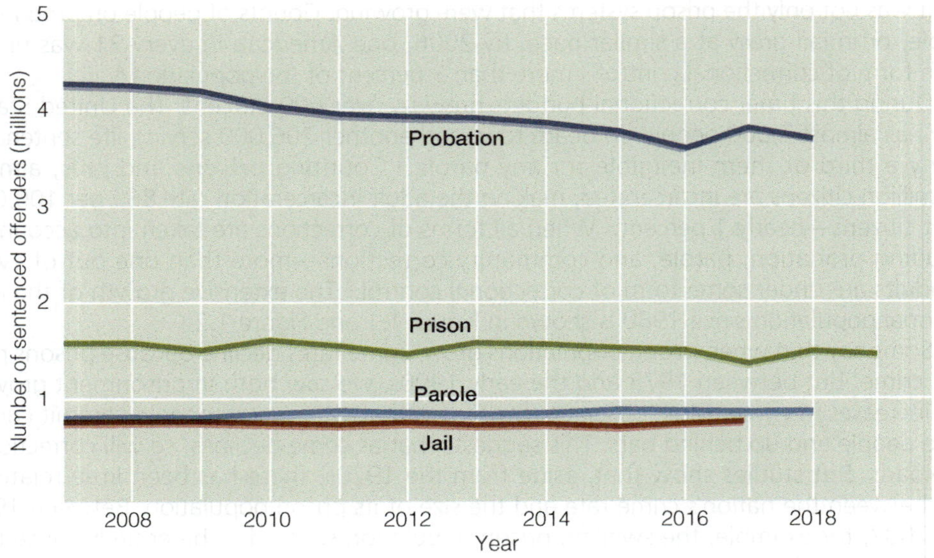

FIGURE 1.2 Correctional Population Contraction in the United States, 2008–2019

After a generation of growth, the correctional system has been declining.

Sources: Latest data available from the Bureau of Justice Statistics correctional surveys, www.ojp.usdoj.gov: Bureau of Justice Statistics, Annual Probation Survey, Annual Parole Survey, Annual Survey of Jails, Census of Jail Inmates, and National Prisoner Statistics Program, 2008–2019.

dropped by more than one-third, yet the corrections system increased by more than 50 percent.[9] A much bigger factor than the drop in crime is that policy makers have been busy reforming the correctional system with the goal of reducing its size. Political leaders all over the country, once the loudest voices for ever-tougher penal policies, are suddenly instead looking for ways to control the size, scope, and costs of the corrections system. One census of prison-related reforms found that 46 of the states have passed legislation designed to reduce the number of people going to or returning to prison and jail.[10] This pattern is true in traditionally conservative states, such as Texas, which has actually closed three prisons,[11] to more-liberal states such as Michigan, which reduced the prison population by 23 percent and closed more than 20 prisons.[12] During 2019, almost two-thirds of the states in the United States had actual reductions in the number of people in prison.[13] Since 2010, in fact, more than half the states have reduced both their imprisonment rates and their crime rates.[14]

These changes reflect a new liberal–conservative consensus that most people who are convicted of nonviolent crimes need not end up in prison. There is a growing idea that the penal system, especially prisons, has grown too much. People all across the political spectrum believe that "mass incarceration" has become a problem in its own right. Concerns about burgeoning probation caseloads and high jail counts have arisen as well. Both liberals and conservatives rightfully worry that the expansion of corrections has affected some groups more than others. African Americans are five times more likely to be in prison than whites; in some states, 5 percent of all black men are in prison.[15] Nearly 12 percent of all African American men 20–40 years old—the age of most fathers—are now locked up. One in six male African Americans has been to prison.[16]

Both liberals and conservatives also share a concern that the cost of corrections, nearly $80 billion per year, is out of line. Prison budgets—by far the most expensive portion of the penal system—grow even when monies for education and other services lag.[17] Probation caseloads and daily jail populations have also grown, and they cost money, too. With growing public concern about the quality of schools and health care, people of all political persuasions are tempted to ask if so much money is needed for corrections. They are especially leery about continuing to invest in what many political leaders, especially conservatives, see as a system that is not as effective as it ought to be.[18]

Corrections, then, is a topic for public debate as never before. A generation ago, most people knew very little about corrections. Prisons were alien "big houses," infused with mystery and located in remote places. The average American had no direct knowledge of "the joint" and no way of learning what it was like. Most people did not even know what probation and parole were, much less have an opinion about their worth.

However, more than 6.6 million Americans are now in the corrections system. This number includes one-third of all African Americans who have dropped out of high school; in fact, 70 percent of this group will go to prison during their lifetime.[19] Add to these numbers the impact on fathers and mothers, brothers and sisters, aunts and uncles, and husbands, wives, and children, and you have an idea of how pervasive corrections is today—especially for poor Americans and people of color.

Further, crime stories dominate our news media. Read any local newspaper or watch any local nightly newscast, and you will encounter a crime story that raises questions about corrections: Should the person have been released? Is the sentence severe enough? Should laws for this type of crime be tougher? In short, corrections now maintains a profound place, not only in the public eye, but also in the public experience. But are the images we form—based on media reports and our own experiences—accurate? Do they tell us all we need to know about corrections?

The coming years will be an exciting period for people interested in corrections. After decades of "get-tough" corrections, today we find ourselves in a new era, characterized by a search for innovative strategies to deal with crime that are more effective and less costly—financially and socially—than the policies that had dominated the landscape for almost 40 years. This is a time when those who study corrections can help shape a new generation of policies and practices. The demand for correctional professionals will continue to grow, but openness to new ideas will be greater than ever before.

People who study corrections want to learn more about the problems that rivet attention. They want to see beyond the three-minute news story, to understand what is happening to people caught in the system. And they suspect that what seems so simple from the viewpoint of a politician arguing for a new law, or from the perspective of a news reporter sharing the latest crime story, may in fact be far more complex for the people involved.

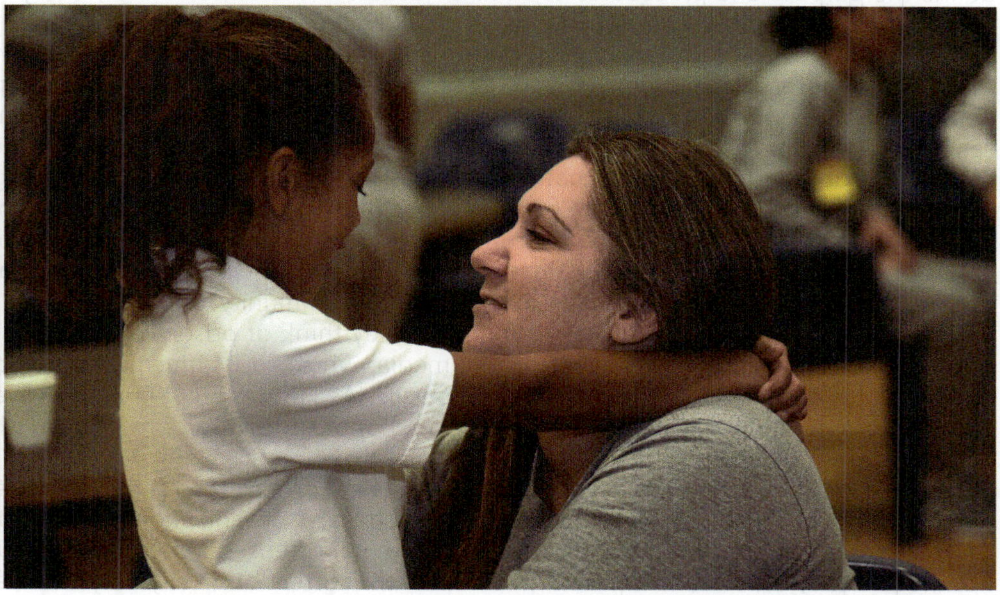

Algerina Perna/Baltimore Sun/TNS/Sipa USA

Clara, aged 8, visits with her mother in Maryland Correctional Institution for Women as a part of Girl Scouts Beyond Bars. Programs such as this help bridge the gap between the community and people in prison.

LO 1

Describe the range of purposes served by the corrections system.

THE PURPOSE OF CORRECTIONS

It is 11:00 A.M. in New York City. For several hours, a five-man crew has been picking up trash in a park in the Bronx. Across town on Rikers Island, the view down a corridor of jail cells shows hands gesturing through the bars as people converse, play cards, share food—the hands of people doing time. About a thousand miles to the south, almost 349 people sit in isolated cells on Florida's death row. In the same state a woman on probation reports to a community control officer. On her ankle she wears an electronic monitoring device that tells the officer if she leaves her home at night. On the other side of the Gulf of Mexico, sunburned Texans in stained work clothes tend crops. Almost due north in Kansas, a grievance committee in a maximum-security prison reviews complaints of guard harassment. Out on the West Coast, in San Francisco, a young man on his way to work checks in with his parole officer and drops off a urine sample. A short 30-minute drive North, in San Quentin prison, students serving time in prison open their text books in a college-level class on Greek Philosophy. All these activities are part of **corrections**. And all the central actors are under correctional authority.

corrections The variety of programs, services, facilities, and organizations responsible for the management of individuals who have been accused or convicted of criminal offenses.

social control Actions and practices, of individuals and institutions, designed to induce conformity with the rules and norms of society.

Punishing people who break society's rules is an unfortunate but necessary part of social life. From the earliest accounts of humankind, punishment has been used as one means of **social control**, of compelling people to behave according to the norms and rules of society. Parents chastise their children when they disobey family rules, groups ostracize individuals who deviate from expected group norms, colleges and universities expel students who cheat, and governments impose sanctions on those who break the law. Of the various ways that societies and their members try to control behavior, criminal punishment is the most formal, for crime is perhaps the most serious type of behavior over which a society must gain control.

In addition to protecting society, corrections helps define the limits of behavior so that everyone in the community understands what is permissible. The nineteenth-century sociologist **Emile Durkheim** argued that crime is normal and that punishment performs the important function of spotlighting societal rules and values. When a law is broken, citizens express outrage. The deviant thus focuses group feeling. As people unite against the law violator, they feel a sense of mutuality or community. Punishing those who violate the law makes people more alert to shared interests and values.

Three basic concepts of Western criminal law—offense, guilt, and punishment—define the purpose and procedures of criminal justice. In the United States, Congress and state legislatures define what conduct is considered criminal.

The police, prosecutors, and courts determine the guilt of a person charged with a criminal offense. The postconviction process then focuses on what should be done with the guilty person. The central purpose of corrections is to carry out the criminal sentence. The term *corrections* usually refers to any action applied to people after they have been convicted and implies that the action is "corrective," or meant to change them according to society's needs. Corrections also includes actions applied to people who have been accused—but not yet convicted—of criminal offenses. Such people are often waiting for action on their cases and are under supervision—sitting in jail, undergoing drug or alcohol treatment, or living in the community on bail.

BIOGRAPHY

EMILE DURKHEIM (1858–1917)

Important French scholar, known as the "Father of Sociology," who argued that criminally involved people and their punishment are functional in society, helping define norms and demonstrating to the public the nature of societal expectations for conformity.

When most Americans think of corrections, they think of prisons and jails. This belief is strengthened by legislators and the media, which focus much attention on incarceration and little on community corrections. As Figure 1.3 shows, however, more than two-thirds of all people under correctional supervision are living in the community on probation or parole.

Corrections thus encompasses all the legal responses of society to some prohibited behavior: the variety of programs, services, facilities, and organizations responsible for managing people accused or convicted of criminal offenses. When criminal justice researchers, officials, and practitioners speak of corrections, they may be referring to any number of programs, processes, and agencies. Correctional activities are

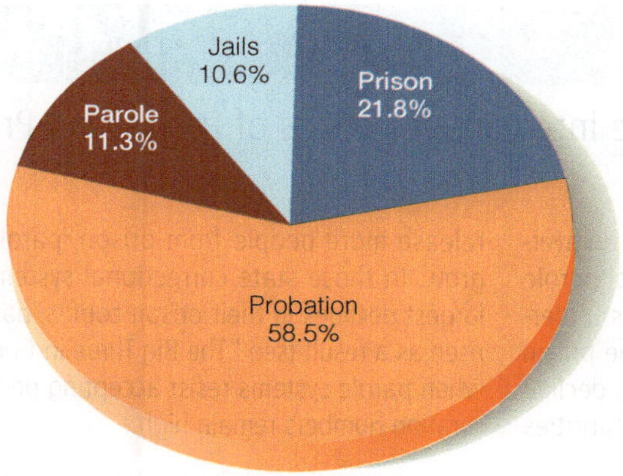

FIGURE 1.3 Percentage of People in Each Category of Correctional Supervision

Sources: Latest data available from the Bureau of Justice Statistics correctional surveys, www.ojp.usdoj.gov: Bureau of Justice Statistics, Annual Probation Survey, Annual Parole Survey, Annual Survey of Jails, Census of Jail Inmates, and National Prisoner Statistics Program.

performed by public and private organizations; involve federal, state, and local governments; and occur in a variety of community and closed settings. We can speak of corrections as a department of the government, a subfield of the academic discipline of criminal justice, an approach to the treatment of those who have broken the law, and a part of the criminal justice system.

Corrections is all these things and more.

LO 2

Define the systems framework and explain why it is useful.

A SYSTEMS FRAMEWORK FOR STUDYING CORRECTIONS

Because it reflects social values, corrections is as complex and challenging as the society in which we live today. Corrections is a legal intervention to deter, to rehabilitate, to incapacitate, or simply to punish or achieve retribution.

Having a framework will help you sort out the complex, multidimensional nature of corrections. In this book we use the concept of the corrections system as a framework for study. A **system** is a complex whole consisting of interdependent parts whose operations are directed toward common goals and are influenced by the environment in which they function. For example, interstate highways make up a transportation system. The various components of criminal justice—police, prosecutors, courts, corrections—also function as a system.

system A complex whole consisting of interdependent parts whose operations are directed toward common goals and are influenced by the environment in which they function.

Goals

Corrections is a complicated web of disparate processes that, ideally, serve the goals of fair punishment and community protection. These twin objectives not only define the purpose of corrections but also serve as criteria by which we evaluate correctional work. Correctional activities make sense when they seem to punish someone fairly or offer some sense of protection. The thought of an unfair or unsafe correctional practice distresses most people.

When these two functions of punishment and protection do not correspond, corrections faces goal conflict. For example, people may believe that it is fair to release people

FOCUS ON

CORRECTIONAL POLICY: The Interconnectedness of Parole and Prison Population Counts

Since 2007, the nation's prison population has dropped an average of 1.2 percent each year. By contrast, the national parole population has increased by .6 percent annually. It is understandable that the parole system would grow when the prison system is declining. One of the ways prison populations decline is through accelerated release from prison. When authorities release more people from prison, parole caseloads naturally grow. In those state correctional systems that have seen the largest declines in their prison counts, parole counts have often risen as a result (see "The Big Three in Corrections"). Conversely, when parole systems resist accepting people from prison, incarceration numbers remain high.

on parole once they have served their sentences, but they may also fear any possible threats that the person poses to the community. Further, such goal conflicts can cause problems in the way the system operates.

Interconnectedness

Corrections can be viewed as a series of processes: sentencing, classification, supervision, programming, and revocation, to name but a few. Processes in one part of the corrections system affect, in both large and small ways, processes in the rest of the system.

For example, when a local jail changes its policies on eligibility for work release, this change will affect the probation caseload. When a parole agency implements new drug-screening practices, the increased number of violators uncovered by the new policy will affect jails and prisons within the system. When writers fail to check their facts for a presentence investigation report, poorly reasoned correctional assignments may result.

These processes all affect one another because people pass through corrections in a kind of assembly line with return loops (see "The Interconnectedness of Parole and Prison Population Counts"). After people are convicted, a selection process determines which ones go where, and why. This sifting process is itself uncertain and often hard to understand. Most, but not all, people convicted of a violent crime are sent to prison. Most, but not all, people who violate probation or parole rules receive a second chance. Most, but not all, people who are caught committing crimes while supervised by correctional authorities will receive a greater punishment than people who were not under supervision during the crime. Figure 1.4 shows examples of interconnections among correctional agencies as they deal with people who have been given different sentences.

Environment

As they process people through the system, correctional agencies must deal with outside forces such as public opinion, fiscal constraints, and the law. Thus, sometimes a given correctional agency will take actions that do not seem best suited to achieving fairness or public protection. At times, correctional agencies may seem to work at odds with one another or with other aspects of the criminal justice process.

Corrections has a reciprocal relationship with its environment. That is, correctional practices affect the community, and community values and expectations in turn affect corrections. For example, if the prison system provides inadequate drug treatment, people return to the community with the same drug problems they had when they were locked up. When citizens subsequently lose confidence in their corrections system, they tend not to spend tax dollars on its programs.

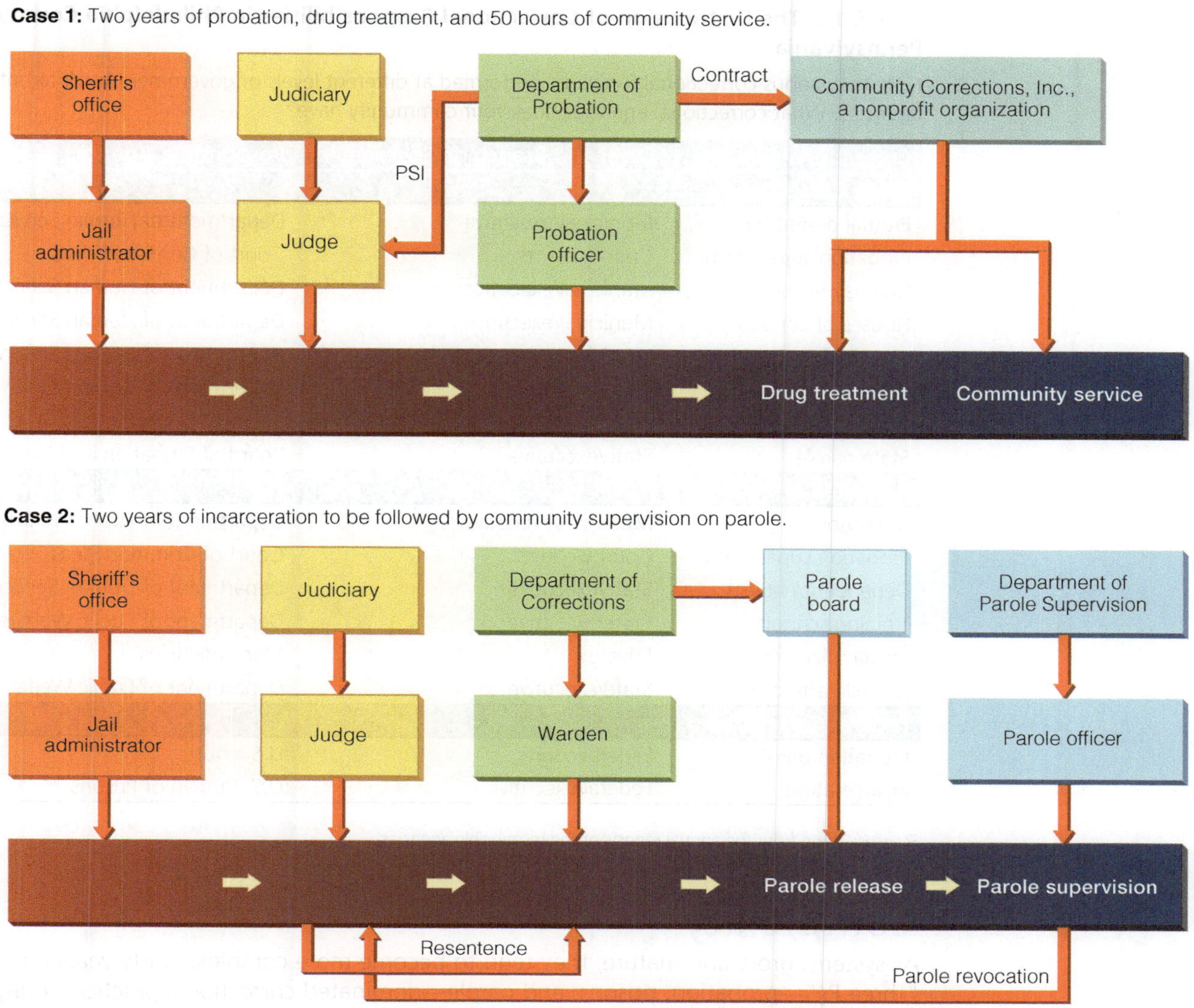

FIGURE 1.4 Interconnectedness of Correctional Agencies in Implementing Sentences
Note the number and variety of agencies that deal with these two cases. Would you expect these agencies to cooperate effectively with one another? Why or why not?

Feedback

Systems learn, grow, and improve according to the feedback they receive about their effectiveness. When a system's work is well received by its environment, the system organizes itself to continue functioning this way. When feedback is less positive, the system adapts to improve its processes.

Although feedback is crucial for corrections, this system has trouble obtaining useful feedback. Success in corrections is best indicated by absence of feedback, such as no new crimes or no prison riots—that is, something that *might* have occurred but did not. Recognizing these absences is difficult at best. By contrast, when corrections fails, everybody knows: The media report new crimes or expose scandals in administration. As a result, corrections systems and their environments tend to overrespond to correctional failure but remain less aware of success.

TABLE 1.1 The Distribution of Correctional Responsibilities in Philadelphia County, Pennsylvania

Note the various correctional functions performed at different levels of government by different agencies. What correctional agencies does your community have?

Correctional Function	Level and Branch of Government	Responsible Agency
Adult Corrections		
Pretrial detention	Municipal/executive	Department of Human Services
Probation supervision	County/courts	Court of Common Pleas
Halfway houses	Municipal/executive	Department of Human Services
Houses of corrections	Municipal/executive	Department of Human Services
County prisons	Municipal/executive	Department of Human Services
State prisons	State/executive	Department of Corrections
County parole	County/executive	Court of Common Pleas
State parole	State/executive	Board of Probation and Parole
Juvenile Corrections		
Detention	Municipal/executive	Department of Public Welfare
Probation supervision	County/courts	Court of Common Pleas
Dependent/neglect	State/executive	Department of Human Services
Training schools	State/executive	Department of Public Welfare
Private placements	Private	Many agencies
Juvenile aftercare	State/executive	Department of Public Welfare
Federal Corrections		
Probation/parole	Federal/courts	U.S. courts
Incarceration	Federal/executive	U.S. Bureau of Prisons

Sources: Taken from the annual reports of the responsible agencies.

Complexity

As systems grow and mature, they tend to become more complex. Thirty years ago, the "three Ps"—probation, prisons, and parole—dominated correctional practice. Today, all kinds of activities come under the heading of corrections, from pretrial drug treatment to electronically monitored home confinement; from work centers, where people can earn money for restitution, to private, nonprofit residential treatment programs.

The complexity of the corrections system is illustrated by the variety of public and private agencies that compose the corrections system of Philadelphia County, Pennsylvania, as Table 1.1 shows. Note that correctional clients are supervised by various service agencies operating at different levels of government (state, county, municipal) and in different branches of government (executive and judicial).

LO 3

Name the various components of the corrections system today and describe their functions.

THE CORRECTIONS SYSTEM TODAY

The U.S. corrections system today employs more than 700,000 administrators, psychologists, officers, counselors, social workers, and others. The federal government, the 50 states, more than 3,000 counties, and uncounted municipalities and public and private organizations administer corrections at an average annual cost of more than $81 billion, according to one recent estimate.[20]

Corrections consists of many subunits, each with its own functions and responsibilities. These subunits—probation offices, halfway houses, prisons, and others—vary in size, goals, clientele, and organizational structure. Some are administered in institutions, others in the community. Some are government agencies; others are private organizations contracted by government to provide specific services to correctional clients. A probation office is organized differently from a halfway house or a prison, yet all three are part of the corrections system and pursue the goals of corrections.

However, there are important differences among subunits of the same general type. For example, the organization of a five-person probation office working closely with one judge in a rural setting differs from that of a more bureaucratized 100-person probation office in a large metropolitan system. Such organizational variety may either help or hinder the system of justice. **Federalism**, a system of government in which power and responsibility are divided between a national government and state governments, operates in the United States. All levels of government—national, state, county, and municipal—are involved in one or more aspects of the corrections system. The national government operates a full range of correctional organizations to handle people convicted of breaking federal laws; likewise, state and local governments provide corrections for people who have broken their laws. However, most criminal justice and correctional activity take place at the state level. Less than 3 percent of individuals on probation and parole, and 9 percent of those in prison, are under federal correctional supervision.[21] (See "The Federal Corrections System Dials Back on Its Agenda of Reform.")

federalism A system of government in which power and responsibilities are divided between a national government and state governments.

FOCUS ON

CORRECTIONAL PRACTICE: The Federal Corrections System Dials Back on its Agenda of Reform

The federal corrections system is larger than any of the state systems, and it handles all violations of federal law. Community corrections, including pretrial services, probation, and parole, are provided by the U.S. Probation and Pretrial Services, which is a part of the U.S. court system. Institutional corrections is operated by the Federal Bureau of Prisons, a part of the U.S. Department of Justice. At last count, there were 92 federal probation offices serving district courts; the U.S. Bureau of Prisons has 110 institutions and 25 residential reentry facilities.

Unlike the situation with state corrections systems, until very recently there has been little pressure to stem the growth of the federal corrections system. Today there are 131,700 people under the supervision of U.S. probation officers, an increase of more than 10 percent over the last five years. People on parole represent less than 10 percent of the total number supervised by probation. There are 209,600 people incarcerated in the federal system, and since 1990 the federal prison system has grown more rapidly than almost any of the 50 state systems. Just under 20 percent of those who are confined in federal prisons are housed in private facilities or local jails under contract with the federal system.

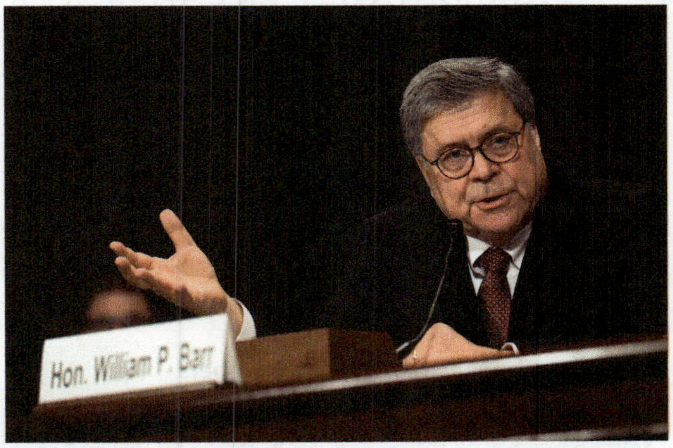

▲ *Serving in the administration of President Donald J. Trump, U.S. Attorney General William P. Barr reversed course on many of the correctional reforms previous administrations had undertaken.*

CORRECTIONAL PRACTICE: The Federal Corrections System Dials Back on its Agenda of Reform (*continued*)

Concerned about this growth, former U.S. Attorney General Eric Holder announced in 2013 the first significant reform of the federal justice system since the establishment of sentencing guidelines in 1984: Under his leadership, federal prosecutors often asked for lower penalties, especially for drug crimes. The federal prison population dropped nearly 10 percent.

Under President Trump, this changed. His first U.S. Attorney General, Jeff Sessions, told federal prosecutors to pursue the most-severe penalties possible, including for drug crimes. Subsequently, AG William P. Barr, reinstituted Federal executions and criticized reformers as "pushing America's cities back toward a more dangerous past."

Joe Biden was elected on a platform of reform for criminal justice. Sensitive to criticisms that his past legislative history as a US Senator includes support for penalties that helped create mass incarceration, he has promised a new, more humane vision for the penal system. Does this signal yet another change for the Federal justice system?

Sources: Dannielle Kaeble and Lauren E. Glaze, *Correctional Populations in the United States, 2016* (Washington, DC: U.S. Bureau of Justice Statistics, 2016); Michael Brice-Sadler, "41 Prosecutors Blast Attorney General Barr for 'Dangerous and Failed' Approach to Criminal Justice," *The Washington Post*, February 13, 2020.

Despite the similarity of behaviors that are labeled criminal, important differences appear from state to state among specific definitions of offenses, types and severity of sanctions, and procedures governing the establishment of guilt and subsequent treatment. In addition, many variations in how corrections is formally organized appear at the state and local levels. The corrections systems in California, Georgia, and Texas handle nearly one-third of all people in state prisons and about one-fourth of all those who are under correctional control in the United States, but each state has developed different organizational configurations to provide corrections (see "The Big Three in Corrections").

FOCUS ON

CORRECTIONAL PRACTICE: The Big Three in Corrections

Three states from three different regions in the United States dominate the corrections scene: Texas, California, and Georgia. They account for more than one-fourth of all people under correctional authority (see Table 1 for a breakdown of the key numbers). Georgia, the smallest of the Big Three, is one-third larger than the next in line (Pennsylvania). These three states stand alone at the top of the list. Each comes by its correctional numbers in different ways, with recent correctional histories that are quite different.

TABLE 1 The Big Three by the Numbers

	Rate/100K Adults	Community	Incarceration
Texas	3,290	482,900	219,600
California	1,770	333,300	200,200
Georgia	6,960	430,800	53,700

Sources: Bureau of Justice Statistics, most recent reports for each state.

TEXAS

Texas supplanted California with the nation's largest prison system in 2012. Not only is the Texas prison system the biggest; everything about Texas criminal justice is "big." The rate of Texans under correctional control is higher than that of any other state in the Union except Georgia and Idaho. More than 10 percent of people on probation in the United States live in Texas. But the story in Texas is changing, and Texas is among the vanguard of states that seek to reduce the number of people in their prisons.

All adult corrections in Texas are housed under the Department of Criminal Justice, which is supervised by a nine-person board appointed by the governor. This department administers corrections through three separate divisions: institutions, parole supervision, and probation. In addition, the parole board reports to the Board of Criminal Justice. The Institutional Division manages all state custodial facilities and monitors the local jails. The Texas Youth Commission handles all juvenile institutions and aftercare. Organized on a county basis, adult probation and juvenile probation are run separately by chief probation officers locally appointed by the county judiciary. Standards for both probation functions are established and monitored by state authority. Adult probation is monitored by the Department of Criminal Justice; juvenile probation is monitored by the Juvenile Probation Commission. Because Texas has more than 200 counties, coordinating the work of these commissions is extremely complicated.

The Texas imprisonment rate was roughly stable during the 1980s. Then, because of a round of punitive sentencing reforms, the Texas incarceration rate doubled between 1990 and 1996, leading the nation. During this time, Texas corrections operated under something of a siege mentality. After losing a series of lawsuits, Texas prisons had a tight population cap, forcing the rest of the system to absorb growing numbers. But decision-making fragmentation made it nearly impossible to develop a coordinated response to the prison overcrowding problem. A federal judge eventually threatened to fine the state more than $500,000 per day if it failed to comply with court-ordered standards. In 2010, when Texas's prison population peaked, the Texas Department of Corrections floated a plan to add 17,000 more prison beds at the cost of almost $1 billion. That led conservatives around the state to take the lead in a broad agenda of criminal justice reform. Since then, the Texas prison population has declined each year, and is now down about 4 percent from the 2010 peak—a number that many Texans are proud of but is less than the national average drop for that same period. For juvenile justice, though, the numbers are almost astonishing: a 76 percent reduction in confinement in the last decade. Texas has now closed four adult prisons and almost all of its juvenile prisons.

Reforms continue to be on the table in Texas, growing from a coalition that includes the "right-on-crime" conservatives and the ACLU liberals. Recent public opinion surveys show strong support for rehabilitation instead of punishments and nonprison alternatives for people convicted of drug crimes and other nonserious felonies. A bipartisan "Cut50" campaign advocates for reducing Texas prison numbers by half. The campaign will try to reduce penalties for low-level drug crimes, and there is talk of raising the age of juveniles from 17 to 18. As oil revenues continue to decline, pressure to constrain the costs of corrections remains high. There is strong public support for reform, which has been helped by substantial drops in Texas crime rates. Texas is "big," not just in size but also in ideas.

CALIFORNIA

California's rate of adults under corrections, 1,770 per 100,000 adults, is below the national average (2,630). The state gets into the Big Three because the state itself is so big. But it has been trying to downsize its correctional system for almost a decade.

In 2011, the state enacted a historically unprecedented approach to reduce dramatically the number of people incarcerated in the state's prison system. In the process, California has dropped its prison count by more than one-fourth since the peak in 2007, a reduction of almost 46,000 people—more than the entire state prison populations of all but seven states. The California story is not only an exemplar in what is possible in prison population reduction, but it also offers a lesson in the public-policy consequences of a change of this magnitude. The system is still large, housing about one in every eleven people in state prisons, but the state has gone from an incarceration rate well above the national average to one of the lowest rates in the West (328 people in prison per 100,000 adult residents, as compared to the national average of 390).

The California adult corrections system is administered by the Adult Authority, and juvenile institutions are administered by the Youth Authority. Both the Adult Authority and the Youth Authority are part of the state government's executive branch. Adult and juvenile probation services are provided by the executive branch at the county level and administered by a chief probation officer. For many years, a portion of the county probation costs was subsidized by the state, but the size of these subsidies started declining in the 1980s. Local taxes pay for jails and probation services, but these taxes have been capped for more than a decade. Local corrections capacity became overloaded when caseloads grew without increases in funding. State correctional facilities were no better off, overcrowded at more than 180 percent capacity. Californians seemed to want to be tough on law violators but didn't want to pay for the repercussions.

In 2006, with every aspect of the corrections system desperately overcrowded, operating with daily chaos, then Governor Arnold Schwarzenegger declared a "state of emergency." Yet his proposed reforms faced deep political resistance, especially from law enforcement. So in 2009 the federal courts stepped in and declared the California system unconstitutional, citing chronic overcrowding, woeful health care, and routine violence. The courts ordered newly installed Governor Jerry Brown to reduce the California prison population by at least 40,000, a requirement affirmed by the U.S. Supreme Court (*Brown v. Plata*). In response, the legislature enacted the California Public Safety Realignment Act in 2011, which devised a new system of sentencing and correctional policies designed to strengthen local correctional capacity and divert a large number of people from the prison system.

Realignment has changed California's correctional numbers. The prison population has dropped by more than 20 percent since 2011. But probation, parole, and local jail counts have also decreased, and the system's overall numbers are down more than 40 percent since Schwarzenegger's original declaration of emergency.

Critics of realignment argue that it has made the public less safe, having put some 18,000 people on the streets who would otherwise have been in prison or jail. These fears were fueled by a small, statewide increase in crime in 2016 as well as a handful of heavily publicized new crimes committed by people released from custody because of realignment. But several careful studies show that violent crime has not been affected by realignment and the small spike in California's crime has since disappeared. Overall, now, crime is down since realignment took effect, and Californians appear to support it. Momentum for cutting down on prisons is so strong that in 2014 Californians overwhelmingly passed Proposition 47, which reduced a list of nonserious felonies to misdemeanors so that people found guilty of them cannot be sent to prison. The fact that felony arrests dropped by more than 50,000 (almost 30 percent) in 2016 foretells continuing reductions in the number of Californians who end up behind bars.

CORRECTIONAL PRACTICE: The Big Three in Corrections (*continued*)

GEORGIA

Georgia joins the Big Three because of the way it uses probation—at a far higher rate than any other state of the union. Its rate of imprisonment is ninth highest in the nation, but its adult probation rate (5,570 per 100,000) is almost twice as high as the next highest state (Rhode Island, at 2,822). The Georgia probation system is, by any standard, massive. About 40 percent of Georgians on probation were placed there for having committed a felony crime—even without misdemeanants, Georgia has among the three highest probation caseloads.

Georgia's prison system has not been declining as rapidly as the rest of the nation. Since its peak in 2009, the prison population has declined by 4 percent, a little more than half the national rate of decline. In the most recent year, the prison population even grew slightly, a sign that the previous reforms may already have run their course.

The state of Georgia administers all institutional corrections through a state-level Department of Corrections, which operates 28 state prisons, four probation revocation centers, and a dozen re-entry offices. The state also has three private prisons. Probation and parole supervision for adults and juvenile is administered by the Department of Community Supervision, which operates dozens of field offices around the state. Juvenile correctional facilities are managed by the Department of Juvenile Justice.

Governor Nathan Deal made criminal justice reform one of his signature policy issues. He was concerned about the large number of citizens who were under correctional authority, and during his eight years in office policies were enacted to reduce some crimes from felonies to misdemeanors, strengthen the role of treatment (including drug courts), and improve re-entry support.

The reforms enacted by Governor Deal were a potent political issue in the 2018 gubernatorial campaign, and Brian Kemp was elected on a get-tough platform in one of the nation's most closely watched elections. He has already started changing the tone of criminal justice, having proposed tougher laws for sex trafficking and gang activity, while reducing funding for the public defender system and specialized courts. The reform trajectory Georgia was once on may have just shifted.

Sources: California: Most recent data available from the U.S. Bureau of Justice Statistics; U.S. Department of Justice; Public Policy Institute of California; *California's Historic Corrections Reforms* (San Francisco, CA: Public Policy Institute of California, 2016); Bradley J. Bartos and Charis E. Kubrin, "Can We Downsize our Prisons and Jails Without Compromising Public Safety?" *Criminology & Public Policy* 17 (no. 3, 2018): 693–715; *Brown v. Plata*, 563 U.S. 2011. Mike Males, *California's 2019 Urban Crime Rate Falls to Record* SF: Center on Juvenile and Criminal justice, May, 2020. Texas: Prison Policy Initiative, www.prisonpolicy.org/profiles/TX.html, 2016; Scott Henson, "Raising the Bars: What's Next for Texas Criminal Justice Reform? *The Observer*, www.texasobserver.org/raising-the-bars-criminal-justice-reform, March 21, 2016; Angela Thielo, Frances T. Cullen, Derek M. Cohen, and Cecilia Chouhy, "Rehabilitation in a Red State: Support for Correctional Reform in Texas," *Criminology & Public Policy* 15 (no. 1, 2016): 137–71. Georgia: Bill Rankin, "Nathan Deal's Criminal Justice Reforms Leave Lasting Legacy," *ACJ*, December 21, 2018; Greg Bluestein and Maya T. Prabhu, "Kemp Pursues a New Criminal Justice Policy, Unnerving Critics," *AJC*, January 22, 2020.

The extent to which the different levels of government are involved in corrections varies by state. The scope of the states' criminal laws is much broader than the federal criminal laws. About 320,000 adults are under federal correctional supervision in more than 100 federal prisons.[22] A recent national count found that the United States holds almost 2.3 million people in 1,833 state prisons, 110 federal prisons, 1,772 juvenile correctional facilities, 3,134 local jails, 218 immigration detention facilities, and 80 Indian Country jails as well as military prisons, civil commitment centers, state psychiatric hospitals, and prisons in the U.S. territories.[23]

The last official count of U.S. prisons listed 110 federal prisons and about 1,000 state prisons. Jails are operated mainly by local governments, but in six states they are integrated with the state prison system.

As noted in Figure 1.5, criminal justice costs are borne by each level of government, with well over 90 percent of correctional costs falling on state and local governments. In most states the agencies of community corrections—probation and intermediate sanctions—are run by the county government and are usually part of the judicial branch. However, in some jurisdictions the executive branch runs them, and in several states this part of corrections is run by statewide organizations.

That the United States is a representative democracy complicates corrections. Officials are elected, legislatures determine the objectives of the criminal law system and appropriate the resources to carry out those objectives, and political parties channel public opinion to office-holders on such issues as law and order. Over time the goals of correctional

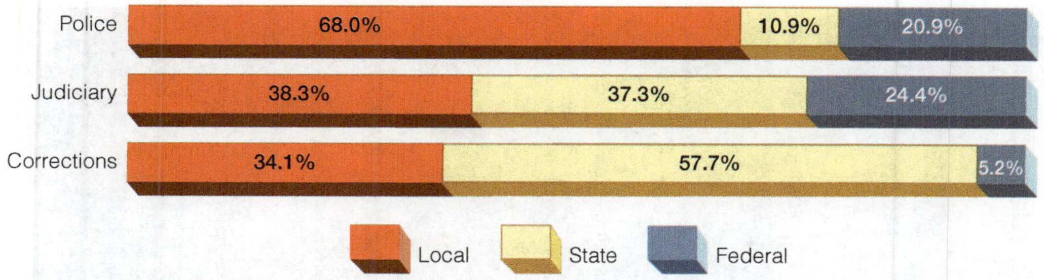

FIGURE 1.5 Distribution of Justice System Expenditures by Level of Government
State and local governments bear the brunt of the costs of correctional activities.

Source: U.S. Bureau of Justice Statistics, Percentage Distribution of Expenditure of the Justice System by Type of Government, Fiscal 2016.

policies have shifted. For example, between 1940 and 1970, corrections was oriented toward liberal rehabilitative policies; between about 1970 and 2000, conservative, get-tough crime control policies have influenced corrections. Now, we are in an era of reform. Questions of crime and justice are thus inescapably public questions, subject to all the pressures and vagaries of the political process.

Clearly, corrections encompasses a major commitment on the part of U.S. society to deal with people convicted of criminal law violations. The increase in the number of people under supervision in the past decade required a major expansion of correctional facilities, staff, and budgets. The size of the system has started to decline, but budgets have remained high in almost all areas of the country.

KEY ISSUES IN CORRECTIONS

LO 4
Identify at least five key issues facing corrections today.

Like all other government services, corrections is buffeted by frequently shifting social and political forces that greatly complicate administration. These forces are also part of what make corrections so interesting to examine. In this section we describe some of the controversies, issues, and themes that arise in the study of corrections. These are divided into three main areas: managing the correctional organization, working with people, and upholding social values.

Managing the Correctional Organization

The ways in which different correctional organizations are managed depend on various factors, including goals, funding, bureaucracy, and interagency coordination.

Goals The theory inherent in the term *corrections*, the assumption that people who have broken the law can be "corrected," faces much dispute. For example, some people believe that most of them can never be rehabilitated, that only social maturation can convince most people to abide by the law. Others argue that the penal system should not be concerned with the future behavior of people who have committed a crime, that the only appropriate response to wrong-doing is punishment. Yet from the end of World War II until the 1970s, the corrective function was so widely accepted that treatment and reform were virtually the only issues in criminal justice deemed worthy of serious attention.

Corrections has constantly faced the challenge of deciding which goals to emphasize. Conflict over goals stems precisely from the shifting forces that directly influence corrections. For example, political ideology often colors the analysis and development of

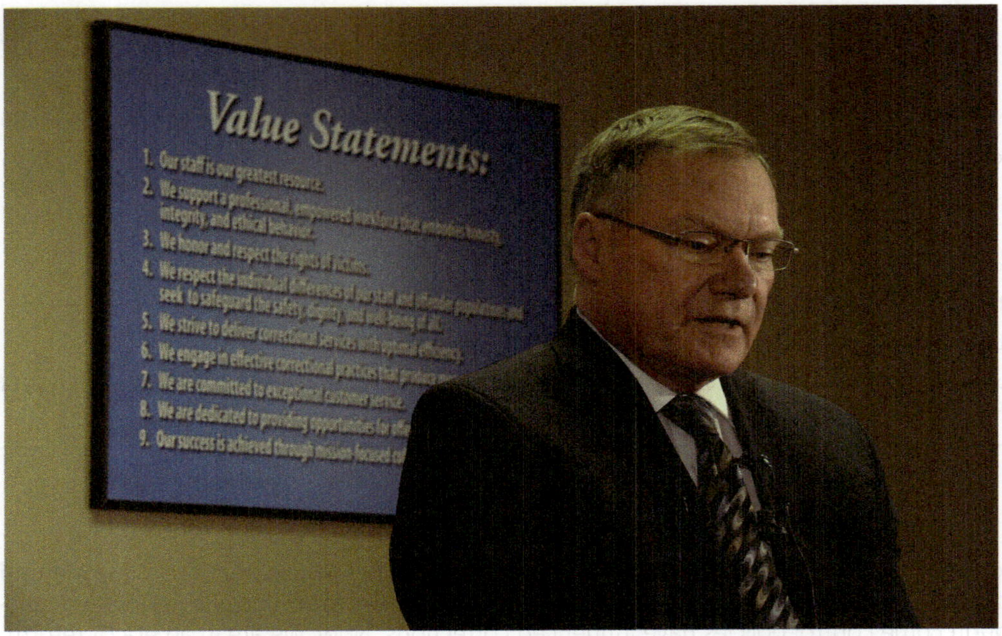

Andy Cross/Getty Images

▲ *Corrections operates under a system of values, and these values can vary from one corrections system to another. How is policy affected by having different values guide different corrections systems?*

correctional policy. Liberals believe that corrections should follow one path; conservatives prefer another. Goals set by conflicting interests do not usually mesh.

In response to conflicting political forces, correctional leaders offer conflicting (or at least divergent) justifications for a given policy in order to maintain an appearance of consensus. For instance, a program of private-industry employment for people in prison can be extolled to liberals as rehabilitative training, to free-enterprise advocates as expansion of the private sector, and to conservatives as a get-tough policy designed to make people put in prison pay the costs of their incarceration. Although this tactic helps preserve support for the prison's industrial operations, it also creates managerial problems for correctional leaders because when the program is implemented, the goals of treatment, profit, and punishment may well conflict.

Further, correctional leaders who state precise objectives risk alienating various important groups or constituencies. Thus, they tend to frame goals as vague generalities, such as "to protect" or "to rehabilitate." The effects of this vagueness extend well beyond public relations; often it is difficult for correctional staff members to make goal-oriented choices because they are unsure of what the leaders want. This conflicted situation has led some observers to argue that corrections does not work to achieve an overriding goal but rather seeks to balance stated and unstated goals so that no single goal is sacrificed.

Funding At all political levels, corrections is only one of many services operated by government and paid for by tax revenues. Thus, corrections must vie for funding not only with other criminal justice agencies but also with agencies supporting education, transportation, social welfare, and so on (see "For Critical Thinking"). Per capita spending on all criminal justice activities ranges from less than $100 in West Virginia to more than $400 in Alaska and New York.

Understandably, corrections does not always receive the funding it needs; people may want garbage collected regularly more than they want quality correctional work performed. Recall, too, that corrections is largely invisible until a problem occurs, such as when a person on parole commits a heinous crime or a prison riot breaks out. An even greater difficulty stems from the perceived undesirability of those corrected; it is not easy to win larger budgets to help people who have broken the law.

Conflict among the branches and levels of government also creates problems for corrections. Local governments are often responsible for correctional programs for people convicted of minor crimes; state governments handle those who will be longer term because of their more-serious crimes. Often the two levels vie for operating funds, and each seeks to avoid responsibility for people supervised by the other. Given this fragmentation, correctional services and programs may overlap.

Officials of the executive branch often complain that legislatures enact correctional codes and prescribe operational responsibilities without providing sufficient funds to carry them out. Both branches complain that court rulings set unfair constraints on their ability to handle assigned caseloads. In developing and implementing policies, correctional agents must consider not only the sociopolitical environment but also the government setting in which corrections functions.

One result of funding squabbles is dispute over organizational "turf." Most probation offices are attached to the judiciary and funded by county governments. Do they then fall within the domain of corrections, or do they belong to the judiciary? Should the sheriff be in charge of transporting people from jail to prison, or should the prison administrators be responsible? To what extent should social service agencies become involved with the needs of correctional clients in a halfway house? Should parole officers or the police be responsible for tracking people down who have violated the conditions of their release?

Struggles for resources also occur between corrections and related social service agencies. A department of corrections may vie with a department of mental health for funds to set up a drug rehabilitation program; both departments may view the new resources as a way to expand. Often, correctional departments take such empire-building actions to keep themselves strong and viable.

FOR CRITICAL THINKING

For many people, the huge cost of corrections, especially prison, is the main reason that it seems like the time has come to reduce the corrections system. But is money alone a sufficient justification for this view? After all, the corrections system is an important public investment through which we achieve justice and promote public safety.

1. Is it fair to let financial pressures determine how much we are willing to spend to promote justice and public safety?
2. Do we need to consider other issues to determine whether the U.S. corrections system is too large?
3. What might some of those reasons be? Are they more important than money?

Bureaucracy Michael Lipsky has provided perhaps the most vivid portrait of the problems facing correctional workers. He coined the term **street-level bureaucrats** to refer to the following:

> Public service workers who interact directly with citizens in the course of their jobs, [including] teachers, police officers and other law enforcement personnel, social workers, judges, public lawyers and other court officers, health workers and many other public employees who grant access to government programs and provide services within them.[24]

street-level bureaucrats Public service workers who interact directly with citizens in the course of their work, granting access to government programs and providing services within them.

Lipsky's provocative generalizations about street-level bureaucrats apply to virtually all individuals who have face-to-face contact with people under the authority of the corrections system. They work with inadequate resources and face ever-increasing demands. Frequently, they find themselves theoretically obligated to provide higher-quality treatment for their clients than they can afford. Thus, street-level bureaucrats soon learn that "with any single client they probably could interact flexibly and responsibly. But if they did this with too many clients, their capacity to respond flexibly would disappear."[25] For example, probation officers may feel obliged to find jobs for their clients. If they took time to do so, however, they could not provide other services. An officer may genuinely desire to work hard for those who show promise, but not for others. Officers facing such conflicts may become alienated from their clients because they cannot satisfy their clients' needs: Maintaining a working relationship proves too frustrating.

Limited resources force administrators of service bureaucracies to carefully monitor the way workers apply their time and energies. Bureaucracies that process people develop categories for their clients, seeking to use personnel or agency resources in the best way and to succeed with some clients, even though they cannot succeed with all.

Lipsky concludes that delivering street-level policy through bureaucracy presents an inherent contradiction. One person delivering service to another suggests human interaction, caring, and responsibility. But delivering service through a bureaucracy suggests detached, inflexible treatment based on limited resources. Conflicting, ambiguous goals, combined with difficulties in measuring work performance, may reduce effectiveness and commitment to the work. Thus, the bureaucratic model guarantees that services are delivered only up to a point and that goals are never fully achieved.

Is Lipsky's conclusion too pessimistic, or just realistic? Certainly, correctional workers and their clients face formidable obstacles. Workers must make daily decisions under conditions of technical uncertainty and sporadic negative feedback; clients must comply both with legal mandates and with less explicit parameters established by the needs of the correctional organization. Yet bureaucratic worker–client relationships offer benefits as well. As their time and tasks grow more structured, workers have less discretion and thus less capacity to abuse their positions. Further, limited organizational resources force agencies to clarify their goals and to direct services toward those people who most need staff time. Given the extensive power of correctional agencies, conditions in bureaucracies may restrain abuse of state power.

Interagency Coordination Managing correctional agencies is further complicated by the fact that most corrections systems comprise several loosely related organizations that are themselves bureaucracies. Thus, decision making is dispersed—no one person can implement the full range of correctional practices. For example, the sheriff who runs the jail and the probation officer who runs the pretrial release program are both affected by jail crowding and delays in sentencing hearings. Even so, they may resist working together because each is busily protecting an area of managerial control. Furthermore, line workers in corrections, those in direct contact with the system's clients, seldom influence organizational policies, even though they must implement those policies daily. Corrections itself cannot determine the type and number of its clients. Others in the criminal justice system, primarily judges, do that, and correctional officials cannot halt or regulate the flow. Thus, the efforts of correctional workers are sometimes sporadic, uncoordinated, or inconsistent merely because various bureaucracies are loosely interconnected. Within the corrections system a great deal of policy is formally interconnected. In some states as many as half or more of all people who go to prison do so because they have violated a requirement of probation or parole; in other states these rule violators are less frequently sent to prison. In other words, the enforcement policies of the supervising agencies help determine prison intake. In most systems, however, prison authorities have little control over policies for enforcing probation rules. Similarly, a probation officer's caseload is determined by the number of people on probation and the length of their probation terms. Even though officers have a finite amount of time for supervision, they generally have little or no control over their caseloads. As people flow through the system after being convicted of a crime—from probation to revocation to prison to work release to parole—one agency determines the workload of the next.

These informal interconnections create an uneasy tension. Agency directors understandably may take steps to protect their piece of the system from encroachment by the rest of it. Each correctional unit commonly insulates itself from the pressures faced by the other units because the others often produce unwanted caseload increases;

for example, crowded jail conditions may encourage judges to put more people on probation.

This isolation makes it more likely that the other units will run into problems resulting from a lack of cooperation and that these problems will haunt all the units when the corrections system as a whole is criticized.

Working with People

"People work" is central to corrections because the raw material of the system consists of people—those who work in the system and those who are under the system's authority. In doing their work, correctional staff must deal with uncertain technologies, engage in exchange relationships with their clients, and follow uncertain correctional strategies.

Professional Versus Nonprofessional Staff The term *staff* in the corrections system refers to probation officers, correctional officers, counselors, and others responsible for the daily management and supervision of people under correctional control. Correctional staff includes both professional and nonprofessional employees. For example, psychologists, counselors, and administrators usually hold at least one college degree. They view themselves as members of various professions, with all the rights that adhere to such callings. They believe they should be able to work without supervision and to make decisions without always consulting rulebooks or guidelines. These professional employees work closely with nonprofessional staff, such as jail or prison correctional officers. The nonprofessional staff members frequently have only a high school education, and they function under close, often paramilitary (military-style) supervision and enforce rules with physical means when necessary. The different perspectives of these two groups and the ways they communicate with each other have caused problems—for example, conflicts over the best ways to deal with people who have broken the law and distrust of each other's motives and expertise—in some types of correctional organizations.

Uncertain Technologies The term **technology** refers to methods of applying scientific knowledge to practical purposes in a particular field. Correctional technologies are not as sophisticated as those of, say, engineering, but their subjects—human beings—are far more complex. Methods of dealing effectively with people who are being "corrected" are highly uncertain. Although knowledge of human behavior has developed significantly during the past century, the validity of the various approaches of treatment—such as group therapy, behavior modification, and anger management—remains in doubt. ("Thinking Outside the Box: Doing What Works" shows one way to deal with uncertain technologies.)

technology A method of applying scientific knowledge to practical purposes in a particular field.

Thus, corrections is expected to implement programs of questionable impact. Correctional organizations face serious problems related to human behavior: Not all those who are released from prison adjust successfully to free society; not all mental health referrals result in emotional adjustment; not all people on probation prove trustworthy. Correctional decisions are prone to error. In fact, correctional organizations may approach the technical problem of human ignorance about humans by seeking to reduce types of error rather than to eliminate error altogether. Further, any organization develops routines just to keep it operating. Like most people, workers in correctional organizations want regular and predictable responsibilities. They do not want to venture into uncharted seas where they may make an uninformed decision and then be penalized for it. Uncertainty declines when people reduce operations to routines—patterns that repeat and thus become familiar. Recognizing these routines is essential for understanding corrections.

THINKING OUTSIDE THE BOX

DOING WHAT WORKS

For much of its history, the field of corrections has based its practices on what might be called ideas of justice—carefully considered hypotheses about what a good corrections system ought to be like. Quite often, these ideas were promoted because their advocates claimed they would be more effective—that they would produce better citizens or deter more crime. But these ideas were seldom put to an empirical test. Generally speaking, whenever traditional correctional strategies have been evaluated, they have been found wanting, even counterproductive. Some of our most cherished ideas simply do not work in practice.

Today, there is an ever-growing evidence base of programs and strategies that have proven effective upon careful evaluation. Descriptions of these approaches are sprinkled throughout this book. Although there is still a great deal to be learned about correctional effectiveness, the truth is we already know a lot about what we should be doing. That does not mean these empirical lessons are always reflected in policy—policy makers seem often to base their choices on ideas of justice rather than evidence. This would never happen in other fields. For example, could you imagine a doctor basing his or her methods on what should work in an ideal world, rather than what does work in practice?

What if correctional policy and practice had to be based on evidence of "what works"? What would happen if correctional leaders had to justify their practices by pointing to specific evidence that strategies either *have* worked in the past or *should* work based on what we know from studies?

Source: National Institute of Justice, *Crime Solutions.gov: Reliable Solutions Real Results*, www.crimesolutions.gov, 2017.

Exchange A key facet of corrections is the degree of interdependence between staff and the people they deal with. The unarmed, outnumbered correctional officer assigned to a prison or jail has surprisingly little raw power with which to exact cooperative behavior. Similarly, a probation officer can do little with a client who resists the officer's influence. Meanwhile, the person in the prison cell depends on the work of the correctional officer, and the person on parole often feels powerless under supervision. Thus, staff and the people they are responsible for are interdependent: To achieve personal goals, each depends on the other. The officer needs cooperation to convince superiors that the officer is performing properly; the person who is in prison needs the officer's recommendation for favorable termination of parole.

exchange A mutual transfer of resources based on decisions regarding the costs and benefits of alternative actions.

The interdependence of people in corrections makes the concept of exchange important to understanding their daily world. **Exchange** occurs when two parties trade promises or concessions that make each person's work easier or more predictable. For example, a person on probation cooperates by reporting regularly and attending an alcohol treatment program; in return, the officer is more likely to overlook incidental, minor violations of probation. Each party's situation is made easier by the voluntary decisions of the other.

Because exchange relations are quite important, they are often subject to informal enforcement. For instance, a someone who is rowdy is removed from his cell and placed in solitary until he "settles down" and recognizes officials' authority. A juvenile on probation is arrested and "detained" (locked up) for the weekend while awaiting a hearing on her truancy from school, even though officials have no intention of revoking her probationary status. Conversely, a guard who is hostile or condescending finds it takes much longer to return people to their cells for the morning count or to quiet down those who are noisy. Subtle and not-so-subtle pressures unceasingly reinforce the need for keepers and the kept to stay aware of each other's needs.

In sum, correctional transactions almost uniformly involve some aspect of worker–client contact and interaction. Because staff members and those they deal with depend on each other to achieve their goals, each person can influence evaluations made by the other. This process must be managed through screening and processing routines, staff training and evaluation programs, and so forth. (See "What Does the Great Experiment in Social Control Cost?")

FOCUS ON

CORRECTIONAL POLICY: What Does the Great Experiment in Social Control Cost?

It has been estimated that the annual budgets of the state and federal correctional agencies total $80.7 billion. For elected officials, the cost of the corrections system is an economic hindrance to the ability to fund other public priorities. For example, in 2014, 11 states spent more on their corrections systems than they did on higher education. Trying to drive down correctional costs is a major motivating factor for many of today's chief executives and legislators.

As big as that $80.7 billion figure is, recent analysts have argued that the heavy U.S. reliance on incarceration to deal with crime carries a host of "hidden" costs—that is, expenditures that show up in other public and private budgets, but not in the corrections budget. They say that a proper accounting of the total costs would include law enforcement and judicial systems, which spent another $92.2 billion annually. But even if the costs of the police and the courts are taken out of the picture, individuals and their families who end up in the corrections system incur significant personal costs: $4.5 billion in civil asset forfeiture, $1.4 billion in court fees, and $2.9 billion in family cash support for people when they are in jail.

While it is often harder to put a dollar figure on the human costs of the U.S. prison system, new research has tried to identify some of the ways that it costs society to have so many people behind bars. These problems include damage to children, families, and communities when individual and collective economic capacity is obstructed.

All of these effects are costly for society, even if a state's budget does not reflect them. Overall, many leading thinkers have begun to agree that there will be significant economic advantages if the U.S. prison system needs to be scaled back.

Sources: Vera Institute of Justice, *The Price of Prisons: What Incarceration Costs Taxpayers* (New York: Author, 2012); Peter Wagner and Bernadette Rabuy, *Following the Money of Mass Incarceration* (Washington, DC: Prison Policy Initiative, 2017); The White House, *Economic Perspectives on Incarceration and the Criminal Justice System* (Washington, DC: Author, 2016).

Uncertainty About Correctional Strategies Throughout the chapters to come we explore an important theme: that correctional workers and managers cannot predict with certainty what effect their choices will have on the system. How does the correctional official organize staff, choose programs, and manage people in them when the consequences of such actions are so ambiguous? Given this uncertainty, organizational theorists say that the correctional environment is unstable and that, as a result, one of management's main concerns is avoiding negative feedback from the community—the courts, political leaders, the public, and so forth.

Because the effectiveness of correctional strategies is so uncertain, organizations often place greater emphasis on secondary technologies in which they have more confidence—the design of a prison's security apparatus, a computer-based tracking system for probation, and so on. But the core work of corrections concerns the interactions of people—staff and people on probation—which will always remain hard to predict and control, no matter what the technology.

There are two points of interest here. First, people in the corrections system are obviously handled in a variety of ways. Who determines what happens to them, and how they make this determination, is a key issue in this book. Second, and even more central, corrections gets its "business" not only from the courts but also from itself. Policies and practices determine how strictly the rules will be enforced, how dire the consequences will be when they are broken, and how much latitude that staff will have in assigning people to programs. See "Do the Right Thing" for more.

Upholding Social Values

LO 5

Discuss what we can learn from the "great experiment in social control."

All these problems combine to make the field of corrections controversial, and therefore engrossing for those who study it. Yet as compelling as these problems may be, they are only a sidelight to the central appeal of the field of corrections. The questions that corrections raises concerning social control are fundamental to defining society

DO THE RIGHT THING

For Governor Wilma James, the most difficult years of the state's fiscal crisis now seem to be over. Her state's Department of Revenue informed her that tax revenue, down recently by as much as 4 percent of the overall budget because of the struggling economy, will now be stable or even up a percent or two. When the crisis was at its height, she saved some money by moving people who were considered low risk into community programs. The move was successful, saving money with no significant impact on overall crime. A few instances of those who had been convicted of serious crimes made public headlines, but the political backlash was almost nonexistent. Some of her staff have argued that the new financial situation means she should return to the earlier policies that led to larger prison populations. But the commissioner of corrections says the program works well enough and could even be expanded, further reducing the cost of the prison system.

WRITING ASSIGNMENT: Write an essay on reducing prison populations. Is this a wise thing to do? Why or why not? How would you approach doing this as a state-level official? What is the best way to reduce the costs of corrections? Is it a short-term problem or a long-term one?

and its values. Seemingly every aspect of the field brings up issues centering on deeply held values about social relations. For example, can the number of people in prisons and jails be reduced without endangering the public? (For one answer to this question, see "What Happened in New York, and What Does It Mean for the United States?") Should corrections be more concerned with punishing people for crimes or with providing programs to help them overcome the problems in their lives that contribute to crime? Is placing surveillance devices in people's homes a good idea or an invasion of privacy? Questions of interest to researchers, students, and citizens hardly end here. Crucial public and private controversies lurk at every turn. In your own studies and throughout your life, you will find you cannot answer the questions inherent in these controversies without referring to your own values and those of society. People who undertake careers in corrections often do so because they find the field an excellent place to express their most cherished values. Probation and parole officers frequently report that their original decision to work in these jobs stemmed from their desire to help people. Correctional officers often report that the aspect of their job they like best is working with people who are in trouble and want to improve their lives. Administrators report that they value the challenge of building effective policies and helping staff perform their jobs better. The field of corrections, then, helps all these individuals to be fully involved with public service and social values. Corrections is interesting to them in part because it deals with a core conflict of values in our society—freedom versus social control—and it does so in ways that require people to work together.

FOCUS ON

CORRECTIONAL POLICY: What Happened in New York, and What Does It Mean for the United States?

There used to be a "Big Four" in corrections (see The "Big Three in Corrections"), with New York having one of the nation's largest prison systems. In fact, in 1999 New York ranked third in prison population. But since then, New York's prison count has decreased by nearly a third. The state now ranks sixth in total number of people in prison. What happened?

The simple story is that New York started sending fewer people to prison and, for many of them, required shorter stays in prison. The story actually centers on what has happened in the state's urban behemoth: New York City.

Twenty years ago, New York City was the main source of people for prison in New York, sending just over 47,000 people to the state prison system while the rest of the state combined sent about 23,000. Today, prison admissions from outside the city have risen by almost a third, to about 30,000, while New York City prison admissions are down by just over 50 percent, to 23,000. That shift more than explains New York's drop from the "Big Four," but what explains the big change?

In New York City, police are arresting far fewer people for drug crimes—a two-thirds drop since 1994. Drug cases now make up barely over 10 percent of the prison population. The drop in violent crime over that same period has translated into a 40 percent drop in felony arrests for violence, and judges send a lower portion of people convicted of felonies to prison. The result: a New York City jail and prison incarceration rate that is today half what it was in 1996. The drop is so dramatic that the city council has voted to close Riker's Island, the city's jail.

The New York City story is an answer to the question "What would happen if prison populations were cut by 50 percent?" For people who worry about public safety, the experience in New York City is instructive. Since 2000, when the city began arresting fewer people and sending fewer of those arrested to state prison, its crime rate has dropped by almost 50 percent.

There is no question that New York City is a unique place. But its history of correctional policy is not unique. Its highest number of prison residents, in 1999, was largely the result of mandatory prison terms for people convicted of drug offenses and long sentences for people who sold drugs and those who were convicted of violent crimes. That is, in many ways, the national story. Could other places reduce their imprisonment rates by 50 percent, like New York City? Some places have already achieved substantial reductions from the peak year of their prison population: Alaska (39 percent) and New Jersey (38 percent) stand out among the dozen states with double-digit reductions. One study has estimated that almost 40 percent of people in U.S. prisons are locked up with little or no public safety benefit.

Sources: Judith A. Greene and Vincent Schiraldi, *Better by Half: The New York City Story of Winning Large-Scale Decarceration While Increasing Public Safety* (Cambridge, MA: Kennedy School of Public Policy, 2016); Jim Parsons, Qing Wei, Christian Henrichson, and Jennifer Trone, *End of an Era? The Impact of Drug Law Reform in New York City* (New York: Vera Institute of Justice, 2015); James Austin and Lauren-Brookes Eisen, *How Many Americans Are Unnecessarily Incarcerated?* (New York: Brennan Center for Justice, 2016); Nazgol Ghandnoosh, *US Prison Decline: Insufficient to Undo Mass Incarceration* (Washington, DC: The Sentencing Project, 2020).

SUMMARY

1 Describe the range of purposes served by the corrections system.

Corrections is a means of social control. It holds people accused of crimes; carries out criminal sentences imposed by courts, including both confinement and community supervision; and provides services for rehabilitation.

2 Define the systems framework and explain why it is useful.

A system is a complex whole consisting of interdependent parts whose operations are directed toward common goals and influenced by the environment in which they function. It is a useful concept because it helps us understand how the various aspects of corrections can affect the others.

3 Name the various components of the corrections system today and describe their functions.

Corrections consists of many subunits. There are both federal and state corrections systems. Institutional corrections include prisons and jails, and they confine people who have been sentenced by the courts (or, in the case of jails, people who are awaiting trial). Community corrections supervises people who are either awaiting trial or have been sentenced by the court but are living in the community. There are also private organizations that provide various services to people under correctional authority. Important differences exist among subunits of the same general type.

4 Identify at least five key issues facing corrections today.

Corrections faces several issues: dealing with conflicting goals, obtaining adequate funding, making the bureaucracy of correctional services more effective, coordinating correctional activity across different agencies, and dealing with correctional uncertainty.

5 Discuss what we can learn from the "great experiment in social control."

The growth in the corrections system has resulted mostly from deliberate policies that have increased the severity of sentences. Changes in crime rates have had little effect on this growth.

KEY TERMS

corrections (*p. 10*)
exchange (*p. 24*)
federalism (*p. 15*)
jail (*p. 7*)
prison (*p. 7*)
social control (*p. 10*)
street-level bureaucrats (*p. 21*)
system (*p. 11*)
technology (*p. 23*)

FOR DISCUSSION

1. Contrast the role of crime with the role of politics in the growth of corrections. Why is this contrast important?
2. What do you see as some of the advantages and disadvantages of the systems concept of corrections?
3. Corrections is a system in which technologies of uncertain validity are used. What are some of the dangers of using these technologies? What safeguards, if any, should be applied?
4. Assume that the legislature has stipulated that rehabilitation should be the goal of corrections in your state. How might people working in the system displace this goal?
5. What does Lipsky mean by the term *street-level bureaucrat*? Give some examples of how street-level bureaucrats act.
6. Suppose you are the commissioner of corrections for your state. Which correctional activities might come within your domain? Which most likely would not?

FOR FURTHER READING

Aviram, Hadar. *Cheap on Crime: Recession Era Politics and the Transformation of American Punishment*. Oakland, CA: University of California Press, 2015. Describes how the great recession of 2008 aligned conservatives with liberals and created a new national consensus for prison reform.

Clear, Todd R., and Natasha Frost. *The Punishment Imperative: The Rise and Failure of the Great Punishment Experiment*. New York: NYU Press, 2013. Describes the basis of the "get-tough" movement and why it is ending.

Cole, George F., Christopher E. Smith, and Christina DeJong. *The American System of Criminal Justice*. 16th ed. Belmont, CA: Wadsworth, 2020. Introduces the U.S. system of criminal justice.

Gottshalk, Marie. *Caught: The Prison State and the Lockdown of American Politics*. Princeton, NJ: Princeton University Press, 2014. An appraisal of the get-tough movement in American politics and a critique of current proposals for reform.

Kubrin, Charis, and Carroll Seron, eds. *The Great Experiment: Realigning Criminal Justice in California and Beyond—The Annals of the American Academy of Political and Social Science*. Special edition, volume 664, March 2016. A series of papers analyzing California's experience with public safety realignment and its implications for reducing incarceration in other states.

Raphael, Steven, and Michael Stoll. *Why Are So Many Americans in Prison*? New York: Russell Sage Foundation, 2013. Detailed analysis of how changes in crime, law enforcement, and especially sentencing led to the unprecedented growth in the U.S. prison system.

Walker, Samuel. *Sense and Nonsense About Crime, Drugs, and Communities*. Boston, MA: Cengage, 2014. Examines crime control practices that do not work and those that have some potential for success.

NOTES

1 Danielle Kaeble and Mary Cowhig, *Correctional Populations in the United States, 2016* (Washington, DC: U.S. Bureau of Justice Statistics, 2018).
2 Jennifer Bronson and E. Ann Carson, *Prisoners in 2017* (Washington, DC: U.S. Bureau of Justice Statistics, 2018), 21.
3 The Annie E. Casey Foundation, *Nearly Six Million Kids Are Impacted by Parental Incarceration*. Baltimore, MD: Annie E. Casey Foundation, November 17, 2017.
4 Kaeble and Cowhig, *Correctional Populations*, 2018.
5 Tracy L. Snell, *Capital Punishment, 2013—Statistical Tables* (Washington, DC: U.S. Bureau of Justice Statistics, 2014).
6 The Sentencing Project, *People Serving Life Exceeds Entire Prison Population of 1970* (Washington, DC: The Sentencing Project, February 2020).

7 Dannielle Kaeble and Lauren E. Glaze, *Correctional Populations in the United States, 2016* (Washington, DC: U.S. Bureau of Justice Statistics, 2018), 4.

8 Ibid., p. 2.

9 FBI, *Uniform Crime Reports* (Washington, DC: U.S. Department of Justice, 1992, 2007, 2016); Tracey L. Snell, *Correctional Populations in the United States, 1992* (Washington, DC: U.S. Bureau of Justice Statistics, 1995).

10 Rebecca Silber, Ram Subramanian, and Maia Spotts, *Justice in Review: New Trends in State Sentencing and Corrections 2014–2015* (New York: Vera Institute of Justice, 2016).

11 Mike Ward, "TDCJ to Consider Layoffs, Prison Closures to Offset Budget Cuts," *Houston Chronicle*, August 18, 2016.

12 Dennis Schrantz, Stephen DeBor, and Marc Mauer, *Decarceration Strategies: How Five States Achieved Substantial Prison Population Reductions* (Washington, DC: The Sentencing Project, 2018).

13 Jennifer Bronson and E. Ann Carson, *Prisoners in 2019* (Washington, DC:U.S. Department of Justice, 2020)

14 Pew Public Safety Performance Project, *National Imprisonment and Crime Rates Continue to Fall* (Washington, DC: Pew Chari- table Trusts, 2016).

15 Ashley Nellis, *The Color of Justice: Racial and Ethnic Disparity in State Prisons* (Washington, DC: Sentencing Project, 2016).

16 Ibid.

17 Suzanne M. Kirchhoff, *Economic Impacts of Prison Growth* (Washington, DC: Congressional Research Service, 2010).

18 See the special issue of *Policy Today* 4 (no. 3, March 2007).

19 Bruce Western, "Recent Trends in Punitive Criminal Justice," paper prepared for the Roundtable on Punitiveness, John Jay College of Criminal Justice, April 2015.

20 Peter Wagner and Bernadette Rabuy, *Following the Money of Mass Incarceration* (Washington, DC: Prison Policy Initiative, 2017).

21 Danielle Kaeble and Lauren Glaze, *Correctional Populations in the United States, 2015* (Washington, DC: U.S. Department of Justice, 2016), 12.

22 Kaeble and Cowhig, *Correctional Populations*, 2018, p. 2.

23 Wendy Sawyer and Peter Wagner, *Mass Incarceration: The Whole Pie 2020* (Northampton, MA: Prison Policy Institute, March 24, 2020).

24 Michael Lipsky, *Street-Level Bureaucracy* (New York: Russell Sage Foundation, 1980), 3.

25 Ibid., pp. 37–38, 81, 99 (quotation from p. 81).

CHAPTER 2

The Early History of Correctional Thought and Practice

Mia2you/Shutterstock.com

Being banned for life from traveling on Royal Caribbean International cruise line may seem odd today, but banishment has a long history as a punishment for crimes.

Still a little intoxicated from a night of drinking, Nick Naydev and his buddies stood on the 11th floor balcony of the cruise ship they were vacationing on. They were docked in Nassau, Bahamas, and it was a beautiful day. As the men gathered around, Naydev climbed up onto the rail, grabbed the overhang above his head to steady himself, and looked over to one of his friends who was videoing the event. After flashing a big smile, Naydev jumped. Some of his friends laughed, apparently in disbelief. Naydev fell approximately 100 feet to the water. He hit the water hard, suffering minor injuries to his neck and tailbone. Shortly after the impact, a nearby boat fished him out of the water. Security personnel on the cruise ship, the Symphony of the Seas, contacted local authorities to report the incident. Naydev and his friends were removed from the ship soon thereafter. The men were probably relieved to learn that the local authorities were not interested in pressing charges. In fact, as Naydev told a reporter, "the police thought the whole situation was amusing."

Officials from the Royal Caribbean International cruise line did not find Naydev's stunt amusing. A Royal Caribbean spokesperson told a reporter, "This was stupid and reckless behavior and he and his companions have been banned from ever sailing with us again." Did Naydev understand the consequences associated with jumping from the cruise ship? Apparently not. In a statement released to the media, Naydev said that he did not think through the stunt. He continued, "My idea was this would be a good laugh for my friends, and I would just swim back to shore and continue my vacation and never thought this would be this serious."[1]

Banning someone from a place as form of punishment is not a new idea. In fact, it is very similar to the practice of banishment that was practiced in Europe for centuries. In England, transporting individuals convicted of crimes to another region, such as Australia, proved quite effective at dealing with overflowing prisons and houses of corrections. Banishment was also more humane than other forms of punishment. Public spectacles were popular, especially during medieval times. Crowds taunted the condemned as the executioner or sheriff conducted whippings, burnings, pilloryings, and hangings on orders of the king or court.

Punishment-as-spectacle was used to control crime and to exhibit the sovereign's power.

But in the 1800s a major change took place in Europe and the United States. Efforts were made to devise a rational, reformative model of criminal sanctions focused on the mind and soul, not the body. With the development of the penitentiary in the 1830s as a place where convicted individuals could reflect on their misdeeds, repent, and prepare for life as crime-free citizens, torture as a public spectacle disappeared. By the 1900s, punishments were carried out within prisons or in the community under the supervision of correctional staff who saw themselves not as instruments of suffering but as social workers, managers, and technicians of reform.

Like other social institutions, corrections reflects the vision and concerns of the larger community. For example, in their post–Revolutionary War idealism, Americans strongly believed that crime could be eliminated from this rich new nation if individuals who had been convicted of committing crimes were isolated from bad influences and encouraged to repent. Similarly, in the early 1900s, inspired by a new faith in the behavioral sciences, penology veered sharply toward a psychological approach to rehabilitating people who committed crimes. As crime rose in the late 1960s, public opinion demanded another shift in correctional policy, toward greater emphasis on crime control.

In this chapter we examine the broad European antecedents to U.S. correctional thought and practice. Chapter 3 will continue this historical overview through an examination of corrections in the United States from colonial times to the present. Later in the book, the history of such specific correctional practices as prison industry, probation, and parole is discussed in greater detail. Let us begin here by examining the correctional practices of earlier times.

LEARNING OBJECTIVES

After reading this chapter, you should be able to . . .

1. Describe the major forms of punishment from the Middle Ages to the American Revolution.
2. Discuss the Enlightenment and how it affected corrections.
3. Identify the contribution of Cesare Beccaria and the classical school.
4. Explain the contribution of Jeremy Bentham and the utilitarians.
5. Discuss the work of John Howard and its influence on correctional reform.

LO 1

Describe the major forms of punishment from the Middle Ages to the American Revolution.

FROM THE MIDDLE AGES TO THE AMERICAN REVOLUTION

The earliest-known comprehensive statements of prohibited behavior include the Sumerian Law of Mesopotamia (3100 B.C.E.) and the Code of Hammurabi, developed by the king of Babylon in 1750 B.C.E. These written codes were divided into sections to cover different types of offenses and contained descriptions of the punishments to be imposed on people who committed crimes. Another important ancestor of Western law is the Draconian Code, which was introduced in Greece in the seventh century B.C.E. This code was the first to erase the distinction between citizens and slaves before the law, and described legal procedures and the forms of punishment: "stoning to death; throwing the offender from a cliff; binding him to a stake so that he suffered a slow death and public abuse while dying; or the formal dedication of the offender to the gods."[2] Lesser punishments included forbidding the burial of people known to be criminally involved and also destroying their houses. In Rome the law of the Twelve Tables (450 B.C.E.) and a code compiled by Emperor Justinian in 534 C.E. helped lay the groundwork for European law. As in Greece and other ancient societies such as Egypt and Israel, Roman law-breakers were made into slaves, exiled, killed, imprisoned, and physically brutalized.[3]

In most of Europe, forms of legal sanctions that are familiar today did not appear until the 1200s. Before that time, Europeans viewed responses to crime as a private affair, with vengeance a duty to be carried out by the person wronged or by a family member. Wrongs were avenged in accordance with the **lex talionis**, or law of retaliation. This principle was the foundation of Anglo-Saxon law until the Norman conquest of England in 1066.

During the Middle Ages, the **secular law** in Europe was organized according to the feudal system.[4] In the absence of a strong central government, crimes among neighbors took on the character of war, and the public peace was endangered as feudal lords sought to avenge one another's transgressions. In response, by the year 1200 a system of **wergild**, or payment of money as compensation for a wrong, had developed in England as a way of reducing the frequency of violent blood feuds. During this period the custom of treating offenses as personal matters to be settled by individuals gradually gave way to the view that the peace of society required the public to participate in determining guilt or innocence and in exacting a penalty.

lex talionis Law of retaliation—the principle that punishment should correspond in degree and kind to the offense ("an eye for an eye and a tooth for a tooth").

secular law The law of the civil society, as distinguished from church law.

wergild "Man money"—money paid to relatives of a murdered person or to the victim of a crime to compensate them and to prevent a blood feud.

Criminal law thus focused on maintaining public order among people of equal status and wealth. Given the parties involved, the main criminal punishments were penance and the payment of fines or restitution. Lower-class individuals who were guilty of committing crimes and were without money received physical punishment at the hands of their masters.

During this same period, the church, as the dominant social institution, maintained its own system of ecclesiastical punishments, which made a great impact on society as a whole. Especially during the Inquisition of the 1300s and 1400s, the church zealously punished those who violated its laws. At the same time, it gave refuge from secular prosecution to people who could claim **benefit of clergy**. In time, benefit of clergy was extended to all literate people.

benefit of clergy The right to be tried in an ecclesiastical court, where punishments were less severe than those meted out by civil courts, given the religious focus on penance and salvation.

From the end of Middle Ages through the 1500s, the authority of government grew, and the criminal law system became more fully developed. With the rise of trade, the breakdown of the feudal order, and the emergence of a middle class, other forms of sanction were applied. In addition to fines, five punishments were most common in Europe before the 1800s: galley slavery, imprisonment, transportation, corporal punishment, and death. As we discuss later, each of these punishments had a specific purpose, and the development of each was linked to ongoing social conditions. Realize that at the time, with neither a police force nor other centralized instruments of order, deterrence was the dominant purpose of the criminal sanction. Thus, before the 1800s, people believed that one of the best ways to maintain order was to intimidate the entire population by publicly punishing convicted individuals. (See "Early Methods of Execution" to review a variety of methods once used to execute the condemned.)

galley slavery Forced rowing of large ships or galleys.

Galley Slavery

Galley slavery was the practice of forcing men to row ships. Now popularly identified with ancient Rome or Greece, galley slavery was not formally abolished throughout Europe until the mid-1700s.[5] However, by the 1500s the practice had begun to wane with the advent of heavy sailing ships. At first used exclusively for slaves or men captured in battle, galley slavery came to be the lot of some convicted men, often as a reprieve from the gallows. According to a 1602 proclamation by Queen Elizabeth I, the galleys were considered more merciful than ordinary civil punishments, even though the oarsmen might remain in chains for life.[6]

Imprisonment

Until the late Middle Ages, prisons were used primarily for the detention of people awaiting trial. In ancient times, individuals who were accused of committing crimes were incarcerated in cages, rock quarries, or even chambers underneath the Roman Forum while they awaited punishment. Short imprisonment as punishment was used in Italy, France, Germany, and England for petty crime, often for those unable to pay their fines or debts.[7] Some individuals who were placed in the medieval prison were "not cast out of urban life"; rather, they were able to roam the city as licensed beggars—debtors seeking settlement of the claims against them—who could plead with their families for sustenance. But for most convicted individuals prior to the 1800s, incarceration provided punishments far greater than mere detention.[8]

Historical Picture Archive/Corbis Historical/Getty Images

During the Middle Ages, punishments were imposed on the body of the individual. Torture was not uncommon, nor did the citizenry condemn its use.

FOCUS ON

CORRECTIONAL PRACTICE: Early Methods of Execution

Over the course of human history, a variety of methods have been used to execute the condemned. In *Discipline and Punish,* Michel Foucault provides an excellent example of medieval punishment by recounting the sentence handed down to Robert-François Damiens, who was convicted of trying to assassinate King Louis XV:

> He is to be taken and conveyed in a cart, wearing nothing but a shift, holding a torch of burning wax weighing two pounds; in the said cart to the Place de Greve, where on a scaffold that will be erected there, the flesh will be torn from his breasts, arms, thighs and calves with red-hot pinchers, his right hand, holding the knife with which he committed the said parricide, burnt with sulphur, and, on those places where the flesh will be torn away, poured molten lead, boiling oil, burning resin, wax and sulphur melted together and then his body drawn and quartered by four horses and his limbs and body consumed by fire, reduced to ashes and his ashes thrown to the winds.

Newspapers reported that Damiens's death was even more horrible than the sentence required. Because the horses were not able to pull him "limb from limb," the executioners resorted to hacking off his arms and legs while he was still alive. Although the most severe forms of executions were usually reserved for individuals convicted of treason, many medieval punishments appear unnecessarily barbaric and violate the laws of humanity by today's standards. What follows are descriptions of seven methods of execution used during centuries past. Unlike in the United States today, people who were subjected to the methods discussed here were executed in public, often in front of large crowds.

BOILED ALIVE

This form of execution involved immersing the condemned in a boiling liquid, such as water, oil, or pitch. The process varied. In some countries the condemned was tied up and immersed up to the neck in liquid that was slowly brought to a boil. In other places the knees of convicted persons were tied to their chests, after which they were tossed headfirst into the boiling liquid. Boiling was used throughout the Far East and Europe for hundreds of years. In the 1300s, executions by boiling in Germany drew considerable crowds of onlookers. In England, boiling was used for the crime of poisoning in the first half of the sixteenth century.

BROKEN ON THE WHEEL

Many variations of this method were practiced over the centuries. One approach involved stretching the condemned over a table or bench, tying him or her down, and placing a large, spiked wheel on top of the body. It was not uncommon for executioners to begin by severing one of the person's hands with an axe. After doing so, the executioner used a large iron bar or hammer to drive the wheel into the person's body, pulverizing bones and ultimately causing death. This method of execution dates back to the second century in the Roman Empire. Such methods were used well into the eighteenth century throughout Western Europe.

BURNED INTERNALLY

This form of punishment entailed pouring some form of liquid, such as boiling pitch or molten lead, down the condemned person's throat. Another approach to internal burning entailed inserting a red-hot iron rod in the person's anus. Although there are recorded instances of burning to death internally in England, this method was rarely used because it was far less fantastic a spectacle relative to hangings and beheadings.

FLAYED ALIVE

This bloody method of execution dates back to at least 200 B.C.E. It was used mostly in China and Turkey, but recorded instances of the practice in Europe also exist. This method entailed taking a sharp, scalpel-like object and methodically stripping the condemned of his or her skin while the victim was still alive. In time, death came upon the skinned person. Castration was also known to be included in this form of execution.

HANGED, DRAWN, AND QUARTERED

This form of execution, called the "three-in-one death penalty," was largely reserved for individuals who had committed the worst crime, treason. The process began by hanging the condemned for a short period of time. After being let down and while still choking and unable to speak, the traitor was stretched out on a table. The executioner, wielding a bladed instrument, would then slit open the stomach and begin removing the intestines with his hands. Sometimes this step was preceded by castration. If the traitor survived the disembowelment, the executioner would extract the heart from the chest. Bodily remnants were burned to ashes in a nearby fire. Finally, the bloody corpse was beheaded and the torso quartered. The body sections were scattered about the locale to remind residents and visitors that the cost of crime was high. This form of execution was used in England from approximately the 1500s to the early 1800s. Versions of this method were also employed in France and in colonial America.

IRON MAIDEN

This coffin-like device was typically made of wood, with a full-length portrait of a woman painted on the doors. Numerous spikes were fastened along the inside of the doors, designed to penetrate the body of the person who was placed in the contraption. Two daggers affixed to the backside of the maiden's head were intended to pierce the eyeballs. After the screaming had subsided, which could take hours, the bottom of the iron maiden would swing open so the bloody and ravaged cadaver could be removed. This method was used in Germany and Spain in the 1500s.

RACK

This tool of execution consisted of two large axles, each arranged some distance apart. The condemned would be placed in between the axles with his wrists attached by rope to the axle above the head. The ankles would be tied with rope to the axle situated near the feet. When the executioners began to turn the axles, the ropes tightened, and the condemned person's body would stretch. The device could be locked to hold the body at a particular point. Ultimately, the stretching continued to a point where the person's knees, elbows, and shoulders dislocated. The rack and similar execution devices were used throughout Europe for centuries. The rack was not used only to kill but also as a means of extracting information from those who were unwilling to divulge it. Capital punishment has been part of the U.S. criminal justice system since its inception, except for a few years in the 1970s when its use was temporarily halted. How do the methods described here compare to current methods of execution, such as the electric chair, hanging, and lethal injection? Would the execution methods used centuries ago better deter crime? Why do you suppose that these early practices were abandoned? Should the public be allowed to witness executions in the United States? Why? Why not?

Sources: Geoffrey Abbott, *Executions: A Guide to the Ultimate Penalty* (West Sussex, UK: Summersdale, 2005); Phil Clarke, Liz Hardy, and Anne Williams, *Executioners: Men and Women Who Kill for the People* (London: Futura, 2008); Michel Foucault, *Discipline and Punish* (New York: Pantheon, 1977), 4.

Conditions in these jails were appalling. Men, women, and children, healthy and sick, were locked up together. The strong preyed on the weak, there was no sanitation, and disease was epidemic. Furthermore, authorities made no provision for the upkeep of people in their custody. Often, the warden viewed his job as a business proposition, selling food and accommodations to his charges. The poor thus had to rely for survival on alms brought to them by charitable people and religious groups.

Attempts to reform prisons began in the 1500s. With the disintegration of feudalism, political power became more centralized, and economies began to shift from agriculture to manufacturing. As links to feudal landlords dissolved, the rural poor wandered about the countryside or drifted to the cities. The emphasis of the Protestant Reformation on the importance of hard work and on the sinfulness of sloth stirred European reformers to urge that some means be found to provide work for the idle poor. Out of these concerns the **house of corrections**, or "workhouse," was born.

In 1553, London's Bishop Nicholas Ridley persuaded Edward VI to donate Bridewell Palace as the first house of corrections. By 1609, each English county was required by law to provide "Bridewells," or houses of corrections. These facilities did not serve merely as a place of detention, as did the jail; they instead combined the main elements of a workhouse, poorhouse, and penal institution. Whereas jails were thought to promote idleness among the incarcerated individuals, the house of corrections was expected to instill "a habit of industry more conducive to an honest livelihood."[9] These individuals—primarily prostitutes, beggars, people convicted of minor crimes, and

FEMALE CONVICTS AT WORK, DURING THE SILENT HOUR, IN BRIXTON PRISON.
(From a Photograph by Herbert Watkins, 170, Regent Street.)

Chronicle/Alamy Stock Photo

In Brixton Prison, women worked under rules of silence during major portions of the day.

house of corrections
Detention facility that combined the major elements of a workhouse, poorhouse, and penal industry by both disciplining individuals who were housed in the facility and setting them to work.

the idle poor such as orphans and the sick—were to be disciplined and set to work. The products made in the house of corrections were to be sold on the market so that the facility would be self-sufficient and not need government subsidy. The term *Bridewell House* came to be used for all versions of the English house of corrections.

Institutions similar to the English house of corrections appeared in Holland, France, Germany, and Italy. Visiting these places in 1775, the English penal reformer John Howard was impressed by their cleanliness, discipline, and emphasis on rehabilitation through Bible study and regularity of habits. A motto carved over the doorway to one institution succinctly defined the authority of the law with regard to the individuals who were housed there: "My hand is severe but my intention benevolent." This motto continued to influence the later development of the penitentiary.

Of the European institutions, the Milan House of Correction, built in 1755, and Ghent's Maison de Force, built in 1772, attracted particular attention. The latter did so because of its design. It was an octagonal building surrounding a central yard. Eight long pavilions radiated from the center, allowing the separation of the individuals who resided there by the seriousness of the crime, by sex, or by status as a member of the noncriminal poor. The imprisoned individuals worked in common areas during the day and were segregated at night.

Conditions in England's Bridewells deteriorated as the facilities increasingly housed criminally involved people rather than the poor. By the 1700s, the labor power provided by the convicted individuals was no longer economically profitable, and the reformative aim of the institution vanished.

The Prison Act of 1865 formally joined the jail and the house of corrections. The resulting institution became known as a prison—a place of punishment for those serving terms of up to two years.[10] As we will see, elements of the houses of corrections were later incorporated into the penitentiary and the industrial prison of the nineteenth century.

Transportation

transportation The practice of transplanting individuals convicted of crimes from the community to another region or land, often a penal colony.

From ancient times, people who have disobeyed the rules of a community have been cast out, or banished (see "For Critical Thinking"). With the breakdown of feudalism and the worsening of economic conditions in the 1600s, **transportation** as punishment increased as prisons and houses of corrections in Europe filled to overflowing. The New World represented a convenient place for England to send convicted individuals.[11] For Russians transported to Siberia, transportation often meant the same as death.

By the early 1600s, the transportation of English convicted individuals to North America became economically important for the colonial companies for whom these people labored.

It also helped relieve the overcrowded prisons of England. By the close of the seventeenth century, English courts had sent about 2,300 men and women to the American colonies. The typical length of sentence was seven years.

The number of people convicted of crimes in England continued to grow. Rather than building more jails to deal with the problem, Parliament decided to increase the number of people sent to colonies with the passage of the Transportation Act of 1718. From 1718 to 1776, an estimated 52,200 English men and women were shipped to the American colonies, nearly 80 percent of whom worked in either Virginia or Maryland. Although these people provided much-needed labor, especially on tobacco farms, Virginia attempted to pass laws

FOR CRITICAL THINKING

The Naydev case discussed at the beginning of the chapter involved a private company banning someone from their cruise ships. Transportation during medieval times involved governments banning convicted people from their homeland. Consider these banishment practices within a historical context.

1. Should judges in the United States today impose banishment as a sentence? Should people be banned from towns? Counties? States? The United States? Explain your answer.
2. What are some of the possible unintended consequences that may result from the practice of banishment? Can you think of a situation where the act of banishment could cause a greater harm than the actual crime being punished?
3. Is the practice of banishment more effective if coupled with other forms of punishment, such as fines or community service? How might the type of punishment applied along with banishment differ by offense type? Would the seriousness of the offense matter?

on several occasions to prevent England from transporting them. Such attempts were always overturned by English authorities. Benjamin Franklin publicly expressed his frustration with the practice of transportation. In 1751 he famously wrote that if the colonies were not allowed to legislate against such importation, then perhaps America should reciprocate by sending shipments of rattlesnakes to England. Not all colonial leaders felt as strongly as Franklin. Indeed, in 1774 George Washington purchased convicted individuals to work on his plantation at Mount Vernon.[12] With the onset of the American Revolution, transportation from England to the colonies was halted.

By this time, questions had also been raised about the appropriateness of the practice. Some critics argued that it was unjust to send people to live in a country where their lives would be easier than at home. But perhaps more importantly, by the beginning of the 1700s American planters had discovered that African slaves were better workers and economically more profitable than the people transported by the English. The importation of black slaves increased dramatically, the prisons of England again became overcrowded, and large numbers of convicted individuals were assigned to live in **hulks** (abandoned ships) along the banks of the Thames.

hulks Abandoned ships that the English converted to hold convicted people during a period of prison crowding between 1776 and 1790.

British transportation began again in 1787, to different locales. Over the next 80 years, 160,000 people were transported from Great Britain and Ireland to New South Wales, Tasmania, and other parts of Australia. As the historian Robert Hughes explains:

> Every convict faced the same social prospects. He or she served the Crown or, on the Crown's behalf, some private person, for a given span of years. Then came a pardon or a ticket-of-leave, either of which permitted him to sell his labor freely and choose his place of work.[13]

However, in 1837 a committee of Parliament reported that, far from reforming people, transportation created thoroughly depraved societies. Critics argued that the Crown was forcing Englishmen to be "slaves until they were judged fit to become peasants."[14] The committee recommended a penitentiary system in which convicted individuals were confined and set to hard labor. This recommendation was only partially adopted; not until 1868 did all transportation from England cease.[15]

Corporal Punishment and Death

Although **corporal punishment** and death have been used throughout history, the sixteenth through eighteenth centuries in Great Britain and Europe were particularly brutal. For example, the German criminal code of 1532 specified that

corporal punishment Punishment inflicted on the convicted person's body with whips or other devices that cause pain.

> An ordinary murderer or burglar merits hanging in chains or beheading with the sword. A woman who murders her infant is buried alive and impaled, a traitor is drawn and quartered. Other grave offenders may be burned to death, or drowned, or set out to die in agony upon the wheel with their limbs smashed.[16]

Because punishment was considered a powerful general deterrent, authorities carried out sanctions in the market square for all to see. Whipping, mutilation, and branding were used extensively, and death was the common penalty for a host of felonies. For example, some 72,000 people were hanged during the reign of Henry VIII (1509–1547), and in the Elizabethan period (1558–1603), vagabonds were strung up in rows of 300–400 at a time.[17] (The modern equivalent would be 15,000–23,000 Americans strung up at once.) Capital punishment could either be a "merciful" instant death (beheading or hanging) or a prolonged death (burning alive or breaking on the wheel). As Pieter Spierenburg notes, prolonged death was practically unknown in England, "although a famous pamphlet of 1701 argued that hanging did not effectively deter potential lawbreakers."[18]

Those who were not executed faced various mutilations—removing a hand or finger, slitting the nostrils, severing an ear, or branding—so that the convicted person could be publicly identified. Such mutilation usually made it impossible for the marked individual to find honest employment. In sum, almost every imaginable torture was used in the name of retribution, deterrence, the sovereignty of the authorities, and the public good.

Hulton Archive/Getty Images

▲ *These people who were transported to Botany Bay in Australia were kept in cages for most of the months-long journey.*

The reasons for the rise in the severity of punishments during this period are unclear but are thought to reflect the expansion of criminal law, the enhanced power of secular authorities, an increase in crime (especially during the eighteenth century), and changes in the economic system. For example, the number of crimes for which the English authorized the death penalty swelled from 50 in 1688 to 160 in 1765 and reached 225 by 1800. Some new statutes made capital crimes of offenses that had previously been treated more leniently, and other laws criminalized certain activities for the first time. But the criminal law, popularly known as the Bloody Code, was less rigid than it seemed; it allowed judicial discretion, and lesser punishments were often given.[19]

London, as well as other cities, doubled in population from 1600 to 1700, although the overall population of England and Wales rose by only 25 percent. Because of the population increases and the accompanying widespread poverty, the incidence of crime in cities ballooned. The rise in the number of prosecutions and convictions may also have represented a response by government and the elite to the threat posed to public order by the suddenly outsized working-class population. As Georg Rusche and Otto Kirchheimer argue, the rise of capitalism led to economic, rather than penal, considerations as the basis for punishment.[20]

ON THE EVE OF REFORM

As noted previously, by the middle of the 1700s England was inflicting capital and corporal punishment extensively, transporting large numbers of people overseas, and facing the problem of overcrowded jails and houses of corrections; however, crime continued its upward curve. England, the most advanced and powerful country in the world, was ready for correctional reform.

At this stage, economic and social factors, particularly concerning labor, began to reshape the nature of penal sanctions. Other important influences stemmed from altered political relationships and changes in the power of the church and the organization of secular authority.

Around the same time, the revolutionaries in the American colonies, with their liberal ideas about the relationship between citizen and government and their belief in human perfectibility, were setting the stage for a shift in penal policies.

In view of all these considerations, we can arbitrarily designate 1770 as the eve of a crucial period of correctional reform on both sides of the Atlantic.

LO 2

Discuss the Enlightenment and how it affected corrections.

THE ENLIGHTENMENT AND CORRECTIONAL REFORM

During the 1700s, Western scholars and social activists, particularly in England and France, engaged in a sweeping reconception of the nature of society. In this remarkable period, known as **the Enlightenment, or the Age of Reason**, new ideas based on rationalism, the importance of the individual, and the limitations of government replaced traditional assumptions. Revolutions occurred in America and France, science made great advances, and the industrial revolution came into full swing.

the Enlightenment, or the Age of Reason A cultural movement in England and France during the 1700s, when concepts of liberalism, rationality, equality, and individualism dominated social and political thinking.

Until the 1700s, European society had generally been static and closed; individuals had their place in a hierarchy of fixed social relationships. The Enlightenment represented a liberal reaction against this feudal and monarchical tradition. The Reformation had already ended the religious monopoly held by the Catholic Church, and the writings of such Protestant thinkers as Martin Luther and John Calvin encouraged a new emphasis on individualism and the social contract between government and the governed. The triumph of William of Orange in the Glorious Revolution of 1688 brought increased power to the English Parliament, and the institutions of representative government were strengthened. The 1690 publication of John Locke's two treatises on government further developed the ideas of a liberal society, as did the writings of the French thinkers Montesquieu and Voltaire.

Finally, advances in scientific thinking led to a questioning attitude that emphasized observation, experimentation, and technological development. Sir Isaac Newton argued that the world could be known and reduced to a set of rules. The scientific revolution had a direct impact on social and political thought because it encouraged people to question established institutions, use the power of reason to remake society, and believe that progress would ultimately bring about a just community.

What impact did these political and social thinkers of the Enlightenment have on corrections? As we have emphasized, ideas about crime and justice are part of larger philosophical and scientific movements. Because of the ideas that gained prominence in the 1700s, people in America and Europe began to rethink such matters as the procedures used to determine guilt, the limits on a government's power to punish, the nature of criminal behavior, and the best ways to reform individuals who commit crimes. Specifically, they began to reconsider how criminal law should be administered and to redefine the goals and practices of corrections. During this period the classical school of criminology emerged, with its insistence on a rational link between the gravity of the crime and the severity of the punishment. Proponents of the social contract and utilitarian philosophies emphasized limitations on the power of government and proposed the need to erect a system of graduated criminal penalties to deter crime. Further, political liberals and religious groups encouraged reform of the prison system.

All these factors produced a major shift in penal thought and practice. Penal codes were rewritten to emphasize adaptation of punishment to the convicted individuals. Correctional practices moved away from inflicting pain on the body of the individual toward methods that would set the person on a path of honesty and right living. Finally, the penitentiary developed as an institution in which criminally involved people could be isolated from the temptations of society, reflect on their offenses, and thus be reformed.

BIOGRAPHY

CESARE BECCARIA (1738–1794)

Italian scholar who applied the rationalist philosophy of the Enlightenment to the criminal justice system.

Of the many individuals who actively promoted the reform of corrections, three stand out: Cesare Beccaria (1738–1794), the founder of what is now called the classical school of criminological thought; Jeremy Bentham (1748–1832), a leader of reform in England and the developer of a utilitarian approach to crime and punishment; and John Howard (1726–1790), the sheriff of Bedfordshire, England, who helped spur changes that resulted in the development of the penitentiary.

Cesare Beccaria and the Classical School

LO 3 *Identify the contribution of Cesare Beccaria and the classical school.*

The rationalist philosophy of the Enlightenment, with its emphasis on individual rights, was applied to the practices of criminal justice by the Italian scholar **Cesare Beccaria** in his 1764 book *On Crimes and Punishments*. He argued that the true aim and only justification for punishment is utility: the safety it affords society by preventing crime.[21] This was the first attempt to explain crime in secular terms instead of religious terms. The book also pointed to injustices in the administration of criminal law. In particular, Beccaria focused on the lack of a rational link between the gravity of given crimes and the severity of punishment. From this movement came **classical criminology**, with main principles as follows:

classical criminology A school of criminology that views behavior as stemming from free will, that demands responsibility and accountability of all perpetrators, and that stresses the need for punishments severe enough to deter others.

1. The basis of all social action must be the utilitarian concept of the greatest good for the greatest number of people.
2. Crime must be considered an injury to society, and the only rational measure of crime is the extent of the injury.
3. The prevention of crime is more important than punishment for crimes. To prevent crime, laws must be improved and codified so that citizens can understand and support them.
4. Secret accusations and torture must be abolished. Further, people accused of a crime have a right to speedy trials and to humane treatment before trial, as well as every right to bring forward evidence on their behalf.
5. The purpose of punishment is crime deterrence, not social revenge. Certainty and swiftness in punishment, rather than severity, best secure this goal.
6. Imprisonment should be more widely employed, and better physical quarters should be provided, with the prison population classified by age, sex, and degree of criminality.

Beccaria summarized the thinking of those who wanted to rationalize the law: "In order for punishment not to be, in every instance, an act of violence of one or many against a private citizen, it must be essentially public, prompt, necessary, the least possible in the given circumstances, proportionate to the crime, dictated by laws."[22]

Beccaria's ideas took hold especially in France; many of them were incorporated in the French Code of 1791, which ranked crimes on a scale and affixed a penalty to each. In the United States, James Wilson, the leading legal scholar of the post–Revolutionary period, credited Beccaria with having influenced his thinking, notably with regard to the deterrent function of punishment. Through Wilson, Beccaria's principles had an important effect on the reform of the penal laws of Pennsylvania, which laid the foundation for the penitentiary movement.[23]

DEA/G. CIGOLINI/De Agostini/Getty Images

Cesare Beccaria, "the father of classical criminology," became so famous for his theories that statues were erected in his honor.

Jeremy Bentham and the "Hedonic Calculus"

Jeremy Bentham, one of the most provocative thinkers and reformers of English criminal law, is best known for his utilitarian theories, often called his "hedonic calculus." Bentham claimed that one could categorize all human

In the early years of the invention of the prison, architects developed competing theories and elaborate drawings in order to depict the ideal way to carry out incarceration.

BIOGRAPHY

JEREMY BENTHAM
(1748–1832)

English advocate of utilitarianism in prison management and discipline who argued for the treatment and reform of convicted individuals.

LO 4

Explain the contribution of Jeremy Bentham and the utilitarians.

actions and, either through pleasurable (hedonic) incentives or through punishment, direct individuals to desirable activities. Supporting this idea was his concept of **utilitarianism**, the doctrine that the aim of all action should be "the greatest happiness of the greatest number." As Bentham noted, an act possesses utility "if it tends to produce benefit, advantage, pleasure, good or happiness ... or to prevent the happening of mischief, pain, evil or unhappiness to the party whose interest is considered."[24] Thus, according to Bentham, rational people behave in ways that achieve the most pleasure while bringing the least pain; they are constantly calculating the pluses and minuses of potential actions.

utilitarianism The doctrine that the aim of all action should be the greatest possible balance of pleasure over pain, hence the belief that a punishment inflicted on a person convicted of committing a crime must achieve enough good to outweigh the pain inflicted.

In Bentham's view, criminally involved individuals were somewhat childlike or unbalanced, lacking the self-discipline to control their passions by reason. Behavior was not preordained, but rather was an exercise of free will. Thus, crime was not sinful, but the result of improper calculation. Accordingly, the criminal law should be organized so that the people would derive more pain than pleasure from a wrongful act. People who considered violating the law, recognizing that legal sanctions were organized according to this scheme, would be deterred from committing antisocial acts.

Bentham sought to reform the criminal laws of England so that they emphasized deterrence and prevention. The goal was not to avenge an illegal act, but to prevent the commission of such an act in the first place. Because excessive punishment was unjustified, the punishment would be no more severe than necessary to deter crime: not "an act of wrath or vengeance," but one of calculation tempered by considerations of the social good and the needs of the convicted person.[25]

Bentham developed plans for a penitentiary based on his utilitarian principles. The design of his "panopticon," or "inspection house," called for a circular building with a glass roof and cells on each story around the circumference. This arrangement would permit a prison inspector in the center of the building to keep out of sight of the convicted people yet view their actions through a system of blinds. Panopticons were never constructed in England; they were proposed in both France and Ireland, but never adopted. Two panopticon-type prisons were actually constructed in the United States. Western State Penitentiary, modeled to some extent on Bentham's ideas, opened in Pittsburgh in 1825. The fullest expression of the style was the prison in Crest Hill, Illinois, where four circular cellhouses were built from 1916 to 1924. Described by an architect as "the most awful receptacle of gloom ever devised,"[26] the panopticon was quickly abandoned.

LO 5

Discuss the work of John Howard and its influence on correctional reform.

John Howard and the Birth of the Penitentiary

Probably no individual did more for penal reform in England than **John Howard**—county squire, social activist, and high sheriff of Bedfordshire. Like many members of the new merchant class, Howard had a social conscience and was concerned about conditions among the poor. On being appointed sheriff in 1773, he exercised the traditional but usually neglected responsibility of visiting the local prisons and institutions. He was shocked by what he saw, especially when he learned that the jailers received no regular salary but made their living from those whom they guarded and that many people who had been discharged by the grand jury or acquitted at their trials were still detained because they could not pay their discharge fees.[27]

Howard expanded his inspections to the prisons, hulks, and houses of corrections outside his jurisdiction in England, and then to those in other parts of Europe. In England the prisons were overcrowded, discipline was lacking, and sanitation was unheard of—thousands died yearly from disease. Even members of the free community feared "prison fever," for the disease often infected courthouse personnel and others in contact with the imprisoned individuals. At the time, seven years of confinement was viewed as a de facto penalty of death.

Ann Ronan Pictures/Print Collector/Getty Images

▲ *John Howard is credited with restoring the peace and persuading mutineers to return to their cells after a revolt in London's Savoy military prison in 1866.*

Howard thought that England should copy some of the prisons he had visited in Belgium, Holland, Germany, and Italy. In particular, he was favorably impressed by the separate confinement of incarcerated individuals at night after their common daytime tasks. Of the Maison de Force, in Ghent, he wrote, "The convicts were properly lodged—fed—clothed—instructed—worked. The utmost regularity, order, cleanliness prevailed; there was no drunkenness; no riot; no excessive misery; no irons, no starvation."[28]

Howard's descriptions of conditions in English penal institutions in his book *The State of Prisons in England and Wales* horrified the public. Of particular concern was the lack of discipline. After his report to the House of Commons, Howard, along with Sir William Blackstone and William Eden, drafted the Penitentiary Act of 1779, a curious amalgam of traditional and progressive ideas that greatly affected penology.

The Penitentiary Act originally called for creating houses of hard labor where people who would otherwise have faced transportation would instead be imprisoned for up to two years. The act was based on four principles set down by Howard: (1) a secure and sanitary structure, (2) systematic inspection, (3) abolition of fees, and (4) a reformatory regimen. People were to be confined in solitary cells at night but were to labor silently in common rooms during the day. The labor was to be "of the hardest and most servile kind, in which Drudgery is chiefly required and where the Work is little liable to be spoiled by Ignorance, Neglect or Obstinancy"—such work as sawing stone, polishing marble, beating hemp, and chopping rags.[29] The legislation further detailed such items as diet, uniforms, and conditions of hygiene.

Howard also helped bring about penal reform in Ireland. While touring Irish prisons in 1786–1787, Howard visited the old Kilmainham Gaol, located in Dublin. He reportedly encountered incarcerated individuals who were intoxicated. These drunkards obtained whiskey from an open window that faced the city street. Following Howard's recommendation, the County of Dublin's Grand Jury built a new prison on elevated ground to improve ventilation and help prevent fever.[30]

Perhaps influenced by his Quaker friends, Howard came to believe that the new penal institution should be a place not merely of industry but also of contrition and penance. The twofold purpose of the penitentiary was to punish and to reform convicted people through solitary confinement between intervals of work, the inculcation of good habits, and religious instruction so that individuals could reflect on their moral duties.

The Penitentiary Act and follow-up legislation passed in 1782 and 1791 attracted political support from a variety of sources. Legalists sought to deter crime, philanthropists wanted to help humanity, conservatives thought products made by imprisoned people would save money, and pragmatic politicians wanted to solve the disquieting prison situation. Philanthropists and other social reformers believed that solitary confinement was the best way to allow convicted individuals to reflect. Bentham agreed because he believed the penitentiary would help deter crime by being onerous to but not destructive of the inhabitant (see "For Critical Thinking").

FOR CRITICAL THINKING

As discussed at the beginning of the chapter, Nick Naydev was banned from all Royal Caribbean cruise ships because of his behavior (leaping about 100 feet into the water from an 11th floor balcony). Doing so will keep Naydev from pulling similar stunts again, and it should also serve as a warning to others contemplating similar actions.

1. Jeremy Bentham argued that effective punishments prevent similar behavior in the future. Do you think that banning who leap from their balconies into the water will prevent such behavior from guests in the future? Explain your answer.
2. Is the ban in the Naydev case proportionate to the seriousness of his offense? Was it unnecessary, too severe, or vengeful? What else could be done to prevent such acts in the future?

WHAT REALLY MOTIVATED CORRECTIONAL REFORM?

Was it just the humanistic concerns of the Quakers and individuals such as Bentham and Howard that prompted this era of criminal law reform, or were other forces at work as well? Apparently, reform sprang as much from the emergence of the middle class as from humanism. The new industrialists may have been concerned about the existing criminal law because, paradoxically, its harshness helped some people who committed crime escape punishment: Jurors would not convict people accused of petty property offenses for which death was prescribed. In petitions to Parliament, groups of businessmen complained that their property was not protected if people who broke the law could expect to escape punishment.[31] They wanted swift and certain sanctions, and their demands coincided with the moral indignation of Bentham, Howard, and other reformers.

Traditional scholarship on corrections has emphasized the humanitarian motives of reformers seeking a system of benevolent justice. However, other scholars have focused on the underlying economic or social factors that account for shifts in correctional policies. They do not accept the standard version that such people as Beccaria, Bentham, and Howard were motivated by concern for their fellow humans when they advocated a particular perspective on the problem of criminality. For example, the revisionists suggest that until 1700 the size of the incarcerated population in England was linked to the economic demand for workers. The penitentiary may thus represent not the product of the humanitarian instincts unleashed by the Enlightenment, but a way to discipline the working class to serve a new industrial society.

Changes took place in England's prisons, and new institutions were constructed along lines suggested by Howard and Bentham, but not until 1842, with the opening of Pentonville in North London, did the penitentiary plan come to fruition. Meanwhile, the concept of the penitentiary had traveled across the Atlantic to the new American republic.

BIOGRAPHY

JOHN HOWARD (1726–1790)

English prison reformer whose book *The State of Prisons in England and Wales* contributed greatly to the passage of the Penitentiary Act of 1779 by the House of Commons.

SUMMARY

1 Describe the major forms of punishment from the Middle Ages to the American Revolution.
From the Middle Ages to the American Revolution, corrections consisted primarily of galley slavery, imprisonment, transportation, corporal punishment, and death.

2 Discuss the Enlightenment and how it affected corrections.
In the latter part of the eighteenth century, the Enlightenment (Age of Reason) brought changes in penal policy. Rather than stressing physical punishment of the convicted individual, influential Enlightenment thinkers such as Beccaria, Bentham, and Howard sought methods for reforming people who committed crimes. The reforms were first proposed in Europe and later fully developed in America.

3 Identify the contribution of Cesare Beccaria and the classical school.
Beccaria applied the rationalist philosophy of the Enlightenment, with its emphasis on individual rights, to the practices of the criminal justice system. Beccaria set forth six principles on which his reforms were based. These principles set the foundation for the classical school of criminology.

4 Explain the contribution of Jeremy Bentham and the utilitarians.
Best known for his utilitarian theories, often called his "hedonic calculus," Bentham claimed that one could categorize all human actions. His idea of *utilitarianism* proposed that the aim of all actions was the "greatest happiness for the greatest number." Criminally involved people were somewhat childlike or unbalanced, lacking the self-discipline to control their passions.

5 Discuss the work of John Howard and its influence on correctional reform.
Howard investigated conditions in European prisons and jails. He was shocked by what he found in English correctional facilities. He rallied legislative interest in reform and was a major proponent of the penitentiary. Parliament passed the Penitentiary Act of 1779 based on Howard's principles: (1) a secure and sanitary structure, (2) systematic inspections, (3) abolition of fees, and (4) a reformatory regimen.

KEY TERMS

benefit of clergy (*p. 33*)
classical criminology (*p. 40*)
corporal punishment (*p. 37*)
galley slavery (*p. 33*)
house of corrections (*p. 36*)
hulks (*p. 37*)
lex talionis (*p. 32*)
secular law (*p. 32*)
the Enlightenment, or the Age of Reason (*p. 39*)
transportation (*p. 36*)
utilitarianism (*p. 41*)
wergild (*p. 32*)

FOR DISCUSSION

1. In what ways have changes in the social, economic, and political environment of society been reflected in correctional policies?
2. How do you suppose that the developments discussed in this chapter eventually brought about the separation of children from others in the prison system?
3. How have the interests of administrators and the organizations they manage distorted the ideals of penal reformers?
4. Some people believe the history of corrections shows a continuous movement toward more-humane treatment of convicted people as society in general has progressed. Do you agree? Why or why not?

5. How may specific underlying social factors have influenced the development of correctional philosophies?

FOR FURTHER READING

Abbott, Geoffrey. *Execution: A Guide to the Ultimate Penalty*. West Sussex, UK: Summersdale, 2005. Describes numerous execution methods that have been used over the centuries and provides information from first-hand accounts.

Cawthorne, Nigel. *Public Executions: From Ancient Rome to the Present Day*. London: Chartwell, 2006. Covers aspects of the various types of public executions used over the centuries.

Diehl, Daniel, and Mark P. Donnelly. *The Big Book of Pain: Torture and Punishment Through History*. Stoud, UK: History Press, 2009. Provides a close-up look at the many punishments and acts of torture used throughout history.

Geltner, G. *The Medieval Prison: A Social History*. Princeton, NJ: Princeton University Press, 2008. Argues that prisons existed in Europe in the thirteenth and fourteenth centuries.

Lyons, Lewis. *The History of Punishment*. London: Amber, 2003. Covers the legal codes and punishments dating from the ancient Code of Hammurabi to modern practices.

Ruhling, Erik. *Infernal Device: Machinery of Torture and Execution*. New York: Disinformation, 2007. Features photographs and artistic renderings of the devices used to inflict pain and end life.

NOTES

1 Amy B. Wang, "A Man Jumped Off a Cruise Ship as a Joke. Royal Caribbean Has Banned Him for Life," https://www.washingtonpost.com/transportation/2019/01/18/man-jumped-off-cruise-ship-joke-royal-caribbean-has-banned-him-life/.

2 Edward M. Peters, "Prisons Before the Prison: The Ancient and Medieval Worlds," in *The Oxford History of the Prison*, edited by Norval Morris and Michael Tonry (New York: Oxford University Press, 1995), 5.

3 Ibid., pp. 3–47.

4 Pieter Spierenburg, *The Spectacle of Suffering* (New York: Cambridge University Press, 1984), 14.

5 Pieter Spierenburg, "The Body and the State: Early Modern Europe," in *The Oxford History of the Prison,* edited by Norval Morris and David J. Rothman (New York: Oxford University Press, 1995), 75.

6 For a description of the treatment of galley slaves, see George Ives, *A History of Penal Methods* (Montclair, NJ: Patterson Smith, 1970), 104.

7 John H. Langbein, "The Historical Origins of the Sanction of Imprisonment for Serious Crime," *Journal of Legal Studies* 5 (1976): 37.

8 G. Geltner, *The Medieval Prison: A Social History* (Princeton, NJ: Princeton University Press, 2008), 4; Peters, "Prisons Before the Prison." See also Roger Matthews, *Doing Time: An Introduction to the Sociology of Imprisonment* (New York: St. Martin's, 1999), 5–9.

9 Adam J. Hirsch, *The Rise of the Penitentiary* (New Haven, CT: Yale University Press, 1992), 14.

10 Matthews, *Doing Time*, p. 8.

11 A. Roger Ekirch, *Bound for America: The Transportation of British Convicts to the Colonies 1718–1775* (New York: Oxford University Press, 1987).

12 Emily Jones Salmon, "Convict Labor During the Colonial Period," *Encyclopedia Virginia,* www.encyclopediavirginia.org/Convict_Labor_During_the_Colonial_Period, November 21, 2013.

13 Robert Hughes, *The Fatal Shore* (New York: Knopf, 1987), 282.

14 Ibid.

15 Ibid., p. 162.

16 Langbein, "Historical Origins," p. 40.

17 Georg Rusche and Otto Kirchheimer, *Punishment and Social Structure* (New York: Russell & Russell, [1939] 1968), 19.

18 Spierenburg, "The Body and the State," p. 54.

19 Michael Ignatieff, *A Just Measure of Pain* (New York: Pantheon, 1978), 27.

20 Rusche and Kirchheimer, *Punishment and Social Structure,* p. 96.

21 Mark M. Lanier and Stuart Henry, *Essential Criminology* (Boulder, CO: Westview, 1998), 67.

22 Harry E. Barnes and Negley K. Teeters, *New Horizons in Criminology* (New York: Prentice-Hall, 1944), 461.

23 Francis Edward Devine, "Cesare Beccaria and the Theoretical Foundation of Modern Penal Jurisprudence," *New England Journal of Prison Law* 7 (1981): 8.

24 Gilbert Geis, "Jeremy Bentham," in *Pioneers in Criminology*, edited by Herman Mannheim (Montclair, NJ: Patterson Smith, 1973), 54.
25 Ignatieff, *Just Measure of Pain*, p. 27.
26 Geis, "Jeremy Bentham," p. 65.
27 Anthony Babington, *The English Bastille* (New York: St. Martin's, 1971), 103.
28 Barnes and Teeters, *New Horizons in Criminology*, p. 481.
29 Ignatieff, *Just Measure of Pain*, p. 93.
30 Pat Cooke, *A History of Kilmainham Gaol, 1796–1924* (Dublin: Office of Public Works, 1995), 7.
31 Michael Russigan, "A Reinterpretation of Criminal Law Reform in Nineteenth-Century England," *Journal of Criminal Justice* 8 (1980): 205.

CHAPTER 3

The History of Corrections in America

dpa picture alliance/Alamy Stock Photo

During the COVID-19 pandemic, prison industries at many institutions started manufacturing personal protective equipment to help combat the virus.

A MAN WEARING GLOVES AND A FACE MASK HUNCHES OVER A SEWING MACHINE, CAREFULLY STITCHING WHITE FABRIC TOGETHER. He and his co-workers are making masks and other protective clothing for criminal justice personnel and first responders to help slow the spread of COVID-19. As employees in a garment shop, these men are especially well positioned to provide much needed protective clothing to combat the virus.

Some people may be surprised to learn that these men are not employees of a traditional clothing factory. Rather, they work for Delaware Correctional Industries (DCI) and are incarcerated at the James T. Vaughn Correctional Center. The DCI employs approximately 4,200 incarcerated individuals who are paid between 25 cents and $2 per hour. DCI provides those incarcerated in Delaware's facilities with opportunities to develop marketable skills that individuals can put to use upon release. Once the shop reaches full capacity, the DCI expects they will produce 500 face masks each week. Commissioner Claire DeMatteis, who heads the state's Department of Corrections, noted that "this initiative by correctional officers and offenders demonstrates that we all want to do our part to help slow the spread of COVID-19."[1]

America gave the world its first penitentiary, an institution created to reform people convicted of committing crimes within an environment designed to focus their full attention on their moral rehabilitation. An important element in early American prisons was labor done by the people imprisoned there. To the Quakers in Pennsylvania, solitary work was viewed as necessary for reforming wayward men. New York prison officials saw labor by those imprisoned not only as a way to reform inhabitants but also as a way to finance prison operations. The use of the penitentiary reflected a major shift in correctional practice away from the brutal public punishments that had once occurred with some regularity. Ideas about both human nature and the purpose of punishment had changed dramatically as well. Although the work of Cesare Beccaria and others affected penal policies throughout much of the Western world, American correctional institutions and practices have developed in decidedly American ways by responding to social and political pressures within the United States.

This chapter surveys the historical changes in correctional thought and practices in the United States. We focus on seven periods: the colonial period, the arrival of the penitentiary, the reformatory movement, the Progressive movement, the medical model, the community model, and the crime control model. As each period is discussed, we emphasize the ways in which correctional goals reflected ideas current at the time.

LEARNING OBJECTIVES

After reading this chapter, you should be able to . . .

1. Describe "The Great Law" of Pennsylvania and note its importance.
2. Compare and contrast the basic assumptions of the penitentiary systems of Pennsylvania and New York.
3. Discuss the elements of the Cincinnati Declaration.
4. Identify the reforms advocated by the Progressives.
5. Discuss the assumptions of the medical model regarding the nature of criminal behavior and its correction.
6. Illustrate how the community model reflected the social and political values of the 1960s and 1970s.
7. Describe the forces and events that led to the present crime control model.

LO 1

Describe "The Great Law" of Pennsylvania and note its importance.

THE COLONIAL PERIOD

During the colonial period most Americans lived under laws and practices transferred from England and adapted to local conditions. In New England the Puritans maintained a strict society, governed by religious principles, well into the middle of the eighteenth century, and they rigorously punished violations of religious laws. As in England, banishment, corporal punishment, the pillory, and death were the common penalties. In 1682, with the arrival of **William Penn**, Pennsylvania adopted "The Great Law," which was based on humane Quaker principles and emphasized hard labor in a house of correction as punishment for most crimes. Death was reserved for premeditated murder. The Great Law survived until 1718, when it was replaced by the Anglican Code, which was already in force in other colonies. The latter code listed 13 capital offenses, with larceny the only felony not punishable by death. Whipping, branding, mutilation, and other corporal punishments were prescribed for other offenses, as were fines. Enforcement of this code continued throughout the colonies until the Revolution.

Unlike England, with its crowded hulks, jails, and houses of correction, the colonies seldom used institutions for confinement.[2] Instead, banishment, fines, death, and the other punishments just mentioned were the norm. As David Rothman writes, the death penalty was common:

> The New York Supreme Court in the pre–Revolutionary era regularly sentenced criminals to death, with slightly more than twenty percent of all its penalties capital ones. When magistrates believed that the fundamental security of the city was in danger, as in the case of a slave revolt in 1741, the court responded with great severity (burning to death thirteen of the rebellion's leaders and hanging nineteen others). Even in less critical times the court had frequent recourse to the scaffold for those convicted of pickpocketing, burglary, robbery, counterfeiting, horse stealing, and grand larceny as well as murder.[3]

BIOGRAPHY

WILLIAM PENN (1644–1718)

English Quaker who arrived in Philadelphia in 1682. Succeeded in getting Pennsylvania to adopt "The Great Law," which emphasized hard labor in a house of correction as punishment for most crimes.

Jails held people awaiting court action or unable to pay their debts. Only rarely were convicted individuals jailed for their whole sentences; the stocks, whipping post, or gallows were the places for punishment. Punishments were public spectacles because "rubbing the noses of offenders in the community context was an essential part of the process of ripping and healing, which criminal justice was supposed to embody."[4] In keeping with the Calvinist doctrine of pre-destination, little thought was given to reforming criminally involved individuals; such people were considered naturally depraved.[5]

THE ARRIVAL OF THE PENITENTIARY

Bettmann/Getty Images

Until the 1800s, Americans followed the European practice of relying upon punishments that were physically brutal, such as flogging and branding.

Until the beginning of the 1800s, America remained sparsely populated and predominantly rural. In 1790 the entire population numbered less than four million, and no city had more than 50,000 inhabitants. By 1830 the rural population had more than doubled, and the urban population had more than tripled. Growth was accompanied by rapid social and economic changes that affected all aspects of life. Colonial life had been oriented toward the local community: Everyone knew everyone else, neighbors helped one another as needed, and the local clergy and the elite maintained social control. In the nineteenth century, however, social problems could no longer be handled with the help of neighbors. In an increasingly heterogeneous urban and industrial society, responsibility for the poor, insane, and criminal became the province of the state and its institutions.

With the Revolution, the ideas of the Enlightenment gained currency (see Chapter 2), and a new concept of criminal punishment came to the fore. This correctional philosophy, based on the ideas of Beccaria, Bentham, and Howard, coincided with the ideals of the Declaration of Independence, which took an optimistic view of human nature and a belief in each person's perfectibility.[6] Social progress was thought possible through reforms to match the dictates of "pure reason." Emphasis also shifted from the assumption that deviance was part of human nature to a view that crime was caused by forces in the environment. The punitive colonial penal system based on retribution was thus held to be incompatible with the idea of human perfectibility.

Reformers argued that if Americans were to become committed to the humane and optimistic ideal of human improvability, they had to remove barbarism and vindictiveness from penal codes and make reformation of the criminally involved the primary goal of punishment. Thomas Jefferson and other leaders of the new republic worked to liberalize the harsh penal codes of the colonial period. Pennsylvania led the way with new legislation that sought "'to reclaim rather than destroy,' 'to correct and reform the offenders,' rather than simply to mark or eliminate them."[7] Several states, including Connecticut (1773), Massachusetts (1785), New York (1796), and Pennsylvania (1786), added incarceration with hard labor as an alternative to such public punishments as whippings and the stocks.

Incarceration, in the tradition of the English workhouse, developed in the immediate aftermath of the Revolution. The **penitentiary**, as conceptualized by the English reformers and their American Quaker allies, first appeared in 1790, when part of Philadelphia's Walnut Street Jail was converted to allow separate confinement. The penitentiary differed markedly from the prison, house of correction, and jail. It was conceived as a place where convicted individuals could be isolated from the bad influences of society and from one another so that, while engaged in productive labor, they could reflect on their past misdeeds, repent, and be reformed. As the word *penitentiary* indicates, reformers hoped that while people were being punished, they would become penitent, see the error of their ways, and wish to place themselves on the right path. They could then reenter the community as useful citizens.

penitentiary An institution intended to isolate individuals convicted of a crime from society and from one another so that they could reflect on their past misdeeds, repent, and thus undergo reformation.

LO 2

Compare and contrast the basic assumptions of the penitentiary systems of Pennsylvania and New York.

The American penitentiary attracted the world's attention, and the concept was incorporated at Millbank and Pentonville in England and in various other locales in Europe. By 1830, foreign observers were coming to America to see this innovation in penology; France sent Alexis de Tocqueville and Gustave Auguste de Beaumont, England sent William Crawford, and Prussia sent Nicholas Julius. By the middle of the century, the U.S. penitentiary in its various forms—especially the Pennsylvania and New York systems—had become world famous.

The Pennsylvania System

As in England, U.S. Quakers set about to implement their humanistic and religious ideas in the new nation; in Philadelphia their efforts came to fruition. For Quakers, penance and silent contemplation could allow one to move from the state of sin toward perfection. The penitentiary thus provided a place where individuals, left on their own, could be reformed.

Quakers were among the Philadelphia elite who in 1787 formed the reformist Society for Alleviating the Miseries of Public Prisoners. Under the Quaker leadership of **Benjamin Rush** and others, including Benjamin Franklin, the society urged that capital and corporal punishment be replaced with incarceration. Members of the Society had communicated with John Howard, and their ideals in many ways reflected his.

BIOGRAPHY

BENJAMIN RUSH
(1745–1813)

Physician, patriot, signer of the Declaration of Independence, and social reformer, Rush advocated the penitentiary as a replacement for capital and corporal punishment.

In 1790 the Society was instrumental in passing legislation almost identical to England's Penitentiary Act of 1779. The 1790 law specified that an institution was to be established in which "solitary confinement to hard labour and a total abstinence from spirituous liquors will prove the most effectual means of reforming these unhappy creatures."[8]

To implement the new legislation, the existing three-story Walnut Street Jail in Philadelphia was expanded in 1790 to include a "Penitentiary House" for the solitary confinement of "hardened and atrocious offenders." The plain stone building housed eight cells on each floor and had an attached yard. Each cell was dark and small—only 6 feet long, 8 feet wide, and 9 feet high. From a small grated window high on the outside wall, captives "could perceive neither heaven nor earth." Those held captive were classified by offense: Individuals deemed too dangerous were placed in solitary confinement without labor; the others worked together in shops during the day under a strict rule of silence and were confined separately at night.[9]

The Walnut Street Jail soon became unmanageable, with crowding a major issue. At one point, upwards of 40 people were housed together in cells measuring 18 square feet.[10] The legislature approved construction of additional institutions for the state: Western Penitentiary on the outskirts of Pittsburgh and Eastern State Penitentiary in Cherry Hill, near Philadelphia.

separate confinement A penitentiary system developed in Pennsylvania in which each convicted individual was held in isolation from other people, with all activities, including craft work, carried on in the cells.

The opening of Eastern State Penitentiary in 1829 marked the full development of the penitentiary system based on **separate confinement**. Eastern was designed by John Haviland, an English immigrant and an acquaintance of John Howard. The newly constructed facility was described at the time as "the most imposing in the United States."[11] Cell blocks extended from a central hub like the spokes of a wheel. Individual cells measured 12 by 8 by 10 feet and had an attached 18-foot-long exercise yard. Cells were furnished with a fold-up metal bedstead, a simple toilet, a wooden stool, a workbench, and eating utensils. Light came from an 8-inch window in the ceiling; the window could be blocked to plunge the cell into darkness as a disciplinary measure. The inhabitants did not see peers; in fact, their only human contact was the occasional visit of a clergyman or prison official.[12] Solitary labor, Bible reading, and reflection on their own behavior were viewed as the keys to providing the imprisoned with the opportunity to repent.

In the years between Walnut Street and Eastern, other states had adopted aspects of the Pennsylvania system. Separate confinement was introduced by Maryland in 1809, by Massachusetts in 1811, by New Jersey in 1820, and by Maine in 1823, but Eastern was the fullest expression of the concept of rehabilitation through separate confinement.

As described by Robert Vaux, one of the original reformers, the Pennsylvania system was based on the following principles:

1. People would not be treated vengefully but should be convinced that through hard and selective forms of suffering they could change their lives.
2. Solitary confinement would prevent further corruption inside prison.
3. In isolation, individuals would reflect on their transgressions and repent.
4. Solitary confinement would be punishment because humans are by nature social beings.
5. Solitary confinement would be economical because people would not need long periods of time to repent; therefore, fewer keepers would be needed, and the costs of clothing would be lower.[13]

CHARLES PHELPS CUSHING/ClassicStock/Alamy Stock Photo

Located outside Philadelphia, Eastern State Penitentiary became the model of the Pennsylvania system of "separate confinement." The building was designed to ensure that each inhabitant remained separated from all human contact so that he could reflect on his misdeeds.

The Pennsylvania system of separate confinement soon became controversial. Within five years of its opening, Eastern endured the first of several investigations carried out over the years by a judicially appointed board of inspectors. The reports revealed that the goal of separate confinement was not fully observed, that physical punishments were used to maintain discipline, and that some convicted individuals suffered mental breakdowns because of the isolation. Eastern was also the target of allegations much more scandalous than merely not following established separate confinement protocol: A report published in 1835 claimed that prison officials regularly used convicted individuals as servants, that widespread theft of prison property (especially food) occurred, and that there were "wild parties and illicit sexual relationships involving staff and possibly inmates."[14] Separate confinement declined by the 1860s, when crowding required doubling up in each cell, yet it was not abolished in Pennsylvania until 1913.[15]

The New York (Auburn) System

Faced with overcrowded facilities such as Newgate Prison, in 1816 the New York legislature authorized a new state prison in Auburn. Influenced by the reported success of the separate confinement of some people in the Walnut Street Jail, the New York building commission decided to erect a portion of the new facility on that model and to authorize an experiment to test its effectiveness. The concept proved a failure—sickness, insanity, and suicide increased markedly. The practice was discontinued in 1824, and the governor pardoned those then held in solitary.

In 1821 **Elam Lynds** was installed as warden at Auburn. Instead of duplicating the complete isolation practiced in Pennsylvania, Lynds worked out a new **congregate system** whereby inhabitants were held in isolation at night but congregated in workshops during the day. Individuals were forbidden to talk or even to exchange glances while on the job or at meals. Lynds was convinced that convicted individuals were incorrigible and that industrial efficiency should be the overriding purpose of the prison. He instituted a reign of discipline and obedience that included the lockstep and the wearing of prison stripes. Furthermore, he considered it "impossible to govern a large prison without a whip. Those who know human nature from books only may say the contrary."[16]

BIOGRAPHY

ELAM LYNDS (1784–1855)

A former army officer, Lynds was appointed warden of the newly opened Auburn prison in 1821. He developed the congregate system and a regimen of strict discipline. Prison inhabitants were known only by their number, wore striped clothing, and moved in lockstep. In 1825 he was commissioned to oversee construction at Ossining (Sing Sing), New York.

congregate system A penitentiary system developed in Auburn, New York, in which prison inhabitants were held in isolation at night but worked with others during the day under a rule of silence.

Interim Archives/Archive Photos/Getty Images

▲ *Early prisons emphasized a congregate system of discipline, obedience, and work. The aim was to teach convicted individuals to submit to authority.*

Whereas people held in the Pennsylvania penitentiaries worked in their cells, those in New York were employed in workshops both as therapy and as a way to finance the institution. Labor for profit through a **contract labor system** became an essential part of Auburn and other northeastern penitentiaries. Through this system of "free" labor, the state negotiated contracts with manufacturers, which then delivered raw materials to the prison for conversion into finished goods. By the 1840s, Auburn was producing footwear, barrels, carpets, carpentry tools, harnesses, furniture, and clothing. During this period, convicted individuals also built the new prison at Ossining-on-the-Hudson (Sing Sing). Wardens that adopted the New York (often called Auburn) system seemed to be more concerned with instilling good work habits and thus preventing recidivism (relapse into crime) than with rehabilitating people.

Debating the Systems

Throughout this era the preferred structure of prison systems was hotly debated. Advocates of both the Pennsylvania and the New York plans argued on public platforms and in the nation's periodicals over the best methods of punishment (see Table 3.1). Underlying the debates were questions about disciplining citizens in a democracy and maintaining conformity to social norms in a society that emphasized individualism. Participants included some of the leading figures of the time. As each state considered new penal construction, it joined the debate.

contract labor system A system under which the labor of convicted individuals was sold on a contractual basis to private employers that provided the machinery and raw materials with which prison residents made salable products in the institution.

What divided the two camps was the way in which reformation was to be brought about. Proponents of the New York system maintained that prison residents first had to be "broken" and then socialized by means of a rigid discipline of congregate but silent labor. Advocates of Pennsylvania's separate system rejected such harshness and, following Howard, renounced physical punishments and any other form of human degradation. The New Yorkers countered that their system cost less, efficiently tapped an available labor source, and developed individuals who would eventually be able to return to the community with the discipline necessary for the industrial age. The Pennsylvanians responded that New York had sacrificed the principal goal of the penitentiary (reformation) to the accessory goal (cost-effectiveness) and contended that exploiting individuals convicted of committing crimes through large-scale industry failed to promote the work ethic and only embittered them.

The Pennsylvania model looked back to an earlier, crafts-oriented, religious society, whereas the New York model looked forward to the emerging industrial age. John Conley argues that the Pennsylvania model lost out because it embraced an outdated labor system. In contrast, the New York system was consistent with the new demands and challenges of

TABLE 3.1 Comparison of Pennsylvania and New York (Auburn) Prison Systems

Goal		Implementation	Method	Activity
Pennsylvania (Separate System)	Redemption through the well-ordered routine of the prison	Isolation, penance, contemplation, labor, silence	Individuals are kept in their cells for eating, sleeping, and working.	Bible reading, working on crafts in cell
New York (Auburn) (Congregate System)	Redemption through the well-ordered routine of the prison	Strict discipline, obedience, labor, silence	Individuals sleep in their cells but come together to eat and work.	Working together in shops making goods to be sold by the state

factory production, which "would provide the state with a means of exploiting the labor of inmates to defray the expenses of the institution and possibly earn a profit for the state."[17] In this sense Auburn served as forerunner of the industrial prison that would dominate until the rise of organized labor in the twentieth century (see "For Critical Thinking").

In addition to clarifying some hazy issues in the writings of Bentham and Howard, this debate contributed to decisions in several states and in Europe about the design and management of penitentiaries. Most European visitors favored the Pennsylvania model, and the First International Prison Congress, held in 1846 in Germany, endorsed it by a large majority. The separate confinement system was soon incorporated in correctional facilities in Germany, France, Belgium, and Holland.

Initially, many American states—New York in 1797, Massachusetts in 1805, and New Jersey in 1836—built penitentiaries with at least a portion devoted to separate confinement, but within a few years of opening they had all shifted to the New York style. By 1840, hard labor organized under the contract system achieved dominance in northeastern penitentiaries.[18]

As prison populations increased, the Pennsylvania system proved too expensive. In addition, the public became concerned by reports that some convicted individuals were going insane because they could not endure long-term solitary confinement. Designs for penitentiary construction during the nineteenth century almost entirely followed the New York model (see Figure 3.1). Yet not until the end of that century did Pennsylvania,

FOR CRITICAL THINKING

We opened this chapter by discussing Delaware Correctional Industries (DCI). This program employs incarcerated individuals who work many different jobs, using different types of tools and machinery. Having incarcerated individuals perform work has been common ever since the first U.S. penitentiary opened. However, the way in which such individuals perform their work has changed over the years.

1. Recall that the separate confinement system in Pennsylvania had people involved in "productive labor" alone in their cells. Could the DCI's garment factory coordinate its confined labor force using the separate confinement system? Explain your answer.
2. In the New York system, prison inhabitants were employed in workshops but were forbidden to talk to one another. To enforce this rule, Warden Elam Lynds advocated using a whip. Would a rule of silence help DCI employees work more efficiently? Because the use of a whip would not be tolerated today, how would you enforce such a rule? What would Elam Lynds think of DCI?
3. How are the people incarcerated in today's prisons different from those who were once confined in the Pennsylvania and New York systems during the early 1800s? How might these differences influence prison work programs? Could a work program be effective for all prison inhabitants regardless of the historical time period? What would such a work program look like?

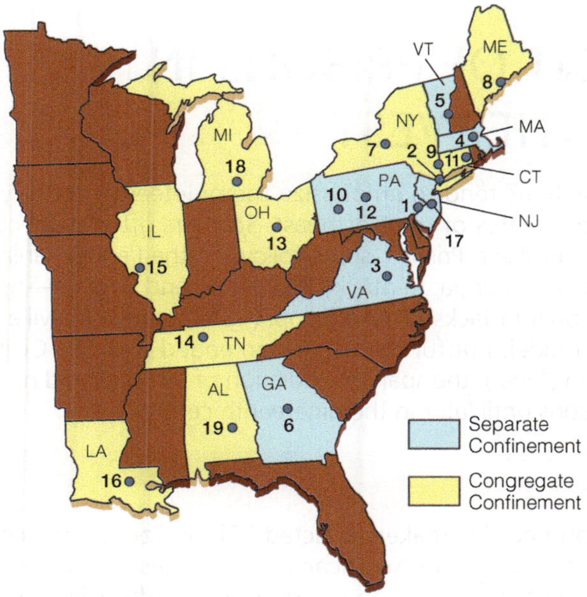

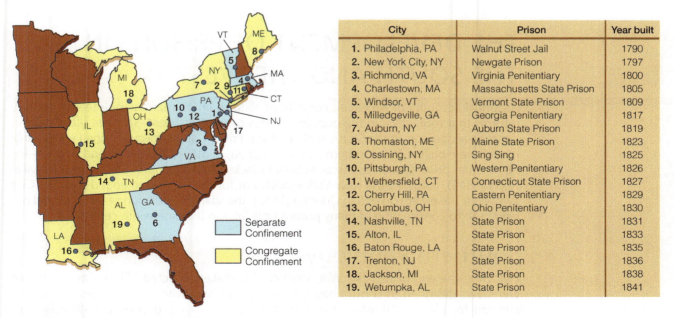

City	Prison	Year built
1. Philadelphia, PA	Walnut Street Jail	1790
2. New York City, NY	Newgate Prison	1797
3. Richmond, VA	Virginia Penitentiary	1800
4. Charlestown, MA	Massachusetts State Prison	1805
5. Windsor, VT	Vermont State Prison	1809
6. Milledgeville, GA	Georgia Penitentiary	1817
7. Auburn, NY	Auburn State Prison	1819
8. Thomaston, ME	Maine State Prison	1823
9. Ossining, NY	Sing Sing	1825
10. Pittsburgh, PA	Western Penitentiary	1826
11. Wethersfield, CT	Connecticut State Prison	1827
12. Cherry Hill, PA	Eastern Penitentiary	1829
13. Columbus, OH	Ohio Penitentiary	1830
14. Nashville, TN	State Prison	1831
15. Alton, IL	State Prison	1833
16. Baton Rouge, LA	State Prison	1835
17. Trenton, NJ	State Prison	1836
18. Jackson, MI	State Prison	1838
19. Wetumpka, AL	State Prison	1841

FIGURE 3.1 Early Prisons in the United States

Source: Norman Johnston, *Forms of Constraint: A History of Prison Architecture* (Urbana: University of Illinois Press, 2000).

FOCUS ON

CORRECTIONAL POLICY: From Eastern State to Pelican Bay: The Pendulum Swings

Eastern State Penitentiary holds the distinction of being the first correctional institution in the world based on the system of separate confinement. When it opened in 1829, men were held in their own cell for the duration of their sentence. Food was passed through a slot in the cell door, there was a small window to let in light, and each man could use the exercise yard attached to the cell. There was no opportunity for human contact except for occasional visits from the chaplain or prison officials. The purpose of these arrangements was to allow the prison inhabitant time to reflect on his misdeeds and, through penitence, correct his life without the distractions of other convicted individuals or the outside world. Not surprisingly, many people held under these conditions of solitary confinement went mad. In 1890 the U.S. Supreme Court condemned the Pennsylvania system, noting that a considerable number of convicted individuals became insane, others committed suicide, and still others survived the ordeal but were not reformed. By the twentieth century, long-term solitary confinement was considered cruel and ineffective.

When the United States experienced a rise in crime in the 1970s, the punishment pendulum swung away from the rehabilitation emphasis of the 1950s toward a much more punitive approach with longer sentences of incarceration. Beginning in the 1980s, solitary confinement roared back into correctional practice. During the 1990s, a number of states and the Federal Bureau of Prisons built "super-max" prisons to hold the most disruptive, violent, and incorrigible individuals. Unlike Pennsylvania's Eastern State Penitentiary, the super-max prison is designed not to transform the person but to contain his behavior.

California's Pelican Bay institution and the federal penitentiary in Florence, Colorado, are examples of prisons designed to hold the "worst of the worst." As with Eastern State Penitentiary, individuals in super-max facilities spend up to 23 hours a day in their 8-by-10-foot concrete cells, in silence and with little human contact. They are shackled whenever they are taken out of their cells—during recreation, showers, and weekend visits (conducted through security glass). Many of the super-max facilities have had to add mental health units to deal with those whose minds deteriorate under the conditions of isolation first used at Eastern and now continued at super-max institutions.

Are there differences between Pennsylvania's separate confinement policy and today's super-max prisons? Should we expect this new approach to succeed where the similar policies of the 1830s failed?

the birthplace of the penitentiary, finally convert to the congregate system. In 1971 Eastern State Penitentiary closed. (See "From Eastern State to Pelican Bay: The Pendulum Swings.")

THE DEVELOPMENT OF PRISONS IN THE SOUTH AND THE WEST

Historical accounts of American corrections tend to emphasize the nineteenth-century reforms that took place in the populous states of the Northeast. Scholars often neglect penal developments in the South and the West. Prisons, some following the Pennsylvania model, were built in four southern states—Georgia, Kentucky, Maryland, and Virginia—by 1817. Later prisons, such as the ones built in Jackson, Mississippi (1842), and Huntsville, Texas (1848), followed the New York model. But further expansion ended with the Civil War. With the exception of San Quentin (1852), the sparse population of the West did not lend itself to construction of many prisons until later in the nineteenth century.

Southern Penology

Following the end of the Civil War, southern lawmakers enacted "Black Codes," which were laws designed to control newly freed African Americans. Such codes established curfews for blacks and made it a crime for them to own a gun or use offensive language around white women.[19] Freed slaves and their descendants were also subject to vagrancy laws that required all individuals to give proof of employment at a moment's notice. Unemployment among all southern men following the Civil War was extremely high, but it was primarily black men who were subjected to the enforcement of vagrancy laws. Once arrested, these men enjoyed almost no rights afforded to arrestees today, such as legal representation.[20] Any conviction, regardless of the crime committed, resulted in harsh punishments.

lease system A system under which people who were convicted of crimes were leased to contractors who provided these individuals with food and clothing in exchange for their labor. In southern states they worked in mines, lumber camps, and factories, and on farms as field laborers.

Because of the devastation of the war and depression in the agriculturally based economy, funds to construct new prisons were scarce. At the same time, southerners faced the task of rebuilding their communities and economy. Given these challenges, a large labor force made up of convicted individuals, and the states' need for revenue, southern states saw the development of the **lease system**. Under this system, imprisoned individuals (most of whom were African Americans) were leased to large corporations, small-time entrepreneurs, and local farmers. Those doing the leasing agreed to pay off these men's fines and fees.[21]

Originating in Massachusetts in 1798, the leasing of convicted individuals to private entities took hold in the South first in Kentucky (1825) and later in other states. Businesses in need of workers could negotiate with the state for the labor and care of these people. This was particularly true in Alabama, Arkansas, Florida, Georgia, Louisiana, and Mississippi.[22] In 1866 Alabama turned over the state prison to a contractor that used the labor of inhabitants to build a railroad through the heart of the state's mineral region.[23] Texas leased the residents of Huntsville Penitentiary to a firm that used them as laborers on railroad construction, wood milling, and cotton picking.[24] As Edgardo Rotman notes, the entities who leased black individuals serving time in prison, "hav[e] no ownership interest in them, exploited them even worse than slaves."[25] Diseases such as tuberculosis and pneumonia regularly sickened and killed large numbers of these people. Accidents and homicides resulted in the deaths of others. As such, death rates soared. Convicted individuals were usually buried in shallow graves around work sites.[26] (See "Do the Right Thing.") The South's agrarian economy and the great number of imprisoned African Americans also provided the basis for state-run plantations that grew crops to feed the prison population and to sell on the market.

Large-scale penal farms developed mainly in the latter half of the century, particularly in Louisiana, Mississippi, and Texas. Upset by the failure of authorities to collect profits from the lessees, the people of Mississippi adopted a constitutional provision to end all contracts by 1895. Prison officials then purchased the 15,000-acre Parchman Farm, which served for many at the time as a model for southern penology.[27] In many southern states, penal farms remain a major part of corrections.

DO THE RIGHT THING

It is 1887. As a legislator, you must vote on a bill to extend or end the contract allowing the Natchez Coal and Mining Company to lease convicted individuals from the state of Mississippi. You know that the contract brings money into the state treasury and relieves the prison system by housing, feeding, and guarding the more than 800 men who are leased to the mining company. But you also know that the working conditions are horrendous and that the death rate is high. Tales of guards beating the men have become a major issue in the state, and journalists have uncovered corruption in the decision to award the contract to the company.

WRITING ASSIGNMENT: Should you vote to extend the leasing contract? What facts might influence you to vote one way or the other? Write a letter to your constituents explaining your position.

Underwood Archives/Archive Photos/Getty Images

Following the Civil War, southern states leased their prisoners to private entrepreneurs to be used as field hands, railroad builders, loggers, and miners.

Western Penology

Settlement in the West did not take off until the California Gold Rush of 1849; only during the latter half of the nineteenth century did most western states enter the Union. Except in California, the prison ideologies of the East did not greatly influence penology in the West. Prior to statehood, people were held in territorial facilities or in federal military posts and prisons. Until Congress passed the Anti-Contract Law of 1887, which restricted the employment of people convicted of federal crimes, leasing programs were used extensively in California, Montana, Oregon, and Wyoming. In their eagerness to become states, some of the last of the territories included anticontract provisions in their new state constitutions.[28]

In 1850 California became the first western state to be admitted to the Union. The old Spanish jails had become inadequate during the Gold Rush, and, "following frontier traditions," the care of convicted people was placed in the hands of a lessee. In 1852 the lessee chose Point San Quentin, a spit of land surrounded by water on three sides. Using the newly acquired labor force, the lessee built two prison buildings. In 1858, when San Quentin became overcrowded and reports of deaths, escapes, and the brutal discipline of the guards came to public attention, the state took over the facility.[29]

The Oregon territory erected a log prison structure in the 1850s, but with rumors of official corruption, it was soon leased to a private company. On joining the Union in 1859, the state discontinued the lease system. In 1866 the legislature decided to build a prison in Salem on the New York plan, which was completed in 1877. Yet, with labor difficulties and an economic depression in the 1890s, responsibility for the prison was again turned over to a lessee in 1895.[30]

THE REFORMATORY MOVEMENT

The ways in which reforms are implemented often do not match the high ideals of social activists. Legislators and governors may be willing to support the espoused goals of change, but putting the ideals into practice requires leadership, money, public support, and innovative administrators. Thus, soon after a given innovation, correctional facilities become overcrowded, discipline wanes, programs are abandoned, and charges of official misconduct erupt. The subsequent investigation typically recommends changes that may or may not be implemented—and the cycle continues.

By the mid-1800s, reformers had become disillusioned with the penitentiary. Neither the New York nor the Pennsylvania systems nor any of their imitators had achieved rehabilitation or deterrence. This failure was seen as resulting from poor administration rather than from weakness of the basic concept. Within 40 years of being built, penitentiaries had become overcrowded, understaffed, and minimally financed. Discipline was lax, brutality was common, and administrators were viewed as corrupt. For example, in 1870 investigators at Sing Sing discovered that "dealers were publicly supplying prisoners with almost anything they could pay for" and that the imprisoned men were "playing all sorts of games, reading, scheming, trafficking."[31] This reality was a far cry from the vision of John Howard and Benjamin Rush.

In 1865 the New York Prison Association commissioned **Enoch Cobb Wines** and Theodore Dwight to undertake a nationwide survey of prisons. After visiting 18 prisons and houses of correction, they published their *Report on the Prisons and Reformatories of the United States and Canada* in 1867. Not one of the prisons they visited viewed reformation of those held there as a primary goal or deployed resources to further reformation. Inadequacies in the physical plants, lack of staff training, and poor administrative practices were in evidence. However, the researchers were most upset by the extent to which corporal punishment was used for discipline. The report emphasized that prisons should prepare residents for release by allowing them to "advance toward freedom by moving through progressively liberal stages of discipline."[32]

BIOGRAPHY

ENOCH COBB WINES (1806–1879)

A guiding force of U.S. corrections starting in 1862, when he became the secretary of the New York Prison Association and served in this role until his death.

Organizer of the National Prison Association in 1870 and a major contributor to the Cincinnati Declaration of Principles.

Across the Atlantic, a controversy arose that directly influenced U.S. corrections. In England, Alexander Maconochie urged the **mark system** of graduated terms of confinement. Penalties would be graded according to the severity of the crime, and people would be released from incarceration according to their performance. A certain number of marks would be given at sentencing, and the imprisoned individuals could reduce the number by voluntary labor, participation in educational and religious programs, and good behavior. Maconochie thus argued for sentences of indeterminate length and a system of rewards. Through these incentives, individuals would be reformed so that they could return to society.

mark system A system in which prison residents are assessed a certain number of marks, based on the severity of their crime, at the time of sentencing. Individuals could reduce their term and gain release by reducing marks through labor, good behavior, and educational achievement.

Maconochie's ideas were not implemented in England. However, in Ireland in 1854 Sir Walter Crofton adopted practices similar to the mark system that came to be known as the Irish or *intermediate* system. Convicted individuals spent a period in solitary confinement and then were sent to public work prisons where they could earn positive marks (rather than removing initial marks against them). When they had enough marks, they were transferred to the intermediate stage, or what today might be called a *halfway house*. The final test was a *ticket-of-leave*, a conditional release that was the precursor of the modern parole system.[33] Again, theory and practice bridged the continents as Maconochie's and Crofton's ideas traveled across the Atlantic.

LO 3

Discuss the elements of the Cincinnati Declaration.

Cincinnati, 1870

By 1870 a new generation of American penal reformers had arisen. Among them were Gaylord Hubbell, warden of Sing Sing, who had observed the Irish system in operation; Enoch C. Wines, secretary of the New York Prison Association; Franklin Sanborn, secretary of the Massachusetts State Board of Charities; and Zebulon Brockway, head of Detroit's Michigan House of Correction. Like the Quakers, these penologists were motivated by humanitarian concerns, but they also understood how prisons operated.

The National Prison Association (NPA, predecessor of the American Correctional Association) and its 1870 meeting in Cincinnati embodied the new spirit of reform. In its famous Declaration of Principles, the association advocated a new design for penology: that prison operations should stem from a philosophy of changing convicted individuals, with reformation rewarded by release. Sentences of indeterminate length would replace fixed sentences, and proof of reformation, rather than mere lapse of time, would be a requirement for release. Classification on the basis of character and improvement would encourage the reformation program. Penitentiary practices that had evolved during the first half of the nineteenth century—fixed sentences, lockstep, rules of silence, and isolation—were now seen as debasing and humiliating.

Given the leadership roles of clergy in the National Prison Association, it is not surprising that, like the activists who had promoted the penitentiary in the 1830s, those gathered at Cincinnati still saw crime as a sort of moral disease that could be treated by efforts at moral regeneration.

Like the Quakers before them, the 1870 reformers looked to institutional life as the way to effective rehabilitation. Individuals convicted of committing crimes would be made into well-adjusted citizens, but the process would take place behind walls. The Cincinnati Declaration could thus in good faith insist that "reformation is a work of time; and a benevolent regard to the good of the criminal himself, as well as to the protection of society, requires that his sentence be long enough for the reformatory process to take effect."[34]

BIOGRAPHY

ZEBULON BROCKWAY (1827–1920)

Reformer who began his career in penology as a clerk in Connecticut's Wethersfield Prison at age 21. In 1854, while superintendent of the Monroe County Penitentiary in Rochester, New York, he began to experiment with ideas on making prisons more rehabilitative. He put his theories to work as the superintendent of Elmira State Reformatory, New York, in 1876, retiring from that institution in 1900.

Elmira Reformatory

The first **reformatory** took shape in 1876 at Elmira, New York, when **Zebulon Brockway** was appointed superintendent. Brockway believed that diagnosis and treatment were the keys to reform and rehabilitation. He questioned each new resident to explore the social, biological, psychological, and "root causes" of his deviance. An individualized work-and-education treatment program was then prescribed. Residents adhered to a rigid schedule

reformatory An institution for young individuals convicted of crimes that emphasized training, a mark system of classification, indeterminate sentences, and parole.

▲ *The reformatory movement emphasized education and training. On the basis of their conduct and achievement, individuals moved toward their release.*

of work during the day, followed by courses in academic, vocational, and moral subjects during the evening. Individuals who did well achieved early release.[35]

Designed for males between the ages of 16 and 30 who had been convicted of their first felony offense, the approach at Elmira incorporated a mark system of classification, indeterminate sentences, and parole. Once the courts had committed an individual to Elmira, the administrators could determine the release date; the only restriction was that the time served could not exceed the maximum prescribed by law for the particular offense.

The indeterminate sentence was linked to a three-grade system of classification. Each person entered the institution at grade 2, and if the individual earned nine marks a month for six months by working hard, completing school assignments, and causing no problems, he could be moved up to grade 1, which was necessary for release. If he failed to cooperate and violated rules of conduct, thus showing poor self-control and an indifference to progress, he would be demoted to grade 3. Only after three months of satisfactory behavior could he reembark on the path toward eventual release.[36] In sum, this system placed "the prisoner's fate, as far as possible, in his own hands."[37]

Elmira's proclaimed success at reforming young men convicted of felonies was widely heralded, and over the next several decades its program was emulated in 20 states. Brockway's annual reports claimed that 81 percent of individuals released from Elmira underwent "probable reformation." An article in the *Journal of the American Social Science Association*, "How Far May We Abolish Prisons?" echoed this optimism. The author's answer to the title question was "to the degree that we put men into reformatories like Elmira, for it reforms more than 80 percent of those who are sent there."[38] Brockway even weathered an investigation into charges of brutality at Elmira, which revealed that the whip and solitary confinement were used there regularly. However, in 1900 he was forced to resign in the face of mounting criticism of his administration.

By 1900 the reformatory movement had spread throughout much of the nation, yet at the outbreak of World War I in 1914, it was already declining. In most institutions the architecture, the attitudes of the guards, and the emphasis on discipline differed little from past orientations. Too often, the educational and rehabilitative efforts took a back seat to the traditional emphasis on punishment. Even Brockway admitted that it was difficult to distinguish between inhabitants whose attitudes had changed and those who merely lived by prison rules. Displaying good behavior became the way to win parole, but this did not mean that the prison residents had truly changed.

Lasting Reforms

Although the ideals of Wines, Brockway, and the other leaders of the reformatory movement were not realized, these men made several major contributions to U.S. corrections. The indeterminate sentence, classification, rehabilitative programs, and parole were first developed at Elmira. The Cincinnati Declaration of Principles set goals that inspired prison reformers well into the twentieth century. More changes were still to come, however: In the mid-nineteenth century, the United States entered a period of significant social change. The nation faced problems arising from two demographic changes: the gradual shift of the population from the countryside to the cities and the influx of immigrants. The stage was set for progressive reforms.

LO 4

Identify the reforms advocated by the Progressives.

THE RISE OF THE PROGRESSIVES

The first two decades of the 1900s, called the Age of Reform, set the dominant tone for U.S. social thought and political action until the 1960s.[39] Industrialization, urbanization, technological change, and scientific advancements had revolutionized the American landscape. A group known as the Progressives attacked the excesses of this emergent society, especially those of big business, and placed their faith in state action to deal with the social problems of slums, adulterated food, dangerous occupational conditions, vice, and crime.

The Progressives, most of whom came from upper-status backgrounds, were optimistic about the possibility of solving the problems of modern society. Focusing in particular on conditions in cities, which had large immigrant populations, they believed that civic-minded people could apply the findings of science to social problems, including penology, in ways that would benefit all. Specifically, they believed that society could rehabilitate the criminally involved through individualized treatment.

Individualized Treatment and the Positivist School

The scholar David Rothman epitomized the Progressive programs in two words: *conscience and convenience*. Progressive reforms were promoted by benevolent and philanthropic men and women who sought to understand and cure crime through a case-by-case approach. They believed that the reformers of the penitentiary era were wrong in assuming that all deviants were "victims of social disorder" and "could all be rehabilitated with a single program, the well-ordered routine" of the prison.[40]

The Progressives thought it necessary to know the life history of each convicted individual and then devise a treatment program specific to that individual. This meant that correctional administrators would need the discretion to diagnose each person, prescribe treatment, and schedule release to the community. From this orientation, the phrase "treatment according to the needs of the offender" came into vogue, in contrast to "punishment according to the severity of the crime," which had been the hallmark of Beccaria and the reformers of the early 1800s.

Rothman argues that because discretion was required for the day-to-day practice of the new penology, correctional administrators responded favorably to it. The new discretionary authority made it easier for administrators to carry out their daily assignments. He also notes that those Progressives committed to incarceration were instrumental in promoting probation and parole, but supporters of the penitentiary used the requirement of discretion to expand the size of the prison population.

The Progressives had faith that the state would carry out their reforms judicially. In the same way that they looked to government programs to secure social justice, they assumed that the agents of the state would help individuals convicted of committing crimes. As Rothman notes,

> In criminal justice, the issue was not how to protect the offender from the arbitrariness of the state, but how to bring the state more effectively to the aid of the offender. The state was not a behemoth to be chained and fettered, but an agent capable of fulfilling

an ambitious program. Thus, a policy that called for the state's exercise of discretionary authority in finely tuned responses was, at its core, Progressive.[41]

positivist school An approach to criminology and other social sciences based on the assumptions that human behavior is a product of biological, economic, psychological, and social factors and that the scientific method can be applied to ascertain the causes of individual behavior.

As members of the **positivist school**, the Progressives looked to social, economic, biological, and psychological rather than religious or moral explanations for the causes of crime, and they applied modern scientific methods to determine the best treatment therapies. Recall that the classical school of Beccaria and Bentham had emphasized a legal approach to the problem, focusing on the act rather than the person. In contrast, the scientific positivist school shifted the focus from the criminal act to the individual. By the beginning of the twentieth century, advances in the biological and social sciences provided the framework for the reforms proposed by the Progressives.

Although the positivist school comprised several theoretical perspectives, most of its practitioners shared three basic assumptions:

1. Criminal behavior is not the result of free will but stems from factors over which the individual has no control: biological characteristics, psychological maladjustments, and sociological conditions.
2. Criminally involved people can be treated so that they can lead crime-free lives.
3. Treatment must center on the individual and the individual's problem.

Progressive Reforms

Armed with their views about the nature of criminal behavior and the need for state action to reform criminally involved individuals, the Progressives fought for changes in correctional methods. They pursued two main strategies: (1) improving conditions in social environments that seemed to be breeding grounds for crime and (2) rehabilitating individuals. Because they saw crime as primarily an urban problem, concentrated especially among the immigrant lower class, the Progressives sought through political action to bring about changes that would improve ghetto conditions: better public health, landlord–tenant laws, public housing, playgrounds, settlement houses, and education. However, because they also believed that criminal behavior varied among individuals, a case-by-case approach was required.[42]

By the 1920s, portions of the Progressives' program were gaining wide acceptance, including probation, indeterminate sentences, and parole. These elements had been proposed at the 1870 Cincinnati meeting, but the Progressives and their allies in corrections implemented them throughout the country[43]:

1. *Probation*. This alternative to incarceration was consistent with the Progressive scheme because it recognized individual differences and allowed convicted individuals to be treated in the community under supervision.
2. *Indeterminate Sentences*. Although the sentences were called "indeterminate," state legislatures nearly always set a minimum and maximum term within which the correctional process of rehabilitation could operate. Fixed sentences were retained for lesser offenses, but during this period more than three-quarters of convicted individuals whose maximum terms exceeded five years were serving indeterminate sentences.
3. *Parole*. Although the idea of parole release had been developed in Ireland and Australia in the 1850s—and Zebulon Brockway had instituted it at Elmira in 1876—not until the mid-1920s did it really catch on in the United States. Like probation, parole expanded greatly during the Progressive period. By the mid-1920s, well over 80 percent of people convicted of felonies in the major industrialized states left prison via parole.[44]

Although the reforms of the Progressives were much criticized, probation, indeterminate sentences, and parole remain dominant elements of corrections to this day. Perhaps, as Rothman suggests, this is because these options provide authority to criminal justice officials and affirm the vitality of the rehabilitative idea.[45] However, these three crucial reforms provided the structure for yet another change in corrections.

THE RISE OF THE MEDICAL MODEL

LO 5

Discuss the assumptions of the medical model regarding the nature of criminal behavior and its correction.

Even before psychiatry began to influence U.S. society, the idea that criminally involved people were mentally ill was popular in correctional circles. At the 1870 Cincinnati congress, one speaker described a typical specimen as

> a man who has suffered under a disease evinced by the perpetration of a crime, and who may reasonably be held to be under the dominion of such disease until his conduct has afforded very strong presumption not only that he is free from its immediate influence, but that the chances of its recurrence have become exceedingly remote.[46]

Certainly, much Progressive reform was based on the idea that people could be rehabilitated through treatment, but not until the 1930s were serious attempts made to implement what became known as the **medical model** of corrections. Under the banner of the newly prestigious social and behavioral sciences, the emphasis of corrections shifted to treating the criminally involved as people whose social, psychological, or biological deficiencies had caused them to engage in illegal activity.

medical model A model of corrections based on the assumption that criminal behavior is caused by social, psychological, or biological deficiencies that require treatment.

One early proponent of the medical model was **Howard Gill**, who became the superintendent of Massachusetts's Norfolk State Prison Colony in 1927. Gill tried to create a "community" of prison inhabitants within secured walls. He helped design Norfolk in the style of a college campus, staffed not only with guards but also with professionals who provided treatment programs: educators, psychiatrists, and social workers. Residents wore ordinary clothing, not prison garb, and participated with staff on advisory councils dealing with matters of community governance. During the Great Depression, Gill's policies came under increasing fire. An escape by four individuals triggered a backlash that led to his removal in 1934. Gill continued his progressive reform work through several prison-related posts in the federal government until he entered academia in 1947.[47]

BIOGRAPHY

HOWARD GILL (1890–1989)

A prison reformer in the Progressive tradition, Gill designed Massachusetts's Norfolk State Prison Colony to be a model prison community. Norfolk provided individual treatment programs and included convicted individuals on an advisory council to deal with community governance.

The concept of rehabilitation as the primary purpose of incarceration took on national legitimacy in 1929, when Congress authorized the new Federal Bureau of Prisons to develop institutions that would ensure the proper classification, care, and treatment of convicted individuals. **Sanford Bates**, the first director of the bureau, had served as the president of the American Correctional Association and promoted the new medical model.

BIOGRAPHY

SANFORD BATES (1884–1972)

The first director of the Federal Bureau of Prisons, Bates advocated prison reform throughout his career. After becoming the president of the American Correctional Association in 1926, he also played an important role in the development of programs in New Jersey and New York.

The 1950s came to be known as the Era of Treatment as many states, particularly California, Illinois, New Jersey, and New York, fell in line with programs designed to reform people. Most other states, as well as political leaders everywhere, adopted at least the rhetoric of rehabilitation, changing statutes to specify that treatment was the goal of their corrections system and that punishment was an outdated concept. Prisons were thus to become something like mental hospitals, rehabilitating and testing people for readiness to reenter society. In many states, however, the medical model was adopted in name only: Departments of prisons became departments of corrections, but the budgets for treatment programs remained about the same. Because the essential structural elements of parole, probation, and the indeterminate sentence were already in place in most states, incorporating the medical model required only adding classification systems to diagnose convicted individuals, as well as treatment programs to reform them.

Initially, the number of psychiatrists and therapeutic treatment programs in corrections was limited, but both increased sharply after World War II. Group therapy, behavior modification, shock therapy, individual counseling, psychotherapy, guided group interaction, and many other approaches all became part of the "new penology." Competing schools of psychological thought debated the usefulness of these techniques, many of which were adopted or discarded before their worth had been evaluated.[48] However, the administrative needs of the institution often superseded the treatment needs of the individual: Prison residents tended to be assigned to the facilities, jobs, and programs that had openings rather than to those that would provide the prescribed treatment. California adopted the medical model more thoroughly than did any other state. In 1944 the administration of Governor Earl Warren authorized the construction of specialized

FOR CRITICAL THINKING

The medical model assumes that people commit crimes because of personal shortcomings, such as social, psychological, or biological deficiencies. Driven by this approach, prisons throughout the United States implemented a variety of prison programs beginning in the 1930s. Work programs remained throughout this time period.

1. What personal deficiencies could be addressed by Delaware Correctional Industries (DCI), discussed at the beginning of this chapter? What other types of rehabilitation programs might prove effective if coupled with work of this type? Explain your answer.
2. Suppose that you are advocating on behalf of DCI to lawmakers who are skeptical of its effectiveness. What would you say to them to change their minds?
3. Classification systems to diagnose and treat convicted individuals emerged along with the medical model. However, critics have noted that the treatment needs of prison residents were usually secondary to the administrative needs. If you were a prison warden in Delaware, what would you do to help ensure that DCI met both the needs of the incarcerated individuals under your ward and the needs of the prison?

prisons and the California Adult Authority. Individuals convicted of felony offenses received indeterminate sentences, the lengths of which were determined by the nine members of the Authority; these nine had almost complete power to classify, distribute, and treat imprisoned individuals, and ultimately to determine their release. California developed a full range of treatment programs, including psychotherapy and group therapy. By the 1970s, many California prisons were in turmoil, the value of treatment programs had come into question, and disparities in the release decisions of the Adult Authority had begun to be questioned. Later, California was one of the first states to move toward determinate sentencing and away from the medical model.[49]

Maryland's Patuxent Institution, which opened in 1955, is probably the best example of a prison built according to the principles of the medical model. Patuxent was founded to treat adults given indeterminate sentences and judged to be "defective delinquents." Its administrators had broad authority to control intake, to experiment with a treatment milieu, and to decide when to release "patients." Throughout the period of incarceration, a patient was diagnosed and treated through a variety of programs and therapies.

Critics of treatment programs in U.S. prisons pointed out that even during the 1950s, when the medical model reached its zenith, only 5 percent of state correctional budgets were allocated for rehabilitation. Although states adopted the rhetoric of the medical model, custody remained the overriding goal of institutions. Some argued that it was impossible to develop the rapport with prison inhabitants that was needed to cure their personality difficulties; others asserted that custody always took precedence over treatment in the daily running of prisons (see "For Critical Thinking").

LO 6

Illustrate how the community model reflected the social and political values of the 1960s and 1970s.

FROM MEDICAL MODEL TO COMMUNITY MODEL

As we have seen, social and political values greatly influence correctional thought and practices. During the 1960s and 1970s, U.S. society experienced the civil rights movement, the war on poverty, and resistance to the Vietnam War. Americans also challenged government institutions dealing with education, mental health, juvenile delinquency, and adult corrections. In 1967 the President's Commission on Law Enforcement and Administration of Justice reported the following:

> Crime and delinquency are symptoms of failures and disorganization of the community.... The task of corrections, therefore, includes building or rebuilding social ties, obtaining employment and education, securing in the larger senses a place for the offender in the routine functioning of society.[50]

This analysis was consistent with the views of **community corrections** advocates, who felt that the goal of the criminal justice system should be the reintegration of convicted individuals into the community.

community corrections A model of corrections based on the assumption that reintegrating the convicted individual into the community should be the goal of the criminal justice system.

AP Images

▲ The prison riot at Attica in 1971 was a watershed moment in correctional history. Prison reformers thought it signaled a new era for better treatment of prison inhabitants, but what actually ensued was a 40-year increase in the size of the U.S. prison population.

The prison riot and hostage taking at New York State's Attica Correctional Facility aided the move toward community corrections. On the morning of September 13, 1971, after four days of negotiations, a helicopter began dropping CS gas (an incapacitating agent) on those milling around in the prison yard. After the gas came a rain of bullets from state police guns, which hit 128 men and killed 29 prison inhabitants and 10 hostages. With the exception of the massacres of Native Americans in the late nineteenth century, it was the "bloodiest one-day encounter between Americans since the Civil War."[51] For many, the hostilities at Attica showed prisons to be counterproductive and unjust. They urged officials to make decarceration through community corrections the goal and pressed for greater use of alternatives to incarceration, such as probation, halfway houses, and community service.

Community corrections called for a radical departure from the medical model's emphasis on treatment in prison. Instead, prisons were to be avoided because they were artificial institutions that interfered with the individual's ability to develop a crime-free lifestyle. Proponents argued that corrections should turn away from psychological treatment in favor of programs that would increase opportunities to become successful citizens. Probation would be the sentence of choice for people convicted of nonviolent crime so that they could engage in vocational and educational programs that increased their chances of adjusting to society. For the small portion of convicted individuals who had to be incarcerated, time in prison would be only a short interval until release on parole. To further the goal of reintegration, correctional workers would serve as advocates for individuals as they dealt with government agencies, providing employment counseling, medical treatment, and financial assistance.

The reintegration idea prevailed in corrections only until the late 1970s, when it gave way to a new punitiveness in criminal justice in conjunction with the rebirth of the determinate sentence. Similar to advocates of previous reforms, supporters of reintegration claim that the idea was never adequately tested. Nevertheless, community corrections remains a significant idea and practice in the recent history of corrections.

THE CRIME CONTROL MODEL: THE PENDULUM SWINGS AGAIN

LO 7

Describe the forces and events that led to the present crime control model.

Beginning in the late 1960s, the public became concerned about rising crime rates. At the same time, studies uncovered concerns about the worth of treatment programs as well as the Progressive assumption that state officials would exercise discretion in a positive way. Critics of rehabilitation attacked the indeterminate sentence and parole, urging that treatment be available on a voluntary basis but that it not be tied to release. In addition, proponents of increased crime control called for longer sentences, especially for people who had made a career out of crime and individuals who had been convicted of violent offenses.

The Decline of Rehabilitation

According to critics of rehabilitation, its reportedly high recidivism rates prove its ineffectiveness. Probably the most influential analysis of research data from treatment programs was undertaken by Robert Martinson for the New York State Governor's Special Committee on Criminal Offenders. He surveyed 231 English-language studies of rehabilitation programs in corrections systems. They included such standard rehabilitative programs as educational and vocational training, individual counseling, group counseling, milieu therapy, medical treatment (plastic surgery, drugs), parole, and supervision. Martinson summarized his findings by saying, "With few and isolated exceptions, the rehabilitative efforts that have been reported so far have had no appreciable effect on recidivism."[52]

Critics of the rehabilitation model have also challenged as unwarranted the amount of discretion given to correctional decision makers to tailor the criminal sanction to the needs of each individual. In particular, they have argued that the discretion given to parole boards to release people is misplaced because board decisions are more often based on the whims of individual members than on the scientific criteria espoused by the medical model.

The Emergence of Crime Control

crime control model of corrections A model of corrections based on the assumption that criminal behavior can be controlled by more use of incarceration and other forms of strict supervision.

As the political climate changed in the 1970s and 1980s, and with the crime rate at historic levels, legislators, judges, and officials responded with a renewed emphasis on a **crime control model of corrections**. By 1980, the problem of crime and how to deal with convicted individuals had become an intense political issue.

The critique of the rehabilitation model led to changes in the sentencing structures of more than half of the states and to the abolition of parole release in many. The new determinate sentencing laws were designed to incarcerate people for longer periods. In conjunction with other forms of punishment, the thrust of the 1980s centered on crime control through incarceration and risk containment.

The punitive ethos of the 1980s and 1990s appeared in the emphasis on dealing more strictly with those convicted of violent crimes, drug dealers, and people who had made a career out of crime. It was also reflected in the trend toward intensive supervision of individuals on probation, the detention without bail of accused people thought to present a danger to the community, reinstitution of the death penalty in 37 states, and the requirement that judges impose mandatory penalties for people convicted of certain offenses or who have extensive criminal records. By the end of the century, the effect of these "get-tough" policies showed in the record numbers of convicted individuals, the longer sentences being served, and the size of the probation population. Some observers point to these policies as the reason why the crime rate has begun to fall. Others ask whether the crime control policies have really made a difference, given demographic and other changes in the United States. Table 3.2, which traces the history of correctional thought and practices in the United States, highlights the continual shifts in focus.

AP Images/Ted S. Warren

▲ *Under the crime control model, prisons would be designed as place of punishment, not rehabilitation, and solitary confinement would be used to enforce the punishment.*

TABLE 3.2 The History of Corrections in America

Note the extent to which correctional policies have shifted from one era to the next and how they have been influenced by various societal factors.

Colonial (1600s–1790s)	Penitentiary (1790s–1870s)	Reformatory (1870s–1890s)	Progressive (1890s–1930s)	Medical (1930s–1960s)	Community (1960s–1970s)	Crime Control (1970s–Present)
Features						
Anglican Code Capital and corporal punishment, fines	Separate confinement Reform of individual Power of isolation and labor Penance Disciplined routine Punishment according to severity of crime	Indeterminate sentences Parole Classification by degree of individual reform Rehabilitative programs Separate treatment for juveniles	Individual case approach Administrative discretion Broader probation and parole Juvenile courts	Rehabilitation as primary focus of incarceration Psychological testing and classification Various types of treatment programs and institutions	Reintegration into community Avoidance of incarceration Vocational and educational programs	Determinate sentences Mandatory sentences Sentencing guidelines Risk management
Philosophical Basis						
Religious law Doctrine of predestination	Enlightenment Declaration of Independence Human perfectability and powers of reason Religious penitence Power of reformation Focus on the act Healing power of suffering	NPA Declaration of Principles Crime as moral disease Criminally involved people as "victims of social disorder"	The Age of Reform Positivist school Punishment according to needs of individuals Focus on the individual Crime as an urban, immigrant ghetto problem	Biomedical science Psychiatry and psychology Social work practice Crime as signal of personal "distress" or "failure"	Civil rights movement Critique of prisons Small is better	Crime control Rising crime rates Political shift to the right New punitive agenda

WHERE ARE WE TODAY?

The time may be ripe for another look at correctional policy. The optimism that once suffused corrections has waned. For the first time in decades, the financial and human costs of the retributive crime control policies of the 1990s are now being scrutinized. States are now facing the fact that incarceration is expensive. Are the costs of incarceration and surveillance justified? Has crime been reduced because of correctional policies? Are we safer today than before? What does the experience of contemporary crime control policies indicate about the future of corrections in the United States?

SUMMARY

1 Describe "The Great Law" of Pennsylvania and note its importance.

With the arrival in 1682 of William Penn, Pennsylvania adopted "The Great Law," which was based on Quaker principles and emphasized hard labor in a house of correction as punishment for most crimes. Death was reserved for premeditated murder.

2 Compare and contrast the basic assumptions of the penitentiary systems of Pennsylvania and New York.

The penitentiary ideal, first incorporated in Pennsylvania, emphasized the concept of separate confinement. Residents were held in isolation, spending their time at craft work and considering their transgressions. In the New York congregate system, prison inhabitants were held in isolation but worked together during the day under a rule of silence.

3 Discuss the elements of the Cincinnati Declaration.
A Declaration of Principles was adopted at the 1870 meeting of the National Prison Association, held in Cincinnati. The declaration stated that prisons should be organized to encourage reformation, rewarding it with release. It advocated indeterminate sentences and the classification of imprisoned people based on character and improvement. The reformers viewed the penitentiary practices of the nineteenth century as debasing, humiliating, and destructive.

4 Identify the reforms advocated by the Progressives.
The Progressives looked to social, economic, biological, and psychological rather than religious or moral explanations for the causes of crime. They advocated the development of probation, indeterminate sentences, treatment programs, and parole.

5 Discuss the assumptions of the medical model regarding the nature of criminal behavior and its correction.
Beginning in the 1930s, reformers put forward the medical model of corrections, which viewed criminal behavior as caused by psychological or biological deficiencies. They held that corrections should diagnose and treat these deficiencies using a variety of programs and therapies. When "well," the individual should be released.

6 Illustrate how the community model reflected the social and political values of the 1960s and 1970s.
During the 1960s and 1970s, dissatisfaction with the medical model led to the development of community corrections. Influenced by the civil rights movement, protests against the Vietnam War, and the war on poverty, reformers held that prisons were to be avoided because they were artificial institutions that interfered with the individual's ability to develop a crime-free lifestyle. People should instead receive opportunities for success in the community, and corrections should emphasize the rebuilding of an individual's ties to the community.

7 Describe the forces and events that led to the present crime control model.
The rise of crime in the late 1960s and questions about the effectiveness of rehabilitative programs brought pressure to shift to a crime control model of corrections, with greater use of incarceration and other forms of strict supervision.

KEY TERMS

community corrections (*p. 64*)
congregate system (*p. 53*)
contract labor system (*p. 54*)
crime control model of corrections (*p. 66*)
lease system (*p. 57*)
mark system (*p. 59*)
medical model (*p. 63*)
penitentiary (*p. 51*)
positivist school (*p. 62*)
reformatory (*p. 59*)
separate confinement (*p. 52*)

FOR DISCUSSION

1. Why do you think the penitentiary first caught on in Pennsylvania and New York? How would you explain the increase in the number of penitentiaries throughout the United States after Eastern State Penitentiary and Auburn Prison began operating?
2. When Americans think of punishment, they usually first think of prisons. What other ways of punishing convicted individuals might the general public find acceptable?
3. How do you think that people convicted of committing crime will be punished in the United States in the future? What established punishments will still be around, and what kinds of new sanctions might emerge?
4. What lessons can today's correctional professionals learn from the historical punishment practices covered in this chapter? Which practices should we not reinstate? Which practices should we consider adopting?

FOR FURTHER READING

Blackmon, Douglas A. *Slavery by Another Name: The Re-Enslavement of Black Americans from the Civil War to World War II*. New York: Doubleday, 2008. Brings to the fore the "Age of Neoslavery" that thrived in many southern states following the Civil War, a big part of which was the development of African American labor camps.

Kann, Mark E. *Punishment, Prisons, and Patriarchy: Liberty and Power in the Early American Republic*. New York: New York University Press, 2005. Presents the view that in the post–Revolution period, reformers coupled their legacy of liberty with a penal philosophy that denied liberty, especially to marginal Americans.

Mancini, Matthew J. *One Dies, Get Another: Convict Leasing in the American South, 1866–1928*. Columbia: University of South Carolina Press, 1996. Chronicles the use of harsh and exploitive leasing programs in the post–Civil War South.

McLennan, Rebecca M. *The Crisis of Imprisonment: Protest, Politics, and the Making of the American Penal State, 1776–1941*. Cambridge and New York: Cambridge University Press, 2008. Identifies and discusses the periods of popular protest, instability, and political crisis that helped shape the history of prison-based punishment in the United States.

Pisciotta, Alexander W. *Benevolent Repression: Social Control and the American Reformatory-Prison Movement*. New York: New York University Press, 1994. Argues that reformatories, although dedicated to humane, constructive, and charitable treatment, worked instead to tame and train criminal elements of the working class.

Sullivan, Larry E. *The Prison Reform Movement: Forlorn Hope*. Boston: Twayne, 1990. A concise history of American penology from the eighteenth century to the present.

NOTES

1 "Vaughn Inmate Workers Switch Gears to make Face Masks," www.delawarestatenews.net/coronavirus/vaughn-inmate-workers-switch-gears-to-make-face-masks, April 3, 2020.

2 David J. Rothman, "Perfecting the Prison: United States, 1789–1865," in *The Oxford History of the Prison*, edited by Norval Morris and David J. Rothman (New York: Oxford University Press, 1995), 112.

3 David J. Rothman, *The Discovery of the Asylum* (Boston: Little, Brown, 1971), 51.

4 Lawrence M. Friedman, *Crime and Punishment in American History* (New York: Basic, 1993), 48.

5 Adam J. Hirsch, *The Rise of the Penitentiary* (New Haven, CT: Yale University Press, 1992), 8.

6 Louis P. Masur, *Rights of Execution* (New York: Oxford University Press, 1989), 24.

7 Gordon S. Wood, *The Radicalism of the American Revolution* (New York: Knopf, 1992), 193.

8 Blake McKelvey, *American Prisons* (Montclair, NJ: Patterson Smith, 1977), 8.

9 Norman Johnston, *Forms of Constraint: A History of Prison Architecture* (Urbana: University of Illinois Press, 2000), 68.

10 Norman Johnston, "Early Philadelphia Prisons: Amour, Alcohol, and Other Forbidden Pleasures," *Prison Journal* 90 (March 2010): 12–23.

11 Negley K. Teeters and John D. Shearer, *The Prison at Philadelphia's Cherry Hill* (New York: Columbia University Press, 1957), 63.

12 Norman Johnston, *Eastern State Penitentiary: Crucible of Good Intentions* (Philadelphia: Philadelphia Museum of Art, 1994).

13 Thorsten Sellin, "The Origin of the Pennsylvania System of *Prison Discipline*," Prison Journal 50 (Spring–Summer 1970): 15–17.

14 Johnston, "Early Philadelphia Prisons," p. 14.

15 Teeters and Shearer, *Prison at Philadelphia's Cherry Hill*, ch. 4.

16 Gustave de Beaumont and Alexis de Tocqueville, *On the Penitentiary System in the United States and Its Application to France* (Carbondale: Southern Illinois University, [1833] 1964), 201.

17 John A. Conley, "Prisons, Production, and Profit: Reconsidering the Importance of Prison Industries," *Journal of Social History* 14 (Winter 1980): 55.

18 Martha A. Myers, *Race, Labor, and Punishment in the New South* (Columbus: Ohio State University Press, 1998), 6.

19 Mary Ellen Curtin, *Black Prisoners and Their World, Alabama, 1865–1900* (Charlottesville: University Press of Virginia, 2000), 6.

20 Douglas A. Blackmon, *Slavery by Another Name: The Re-Enslavement of Black Americans from the Civil War to World War II* (New York: Doubleday, 2008).

21 Ibid., p. 2.

22 Matthew Mancini, *One Dies, Get Another: Convict Leasing in the American South, 1866–1928* (Columbia: University of South Carolina Press, 1996); Myers, *Race, Labor, and Punishment*, p. 8.

23 Curtin, *Black Prisoners*, p. 63.

24 Donald R. Walker, *Penology for Profit: A History of the Texas Prison System 1867–1912* (College Station: Texas A&M University Press, 1988).

25 Edgardo Rotman, "The Failure of Reform, United States, 1865– 1965," in *The Oxford History of the Prison*, edited by Norval Morris and Michael Tonry (New York: Oxford University Press, 1995), 176.
26 Blackman, *Slavery by Another Name*, p. 2.
27 McKelvey, *American Prisons*, pp. 213–14; William Banks Taylor, *Down on Parchman Farm* (Columbus: Ohio State University Press, 1999).
28 McKelvey, *American Prisons*, p. 229.
29 Shelley Bookspan, *A Germ of Goodness: The California State Prison System, 1851–1944* (Lincoln: University of Nebraska Press, 1991), 6–14.
30 McKelvey, *American Prisons*, pp. 228–33.
31 David J. Rothman, *Conscience and Convenience* (Boston: Little, Brown, 1980), 18.
32 Rotman, "Failure of Reform," p. 172.
33 Elizabeth Eileen Dooley, "Sir William Crofton and the Irish or Intermediate System of Prison Discipline," *New England Journal of Prison Law* 575 (Winter 1981): 55.
34 Rothman, *Conscience and Convenience*, p. 70.
35 Rotman, "Failure of Reform," p. 174.
36 Alexander W. Pisciotta, *Benevolent Repression: Social Control and the American Reformatory-Prison Movement* (New York: New York University Press, 1994), 20.
37 Ibid., p. 41.
38 W. M. F. Round, "How Far May We Abolish Prisons?" *Journal of the American Social Science Association* 325 (1897): 200–01, as cited in Rothman, *Conscience and Convenience*, p. 55.
39 Richard Hofstader, *The Age of Reform* (New York: Knopf, 1974).
40 Rothman, *Conscience and Convenience*, p. 5.
41 Ibid., p. 60.
42 Ibid., p. 53.
43 Ibid., p. 99.
44 Rotman, "Failure of Reform," p. 183.
45 Rothman, *Conscience and Convenience*, p. 99.
46 Quoted in Jessica Mitford, *Kind and Usual Punishment* (New York: Knopf, 1973), 96.
47 Thomas C. Johnsen, "Howard Belding Gill," *Harvard Magazine*, September–October 1999, p. 54.
48 Karl Menninger, *The Crime of Punishment* (New York: Viking, 1969), 19.
49 Larry E. Sullivan, *The Prison Reform Movement: Forlorn Hope* (Boston: Twayne, 1990), 71.
50 U.S. President's Commission on Law Enforcement and Administration of Justice, *The Challenge of Crime in a Free Society* (Washington, DC: U.S. Government Printing Office, 1967), 7.
51 New York State Special Commission on Attica, *Attica: The Official Report of the New York State Special Commission on Attica* (New York: Bantam, 1972), xi.
52 Robert Martinson, "What Works? Questions and Answers About Prison Reform," *Public Interest* 35 (Spring 1974): 22.

CHAPTER 4

Contemporary Punishment

Jefferson Siegel/Pool/Sipa USA

Our images of the punishment system are sometimes turned upside down when celebrities, such as Harvey Weinstein, get arrested.

MOVIE PRODUCER HARVEY WEINSTEIN MAKES HIS WAY PAST A GROUP OF REPORTERS AND PHOTOGRAPHERS WHO DOCUMENT HIS EVERY MOVE.

Today, he is not attending a movie premier, nor is he at an awards ceremony for one of his films. Instead, he is a defendant who will be sentenced for his crimes. Approximately two weeks prior, Weinstein was convicted of two felony offenses, involving sex crimes against women.

Prosecutors argued that Weinstein had used his power and status in the movie business to victimize young women. Joan Illuzzi, the lead prosecutor in the case, said that Weinstein "held the dreams of many people in his hand" and that these young "dreamers were not even people to him." At trial, Weinstein was convicted of first-degree criminal sexual act and third-degree rape for his actions. However, he was also acquitted of two more serious charges of predatory sexual assault.

Presiding over the case was Justice James A. Burke. Weinstein, who had no prior criminal convictions, was sentenced to 23 years in prison. Burke could have given the defendant as little as five years, but noted that the prosecution's case held sway, stating "[t]here is evidence before me of other incidents of sexual assault involving a number of women, all of which are legitimate considerations for sentence." While the prosecutors applauded Burke's decision, members of Weinstein's defense team objected to the length of the prison term and said that some murderers receive lighter sentences.[1]

Crucial to every decision in the criminal justice process is the question "Is it just?" Should Harvey Weinstein have been given less time in prison, put on house arrest, or some mix of sanctions? Did justice serve those harmed by Weinstein's crimes? Did the sentence support society's need for the maintenance of right conduct? What rationale governed the judge's sentencing decision?

These types of questions are central to the mission of corrections. In this chapter, we examine the goals of corrections, identify the different forms of the criminal sanction, and discuss the sentencing process. As we explore these topics, we will examine their links to one another and to the historical and philosophical issues developed in Chapters 2 and 3.

LEARNING OBJECTIVES

After reading this chapter, you should be able to . . .

1. Discuss the goals of punishment.
2. Identify the different forms of the criminal sanction.
3. Explain how different factors affect the sentencing process.
4. Discuss the problem of unjust punishment.

THE PURPOSE OF CORRECTIONS

Rationales for punishment are influenced by the broad philosophical, political, and social themes of their era. Prevailing ideas about the causes of crime are closely tied to questions of responsibility and hence to the rationale for specific sanctions. As explained in Chapter 2, the ideas of the classical school of criminology, founded by Cesare Beccaria, squared nicely with the concepts of the Age of Reason, as did Jeremy Bentham's utilitarianism. In the context of the times, "making the punishment fit the crime" was more humane because it sought to do away with the brutal punishments often inflicted for trivial offenses. With the rise of science and the development of positivist criminology toward the end of the 1800s, new beliefs emerged about criminal responsibility and the desirability of designing punishment to meet the needs of the individual. The positivists considered criminal behavior to be the result of sociological, psychological, or biological factors and therefore directed correctional work toward rehabilitating people through treatment. Before further examining the goals of the criminal sanction, we should consider what the term *punishment* actually means. Herbert Packer argues that punishment is marked by these three elements:

1. An offense.
2. The infliction of pain because of the commission of the offense.
3. A dominant purpose that is neither to compensate someone injured by the offense nor to better the convicted person's condition but to prevent further offenses or to inflict what is thought to be deserved pain on the individuals who commit crime.[2]

Note that Packer emphasizes two major goals of criminal punishment: inflicting deserved suffering on convicted persons and preventing crime.

LO 1
Discuss the goals of punishment.

Criminal sanctions in the United States have four goals: retribution (deserved punishment), deterrence, incapacitation, and rehabilitation. In Chapter 22 we describe the movement to make restorative and community justice a fifth goal of the criminal sanction. Here, as we discuss each of the four traditional justifications for punishment, bear in mind that although judges often state publicly that their sentencing practices accord with a particular goal, conditions in correctional institutions or the actions of probation officers may be inconsistent with that goal. Thus, sentencing and correctional policies may be carried out in such a way that no one goal dominates or, in some cases, that justice itself is not demonstrably served.

Retribution (Deserved Punishment)

retribution Punishment inflicted on a person who has infringed on the rights of others and so deserves to be penalized. The severity of the sanction should fit the seriousness of the crime.

Retribution is punishment inflicted on a person who has violated a criminal law and so deserves to be punished. The Biblical expression "an eye for an eye, a tooth for a tooth" illustrates the philosophy underlying retribution. Retribution means that those who commit a particular crime should be punished alike, in proportion to the gravity of the offense or to the extent to which others have been made to suffer. Retribution is deserved punishment; convicted individuals must "pay their debts." This idea focuses on the offense alone, not the person's future acts or some other purpose such as reform or deterrence. Criminally involved people must be penalized for their wrongful acts, simply because fairness and justice require that they be punished.

With the Age of Reason and the development of utilitarian approaches to punishment, the idea of retribution lost much of its influence (see Chapter 2). However, some scholars claim that the desire for retribution is a basic human emotion. They maintain that if the state does not provide retributive sanctions to reflect community revulsion at offensive acts, citizens will take the law into their own hands to punish people who break the law. In this view, the failure of government to satisfy the people's desire for retribution could produce social unrest. Retribution helps the community emphasize the standards it expects all members to uphold.

This argument may not be valid for all crimes, however. If a rapist is inadequately punished, then the victim's friends, family, and other members of the community may be tempted to exact their own retribution. How about a young adult who uses recreational drugs? If the government failed to impose retribution for this offense, would the community care? The same apathy may hold true with respect to people who commit other small, nonviolent crimes. But even in these seemingly trivial situations, retribution may be useful and necessary to remind the public of the general rules of law and the important values that it protects.

Since the late 1970s, retribution as a justification for the criminal sanction has aroused new interest. This has occurred largely because of dissatisfaction with the philosophical basis and practical results of rehabilitation. Using the concept of "just deserts" (or deserved punishment) to define retribution, some theorists argue that one who infringes on the rights of others deserves to be punished. This approach is based on the philosophical view that punishment is a moral response to harm inflicted on society. Put differently, basic morality demands that wrongdoers be punished. Andrew von Hirsch, a well-known punishment scholar, says that "the sanctioning authority is entitled to choose a response that expresses moral disapproval: namely, punishment."[3] The deserved-punishment approach requires that sanctions be administered only to exact retribution for the wrong inflicted and not primarily to achieve other goals, such as deterrence, incapacitation, or rehabilitation.

Deterrence

Many people think of criminal punishment as a way to affect the future choices and behavior of individuals. Politicians frequently talk about being "tough on crime" in order to send a message to people considering the commission of a crime. This approach goes back to the eighteenth century. Recall from Chapter 2 that Jeremy Bentham was struck by what seemed to be the pointlessness of retribution. Other reformers adopted his theory of utilitarianism, which holds that human behavior is governed by the individual's calculation of the benefits versus the costs of one's acts. Before stealing money or property, for example, such individuals consider the punishment that others have received for similar acts and are thereby deterred.

Modern thinking distinguishes two types of deterrence.[4] **General deterrence** presumes that members of the general public will be deterred by observing the punishments of others and will conclude that the costs of crime outweigh the benefits. For general deterrence to be effective, the public must be constantly reminded about the likelihood and severity of punishment for various acts. They must believe they will be caught, prosecuted, and given a specific punishment if they commit a particular crime. Moreover, the punishment must be severe enough to impress them well enough to avoid committing crimes.

general deterrence Punishment that is intended to be an example to the general public and to discourage the commission of offenses by others.

By contrast, **specific deterrence** (also called **special** or **individual deterrence**) targets the decisions and behavior of people who have already been convicted. In this approach, the amount and kind of punishment are calculated to discourage the individual from repeating the offense. The punishment must be sufficiently severe to make the person conclude that "The consequences of my crime were painful. I won't commit that crime again because I don't want to risk being punished again."

specific deterrence (special or individual deterrence) Punishment inflicted on convicted individuals to discourage them from committing future crimes.

The concept of deterrence poses obvious difficulties. Deterrence assumes that all people act rationally and think before they act. It does not account for the many people who commit crimes under the influence of drugs or alcohol, those who suffer from psychological problems or mental illness, or those who violate the law when in an extreme emotional state. In other cases the low probability of being caught defeats both general and specific deterrence. To be generally deterrent, punishment must be perceived as fast, certain, and severe—but it does not always happen this way.

Knowledge of the effectiveness of deterrence is limited. For example, social science cannot measure the effects of general deterrence; only those who are not deterred come to the attention of researchers. A study of the deterrent effects of punishment would have to examine the impact of different forms of the criminal sanction on various potential lawbreakers. How can anyone determine how many people—or even if *any* people—stopped themselves from committing a crime because they were deterred by the prospect of prosecution and punishment? Therefore, while legislators often cite deterrence as a rationale for certain sanctions, no one really knows the extent to which sentencing policies based on deterrence achieve their objectives.

Incapacitation

incapacitation Depriving a person of the ability to commit crimes against society, usually by detaining the person in prison.

Incapacitation assumes that society can, by detention in a correctional facility or by execution, remove a person's capacity to commit further crimes. Many people express such sentiments by urging, "Lock 'em up and throw away the key!" In primitive societies, banishment from the community was the usual method of incapacitation. In early America, convicted people often agreed to move away or to join the army as an alternative to some other form of punishment. Today, imprisonment is the usual method of incapacitation. People can be confined within secure institutions and effectively prevented from committing additional harm against society for the duration of their sentence. Capital punishment is the ultimate method of incapacitation.

Any sentence that physically restricts an individual can have an incapacitating effect, even when the underlying purpose of the sentence is retribution, deterrence, or rehabilitation. However, sentences based primarily on incapacitation are future oriented. Whereas retribution requires focusing on the person's harmful act, incapacitation looks at the individual's potential actions. If the person is likely to commit future crimes, then the judge may impose a severe sentence—even for a relatively minor crime.

Under the theory of incapacitation, for example, a woman who kills her abusive husband as an emotional reaction to his verbal insults and physical assaults could receive a light sentence. As a one-time impulse killer who felt driven to kill by unique circumstances, she is not likely to commit additional crimes. By contrast, someone who shoplifts merchandise from a store and has been convicted of the offense on 10 previous occasions may receive a severe sentence. The criminal record and type of crime indicate that he or she will commit additional crimes if released. Thus, incapacitation focuses on characteristics of convicted individuals instead of characteristics of their offenses.

Does it offend the American sense of justice that a person could receive a harsher sentence for shoplifting than for manslaughter? Questions also arise about how to determine the length of sentences. Presumably, incarcerated individuals will not be released until the state is reasonably sure that they will no longer commit crimes. But can we ever be completely sure about what someone will do in the future? And, finally, on what grounds can the state punish people for acts that the state believes they will commit in the future?

selective incapacitation Making the best use of expensive and limited prison space by targeting for incarceration those people whose incapacity will do the most to reduce crime in society.

In recent years, greater attention has been paid to the concept of **selective incapacitation**, whereby individuals who repeat certain kinds of crimes are sentenced to long prison terms. Decades of criminological research have consistently shown that a relatively small number of people commit a large number of violent and property crimes. Thus, these "career criminals" should be locked up for long periods.[5]

Although the idea of confining or closely supervising people with repeat criminal convictions is appealing, it is also quite expensive to do so. In addition, selective incapacitation raises several moral and ethical questions. Because the theory looks at aggregates—the total harm caused by a certain type of crime versus the total suffering to be inflicted to reduce its incidence—policy makers may tend to focus on cost–benefit comparisons, disregarding serious issues of justice, individual freedom, and civil liberties.

Rehabilitation

rehabilitation The goal of restoring a convicted person to a constructive place in society through some form of vocational or educational training or therapy.

Rehabilitation has the goal of restoring a convicted person to a constructive place in society through some form of vocational or educational training or therapy. Many people believe that rehabilitation is the most appealing modern justification for use of the criminal sanction. They want individuals to be treated and resocialized so they will lead a crime-free, productive life. Over the last century, rehabilitation advocates have argued that techniques are available to identify and treat the causes of criminal behavior. If a person's criminal behavior is assumed to result from some social, psychological, or biological deficiency, the treatment of the disorder becomes the primary goal of corrections.

The goal of rehabilitation is oriented solely toward the convicted individual and does not imply any consistent relationship between the severity of the punishment and the gravity of the crime. People who commit lesser offenses may receive long prison sentences if experts believe that such people need a long period to become rehabilitated. By contrast, a murderer may win early release by showing signs that the psychological or emotional problems that led to the killing have been corrected.

According to the concept of rehabilitation, convicted individuals are treated, not punished, and will return to society when they are reformed. Consequently, judges should not set a fixed sentence but one with a maximum and minimum term so that parole boards may release somebody when he or she has been rehabilitated. Such sentences are known as indeterminate sentences. The indeterminate sentence is justified by the belief that if incarcerated people know when they are going to be released, they will not make an effort to engage in the treatment programs prescribed for their rehabilitation. If, however, they know they will be held until reformed, they will cooperate with counselors, psychologists, and other professionals seeking to treat their problems.

From the 1940s until the 1970s, the goal of rehabilitation was so widely held that treatment and reform of people convicted of violating the law were generally regarded as the only issues worthy of serious attention. Experts assumed that crime was caused by problems affecting individuals and that modern social sciences had the tools to address those problems. Since the 1970s, however, studies of rehabilitative programs have challenged the idea that we really know how to reform people who break the law.[6] Moreover, scholars no longer take for granted that crime is caused by identifiable, solvable problems such as poverty, lack of job skills, low self-esteem, and hostility toward authority. Instead, some argue that one cannot identify the cause of criminal behavior. And still others believe that coerced prison treatment programs are a waste of valuable resources.

Clearly, many legislatures, prosecutors, and judges have abandoned the rehabilitation goal in favor of retribution, deterrence, or incapacitation. Yet on the basis of opinion polls, researchers have found public support for rehabilitative programs.[7]

New Approaches to Punishment

During the past decade, many people have called for shifts away from punishment goals that focus either on the convicted person (rehabilitation, specific deterrence) or the crime (retribution, general deterrence, and incapacitation). Some have argued that the current goals of the criminal sanction leave out the needs of the crime victim and the community. Crime has traditionally been viewed as violating the state, but people now recognize that a criminal act also violates the victim and the community. In keeping with the focus of police, courts, and corrections on community justice (see Chapter 22), advocates are calling for **restoration** to be added to the goals of the criminal sanction.

restoration Punishment designed to repair the damage done to the victim and community by a person's criminal act.

The restorative perspective views crime as more than a violation of penal law. The criminal act practically and symbolically denies community by breaking down trust among citizens. Restoration requires that the community determine how best to communicate that nobody is above the law and that victims are not beneath its reach. Crime victims suffer losses involving damage to property and self. The primary aim of criminal justice should be to repair these losses. Crime also challenges the essence of community, to the extent that community life depends on a shared sense of trust, fairness, and interdependence.

Critics say that the retributive focus of today's criminal justice system denies the victim's need to be acknowledged and isolates community members from the conflict between the person who broke the law and the victim. By shifting the focus to restorative justice, sanctions can provide ways for the convicted individual to repair harm. However, others warn that society should approach restorative justice with caution because many procedural safeguards, such as legal representation and the presumption of innocence, may be impaired.[8] Restoration-oriented programs take many forms, most involving the participation of the convicted individual, the victim, and the community. The person who violated the law must take responsibility for the offense, agree to "undo" the harm through restitution, and affirm a willingness to live according to the law. The victim must specify the harm of the offense and the resources necessary to restore the losses suffered; the victim must also lay out the conditions necessary to diminish any fear or resentment toward the person who caused them harm. The community helps with the restorative process by emphasizing to the convicted individual the norms of acceptable behavior, providing support to restore the victim, and offering opportunities for the convicted person to perform reparative tasks for the victim and the community. Finally, it provides ways for the convicted individual to get the help needed to live in the community crime free.[9]

Research suggests that restoration-oriented programs can be effective. For example, a meta-analysis conducted by Lawrence Sherman and his colleagues showed that these programs reduce recidivism among convicted individuals. The authors conclude that restorative justice conferences can promote desistence from crime among program participants.[10]

Criminal Sanctions: A Mixed Bag?

How should society justify the use of criminal sanctions? Should the purpose be deterrence or incapacitation? What about retribution and rehabilitation? Justifications for specific sanctions usually overlap. A term of imprisonment may be philosophically justified by its primary goal of retribution but also serve the secondary functions of deterrence and incapacitation. General deterrence is such a broad concept that it adapts to the other goals, except possibly rehabilitation.

In restorative justice programs, people who have broken the law get an opportunity to take responsibility for the harm they have caused in ways that go beyond merely being punished.

Joseph Rodriguez/Redux

However, rehabilitation clearly conflicts with the other goals. For example, the deterrent power of incarceration depends primarily on being unpleasant. If incarceration consists mainly of a pleasant rehabilitative experience, it loses its deterrent power. By the same token, the more unpleasant prison life is, the less suitable an environment it is for most rehabilitation programs.

Trial judges carry the heavy burden of fashioning a sentence that accommodates these values in each case. A judge may sentence a forger to a long prison term as an example to others, even though this person poses little threat to community safety and probably does not need correctional treatment. The same judge may impose a shorter sentence on a youthful individual who has committed a

TABLE 4.1 Hypothetical Punishments for Harvey Weinstein

At sentencing, the judge usually gives reasons for the punishment imposed. Here are some statements Justice James Burke *might* have made, depending on the correctional goal he wanted to promote.

Goal	Judge's Statement
Retribution	I am imposing this sentence because you deserve to be punished. Your criminal behavior in this case is the basis for your punishment. Justice requires me to impose a sanction that reflects the value the community places on right conduct.
Deterrence	I am imposing this sentence so that your punishment will serve as an example and deter others who may contemplate similar actions. In addition, I hope that the sentence will deter you from ever again committing such an act.
Incapacitation	I am imposing this sentence so that you will be unable to violate the law while under correctional supervision. You do not appear likely to commit a similar offense in the future, so selective incapacitation is not warranted.
Rehabilitation	The trial testimony of the psychiatrists and the information contained in the presentence report make me believe that aspects of your personality led you to violate the law. I am therefore imposing this sentence so that you can be treated in ways that will rectify your behavior so you will not break the law again.

serious crime but may be a good candidate for rehabilitation if quickly reintegrated into society.

To see how these goals might be enacted in real life, consider again the sentencing of Harvey Weinstein. Table 4.1 shows various hypothetical sentencing statements that Justice James A. Burke might have given, depending on prevailing correctional goals.

As we next consider the ways in which these goals are applied through the various forms of punishment, keep in mind the underlying goal or mix of goals that justifies each form of sanction (see "For Critical Thinking").

FOR CRITICAL THINKING

As discussed at the beginning of the chapter, Harvey Weinstein was sentenced to 23 years in prison after being convicted of two felonies involving sexual offenses against two women.

1. Do you believe that Weinstein's sentence will serve as a general deterrent? Explain your answer.
2. Does the sentence imposed on Weinstein achieve any other correctional goals, such as retribution or rehabilitation? If you were the judge, how would you alter Weinstein's sentence so that other goals might be better achieved?

FORMS OF THE CRIMINAL SANCTION

Incarceration, intermediate sanctions, probation, and death are the ways that the criminal sanction, or punishment, is applied in the United States. Most people think of incarceration as the usual punishment. As a consequence, much of the public believes that people who break the law and receive anything less than incarceration, such as probation, are "getting off." However, community-based punishments such as probation and intermediate sanctions are imposed far more often than prison sentences.

LO 2
Identify the different forms of the criminal sanction.

Many judges and researchers believe that the sentencing structures in the United States are both too severe and too lenient. That is, many people who do not warrant incarceration are sent to prison, and many who should be given more-restrictive punishments receive minimal probation supervision.

Advocates for more-effective sentencing practices increasingly support a range or continuum of punishment options, with graduated levels of supervision and harshness. They argue that by using this type of sentencing scheme, authorities can reserve expensive prison cells for violent individuals. At the same time, less restrictive community-based

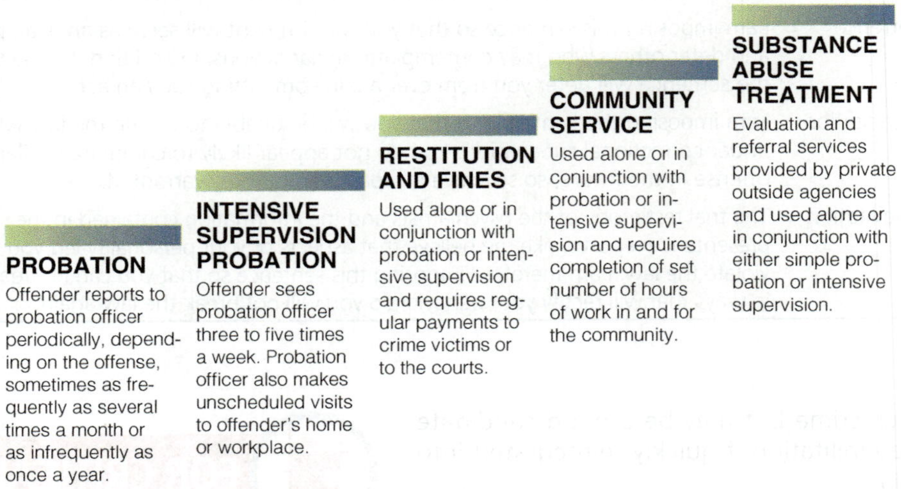
SUBSTANCE ABUSE TREATMENT
Evaluation and referral services provided by private outside agencies and used alone or in conjunction with either simple probation or intensive supervision.
COMMUNITY SERVICE
Used alone or in conjunction with probation or intensive supervision and requires completion of set number of hours of work in and for the community.
RESTITUTION AND FINES
Used alone or in conjunction with probation or intensive supervision and requires regular payments to crime victims or to the courts.
INTENSIVE SUPERVISION PROBATION
Offender sees probation officer three to five times a week. Probation officer also makes unscheduled visits to offender's home or workplace.
PROBATION
Offender reports to probation officer periodically, depending on the offense, sometimes as frequently as several times a month or as infrequently as once a year.

FIGURE 4.1 Escalating Punishments to Fit the Crime
This list includes generalized descriptions of many sentencing options used in jurisdictions across the country.

Source: *Seeking Justice: Crime and Punishment in America* (New York: Edna McConnell Clark Foundation, 1997), 32–33.

programs can be used to punish nonviolent people. As Figure 4.1 shows, simple probation lies at one end of this range, and traditional incarceration lies at the other. A range of sentencing options allows judges greater latitude to fashion sentences that reflect the severity of the crime and the risk and needs of the person.

There is no standard approach to sentencing and corrections. Some states use parole release; some have abolished it. Many states have sentencing guidelines, others have determinate sentences, and some still use indeterminate sentences. Mandatory minimums, three-strikes laws, and truth-in-sentencing have affected all jurisdictions.

As we examine the various forms of criminal sanctions, bear in mind that complex problems are associated with applying these legally authorized punishments. Although the penal code defines the behaviors that are illegal and specifies the procedures for determining guilt, the legal standards for sentencing—for actually applying the punishment—have not been as well developed. In other words, the United States has no common laws of sentencing. Thus, judges have discretion in determining the appropriate sentence within the parameters of the penal code.

Incarceration

Imprisonment is the most visible penalty imposed by U.S. courts. At year-end 2017 about 1.49 million Americans were in federal and state prisons.[11] Many people think that imprisonment significantly deters people who are considering breaking the law. However, incarceration is expensive. It also creates problems of reintegrating people back into society upon their release.

DAY REPORTING
Clients report to a central location every day where they file a daily schedule with their supervision officer showing how each hour will be spent —at work, in class, at support group meetings, etc.

HOUSE ARREST AND ELECTRONIC MONITORING
Used in conjunction with intensive supervision; restricts offender to home except when at work, school, or treatment.

HALFWAY HOUSE
Residential settings for selected inmates as a supplement to probation for those completing prison programs and for some probation or parole violators. Usually coupled with community service work and/or substance abuse treatment.

BOOT CAMP
Rigorous military-style regimen for younger offenders, designed to accelerate punishment while instilling discipline, often with an educational component.

PRISONS AND JAILS
More-serious offenders serve their terms at state or federal prisons, while county jails are usually designed to hold inmates for shorter periods.

In penal codes, legislatures stipulate the type of sentences and the amount of prison time that may be imposed for each crime. Three basic sentencing structures are used: (1) indeterminate sentences, (2) determinate sentences, and (3) mandatory sentences. Each type of sentence makes certain assumptions about the goals of the criminal sanction, and each provides judges with varying degrees of discretion.

Indeterminate Sentences When the goal of rehabilitation dominated corrections, legislatures enacted **indeterminate sentences** (often termed *indefinite sentences*). In keeping with the goal of treatment, indeterminate sentencing gives correctional officials and parole boards significant control over the amount of time that a person serves. Penal codes with indeterminate sentencing stipulate a minimum and maximum amount of time to be served in prison (for example, 1–5 years, 3–10 years, 10–20 years, 1 year to life, and so on). At the time of sentencing, the judge informs the convicted individual about the range of the sentence and that he or she will probably be eligible for parole at some point after the minimum term has been served. The parole board decides the actual release date.

indeterminate sentence
A period of incarceration with minimum and maximum terms stipulated so that parole eligibility depends on the time necessary for treatment; it is closely associated with the rehabilitation concept.

Determinate Sentences In the 1970s, dissatisfaction with the rehabilitation goal and support for the concept of retribution (deserved punishment) led many legislatures to shift to **determinate sentences**. With a determinate sentence, a convicted individual is imprisoned for a specific period (for example, 2 years, 5 years, 10 years) that is determined by the legislature. At the end of the term, minus credited good time (discussed later in this chapter), the person is automatically freed. The time of release is tied neither to participation in treatment programs nor to a parole board's judgment concerning the

determinate sentence
A fixed period of incarceration imposed by a court; it is associated with the concept of retribution or deserved punishment.

individual's likelihood of returning to criminal activities. This sentencing policy is based on the assumption that state legislatures are able to make effective sentencing determinations, although well-known sentencing scholar Brian Johnson argues that "elected officials are unlikely to have the expertise, available time, or legal knowledge to adequately codify, monitor, and regulate systems of fixed determinate punishments."[12]

Some determinate-sentencing states have adopted penal codes that stipulate a specific term for each crime category. Others allow the judge to choose the amount of time to be served from within a range. Some states emphasize a determinate **presumptive sentence**; the legislature or a commission specifies a term based on a time range (for example, 14–20 months) into which most cases should fall. Only in extenuating circumstances can judges depart from the recommended ranges. Whichever sentencing scheme is used, the convicted individual theoretically knows at sentencing the amount of time to be served.

presumptive sentence
A sentence for which the legislature or a commission sets a minimum and maximum range of months or years. Judges are to fix the length of the sentence within that range, allowing for special circumstances.

mandatory sentence
A sentence stipulating that some minimum period of incarceration must be served by people convicted of selected crimes, regardless of background or circumstances.

Mandatory Sentences Politicians and the public have continued to complain that too many people are released before serving terms that are long enough, and legislatures have responded. All states and the federal government now require **mandatory sentences** (often called *mandatory minimum sentences*) that stipulate some minimum period of incarceration that people convicted of selected crimes must serve. The judge may not consider either the circumstances of the offense or the background of the convicted person, and the judge may not impose sentences that do not involve incarceration. Mandatory prison terms are most often specified for violent crimes, drug violations, people with many previous convictions, or crimes involving firearms.

The three-strikes laws now adopted by several states and the federal government provide one example of mandatory sentencing. These laws require that judges sentence individuals who have three felony convictions (in some states two or four convictions) to long prison terms, sometimes to life without parole. Research shows that California's three-strikes law has increased the size of the prison population. Many of these individuals received their third strike for nonviolent crimes, and these people are disproportionately African American and Latino.[13] This law has also resulted in a substantial aging of the prison population that will eventually result in soaring health care costs.[14] Research shows that such laws have had little impact on reducing rates of serious crime (see "Myths in Corrections" for more).[15]

In 2003 the U.S. Supreme Court, in two 5–4 rulings, upheld California's three-strikes law. The plaintiffs in both cases argued that their third felonies were minor and that their long sentences were unconstitutional "cruel and unusual" punishments. Leondro Andrade's third felony was for stealing two videotapes, for which he was sentenced to 50 years without the possibility of parole. Gary Ewing's theft of golf clubs earned him a sentence of 25 years to life. Justices in the majority said that the California law reflected a legislative judgment and that the Court should not second-guess this policy choice. The four justices in the minority argued that there was a "gross" disparity between the pettiness of the crimes and the severity of the sentences.[16]

In November 2012, voters in California approved Proposition 36, changing the provisions of the state's three-strikes law in two important ways. The new law requires that people receiving a third strike must be convicted of serious or violent felonies to be eligible for a sentence of 25 years to life. It also allows certain individuals serving life sentences under the old law to petition the court to request resentencing. These people are eligible for resentencing if the court finds that they do not pose an unreasonable risk of harm to society. In 2015 it was announced that the number of people serving "three-strikes" sentences fell to a 15-year low in California—from 8,900 in 2012 to 6,900 in 2015. This substantial reduction was attributed to changes resulting from the passage of Proposition 36.[17]

Faced with prison overcrowding and constricted budgets, officials are apparently now having second thoughts about mandatory sentences. In many states, mandatory minimum drug laws have come under attack. Well-known criminal justice policy expert Michael Tonry contends that "mandatory penalties are an idea whose time long ago passed."[18]

MYTHS in Corrections

Three Strikes and You're Out

THE MYTH: Three-strikes laws that require judges to sentence people with three felony convictions to long prison terms, such as life without parole, deter people who are thinking about breaking the law and reduce the violent crime rate.

THE REALITY: Research shows that after taking into account how often three-strikes laws are used and considering other factors related to crime, three-strikes laws have virtually no effect on violent crime.

Source: Robert Nash Parker, "Why California's 'Three Strikes' Fails as Crime and Economic Policy, and What to Do," *California Journal of Politics and Policy* 5 (July 2012): 206–31.

The Sentence Versus Actual Time Served Regardless of the discretion that judges have to fine-tune the sentences they give, the prison sentences that are imposed may bear little resemblance to the amount of time served. In reality, parole boards in indeterminate-sentencing states have broad discretion in release decisions once the person has served a minimum portion of the sentence.

Most states have provisions for **good time**, by which days are subtracted from the minimum or maximum sentence for good behavior or for participating in various types of vocational, educational, or treatment programs. Correctional officials consider these policies necessary for maintaining institutional order and reducing crowding. The possibility of receiving good-time credit provides an incentive for incarcerated individuals to follow institutional rules. Prosecutors and defense attorneys also take good time into consideration during plea bargaining. In other words, they think about the actual amount of time that a particular individual is likely to serve.

good time A reduction of a person's prison sentence, at the discretion of the prison administrator, for good behavior or for participation in vocational, educational, and treatment programs.

intermediate sanctions A variety of punishments that are more restrictive than traditional probation but less severe and costly than incarceration.

The amount of good time one can earn varies among the states, usually from 5 to 10 days a month. In some states, once 90 days of good time are earned, these credits are vested; that is, they cannot be taken away as a punishment for misbehavior. Those who then violate the rules risk losing only days not vested.

Judges in the United States often prescribe long periods of incarceration for serious crimes, but good time and parole reduce the amount of time spent in prison. For example, the average length of a state prison sentence is 6.4 years, of which individuals serve 45.5% of these sentences. The percentage of time served varies by the seriousness of the offense committed. For example, individuals sentenced for violent offenses, on average, serve a greater proportion of their sentence than those who committed drug and property crimes.[19]

Truth-in-Sentencing *Truth-in-sentencing* refers to laws that require people to serve a substantial proportion (usually 85 percent for violent crimes) of their prison sentence before being released on parole. These laws have three goals: (1) providing the public with more-accurate information about the actual length of sentences, (2) reducing crime by keeping convicted individuals in prison for longer periods, and (3) achieving a rational allocation of prison space by prioritizing the incarceration of people who commit certain type of crime (such as violent offenses). Critics maintain that truth-in-sentencing increases prison populations at a tremendous cost.

Intermediate Sanctions

Prison crowding and the low levels of probation supervision have spurred interest in the development of **intermediate sanctions**, punishments less severe and costly than prison but more restrictive than traditional probation. Intermediate sanctions provide a variety of restrictions on freedom, such as fines or other monetary sanctions, home confinement, intensive probation supervision, restitution to victims, community service, boot camp, and forfeiture of possessions or illegally gained assets.

Advocates of intermediate punishments stipulate that these sanctions should be used in combination in order to reflect the severity of the offense, the characteristics of the convicted person, and the needs of the community. In addition, intermediate punishments must be supported and enforced by mechanisms that take seriously any breach of the conditions of the sentence. Too often, criminal justice agencies have devoted few resources to enforcing sentences that do not involve incarceration. If the law

Electronic monitoring is an intermediate sanction for people who are not seen as a risk to the public.

does not fulfill its promises, individuals may believe that they have "beaten" the system, which makes the punishment meaningless. Citizens viewing the system's ineffectiveness may develop the attitude that nothing but stiffer sentences will work (see Chapter 9 for a full discussion of intermediate sanctions).

Probation

probation A sentence allowing the convicted individual to serve the sanctions imposed by the court while he or she lives in the community under supervision.

The most frequently applied criminal sanction in the United States is **probation**, a sentence that a convicted person serves in the community under supervision. An estimated 55.5 percent of adults under correctional supervision are on probation (approximately 3.67 million adults).[20] Probation is designed to maintain supervision of individuals while they try to straighten out their lives. As a judicial act, granted by the grace of the state, probation is not extended as a right. Conditions are imposed specifying how an individual will behave throughout the length of the sentence. People on probation may be ordered to undergo regular drug tests, abide by curfews, enroll in educational programs or remain employed, stay away from certain parts of town or certain people, or meet regularly with probation officers. If the conditions of probation are not met, the supervising officer may recommend to the court that the probation be revoked and that the remainder of the sentence be served in prison. Probation may also be revoked for committing a new crime. (See Chapter 8 for a full discussion of probation.)

shock probation A sentence by which an individual is released after a short incarceration and resentenced to probation.

Although people who are on probation serve their sentences in the community, the sanction is often tied to incarceration. In some jurisdictions the court can modify a person's prison sentence, after a portion is served, by changing it to probation. This is often referred to as **shock probation** (or *split probation*). An individual is released after a period of incarceration (the "shock") and resentenced to probation. A person who is on probation may be required to spend intermittent periods, such as weekends or nights, in jail. Whatever the specific terms of the probationary sentence, it emphasizes guidance and supervision in the community.

Probation is generally advocated as a way of rehabilitating people whose crimes are less serious or whose past records are clean. It is viewed as both less expensive and more effective than imprisonment, which may embitter convicted individuals with less experience breaking the law and also mix them with hardened residents so that they learn more-sophisticated criminal techniques.

Death

Although other Western democracies abolished the death penalty years ago, the United States continues to use it. Capital punishment was imposed and carried out regularly before the late 1960s. Amid debates about the constitutionality of the death penalty and with public opinion polls showing increasing opposition to it, the U.S. Supreme Court suspended the use of the death penalty from 1968 to 1976. The Court eventually decided that capital punishment does not violate the Eighth Amendment's prohibition on cruel and unusual punishments. Executions resumed in 1977 as a majority of states began, once again, to sentence murderers to death.

The number of people facing the death penalty increased dramatically for over two decades, as Figure 4.2 reveals. Over the last several years this increase has leveled off. On January 1, 2020, 2,620 people awaited execution in the United States. About one-half of those on death row are in the South. The state with the largest death row population is California (725 people in 2020).[21] Since 1976 the annual number of executions has never exceeded 98 (in 1999). Is this situation the result of the appeals process or of the lack of will on the part of political leaders and a society that is perhaps uncertain about the taking of human life? The death penalty may have more significance as a political symbol than as a deterrent to crime.

In May 2019 the legislature in New Hampshire voted to repeal the state's capital punishment law. New Hampshire became the ninth state in the last 15 years to do so. The new law applies to future cases. After voting in support of the repeal, Representative Renny Cushing stated, "I think it's important the voices of family members who oppose the death penalty

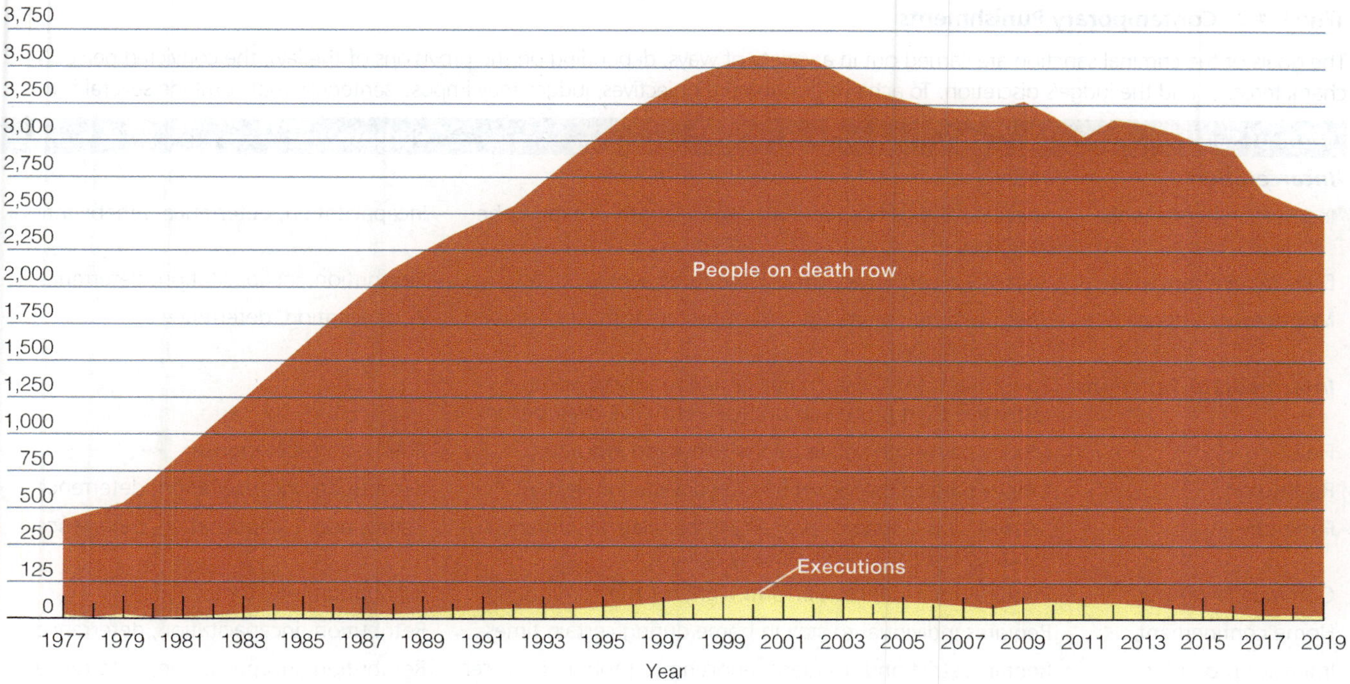

FIGURE 4.2 People Under Sentence of Death and People Executed, 1977–2019

Since 1976, hundreds of new individuals have been added to death row each year, yet the number of executions has never been greater than 98. What explains this situation?

Source: Death Penalty Information Center, www.deathpenaltyinfo.org, April 9, 2020.

were heard, the voices of law enforcement who recognize that the death penalty doesn't work in terms of public safety, and the voices of the people in the state that know the death penalty is an abhorrent practice were all heard today by the Legislature."[22] Governors of other states have taken similar action. For example, California's governor, Gavin Newsom, halted executions in 2019, arguing that the law "has discriminated against defendants who are mentally ill, black and brown, or can't afford expensive legal representation."[23]

The number of executions carried out annually in the United States has dropped steadily between 2009 and 2019 (from 52 to 22).[24] Will the United States eventually join the other industrial democracies and stop executing people? This is an important question, which is addressed in Chapter 20.

Forms and Goals of Sanctions

The criminal sanction takes many forms, and individuals are punished in various ways to serve various purposes. Table 4.2 summarizes how these sanctions operate and how they reflect the underlying philosophies of punishment. Note that incarceration, intermediate sanctions, probation, and death can each be used to achieve one or more punishment goals. As you examine the sentencing process, notice how judges use their discretion to set the punishment within the provisions of the law and the characteristics of the convicted individual.

In recent years, more and more attention has been directed toward "invisible punishments," which include a variety of sanctions that are applied to convicted people that are not always readily apparent to members of the general public. These invisible punishments include (1) allowing termination of parental rights, (2) establishing a felony conviction as grounds for divorce, (3) restricting access to certain occupations, (4) barring those convicted of felonies from public welfare programs and benefits (such as public housing, student loans, and food-purchasing assistance), and (5) denying people convicted of felonies the right to vote.[25]

TABLE 4.2 Contemporary Punishments

The goals of the criminal sanction are carried out in a variety of ways, depending on the provisions of the law, the convicted person's characteristics, and the judge's discretion. To achieve punishment objectives, judges may impose sentences that combine several forms.

Form of Sanction	Description	Purpose
Incarceration	Imprisonment	
Indeterminate sentence	Specifies a maximum and minimum length of time to be served	Incapacitation, deterrence, rehabilitation
Determinate sentence	Specifies a certain length of time to be served	Retribution, incapacitation, deterrence
Mandatory sentence	Specifies a minimum amount of time that must be served for given crimes	Incapacitation, deterrence
Intermediate Sanctions	Punishment for those crimes requiring sanctions more restrictive than probation but less restrictive than prison	
Fine	Money paid to the state by the convicted individual	Retribution, deterrence
Restitution	Money paid to the victim by the convicted individual	Retribution, incapacitation, deterrence
Forfeiture	Seizure by the state of property either illegally obtained or acquired with resources illegally obtained	Retribution, incapacitation, deterrence
Community service	Requires individual to perform work for the community	Retribution, deterrence
Home confinement	Requires individual to stay in home during certain times	Retribution, incapacitation, deterrence
Intensive probation	Requires strict and frequent reporting to probation officer	Retribution, incapacitation, deterrence
Boot camp/Shock probation	Short-term institutional sentence emphasizing physical development and discipline, followed by probation	Retribution, incapacitation, deterrence
Probation	Allows individual to serve a sentence in the community under supervision	Retribution, incapacitation, rehabilitation
Death	Execution	Retribution, incapacitation, deterrence

felon disenfranchisement
A term used to describe laws that either temporarily or permanently restrict the voting rights of individuals convicted of felony offenses.

Much of the debate regarding invisible punishments has centered on voting rights. The process of either permanently or temporarily denying convicted individuals the right to vote is referred to as **felon disenfranchisement**. Many states have disenfranchisement laws in place. Some of these laws restrict voting rights only while people are serving prison terms, but other laws apply to both people who are in prison and on parole. Still others apply to people on probation as well. In a small number of states, voting rights are restricted for incarcerated individuals, people on parole, individuals under probation supervision, and individuals who have completed their felony sentences. In some states, voting rights can be reestablished after a waiting period, the length of which varies from state to state.

Those who are critical of disenfranchisement laws are quick to point out the large number of people affected by them. One study estimates that 6.1 million Americans are disenfranchised because of a felony conviction, which translates to about 1 of every 40 adults in the voting-age population. The estimates are even more alarming when the adult African American population is considered: 1 of every 13 individuals is prohibited from voting (about 7.4 percent of the adult African American population).[26] The map provided in Figure 4.3 shows how disenfranchisement practices vary widely across the states.

Opponents of felon disenfranchisement argue that such laws stifle reintegration efforts because they send people who are returning to the community from prison the message that they have not fully repaid their debt to society. Critics also allege that such laws have actually changed the outcomes of several elections across the United States. Supporters of laws restricting voting rights argue that disenfranchisement is necessary to encourage reform. Put simply, requiring people returning to society from prison to wait several years before having their voting rights reinstated provides them with the opportunity (and provides an incentive) to show they deserve to exercise this right.[27]

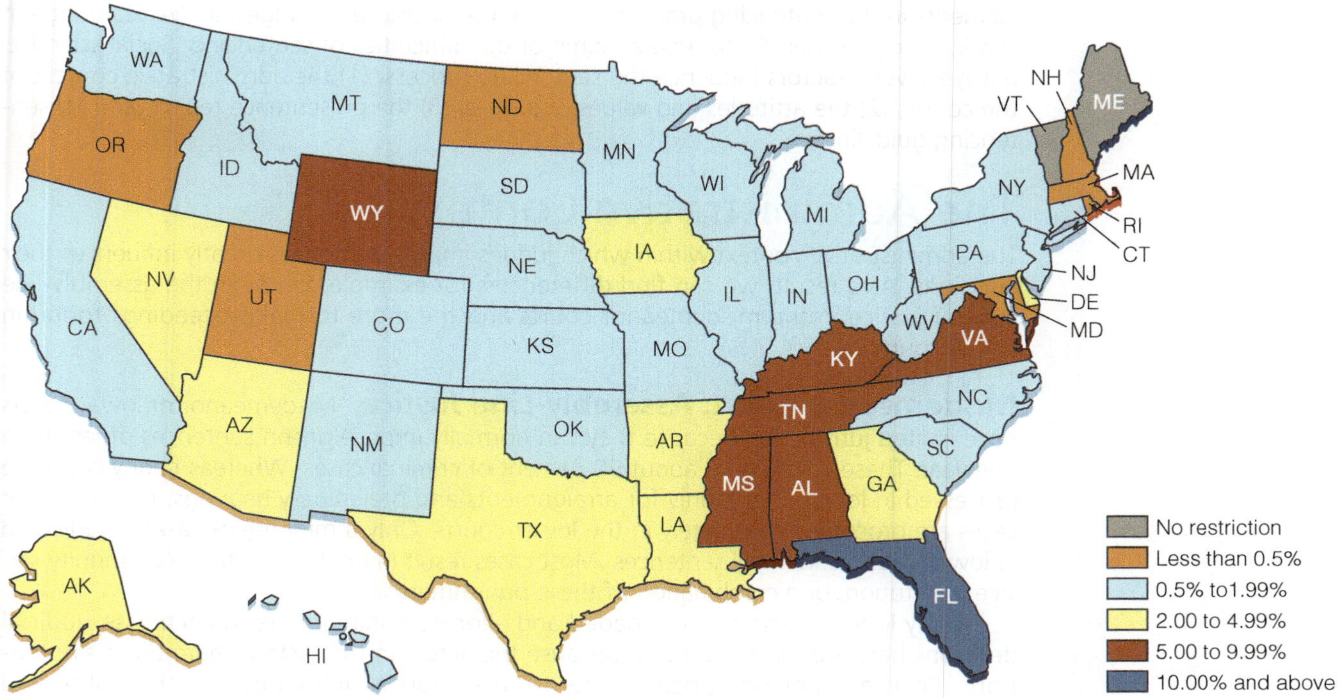

FIGURE 4.3 Rate of Felon Disenfranchisement as Percentage of Voting-Age Adult Population

What accounts for the varying rates of disenfranchisement across states?

Source: Christopher Uggen, Ryan Larson, and Sarah Shannon, *6 Million Lost Voters: State-Level Estimates of Felon Disenfranchisement in the United States, 2016* (Washington, DC: The Sentencing Project, 2016), 15.

THE SENTENCING PROCESS

LO 3

Explain how different factors affect the sentencing process.

Regardless of how and where the decision is made—misdemeanor court or felony court, plea bargain or adversarial context, bench trial or jury trial—judges are responsible for imposing sentences. The often-difficult task of sentencing involves more than applying clear-cut principles to individual cases (see "For Critical Thinking").

Legislatures establish the penal codes which set forth the sentences that judges may impose. These laws generally give judges discretion in sentencing. Judges may combine various forms of punishment in order to tailor the sanction to the individual. For example, the judge may specify that the prison terms for two charges are to run either concurrently (at the same time) or consecutively (one after the other), or that all or part of the period of imprisonment may be suspended. In other situations the convicted person may receive a combination of a suspended prison term, probation, and a fine. Judges may also suspend a sentence as long as the individual stays out of trouble, makes restitution, or seeks medical treatment. They may also delay imposing any sentence but retain the power to set penalties at a later date if the person misbehaves.

When a judge gazes at a convicted man or woman and pronounces sentence, what thinking has gone into his or her decision? Within the discretion allowed by the code, various

FOR CRITICAL THINKING

As was noted at the start of the chapter, Harvey Weinstein was sentenced to 23 years in prison. Some people familiar with this case probably disagree with the sentence that was imposed.

1. If you were the sentencing judge, would you include any intermediate sanctions in Weinstein's sentence? House arrest? Community service? Describe how you would fashion his sentence, and identify the correctional goal(s) it would achieve.
2. Do you think Harvey Weinstein should have been sentenced to a shorter term of incarceration? How long should he serve? What factors associated with the case should influence the length of his imprisonment?

elements in the sentencing process influence the decisions of judges. In "A Trial Judge at Work," Judge Robert Satter relates some of the difficulties of sentencing. Social scientists believe several factors influence the sentencing process: (1) the administrative context of the courts, (2) the attitudes and values of judges, (3) the presentence report, and (4) sentencing guidelines.

The Administrative Context

The administrative context within which judges impose sentences greatly influences their decisions. As a result, we can find differences, for example, between the assembly-line style of justice in the misdemeanor courts and the more formal proceedings found in felony courts.

Misdemeanor Court: Assembly-Line Justice Misdemeanor or lower courts have limited jurisdiction because they can normally impose prison sentences of less than one year. These courts hear about 90 percent of criminal cases. Whereas felony cases are processed in lower courts only for arraignments and preliminary hearings, misdemeanor cases are processed completely in the lower courts. Only a minority of cases adjudicated in lower courts end in jail sentences. Most cases result in fines, probation, community service, restitution, or a combination of these punishments.

Many lower courts are overloaded and allocate minimal time to each case. Judicial decisions here are mass-produced because the actors in the system share three assumptions. First, any person appearing before the court is guilty because the police and

FOCUS ON

PEOPLE IN CORRECTIONS: A Trial Judge at Work: Judge Robert Satter

I am never more conscious of striving to balance the scales of justice than when I am sentencing the convicted. On one scale is society, violated by a crime, on the other is the defendant, fallible, but nonetheless human. . . .

George Edwards was tried before me for sexual assault, first degree. The victim, Barbara Babson, was a personable woman in her late twenties and a junior executive in an insurance company. She described on the stand what had happened to her:

> I was returning to my Hartford apartment with two armloads of groceries. As I entered the elevator, a man followed me. He seemed vaguely familiar but I couldn't quite place him. When I reached my floor and started to open my door, I noticed him behind me. He offered to hold my bags. God, I knew right then I was making a mistake. He pushed me into the apartment and slammed the door. He said, "Don't you know me? I work at Travelers with you." Then I remembered him in the cafeteria and I remembered him once staring at me. Now I could feel his eyes roving over my body, and I heard him say, "I want to screw you." He said it so calmly at first, I didn't believe him. I tried to talk him out of it. When he grabbed my neck, I began to cry and then to scream. His grip tightened, and that really scared me. He forced me into the bedroom, made me take off my clothes.

"Then," she sobbed, "he pushed my legs apart and entered me."
"What happened next?" the state's attorney asked.

> He told me he was going to wait in the next room, and if I tried to leave he would kill me. I found some [pieces of] cardboard, wrote HELP! on them, and put them in my window. But nobody came. Eventually I got up the courage to open the door, and he had left. I immediately called the police.

Edwards's lawyer cross-examined her vigorously, dragging her through the intimate details of her sex life. Then he tried to get her to admit that she had willingly participated in sex with the defendant. . . .

Edwards took the stand in his own defense. A tall man with bushy hair, he was wearing baggy trousers and a rumpled shirt. In a low voice he testified that the woman had always smiled at him at work. He had learned her name and address and gone to her apartment house that day. When he offered to help her with her bundles, she invited him into her apartment. She was very nice and very willing to have sex. He denied using force. I did not believe him. I could not conceive that Miss Babson would have called the police, pressed the charges, and relived the horrors of the experience on the stand if the crime had not been committed as she testified. The jury did not believe him either. They readily returned a verdict of guilty. First-degree sexual assault is a class B felony punishable by a maximum of twenty years in the state prison. If I had sentenced Edwards then, I would have sent him to prison for many years. But sentencing could take place only after a presentence report had been prepared by a probation officer....

Before the rescheduled date, I had weighed the factors, made up my mind, and lived with my decision for several days. In serious criminal cases I do not like to make [a] snap judgment from the bench. I may sometimes allow myself to be persuaded by the lawyers' arguments to reduce a preconceived sentence, but never to raise it....

I gaze out the courtroom window, struggling for the words to express my sentence. I am always conscious that the same sentence can be given in a way that arouses grudging acceptance or deep hostility.

> Mr. Edwards, you have committed a serious crime. I am not going to punish you to set an example for others, because you should not be held responsible for the incidence of crime in our society. I am going to punish you because, as a mature person, you must pay a price for your offense. The state's attorney asks for twenty years because of the gravity of the crime. Your attorney asks for a suspended sentence because you are attempting to deal with whatever within you caused you to commit the crime. Both make valid arguments. I am partially adopting both recommendations. I herewith sentence you to state prison for six years.

Edwards wilts. His wife gasps. I continue.

> However, I am suspending execution after four years. I am placing you on probation for the two-year balance of your term on the condition that you continue in psychiatric treatment until discharged by your doctor. The state is entitled to punish you for the crime that you have committed and the harm you have done. You are entitled to leniency for what I discern to be the sincere effort you are making to help yourself.

Edwards turns to his wife, who rushes up to embrace him. Miss Babson nods to me, not angrily, I think. She walks out of the courtroom and back into her life. As I rise at the bench, a sheriff is leading Edwards down the stairwell to the lockup.

Did Judge Satter strike the appropriate balance in this case? If you were judging this case, how would you sentence Edwards? What facts from the case would you consider when making your decision?

Source: Robert Satter, *Doing Justice: A Trial Judge at Work* (New York: Simon & Schuster, 1990), 170–81.

prosecution have presumably filtered out doubtful cases. Second, the vast majority of people charged with a crime will plead guilty. Third, those charged with minor offenses will be processed in volume, with dozens of cases being decided in rapid succession within a single hour. The citation will be read by the clerk, a guilty plea entered, and the sentence pronounced by the judge for one person after another.

People whose cases are processed through the lower-court assembly line may seem to receive little or no punishment. However, people who get caught in the criminal justice system experience other punishments, whether or not they are ultimately convicted. Time spent in jail awaiting trial, the cost of a bail bond, and days of work lost make an immediate and concrete impact. Some people may even lose their jobs or be evicted from their homes if they fail to work and pay their bills for just a few days. For most people, simply being arrested is devastating. Measuring the psychological and social price of being stigmatized, separated from family, and deprived of freedom is impossible.[28]

Felony Courts Felony cases are processed and convicted individuals are sentenced in courts of general jurisdiction. Because of the seriousness of the crimes, the atmosphere is more formal and generally lacks the chaotic, assembly-line environment of misdemeanor courts. Caseload burdens can affect how much time is devoted to individual cases. Exchange relationships among courtroom actors can help with arranging plea bargains and shape the content of prosecutors' sentencing recommendations. That is, sentencing decisions are ultimately shaped, in part, by the relationships, negotiations, and agreements among the prosecutor, defense attorney, and judge. Table 4.3 shows the types of felony sentences imposed for different offense classifications.

Attitudes and Values of Judges

All lawyers recognize that judges differ from one another in their sentencing decisions. The differences can be explained in part by the conflicting goals of criminal justice, by administrative pressures, and by the influence of community values. Sentencing decisions

TABLE 4.3 Types of Felony Sentences Imposed by State Courts

Note that although we often equate a felony conviction with a sentence to prison, nearly a fourth of people convicted of a felony receive probation.

Most Serious Conviction	Prison	Jail	Probation
All offenses	42%	33%	24%
Violent offenses	57	27	16
Property offenses	42	33	25
Drug offenses	34	37	28
Weapon offenses	53	28	19

Source: Brian Reaves, *Felony Defendants in Large Urban Counties, 2009—Statistical Tables* (Washington, DC: U.S. Government Printing Office, 2013), 29.

also depend on judges' attitudes about the convicted person's blameworthiness, the protection of the community, and the practical implications of the sentence.

Blameworthiness concerns such factors as offense severity (such as violent crime or property crime), the person's criminal history (such as recidivist or first timer), and role in commission of the crime (such as leader or follower). For example, a judge might impose a harsh sentence on an individual who has repeatedly broken the law in the past or who organized others to commit serious crimes.

Protection of the community is influenced by similar factors, such as dangerousness, recidivism, and offense severity. However, it focuses mostly on the need to incapacitate convicted individuals or to deter people who are thinking about breaking the law.

Finally, the practicality of a sentence can affect judges' decisions. For example, judges may take into account the person's ability to "do time," as in the case of an elderly person. They may also consider the impact on the individual's family; a mother with children may call for a different sentence than a single woman would. Finally, costs to the corrections system may play a role in sentencing, as judges consider the size of probation caseloads or prison crowding.

The Presentence Report

presentence report Report prepared by a probation officer, who investigates a convicted person's background to help the judge select an appropriate sentence.

Even though sentencing remains the judge's responsibility, the **presentence report** is an important ingredient in the judicial mix. Usually, a probation officer investigates the convicted person's background, criminal record, job status, and mental condition to suggest a sentence that is in the interests of both the convicted person and society. Although the presentence report serves primarily to help the judge select the sentence, it also helps in the classification of convicted individuals for treatment planning and risk assessment. In the report, the probation officer makes judgments about what information to include and what conclusions to draw from that information. In some states, however, probation officers present only factual material to the judge and make no sentencing recommendation. Because the probation officer does not necessarily follow evidentiary rules, presentence reports include hearsay statements as well as firsthand information. (See Chapter 8 for an example of a presentence report.)

Although presentence reports are represented as diagnostic evaluations, critics point out that they are not scientific and often reflect stereotypes. Research has shown that the nature of the offense and the prior criminal record are what largely influence probation officers' final sentencing recommendation in presentence reports. Officers begin by reviewing the case and typing the accused person as one who should fit into a particular sentencing category. Investigations are then conducted mainly to gather further information to support the initial decision.

The presentence report is one means by which judges ease the strain of decision making. The report lets judges shift partial responsibility to the probation department.

Because a substantial number of sentencing alternatives are available to judges, they often rely on the report for guidance. But two questions often arise: (1) Should judges rely so much on the presentence report? and (2) Does the time spent preparing it represent the best use of probation officers' time? "Do the Right Thing" illustrates some of the difficulties faced by a judge who must impose a sentence with little more than the presentence report to consider.

DO THE RIGHT THING

Seated in her chambers, Judge Carla Tolle read the presentence investigation report of the two young men she would sentence when court resumed. She had not heard these cases. As often happened in this overworked courthouse, the cases had been given to her only for sentencing. Judge Mark Krug had handled the arraignment, plea, and trial.

The two men had held up a convenience store early in the morning, terrorizing the young manager and taking $47.50 from the till. As she read the reports, Judge Tolle noticed that they looked pretty similar. Each of them had dropped out of high school, had held a series of low-wage jobs, and had one prior conviction for which probation had been imposed. Each had been convicted of Burglary 1, robbery at night with a gun. Then she noticed the difference. David Breen had pleaded guilty to the charge in exchange for a promise of leniency. Richard Lane had been convicted on the same charge after a one-week trial. Judge Tolle pondered the decisions that she would soon have to make. Should Lane receive a stiffer sentence because he had taken the court's time and resources? Did she have an obligation to impose the light sentence recommended for Breen by the prosecutor and the defender?

There was a knock on the door. The bailiff stuck his head in. "Everything's ready, Your Honor."

"Okay, Ben, let's go."

WRITING ASSIGNMENT: Put yourself in Judge Tolle's shoes and render a decision in the Breen and Lane cases. First, provide your sentencing decision. Next, discuss the factors that you considered during the decision-making process. Finally, explain which factors influenced you the most and why.

Sentencing Guidelines

Since the 1980s, many states and the federal courts have adopted **sentencing guidelines** in hopes of reducing disparity in sentencing for similar offenses, increasing and decreasing punishments for certain types of convicted individuals and offenses, establishing truth-in-sentencing, reducing prison crowding, and making the sentencing process more rational.[29] Although statutes provide a variety of sentencing options for particular crimes, guidelines point the judge to more-specific actions that have been given previously in similar cases. The range of sentencing options provided for most offenses allows for the seriousness of the crime and the individual's criminal history. In some states guidelines are used for intermediate sanctions.

Legislatures and—in some states and the federal government—commissions construct sentencing guidelines as a grid of two scores. As shown in Table 4.4, one dimension relates to the seriousness of the offense, the other to the individual's criminal history. The person's score is obtained by totaling the points allocated to such factors as the number of juvenile, adult misdemeanor, and adult felony convictions; the number of times incarcerated; his or her status at the time of the last offense, whether on probation or parole or escaped from confinement; and employment status or educational achievement. Judges look at the grid to see what sentence should be imposed on a particular individual who has committed a specific offense. Judges may go outside of the guidelines if aggravating or mitigating circumstances exist; however, they must provide a written explanation of their reasons for doing so.

sentencing guidelines An instrument developed for judges that indicates the usual sanctions given previously for particular offenses.

Sentencing guidelines are expected to be reviewed and modified periodically so that recent decisions will be included. Given that guidelines are constructed on the basis of past sentences, some critics argue that because the guidelines reflect only what has happened, they do not reform sentencing.

One impact of guidelines is that sentencing discretion has shifted from the judge to the prosecutor.[30] The ability of prosecutors to choose the charge and to plea bargain has affected persons accused of a crime: They now realize that they must plead guilty and cooperate in order to avoid the harsh sentences specified for some crimes (such as operating a continuing criminal enterprise). In fact, federal drug laws give prosecutors discretion to ask judges to give sentence reductions for individuals who have provided "substantial assistance in the investigation or prosecution of another person."[31]

TABLE 4.4 Minnesota Sentencing Guidelines Grid (Presumptive Sentence Length in Months)

The italicized numbers within the grid denote the range within which a judge may sentence without the sentence being deemed a departure. Adjudicated individuals with stayed felony sentences may be subject to local confinement.

LESS SERIOUS ↑ ↓ MORE SERIOUS	LESS SERIOUS ← → MORE SERIOUS CRIMINAL HISTORY SCORE 0	1	2	3	4	5	6 or more
Murder, second degree (intentional murder; drive-by shootings)	306 *261–367*	326 *278–391*	346 *295–415*	366 *312–439*	386 *329–363*	406 *346–480*[a]	426 *363–480*[a]
Murder, third degree Murder, second degree (unintentional murder)	150 *128–180*	165 *141–198*	180 *153–216*	195 *166–234*	210 *179–252*	225 *192–270*	240 *204–288*
Assault, first degree Controlled substance crime, first degree	86 *74–103*	98 *84–117*	110 *94–132*	122 *104–146*	134 *114–160*	146 *125–175*	158 *135–189*
Aggravated robbery, first degree Controlled substance crime, second degree	48 *41–57*	58 *50–69*	68 *58–81*	78 *67–93*	88 *75–105*	98 *84–117*	108 92–129
Felony DWI	36	42	48	54 *46–64*	60 *51–72*	66 *57–79*	72 *62–86*
Assault, second degree Felon in possession of a firearm	21	27	33	39 *34–46*	45 *39–54*	51 *44–61*	57 *49–68*
Residential burglary Simple robbery	18	23	28	33 *29–39*	38 *33–45*	43 *37–51*	48 *41–57*
Nonresidential burglary	12[b]	15	18	21	24 *21–28*	27 *23–32*	30 *26–36*
Theft crimes (over $2,500)	12[b]	13	15	17	19 *17–22*	21 *18–25*	23 *20–27*
Theft crimes ($2,500 or less) Check forgery ($200–$2,500)	12[b]	12[a]	13	15	17	19	21 *18–25*
Sale of simulated controlled substance	12[b]	12[a]	12[a]	13	15	17	19 *17–22*

☐ Presumptive commitment to state imprisonment. First-degree murder is excluded from the guidelines by law and continues to be a mandatory life sentence.
☐ Presumptive stayed sentence; at the discretion of the judge, up to a year in jail and/or other nonjail sanctions can be imposed as conditions of probation. However, certain offenses in this section of the grid always carry a presumptive commitment to state prison.

[a]M.S. § 244.09 requires the Sentencing Guidelines to provide a range of 15% downward and 20% upward from the presumptive sentence. However, because the statutory maximum sentence for these offenses is no more than 40 years, the range is capped at that number.
[b]One year and one day.

Sentencing guidelines have led to the development of a rich body of appellate case law. Until the advent of guidelines, the right of convicted individuals or prosecutors to appeal the terms of a sentence was limited. Challenges of judicial interpretations of the guidelines have now increased so that a common law of sentencing is developing. In most states, either party may appeal any departures from the guidelines. For example, if the guidelines call for a 36-month prison sentence and the judge imposes 60 months, the convicted person can appeal.[32] Whereas in 1975 virtually all appeals challenged only the conviction, today sentencing issues may be the sole or primary basis for appeal.

The Future of Sentencing Guidelines

In 2005 the U.S. Supreme Court transformed criminal sentencing by returning much of the discretion that was taken from federal judges in 1984 with the institution of sentencing guidelines. The Court presented its 5–4 decision, *United States v. Booker*, in two parts.[33] In the first part the justices said that the guidelines violated the right to trial by jury because judges had the power to make factual findings that increased sentences beyond the maximum that would be supported by the evidence presented to the jury. Freddie J. Booker had been convicted of intending to distribute at least 50 grams of cocaine base, for which the guidelines recommended a sentence of 20 to just over 22 years. However, the judge imposed a 30-year sentence because he learned that Booker had distributed 10 times that amount of cocaine in the weeks prior to his arrest, a fact that had not been presented to the jury. The majority of the justices said that this violated the Sixth Amendment.

In the second part of the *Booker* decision, the justices said that the guidelines should be treated as discretionary rather than mandatory. Justice Breyer, writing for the majority in this portion of the decision, said that judges should consult the guidelines and take them into account. The guidelines should be understood as being advisory and could be appealed for reasonableness. Some observers noted that judges would still rely heavily on the guidelines, while others said that such an advisory system would give federal trial judges more sentencing power than ever.[34]

The *Booker* case is one in a series of decisions that have thrown into doubt the constitutionality of the federal sentencing guidelines and those of many states. For most observers it was the logical outcome of a line of legal development that began with *Apprendi v. New Jersey* (2000). In that case the U.S. Supreme Court invalidated New Jersey's hate-crime statute, which increased the sentence for an ordinary crime if the judge found that the act was motivated by bias. The Court said that, other than a previous conviction, "any fact that increases the penalty for a crime beyond the prescribed statutory maximum must be submitted to a jury and proved beyond a reasonable doubt."[35] Until the *Apprendi* decision, many state and federal drug indictments did not specify a quantity of drugs in the indictment, allowing the judge to include that information in calculating the sentence. Typically, drug laws impose a series of escalating sentences, depending on drug quantity. Questions were immediately asked about the constitutionality of these laws.

In 2004 the U.S. Supreme Court, following the rationale established in *Apprendi*, struck down the state of Washington's sentencing guidelines (*Blakely v. Washington*), which permitted judges to enhance a sentence by using information that had not been proved beyond a reasonable doubt to a jury.[36] In this case the judge added 37 months to the sentence for kidnapping; as justification, the judge cited "deliberate cruelty," a finding not supported by admissions in Blakely's plea bargain and not proved before the jury. Writing for the 5–4 majority, Justice Scalia said that this provision of the guidelines violates the right to trial by jury because "the judge's authority to sentence derives wholly from the jury's verdict."[37] Quickly following the Court's announcement of the *Blakely* decision, several federal judges declared the federal sentencing guidelines to be unconstitutional.[38]

Although the *Booker* decision might seem to end federal and state guidelines, members of the House of Representatives and the Senate indicated that there would be a renewed struggle between the congressional and judicial branches regarding sentencing policies.[39] Conservatives have been highly critical of judges who have imposed sentences lighter than those called for in the guidelines, while liberals have argued that judges must have the discretion to tailor the punishment to fit the individual and the crime (see "For Critical Thinking"). Sentencing guidelines and efforts to restrict the discretion of judges are not yet over.

FOR CRITICAL THINKING

A variety of factors influence a judge's decision during the sentencing process. Assume that you are the sentencing judge in the Harvey Weinstein case presented at the beginning of this chapter, and consider the following questions:

1. Research shows that most judges are influenced by their assessment of the individual's blameworthiness. Two important elements in determining blameworthiness are the severity of the offense and the role that the convicted person played in the commission of the crime. In the Weinstein case, would either of these two components of blameworthiness cause you to impose a harsher sentence?
2. Would you let the presentence report influence your sentencing decision? If so, what information in the presentence report would be most influential as you make your decision? Weinstein's background? Lack of criminal record? Job status? Mental condition?

UNJUST PUNISHMENT

Unjust punishment can occur because of sentencing disparities and wrongful convictions. The prison population in most states contains a higher proportion of African American and Hispanic men than appears in the general population. Are these sentencing disparities caused by racial prejudices and discrimination, or are other factors at work? Wrongful conviction occurs when an innocent person is nonetheless found guilty by plea or verdict. It also includes those cases in which the conviction of a truly guilty person is overturned on appeal because of due process errors.

LO 4

Discuss the problem of unjust punishment.

Sentencing Disparities

sentencing disparity
Divergence in the lengths and types of sentences imposed for the same crime or for crimes of comparable seriousness when no reasonable justification can be discerned.

A central question is whether gender, racial, ethnic, or class sentencing disparity is the result of discrimination. **Sentencing disparity** occurs when widely divergent penalties are imposed on individuals with similar criminal histories who have committed the same offense, but no reasonable justification can be discerned for the disparity. As shown in Figure 4.4, the incarceration rate for white individuals is lower in many states when compared to African Americans.

In contrast, discrimination occurs when criminal justice officials either directly or indirectly treat people differently because of their race, ethnicity, gender, or class. The fact that African Americans and Hispanics receive harsher punishments than do whites may simply mean that minorities happen to commit more-serious crimes than do whites; if true, this would account for the sentencing disparity. However, if officials singled out members of these groups for harsh punishment because of their race or ethnicity, that would be discrimination.

The research on racial disparities in sentencing has failed to produce consistent results. Overall, however, the weight of the evidence indicates that African American and Hispanic

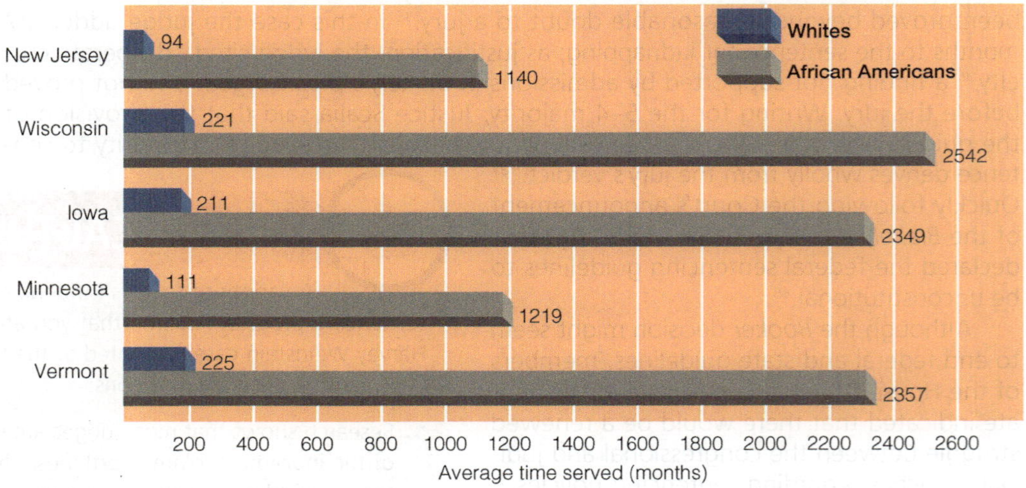

FIGURE 4.4 State Incarceration Rates, by Race

In every state, whites are incarcerated at lower rates than African Americans. This figure provides incarceration rates (per 100,000 population) for states with the greatest racial differences. Why are there such differences between racial groups?

Source: Ashley Nellis, *The Color of Justice: Racial and Ethnic Disparity in State Prisons* (Washington, DC: The Sentencing Project, 2016), 8.

individuals are disadvantaged when it comes to sentencing decisions in that, compared to whites, they are more likely to be incarcerated and less likely to benefit from downward departures from sentencing guidelines.[40] A meta-analysis consisting of 71 published studies found evidence that racial disparities in sentencing are present in cases involving drug offenses and imprisonment.[41]

Do sentencing disparities stem from the prejudicial attitudes of judges, police officers, and prosecutors? Are African Americans and Hispanics viewed as threats when they commit crimes of violence and drug selling, which are thought to be spreading from the inner city to the suburbs? Are enforcement resources distributed so that certain groups are subject to closer scrutiny than others?

Scholars have pointed out that the relationship between race and sentencing is complex and that judges consider many defendant and case characteristics. According to this view, judges assess not only the legally relevant factors of blameworthiness, dangerousness, and recidivism risk, but also race, gender, and age characteristics. The interconnectedness of these variables, not judges' negative attitudes, is what culminates in the disproportionately severe sentences given to young African American men.[42] Laws dealing with the possession and sale of crack cocaine raise interesting questions regarding sentencing disparity and racial discrimination, as discussed in "Politics and Sentencing: The Case of Crack Cocaine."

Wrongful Convictions

A serious dilemma for the criminal justice system concerns people who endure **wrongful conviction**. Whereas the public expresses much concern over those who "beat the system" and go free, people pay comparatively little attention to those who are innocent yet are still convicted.

wrongful conviction A conviction that occurs when an innocent person is found guilty by either plea or verdict.

The development of DNA (deoxyribonucleic acid) technology has increased the number of people exonerated by science. This technology compares the DNA of the suspected person with the DNA in biological substances found on the victim or at the crime scene. As of April 2020, there have been 367 criminal cases in which the convicted person was exonerated because of DNA evidence. Those exonerated spent an average of 14 years in prison. This translates to approximately 5,097 years behind bars for this group. The majority of individuals (roughly 61 percent) who have been exonerated since 1989 are African American.[43]

Over the past decade the number of "innocence projects" has mushroomed nationally. These projects have played a key role in exonerating incarcerated individuals through DNA testing, pressing states to pass postconviction DNA statutes, implementing video-recorded interrogations in police departments, and reforming eyewitness identification procedures.

Why do wrongful convictions occur? Experts usually cite such factors as eyewitness error, improper or invalidated forensic techniques, false confessions, perjured testimony, unethical conduct by police and prosecutors, inadequate counsel, and unreliable informants.[44] Beyond the fact that the real culprit is presumably still free in such cases, the standards of our society are damaged when an innocent person has been wrongfully convicted.

It is very difficult to determine the number of people wrongfully convicted each year in the United States. A study conducted by Robert Ramsey and James Frank asked criminal justice professionals (prosecutors, defense attorneys, judges, and police officers) to estimate how frequently wrongful convictions occur in felony cases. The results indicate that professionals believe such errors occur in 0.5 percent to 1 percent of felony cases in the legal jurisdiction in which they work, and in 1 percent to 3 percent of felony cases nationwide. These same people indicated that a wrongful conviction rate of less than 0.5 percent was acceptable.[45]

FOCUS ON

CORRECTIONAL POLICY: Politics and Sentencing: The Case of Crack Cocaine

The American public first heard about crack cocaine in the mid-1980s. The media reported that it was extremely addictive and cheaper than the powdered form of cocaine. Fear soon spread that crack was not only the drug of choice in the ghetto but was also being used by middle-class, suburban Americans. To address the problem, Congress passed the Anti-Drug Abuse Act in the fall of 1986. The law specified that conviction for possession or distribution of 5 grams of crack cocaine would mean a mandatory five-year sentence with no parole. Possession of greater amounts could lead to a life sentence with no chance of parole. At that time people did not seem to notice that the crack penalty equaled a 100:1 ratio, compared with conviction for possession or distribution of the more expensive powdered cocaine.

The impact of the 1986 law was immediate. From 1988 to 1989, the number of individuals incarcerated for drug offenses shot up by more than 5,500, at the time the largest one-year increase ever recorded by the Federal Bureau of Prisons. By 2008, nearly 20,000 people incarcerated in federal prisons were serving sentences for crack cocaine offenses. Approximately 82 percent of people sentenced in federal court for dealing crack were African American. The disparity between punishments for crack and powdered cocaine offenses soon became a major issue for African Americans.

In 2007 the U.S. Supreme Court ruled that federal judges could use discretion to shorten prison terms for offenses involving crack cocaine. The ruling was intended to reduce the disparity between crimes involving crack and powdered cocaine. Then, in 2010, Congress passed the Fair Sentencing Act. This law greatly reduces the powder-to-crack sentencing ratio (from 100:1 to 18:1). The law also eliminates the five-year mandatory minimum sentences for possession of 28 grams or less of crack cocaine with the intent to distribute. The law is not retroactive. This means that approximately 9,000 people in federal prisons who were convicted of crack offenses (a large portion of whom are African American) remained in prison after the law passed.

Members of the Obama administration recognized that the old law and its 100:1 ratio were unjust. Although they favored legislative remedies, such as passing a law that would make the Fair Sentencing Act retroactive for some individuals convicted of crack offenses, lawmakers never acted. President Obama took action and encouraged people serving long prison sentences for crack cocaine to apply for clemency. Many of the punishments reduced by Obama during his term included those incarcerated for crimes involving crack.

More recently, The First Step Act was signed into law. Among other things, this law allows individuals sentenced under the old law and its 100:1 ratio who are considered low risk and have good conduct records to apply for sentence reductions.

Why has it taken so long for lawmakers to address this perceived injustice? Should elected officials further reduce the crack-to-powder sentencing ratio? If so, what should the ratio be?

Sources: Allie Malloy and Kevin Liptak, "Obama Commutes 330 Sentences, Most in Single Day," CNN.com, January 20, 2017, www.cnn.com/2017/01/19/politics/obama-commutes-330-sentences-most-in-single-day; "At Long Last, a Measure of Justice for Some Drug Offenders," *The New York Times*, June 11, 2019, https://www.nytimes.com/2019/06/11/opinion/first-step-act-drug-offenders.html.

How should the wrongfully convicted be compensated for the time they spent in prison? What is the value of a life unjustly spent behind bars? Increasingly, legislatures have had to face these questions. Thirty-five states and the federal government now have laws to provide compensation. A majority of states with laws to compensate individuals who were wrongfully convicted provide $50,000 or more for each year of incarceration. But these laws vary. For example, some states provide more financial compensation if the individual served time on death row. And some states also provide exonerees with non-monetary services, such as medical expenses, housing assistance, counseling, and other re-entry services.[46] Does any amount of money compensate for missing your child's first day of school or not being with your parents when they die? Compensation can be much higher when in the hands of a jury. In 2019 a federal jury in Massachusetts awarded a man who spent 27 years in prison for a murder he did not commit $27 million.[47]

The U.S. Supreme Court has weighed in on the matter of lawsuits filed by exonerated individuals. The case involved John Thompson, who was convicted of armed robbery and, in a later trial, murder. Two attorneys who were working to save Thompson from the death penalty uncovered blood evidence that was withheld by the prosecution during the murder trial. The evidence proved Thompson's innocence. Prosecutors confessed to the misconduct, the armed robbery conviction was thrown out, and another murder trial was held that resulted in an acquittal. In all, Thompson was incarcerated for 18 years, 14 of which were spent on death row; he once came within weeks of execution. Thompson sued the district attorney's office. The jury in the case awarded him $14 million. However, the U.S. Supreme Court ruled that Thompson could not demonstrate that the district attorney exercised a pattern of deliberate indifference with regard to how he instructed and trained his staff on the matter of sharing evidence with the defense.[48]

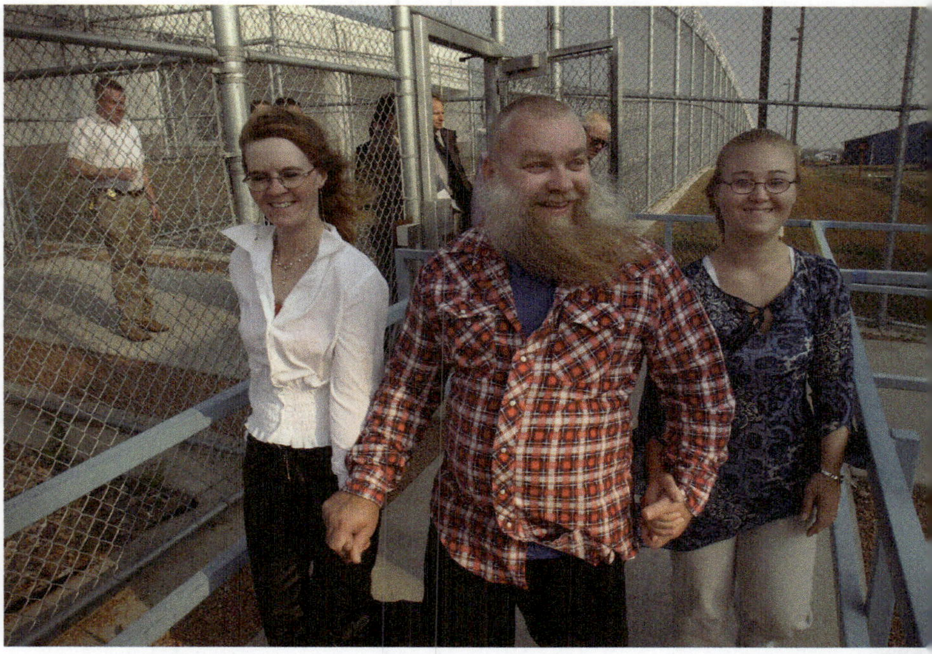

Jeffrey Phelps/Milwaukee Journal Sentinel via USA TODAY

▲ *Steven Avery, accompanied by his sister and daughter, leaves a Wisconsin correctional facility after his murder conviction was overturned—but he spent 18 years in prison waiting for this day.*

Whether unjust punishments result from racial discrimination or from wrongful conviction, they do not serve the ideals of justice. Unjust punishments raise fundamental questions about the criminal justice system and its links to the society that it serves.

SUMMARY

1 Discuss the goals of punishment.

In the United States, criminal sanctions have four goals. Retribution (or deserved punishment) entails punishing a convicted person because he or she deserves to be penalized. Deterrence involves administering punishment to discourage members of the general public (general deterrence) and the convicted person (specific deterrence) from committing future crimes. Incapacitation keeps people from committing future crimes by incarcerating them or putting them to death. Rehabilitation attempts to restore the convicted individual to a constructive place in society through the use of educational or vocational training or therapy.

2 Identify the different forms of the criminal sanction.

Four forms of criminal sanction are used in the United States: incarceration, intermediate sanctions, probation, and death. Incarceration can take place in a jail or prison. A variety of sentencing structures are used (indeterminate, determinate, and mandatory). Intermediate sanctions are penalties that are more severe than probation but less severe than incarceration. Judges use these sanctions in combination in order to reflect the severity of the crime, the characteristics of the person, and the needs of the community. Probation is a sentence that the individual serves in the community. Conditions are imposed specifying how an individual is to behave throughout the sentence. If the conditions are not met, the supervising officer may recommend to the court that probation be revoked. Death is the least frequently used sanction. The death penalty may have more significance as a political symbol than as a deterrent to crime.

3 Explain how different factors affect the sentencing process.
Several factors influence the sentencing process. First, the administrative context of the courts plays a role in sentencing. Misdemeanor courts are run like an assembly line. Because judges hear a large number of cases on a daily basis, they allocate minimal time to each case. In felony courts the crimes are more serious and the proceedings more formal. Second, sentencing decisions depend on judges' values and attitudes about the convicted individual's blameworthiness, which includes such factors as the severity of the offense, the person's criminal history, and the person's role in commission of the crime. Third, the presentence report, usually prepared by a probation officer, provides background information about the individual that helps the judge select the sentence. Finally, sentencing guidelines provide judges with information on the usual sanctions given previously to particular offenses. Sentencing guidelines are intended to reduce disparity in sentencing people who commit similar crimes, establish truth-in-sentencing, and make the sentencing process more rational.

4 Discuss the problem of unjust punishment.
Unjust punishments can occur because of sentencing disparities and wrongful convictions. Sentencing disparity occurs when widely divergent penalties are imposed on people with similar criminal histories who have committed the same offense but when no reasonable justification can be discerned for the disparity. Wrongful conviction occurs when an innocent person is found guilty by either plea or verdict. DNA evidence has helped exonerate innocent people who have been wrongly convicted. To create a system that is more just, reformers want to reduce sentencing disparities and wrongful convictions.

KEY TERMS

determinate sentence (*p. 81*)
felon disenfranchisement (*p. 86*)
general deterrence (*p. 75*)
good time (*p. 83*)
incapacitation (*p. 76*)
indeterminate sentence (*p. 81*)
intermediate sanctions (*p. 83*)
mandatory sentence (*p. 82*)
presentence report (*p. 90*)
presumptive sentence (*p. 82*)
probation (*p. 84*)
rehabilitation (*p. 76*)
restoration (*p. 77*)
retribution (*p. 74*)
selective incapacitation (*p. 76*)
sentencing disparity (*p. 94*)
sentencing guidelines (*p. 91*)
shock probation (*p. 84*)
specific deterrence (special or individual deterrence) (*p. 75*)
wrongful conviction (*p. 95*)

FOR DISCUSSION

1. Should one goal dominate how judges assign criminal sanctions? If not, how would you organize the different goals? By the amount of harm that a person who commits a crime causes? By an individual's criminal history? By some other factor?
2. Can all individuals convicted of a crime be rehabilitated? What kinds of individuals are most likely to benefit from rehabilitation efforts? How should the corrections system deal with people who are difficult to rehabilitate?
3. How much discretion should judges, prosecutors, and parole board members have in administering the criminal sanction? Should one of these positions enjoy higher levels of discretion relative to the others? If yes, what justifies such a view?
4. Suppose you are a state lawmaker. What factors would influence your vote on how criminal sanctions should be used? What factors would you ignore?
5. How would you respond to the argument that individuals who are wrongfully convicted are simply casualties of the war on crime? How would you feel if your friend or relative was wrongfully convicted? If you had a friend who was exonerated of a crime that he or she did not commit, what government compensation would be best?

FOR FURTHER READING

Easton, Susan, and Christine Piper. *Sentencing and Punishment: The Quest for Justice*. London and New York: Oxford University Press, 2016. A comprehensive examination of the current debates on sentencing and punishment in the United Kingdom.

Gould, Jon B. *The Innocence Commission: Preventing Wrongful Convictions and Restoring the Criminal Justice System*. New York: New York University Press, 2007. Examines 12 cases of wrongful conviction in Virginia and points to ways that similar mistakes can be avoided in the future.

Hood, Roger G., and Carolyn Hoyle. *The Death Penalty: A Worldwide Perspective*. London and New York: Oxford University Press, 2008. Provides a global assessment of capital punishment.

Loury, Glenn C. *Race, Incarceration, and American Values*. Cambridge, MA: MIT Press, 2008. Presents the argument that the growing use of incarceration in the United States is not a result of rising crime rates, but instead a product of a generation-old decision to become more punitive as a society.

Manza, Jeff, and Christopher Uggen. *Locked Out: Felon Disenfranchisement and American Democracy*. London and New York: Oxford University Press, 2006. Provides an examination of the political, legal, and sociohistorical context of felon disenfranchisement in the United States.

Spohn, Cassia C. *How Do Judges Decide? The Question for Fairness and Justice in Punishment*. 2nd ed. Thousand Oaks, CA: Sage, 2009. A comprehensive overview of punishment, the sentencing process, disparity in sentencing, and sentencing reform.

NOTES

1 Jan Ransom, "Harvey Weinstein's Stunning Downfall: 23 Years in Prison," *The New York Times*, www.nytimes.com/2020/03/11/nyregion/harvey-weinstein-sentencing.html, March 11, 2020.

2 Herbert L. Packer, *The Limits of the Criminal Sanction* (Stanford, CA: Stanford University Press, 1968), 33–34.

3 Andrew von Hirsch, *Doing Justice* (New York: Hill & Wang, 1976), 49.

4 Kristie R. Blevins, Leah E. Daigle, and Tamara D. Madensen, "The Empirical Status of Deterrence Theory: A Meta-analysis," in *Taking Stock: The Empirical Status of Criminological Theory—Advances in Criminological Theory*, vol. 15, edited by Francis T. Cullen, John Paul Wright, and Kristie R. Blevins (New Brunswick, NJ: Transaction, 2006), 367–95.

5 Kathleen Auerhahn, *Selective Incapacitation and Public Policy* (Albany, NY: State University of New York Press, 2003).

6 Robert Martinson, "What Works? Questions and Answers About Prison Reform," *Public Interest* 35 (Spring 1974): 25–54.

7 Francis T. Cullen, Bonnie S. Fisher, and Brandon K. Applegate, "Public Opinion About Punishment and Corrections," in *Crime and Justice: A Review of Research*, vol. 27, edited by Michael Tonry (Chicago: University of Chicago Press, 2000), 1–79.

8 Leena Kurki, "Restorative and Community Justice in the United States," in *Crime and Justice: A Review of Research*, vol. 27, edited by Michael Tonry (Chicago: University of Chicago Press, 2000), 235–303.

9 Kathleen Daly and Gitana Proietti-Scifoni, "Reparation and Restoration," in *The Oxford Handbook of Crime and Criminology*, edited by Michael Tonry (New York and Oxford: Oxford University Press, 2011), 207–53.

10 Lawrence W. Sherman, Heather Strang, Evan Mayo-Wilson, Daniel J. Woods, and Barak Ariel, "Are Restorative Justice Conferences Effective in Reducing Repeat Offending? Findings from a Campbell Systematic Review," *Journal of Quantitative Criminology* 31 (March 2015): 1–24.

11 Jennifer Bronson and E. Ann Carson, *Prisoners in 2017* (Washington, DC: U.S. Government Printing Office, 2019), 3.

12 Brian D. Johnson, "Sentencing." In *The Oxford Handbook of Crime and Criminology*, edited by Michael Tonry (New York and Oxford: Oxford University Press, 2011), 703–04.

13 Scott Ehlers, Vincent Schiraldi, and Jason Ziedenberg, *Still Striking Out: Ten Years of California's Three Strikes* (Washington, DC: Justice Policy Institute, 2004).

14 Kathleen Auerhahn, "Selective Incapacitation, Three Strikes, and the Problem of Aging Prison Populations: Using Simulated Modeling to See the Future," *Criminology and Public Policy* 1 (2002): 353–88.

15 Robert Nash Parker, "Why California's 'Three Strikes' Fails as Crime and Economic Policy, and What to Do," *California Journal of Politics and Policy* 5 (2012): 206–31.

16 *Lockyer, Attorney General of California v. Andrade*, 538 U.S. 63 (2003); *Ewing v. California*, 538 U.S. 11 (2003).

17 Phillip Reese, "Number of California Inmates Serving Time on 'Three-Strikes' Falls to 15-Year Low," *Sacramento Bee*, www.sacbee.com/site-services/databases/article72913277.html, April 21, 2016.

18 Michael Tonry, "Criminology, Mandatory Minimums, and Public Policy," *Criminology and Public Policy* 5 (2006): 54.

19 Danielle Kaeble, *Time Served in State Prison, 2016* (Washington, DC: U.S. Government Printing Office, 2018).

20 Danielle Kaeble and Mary Cowhig, *Correctional Populations in the United States, 2016* (Washington, DC: U.S. Government Printing Office, 2018), 2.

21 "Facts About the Death Penalty," *Death Penalty Information Center*, https://files.deathpenaltyinfo.org/documents/pdf/FactSheet.f1585003454.pdf, April 17, 2020.
22 "New Hampshire Becomes 21st State to Abolish Death Penalty," *Death Penalty Information Center*, https://deathpenaltyinfo.org/news/new-hampshire-becomes-21st-state-to-abolish-death-penalty, May 30, 2019.
23 "California Governor Announces Moratorium on Executions," Death Penalty Information Center, https://deathpenaltyinfo.org/news/california-governor-announces-moratorium-on-executions, March 13, 2019.
24 "Facts About the Death Penalty," *Death Penalty Information Center*, https://files.deathpenaltyinfo.org/documents/pdf/FactSheet.f1585003454.pdf, April 17, 2020.
25 Jeremy Travis, "Invisible Punishment: An Instrument of Social Exclusion," in *Invisible Punishment: The Collateral Consequences of Mass Imprisonment*, edited by Marc Mauer and Meda Chesney-Lind (New York: New Press, 2002), 17–18.
26 Christopher Uggen, Ryan Larson, and Sarah Shannon, *6 Million Lost Voters: State-Level Estimates of Felon Disenfranchisement, 2016* (Washington, DC: The Sentencing Project, 2016).
27 Hans A. von Spakovsky, "Ex-cons Should Prove They Deserve the Right to Vote," *Heritage Foundation*, www.heritage.org/research/commentary/2013/3/excons-should-prove-they-deserve-the-right-to-vote, March 15, 2013.
28 Malcolm M. Feeley, *The Process Is the Punishment* (New York: Russell Sage Foundation, 1979).
29 U.S. Department of Justice, *Sentencing Guidelines: Reflections on the Future* (Washington, DC: U.S. Government Printing Office, 2001), 2.
30 John Wooldredge and Timothy Griffin, "Displaced Discretion Under Ohio Sentencing Guidelines," *Journal of Criminal Justice* 33 (2005): 301.
31 *2011 Federal Sentencing Guidelines Manual*, www.ussc.gov/Guidelines/2011_Guidelines/Manual_HTML/5k1_1.htm, March 31, 2014.
32 Cassia Spohn, *How Do Judges Decide?* (Thousand Oaks, CA: Sage, 2002), 229.
33 *United States v. Booker*, 543 U.S. 220 (2005).
34 Jan Crawford Greenburg, "High Court Voids Mandatory Sentencing in Federal Courts," *Chicago Tribune*, January 13, 2005, p. 1.
35 *Apprendi v. New Jersey*, 500 U.S. 466 (2000).
36 *Blakely v. Washington*, 124 S. Ct. 2531 (2004).
37 Linda Greenhouse, "Justices, in 5–4 Vote, Raise Doubts on Sentencing Rules," *The New York Times*, June 26, 2004, p. 1.
38 Adam Liptak, "U.S. Judge Overturns Guidelines for Sentences," *The New York Times*, June 30, 2004, A4.
39 Carl Hulse and Adam Liptak, "New Fight Over Controlling Punishments Is Widely Seen," *The New York Times*, January 13, 2005, p. A29.
40 Johnson, "Sentencing," 711.
41 Ojmarrh Mitchell, "A Meta-analysis of Race and Sentencing Research: Explaining the Inconsistencies," *Journal of Quantitative Criminology* 21 (2005): 439–66.
42 Samuel Walker, Cassia Spohn, and Miriam DeLone, *The Color of Justice* (Belmont, CA: Wadsworth 1996), 154.
43 "DNA Exonerations in the United States," *innocenceproject.org*, www.innocenceproject.org/dna-exonerations-in-the-united-states, April 19, 2020.
44 Jon B. Gould and Richard Leo, "One Hundred Years Later: Wrongful Convictions After a Century of Research," *Journal of Criminal Law and Criminology* 100 (2010): 825–68.
45 Robert J. Ramsey and James Frank, "Wrongful Conviction: Perceptions of Criminal Justice Professionals Regarding the Frequency of Wrongful Conviction and the Extent of Systematic Errors," *Crime and Delinquency* 53 (2007): 436–70.
46 "Compensating the Wrongly Convicted," innocenceproject.org, www.innocenceproject.org/compensating-wrongly-convicted, April 19, 2020.
47 Karen Brown, "Jury Awards $27 Million to Massachusetts Man Wrongfully Convicted of Murder," npr.org, https://www.npr.org/2019/10/02/765786518/jury-awards-27-million-to-massachusetts-man-wrongfully-convicted-of-murder, , October 2, 2019.
48 *Connick v. Thompson*, 563 U.S. (2011).

CHAPTER 5

The Law of Corrections

At the Green Bay Correctional Institution, prisoners who tested positive for COVID-19 were isolated and those who were exposed were quarantined.

IN THE EARLY MONTHS OF 2020, THE COVID-19 PANDEMIC BEGAN TO POSE CHALLENGES TO BOTH PRIVATE AND PUBLIC INSTITUTIONS IN THE UNITED STATES. Many businesses were forced to close their doors. Universities moved their classes online. Hospitals in some parts of the country were flooded with patients, many of whom required specialized equipment like ventilators to treat. It quickly became apparent that health care services in some cities were ill-prepared to combat the virus. Not long into the crisis, people started to ask questions about the well-being of those who are incarcerated in correctional facilities. COVID-19 posed an especially difficult problem for corrections officials. Many of the strategies employed to combat the virus were untenable in prison settings. For example, "social distancing" is impossible to achieve in crowded facilities and alcohol-based hand sanitizer is considered contraband in prison.

In an attempt to slow the spread of COVID-19 behind the prison walls, a group of reformers in California filed a motion asking a federal three-judge panel to reduce the prison population. The panel ultimately rejected the motion, ruling that they did not have the authority to consider it. Acknowledging the serious nature of the issue at hand, the panel stated: "We take no satisfaction in turning away Plaintiffs' motion without reaching the important question of whether Defendants have implemented constitutionally adequate measures to protect the inmates of California's prisons from the serious threat posed by this unparalleled pandemic." A spokesperson for the California Department of Corrections and Rehabilitation (CDCR) reassured the public that the "CDCR has taken significant steps to address the safety and well-being of inmates and staff during the COVID-19 pandemic." Only time will tell whether the measures implemented by state authorities will effectively protect corrections personnel and those who are incarcerated from COVID-19.[1]

For a large portion of U.S. history, the federal courts did not interfere with prison operations, largely maintaining a "hands-off policy." People in prison, it was believed, had very few (if any) constitutional rights. This approach came to an end in the 1960s. Under the leadership of Chief Justice Earl Warren, the U.S. Supreme Court ruled that suits against state officials, such as prison wardens and their subordinates, could be heard in the federal courts. Incarcerated individuals started to enjoy a limited set of constitutional rights and could seek relief for violations, such as inadequate medical care and brutality by prison officials, by filing suit in the federal courts.

Federal and state courts are not just concerned about claims by incarcerated individuals that their rights have been violated: Judges have also insisted that the rights of people on probation or parole be respected. In some jurisdictions the courts have declared entire corrections systems to be operating in ways that violate the Constitution. The courts have also ruled on claims by correctional personnel regarding employment discrimination, affirmative action, collective bargaining, and liability for job-related action.

In this chapter we examine the legal foundations on which correctional law is based, analyze the constitutional rights of convicted individuals, and explore the rights and liabilities of correctional personnel.

LEARNING OBJECTIVES

After reading this chapter, you should be able to . . .

1. Discuss the foundations that support the legal rights of incarcerated individuals.
2. Explain the role of the U.S. Supreme Court in interpreting correctional law.
3. Discuss the constitutional rights of incarcerated individuals.
4. Identify the alternatives to litigation.
5. Explain the rights of individuals under community supervision.
6. Discuss how the law affects correctional personnel.

LO 1

Discuss the foundations that support the legal rights of incarcerated individuals.

THE FOUNDATIONS OF CORRECTIONAL LAW

Four foundations support the legal rights of individuals under correctional supervision: (1) constitutions, (2) statutes, (3) case law, and (4) regulations. Most correctional litigation has involved rights claimed under the U.S. Constitution. State constitutions generally parallel the U.S. Constitution but sometimes confer other rights. Legislatures are free to grant additional rights to convicted individuals and to authorize correctional departments to adopt regulations that recognize those rights.

Constitutions

constitution Fundamental law contained in a state or federal document that provides a design of government and lists basic rights for individuals.

Constitutions contain basic principles and procedural safeguards, and they describe the institutions of government (legislature, judiciary, and executive), the powers of government, and the rights of individuals. Constitutional rights are basic protections held by individuals against improper limitations of their freedom. For example, the first 10 amendments to the U.S. Constitution, known collectively as the Bill of Rights, provide protection against government actions that would violate basic rights and liberties. Several have a direct bearing on corrections because they uphold freedom of religion, association, and speech; limit unreasonable searches and seizures; require due process; and prohibit cruel and unusual punishments.

States have their own constitutions that contain protections against state and local governments. During the early 1960s the U.S. Supreme Court decided to require state governments to respect most of the rights listed in the Bill of Rights; before that time the Bill of Rights protected citizens only against actions of the federal government. As a result of Supreme Court decisions, the power of all government officials is limited by the U.S. Constitution and their own state constitution.

The courts of each state are empowered to declare correctional conditions and practices in violation of either the state or the federal constitution. Although most state constitutions do not give convicted persons any greater rights than those granted by the U.S. Constitution, some do.

When convicted of a crime, an individual does not lose all his or her constitutional rights. However, some rights may be limited when they are outweighed by legitimate government interests and when the restriction is reasonably related to those interests. The courts have recognized three specific interests as justifying some restrictions on the constitutional rights of imprisoned individuals: (1) the maintenance of institutional order, (2) the maintenance of institutional security, and (3) the rehabilitation of convicted individuals. Thus, on a case-by-case basis the courts must ask the following question: Are proposed restrictions reasonably related to preserving these interests? Later in this chapter we discuss specific amendments to the U.S. Constitution and decisions of the U.S. Supreme Court regarding prisoners' rights.

Statutes

Statutes are laws passed by legislatures at all levels of government. Within the powers granted, the U.S. Congress is responsible for statutes dealing with problems concerning the entire country. Thus, laws passed by Congress define federal crimes and punishments, allocate funds for criminal justice agencies of the national government, and authorize programs in pursuit of criminal justice policies. Each state legislature enacts laws that govern the acts of its governments (state and local) and individuals within their borders, and enacts laws that fund state agencies such as corrections. The penal codes of the national and state governments contain statutes defining criminal behavior.

statute Law created by the people's elected representatives in legislatures.

Statutes are written in more specific terms than are constitutions. Nonetheless, courts must often interpret the meaning of terms and rule on the legislature's original intent. State legislatures may grant specific rights to convicted individuals beyond those conferred by the state constitutions or the U.S. Constitution. Some state laws have created "liberty interests" that cannot be denied without due process of law. Some states have also enacted "right-to-treatment" legislation and other statutes that charge correctional officials with particular duties. Incarcerated individuals may sue officials who fail to fulfill their statutory duties and obligations. If such claims are upheld, complainants may be entitled to collect monetary damages from the responsible officials or to receive a court ruling ordering a practice stopped.

Case Law

Court decisions, often called **case law**, are a third foundation of correctional law. The United States operates under a common-law system in which judges create law or modify existing law when they rule in specific cases. In deciding the cases presented to them, U.S. judges are guided by constitutional provisions, statutes, and decisions in other cases. These prior rulings, also known as **precedent**, establish legal principles used in making decisions on similar cases. When such a case arises, the judge looks to the principles arising from earlier rulings and applies them to the case being decided. The judge's ability to adjust legal principles when new kinds of situations arise makes the common law, or case law, flexible so that it can respond to changes in society.

case law Legal rules produced by judges' decisions.

precedent Legal rules created in judges' decisions that serve to guide the decisions of other judges in subsequent similar cases.

Constitutions often have phrases that lack clear, definite meanings. Consider the Eighth Amendment's phrase *cruel and unusual punishments*, which judges have interpreted differently in various cases. In *Ford v. Wainwright* (1986), the U.S. Supreme Court was asked to consider whether it was cruel and unusual punishment to execute an individual who became mentally ill while incarcerated. The Court concluded that the Eighth Amendment prohibits the state from executing a person who is insane, ruling that executing an insane person has little retributive value, has no deterrence value, and simply offends humanity.[2] With this decision, *Ford v. Wainwright* became a precedent (and part of case law) that judges are to use when the pending execution of a mentally ill person is challenged. More recently, the Court also addressed whether a condemned individual can be executed if they no longer remember committing the crime because of a mental disability, such as brain damage due to a stroke. The Court ruled that an inability to remember the crime does not prohibit the state from carrying out an execution. However, if the individual in question does not rationally understand the reasons for the execution, the sentence cannot be carried out.[3] Accordingly, we should expect this more recent ruling to also become a precedent when the execution of a person who suffers from severe cognitive dysfunction is contested.

Regulations

Regulations are rules made by federal, state, and local administrative agencies. The legislature, president, or governor gives agencies the power to make detailed regulations governing specific policy in areas such as health, safety, and the environment.

regulations Legal rules, usually set by an agency of the executive branch, designed to implement in detail the policies of that agency.

BIOGRAPHY

EARL WARREN (1891–1974)

The fourteenth chief justice of the United States (1953–1969), Earl Warren began his public career in 1919 as the district attorney of Alameda County, California. He was elected California's attorney general in 1938 and governor in 1942, then twice reelected. President Dwight Eisenhower later appointed him as chief justice. Under his leadership, the Court had a major impact on U.S. law and provided support and impetus for significant social changes.

A department of corrections may create regulations regarding the personal items that individuals may have in their cells, when they can have visitors, how searches are to be carried out, the ways that disciplinary procedures will be conducted, and so forth. Often, these regulations are challenged in court. For example, weekend visiting hours in some prisons are regulated so that half of the incarcerated are eligible for a visit on Saturday and the other half on Sunday. This is justified because of the great numbers who swamp the visiting area on weekends. However, a challenge to the regulation might be mounted by those who for religious reasons cannot travel on the designated day.

Regulations are a form of law that guides the behavior of correctional officials. Regulations are often the basis of legal actions filed by prison residents and correctional employees, who may claim that the regulations violate constitutional protections or statutes or that officials are not following the regulations.

CORRECTIONAL LAW AND THE U.S. SUPREME COURT

For most of U.S. history, the Bill of Rights was interpreted as protecting individuals only from acts of the federal government. These important constitutional rights were viewed as having no bearing on cases where citizens felt unjustly abused by state and local laws. This meant that the Bill of Rights had little influence over criminal justice because the vast majority of cases are in state courts and state corrections systems.

The Fourteenth Amendment, ratified in 1868, barred states from violating a person's right to "due process" and "equal protection" of the law. But not until the 1920s did the U.S. Supreme Court begin to name specific rights that the Fourteenth Amendment protected from infringement by states. Only during the 1960s, under the leadership of Chief Justice Earl Warren, did the Court begin to require that state officials abide by the specific provisions of the Bill of Rights.

hands-off policy A judicial policy of noninterference concerning the internal administration of prisons.

Prior to the 1960s the courts maintained a **hands-off policy** with respect to corrections. Judges in some states applied their states' constitutions to correct abuses in jails and prisons. However, most judges followed the belief of the Virginia judge in *Ruffin v. Commonwealth* (1871) that incarcerated individuals did not have rights.[4] Judges also argued that the separation of powers among the three branches of government prevented them from interfering in the operations of any executive agency. Judges supposed that because they were not penologists, their intervention in the internal administration of prisons would disrupt discipline.

LO 2

Explain the role of the U.S. Supreme Court in interpreting correctional law.

The End of the Hands-off Policy

Although prior to the 1960s individual state court judges occasionally ordered sheriffs and prison officials to change conditions and policies in specific correctional facilities, the U.S. Supreme Court decision in *Cooper v. Pate* (1964) signaled the end of the hands-off policy.[5] The Court said that through the Civil Rights Act of 1871 (referred to here as Section 1983), people held in state prisons were *persons* whose rights are protected by the Constitution. The act imposes **civil liability** on any person who deprives another of constitutional rights. It allows suits against state officials to be heard in the federal courts. Because of *Cooper v. Pate*, the federal courts now recognize that incarcerated individuals may sue state officials over such things as brutality by guards, inadequate nutrition and medical care, theft of personal property, and the denial of basic rights.[6]

civil liability Responsibility for the provision of monetary or other compensation awarded to a plaintiff in a civil action.

At the time, the federal courts were seen as being more likely to rule in the plaintiff's favor than were the state courts. By allowing incarcerated individuals to express grievances to parties outside the institution, the absolute power that prison officials wielded was severely curbed and the prison society was far less isolated from larger society.

Although Section 1983 is the most commonly used legal action to challenge prison and jail conditions, incarcerated individuals may also seek relief by filing a **habeas corpus** petition. This is an ancient legal writ by which plaintiffs (those already in prison or those temporarily detained there prior to trial) ask the courts to examine the legality of their imprisonment and ask for release from illegal confinement. In recent years the Supreme Court has issued several decisions limiting opportunities for incarcerated individuals to file habeas corpus petitions. In 1996 Congress passed the Anti-Terrorism Act, which imposes a one-year limit from the time of conviction to file a federal habeas petition. It also passed the Prison Litigation Reform Act, which makes filing lawsuits more difficult for incarcerated individuals, especially if they have previously had cases dismissed as frivolous. The Military Commissions Act of 2006 restricts unlawful enemy combatants from filing habeas petitions. In 2008, however, the U.S. Supreme Court ruled that the 2006 restrictions were unconstitutional.[7]

habeas corpus A writ (judicial order) asking a person holding another person to produce this person and to give reasons to justify continued confinement.

The number of habeas corpus petitions filed in federal courts by people held in federal and state prisons decreased from 18,329 in 2015 to 17,411 in 2017 (see "Myths in Corrections"). Figure 5.1 presents trends in prisoner habeas corpus petitions since 1966.

Remember that plaintiffs filing habeas petitions are asking to be released from illegally imposed confinement, whereas the Section 1983 civil rights cases seek improvements in prison conditions, return of property, or compensation for abuse by officers. Merely filing

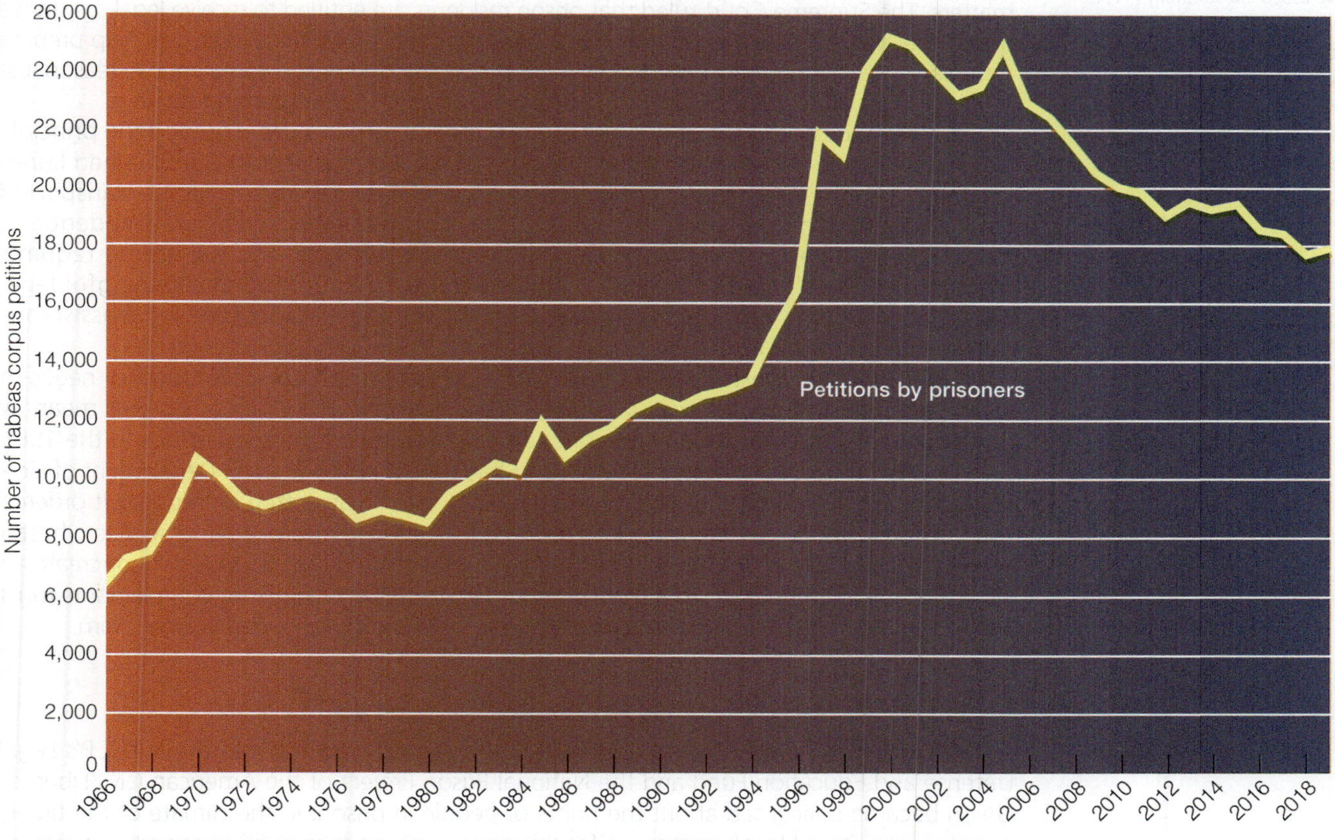

FIGURE 5.1 Trends in Prisoner Habeas Corpus Petitions Filed in U.S. District Courts

A higher number of habeas corpus petitions are filed by people incarcerated in state prisons. This is partially because of the larger number of individuals housed in state facilities compared with the number in federal institutions.

Sources: Bureau of Justice Statistics, *Sourcebook of Criminal Justice Statistics, 1977* (Washington, DC: U.S. Government Printing Office, 1978), Table 5.28; Ann L. Pastore and Kathleen Maguire, eds., *Sourcebook of Criminal Justice Statistics*, Table 5.65.2012, www.albany.edu/sourcebook/pdf/t5652012.pdf, February 18, 2014; United States Courts, *Judicial Business 2019 Tables*, Table C-3, https://www.uscourts.gov/statistics/table/d/statistical-tables-federal-judiciary/2019/12/31, April 22, 2020.

MYTHS in Corrections

Habeas Corpus

THE MYTH: The right of writs of habeas corpus is abused by today's plaintiffs.

THE REALITY: Although the number of habeas petitions has increased dramatically since the mid-1970s, so too has the incarceration rate. In 1975, 8,534 habeas petitions were filed. In that same year the combined federal and state prison population was 240,943. That equals 35 petitions per 1,000 people in prison. The prison population at the end of 2017 was much larger: an estimated 1.49 million people. The number of habeas petitions has also increased substantially (17,411 filings). However, after adjustments are made for prison population growth, the rate of filing has actually decreased to nearly 12 petitions per 1,000 people in prison.

Sources: Ann L. Pastore and Kathleen Maguire, eds., *Sourcebook of Criminal Justice Statistics,* Table 5.65.2012, www.albany.edu/sourcebook, February 18, 2014; United States Courts, *Judicial Business 2019 Tables*, Table C-3, https://www.uscourts.gov/statistics/table/d/statistical-tables-federal-judiciary/2019/12/31, April 22, 2020.

a case in court does not mean that it will be heard, however: A large number of Section 1983 cases are dismissed because the plaintiff did not follow the court's rules or because there was no evidence of a constitutional rights violation. Very few cases actually go to trial and are decided in favor of the plaintiff. The number of Section 1983 cases increased from 26,753 cases in 2015 to 28,454 cases in 2017.[8]

Prisoner-inspired litigation skyrocketed after *Cooper v. Pate*. In federal courts alone, the number of suits brought by incarcerated individuals held in state prisons rose from 218 in 1966 to a high of 40,569 in 1995. Additional cases, of course, were filed in state courts. This onslaught of prisoner litigation drew criticism from correctional officials who said they spent time and resources responding to the suits, conservatives who opposed federal intervention in prison administration, and legislators who argued that judges should refrain from making public policy.[9]

Access to the Courts

Supreme Court decisions that eased prisoner access to the courts assisted this increase in filings. Until the 1970s, many states limited communication between incarcerated individuals and their attorneys, prohibited jailhouse lawyers, and did not provide prison law libraries. These limitations were imposed on the grounds of institutional security, but those who are incarcerated need access to the courts to ensure that officials have followed the law.

The leading case on access to courts is *Johnson v. Avery* (1969).[10] Johnson was disciplined for violating a regulation prohibiting one prison resident from assisting another with legal matters. The Supreme Court ruled that prison residents are entitled to receive legal assistance from other incarcerated individuals unless alternative resources are provided to help prepare necessary legal documents. However, the Court said that the prison could impose reasonable regulations on "jailhouse lawyers" in keeping with the need for order and security.

In a second case, *Bounds v. Smith* (1977), the Supreme Court extended the principle of prisoner access by addressing the question of law libraries. North Carolina had libraries in only 7 of its 77 prisons. People incarcerated in these facilities could be transported to a library for one day of legal research. The Court ruled that this was inadequate, holding that "the fundamental constitutional right of access to the courts requires prison authorities to assist inmates in the preparation and filing of meaningful legal papers by providing prisoners with adequate law libraries or adequate legal assistance from persons trained in the law."[11]

But is the mere presence of a law library enough to satisfy the constitutional needs of incarcerated individuals for access to the courts? What did the Court in *Bounds* mean by "adequate legal assistance"? The Supreme Court addressed these questions in the 1996 case of *Lewis v. Casey*.[12] A lower federal court had held that the Arizona Department of Corrections was not providing adequate legal assistance to incarcerated individuals. It ordered more training for library staff, updating of legal materials, photocopying services, better access to the library, and so forth. In its ruling, the Court said that *Bounds* did not create an abstract, freestanding right to a law library or legal assistance but that complainants must show that the inadequacy of the library hindered their efforts to pursue a legal claim.

The Prisoners' Rights Movement

As an outgrowth of the civil rights movement, organizations such as the NAACP's Legal Defense and Education Fund and the National Prison Project of the American Civil Liberties Union became concerned about the rights of people in prison. In the climate of the times, many groups placed legal protections for this group high on their political agendas. It was no longer unheard of for incarcerated individuals to sue wardens or commissioners of corrections.

The first successful prisoners' rights cases involved the most excessive prison abuses: brutality and inhuman physical conditions. In 1967, for example, the Supreme Court invalidated a Florida man's confession of rioting after he had been thrown naked into a "barren cage," filthy with human excrement, and kept there for 35 days.[13] The notorious Cummins Farm Unit of the Arkansas State Prison (depicted in the film *Brubaker*) was

20th Century Fox Film Corp./Everett Collection

Movies about prison are popular in American culture. Robert Redford starred in Brubaker, the story of Tom Murton, who reformed the Arkansas prison system.

declared in violation of the Eighth Amendment by a federal district court in 1971. In that case the judge, noting that Arkansas relied on trusties (prison residents who serve as "guards") for security, ruled that leaving people open to "frequent assaults, murder, rape, and homosexual conduct" was unconstitutional.[14]

By the end of the 1970s, federal judges had imposed changes on prisons and jails in nearly every state. In addition, important decisions were made requiring due process in probation and parole. By 1990, most of the worst abuses had been corrected, and judges stopped expanding the number and nature of prisoners' rights. As Malcolm Feeley and Edward Rubin note, "Over the course of a single decade, the federal courts fashioned a comprehensive set of judicially enforceable rules for the governance of American prisons."[15]

We have seen that over the past four decades, imprisoned people have pursued rights guaranteed in the U.S. Constitution by filing Section 1983 petitions (42 U.S.C. 1983) in the federal courts (see "For Critical Thinking"). They have asserted that civil rights found in the Bill of Rights have been violated. We now examine the case law that has evolved as the Supreme Court has considered such claims.

FOR CRITICAL THINKING

We opened this chapter by discussing how a group of individuals filed a motion asking a panel of federal judges to make changes to the California prison system to protect incarcerated individuals and staff from COVID-19. This case could have resulted in the federal judiciary directing the executive branch of government regarding correctional matters.

1. When it comes to correctional issues, should the federal courts possess more authority than the other branches of government? Should legislative bodies pass laws attempting to limit the authority of the courts over correctional matters? Explain your answer.
2. Section 1983 allows incarcerated individuals to sue state officials who deprive them of their constitutional rights. How, if at all, should lawsuits by incarcerated people be limited? Should a person who files numerous frivolous lawsuits have this right taken away? How many bad lawsuits would an imprisoned individual have to file before losing access to the courts? Should the federal courts establish some sort of process to screen out ridiculous lawsuits? What would such a process look like? (Some of these questions were addressed by the Prison Litigation Reform Act of 1996, which you will learn more about later in the chapter.)
3. As a society, how concerned should we be with prisoners' rights? Do these rights convey a message to the rest of the world? What about countries that we are encouraging to improve their human rights records? How great is the cost of providing incarcerated individuals with a limited set of constitutional rights and the means with which to protect them?

LO 3

Discuss the constitutional rights of incarcerated individuals.

CONSTITUTIONAL RIGHTS OF THE INCARCERATED

The rights applicable to incarcerated individuals are essentially summarized in a handful of phrases in four of the amendments to the U.S. Constitution. Three of these—the First, Fourth, and Eighth Amendments—are part of the Bill of Rights. The fourth, the Fourteenth Amendment, became effective in 1868. In this section we present the text of these amendments and discuss the rights under them in more detail.

Realize that constitutional rights are not absolute and may conflict with the broader needs of society. Courts must examine government rules to determine exactly which behaviors have been infringed upon and which have not. The Supreme Court did not fully address these boundaries with regard to prisoners' rights until 1987. Because guidance from the higher courts was lacking, many of the tests developed by the lower courts to resolve these cases were contradictory.

Some lower courts have held rules in conflict with First Amendment protections to be unconstitutional unless they were the **least restrictive methods** of dealing with an institutional problem. For example, a court struck down the punishment of incarcerated individuals for writing inflammatory political tracts because officials could have merely confiscated the material.[16] Other courts have stated that a right may be limited if it interferes with a **compelling state interest** such as the goal of maintaining security. A rule prohibiting the receipt of photographs of nude wives and girlfriends was found unconstitutional. The court ruled that the right to receive such photographs was protected; however, because other individuals might be aroused by the sight of them, a rule against their display would have been proper as a security measure.[17] Limitations on the receipt of certain publications have also been upheld on the grounds that such publications present a **clear and present danger** "to the security of a prison, or to the rehabilitation of prisoners."[18]

least restrictive methods Means of ensuring a legitimate state interest (such as security) that impose fewer limits to prisoners' rights than do alternative means of securing that end.

compelling state interest An interest of the state that must take precedence over rights guaranteed by the First Amendment.

clear and present danger Any threat to security or to the safety of individuals that is so obvious and compelling that the need to counter it overrides the guarantees of the First Amendment.

rational basis test Requires that a regulation provide a reasonable, rational method of advancing a legitimate institutional goal.

With courts using different methods to distinguish constitutional from unconstitutional policies, the Supreme Court needed to set standards. Guidance for the lower courts was first enunciated in *Turner v. Safley* (1987), in which the Court upheld a Missouri ban on correspondence among prison inhabitants in different correctional institutions. Justice O'Connor, writing for a 5–4 majority, said that such a regulation was valid only if it was "reasonably related to legitimate penological interests."[19] She specified the four elements of the **rational basis test:**

1. There must be a rational connection between the regulation and the legitimate interest put forward to justify it.
2. There must be alternative means of exercising the right that remain open to people serving prison sentences.
3. There must be a minimal impact of the regulation on correctional officers and other individuals serving prison sentences.
4. There must be a no-less-restrictive alternative available.

This test is the current standard for the analysis of not only First Amendment claims but other constitutional claims as well.

The First Amendment

> **Amendment I:** *Congress shall make no law respecting an establishment of religion, or prohibiting the free exercise thereof; or abridging the freedom of speech, or of the press; or the right of the people peaceably to assemble, and to petition the government for a redress of grievances.*

Since the 1940s, the Supreme Court has maintained that the First Amendment holds a special position in the Bill of Rights because it guarantees those freedoms essential in a democracy.

TABLE 5.1 Selected Interpretations of the First Amendment as Applied to People in Prison

The Supreme Court has made numerous decisions affecting prisoners' rights to freedom of speech and expression and freedom of religion.

Case	Decision
Fulwood v. Clemmer (1962)	The Muslim faith must be recognized as a religion, and officials may not restrict members from holding services.
Gittlemacker v. Prasse (1970)	The state must give incarcerated individuals the opportunity to practice their religion but is not required to provide a member of the clergy.
Cruz v. Beto (1972)	People who adhere to other than conventional beliefs may not be denied the opportunity to practice their religion.
Procunier v. Martinez (1974)	Censorship of mail is permitted only to the extent necessary to maintain prison security.
Kahane v. Carlson (1975)	An Orthodox Jewish person has the right to a diet consistent with his or her religious beliefs while incarcerated unless the government can show cause why it cannot be provided.
Theriault v. Carlson (1977)	The First Amendment does not protect so-called religions that are obvious shams, that tend to mock established institutions, and whose members lack religious sincerity.
O'Lone v. Estate of Shabazz (1987)	The rights of Muslims are not violated when work makes it impossible for them to attend religious services if no alternative exists.
Turner v. Safley (1987)	Incarcerated individuals do not have a right to receive mail from one another, and this mail can be banned if "reasonably related to legitimate penological interests."
Beard v. Banks (2006)	Prison policies that deny magazines, newspapers, and photographs to the most incorrigible residents in the prison system in an effort to promote security and rule compliance are constitutional.

Because of the preferred position of this amendment, it is not surprising that some of the early prisoners' rights cases concerned rights protected by it: access to reading materials, noncensorship of mail, and freedom of religious practice. Table 5.1 shows some of the most significant cases decided under this amendment.

Speech Since the 1970s, courts have extended the rights of freedom of speech and expression to incarcerated individuals, requiring correctional administrators to show why restrictions on these rights must be imposed. For example, in 1974 the Supreme Court ruled that censorship of mail was permissible only when officials could demonstrate a compelling government interest in maintaining security.[20] The result has been a marked increase in communications between people in prison and the outside world. However, the decision in *Turner v. Safley* allowed Missouri to ban correspondence between individuals incarcerated at different institutions as a means of combating prison gangs and communicating escape plans.[21] The Court reaffirmed this in 2001 when it said that regulations concerning mail are valid if they meet the *Turner* test, without regard to whether the letters contain information relevant to a legal case.[22]

The right of free speech also includes access to publications. Incarcerated individuals generally receive books and magazines only directly from the publisher. The Pennsylvania Department of Corrections (PDC) instituted a ban on such periodicals in its Long Term Segregation Unit, which requires those in prison to remain in their cells 23 hours per day. PDC officials noted that doing so was necessary for rehabilitative and security purposes. They argued that depriving individuals of these materials provides an incentive for good behavior and helps improve security because people cannot use such materials to start cell fires or use them to throw feces on unsuspecting officers. The Court said that the PDC's justifications were sufficient, and it noted the need to induce law-abiding behavior among the most difficult residents.[23]

Religion The First Amendment prevents Congress from making laws respecting the establishment of religion or prohibiting its free exercise. Cases concerning the free exercise of religion have caused the judiciary some problems, especially when the practice in question may interfere with prison routine and the maintenance of order.

The growth of the Black Muslim religion in prisons set the stage for suits demanding that this group be granted the same privileges as other faiths (special diets, access to clergy and religious publications, and opportunities for group worship). In the 1960s many wardens believed that the Muslims were a radical political group posing as a religion. They did not grant them the benefits extended to people who practiced conventional religions.

In an early case (*Fulwood v. Clemmer*, 1962), a federal court ruled that officials must recognize the Black Muslims as a religion and allow them to hold worship services as followers of other faiths do. It did not accept the view that the Black Muslims posed a "clear and present danger."[24] In another religion case (*Cruz v. Beto*, 1972), the Supreme Court declared that a Buddhist must be given reasonable opportunities to practice his or her faith, like those given others belonging to religions more commonly practiced in the United States.[25]

However, in *O'Lone v. Estate of Shabazz* (1987), the Court ruled that a Muslim's free-exercise rights were not violated by prison officials who would not alter his work schedule so that he could attend Friday afternoon Jumu'ah services.[26] Shabazz's assignment took him outside the prison, and officials claimed that returning him for services would create a security risk. The justices ruled that the policy was related to a legitimate penological interest.

Muslim, Orthodox Jew, Native American, and others have gained some of the rights considered necessary for the practice of their religions. Court decisions have upheld prisoners' rights to be served meals consistent with religious dietary laws, to correspond with religious leaders and possess religious literature, to wear a beard if one's belief requires it, and to assemble for services. In sum, members of religious minorities have broken new legal ground on First Amendment issues.

Religious freedom is a continuing issue, as seen in the Religious Freedom Restoration Act of 1993 (42 U.S.C. 2000bb). This legislation came in response to a Supreme Court decision, unrelated to corrections, upholding denial of unemployment compensation to two drug treatment counselors dismissed for using peyote during a Native American religious ceremony.[27] Religious leaders immediately became concerned that the Court had weakened First Amendment protections for believers. A broad coalition of groups pressured Congress to restore the requirement that the government must show a compelling interest before it can limit the free exercise of religion. To some, the act undermined the *Turner* and *Shabazz* decisions. In 1997, however, the Supreme Court declared that Congress did not have the authority to enact such legislation (*City of Boerne v. Flores*).[28] To overcome the Court's objections, Congress passed the Religious Land Use and Institutionalized Persons Act in 2000 (RLUIPA). Although much of the litigation surrounding the act concerns land-use regulations and churches' use of their property (as in the *Flores* case), Section 3 prevents government from imposing "substantial burden on a person residing in or confined to an institution." In 2015 the Court ruled unanimously that Arkansas prison officials violated the RLUIPA when they prevented an incarcerated Muslim man from growing a half-inch beard, which is required according to his religious beliefs. Many other state prison systems allow such beards without any problems.[29]

The Fourth Amendment

Amendment IV: *The right of the people to be secure in their persons, houses, papers, and effects, against unreasonable searches and seizures, shall not be violated, and no warrants shall issue but upon probable cause, supported by oath or affirmation, and particularly describing the place to be searched, and the persons or things to be seized.*

TABLE 5.2 Selected Interpretations of the Fourth Amendment as Applied to People in Prison

The Supreme Court has often considered the question of unreasonable searches and seizures.

Case	Decision
Lanza v. New York (1962)	Conversations recorded in a jail visitor's room are not protected by the Fourth Amendment.
United States v. Hitchcock (1972)	A warrantless search of a cell is not unreasonable, and documentary evidence that is found there is not subject to suppression in court. It is not reasonable to expect a prison cell to be accorded the same level of privacy as a home or automobile.
Bell v. Wolfish (1979)	Strip searches, including searches of body cavities after contact visits, may be carried out when the need for such searches outweighs the personal rights invaded.
Hudson v. Palmer (1984)	Officials may search cells without a warrant and seize materials found there.

The Fourth Amendment was designed to protect areas of privacy from government intrusion such as searches. However, on being confined in a correctional institution, people surrender most of their rights to privacy. The amendment prohibits only "unreasonable" searches and seizures. Thus, regulations viewed as reasonable to maintain security and order in an institution may be justified. Table 5.2 outlines some of the Supreme Court's Fourth Amendment opinions. They reveal the fine balance between the right to privacy and institutional need.

Two principal types of searches occur in prisons: searches of cells and searches of persons. In *Hudson v. Palmer* (1984) the Supreme Court made clear that the Fourth Amendment does not apply within the confines of the prison cell. However, the Court noted that this does not necessarily mean that incarcerated individuals have no protections against the harmful consequences of some searches. For example, if the individual's property is damaged or destroyed, he or she can file a lawsuit against the correctional officers.[30]

Searches of the person may be conducted at different levels of intrusiveness: metal detectors, pat-down searches of clothed individuals, visual "strip" (nude) searches, and body cavity searches. Correctional administrators must craft regulations to demonstrate clearly that the level of intrusiveness is related to a legitimate institutional need and not conducted with the intent to humiliate or degrade.[31]

The most-intrusive personal searches involve body cavity examinations, which may require a visual or digital examination of the person's body openings, an X-ray, or the forced taking of a laxative if it is believed that contraband has been hidden in the body. For example, individuals housed in Federal Bureau of Prisons facilities, including those in pretrial detention, are required to expose their body cavities for visual inspection following every contact visit with a person from outside the institution. In *Bell v. Wolfish* (1979), judges argued that this requirement violated the Fourth Amendment. However, in a 5–4 decision the Supreme Court said that "balancing the significant and legitimate security interests of the institution against the privacy interests of the inmates, we conclude that they can [conduct the searches]."[32] The prisoners' privacy rights could be suspended for security purposes. To justify a digital examination to probe the anus or vagina, however, the courts have ruled that there must be reasonable suspicion based on factual circumstances. For example, if an officer observes an incarcerated person receiving a small packet from a visitor and it is not found after pat-down and strip searches, a body cavity search may be justified.[33]

With the employment of both male and female correctional officers in all institutions, lawsuits have been brought to stop opposite-sex officers from viewing and searching the bodies of prison residents. Some courts have ruled that staff members of one sex may not supervise individuals of the opposite sex during bathing, use of the toilet, or strip searches.[34] Here, the inconvenience of ensuring that the officer is of the same sex as the incarcerated individual does not justify the intrusion. Yet the courts have upheld the authority of female guards to pat down male residents, excluding the genital area.[35] Complicating this issue is the concern that not allowing male or female officers to carry out the same job responsibilities, such as opposite-sex searches, violates nondiscrimination laws.

In general, the courts have favored the security and safety interests of prison officials when dealing with search and seizure issues. Only the most intrusive physical searches have come under scrutiny and must be justified on the grounds that officers expected to find contraband.

The Eighth Amendment

> **Amendment VIII:** *Excessive bail shall not be required, nor excessive fines imposed, nor cruel and unusual punishments inflicted.*

The Constitution's prohibition of cruel and unusual punishments has been tied to the need for decent treatment and minimal health standards. The courts have applied three principal tests under the Eighth Amendment to determine whether conditions are unconstitutional: (1) whether the punishment shocks the general conscience of a civilized society, (2) whether the punishment is unnecessarily cruel, and (3) whether the punishment goes beyond legitimate penal aims. Table 5.3 summarizes some of the major Eighth Amendment cases.

totality of conditions The aggregate of circumstances in a correctional facility that, when considered as a whole, may violate the protections guaranteed by the Eighth Amendment, even though such guarantees are not violated by any single condition in the institution.

Federal courts have ruled that although some aspects of prison life may be acceptable, the combination of various factors—the **totality of conditions**—may be such that life in the institution constitutes cruel and unusual punishment. This concept developed from the 1976 decision in *Pugh v. Locke*. Here, Federal District Court Judge Frank M. Johnson Jr., found that "the evidence ... establishes that prison conditions [in Alabama] are so debilitating that they necessarily deprive inmates of any opportunity to rehabilitate themselves or even maintain skills already possessed."[36]

TABLE 5.3 Selected Interpretations of the Eighth Amendment as Applied to Prison Residents

The Supreme Court is called on to determine whether correctional actions constitute cruel and unusual punishment.

Case	Decision
Estelle v. Gamble (1976)	Deliberate indifference to serious medical needs of prison residents constitutes the unnecessary and wanton infliction of pain, and thus violates the Eighth Amendment.
Ruiz v. Estelle (1980)	Conditions of confinement in the Texas prison system are unconstitutional.
Rhodes v. Chapman (1981)	Double-celling and crowding do not necessarily constitute cruel and unusual punishment. It must be shown that the conditions involve "wanton and unnecessary infliction of pain" and are "grossly disproportionate" to the severity of the crime warranting imprisonment.
Whitley v. Albers (1986)	A prison resident mistakenly shot in the leg during a disturbance does not suffer cruel and unusual punishment if the action was taken in good faith to maintain discipline rather than for the mere purpose of causing harm.
Wilson v. Seiter (1991)	Plaintiffs must not only prove that prison conditions are objectively cruel and unusual but also show that they exist because of the deliberate indifference of officials.
Overton v. Bazetta (2003)	Regulations suspending visiting privileges for two years for those who have "flunked" two drug tests do not constitute cruel and unusual punishment. The regulations relate to legitimate penological interests.

When brutality, unsanitary facilities, overcrowding, and inadequate food have been found, judges have used the Eighth Amendment to order sweeping changes and, in some cases, to take over the administration of entire prisons or corrections systems. In these cases, wardens have been ordered to follow specific procedures and to spend money on certain improvements.

Several dramatic cases demonstrate this point. In Georgia, for example, prison conditions were shown to be so bad that judges demanded change throughout the state.[37] In *Ruiz v. Estelle* (1980), described more fully in "The Impact of *Ruiz v. Estelle*," the court ordered the Texas prison system to address unconstitutional conditions. Judicial supervision of the system continued for a decade, finally ending in 1990.

In *Hutto v. Finney* (1978), the Supreme Court upheld a lower court's decision that confinement in Arkansas's segregation cells for more than 30 days was cruel and unusual. In that decision the Court also summarized three principles with regard to the Eighth Amendment:

1. Courts should consider the totality of conditions of confinement.
2. Courts should specify in remedial orders each factor that contributed to the violation and that required a change in order to remove the unconstitutionality.
3. Where appropriate, courts should enunciate specific minimum standards that, if met, would remedy the total constitutional violation.[38]

However, the Court has indicated that unless extreme conditions are found, courts must defer to correctional officials and legislators. Yet the federal courts have intervened in states where institutional conditions or specific aspects of their operation violate the Eighth Amendment.

Of particular concern to correctional officials are court orders requiring an end to prison crowding. For example, the courts have stated that cells must afford each person at least 60 square feet of floor space. However, in *Rhodes v. Chapman* (1981) the Supreme Court upheld double-bunking (two individuals in a cell designed for one person) in Ohio as not constituting a condition of cruel and unusual punishment. To prove violation of the Eighth Amendment, the Court noted, it must be shown that the punishment either "inflicts unnecessary or wanton pain or is grossly disproportionate to the severity of the crime warranting punishment." Unless the conditions in the Ohio prison were "deplorable" or "sordid," the Court declared, the courts should defer to correctional authorities.[39]

The Eighth Amendment also addresses the use of force by correctional officers. In *Wilkins v. Gaddy* (2010) a man held in a North Carolina state prison alleged that officers punched, kicked, kneed, and choked him, causing lower back pain, elevated blood pressure, and mental anguish, among other ailments. The lower courts ruled that the noted injuries were too minimal and dismissed the case. The Supreme Court accepted the case and ruled that two factors must be considered when evaluating use-of-force suits: (1) the extent of injuries alleged by the complainant and (2) the officer's state of mind. Regarding the latter, courts must determine whether the force was applied to restore order or done maliciously—simply to cause

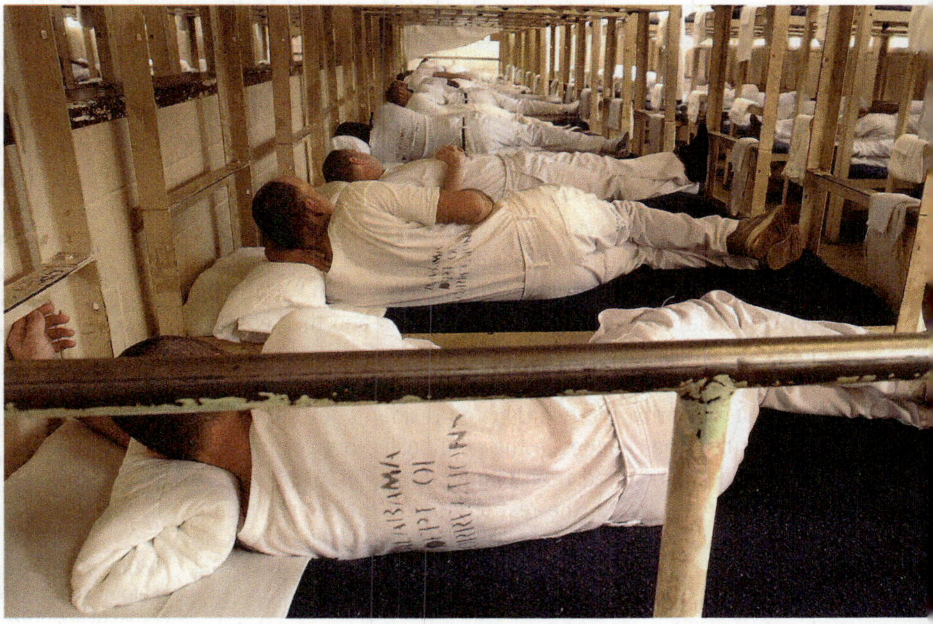

© TAMIKA MOORE, Montgomery Advertiser via Imagn Content Services, LLC

▲ *Overcrowding of prisons and jails can create conditions so problematic that they violate the Eighth Amendment to the Constitution.*

FOCUS ON

CORRECTIONAL POLICY: The Impact of *Ruiz v. Estelle*

In December 1980 William W. Justice, a federal judge for the Eastern District of Texas, issued a sweeping decree against the Texas Department of Corrections. He ordered prison officials to address a host of unconstitutional conditions, including overcrowding, unnecessary use of force by personnel, inadequate numbers of guards, poor health care practices, and a building-tender system that relied on a select group of incarcerated individuals to maintain order inside the prison walls.

Eastham is a large maximum-security institution housing convicted individuals over the age of 25 who have been in prison three or more times. It is tightly managed and has served as the depository for troublemakers from other Texas prisons. To help control this difficult population, the staff used to rely on a select group of prison residents known as building tenders (BTs). By co-opting the BTs with special privileges, officials could use them and their assistants, the turnkeys, to handle problematic individuals serving their sentences at the facility.

In May 1982 Texas signed a consent decree, agreeing to dismantle the building-tender system by January 1983. BTs were reassigned to ordinary prison jobs; stripped of their power, status, and duties; and moved to separate cell blocks for their protection. At the same time, Eastham received 141 new officers, almost doubling the guard force, to help pick up the slack. These reforms were substantial and set off a series of shifts that fundamentally altered the prison society.

With the removal of the BTs and turnkeys, with restrictions on the unofficial use of force by guards, and with the institution of a prisoner discipline system emphasizing due process, fairness, and rights, the traditional social structure of Eastham came under severe strain. Major changes took place within the prison community related to interpersonal relations between the guards and residents, the social organization of prison life, and the guard subculture and work role.

GUARDS AND THE GUARDED

Formerly, ordinary individuals serving time had been subject to an all-encompassing, totalitarian system in which they were "dictated to, exploited, and kept in submission." But with the new relationship between the keepers and the kept, the latter challenged the authority of correctional officers and were more confrontational and hostile. In response to the assaults on their authority, the guards cited residents for infractions of the rules. The changes in the relationship between guards and residents resulted from many factors. First, there were more guards. Second, the restrictions on the guards meant that physical reprisals were not feared. Third, the guards no longer had the BTs to act as intermediaries. Finally, the social distance between guards and residents had diminished. This last factor is important because one result of the civil rights movement is that incarcerated individuals were no longer viewed as "nonpersons." They now had rights and could invoke due process rules to challenge decisions of guards and other officials. As a result, guards had to "negotiate, compromise, or overlook many difficulties with inmates within the everyday control system."

REORGANIZATION WITHIN PRISON SOCIETY

The purging of the BT–turnkey system created a power vacuum characterized by uncertainty. One outcome was a rise in the amount of violence. Whereas in the past the BTs had helped settle disputes among prison residents, during the postreform period these conflicts more often led to violence in which weapons were used. Violent self-help became a social necessity. As personal violence escalated, so did gang activities. Gang members knew that they had to have the assistance of others if they were threatened, assaulted, or robbed. For those men not in gangs, heightened levels of personal insecurity meant that they had to rely on themselves and avoid contact with their potentially troublesome neighbors.

GUARD SUBCULTURE AND WORK ROLE

The court-ordered reforms brought Eastham's operations more in line with the constitutional requirements of fairness and due process, but disrupted an ongoing social system. Before the *Ruiz* decision, the prison had been run on the basis of paternalism, coercion, dominance, and fear. Guards exercised much discretion over the people they supervised, and they used the BTs to help maintain order and to provide information. With the removal of the BTs, guards were assigned to cell-block duty for the first time, placing them in close contact with the incarcerated. The fact that most of the guards were new to prison work meant that they were hesitant to enforce order. Many officers believed that because they could not physically punish individuals and have their supervisors back them up, it was best not to enforce the rules at all. They thought that their authority had been undermined and that the new disciplinary process was frustrating. Many preferred simply to look the other way.

During the transition to a new bureaucratic–legal order, levels of violence and personal insecurity increased. Authority was eroded, combative relations between prison residents and officers materialized, and gangs developed to provide security and autonomy for members. Judicial supervision of the Texas prison system as a result of this case lasted for a decade and ended on March 31, 1990.

Source: Adapted from James W. Marquart and Ben M. Crouch, "Judicial Reform and Prisoner Control: The Impact of *Ruiz v. Estelle* on a Texas Penitentiary," *Law and Society Review* 19 (1985): 557–86. See also *Ruiz v. Estelle*, 503 F.Supp. 1265 (S.D.Tex. 1980).

harm. Interestingly, the Court had identified these two factors in a 1992 case (*Hudson v. McMillian*).[40] In 2010, while correcting the actions of the lower courts and ruling in favor of the plaintiff, the Supreme Court concluded that "an inmate who is gratuitously beaten by guards does not lose his ability to pursue an excessive force claim merely because he has the good fortune to escape without serious injury."[41]

The Fourteenth Amendment

> **Amendment XIV:** *All persons born or naturalized in the United States, and subject to the jurisdiction thereof, are citizens of the United States and of the state wherein they reside. No state shall make or enforce any law which shall abridge the privileges or immunities of citizens of the United States; nor shall any state deprive any person of life, liberty, or property without due process of law; nor deny to any person within its jurisdiction the equal protection of the laws.*

One word and two clauses of the Fourteenth Amendment are relevant to the question of prisoners' rights. The relevant word is *state*, which is found in several clauses. Recall that by the 1970s the Supreme Court had ruled that, through the Fourteenth Amendment, the Bill of Rights restricts state governments.

The first important clause concerns procedural due process. **Procedural due process** requires that all individuals be treated fairly and justly by government officials and that decisions be made according to procedures prescribed by law. Incarcerated individuals sometimes file claims based on the due process clause when they believe that state statutes or administrative procedures have not been followed regarding parole release, intraprison transfers, transfers to administrative segregation, or disciplinary hearings, for example.

The second important clause is the **equal protection** clause. Claims that incarcerated individuals have been denied equal protection of the law involve issues of racial, gender, or religious discrimination.

procedural due process The constitutional guarantee that no agent or instrumentality of government will use any procedures other than those procedures prescribed by law to arrest, prosecute, try, or punish any person.

equal protection The constitutional guarantee that the law will be applied equally to all people, without regard for such individual characteristics as gender, race, and religion.

Due Process in Prison Discipline

Administrators have the discretion to discipline individuals who break prison rules. Until the 1960s, disciplinary procedures could be exercised without challenge because the person was physically confined, lacked communication with the outside, and was legally in the hands of the state. In addition, formal rules of prison conduct either did not exist or were vague. For example, disrespect toward a correctional officer was an infraction, but the characteristics of "disrespect" were not defined. The word of the correctional officer was accepted, and the person who was incarcerated had little opportunity to challenge the charges.

In a series of decisions in the 1970s, the Supreme Court began to insist that procedural due process be part of the most sensitive of institutional practices: sending individuals to solitary confinement and taking away good-time credit for misconduct.

The 1974 case of *Wolff v. McDonnell* extended certain due process rights.[42] The Supreme Court specified that when a person faces serious disciplinary action that may result in segregation or the withdrawal of good time, the state must follow certain minimal procedures that conform to the guarantee of due process:

1. The accused person must be given 24-hour written notice of the charges.
2. The accused person has the right to present witnesses and documentary evidence in defense against the charges.
3. The accused person has the right to a hearing before an impartial body.
4. The accused person has the right to receive a written statement from that body concerning the outcome of the hearing.

However, the Court also recognized the special conditions of incarceration. The Court further stated that incarcerated persons do not have the right to cross-examine witnesses and that the evidence presented by the individual shall not be unduly hazardous to institutional safety or correctional goals.[43]

TABLE 5.4 Selected Interpretations of the Fourteenth Amendment as Applied to People in Prison

The Supreme Court has ruled concerning procedural due process and equal protection.

Case	Decision
Lee v. Washington (1968)	The law in Alabama used to segregate white from black individuals in jails and prisons is unconstitutional.
Wolff v. McDonnell (1974)	The basic elements of procedural due process must be present when decisions are made concerning the disciplining of an individual who is in prison.
Baxter v. Palmigiano (1976)	Although due process must be accorded, an individual has no right to counsel in a disciplinary hearing.
Vitek v. Jones (1980)	The involuntary transfer of an incarcerated individual to a mental hospital requires a hearing and other minimal elements of due process such as notice and the availability of counsel.
Sandin v. Conner (1995)	Prison regulations do not violate due process unless they place atypical and significant hardships on a resident.

As a result of the Supreme Court's decisions, some of which are outlined in Table 5.4, prison officials have established rules that provide some elements of due process in disciplinary proceedings. In many institutions a disciplinary committee receives charges, conducts hearings, and decides guilt and punishment. Such committees usually include administrative personnel, but sometimes they also include prison residents or citizens from the outside. Even with these protections, incarcerated individuals are still relatively powerless and may risk further punishment if they challenge the warden's decisions too vigorously.

Equal Protection In 1968 the Supreme Court firmly established that racial discrimination may not be official policy within prison walls.[44] Segregation may be justified only as a temporary expedient during periods when violence between races is demonstrably imminent. In *Johnson v. California* (2005) the Court justified desegregation in prison by ruling that (1) the use of racial classifications is subject to strict scrutiny analysis, (2) segregation potentially leads to stigmatization, and (3) segregation may promote race-based violence.[45]

Equal protection claims have also been upheld in relation to religious freedoms and access to reading materials of interest to racial minorities. For instance, the cases brought by members of the Black Muslim religion, discussed previously, concerned both the First Amendment right to religious freedom and the Fourteenth Amendment right to equal protection.

Some recent cases concerning equal protection deal with issues concerning female prison inhabitants. Although the U.S. Supreme Court has yet to rule, state and lower federal courts have considered several relevant cases. In *Pargo v. Elliott* (1995), convicted females in Iowa argued that their equal protection rights were violated because programs and services were not at the same level as those provided to males who were incarcerated in Iowa's facilities. The federal court ruled that because of differences and needs, identical treatment is not required for men and women. It was concluded that there was no evidence of "invidious discrimination."[46]

A Change of Judicial Direction

The early years of the prisoners' rights movement brought noteworthy victories. As noted previously, the Supreme Court's decision in *Cooper v. Pate* (1964) allowed incarcerated individuals to sue state officials in the federal courts when their constitutional rights had been denied. But it was not until 1974, in *Wolff v. McDonnell*, that the Court "provided the kind of clarion statement that could serve as a rallying call for prisoners' rights advocates."[47] In that case Justice Byron White, speaking for the Court, wrote the following:

> Lawful imprisonment necessarily makes unavailable many rights and privileges of the ordinary citizen, a retraction justified by the considerations underlying our penal system. ... But though his rights may be diminished by the needs and exigencies of the institutional environment, a prisoner is not wholly stripped of constitutional protections when he is imprisoned for crime.[48]

The language used by the Court here and in several subsequent cases provided the movement with a symbolic lift. It gave prisoners' rights advocates the feeling that the Supreme Court was backing their efforts.

During the past 30 years the Supreme Court has been less supportive of the expansion of prisoners' rights, and a few decisions reflect a retreat. In *Bell v. Wolfish* (1979) the Court asked if the particular restrictions under question were intended as punishment or as an "incident of some other legitimate governmental purpose." The justices also seemed to take great pains to say that "prison administrators should be accorded wide-ranging deference in the adoption and executing of policies."[49] This ruling was followed by *Rhodes v. Chapman* (1981), in which the Court held that to prove an Eighth Amendment violation, the complainant must show that the punishment was unnecessary or out of proportion to the prison-rule violation. Again, the justices said that in most cases the courts should defer to correctional authorities.[50]

Does the emergence of the doctrine that "due deference" must be given to administrators to run their prisons signify a return to the hands-off policy? Justices seem unwilling to intervene in problems of administration, but they have expressed a willingness to hear cases involving substantive rights issues, as in the following 1985 federal circuit court opinion:

> In the great majority of cases it would be sheer folly for society to deny prison officials discretion to act in accordance with their professional judgment. At the same time it would be an abrogation of our responsibility as judges to assume (or, more precisely, to reassume) a "hands-off" posture, requiring categorical acquiescence in such judgments.[51]

The concept of deliberate indifference surfaced in *Daniels v. Williams* (1986). Here the Court said that an incarcerated individual could sue for damages only if officials had inflicted injury intentionally or deliberately.[52] This reasoning was extended in the 1991 case of *Wilson v. Seiter*, where the Court ruled that a resident's conditions of confinement are not unconstitutional unless it can be shown that administrators had acted with "deliberate indifference" to basic human needs.[53] The opinion cites *Estelle v. Gamble* (1976) and *Whitley v. Albers* (1986) to present other Eighth Amendment cases requiring a showing of correctional officials' motives in order to prove a constitutional violation.[54]

Many scholars believe that the deliberate-indifference requirement indicates a shift from the use of objective criteria (proof that the convicted individual suffered conditions protected by the Eighth Amendment) to subjective criteria (the state of mind of correctional officials, namely, deliberate indifference) in determining whether prison conditions are unconstitutional.

Besides upholding deliberate indifference, more recent rulings and laws have also limited access to the federal courts, suggesting that the number of prisoners' rights cases will continue to decrease. For example, in *McCleskey v. Zant* (1991) the Court ruled that all habeas corpus claims must be raised in the initial petition.[55] Also, in *Coleman v. Thompson* (1991) the Court stated that a habeas petition should not be considered even when attorney error resulted in violations of state procedural rules.[56] Thus, although people in prison have a right to access to the courts via law libraries and the assistance of others, the reality is that access has been diminished, especially for those people who lack counsel and are likely to be tripped up by the stricter procedural rules (see "For Critical Thinking").

After years of lobbying by governors and state attorneys general, Congress passed the Prison Litigation Reform Act (PLRA) in 1996. The PLRA has made it more difficult for incarcerated individuals to file civil rights lawsuits and for judges to make decisions affecting prison operations. Regarding judicial intervention, the act limits the authority of federal judges to order remedies and maintain supervision over correctional institutions as a result

FOR CRITICAL THINKING

As noted at the outset of this chapter, the federal courts can mandate changes in state prison operations. However, several reform initiatives have sought to restrict lawsuits filed in federal courts. This chapter has discussed a number of different constitutional rights and mechanisms that can be used by imprisoned people to protect said rights.

1. In the future, which prisoners' rights might be targeted for restriction? Will free speech and the exercise of religion rights be narrowed? Will protections against searches of the person be removed? Will due process in prison discipline be curtailed? Or is it possible that the courts may expand prisoners' rights in the future?
2. Are additional restrictions likely to be placed on Section 1983 suits? Are such restrictions necessary? Explain your answer.
3. Do Section 1983 suits serve any purpose beyond holding prison officials accountable for violating prisoners' constitutional rights? Are prison officials deterred from misconduct out of fear that they will be sued? Can these lawsuits be used to harass prison officials?

of civil rights lawsuits. Judges' orders affecting prisons automatically expire after two years unless new hearings are held to demonstrate that rights violations continue to exist. The act has also made it more difficult for incarcerated individuals to file a civil rights suit because they are first required to exhaust all administrative remedies to resolve a grievance and to recover compensation for mental or emotional injury. In addition, they are prohibited from filing additional civil rights lawsuits if they previously had three lawsuits dismissed as frivolous. The only exception to this rule is if they need to file lawsuits when they are in imminent danger of serious physical harm. Thus, a person who has three prior dismissals cannot file a civil rights lawsuit about a new violation of religious freedom rights because such rights do not concern his or her safety. As shown in Figure 5.2, the number of Section 1983 lawsuits filed in federal courts has dropped substantially since the act was passed. Interestingly, during this same time period the prison population increased dramatically (from 1.13 million in 1996 to 1.49 million in 2017).

Various aspects of the PLRA have been challenged in court, but the U.S. Supreme Court has endorsed the provisions of the law. For example, in *Booth v. Churner* (2001) the Court ruled that a prison resident seeking monetary damages must first complete available prison administrative processes before filing a lawsuit, even if that process does not make provisions for awarding monetary damages.[57] In 2007 the Court ruled that various procedural rules implemented by lower courts, such as rules intended to enforce the PLRA's exhaustion requirement, are not required by the act and that imposing them exceeds proper judicial limits.[58] More recently, the Court unanimously rejected a petitioner's claim that indigents who cannot afford to pay court filing fees in full can be forced to pay only 20 percent of their monthly income, even in the event that they have filed multiple section 1983 cases.[59]

Has the PLRA discouraged meritless lawsuits? It is hard to tell. But critics point out that if this was the case, then we would expect that those cases that have been filed, which are presumably more meritorious, to succeed more frequently than cases filed before the act was passed—a time in which the federal courts were allegedly clogged with frivolous lawsuits. But the success rate following passage has actually decreased, suggesting that meritless cases are not being filtered out.[60] Critics charge that the PLRA has "tilted the playing field against prisoners across the board" by denying equal protection to individuals incarcerated in prisons, jails, and juvenile facilities.[61]

Historically speaking, the Rehnquist Court era (1986–2005) was a period in which "the Supreme Court firmly halted the expansion of constitutional rights for offenders."[62] Although the Supreme Court and Congress may be less sympathetic toward prisoners' claims, the lower federal courts and many state courts continue to support judicial intervention to uphold civil rights. A return to a strict hands-off policy seems highly unlikely, but greater deference is being given to prison administrators.

The Impact of the Prisoners' Rights Movement

The prisoners' rights movement can probably be credited with general changes in U.S. corrections since the late 1970s. The most obvious changes are improvements in institutional conditions and administrative practices. Law libraries and legal assistance are now

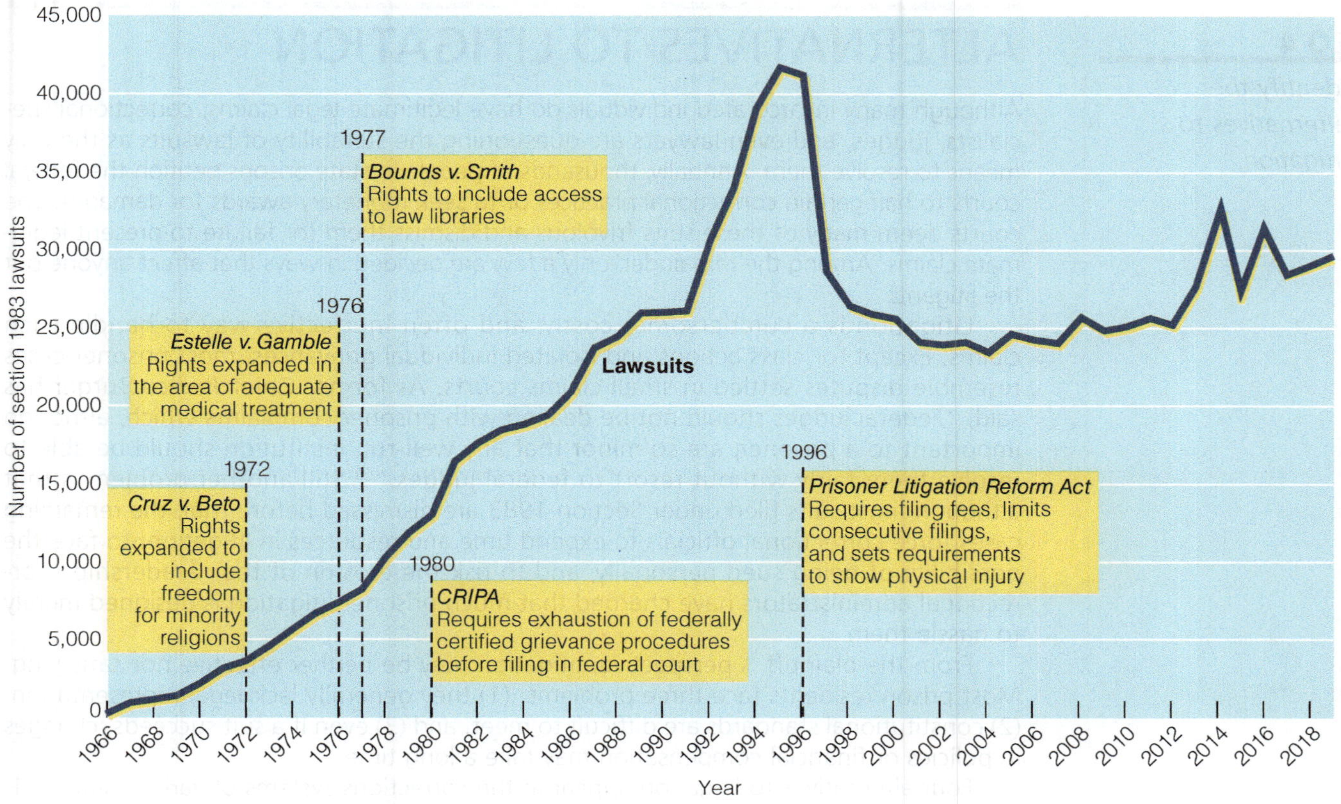

FIGURE 5.2 Section 1983 Lawsuits

The number of Section 1983 lawsuits brought by individuals incarcerated in state prisons has dropped dramatically since the passage of the Prison Litigation Reform Act of 1996.

Sources: Bureau of Justice Statistics, *Sourcebook of Criminal Justice Statistics, 1977* (Washington, DC: U.S. Government Printing Office, 1978), Table 5.28; Ann L. Pastore and Kathleen Maguire, eds., *Sourcebook of Criminal Justice Statistics*, Table 5.65.2012, www.albany.edu/sourcebook, February 18, 2014; United States Courts, *Judicial Business 2019 Tables*, Table C-3, https://www.uscourts.gov/statistics/table/d/statistical-tables-federal-judiciary/2019/12/31, April 22, 2020.

generally available, communication with the outside is easier, religious practices are protected, complaint procedures have been developed, and due process requirements are emphasized. People in solitary confinement undoubtedly suffer less neglect than they did before. Overcrowding remains a problem in some states, but the conditions of prison life have greatly improved.

Although individual cases may have made only a dent in correctional bureaucracies, real changes have occurred over time. The prisoners' rights movement has clearly influenced correctional officials. The threat of lawsuits and public exposure has placed many in the correctional bureaucracy on guard. For example, wardens and their subordinates may now be refraining from traditional disciplinary actions that might result in judicial intervention. One can argue whether or not such changes will ultimately prove useful. On the one hand, this wariness may have merely further bureaucratized corrections, requiring staff to protect themselves from lawsuits by preparing extensive and time-consuming documentation of their actions. On the other hand, judicial intervention has forced corrections to rethink existing procedures and organizational structures. As part of the wider changes in the "new corrections," new administrators, increased funding, reformulated policies, and improved management procedures have, at least in part, been influenced by the prisoners' rights movement. The actual impact of extending constitutional rights to incarcerated individuals has not yet been measured, but evidence suggests that court decisions have had a broad effect.

LO 4

Identify the alternatives to litigation.

ALTERNATIVES TO LITIGATION

Although many incarcerated individuals do have legitimate legal claims, correctional specialists, judges, and even lawyers are questioning the suitability of lawsuits as the only means to resolve them. Annually, thousands of people in state prisons petition the federal courts to halt certain correctional practices or to seek monetary awards for damages. The courts deem many of these suits frivolous and dismiss them for failure to present legitimate claims. Among the remainder, only a few are decided in ways that affect anyone but the litigant.

Litigation is a cumbersome, costly, and often ineffective way to handle such claims. Except for class actions and isolated individual grievances, most prisoner cases resemble disputes settled in small claims courts. As former Chief Justice Burger has said, "Federal judges should not be dealing with prisoner complaints which, although important to a prisoner, are so minor that any well-run institution should be able to resolve them fairly without resort to federal judges."[63] Still another problem is that although most suits filed under Section 1983 are dismissed before trial, the remaining cases force correctional officials to expend time and resources in litigation, to face the possibility of being sued personally, and to risk the erosion of their leadership. Correctional administrators have charged that much prisoner litigation is designed merely to hassle them.

From the plaintiff 's perspective, litigation may be neither effective nor satisfying. Most prison residents face three problems: (1) they generally lack legal representation, (2) constitutional standards are difficult to meet, and (3) even if a suit succeeds, changes in policies or financial compensation may take a long time.

Four alternatives to litigation appear in the corrections systems of various states: (1) grievance procedures, (2) use of an ombudsman, (3) mediation, and (4) legal assistance. All are designed to solve problems before people feel compelled to file a suit, but mediation and legal assistance can also be invoked after a suit has been initiated.

Grievance Procedures

Although informal procedures for hearing prison residents' complaints have existed for many years, only since the mid-1970s have formal grievance mechanisms been widely used. All states and the Federal Bureau of Prisons now have grievance procedures.

Most corrections systems use a three-step grievance process. A staff member or committee in each institution usually receives complaints, investigates them, and makes decisions. If the complainant is dissatisfied with the outcome, he or she may appeal the case to the warden and ultimately to the commissioner of corrections. Reports indicate that some grievances are more easily resolved than others. For example, many individuals in prison complain that they are not receiving proper medical treatment, but because medical personnel can usually document the treatment provided, such complaints normally subside. The many complaints of lost personal property are another matter. Most involve items deposited at the reception center at the time of arrival but not transferred with the individual to another institution. Staff members often cannot account for missing property, and the process for receiving compensation for property lost or damaged can be complicated. Probably the most difficult situation to resolve is alleged brutality by a guard. Such a complaint virtually always comes down to the incarcerated person's word against the officer's because staff members rarely testify against other officers.

The grievance procedure can help defuse tensions in correctional facilities. It also serves as a management tool. By attentive monitoring of the complaint process, a warden can discern patterns of discontent among the imprisoned that may warrant actions to prevent the development of deeper problems.

The Ombudsman

Ombudsman programs are dispute-resolution mechanisms in corrections. Begun in Sweden, such programs have been used successfully throughout the United States for more than two decades. An **ombudsman** is a public official with full authority to investigate citizens' complaints against government officials.

ombudsman A public official who investigates complaints against government officials and recommends corrective measures.

Ombudsman programs succeed if incarcerated individuals have quick and easy access to the office. When prison residents respect their ombudsman, his advice on the merits of grievances may help reduce the number of frivolous claims; when ombudsmen see merit in claims, they can try to convince authorities that it would be in their interest to resolve the matters out of court.

Mediation

Mediation is a consensual and voluntary process in which a neutral third party assists disputants in reconciling their differences. The informality of the process stands in contrast to the complex, cumbersome procedures of the courtroom. Proponents point out that in the mediation process, straightforward questions can be asked so that underlying issues can be explored. This feature offers a special advantage to disputants, most of whom would not have counsel were they to take their cases to court. Mediation is particularly effective when the essence of a complaint is not a conflict of abstract principles but a problem requiring an administrative solution. However, mediation has not lived up to its potential in the correctional arena because in many cases neither party seems willing to be bound by the decision.

mediation Intervention in a dispute by a third party to whom the parties in conflict submit their differences for resolution and whose decision (in the correctional setting) is binding on both parties.

FOCUS ON

PEOPLE IN CORRECTIONS: The Best Jailhouse Lawyer in America?

In January 2004, Seth Waxman, an attorney who once served as solicitor general of the United States, rushed to the phone to call his colleague, Shon Hopwood. The news that Waxman wanted to share was good. The U.S. Supreme Court had just handed down a 9–0 ruling in support of a petition authored by the two men. Truth be told, it was something of a small miracle that the Court heard the petition in the first place. After all, the Court receives several thousand petitions each year. In 2004 it selected only eight of them to hear. Where was Hopwood? What was he doing? He wasn't holed up in a fancy New York City law office preparing another petition. He was serving 13 years in a federal prison for robbing banks.

Between 1997 and 1998, Shon Hopwood robbed five rural Nebraska banks. No one was ever physically injured during the heists, nor did Hopwood get away with millions of dollars. But bank robbery is a serious crime. The judge hearing the case, Richard Kopf, noted that Hopwood had instilled considerable fear in the bank employees. Addressing the court during the sentencing phase of the trial, Hopwood promised to change his ways. Judge Kopf responded, "We'll know in about 13 years if you mean what you say."

While in prison, Hopwood worked in the law library, helping other prison residents with their cases and studying the law. When he first took the job, he did not have grand aspirations to one day practice law. To the contrary, he just wanted to get out of the prison kitchen. The working conditions there were miserable. In 2002 Hopwood prepared his first petition, which the Supreme Court agreed to hear. Then in 2005 the Court agreed to hear another petition prepared by Hopwood. Matt Jones, associate director of the Office of State's Attorneys Appellate Prosecutor, commented that to have one of your petitions heard by the Supreme Court is "remarkable" but to have a second one heard is "mind blowing." Hopwood is also credited with helping many other convicted individuals from various states with their cases.

When asked why he robbed five banks, Hopwood said that he was a "stupid and immature kid" whose life lacked direction. He was released from prison in 2008. In 2009 he married a high school classmate. Hopwood graduated from the University of Washington in 2014 with a law degree. After working as a clerk in the D.C. circuit court, Hopwood assumed a faculty position at the Georgetown University Law Center, where he also received a postgraduate degree in law.

Sources: Adam Liptak, "A Mediocre Criminal, but an Unmatched Jailhouse Lawyer," *The New York Times*, February 9, 2010, www.nytimes.com/2010/02/09/us/09bar.html; Pam Adams, "Former Pekin Inmate Turns Life Around After Supreme Court Cases," pjstar.com, September 26, 2010, www.pjstar.com/news/tricounty/x1319753156/Former-Pekin-inmate-turns-life-around-after-Supreme-Court-cases; Michael Santos, "The Inspiring Story of an Ex–Bank Robber Who Turned into America's Best Jailhouse Lawyer," *Business Insider*, www.businessinsider.com/the-inspiring-story-of-an-ex-bank-robber-who-turned-into-americas-best-jailhouse-lawyer-2015-4, April 7, 2015.

Legal Assistance

As noted previously, the Supreme Court has emphasized that incarcerated individuals must have access to legal resources so that they can seek postconviction relief.[64] Since the early 1970s, several legal-assistance mechanisms have been developed in correctional institutions, including staff attorneys to assist incarcerated individuals with their legal problems, jailhouse lawyers, and law school clinics (see "The Best Jailhouse Lawyer in America?").

Providing legal assistance may seem counterproductive if the goal of correctional administrators is to avoid litigation, but lawyers do more than simply help incarcerated individuals file suits. They also advise on the legal merits of complaints and thus can discourage frivolous suits. Further, counsel can help determine the underlying issues of a complaint and therefore frame questions in legal terms.

LAW AND COMMUNITY CORRECTIONS

Although public attention and most correctional law concerns prisons and jails, a majority of convicted individuals are supervised in the community. However, as with individuals in prison, individuals under correctional supervision in the community do have rights, and courts have addressed issues concerning due process and searches and seizures.

As discussed in Chapter 4, probation is a type of community sentence, and people on parole are individuals released to community supervision after spending a portion of their sentence in prison. Probation is imposed by a judge and is administered by probation officers. Parole is usually granted by a parole board and is administered by parole officers. Eligibility for parole is stated in the law, as are the release criteria. Even in those states with determinate sentencing and mandatory release, people on parole receive supervision for a specified length of time.

There is no *right* to parole. In *Greenholtz v. Inmates of the Nebraska Penal and Correction Complex* (1979), the U.S. Supreme Court made clear that the state grants release on parole and that individuals do not have a right to be conditionally released before the expiration of a sentence.[65] Supporting the authority of parole and pardons boards, the Court ruled in *Connecticut Board of Pardons v. Dumschat* (1981) that an incarcerated individual did not have a right to learn why his request for commutation (reduction) of his life sentence was denied. Dumschat claimed that he had some expectation of commutation because three-quarters of lifers in that state received commutation and thereby became eligible for parole.[66] In 2011 the Court revisited the issue in response to the Ninth Circuit Court of Appeals order that parole be granted to several incarcerated individuals, some of whom were convicted of murder. The Court reversed the lower court's ruling (*Swarthout v. Cooke*, 2011). Writing for the majority, Justice Anthony Kennedy stated that "there is no right under the Federal Constitution to be conditionally released before the expiration of a valid sentence, and the States are under no duty to offer parole to their prisoners."[67]

LO 5

Explain the rights of individuals under community supervision

Constitutional Rights of People on Probation or Parole

While in the community on probation or parole, individuals must live according to conditions specified at the time of their sentencing or parole release. Should these conditions be violated, community supervision may be revoked and the person sent to prison for the remainder of the sentence, meaning that this group of people does not enjoy the constitutional rights of ordinary citizens. As Justice Scalia said, "It is always true of probationers (as we have said it to be true of parolees) that they do not enjoy 'the absolute liberty to which every citizen is entitled, but only ... conditional liberty properly dependent on observation of special restrictions.'"[68]

The conditions placed on these people may interfere with their constitutional rights. Such conditions typically limit the right of free association by denying them contact with their crime partners or victims. But courts have struck down conditions preventing people on parole from giving public speeches and receiving publications. The case of *Griffin v. Wisconsin* (1987) provides a good example of the clash between the Bill of Rights and community corrections.[69] Learning that Griffin might have a gun, probation officers searched his apartment without a warrant. The Supreme Court noted the practical problems of obtaining a search warrant while Griffin was under supervision. The Court said that the probation agency must be able to act before the supervised individual damages himself or society. In Griffin's case the Court felt that the agency had satisfied the Fourth Amendment's reasonableness requirement.

In a 1998 case, *Pennsylvania Board of Probation and Parole v. Scott*, a closely divided Court ruled that evidence that would be barred by the exclusionary rule from use by the prosecution in a criminal trial can be used in parole-revocation hearings.[70] Officers, without a search warrant, found guns in the home of a paroled murderer who was barred from owning weapons. The Court upheld revocation of the individual's parole. A unanimous Supreme Court later upheld a condition of probation that required the individual to submit to searches at any time, with or without a warrant.[71] More recently, the case of *Samson v. California* (2006) involved a police officer who stopped and searched a motorist he knew was on parole. The officer found methamphetamines in the car.

At trial, the defense argued that the drugs were inadmissible as evidence because the officer did not have a warrant. The trial court denied the defense motion. Later the Supreme Court ruled that because people on parole, who are by definition in the legal custody of the state, have reduced privacy rights and because Samson signed a written consent to suspicionless searches by a parole or peace officer, the warrantless search was constitutional.[72]

Revocation of Probation and Parole

When people on probation or parole do not obey their conditions of release, they may be sent to prison. As fully discussed in Chapters 8 and 16, if the person under supervision commits another crime, probation or parole will likely be revoked. For minor violations of the conditions (such as missing an Alcoholics Anonymous meeting), the supervising officer has discretion as to whether to ask for revocation.

The Supreme Court has addressed the question of due process when revocation is being considered. In *Mempa v. Rhay* (1967) the justices determined that a person on probation had the right to counsel in revocation and sentencing hearings before a deferred prison sentence could be imposed.[73] In *Morrissey v. Brewer* (1972) they ruled that people facing parole revocation must be given due process through a prompt informal inquiry before an impartial hearing officer.[74] The Court required a two-step revocation hearing process. In the first stage, a hearing officer determines whether there is probable cause that a violation has occurred. Paroled individuals have the right to be notified of the charges against them, to know the evidence against them, to be allowed to speak on their own behalf, to present witnesses, and to confront the witnesses against them. In the second stage, the revocation hearing, the paroled individual must receive a notice of charges and the disclosed evidence of the violation. He or she may cross-examine witnesses. The hearing body determines if the violation is sufficiently severe to warrant revocation. It must give the paroled individual a written statement outlining the evidence and giving reasons for the decision.

In the following year the Supreme Court applied the *Morrissey* procedures to probation revocation proceedings in *Gagnon v. Scarpelli* (1973).[75] But in *Gagnon* the Court also looked at the right to counsel. It ruled that there was no absolute requirement but that in some cases people on probation or parole might request counsel, which should be allowed on a case-by-case basis depending on the complexity of the issues, mitigating circumstances, and the competence of the convicted individual.

LO 6

Discuss how the law affects correctional personnel.

LAW AND CORRECTIONAL PERSONNEL

Just as law governs relationships among correctional personnel, prison residents, people on probation, and those released on parole, laws and regulations also define the relationships between administrators and their staff. With the exception of those working for private and nonprofit organizations, correctional personnel are public employees. In this section we look at two important aspects of correctional work. First, as public employees, all correctional employees are governed by civil service rules and regulations. Second, correctional clients may sue state officials under Section 1983 of the United States Code. We will examine the liability of correctional personnel with regard to these suits.

Civil Service Laws

From the time a public employee is recruited until he or she leaves public service, civil service rules and regulations govern the work environment. Civil service laws set the procedures for hiring, promoting, assigning, disciplining, and firing public employees. Such laws protect public employees from arbitrary actions by their supervisors. Workplace rules also develop through collective-bargaining agreements between unions and the government. Where correctional personnel can join unions, the bargaining process develops rules concerning assignments, working conditions, and grievance procedures. These agreements carry the force of law.

Like their counterparts in the private sector, government employees are protected from discrimination. With the Civil Rights Act of 1964, Congress prohibited employment discrimination based on race, gender, national origin, and religion. Subsequent federal legislation prohibits discrimination against people with disabilities (Americans with Disabilities Act) and age discrimination (Age Discrimination in Employment Act). States have their own antidiscrimination laws. All such laws have increased the number of minorities and women who work in corrections.

Unlike many public employees, those who work in corrections face a difficult position. Convicted persons have not chosen to be incarcerated or to be supervised in the community. Thus, they do not look on correctional personnel as offering them assistance. Correctional employees must assert authority to control the behavior of individuals who have shown that they lack selfcontrol and/or have little regard for society's rules. Whether in prison, in a probationer's home, or on the street, this responsibility creates pressures and difficult—sometimes dangerous—situations.

Correctional personnel also face pressures from their supervisors. If they expect to succeed in their job and gain promotions, they must carry out their duties in a professional manner that will please their supervisors, who may not always appreciate the quick decisions that must be made on the "front line."

Liability of Correctional Personnel

As noted, in *Cooper v. Pate* (1964) the Supreme Court said that Section 1983 provides a means not only for incarcerated individuals but also for people on probation and parole to bring lawsuits against correctional officials. The statute says that "any person" who deprives others of their constitutional rights while acting under the authority of law may be liable in a lawsuit.[76]

In subsequent decisions the Court further clarified the meaning of Section 1983. In *Monell v. Department of Social Services of the City of New York (1978)*, the Court said that individual officers and the agency may be sued when the agency's "customs and usages" violate a person's civil rights. If an individual can show that harm was caused by employees whose wrongful acts were the result of these "customs, practices, and policies, including poor training and supervision," then the employees can be sued.[77] This position was strengthened in *Hope v. Pelzer* (2002). The Court denied qualified immunity to Alabama correctional officials who had handcuffed an incarcerated individual to a hitching post in the prison yard and denied him adequate water and bathroom breaks. The decision emphasized that a reasonable officer would have known that using a hitching post in this manner was a violation of the Eighth Amendment prohibition on cruel and unusual punishments.[78] (See "Do the Right Thing" for another example.)

With the increased use of private prisons, questions have arisen about the liability under Section 1983 of private contractors. Correctional Services Corporation, which operated a community center under contract with the Federal Bureau of Prisons, was sued for a civil rights violation for making an incarcerated person with a heart condition climb five flights of stairs instead of permitting him to use an elevator; this triggered a heart attack and a fall on a staircase. The Court held in a 5–4 ruling that a Section 1983–type action could not be brought against the contractor. The complainant should have filed a grievance through the Bureau of Prison's administrative process or brought a regular tort lawsuit for injunctive relief.[79]

In Section 1983 litigation, correctional employees may be sued as individuals in their personal capacity, as opposed to their official capacity as a state employee. Usually, attorneys for the state will defend the case, and most states will assume responsibility for any financial damages awarded the plaintiff. However, if the court finds the employee to have acted intentionally or maliciously or to have committed a criminal act against a client, he or she may be responsible for paying the legal defense and the damages that the jury awards.

How should correctional workers protect themselves from civil rights suits? Clair Cripe, formerly the general counsel of the Federal Bureau of Prisons, suggests five rules for correctional employees:

1. Follow agency policies and the instructions of supervisors. By following policies, the staff member will be in step with the professional expectations of the agency's management. From a legal standpoint, the employee should follow the policies to ensure compliance with legal standards and avoid lawsuits.
2. Obtain good training. Staff members need to know the areas of their performance that expose them the most to liability.

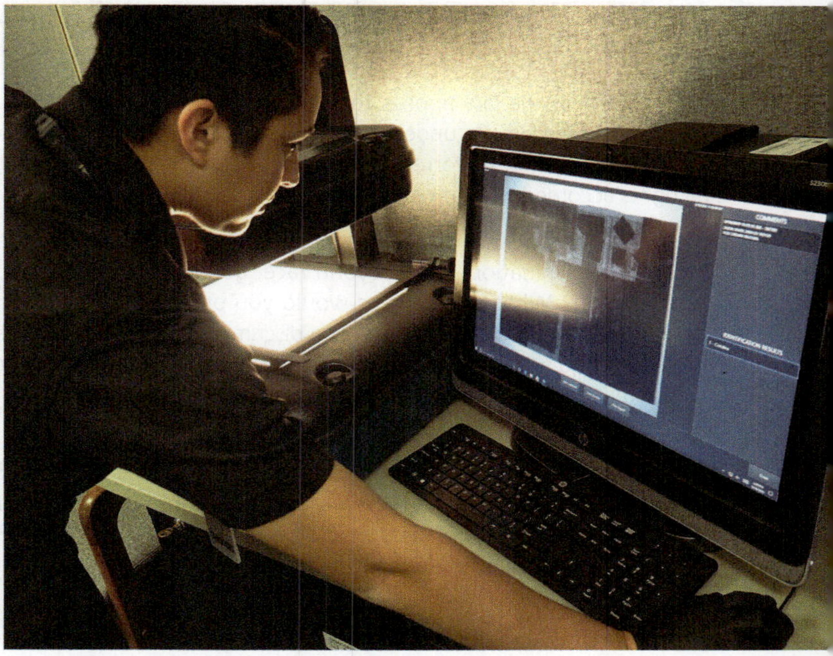

Prison officials try to control contraband by scanning the mail that enters facilities for drugs and other banned items.

DO THE RIGHT THING

Federal District Court Judge Scott Wolfe sits quietly in his chambers reviewing documents from a recent case. The lawsuit was brought by Patrick Haynes, incarcerated in a state prison, who prevailed in a retaliatory discipline claim under Section 1983 against Sergeant Tom Bloom and two other correctional officers.

Haynes had been placed in administration segregation after assaulting a correctional officer. He had thrown a container filled with urine and feces in the face of the unsuspecting officer, who had recently written him up on a misconduct charge. Shortly after "lights out" that evening, Sergeant Bloom and the two officers entered Haynes's cell, restrained him, and forcibly inserted a broom handle into his rectum. Haynes was found in his cell in the morning by day-shift officers. He was quickly transferred to the prison infirmary.

After a bench trial, Judge Wolfe ruled in Haynes's favor. The only matter to be resolved is the amount of punitive damages, the monetary compensation that Bloom and the other officers will have to pay Haynes as punishment for their wrongdoing.

WRITING ASSIGNMENT: If you were in Judge Wolfe's position, how much would you award Haynes in punitive damages? What factors would weigh most heavily in your decision? What if Haynes's injuries were permanent? Would Haynes's age, sentence length, or criminal history influence your decision?

FOR CRITICAL THINKING

Just as the law applies to those in correctional institutions and convicted individuals under community supervision, the law also regulates the behavior of correctional staff. It is conceivable, then, that legal rights accorded to staff could be curtailed or expanded.

1. Can an argument be made to expand correctional staff protections against discrimination to go beyond race, gender, national origin, and religion? What other status would you protect? Explain your answer. Should statutes regarding age discrimination and discrimination against disabled people be applied to correctional settings that are potentially violent? Why or why not?
2. Should the civil liability of prison officials be expanded beyond the violation of constitutional rights? What about prison services and amenities? Should incarcerated individuals be able to sue prison officials who do not provide access to educational programming? How do you feel about lawsuits against prison staff because the food is bland?

3. Become familiar with the law directly affecting the job. This is true whatever the specialty—casework, security, health care, probation, parole, or institutional programs.
4. To ensure a good defense when being sued, find a good mentor. Although correctional workers receive formal training, they gain on the job much knowledge of how things "really" work.
5. Keep good records. If correctional employees are called to testify at a trial or grievance hearing, good records are invaluable.[80]

Although huge financial settlements make headlines and the number of Section 1983 filings is large, few cases come to trial, and very few correctional employees must personally pay financial awards to plaintiffs. However, no correctional employee wants to be involved in such legal situations. Not only are they time-consuming and emotionally draining, but the mere fact of being sued can seriously damage a professional career (see "For Critical Thinking").

SUMMARY

1 Discuss the foundations that support the legal rights of incarcerated individuals.

Four foundations support the legal rights of individuals under correctional supervision. Constitutions not only provide the design of the government but also list the basic rights of individuals. Individuals do not lose all of their constitutional rights after being convicted of a crime. However, some of the rights of incarcerated individuals are outweighed by legitimate government interests (maintaining institutional order, maintaining institutional security, and rehabilitation programs). Statutes are laws passed by elected officials in legislatures. Statutes may provide specific rights to individuals who are incarcerated beyond those conferred by state constitutions or the U.S. Constitution. Case law refers to the legal rules produced by judges. Prior judicial rulings serve to guide the decisions of other judges who must rule on similar cases. Finally, regulations are rules set by agencies in the executive branch of government. For example, a department of corrections may create regulations on the type of personal items that prison inhabitants are allowed to have in their cells.

2 Explain the role of the U.S. Supreme Court in interpreting correctional law.

Traditionally, the U.S. Supreme Court maintained a hands-off policy with respect to corrections. Because incarcerated individuals were viewed as not having rights, judges did not interfere with prison operations. In the 1960s, however, this policy was abandoned, and the Court issued a series of decisions that broadly outlined the rights of the incarcerated, including providing people in state and federal prisons with access to the federal courts to sue prison officials for denying them basic rights. Today's Court is comparatively less active in correctional matters, but it occasionally rules on cases to clarify constitutional issues in correctional settings.

3 Discuss the constitutional rights of incarcerated individuals.

The rights of convicted individuals can be summarized in a handful of phrases in four amendments to the U.S. Constitution—the First, Fourth, Eighth, and Fourteenth. The First Amendment addresses rights related to access to reading materials, noncensorship of mail, and freedom of religious practices. The Fourth Amendment provides protection against government intrusion (searches and seizures). However, people surrender most of their privacy rights when they enter prison. In correctional facilities, the Fourth Amendment concerns searches of cells and searches of persons. The Eighth Amendment protects convicted individuals against cruel and unusual punishments. The federal courts have intervened in states where prison conditions or specific aspects of their operation were found to violate the Eighth Amendment. Finally, the Fourteenth Amendment helps to ensure procedural due process and equal protection. These two clauses of the Fourteenth Amendment are very important when incarcerated individuals are disciplined for violating institutional rules.

4 Identify the alternatives to litigation.

Four alternatives to litigation are present in the corrections systems of various states. Grievance procedures usually involve a three-step process: (1) an incarcerated person files a complaint, (2) a prison staff member (or grievance officer) investigates the matter, and (3) the investigator issues a decision. Another alternative, the ombudsman, involves an official who receives complaints, investigates, and recommends corrective measures. The effectiveness of this approach is contingent on whether the prison residents respect the ombudsman. Mediation entails a third party reviewing the matter and making a decision that is usually binding on both prison officials and incarcerated persons. This approach is most effective when the complaint involves a problem that requires an administrative solution. Finally, legal assistance by staff attorneys, jailhouse lawyers, and law school clinics can advise incarcerated individuals on the legal merits of their complaints and assist them in framing their complaints in legal terms.

5 Explain the rights of individuals under community supervision.

Like residents of correctional facilities, convicted individuals in the community also have rights, but not the same rights as ordinary citizens. For example, various conditions are placed on individuals on parole, such as limiting their right to associate with their partners in crime and with victims. In instances when parole supervision is being revoked, individuals possess various due process rights. For example, these people have the right to be notified of the charges against them, to know the evidence against them, to speak on their own behalf, to present witnesses, and to confront the witnesses against them. As for the right to counsel, the Supreme Court has ruled that it should be allowed on a case-by-case basis.

6 Discuss how the law affects correctional personnel.

Law and regulations define the relationships between prison administrators and their staff. All correctional employees working in public prisons are governed by civil service rules and regulations. Civil service laws set the procedures for hiring, promoting, assigning, disciplining, and firing public employees. Such laws protect public employees from arbitrary actions by their supervisors. Workplace rules also develop through collective-bargaining agreements between unions and the government. A second way that the law affects correctional personnel relates to the ability of convicted individuals to sue correctional officials under Section 1983 of the United States Code. Section 1983 provides a means not only for incarcerated individuals but also people on probation or parole to bring lawsuits against correctional officials. The statute says that "any person" who deprives others of their constitutional rights while acting under the authority of law may be liable in a lawsuit. Few of these cases come to trial, and very few correctional employees must personally pay financial awards to plaintiffs.

KEY TERMS

case law (*p. 105*)
civil liability (*p. 106*)
clear and present danger (*p. 110*)
compelling state interest (*p. 110*)
constitution (*p. 104*)
equal protection (*p. 117*)
habeas corpus (*p. 107*)
hands-off policy (*p. 106*)
least restrictive methods (*p.110*)
mediation (*p. 123*)
ombudsman (*p. 123*)
precedent (*p. 105*)
procedural due process (*p. 117*)
rational basis test (*p. 110*)
regulations (*p. 105*)
statute (*p. 105*)
totality of conditions (*p. 114*)

FOR DISCUSSION

1. What difficulties might you, as a correctional officer, foresee in attempting to run your unit of the institution while at the same time upholding the legal rights of the residents?
2. Suppose that you are a prison warden. A group of incarcerated individuals calling themselves the "Sun Devils" claims that they are a religious organization. They request that the institution grant them permission to chant at the sun at noon each day as part of their First Amendment rights. How would you determine whether you must grant this request?
3. Should convicted people under parole supervision enjoy the same constitutional rights as law-abiding citizens? If not, which rights should be withheld? Should these rights be granted after a person successfully completes parole?
4. Which of the following alternatives to litigation—grievance procedures, ombudsman, and mediation—do you believe is most effective in maximum-security prisons for men? What factors make these alternatives less effective at resolving complaints?
5. As a correctional officer, what steps would you take to protect yourself from lawsuits? How can prison officials limit the number of lawsuits filed by incarcerated individuals?

FOR FURTHER READING

Anderson, Lloyd C. *Voices from a Southern Prison*. Athens: University of Georgia Press, 2000. A case study of the 10-year litigation to reform the Kentucky State Reformatory as seen through the eyes of the three people who brought the litigation, as well as the perspective of the judge, the reform-minded head of the Kentucky corrections system, and a journalist.

Belbot, Barbara, and Craig Hemmens. *The Legal Rights of the Convicted*. El Paso, TX: LFB Scholarly Publishing, 2010. This book provides a comprehensive review of the many different legal aspects of corrections.

Carroll, Leo. *Lawful Order: A Case Study of Correctional Crisis and Reform*. New York: Garland, 1998. An examination of the Rhode Island prison system over a 25-year period, focusing on the impact of *Palmigiano v. Garrahy*.

Cripe, Clair A., and Michael G. Pearlman. *Legal Aspects of Corrections Management*. 2nd ed. Boston, MA: Jones & Bartlett, 2005. A textbook geared primarily to correctional administrators.

Hopwood, Shon, and Dennis Burke. *Law Man: My Story from Robbing Banks, Winning Supreme Court Cases, and Finding Redemption*. New York: Crown, 2012. A memoir of a convicted bank robber who became one of the most successful jailhouse lawyers in U.S. history.

Smith, Christopher E. *Law and Contemporary Corrections*. Belmont, CA: Wadsworth, 2000. A text that examines the law as applied to prisons, probation, parole, and correctional personnel.

NOTES

1 Alexei Koseff, "Coronavirus Behind Bars," *San Francisco Chronicle*, https://www.sfchronicle.com/politics/article/Federal-panel-rejects-bid-to-free-prisoners-to-15179850.php, April 5, 2020.

2 *Ford v. Wainwright*, 477 U.S. 399 (1986).

3 *Madison v. Alabama*, 586 U.S. ___(2019).

4 *Ruffin v. Commonwealth*, 62 Va. 790 (1871).

5 Christopher E. Smith, "The Prison Reform Litigation Era: Book-Length Studies and Lingering Research Issues," *Prison Journal* 83 (September 2003): 337–58.

6 Note that people in federal prisons cannot use Section 1983 to bring suits charging officials with violating their constitutional rights. But the Supreme Court in *Bivens v. Six Unknown Federal Narcotics Agents*, 403 U.S. 388 (1971), and later cases has allowed people in federal prisons to sue officials. These types of actions are called "*Bivens* suits," not Section 1983 actions.

7 *Boumediene v. Bush*, 553 U.S. 723 (2008).

8 United States Courts, *Judicial Business* 2017 Tables, Table C-3, https://www.uscourts.gov/statistics/table/c-3/statistical-tables-federal-judiciary/2017/12/31, retrieved April 26, 2020.

9 John A. Fliter, *Prisoners' Rights: The Supreme Court and Evolving Standards of Decency* (Westport, CT: Greenwood, 2001), 1–4.

10 *Johnson v. Avery*, 393 U.S. 413 (1969).

11 *Bounds v. Smith*, 430 U.S. 817 (1977).

12 *Lewis v. Casey*, 64 U.S.L.W. 4587 (1996).

13 *Brooks v. Florida*, 389 U.S. 413 (1967).

14 *Holt v. Sarver*, 442 F.2d 308 (8th Cir. 1971).

15 Malcolm M. Feeley and Edward Rubin, *Judicial Policy Making and the Modern State: How the Courts Reformed America's Prisons* (New York: Cambridge University Press, 1998), 14.

16 *Brown v. Wainwright*, 419 F.2d 1308 (5th Cir. 1969).

17 *Pepperling v. Crist*, 678 F.2d 787 (9th Cir. 1982). However, the U.S. Court of Appeals for the Seventh Circuit, in *Trapnell v. Riggsbuy*, 622 F.2d 290 (7th Cir. 1980), found absolute prohibition a "narrowly drawn and carefully limited response to a valid security problem."

18 *Sostre v. Otis*, 330 F.Supp. 941 (S.D.N.Y. 1971).

19 *Turner v. Safley*, 482 U.S. 78 (1987).

20 *Procunier v. Martinez*, 416 U.S. 396 (1974).

21 *Turner v. Safley*, 482 U.S. 78 (1987).

22 *Shaw v. Murphy*, 532 U.S. 223 (2001).

23 *Beard v. Banks*, 548 U.S. 521 (2006).

24 *Fulwood v. Clemmer*, 206 F.Supp. 370 (D.C. Cir. 1962).

25 *Cruz v. Beto*, 450 U.S. 319 (1972).

26 *O'Lone v. Estate of Shabazz*, 482 U.S. 342 (1987).

27 *Employment Division of Oregon v. Smith*, 494 U.S. 872 (1990).

28 *City of Boerne v. Flores*, 117 S. Ct. 2157 (1997).

29 *Holt v. Hobbs*, 135 S. Ct. 853 (2015).

30 *Hudson v. Palmer*, 468 U.S. 517 (1984).

31 *Smith v. Fairman*, 678 F.2d 52 (7th Cir. 1982).

32 *Bell v. Wolfish*, 441 U.S. 520 (1979).

33 *United States v. Oakley*, 731 F.Supp. 1363 (S.D. Ind. 1990).

34 *Lee v. Downs*, 641 F.2d 1117 (4th Cir. 1981).

35 *Smith v. Fairman*, 678 F.2d 52 (7th Cir. 1982).

36 *Pugh v. Locke*, 406 F.2d 318 (1976).

37 Bradley S. Chilton, Prisons Under the Gavel: *The Federal Court Takeover of Georgia Prisons* (Columbus: Ohio State University Press, 1991).

38 *Hutto v. Finney*, 98 S. Ct. 2565 (1978).

39 *Rhodes v. Chapman*, 452 U.S. 337 (1981).

40 *Hudson v. McMillian*, 503 U.S. 1 (1992).

41 *Wilkins v. Gaddy*, 559 U.S. 34 (2010).

42 *Wolff v. McDonnell*, 418 U.S. 539 (1974).

43 Ibid.

44 *Lee v.* Washington, 390 U.S. 333 (1968).

45 *Johnson v. California*, 543 U.S. 499 (2005). For a discussion on the legal aspects, court rulings, and practice of prison segregation, see Chad R. Trulson, James W. Marquart, Craig Hemmens, and Leo Carroll, "Racial Segregation in Prisons," *Prison Journal* 88 (June 2008): 270–99.

46 *Pargo v. Elliott*, 49 F.3d 1355 (1995).

[47] James B. Jacobs, *New Perspectives on Prison and Imprisonment* (Ithaca, NY: Cornell University Press, 1983), 42.
[48] *Wolff v. McDonnell*, 418 U.S. 539 (1974).
[49] *Bell v. Wolfish*, 441 U.S. 520 (1979).
[50] *Rhodes v. Chapman*, 452 U.S. 337 (1981).
[51] *Abdul Wali v. Coughlin*, 754 F.2d 1015 (2nd Cir. 1985).
[52] *Daniels v. Williams*, 474 U.S. 327 (1986).
[53] *Wilson v. Seiter*, 111 S. Ct. 2321 (1991).
[54] *Estelle v. Gamble*, 429 U.S. 97 (1976); *Whitley v. Albers*, 475 U.S. 312 (1986).
[55] *McCleskey v. Zant*, 111 S. Ct. 1454 (1991).
[56] *Colman v. Thompson*, 111 S. Ct. 2546 (1991).
[57] *Booth v. Churner*, 532 U.S. 731 (2001).
[58] *Jones v. Bock*, 549 U.S. 199 (2007).
[59] *Bruce v. Samuels*, 577 U.S. (2016).
[60] David Fathi, *No Equal Justice: The Prison Litigation Reform Act in the United States* (New York: Human Rights Watch, 2009).
[61] Ibid., p. 3.
[62] Christopher E. Smith, "Prisoners' Rights and the Rehnquist Court Era," *Prison Journal* 87 (December 2007): 473.
[63] Warren E. Burger, "Chief Justice Burger Issues Year-End Report," *American Bar Association Journal* 62 (1976): 189–90.
[64] *Johnson v. Avery*, 393 U.S. 499 (1969).
[65] *Greenholtz v. Inmates of the Nebraska Penal and Correction Complex*, 442 U.S. 1 (1979).
[66] *Connecticut Board of Pardons v. Dumschat*, 452 U.S. 458 (1981).
[67] *Swarthout v. Cooke*, 562 U.S. 555 (2011).
[68] *Griffin v. Wisconsin*, 483 U.S. 868 (1987).
[69] Ibid.
[70] *Pennsylvania Board of Probation and Parole v. Scott*, 524 U.S. 357 (1998).
[71] *United States v. Knights*, 534 U.S. 112 (2001).
[72] *Samson v. California*, 547 U.S. 843 (2006).
[73] *Mempa v. Rhay*, 389 U.S. 128 (1967).
[74] *Morrissey v. Brewer*, 408 U.S. 471 (1972).
[75] *Gagnon v. Scarpelli*, 411 U.S. 778 (1973).
[76] *Cooper v. Pate*, 378 U.S. 546 (1964).
[77] *Monell v. Department of Social Services of the City of New York,* 436 U.S. 658 (1978).
[78] *Hope v. Pelzer*, 536 U.S. 730 (2002).
[79] *Correctional Services Corporation v. Malesko*, 534 U.S. 61 (2001).
[80] Cripe, Clair A., and Michael G. Pearlman, *Legal Aspects of Corrections Management*, 2nd ed. (Boston: Jones & Bartlett, 2005), 75–77.

CHAPTER 6

The Correctional Client

Actress Felicity Huffman heading from court after pleading guilty to fraud in a college admissions scandal that shocked the nation. Many types of people, facing a wide range of circumstances, can end up in trouble with the law because of bad decisions.

FELICITY HUFFMAN IS A STAR. She had a leading role in the long running TV drama, *Desperate Housewives,* for which she received an Emmy; she also has a Golden Globe Award, three Screen Actors Guild Awards, and an Oscar nomination. She is undoubtedly an actor of notoriety and talent.

She is also a felon and is—as of October 25, 2019—formerly incarcerated. That was the day she walked out of a federal prison in Dublin, California, after having served most of a 14-day sentence for mail fraud, a federal crime. She pled guilty to charges that she paid $15,000 to have a proctor of her daughter's SAT test correct some of the wrong answers before the test was scored.[1]

Huffman was just one of over 600,000 people who were released from prison in 2019; one of about 10 million that year in America brought into one part of or another of the correctional system on criminal charges. She is undoubtedly atypical in many respects. Her arrest made national headlines. She is wealthy, privileged, and well-connected. Few, indeed, of the millions who get caught up in the corrections system can make any of those claims. Those who enter the corrections system are overwhelmingly poor, disproportionately people of color, and decidedly without "connections."

But she is like all of them in one respect. She thought she could break the law and get away with it. This is not a rare attribute, and experience suggests that under the right circumstances, all of us are capable of breaking the law. People who end up in the corrections system are often guilty of more serious offenses or more frequent offending, but it is also the case that their distinguishing characteristic is basically that they got caught.

There are so many clients of corrections, in fact, that chances are someone in this class with you, studying corrections, has been incarcerated. In fact, it is likely that more than one of your class members have been to jail, probably just an overnight stay for some public order infraction or another. Perhaps one of your classmates has been to prison as well and has now joined you in studying the system that once held him—or, less likely, her—captive. It may strike you as odd to think that someone you see almost every day might have been locked behind bars, but statistics say that in a typical group of 30 or so young adults, at least one has likely been locked up, usually for a minor offense. As noted in Chapter 1, almost 3 percent of all adults in the United States are currently under some form of correctional control. This large group extends into all kinds of households, neighborhoods, and social groups.

Still, the idea that one of "us" might be under correctional authority can be unsettling. (See "Inmates, Offenders, Prisoners, Probationers, and Parolees—They Are All People.") We are used to thinking of people who break the law as somehow different from "normal" citizens, so when we encounter someone who has been on probation or imprisoned, we wonder about how that person received a criminal sentence and also about our preconceptions of people who break the law. Who are they? What gets them into trouble? What should we think of them?

As we have seen, anyone can get into trouble. So when we ask the question "What are people who break the law like?" one answer is that they can be like any of us. Yet when we look at them as a group, we see that while they come from every walk of life, in fact the powerful and wealthy rarely encounter the criminal justice system. The typical client of the criminal justice system is a young, male minority member from a poor neighborhood. For example, African Americans make up less than one-seventh of the U.S. population but nearly half of the accused and convicted people in the justice system. Men as a group constitute less than half of the general population but are nearly nine-tenths of the justice system population. Almost half of those entering state prisons are between 18 and 27 years old.

In this chapter we examine why correctional clients seem to differ so markedly from the general population. The reasons are not clear, but they generally have to do with the selection process that determines who gets charged, prosecuted, and convicted. Exactly how this selection process produces the subjects for corrections is a matter of some controversy.

LEARNING OBJECTIVES

After reading this chapter, you should be able to . . .

1. Explain how the criminal justice system operates as a large selection process to determine who ends up in the corrections system.
2. Describe some of the main similarities and differences between the general population and people who end up under correctional authority.
3. Identify different types of clients in the corrections system and the kinds of problems they pose for corrections.
4. Describe the classification process for people under correctional authority and explain why it is important.
5. Discuss important problems and limitations in classifying people under correctional authority.

FOCUS ON

CORRECTIONAL POLICY: Inmates, Offenders, Prisoners, Probationers, and Parolees—They Are All People

Language matters. Words matter. Names matter. Terms that are conventional at one time are seen to be problematic upon deeper, later analysis. For example, though the term *mental retardation* was once common, we now say *developmental disability.* Getting language right is important because terminology can be disrespectful; it can also be hurtful. Some terms connote stereotypes and serve as pejorative labels.

In the field of corrections, there is a growing recognition that terms like *inmate* and *offender* can also promote stereotypes and put labels on people that become the lens through which everything they do is interpreted. Some of these labels take on a permanent kind of power over a person's life: It is often hard for a person to overcome a label such as *offender* or *inmate* because when a person is described this way, the term itself takes on more importance than it deserves. Too often, people relate to someone who is an "ex-offender" through the label in ways that can make it difficult to overcome. People who have broken the law sometimes say, "What I did was wrong. I take responsibility for it. But I want to be able to put it behind me so that I can move on with my life. I don't want to always be known by my worst judgment ever. Nobody does."

Experts now recognize that some labels can be misused. In fact, people who are being processed by the corrections system are exactly that: people. Across the corrections world, there is a growing appreciation for the way the picture changes when phrases such as *people in prison* replace terms such as *inmates* and *offenders.*

…OR THE CORRECTIONS SYSTEM

LO 1

Explain how the criminal justice system operates as a large selection process to determine who ends up in the corrections system.

The process leading to conviction might suggest that becoming a correctional client is quite difficult—as if corrections had to be "broken into," like a career. There is some truth to this idea. As Figure 6.1 shows, we can view the criminal justice system as a filtering process because it operates as a large client-selection bureaucracy. At each stage, some

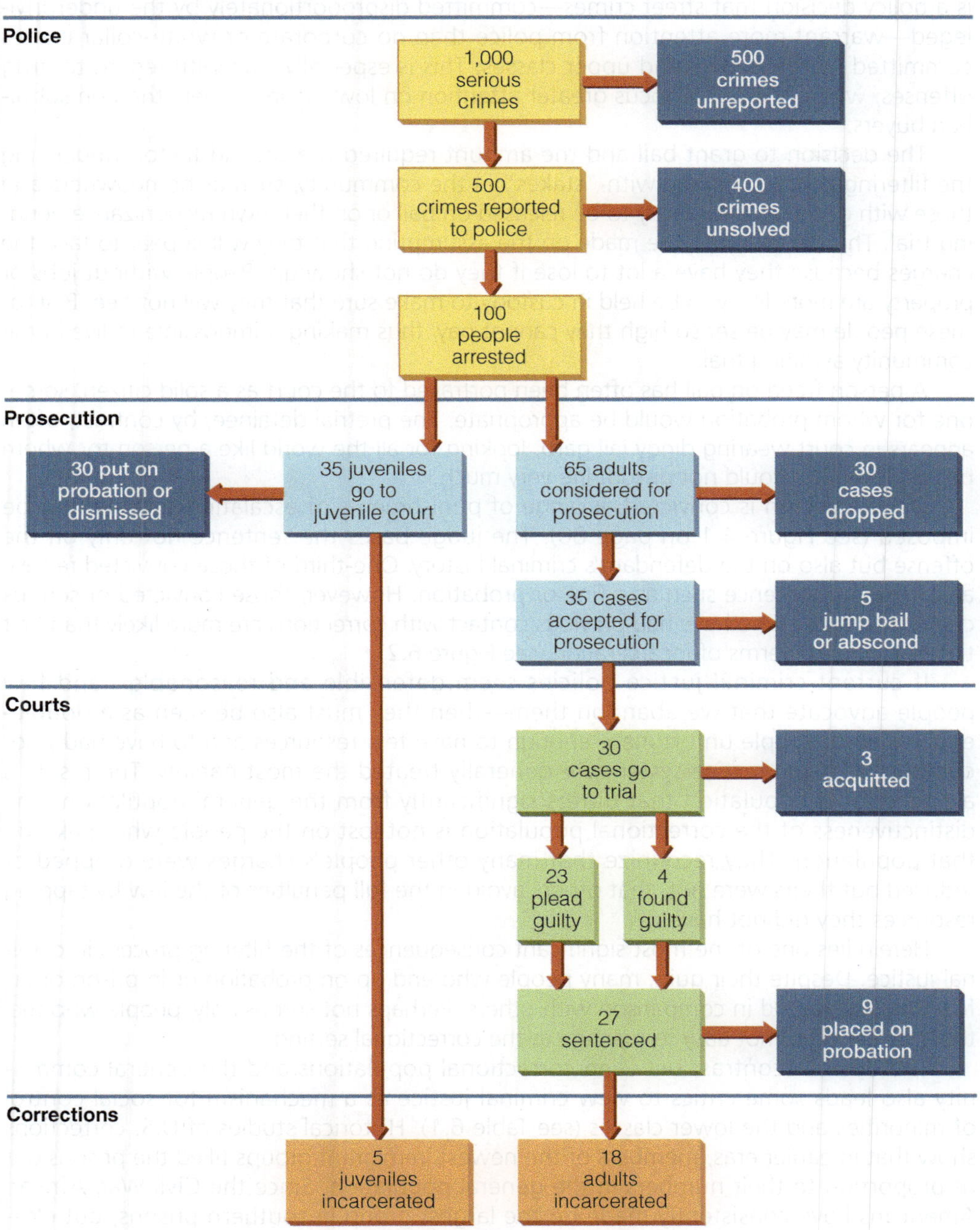

FIGURE 6.1 Criminal Justice as a Filtering Process

Decisions at each point in the system result in some cases being dropped while others are passed on to the next point. Are you surprised by the small portion of cases that remain?

Sources: Data in this figure have been drawn from many sources, including the U.S. Bureau of Justice Statistics.

individuals are sent on to the next stage while others are either released or processed under changed conditions. Note that few people who are arrested are then prosecuted, tried, and convicted. Some go free because the police decide that a crime has not been committed or that the evidence is not sound. The prosecutor may decide that justice would be better served by sending the individual to a substance abuse clinic. Many people will plead guilty, the judge may dismiss charges against others, and the jury may acquit a few. Thus, the criminal justice system is often described as a filtering process or a funnel—many cases enter it, but only a few result in conviction and punishment. These few are the clients of corrections.

What other factors can influence who becomes a correctional client? One factor is a policy decision that street crimes—committed disproportionately by the underprivileged—warrant more attention from police than do corporate or white-collar crimes committed by the middle and upper classes. This is especially true with regard to drug offenses, where the police focus greater attention on low-income sellers than on suburban buyers.

The decision to grant bail and the amount required is a second factor influencing the filtering process. People with "stakes" in the community, such as homeowners and those with good jobs, are likely to be released on bail or on their own recognizance pending trial. This decision may be made on the assumption that they will appear to face the charges because they have a lot to lose if they do not show up. People without jobs or property are more likely to be held in custody to make sure that they will not flee. Bail for these people may be set so high they cannot pay, thus making it impossible to live in the community awaiting trial.

LO 2

Describe some of the main similarities and differences between the general population and people who end up under correctional authority.

A person freed on bail has often been portrayed to the court as a solid citizen, someone for whom probation would be appropriate. The pretrial detainee, by contrast, often appears in court wearing dingy jail garb, looking for all the world like a person for whom being locked up would not disrupt life very much.

Once a person is convicted, a range of punishments of escalating severity may be imposed (see Figure 4.1 on page 80). The judge bases the sentence not only on the offense but also on the defendant's criminal history. One-third of those convicted receive a community sentence such as a fine or probation. However, those convicted of serious crimes and those who have had previous contact with corrections are more likely than first timers to receive terms of incarceration (see Figure 6.2).

If current criminal justice policies seem defensible and reasonable—and few people advocate that we abandon them—then they must also be seen as a double-edged sword: People unfortunate enough to have few resources and to have had prior contacts with the justice system are generally treated the most harshly. The result is a correctional population that differs significantly from the general population. The distinctiveness of the correctional population is not lost on the people who make up that population. They recognize that many other people's charges were dropped or reduced but theirs were not, that others avoided the full penalties of the law by tapping resources they did not have.

Herein lies one of the most significant consequences of the filtering process in criminal justice: Despite their guilt, many people who end up on probation or in prison or jail feel unjustly treated in comparison with others. Perhaps not surprisingly, people who feel this way are often not easy to manage in the correctional setting.

The obvious contrast between correctional populations and the general community also leads some critics to view criminal justice as a mechanism for social control of minorities and the lower classes (see Table 6.1). Historical studies of U.S. corrections show that in earlier eras, members of the newest immigrant groups filled the prisons out of proportion to their numbers in the general population. Since the Civil War, African Americans have consistently made up the largest group in southern prisons, but elsewhere the largest group has changed over time: first Germans, Irish, and Italians, and today African Americans and Hispanics. There is recent evidence that the gap between Whites and Blacks has been declining, as the prison population has also declined.[2] Even

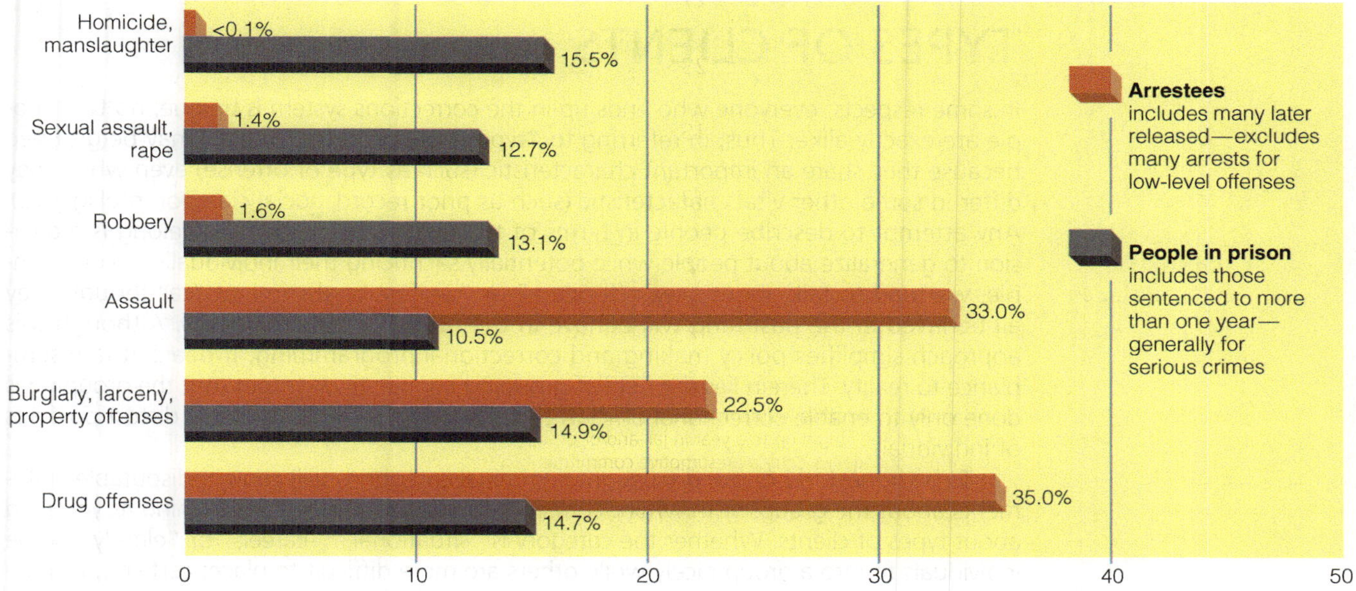

FIGURE 6.2 Percentages of People Arrested and Imprisoned for Serious Offenses in Six Categories

The justice system acts as a selection filter, increasingly bringing more-serious cases forward for more-severe punishments.

TABLE 6.1 Comparison of Gender and Race/Ethnicity of People Under Different Types of Correctional Supervision

These numbers show the percentage of those who receive probation, jail time, or prison sentences in two categories: gender and race/ethnicity. Women tend to spend far less time incarcerated than do men and are more likely to receive probation. Keep in mind that although the percentages of whites and blacks here are similar, the black percentages represent a much larger proportion of the African American community than the white percentages do of the white population.

	Probation	Jail	Parole	Prison
Male	75%	85%	87%	93%
Female	25	15	13	7
White	55	50	45	30
Black	28	34	38	33
Hispanic	14	15	15	23
Other	3	2	2	14

Sources: Jennifer Bronson and E. Ann Carson, *Prisoners in 2017* (Washington, DC: U.S. Bureau of Justice Statistics, 2015); U.S. Bureau of Justice Statistics, *Jails Inmates in 2017;* U.S. Bureau of Justice Statistics, *Probation and Parole in the United States, 2016.*

so, African Americans still end up in prison in numbers disproportionate to their size in the regular population.

If many correctional clients share characteristics of social class, race, and sex, they also have important differences. In the sections that follow we classify correctional clients according to some of those differences and discuss the implications of such classifications for correctional programming.

TYPES OF CLIENTS

In some respects, everyone who ends up in the corrections system is unique; no two people are exactly alike. Thus, in referring to "types" of clients, individuals may be grouped because they share an important characteristic (such as type of offense) even when they differ in some other vital characteristic (such as prior record, social class, or intelligence). Any attempt to describe people in terms of the groups to which they belong is a decision to generalize about people while potentially sacrificing their individualism. For example, we tend to talk about "sex offenders" or "professional criminals" as though they all behaved in the past (and will behave in the future) in the same way. Although this approach simplifies policy making and correctional programming, it bears little resemblance to reality. Therein lies the peril of grouping people: If we forget that the grouping is done only to enable correctional officials to take action, we will inevitably distort portraits of individuals.

To be honest, then, our discussion of criminal categories will contain disputable statements about the groups with whom corrections must work. Keep this in mind as you read about types of clients. Whether the category is "situational," "career," or "elderly," some individuals fit into a group nicely while others are more difficult to place; certainly, all individuals within a group will vary in some respects.

The groupings are made for our convenience; we call them "types" even though few people rigidly fit the category. We choose these categories because they are the broad types that corrections must manage and whose general characteristics influence the kind of work required. To illustrate each type, we offer a series of personal stories. Each story is true; some are classics, like the story of Johnnie Baxstrom, about whom the U.S. Supreme Court once deliberated. There are a few old friends, like Archie and Mary Lou, whose stories we have used over the years; even though their stories are decades old, their lives still reflect those of many of the mostly faceless people who go through the corrections system today. We also introduce our good friend Michael Santos, who was once incarcerated in the federal prison system and whose writing appears throughout this book. We tell these stories, current and historical, to give a human face to the people who go through the corrections system. Even the most troubling stories illustrate a central point about corrections—it is a system of people whose lives have depth and meaning well beyond the convenient labels that we use to characterize their crimes.

LO 3

Identify different types of clients in the corrections system and the kinds of problems they pose for corrections.

Situational Clients

Most people convicted of a felony are not arrested again. Some studies estimate that this is true for 80 percent of first-timers. Of course, some undoubtedly commit further crimes and are simply never caught, but most do not commit a second offense. The person entering the corrections system and having committed what appears to be a one-time offense fits the definition of the **situational client**. In their classic study, Martin Haskell and Lewis Yablonsky described this type as one who (1) confronted a problem requiring action, (2) took action that violated the criminal law, (3) was caught and given a criminal status, and (4) until the time of the offense, was committed to the normative system of our society and was indistinguishable from other people.[3] Thus, the situational client "made a mistake" and "paid a debt to society" for that mistake.

situational client A person who in a particular set of circumstances has violated the law but who is not given to criminal behavior under normal circumstances and is unlikely to repeat the offense.

The situational type of client presents many problems for corrections. First, the crime is usually a serious, violent crime (often murder or aggravated assault), and the person who committed it usually knew the victim well (often a spouse or other family member). For such a crime, a severe punishment is thought appropriate. Even though only an extremely small percentage of murderers commit murder again, society's fear of people who commit situational crimes, together with outrage at the offense, often results in lengthy incarceration.

For many situational clients, there is little for corrections to do. Many of them have a positive orientation toward accepted social values, a solid work history, and good basic employment skills. Other situational clients faced hardships that fueled their criminality, and going to prison is a first step in alleviating those hardships (see "Cyntoia's Story"). The prognosis for successful readjustment while on parole is extremely good. However, other than help in adjusting to the life crisis of imprisonment, and maybe taking advantage of some positive programming, the correctional agenda for situational clients is limited. Situational clients may participate in programs as a means of self-improvement, but their time under correctional authority remains mainly a matter of simply serving the sentence.

Situational clients are always good targets for early release because they pose little threat to the public. However, granting them early release opens the corrections system to criticism because citizens inevitably react to what they see as "coddling" a person who has committed a very serious crime. Furthermore, the one situational client out of twenty who murders again can destroy the careers of the officials who allowed parole. Therefore, these people often remain in prison while others, those who actually represent more threat to society but less threat to corrections, are released.

Clients with Careers in Crime

One of the most slippery concepts in the classification of people into "types" is the so-called "career criminal." When the criminologist Walter Reckless first developed the idea of the **career criminal**, he had in mind a specific set of attributes:

career criminal A person who sees crime as a way of earning a living, who has numerous contacts with the criminal justice system over time, and who may view the criminal sanction as a normal part of life.

1. Crime is his way of earning a living, his main occupation.
2. He develops technical skills useful to the commission of his crimes.
3. He started as a delinquent child and progressed toward criminality.
4. He expects to do some time in prison as a "cost" of doing this type of work.
5. He is psychologically normal.[4]

FOCUS ON

PEOPLE IN CORRECTIONS: Cyntoia's Story

When Cyntoia Brown was 2, she was put up for adoption by her mother, an alcoholic and crack cocaine addict. Her new home was a loving one, but Cyntoia never adjusted well. Her growing up was punctuated by frequent victimization by her peers. She had regular contact with juvenile justice authorities, eventually resulting in a commitment to Woodland Hills Youth Development Center in Nashville. At age 16, she escaped Woodland Hills and ended up on the streets, using drugs herself. Soon enough she hooked up with a pimp named Garion L. McGlothen, whose nickname was "Kut-throat." Kut repeatedly threatened her and eventually forced her into prostitution.

On August 6, 2004, Brown met 43-year-old Johnny Michael Allen in a Nashville parking lot. Allen offered $150 for her to have sex with him, and she got in Allen's car and accompanied him to his home. That night, after Allen fell asleep, she shot him in the back of the head. Law enforcement officials claimed her motive was robbery, and some of Brown's later actions seem to support that claim. Brown said she shot Allen because she was afraid he was going to get one of his guns and kill her.

She was tried as an adult and sentenced to life in prison—eligible for parole in 2055. Once inside prison, she began to blossom. She obtained an AA degree from Lipscomb University with a 4.0 average. Public figures such as Kim Kardashian West and Rihanna advocated for her release. In 2011, a documentary was made of her life, and a host of advocates, local and national, began to appeal to then Governor Bill Haslam to grant her clemency.

Haslam granted her clemency in August of 2019, saying, "society was better off with Cyntoia out of prison." On August 7, almost 15 years to the day after the murder, Cyntoia Brown was released from her Tennessee prison.

Given all that has passed, it seems extremely unlikely that the circumstances leading up to Cyntoia Brown's crime will repeat themselves.

Source: Christina Houser, "Cyntoia Brown Is Freed from Prison in Tennessee," *The New York Times*, August 7, 2019.

Reckless attributed these characteristics to a small group of people who work at crime, including organized-crime figures, those who specialize in white-collar crime, and those who spend their lives laboring at an illegal occupation (see "Archie's Story"). However, the conception of career criminals has recently changed. Given research ranging from studies of a group of men born in Philadelphia in 1958 to interviews with convicted and imprisoned adults in California, Texas, and Michigan, scholars in the 1980s concluded that a small group of criminally active people commit a majority of all crimes.[5] This has led to a significant shift in thinking about the career criminal type. Instead of applying the term to someone whose work is crime, policy makers began to use it to refer to anyone with several convictions or arrests. Thus, a person with as few as three or four convictions is now commonly labeled a "career criminal," under the assumption that such a person is responsible for a much larger number of crimes than the arrest record indicates. This may seem a bit odd to most of us; we would hardly call our own jobs a career if we had been seen at work only three or four times.

Of course, many individuals who are repeatedly convicted admit to more crimes, sometimes many more than the handful for which they are being punished. For example, Peter Greenwood's famous study of robbers found that as many as half of those with

FOCUS ON

PEOPLE IN CORRECTIONS: Archie's Story

Archie left home at age 13 and traveled around the country as a transient, sometimes supporting himself as a truck driver. Archie claims to have committed about 500 burglaries, 500 auto thefts, and 5 robberies before his eighteenth birthday. Of them, he was arrested for only one robbery. As he was not convicted, however, he has no juvenile record. Even in this early phase of his criminal career, Archie was quite sophisticated in his MO (*modus operandi*, or "method of operating"). He used theatrical makeup to disguise himself for his burglaries and robberies, including contact lenses of various colors. He recalls being fairly violent and obsessed about his small size. He injured one of his robbery victims when the man tried to resist.

Archie's first incarceration did not come until his mid-thirties. For this conviction he served several years in a California prison. Although his rap sheet shows nine arrests for drug violations and petty theft, the only serious prison time he served before his present term was for an auto theft conviction.

Before his first incarceration, Archie was employed much of the time, but his main source of income was crime. Between his eighteenth birthday and his first incarceration, he estimates that he committed about 100 grand thefts, 100 burglaries, and 12 robberies. His average take per robbery was about $2,500. He was never arrested for any of these crimes. His wife was a heroin addict, and he used the loot mainly to support her drug habit and for partying.

The main targets of Archie's robberies were savings and loan banks or payroll offices. His MO was to disguise himself in full theatrical makeup and to enter the savings and loan carrying a sawed-off shotgun, which he would point at a young female employee.

The main targets of Archie's burglaries were pawnshops or businesses. His few residential burglaries were at private homes where an informer had told him a valuable collection or large sums of money were kept. His typical MO was to make the acquaintance of the prospective victim and gain access to his home to learn where the valuables were kept. Within a month after befriending the victim, Archie would burglarize his house. He also performed insurance fraud burglaries in which the "victim" would indicate the articles he wanted stolen. Archie would burglarize the house at a prearranged time, stealing the articles that had been specified and selling them to a fence. The fence would profit, Archie would profit, and the insurance company would reimburse the victim for the items stolen.

Archie reports having shot victims when they tried to resist, in both burglaries and robberies. He also mentions having retaliated against two heroin addicts who were friends of his wife and who apparently had tried to kill him. Archie says that both were seriously injured. Archie relates that his first conviction and incarceration occurred because his wife informed on him when he was trying to stop her from using drugs.

After release from the first incarceration, in his late thirties, Archie remained on the street about five years before being incarcerated for his present term. During this period he committed only four robberies, at large stores or markets, and they yielded very large amounts of money. As in his earlier years, he engaged in elaborate planning for each crime. Archie was convicted by a jury on two counts of armed robbery with a prior felony conviction, and he is serving two concurrent sentences of five-to-life; he is also serving two consecutive five-to-life sentences for use of a firearm in these robberies.

Source: Joan Petersilia, Peter W. Greenwood, and Marvin Lavin, *Criminal Careers of Habitual Felons* (Washington, DC: U.S. Government Printing Office, 1978), 100–01.

multiple convictions for robbery admitted to having committed a large number of robberies for which they had not been caught.[6] Undeniably, this small minority made something of a career out of that crime. Still, many repeaters—almost half of Greenwood's sample, for instance—are not committing crimes at these high rates. That is, the mere existence of multiple convictions does not imply a career in crime as Reckless defines it; the person may simply be a frequent lawbreaker who shifts from one type of crime to another.

Why, then, this recent trend to paint the picture of the "career criminal" type with such a broad brush? Part of the answer has to do with political pressures. With the devaluation of rehabilitation in the 1970s came renewed confidence in incapacitation as the appropriate correctional course. But if incapacitation was the political catchword, what group would be the target? Previous studies had unearthed so few career criminals that this notion was not promising for crime control hard-liners. If the career criminal concept could be expanded to include virtually all crime repeaters, however, then the target group for this newly popular policy would be large indeed.

Corrections has borne the cost of this conceptual shift. Much as in the case of violent situational criminal types, pressure has grown to keep repeaters in prison longer to prevent them from pursuing their predatory "careers." Yet these criteria result in people being misclassified as career criminals when they are neither professionals nor persistent. This can contribute to prison overcrowding. California's three-strikes legislation specifies a sentence of 25 years to life for any third felony conviction. The law is meant to catch career criminals early in their careers, but critics point out that it ends up putting a large number of petty repeaters behind bars for a very long time.

Without question, our prisons hold some career criminals—professionals committed to lives of crime. But we must examine the accuracy of the overall label and recognize that any decision to classify people as "career criminals" has social and political significance.

MYTHS in Corrections

Violence by People Who Commit Sex Crimes

THE MYTH: People who commit violent sex crimes typically victimize unsuspecting strangers.

THE REALITY: Most sex crimes occur between people who are acquainted with each other and involve coercion but not violence.

Source: Karen Terry, *Sexual Offenses and Offenders: Theory, Practice and Policy* (Belmont, CA: Wadsworth, 2006).

sex crimes Sexual acts prohibited by law, such as rape, child molestation, or prostitution, motivated by economic, psychological, or situational reasons.

Clients Convicted of Sex Crimes

Although a wide array of legislation regulates sexual conduct, corrections commonly deals with people convicted of three basic types of **sex crimes**: (1) rape (sexual assault), (2) child molestation (pedophilia), and, to a lesser extent, (3) prostitution. Each class of sex crimes has a variety of economic, psychological, and situational motivations, and for each the correctional response is deeply influenced by prevailing public opinion about the crimes themselves. (See "Myths in Corrections" for more.)

At sentencing William Gallagher said he tried to rob a bank in order to get back to prison. A career criminal, Gallagher has spent much of his life in prison and felt out of place in the community.

© Angela Peterson/Milwaukee Journal Sentinel

Rape With the resurgence of feminism in the 1960s and 1970s, the justice system's response to rape became a major political issue. Indeed, to discuss rape under the heading of "sex offenses" risks ignoring that it is primarily an act of violence against women. In her classic study *Against Our Will,* Susan Brownmiller persuasively argued that rape needs to be reconceptualized; it is not a sex crime but a brutal personal assault: "To a woman the definition of rape is fairly simple. . . . A deliberate violation of emotional, physical and rational integrity and . . . [a] hostile, degrading act of violence."[7] When rape is placed where it truly belongs, within the context of modern criminal violence and not within the purview of archaic masculine codes, the crime retains its unique dimensions, taking its place with armed robbery and aggravated assault. The link between lethal violence and sexual assault was first established when a study a generation ago found that about half of all murders of women were committed by acquaintances and that two-thirds of those by strangers occurred in the process of sexual assaults.[8]

The widespread reconception of rape—the recognition that it is not sexually motivated but represents a physical intrusion fueled by a desire for violent coercion—led to two broad shifts in criminal justice. The first was a move to redefine the crime of rape as a gender-neutral "sexual assault" or even as a special case of the general crime of assault. The second shift was a trend toward harsher sentences for people convicted of rape. The sexual assault case presents particular difficulties for correctional management. Those clients who have been truly violent often prove to be a security risk inside the prison because the same irrational attitudes and unpredictable behavior patterns displayed before conviction might also occur during incarceration. More likely, however, this person will become a target for violence. In the prison subculture, "crazies," including many who are serving time for rape, are near the bottom of the pecking order. They are commonly subjected to humiliating physical and sexual attacks as a form of prison domination. Thus, whether unpredictably violent or predictably vulnerable to attack, the person who has been convicted of sexual assault is a security risk.

Child Molestation Few crimes are so uniformly reviled or carry so great a stigma as child molestation. However, only in recent years, with more open discussion of sexual issues, have scholars focused significantly on people convicted of this crime.

The picture of child molestation that emerges is often more tragic than disgusting. As many as 90 percent of people convicted of child molestation were themselves molested as children, and people convicted of sex crimes are about twice as likely as others in the prison system to report having been sexually victimized as a child.[9] Child molestation is a complex crime involving many factors; it ordinarily stems from deep feelings of personal inadequacy on the part of the perpetrator. As many as 20 percent of people convicted of child molestation are over 50 years old, and many cases involve ambivalent feelings of attachment between adults and children that gradually become converted into sexual contact. Many people who molest children are of borderline intelligence. Some victims of molestation are confused by the crime and feel guilty about it because of their emotional attachment to the people who molested them. They are usually aware that the act is "wrong" or "bad." If the act arouses pleasurable feelings, the situation is further complicated.

Someone convicted of child molestation is often the most despised person in court and in prison. Once incarcerated, men who are convicted of this crime are almost certain to be the target of repeated threats, physical violence, and routine hostility from others. Moreover, because most prison systems have few treatment options for them, the prison experience is typically quite bleak. To deal with these issues, some states have set aside special institutions or cell blocks for people convicted of child-related sex crimes to ensure their safety.

Prostitution Prostitution is more an economic than a sexual crime; in other words, it is an illegal business transaction between a service provider and a customer. Public opinion about prostitution is ambivalent; public policy seems to fluctuate between "reform" legislation designed to legalize and regulate prostitution and wholesale police roundups of "hookers and pimps" to "clean up" the streets. The AIDS epidemic fueled renewed concern about prostitutes' transmission of the disease. In response, some courts have ordered infected prostitutes to refrain from practicing their trade. In any event, prostitution exists (even flourishes) in virtually every section of the country, and when prostitutes or their pimps are punished, the sentence is generally probation or a fine.

Studies of female street prostitutes have found that many began their work at young ages, often having been raised in dysfunctional families, brought up without parents in

FOCUS ON

PEOPLE IN CORRECTIONS: Harvey's Story

Harvey Weinstein celebrated—if that's the word—his 68th birthday in the maximum-security wing of Wende Correctional Facility, one of New York State's strictest prisons. He was a few months into his 23-year sentence, when he tested positive for COVID-19, so his circumstances, already difficult, became even more stark, as stringent procedures to further isolate him from the general population were tacked onto his already routine segregation.

It was not always like this. Less than three years earlier, Harvey had been among the most powerful men in Hollywood and Broadway. A co-founder of Miramax pictures, one of the industry's most successful production companies for independent films, he had won an Oscar for producing the film *Shakespeare in Love*, and had received seven Tony awards for various Broadway productions.

In October of 2017, *The New York Times* and *The New Yorker* broke stories of more than a dozen women accusing him of using his powerful position to force sexual relations with women. The stories varied in their particulars, but all had the same theme. The women came to him seeking parts in shows he was producing, he created situations in which they were alone with him, and then he forced them to engage in sex with him. They all reported they felt cornered, felt he had power over them, and threatened directly or indirectly that their careers depended upon them accommodating him sexually.

After nine months of investigation, Cy Vance, Jr., the Manhattan District Attorney, announced that he was being charged with multiple counts of rape, criminal sex act, sex abuse, and sexual misconduct involving two of his victims. After a six-week jury trial, he was convicted of one count of criminal sexual assault in the first degree and one count of rape in the third degree. The court sentenced him to 23 years.

Harvey does not dispute the sexual encounters, but claims they were all consensual. Experts say that one of the classic rationalizations used by people who commit sexual assaults is that "she wanted it." His pattern of repeated sexual violations of women who were vulnerable to his status and power is one of the oldest stories in the book of rape.

The charges against Harvey drew national attention, and helped the viral spread of the *#MeToo movement*, in which thousands of women went public with their experiences of many types of sexual exploitation and violation at the hands of men in their lives—often men they knew rather than strangers.

an atmosphere of drug use and sexual assault. Their occupation places them at very high risk of sexually transmitted diseases and violent victimization. They have high rates of repeated contact with the criminal justice system, and even though their lifestyle contains a great deal of trauma and health challenges, including substance abuse, they often do not seek treatment.[10] Many prostitutes have children, though they do not have custody of them.[11] Child prostitution is a special version of this problem because the sexual exploitation of these children has such a lasting impact on them.

Because prostitution is an economic crime, correctional caseworkers must find a substitute vocation for people convicted of this crime. This is not easy, for prostitutes often lack education and marketable skills, and many are addicted to drugs. Further, many attempt to leave the trade, but few succeed until age, illness, or disability renders them less productive. Because prostitution is more a nuisance than a threat to the public, caseworkers tend to accord such cases low priority, as do the courts and prosecutors. Therefore, prostitution often receives marginal enforcement of laws and indifferent punishment.

Concern About Sex Crimes When John E. Couey abducted nine-year-old Jessica Lunsford from her bedroom in the middle of the night, raped her, and eventually murdered her, a nation watched the case with horror. Couey had a long criminal record with over 24 arrests, including a conviction for the assault of a woman during a burglary for which he was sentenced to 10 years. The sight of Couey idly scribbling on a notepad as the most gruesome facts of his crime were put in evidence—little Jessica had been repeatedly raped and was buried alive, suffocating to death in a plastic bag—galvanized a response to deal with what are referred to as "sexually violent predators," people who repeatedly victimized others sexually and seemed incapable of stopping themselves from escalating their violence. It seems that too many people who commit sex crimes become recidivists because treatment fails.

Partly in response to fears about repeat sexual violence committed by sexually violent predators, new laws call for a range of close controls to be placed on people convicted of sex crimes, from broad community notification when they move into a neighborhood after release from prison to GPS monitoring of their whereabouts 24 hours per day. In recent years, 16 states have enacted sexually violent predator statutes. These laws are based on the belief that society needs a way to keep potentially dangerous "perverts" off the streets after their sentences have been served. Many states place them under longer terms of intense supervision, while other states have imposed tougher sentencing measures. All states now have laws requiring public notification when people convicted of violent sex crimes are paroled. The most drastic type of legislation allows correctional authorities to propose indefinite "civil commitment" of people classified as "sexually violent predators," which in practice means they will be confined for life (or until cured) in a mental institution devoted to them. These new laws seem harsh, but the courts have not overturned them, even though studies show they have very limited effects on serious sexual crimes.[12]

Concern about sex crimes is understandable but not always completely appropriate. One of the most authoritative studies, conducted on more than 20,000 people who had been convicted of sex crimes and released from prison, found that they were three times more likely than others to be rearrested for rape within nine years of their release.[13] Yet this figure could be misleading because the actual rate of these arrests is small: Only 7.7 percent of the 20,000 were rearrested for rape, compared to 2.3 percent of all people released from prison in that time period. To complicate matters further, this group was far less likely to be rearrested for *any* kind of offense; 67 percent of them had a new arrest after nine years, compared with 84 percent of people released from prison on a nonsex crime. Another study has found that juveniles who are convicted of sex-related crimes are no more likely to be arrested for sex crimes as adults than are other juvenile delinquents.[14] So while it is clear that people convicted of sex crimes pose a different kind of risk than others, it is equally clear that many of them can and do reenter society successfully after release from prison.

sex offender registry
A public website that lists the names, addresses, and crimes of people who have convicted of specified sex crimes; sometimes neighbors are notified when a person living nearby is on such a website.

One widespread change in the response to people convicted of sex crimes has been the creation of **sex offender registries**. In these registries, people who are convicted of certain sex crimes are listed on publicly available websites, and neighbors are often notified when a person living nearby is on such a website. The popularity of sex offender registries has grown rapidly, with as many as 750,000 names.[15] The idea is that people will be able to protect themselves if they know that a neighbor has a record for a sex crime. But the effectiveness of the approach is questionable. One study found that the implementation of sex offender registries had no impact on the number of sex crimes.[16] Legislatures have also tried to restrict the places where people convicted of sex crimes can live, after release from prison. These laws tend to concentrate people with sex crime histories in impoverished areas,[17] and they fail to reduce the risk of repeat sexual crimes outside of those areas.[18]

The new laws are quite popular, but they raise important questions about the reach of the laws and fairness in dealing with people who commit sex crimes. On the one hand, research has not shown promising results for treatment programs. This suggests that civil-commitment programs are not likely to help those sent there. Indeed, there appear to be problems in the management of some civil-commitment centers, with poorly trained staff and difficulties in maintaining control. On the other hand, public alarm may be overblown. Studies consistently show that those convicted of sex crimes have lower than average rates of new crimes after they have served their sentences; indeed, they even appear to have low rates of new *sex* crimes: The average person caught for a sex crime neither specializes in that type of crime nor is persistent in any type of crime, generally. The John E. Coueys of this world are extremely rare, and it turns out that trying to predict who they are is nearly impossible (see the section on classification later in this chapter).

Substance Abusers

Substance abuse and addiction fundamentally influence the nature of the correctional population. As noted by the National Center on Addiction and Substance Abuse, crime and alcohol/ drug abuse in America are joined at the hip. Its study found that four out of five people in jail and prison "had been high when they committed their crimes, had stolen to support their habit or had a history of drug and alcohol abuse that led them to commit crime."[19]

Criminal law typically distinguishes between the use of illegal drugs and the illegal use of alcohol. In the case of drugs, any unauthorized possession of a controlled substance is prohibited. Laws against the mere possession of some drugs are so strict that prison terms are mandatory for such offenses in the federal system as well as in many states. In contrast, possession of alcohol is prohibited only for minors. The criminal justice system becomes involved in situations related to alcohol abuse primarily because of a person's conduct under the influence of alcohol. Because the difference between drug-related crime and alcohol-related crime is important for correctional policy, we discuss them here separately.

Drug Abuse Our culture is a drug-using culture, from aspirin and caffeine to marijuana and cocaine. Not surprisingly, then, substance abuse figures prominently in criminal behavior (see "Mary Lou's Story"). Nearly one-third of people in state prisons serving time

FOCUS ON

PEOPLE IN CORRECTIONS: Mary Lou's Story

Mary Lou looks much older than her 25 years. She was brought up in Chicago in a family of six children, where the only income was her mother's monthly welfare check. She is now approaching the time of her release from prison after serving a sentence for driving the getaway car involved in the armed robbery of a drugstore.

A school dropout at age 16, Mary Lou met Frankie, a flashy dude who seemed to have money to spend yet was always on the street. Soon she was doing drugs with Frankie, and even though her girlfriends warned her that he was a junkie and a pimp, she moved into his apartment; by then, she had graduated to heroin. During their first weeks together, they were high much of the time—sleeping through the morning, getting a fix, then cruising the streets in Frankie's Buick, dropping in at bars and apartments to visit what seemed like an endless number of his friends.

When Frankie's money ran low, he told Mary Lou she was going to have to "hustle" if she expected to live with him. She told him she wouldn't and moved in with a girlfriend. Within a day, she was feeling so bad that she had to borrow money for a fix. Faced with her habit and an empty pocketbook, Mary Lou hustled. She turned two tricks the first night, but her second customer beat her up. Shaken by the experience and hurting for heroin, she returned to the only person she thought could help her—Frankie. He was not happy to see her because another girl had already taken her place, but he agreed to help if she would hustle for him. During the next six months she was able to make enough money to retain Frankie's protection and to support her habit.

With the onset of winter, the streets of Chicago turned cold, and the supply of heroin on the streets suddenly tightened in response to a strong law enforcement effort. By this time both Mary Lou and Frankie were heavy users. After two frantic days of trying to find affordable heroin, Frankie decided to rob a drugstore. In a haze, Mary Lou drove him to the store, parked in an alley, and waited while Frankie, armed with a gun, entered the store. Within minutes he came dashing back, a burglar alarm blaring in his wake. Mary Lou gunned the Buick down the alley and into the street, where it struck another car. Frankie jumped out and ran off. A stunned Mary Lou just sat behind the wheel while a crowd formed and an officer arrived to investigate the accident.

It took very little detective work for the police to link the collision to the robbery. They arrested Frankie back at his apartment and took him to the station house for booking. Mary Lou was already there when he was brought in. Held in the Cook County jail awaiting court action, she endured agonizing withdrawal from heroin.

At the suggestion of her public defender, Mary Lou pleaded guilty to a reduced charge of abetting an armed robbery and was sentenced to a three- to five-year term.

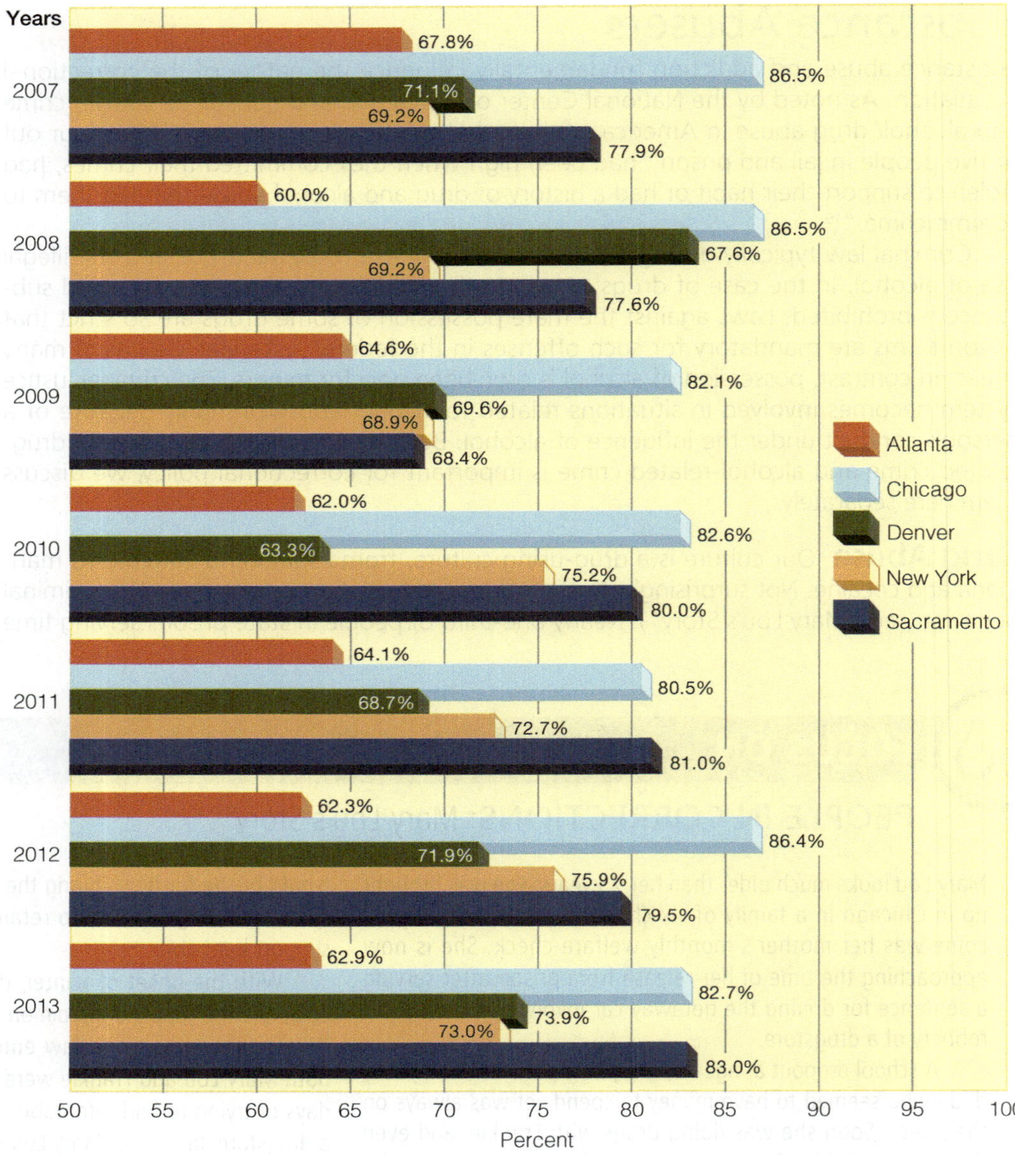

FIGURE 6.3 Drug Use by Male Booked Arrestees in Five U.S. Cities

Drug use among the arrested population has been fairly stable in key cities nationally.

Source: National Institute of Justice, *ADAM II: 2013 Annual Report* (Washington, DC: U.S. Government Printing Office, 2015).

for violent offenses were under the influence of an illegal drug when they committed the crime.[20] As Figure 6.3 shows, the majority of people arrested in five U.S. cities tested positive for an illegal drug at the time of their arrest.

drug abuse The disruption of normal living patterns by the use of illegal chemical substances to the extent that social problems develop, often leading to criminal behavior.

Drug abuse is now the leading cause of death for people in the United States under the age of 50.[21] It presents both treatment and management problems for corrections. Many people have been convicted for possession or sale of drugs or for some other crime that was committed as a result of drug use. In all of these cases, correctional personnel must address the effects of drug dependency while the client is in detention, on probation, in prison, or on parole. Drug abuse also represents a potential control problem for correctional staff because of a high likelihood that people who continue to use drugs will eventually be rearrested.

The street addict's life is structured by the need to get money to support the habit, and that need often leads to property crime. Studies of the relationship between drugs and crime have found that although much of the money for supporting a drug habit may be legitimately obtained, a high proportion of drug users admit to income-generating crimes. Even if an addict supports only a small fraction of the habit's cost through crime, this can translate into many violations.

Habits costing $50–$150 a day are not uncommon. Because stolen goods are fenced at much less than their market value, an addict must steal goods worth several times the cost of the drug just to support the habit.[22] Robbery is more directly lucrative than theft but also chancier: There is always a risk of violence, and the victim may have little cash.

Treatment programs for people who compulsively or habitually use drugs do not have high success rates, and some are controversial. As the social movement against heroin grew in the 1950s and 1960s, support for clinical treatment of addiction also grew, and drug treatment facilities were opened to house addicts as a special population. Civil-commitment procedures were often used to send people addicted to drugs from court to such facilities, where their incarceration term frequently exceeded what they would otherwise have received. Evaluations of these programs showed dismal results, with long-term abstinence rates around 10 percent.

Thus, substance abuse represents a serious dilemma for corrections. By definition, the behavior is compulsive and likely to be repeated. Although the mere act of drug abuse is not considered a serious offense, the collateral acts of crime and violence are considered quite serious.

Since the 1980s, federal policies have sought to combat drug abuse by providing tougher criminal sanctions. Punishments for drug possession and sales were made considerably harsher, especially in the federal courts, where sentences of 10 years or longer became routine. There was also a renewed emphasis on treatment for drug addiction, and some of these prison-based programs had better results than the earlier civil-commitment programs did. However, most experts believe that the dual-track strategy of punishment and treatment has not appreciably lowered drug abuse, and recent research indicates that going to prison does not reduce recidivism rates for moderate drug abusers.[23]

More recently, reform efforts have sought to deliver drug treatment services to people who remain in the community, diverted from prison and jail. Typically offered under the oversight of a special court called a drug court, this approach carefully monitors a person's progress in treatment and often eliminates the criminal charges when a person succeeds in treatment. Drug courts have had broad success as an alternative to incarceration and traditional correctional programs.[24]

Methamphetamine and opioids Throughout history, drug abuse has been associated with urban areas. In the last decade, however, the United States has seen an epidemic of opioid and methamphetamine abuse that predominates in rural America. **Methamphetamine** (called "meth") is a highly addictive stimulant that is made illicitly in labs by "cooking" the parent drug, amphetamine (used legally to treat attention deficit disorder). **Opioids** are various prescription drugs used to treat pain, especially chronic pain.

Methamphetamine Highly addictive stimulant that is made from amphetamine.

Opioid Any of a range of prescription pain killers.

The meth wave began in the 1990s, and accelerated at the turn of the century. Initially, meth was supplied by an estimated 15,000 domestic labs. By the time meth became big business, aggressive U.S. law enforcement had shut down most of the local labs, and Mexico has risen to become the major supplier of meth to U.S. users. Smoking or injecting methamphetamine provides a brief, pleasurable high—a "rush" that quickly subsides into an enduring "high." The long-term side effects of a meth habit include memory loss, aggression, psychotic behavior, damage to the cardiovascular system, malnutrition, and severe dental problems. In the most recent year for which we have data, about 1.6 million Americans reported using meth,[25] and the frequency of meth use has increased six-fold since 2013.[26] Behavioral treatments (see pp. 372 in Chapter 14) have proven effective in treating meth addiction.

Opioid abuse is newer to the scene. The opioid crisis began when pharmaceutical manufacturers of painkillers convinced the medical profession that their use could not be addictive. They also heavily marketed painkillers to doctors, who started prescribing them much more often—even for routine situations. At least one out of every five patients for which painkillers became prescribed began to misuse them, and about half of that group became addicted. Some opioid addicts graduated to heroin, but others simply continued to use the drugs in increasing quantities, eventually leading to an overdose. The problem of opioid abuse became so severe that the rate of overdoses doubled every year between 2013 and 2017, and by 2018, 128 people a day were dying from opioid overdose.[27]

For years, pharmaceutical companies had aggressively marketed opioids, but when the evidence of addiction became clear, authorities began to place more stringent controls on prescription and use. Producers also developed a powerful synthetic opioid, called **fentanyl**—50 times more powerful than heroin and 100 times more powerful than morphine. Access to fentanyl has accelerated the lethality of opioid misuse, and put it at the very top of the dangerous drug list. Treatment approaches usually begin with medical help to overcome the effects of withdrawal, followed by drugs (such as methadone) that suppress the craving in combination with behavior therapy to reinforce new habits.

Fentanyl A powerful, synthetic opioid.

Alcohol Abuse Unlike marijuana, heroin, and other controlled substances, alcohol is widely available and relatively inexpensive, and its consumption is an integral part of life in the United States. Only when alcohol leads to problems such as unemployment, family disorganization, and crime does society become concerned (see "Henry's Story").

The **alcohol abuse** problem translates into crime much less directly than that of the drug user. Where many addicts must engage in a criminal act just to get the drug of their choice, the alcoholic need only go to the corner store. However, alcoholics produce far-more-disastrous consequences than heroin addicts do. According to some estimates, alcohol use contributes to almost 100,000 deaths annually, about six times the total number of homicides reported to the police. Alcohol is more closely associated with crimes of violence than is any illegal drug, and the number of alcohol-related traffic fatalities is about the same as the number of homicides. Alcohol use impairs coordination and judgment, reduces inhibitions, and confuses understanding; criminal acts can easily follow. Thus, a drunk's drive home may become vehicular homicide, a domestic dispute may become aggravated assault, a political debate or quarrel over money may become disorderly conduct, and a night of drinking may lead to burglary or auto theft.

alcohol abuse The disruption of normal living patterns caused by high levels of alcohol use, frequently leading to violations of the law while under the influence of alcohol or in attempting to secure it. Chronic alcohol abusers are generally referred to as alcoholics.

Although research on alcohol abuse has focused on the incarcerated, this problem appears in other correctional environments as well. Like drug abusers, alcoholics present problems for probation officers, community treatment providers, and parole officers. Because some alcoholics become assaultive when they drink, dealing with them is neither pleasant nor safe.

Other problems are related to the treatment of alcohol abusers. To some extent, these problems stem from Americans' generally ambivalent attitude toward alcohol use, which is seen as recreational behavior rather than deviance. Consequently, treatment programs seem to work best when they focus on getting people to recognize the problems that arise from their own patterns of alcohol abuse rather than on "the evils of alcohol" per se. This is one reason why the program of Alcoholics Anonymous (AA) has consistently proved among the most successful of treatment methods: It provides intensive peer support to help people face their own personal inability to manage alcohol use. Recent studies also suggest that drug therapies (such as Naltrexone) can help prevent relapse for people who have stopped drinking.[28]

Despite its general success, AA alone may be of limited usefulness in criminal justice. AA views itself as a strictly voluntary treatment program; individuals must want to help

FOCUS ON
PEOPLE IN CORRECTIONS: Henry's Story

Henry Earl has been called "the world's most arrested man." By the age of 64, he had been arrested about 1,500 times as an adult—an average of just over three arrests a month. It has been estimated that Earl has spent more than 6,000 days in jail—the equivalent of more than 16 years behind bars.

Earl, who lives in Kentucky, was first arrested in July of 1970 for carrying a concealed weapon—one of 33 arrests in the 1970s. His arrest record accelerated over the years, mostly for alcohol-related offenses such as drunk and disorderly. The pattern of offending since has been almost as predictable as clockwork. He is found in some state of public intoxication, perhaps sleeping on a bench or in an alleyway. He is arrested and brought to jail, where he spends a day or two awaiting a court hearing. He pleads guilty and is sentenced. For years, his typical sentence was a few days in jail, but recently judges have started imposing longer terms of two to three months. Once released, he finds himself back on the streets and soon is drunk again.

A few years ago, a Lexington television station, WKYT, did a story on his 1,000th arrest. The story astonished many viewers, with reactions ranging from "This man is a homeless alcoholic who needs help" to "When will enough be enough?" Ironically, the news story underestimated his arrest record by almost a third. Since that time, a popular crime blog, the Smoking Gun, has been keeping track of his continuing contact with the criminal justice system. Most recently, Earl spent both Thanksgiving and Christmas in the local jail—on different charges.

Source: Adapted from the Smoking Gun, www.thesmokinggun.com /buster/henry-earl-jail-sentence-674512.

themselves. This often clashes with the coercive nature of treatment in corrections, which may require attendance at AA meetings as a condition of the sentence. The poor fit between AA's voluntary peer group structure and the involuntary nature of corrections may explain why AA has had only mixed success for people convicted of public drunkenness.

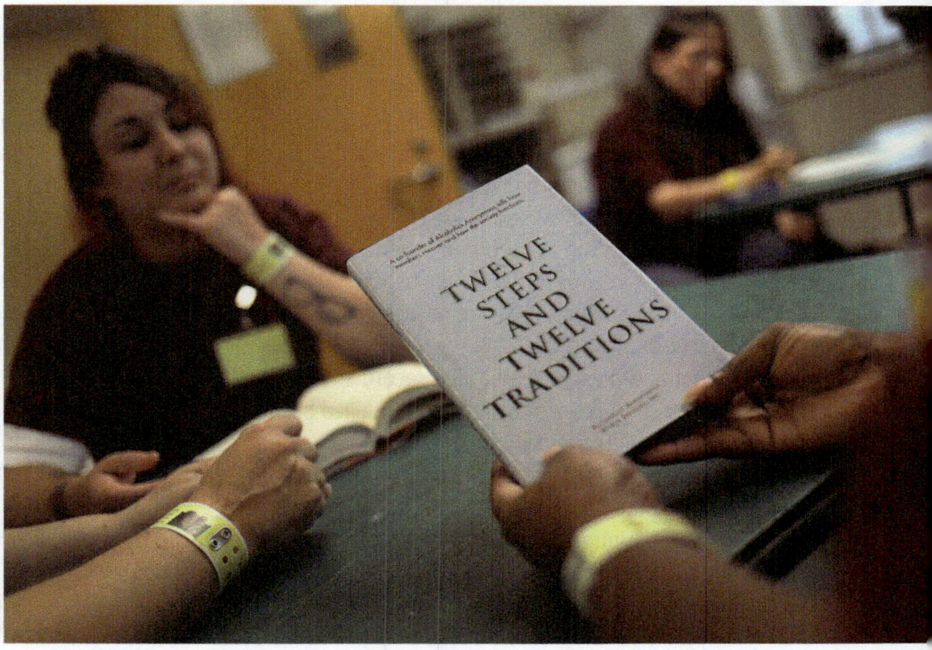

John Moore/Getty Images News/Getty Images

Twelve-step programs are common in correctional facilities—they help substance abusers prevent relapse into various addictions, such as alcohol, narcotics, and sex.

Clients with Mental Illnesses

When he was 25, Michael Megginson was arrested for stealing a cell phone and sent to New York City's jail at Rikers Island. There he became disruptive, getting into fight after fight. His bones were broken in altercations with staff. He was thought to be one of the most violent people incarcerated in Rikers. But he also hurt himself, cutting himself and attempting suicide, and he had psychotic episodes, trashing his cell. None of this was really new. Even though he never had a diagnosis that stuck, Megginson had been under acute psychiatric care since the age of 6, confined at least 20 times whenever his uncontrollable rage overtook him. For a while, he had been barely coping on the streets. But once he was forced to deal with the emotional and physical strains of jail, he deteriorated rapidly.[29]

Some surveys of mental health problems in prisons and jails are more than a decade old, but their prevalence estimates remain valid today, the serious mental illnesses afflict almost 200,000 people in prison and more than 125,000 people in jails. They estimated that almost 800,000 people in prisons and almost 500,000 in jails suffered from some form of mental health problem.[30]

Few images disturb people more than that of the "crazy," violence-prone individual whose acts seem random, senseless, or even psychopathic. To understand such people better, correctional professionals often roughly classify them as "disturbed" or as having a **mental illness**— people whose rational processes do not seem to operate in normal ways (see "Johnnie's Story"). People who have serious mental illnesses are often less able than others to think realistically about their conduct, including criminal conduct. While it is clear that problems of mental illness are important in corrections, the centrality of mental illness to criminal behavior should not be overstated. It is important not to stereotype people with mental illnesses as "dangerous" because that is also not necessarily the case. Very few of those who have a mental illness are violent or psychopathic, and those who are account for an extremely small fraction of all violent crimes.

mental illness A health condition involving changes in thinking, emotion, and/or behavior that can cause problems in social, work, or family activities.

Even so, daily headlines bring our attention to the problem of mental illness. When Dylann Roof killed nine worshippers at South Carolina's Emanuel African Methodist Episcopal Church in June 2015, he claimed his racist beliefs were the motivation:

FOCUS ON

PEOPLE IN CORRECTIONS: Johnnie's Story

Johnnie Baxstrom, a black male, was born on August 12, 1918, in Greensboro, North Carolina. He quit school in the eleventh grade at the age of 17. As described by his hospital notes, throughout his childhood "he had what he termed 'fainting headaches.'" He said that it felt as though someone were beating on the side of his temple, and he would black out in school. He was hospitalized from May 29 to June 8, 1956, for head injury. Diagnosis: "Idiopathic Epilepsy and residuals from Bilateral Subdural Hematoma, following skull fracture."

Baxstrom had a very irregular job record showing that he worked only for short times at a variety of unskilled positions. He did have a good military record; he entered the armed forces in September 1943 and received an honorable discharge in March 1946. He was married three times.

Baxstrom's criminal record is a lengthy list of drinking and property offenses. However, his first offense did not occur until he was 30, which was two years after he got out of the military service and while he was living with his second wife. He was charged with assaulting a female with a dangerous weapon, but the case was never disposed of in the courts. Again in 1950, he was arrested on two counts of assault and one of larceny in Baltimore. He was found not guilty of all charges. His first conviction occurred six months later. He received a 12-month sentence on the road gang for an "affray [offensive] assault on a female." Over the next few years, Baxstrom appears to have taken up a wandering lifestyle involving no work. Between 1951 and 1958, when he was sentenced to Attica, he was arrested 12 times for such things as trespassing on Southern Railway property, drunkenness, vagrancy, disorderly conduct, intoxication, and one time for robbery for which he received and served a one-year sentence in the Maryland House of Corrections.

On October 21, 1958, Baxstrom was arrested in Rochester, New York, for attacking a police officer with an ice pick. According to hospital records, he stabbed the officer in the face, forehead, and collarbone. Apparently, Baxstrom was drinking in a bar where he got into a fight with another patron. During the fight Baxstrom pulled a knife or ice pick and stabbed the other combatant. This man turned out to be a police officer in civilian clothes. For this act, Baxstrom received a two-and-a-half- to three-year sentence. The conviction was for second-degree assault. He was admitted to Attica State Prison.

While in Attica, Baxstrom was reported to "often have epileptic fits during which he was aggressive and assaultive. He also used obscene language." Because of this, he was transferred administratively to Dannemora Prison on a civil commitment. In 1966, in a landmark case, the U.S. Supreme Court (383 U.S. 107) held that an administrative civil commitment to a mental hospital without basic due process of law was unconstitutional.

Source: H. J. Steadman and J. J. Cocozza, *Careers of the Criminally Insane* (Lexington, MA: Lexington, 1974), 43–45. Reprinted by permission.

"I felt like I had to do it, and I still do feel like I had to do it." This is certainly not normal thinking, and it is wildly abnormal behavior. It is hard for us to believe that a person of sound mind would do such a thing. But is it a mental illness? Or is it just, as some of the victim's family members said at sentencing, "the worst kind of evil"?[31]

Roof committed his crime in cold blood and was sentenced to death. He refused to allow consideration of his mental health status in the trial or the sentencing hearing. But we cannot look at his actions without thinking that mental illness is at least a factor in his motivation for such an extreme act.

There is some overlap between what we described as the career criminal and the so-called psychopath. Both engage in frequent criminal activity. The intended distinction between them is made clear in the original description of the psychopathic individual: "an asocial, aggressive, highly impulsive person, who feels little or no guilt and is unable to form lasting bonds of affection with other human beings."[32] Thus, this person lacks attachment to people or rules, whereas a career criminal is motivated by economic gain. However, in practice this distinction is problematic because it presumes knowledge of another person's private thoughts. Who can prove that another individual never feels love, affection, or guilt and should therefore be labeled psychopathic? Who can prove that the same individual might not also be motivated by material gain?

The central problem with the mental health model of criminality is that we cannot observe people's minds; we can only infer their inner feelings and thoughts from their behavior. When we see people behaving in outrageous or bizarre ways, we are tempted to conclude that their mind or emotions work in strange ways. We call these people "sick" or "emotionally ill" even when there is no evidence of an illness, in the sense of the flu or other physical disease. In earlier times, deities, witches, and instincts were considered to cause a variety of odd or criminal behaviors. As Thomas Szasz has argued, today we use the term *mental illness* to explain behaviors we do not understand, even if the behavior is not caused by a "disease of the brain."[33]

Our need to explain some criminal behavior as mental illness can easily lead us to overgeneralize and ascribe mental illness to all people who engage in crime. In 1969 the National Commission on the Causes and Prevention of Violence recognized the problem when it concluded famously that (1) research evidence does not support the popular idea that the mentally ill are overrepresented in the population of those who commit violent crime and that (2) people identified as mentally ill generally pose no greater risk of committing violent crimes than does the population as a whole.[34] Recent research has shown that upon release from prison, people diagnosed as mentally ill tend to commit fewer serious crimes than those without the diagnosis because people with mental illness pose such a lower risk of violence than the average person on parole. However, when compared to other low-risk individuals, those with a mental illness actually commit more-serious crimes.[35] So providing treatment to correctional clients with mental illness is a high priority.

This conclusion underscores the problem for corrections that comes with mental illness: A person's mental health condition is often a separate issue from criminality, and dealing with a person's criminality may not require treatment of mental illness. In other words, the fact that a person has mental or emotional problems does not necessarily mean that he or she will continue to break the law until the mental or emotional problems are resolved. But for those who suffer from a mental illness, obtaining and maintaining treatment can be important. Foregoing treatment and failing to take medication prescribed to treat mental illness are each risk factors for arrests.

Why do some people become mentally ill while serving their terms? We must recognize that incarceration is stressful, even for the emotionally strong. People serving time lose contact with families and other sources of emotional support. Often they feel humiliated by being convicted and sentenced to prison. Then they must face the strains of prison life, which are often augmented by unsafe and burdensome prison conditions. For some, the strain proves too much—they lose their emotional stability.

Institutional care for people with mental illnesses has paralleled historical shifts in corrections. There were early efforts to separate people with mental illnesses from others who were incarcerated, but not until 1859 did the first institution built specially for such people, the New York State Lunatic Asylum for Insane Convicts, open near Auburn Prison. The facility held both convicted and nonconvicted patients, and it later received patients judicially transferred from civil hospitals.

Today, all states have either separate facilities for convicted individuals who are mentally ill or sections of mental hospitals reserved for them. In some states the department of corrections controls these institutions, and in others the department of mental health does. In the coming decade, corrections will face an increased number of clients with mental illnesses. Much of the increase is related to a major policy shift in the mental health field: **deinstitutionalization**. With the availability of drugs that inhibit aberrant behavior, it became possible to release a multitude of mental patients to the community. Unfortunately, some former patients fail to take their medication and then commit deviant or criminal acts. Because of their behavior, some are shuttled back and forth between the mental hospital and jail or prison.

deinstitutionalization The release of a mental patient from a mental hospital and his or her return to the community.

Clients with Developmental Disabilities

The 43-year-old man entered the Dunkin' Donuts shop, approached the counter, and demanded, "All your money and a dozen doughnuts." With his finger pointed inside his pocket, he announced that he had a gun and would use it. When the police arrived, they found the man standing outside the shop eating the doughnuts—just as they had found him after several previous holdups. The man's name is Eddie; he has an IQ of 61. He has served prison sentences for this type of offense, but almost immediately upon release he commits another such crime.

Ron, a 33-year-old man who functions at the level of a 10-year-old, was sentenced to a five-year prison term for bank robbery. He was easily identified by the police because he had signed his name on the holdup note he had given to the teller.

Charlie, who has an IQ of 85, set fire to a trash barrel in the hallway of his apartment building. A psychotic tenant, panicked by the smoke, jumped out of the window and was killed by the fall. Charlie was charged with murder.

These cases point to another problematic type of person for the corrections system: the person who has a **developmental disability**, sometimes referred to as a "learning disability." An estimated 2 to 3 percent of the people in the United States have a developmental disability (having IQs below 70). Among the correctional population, the proportion is much higher. Like other Americans, people who have a developmental disability commit crimes, but there is no proven link between that disability and a propensity for criminal behavior. Their criminality may result from the fact that they do not know how to obtain what they want without breaking the law (see "Donald's Story"). It may also result from the fact that they are easily duped by people who think that deviant behavior is a joke or who use them to secure something illicitly for themselves. The developmentally disabled are also disproportionately poor, so if they need or want something, they may commit a crime to get it. Further, because they cannot think quickly, they get caught more often than others.

developmental disability The inability to learn or develop skills at the same rate as most other people because of a problem with the brain.

The majority of the offenses committed by people with developmental disabilities are classified as property or public-order crimes. This is not to say that they do not also commit serious violent crimes; among the incarcerated, people who are developmentally disabled commit higher rates of homicide and other crimes against persons. Because of the special circumstances that are often involved when people who are developmentally disabled commit a very serious crime, numerous states have prohibited their execution, regardless of the nature of the crime. In 2002 the U.S. Supreme Court ruled in *Atkins v. Virginia* that executing a person who is developmentally disabled violates the Eighth Amendment of the U.S. Constitution (prohibiting cruel and unusual punishment), making this a nationwide law.[36]

FOCUS ON

PEOPLE IN CORRECTIONS: Donald's Story

Donald stole to survive. Often he took food from grocery stores. Sometimes he broke into diners to cook meals for himself in the middle of the night.

"I'd never break into anybody's house," Donald said. "That would be wrong. People have to work too hard for their money. I only break into stores." He doesn't understand that when he steals from businesses, he hurts the people who own them. He has a mental disability.

Donald, whose IQ is in the 60s (100 is normal), spent most of his life in Ladd School, Rhode Island's institution for people with mental disabilities. In 1967, when he was 24 years old, he was released and given a job washing dishes in an East Greenwich, Rhode Island, restaurant.

"It wasn't enough money," said Donald. "It was only $30 a week. If I paid for my room, I couldn't eat. So I quit. I had to survive somehow, so I would go out and steal. I didn't know how to do no job." When asked why he didn't go on welfare, he replied, "I didn't know about that stuff. Nobody ever told me anything about it. It's hard to get on welfare. You have to write stuff on papers."

Donald's court records show that his arrests came one after the other. One was for breaking into a diner and stealing 35 cents. At one point, Donald found a job at a Providence laundry, and for a few months the break-ins stopped.

"All I did was fold clothes from the dryer," he recalled. "There was me and another guy. Then they decided one person could do it, and they got rid of my helper. I got scared. I couldn't do it alone. So I just quit."

So it was back to the break-ins.

Donald often got caught and was continually before the courts. But the judges never knew what to do with him; Rhode Island has no program for the developmentally disabled. Sometimes they put him on probation, and on several occasions, they sent him to the state mental hospital for observation.

But no one helped Donald get a job. Finally, the judges lost patience and started sending Donald to prison. He has served at least three prison sentences, although court records are unclear and Donald is not sure there were not more. He is not good with numbers. When asked, he didn't know his age, which is 37.

On July 30, 1978, police records show that Donald was out of prison again. At 10:02 that night, a burglar alarm went off at a Providence factory building. Police found Donald hiding behind a door with a glass cutter in his pocket. As usual, Donald confessed. "I felt like getting some money," he told police. "I didn't know where to get it. Then I tried to get it in there."

A sympathetic judge put Donald on probation on the condition that he voluntarily live at the state mental hospital until a better arrangement could be made for him. Since then, Donald hasn't done any stealing. "Don't need to," he said. "I eat for free now."

Every weekday, after breakfast at the mental hospital, Donald takes the bus to downtown Providence and walks the streets looking for a job. He's been doing it for more than a year now, without success.

"If only I can get a job, maybe I can get out of the hospital," he said. "But I can't read and write. I can't do the forms. They ask you where you live. I live in a nuthouse. They ask about your last job." What's his future? "I don't know," he said. "I don't want to steal no more. It ain't worth it. I wish when I got in trouble a cop had shot me. So I wouldn't have to do it no more."

Source: B. DeSilva, "Donald's Story," *Corrections Magazine*, August 1980, p. 27. Reprinted by permission of the Edna McConnell Clark Foundation.

Programs that deal with people who have developmental disabilities have focused on deinstitutionalization. Like those with mental illnesses, when those with developmental disabilities are returned to the community, they are often expected to live, work, and care for themselves with minimal supervision. Yet when they have difficulty adjusting to the rules of the community, they again come to the attention of the criminal justice system.

What can corrections do for or with this special group? Obviously, the usual routines of probation, diversion, incarceration, and community service will not work. People with developmental disabilities are often not comfortable with change, are difficult to employ outside of sheltered workshops, and are not likely to improve significantly in terms of mental condition or social habits. When they violate probation or break prison rules, they are further penalized. While incarcerated, they are often the butts of practical jokes and exploited as scapegoats or sexual objects. Recent litigation has called attention to the fact that those with developmental disabilities require special programs, and the Americans with Disabilities Act (ADA) provides federal oversight to local correctional programs for them.

Correctional programs for people with developmental disabilities need to be appropriate. In many prisons and jails, they are segregated from the regular population, along with others who have special needs. This strategy has been criticized because they are sometimes preyed on by others in the unit. In several states, such as Massachusetts and Texas, there are programs within probation and parole to provide additional assistance and services to people who are developmentally disabled. Day reporting centers are used in some states, as are halfway houses. These programs aim at helping people who are developmentally disabled gain the skills and discipline they need to live independent and crime-free lives.

Some observers believe that people with developmental disabilities are not really criminally oriented but instead lack training in how to live in a complex society; they belong not in prison but in a treatment facility where they can learn rudimentary life skills. Criminal justice practitioners often argue that people who are developmentally disabled constitute a mental health problem, but because they have committed crimes, mental health agencies do not want them. Thus, they are shunned by both camps and get little help from either.

Clients with HIV/AIDS

Human immunodeficiency virus (HIV) and its full-blown symptomatic stage, acquired immune deficiency syndrome (AIDS), have a major impact on U.S. corrections. This remains true, even though the most recent data show that rates of HIV and AIDS in prisons and jails are on the decline. Between 1998 and 2015, the number of HIV-positive people in state prisons declined from 24,910 to 15,610 (1.2 percent of the total prison population, down from 2.3 percent in 1998). In 2015, 45 people in state prisons died of AIDS, down from 1,010 in 1995. Today, HIV rates and death rates in U.S. prisons are very similar to those of the nation as a whole.[37]

The correctional client with HIV or AIDS confronts probation and parole officers with several problems. For jail and prison administrators, the problems stem mainly from policy issues concerning the people under their supervision. Institutional administrators must develop policies covering such matters as finding ways to prevent disease transmission, housing those who are infected, and providing medical care for people in the last stages of AIDS. In determining what actions should be taken, administrators have found that a host of legal, political, budgetary, and attitudinal factors limit their ability to make the best decisions (see "Mike's Story").

The long incubation period of the disease—the time between infection and the appearance of outward symptoms—also makes preventing the spread of AIDS difficult. Carriers may engage in unsafe drug taking and sex without knowing they are infecting others. Although most HIV-positive correctional clients were infected before they were incarcerated, transmission within the institution remains a concern.

When a person exhibits AIDS-related symptoms, the response usually includes confinement in a hospital or infirmary. In some states (such as New Jersey), these people are placed in a hospital in the community; in other states (such as California), they are placed in a correctional medical facility. States with a large number of people carrying the virus follow the policy of segregated housing, even when those people show no active symptoms of AIDS. For example, California now houses all who are HIV-infected in a wing of the Correctional Medical Facility at Vacaville to prevent transmission and to provide medical and counseling services to the group in the most effective way.

Medical services for AIDS patients are costly, ranging from $50,000 to $145,000 annually per patient; in some high-cost areas, extended acute medical care can run as high as $300,000. States with a large number of HIV-positive and AIDS-infected people in prison face costs that could easily constitute a major portion of their entire correctional budgets. But medical care and social acceptance have now advanced to the point that dealing with the medical needs of the HIV positive in prison is not markedly different than outside, and the prognosis is also similar.

FOCUS ON

PEOPLE IN CORRECTIONS: Mike's Story

Mike Camargo lay in his hospital bed in the prison ward of Bellevue Hospital in New York City. Camargo was a pretrial detainee accused of selling drugs to an undercover police officer the previous summer. When he was conscious, he felt sharp, stabbing pains in his arms and feet. He could hardly move, much less sit up. Camargo was told that he suffered from pneumonia and toxoplasmosis.

Six weeks later he was transferred to an intensive-care unit of the hospital. He had gone into shock because the bacteria growing in his brain deprived his nervous system of necessary oxygen. His inability to breathe was also caused by other bacteria clogging his heart valves. Mike Camargo's life had been spent in petty crime as a small-time drug dealer. The cops had caught him more than once, and he had served several sentences. Now he was dying of AIDS.

Later that year, Camargo's presence was required for a court appearance before Justice Sheindlin of the Supreme Court of New York in the Bronx. Dr. Jonathan Cohn, Camargo's attending physician at Bellevue Hospital, was subpoenaed by Camargo's lawyer to explain the defendant's absence. Cohn was placed under oath, and he then graphically explained to the court why he believed that Camargo's deteriorating condition made continuing prosecution futile.

Over the prosecutor's objection, the court granted Camargo's motion to dismiss in the interest of justice. Justice Sheindlin explained to the prosecutor that although Camargo was a recidivist, it was doubtful he could be regarded as a threat to the safety or welfare of society. To impose incarceration on this minor drug dealer would be absurd given his imminent death. Further, the court noted that no sentence would compare with the many diseases now attacking him.

The typical AIDS situation is much like Mike Camargo's: He was in his early thirties. He was an intravenous drug user who had been incarcerated for a drug-related crime. And he died of AIDS-related pneumonia.

Source: Adapted from Patricia Raburn, "Prisoners with AIDS: The Use of Electronic Processing," *Criminal Law Bulletin*, May–June 1988, pp. 213–14. Reprinted by permission. Copyright © 1988 by Warren, Gorham & Lamont Inc., 210 South Street, Boston, MA 02111.

Elderly Clients

Crime—at least predatory street crime—is the province of young men. In visiting a prison, one is struck by the predominant numbers of young men, especially minorities. America's prison population has traditionally been young and poor, but in recent years it has been aging. In 2017 U.S. prisons and jails held 171,336 people over 55 years old,[38] more than an eleven-fold increase since 1981. In 1974 only about one-sixth of the prison population was 40 or older; 43 years later, that proportion had ballooned to more than two-fifths. If current trends continue, there may be as many as 400,000 people in prison 55 years old or older by the year 2030.[39] A year of incarceration for a person over 55 is twice as expensive as that of a younger person, mostly as a result of medical costs—and one year for an elderly person in prison costs one-and-a-half times more than the average American household *earns* in a year.

The prison population is growing older for two reasons. First, sentencing practices have changed. Consecutive, often lengthy sentences for heinous crimes, long mandatory minimum sentences, and life sentences without parole mean that more people who enter prison will spend most or all of the rest of their lives behind bars. Second, and perhaps more important, the drug war of the 1980s brought into prison a larger number of people earlier in their lives, and many of them have been released only to return to prison, maintaining a large but aging prison population.[40] This latter fact is important because it suggests that without the drug war, not only would prison populations have been smaller, but they would not be aging as rapidly.

The elderly in prison can be divided into three general groups. Most were young when they first entered prison, facing very long terms for particularly serious crimes such as murder or brutal sexual assault (see "Dennis's Story"). A few first enter prison in their old age, usually convicted of either financial crimes such as embezzlement or sexual assaults such as child molestation. Finally, there are those who are doing "life on the installment plan," people who have been in prison multiple times and are returning on yet another conviction. Many elderly people behind bars pose a very low risk to the community—arrest rates for those who have served their time and are released in their fifties are about one-tenth that of the average person released from prison.[41] The Vera Institute of Justice

FOCUS ON

PEOPLE IN CORRECTIONS: Dennis's Story

For 44 years, Dennis Whitney's world has consisted largely of steel bars, razor wire, and a metal bed with a three-inch mattress. He has grown old in prison, doing hard time for two murders committed when he was 17. And with time have come the ravages of age: Whitney, 61, has undergone two costly angioplasties at state expense to clear narrowed or blocked blood vessels, and he needs a third such procedure.

Whitney was condemned to die for two 1960 murders and admitted to five other slayings. He spent 12 years on death row and came within two days of dying in the electric chair before his sentence was commuted to life in prison in 1972, when the U.S. Supreme Court declared Florida's death penalty law unconstitutional.

He comes up for parole again next fall after being turned down time after time in the past 14 years.

"If they turn me down, I'm just going to let the state take care of me the rest of my life," he said. "I'm well fed, well clothed, and well taken care of."

Source: Adapted from "Elderly Inmates Swell Prisons, Driving up Health Care Costs," *USA Today*, www.usatoday.com/news /nation/2004–02-28 -elderly-inmates_x.htm, February 2, 2004.

has recommended that release from prison should be considered for every person behind bars who is more than 55 years old.

Although recent attention has focused on the elderly in prison, increasing numbers of seniors are also among those on probation and parole. Probation has always had to deal with elderly people whose low-level public-order, property, and motor vehicle crimes have enabled them to be given community sentences. But, like other elderly poor, these individuals typically have special needs for employment, housing, and the maintenance of family ties. In many cases, probation officers must provide extra supervision to ensure that elderly clients adhere to the conditions of their sentence.

Corrections also faces a huge increase in the number of elderly people on parole, as those who were imprisoned in their youth for long terms are released to community supervision. Imagine the problems faced by, say, a 55-year-old, poorly educated, unskilled man who has spent the last 15–20 years behind bars. Parole faces the challenge of helping people like these make the transition to living in a society that they have not confronted for more than a decade.

The most obvious special characteristic of the elderly within corrections is personal health. People who grow old in prison have increasing trouble handling the physical strains of prison life, and the aged usually need increased medical care. The elderly also have different social interests. Whereas most of those in prison enjoy physical sports and competitive recreation, those who are older, like their counterparts on the outside, often prefer solitude and less strenuous interaction. These differences between the elderly and the rank and file translate into significantly greater operating costs for the former because of the need for special health, recreational, and housing services.

In the exercise room at the Chronic Care Unit of Dixon Correctional Center, resident caregiver Eugene McDaniel works with Lambert Knoll, who lives in Illinois' only hospice program in a prison.

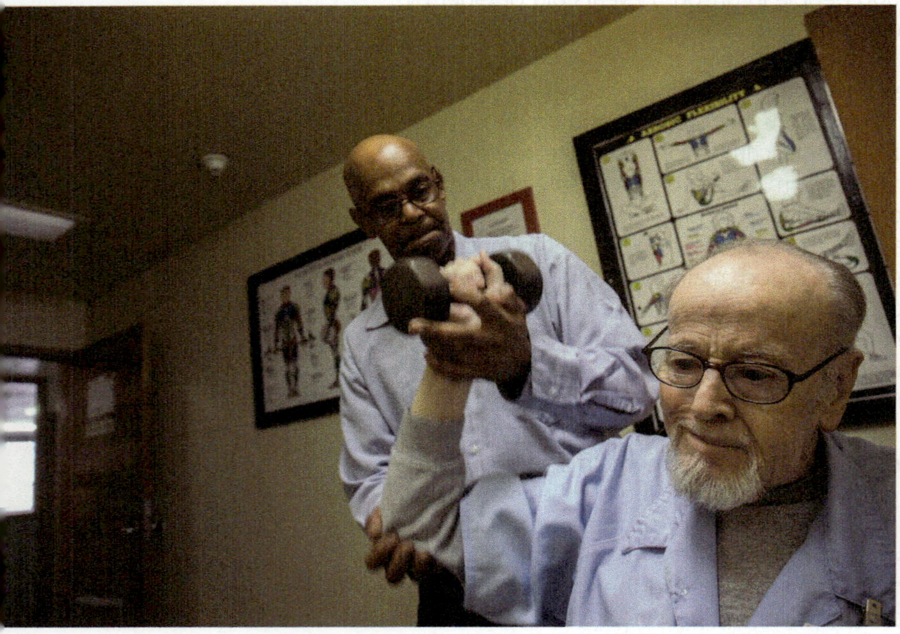

Zbigniew Bzdak/Chicago Tribune/MCT/Sipa USA

Even though a large number of elderly people who are in prison have committed quite serious crimes, studies indicate that age reduces the chance that a person will violate prison rules. The elderly are often more stable and dependable than their youthful counterparts, and they frequently occupy positions of trust within the prison.

Upon release, they typically pose little risk to the public. The adjustment problem facing most people released from prison at advanced ages has to do with the way that extended prison terms tend to promote institutionalization. When a person spends many years in prison, the routines of the prison become debilitating. The prison regime controls every hour of the day and takes away most personal autonomy and decision making. After years of being told what to do almost every waking hour, a person may find it difficult to relearn how to make even the simplest decisions.

Long-Termers

More people serve long sentences in the United States than in any other Western nation (see "Michael's Story"). The median sentence is now more than two years, and people convicted of violent crimes get a median sentence of about four years.[42] About 24 percent of all those who go to prison have sentences of more than 25 years, and another 9 percent have life sentences. Most **long-termers** have been convicted of violent crime or drug distribution. These are often the same people who will become elderly inside prison walls, with all the attendant problems just discussed. Those who are returned to the community

long-termer A person who serves a lengthy period in prison, such as 10 years or more, before his or her first release.

FOCUS ON

PEOPLE IN CORRECTIONS: Michael's Story

Just after his twenty-fourth birthday, Michael Santos was sentenced to 45 years in prison on nonviolent continuing criminal enterprise charges for his participation in cocaine trafficking. Under U.S. Sentencing Commission guidelines, which were expressly designed to deal harshly with drug dealers, Santos expected to serve at least 85 percent of the sentence: over 38 years. He should have been in his sixties when he was released. But Michael Santos was an exceptional person while he was behind bars. He wrote books and articles (and essays that appear in this text) about the experience of criminal justice. Some of his sentence was commuted. He was released in August 2012, at the age of 50, having been in prison for more than a quarter century.

Michael Santos's case illustrates a correctional trend particular to the United States—more people serving long terms. His sentence was an almost unimaginable length of time. For many of you reading this book, it is more than two times your current age. What must it mean to a man in his twenties to hear a judge impose such a sentence? How can a person face it?

In a recent scholarly paper on the topic, Santos mused on some of the dread and distress he felt facing his future: "Would my life be reduced to a prison registration number, being counted periodically as I waited for paint to peel off prison walls and years to pass away?"

Long-termers must confront three main areas of concern. First, there is the inevitable shock, dismay, and sense of injustice on hearing the sentence pronounced. Even when lawyers have prepared their client for the worst, something ruinous occurs when the judge reads the sentence aloud. And even when the crime has been particularly heinous, the person experiences disbelief and angry disheartenment on hearing the penalty, as though in some way it were disconnected from the crime itself.

Second, there is the problem of personal loss. Santos realized that the long term was "likely to rip apart my relationships." He had married only a few months before his arrest, and he had little hope that the marriage could survive the fissure of imprisonment. But even if the marriage did not end, he had to wonder about what its quality would be—its intimacy and its potential for meaningful family life with no children and restricted contact. No matter how much love was present, it seemed woefully inadequate to overcome the abyss of 45 years in prison.

Whenever Santos wondered about the future, he had countless others to advise him of the possibilities: mates who had long since abandoned their partners in painful, often acrimonious splits, or children who felt that their fathers had deserted them, an accusation nearly impossible to dispute from behind the prison walls. Even the salvaged relationships seemed strained and unappealing.

Third, there is the challenge of finding meaningful ways to while away the interminable hours among society's outcasts. Like most long-termers, Santos spent the first years involved in legal wrangles, trying to overturn his conviction or obtain clemency. But after these initial years, "an ocean of depression swallowed me." The biggest battle was simply how to cope, how to escape the inviting sinkhole of hopelessness.

Today, Michael Santos has restarted his life. He is a doctoral student, a motivational speaker, an author—and a productive citizen.

Source: Adapted from various writings from Michael G. Santos, including his blog: http://michaelsantos.com/blog.

FOR CRITICAL THINKING

Michael Santos served a very long sentence for his crime of selling drugs. Some say that long sentences such as this are inherently unjust. Others believe that long sentences are necessary to demonstrate public disapproval of serious criminal acts. Still others think that long sentences should be used only when necessary to protect the community.

1. Are sentences that lock people up for decades defensible?
2. If not, why not? If so, under what conditions should they be imposed, and why?

at perhaps age 55 following 20 years of incarceration face daunting prospects in terms of adjustment, employment, and housing.

There is no one standard way that a long-termer reacts to the time in prison. Studies show substantial differences in the way the long-termer responds, with some people but not others experiencing severe stress, depression, and other health problems. When severe emotional stress occurs, it tends to take place earlier rather than later in the sentence. Many long-termers eventually come to grips with their situation, and find a way to make the later stages of their sentences meaningful and productive.[43]

Long-termers are not generally seen as control problems—they are charged with disciplinary infractions about half as often as are short-termers—but they do present a management problem for prison administrators. Program managers have to find ways of making prison life livable for those who are going to be there a long time.

Military Veterans

It has been estimated that about 8 percent of people who are incarcerated are military service veterans.[44] There are no comparable statistics for military veterans in noncustodial corrections, but the numbers are most likely similar. If that is the case, more than 200,000 veterans are behind bars, and at least a half million are on probation or parole. Given the many years of U.S. military involvement in the Middle East, veterans involved in the justice system have been recognized as a client group that poses a particular set of concerns.

It is often assumed that the strains of combat make young men more susceptible to criminal activity—in particular, combat tours in areas where terrorism is widespread and the "enemy" looks and acts like ordinary citizens. Research shows that this assumption does not hold up. Although most veterans who are involved in the justice system served in the military during times of war, only about one-fifth of them actually saw combat duty. Likewise, military veterans have an incarceration rate that is about one-half that of nonveterans.[45] So although veterans are a major subgroup of the correctional population, they do not represent, as a whole, a population of high risk to the public.

Military veterans represent a special subgroup of people in prison. Often their crimes stem from the emotional distress that comes from trauma experienced during military actions during wartime.

John Moore/Getty Images

That is not to say that a person's status as a veteran is irrelevant to the correctional system once a veteran gets in trouble with the law. For many veterans, as for a large proportion of people in the corrections system, substance abuse lies at the heart of their reasons for breaking the law. But for veterans, there can be the additional burden of post-traumatic stress disorder (PTSD)—the extreme feeling of stress or anxiety, brought on by exposure to the dangers of combat, that continues long after the dangers have subsided. Veterans who experience PTSD will often try to dull the pains by overuse of alcohol or other drugs, a coping mechanism that can lead to involvement in the criminal

FOCUS ON

PEOPLE IN CORRECTIONS: Christopher's Story

In his last year of service in the Marine Reserves, Christopher Boyd was sent to Iraq, where he served as a driver. His job was to escort convoys and sweep for land mines, always keeping an eye out for hidden roadside bombs.

In January 2004 he was stationed about 100 miles from Fallujah, an insurgent stronghold, when his company went on a raid. He drove a Humvee carrying nine combat Marines. The raid itself turned out to be uneventful, but on their way back to the base they were attacked and pinned down in a 20-minute firefight with enemy soldiers they could not see in the darkness. Just as the shooting died down and they got going again, the Humvee was suddenly hit by a rocket-fired grenade. Somehow, Boyd kept the Humvee going and got it back to the base, but not before four Marines were killed and five others wounded. Boyd was unhurt.

When Boyd went back home to Virginia, he returned to his job at a Frito-Lay plant. But he had trouble sleeping, and he had recurrent nightmares. The only way he could go to sleep and avoid the nightmares was to drink until he passed out, which he began doing regularly. His family saw him change; he became withdrawn, negative, and easily angered. He stopped spending time with his two children. He started carrying a gun.

One Saturday morning in 2008, Boyd finished his shift and began to drink heavily, later going with a friend to a party. He blacked out in the friend's car, sitting outside the party. When he came to, he was in a police car, on his way to jail. The police said that he had shot his friend in the chest. Miraculously, the friend lived. To this day, Boyd remembers nothing about the shooting.

Boyd was sentenced to five years in prison.

Source: Adapted from Matthew Wolfe, "From PTSD to Prison: Why Veterans Become Criminals," *Daily Beast*, www.thedailybeast.com/articles/2013/07/28/from-ptsd-to-prison-why-veterans-become-criminals.html, July 28, 2013.

justice system (see "Christopher's Story"). Other side effects of PTSD are that a veteran will find it hard to keep a job, and interpersonal relations with loved ones can become strained, leading to isolation—and sometimes, ultimately, homelessness. Taken together, these factors make it easy to understand why veterans ought to be seen as a special subgroup within the correctional population, even though they may otherwise look like the general correctional population in terms of age, social class, and ethnicity.[46]

In general, because the experiences that many veterans have had in the military are a source of their legal trouble, treatment programs for veterans can be more effective if they are specially designed for that group. For example, substance abuse treatment is thought to be more effective when veterans' specialists carry it out. This kind of thinking has led to the development of the Health Care for Reentry Veterans (HCRV) program, administered by the Veterans Health Administration (VHA), which focuses on helping veterans who are at risk of incarceration. There has also been a movement to establish veterans' treatment courts to provide special services for veterans in the justice system.

LO 4

Describe the classification process for people under correctional authority and explain why it is important.

CLASSIFYING PEOPLE IN THE CORRECTIONS SYSTEM: KEY ISSUES

Our descriptions of these "types" of people who commit crimes should make clear that several factors frustrate attempts to classify corrections' clients. Problems center on overlap and ambiguity in classification, the programmatic needs of corrections, behavioral probabilities, sociopolitical pressures, and individual distinctions.

Overlap and Ambiguity in Classification

Some people convicted of sex crimes may also be alcoholics; some situational crimes are committed by people with emotional problems (perhaps even stemming from their new status under the law); some people with repeated criminal convictions may also be addicts. A classification system that has so much overlap cannot give correctional decision makers much guidance about appropriate treatment. Should a drug-addicted multiple burglar be treated as a career criminal or as an addict?

classification systems
Specific sets of objective criteria, such as offense histories, previous experiences in the justice system, problems in life circumstances, and substance abuse patterns, applied to all clients to determine the best correctional programs.

To combat ambiguities in classification, correctional administrators have started using **classification systems.** These systems apply a set of objective criteria to everyone in the corrections system in order to arrive at an appropriate classification. The criteria usually include such factors as current and prior offense histories, previous experiences in the justice system, problems in life circumstances, and substance abuse patterns. By using objective criteria, these systems reduce the unreliability of the correctional classification, and by limiting the criteria to a few relevant facts, the systems avoid overlap.

Offense Classifications and Correctional Programming

LO 5
Discuss important problems and limitations in classifying people under correctional authority.

Some critics argue that the most important requirement for any correctional classification system is that it should improve our ability to manage and treat clients effectively. If the categories described leave many correctional programming decisions unresolved, what good are they?

When one considers people under correctional authority, a normal response is to ask first about the person's crime and then about the person's criminal history. The ten "types" of clients we have described probably constitute 80 percent or more of the people managed by corrections, yet in each case the category is so broad that it does not answer the important question: How should a person fitting this "type" be managed? Broad categories can help portray the nature of people falling in that category, but the programmatic needs of corrections require much narrower and more-precise classification systems. Most important, perhaps, corrections must be able to determine the client's potential risk to correctional security and to the community.

Behavioral Probabilities

Human behavior may be impossible to predict, but we can certainly make educated guesses about a person's likely future behaviors. Thus, we can say confidently that a five-time check forger is likely to commit a similar offense again, just as a first-timer is unlikely to repeat the offense. We know, of course, that the check forger may stop after the fifth time, just as the first-timer may get rearrested. But, on average, our educated guesses will more often than not be right. This is defined as a "probabilistic" approach to classification—nothing is thought of as "certain," but some things are more likely than not.

Recent classification systems have included probabilistic concepts. Officials try to see which client characteristics are associated with reinvolvement in crime. The approach resembles the one used by automobile insurance companies, whose actuaries recognize that even though many teenagers do not have accidents, teenagers as a group have much higher accident rates than do adult drivers. Therefore, teenagers pay higher premiums because they represent a greater risk.

Similarly, correctional clients who have characteristics associated with higher risk can be classified as more likely to pose a threat and so can be required to pay a penological "premium": higher bail or no bail, closer supervision on probation or parole, tighter security in institutions, and so on.

Sociopolitical Pressures

One of the most frustrating aspects of correctional classification is that the public response to crime frequently makes classification an emotionally charged issue. As a result, when setting out its programs, corrections often must respond to changing public demands.

At one time or another, each correctional type we have described has endured intense public hostility. In the 1940s and 1950s, for instance, public outrage over narcotics led to stiff penalties for their sale and promoted the establishment of addiction hospitals across the United States. In the 1950s and 1960s, public concern about the "psychopath" led to the establishment of long-term treatment facilities just for the "dangerous individual," such as Maryland's famous Patuxent Institution. In the 1980s, concerns about crack cocaine and heroin led to mandatory prison sentences for people convicted of drug crimes. A few years ago, attention focused on people called "high-rate offenders," and policies sought to incapacitate them selectively or collectively.

In each case, public alarm about crime has produced new labeling patterns in the criminal justice system, with special handling mandated for all those who match the label. However, difficulties arise because the labels are often broadly applied (partly because of the overlap in any classification system) and because the handling is usually more severe than is necessary. Those who object to the frequent "reform" movements in corrections recognize that misapplying labels can do great harm. Yet in many instances the accuracy of the label and its application matter little to correctional policy makers, who face the worse problem of having to respond to the public demand for "action" to "crack down" on one type of crime or another. The problem is more political than penological.

Distinctions in Classification Criteria

We all classify the people around us. We think, *John is a Democrat, Nancy is a nice person, Tim is untrustworthy*, and so on. We realize that these terms do not fully describe the individuals but serve only as rough labels that help us gauge how they may behave or think in a given situation. In reality, we know that sometimes John may sound like a Republican, Nancy may be grumpy, and Tim may keep his word. Certain tendencies may characterize a person's behavior, but habits are seldom absolutely consistent.

Given the variability of human behavior, correctional classification must be seen as a rough way of grouping people. Being precise about the criteria used for grouping is equally important. Three general kinds of criteria are used to classify people who are under correctional authority:

1. Offense criteria classify people by the seriousness of the crime committed.
2. Risk criteria classify people by the probability of future criminal conduct.
3. Program criteria classify people by the nature of correctional treatment appropriate to each person's needs and situation.

Different criteria lead to different correctional practices. That is, if we apply offense criteria, the suggested correctional strategy will differ from the consequence suggested by applying the risk or program criteria. For example, many people who committed serious crimes most likely will not do so again, many who have few treatment needs still represent a risk to the community, and so on. Thus, corrections systems need to apply all three classification criteria to determine the most appropriate way to manage any given population of clients.

SUMMARY

1 Explain how the criminal justice system operates as a large selection process to determine who ends up in the corrections system.

We can view the criminal justice system as a filtering process because it operates as a large client-selection bureaucracy. At each stage, some people are sent on to the next stage, while others are either released or processed under changed conditions. Note that few individuals who are arrested are then prosecuted, tried, and convicted. Some go free

2 Describe some of the main similarities and differences between the general population and people who end up under correctional authority.

Historical studies of U.S. corrections show that in earlier eras, members of the newest immigrant groups filled the prisons out of proportion to their numbers in the general population. Since the Civil War, African Americans have consistently made up the largest group in southern prisons, but elsewhere the largest group has changed over time:

because the police decide that a crime has not been committed or that the evidence is not sound. The prosecutor may decide that justice would be better served by sending the person to a substance abuse clinic. Many people will plead guilty, the judge may dismiss charges against others, and the jury may acquit a few. Thus, the criminal justice system is often described as a filtering process or a funnel—many cases enter it, but only a few result in conviction and punishment. These few are the clients of corrections. first Germans, Irish, and Italians, and now African Americans and Hispanics. Although this idea of ethnic succession is not entirely consistent with recent research, our prisons and jails undeniably hold disproportionate numbers of poor, disadvantaged, and minority citizens.

3 **Identify different types of clients in the corrections system and the kinds of problems they pose for corrections.**
This chapter presents ten main types of people under correctional authority: situational clients, career criminals, people convicted of sex offenses, people convicted of substance abuse crimes, clients with mental illnesses, clients with developmental disabilities, clients with HIV/AIDS, elderly clients, long-termers, and military veterans. Each group has its own special characteristic that creates treatment and management issues for correctional authorities. The main issues that differentiate these types are (1) the risk they represent to the community, (2) their need for special kinds of correctional programming, and (3) distinctions that need to be made among people within each group.

5 **Discuss important problems and limitations in classifying people under correctional authority.**
Five main challenges to the classification of correctional clients have been identified: overlap and ambiguity in correctional classifications, correctional programming, behavioral probabilities, sociopolitical pressures, and distinctions in classification criteria. There are no easy solutions for any of these problems, but the success of correctional classification systems depends on minimizing the negative implications of each challenge.

4 **Describe the classification process for people under correctional authority and explain why it is important.**
Correctional authorities need to answer a question about every person under their supervision: "How should this person be managed?" Broad categories can help portray their nature, but the programmatic needs of corrections require much narrower and more precise classification systems. In particular, corrections must be able to identify the person's potential risk to correctional security and to the community. This is the purpose of classification. In classifying people, correctional administrators put them into groups based on the seriousness of their offense, the security risks they pose to the prison, and their treatment needs.

KEY TERMS

alcohol abuse (*p. 150*)
career criminal (*p. 141*)
classification systems (*p.162*)
deinstitutionalization (*p. 154*)
developmental disability (*p. 154*)
drug abuse (*p. 148*)
fentanyl (*p. 150*)
long-termer (*p. 159*)
mental illness (*p. 152*)
methamphetamine (*p. 149*)
opioid (*p. 149*)
sex crimes (*p. 143*)
sex offender registry (*p. 146*)
situational client (*p. 140*)

FOR DISCUSSION

1. Is the process by which correctional clients are selected discriminatory? What might be done to reduce actual or perceived discrimination?
2. How does the classification of correctional clients reflect the fragmentation of corrections?

3. What role should public opinion play in categorizing various people for the purpose of punishing them?
4. Is classifying people who have been convicted of a crime according to the probability of future criminal conduct a good idea? What are the dangers of the practice? What are its advantages?
5. What policy recommendations would you make with regard to the way career criminals are handled?

FOR FURTHER READING

Drucker, Ernest. *A Plague of Prisons: The Epidemiology of Mass Incarceration in America*. New York: New Press, 2013. Describes the contribution of drug sentencing laws to the problem of mass incarceration.

Human Rights Watch. *Ill Equipped: U.S. Prisons and Offenders with Mental Illness*. New York: Author, 2003. Describes case studies of the "crisis" in mental health treatment in U.S. prisons and provides a series of recommendations for improvement of care.

Macy, Beth. *Dopesick: Dealers, Doctors, and the Drug Company that Addicted America*. Boston: Little Brown, 2018. Exposes the causes and consequences of the opioid crisis.

Mauer, Marc, Ashley Nellis, and Kerry Myers. *The Meaning of Life: The Case for Abolishing Life Sentences*. New York: New Rutgers Press, 2018. A critical study of the imposition of life sentences accompanied by stories of people serving life terms.

Terry, Karen J. *Sexual Offenses and Offenders: Theory, Practice, and Policy*. 2nd ed. Boston: Cengage, 2012. Covers deviant sexual behavior, types of sex crimes, theories of sexual criminality, treatment, and management and supervision policies.

Toch, Hans, *Violent Men: An Inquiry into the Psychology of Violence*. New York: American Psychological Association, 2017.

NOTES

1 Kate Taylor, "Parents Paid to Open College Doors, Now They're Spending to Limit Prison Time," *The New York Times*, October 22, 2019.

2 John Gramlich, *The Gap Between the Number of Blacks and Whites in Prison is Shrinking* (Philadelphia: Pew Research Center, April 30, 2019).

3 Martin R. Haskell and Lewis Yablonsky, *Criminology: Crime and Criminality* (Chicago: Rand McNally, 1974), 264.

4 Walter C. Reckless, *The Crime Problem* (New York: Appleton-Century-Crofts, 1961), 153–77.

5 Alfred Blumstein, Jacqueline Cohen, Jeffrey Roth, and Christy Visher, *Criminal Careers and "Career Criminals"* (Washington, DC: National Academy of Sciences, 1986).

6 Peter Greenwood, *Selective Incapacitation* (Santa Monica, CA: RAND, 1982).

7 Susan Brownmiller, *Against Our Will* (New York: Simon & Schuster, 1975), 376–77.

8 Lawrence A. Greenwood, *Sex Offenses and Offenders: An Analysis of Data on Rape and Sexual Assault* (Washington, DC: U.S. Government Printing Office, 1997).

9 Ibid., p. 23.

10 Ronet Bachman, Samantha Rodriquez, Erin M. Kerrison, and Chrisanthi Leon, "The Recursive Relationship Between Substance Abuse, Prostitution, and Incarceration: Voices from a Long-Term Cohort of Women," *Victims and Offenders* 14 (no. 5, 2019), 587–605.

11 Rene Love, "Street Level Prostitution: A Systematic Literature Review," *Issues in Mental Health Nursing* 36 (no. 8, 2015), 568–77.

12 Jeffrey C. Sandller and Naomi J. Freeman, "Evaluation of New York State's Sex Offender Civil Management Assessment Process Outcomes," *Criminology & Public Policy* 16 (no. 3, 2017), 913–36.

13 Mariel Alper and Matthew R. Durose, *Recidivism of Sex Offenders Released from Prison: A Nine-Year Follow-up (2005–2014)* (Washington, DC: U.S. Government Printing Office, 2019).

14 Franklin E. Zimring, Wesley G. Jennings, Alex R. Piquero, and Stephanie Hays, "Investigating the Continuity of Sex Offending: Evidence from the Philadelphia Birth Cohort," *Justice Quarterly* 26 (no. 1, March 2009): 58–76.

15 Trevor Hoppe, "Punishing Sex: Sex Offenders and the Missing Punitive Turn in Sexuality Studies," *Law & Social Inquiry* 41 (no. 3, summer 2016): 573–94.

16 Jeff A. Bouffard and LaQuana N. Askew, "Time-Series Analysis of the Impact of Sex Offender Registration and Notification Implementation and Subsequent Modifications on Rates of Sexual Offenses," *Crime and Delinquency 65* (no. 11, 2019), 1483–1512.

17 Jason Rydberg, Eric Grommon, Beth M. Huebner, and Breanna Pleggenkuhle, "Examining Correlates of Sex Offender Residence Restriction Violation Rates," *Journal of Quantitative Criminology* 33 (2017), 347–69.

18 Melanie Clark Mogavero and Leslie W. Kennedy, "The Social and Geographic Patterns of Sexual Offending: Is Sex Offender Residence Restriction Legislation Practical?" *Victims & Offenders* 12 (2017), 401–33.

19 National Institute of Justice, *ADAM II: 2013 Annual Report* (Washington, DC: U.S. Government Printing Office, 2015).

20 Helene R. White and Rolf Loeber, *Substance Abuse and Criminal Offending: Policy Brief* (New Brunswick, NJ: Rutgers University Center for Behavioral Health Services and Criminal Justice Research, 2009).

21 The National Center on Addiction and Substance Abuse, *Ending the Opioid Crisis: A Practical Guide for State Policy Makers* (New York: National Center on Addiction and Substance Abuse, 2019).

22 Richard B. Felson and Jeremy Staff, "Committing Crime for Drug Money," *Crime & Delinquency* 63 (no. 4, 2017), 375–90.

23 Ojmarrh Mitchell, Joshua C. Cochran, Daniel P. Mears, and William D. Bales, "The Effectiveness of Prison for Reducing Drug Offender Recidivism: A Regression Discontinuity Analysis," *Journal of Experimental Criminology* (no. 1, 2017), 1–27.

24 Brook W. Kearly, *Long-Term Effects of Drug Court Participation: Evidence from a 15-Year Follow-up of a Randomized Controlled Trial*. Doctoral Dissertation, University of Maryland.

25 National Institute of Drug Abuse, *Opioid Overdose Crisis* (Bethesda, MD: National Institute of Health, 2020).

26 R. K. Twillman, E. Dawson, L. LaRue, M. G. Guevara, P. Whitley, and A. Huskey, "Evaluation of Trends of Near-Real-Time Urine Drug Test Results for Methamphetamine, Cocaine, Heroin, and Fentanyl." *JAMA Netw Open.* 3 (no. 1, 2020), e1918514. doi:10.1001/jamanetworkopen.2019.18514.

27 National Institute of Drug Abuse, *Methamphetamine* (Bethesda, MD: National Institute of Health, 2019).

28 Joshua D. Lee, Peter D. Friedmann, Timothy W. Kinlock, et al., "Extended-Release Naltrexone to Prevent Opioid Relapse in Criminal Justice Offenders," *New England Journal of Medicine* 373 (no. 13, 2016): 1232.

29 Michael Winerip and Michael Schwirtz, "Trapped in a Loop," *The New York Times*, April 12, 2015, B1, B6–B7.

30 Office of Research and Public Affairs, Treatment Advocacy Center, *Serious Mental Illness Prevalence in Jails and Prisons* (Arlington, VA: Treatment Advocacy Center, 2016).

31 Khushbu Shah and Eliott C. McLaughlin, "Victim's Dad Warns Dylann Roof: 'Your Creator . . . He's Coming for You,'" CNN, January 11, 2017.

32 William McCord and Joan McCord, *The Psychopath* (New York: Van Nostrand, 1964), 2.

33 Thomas S. Szasz, *Law, Liberty, and Psychiatry* (New York: Macmillan, 1963), 12.

34 U.S. National Commission on the Causes and Prevention of Violence, *Crimes of Violence* (Washington, DC: U.S. Government Printing Office, 1969), 444.

35 Michael Ostermann and Jason Matejkowski, "Estimating the Impact of Mental Illness on Costs of Crimes," *Criminal Justice and Behavior* 20 (no. 10, 2013): 1–21.

36 *Atkins v. Virginia*, 536 U.S. 304 (2002).

37 Laura M. Maruschak and Jennifer Bronson, *HIV in Prisons, 2015* (Washington, DC: Bureau of Justice Statistics, 2019).

38 Jennifer Bronson and E. Anne Carson, *Prisoners in 2017* (Washington, DC: Bureau of Justice Statistics, 2016).

39 American Civil Liberties Union, *At America's Expense: The Mass Incarceration of the Elderly* (New York: Author, 2012).

40 Lauren C. Porter, Shawn D. Bushway, Hui-Shien Tsao, and Herbert L. Smith, "How the U.S. Prison Boom Has Changed the Age Distribution of the Prison Population," *Criminology* 54 (no. 1, February 2016): 30–55.

41 American Civil Liberties Union, *At America's Expense.*

42 Brian Reaves, *Felony Defendants in Large Urban Counties, 2009* (Washington, DC: Bureau of Justice Statistics, 2013), 25.

43 Ben Crewe, Susie Hulley, and Serena Wright, "Swimming with the Tide: Adapting to Long-Term Imprisonment," *Justice Quarterly*, 34 (no. 3, 2017), 517–41.

44 Bronson, Jennifer, E. Ann Carson, and Margaret Noonan, *Veterans in Prison and Jail, 2011–12* (Washington, DC: U.S. Department of Justice, 2015).

45 Jack Tsai, Robert A. Rosenheck, Wesley J. Kasprow, and James F. McGuire, "Risk of Incarceration and Other Characteristics of Iraq and Afghanistan Era Veterans in State and Federal Prisons," *Psychiatric Services* 64 (no. 1, January 2013).

46 William B. Brown, Robert Stanulis, Bryan Theis, et al., "The Perfect Storm: Veterans, Culture, and the Criminal Justice System," *Justice Policy Journal* 10 (no. 2, 2013); see also William B. Brown, "From War Zones to Jail: Veteran Reintegration Problems," *Justice Policy Journal* 8 (no. 1, 2011).

PART TWO

Correctional Practices

Although the public views the corrections system as primarily concerned with prisons and jails, more than two-thirds of the people under correctional authority are supervised in the community. In Part 2, "Corrections Practices," we examine correctional practices in both the community and institutions. The chapters that follow are organized to cover the ways that people processed by the corrections system are dealt with, from start to finish—from jail detention to sentences of probation, intermediate sanctions, or incarceration, to release and reentry into the community. By focusing on the day-to-day practices of corrections, Part 2 shows correctional professionals in action.

GUEST PERSPECTIVE

The Big Set Back: Collateral Consequences of Criminal Convictions

MICHELLE DANIEL JONES

Michelle Daniel Jones

When a person leaves prison we tend to think that the sentence is over, their debt to society paid. In fact, it is quite the opposite. As Michelle Alexander says in *The New Jim Crow,* "Today, a criminal freed from prison has scarcely more rights, and arguably less respect, than a freed slave or a black person living 'free' in Mississippi at the height of Jim Crow."

Across the nation, people who leave prison contend with the debilitating consequences stemming from their criminal convictions. In its *Collateral Consequences Project*, the American Bar Association (ABA) has identified nearly 48,000 laws that directly affect the opportunities afforded those who are newly released from prison, half of which are job-related.[1] Securing employment has always been crucial to reducing recidivism, and yet free society is only now becoming aware of how debilitating collateral consequences are to those reentering from prison. The Collateral Consequences Project grew from urgings by the ABA and the Uniform Law Commission to "identify and codify collateral sanctions," across the nation, an effort that took five years to complete. It had become apparent that there were many barriers to full citizenship the newly released experienced, but because they were scattered across various state and federal statutes, state and local regulatory codes, as well as local rules and policies, the full impact of the penalties for criminal convictions was never fully appreciated.

Collateral consequences are legion. They make people ineligible for a wide range of employment and occupational licenses such as nurses, lawyers, plumbers, bartenders, and beauticians. They also include the ineligibility for public housing, government contracts, pension benefits, and welfare benefits. In most states, a felony conviction or prison term takes away the right to vote, right to hold an office of public or private trust, be a public service volunteer, and sit on a jury. There may be the loss of parental rights, the right to travel freely, live in certain parts of town or live with family members who are on parole/probation. Non-citizens can be deported. People who have been incarcerated often do not qualify for bonded positions, such as insurance agents, bail bondsmen, private detectives, and even some bonded commercial janitorial positions. They are not permitted a license to carry a firearm.

Most collateral consequences are applied across the board rather than on a case-by-case basis. Imagine an eighteen-year-old high school student who was convicted of having consensual sex with a sixteen-year-old. This eighteen-year-old will be required to register as a sex offender for life, no different than someone convicted of pedophilia. These collateral consequences affect so many people in ways that are hard to mitigate. The technology of social media sites and easy background checks has added to the difficulty in overcoming collateral consequences. It is in this way that collateral consequences are usually harsher than the sentence originally imposed by a judge.

These collateral consequences are experienced as a kind of violence that threatens those who have been incarcerated at the very core of their being. The institutions that control access to desired goods and social status affix labels to people who have been in prison and then use those labels to justify excluding them from access. This applies to the growing millions with criminal records. It has been referred to as "biographic mediation": lifelong discrimination is made possible by the way labels justify stigma.[2] Social institutions relate to people through those labels, and they force people living under those labels to live lives constrained by the exclusion those labels justify. From this vantage point, institutions claim to speak authoritatively about personal history because they create the frameworks within which the formerly incarcerated must tell their stories. The institutionalization of organized prejudice and discrimination disorients the incarcerated and formerly incarcerated by claiming that who they are boils down to a label, and the label denies access that everyone else enjoys.

The bottom line is that the post-incarcerated experience is one of an automatic reduction of full citizenship rights upon release, leaving people subject to "unlimited discrimination" and "social stigmatization" that makes recidivism more likely. After incarceration, people who leave prison are socially defined as different from everyone else, are judged at every turn in light of that definition, by those inside and outside of the corrections framework. They are under hyper-surveillance, tested and judged in such a way that, though they have been released from prison, they are nevertheless still captured. Collateral consequences of criminal convictions are at the heart of why the completion of a sentence does not equal freedom or a debt paid, but is actually a hobbled state of what Ruth Wilson Gilmore has aptly called "unfreedom."[3]

CHAPTER 7

Jails: Detention and Short-Term Incarceration

Kathleen Merchant stands by the sign for her place of employment, Project Lia, in the Circle City Industrial Complex in Indianapolis. The Bail Project, a national nonprofit, paid her $500 bail and helped her get a job. Her case was later dismissed.

THERE ARE ALMOST A HALF MILLION PEOPLE IN JAIL IN THE UNITED STATES BECAUSE THEY ARE AWAITING TRIAL. Almost all of them are there because they cannot afford the bail set by the court—for many of them, even putting up $200 would enable them to be freed from jail. To many people, this doesn't seem fair. It means that impoverished people who end up in jail have to stay there, while those with money—even a little money—can go free.

In 2012, New York State enacted the Charitable Bail Act that enabled charities to put up bail on behalf of people charged with misdemeanors with bail set at $2,000 or less. A group of reformers established the Brooklyn Community Bail Fund (BCBF), which started putting up the bail money for selected people awaiting trial in New York City Jails. To date, the fund has paid for the release of over 4,000 people—averaging $1,100 per case. Ninety-five percent of their clients show up for court hearings. When they do, the bail money is returned to the Community Bail Fund coffers, to be used for the next person. Free to fight the charges against them, BCBF clients are three times more likely either to have their charges dropped or to avoid being sentenced to jail. The approach has been so successful that versions of the community bail fund have started up in dozens of other big cities around the country.[4]

The Brooklyn Community Bail Fund story is but one example of a reform movement for America's jails that is sweeping the nation. It seems as though students who are interested in improving corrections during their coming careers could find no area that more obviously needs reform than U.S. jails. Until very recently, the problems of jails have been neglected by scholars and officials and mostly ignored by the public. Typically jam-packed and frequently brutalizing, jails almost never enhance life. Many criminal justice researchers agree that of all correctional agencies, jails have been the oldest, most numerous, most criticized, and most stubbornly resistant to reform.

Jails are a strange correctional hybrid: part detention center for people awaiting trial, part penal institution for people sentenced on misdemeanor charges, part refuge for social misfits taken off the streets. Jails hold men, women, and juveniles who have been accused of violating the law. Jails are the traditional dumping ground not only for people involved in traditional criminal activities but also for petty hustlers, derelicts, drug addicts, prostitutes, people with mental illnesses, and disturbers of the peace, mainly from the poorer sections of cities.

Further, conditions in many jails are getting worse because people convicted of a felony are held there while awaiting vacancies in overcrowded state prisons. Therefore, scholars, administrators, policy makers, and elected officials agree that using jail as punishment for breaking the law should be avoided whenever possible. Yet jail represents nearly all Americans' initial contact with corrections. For many people, this will be their only time in a correctional institution, and the impression it leaves will greatly influence their views of the criminal justice system.

With an estimated 10.7 million jail admissions per year, more people directly experience jails than experience prisons, mental hospitals, and halfway houses combined.[5] Even if we consider that some portion of this total is admitted more than once, probably at least 7–8 million people are detained in a jail at some time during the year.

In this chapter we examine problems of operating jails and how some individuals avoid pretrial detention. We also raise questions about the role of corrections in this type of facility, where too many people sit idle without access to treatment and rehabilitative programs.

LEARNING OBJECTIVES

After reading this chapter, you should be able to . . .

1 Describe the history of the jail and its current function in the criminal justice system.

2 Describe who is in jail and why they are there.

3 Discuss the kinds of jails in the United States.

4 List the main issues facing jails today.

5 Outline the problem of bail and list the main alternatives to bail.

6 Explain the problems of jail administration.

7 Describe new developments in jails and jail programs.

8 Critically assess the future of the jail.

THE CONTEMPORARY JAIL: ENTRANCE TO THE SYSTEM

Jails are the entryway to corrections. They house both the people who are awaiting trial and those who have been sentenced for a crime, usually serving one-year terms or less. People appealing sentences are often held in jail as well, as are those awaiting transfer to other juris dictions. Nationally, about 738,400 people are under jail authority on any given day; more than nine-tenths of them are behind bars, with the remainder under some form of community release.[6]

Some people argue that jails lie outside corrections. For one thing, they claim that most of the nation's 3,163 jails (operated in 2,872 jurisdictions)[7] are really a part of law enforcement because most are administered by sheriffs. For another, they note that people who have been sentenced make up only about half of the jail population and that people being held for trial, who compose most of the other half, should not fall within the scope of correctional responsibility. Finally, they suggest that because so many jails have neither treatment nor rehabilitative programs, they should be excluded from corrections.

We believe that jails are an important part of corrections and demonstrate many complexities of the system. Typically administered by locally elected officials, jails are buffeted by the local politics of taxation, party patronage, and law enforcement. Jail practices also affect probation, parole, and prison policies.

Jails are perhaps the most frustrating component of corrections for those who want to provide treatment programs to people who have committed crimes. Of the enormous numbers of people in jail, many need a helping hand. But the unceasing human flow usually does not allow time for such help—nor are the resources available in most instances.

Origins and Evolution

LO 1

Describe the history of the jail and its current function in the criminal justice system.

Jails in the United States descend directly from feudal practices in twelfth-century England. At that time, an officer of the crown, the *reeve*, was appointed in each *shire* (what we call a county) to collect taxes, keep the peace, and operate the *gaol* (jail). The *shire reeve* (from which the word *sheriff* evolved), among other duties, caught and held in custody people accused of breaking the king's law until a formal court hearing determined guilt or innocence. With the development of the workhouse in the sixteenth century, the sheriff took on added responsibilities for vagrants and the unemployed who were sent there. The sheriff made a living by collecting per diem fees and by hiring out prison labor.

English settlers brought these traditions and institutions with them to the American colonies. After the Revolution, the local community elected law enforcement officials—particularly sheriffs and constables—but the functions of the jail remained unchanged. Jails were used to detain accused persons awaiting trial, as well as to shelter misfits who could not be taken care of by their families, churches, or other groups.

The jails were often in the sheriffs' homes and run like the sheriffs' households. Residents were free to dress as they wished and to contribute their own food and necessities: "So long as they did not cost the town money, inmates could make living arrangements as pleasant and homelike as they wished."[8] Local revenues paid room and board for those who could not make independent contributions.

In the 1800s the jail began to change in response to the penitentiary movement. Jails retained their pretrial detention function but also became facilities for people serving short terms, as well as housing vagrants, debtors, beggars, prostitutes, and those with mental illnesses. Although the **fee system** survived, other changes took place. The juvenile reformatory movement and the creation of hospitals for the criminally insane during the latter part of the nineteenth century siphoned off some former jail inhabitants. The development of probation reduced reliance on jail, as did adult reformatories and state farms. However, even with these innovations, most accused and convicted people were held in jail. This pattern has continued into contemporary times.

fee system A system by which jail operations are funded by a set amount paid each day per person held.

Population Characteristics

LO 2

Describe who is in jail and why they are there.

Not until 1978 did the Bureau of the Census conduct a complete nationwide census of jails for the Bureau of Justice Statistics. Repeated every five years by local officials, this census contains information on jail population counts beyond arraignment (that is, usually more than 48 hours). Excluded from the count are people in federal and state facilities. An annual survey of the top one-third largest jails, which hold about 75 percent of imprisoned people, supplements these five-year nationwide counts.

The most recent National Jail Census shows that about 84 percent are men, nearly two-thirds are under 35 years old, half are white, and most have little education and a very low income.[9] The demographic characteristics of the jail population differ from those of the national population in many ways: People in jail are younger and disproportionately African American, and most are unmarried (see Figure 7.1).

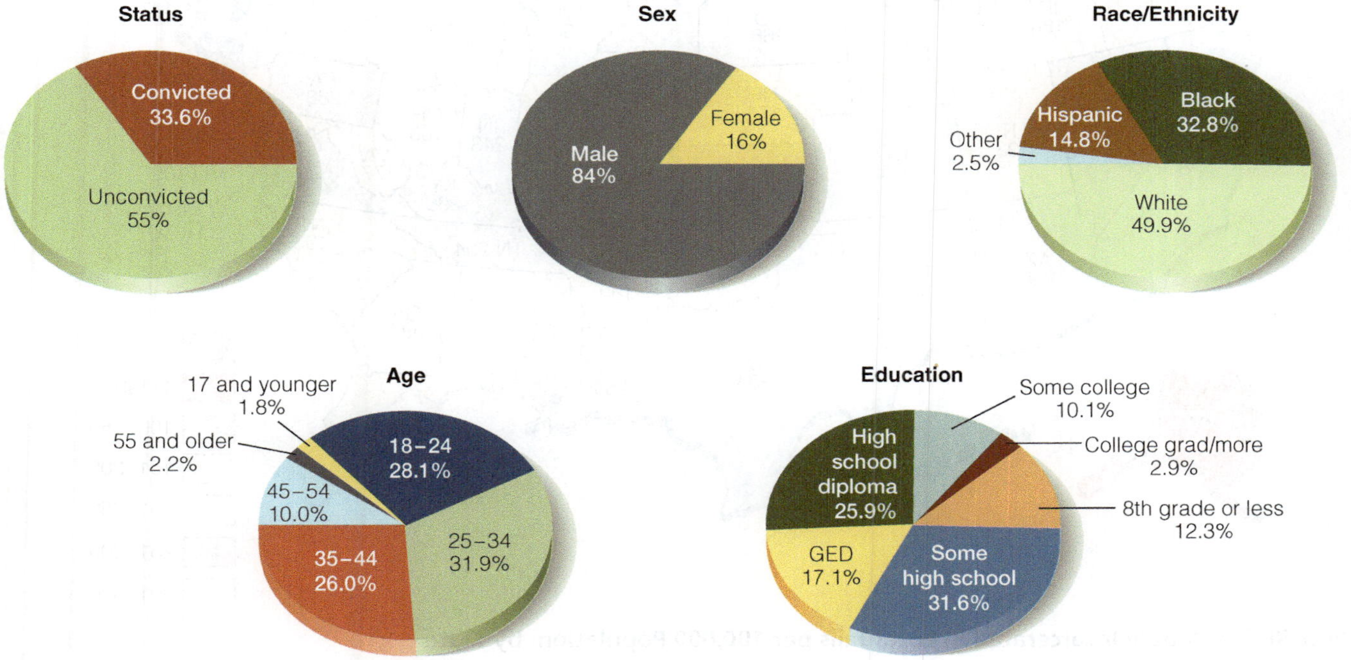

FIGURE 7.1 Characteristics of Adults in U.S. Jails

Compared with the U.S. population as a whole, jails are disproportionately inhabited by men, minorities, the poorly educated, and those with low incomes.

Sources: Zhen Zeng, *Jail Inmates in 2018* (Washington, DC: Bureau of Justice Statistics, March 2020); William J. Sabol and Todd D. Minton, *Jail Inmates at Midyear 2007* (Washington, DC: Bureau of Justice Statistics, June 2008).

As with prisons, jail populations vary from region to region and from state to state. The proportion of a state's population in jail, known as the *jail rate*, is high in the West and South (see Figure 7.2). In many states where prisons are filled to capacity, people sentenced for felonies sit in jails, awaiting transfer.

One of the most concerning problems in jails is the rate of incarceration for African Americans. Figure 7.3 shows the changes in these rates from 1990 to 2018; much of the growth in jail population between 1990 and 2010 was due to a huge increase in the number of African Americans in jails. The gap peaked in 2018, when African Americans were jailed at a rate four times that of Whites and almost three times that of Hispanics. In the last decade, however, the gap between Whites and African Americans has been declining, while the gap between Whites and Hispanics has disappeared, as the jail rate for Whites has slowly grown. Even so, the jail rate for African Americans remains more than three times that of either group. As we discuss in Chapter 19, the rate of incarceration for African Americans is now dropping relative to the white rate; this trend applies to all of corrections, not just jails.

LO 3

Discuss the kinds of jails in the United States.

Administration

Of the 3,163 (city, county, or privately operated) jails in the United States, 80 percent have a county-level jurisdiction, and most are administered by an elected sheriff. An additional 600 or so municipal jails are in operation. Only in six states—Alaska, Connecticut, Delaware, Hawaii, Rhode Island, and Vermont—are jails for adults

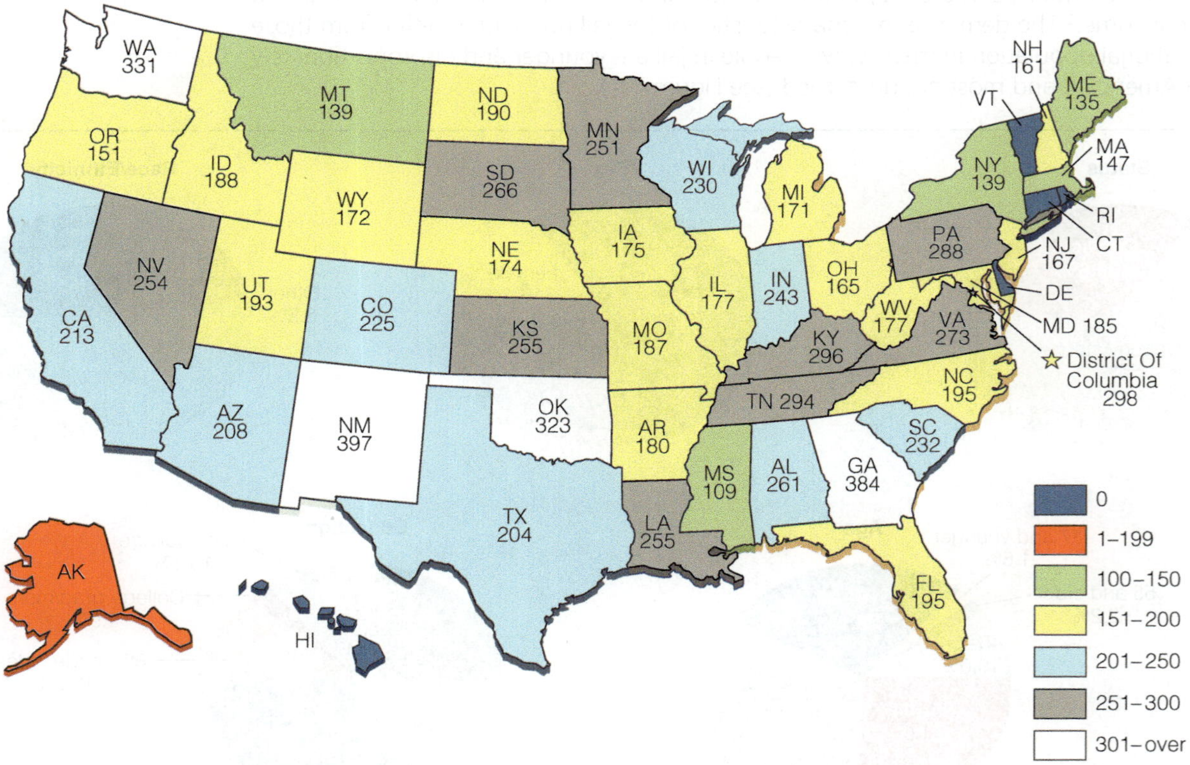

FIGURE 7.2 People Incarcerated in Local Jails per 100,000 Population, by State

What accounts for the fact that incarceration rates in jails differ from state to state?

Note: Six states—Alaska, Connecticut, Delaware, Hawaii, Rhode Island, and Vermont—have integrated jail–prison systems; therefore, information for these states is not given.

Source: Prison Policy Initiative, Correctional Control 2018: Incarceration and Supervision by State. https://www.prisonpolicy.org/reports/correctionalcontrol2018_data_appendix.html.

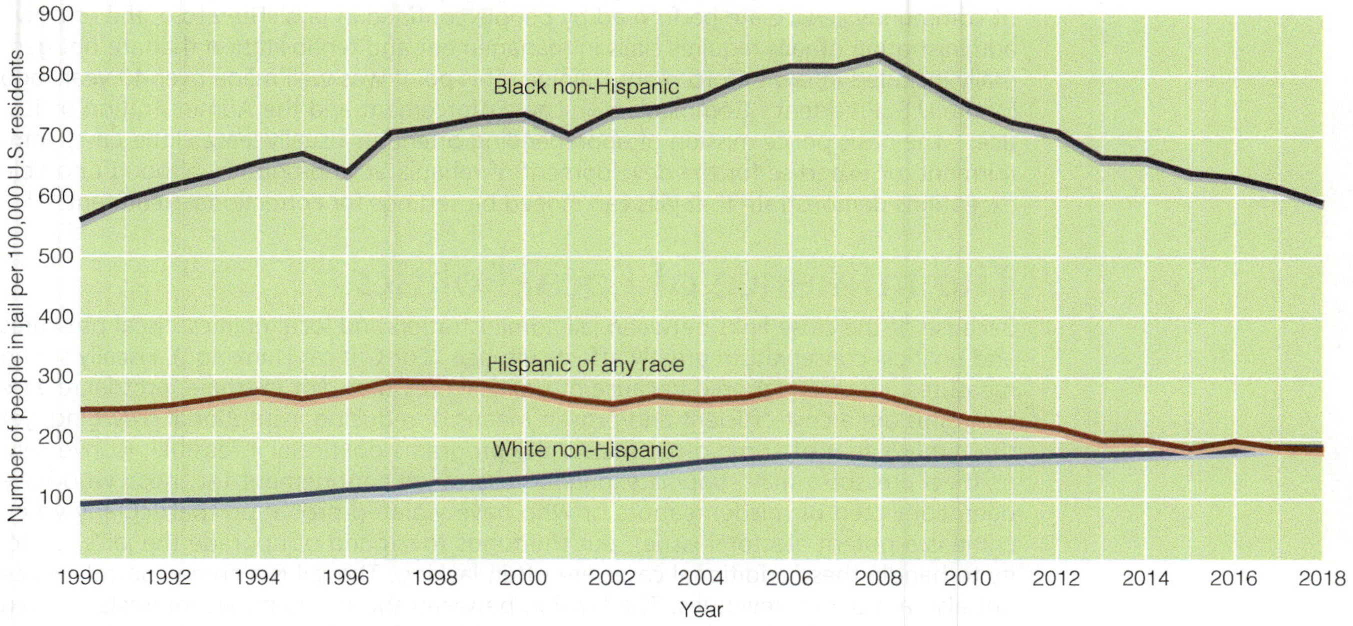

FIGURE 7.3 Jail Incarceration Rates by Race and Ethnicity, 1990–2018

What can explain the phenomenal increase in the incarceration rate of African Americans?

Source: Zhen Zeng, *Jail Inmates in 2018* (Washington, DC: U.S. Bureau of Justice Statistics, 2020).

administered by state government.[10] There are also an estimated 13,500 police **lockups** (or drunk tanks) and similar holding facilities authorized to detain people for up to 48 hours. At most recent counting, the Federal Bureau of Prisons operated 12 jails for the detained only, holding about 12,000 people. There are also 218 immigration detention facilities, 80 Indian Country jails, and 39 privately operated jails, under contract to state or local governments.[11]

lockup A facility authorized to hold people before court appearances for up to 48 hours. Most lockups (also called drunk tanks or holding tanks) are administered by local police agencies.

Jails serve every part of the United States, but because much of the country is sparsely populated, most jails have a rated capacity to hold fewer than 250 people. The 152 jails holding 1,000 or more people represent just over 5 percent of all jails, but they hold more than 40 percent of the nation's daily jail population.[12] The 10 largest U.S. jails hold 10 percent of the total national jail population, but it would be a mistake to think that jails are predominantly an urban concern. Small county jail populations have been growing at a much faster rate than their urban counterparts. In 1970 small county jails held about one-fourth of the nation's jail population. Today they hold more than four-fifths of the total population.[13] This shift has a lot to do with new jail construction in small and medium-sized jurisdictions, largely as a result of legal actions taken against substandard jails that needed to be replaced.

As facilities to detain accused people awaiting trial, jails customarily have been run by law enforcement agencies. We might reasonably expect that the agency that arrests and transports people to court should also administer the facility that holds them. Typically, however, neither sheriffs nor deputies have much interest in corrections. They often think of themselves as police officers and of the jail as merely an extension of their law enforcement activities. In some major cities, municipal departments of correction, rather than the police, manage the jails.

Many experts argue that jails have outgrown police administration. Jails no longer serve simply as holding places but now represent one of the primary correctional facilities in the criminal justice system. In fact, much correctional work is directed toward people housed in jails. Probation officers conduct presentence investigations in jails, people who abuse alcohol and drugs receive treatment in many facilities, and many hours of community service are performed by people confined in jails. Therefore, the effective administration of jails requires skills in management and rehabilitation that are not generally included in law enforcement training. This point was well made over 40 years ago by the U.S. President's Commission on Law Enforcement and the Administration of Justice: "The basic police mission of apprehending offenders usually leaves little time, commitment, or expertise for the development of rehabilitative programs, although notable exceptions demonstrate that jails can indeed be settings for correctional treatment."[14]

The Influence of Local Politics

Because of the close links between jail administration and local politics, fiscal pressures and political conservatism greatly affect jails (see "For Critical Thinking"). Fiscally sound measures are often ignored because of political pressures. For example, pretrial release programs are a cost-efficient and proven means of reducing institutional crowding, yet the public's fear of crime often makes the programs politically infeasible. Conversely, political pressures may support expanded use of jail confinement for those who have been convicted of misdemeanors or who have violated probation (particularly when crime is a potent electoral issue), but the funds to expand or upgrade the jail's capacity to handle these additional cases are often lacking. The jail is a crime control service but also a drain on revenues. The tension between these two public interests is often expressed in local debates over capital expenditures for jail construction. Because revenues are often insufficient, many jails are overcrowded and cannot house everyone who has been sent to jail, so a portion end up being released or placed in other facilities.

It is very hard to wrest control of local facilities away from a politically sensitive office such as that of sheriff or police chief. Jail employees constitute a large block of political patronage for elected officials to distribute to political supporters. Political appointees spend most of their time administering the jail, but during political campaigns they hustle votes and money for their bosses. Even when jail employees are civil servants, political considerations can affect hiring and promotion. Because few politicians willingly surrender control over such a potential political force as the jail, change is slow. See "Careers in Corrections" for more about what it means to work in a local jail.

FOR CRITICAL THINKING

Everywhere in the United States, sheriffs have to run for office. That means they must convince voters they care about public safety and other high-priority voter issues. But because many sheriffs also run local jails, they are responsible for maintaining safe and effective facilities. Sometimes, jail safety and humaneness are not high priorities for local voters. That means that the kinds of public policies that may attract votes, such as "getting tough on people in jail," may not contribute to effective and humane conditions. In other words, there may be conflicts between what it takes to get elected and what it takes to be a good jail administrator.

1. Should the head of the jail be an elected official?
2. What are the advantages of electoral accountability for a person who is a jail administrator? What are the disadvantages?

Regional Jails

Most local jails are located away from major population centers, and at least one-third hold as few as 30 people. Although the state may provide a portion of their operating funds, the smallest jails lack essential services, such as medical care, that must be provided no matter how few people may need them.

One recent trend designed to remedy these problems is regionalization: the creation of combined municipal–county or multicounty jails. This multi-jurisdictional or **regional jail**, fiscally sound though it may be, has been slow to catch on because it negatively affects several interest groups. Local political and correctional leaders do not want to give up their autonomy or their control over patronage jobs, and reformers often object to moving local residents to places that are sometimes far away from their communities. Citizens who oppose having regional jails "in their backyard" make finding locations to build these jails difficult. Nevertheless, the number of jail jurisdictions in the United States has actually dropped by more than 6 percent since 1999.[15]

regional jail A facility operated under a joint agreement between two or more government units, with a jail board drawn from representatives of the participating jurisdictions and having varying authority over policy, budget, operations, and personnel.

CAREERS IN CORRECTIONS

Correctional Officer—Local Jails

Nature of the Work

Most jails are operated by county governments, and three-quarters of them are under the jurisdiction of an elected sheriff. The approximately 175,000 correctional officers in the jail system admit and process more than 7 million people per year in either pretrial or sentenced categories. Officers must supervise individuals during the postarrest phase, when they may be most stressed, violent, and dangerous. The constant turnover of the jail population is an additional problem in terms of maintaining security and stability.

Required Qualifications

Candidates for employment must be at least 18 or 21 years of age (the minimum age varies), be a U.S. citizen, have a high school education, have no felony convictions, and have some work experience. They must be in good health and meet formal physical fitness, eyesight, and hearing standards. Some local departments provide training for officers according to criteria set by the American Jail Association. In some states, regional training academies are available to local correctional agencies. On-the-job training is a major resource for officer candidates.

Earnings and Job Outlook

Job opportunities for correctional officers employed in county jails depend on local budgetary constraints even in the face of increases in the jail population, but job growth is expected to be about 9 percent during this decade. Salaries for entry-level correctional officers vary greatly, with the highest being in the Northeast and the lowest in the rural South. Median annual wages of correctional officers and jailers are $44,830. The lowest 10 percent earned less than $31,140, and the highest 10 percent earned more than $76,760.

More Information

Source: U.S. Bureau of Labor Statistics, www.bls.gov/oes/current/oes333012.htm. For more information, see the website of the *Occupational Outlook Handbook* and search for "Correctional Officers."

FOCUS ON

PEOPLE IN CORRECTIONS: Jimmy's First Day in Jail

Jimmy James sat in the back of the Mountain View police car, his hands cuffed behind his back. He had never been arrested before, and thoughts about jail tormented his mind. When Jimmy saw news reports depicting the crowded conditions and violence, he didn't pay much attention. The trauma of confinement was the furthest thing from his mind. Yet he found trouble by downloading nude pictures from the Internet. Facts later revealed that the girls in the pictures were underage, and Jimmy now faced felony charges for child pornography.

The police officers drove in to a basement garage and parked their vehicle. After one of the officers opened the car's rear door, Jimmy stepped out, his heart pounding. The officer gripped Jimmy by the handcuff, making him feel as if he were a dog on a leash. The officer guided Jimmy into an elevator. When the door opened again, Jimmy saw the madness of the large King County Jail.

Jimmy's legs shook as he walked into the jail's administrative area. His first stop was booking. To his right were prisoners packed in a series of open holding cages. The cages resembled the dog pound, he thought, though instead of yelping and barking dogs, Jimmy heard the blustering cacophony that came from scores of young, seemingly angry men. He hoped the officers would not lock him inside with the other prisoners.

As the jail staff took Jimmy into custody, the officers lost interest in him. He was fingerprinted, positioned for his mug shot, and then led toward the bullpens.

"Can I go into that one?" Jimmy gestured toward the bullpen that held only three prisoners seated on a bench, each of whom looked contrite.

"No can do," the jailer said. "That's the misdemeanor tank. You're in with the felons, Class A."

The jailer unlocked the gate to the most crowded cage. "Step inside," the jailer ordered.

Jimmy hesitated, and the prisoners taunted him. "Step inside, bitch," he heard one prisoner yell. "Don't get scared now. What is it homey, you too good to be in here with us?"

"Get in," the jailer ordered.

Jimmy walked into the cage. Once the jailer locked the gate behind him, Jimmy passed his cuffs through the bars and the jailer freed his wrists. Then the jailer walked away, leaving the prisoners to themselves.

The crowd of strangers frightened Jimmy. He was 21, shorter than average height with a slender build. His sandcolored hair was thinning prematurely. He didn't have anywhere to sit, so he walked toward the back of the cell and leaned against the wall.

PEOPLE IN CORRECTIONS: Jimmy's First Day in Jail (*continued*)

A larger prisoner stepped toward Jimmy. "What up, big dog?"

Jimmy didn't know how to respond. He nodded his head.

"Where you from?"

Jimmy didn't want to talk to anyone. He stood silent against the wall, with hunched shoulders and bowed his head toward the floor.

"I'm sayin'," the aggressive prisoner persisted, "you ain't tryin' to talk?"

Jimmy kept silent.

"Okay, okay," the prisoner said. "I feel ya. But check dis out. Wussup wit dat watch?"

Jimmy looked up, realizing his efforts at disappearing were not working. "What do you mean?"

"I'm sayin', wassup wit dat watch? You know some'nes gonna take it up off you once you get to the block."

"Why?"

"You's in jail, fool. Straight gangstas up in here. Best let me hold it for you. I'm a take care it, make sure you get it back when your daddy post bail."

Jimmy thought for a split second. He didn't want any problems. The watch wasn't fancy, just a simple digital model with an alarm. Knowing he probably wouldn't see it again, he unfastened the Velcro band and handed it over.

"Dat's wassup, homey," the prisoner strapped the prize on his wrist. "I'm a take good care you up in here. What dey got you up in here for, youngun?"

"Internet porn."

"Internet porn. Wus dat?"

"Internet porn, you know, downloading nude pictures from the web."

"They be lockin' mothafuckas up for dat?"

"Well, the models were underage."

The prisoner smiled. "Oh, you be likin' dem kids."

"I didn't know the models were underage."

"Uh-huh. Was dey little girls or little boys?"

"They were young women. I'm not gay, you know."

"Ain't no one sayin' you was gay. I's just axin', dat's all. But check dis out, youngun. When we gets up on da block, don't be talkin' 'bout your case. Just stay close to me. I'm a look out for ya."

The jailer returned to the bullpen. He unlocked the gate and called names to step out. Jimmy made his way through the crowd, as did his unnamed protector. The jailer handed the men a roll of dingy sheets, a threadbare blanket, and a brown sack that held two pieces of white bread with bologna. The prisoners marched through the jail's corridor, passing through various sliding gates until they reached a housing unit. "Grab a mat," the jailer ordered, "and find yourself a home on the floor."

Jimmy couldn't believe he would have to live in such conditions. Sleeping mats were everywhere. A list on the wall posted 30 names waiting for cell space. The bathrooms were open, lacking a modicum of privacy. A stench of dried urine permeated the air. Noise from table games, aggressive voices, and a television blasting rap songs contributed to the frenetic energy in the housing unit.

He would go crazy if he had to stay in jail long, Jimmy thought.

"Don't even sweat it," the larger prisoner said. "We goin' crash right here. I'm a look out for ya, youngun."

Jimmy quivered. He sat on the mat that he had dropped, held his knees, and waited, afraid for what might happen next.

PRETRIAL DETENTION

Imagine that you have been arrested by the police and accused of a crime. They have handcuffed you, read you your rights, and taken you to the station for booking. Frightened, you have a hundred questions, but the police treat you as if your fears were irrelevant to their work. You may be angry with yourself for what you have done. You may be frustrated that you cannot seem to control the flow of procedure: fingerprints, mug shots, long waits while detectives and prosecutors discuss you without acknowledging your presence. Slowly you begin to understand that you have acquired a new status: "accused offender."

Then you are taken to the detention section of the jail. If it is an advanced facility, you are placed in a holding room for an intake interview. There your situation is explained to you, you are asked questions about your background that will help determine how best to manage you while you are in jail, and you are told what you can expect next. If, however, you are in one of many jails with no formal intake procedure, you are simply put in the holding tank. If you are a man, strangers likely will be in the cell with you, men whose stories you do not know and whose behavior you cannot predict. If you are a woman, you will more likely be by yourself. In either case, once the guard leaves, you are on your own behind bars, and the full extent of your situation begins to sink in. This can be an especially trying period for those people who are thrust into a hostile and threatening environment.

In such circumstances, many people panic. In fact, the hours immediately following arrest are often a time of crisis, stemming from the arrested person's sense of vulnerability and hopelessness, fear of lost freedom, and sheer terror. Over one-third of the deaths that occur in jails are suicides. Not surprisingly, most of these suicides happen within the first 6–10 hours after lockup, and most psychotic episodes occur during or just after jail intake.

Other factors can exacerbate the crisis brought on by arrest and detention. Often the person who has been arrested is intoxicated or on drugs, a state that may have contributed to the crime for which the person is being held. Sometimes the criminal behavior stems from an emotional instability that may worsen in detention. Especially for the young, the oppressive reality can trigger debilitating depression.

Unquestionably, one of the most crucial times is the period immediately following arrest. (See "Jimmy's First Day in Jail.") People differ in their need for help during this period. Those under the influence of a mind-altering substance need time to overcome its effects; others need to be left alone; still others need communication and advice. Jails lack the programmatic flexibility to accommodate the range of needs. However, the early confinement period also represents a mental health opportunity because an individual in crisis is most likely to respond positively to efforts of help. Unfortunately, the jail is not ordinarily well suited to provide aid in the first hours of detention. Elaborate mental health measures are neither feasible nor necessarily required. However, even simple human contact—conversation with correctional staff, involvement in some activity, communication about what the person is likely to be experiencing—is frequently enough to reduce many initial anxieties.

Special Problems of People Held for Trial

LO 4

List the main issues facing jails today.

Beyond the initial crisis of being arrested and jailed, people who are detained for an extended period often face serious problems. The most significant are mental health problems, substance dependency, medical needs, and legal problems. Because so many people housed in jail have these problems, local jails have often been referred to as the social agency of last resort.

Yet it is not easy for a jail to meet the needs of the people who are sent there. The most important issue is turnover. The average stay in jail is 25 days, and that makes coherent programming difficult to carry out. In fact, for most jails, half of the population turns over every week.[16]

Mental Health Problems Growing attention is being paid to the mental health of people in jail whose behavior, while not seriously criminal, is socially bizarre—those who are only partially clothed, who speak gibberish or talk loudly to themselves, who make hostile gestures, and so on. These people, whose behavior is unpredictable and to some extent uncontrollable, were once transported to mental institutions, where they could be treated. But with the nationwide deinstitutionalization movement they have become outpatients of society, and they often spend time in jail instead of receiving the psychiatric treatment they once might have received.

In fact, some people say jails have replaced mental institutions for dealing with serious mental illness. One study found that in every U.S. county that had both a jail and a mental health hospital, the jail held more people with serious mental health issues than did the hospital.[17]

Recent estimates are that almost half of those in jail have a history of mental problems; just over one-fourth are currently experiencing severe psychological distress. (See Figure 7.4.) Of the latter group, nearly 40 percent receive no treatment at all.[18]

Observers say that the percentage of people in jail who are considered to have a mental illness is increasing.[19] However, police have few alternatives to confinement for people who behave oddly or self-destructively, even if they are basically just nuisances. Moreover, unstable people often respond to the stress of jail with emotional outbursts and irrational behavior. Jails not only draw from but also add to the ranks of the mentally disturbed.

The most common treatment given to people in jail who have a history of mental illness is some sort of prescription medication. About two-fifths of the mentally ill in jail receive some form of counselling.[20] But most jails have limited rehabilitative staff, and the vast majority of rehabilitative personnel lack training to deal with severe cases of mental and emotional stress, particularly when threats of self-injury are involved. Consequently, people with mental illnesses too often languish in jails, where they are abused by their peers, misunderstood by correctional workers, and left untreated by professional personnel.

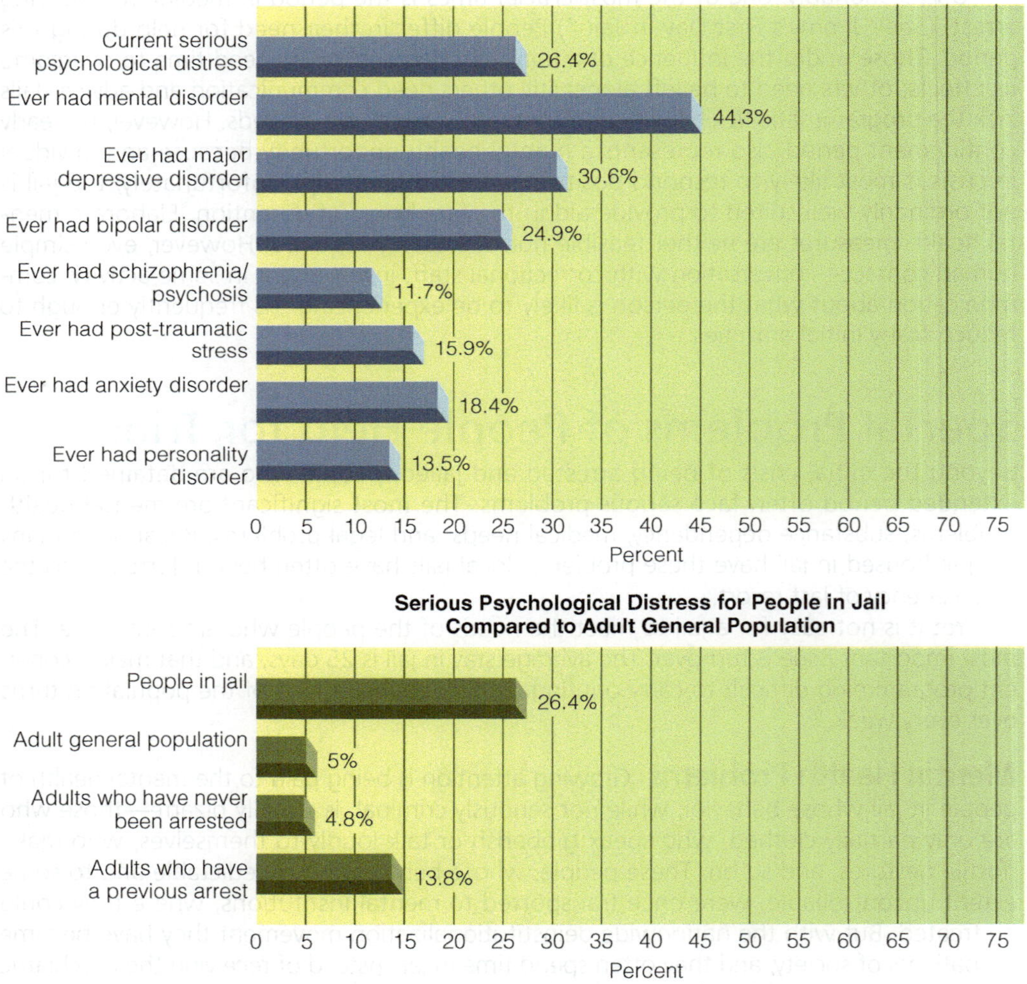

FIGURE 7.4 Percentage of People in Jail with Mental Health Symptoms

People in jails exhibit a wide range of mental health problems.

Source: Jennifer Bronson and Marcus Berzofsky, *Indicators of Mental Health Problems Reported by Prisoners and Jail Inmates, 2011–2012* (Washington, DC: Bureau of Justice Statistics, 2017).

The news is not all bad, however; some positive steps have been taken to divert the mentally ill from jail. Many jails now screen new arrivals for mental health problems, with specially trained counselors interviewing and evaluating people held for trial. Those with mental health problems are usually referred to local social service agencies for treatment and may be diverted from criminal prosecution in order for treatment to proceed.

Substance Dependency Nationally, half of all people placed in jail are under the influence of alcohol or an illegal drug at the time of arrest, and nearly two-thirds, more than 400,000, have a history of substance abuse. More than half of those entering jail have a history of failed drug treatment, often during previous jail or probation terms.[21] In a study of four large cities, 60–85 percent of all people arrested tested positive for illicit substances at the time of arrest.[22]

The most dramatic problems posed by drug abuse occur during withdrawal, when the addict's body reacts to the loss of the substance on which it has grown dependent. Both alcoholics and drug addicts suffer withdrawal, but it is especially painful for the latter group and may last as long as a week. Addicts may attempt suicide to escape the pains of withdrawal, and a higher percentage of drug addicts than nonaddicts succeed in the attempt. Early identification of the drug addict is therefore a high priority in jails, for withdrawal symptoms can be assuaged by methadone maintenance or release to an addiction treatment facility.

Despite the shortness of most stays in jail, treatment programs designed especially for jails have shown some success. There is a great need for substance abuse treatment in jails, but less than one-fifth of those who need such treatment receive it while there.[23] The most recent survey shows that more than 80 percent of those in jail have used some illegal drug, with one-third to one-half having used stimulants and opiates. (See Figure 7.5.) From one-fifth to one-third report regular use of these drugs.[24] The most recent surveys are a decade old, and so methamphetamine and opioid use may have grown since then.

Every jail regularly houses alcoholics, many of whom, during the initial hours of confinement, are physically sick, hallucinating, and paranoid. These symptoms tend to be viewed as inconveniences rather than as conditions requiring treatment, even though a severe alcoholic in withdrawal can become sick enough to die. For that reasons, since the first detoxification center in the United States was established in St. Louis, in 1966, the national trend has been toward treating public drunkenness as more of a medical than a criminal problem. These detox centers are quasi-voluntary facilities for chronic alcoholics, many of whom have no other place to go. The centers provide shelter, medical care, food, clothing, and counseling for residents, most of whom are taken there by police.

Medical Needs People in jail have many medical needs, ranging from minor scrapes and bruises sustained during arrest and booking to major injuries sustained during the crime and its aftermath. To these injuries can be added the routine health deficiencies of any lower-class citizen: infections, poor nutrition, lack of dental care, and so forth. Taken together, more than one-third of those in jail report a physical ailment of some sort.[25] Even so, almost half of the nation's jails do not screen routinely for infectious diseases, such as tuberculosis.[26] Just over 1,000 people die in jail annually, most often from illnesses such as heart disease, which accounts for over one-fourth of jail deaths. Nearly one-third of jail deaths are suicides, connected to mental illness. One-tenth result from drug or alcohol overdose.[27]

In 2020, the international pandemic of COVID-19 hit jails particularly hard. The preferred remedy—social distancing—is simply not possible in the jail setting. People are confined in close proximity with one another, and staff must interact with them routinely. The underlying health conditions that make the virus more lethal afflict those who are incarcerated in jails at a high rate. Officials looked at the jail as a kind of incubation engine for spreading the virus. Within a few days, there were reports of increasing numbers of COVID-19 confirmed cases among both staff and the confined. Jail administrators readily admitted that they had no capacity to deal with anyone who got severely ill, and as staff started calling out sick, the ability to create conditions needed to halt the spread of the virus was reduced. Many jails started releasing people accused of low-level crimes, as well as anyone whose health conditions increased their risk of death from the disease. One estimate held that almost 54,000 people were released from the nation's jails due to COVID-19 concerns in just the first three months of the pandemic.[28] The population at New York City's main jail, Rikers Island, dropped by one-fourth in two months.[29] As people study how the pandemic affected jails, the implications of COVID-19 and similar diseases are becoming clearer.[30]

For the most part, citizens who end up in jail, on either charges or sentences, lack medical insurance, so whatever medical care they receive is provided by the jail itself. Almost 60 percent of America's jails make people incarcerated there pay for at least some of the medical care they receive; two-thirds of those require payment for all services. Forty percent provide the health care through on-site staff or other government employees. Even in the jails that seek to address health problems, services are problematic, and many residents have complained about the quality of care being offered.

Legal Needs People held for trial need access to legal assistance. In the emotionally stressful postarrest period, they need information about what will happen prior to their trial. They also need legal help in securing release through bail or diversion. If release is not possible, they must have help in preparing their case, negotiating with the prosecutor about charges, or directing their attorney to people who may provide an alibi or exonerating evidence. Not surprisingly, research consistently shows that people held in jail until trial suffer a disadvantage in preparing their defense. People in jail are likely to need a public defender, an appointed counsel, or an attorney provided by contract. Unfortunately, because they must process large numbers of cases for relatively small fees, criminal defense attorneys cannot spend much time locating witnesses, conducting investigative interviews, and preparing testimony. So for many people held for trial, these essential defense plans are only partially pursued.

They can expect to spend long periods without seeing an attorney. In fact, most have only one or two hurried conversations with their attorneys before they appear in court. To add insult to injury, they are brought to court in shackles and jail-issue clothing, in dramatic contrast to well-groomed people who have been able to remain free. Some of those held for trial who were once employed have long since been fired. In short, they have relatively dim prospects.

The Rights of People Detained for Trial Unlike people serving time, people in this group have not been convicted of the crimes for which they are being held. Technically, they are innocent, yet they are detained under some of the worst conditions of incarceration. In the 1970s several courts reasoned that such people should suffer no more restrictions than are necessary to ensure their presence at trial and that their legal protections should exceed those of the sentenced.

However, in 1979 the U.S. Supreme Court overruled the lower courts by limiting pretrial detainees' rights. As discussed in Chapter 5, the Court in *Bell v. Wolfish* ruled that conditions can be created to make certain that detained people are available for trial and that administrative practices designed to manage jails and to maintain security and order are constitutional.[31] The justices said that restrictions other than those that ensure court appearance may legitimately be imposed on people held for trial and that when jail security, discipline, and order are at stake, they may be treated like others in jail.

Release from Detention

One of the most startling facts about U.S. jails is that so many of their occupants are awaiting trial. For many, this pretrial detention will last a long time: The most recent national data available show that the average delay between arrest and sentencing is more than six months. For those charged with a felony, the average delay between arrest and adjudication is 111 days.[32] In urban jails the wait is often longer because of heavy court backlogs. Remarkably, despite the constitutional right to a speedy trial, in some court systems people can expect to languish in jail for a year or more before their cases come to trial.

The hardship of pretrial detention exerts pressure on accused people to waive their rights and plead guilty. Further, it undermines their defense. And delay, often a useful defense tactic because it can weaken the prosecutor's case, imposes a further penalty on the detained person.

Small wonder, then, that recent years have seen a major emphasis on programs to enable release for those awaiting trial. Rates of pretrial release have gradually grown from less than 50 percent in the early 1960s to nearly 90 percent in some of today's largest urban areas. (See Focus: Pretrial Reform Is Sweeping the Nation.) Nationally, the percentages of pretrial release ranged from 12 percent for people brought into federal courts for immigration violations to 71 percent for people charged with property crimes. However, in the nation's largest counties, 62 percent of people awaiting trial on felony charges are released prior to the disposition of their case, half of them within a day.[33] Even so, the proportion of people in jail who are there because they are awaiting trial has increased from about one-half to two-thirds in the last 10 years.[34]

Paradoxically, jail crowding may have exacerbated the problem of pretrial populations. As mentioned, the 1990s saw a trend of closing down old, dilapidated jails and replacing them with newer, larger facilities. The proportion of jail population that is housed in large jails (with over 2,000 capacity) has almost doubled since 1993. Jail capacity has increased nationally by more than one-third.[35] Many of the new spaces, though, are taken not by people sentenced to jail but by people being held for trial. The irony is that the expansion in jail capacity was met by an increase in demand for jail space, so that jails now hold about the same number of people they did 15 years ago, even though the rest of corrections is declining.

FOCUS ON

CORRECTIONAL POLICY: Pretrial Reform Is Sweeping the Nation

For almost as long as there have been local jails, they have been the stepchild of the criminal justice system: overlooked and neglected. It seems as though it was always easier to interest policy makers in reforms of other parts of the system. The jails stayed pretty much as they always were: ignored, underfunded, and understaffed.

Then came the Great Punishment Experiment that started in the 1970s. Correctional intake grew steadily for years. By the 1980s, jails began to feel the pressure of burgeoning numbers of those awaiting trial as well as those sentenced on low-level offenses. As prison systems strained beyond capacity, jails were often forced to pick up the slack. By the 1990s, jails almost everywhere were seriously overcrowded and under legal scrutiny.

State prison systems were also overcrowded, but their solution was straightforward: build more prisons. Building new local jails was a more difficult proposition, because the tax base is not as large. Nevertheless, many jurisdictions sacrificed other priorities in order to build newer and larger jails, hoping this would solve the problem. Their elected officials were dismayed when the jail crowding problems returned, often within months of opening the new facility.

This experience has led to a new generation of jail reform, one which seeks to keep a lid on the jail population. Too many defendants sit in jail because they could not raise funds for bail. So many places have expanded alternatives to bail and reduced the use of cash bail. Three states—California, New York, and New Jersey—have eliminated cash bail for large subgroups of defendants. Specialized treatment courts for drug abuse, mental health, and veterans have reduced the number of jail sentences.

After generations of neglect, jail reform is on the table almost everywhere. The case for jail reform remains strong, however. Prison and community corrections populations have been declining, but jail populations have not. Two-thirds of those in jail are innocent, awaiting trial. The time is right for comprehensive jail reform.

Source: Chris Mai, Mikelina Belaineh, Ram Subramanian, and Jacob Kang-Brown, *Broken Ground: Why America Keeps Building More Jails and What It Can Do Instead* (New York: Vera Institute of Justice, 2019).

LO 5

Outline the problem of bail and list the main alternatives to bail.

THE BAIL PROBLEM AND ALTERNATIVES

bail An amount of money, specified by a judge, to be posted as a condition for pretrial release to ensure appearance of the accused individual at trial.

When someone is arrested for a crime, the court seeks to ensure that he or she will appear at the appointed time to face charges. Judges have traditionally responded to this need by requiring that the person post **bail**, normally ranging from $1,000 to $25,000 (although higher amounts may be required), to be forfeited if the accused individual fails to appear. See Figure 7.5 to see the most recent study of median bail amounts for people accused of a felony.

Dissatisfaction with the bail process stems from several factors. First, many people who want to post bail—in some studies over 90 percent of those who are held for trial—are effectively indigent and cannot afford bail. Second, money is a weak incentive for appearance in court in many cases because the people who can afford bail are the ones most likely to appear at trial without the threat of its forfeiture. Perhaps the most disquieting factor is that human freedom can be had for a price. Imprisoning people merely because they are too poor to pay for their release seems antithetical to our cultural ideals and our concept of justice. These are some of the reasons that Federal Judge Lee H. Rosenthal declared the Harris County (Houston), Texas, bail system "fundamentally unfair" to the poor and ordered the county to release people who were accused of misdemeanors but were not able to post bail.[36]

To avoid the problems of bail, some jurisdictions have increased the use of citations and summonses. For nonserious offenses, police can give the accused person a "ticket" specifying a court appearance date and thus avoid having to take him or her into custody. Experiments with this approach indicate that it effectively reduces demands for short-term detention space. See Figure 7.6 for more on pretrial release.

Release on Recognizance

release on recognizance (ROR) Pretrial release option used when the judge believes the person's ties in the community are sufficient to guarantee his or her appearance in court.

By far the most successful alternative approach allows people to be released solely on their promise to appear at trial, a practice known as **release on recognizance (ROR)**. ROR programs assume that ties to the community (residence, family, employment) give people an incentive to keep their promise to appear and to retain their status in the community.

day reporting center A facility where people under pretrial release or with probation violations can attend daylong intervention and treatment sessions.

People released on recognizance frequently have higher appearance rates than do people freed through various bail programs; they also have lower rearrest rates and higher rates of sentences to probation rather than prison. ROR programs have demonstrated clearly that the vast majority of accused people can be safely released into the community on their promise to return for trial. Loss of bail is an unnecessary threat. The rate of willful failure to appear in most jurisdictions is normally less than 5 percent.

electronic monitoring Community supervision technique, ordinarily combined with home confinement, that uses electronic devices to maintain surveillance.

Despite the benefits of ROR, questions arise. Because ROR requires that people have ties to the community, only a portion of defendants can participate. One national analysis of ROR found that women are more likely than men to be released and that African Americans are less likely to be released than whites, especially in the West and South.

Some jurisdictions have begun to experiment with pretrial release under some form of supervision. Nationally, over 57,900 people are under some form of supervised release. Many are supervised by probation officers or other counselors through pretrial supervision, others attend **day reporting centers**, others perform community service (discussed more fully in Chapter 9), or are under **electronic monitoring**.

pretrial diversion An alternative to adjudication in which the accused person agrees to conditions set by the prosecutor (for example, counseling or rehabilitation) in exchange for withdrawal of charges.

Pretrial Diversion

As an alternative to adjudication, **pretrial diversion** began with the belief that formally processing people through the criminal justice system is not always beneficial. Each of the three main reasons advanced in support of pretrial diversion has provoked controversy:

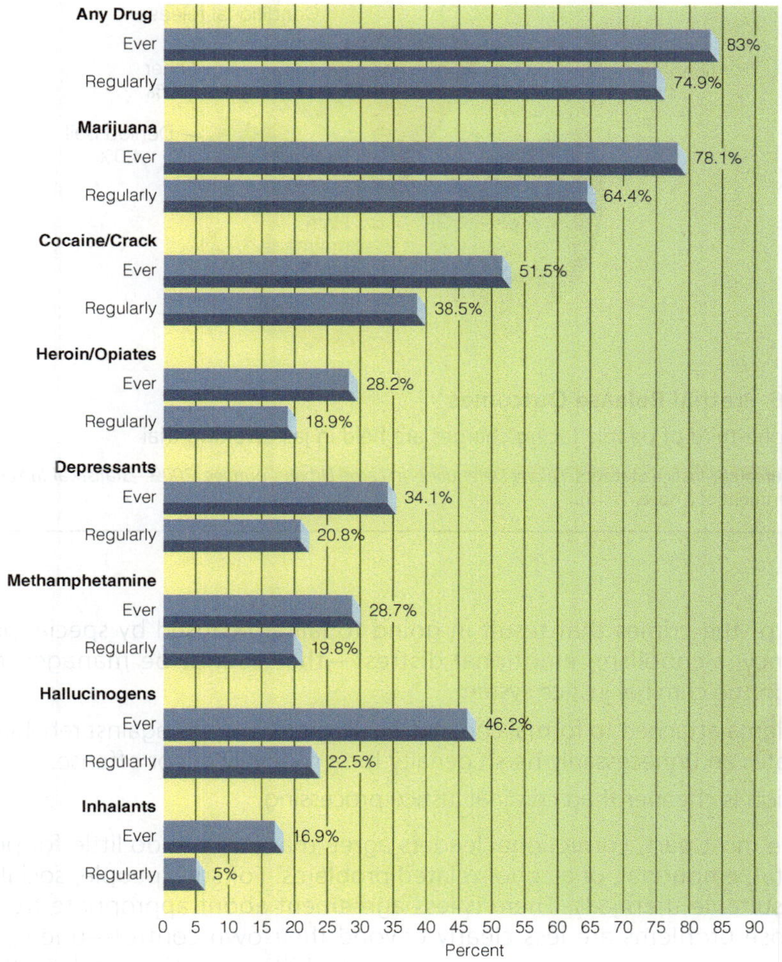

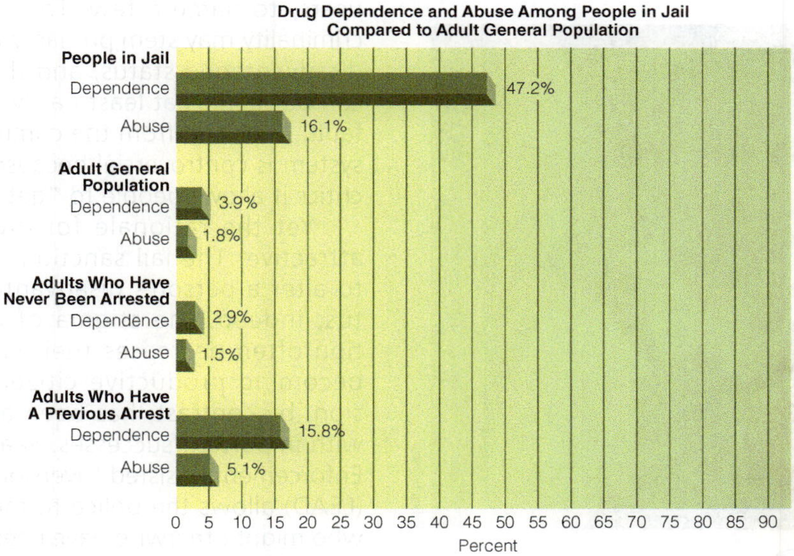

FIGURE 7.5 Median Bail Amount for People Accused of Felonies, 2009

Most judges set low bail amounts for people facing felony charges, yet even these amounts are hard for some people to raise.

Source: U.S. Bureau of Justice Statistics, *Felony Defendants in Large Urban Counties, 2009—Statistical Tables* (Washington, DC: U.S. Department of Justice, 2013), 7.

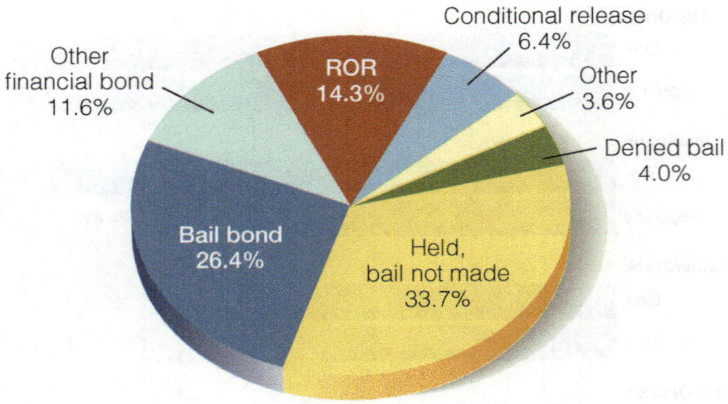

FIGURE 7.6 Pretrial Release Outcomes

More than one-third of people facing charges are held in jail awaiting trial.

Source: U.S. Bureau of Justice Statistics, *Felony Defendants in Large Urban Counties, 2009—Statistical Tables* (Washington, DC: U.S. Department of Justice, 2013).

1. Many of the crimes that result in going to jail are caused by special problems—vagrancy, alcoholism, emotional distress—that cannot be managed effectively through the criminal justice system.
2. The stigma attached to formal criminal labeling often works against rehabilitation and promotes an unnecessarily harsh penalty for a relatively minor offense.
3. Diversion is cheaper than criminal justice processing.

For the most part, correctional leaders agree that jails can do little for people who have mental, emotional, or alcohol-related problems. For such people, social programs are more suitable than jails. There is less agreement about appropriate treatment for those whose problems are less clearly beyond their own control—unemployed and unskilled youths, and multiple-drug users, to name a few. Their marginal criminality may stem primarily from their disadvantaged status, and their status can be seen as at least partly their own fault. Diversion from the criminal justice system is controversial because to some critics it allows people to "get off easy."

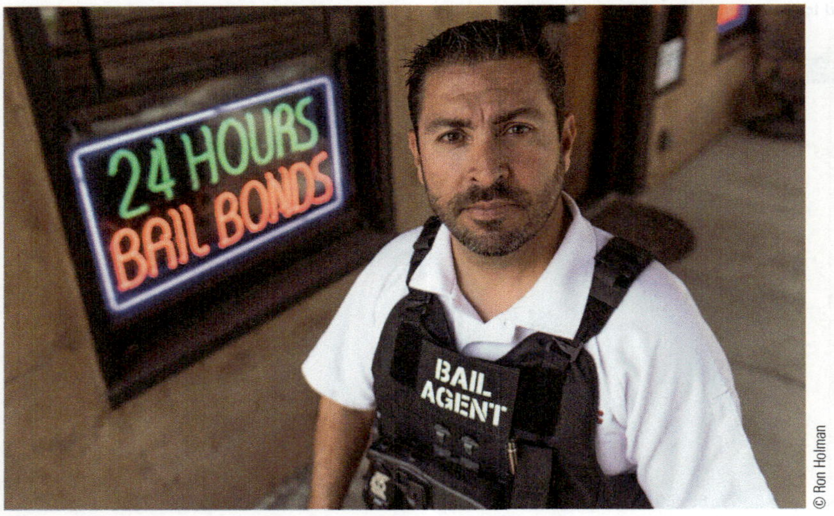

▲ *Visalia bail bondsman Scott James is one of many across California affected by the elimination of cash bail effective in 2019.*

Yet the rationale for diversion is attractive. The jail sanction does little to alter a person's disadvantaged status; indeed, the stigma of a conviction often decreases their chances of becoming productive citizens. Diversion, by contrast, has been associated with important successes. Seattle's Law Enforcement Assisted Diversion Program (LEAD) allows the police to take people who might otherwise have been arrested to social services agencies—homeless shelters, drug treatment programs, hospitals—instead of jail. This approach has been credited with a substantial reduction in repeat arrests, a reduction in the problems that led to the original arrest, and major savings in costs.[37]

One problem of pretrial diversion programs, however, highlights a persistent problem of criminal justice reform. Innovations designed to reduce the overall intrusiveness of the system, no matter how well intentioned, often backfire and instead expand its capacity for social control. The process, called "**widening the net,**" occurs when a new program is applied to people who ordinarily would have gotten a less severe punishment; rather than diverting people from punishment, it increases the scope of corrections.

widening the net Increasing the scope of corrections by applying a diversion program to people charged with offenses less serious than those of the people the program was originally intended to serve.

If pretrial diversion programs are to meet their objectives, they must be applied to people who would otherwise be treated more harshly. This is not easy to accomplish because many criminal justice system officials distrust programs that are more lenient or more oriented to community service than are their current practices.

Conduct During Pretrial Release

People who are awaiting trial would seem to have a special incentive to behave well. If they show up for court with a job and prospects for a good future, it will be harder for a judge to impose a sentence of confinement. If they show they can adjust well to the community during the period between the arrest and the trial, then the judge will likely take that into account when imposing a sentence.

It may be surprising, then, that many people do not behave well during their period of release before trial. While the vast majority—78 percent—of individuals on some form of pretrial release show up for every court hearing, more than one in five do not. These are called **absconders**; unless there is some good reason that they missed the court date, a warrant is sent out for their arrest, and they are considered fugitives. Nationally, nearly one-fourth of these fugitives (3 percent of all people accused of a crime) remain at large at least one year after they were supposed to have had their trial.[38]

absconders People who fail to appear for a court date for no legitimate reason.

The failure to appear for trial is not the only form of misbehavior that happens when people are released before trial. Almost one in five (16 percent) of all people released while awaiting trial are rearrested before their trial date arrives, half of them for a felony.[39] The high arrest rate of these people represents a significant concern to those interested in jail reform, who may wonder if some sort of supervision or treatment program would help keep these numbers down. They also see that high rates of arrests for this population lead to questions about the effectiveness of the pretrial system. Moreover, when people who are released before trial fail to appear or get rearrested, one result is that the sentence on their original charges becomes more severe.[40]

Preventive Detention

Even as ROR and other prerelease programs have moved forward, the heightened public concern about misconduct by people who are released while awaiting trial has led to a political movement to prevent pretrial release, especially release on bail. With **preventive detention**, people who are regarded as dangerous or likely to commit crimes while awaiting trial are kept in jail for society's protection. In 1984 the Comprehensive Crime Control Act authorized the holding of an allegedly dangerous person without bail if the judge finds that no conditions of release would ensure the individual's appearance at trial and at the same time ensure the safety of the community.

preventive detention Detention of an accused person in jail to protect the community from crimes that he or she is considered likely to commit if set free pending trial.

The notion of the need for protection from people accused of committing a crime has been subjected to sustained analysis. Many scholars believe that holding in custody a person who has not been convicted of a crime but who someone thinks might commit a crime violates the due process provisions of the Constitution. Others argue that the practice is impractical and potentially nefarious. And as we have seen, fewer than one in five of all people who are released pending trial are arrested for another crime before trial, and many of those are not convicted of the new crime. One analysis of more than 100,000 pretrial releases found that judges often detain the wrong people.[41]

To assist judges, social scientists have developed risk assessment tools that employ systematic criteria to determine how much risk a defendant represents. One of the most widely used risk assessment devices, the **Public Safety Assessment** (PSA), classifies defendants according to their likelihood of failing to show up in court after being

Public Safety Assessment A check-off system that provides an objective rating of a person's likelihood to fail to show up for court hearings and the likelihood that the person will be rearrested before those court hearings.

released and their likelihood of getting arrested before their court date.[42] The PSA is controversial, partly because judges resist what they see as encroachments on their judicial discretion. Other critics point out that the PSA makes criminal risk as aspect of the pretrial release decision, when the only issue should be a person's likelihood of absconding before trial.

Political pressure to incorporate the public's safety concerns into release decisions has become so strong that well over half of the states have laws allowing preventive detention. The U.S. Supreme Court approved preventive-detention practices in *Schall v. Martin* (1984) and *United States v. Salerno* (1987).[43]

MYTHS in Corrections

Jails Are for People Convicted of Misdemeanors

THE MYTH: Jail sentences are more common for people convicted of misdemeanors than they are for people convicted of felonies.

THE REALITY: Nearly 40 percent of people accused of committing a felony are eventually sentenced to jail, a rate that is almost the same as prison sentences for misdemeanors.

Source: Brian A. Reaves, *Felony Defendants in Large Urban Counties, 2009—Statistical Tables* (Washington, DC: U.S. Bureau of Justice Statistics, 2013), 28.

PEOPLE SENTENCED TO JAIL

People who have been sentenced to jail by the court present special difficulties for the correctional administrator, mainly because of the short duration of the term and the limitations of the jail's physical plant. By definition, jail terms are shorter than prison terms—typically 30–90 days for a misdemeanor. People convicted of a felony commonly serve from six months to a year, and on some occasions (those convicted of sexual assault or robbery, for example) they will serve two years or more. (See "Myths in Corrections.") In many cases the sentence ultimately imposed is "time served" because the judge believes that the time already spent in pretrial detention—when under the law the person was presumed innocent—is sufficient, or more than sufficient, punishment for the offense committed. The real punishment is not the sentence but rather the impact of the unpleasant, costly, and harmful conditions of life behind bars from arrest up to case disposition. In short, the process is the punishment.

Of those sentenced to additional jail time, people convicted of misdemeanors constitute the forgotten component of local criminal justice operations. Over half are under criminal justice system supervision at the time of their arrest: probation, parole, or pretrial release. Nearly three-quarters have previously been sentenced to probation or confinement (see "Thinking Outside the Box").

They also have a range of treatment needs. Problems related to illegal drug use, unemployment, and poverty afflict large portions of the jailed population. Many suffer from physical or emotional trauma. Most lack educational credentials, and basic literacy skills.

Their short terms make education and treatment difficult. For example, people in jail can rarely earn a high school equivalency diploma in one or two months, and prospects for continued education after release are dim. Similar impracticalities are inherent in job-training programs, which may require 25–30 weeks to complete. In addition, job-placement prospects are spotty for people with jail records, many of whom do not have the help of a parole or probation officer in looking for work. Treatment programs for the mentally ill, the emotionally disturbed, and alcoholics and drug addicts suffer from the same time constraints.

The jail facility also limits program opportunities. Jobs within the institution are few, and most people have a lot of idle time. Those assigned to work details find the labor menial and monotonous: janitorial, kitchen, and laundry tasks. Still, they are lucky. The vast majority simply languish in small cells. Recreational options may consist of a small library of donated books, some table tennis facilities, and a few card tables; few jails have basketball courts, weight rooms, and the like. Whatever the resources, recreational time is carefully rationed. Contact with friends and relatives is the only thing that sustains many people in jail, but visiting hours are often limited to a few minutes each week.

In sum, with isolated exceptions, jail time is the worst kind of time to serve as a correctional client. For corrections, jail is an expensive and largely ineffective proposition—a revolving door that leads nowhere.

FOCUS ON

PRACTICE: Jails in Indian Country

In the United States, there are 326 Indian reservations—designated areas of land managed by a recognized Indian tribe under the administrative authority of the U.S. Bureau of Indian Affairs. In these areas, the governing authority is typically a tribal council which exercises limited legal sovereignty for the enforcement of law on reservation land. While a state's criminal law applies generally within the boundaries of a given reservation, the tribe members living on reservations also establish tribal law that applies to people living on the reservation or doing business there. Those laws are enforced by tribal agencies of justice—police, courts, and corrections. In 2020, the U.S. Supreme Court upheld the integrity of tribal-run justice systems for crimes committed on reservation land.[44]

Tribal justice systems currently run over 90 detention centers, which at last count held 2,540 people awaiting trial in a tribal court or serving imposed by that court. Collectively, these jails operate at about 60 percent capacity. Tribal land jail populations have grown 43 percent since 2000.

Compared to local jails, tribal jails do not hold people as long: the average length of stay in tribal facilities is 8 days; in local jails the average stay is 25 days. One-third of those in tribal jails have been charged with some form of substance abuse—public intoxication or drug possession. Domestic violence and assault account for another one-fourth of the charges.

Tribal jails employ 1,810 workers; 70 percent of these handle direct custody, while 7 percent provide educational and treatment services. Recently, tribal leaders have recognized the need for improved services for people who flow through the tribal justice system. One group of elders said:

> Our children are taking their lives, our families are being torn apart, our cultural values are being challenged more than ever before, all because of alcohol, and drug abuse, violence and suicide, and we need to act now to stop this destruction.

In order to stem this tide of harm, new programs have been developed to divert people from jail in order to provide integrated services of prevention, intervention, treatment, and recovery. The goal is to reduce high rates of recidivism and prevent intergenerational patterns of substance abuse and violence.

Sources: Todd D. Minton and Mary Cowhig, *Jails in Indian Country 2016* (Washington, DC: Bureau of Justice Statistics, 2017); Bureau of Indian Affairs, Office of Justice Services, https://www.bia.gov/bia/ojs (2020); Jeffrey T. Ulmer and Mindy S. Bradley, "Jails in Indian Country: Ironies of Federal Punishment of Native Americans," *Justice Quarterly* 35 (2018), 751-81.

THINKING OUTSIDE THE BOX

JAILS' FREQUENT FLYERS

Anyone who works at a jail will attest that a small number of people cycle in and out many times in a short period of time. Sometimes called "frequent flyers," these people have almost never committed serious crimes, and they rarely pose a risk to the community. They are disruptive people: often intoxicated, often on the streets with no place to go. For example, in New York City, up to 60 percent of people who are homeless are rearrested within a year of being released from jail.

This problem has led some experts to propose what they call "frequent flyer programs." These approaches begin with research—just who are the people who enter and leave jails so often, sometimes dozens of time in a year? Then the research must be assessed—what are the problems underlying a person's going to jail so frequently? The ultimate goal of this research is to prescribe a strategy or program that will deal with those problems and help keep the person out of jail. What kind of treatment do you think such a program would prescribe? What results might you expect? How much should social science research be able to tailor individual sentences?

Sources: Craig Davis, "How Police and Mental Health Professionals Work Together in Framingham," *Metro West Daily News*, October 28, 2012; Richard R. Peterson, "Re-arrests of Homeless Defendants in New York City," *Criminal Justice Agency Research in Brief* 39 (February 2016).

To ameliorate these problems, reformers have begun to emphasize the importance of carefully planned and supported reentry programs. Jail administrators are to begin preparing for a sentenced person's release from the first day of confinement,[45] and partnerships with community supervision agencies are encouraged in order to provide more support for the person who is returning to the community from the jail.[46]

LO 6

Explain the problems of jail administration.

ISSUES IN JAIL MANAGEMENT

U.S. jails are faced with numerous problems, many of them age-old: lack of programs, poor financial resources, antiquated facilities, and so on. Here we discuss five of the most important issues related to jail: legal liability, jail standards, personnel matters, jail crowding, and the jail facility itself.

Legal Liability

As discussed in Chapter 5, jail employees may be legally liable for their actions (42 U.S.C. 1983). Whenever a government official (such as a correctional officer) uses his or her authority to deprive a citizen of civil rights, the victim can sue the official to halt the violation and to collect damages (both actual and punitive) and recoup legal costs. Supervisors, including wardens, can also be liable for the actions of staff members—even if they were not aware of those actions—if it can be shown that they should have been aware. A lack of funds does not excuse an administrator from liability for failing to train staff sufficiently or to provide basic, constitutionally required custodial arrangements. Local governments that administer the jails are also liable for injurious conduct.

Many people believe that court decisions awarding civil judgments under Section 1983 are an open invitation to sue, and the frequency of suits filed by people in prison has certainly increased. Just about every conceivable aspect of the conditions of incarceration has been litigated, from hours of recreation to quality of food. The most successful suits have been those showing that an employee's action has contributed to harming someone. But jail conditions have also been the subject of suits, especially when substandard safety mechanisms result in injury or death.

The threat of litigation has forced jails to develop basic humane practices for management. Civil damages and legal fees of more than $1 million have been awarded often enough to draw the attention of sheriffs, jail managers, and local government officials. Budgets for jails have been increased to reflect the additional costs of developing training programs, classification procedures, and managerial policies to prevent actions leading to liability suits.

Jail Standards

One of the best ways to reduce litigation is to develop specific standards for the practices and procedures that routine jail operations entail. Standards are important for at least three reasons. First, they indicate proactive criteria for jail management, which help eliminate the "Monday morning quarterback" (rehashed in hindsight) aspect of much litigation. If jails are following standard procedures, they cannot be held as accountable as they otherwise would for problems experienced during incarceration. Second, standards provide a basis by which administrators can evaluate staff performance: They need merely determine whether staff are complying with operational standards. Third, standards aid the planning and evaluation of jail programs by giving program managers a target to consider in their work.

Even so, authorities are uncertain about the best way to design and implement jail standards. Some experts argue that standards should be binding. Generally, this means that an oversight agency visits each jail in the state and determines whether its programs are consistent with the standards. Jails that fail to comply with standards are given a deadline by which to meet them. If they do not, they may be fined—or even closed down.

Other experts argue that because jails differ so much in size and needs and because so many of them suffer from underfunding and inadequate facilities, holding all jails accountable for meeting the same inflexible set of standards is unreasonable. These experts push for voluntary guidelines by which program goals for jail operations would be set by groups such as the American Correctional Association and monitored by teams of professionals.

The bottom line is that if jail administrators do not implement standard practices, the courts will intervene. Even new jails are not immune to this problem. In the late 1980s, jails commonly came under court orders soon after opening, and sometimes even before opening.

Personnel Matters

Local correctional workers are among the most poorly trained, least-educated, and worst-paid employees in the criminal justice system. Many take custodial positions on a temporary basis while awaiting an opening in the ranks of the sheriff 's law enforcement officers. According to the last jail census, there are approximately 221,600 jail employees, serving as correctional officers, administrators, and in clerical, maintenance, education, and professional staff roles. Almost 80 percent of jail employees serve as correctional officers.[47]

Personnel problems facing jail administrators stem from several factors, but the primary one is probably a combination of low pay and poor working conditions. Local correctional workers earn substantially less than firefighters and police officers in the same jurisdiction. And whenever these correctional workers can, they leave for better-paying jobs with less stressful working conditions. However, many correctional employees have only limited education and do not fare well in competition for better positions, so they must stay where they are.

Understaffing further exacerbates these poor working conditions. Jails are 24-hour operations. Assuming that the typical jurisdiction has a 40-hour workweek with normal holidays and leave time, nearly five full-time employees are required to fill one position around the clock. The national ratio of the confined to custodial employees in jails is about 4.2 to 1, which translates to about 25 to 1 for each staff workday. In essence, each jail employee must be able to control 25 people or more, which helps account for the common practice of simply locking the doors and leaving people in their cells all day. Not surprisingly, local correctional workers are often an unhappy bunch. Turnover is extraordinarily high, with many jails reporting complete staff turnover every two or three years. The effects are disastrous. No matter what the level of staffing, proper security must be maintained in the jail, so there is pressure to move new employees directly into the ranks, despite the fact that training at a state academy may last 30–60 days—and classes may not start for several months. The dilemma is obvious and has prompted the Jail Division of the National Institute of Corrections in Longmont, Colorado, to make the training of jail staff instructors a high national priority. This strategy seeks to increase the number of qualified trainers for jail workers so that no new employee lacks the necessary preparation for the assignment. At best, however, this is a stopgap. In the long run, society must improve pay rates and working conditions to make jail employment more attractive.

Jail Crowding

The number of people confined in jails reached nearly crisis proportions in the early 1990s. The jail population, which had remained fairly stable during the 1970s, more than doubled between 1983 and 1993, and it has increased by three-quarters since 1993. During the heaviest growth period—the 1980s and early 1990s—jail crowding became a nationwide problem. Hundreds of jails were forced to close as a result of litigation, and many jails had to operate under a court order of one type or another.

This crowding led to serious problems in jail management, including inadequate supervision, increased violence, idleness, and exposure to mental and physical trauma. Tempers flare in close quarters, and the merely vulnerable become likely victims. These circumstances are especially problematic, because most of the people subjected to them have not yet been tried and must be presumed to be innocent.

Faced with crowding as a crisis, leaders began to develop strategic solutions. Two involved people detained before trial: (1) increasing the availability of release options, such

FOCUS ON

CORRECTIONAL POLICY: Closing Rikers Island—One of America's Most Famous Jails

At one time, Rikers Island, New York City's jail, was among the largest jails in the United States. In 1992, at the height of the city's crack epidemic, the daily population of Rikers was 21,500, and the annual intake exceeded 111,000. The jail was also notorious: Everyone knew that doing time at Rikers was tough and that there was plenty of violence between rival gangs and between staff and the people who were incarcerated there.

Then the numbers started dropping. As the city's crime rate plummeted every year for two decades, so did the need for the city's jail to hold people arrested for crime. And even though New York City began to use misdemeanor arrests (usually calling for jail time instead of prison time) for crimes that used to provoke a felony record, the Rikers Island correctional population continued to plummet. By 2017, the average daily population was less than half the level 25 years earlier.

Over the years, the jail had become tainted by what seemed like myriad daily scandals. Allegations included systematic brutality by corrections officers, sexual misconduct by male staff against female staff, mistreatment of the mentally ill, collusion with gangs, and financial corruption. Some began referring to Rikers as "the most notorious jail in America."

In 2014 *The New York Times* ran a special investigative series documenting over 100 cases of abuse. This prompted a U.S. Department of Justice investigation of civil rights violations at Rikers that concluded there was a "deep-seated culture of violence" at the jail carried out by corrections officers who did their jobs without fear of reprimand. After the report was made public, people began saying the jail was a hopeless catastrophe and needed to be closed.

The last straw was a scandal that made national news and dominated local headlines. When Kalief Browder was 16, he was arrested by the police, accused of stealing a backpack—a charge that he denied. He ended up at Rikers, unable to afford bail of $3,000. Brower refused multiple offers to plead guilty and be released, insisting he was innocent. Over his three years in Rikers, Browder was targeted for violence on multiple occasions, attempted suicide more than once, and spent much of his time in solitary confinement, where he experienced bouts of mental illness. The shocking fact was that he had never been charged with a crime. Finally, after 31 court appearances, the district attorney agreed to dismiss the charges. Browder went home emotionally damaged and depressed. His case, which was featured in a documentary by rapper Jay Z, fueled public outrage.

In 2016 Bill DeBlasio, New York's mayor, formed a blue-ribbon committee to suggest ways to reform Rikers. The report, released in 2017, concluded that New York City's justice system would be improved by closing the jail down. People awaiting trial would be held at several detention centers located near the city's criminal courts. Short sentences would be eliminated. Alternative punishments would be enhanced, and community justice would be expanded.

Will Rikers be closed? Law enforcement unions have vowed to fight the proposal, but the reaction of the public has been positive. Everyone realizes that a lot of planning must take place before a place like Rikers can be shuttered. But the work is under way.

Source: Independent Commission on New York City Criminal Justice and Incarceration Reform, *A More Just New York City* (New York: Author, 2017).

as ROR and supervised release, and (2) speeding up trials. Other ameliorative measures were directed toward people serving time and include work release sentences, which at least relieve crowding for part of the day. Jail crowding remains a problem in many local jurisdictions—one in five jails currently houses numbers above its rated capacity. But nationally, the problem of crowding has eased, as the nation's jail capacity is one-fourth higher than its daily population count.[48]

Oddly, building new jails—or increasing the capacity of existing facilities—has had only some effect on the problem of crowding. Wide variations exist among jurisdictions in patterns of jail use—some jails are heavily used, others less so. It used to be that large jails in urban centers suffered from the most crowding, but that is no longer the case. Today, it is the mid-size jails—holding between 250 and 500 people at a time—that face the heaviest population pressure. One in three of these mid-size jails is over-capacity, compared to only one out of thirteen large urban jails (holding over 2,500). In many of these mid-size jurisdiction, new jails have been built to replace obsolete, overcrowded predecessors. Frequently, these new jails opened up with expanded capacity, and yet they were soon again overcrowded.

The challenge is how to handle large numbers of "pass-through" populations—people who have been arrested and people who are being held for trial. The failure to quickly move this population back out into the community may explain much of today's crowding. The solution to crowding is not as much jail capacity as it is jail policy.

There are other reasons why jail expansion is not as popular as it once was. Building new facilities is extremely expensive, costing on average $40,000–$50,000 per cell—meaning that a facility for 1,000 can cost $50 million to build and another $25 million annually to run. At a time when local governments are pressed to fund other priorities, such as education and health care, these costs seem extravagant. This is especially true because most people who go to jail do not return to the community as more-capable citizens, so the jail acts more like a revolving door than a correctional service. In short, while jail growth has been a major dynamic in correctional policy for nearly 30 years, policy makers increasingly desire to stem this growth and look for other ways to deal with minor criminal activity and with people who are awaiting trial.[49]

The Jail Facility

LO 7

Describe new developments in jails and jail programs.

New jails are expensive structures; at their most expensive, they can cost as much as $100,000 per cell to build—and perhaps $200,000 per cell when financing is taken into consideration. Running a physically outmoded jail can be more expensive still.

In many older jails even such basic items as radios and television sets are lacking. With idle time, poor physical security, and little or no chance to participate in programs, people are often cheek to jowl, day in and day out. Crowded cells make for threatening environments that may translate into potentially costly lawsuits. Often the only way to counteract poor security in older jails is to hire extra staff. For these reasons and others, many jurisdictions have turned toward what is called the **new-generation jail**. This jail, through its unique design and set of programs, attempts to use the physical plant to improve the staff 's ability to manage and interact with the incarcerated population and to provide services. Three general concepts are employed: podular design, interaction space, and personal space.

new-generation jail A facility with a podular architectural design and management policies that emphasize interactions with staff and provision of services.

The **podular unit** (derived from *pod* and *modular*) is a living area for a group that defines a post or a watch. The podular unit replaces the old cell blocks. Twelve to 25 individual cells are organized into a unit (the pod) that serves as a self-contained mini-jail. Typically, the cell doors open into a common living area where those in the pod can congregate.

podular unit Self-contained living areas designed to hold 12–25 people, composed of individual cells for privacy and open areas for social interaction. New-generation jails are made up of two or more pods.

The new-generation jail tends to reinforce interaction of various sorts. For example, the residents have greater freedom to interact socially and recreationally with one another, and correctional staff are in direct physical contact with them throughout the day, an approach called **direct supervision**. In older jails, bars and doors separate correctional officers from the confined population; the new-generation jail places them in the same rooms. People are given personal space and may stay in their individual cells to pursue their own interests when they wish. They may even have keys to their own quarters within the pod.

direct supervision A method of correctional supervision in which staff members have direct, continual physical interaction with people confined in the jail.

The new structure offers several advantages over older jails. First, its economics are flexible. When jail populations are low, whole pods can be temporarily shut down, saving personnel and operational costs. Second, minimum standards for recreation time and nonlockup time can be met routinely without costly construction or renovation. Third, supervising the staff is less demanding, for staff have greater autonomy to manage their pods. Fourth, policy makers have learned that new-generation jails are as much as 20 percent cheaper to construct, and they provide more-effective security and supervision. Finally, there is some evidence that the new-generation concept results in less violence and fewer infractions, leaving staff feeling more secure in their work.

However, the greatest advantages are programmatic. In larger jails, pods can serve specialized groups who share a need, such as for remedial educational services, or who for any reason (for example, AIDS, gang affiliation, or offense type) need to be segregated from the rest of the jail population. Thus, the needs of the confined can become a more significant factor in the nature of the jail experience.

Placing correctional staff in closer contact with the jail population also has benefits. People in jail often show symptoms of depression or behave disruptively because of stress or the emotional strain of confinement; this can become more troublesome without appropriate staff response. When correctional officers are physically closer to those they supervise, they can more readily become aware of feelings or behavior that may require attention. Further, the physical structure can potentially moderate conflict. When officers and residents get to know one another better, more-positive interactions occur. Thus, in the long run the new-generation jail is thought to be one way to help overcome the correctional officer's traditional isolation.

therapeutic justice A philosophy of reorienting the jail experience from being mostly punitive to being mostly rehabilitative.

More recently, the concept of the new-generation jail has evolved to embrace the idea of **therapeutic justice**, a philosophy of reorienting the jail experience from being mostly punitive to being mostly rehabilitative. (See "Women in Jail" for more.)

In the 1980s, administrators became enamored of the tight management approaches that the criminologist John DiIulio advocated (see Chapter 13). DiIulio's "control model" emphasizes running prisons safely and securely. The control model asserts that a manager's first priority is to exert total control over the population at all times. This control is achieved by isolating people as much as possible and limiting interpersonal contact. However, research on the new-generation jail has called his ideas into question, at least as concerns the jail. Studies show that an alternative "employee investment" approach, in which everyone in the jail system is seen as a potential resource to be developed rather than a potential problem to be controlled, is more successful in achieving the results that DiIulio sought with his control model. This is one reason that many experts now agree that the direct-supervision jail offers the best route toward improved staff morale, reduced staff sick leave, reduced injuries across the board—and even reduced maintenance costs.

Despite its advantages, all is not well with the new-generation jail. For one thing, it is hard to sell the concept to a public that underestimates the painfulness of the jail experience and sees the new system as a means of "coddling criminals." That more than half of those confined in jail have *not* yet been convicted of a crime does not dampen the public's desire for harsh punishment. Jail administrators need to inform political decision makers about the fiscal and programmatic advantages of the new jail.

A second problem is more troubling: Many new jails become outmoded between the planning stage and completion of construction. Legal standards may change, creating new requirements for cell space, recreational space, visitation areas, and the like. Inadequate attention may have been given to possible programmatic needs. Often, the very existence of a new jail leads to such an enthusiastic response by judges and other criminal justice officials that the new facility quickly becomes crowded.

Finally, the number of cells that should be built into a new jail is controversial. Planners often argue that new jails need to be more spacious than old jails to accommodate the growing numbers of people sent there. Architects pleading for large jails often use projections of burgeoning jail populations to support expansion. Critics respond that jail populations grow to meet available capacity, and they cite numerous new jails of doubled capacities that became overcrowded the day they opened. There is a need, they say, for policies to keep jail populations under control as well as facilities to house those populations.[50]

community model for jails An innovative model for jail administration that promotes a sense of community across the board, while using community to promote rehabilitation.

The Center of Therapeutic Justice, an advocacy group specializing in jail reform, has recently presented another approach to managing jails, called the **community model**. The community model is created by building a prosocial, self-governing podular-style unit within the jail. In this unit the norm of mutual aid is taught and reinforced, and all the people in the jail work together to create a culture based on positive community values, such as self-control, interpersonal competence, and abstinence from substance abuse. The community model replaces the conflict of the traditional jail with a spirit of cooperation and support, and in doing so promotes long-term behavior change.

The community model is usually not initially a jail-wide phenomenon. Instead, it develops in a separate part of the jail. This demonstrates to everyone the possibilities it offers for a better jail culture and environment. The model incorporates treatment approaches that have been proved effective, and it builds into them a democratically elected program

FOCUS ON

CORRECTIONAL PRACTICE: Women in Jail

In 1970 only about 8,000 women were locked up in U.S. jails. Today that number exceeds 100,000—a larger increase in incarceration rates than for any other social group.

How did this happen? Experts say as the general "get-tough" movement gained footing in the 1970s and 1980s, women started receiving more-severe handling by police, prosecutors, and judges. In particular, as the drug war accelerated, women who might once have been handled leniently began to get the full brunt of the law. Finally, social problems such as domestic violence, homelessness, and drug addiction have contributed to the growth of the number of women in jails.

There are important ways in which jail for women is a different policy problem than that for men. For one thing, more than 80 percent of women in jail are there for nonviolent crimes. Almost two-thirds were unemployed at the time of the arrest. Half report medical problems requiring a doctor, and one-third have been previously diagnosed with a serious mental illness. Almost 9 in 10 have been the victim of a sexual assault, and more than two-thirds have experienced violent assault by an intimate partner.

Experts point out the special problems women can face in jail. Most jail classification systems are built for men; most jail programs are also based on men's needs. And yet women will have needs related to reproductive health, including some women who are pregnant when they go to jail. Many women have significant responsibility for child care, and the strain on their families can be severe. Also, women can have a stronger, more problematic emotional response to jail. Taken together, the many ways in which jail poses a different kind of experience for women mean that it is important to take account of those issues when women go to jail.

The national trends in this area have been changing, too. The proportion of all arrests that involve women has more than doubled since 1960. Since the 1990s, the rate of incarceration of women actually grew faster than that of men. And this has been even more true for rural jails, where women's incarceration rates have nearly doubled in the last 15 years, a time period when urban jail incarceration rates have actually dropped.

All of this suggests that jail policies for women cannot simply be the same policies that are applied to men. The issues women face are different enough that a special kind of correctional policy for women makes sense. For too long, the special issues faced by women have been overlooked.

Source: Elizabeth Swavala, Kristine Riley, and Ram Sabramian, *Overlooked: Women and Jails in an Era of Reform* (New York: Vera Institute of Justice, 2016).

based on building motivation, compliance, and a positive attitude toward the hard work of creating a community and strengthening personal responsibility. After the community model is fully developed, it is less expensive to run than the traditional jail, and its proponents claim that it reduces violence and increases program participation—with the promise of long-term change and lower rates of recidivism.[51]

THE FUTURE OF THE JAIL

LO 8

Critically assess the future of the jail.

Few government functions in the United States are under assault from as many camps as is the jail. Reform groups call for more-humane jail conditions; the media expose jails as cruel, crowded, and counterproductive; people sent to jail sometimes end up suing their keepers for mistreatment, often successfully; and experts describe jails as failures, and local officials find them expensive.

In some respects, the jail's importance to the criminal justice system has seldom been greater than it is today. As local governments experiment with ways to improve the credibility of the criminal justice system, solutions seem inevitably to involve the jail—for work release, for enforcing court orders for people on probation, for new laws against drunkenness, and for other initiatives. Local decision makers have more control over jails and jail policy than over facilities operated by state correctional agencies.

Moreover, the jail is an expensive item in county and municipal budgets. The average cost of a day in jail varies greatly, but for a large urban jail it can be quite high. A day in New York City's Rikers Island—the nation's most expensive stay—costs $228, and the next-most expensive, the Multnomah County (Portland, Oregon) jail, is no bargain

© Richard B. Levine

▲ *The entrance to Rikers Island, the New York City jail. Notorious as a place of violence and despair, reformers have been able to convince the city to set a schedule for it to close.*

at $103 per day. Even in the "cheap" jails, with daily costs under $30, the price adds up, as one bed can cost $10,000 per year. (See "Do the Right Thing" for more.)[52]

For many of these municipalities the overall costs of jail place a major strain on budgets. One-fourth of the Harris County (Houston) annual budget goes to law enforcement, with more than three-quarters of a million dollars spent daily on sentenced and unsentenced people held in jail.[53] Over the last quarter-century, jail costs have grown 50 percent faster than all other municipal criminal justice costs.

Perhaps because of the jail's budgetary costs and system centrality, two general trends—if they continue—bode well for its future. First, many jurisdictions have renovated or replaced jail facilities since the early 1970s. The overwhelming difficulties associated with decrepit physical plants are at least partially overcome by this new construction. Second, many jurisdictions are joining together to build and maintain a single jail to serve their collective needs. Although political problems abound in such an arrangement—politicians resist giving up authority over jail budgets—this movement seems to be gaining adherents.

DO THE RIGHT THING

Local justice systems are strapped for cash. Douglas A. Valeska II, the head prosecutor in Henry County, Alabama, had a solution. After all, he is the person who decides what to charge people with when they are arrested. He makes the bail recommendations to the court. These two decisions—the charge and the bail level—are what determines whether people have to sit in jail awaiting trial. What if he established a diversion program that enabled people to get their charges dismissed—and getting into the diversion program would involve a "program fee" of a couple of thousand dollars? This could solve a few problems all at once. It would enable people to avoid the stigma of a criminal conviction. It would raise money for the county justice system to use for other things. People who commit petty crimes would benefit, and the county would as well.

Critics have complained. They say that it is unfair for well-to-do people to be able to buy their way out of jail and the consequences of a criminal conviction. In Henry County, the program often results in diversion for whites and jail for blacks. Critics also say that Valeska piles the penalties onto the people who don't pay for diversion, and the result is that petty crimes get severe punishment—for those who don't pay. Valeska's supporters claim that he has uncovered a new source of revenue that comes only from those who can afford it; people who cannot afford it don't have to choose it.

You are a jail administrator, running a jail that is in financial trouble. A diversion program promises to provide funds for things that you really need—training for staff, new computers and software, security upgrades for the jail. The local prosecutor has asked if you want her to start up a diversion strategy along the lines of the one in Henry County.

Source: Shaila Dewan and Andrew L. Lehren, "An Alabama Prosecutor Sets the Penalties and Fills the Coffers," *The New York Times*, December 13, 2016, pp. 1, 14.

WRITING ASSIGNMENT: Should local diversion programs have entry fees that provide funds to improve local justice system capacity? What are the ethics of this policy? Write a memo to the prosecutor explaining your position.

SUMMARY

1 Describe the history of the jail and its current function in the criminal justice system.
Jails in the United States descend from feudal practices in twelfth-century England, in which the *shire reeve* (from which the word *sheriff* evolved) caught and held in custody people accused of breaking the king's law. English settlers brought these traditions and institutions with them to the colonies. Today, jails are the entryway into the criminal justice system and a place of confinement for less-serious law violators.

2 Describe who is in jail and why they are there.
There are two main groups of people in jail: those who are awaiting trial and those who are sentenced to terms of confinement of less than a year. Both populations are mostly young men, particularly young men of color. The majority of those in jail are serving sentences for crimes, with the remainder awaiting adjudication of charges (including probation and parole revocation).

3 Discuss the kinds of jails in the United States.
The smallest jails are police lockups. Most other jails are run by county governments, although there are also municipal jails under the authority of the larger cities. In some areas, regional jails serve multiple city and county governments.

4 List the main issues facing jails today.
Jails struggle with the need to provide services to people who are awaiting trial, in part because their stay may be of a short duration and also that they are not yet convicted of any crimes. Jails also face issues affecting their residents, especially mental health problems, substance abuse, medical problems, and legal needs.

5 Outline the problem of bail and list the main alternatives to bail.
Being held on bail is damaging to a person's life circumstances, as well as being detrimental to his or her chances at trial and sentence. Financial bail systems discriminate against the poor, who constitute the vast majority of the people in jail. Bail alternatives, such as release on recognizance and pretrial diversion, apply to only a portion of those awaiting trial.

6 Explain the problems of jail administration.
Jail administrators are legally liable for the treatment of people incarcerated in their facility. They must meet certain written standards, even if their facility lacks sufficient funds to meet them. Because jails often pay their employees less than other justice-related institutions do, recruiting and retaining high-quality personnel remains difficult. Finally, jail crowding and outmoded jail facilities make maintaining good programs extremely difficult.

7 Describe new developments in jails and jail programs.
To deal with the problems of jails, there has been a recent movement to increase the use of the new-generation jail, in which jail residents are kept in podular units instead of cells and security is maintained by direct supervision methods. Another new idea is to implement the community model for jails.

8 Critically assess the future of the jail.
Although jails are an expensive part of local government budgets, they are widely neglected by scholars and officials, and the public knows little about them. The prospects of jails are looking up, though, because of extensive efforts to renovate old jails and build new ones, and to design these replacements in ways that offer better services and improved security.

KEY TERMS

absconders (*p. 187*)
bail (*p. 184*)
community model for jails (*p. 194*)
day reporting center (*p. 184*)
direct supervision (*p. 193*)
electronic monitoring (*p. 184*)
fee system (*p. 173*)
lockup (*p. 175*)
new-generation jail (*p. 193*)
podular unit (*p. 193*)
pretrial diversion (*p. 184*)
preventive detention (*p. 187*)
Public Safety Assessment (*p. 187*)
regional jail (*p. 176*)
release on recognizance (*ROR*) (*p. 184*)
therapeutic justice (*p. 194*)
widening the net (*p. 187*)

FOR DISCUSSION

1. How do local politics affect jail administration? Should political influence be as extensive as it is? Does it help or hinder good correctional practices?
2. What special problems and needs do people in jail have? Why? What problems do these needs pose for jail administrators?
3. What are the pros and cons of preventive detention? How might it affect crime control? Due process?
4. How would you balance tensions between jail management and public safety?
5. What are some problems you would expect to encounter if you were in charge of providing rehabilitative programs in a jail?

FOR FURTHER READING

Buser, Mary E, *Lockdown on Rikers: Shocking Stories of Abuse and Injustice at New York's Notorious Jail*. New York: St Martin's Press, 2015. Award winning expose of problems and prospects for women doing time at Rikers Island.

Cornelius, Gary. *The American Jails: Cornerstone of Modern Corrections*. Upper Saddle River, NJ: Prentice-Hall, 2007. A contemporary critical assessment of the state of jails in the United States and the new directions in jail policy and practice.

Goldfarb, Ronald. *Jails: The Ultimate Ghetto*. Garden City, NY: Doubleday, 1975. Classic and still accurate critique of the U.S. jail.

Irwin, John. *The Jail*. Berkeley, CA: University of California Press, 1985. Classic description of the jail experience and personal reactions to it.

Mai, Chris, Mikelina Belaineh, Ram Subramanian, and Jacob Kang-Brown. *Broken Ground: Why America Keeps Building More Jails and What It Can Do Instead*. New York: Vera Institute of Justice, 2019.

Schwartz, Sunny. *Dreams from the Monster Factory: A Tale of Prison, Redemption, and One Woman's Fight to Restore Justice to All*. New York: Scribner, 2009. Describes the "Resolve to Stop the Violence" project in a San Francisco jail, an approach that creates a philosophy of empowerment and accountability.

Subramanian, Ram, Ruth Delaney, Stephen Roberts, et al. *Incarceration's Front Door: The Misuse of Jails in America*. New York: Vera Institute of Justice, 2015. A high-quality literature review and broad-scale critique of the problems of jails in the United States and recommendations for reform.

NOTES

1 National Inventory of Collateral Consequences of Conviction. *https://niccc.csgjusticecenter.org/*. Originally organized by the American Bar Association in accordance with the UNIFORM COLLATERAL CONSEQUENCES OF CONVICTION ACT § 4 (2010).

2 Jones, Michelle. "Biographic Mediation and the Formerly Incarcerated: How Dissembling and Disclosure Counter the Extended Consequences of Criminal Convictions," Special Issue—Biographic Mediation: On the Uses of Personal Disclosure in Bureaucracy and Politics. *Biography: An Interdisciplinary Quarterly* 42 (no 3, November 2019): 486–513.

3 "Unfreedom," as termed by Ruthie Gilmore Wilson, means a precarious state of life, bare life, holistically threatened by external forces operating upon the post-incarcerated ensuring the destruction of their opportunity.

4 Brooklyn Community Bail Fund, *2015–16 Annual Report* (New York: Brooklyn Community Bail Fund, 2016). https://brooklynbailfund.org.

5 Zhen Zeng, *Jail Inmates in 2018* (Washington, DC: U.S. Bureau of Justice Statistics, 2020), 3.

6 Ibid.

7 Todd D. Minton, *Census of Jails: Population Changes, 1999–2013* (Washington, DC: U.S. Bureau of Justice Statistics, 2015).

8 David Rothman, *Discovery of the Asylum* (Boston: Little, Brown, 1971), 56.

9 U.S. Bureau of Justice Statistics, *Statistical Tables*, March 2009, 5; see also Minton and Zeng, *Jail Inmates*, p. 4; Zhen Zeng, *Jail Inmates in 2018* (Washington, DC: U.S. Bureau of Justice Statistics, 2020).

10 James Stephan and Georgette Walsh, *Census of Jail Facilities* (Washington, DC: U.S. Bureau of Justice Statistics).

11 Minton, *Census of Jails*, p. 20.

12 R. Zhen Zeng, *Jail Inmates in 2018* (Washington, DC: U.S. Bureau of Justice Statistics, 2020), 7.

13 Ram Subramanian, Christian Henrichson, and Jacob Kang-Brown, *In Our Own Backyard: Confronting Growth and Disparities in American Jails* (New York: Vera Institute of Justice, 2015).

14 U.S. President's Commission on Law Enforcement and the Administration of Justice, *Task Force Report: Corrections* (Washington, DC: U.S. Government Printing Office, 1967), 79.

15 Compare Stephan and Walsh, *Census of Jail Facilities*, p. 4., to Zeng, *Jail Inmates in 2018*.

16 Zeng, *Jail Inmates in 2018*, p. 8.

17 E. Fuller Torrey, Mary T. Zdanowicz, Aaron D. Kennard, et al., *More Mentally Ill Persons Are in Jails and Prisons Than Hospitals: A Survey of the States* (Arlington, VA: Treatment Advocacy Center, 2010).
18 Jennifer Bronson and Marcus Berzofsky, *Indicators of Mental Health Problems Reported by Prisoners and Jail Inmates, 2011–2012* (Washington, DC: Bureau of Justice Statistics, 2017).
19 Fuller Torrey, Mary T. Zdanowicz, Aaron D. Kennard, et al. *The Treatment of Persons with Mental Illness in Prisons and Jails: A State Survey* (Arlington, VA, Treatment Advocacy Center, 2014).
20 Bronson and Berzofsky, *Indicators of Mental Health Problems*, p. 8.
21 Jennifer Bronson, Jessica Stroop, Stephanie Zimmer, and Marcus Berzofsky, *Drug Use, Dependence, and Abuse Among Prisoners and Jail Inmates, 2007–2009* (Washington, DC: Bureau of Justice Statistics, 2017).
22 Office of National Drug Control Policy, *ADAM II: 2013 Annual Report* (Washington, DC: Executive Office of the President, 2014).
23 Ram Subramanian, Ruth Delaney, Stephen Roberts, et al., *Incarceration's Front Door: The Misuse of Jails in America* (New York: Vera Institute of Justice, 2015), 13.
24 Bronson, Stroop, Zimmer, and Berzofsky, *Drug Use, Dependence, and Abuse*, p. 5.
25 Subramanian, Delaney, and Roberts, *Incarceration's Front Door*, p. 15.
26 Karishma A. Chari, Alan E. Simon, Carol J. DeFrances, and Laura Maruschak, *National Survey of Prison Health Care: Selected Findings* (Washington, DC: National Center for Health Statistics, 2016).
27 E. Ann Carson and Mary P. Cowhig, *Mortality in Local Jails, 2000–2016*. (Washington, DC: U.S. Bureau of Justice Statistics, 2020).
28 UCLA COVID-19 Behind Bars Project: https://docs.google.com/spreadsheets/d/1X6uJkXXS-O6eePLxw2e4JeRtM41uPZ2eRcOA_HkPVTk/edit#gid=1678228533.
29 New York City Criminal Justice Agency, *New York City Jail Population Reduction in the Time of COVID-19* (New York: CJA, May 25, 2020). http://criminaljustice.cityofnewyork.us/wp-content/uploads/2020/04/MOCJ-COVID-19-Jail-Reduction.pdf.
30 Cary Aspinwall, Kari Blakinger, Abbie Van Sickle, and Christie Thompson, "Coronavirus Transforming Jails Across the Country," *The Marshall Project*, March 21, 2020.
31 *Bell v. Wolfish*, 441 U.S. 520 (1979).
32 Brian A. Reaves, *Felony Defendants in Large Urban Counties*, 2009 (Washington, DC: U.S. Bureau of Justice Statistics, 2013), 6.
33 Thomas H. Cohen, *Pretrial Release and Misconduct in Federal District Courts, 2008–2010* (Washington DC: U.S. Bureau of Justice Statistics, 2012).
34 Zhen Zeng, *Jail Inmates in 2018*, p. 6.
35 Ibid, p. 7.
36 Gabrielle Banks, "Federal Judge: Harris Co. Bail System Unfair to Poor, Low-Level Defendants," *Houston Chronicle*, April 29, 2017.
37 Sima L. Clifasefi, Heather S. Lonczak, and Susan E. Collins, "Seattle's Law Enforcement Assisted Diversion (LEAD) Program: Within-Subjects Changes on Housing, Employment, and Income/Benefits Outcomes and Associations With Recidivism," *Crime & Delinquency* 63 (no. 4, 2017), 429–45; Susan E. Collins, Heather S. Lonczak, and Sima L. Clifasefi, "Seattle's Law Enforcement Assisted Diversion (LEAD) Program: Program Effects on Criminal Justice and Legal System Utilization and Costs," *Journal of Experimental Criminology* 15 (no. 2, 2019), 201–11.
38 Reaves, *Felony Defendants*, p. 21.
39 Ibid.
40 James C. Oleson, Christopher T. Lowenkamp, John Wooldredge, Marie Van Nostrand, and Timothy P. Cardigan, "The Sentencing Consequences of Federal Pretrial Supervision," *Crime & Delinquency*, 63 (3, 2017), 313–33.
41 Shima Baradaran and Frank L. McIntyre, "Predicting Violence," *Texas Law Review* 90 (no. 3, February 2012), 497–570.
42 National Partnership for Pretrial Justice, *Advancing Pretrial Justice*. April 2020. https://www.psapretrial.org.
43 *Schall v. Martin*, 467 U.S. 253 (1984); *United States v. Salerno*, 481 U.S. 739 (1987).
44 *McGirt v Oklahoma* argued May 11, 2020—decided July 9, 2020.
45 Jeff Mellow, Debbie Mukamal, Stefan LoBuglio, et al., *The Jail Administrator's Toolkit for Reentry* (Washington, DC: Urban Institute, 2008).
46 Andrea Woods and Portia Allen-Kyle, *A New Vision for Pretrial Justice in the United States* (New York: American Civil Liberties Association, March, 2019).
47 Zeng, *Jail Inmates in 2018*.
48 Ibid, p. 8.
49 Amanda Petteruti and Nastassia Walsh, *Jailing Communities: The Impact of Jail Expansion and Effective Public Strategies* (Washington, DC: Justice Policy Institute, 2008).
50 Chris Mai, Mikelina Belaineh, Ram Subramanian, and Jacob Kang-Brown, *Broken Ground: Why America Keeps Building More Jails and What It Can Do Instead* (New York: Vera Institute of Justice, 2019).
51 Lance Forsythe, Aretha Hicks, Penny B. Patton, and V. Morgan Moss, "Center for Community Justice's Community Model: The Jail Administrator's Best Friend," *American Jails* (January–February 2006), 35–41.
52 National Association of Counties. *State Prisoners in County Jails* (Lexington, KY: Author, 2010).
53 Jesse Bogan, "America's Jail Crisis," *Forbes*, www.forbes.com/2009/07/10/jails-houston-recession-businessbeltway-jails.html, July 13, 2009.

CHAPTER 8

Probation

© Mitsu Yasukawa/Northjersey.com via Imagn Content Services, LLC

Ricky Salazar of Paterson, NJ is on probation. He is also a public advocate for people under criminal justice authority to be able to vote. New Jersey's Governor Phil Murphy has called for reform of the state's felony disenfranchisement laws, and New Jersey has recently responded by passing laws that enable people on probation and parole to vote.

EVERYONE SEEMS TO BE TAKING A NEW LOOK AT PROBATION. As more people question the wisdom of mass incarceration, they look to probation to help ease the pressure created by large prison populations. The stakes are high. One economic policy think tank has estimated that up to $15 billion could be saved by using probation more often for people convicted of nonviolent crimes.[1]

After years—decades, really—of neglect and irrelevance, probation is suddenly brimming with new ideas. It seems that in every corner of the country, some new probation model is being advanced: HOPE Probation in Honolulu, Public Safety Realignment in California (see Chapter 1, pp. 12 and 17), RECLAIM Ohio in Chapter 8, the Robina Institute's "Rethinking Probation" model, and EXIT's plan for the future of probation—just to name a few. (See the Focus boxes throughout this chapter.)

But is probation up to the task?

Most people would say that probation needs to change. Although few citizens or political leaders give it much respect, it is by far the most extensively used form of corrections in the United States. Over half of all adults under correctional authority are serving probation sentences. In early 2017, this included more than 3.5 million people, or about two and one-half times the number of adults in prisons.[2] Escalating prison growth has captured the public's attention, but since 1985 the U.S. probation population has actually grown at a faster rate than the incarcerated population.

In fact, while it is well-known that U.S. prison populations are abnormally high compared to the rest of the world, many people are surprised to learn that U.S. probation rates are perhaps even more extreme. The U.S. probation rate is 1,389 per 100,000 citizens, or 1.5 percent of the population. Only Turkey (1,212 per 100,000 citizens) comes close to our rate; the third-highest probation rate in the world is Latvia (817 per 100,000 citizens), whose rate is lower than all but seven of the U.S. states. (In the state of Georgia, more than 5 percent of adults are on probation.) Notably, the European average probation rate is *one-fifth* that of the United States.[3] It has been argued that when probation is included in the mix, America's system of mass incarceration starts to emerge more clearly as a system of mass penology of all types.[4]

Despite the wide use of probation, media critics tend to give it short shrift, often portraying it as a "slap on the wrist." This notion is so widespread that a well-known scholarly work on correctional policy once referred to probation as "a kind of standing joke."[5] These views sharply contrast with official policies. For example, during the past decade alone the government devoted over a quarter of a billion dollars in federal funds to improve and expand probation, and supervision in the community is becoming the sanction for more and more people who have committed crimes. Further, advocates of intermediate sanctions point to probation as the base on which to build greater punishments.

What is really true about probation? How effective is it? How important is it today? In this chapter we describe the function of probation in corrections and review numerous studies of probation supervision and court services. Although in today's correctional environment probation is increasingly coupled with a variety of intermediate sanctions, in this chapter we consider traditional probation services. (Intermediate sanctions are covered in Chapter 9.)

Our review will demonstrate that, as in most other areas of corrections, probation agencies work amid social and political ambivalence about punishment. This ambivalence, together with uncertainty about treatment methods, leaves probation in a quandary: We ordinarily rely heavily on it in sentencing, but we show limited confidence in its corrective capacities.

LEARNING OBJECTIVES

After reading this chapter, you should be able to . . .

1. Describe the history and development of probation, including how it is organized today.
2. Describe the two functions of probation.
3. Discuss the purpose and content of the presentence investigation report.
4. List the major issues involved in the presentence investigation.
5. Describe the dynamics that occur among the probation officer, the person on probation, and the probation bureaucracy.
6. Identify the different kinds of probation conditions and explain why they are important.
7. Define *recidivism* and describe its importance to probation.
8. Define *evidence-based practice* and discuss its importance to probation.
9. Describe what is known about the effectiveness ofprobation supervision.
10. Discuss the revocation of probation, including "technical" revocation.

LO 1

Describe the history and development of probation, including how it is organized today.

THE HISTORY AND DEVELOPMENT OF PROBATION

Probation is the idea that in lieu of imprisonment, a person is allowed to serve a sentence while living in the community under supervision, demonstrating a willingness to abide by its laws. In this country, probation began with the innovative work of **John Augustus**, who was the first to provide bail for people under the authority of the Boston Police Court, in 1841. However, the roots of probation lie in earlier attempts, primarily in England, to mitigate the harshness of the criminal law.

BIOGRAPHY

JOHN AUGUSTUS
(1785–1859)

A Boston boot-maker known as the first probation officer. In helping people brought before the Boston courts, he acted as counsel, provided bail, and found housing for them.

Benefit of Clergy

From the 1200s until the practice was abolished in 1827, people accused of serious offenses in England could appeal to the judge for leniency by reading in court the text of Psalm 51. The original purpose of this benefit of clergy was to protect people under church authority, such as monks and nuns, from the power of the king's law. Because this benefit was gradually extended to protect ordinary citizens from capital punishment, Psalm 51 came to be known as the "neck verse." The requirement that the person be able to read favored the upper social classes. Eventually, common thugs memorized the verse so they could pretend to read it before the court and thus avail themselves of its protection; judges then became more arbitrary in granting the benefit. In the United States, benefit of clergy was criticized because of its unequal application and baffling legal character—charges often directed at probation today.

Judicial Reprieve

judicial reprieve A practice under English common law whereby a judge could suspend the imposition or execution of a sentence on condition of good behavior.

Judges have long understood the need to grant leniency on occasion, and they regularly seek ways to deflect the full punitive force of the law. In nineteenth-century England, **judicial reprieve** became widespread. Upon request, the judge could suspend either the imposition or execution of a sentence for a specified length of time on condition of good behavior. At the end of that time, the Crown could give a pardon.

In the United States, judicial reprieve took a different form and led to a series of legal controversies. Rather than limiting the duration of the reprieve, many judges suspended imposition of punishment as long as the person's behavior remained satisfactory. The idea was that a person who remained crime-free need not fear the power of the court; however, someone who committed another crime was subject to punishment for both crimes.

In 1916 the U.S. Supreme Court declared the discretionary use of such indefinite reprieves unconstitutional.[6] The Court recognized the occasional need to suspend a sentence temporarily because of appeals and other circumstances, but it found that indefinite suspension impinged on the powers of the legislative and executive branches to write and enforce laws. With this decision, the practices of probation became subject to the provisions of the states' penal codes.

In this austere building in the 1830s, Judge Peter Oxenbridge Thatcher of the Boston Municipal Court originated the practice of recognizance, which led to the development of probation.

Recognizance

In a search for alternative means to exercise leniency in sentencing, nineteenth-century judges began to experiment with extralegal forms of release. Much of this innovation occurred among the Massachusetts judiciary, whose influence on modern probation was enormous.

One of the trailblazers was Boston Municipal Court Judge Peter Oxenbridge Thatcher, the originator of the practice of **recognizance**. In 1830 Thatcher sentenced Jerusha Chase "upon her own recognizance for her appearance in this court whenever she was called for."[7] In 1837 Massachusetts made recognizance with monetary sureties into law. What made this important was the implied supervision of the court—the fact that the person's whereabouts and actions were subject to court involvement.

recognizance A formally recorded obligation to perform some act (such as keep the peace, pay a debt, or appear in court when called) entered by a judge to permit a person who has been charged with or convicted of a crime to live in the community, often on posting a sum of money as surety, which is forfeited by nonperformance.

Both reprieve and recognizance aimed at humanizing the criminal law and mitigating its harshness. The practices foreshadowed the move toward individualized punishment that would dominate corrections a century later. The major justifications for probation—flexibility in sentencing and individualized punishment—already had strong support. Yet an institutionalized way of performing recognizance functions was still needed.

As the first probation officer, John Augustus was the first to formalize court leniency. Because his philanthropic activities made Augustus a frequent observer in the Boston Police Court, the judge deferred sentencing a man charged with being a common drunkard and released him into Augustus's custody. At the end of a three-week probationary period, the man convinced the judge that he had reformed, therefore receiving a nominal fine.

Besides being the first to use the term *probation,* Augustus developed the ideas of the presentence investigation, supervision conditions, social casework, reports to the court, and revocation of probation. He screened his cases "to ascertain whether the prisoners were promising subjects for probation, and to this end it was necessary to take into consideration the previous character of the person, his age, and the influences by which he would in future be likely to be surrounded."[8] Augustus's methods were analogous to casework strategies: He gained his clients' confidence and friendship, and by helping them get a job or aiding their families in various ways, he helped them reform.

© Robert McGraw/Gazette

▲ *Probation officers work closely with judges and other court officers to help the justice system work more smoothly and to improve the quality of information for judicial decision-making.*

The Modernization of Probation

Probation eventually extended to every state and federal jurisdiction. As it developed, the field underwent a curious split. Augustus and his followers had contributed a humanitarian orientation that focused on reformation. In contrast, the new probation officers were drawn largely from the law enforcement community—retired sheriffs and policemen—who had their own orientation.

The strain between the so-called law enforcer role of probation, which emphasizes surveillance with close control on behavior, and the social worker role, which emphasizes provision of supportive services, continues today—with no resolution in sight. Advocates of the law enforcement model argue that conditions for community control must be realistic, individualized, and enforceable. Proponents of the social work model believe that supervision must include treatment to help the person become a worthwhile citizen. Each view has dominated at one time or another in the past half-century.

In the 1940s, leaders in probation and other correctional branches began to embrace ideas from psychology about personality and human development. Probation began to emphasize a medical model, with rehabilitation as its overriding goal.

This new focus moved probation work—or at least its rhetoric—to a more professional approach. Although only a very small number of probation departments fully implemented this approach, the ideas underlying it dominated the professional literature.

The medical model remained influential through the 1960s, when the reintegration model came to the fore. This model assumed that crime is a product of poverty, racism, unemployment, unequal opportunities, and other social factors. Probation was seen as central because it was the primary existing means of working with the person's problems in the context where the problems occur—the community. Methods of probation began to change from direct service (by psychological counseling) to service brokerage: After being assessed, clients were put in touch with appropriate community service agencies. Government studies heralded the reintegrative approach, and federal funds were shifted to community-based correctional agencies (discussed in Chapter 9), including probation agencies.

In the latter part of the 1970s, thinking about probation changed again in a manner that continues to this day. The goals of rehabilitation and reintegration have given way to an orientation widely referred to as *risk management*. The goal here is to minimize the probability of a new offense, especially by applying tight controls over the person's activities and maintaining careful surveillance. Risk management combines values of the just deserts model of the criminal sanction with the idea that the community deserves protection.[9]

Today, people are placed on probation in one of three ways. Most commonly, judges impose a sentence of probation directly (applying to a majority of those on probation). Often, a judge imposes a sentence of incarceration (prison or jail) that is suspended pending compliance with conditions set by the judge and monitored by probation. Sometimes, the court will require that some period of incarceration be served prior to probation; this is called a "split sentence."

This last option was quite popular in the 1990s, but its use has waned in the last few years. This may be because many people are in jail while awaiting trial or because prison space is limited. In addition, judges may use other sentencing arrangements, including the following:

1. *Modification of sentence:* The original sentencing court reconsiders the prison sentence shortly after it is imposed and modifies it to probation.
2. *Shock incarceration:* A person sentenced to incarceration is released after a period of confinement (the shock) and resentenced to probation.
3. *Intermittent incarceration:* A person on probation spends weekends or nights in a local jail.

Who gets probation? In the past it was thought that probation should be reserved for people being convicted for the first time who had committed lesser crimes. This has changed over time so that today 59 percent of people placed on probation have been convicted of a felony, and about one-fifth have been convicted of a violent crime.[10] The characteristics of people on probation are shown in Figure 8.1. (See also "Myths in Corrections.")

Clearly, probation practices reflect the social forces of the time. For instance, the emphasis on psychiatric social work flowed naturally from the idea of corrections as reformative, a vision held by religious and social reformers of the day. Further, the reintegration movement represented a shift from imprisonment toward services such as job training and education. This was consistent with President Lyndon Johnson's vision of the Great Society, which would create equal opportunities for all citizens and eliminate discrimination,

MYTHS in Corrections

Who Is on Probation?

THE MYTH: Probation is a sanction that is reserved for low-level crimes.

THE REALITY: Compared with people in prison, twice as many people on probation have been convicted of assault, and one-third more have been convicted of burglary. Further, the number of people convicted of sexual assault is 80 percent of the number in prison for that offense.

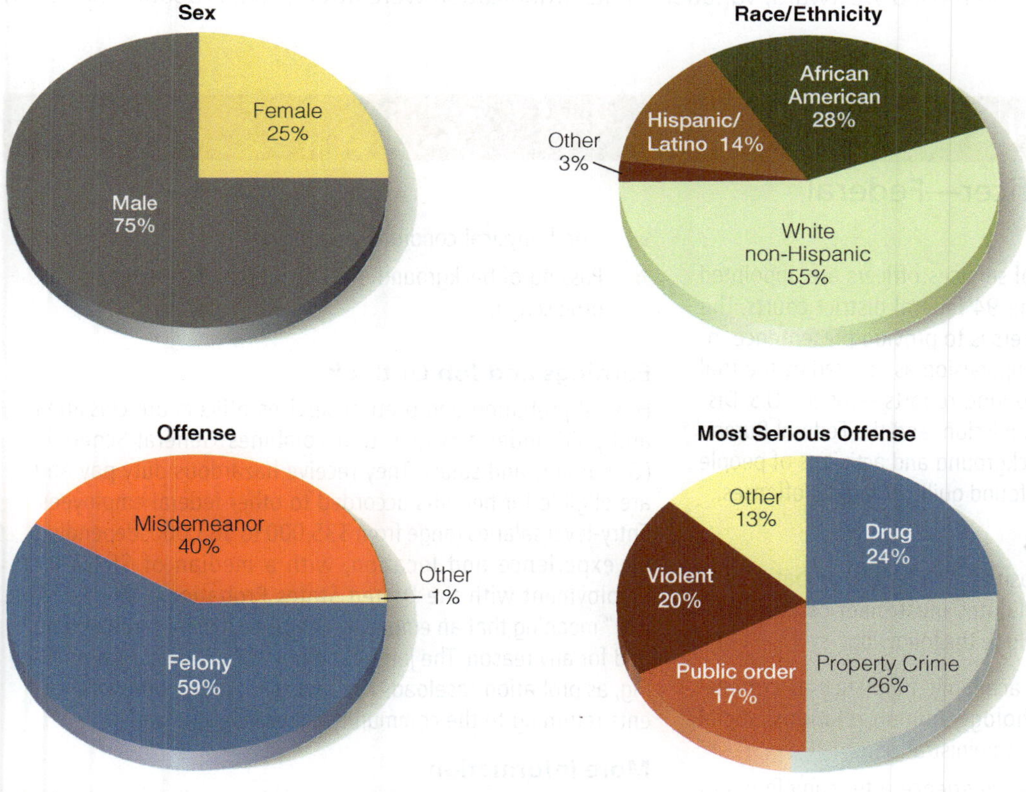

FIGURE 8.1 Characteristics of Adults on Probation

Although probation was originally used mainly for first-timers convicted of lesser crimes, many of today's clients have been sentenced for felonies and other serious offenses.

Source: Danielle Kaeble, *Probation and Parole in the United States, 2016* (Washington, DC: Bureau of Justice Statistics 2018), 5.

poverty, and injustice. When the Great Society failed to materialize, attention turned to the responsibility of society to protect its citizens from crime. Thus, the recent emphasis on risk management sprang from widespread public demands that the justice system be streamlined and that it focus on reducing crime. Many see combining probation with periods of incarceration as a way to make probation "tougher" and more effective at reducing crime.

community justice A model of justice that emphasizes reparation to the victim and the community, approaching crime from a problem-solving perspective, and citizen involvement in crime prevention.

Today, there has been a growing interest in probation's role as a part of **community justice**, a philosophy that emphasizes reparation to the victim and the community, problem-solving strategies instead of adversarial procedures, and increased citizen involvement in crime prevention. By breaking away from traditional bureaucratic practices, community justice advocates hope to develop a more flexible and responsive form of local justice initiatives—and many see probation as leading the way. (See Chapter 22 for more.)

THE ORGANIZATION OF PROBATION TODAY

Originating in court, the first probation agencies were units of the judicial branches of city and county governments, primarily in the eastern United States. The first full-time federal probation officer was appointed in 1927. "Careers in Corrections" offers a view of work as a federal probation officer (compare this with the Careers feature on state and county probation officers later in the chapter). As the idea of probation caught on and moved westward, variations in its organization were attempted. Probation has been

CAREERS IN CORRECTIONS

Probation Officer—Federal

Nature of the Work

Federal probation and pretrial services officers are appointed by the judiciary in each of the 94 federal district courts. The primary mission of these officers is to provide presentence investigations and community supervision as ordered by the trial court. The work includes preparing reports—for the U.S. District Court, the U.S. Parole Commission, and the Federal Bureau of Prisons—regarding the background and activities of people charged with or having been found guilty of federal offenses.

Required Qualifications

To qualify for an entry-level position as a federal probation and pretrial services officer, candidates must meet certain minimum requirements, which include the following:

- Bachelor's degree in an academic field such as criminal justice, sociology, psychology, human relations, social work, business, or public administration.
- Progressively responsible experience after completion of the bachelor's degree in such fields as probation, pretrial services, parole, or corrections, or work in addiction treatment. A master's degree in one of the accepted fields may be substituted for the required work experience.
- Good physical condition and health.
- Passing of background investigation andpre-employment drug screen.

Earnings and Job Outlook

Federal probation and pretrial services officers are classified and paid under a system that combines General Schedule (GS) grades and salary. They receive hazardous duty pay and are eligible for benefits accorded to other federal employees. Entry-level salaries range from $35,000 to $83,000, depending on experience and location, with a median of $51,240. Employment with the United States Probation Office is "at will," meaning that an employee can be terminated at any time and for any reason. The job outlook for these officers is promising, as probation caseloads rise and the number of federal clients returning to the community increases.

More Information

You can obtain additional information about this occupation from the Occupational Career Outlook Handbook website: Probation Officer Careers, Jobs, and Training Information.

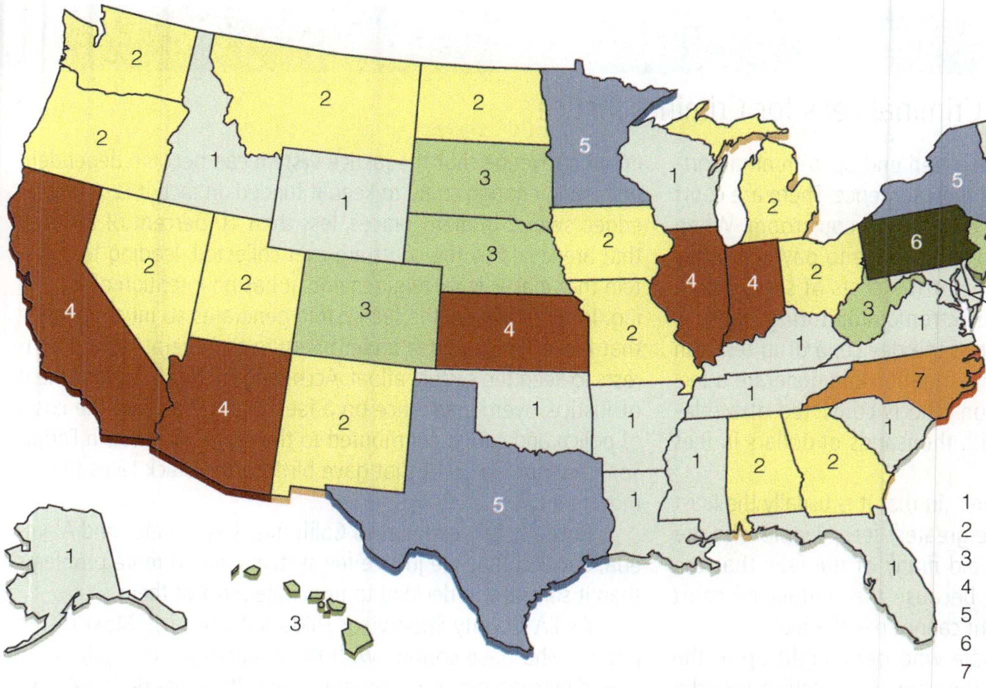

	Adult Probation	Juvenile Probation
1	State executive	State executive
2	State executive	Local judiciary
3	State judiciary	State judiciary
4	Local judiciary	Local judiciary
5	Local executive	Local executive
6	Local executive	Local judiciary
7	State executive	State judiciary

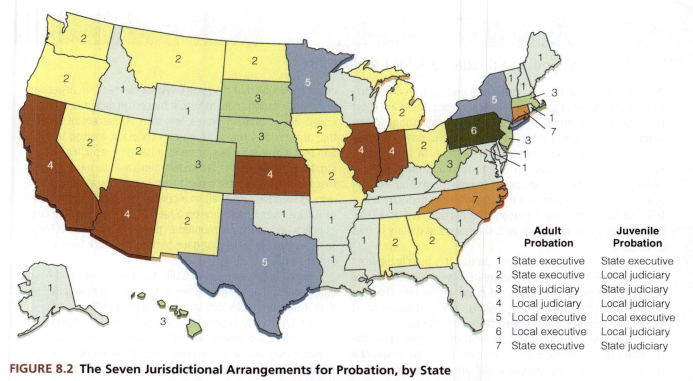

FIGURE 8.2 The Seven Jurisdictional Arrangements for Probation, by State

The organization of probation varies depending on the traditions and politics of state and local governments.

Source: American Correctional Association, *2010 Directory of Adult and Juvenile Correctional Departments, Institutions, Agencies, and Probation and Parole Authorities*

placed in the executive branch, it has been subjected to statewide unification, and it has been consolidated with parole. Figure 8.2 shows the seven jurisdictional patterns of probation organization nationwide, including the differing arrangements for adult and juvenile probation.

The organization of probation involves three issues concerning whether it should be (1) centralized or decentralized, (2) administered by the judiciary or the executive branch, and combined with parole services or not.

Should Probation Be Centralized or Decentralized?

The centralization issue concerns the location of the authority that administers probation services. Proponents of decentralization argue that an agency administered by a city or county instead of a state is smaller, more flexible, and better able to respond to the unique problems of the community. Because decentralized probation draws its support from the community and the local government, it can offer more-appropriate supervision for its clients and make better use of existing community resources than centralized probation can.

In contrast, centralization places authority for a state's probation activities in a single state-wide administrative body. Proponents of this approach assert that local probation has tended to follow outdated practices and to lack professionalism. State agencies, they argue, are larger, can train staff to take a variety of roles, and can implement broader programs with greater equality in supervision and services. (For information on how California's state legislature has treated probation, see "California Public Safety Realignment.")

FOCUS ON

POLICY: Ending Criminal Fees for Criminal Justice

When people break the law, they often end up with an assortment of justice fees tacked onto their sentence. There are court fees that pay for some of the cost of the courtroom. When people are placed on probation, many have to pay a monthly probation fee to reimburse some of the costs of supervision. For those who are placed on electronic monitoring, there is usually a rental fee for the cost of the device; a drug test can result in a fee; a presentence investigation can generate a fee. It is not uncommon for a person who is convicted of a relatively minor crime to end up with thousands of dollars in fees to be paid.

The justice fee system is ironic, in that it is usually the least serious crimes that generate the greatest fees. People who are sentenced to prison usually avoid many of the fees that the everyday misdemeanants face, because the sentencing court knows that people in confinement cannot pay the fees.

Yet neither can most people who get caught up in the criminal justice system, even if they are sentenced to spend a day behind bars. Most people in jail are there because they cannot afford to put up bail—often as little as 10 percent of 5,000. It is no surprise that many fees go unpaid, causing a crisis of credibility. After all, if a person is otherwise doing well, but cannot afford to pay the fees, is it really in anyone's interests to send them back to jail?

Advocates of the fee system argue that it is simply fair to make the people who break the law pay for the costs of enforcing the law. Why should the taxpayer bear the full brunt of an expensive criminal justice system?

But the fee system makes it harder for people who have broken the law to get their lives back on track. It also generates enough revenue that the justice system can become dependent on having enough crime to keep it funded. In fact, it is a double-edged sword. In many places, less than 10 percent of the fees that are levied by the court are ever collected, leading to a system that makes legal requirements it has no intention of enforcing. In other places, the fee system generates so much revenue that law enforcement is under pressure to generate enough arrests to keep the system afloat. According to the U.S. Department of Justice, overdependence on a fee system that paid the costs of police and courts contributed to the police violence in Ferguson, Missouri, in 2014 that gave birth to the Black Lives Matter movement.

Recently two counties in California, Los Angeles and Alameda, decided that the justice fee system created more problems than it solved, and decided to terminate most of them.

As LA County Supervisor Hilda Solis put it, "Most of the people who have contact with the criminal justice system are already struggling to make ends meet. It's most definitely not the purpose of the justice system to punish poor people for their poverty."

Today, many observe it is time for the fee system to go. What is happening in California may be a bellwether for the rest of the nation.

Sources: Jacki Botts, "Los Angeles County Eliminates Criminal Fees. Will the Rest of California Follow?" *CalMatters*. Published online: February 19, 2020; Peter Hegarty, "Alameda County Eliminates Some Criminal Justice Fees that Saddle Inmates," *East Bay Times*, November 21, 2018; U.S. Department of Justice, *Investigation of the Ferguson Police Department* (Washington, DC: U.S. Department of Justice, March 2015).

Who Should Administer Probation?

Although the recent trend has been away from judicially administered probation, many observers (especially those who seek greater accountability in probation) believe that the probation function rightfully belongs under the judiciary. The usual claim is that under judicial administration, probation is more responsive to the desires of the sentencing judge, who is more likely to scrutinize supervision when it is performed by judicial employees. Also, the morale of probation officers who work closely with judges may be higher than that of other probation officers.

Proponents of placing probation under the executive branch argue that the judiciary is ill prepared to manage a human services operation. To coordinate and upgrade the quality of a human services operation such as probation requires the full attention of professional public administrators. It is argued that placing probation under the executive branch results in better allocation of probation services, increased interaction and administrative coordination between corrections and allied human services, increased access to the legislature and the budgeting process, and more-appropriate service priorities.

Should Probation Be Combined with Parole?

Both probation and parole supervise people who are serving portions of their sentences in the community. Indeed, the growth in the use of split sentences and shock probation means that probation often begins after a jail or even prison term—just as with parole.

Because of these similarities, many states have placed probation and parole functions under a single agency, which promotes more-efficient hiring and training practices. Arguably, such comprehensive approaches also promote the professionalization of community supervision officers.

However, some experts suggest that subtle but important distinctions between the clients of probation and parole are hard to sustain in a unified system. People on probation are usually less deeply involved in criminal lifestyles, while people on parole face serious problems in reentering the community after longer incarceration (see Chapter 16). These differences call for different handling, which some people believe can best be done by separate agencies.

No solution to the problem of how to organize probation is at hand. Rather than searching for a single "best" way to organize probation, considering how it will work in a given state or region may be more fruitful. For example, in jurisdictions with a tradition of strong local government, decentralized probation under the executive branch may be best, whereas states with a strong central bureaucracy or strong judiciary may choose to place probation there. Figure 8.3 shows that states vary dramatically in their use of probation. Further, no clear pattern has appeared in the relationship between the way probation is organized and how frequently it is used.

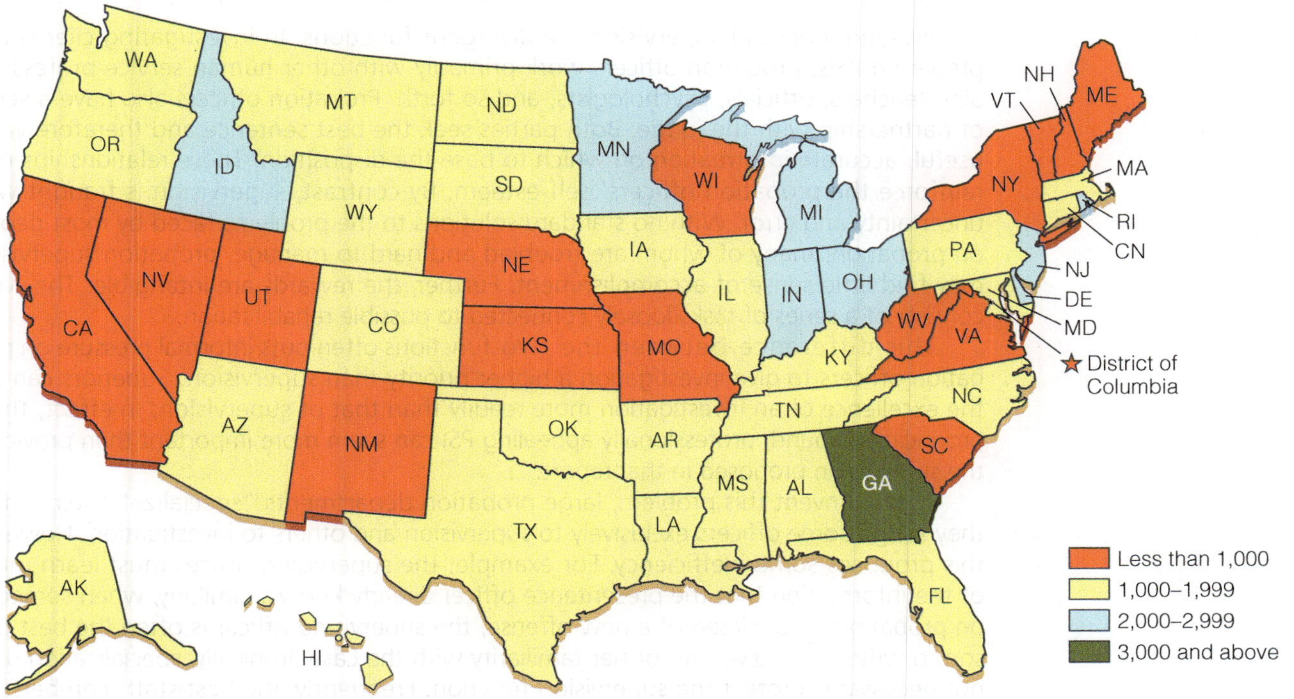

FIGURE 8.3 State Variations in the Use of Probation

Some states make greater use of probation as a criminal sanction than others. Unlike incarceration rates, which are higher in the southern and western states, there is no regional pattern in probation use.

Source: Danielle Kaeble, *Probation and Parole in the United States, 2016* (Washington, DC: Bureau of Justice Statistics, 2018), Appendix: Table 2.

LO 2

Describe the two functions of probation.

THE DUAL FUNCTIONS OF PROBATION: INVESTIGATION AND SUPERVISION

presentence investigation (PSI) An investigation and summary report of a convicted person's background that helps the judge decide on an appropriate sentence. Also known as a presentence report.

Probation officers have traditionally performed two major functions: investigation and supervision. Regardless of the specifics of a given probation agency's structure or practices, certain aspects of investigation and supervision are uniform.

Investigation involves the preparation of a **presentence investigation (PSI)**, which the judge uses in sentencing a person who has been convicted of a crime. Typically, the court orders the PSI after the conviction (often on a guilty plea). Before the sentencing date, the probation officer conducts the investigation and prepares the PSI.

The PSI process typically begins with an interview to obtain basic background information on the person to be sentenced. The probation officer then seeks to verify, clarify, and explore the information derived (or omitted) from the initial interview. The final PSI document summarizes and evaluates the officer's findings, and often recommends a sentence.

Supervision begins once the person is sentenced to probation. Supervision policies and practices vary greatly among agencies but usually involve three steps:

1. The probation officer establishes a relationship with the client and defines the roles of the officer and the expectations for the client.
2. The officer and client establish supervision goals that comply with conditions established by the court (often directed at helping overcome significant needs or problems in the client's life).
3. On the basis of the client's response to supervision, the officer decides how to terminate probation. Options include early termination because of satisfactory adjustment, termination because the sentence has expired, or revocation because of a new conviction or violation of probation conditions set by the judge or probation officer.

Investigation and supervision are divergent functions. In investigating clients and preparing PSIs, probation officers work primarily with other human service professionals—teachers, officials, psychologists, and so forth. Probation officers also have a sense of partnership with the judge: Both parties seek the best sentence and therefore value useful, accurate information on which to base the disposition. These relationships may reinforce the probation officers' self-esteem. By contrast, supervision is fraught with uncertainty and error. With no standard solutions to the problems faced by most people on probation, many of whom are troubled and hard to manage, probation supervisors may find little sense of accomplishment. Further, the rewards are intangible: The work consists of a series of tasks loosely connected to possible rehabilitation.

This difference between the two functions often puts informal pressure on probation officers to give investigation a higher priority than supervision. Superiors can see the excellence of an investigation more readily than that of supervision; in effect, then, producing a sound, professionally appealing PSI can seem more important than providing the supervision proposed in that report.

To circumvent this problem, large probation departments "specialize" their staff—they assign some officers exclusively to supervision and others to investigation. However, this produces some inefficiency. For example, the supervising officer must learn much of the information that the presentence officer already knows. Similarly, when someone on probation is convicted of a new offense, the supervising officer is often the best person to write a PSI, given his or her familiarity with the case. Ironically, specialization does not necessarily protect the supervision function. Frequently, the best staff members are assigned to the PSI units, and top priority is given to maintaining an adequate PSI workforce, even in the face of unwieldy supervision caseloads.

In any case, a probation system whose workers are specialized is much easier to manage. Such a system enhances accountability for the timeliness and accuracy of PSIs and more easily ensures the operation of supervision routines according to agency policies. Therefore, the trend is toward specialization of these functions, almost as if they were two different jobs.

The Investigative Function

LO 3

Discuss the purpose and content of the presentence investigation report.

As noted earlier, the presentence investigation serves mainly to help the judge select an appropriate sentence. It also helps with the eventual classification decisions that must be made regarding probation, incarceration, and parole agencies; it aids treatment planning and parole decisions; and it serves as a document for systematic research.

Purpose Apart from its many other uses, the PSI plays its most important role in the sentencing process. This is especially true because there are no uniformly accepted guidelines or rationales for sentencing. Individual judges, even in the same court system, may weigh factors in the case differently. The PSI must therefore be comprehensive enough to provide necessary information to judges with a variety of sentencing perspectives.

The rehabilitative goal requires assessment of treatment needs. The consensus is that imprisonment has limited rehabilitative value, so in practice a commitment to rehabilitation poses two questions: (1) are there special problems, circumstances, or needs that led to the criminal behavior? and (2) can these problems be overcome by community services combined with careful supervision to prevent further criminal involvement?

The increasingly popular goal of community protection leads to other questions. With risk management in mind, the probation officer assesses the likelihood of continued criminal behavior if the individual is allowed to remain in the community. Estimates of risk are based on degree of prior criminal involvement, stability of the person's lifestyle, and pattern of prior adjustment to correctional treatment.

In practice, two circumstances constrain the influence of the PSI in sentencing. First, because goals are unclear, judges often seek some balance between rehabilitation and risk management. Rather than pursue a single value in sentencing, judges ordinarily ask a more complicated question: If the person's risk to the community is low, is there some rehabilitative reason to keep him or her in the community—a reason strong enough to overcome the objection that probation tends to depreciate the seriousness of the crime?

The second constraint is plea bargaining. When the sentence is proposed in the process of negotiation between the prosecutor and the defense attorney, the role of the PSI is altered. Instead of helping the judge decide the case, the PSI helps determine whether the negotiated agreement is appropriate. To counter this problem, some probation officials argue that PSIs should be written before the initial plea. Although support exists for this innovation, it is unclear whether in the long run PSIs written before plea bargaining would be feasible for most cases.

According to some, such continued constraints mean that the PSI's importance is vastly overestimated. Often, they say, the sentence is determined by facts about the case—the offense, the plea agreement—that are far more obvious than anything the PSI can uncover. Others argue that the traditional PSI is a relic of the medical model of corrections, when judges relied on clinical assessments of people awaiting sentencing. Small wonder that so many judges simply scan a PSI for a few relevant facts so they can make sure that their intended decision makes sense.

LO 4

List the major issues involved in the presentence investigation.

Contents For many years the ideal PSI was thought to be a lengthy narrative description of the circumstances of the crime and the defendant's situation, culminating in a recommendation for sentencing and a justification for that recommendation. Early PSI-writing manuals stressed length and breadth of coverage. Now, however, people are questioning the assumption that more is better. Information theory suggests that PSIs that are short and to the point are not necessarily less useful than long ones.

A shortened, directed, and standardized PSI format is becoming more common (see "Sample Presentence Report"). This approach may seem less professional, but in practice it places even greater responsibility on the probation officer. It requires the officer to know the case and the penal code well enough to know precisely what information the judge will require to evaluate the sentencing options.

To be useful, PSIs must offer valid and reliable information. Two techniques improve validity and reliability: verification and objectivity. *Verification* occurs when PSI information

FOCUS ON

CORRECTIONAL PRACTICE: Sample Presentence Report

State of New Mexico
Corrections Department
Field Service Division
Santa Fe, New Mexico 87501
Date: January 4, 2022
To: The Honorable Manuel Baca
From: Presentence Unit, Officer Brian Gaines
Re: Richard Knight

Appearing before Your Honor for sentencing is 20-year-old Richard Knight who, on November 10, 2021, pursuant to a Plea and Disposition Agreement, entered a plea of guilty to Aggravated Assault Upon a Peace Officer (Deadly Weapon) (Firearm Enhancement), as charged in Information Number 10-5736900. The terms of the agreement stipulate that the maximum period of incarceration be limited to one year, that restitution be made on all counts and charges whether dismissed or not, and that all remaining charges in the Indictment and DA Files 39780 be dismissed.

PRIOR RECORD

The defendant has no previous convictions. An arrest at age 15 for disorderly conduct was dismissed after six months of "informal probation."

EVALUATION

The defendant is an only child, born and raised in Albuquerque. He attended West Mesa High School until the 11th grade, at which time he dropped out. Richard declared that he felt school was "too difficult" and that he decided that it would be more beneficial for him to obtain steady employment rather than to complete his education. The defendant further stated that he felt it was "too late for vocational training" because of the impending one-year prison sentence he faces, due to the Firearm Enhancement penalty for his offense.

The longest period of time the defendant has held a job has been for six months with Frank's Concrete Company. He has been employed with the Madrid Construction Company since August 2021 (verified). Richard lives with his parents, who provide most of his financial support. Conflicts between his mother and himself, the defendant claimed, precipitated his recent lawless actions by causing him to "not care about anything." He stressed the fact that he is now once again "getting along" with his mother. Although the defendant contended that he doesn't abuse drugs, he later contradicted himself by declaring that he "gets drunk every weekend." He noted that he was inebriated when he committed the present offense.

In regard to the present offense, the defendant recalled that other individuals at the party attempted to stab his friend and that he and his companion left and returned with a gun in order to settle the score. Richard claimed remorse for his offense and stated that his past family problems led him to spend most of his time on the streets, where he became more prone to violent conduct. The defendant admitted being a member of the 18th Street Gang.

RECOMMENDATION

It is respectfully recommended that the defendant be sentenced to three years' incarceration and that the sentence be suspended. It is further recommended that the defendant be incarcerated for one year as to the mandatory Firearm Enhancement and then placed on three years' probation under the following special conditions:

1. That restitution be made to Juan Lopez in the amount of $662.40
2. That the defendant either maintain full-time employment or obtain his GED [general equivalency diploma]
3. That the defendant discontinue fraternizing with the 18th Street Gang members and terminate his own membership in the gang

is cross-checked with some other source for accuracy. If the client claims during the PSI interview that he or she has no drinking problem, for example, the investigator checks with others such as the family, friends, and employer before writing "No apparent problem" in the PSI.

Objectivity is aided by avoiding vague conclusions about the case. For instance, rather than describe the client as *immature* (a term subject to various interpretations), the PSI writer might describe patterns of behavior that suggest immaturity: poor work attendance, lack of understanding of the seriousness of the offense, and so forth.

The victims' rights movement of the 1970s included an emphasis on having the PSI provide detail about the impact of the crime on the victim. Called the **victim impact statement**, this new section of the standard PSI required the probation officer to interview the victim and determine, in the victim's own words, the damage caused by the crime. Victims' advocates claimed that adding these statements to the PSI would let the judge better appraise the seriousness of the crime and choose the most appropriate sentence.

victim impact statement A description in a PSI of the costs of the crime for the victim, including emotional and financial losses.

Critics are worried that the judge would be unfairly prejudiced by articulate victims and those who overestimated their true losses. However, experience has shown that the addition of victim impact statements to PSIs has not increased the willingness of judges to impose harsh sentences.

Recommendations Sentencing recommendations in PSIs are controversial because a person without authority to sentence is nevertheless suggesting what the sentence should be. For this reason, not all probation systems include it in the PSI. Yet there is a well-established tradition of sentence recommendations by nonjudicial court actors; normally, the judge solicits recommendations from the defense and prosecution, as well as from the probation officer. What the probation officer says may carry extra weight because it is presumably an unbiased evaluation of the situation based on thorough research by someone who understands the usefulness of probation and is familiar with community resources. These considerations may explain why judges so often follow the recommendations in the PSI.

The congruence of the PSI recommendation and the sentences ranges from 70 to over 90 percent. Of course, it is hard to know whether judges are following the officers' advice or whether the officers' experience has given them the ability to come up with recommendations that the judges will select. If the reason for the congruence between the probation officer's recommendations and the sentences imposed is the judge's confidence in the officer's analysis, that confidence may be misplaced. One evaluation found that "in only a few instances did people recommended for probation behave significantly better than those recommended for prison."[11] The study speculated that perhaps this prognostic inaccuracy arose because officers did not have time to verify information reported in the PSI because of their heavy caseloads.

The recommendation may be most useful when a plea-bargaining agreement includes a sentence. In such cases the PSI is a critical check on the acceptability of the negotiated settlement, permitting the judge to determine whether any factors in the offense or in the person's background might indicate that the agreement should be rejected.

Disclosure In view of the importance of the PSI to the sentencing decision, one would think that the defense would have a right to see it. After all, it may contain inadvertent irrelevancies or inaccuracies that the defense would want to dispute at the sentencing hearing.

Nevertheless, in many states the defense does not receive a copy of the report. The case most often cited in this regard is *Williams v. New York* (1949), in which the judge imposed a death sentence on the basis of evidence in the confidential PSI despite the jury's recommendation of a life sentence.[12] The U.S. Supreme Court upheld the judge's decision to deny the defense access to the report, although without such access the defense was incapable of challenging its contents at the sentencing hearing.

Cases and state law since 1949 have reduced the original restrictive impact of *Williams*. For example, at least one circuit court has held that the PSI cannot refer to illegally seized evidence excluded from a trial.[13] Sixteen states require full disclosure of the PSI; in the other states, the practice is generally to "cleanse" the report and then disclose it. Cleansing involves deleting two kinds of statements that should not be shared with the client: (1) confidential comments from a private citizen that, if known by the client, might endanger the citizen, and (2) clinical statements or evaluations that might be psychologically damaging to the client if disclosed. Many judges allow the defense to present a written challenge of any disclosed contents of the PSI.

Private PSIs Private investigative firms have recently begun to provide judges with PSIs. These firms work in one of two ways. Some contract with the defense to conduct comprehensive background checks and provide judges with creative sentencing options as alternatives to incarceration. In this approach, often called **client-specific planning**, the firm serves as a defendant's advocate at the sentencing stage. In the second approach, the court hires a private investigator to provide a neutral PSI.

client-specific planning Process by which private investigative firms contract with the person who was convicted to conduct comprehensive background checks and suggest to judges creative sentencing options as alternatives to incarceration.

FOCUS ON

PRACTICE: Technology and Probation

As the world is being changed by the growing use of social apps in everyday life, so is probation.

Probation officers have always used phones in their work. They routinely make calls to clients, partnering social services agencies, other law enforcement agencies, employers, and many others as they carry out their dual functions of investigation and supervision. For many years, this was a part of the desk job portion of the probation officer's day. Today, however, like everyone else, probation officers are always with their phones. It has changed the way they work.

Many probation officers use their phones to text clients, reminding them of appointments and court dates. Studies show that text reminders significantly reduce the rates of missed appointments and court date no-shows. Smart phones can be used for short, unplanned face-time interviews with clients, and the camera on a phone can be used to verify which family members are in the company of a client at any given time.

Recently, the National Science Foundation and the National Institute of Justice have announced grants to test whether GPS technology and "artificial intelligence" (AI) systems in phones can be adapted to improve support for people under community supervision.

The GPS systems let probation officers know of client's comings and goings, which is an obvious improvement in the capacity of surveillance. AI can help learn what strategies work best for people on probation and parole. Both grant programs are designed to see if technology can help in services, not just control.

"For too long, we've focused on catching offenders when they screw up. It used to be 'Tail, nail and jail,'" says Ron Corbett, project co-director and former commissioner of the Massachusetts Probation Service.

Technology is here to stay. It is easy to see how the new technologies can be used to increase the surveillance and control functions of probation supervision. Can it become a central part of improving the way probation provides services?

Sources: April Pattavina and Ron Corbett, "How Smartphone Technology Can Link the Theoretical, Policy, and Practical Contexts of Supervision Reform: Voices from the Field," *Victims & Offenders* 14 (no. 7, 2019): 777–92; Katharine Webster, "How Next-gen Electronic Monitoring Could Aid Probation and Parole Officers," *CorrectionsOne.Com*, November 7, 2017; Brannon Green and Christopher Rigano, *Specialized Smartphones Could Keep Released Offenders on Track for Successful Reentry*. National Institute of Justice, April 20, 2020. https://nij.ojp.gov/topics/articles/specialized-smartphones-could-keep-released-offenders-track-successful-reentry?utm_source=govdelivery&utm_medium=email&utm_campaign=articles.

Privately conducted PSIs have sparked controversy. Because the client pays for this service, many people view it as an unfair advantage for the upper- and middle-class individuals who can afford the special consideration the advocacy report provides. These concerns are well taken; as advocates of private PSIs point out, their reports often result in less severe sentences for their clients. (For another take on private probation services, see "The 'Client-Funded' Model for Probation.")

The neutral private PSI also raises serious issues. Proponents say that private investigators do what the probation department does—only better. Yet critics question whether private firms ought to be involved in the quasi-judicial function of recommending sentences. They say the liability of private investigators for the accuracy and relevance of the information that they provide to courts is unclear. Also, private PSIs, when purchased by the court, probably cost taxpayers more than do the traditional alternatives.

LO 5

Describe the dynamics that occur among the probation officer, the person on probation, and the probation bureaucracy.

The Supervision Function

People placed on probation supervision come from a mix of backgrounds, and the charges against them represent a range of seriousness. Compared with those in prison and jail, people on probation are more likely to be white and slightly more likely to be female (see Table 8.1). Of the 3.7 million on probation, half had at least one conviction before they were arrested on the charge leading to probation. The variety of people on probation calls for a range of supervision strategies.

As in the case of PSIs, probation supervision follows universally accepted standards. Indeed, both probation officers and clients generally enjoy wide latitude. To show how

TABLE 8.1 Ethnicity and Sex of People on Probation and People in Jail and Prison

Compared to people confined in prison or jail, people on probation are more likely to be white and female.

	Ethnicity				Sex	
	White	Amer	Hispanic	Other	Male	Female
Probation	55%	30%	13%	2%	75%	25%
Jail	50	33	15	2	85	16
Prison	33	36	25	6	93	7

Sources: *Probation and Parole in the United States, 2017-2018.*

LO 6

Identify the different kinds of probation conditions and explain why they are important.

this latitude is exercised in practice, we describe the three major elements of supervision: the officer, the client, and the bureaucracy.

The Officer The probation officer faces role conflict in virtually every aspect of the job. Most of this conflict has its genesis in the uneasy combination of two responsibilities: (1) enforcing the law and (2) providing services. Although the responsibilities may be compatible, they often are not.

power The ability to force a person to do something he or she does not want to do.

authority The ability to influence a person's actions in a desired direction without resorting to force.

The chief conflict between the officer's two roles arises from the use of power and authority. In human relations these terms have very specific meanings. **Power** is the ability to force a person to do something he or she does not want to do. **Authority** is the ability to influence a person's actions in a desired direction without resorting to force. Thus, a person who chooses to exercise power in a relationship can almost always be shown to lack authority.

The problem of power and authority is a thorny one for probation officers. Officers are expected to exercise the power of law in controlling those under their supervision. This is one reason that in many jurisdictions probation officers are legally classified as "peace officers," with the power of arrest. Yet the actual power of the role is less than it seems: Short of exercising their formal power to arrest or detain their clients, probation officers can normally do little to force them to comply with the law. And the powers of arrest and revocation are themselves carefully constrained by case law and statutes.

Blend Images/John Fedele/Getty Images

▲ *Field work is a key responsibility of probation officers—making sure that everything is as it should be at the home and workplace of the person on probation.*

The lack of substantive power explains why probation officers rely heavily on their authority: It is a more efficient and ultimately more effective tool. The techniques of authority in probation are like those in social casework, but many people question their applicability in a role permeated by the power of law. They point out that the principles of social work have long been based on self-determination, which lets clients decide the nature, goals, and duration of the intervention—a condition not always feasible in the probation setting.

Despite such skepticism, professionals have tried to understand how probation officers might use authority as a positive tool. These officers use three different types of authority in their work:

1. Irrational authority, based solely on power
2. Rational authority, derived from the officer's competence in deciding on the best approach to take
3. Psychological authority, the most influential type, reflecting acceptance by both client and officer of each other's interest in jointly determined goals and strategies of supervision

The most effective probation officers combine all three types of authority rather than resorting to the formal power of their role. This concept is difficult to execute. The officer is attempting to gain the client's trust and confidence so that, guided by a measure of rational or (better) psychological authority, the client will change patterns that tend to promote involvement in crime. Yet both parties know that the officer can wield raw power should the client falter. Often the message is simply "Let me help you—or else!" This kind of mixed message leads to manipulation by both officer and client and can make the supervision relationship seem inconsistent.

In response to the complicated nature of their authority, probation officers often define their role in very simplistic terms, as if choosing between two incompatible sets of values: protecting the public versus helping the person on probation, enforcing the law versus doing social work, and so on. But such simplistic classification does not resolve the ambiguities of the probation officer's job. Frequently, the officer is given only vague guidelines for supervision, resulting in wide disparities at times.

motivational interviewing A method for increasing the effectiveness of correctional treatment by having the probation officer interact with the client in ways that promote the client's stake in the change process.

Recently, probation specialists have argued that probation officers' roles can best be melded through a technique referred to as **motivational interviewing**. This is a way of interacting with clients that was first developed for people addicted to drugs, but it has been extended to apply to a large number of involuntary clients. Motivational interviewing involves a variety of interpersonal techniques that increase the effectiveness of correctional treatment by having the probation officer interact with the client in ways that promote the client's stake in the change process. The strategy promises to do the following:

- Help the officer get "back into the game" of behavior change
- Identify effective tools for handling resistance and help keep difficult situations from getting worse
- Keep the probation officer from doing all the work
- Place the responsibility for behavior change on the client[14]

Even for the most effective probation officers, however, role conflict makes the job difficult. Probation officers are now held accountable for any abridgment of the community's safety resulting from acts of commission or omission in performing their duties. In practice, this means they must make reasonable efforts to monitor the behavior of clients and to exercise caution with those whose backgrounds make them potential risks to the community. The most famous case that established this principle involved a man convicted of sexual assault. His probation officer helped him get a job as a maintenance worker in an apartment complex, giving him access to keys to various apartments. In placing him, the officer withheld his client's past record from the employer. The client sexually assaulted several apartment residents, who later sued the probation officer for covering up his record. The court decided in favor of the victims, ruling that probation officers are indeed liable for their conduct as government employees.[15]

The liability of probation officers (and parole officers as well) is an area of law not yet well formulated. This issue has certainly made operational procedures in probation more important than ever. To defend against possible allegations of misconduct, probation officers need to document their actions so that they can meet any potential challenge. See "Careers in Corrections" for more on the work of state and county probation officers.

The Client The way the person on probation responds to supervision strongly influences the overall effectiveness of probation. Some people respond favorably to probation and get along well with their probation officers; others are resentful or resistant.

The response to being on probation depends in part on the reaction to the probation officer's power. Most people on probation believe they have little effect on the supervision process. Although probation officers' real power is limited by law and bureaucracy, the officer may seem to have a commanding role. Officers decide on the style of supervision—whether supportive or controlling—and the client has little direct influence on even this decision. Therefore, people on probation often perceive themselves as relatively powerless in the face of potentially arbitrary decisions by the officers.

Clients thus commonly resent their status, even when most people think they should be grateful for "another chance." In response, many probation officers try to involve the client in determining goals and strategies and in actively solving problems, rather than simply requiring participation in certain services or assistance. Such strategies are aimed at reducing the perceived discrepancy between the power of the officer and the powerlessness of the client.

The Bureaucracy All supervision activities take place in the context of a bureaucratic organization, which imposes both formal and informal constraints. *Formal*

CAREERS IN CORRECTIONS

Probation Officer: State and County

Nature of the Work

State and county probation officers have two main functions. First, they conduct investigations and write reports and recommendations for the courts, keeping the judge up to date on the client's compliance with the conditions of the probation terms. Second, they supervise the client's adjustment to the community, maintaining contact with him or her and providing guidance based on the client's risk levels and specific needs. Officers are usually required to spend more time with clients who need more rehabilitation and counseling or with those who pose a higher risk than others. Agencies and jurisdictions can also determine the maximum number of cases an officer is allowed to manage. Officers may handle anywhere from 20 to 100 cases at any given time.

Required Qualifications

Prospective probation officers are expected to have a four-year degree in criminal justice, social work, or some other related field, though specific requirements vary among states. A master's degree or related work experience is recommended and even required by some employers. Written, psychological, physical, and oral testing is ordinarily part of the application process, and good mental and physical health is a prerequisite to working as a probation officer. People who have been convicted of a felony may be disqualified from this field of employment. Computer-related knowledge and skills are helpful, and strong interpersonal abilities are needed as well because probation officers interact with a wide range of people in the pursuit of their duties. Because of the large number of reports that a correctional treatment specialist or probation officer will produce over his or her career, candidates should possess strong writing skills. Newly hired officers and specialists receive additional on-the-job training for up to one year after being hired.

Earnings and Job Outlook

Recent statistics show that probation officers earned $54,290 in 2019. The middle 50 percent earned between $35,990 and $60,430. The top 10 percent earned greater than $78,210, while the lowest 10 percent brought in less than $29,490. Higher wages tend to be found in urban areas. The employment growth rate for probation officers and correctional treatment specialists is expected to be average. However, many officers and specialists are projected to retire soon, creating many job opportunities in addition to those generated by natural job growth.

More Information

Information about state and county employment opportunities can be found at various state and local official probation websites, including the website for the Career Center of the American Probation and Parole Association.

standard conditions Constraints imposed on all probation clients, including reporting to the probation office, reporting any change of address, remaining employed, and not leaving the jurisdiction without permission.

punitive conditions Constraints imposed on some probation clients to increase the restrictiveness or painfulness of probation, including fines, community service, and restitution.

treatment conditions Constraints imposed on some probation clients to force them to deal with a significant problem or need, such as substance abuse.

constraints are the legal conditions of probation, whether standard, punitive, or treatment; these are set by the court or written into law. **Standard conditions**, imposed on everyone on probation, include reporting to the probation office, notifying the agency of any change of address, remaining gainfully employed, and not leaving the jurisdiction without permission. **Punitive conditions**, including fines, community service, and some forms of restitution, are designed to increase the restrictiveness or painfulness of probation. A punitive condition usually reflects the seriousness of the offense. **Treatment conditions** force the client to deal with a significant problem or need, such as substance abuse. A person on probation who fails to comply with a condition is usually subject to incarceration; thus, one main purpose of the officer's supervision is to enforce compliance with the conditions.

In spite of conceptual distinctions, in practice, the rationale for different conditions can become blurred. Standard conditions regarding drug treatment may be imposed because they are thought to increase the impact of drug treatment; restitution may be seen as an important part of a client's change in attitude. In fact, it may be that paying restitution results in lower rearrest rates, suggesting that it can be both a punitive and a treatment condition.[16] Moreover, there is some evidence that young African Americans on probation receive more restrictive conditions than their counterparts.[17]

Until recently, most probation agencies had to enforce large numbers of conditions of all types, perhaps because the sentencing judges believed that the more conditions they imposed, the greater the control they had. In fact, the reverse is often true: With numerous conditions, some quite meaningful and others not, all the conditions can lose credibility. When someone on probation disobeys a trivial condition, the probation officer may well choose to look the other way, leading the client to wonder if *any* conditions will be enforced. Moreover, scattershot conditions cloud the officer's authority and sometimes undermine the overall plan of assistance. The formal constraints imposed by the organizational policy often pale before the *informal constraints* imposed by bureaucratic pressures. Three such pressures are (1) case control, (2) case management structure, and (3) competence.

Case control pressures emerge because judges, prosecutors, administrators, and community members all expect probation officers to "make" clients abide by the conditions and legal requirements of probation. But the officer can do little to "make" the person on probation cooperate, for real power (such as the threat of revocation) is usually limited. Consequently, officers must rely on their discretion and individual supervision style, often minimizing or deliberately ignoring formal requirements in order to promote cooperation.

Similarly, the often large caseloads that bureaucracies generate and the unpredictability of the job produce a need for case management structure. This is achieved by documenting the officer's activities and by maintaining such routines as scheduled reporting days (for office visits) and field days (for home visits). But regular schedules do not always meet the demands of the caseload, nor do established operating procedures always lead to positive results. Such structure can limit the officer's creativity and intensity, as well as the agency's overall responsiveness.

Finally, the pressure for competence that a correctional bureaucracy exerts can demoralize a probation staff. Officers simply cannot manage all their cases effectively—there is no surefire approach to take with everyone on probation. Further, the officer typically receives little feedback about successes but much about failures. The result is an unintentional but systematic attack on the officer's sense of competence. Many officers react with cynical, defensive stances: Clients cannot be changed unless they want to be, people on probation are losers, and so forth. When several probation officers within an office develop this kind of cynicism, their negativism can pollute the whole working atmosphere.

In sum, the informal world of supervision is best understood as a complex interaction between officers (who vary in style, knowledge, and philosophy) and clients (who vary in responsiveness and need for supervision) in a bureaucratic organization that imposes significant formal and informal constraints on the work.

THE EFFECTIVENESS OF SUPERVISION

LO 7
Define recidivism and describe its importance to probation.

In light of such complexity, the effectiveness of probation supervision is difficult to assess. It depends on several factors: the skills of the officer, the availability of services such as employment counseling or drug treatment, and the needs and motives of the client. For many years, experts believed that reducing probation officers' caseloads could make supervision more effective. They reasoned that smaller caseloads would let officers devote more attention to each case, improving services. Frequently cited standards called for caseloads of 35–50, although such figures had never been justified by empirical study. During the 1960s and 1970s, dozens of experiments were conducted to find the optimal caseload. Yet subsequent reviews of those studies showed that caseload reduction did not significantly reduce **recidivism**—the return of a former correctional client to criminal behavior, as measured by new arrests or other problems with the law—among adult clients.

recidivism The return of a former correctional client to criminal behavior, as measured by new arrests or other problems with the law.

Why didn't smaller caseloads improve supervision effectiveness? Perhaps the assumption that "more supervision is better supervision" was too simplistic. Many factors—including the overall supervision experience, classification, officers' competence, treatment types, and policies of the probation agency—contribute to effectiveness more than does caseload. It now seems that caseload size matters when probation officers are using evidence-based methods. A recent study found that reducing the size of a caseload, by itself, had no effect. However, when the officers employed evidence-based strategies with a smaller caseload, the results did improve significantly.[18] (See "The New York City Opportunity Probation Model.")

Case Management Systems

Case management systems help focus the supervision effort of probation officers on client problems, which are identified using a standardized assessment of probationer risks and needs. In 1980 the National Institute of Corrections (a division of the Federal Bureau of Prisons) developed what it calls a "model system" of case management. This model has four principal components—statistical risk assessment, systematic needs assessment, contact supervision standards, and case planning—each designed to increase the effectiveness of probation supervision:

1. *Statistical risk assessment:* Because fully accurate predictions are impossible, there is pressure to assess risk conservatively—to consider the client a risk even when the evidence is ambiguous. This tendency toward overprediction (estimating that a person's chance of being arrested is greater than it actually is) means that officers will spend time with clients who actually need little supervision. The use of statistically developed risk assessment instruments reduces overprediction and improves the accuracy of risk classifications.
2. *Systematic needs assessment:* Subjective assessments of clients' needs often suffer from probation officers' biases and lack of information. With systematic needs assessment, officers can more consistently and comprehensively address clients' problems by evaluating them according to a list of potential needs.
3. *Contact supervision standards:* Probation officers understandably tend to avoid "problem" clients and spend more time with cooperative ones. Ideally, however, those who pose the greatest risk and have the greatest needs require the most time. Based on the two assessments, people are classified into supervision levels. Each level has a minimum supervision contact requirement, with the highest-risk or highest-need cases receiving the most supervision.
4. *Case planning:* The broad discretion given to probation officers to supervise their clients can lead to idiosyncratic approaches. When a probation officer must put the supervision plan in writing, the result is likely to be a better fit between the client's problems and the officer's supervision strategy. (See "Sample Supervision Plan" for more.) In addition, the officer's work is more easily evaluated.

FOCUS ON

POLICY: A New Vision for Probation

Recently, a group calling themselves Executives Transforming Probation and Parole (EXIT), comprised of more than 40 of the most prominent leaders in probation services, published a *Statement on the Future of Probation & Parole in the United States.* The opening part of the statement identifies the problem with community supervision today:

> *Every day in the United States, 4.5 million people are under probation or parole supervision, more than twice as many people as are incarcerated. This figure is nearly a four-fold increase since 1980 and represents more people than live in half of all U.S. states. Originated in the 19th century as a rehabilitative front-end alternative to incarceration (probation) or back-end release valve for incarcerated individuals who were believed to be rehabilitated (parole), community supervision has now become overly burdensome, punitive and a driver of mass incarceration, especially for people of color.*
>
> *Mass supervision has taken an enormous human and fiscal toll. Close to half (45 percent) of people entering prison in America were on probation or parole at the time of their current incarceration. Meanwhile, a quarter of those entering prison are incarcerated for technical violations, like staying out past curfew or missing appointments, disrupting their lives and costing taxpayers $2.8 billion annually. Community supervision and revocations disproportionately affect people of color. For example, while one in 55 adults in America are under probation and parole supervision, that proportion jumps significantly for black people, one in 23 of whom are under supervision.*
>
> *Probation and parole have grown far too large because people are being supervised who should not be and are being kept on supervision for far too long. For those under community supervision, it is often too punitive and focused on suppression, surveillance, and control, rather than well-being and growth. Far from being an aid to community reintegration as originally designed, community supervision too often serves as a tripwire to imprisonment, creating a vicious cycle of reincarceration for people under supervision for administrative rule violations that would rarely lead someone not under supervision into prison.*
>
> ***As people who run or have run community supervision throughout the country and others concerned with mass supervision, we call for probation and parole to be substantially downsized, less punitive, and more hopeful, equitable and restorative.***

EXIT goes on to call for reforms that would, among other things:

- reduce the length of supervision terms to keep them 18 months or under, in most cases;
- eliminate return to prison for technical revocations that involve no new crimes;
- divert more people from probation and parole, when they do not need the assistance provided by these agencies;
- eliminate supervision fees;
- eliminate boilerplate supervision conditions, and tailor conditions to the circumstances of the client;
- reorient community supervision so it supports a person's community reentry rather than enforces compliance with a laundry list of conditions—services not surveillance; and
- involve the affected community in the priorities of services probation and parole provide.

Read the full statement here: https://justicelab.columbia.edu/news/launching-exit-executives-transforming-probation-and-parole

This five-part model has enjoyed widespread support from probation and parole administrators as an evidence-based strategy. Risk assessment tools have been validated on a wide variety of client populations.[19] It has come to be considered standard practice in virtually every large probation agency in the United States, and several other countries have adopted it.

Recent research has pointed to new ways that case management systems can improve probation's effectiveness. Computer-based methods for risk forecasting have been developed that improve the accuracy of predictions of reoffending.[20]

FOCUS ON CORRECTIONAL PRACTICE: Sample Supervision Plan

SUPERVISION PLAN

Client Richard Knight

Probation Officer Brian Gaines

Supervision Level ________High

___X____Regular

________Minimum

Richard Knight will:

1. Provide check stubs showing monthly restitution payment of $50.
2. Obtain GED assessment from Nuestra Familia Educational Center.
3. Complete job-training course at New Mexico Technical High School.
4. Keep curfew of 8 P.M. on weekdays and 10 P.M. on weekends.

Signed: Richard Knight

Probation Officer: Brian Gaines

Client: Richard Knight

Date: January 6, 2021

Structured case management systems help probation staff decide which supervision approach that clients need most: intensive supervision, special services, or traditional probation monitoring.[21] When clients are placed in the most appropriate supervision approach, probation effectiveness increases. When risk factors can be changed by supervision strategies, the chances of recidivism have been shown to decline for all but the low-risk clients.[22]

Some probation officers do not like the case management approach. They feel that it constrains their ability to be creative in supervising clients. They also do not like the mechanistic way the "paperwork" makes them justify their decision making. Many probation officers eventually become perfunctory in the way they fill out the case management forms, not really paying much attention to them.

Evidence-Based Supervision

LO 8

Define evidence-based practice and discuss its importance to probation.

Researchers have begun to investigate systematically the differences between programs that work—that is, programs that reduce recidivism—and those that do not. This endeavor is called **evidence-based practice**. Studies suggest that among the most important characteristics of probation programs, four stand out:

evidence-based practice Using correctional methods that have been shown to be effective by well-designed research studies.

- Focusing the program on high-risk clients (risk principle)
- Providing greater levels of supervision to higher-risk clients (supervision principle)
- Providing treatment programs designed to deal with the problems that produce the higher risk level (treatment principle)
- Making referrals to treatment programs (referral principle)[23]

These "effectiveness" principles matter greatly in the design of probation-supervision programs. In one study of 66 community-based programs in Ohio, for example, meeting these principles was found to be an important determinant of each program's overall effectiveness. Just as important, failing to follow these principles often meant programs did *worse*. One of the key findings of this line of research is that surveillance-oriented supervision programs do not seem to work very well. By comparison, the evidence-based approach, when it seeks to prepare clients for postsupervision lives as regular citizens, has been shown to reduce rates of rearrest by almost one-third.[24]

Overall, the evidence-based movement in community supervision has tended to support the value of programs when they are applied to high-risk clients and when they include methods that are designed to reduce the risk.[25] Some people suggest that this line of research supports a range of specialized services for clients with special types of problems. Despite strong support for the use of case management systems, most probation officers still do not use these principles.

Specialized Supervision Programs

The needs of probation clients vary dramatically. People with histories of sex offenses require different supervision strategies than do those with substance abuse problems. People who have mental illnesses must be handled differently from those whose criminal background is limited to property crimes. However, because caseloads often exceed 100 per officer, agencies sometimes group clients with similar problems into a single caseload. This specialization allows the probation officer to develop more expertise in handling each problem, and it promotes a concentrated supervision effort.

Studies show that this approach has promise. For example, employment-counseling programs and support services improve employment possibilities, and specialized treatment for people convicted of sex offenses reduces their recidivism. Specialized services have been found to be more effective than traditional services for otherwise difficult subgroups of clients, including domestic violence cases[26] and individuals with mental illness.[27]

Recent interest in the problem of substance abuse has increased the attention given to clients affected by drugs and alcohol. Several specialized programs designed to combat drug use typically take advantage of new techniques for drug surveillance and treatment. Among the most important of these new methods is the **drug court**. Drug courts focus on providing supervision and control for people who are convicted of crimes stemming from drug abuse. The focus of the drug court is to maintain abstinence from illegal substances, though there is also emphasis on employment and other social services. Studies have found that using drug courts can reduce rates of new criminality, but when stiffer penalties for those who are arrested is factored in, there is no net reduction in the amount of incarceration.[28] There is also some evidence that police are more likely to make minor drug arrests after a drug court is created, possibly because they believe the person will get treatment.[29]

drug court A special court for people convicted of drug-abuse-related crimes.

urinalysis Technique used to determine whether someone is using drugs.

Antabuse A drug that when combined with alcohol causes violent nausea; it is used to control a person's drinking.

methadone A drug that reduces the craving for heroin; it is used to spare addicts from painful withdrawal symptoms.

Drug courts often use special technologies for enforcing abstinence. **Urinalysis** determines if a person is using drugs. **Antabuse**, a drug that stimulates nausea when combined with alcohol, inhibits drinking. **Methadone**, a drug that reduces craving for heroin, spares addicts from painful withdrawal symptoms. These approaches are often combined with close surveillance in order to reinforce abstinence during probation.

Another new specialized program pairs the probation officer more closely with street police officers. Officers who work in tandem with the police are often given caseloads of especially tough clients. The police liaison allows for more effective searches and arrests, and gives probation officers access to police information.

The difficulty with specialized supervision programs is what to do with the "ordinary" person on probation, slated for traditional services. Often, probation officers regard "regular" probation as a less attractive function, and conflict among the specialized units can become a serious management problem. As a consequence, such programs, even when successful, require extensive managerial support.

Even so, specialization of supervision will likely continue to grow in popularity. One reason has to do with an increasing recognition of the seriousness of the problems faced by people on probation and parole. In one sample of probation clients, 40 percent were under the influence of alcohol at the time of their offense, and 14 percent had been using illegal drugs.[30] Statistics such as these point to the importance of providing specialized programs for probation clients whose problems with drugs or alcohol lead to repeated criminality and revocation.

Performance-Based Supervision

Questions about the effectiveness of community supervision have spawned **performance-based supervision**, an approach that emphasizes "results" in setting priorities and selecting activities. The focus on results affects both the strategies and the agencies of client supervision. (See "The Robina Institute Reimagines Probation.")

performance-based supervision An approach to probation that establishes goals for supervision and evaluates the effectiveness of meeting those goals.

The performance-based movement has called for a new emphasis on public safety in probation. Rather than promoting an amorphous belief in "rehabilitation," this new philosophy of probation squarely accepts responsibility for adopting approaches that help enhance the safety of the public. By accepting public safety as a primary aim, probation leaders recognize the critical role that probation can play not just in reducing crime but also in enriching communities by contributing to a sense of personal security and quality of life.

Probation organizations that adopt a performance-based orientation express the focus on public safety in two ways. First, they choose supervision strategies that reflect what is known about the effectiveness of supervision. In most cases this means providing the greatest attention to the highest-risk cases, emphasizing the reduction of the kinds of problems that most contribute to crime, and consistently reinforcing crime-free behaviors. Second, they set goals for improved supervision outcomes with their clients. Measuring whether these goals are accomplished gives the probation administrator the ability to know if the supervision methods are "performing correctly" or need to be changed.

FOCUS ON

CORRECTIONAL POLICY: The Robina Institute Reimagines Probation

The Robina Institute of Criminal Law and Criminal Justice at the University of Minnesota has recently begun a long-term investigation of probation in the United States. The aim is to develop a better understanding of what is problematic about probation today, and then to recommend a series of reforms that would make probation better.

At the core of the institute's critique of probation is that probation tries to do too much. Probation is used for too many people, when lesser sanctions such as fines or community service would suffice. Too many conditions are applied to people who are placed on probation, with the result that failure to abide by the many conditions becomes much more likely. Probation terms are too long, again increasing the odds of failure. Reimagining probation entails putting into place a series of new priorities:

1. *Who gets probation?* Probation is too often designated by what it is *not*—it is *not* prison. Instead of this negative definition, probation should mean something positive: It is a criminal sanction that takes place in the community, used because a community-based sanction is often the best way to ensure that a person will not pose a risk to public safety.
2. *What conditions does probation enforce?* Conditions should be carefully tailored to address the public-safety concerns each case represents. There should be very few "standard" conditions that apply to every person on probation; rather, conditions should be customized to fit the specific factors in a person's situation that contribute to risk of new criminality. The test should be that failure to comply with the conditions raises reasonable questions of direct risk to the public.
3. *When is probation revoked?* Probation should be revoked only in the face of a new crime. Conditions that fall short of a new crime can be enforced when the misbehavior presents a proximate and serious risk to the community. Violations of conditions that fall short of new crimes should be enforced with graduated sanctions such as restrictions on freedom rather than return to prison.
4. *How long does probation last?* Probation terms should be short: six months or a year, and rarely more than two years.

Probation, reimagined in this way, is less intrusive, more focused on legitimate interests of public safety, and less likely to contribute to problems of mass incarceration.

Sources: Cecilia Klingele, "Rethinking the Use of Community Supervision," *Journal of Criminal Law and Criminology* 103 (no. 4, 2013): 1015–69; Ronald P. Corbett, Jr., "The Burdens of Leniency: The Changing Face of Probation," *Minnesota Law Review* 99 (no. 5, 2015): 1697–733.

In short, the performance movement shifts the focus of supervision plans from activities to results—from what probation officers do to what they accomplish. The test of probation, in this circumstance, is how well the sentence turns out in the end (see "Thinking Outside the Box").

LO 9

Describe what is known about the effectiveness ofprobation supervision.

Is Probation Effective Regardless?

Almost all studies of the effectiveness of probation supervision compare different probation strategies. They often find no difference in outcomes, and even when there is a difference, it is typically modest. The frequency of such weak results for probation studies leads some scholars to conclude that probation "doesn't work" or that its effects are minimal at best. This often makes prison seem a more powerful option by comparison, even if it is much more expensive than probation.

Again, these studies almost always compare one kind of probation to another. They do not compare probation with "doing nothing" because doing nothing is not a reasonable option. Yet what if probation is considerably better than "doing nothing"? What if the various *methods* of probation vary little in their impact, but probation itself works?

We have no completely convincing studies of this question. (What judge would want to engage in an experiment where a sentence of "nothing" was routinely given to a random sample of people convicted of a felony?) But a recent study suggests that probation works perhaps far better than most people might suspect. Designed to find out whether the personal relationships of clients affected their likelihood of being arrested, the study followed a sample of individuals for the first eight months of their probation term. The study found that a few case factors predicted the likelihood of new criminal behavior (carrying guns or using drugs or alcohol) but that overall, the entire sample exhibited a large and abrupt reduction in criminal activity immediately

THINKING OUTSIDE THE BOX

MACHINES RUNNING PROBATION SUPERVISION

Risk classification is almost a uniform practice in probation today. While the formats are different and the variables used to assess risk also vary from one instrument to another, they all have the same basic form: The officer completes the form by checking off a standard set of boxes; the boxes are added up to suggest a supervision risk level.

It is not surprising that probation officers sometimes make mistakes when they fill out risk forms. They check off an incorrect box; they add the boxes incorrectly. These errors can affect the recommended supervision risk level. How big of a problem is this?

Researchers have shown that mistakes can result in serious errors in misclassifying people on probation. Human error happens often enough that probation may be unfairly applying close supervision to some clients while mistakenly ignoring others who should receive closer supervision.

It turns out that machines can help. In terms of scoring items on a risk assessment, machines can input data from electronic files and make sure that objective factors such as prior record and education level are accurately scored. Also, machines never make addition errors. Once a machine has classified a risk level accurately, it can also suggest priorities for supervision goals. A machine can help highlight which risk issues are most problematic, and it can provide estimates of which supervision goals will be most effective at reducing risk. In fact, studies show that automated risk instruments make fewer errors, provide more reliable risk classifications, and—in the long run—save money.

Of course, human judgment can never be completely removed from the probation supervision process. But human error can be minimized. And machines can provide invaluable guidance about the best courses of action.

Sources: Grant Duwe and Michael Rocque, "Effects of Automating Recidivism Risk Assessment on Reliability, Predictive Validity and Return on Investment," *Criminology & Public Policy* 16 (no. 1, February 2017): 235–70; Ira M. Schwartz, Peter York, Mark Greenwald, et al., "Using Predictive Analytics and Machine Learning to Improve the Accuracy and Performance of Juvenile Risk Assessment Instruments," in *Handbook on Risk and Need Assessment: Theory and Practice,* edited by Faye S. Taxman (New York: Routledge, 2017).

following being placed on probation, and the initial reduction lasted the duration of the study. This reduction in criminality had little to do with life circumstances but instead appeared to be a general effect of the probation sentence.[31]

This work is bolstered by a recent study reported by the New York City Criminal Justice Agency that compared traditional New York City probation, more heavily funded "alternatives to incarceration" (such as those discussed in Chapter 9), and jail. The researchers concluded that when it came to preventing new arrests, probation was as effective as lauded "alternative" sanctions and more effective than jail.[32] Another study compared probation supervision with imprisonment for people convicted of drug crimes; it concluded that the people placed on probation had fewer arrests and convictions, even accounting for the time that the prison group spent behind bars.[33]

A few studies are not enough to prove a point, but the result is good news for probation. It may be that the fact of simply being on probation matters more than the kind of probation implemented.

REVOCATION AND TERMINATION OF PROBATION

LO 10

Discuss the revocation of probation, including "technical" revocation.

Probation status ends in one of two ways: (1) the person successfully completes the period of probation, or (2) the person's probationary status is revoked because of misbehavior. Revocation can result from a new arrest or conviction or from a *rules violation,* a failure to comply with a condition of probation. Rules violations that result in revocations are referred to as **technical violations**.

technical violation The failure to abide by the rules and conditions of probation (specified by the judge), resulting in revocation of probation.

Revocations for technical violations are somewhat controversial because behaviors that are not ordinarily illegal—changing one's residence without permission, failing to attend a therapy program, neglecting to report to the probation office, and so forth—can result in incarceration. Some years ago, technical violations were common whenever clients were uncooperative. Today, probation is revoked when the rules violation persists or poses a threat to the community. Probation officers have broad discretion to investigate potential rules violations and even new crimes. The U.S. Supreme Court has ruled that people on probation may be searched when the probation officer has a "reasonable suspicion" that a crime or rules violation may have occurred.[34] This means that probation officers do not need search warrants, nor do they have to have "probable cause" to believe a crime has occurred, the higher standard for searches that applies to citizens who are not under correctional supervision.

Although patterns vary across the country, the most common reason for a revocation is a new offense by the client. Sometimes the court waits for conviction on the new offense before revoking probation, but if the offense is serious enough, probation is immediately revoked. In such cases a technical violation is alleged, even though the real basis for revocation is the new offense. (See "Sample Revocation Form" for a look at a technical violation.)

According to most studies of probation revocation, from one-fifth to one-third of people on probation fail to abide by the terms of their probation. However, a widely publicized RAND Corporation study found much higher rates of violation, raising the concern of probation administrators. For 40 months the RAND researchers followed a sample of individuals from two urban California counties who had been placed on probation for violent crimes and property crimes. More than one-third were reincarcerated for technical violations or new offenses; of these, 65 percent were arrested for a felony or misdemeanor, and 51 percent were actually convicted of a crime. In other words, many of these probation "failures" remained on probation after their convictions, even though the crimes were often serious. This study found that once a person

FOCUS ON

CORRECTIONAL POLICY: Sample Revocation Form

ORDER OF REVOCATION, STATE OF NEW MEXICO

In the 1st District Court of New Mexico, Santa Fe

Defendant: Richard Knightt
Case Number: 2010-00235
Matter: *State of New Mexico v. Richard Knight*
Date: April 15, 2021

The above-named defendant has been charged with the violation of probation, as follows:

1. Failure to make restitution as ordered by the court
2. Association with the 18th Street Gang in violation of the order of the court

On ____January 4, 2021____ the defendant was convicted of the crime of Aggravated Assault Upon a Peace Officer (Deadly Weapon) (Firearm Enhancement), as charged in Information Number 110-5736900______ and was notified of his rights, and given a copy of the probation order of the court.

On March 23, 2021, Probation Officer informed the court of probable cause that the probationer was in violation of the following probation conditions:

1. That restitution be made to Juan Lopez in the amount of $662.40
2. That the defendant discontinue fraternizing with the 18th Street Gang members and terminate his own membership in the gang

Defendant was (1) provided with a copy of the alleged violations, (2) informed that any statement s/he made could be used against him/her, (3) informed of the right to obtain assistance of counsel and to have one provided if indigent, and (4) informed of the date of the probation revocation hearing. Pursuant to this allegation, the defendant: Pursuant to this allegation, the defendant:

__X__ admitted the violations
_____ asked for a hearing on the charges
__X__ waived counsel
_____ sought the assignment of counsel due to indigent status

The court finds that

__X__ sufficient evidence exists to support the allegation of a violation of probation
_____ the evidence of a violation of probation is insufficient

In finding that a violation of probation has occurred, the court relied on the following evidence: testimony by the probation officer that restitution had not been paid; testimony by the probation officer that he observed the defendant in the company of gang members; admission under oath by the defendant that these allegations were true.

Based on the court's finding of a violation of probation, the following sentence is ordered:

1. A jail term of 30 days
2. Attendance in the Gang Violence Reduction Program of the probation department
3. Intensive probation supervision following release jail

Signed: *Judge Manuel Baca*

is placed on probation, serious misbehavior does not necessarily result in removal from the community.[35]

Other follow-up studies have supported the overall results of the RAND study. When we look at annual exits from probation, we see a similar picture: Figure 8.4 displays the most recently available statistics showing the ways in which people on probation in the United States ended their terms. Note that about two-thirds completed their terms successfully. (For more on new practices in probation revocation, see "Is There Hope for HOPE Probation?")

Replications of this type of follow-up study outside of "big corrections" states such as California and Texas have found somewhat lower levels of serious misbehavior by people on probation. Perhaps probation works well in some areas but less well in others, partly depending on the nature of the person placed on probation, which can vary dramatically from place to place. Probation agencies that supervise more-serious cases can be expected to have higher rates of revocation. In locations where clients have serious criminal histories, some probation departments have begun to collaborate with police departments to improve the public-safety effectiveness of both agencies.

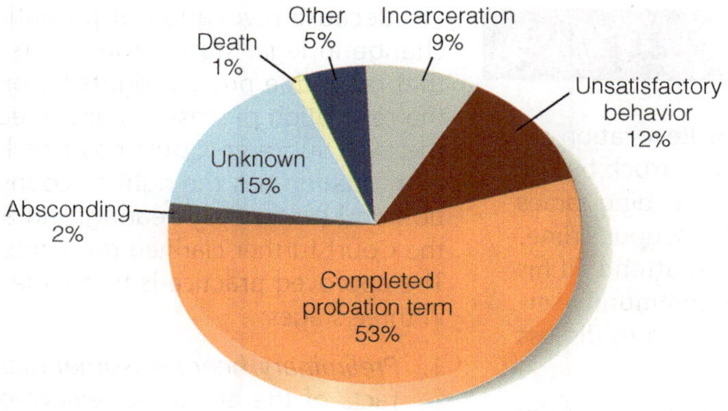

FIGURE 8.4 Termination of Probation in the United States*

Most people who finish their probation terms do so satisfactorily, but about one in six ends up in prison.

*Does not total 100% because of rounding.

Source: *Probation and Parole in the United States, 2012* (Washington, DC: U.S. Bureau of Justice Statistics, 2013).

FOCUS ON

CORRECTIONAL POLICY: Is There Hope for HOPE Probation?

It all began when Hawaii judge Steven Alm became frustrated with the long line of probation revocations he kept seeing, some of them the ninth or tenth violation. Working with local probation administrators, Judge Alm developed a new approach based on an enforcement strategy that was "certain, swift, and fair: CSF." Thus was born Hawaii's Opportunity Probation with Enforcement (HOPE). When the results first came in, policy makers who favored "tough" probation started to crow: It seemed that a tough, no-nonsense probation approach that made threats it was willing to carry out could really work.

The CSF strategy begins with a stern warning offered by the court: "The first dirty urine or missed appointment and you will be back in jail, only to come out back on probation and start over again." Clients who violate their probation are taken before the judge the day of the violation and go straight to jail for about a week; then they come back out on probation. The idea is to make sanctions credible but not draconian, and to force people on probation to choose through their own behavior whether they go to jail or not. Dirty urines result in rapid court hearings and immediate jail terms, all of which occur within a couple of days. Jail terms are short—the theory being that swift and certain penalties are more effective than slow, sporadic, and severe ones.

The evaluation of Project HOPE had impressive results. Compared to a control group, HOPE clients had fewer dirty urines, fewer missed appointments, and fewer arrests, and spent less time behind bars. These results were so impressive that the U.S. Department of Justice promoted widespread dissemination of the HOPE model, with at least 40 programs up and running within the first five years.

Evaluations of these replications of HOPE have produced mixed results. At least one project, a statewide strategy in Washington, had results similar to those in Hawaii. But of all the major evaluations of HOPE, fewer than one-third have reported positive results. The largest study, a federally funded national replication, found that HOPE probation did not produce fewer arrests or less time in confinement in any of the places where it was tried—and it cost more money than regular probation.

Some people remain enthusiastic about the "certain, swift, and fair" approach to enforcing probation rules. After all, the results in some places have been notable. But other experts say that HOPE is "hopeless" as long as there are no services provided—the real difference, they say, comes when probation gives priority to services instead of enforcement.

Source: Daniel Nagin, ed., "HOPE Collections," *Criminology & Public Policy* 15 (no. 4, November 2016); Alexander J. Cowell, Alan Barnosky, Pamela K. Lattimore, Joel K. Cartwright, & Matthew DeMichele, "Economic Evaluation of the HOPE Demonstration Field Experiment." *Criminology & Public Policy* 17 (no. 4, 2018): 875–99.

DO THE RIGHT THING

As you look over the Recommendation for Revocation report sent to you by Officer Sawyer, you are struck by the low-level technical violations used to justify sending James Ferguson, who has not been convicted of a serious crime, to prison. Sawyer cites Ferguson's failure to attend all his drug treatment sessions, to complete his community service, and to pay a $500 fine. You call Sawyer in to discuss the report.

"Bill, I've looked over your report on Ferguson, and I'm wondering what's going on here. Why isn't he fulfilling the conditions of his probation?"

"I'm really not sure, but it seems he just doesn't want to meet the conditions. I think he's got a bad attitude, and I don't like the guys he hangs around with. He's always mouthing off about the 'system' and says I'm on his case for no reason."

"Well, let's look at your report. You say that he works for Capital Services cleaning offices downtown from midnight till 8 a.m. yet has to go to the drug programs three mornings a week and put in 10 hours a week at the Salvation Army Thrift Store. Is it that he isn't trying, or does he have an impossible situation?"

"I think he could do it if he tried, but also, I think he might be selling cocaine again. Perhaps he needs to get a taste of prison."

"That may be true, but do you really want to revoke his probation?"

WRITING ASSIGNMENT: What's going on here? Is Sawyer recommending revocation because of Ferguson's attitude and the suspicion that he is selling drugs again? Do the technical violations warrant prison? Write a memo explaining what you would recommend and why if you were Ferguson's probation officer.

Because revocation of probation is a serious change in legal status, the courts have required that basic due process rights be observed during the revocation process. As discussed in Chapter 5, the U.S. Supreme Court has ruled that a person on probation has the right to counsel at a revocation and sentencing hearing.[36] In a later decision the Court further clarified revocation procedures.[37] The approved practice is to handle the revocation in three stages:

1. *Preliminary hearing (sometimes waived):* The facts of the arrest are reviewed to determine if there is probable cause that a violation has occurred.
2. *Hearing:* The facts of the allegation are heard and decided. The probation department presents the evidence to support the allegation, and the client has an opportunity to refute the evidence. Specifically, he or she has the right to see written notice of the charges and the disclosure of evidence of the violation, to testify and to present witnesses and evidence to contradict the allegations, to cross-examine adversarial witnesses, to be heard by a neutral and detached officer, and to review a written statement of findings. Unless unusual grounds exist to deny counsel, the client also has the right to an attorney.
3. *Sentencing:* With an attorney present, the judge decides whether to impose a term of incarceration and, if so, the duration of the term. This stage is more than a technicality because after a minor violation, probation is often reinstated with greater restrictions.

For those who successfully complete probation, the sentence is terminated. Ordinarily, the client is then a completely free citizen again, without obligation to the court or to the probation department.

PROBATION IN THE COMING DECADE

Many dramatic changes are coming in probation. Caseloads of traditional probation are growing well beyond reasonable management: 200- and even 300-person caseloads are not unusual. In many locales, traditional probation has seen deterioration in the quality of supervision because of the loss of staff and the increase in cases. Yet the importance of probation for public safety has never been greater. Studies now suggest that being granted probation actually makes people *less* likely to commit new crimes than if they had been sent to prison.[38] As a result of the renewed emphasis on public safety, many agencies have also experienced a resurgence of intensive and structured supervision for high-risk cases (see Chapter 9). Technology expands the degree of surveillance and control that departments can bring to bear on their more-serious clients.

Since that first day in 1841 when John Augustus looked for a better way of working with people who had just been convicted, probation has continued to grow. What was once known as an "alternative to incarceration" is now the most common sentencing option used by judges all across the United States.

During the last 25 years, probation has gone through three major changes in emphasis, from rehabilitation to surveillance to risk management. Probation now finds itself on the brink of what could be another major directional change. More and more jurisdictions are indicating that probation must take responsibility for the desired behavioral changes in its clients.

This situation leaves us with two increasingly divergent types of probation in the future. One is largely a paper exercise. Whatever services are provided will be done through brokerage: The probation officer serves as a referral agent, involving the person on probation in single-focus community service agencies (such as drug treatment programs) that work with a variety of community clients, not just those under correctional supervision. In the second type of probation, the remaining clients—a minority of the total caseload, to be sure—will be watched closely and will receive first-rate supervision and control from highly trained professionals working with reasonable levels of funding and programmatic support.

The use of brokerage is not necessarily a bad idea. Proponents argue that specialists can provide treatment superior to what a generalist can offer and that communities ought to provide such assistance anyway. Yet community agencies are not always quick to offer services to people under legal authority; they prefer to work with voluntary clients, not those who avail themselves of services only under threat of the law.

Probation administrators are also changing the way they want to be evaluated. Most of the time—and in most of the studies cited in this chapter—probation's effectiveness is determined by rearrest rates: High rates are seen as a sign of ineffective supervision. Yet administrators know that high rearrest rates can also mean that staff is watching high-risk clients vigilantly, something that most citizens would applaud. From this viewpoint, recidivism rates do not offer the sole means of evaluating a probation department.

Instead, some believe that probation should also be evaluated by a series of "performance indicators" that better reveal whether probation is doing its job. These indicators include numbers of community service projects performed by people on probation, amount of probation fees and restitution collected, employment rates, amount of taxes paid, and days free of drug use. However, detractors claim that even if these performance indicators are high, the public is interested in crime as a bottom line—and that means recidivism rates matter most.

In many respects, then, probation finds itself at a crossroads. Although its credibility is probably as low as it has ever been, its workload is growing dramatically and, in view of the crowding in prisons and jails, will probably continue to do so. Under the strain of this workload and on-again, off-again public support, probation faces a serious challenge: Can its methods of supervision and service be adapted successfully to high-risk cases? Many innovations are being attempted, but it is unclear whether such new programs actually improve probation or detract from it. Certainly they expand the variety of probation sanctions, making them more applicable to more people on probation. But do they strengthen the mainstream functions of probation—investigation and supervision? These functions must be improved for probation to succeed in its current challenge.

FOR CRITICAL THINKING

Ohio's chief justice, Maureen O'Connor, has made a case for expanded use of probation. She says it will both save money and increase public safety.

1. What do you think of this argument?

2. Is it fair to expect probation to save money *and* increase safety?

3. What will have to happen for probation to rise to this challenge?

SUMMARY

1 Describe the history and development of probation, including how it is organized today.

Probation stems from European practices that attempted to alleviate the harshness of the criminal law. In the United States, probation goes back to the 1830s, when John Augustus volunteered to "stand bail" for people in the Boston Police Court. Today probation exists as a sentencing option in every state in the nation, operated by courts or by correctional departments.

2 Describe the two functions of probation.

Probation officers have traditionally performed two major functions: investigation and supervision. Investigation involves the preparation of a presentence investigation (PSI), which the judge uses in sentencing someone. Supervision begins once the person is sentenced to probation, and it involves establishing a relationship with the client, setting supervision goals to help in compliance with conditions established by the court, and deciding how to terminate probation on the basis of the client's response to supervision.

3 Discuss the purpose and content of the presentence investigation report.

The PSI plays its most important role in the sentencing process. Because individual judges, even in the same court system, may weigh factors in a case differently, the PSI must be comprehensive enough to provide necessary information to judges with varying sentencing perspectives. A shortened, directed, and standardized PSI format is becoming more common. This approach places greater responsibility on the probation officer, who must discern precisely what information the judge will require to evaluate the sentencing options.

4 List the major issues involved in the presentence investigation.

PSIs present three major issues: (1) Whether to make sentencing recommendations. These are controversial because a person without authority to sentence is nevertheless suggesting what the sentence should be. For this reason, not all probation systems include it in the PSI. (2) Whether to disclose the contents of the PSI to the defense. In many states the defense does not receive a copy of the report. In the other states the practice is generally to "cleanse" the report of confidential comments and clinical statements, then disclose it. (3) Whether private investigative firms ought to be allowed to provide judges with PSIs paid for by the defense. In this approach the firm serves as an advocate at the sentencing stage.

5 Describe the dynamics that occur among the probation officer, the person on probation, and the probation bureaucracy.

Probation officers face role conflict in that they must both enforce the law and provide assistance. The responsibilities are often incompatible. The client's response to supervision depends in part on his or her perception of the officer's power. Most people on probation believe that they have little effect on the supervision process. Although probation officers' real power is limited by law and bureaucracy, these people seem to occupy a commanding role. All supervision activities take place in the context of a bureaucratic organization, which imposes both formal and informal constraints. Formal constraints are the legal conditions of probation.

6 Identify the different kinds of probation conditions and explain why they are important.

Standard conditions, imposed on all probation clients, include reporting to the probation office, notifying the agency of any change of address, remaining gainfully employed, and not leaving the jurisdiction without permission. Punitive conditions, including fines, community service, and some forms of restitution, are designed to increase the restrictiveness or painfulness of probation. A punitive condition usually reflects the seriousness of the offense. Treatment conditions force the client to deal with a significant problem or need, such as substance abuse.

7 Define *recidivism* and describe its importance to probation.

Recidivism is the return of a former correctional client to criminal behavior, as measured by new arrests or other problems with the law. It is the basis on which we decide if a probation strategy is working or not.

8 Define *evidence-based practice* and discuss its importance to probation.

Evidence-based practice centers on an understanding of the differences between programs that work—that is, programs that reduce recidivism—and those that do not. Studies suggest that among the most important characteristics of programs for probation clients, four stand out: focusing (1) the program on high-risk individuals (risk principle), (2) providing greater levels of supervision to higher-risk clients (supervision principle), (3) providing treatment programs designed to deal with the problems that produce the higher risk level (treatment principle), and (4) making referrals to treatment programs (referral principle).

9 Describe what is known about the effectiveness of probation supervision.

Studies of the effectiveness of probation supervision find little or no difference in outcomes for different probation strategies. This often makes prison seem a more powerful option by comparison, even though it costs much more than probation. But some recent studies suggest that probation works perhaps far better than most people might suspect. In preventing new arrests, probation may be as effective as lauded "alternative" sanctions and more effective than jail or prison.

10 Discuss the revocation of probation, including "technical" revocation.

Probation status ends in one of two ways: (1) the person completes the period of probation, or (2) the person's probationary status is revoked because of misbehavior. Revocation of parole can result from a new arrest or conviction or from a rules violation, a failure to comply with a condition of probation. Rules violations that result in revocations are called technical violations; these are somewhat controversial because behaviors that are not ordinarily illegal can result in incarceration.

KEY TERMS

Antabuse (*p. 222*)
authority (*p. 215*)
client-specific planning (*p. 213*)
community justice (*p. 206*)
drug court (*p. 222*)
evidence-based practice (*p. 221*)
judicial reprieve (*p. 203*)
methadone (*p. 222*)
motivational interviewing (*p. 216*)
performance-based supervision (*p. 223*)
power (*p. 215*)
presentence investigation (*PSI*) (*p. 210*)
punitive conditions (*p. 218*)
recidivism (*p. 219*)
recognizance (*p. 203*)
standard conditions (*p. 218*)
technical violation (*p. 225*)
treatment conditions (*p. 218*)
urinalysis (*p. 222*)
victim impact statement (*p. 212*)

FOR DISCUSSION

1. Why is there so much interest in probation today? How does the use of probation affect the corrections system? Why is it used so extensively?
2. How does the presentence investigation report affect accountability for the sentence that is imposed?
3. How do you think the investigative and supervisory functions of probation can be most effectively organized? What would the judges in your area say about your proposal? What would the department of corrections say?
4. Given the two major tasks of probation, how should officers spend their time? How do they actually spend their time?
5. Why might some people on probation be kept in the community after a technical violation rather than having their probation revoked?

FOR FURTHER READING

Corbett, Ronald P., Jr, and Kevin R. Reitz. *Profiles in Probation Revocation*. Minneapolis, MN: University of Minnesota Robina Institute, 2015. Summaries of state statutes and policies regarding the revocation of probation.

DeMichele, Matthew, and Adam K. Matz. *APPA's CARE Model: A Framework for Collaboration, Analysis, Reentry, and Evaluation: A Response to Street Gang Violence*. Lexington, KY: American Probation and Parole Association, 2013. A description of the American Probation and Parole Association's strategy for probation supervision.

Hardy, Jason, *The Second Chance Club: Hardship and Hope After Prison*. New York: Simon & Schuster, 2020. An autobiographical account of probation and parole work in some of Louisiana's toughest neighborhoods.

Pew Charitable Trust. *Policy Reforms Can Strengthen Community Supervision*. Philadelphia, PA: Author, 2020. A manual for implementing the best practices of probation supervision.

Pew Center on the States. *The Impact of California's Probation Performance Incentive Funding Program.* Washington, DC: Author, 2012. A study of how California's Public Safety Realignment affected probation services.

Taxman, Faye S., ed. *Handbook on Risk and Need Assessment: Theory and Practice.* New York: Routledge, 2017. Selections providing the most recent research on the use of risk and needs systems in community supervision.

NOTES

1 John Schmitt, Kris Warner, and Sarika Gupta, *The High Budgetary Cost of Incarceration* (Washington, DC: Center for Economic Policy Research, 2010).

2 Daniel Kaeble and Mariel Alper, *Probation and Parole in the United States, 2017-2018*. (Washington: U.S. Bureau of Justice Statistics. 2020).

3 Mariel Alper, Alessandro Corda, and Kevin R. Reitz, *Data Brief: American Exceptionalism in Probation Supervision* (Minneapolis, MN: Robina Institute, 2016).

4 Michelle Phelps, "Mass Probation: Toward a More Robust Theory of State Variation in Punishment," *Punishment & Society* 19 (no. 1, 2017): 53–73.

5 Robert Martinson, "California Research at the Crossroads," *Crime and Delinquency* 22 (April 1976): 191.

6 *Ex parte United States*, 242 U.S. 27 (1916); often referred to as *Killits*.

7 *John Augustus, First Probation Officer* (New York: Probation Association, 1939), 30. First published as John Augustus, A Report of the Labors of John Augustus, *for the Last Ten Years, in Aid of the Unfortunate* (Boston, MA: Wright & Hasty, 1852).

8 Ibid., p. 34.

9 Michele S. Phelps, "The Curious Disappearance of Sociological Research on Probation Supervision," *Criminal Justice Law Enforcement Annual*, vol. 2 (New York: AMS, 2015): 1–30.

10 Kaeble, *Probation and Parole in the United States, 2016*.

11 Joan Petersilia, Susan Turner, James Kahan, and Joyce Peterson, *Granting Felons Probation: Public Risks and Alternatives* (Santa Monica, CA: RAND, 1985), 39, 41.

12 *Williams v. New York*, 337 U.S. 241 (1949).

13 *Verdugo v. United States*, 402 F.Supp. 599 (1968).

14 For a summary of motivational interviewing, see William R. Miller and Stephen Rollnick, *Motivational Interviewing: Helping People Change,* 3rd ed. (New York: Guilford, 2013).

15 *Rieser v. District of Columbia*, 21 Cr.L. 2503 (1977).

16 R. Barry Ruback, Lauren K. Knoth, Andrew S. Gladfelter, and Brendan Lantz, "Restitution Payment and Recidivism: AS Experiment," *Criminology & Public Policy* 17 (no. 4, 2018): 789–813.

17 Anat Kimchi, "Investigating the Assignment of Probation Conditions: Heterogeneity and the Role of Race and Ethnicity," *Journal of Quantitative Criminology* 35 (no. 4, 2019): 715–45.

18 Jalbert, Sarah Kuck, William Rhodes, Michael Kane, et al., *A Multisite Evaluation of Reduced Probation Caseload Size in an Evidence-Based Practice Setting* (Washington, DC: National Institute of Justice, 2011).

19 Zachary Hamilton, Elizabeth Thompson Tellefsbol, Michael Camagna, and Jacqueline von Wormer, "Customizing Criminal Justice Assessment," in *Handbook on Risk and Need Assessment: Theory and Practice*, edited by Faye S. Taxman (New York: Routledge, 2017), 333–78.

20 Grant Duwe and Michael Rocque, "Effects of Automating Recidivism Risk Assessment on Reliability, Predictive Validity and Return on Investment," *Criminology & Public Policy* 16 (no. 1, February 2017): 235–70.

21 Faye S. Taxman and Michael S. Caudy, "Risk Tells Us Who, But Not What or How: Empirical Assessment of the Complexity of Criminogenic Needs to Inform Correctional Programming," *Criminology & Public Policy* 14 (no. 1, February 2015): 71–104.

22 Thomas H. Cohen, Christopher T. Lowenkamp, and Scott Van Benschoten, "Does Change in Risk Matter? Examining Whether Changes in Offender Risk Characteristics Influence Recidivism Outcomes," *Criminology & Public Policy* 15 (no. 2, May 2016): 264–96.

23 Meghan Guevara and Judith Sachwald, "On the Shoulders of Giants: A Vision of an Evidence-Based Organization," *Perspectives* 34 (no. 4, 2010): 52–63.

24 For a summary of the literature, visit the Evidence-Based Practice Society website: https://www.ebpsociety.org/blog/education/338-evidence-based-practices-corrections.

25 Michael L. Predergast, Frank S. Pearson, Deborah Podus, et al., "The Andrews Principles of Risk, Needs, and Responsivity as Applied in Drug Treatment Programs: A Meta-analysis of Crime and Drug Use Outcomes," *Journal of Experimental Criminology* 9 (no. 3, September 2013): 275–300.

26 Matthew T.DeMichele, Ann Crowe, Andrew Klein, and Doug Wilson, " 'What Works' in the Supervision of Domestic Violence Offenders: Promising Results from a Study in Rhode Island," *Perspectives* 30 (no. 1, Summer 2006): 46–57.

27 Jennifer L. Skeem and Paula Emke-Francis, "Probation and Mental Health: Responding to the Challenges," Perspectives 28 (no. 3, Summer 2004): 22–27. See also *Mental Health Probation Officers: Stopping Justice-Involvement Before Incarceration* (Policy Brief, Center for Behavioral Health Services and Criminal Justice Research, 2010).

28 Brook Kearly, and Denise Gottfredson, "Long Term Effects of Drug Court Participation: Evidence from a 15-year Follow-up of a Randomized Controlled Trial," *Journal of Experimental Criminology* 16 (no. 3, 2019); 27–47.

29 David R. Lilley, "Did Drug Courts Lead to Increased Arrest and Punishment for Minor Drug Offenses?" *Justice Quarterly* 34 (no. 4, 2017): 674–98.

30 BJS *Special Report*, March 1998, p. 1.

31 Doris Layton-MacKenzie and Spencer De Li, "The Impact of Formal and Informal Social Controls on the Criminal Activities of Probationers," *Journal of Research in Crime and Delinquency* 39 (no. 3, August 2002): 243–76.

32 Jukka Savolainen, *The Impact of Felony ATI Programs on Recidivism* (New York: New York City Criminal Justice Agency, 2003).

33 Cassia Spohn and David Holleran, "The Effect of Imprisonment on Recidivism Rates of Felony Offenders: A Focus on Drug Offenders," *Criminology* 40 (no. 2, May 2002): 297–328.

34 *United States v. Knight* (00-1260), 534 U.S. 112 (2001).

35 Petersilia et al., *Granting Felons Probation*, p. 39.

36 *Mempa v. Rhay*, 389 U.S. 128 (1967).

37 *Gagnon v. Scarpelli*, 411 U.S. 778 (1973).

38 Paul Nieuwbeerta, Daniel S. Nagin, and Arjan A. J. Blokland, "Assessing the Impact of First-Time Imprisonment on Offenders' Subsequent Criminal Career Development: A Matched Samples Comparison," *Journal of Quantitative Criminology* 25 (no. 3, September 2009): 227–57.

CHAPTER 9

Intermediate Sanctions and Community Corrections

© Jon Stinchcomb/News Herald

Judge Bruce Winters, right, presents a certificate of graduation to Kylie Zunk, who completed the Ottawa County Drug Addiction Treatment Alliance Program. Drug Courts are an example of the kinds of community correctional programs have become popular alternatives to either jail or probation.

THE ACRONYM IS "EBP."

It stands for *Evidence-Based Practice*. It is the dominant paradigm in correctional practice today. But nowhere is it more important than in the field of community corrections. (See Focus on Correctional Practice: Evidence-Based Corrections.)

In fact, it can be fairly said that the concept of community corrections was brought into existence because of evidence: that prisons are expensive, and that community-based alternatives to prison are not only cheaper, but often are more effective, too. Yet the primary alternative to a prison sentence—probation—also suffered from a problem of evidence of a different kind. Probation worked well enough. But judges were often hesitant to use it, because it seemed too "soft" for many of the people they were about to sentence.

What was missing, people thought, was an array of correctional methods that were not as restrictive as prison but offered a greater level of control than traditional probation. These soon came to be known as "intermediate sanctions," sentencing alternatives that were neither prison nor probation, but something in between. Part of what set these new correctional strategies apart from the traditional approaches was the idea that they would be based on "what works" rather than simply what sounds good. The new correctional methods would be studied. The ones that succeeded would be more widely emulated. Those that failed would be reformed or eliminated. The era of Evidence-Based Practice was born.

LEARNING OBJECTIVES

After reading this chapter, you should be able to . . .

1. Explain the rationale for nonincarceration penalties.
2. Explain the rationale for intermediate sanctions.
3. Illustrate the continuum-of-sanctions concept.
4. Describe some of the problems associated with intermediate sanctions.
5. List the various types of intermediate sanctions and who administers them.
6. Explain what it takes to make intermediate sanctions work.
7. Assess the role of the new correctional professional.
8. Explain how community corrections legislation works and evaluate its effectiveness.
9. Assess the future of probation, intermediate sanctions, and community corrections.

LO 1

Explain the rationale for nonincarceration penalties.

INTERMEDIATE SANCTIONS IN CORRECTIONS

Prison is expensive, no doubt about it. More than $80 billion is spent on corrections each year.[1] Over 90 percent of that goes to pay for incarceration, even though more than two-thirds of people under correctional authority are under community supervision. A year behind bars costs 25–50 times as much as a year on probation. In many states the correctional budget exceeds the higher-education budget. Years of growth in prison expenditures have often been matched by an equivalent drop in education dollars.

More and more, policy makers look at the prison budget and wonder if there is a less expensive way to carry out punishments. Especially in times when state-level revenues are tight and governors face the possibility of having to cut popular health and education programs, prison costs come under scrutiny.

Undeniably, prison is more expensive than probation because it provides total control over a person's life in a way probation cannot. For this reason, people who want to save money by doing something less expensive than prison have been uneasy with probation as the only alternative. As Norval Morris and Michael Tonry have noted, "Prison is used excessively; probation is used even more excessively; between the two is a near vacuum of purposive and enforced punishments."[2]

Judges know that prison is often too much and probation is just as often not enough. For first-timers convicted of nonviolent crimes who have solid links to the community such as a good job, judges generally feel comfortable with a probation term. But the truly first-time, nonviolent felony case is unusual. Much more commonly, a felony conviction is not the person's first crime. Too often, probation or some other sanction has been tried before, and the person has ended up in trouble again.

Just as often, the crime is serious but not alarming. For instance, the person was caught once again using drugs (or was implicated in another theft or was caught with an illegal handgun or got drunk and got in a fight). What good would another term of probation do? What message would it send?

Yet just as clearly, a prison term makes little sense. The 30 months or so of a frequent sentence will require $50,000 or more from the taxpayer; this seems expensive in view of the minor costs of the crime itself. Further, people who go to prison do not have better prospects of making it than do people who remain in the community.

There are other considerations. Most people accused of a crime have dependents—a spouse and/or children—and what will happen to them when the person goes to prison? Many studies have shown that children and families suffer many hardships, ranging from financial to psychological, when a loved one is incarcerated.[3] One of those hardships costs everyone in the long run: In the United States, children of people who go to prison are more likely than others to end up in trouble with the law and eventually land in prison themselves.

And what about the victims? They may seem to want the toughest penalty the law provides, but getting the judge to choose a prison sentence will gain little for the victim. Too many victims leave court feeling alienated from justice, whatever the sentence. Further, they all face the uphill battle of recovering from the emotional and practical costs of crime, a battle that the sentence does little to help. At least people on probation can be ordered to pay restitution. With probation officers' caseloads often 100 or more, what can one realistically expect?

Finally, many types of nonprison sentences seem to lead to lower recidivism rates. Perhaps going to prison makes people less likely to obey the law, or staying in the community makes adjustment to a law-abiding life easier. But if the idea is to help people turn their lives around, in most cases the judge wants a far better choices than sending them to prison.

For all of these reasons, our society benefits from choices that fall between probation and prison—intermediate sanctions that are more exacting than probation but less costly and with fewer collateral consequences than prison. In this chapter we present and analyze nonprobation programs designed to keep people who have been convicted of crimes in local community corrections instead of prisons.

THE CASE FOR INTERMEDIATE SANCTIONS

LO 2

Explain the rationale for intermediate sanctions.

The enormous cost of incarceration is a powerful practical argument for community-based alternatives. But there are other reasons that we need a range of correctional strategies between probation and imprisonment, including these: (1) imprisonment is too restrictive, (2) traditional probation does not work, and (3) justice is well served by having options in between. In the following sections we explore these arguments in more detail.

Unnecessary Imprisonment

Americans have traditionally tended to equate prison with punishment. When someone is sentenced to something other than prison, many people suspect that the person "got off"; similarly, a person who receives a short prison sentence is thought to have "gotten a break." Yet to treat prison as the primary means of punishment is wrong on two grounds.

First, most sanctions in Western democracies do not involve imprisonment. In the United States, probation is the most common sanction: For every person in prison or jail, three are on probation or parole. In Europe this is even more evident. For example, Germany imposes fines as a sole sanction on two-thirds of those convicted of property crimes; in England the figure approaches half. Community service is the preferred sanction for property crimes in England. Further, Sweden, the Netherlands, France, Austria—and virtually every other European Common Market country—use such sanctions far more than incarceration. Because nonprison sanctions are a worldwide phenomenon, it makes little sense to think of them as lack of punishment.

Second, prison is simply not effective in most cases. We expect prison to deter someone from a life of crime, but evidence speaks to the contrary. A host of recent studies now show that people who go to prison do worse after their release than they would have done under a sentence to a community penalty.[4] Along these lines, public sentiment about nonprison punishment appears to be changing. A recent national survey sponsored by the Pew Charitable Trusts found strong public support for reducing the prison population (see Figure 9.1).

If prison is neither the most common nor the most effective sanction, why does it dominate our thinking on punishment? Perhaps it is time to recognize that corrections can and should develop nonincarcerative sanctions that fill the gap between prison and probation.

Limitations of Probation

As we mentioned in Chapter 8, probation may not work with everyone. Because many probation officers handle 100 or more cases at a time, the average person on probation gets maybe 15 minutes of contact per week—hardly meaningful supervision. Further, in many cases this supervision does not really address problems that matter. The probation officer may check the person's pay stubs and test for drug use. But in the limited time available, little may happen to help the person achieve a change in lifestyle.

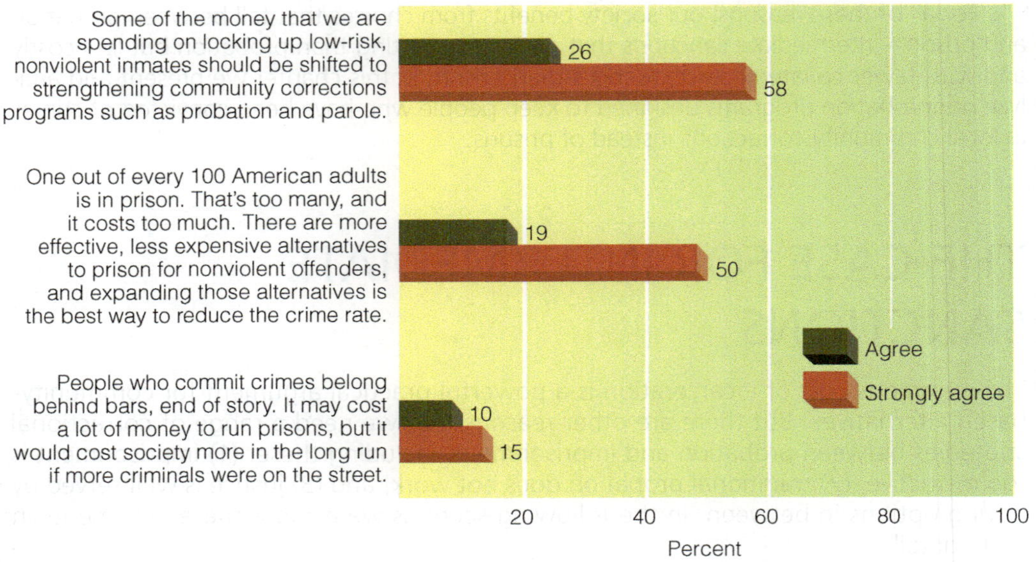

FIGURE 9.1 Public Opinion About Punishment

A majority of Americans approve of intermediate sanctions for most kinds of nonviolent crimes.

Source: Pew Center for the States, *Public Opinion on Sentencing and Corrections Policy in America* (Washington, DC: Author, 2012).

Intermediate sanctions can improve traditional probation supervision in two ways. First, they can intensify supervision. Second, they can provide specialized programs better suited to more-important needs.

Improvements in Justice

Judges sometimes complain that their sentencing choices are limited. They face the need to sentence people whose cases do not warrant prison but for whom probation seems inadequate. Developing an array of sanctions between these two extremes lets judges better match the sentence to the crime. Similarly, when supervision conditions are broken, some response is needed to maintain the credibility of the rules. However, sending the violator to prison for behavior that is not otherwise criminal seems unwarranted.

continuum of sanctions A graded range of correctional management strategies based on the degree of intrusiveness and control, along which a client is moved based on his or her response to those correctional programs.

Finally, intermediate sanctions allow a closer tailoring of the punishment to the situation. Sometimes, a fine is adequate punishment. Other situations may call for a drug treatment program. In still other cases, a period of home confinement will be sufficient. In sum, intermediate sanctions, tailored to fit the specific circumstances, may provide the greatest justice. This may be one reason why public opinion surveys so consistently find support for intermediate sanctions as alternatives to prison and traditional probation.

LO 3

Illustrate the continuum-of-sanctions concept.

CONTINUUM OF SANCTIONS

Intermediate sanctions fit the concept of the **continuum of sanctions**—a range of punishments that vary in intrusiveness and control, as shown in Figure 9.2. Probation plus a fine or community service may be appropriate for minor offenses, whereas six weeks of boot camp followed by intensive probation supervision may be right for serious crimes.

The continuum-of-sanctions concept also incorporates a range of correctional management strategies that vary in intrusiveness and control. Clients are initially assigned to a level of control, depending on the seriousness of their offense and their prior record. They may then move to a less or a more restrictive level, depending on how well they do at each level. For example, a person might start with a 7:00 P.M.

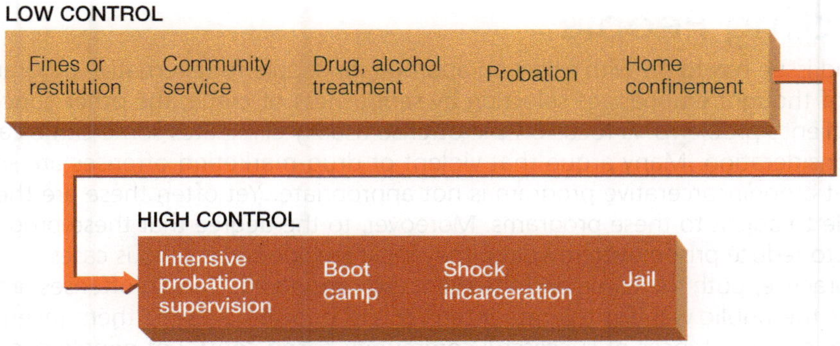

FIGURE 9.2 Continuum of Sanctions

Judges may use a range of intermediate sanctions, from those exerting a low level of control to those exerting a high level.

curfew, a community service obligation, and mandatory treatment programs on the weekends. If those restrictions are satisfactorily met for six months, the person might have the curfew rescinded.

Many jurisdictions have developed a continuum of sanctions, and its advantages now seem plain. First, it increases the corrections system's flexibility. As jails and prisons become more crowded, some clients can be moved to less restrictive options, such as work release programs. Second, it allows more-responsive management of individuals. Thus, if a person on regular probation is not reporting, a brief home confinement can be followed by a return to probation. Finally, it costs less than other alternatives.

Both state and county agencies can benefit from using a continuum of sanctions. Further, this approach can be either codified into law or operated as a practice agreed to by the various correctional agencies. For instance, in Maricopa County, Arizona, the combined resources of multiple agencies—the jail, treatment centers, and probation—are used to develop the punishment system along a continuum of sanctions. This meets the same aims as the state of Delaware's sentencing accountability system, but it is neither a part of penal law nor operated by a single state agency.

PROBLEMS WITH INTERMEDIATE SANCTIONS

LO 4

Describe some of the problems associated with intermediate sanctions.

Despite the growing range of available alternatives to incarceration and parole, all is not well with the intermediate sanctions movement. Problems arise in selecting which agencies will operate the process and which people will receive the sanctions. Further, intermediate sanctions often inappropriately "widen the net."

Selecting Agencies

Administrators of such traditional correctional agencies as jails, prisons, probation, and parole often argue that they should also administer intermediate sanctions. They claim to have the staff and the experience to design new programs for special subgroups, and they suggest that to maintain program coherence, they ought to operate all correctional processes. Critics counter that because traditional correctional organizations must give the highest priority to traditional operations, they cannot adequately support midrange alternatives. Therefore, new agencies, both public and private, should run intermediate programs. Others believe that intermediate sanctions programs will inevitably be controlled by the probation and prison systems—especially because these systems need intermediate sanctions to resolve swollen caseloads and overcrowded facilities.

Selecting People

A second issue has to do with selecting appropriate people for alternative programs. One school of thought emphasizes selection by seriousness of crime; the other concentrates on the client's problems. A focus on the offense usually eliminates some crime categories from consideration. Many argue that violent or drug-marketing offenses are so abhorrent that a nonincarcerative program is not appropriate. Yet often these are the people best able to adjust to these programs. Moreover, to the degree that these programs are needed to reduce prison overcrowding, they must include some serious cases.

In practice, both the crime and the client are considered. Certain offenses are so serious that the public will not tolerate intermediate punishments for them (even though there are many instances of successful community-based control of people convicted of murder and other serious crimes). At the same time, judges want programs to respond to the needs of the people they sentence.

stakes The potential losses to victims and to the system when someone recidivates; stakes include injury from violent crimes and public pressure resulting from negative publicity.

Underlying this issue is the thorny problem of **stakes**. Most of us would be willing to bet $1 on a 1-in-10 chance of winning $10, yet few of us would be willing to bet $1,000 on a 1-in-10 chance of winning $10,000. The odds are the same, but we stand to lose so much more in the second case. Similarly, intermediate sanctions programs are often unwilling to accept people convicted of serious crimes, particularly violent crimes, even though the chances of them successfully completing a program may be quite good. If one of them commits a new serious crime, the damage to the community and—through negative publicity—to the corrections system can be substantial. With some high-profile cases, the stakes are simply too high, regardless of the amount of risk.

Widening the Net

A third major problem with selecting people for intermediate sanctions is widening the net (see Chapter 7). In some ways this problem is potentially the most damaging because it strikes at the very core of the intermediate sanctions concept. Critics argue that instead of reducing the control over people's lives, the new programs have actually increased it. You can readily see how this might occur. With the existence of an alternative at each possible point in the system, the decision maker can select a more intrusive option than ordinarily would have been imposed. For instance, community service can be added to probation; shock incarceration can be added to a straight probation term.

Available evidence reveals that implementing intermediate sanctions has had three consequences:

1. *Wider nets:* The reforms increase the proportion of people in society whose behavior is regulated or controlled by the state.
2. *Stronger nets:* By intensifying the state's intervention powers, the reforms augment the state's capacity to control people.
3. *Different nets:* The reforms create new jurisdictional authority or transfer it from one agency or control system to another.

LO 5

List the various types of intermediate sanctions and who administers them.

VARIETIES OF INTERMEDIATE SANCTIONS

How the various sanctions programs relate to one another depends on the jurisdiction running them. For example, one county may use intensive supervision in lieu of a jail sentence; another may use it for probation violators. We have organized our description of the main types of intermediate sanctions according to which agencies administer them—the judiciary, probation departments, or correctional departments.

Sanctions Administered by the Judiciary

The demand for intermediate sanctions often comes from judges dissatisfied with their sentencing options. In courts that have managerial authority over probation, this discontent has translated into new probation programs. Other courts have sought to expand their sentencing options by relying more on programs within their control, such as pretrial diversion, fines, forfeiture, community service, and restitution. These programs aim primarily at reducing trial caseloads, especially focusing on less serious cases that need not tie up the court system. The programs also seek to impose meaningful sanctions without incarceration.

Pretrial Diversion The functions of pretrial diversion, especially as a jail alternative, are examined in Chapter 7. Because courts have extremely broad discretion in the pretrial phase of adjudication, some have sought to apply this discretion to a greater range of cases.

Pretrial-diversion programs typically target petty drug crime. A new strategy in Wayne County (Detroit), Michigan, exemplifies this practice. People arrested for first-time drug possession are "fast-tracked" into drug treatment programs within hours of arrest. They are promised that if they successfully complete the drug treatment program, the charges against them will be dropped. This kind of treatment-based diversion program depends on cooperation between the court and the prosecution. Judges indicate their willingness to delay trial if prosecutors are willing to drop charges after the person has demonstrated a change in lifestyle. See "Myths in Corrections" for more about drug treatment as diversion.

MYTHS in Corrections

Hopeless Cases

THE MYTH: Persistent, low-level drug addicts are so down-and-out, so hopeless, that there is really nothing to be done to help them.

THE REALITY: Targeted programs that provide treatment and services for people who are homeless and addicted to drugs—cycling in and out of the justice system on low-level crimes—can reduce recidivism rates by up to 60 percent.

Source: Susan E. Collins, Heather S. Lonczak, and Seema L. Clifasefi, *LEAD Program Evaluation: Recidivism Report* (Seattle: University of Washington— Harborview Medical Center, 2015).

Fines Over $1 billion in fines is collected annually in the United States. Yet, compared with many Western democracies, the United States makes little use of fines as the sole punishment for crimes more serious than motor vehicle violations; the latest national data available show that about 1 percent of people convicted of a felony receive a fine as the sole penalty.[5] Instead, fines are typically used with other sanctions, such as probation and incarceration. For example, it is not unusual for a judge to impose two years' probation and a $500 fine.

Many judges cite the difficulty of enforcing and collecting fines as the reason they do not make greater use of this punishment. They note that the people handled by the court system tend to be poor, and many judges fear that fines would end up being paid from the proceeds of additional illegal acts. Indeed, there is evidence that the imposition of a fine can lead to higher rates of rearrest.[6] Other judges are concerned that relying on fines as an alternative to incarceration would let the more affluent "buy" their way out of jail while forcing the poor to serve time.

In Europe fines are used extensively, are enforced, and are normally the sole sanction for a wide range of crimes. The amounts are geared to both the severity of the offense and the financial resources of the convicted person. To deal with the concern that fines exact a heavier toll on the poor than on the wealthy, Sweden and Germany have developed the **day fine**, which bases the size of the penalty on one's income. For example, a person making $36,500 a year and sentenced to 10 units of punishment would pay $3,650; a person making $3,650 and receiving the same penalty would pay $365 (see "For Critical Thinking"). On the other hand,

day fine A criminal penalty based on the amount of income a person earns in a day's work.

FOR CRITICAL THINKING

Fines and restitution are two of the most commonly used intermediate sanctions. Advocates say they enable a person to be held accountable for a crime without having to impose a term of incarceration. But critics point out that financial penalties can inadvertently favor people who have greater means, and work against the poor. Moreover, financial penalties tend to stack up, leaving people forever dealing with the consequences of their conviction because their money problems keep them in trouble.

1. Do fines work in favor of the rich? What can be done about that?
2. Is it fair to impose monetary penalties that also affect family member quality of life?
3. Is it fair to victims to impose restitution as a sentence when it is clear that a person will never be able to afford to pay it?
4. Does it make sense to stack on financial penalties? At what point does the use of financial penalties become counterproductive?

Source: Karin D. Martin, Sandra Susan Smith, and Wendy Still, "Shackled to Debt: Criminal Justice Financial Obligations and the Barriers to Re-entry They Create," *New Thinking in Community Corrections Paper No. 4* (Washington, DC: National Institute of Justice, 2017).

because fines are so problematic for so many of the very poor who go through the justice system, some jurisdictions are eliminating them altogether. (See Focus on Policy: Ending Criminal Fees for Criminal Justice, in Chapter 8.)

Forfeiture With the passage of the Racketeer Influenced and Corrupt Organizations Act (RICO) and the Continuing Criminal Enterprise Act (CCE) in 1970, Congress resurrected forfeiture, a criminal sanction that had lain dormant since the American Revolution. Through amendments in 1984 and 1986, Congress improved ways to implement the law, making prosecution easier. Similar laws are now found in several states, particularly with respect to controlled substances and organized crime.

forfeiture Government seizure of property and other assets derived from or used in criminal activity.

Forfeiture, in which the government seizes property derived from or used in criminal activity, can take both civil and criminal forms. Under civil law, property used in criminal activity (for example, automobiles, boats, or equipment used to manufacture illegal drugs) can be seized without a finding of guilt. Under criminal law, forfeiture is imposed as a consequence of conviction and allows the courts to impound various assets related to the crime. These assets can be considerable. In 2019 a total of $2.2 billion in assets were seized under asset forfeiture laws—two-thirds the total losses of all the burglaries that same year.[7]

However, forfeiture is controversial. When money like this is involved, it can create perverse incentives for law enforcement to handle certain cases, just because they will lead to money being forfeited. Critics also argue that confiscating property without a court hearing violates citizens' constitutional rights. In 1993 the U.S. Supreme Court restricted the use of summary forfeiture. Now the use of this sanction has waned.[8]

community service Compensation for injury to society by the performance of service in the community.

restitution Compensation for financial, physical, or emotional loss caused by the crime, in the form of either payment of money to the victim or to a public fund for crime victims, as stipulated by the court.

Community Service and Restitution

Although for years judges have imposed community service and restitution, few judges have used them as exclusive sanctions. Recently, with prisons overcrowded and judges searching for efficient sentencing options, interest in these sanctions has increased.

© Matthew Berry/Eagle-Gazette

▲ *Community service replaces jail terms with work assignments that benefit the community. Here, Anthony Diles helps renovate a school in Lancaster, PA as part of his sentence.*

Community service requires the performance of a specified number of hours of free labor in some public service, such as street cleaning, repair of run-down housing, or hospital volunteer work. **Restitution** is compensation for financial, physical, or emotional loss caused by the crime, in the form of either payment of money to the victim or to a public fund for crime victims.

Both alternatives rest on the assumption that a person can atone for the crime with a personal or financial contribution to the victim or to society. They have been called *reparative alternatives* because they seek to repair some of the harm done. Such approaches have become popular because they force a positive contribution to be made to offset the damage, thus satisfying a common public desire that people not "get away" with their crimes.

The effectiveness of these programs is mixed. Studies have found that, without such programs, many—perhaps most—of the people who were ordered to provide community service and restitution would have been punished with a traditional probation sentence. This does not speak strongly to community service being a real solution for correctional crowding. Moreover, people made to pay restitution experience it as both punitive and rehabilitative. And people sentenced to community service may end up having lower rearrest rates than would be expected if they had been sentenced differently.

In sum, community service and restitution show that simply implementing a so-called alternative does not always achieve the aims of intermediate sanctions. In order not to widen the net, careful attention must be paid to selecting appropriate people for these programs. Judicial decision making must be controlled to ensure that people who enter the programs are those who otherwise would have been incarcerated.

Sanctions Administered by Probation Departments

One basic argument for intermediate sanctions is that probation, as traditionally practiced, is inadequate for a large portion of people convicted of crimes, particularly serious crimes. Probation leaders have responded to this criticism by developing new intermediate sanctions programs and expanding old ones. New programs often rely on increased surveillance and control. Often, old programs are revamped to become more efficient and expanded to fit more people.

Day Reporting (Treatment) Centers Recently, as prisons became more and more crowded, judges grew reluctant to incarcerate probation violators except when the violation involved a new crime. As a result, people on probation in some jurisdictions came to realize that they could disregard probation rules with relative impunity. Probation administrators found that the lack of credibility with clients severely hampered their effectiveness.

The solution seemed to be the development of probation-run enforcement programs. For example, Georgia has experimented with **probation centers**, where persistent probation violators reside for short periods. Massachusetts and New York City have instituted *day reporting centers,* where violators attend daylong intervention and treatment sessions (see Chapter 7). Minnesota and other states have established **restitution centers**, where those who fall behind in restitution are sent to make payments on their debt.

probation center Residential facility where persistent probation violators are sent for short periods of time.

restitution center Facility where people who fall behind in restitution are sent to make payments on their debt.

All of these types of centers are modeled after an innovation developed in Great Britain in the 1970s. In the United States these facilities vary widely, but all provide a credible option for probation agencies to enforce conditions when prisons are overcrowded. All of them, regardless of specific type, are usually referred to as day reporting centers. Most day reporting centers use a mix of common correctional methods. For example, some provide a treatment regimen comparable to that of a halfway house—but without the problems of running a residential facility. Others provide contact levels equal to or greater than intensive supervision programs, in effect creating a community equivalent to confinement.

The most sophisticated study of day reporting centers to date does not support this approach. A three-year follow-up of almost 3,000 participants in day reporting centers found that they did worse on all outcome measures: rearrest, reconviction, and return to prison.[9] One problem common to newly established intermediate sanctions programs is that stringent eligibility requirements result in small numbers of cases entering the program.

Day reporting centers are growing in popularity faster than evidence concerning their effectiveness, with hundreds of programs now operating in more than half of the states. If they do not affect recidivism, then the ultimate test of these programs will involve two questions: (1) how much do they improve probation's credibility as a sanction? and (2) how well do they combat jail and prison crowding?

intensive supervision probation (ISP) Probation granted with conditions of strict reporting to a probation officer who has a limited caseload.

Intensive Supervision

Intensive supervision probation (ISP) seems ideally suited to the pressures facing corrections. Because ISP targets those who are subject to incarceration, it should help alleviate crowding; because ISP involves strict supervision, it responds to community pressures to be in control.

What constitutes intensive supervision? Even the most ambitious programs require only daily contacts between probation officers and those they are supervising. Such contacts, which can last 10 minutes or less, never occupy more than a minuscule portion of the client's waking hours. So, no matter how intensive the supervision, substantial trust must still be placed in the person on probation.

Early evaluations of ISP programs in Georgia, New York, and Texas found that intensive supervision can reduce rearrest rates. Nevertheless, these programs were not received without controversy. For one thing, the low number of rearrests came at a cost. All evaluations of intensive supervision found that, probably because of the closer contact, probation officers uncovered more rules violations than they did in regular probation. Therefore, ISP programs often had higher technical failure rates than did regular probation, even though ISP clients had fewer arrests.

This was precisely what researchers found in a series of important experiments testing ISP effectiveness. People on probation in California were randomly assigned to either ISP or regular supervision. Results indicated no differences in overall rearrest rates but substantial differences in probation failure rates. ISP clients did much worse under the stricter rules—possibly because ISP makes detecting rules violations easier.[10] Later studies also found that ISP did not result in lower rates of revocation.[11] In sum, these programs not only failed to reduce crime but actually cost the public more than if the programs had not been started in the first place.

Despite questions about the effectiveness of ISP, the approach has enjoyed wide support from correctional administrators, judges, and even prosecutors. The close supervision has revitalized the reputation of probation in the criminal justice system. It has also demonstrated probation's ability to enforce strict rules, ensure employment, support treatment programs, and so forth. Given the positive public relations, ISP is likely here to stay.

Although intensive supervision may satisfy public demands for control measures, the people placed on probation continue to need various forms of assistance. Many of them face serious personal problems—unemployment, emotional and family crises, substance abuse—that require service or treatment. Therefore, officers still have to juggle the roles of helper and controller. On paper the conflicts between these roles in ISP programs may seem less extreme, but in practice they may well continue and perhaps be exacerbated by the mixed messages of the programs.

home confinement Sentence whereby people serve a term of incarceration in their own home.

Home Confinement

Under **home confinement**, people are sentenced to incarceration but serve their term in their own home. Variations are possible. For instance, after a time some might be allowed to go to work or simply leave home for restricted periods during the day; others might be allowed to maintain employment for their entire sentence. Whatever the details, the concept involves using the person's residence as the place of punishment.

On the surface, the idea of home confinement is appealing. It costs the state nothing for housing; the client pays for lodging, subsistence, and often even the cost of an electronic monitor. More importantly, significant community ties can be maintained—to family, friends (restricted visitation is ordinarily allowed), employers, and community groups. The punishment is more visible to the community than when the sentence is prison. The goals of reintegration, deterrence, and financial responsibility are served simultaneously. When people know a little bit about home confinement, they tend to favor it for many kinds of crimes. To illustrate how powerful this can be, some criminal justice college classes require students to stay at home for an entire 24-hour period. Students generally learn that a long stay at home would be quite a penalty. Evaluations of home confinement suggest that the home confinement can be an effective way of helping people transition from confinement to release to the community.[12] However, as a direct sentence, the value of home confinement seems to wear off after a few months; it is increasingly difficult to enforce detention conditions as the sentence rounds into its second half-year. The program seems best suited to low-risk cases who have relatively stable residences.[13]

Electronic Monitoring One of the most popular approaches to probation supervision is surveillance by electronic monitors. The use of electronic monitors more than doubled since 2005.[14] Electronic monitoring is ordinarily combined with and used to enforce home confinement. The total number of people currently under monitoring is difficult to estimate because the equipment manufacturers consider this to be privileged information, but one estimate holds that there are almost 100,000 people under electronic monitoring in the criminal justice system.[15] For most of these people, monitoring is a condition of a probation sentence.

Two basic types of electronic-monitoring devices exist. Passive monitors respond only to inquiries; most commonly there is an automated telephone call from the probation office, and the device has to be placed on a receiver attached to the phone. Active devices send continuous signals that are picked up by a receiver; a computer notes any break in the signal.

Advances in the technology will soon make passive monitors obsolete. The coming generation of devices will be smaller and less awkward to wear. The data they send will be combined with mapping data to show the exact whereabouts at any given time of the person being monitored, including whether the person has ventured into a restricted area and whether there is another person under monitor control close by. The companies that provide electronic monitoring advocate that a "new generation" of devices and programs will more closely integrate monitoring into treatment aspects of programs, rather than just providing surveillance.[16] The chances for a deeper penetration into the life of a person who is on the streets seem already upon us.[17]

Advocates of these systems point out that they are tougher than probation and cheaper than incarceration (a per diem cost of $6–$20 for electronic monitoring versus $40–$90 for jail), especially because the client often pays to use the system.[18] Yet even if most of the 14,200 people under electronic monitoring as a condition of a jail sentence have been truly diverted from confinement, that is only around 1.7 percent of the total jail population.[19] Nonetheless, these systems are more humane than prison or jail because people under surveillance can keep their jobs and stay with their families. In addition, probation officers are free to spend more time providing services rather than carrying out surveillance.

Studies of electronic monitoring show that they hold promise for achieving important correctional goals. Florida's community control cases have lower rearrest rates than people sentenced to jail, and this large program of electronic monitoring is believed to save the state a considerable amount of money, though studies in other states have not been as positive.[20] An electronic monitoring experiment in San Diego for people convicted of sex crimes found higher rates of compliance with registry laws and lower rearrest rates, suggesting that electronic monitoring could be successful with this kind of conviction, which typically results in a prison sentence.[21] A large field study in Denmark found that electronic monitoring proved less harmful than prison for people under correctional control, indicating that it is a more humane alternative.[22]

Some observers oppose electronic monitoring because only people who own telephones and who can afford the $25–$100 per week that these systems cost to rent are eligible. In addition, confinement to the home is no guarantee that crimes will not occur. Many crimes—child abuse, drug sales, and assaults, to name a few—commonly occur in residences.

Moreover, the reliability of these devices has recently become an issue. Some people have figured out how to remove the monitors without detection; others have been arrested at the scene of a crime—even though the monitoring system indicated that they were safely at home. Monitors can also intrude on the privacy of the family and be unduly stressful for the family.

Despite these drawbacks, the use of electronic monitoring will likely continue to increase, along with technological advances. Recently, global positioning systems (GPS), which use satellite tracking devices to monitor whereabouts, have become more feasible. These new approaches provide 24-hour verification of a person's exact location.

Sanctions Administered by Correctional Departments

Correctional agencies have had to develop intermediate sanctions to manage their burgeoning caseloads. Some correctional agencies rely on electronic monitoring to support an early-release program, but shock incarceration and boot camps are the two most common responses to overcrowding.

shock incarceration A short period of incarceration (the "shock"), followed by a sentence reduction.

Shock Incarceration The fact that the deterrent effect of incarceration wears off after a very short term of imprisonment has led to experimentation with **shock incarceration**. The person is sentenced to a jail or prison term; then, after 30–90 days, the judge reduces the sentence. The assumption is that the jail experience will be so distasteful that the person will be motivated to "stay clean."

Shock incarceration is controversial. Its critics argue that it combines the undesirable aspects of both probation and imprisonment. People who are incarcerated lose their jobs, have their community relationships disrupted, acquire the convict label, and are exposed to the brutalizing experiences of the institution. Further, the release to probation reinforces the idea that the system is arbitrary in decision making and that probation is a "break" rather than a truly individualized supervision program. It is hard to see how such treatment will not be demeaning and embittering. As we pointed out at the opening of this chapter, many studies of shock incarceration showed no improvement in recidivism rates. Nonetheless, interest has remained high, leading to a new form of the shock technique called boot camp.

boot camp A physically rigorous, disciplined, and demanding regimen emphasizing conditioning, education, and job training, designed primarily for the young.

Boot Camp One variation on shock incarceration is the **boot camp**, in which young people serve a short institutional sentence and then go through a rigorous, paramilitary regimen designed to develop discipline and respect for authority. The daily routine includes strenuous workouts, marches, drills, and hard physical labor.

Proponents of boot camp argue that many young people get involved in crime because they lack self-respect and cannot order their lives. Consequently, the boot camp model targets young first-timers who seem to be embarking on a path of sustained criminality. Evaluations show that those who are given boot camp may improve in self-esteem. But critics argue that military-style physical training and the harshness of the experience do little to overcome problems that get inner-city youths in trouble with the law. In fact, follow-ups of boot camp graduates show they do no better than others after release. This ineffectiveness has led several authorities to close their boot camps. Even more troubling are the charges of fatal physical abuse that, in some states, have led to the closing of all of their boot camps.

Studies show that only boot camps that are carefully designed, target the right people, and give them rehabilitative services are likely to save money and reduce recidivism.[23] Too many boot camps overemphasize discipline, to the detriment of the graduates. In fact, in Maricopa County, Arizona, a special group had to be set up for boot camp graduates because their failure rates were so high after leaving the program.

▲ *Gaylia Mills earned release from the Flowood Restitution Center in Jackson, MS, by earning $2,893, working at a drive-in restaurant while living at the Center. Her restitution order came after she violated the terms of her probation on a drug possession charge.*

Do boot camps work? There is no firm answer, but results to date have not been promising.[24] Perhaps job training and education would be more beneficial than physical training. The intentionally harsh tactics of boot camp are brutal, especially for impressionable young people, and even when these tactics are combined with a heavy emphasis on rehabilitation programming, they appear to fail to reduce rearrest rates. Nevertheless, the approach has proved popular with a public that is searching for new ways to deal with crime.

MAKING INTERMEDIATE SANCTIONS WORK

LO 6

Explain what it takes to make intermediate sanctions work.

Intermediate sanctions have not been used long enough to allow a complete evaluation of their effectiveness. Only a few of the hundreds of programs attempted since the mid-1980s have been studied. Summaries of the value of intermediate sanctions note frequent failures to achieve goals, but that certainly does not mean the idea should be abandoned.

One evaluation problem is that intermediate sanctions often profess lofty goals such as improving justice, saving money, and preventing crime. Yet the limited record on intermediate sanctions suggests that these goals are not always accomplished. If intermediate sanctions are to work, they must be carefully planned and implemented. Even then they must overcome obstacles and resolve such issues as sentencing philosophies and practices, selection criteria, and surveillance and control methods.

Sentencing Issues

The most important issue concerning the use of intermediate sanctions has to do with sentencing philosophy and practice. In recent years, greater emphasis has been placed on deserved punishment: the idea that similar offenses deserve penalties of similar severity. Intermediate sanctions could potentially increase the number of midrange punishments and thereby improve justice.

Yet advocates of deserved punishment argue that it is not automatically evident how intermediate sanctions compare with either prison or probation in terms of severity, nor is it clear how they compare with one another. For example, placing someone on intensive probation while ordering someone else to pay a heavy fine may violate the equal punishment rationale of just deserts.

When intermediate sanctions are used to reduce prison crowding, the issue becomes even murkier. For example, is it fair for some to receive prison terms while others receive the intermediate sanction alternative?

For intermediate sanctions to be effective, exchange rates consistent with the **principle of interchangeability** must be developed so that one form can be substituted for or added to another form. In other words, different forms of intermediate sanctions must be calibrated to make them equivalent as punishments despite their differences in approach. For example, 2 weeks of jail might be considered equal to 30 days of intermittent confinement or 2 months of home confinement or 100 hours of community service or 1 month's salary.

principle of interchangeability The idea that different forms of intermediate sanctions can be calibrated to make them equivalent as punishments despite their differences in approach.

Advocates say that, in terms of intrusiveness, a short prison sentence can be roughly equivalent to some intensive supervision programs or residential drug treatment and that various forms of intermediate sanctions can be made roughly equivalent to one another. It is clear, both from studies and from experience, that some people would rather be in prison than be placed on tough intermediate sanctions. Thus, one can design intermediate sanctions that equal incarceration in terms of intrusion, thereby upholding the principles of deserved punishment.

Yet these studies are troubling in that they find substantial differences across racial groups in the preference for prison over intermediate sanctions. For example, African

Americans and Hispanics are more likely than whites to rate prison as preferable to an intermediate sanction. This raises a concern that widespread adoption of intermediate sanctions may further exacerbate racial disparities in prison populations.

In practice, some observers have tried to structure this principle of interchangeability by describing punishment in terms of units: A month in prison might count as 30 units; a month on intensive supervision might count as 10. Thus, a year on ISP would be about the same as a four-month prison stay. To date, no one has designed a full-blown system of interchangeability, though both the federal sentencing guidelines and those in Oregon embrace the concept of punishment units. The future will likely bring attempts to create interchangeability based on the relative weights of punishments.

Selection Issues

If intermediate sanctions are to work, they must be reserved for the right cases; which clients are chosen, in turn, depends on a program's goals. No matter what the program's goals, however, intermediate sanctions must be made available regardless of race, sex, or age.

The Target Group Intermediate sanctions have two general goals: (1) to serve as a less costly alternative to prison and (2) to provide a more effective alternative to probation. To meet these goals, intermediate sanctions managers search for appropriate cases to include in their program—often a difficult task. But there are plenty of people who are prison-bound yet who seem to be appropriate candidates for intermediate sanctions.

Because of judges' reluctance to divert people from prison, many intermediate sanctions programs billed as prison alternatives actually serve as probation alternatives. As an example, consider boot camp programs, which are usually restricted to first-timers, age 16–25, who have been convicted of property crimes. Boot camp, then, cannot be considered an effective prison alternative because young first-timers convicted of property crimes seldom go to prison. Probation alternatives (often called probation enhancements) face a similar problem. Theoretically, they should be restricted to the highest-risk cases on probation—those needing the most surveillance and control. Typically, however, the conservatism inherent in new programs makes the truly high-risk cases ineligible for the program.

Clearly, when intermediate sanctions are applied to the wrong target group, they cannot achieve their goals. When prison alternatives are applied to nonprison cases, they cannot save money. When probation-enhancement programs are provided to low-risk clients, they cannot reduce much crime.

One possible solution is to use intermediate sanctions as a backup for clients who fail on regular probation or parole. This practice would increase the probability that the target group is composed of high-risk clients and the prison-bound.

Problems of Bias Race, sex, and age bias are of particular concern for intermediate sanctions. Because getting sentenced to an intermediate sanction involves official (usually judicial) discretion, the concern is that white, middle-class cases will receive less harsh treatment than will other groups. In fact, unless program administrators work hard to widen their program's applicability, nonwhites will be most likely to remain incarcerated rather than receive alternative sanctions, and minorities may be more likely to face tougher supervision instead of regular probation.

Alternative sanctions also tend to be designed for men, not women. One could argue that this is reasonable because men make up over 80 percent of the correctional population, but the patently unfair result may be that special programs are available only to men. Moreover, some experts on women who have committed crimes challenge the design of intermediate sanctions, which are often based on tough supervision. They argue that measures for many women should instead emphasize social services.

Solutions to the problem of bias are neither obvious nor uncontroversial. Most observers recognize that some discretion is necessary in placing people in specialized programs. They believe that without the confidence of program officials, people are more likely to fail. This means that automatic eligibility for these programs may not be a good idea. It may be necessary to recognize the potential for bias and to control it by designing programs especially for women, for example, making certain that cultural factors are taken into account in selecting people for these programs.

USING SURVEILLANCE AND CONTROL IN COMMUNITY CORRECTIONS

People who are in prison are always being watched, and they have extreme limits placed on their freedom. In order to be palatable as alternatives to imprisonment, many intermediate sanctions use heightened surveillance and control as a means of demonstrating that intermediate sanctions can also be onerous. The rhetoric of "tough" supervision is designed to instill confidence in a doubting public that keeping people in the community will pose no threat.

Surveillance has other goals as well. Without some degree of surveillance, treatment providers cannot know for sure if a given treatment is working. The providers argue that some form of drug use surveillance, for instance, is essential to any drug treatment program. Deterrenceminded people argue that tough surveillance deters crime in two ways: (1) it makes people less willing to decide to commit a crime because they are being watched so closely, and (2) it catches people still active in crime earlier in their recidivism.

Community corrections uses four general types of control strategies: drugs, electronics, human surveillance, and control programs. They may be used either separately or in combination.

Drug Controls

It is perhaps ironic that a society so concerned about drug abuse uses chemicals as one of the main strategies for controlling human behavior. A long tradition of prescribing drugs for precisely this purpose exists in the United States. Five drugs illustrate the kind of control regimen that is available by using chemicals:

1. Antabuse is frequently given to alcohol abusers. Antabuse blocks the metabolism of alcohol, so if a person on Antabuse drinks, he or she will experience unpleasant side effects, such as severe nausea. The drug is controversial because it is seldom taken voluntarily and its side effects are so undesirable.
2. Sometimes called "chemical castration," the drug Depo-Provera constrains the male sexual response. It is used to reduce or eliminate the sex drive of men convicted of certain sex offenses. The drug is fairly effective in eliminating the capacity to sustain an erection, but it does nothing to counter the aggression inherent in sex offenses.
3. Chlorpromazine (trade names include Thorazine and Largactil) has long been prescribed for people suffering from certain psychotic disorders, such as schizophrenia. Chlorpromazine is a drug designed to help people think more clearly. It may also reduce hallucinations experienced by people with schizophrenia, as well as the likelihood of them engaging in violence toward themselves or others.
4. For clients who suffer from depression, the drug Prozac is often prescribed. Widely used, this drug decreases the low, sad feelings that accompany depression. (Zoloft and Paxil are also used, though less frequently.)

5. To treat opioid addiction, naltrexone and buprenorphine are often prescribed, usually through treatment programs in the community, although some parole systems use long-acting shots for people released from prison.

These examples illustrate the range of problems addressed through drugs and the variety of physical, biological, and emotional responses that these drugs produce. The examples also show the controversial nature of chemical controls—they often have adverse side effects, and their effectiveness is sometimes questionable.

Electronic Controls

Perhaps the most important penological innovation of the 1980s was electronic monitoring. As we saw earlier in the chapter, the idea of electronic monitoring has many advantages: It represents "high-tech" corrections, and it costs less than prison. This technology is becoming particularly popular in community supervision of people convicted of sex crimes.

The electronic age has made possible a quantum leap in surveillance technology. For example, the technology now exists for visual monitoring via telephone lines. Therefore, video screens can be used to ensure that the person is actually at home during the phone call. The probation officer can simply make a call and then conduct a face-to-face interview without ever leaving the office.

Consider also the technology of the "electric fence" that is now used to confine some dogs. It establishes a perimeter (usually the yard) outside of which the dog may not venture without getting an electric shock. This kind of technology might be easily adapted to keep selected individuals away from schools, bars, or other areas. In theory, at least, it could allow extensive freedom within the necessary restrictions.

Some states require people released from prison who have criminal histories for sex crimes to receive some form of parole supervision for life. Another application of technology allows correctional officials to monitor the computer and Internet use of people convicted of sex crimes and to restrict access to sexually explicit websites, under the theory that such websites stimulate the desire for repeat sexual offending.

Human Surveillance Controls

Unlike the technological advances of electronics and drugs, personal contact allows the correctional worker to process an array of subtle information—body language, attitudes, odors, and so forth. When it comes to surveillance, no approach can fully supplant the basic strategy of increasing contact with the experienced correctional worker.

Intensive supervision systems have been used to increase both the frequency and the diversity of this surveillance contact. What makes the surveillance effective is not just how much contact there is but how diverse it is. Clients are seen at the office, in their homes, and at work; they are seen at regular intervals and in "surprise" visits. The dominant effect is an aura of surveillance in which no aspect of the person's life is totally free of potential observation.

In short, through routine and random contacts, the correctional officer can observe a wide range of behavior in a broad array of situations. Increasing this capacity yields a deeper confidence that there is compliance with the law.

One of the most recent trends is to empower everyday citizens to perform their own surveillance. All 50 states now have sex offender registries, and both law enforcement and the general public have access to much of the data on these registries. Sex offender notification laws enable neighbors to keep an eye on any people living near them who have been convicted of a sex crime. Similar measures being considered include sex offender license plates and public access to GPS monitoring. These programs have proved very popular, even though their results have sometimes been problematic. In Chicago, for example, housing restrictions placed on people with sex crime histories can exclude them from vast sections of the neighborhoods where most of them can afford to live, and as a consequence many live in places that violate the restrictions because of proximity to a school or day-care center.[25]

Programmatic Controls

The most widely used techniques of surveillance and control are established elements of treatment programs. Drug testing is a good example. In these programs, urine samples are routinely taken to test for drug use. Normally, a urine sample has to be submitted (with a correctional worker watching as it is "produced" to ensure whose urine it is) and then sent to a lab for testing. Recently, on-the-spot tests have been developed to overcome the problem of delays in test results.

Programs also sometimes provide for systems of surveillance and control to support treatment. Vermont's Relapse Prevention Program trains the client to be aware of potential "signals" that indicate a return to deviant sexual behavior, and selected individuals living in the client's personal community—family, friends, therapists, and coworkers—are taught to look for the same signs. In effect, these people become additional eyes and ears for the correctional worker, who regularly contacts them to see if the person is exhibiting behavioral changes that should concern the authorities. Similarly, electronic monitoring is being tested to aid programs for school truants and for people who have been ordered to pay child support.[26]

THE NEW CORRECTIONAL PROFESSIONAL

LO 7
Assess the role of the new correctional professional.

Without a doubt, the advent of intermediate sanctions has changed the work world of the professional in corrections. The long-standing choice between prison and probation now includes community and residential options that run the gamut from tough, surveillance-oriented operations to supportive, treatment-based programs. The kinds of professionals needed to staff these programs vary from recent college graduates to experienced and well-trained mental health clinicians. However, three major shifts in the working environment of the new correctional professional are central to this growth.

First, nongovernment organizations have emerged to administer community corrections programs. Hundreds of nonprofit agencies now dot the correctional landscape. These organizations contract with probation and parole agencies to provide services to clients in the community.

Second, an increased emphasis on accountability has reduced individual discretion. Professionals currently work within boundaries, often defined as guidelines, that specify policy options in different case types. For instance, a staff member may be told that each client must be seen twice a month in the office and once a month in the community and that each time a urine sample must be taken. Rules such as these not only constrain discretion but also provide a basis for holding staff accountable.

Third, the relationship between the professional and the client has become less important than the principles of criminal justice that underlie that relationship. Instead of training in psychology and counseling, for instance, the new correctional professional receives training in law and criminal justice decision making. This means that the sources of job satisfaction have shifted from helping people with their problems toward simply shepherding them through the system.

Perhaps the most important change is the advent of Evidence-Based Practice, mentioned at the opening of this chapter. The new correctional professional is expected to be comfortable working with discretion that is structured by years of study of "what works." (See Focus on Correctional Practice: Evidence-Based Practice.) The job has always been one in which it was important to learn from experience. But now the experiences that shape the work include a host of studies that provide the guidance, not just the day-to-day lessons of the job.

Thus, the new correctional professional is more accountable for decision making and is more oriented toward the system in carrying out agency policy. This has significant

FOCUS ON

CORRECTIONAL POLICY: RECLAIM Ohio?

RECLAIM (Reasoned and Equitable Community and Local Alternatives to the Incarceration of Minors) Ohio is a funding strategy that encourages evidence-based practices in local juvenile justice systems, especially probation. Juvenile courts develop or purchase a range of community-based options to meet the needs of local juveniles. When the system diverts youths from Ohio Department of Youth Services (DYS) institutions, courts get special funds to manage the youths locally through RECLAIM.

RECLAIM was created on July 1, 1993, to meet the need for better local alternatives for juvenile courts to stem overcrowding in Ohio's youth institutions. County-level juvenile courts receive a yearly allocation of funds from DYS for the local treatment of at-risk youths. The allocation is based on the number of juveniles processed through the court system and is reduced on a per capita basis for every youth from that county who is incarcerated. The highest allotments go to those counties with a large volume of juvenile justice activity but a low number of referrals to state facilities. Keeping youths locally is good fiscal policy for Ohio counties. Each month, after the court's total incarceration costs are subtracted from the monthly allocation, any remaining funds are paid to the court for use in community-based programming.

RECLAIM Ohio has changed juvenile justice in that state. More youths today are being served locally; fewer families are broken. The DYS population declined from 2,600 in May 1992 to about 400 in December 2015. The number of juveniles arrested for crimes has dropped by half, and the rate at which those youths are placed in juvenile institutions has decreased by more than 40 percent. This means that DYS institutions are less crowded, so staff can concentrate treatment and rehabilitative efforts on more-serious, felony-level youths.

At the same time, local probation has received an influx of resources to mount an array of new and evidence-based programs. More than 80 percent of RECLAIM clients succeed on probation, and they have far lower rearrest rates than youths who were sent to DYS institutions. RECLAIM has done what so many systems try to do but fail: shift resources from institutional corrections to community corrections, reducing recidivism and increasing the quality of programming across the board.

Source: Adapted from Ohio Department of Youth Services, http://dys.ohio.gov/Portals/0/PDFs/CommunityPrograms/RECLAIM_Ohio/RECLAIM_Ohio_Statistics_2015.pdf.

implications for the motivation and training of staff, but it also means that in the traditional three-way balance among clients, staff, and the bureaucracy, the last has grown in importance. (See "Careers in Corrections" to learn about one type of correctional professional: addiction treatment specialist.)

LO 8

Explain how community corrections legislation works and evaluate its effectiveness.

COMMUNITY CORRECTIONS LEGISLATION

Most correctional clients in the United States are under state or county authority. Corrections systems located only a few miles apart can vary dramatically in philosophy and practice because of differences in community values, interests, and politics. In most states, judges, prosecutors, and sheriffs are elected by voters in each county. These officials have extensive discretion concerning the disposition of cases. Their decisions often reflect the political and social realities of their community. For instance, a person who crosses the border from Utah to Nevada goes from a state with one of the lowest incarceration rates in the United States to a state with one of the highest, even though their crime rates are nearly identical.

The differences in the style and philosophy of correctional programs in different localities reflect a basic truth about law and order: Beliefs about right and wrong, as well as values about how to deal with wrongdoers, differ from one locality to the next. Over the years the concept of community corrections has revolved around many themes, but one core idea has endured—that local governments know best how to deal with their own crime problems. As such, local and state laws reflect unique ways of implementing community corrections, even though they share similar goals. As we will see in the following discussions, the implementation and evaluation of community corrections must take local differences into account.

FOCUS ON

CORRECTIONAL PRACTICE: Evidence-Based Practice

The term *Evidence-Based Practice* has become a correctional acronym EBP. The idea that professional practices should be evidence-based originated in medicine, when professionals argued that decision making should be based on scientifically robust evidence, rather than intuition or tradition. The idea is that when decisions are based on scientific knowledge rather than gut instinct, they generally turn out better.

In corrections, the EBP paradigm has been slow to take hold; in part, because there is so much discretion in the decisions most correctional staff have to make. But a solid foundation of studies establishes an evidence-based framework for the way correctional systems and staff should interact with their clients. Recently, the National Institute of Corrections (a division of the Federal Bureau of Prisons) summarized the five basic principles of EBP with the clients of corrections:

1. Assess risk systematically—use systematic assessments to determine the client's level of risk, and then focus on cases posing higher rather than lower risk.
2. Enhance motivation to change—use interviewing techniques that improve the client's desire to overcome the problems that lead to crime.
3. Target interventions—systematically assess the problems that are known to lead to more crime, and focus supervision on those problems.
4. Increase positive reinforcements—make sure to provide positive inducements when the client is making progress.
5. Engage community support—make sure that community resources (agencies and other groups) are providing support, too.

In addition to these five principles with clients, there are three EBP principles for staff:

1. Train and give direction—help the staff to understand the principles of EBP and provide training and direction on how to use those principles in daily work.
2. Measure relevant processes and practices—evaluate staff on how well they implement the techniques of EBP.
3. Use feedback—evaluate programs and strategies to make sure they work.

These principles are widely accepted today as being the state-of-the-art for corrections professionals. But they are not etched in stone. That is the secret of EBP. As new evidence comes along, what is considered EBP gets amended and improved.

Source: National Institute of Corrections, *Evidence-Based Practices (EBP)*. https://nicic.gov/evidence-based-practices-ebp (accessed May 17, 2020).

CAREERS IN CORRECTIONS

Addiction Treatment Specialist

Nature of the Work

Drug and alcohol abuse is a major problem that is often linked to criminal behavior. Correctional addiction treatment specialists, also known as clinical social workers or addiction counselors, may work with clients either in prisons or in community health organizations. Addicted clients are usually referred to treatment by the courts or by probation, prison, or parole authorities. Addiction treatment is a major component of community corrections.

Addiction treatment specialists assess and treat individuals with substance problems, including abuse of alcohol or drugs. They develop treatment plans by examining a case's institutional files and gathering information from family members and other counselors. Treatment is through individual and group therapy in either outpatient or residential settings. Twelve-step programs are often incorporated into the treatment regimen.

Required Qualifications

A bachelor's degree in social work and training in addiction therapies are normally the minimal requirements for entry into this position. Some states require a master's degree, certification in addiction treatment, and supervised work experience.

Earnings and Job Outlook

The U.S. Bureau of Labor Statistics expects that the demand for treatment specialists will grow rapidly over the next decade because substance abusers are increasingly being placed into community treatment programs instead of being sent to prison. The median annual salary for a substance abuse and behavioral disorder counselor was $46,240 in 2019.

More Information

You can obtain additional information about this occupation from the website of the U.S. Bureau of Labor Statistics Occupational Outlook Handbook.

Reducing Reliance on Prison

Community corrections legislation is best understood in terms of its goal to reduce reliance on prisons. In pursuit of this goal, it embraces a wide spectrum of alternatives to incarceration among which judges and other criminal justice system officials can choose.

In the late 1960s and early 1970s, several states considered legislation that would establish financial and programmatic incentives for community corrections. For example, in 1965 California passed the Probation Subsidy Act, which sought to reimburse counties for maintaining correctional clients in the local corrections system instead of sending them to state facilities. Lawmakers developed a formula to determine the number who ordinarily would be sent to state institutions and to pay the counties a specified sum for each one not sent to prison. The counties could then use the money to strengthen probation and other local correctional services in order to handle the additional numbers. (See "Thinking Outside the Box.")

THINKING OUTSIDE THE BOX

USING COST–BENEFIT ANALYSIS TO DECIDE ON CORRECTIONAL PROGRAMS

It is now possible to analyze programs in terms of their "cost–benefit ratio." A cost–benefit ratio is a statistic that shows how much benefit is received by a program or correctional strategy for each dollar that it costs. The cost–benefit ratio enables us to compare two different programs in terms of payoff. For example, an expensive correctional program may be so effective that it is worth what it costs; likewise, a much cheaper correctional program may be preferable, even if its outcomes are slightly less desirable.

Policy makers calculate cost–benefit ratios for correctional programs by putting a price tag on the crimes a person commits when a program fails, then comparing the costs of two different programs in terms of both their program costs and the cost differences of their outcomes. Analysts who specialize in this kind of work point out that policy makers often employ programs with unfavorable cost–benefit ratios because they like something about the program. For example, boot camps have problematic cost–benefit ratios because people who go to boot camps do no better than people who are on regular probation. By contrast, people who get multi-systemic family therapy have much better cost–benefit ratios than people who simply go to jail. In the long run, some say, cost–benefit ratios should be used to decide which programs that correctional systems should employ.

Source: Adapted from Patricio Dominquez and Steven Raphael, "The Role of the Cost-of-Crime Literature in Bridging the Gap Between Social Science Research and Policy Making Potentials and Limitations," *Criminology & Public Policy* 14 (no. 4, November 2015): 589–632.

In 1973 Minnesota passed the Comprehensive Community Corrections Act, which funded local corrections systems with money saved by state corrections when individuals were not sentenced to state facilities. Colorado in 1976 and Oregon in 1978 passed legislation patterned after Minnesota's law. The experiences of these pioneering states in community corrections were so well regarded that by 1995, more than half of U.S. states had passed community corrections legislation. (See Focus on Correctional Policy: RECLAIM Ohio? as an example.) By 2007, the vast majority of states had done so, as shown in Figure 9.3.

Community corrections legislation is based on the idea that local justice systems have little incentive to keep their own community members in local corrections. State-administered institutions are funded by state tax revenues, and it costs communities little to send large numbers of cases there. In contrast, it costs local citizens much more to keep clients in jail or on local probation because their taxes pay for those services.

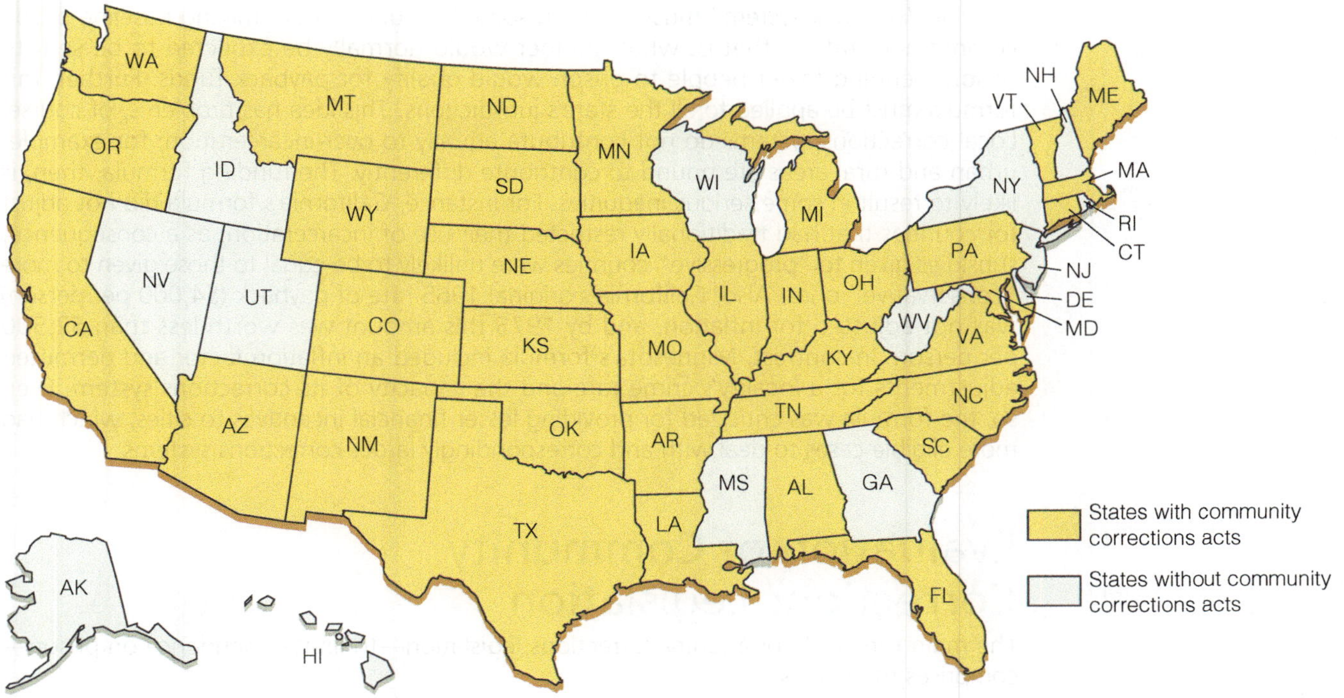

FIGURE 9.3 States with Community Corrections Acts

Many states provide financial incentives for local governments to keep people in local correctional agencies instead of sending them to state prisons.

Source: Mary Shilton, "Community Corrections Acts by State," http://centerforcommunitycorrections.org/?page_id=78, September 24, 2009.

Yet incarceration in a state prison costs substantially more than local incarceration or probation (see Table 9.1). In the long run, centralized, state-administered punishments seem to be more expensive than local corrections. If we also acknowledge that many people are sentenced to state prison when this extreme punishment is not necessary, we can easily see that the financial incentives that favor imprisonment run contrary to good correctional policy.

TABLE 9.1 Costs of Incarceration and Intermediate Sanctions in Four States

In a study of Colorado, North Carolina, Ohio, and Virginia, intermediate sanctions proved far less expensive than imprisonment.

Correctional Method	Cost per Year per Person
Prison	$28,809
Jail	20,227
Probation	1,352
Intensive supervision	3,708
Community service	4,646
Day reporting	4,465
House arrest	651
Electronic monitoring	3,256
Halfway house	20,227
Boot camp	38,384

Source: Based on data from *Seeking Justice: Crime and Punishment in America* (New York: Edna McConnell Clark Foundation, 1997), 34. Adjusted for 2020 inflation by the authors.

The "payback system" must establish some formula for determining baseline prison commitment rates—that is, what number would normally be expected to be sent to prison. Sending fewer people to prison would qualify for payback funds. Further, this formula must be applied to all the state's jurisdictions. This idea has problems, of course. Local corrections systems do not contribute equally to over-incarceration; for example, urban and rural areas are bound to contribute differently. The funding formula, then, is likely to result in some serious inequities. For instance, California's formula did not adjust for counties that had traditionally restricted their use of incarceration; as a consequence, subsidies given to "progressive" counties were unlikely to be equal to those given to more "conservative" ones. Also, California's original 1965 rate of payback ($4,000 per person) was not adjusted for inflation, and by 1975 this amount was worth less than $2,500 per person. In contrast, Minnesota's formula included an inflation factor and permitted adjustments for a locality's crime rate and the capacity of its corrections system. Even so, the formula was criticized for providing lesser financial incentives to cities, which had more eligible cases to deal with and correspondingly larger corrections systems.

Evaluation of Community Corrections Legislation

The main thrust of community corrections legislation—to limit dependence on prison—comprises three aims:

1. To reduce the rate and number of people sentenced to state correctional facilities
2. To reduce tax revenues spent on corrections by transferring both the costs and the funding to less-expensive local correctional facilities
3. To reduce prison populations

Have these aims been achieved? The answer is complicated.

Early evaluations of California's Probation Subsidy Act showed that both adult and juvenile commitments to state facilities decreased immediately following the enactment of the probation subsidy. People who ordinarily would have gone to state facilities were being handled by local correctional agencies at the county level. For reformers, however, the news was not all good. In these local justice systems, the general intrusiveness of corrections increased for both adults and juveniles. More were given jail terms, and more received tighter control through commitment to local drug treatment and mental health facilities. Thus, the overall effect of the subsidy was primarily to transfer incarceration from state-funded prisons to state-subsidized local corrections—hardly a resounding victory for community corrections advocates.

In those early years, community corrections acts did not have much impact on the growth in imprisonment. In most states that enacted such legislation, prisons remained crowded. Parole decisions have become more conservative in some states, counterbalancing modest reductions in commitments achieved by community corrections legislation. Critics argue that the community corrections movement has offered only a surface shift in policies that emphasize incarceration, while the talk of community corrections reform enables the correctional field to continue its costly practices while creating an image of fiscal responsibility.

Yet it would be a mistake to say that community corrections legislation has failed. Recent efforts have provided more-robust incentives to move cases out of traditional prison and into other correctional methods. In Ohio, for example, comprehensive evaluations have demonstrated that RECLAIM Ohio has reduced the number of youths in prison. However, those results are not entirely conclusive.[27] An evaluation of California's enhanced system of community corrections showed a major reduction in the number of people in prison as well as double-digit drops in crime.[28] All studies have found that some cases were shifted to local corrections, which is encouraging. The problem is this: How can administrators control local correctional programs to ensure that prison commitments are actually reduced under the new policies, as the legislation intended? The community

FOCUS ON CORRECTIONAL POLICY: Community Corrections Today

Community corrections is changing. With all the action we have seen in the area of probation, community corrections, and intermediate sanctions, scholars think it is important to return to the values that should undergird the work. Here is a short list of recommendations that one team of scholars has suggested for "reinventing community corrections":

I. Incentivize the use of community corrections.

Recommendation 1: Dispute that imprisonment is the only appropriate response to a conviction.

Recommendation 2: Subsidize the use of community corrections.

Recommendation 3: Make communities pay to use prisons.

II. Focus on recidivism.

Recommendation 4: Hold correctional officials accountable for lowering recidivism.

Recommendation 5: Practice evidence-based programming.

Recommendation 6: Use technology to enhance treatment.

Recommendation 7: Create information that can guide programs.

III. Do less harm.

Recommendation 8: Leave low-risk cases alone whenever possible.

Recommendation 9: Reduce the over-control of people under correctional authority.

Recommendation 10. Help people who have been convicted of crimes to be redeemed.

Source: Adapted from Frances T. Cullen, Cheryl Lero Jonson, and Daniel P. Mears, "Reinventing Community Corrections," *Crime and Justice* 46 (no. 1, 2017).

corrections acts that allow local government to contract with private, nonprofit businesses that provide services claim that they create private jobs while reducing commitments to prison, and this aspect of community corrections acts may benefit all concerned.

Certainly, community corrections is no panacea. The desire to reduce the number of people in prison must be supported by procedures to control the manner in which cases are handled in local programs. (See "Community Corrections Today" for one set of suggestions.)

LO 9

Assess the future of probation, intermediate sanctions, and community corrections.

THE FUTURE OF INTERMEDIATE SANCTIONS AND COMMUNITY CORRECTIONS

What does the future hold for intermediate sanctions and community corrections? Certainly, those who support these programs must address three recurring problems.

First, some way must be found to overcome the seemingly immutable tendency of the criminal justice system to resist placing people in less restrictive options and to keep increasing the level of corrections. As we have seen, studies of nonprison alternatives find that even the most successful programs enroll only a minority of people who would otherwise have been incarcerated. The usual pattern is first to place a person in prison and then to release the person to the community. New alternative programs are filled with people who formerly would have been placed on regular probation. Nonprison programs, whether intermediate sanctions or community corrections programs, must improve their ability to obtain the kinds of cases for which they are intended.

Second, community support for these programs must increase. Too often, citizens fear having the people who have been convicted of crimes live in their midst. Active measures must be taken to allay those fears, to help citizens become comfortable with a correctional mission that recognizes a wide array of programs rather than favoring incarceration.

Third, the purposes of these sanctions must be clarified. No program can operate successfully for long without clearly defined goals. The goals of most programs today state vague and often competing generalizations: rehabilitation, reduction of overcrowding, protection of the community, reintegration, cost-effectiveness, and so on. Although no legitimate government operation can reject any of these considerations, officials must prioritize and clarify some of their objectives before these new forms of correctional functions can take their rightful place as core operations in the overall system.

SUMMARY

1 Explain the rationale for nonincarceration penalties.
Per year, incarceration costs between 25 and 50 times as much as probation. For certain crimes, prison is too harsh a punishment and probation not harsh enough. Neither probation nor prison guarantees that a person will "make it" once his or her term is served. Further, children and families suffer financial, psychological, and other hardships when one of their loved ones goes to prison. Many victims leave court feeling alienated from justice, whatever the sentence. Finally, a range of nonprison sentences seem to lead to lower recidivism rates. For all of these reasons, there needs to be a choice between probation and prison—some intermediate sanction that is more exacting than probation but less costly and with fewer collateral consequences than prison.

2 Explain the rationale for intermediate sanctions.
Intermediate sanctions have arisen because many people believe that a sentence of probation is not strict enough but prison is too extreme. To implement intermediate sanctions, many jurisdictions have developed the continuum-of-sanctions concept, which offers a range of correctional options between prison and probation. To be effective, intermediate sanctions have to target the right group and place less emphasis on surveillance and control and more emphasis on services.

3 Illustrate the continuum-of-sanctions concept.
Corrections systems have developed a range of punishments that vary in intrusiveness and control, providing choices that fall between probation and prison. Probation plus a fine or community service may be appropriate for minor offenses, whereas six weeks of boot camp followed by intensive probation supervision may be right for serious crimes.

4 Describe some of the problems associated with intermediate sanctions.
Problems with intermediate sanctions center on selecting appropriate agencies to run them, selecting the right people to place in them, and avoiding widening the net.

5 List the various types of intermediate sanctions and who administers them.
Courts offer pretrial diversion, fines, forfeiture, community service, and restitution; probation departments offer day reporting centers, intensive supervision, home confinement, and electronic monitoring; correctional departments offer shock incarceration and boot camps.

6 Explain what it takes to make intermediate sanctions work.
To make intermediate sanctions work, there must be interchangeability of sanctions so that penalties in the community can be compared with penalties in confinement. The right people need to be selected for the right programs, and problems of bias must be avoided. Surveillance and control must be carefully used so that sanctions do not backfire.

7 Assess the role of the new correctional professional.
New correctional professionals can work within a context of strong bureaucratic guidelines and high expectations of accountability. They are at ease dealing with nongovernment agencies, and they possess a range of skills at motivating clients to use an array of correctional services.

8 Explain how community corrections legislation works and evaluate its effectiveness.
When communities keep people locally instead of sending them to prison, they save the state money. Community corrections legislation gives the money that was saved back to these communities to fund local programs that manage those clients. These strategies work when the cost incentives are large enough to reward communities for keeping people locally and when jail is not used as a replacement for prison.

9 Assess the future of probation, intermediate sanctions, and community corrections.
Community-based correctional approaches face challenges in getting public support for keeping people in community programs instead of sending them to incarceration. These applications must clarify their mission and become more-crucial components of the correctional array of programs. Justice reinvestment strategies offer one viable way of doing this.

KEY TERMS

boot camp (*p. 246*)
community service (*p. 242*)
continuum of sanctions (*p. 238*)
day fine (*p. 241*)
forfeiture (*p. 242*)
home confinement (*p. 244*)
intensive supervision probation (*ISP*) (*p. 244*)
principle of interchangeability (*p. 247*)
probation center (*p. 243*)
restitution (*p. 242*)
restitution center (*p. 243*)
shock incarceration (*p. 246*)
stakes (*p. 240*)

FOR DISCUSSION

1. How do intermediate sanctions work better—as a way of improving on probation or as a way of avoiding the negatives of imprisonment? Why?
2. Should intermediate sanctions be run by traditional probation and prison systems or by new agencies seeking to serve as alternatives to them?
3. What does the California probation subsidy program tell us about the interdependence of various elements of corrections?
4. Why do states with similar crime rates sometimes have different incarceration rates?
5. Do you think that intermediate sanctions are acceptable to the general public in the current political climate?

FOR FURTHER READING

Byrne, James M., Arthur J. Lurigio, and Joan Petersilia. *Smart Sentencing: The Emergence of Intermediate Sanctions.* Newbury Park, CA: Sage, 2005. Explores various issues in the design and implementation of intermediate sanctions programs, with special reference to programs in the United States.

Griffin, Patricia A., Kirk Heilbrun, Edward P. Mulvey, et al. *The Sequential Intercept Model and Criminal Justice: Promoting Community Alternatives for Individuals with Serious Mental Illness.* New York: Oxford University Press, 2015. A description of the theory and impact of the Sequential Intercept Model (SIM) for dealing with justice-involved people who suffer from serious mental illness.

May, David C., and Peter B. Wood. *Ranking Correctional Punishment: Views from Offenders, Practitioners, and the Public.* Durham, CA: Carolina Academic Press, 2010. Presents the results of a series of studies in which people compared the punitiveness of prison sentences, probation sentences, and the range of intermediate sanctions in between.

Morris, Norval, and Michael Tonry. *Between Prison and Probation: Intermediate Punishments in a Rational Sentencing System.* New York: Oxford University Press, 1990. Original and classic description of intermediate punishments that can sanction people more severely than can nominal probation but less severely than incarceration.

Nellis, Mike, Kristel Beyens, and Dan Kaminski. *Electronically Monitored Punishment: International and Critical Perspectives.* New York: Routledge, 2012. Up-to-date assessment of the scope and impact of electronically monitored community punishments.

Roman, John K., Terence Dunworth, and Kevin Marsh, eds. *Cost–Benefit Analysis and Crime Control.* Washington, DC: Urban Institute Press, 2010. A series of papers that describe ways to assess the cost–benefit outcomes of crime control strategies, with several examples of correctional crime control approaches.

Worrall, Anne, and Clare Hoy. *Punishment in the Community: Managing Offenders, Making Choices.* Portland, OR: Willan, 2005. A critical assessment of the programs and policies of community-based programs, with special attention given to the United Kingdom.

NOTES

1 Diane Whitmore Schanzenbach, Ryan Nunn, Lauren Bauer, et al., *Twelve Facts About Incarceration and Prisoner Reentry* (Washington, DC: Brookings Institution Hamilton Project, 2016).

2 Norval Morris and Michael Tonry, Between Prison and Probation: Intermediate Punishments in a Rational Sentencing System (New York: Oxford University Press, 1990), 3.

3 Sara Wakefield and Christopher Wildeman, Children of the Prison Boom: Mass Incarceration and the Future of American Inequality (New York: Oxford University Press, 2013).

4 Daniel S. Nagin, Francis T. Cullen, and Cheryl Lero Jonson, "Imprisonment and Reoffending," *Crime and Justice* 38 (no. 1, 2009): 115–200. See also Amy Elizabeth Lerman, "The People Prisons Make: Effects of Incarceration on Criminal Psychology," in *Do Prisons Make Us Safer? The Benefits and Costs of the Prison Boom,* edited by Steven Raphael and Michael Stoll (New York: Russell Sage Foundation, 2009), 151–76; William D. Bales and Alex R. Piquero, "Assessing the Impact of Imprisonment on Recidivism," *Journal of Experimental Criminology* 8 (2012): 71–101; Francis T. Cullen, Cheryl Lero Jonson, and Daniel S. Nagin, "Prisons Do Not Reduce Recidivism: The High Cost of Ignoring Science," *Prison Journal* 91 (no. 3, September 2011): 48–65; Damon M. Petrich, Travis C. Pratt, Cheryl Lero Jonson, and Francis T. Cullen, "A Revolving Door? A Meta-Analysis of the Impact of Custodial Sanctions on Reoffending" *Criminology & Public Policy*, forthcoming, 2020.

5 U.S. Department of Justice, *Felony Defendants in Large Urban Counties* (Washington, DC: U.S. Government Printing Office, 2008), 32.

6 Alex Piquero and Wesley G. Jennings, "Research Note: Justice System–Imposed Financial Penalties Increase the Likelihood of Recidivism in a Sample of Juvenile Offenders," *Youth Violence and Juvenile Justice* (September 2016): 1–16.

7 U.S. Department of Justice, *Asset Forfeiture Management Program Annual Report* (Washington, DC: U.S. Department of Justice 2019); *FBI Uniform Crime Reports, 2018; see also* Dick M. Carpenter II, Lisa Knepper, Angela C. Erickson, and Jennifer McDonald, *Policing for Profit,* 2nd ed. (Alexandria, VA: Institute for Justice, 2015).

8 *Austin v. United States*, 61 Lw. 4811 (1993).

9 Jordon M. Hyatt and Michael Ostermann, "Better to Stay Home: Evaluating the Impact of Day Reporting Centers on Offending," *Crime & Delinquency* 65 (no. 1, 2017): 94–121.

10 Joan Petersilia and Susan Turner, Intensive Supervision for High-Risk Offenders: Three California Experiments (Santa Monica, CA: RAND, 1990).

11 Jordan M. Hyatt and Geoffrey C. Barnes, "An Experimental Evaluation of the Impact of Intensive Supervision on the Recidivism of High-Risk Probationers," *Crime & Delinquency* 63 (no. 1, 2017): 3–38.

12 Jessica Bouchard and Jennifer S. Wong, "The New Panopticon? Examining the Effect of Home Confinement on Criminal Recidivism," *Victims & Offenders* 13 (no. 5, 2017): 589–608.

13 Office of Juvenile Justice and Delinquency Prevention, *Home Confinement and Electronic Monitoring: Literature Review* (Washington, DC: U.S. Department of Justice, October 2–14, 2014), https://www.ojjdp.gov/mpg/litreviews/Home_Confinement_EM.pdf.

14 Stephanie Fahey, Adam Gelb, John Gramlich, and Phil Stevenson, *Use of Offender-Tracking Devices Expands Sharply* (Washington, DC: Pew Charitable Trusts, 2016).

15 Electronic Frontier Foundation, *Street-Level Surveillance: Electronic Monitoring*, https://www.eff.org/pages/electronic-monitoring (accessed May 17, 2020).

16 Nuno Caiado, "The Third Way: An Agenda for Electronic Monitoring in the Next Decade," *Journal of Offender Monitoring* 24 (no. 1, 2012): 5–10.

17 Urs Hunkeler, "New Generation of EM Technology: Soon Too Many Sensors?" *Journal of Offender Monitoring* 26 (no. 2, 2015): 6–9.

18 Laura Taylor, "GPS: Frequently Asked Questions," *Journal of Offender Monitoring* 25 (no. 1, 2013): 18.

19 Minton and Zeng, *Jail Inmates.*

20 William D. Bales, Karen Mann, Thomas G. Blomberg, et al., "Electronic Monitoring in Florida," *Journal of Offender Monitoring* 22 (no. 2, 2011): 5–12.

21 Susan Turner, Alyssa W. Chamberlain, Janette Jesse, and James Hess, "Does GPS Improve Recidivism Among High Risk Sex Offenders? Outcomes for California's GPS Pilot for High Risk Sex Offenders," *Victims & Offenders* 10 (no. 1, January 2015): 1–28.

22 Lars H. Anderson and Signe H. Anderson, "Effect of Electronic Monitoring on Social Welfare Dependence," *Criminology & Public Policy* 13 (no. 3, August 2014): 349–80.

23 Megan C. Kurlychek and Cynthia A. Kempinen, "Beyond Boot Camp: The Impact of Aftercare on Offender Reentry," *Criminology & Public Policy* 5 (no. 2, 2006): 363–88.

24 David B. Wilson, Doris L. MacKenzie, and Faw Ngo Mitchell. "Effects of Correctional Boot Camps on Offending." *Campbell Systematic Reviews* 1. http://www.campbellcollaboration.org/lib/download/3/.

25 Lorine A. Hughes and Keri B. Burchfield, "Sex Offender Residence Restrictions in Chicago: An Environmental Injustice?" *Justice Quarterly* 25 (no. 4, December 2008): 647–73.

26 See Rhonda Zingraff, Sheenagh Lopez, and Jennifer McCoy, "Evidence Favors Electronic Monitoring for Improvements in Child Support Collections," *Journal of Electronic Monitoring* 21 (no. 1, January 2009): 5–9; Peter A. Michel, "Truancy Reduction: An Emerging Application for Electronic Monitoring," *Journal of Electronic Monitoring* 21 (no. 2, March 2009): 12–15.

27 Ryan Gies, "RECLAIM Ohio: Still Promoting Reform After 20 Years," www.nccdglobal.org/blog/reclaim-ohio-still promoting -reform-after-20-years, April 21, 2014.

28 California Board of State and Community Corrections, *Performance Metrics for Community Corrections* (Sacramento: Author, 2015).

CHAPTER 10

Incarceration

Photo/FBI

James Morales, who escaped from a private prison in Rhode Island, was accused in a series of crimes immediately following his escape.

JAMES MORALES APPEARED IN COURT AFTER BEING INDICTED BY A FEDERAL GRAND JURY

Morales was charged with escape from the Donald W. Wyatt Detention Facility, which is a privately run prison located in Central Falls, Rhode Island. At the time of his escape, Morales was awaiting trial for weapons violations. Specifically, it is alleged that he broke into an Army Reserve armory and stole several automatic and semiautomatic firearms. Video from the prison's security cameras revealed how Morales broke out. He was able to climb up a basketball hoop, cut a hole in the fence, and then make his way through razor wire. After breaking free, Morales drove to Massachusetts in a stolen car.[1]

The escape received a lot of media attention, and many questions about the case arose. How could somebody escape from a maximum-security detention facility? Why did it take hours before prison officials noticed that Morales was missing? Why weren't local law enforcement officials notified immediately? Did the fact that the prison was operated by a private corporation contribute in any way to the escape? For example, were fewer prison officers employed to ensure adequate profit margins? These are legitimate questions. The public entrusts prison officials to protect them, especially from people who are known to be violent. This is not a small undertaking; there are nearly 1.49 million people currently housed in federal and state correctional institutions.[2]

Although Morales was captured just five days after his escape, he is accused of committing several crimes during that time. For example, once he arrived in the greater Boston metropolitan area, law enforcement officials believe that Morales attempted to rob two area banks. Ultimately, Morales was apprehended by a state trooper, Joseph Merrick, who chased the fugitive on foot for two blocks before making the arrest.[3]

Media reports suggest that the Morales escape was not the first time the relatively new facility (built in 1993) received negative attention. Two high-profile lawsuits, both of which alleged mistreatment by prison staff, resulted in monetary settlements. Attention in the Morales incident was focused on prison officer staffing levels. Specifically, the facility is designed for 140 officers to oversee the 500 or more people incarcerated at the facility. However, at the time of the escape, only about 100 officers were employed there.[4] This case brings up important questions regarding the organization of correctional institutions in the United States, including these: What role does the federal government play in prison operations? How do states operate prisons? How are prisons designed? Where are prisons located? How does prison privatization work? What are the characteristics of people in the nation's prisons? This chapter explores these questions by focusing primarily on the incarceration of male adults, who make up approximately 92.5 percent of the state and federal prison population.[5]

LEARNING OBJECTIVES

After reading this chapter, you should be able to . . .

1. Explain how today's prisons are linked to the past.
2. Discuss the goals of incarceration.
3. Explain the organization of incarceration.
4. Discuss the factors that influence the classification of prisons.
5. Explain who is in prison.

FOCUS ON

PEOPLE IN CORRECTIONS: Realization

Stainless-steel handcuffs snugly fastened around subdued wrists. Waiting at an outer gatehouse. Watching the uniformed reception officer dispassionately size me up. Then escorted past double fences, inner fences, through steel doors, electronic steel grilles into the inner sanctum of concrete and steel.

Fear. The kind that chews at the stomach and makes the fingers tremble. Fear of known and unknown hidden dangers.

The atmosphere is tense and strange. Still wearing street-side clothes, I am a curiosity. After a number of rights and lefts and double-locked stairways, we come to Admitting and Processing.

Catalogued, tagged, photographed, and deloused. Issued, not issued, acceptable, not acceptable, and then ordered into a cell slightly bigger than a walk-in closet. When that door slams shut, an ache of mental and emotional pain seizes the senses brutally and completely.

Hearing the cell door slam shut the first time, there is a gripping realization, almost spiritual for some, that the consequences of crime are terribly real. Every memory, all of the past, good and bad, returns to haunt. Every single indelible moment is etched upon the mind's eye at some point, and painful memories invade conscious thought. The act, the arrest, pretrial and trial, conviction and sentencing, and most of all the last three hours flood involuntarily into mind and heart.

I look around at the cool, unforgiving gray concrete walls and feel the hopelessness. The helplessness of my predicament. The accommodations are welded and brazed and anchored into the concrete to last for years of use.

The gnawing fear that has been building steadily since hearing the door slam shut prompts me to jump up and test the door to see if it's really locked. It is.

Coming to terms with this reality begins one of the many emotional storms raging inside me. The raw fear penetrates and subsides, and the fight to control myself from crying out or pleading like a small child is a constant struggle.

This sensation of being torn apart from within by conflicting emotions vying for control is the most frightening human experience known. Nothing compares to the realization that I am being confined and controlled so totally. "Oh, God, no," I cry to myself. "Please don't let this be!"

After two hours the door slides back and a shout—"Chow!"—is heard. Steel doors slam, keys clang, and there is the shuffling of hundreds of feet. The strange, listless, angry, and embittered faces of the others offer painful insight into this subculture.

Lock in! 8:30 p.m. Until the morning meal, that door will be locked. Can I make it? The struggle rages again as I feel tears well up behind fatigued eyes. After two hours a uniformed arm pokes a flashlight into the cell for a moment and withdraws. Counted, and counted and counted again, I am among the best-monitored individuals outside an intensive-care unit in the country. More than a half-dozen times a day I am counted to ensure that I still suffer. In addition, clothes, underwear, property, and every file about me bears the assigned number that was issued during the processing.

I didn't know until this day that it was possible to tag, count, and store human beings like merchandise in a warehouse. Yet in this modern maximum-security "correctional institution," the insidiously antiseptic ritual of accepting an individual and transforming him into a number is as normal as sending youngsters on their way to school every morning on a yellow bus.

The consequences, again, become sparklingly clear and real. By committing a crime, I have plunged headlong into this nightmare of living death. I am condemned and I am so sorry; God, I'm sorry. I look around and realize there is no one to tell it to. In that moment I come to the realization that I have been forsaken. I have been cast out of a free society and branded with a number, never to achieve a position of trust or a level of responsibility that I might be capable of. I have come to the place of punishment and proved that the criminal justice system is alive and well in America.

I, the convicted, the incarcerated, come face-to-face with all these truths, only to sit mute upon my bunk, isolated by a society I so desperately want to apologize to.

Source: Written especially for this text by Wayne B. Alexander, convicted of murder and other crimes.

LO 1

Explain how today's prisons are linked to the past.

LINKS TO THE PAST

Reformers are frustrated by the sheer durability of prisons. For example, the oldest prison in America—New Jersey's State Prison in Trenton, which opened in 1798 and was rebuilt in 1836— is still in use. Structures of stone and concrete are not easily redesigned when correctional goals change. Elements of major reform movements can still be found within the walls of many older prisons. In line with the Quakers' belief that convicted individuals could be redeemed only if removed from the distractions of the city, many correctional facilities still operate in rural areas—for example, Stateville (Illinois), Attica (New York), and Walla Walla (Washington)—far from most of the families, friends, and communities of those who are incarcerated there. Although many modern prisons feature "campus" settings, the stronghold remains the primary architectural style. Life on the "inside" varies with the type and locale of the institution and the characteristics of the incarcerated. Yet a prison is still a prison, whatever it is called and however it is constructed (see "Realization").

The image of the "big house," popularized in countless movies and television shows, is still imprinted on the minds of most Americans, although it has long ceased to be a realistic portrayal—if indeed it ever was. Moreover, much social science literature about prison society is based on studies conducted in big houses, or maximum-security prisons, during the 1950s. Fictional depictions of prison life are typically set in the big-house fortress, where the residents are tough and the guards are just as tough or tougher. But U.S. correctional institutions have always been more varied than the movies portray them.

Although big houses were very common in much of the country during the first half of the twentieth century, many prisons, especially in the South, did not conform to this model. Racial segregation was maintained, prison residents were used as farm labor, and the massive walled structures were not as common as in the North.

The typical big house of the 1940s and 1950s was a walled prison with large, tiered cell blocks, a yard, shops, and industries. The clients, in an average population of about 2,500 per institution, came from both urban and rural areas, were usually poor, and, outside the South, were predominantly white. The prison society was essentially isolated; access to visitors, mail, and other communication was restricted. Prisoners' days were very structured, and guards enforced the rules. There was a basic division between residents and staff; rank was observed and discipline maintained. In the big house, few treatment programs existed; custody was the primary goal.

During the 1960s and early 1970s, when the rehabilitation model was dominant, many states built new prisons and converted others into "correctional institutions." Treatment programs administered by counselors and teachers became a major part of prison life, although the institutions continued to give priority to the custody goals of security, discipline, and order.

The civil rights movement of the early 1960s profoundly affected people in prison, especially minorities. Prison residents demanded their constitutional rights as citizens and greater sensitivity to their needs. As discussed in Chapter 5, the courts began to take notice of the legal rights of the imprisoned. As incarcerated individuals gained more legal services, the traditional judicial hands-off policy evaporated. Suddenly,

Everett Collection

Movies in the 1940s and 1950s portrayed the prisons of that era as maximum-security institutions—which they were. Today, there are many types of prisons, most of which bear little resemblance to the movie images from that era.

administrators had to respond to the directives of the judiciary and run the institutions according to constitutional mandates.

During the past 50 years, as the population of the United States has changed, so has the prison population. The number of African Americans and Hispanics in prison has greatly increased. More people in prison come from urban areas, and more have been convicted of drug-related and violent offenses. Incarcerated members of street gangs, which are often organized along racial lines, frequently regroup inside prison and contribute to elevated levels of violence. Another major change has been the number of correctional officers who are members of public employee unions, along with their use of collective bargaining to improve working conditions, safety procedures, and training.

Further, the focus of corrections has shifted to crime control, which emphasizes the importance of incarceration. As a result, the number of people in prison has increased. Some politicians argue that prison residents have it too "cushy" and that prisons should return to the strict regimes found in the early twentieth century. Many states have removed educational and recreational amenities from their institutions.

As the number of people in America's prisons increased substantially over the past three decades, tensions built within the overcrowded institutions. Although today's correctional administrators seek to provide humane incarceration, they must struggle with limited resources. The modern prison faces many of the difficult problems that confront other parts of the criminal justice system: racial conflicts, legal issues, limited resources, and growing populations. Despite these challenges, can prisons still achieve their objectives? The answer to this question depends, in part, on how we define the goals of incarceration.

LO 2

Discuss the goals of incarceration.

THE GOALS OF INCARCERATION

Citing the nature of those who are imprisoned and the need to protect the staff and the community, most people consider security the dominant purpose of a prison. High walls, razor wire, searches, checkpoints, and regular population counts serve the security function: Few people escape. More important, such features set the tone for the daily operations. Prisons are expected to be impersonal, quasi-military organizations where strict discipline, minimal amenities, and restrictions on freedom carry out punishment.

Three models of incarceration have predominated since the early 1940s: custodial, rehabilitation, and reintegration. Each reflects one style of institutional organization.

custodial model A model of correctional institutions that emphasizes security, discipline, and order.

rehabilitation model A model of correctional institutions that emphasizes the provision of treatment programs designed to reform the individual.

1. The **custodial model** assumes that people have been incarcerated for the purpose of incapacitation, deterrence, or retribution. It emphasizes security, discipline, and order, which subordinate the client to the authority of the warden. Discipline is strict, and most aspects of behavior are regulated. This model prevailed in corrections before World War II, and it continues to dominate most maximum-security institutions.
2. The **rehabilitation model**, developed during the 1950s, emphasizes treatment programs designed to reform the individual. According to this model, security and housekeeping activities are preconditions for rehabilitative efforts. As all aspects of the organization should be directed toward rehabilitation, professional treatment specialists enjoy a higher status than do other employees. Treatment programs exist in most contemporary institutions. But since the rethinking of the rehabilitation goal in the 1970s, very few prisons continue to conform to this model.

3. The **reintegration model** is linked to the structures and goals of community corrections. Recognizing that prison residents will be returning to society, this model emphasizes maintaining offenders' ties to family and community as a method of reform. Prisons following this model gradually give incarcerated individuals greater freedom and responsibility during their confinement, moving them to halfway houses or work release programs before releasing them under some form of community supervision.

reintegration model A model of correctional institutions that emphasizes maintenance of the individual's ties to family and the community as a method of reform, in recognition of the fact that the individual will be returning to the community.

Although one can find correctional institutions that conform to each of these models, most prisons are mainly custodial. Nevertheless, treatment programs do exist, and even some of the most custodial institutions attempt to prepare people for reentry into free society. Because prisons are expected to pursue many different and often incompatible goals, it would seem that they are almost doomed to fail. Many people believe that the mission of prisons is confinement and that the basic purpose of imprisonment is to punish the residents fairly, without undue suffering, through terms of confinement proportionate to the seriousness of the crimes. If the purpose of prisons is punishment through confinement under fair and just conditions, what are the implications for correctional managers? (See "For Critical Thinking.") Following these criteria, what measures should we use to evaluate prisons?

FOR CRITICAL THINKING

We opened this chapter by discussing the escape that took place at the Wyatt Detention Facility. It was noted that the institution had experienced other problems in the past, including lawsuits alleging staff abuse.

1. If you were named the new warden at the Wyatt Detention Facility following the escape, what model of incarceration would you practice? Explain the benefits of your selection, and discuss why you did not choose one of the other two models.
2. Do you believe that attempting to follow more than one model of incarceration, such as the custodial model and the rehabilitation model, can result in unsafe and disorderly prison environments? Discuss whether it is possible for this kind of situation to contribute to escape attempts.

ORGANIZATION FOR INCARCERATION

LO 3

Explain the organization of incarceration.

All 50 states and the federal government operate prisons. People who have committed crimes are held in approximately 1,300 confinement facilities, nearly 92 percent of which are operated by the states, and the remainder by the federal government and private companies. The largest percentage of state confinement facilities are located in the South (47 percent), with 20 percent located in the Midwest, 18.5 percent in the West, and 14.5 percent in the Northeast.[6] For the most part, prisons, as distinguished from jails, house people convicted of felonies and people convicted of misdemeanors that carry a sentence of more than one year. However, note that various state governments and the federal government differ in terms of bureaucratic organization for incarceration, number and types of institutions, staffing, and size of prison populations. We now look at the federal and state systems in turn.

The Federal Bureau of Prisons

In 1930 Congress created the Federal Bureau of Prisons within the Department of Justice. The bureau was responsible for "the safekeeping, care, protection, instruction, and discipline of all persons charged or convicted of offenses against the United States." At year-end 1930, shortly after the bureau was created, there were 14 federal prisons housing about 13,000 people. Today the bureau is highly centralized, with a director (appointed by the president), six regional directors, and a staff of over 36,000 who supervise an incarcerated population of about 170,000. To carry out its tasks, the bureau has a network of more than 120 institutions.[7]

The jurisdiction of federal criminal law, unlike that of the states, is restricted to crimes involving interstate commerce, certain serious felonies, violations of other federal laws, and crimes committed on federal property. Historically, federal prisons have housed bank robbers, extortionists, people who commit mail fraud, and arsonists. Between 1940 and 1980 the federal prison population remained fairly stable, hovering around 24,000 people. The explosion of the federal prison population in the 1980s to almost 58,000 individuals was caused by the initiation of the war on drugs and the Sentencing Reform Act of 1984. The number of people convicted of drug offenses in federal prisons has steadily increased. These residents currently constitute over one-half of the federal inmate population. The Sentencing Reform Act established determinate sentencing, reduced good time, and abolished parole, which substantially increased the average length of imprisonment.

There are fewer people in federal prisons for violent offenses than in most state institutions. Federal clients are often a more sophisticated type, from a higher socioeconomic class, than the typical state client. Interestingly, approximately 31,000—about 18.5 percent—of people held in federal prisons are citizens of other countries.[8] The International Prisoner Transfer Program permits the United States to transfer some incarcerated foreign nationals to their home countries. Among the conditions of eligibility include: the individual must be a citizen or national of a foreign country that has a treaty relationship with the United States; the individual did not commit a military offense; the individual has not been sentenced to death; the individual did not commit a political offense; and the individual has at least 6 months left on their sentence.[9] Figure 10.1 presents some key characteristics of individuals held in federal prisons.

The federal government does not have enough pretrial detention space to house most people accused of violating the federal criminal law, so a majority of pretrial detainees are housed in state or local facilities on a contractual basis. The U.S. Marshals Service is responsible for placing these people. Although all 50 states have laws requiring their correctional facilities to accept federal pretrial detainees, the marshals typically enter into intergovernmental service agreements with receptive jails. Local officials fear that sophisticated people in federal prisons will bring lawsuits challenging the conditions of their confinement and believe that federal officials expect the higher federal standards to be maintained at local expense.

The Bureau of Prisons currently operates 122 institutions that are classified using five security levels: minimum, low, medium, high, and administrative. The bureau has one "super-max" prison, located in Florence, Colorado, that houses convicted individuals deemed to be the most dangerous. The bureau is organized so that the wardens report to one of the regional offices. Regional office staff deal with a variety of matters, including health and psychological services, financial management, inmate discipline, and food service. Technical assistance is also provided to institutional and community corrections personnel by regional office staff.

The bureau provides many self-improvement programs to imprisoned people, including vocational training, education, anger management, and life skills training. The Federal Prison Industries (FPI) is a correctional program that employs incarcerated individuals in FPI factories. The objective is to teach them job skills. Workers receive pay and can even earn bonuses if their performance merits it. Incarcerated individuals who are not part of FPI are still required to work, unless they are deemed a security threat or have a medical condition that prevents them. They work at institutional jobs such as groundskeeping and food service.[10]

State Prison Systems

Although states vary considerably in how they organize corrections, the executive branch of each state government administers its prisons. This point is important because probation is often part of the judiciary, parole may be separate from corrections, and in most states jails are run by county governments.

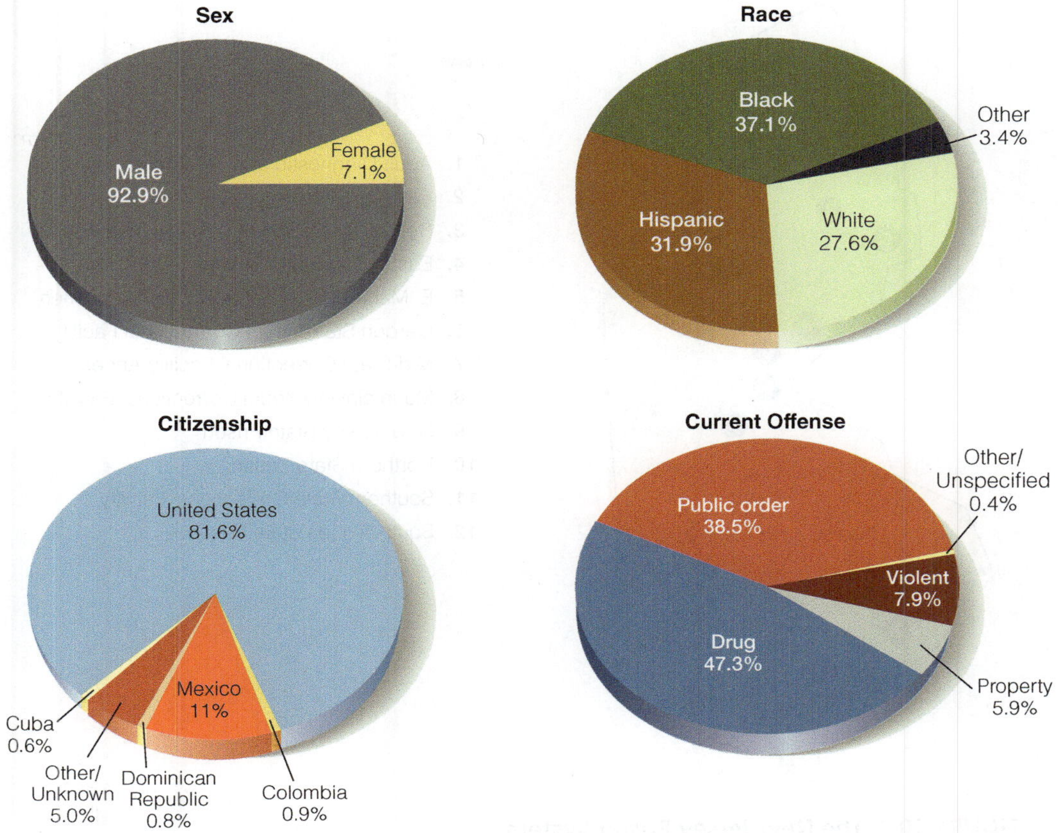

FIGURE 10.1 Who Is in Federal Prison?

Individuals serving sentences in federal prison tend to be male, white, convicted of drug offenses, and U.S. citizens.

Sources: "Inmate Statistics," https://www.bop.gov/about/statistics, May 1, 2020; Jennifer Bronson and E. Ann Carson, *Prisoners in* 2017 (Washington, DC: U.S. Government Printing Office, 2019).

Commissioners of corrections, normally appointed by state governors, are responsible for the operation of prisons. As discussed in Chapter 13, each institution is administered by a *warden* (often called a *superintendent*), who reports directly to the commissioner or a deputy commissioner for institutions. The number of employees in state correctional agencies is estimated to be upwards of 390,000 people—administrators, officers, and program specialists.[11]

To a great extent, the total capacity of a state's prisons reflects the size of the state's population. As discussed in Chapter 18, however, the number of individuals incarcerated in a state's institutions reflects more than just crime rates and social factors. Sentencing practices, legislative appropriations for corrections, and politics can also affect incarceration rates.

In addition to organization, states vary considerably in the number, size, type, and location of correctional facilities. For example, Louisiana's state penitentiary at Angola has a population of more than 5,000, whereas institutions for convicted individuals with special problems frequently house fewer than 100. Some states (such as New Hampshire) have centralized incarceration in a few institutions, and other states, such as California, New York, and Texas, have a wide mix of sizes and styles—secure institutions, diagnostic units, work camps, forestry centers, and prerelease centers. For example, New Jersey has 12 institutions, including a youth facility, a women's prison, and a reception and assignment facility (see Figure 10.2).[12]

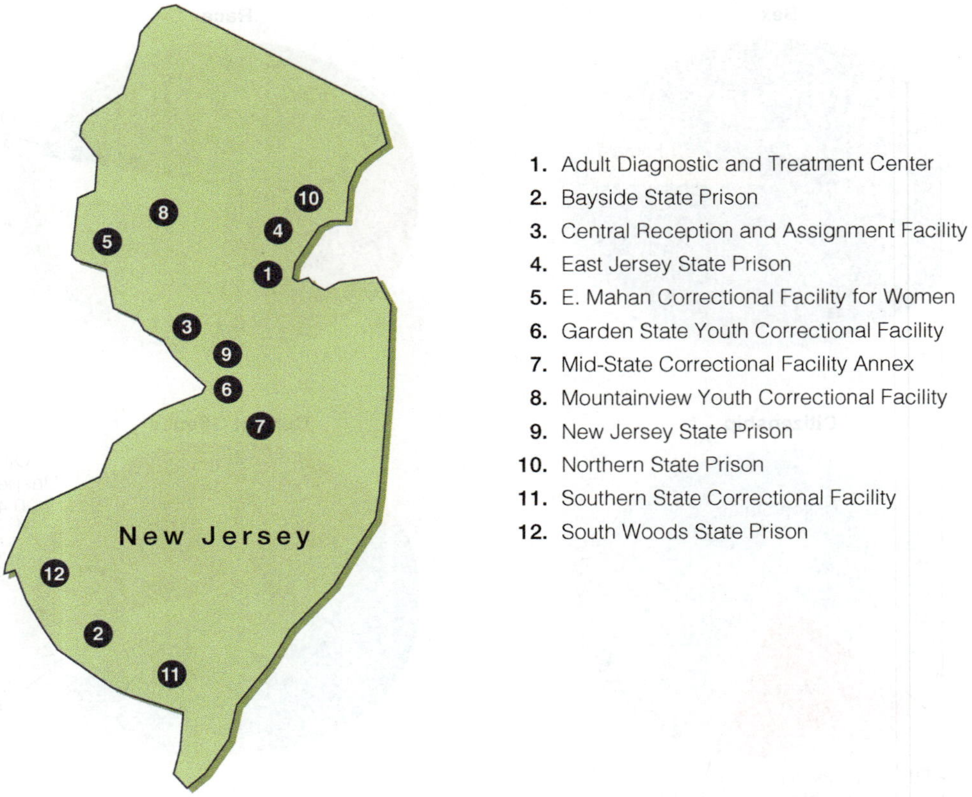

FIGURE 10.2 The New Jersey Prison System

In New Jersey the number and variety of institutions for people convicted of felonies are typical of most medium-size states. What factors might influence the location of penal institutions?

Source: New Jersey Department of Corrections, www.state.nj.us/corrections/pages/index.shtml, May 1, 2020.

THE DESIGN AND CLASSIFICATION OF PRISONS

Since the era of John Howard in England and the Quakers in Philadelphia, penologists have pondered the optimal design of prisons. In all eras, attempts have been made to design correctional institutions that would advance the prevailing purpose of the criminal sanction. In this section we discuss some of the changes and concepts in prison design. A cardinal principle of architecture is that form follows function: The design of a structure should serve the structure's purpose. During the early 1800s some English and American architects specialized in designing penitentiaries that would accommodate contemplation, industry, and isolation, thought to be the necessary conditions for moral reform. Efforts during the penitentiary era were directed at building institutions that would promote penance. When prison industry became the focus after the Civil War, a different design was proposed to enhance the efficiency of the workshops. When punishment through custody reigned supreme, the emphasis was on the fortress-like edifice that ensured security. And during the rehabilitation era of the 1950s and 1960s, new prisons were built in styles thought to promote treatment.

The design and operational characteristics of today's prisons vary considerably from state to state. Some states and the federal government have created smaller facilities. But even with the prison-building boom of the 1990s, many institutions remain old and large.

The antiquated megaprisons found in many states have all the maintenance and operational problems of old, heavily used buildings.

Today's Designs

The buildings constructed to suit the purposes of one era often cannot be easily adapted to suit those of succeeding eras or changes in the sizes and characteristics of prison populations. At the same time, prisons are built to last, which means that form may not continue to serve function. Unlike the nineteenth-century prisons, which were designed as grand fortresses, today's construction is greatly influenced by cost. From a distance, the modern correctional facility resembles a hospital or suburban high school. It has no guard towers because guards are expensive. It has no walls; sensor-controlled cyclone fencing with razor wire is cheaper.

Four basic models account for the designs of most U.S. prisons.

The Radial Design Prisons of the early nineteenth century tended to follow the **radial design** of Eastern Penitentiary (see Figure 10.3a). A control center at the hub makes it possible to monitor movement. From this central core, one or more "spokes" can be isolated from the rest of the institution if trouble erupts. Even though Auburn Prison was administered to contrast with the separation and silence practiced at Eastern, it also had the radial design. At other present-day locations, such as Leavenworth (Kansas) and Rahway and Trenton (New Jersey), the old design persists, but few newer prisons have been built to such specifications.

radial design An architectural plan by which a prison is constructed in the form of a wheel, with "spokes" radiating from a central core.

The Telephone-Pole Design In a prison based on the **telephone-pole design**, a long central corridor (the pole) serves as the means for residents to go from one part of the institution to another (see Figure 10.3b). Jutting out from the corridor are cross-arms, each containing the prison's functional areas: housing, shops, school, recreation area, and so on. The central pole allows continuous surveillance as well as independently controlled access to each functional area.

The telephone pole is the design most commonly used for maximum-security prisons in the United States. For example, Marion (Illinois) and Somers (Connecticut) are designed in this fashion. Built for custody, these prisons can house people according to classification levels, with certain housing areas designated for those with special needs, for those whose conduct merits extra privileges, and so on.

telephone-pole design An architectural plan for a prison calling for a long central corridor crossed at regular intervals by structures containing the prison's functional areas.

The Courtyard Style Some of the newer correctional facilities, including some maximum-security prisons, are built in the **courtyard style** (see Figure 10.3c). In these facilities the functional units of a prison are housed in separate buildings constructed on

courtyard style An architectural design by which the functional units of a prison are housed in separate buildings constructed on four sides of an open square.

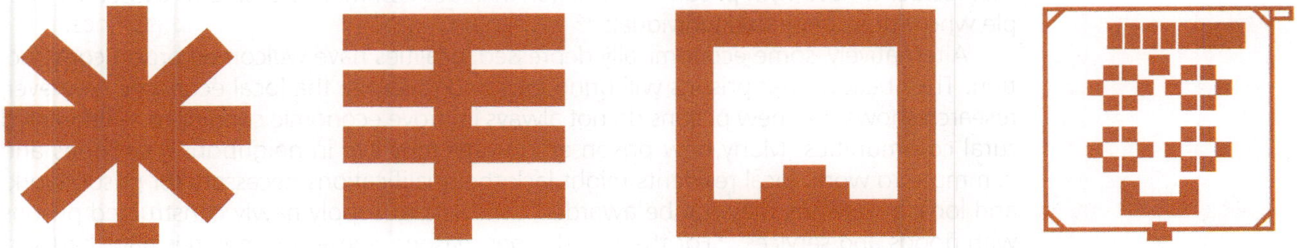

a. Radial design
b. Telephone-pole design
c. Courtyard style
d. Campus style

FIGURE 10.3 Prison Designs Used in the United States

These four basic designs are used throughout the country for most prisons housing adults convicted of felonies. Each style has certain features related to the goals of "keeping and serving" the prison population. How does architecture influence the management of these institutions?

four sides of an open square. Movement along the corridors, which is common in the telephone-pole design, is replaced by movement across the courtyard to the housing units and other functional areas. In some facilities of this type, such functional units as the dining hall, gym, and school are located in the yard area.

campus style An architectural design by which the functional units of a prison are individually housed in a complex of buildings surrounded by a fence.

The Campus Style A design long used for juvenile and women's correctional facilities, the **campus style** has been used for some newer institutions for men as well (see Figure 10.3d). Relatively small housing units are scattered among the shops, school, dining hall, and other units of the facility. This style is thought to be an important development not only because of the humane features of the design but also because individual buildings can be used more flexibly. As in courtyard-style prisons, residents and staff must go outdoors to get from one part of the facility to another. Although the campus style might appear to provide less security than more-conventional facilities, modern prison fences keep escapes to a minimum. Most facilities of this type serve medium- and minimum-security populations.

Surprisingly little research looks into whether architectural design affects levels of inmate misconduct. A study conducted by Robert Morris and John Worrall compared rule violations between individuals incarcerated in campus-style design and telephone-pole design prisons. The authors used a random sample of imprisoned males from 30 Texas state prisons. Interestingly, their findings showed that architectural design was not associated with violent forms of misconduct. As for nonviolent rule violations, however, the campus-style design was related to property and security-related violations.[13] Although the study was limited to only two architectural designs, the results provide some indication that prison design can influence inmate behavior.

The Location of Prisons

Most prisons for adults are located in rural areas. Originally, the rationale was that those serving prison sentences would more readily repent if isolated from urban distractions and family contacts. When more prisons were built later in the nineteenth century, the country setting was retained because the institutions maintained farms that contributed to their self-sufficiency. Now, even though most people in prison come from cities and reintegration is an important correctional goal, new institutions are still being built in the countryside. Many view this as counterproductive because urban families have difficulty visiting their loved ones in rural prisons and meaningful work or educational release programs are impractical.

Although the choice of rural settings stems partly from land costs, political factors also figure in the decision. Many citizens believe that people convicted of serious offenses should be incarcerated, but not in their community. This attitude is often referred to as the NIMBY syndrome (Not in My Back Yard!). Some people fear that a prison will lower property values; this concern prevents criminal justice planners from locating facilities in areas that have the resources and will to oppose prison construction. Another concern that residents have with prison construction includes community problems caused by people who visit incarcerated individuals.[14]

Alternatively, some economically depressed localities have welcomed prison construction. They believe that prisons will bring jobs and revitalize the local economy. However, research shows that new prisons do not always improve economic conditions in depressed rural communities. Many new prison employees may live in neighboring counties and commute to work, local residents might lack the qualifications necessary for prison work, and local businesses may not be awarded contracts to supply newly constructed prisons with goods and services.[15] For these and other reasons, some communities have had second thoughts about the impact of prisons on their economic development.

LO 4

Discuss the factors that influence the classification of prisons.

The Classification of Prisons

State prisons for men are usually classified according to the level of security deemed necessary: maximum, medium, and minimum. Many states and the federal government have created super-maximum-security facilities, which are frequently called "super-max" prisons. These facilities are designed to hold the most-disruptive, violent, and incorrigible men. California's Pelican Bay State Prison and Virginia's Red Onion State Prison are examples of prisons designed to hold the "toughest of the tough" and the "worst of the worst." There is considerable public support for these institutions. Daniel Mears and his colleagues found that 82 percent of the public either support or strongly support the use of super-max prisons to handle violent or disruptive men.[16]

With changes in the number of people in prison and their characteristics, the distinction between maximum and medium security has disappeared in some systems. Crowding has forced administrators to use medium-security facilities to house individuals requiring maximum security. Some penologists believe that many individuals now in maximum-security facilities could be housed at lower levels. Others argue that the higher security level is necessary given the tough orientation of today's prison residents. They also argue that prison space is so expensive that it must be used cost-effectively.

Most states have so few women in prison that they are all housed in one institution; those who require higher levels of security are segregated. In contrast, incarcerated men are assigned to a specific type of facility depending on a variety of factors, including the seriousness of the offense, the possibility of an attempt to escape, and the potential for violent behavior. Because many states do not have an institution designed for each level of security, a facility is often divided into sections for different categories of residents. Such facilities are referred to as "multi-level" facilities. There are no national design or classification standards, so a maximum-security facility in one state may be run as a medium-security facility in another. Nevertheless, some generalizations can be made.

The Maximum-Security Prison Usually an imposing structure surrounded by high stone walls studded with guard towers, the **maximum-security prison** (sometimes called a *closed custody prison*) is designed to prevent escapes and to deter individuals from harming one another. There are 355 such facilities in the United States that house about 38 percent of all state prison residents.[17]

maximum-security prison A prison designed and organized to minimize the possibility of escapes and violence; to that end, it imposes strict limitations on the freedom of residents and visitors.

Residents live in cells, each with its own sanitary facilities. The barred doors may be operated electronically so that an officer can confine all clients to their cells with the flick of a switch. Because the purpose of this type of facility is custody and discipline, it embraces a military-style approach to order. People in prison follow a strict routine. Head counts are frequent, and surveillance of behavior—often through closed-circuit television—eliminates privacy.

These structures are built to last. Many that were built around the end of the nineteenth century, when custody was the dominant model of incarceration, are still in use even though their design makes it difficult to adapt many of them to rehabilitation and reintegration. Some of the most well-known prisons, such as Attica (New York) and Stateville (Illinois), are maximum-security facilities.

The Medium-Security Prison There are 438 **medium-security prisons** in the United States, holding 43 percent of state-level prison residents.[18] From the outside these facilities resemble maximum-security prisons, but they are organized differently, and the inmate routines are less rigid. Clients have more privileges and contact with the outside world through visitors, mail, and access to radio and television. Medium-security prisons usually place greater emphasis on work and rehabilitative programs. Although the convicted individuals may have committed serious crimes, they are not perceived as intractable or hardened. Some of the newer medium-security facilities have a campus or courtyard style, although the razor-wire fences, guard towers, and other security devices remain. In some states, a medium-security prison seems much closer to maximum than to minimum security.

medium-security prison A prison designed and organized to prevent escapes and violence, but in which restrictions on residents and visitors are less rigid than in maximum-security facilities.

The Minimum-Security Prison The **minimum-security prison** (926 facilities housing 19 percent of state-level prison residents) houses the least-violent clients, long-term felony-convicted individuals with clean disciplinary records, and residents who have nearly completed their term.[19] The minimum-security prison lacks the guard towers and

minimum-security prison A prison designed and organized to permit residents and visitors as much freedom as is consistent with the concept of incarceration.

▲ *Most "trustees" serve time under a reduced security level that enables them to do necessary prison labor outside the walls.*

walls usually associated with correctional institutions. Often, chain-link fencing surrounds the buildings. People usually live in dormitories or even in small private rooms rather than cells. There is more personal freedom: Residents may have television sets, choose their own clothes, and move about casually within and among the buildings. The system relies on rehabilitation programs and offers opportunities for education and work release. It also offers reintegration programs and support to those who are preparing for release. Some states and the Federal Bureau of Prisons operate minimum-security prison camps where convicted individuals work on forest conservation and fight wildfires. To the outsider, minimum-security prisons may seem to enforce little punishment, but the clients remain segregated from society, and their freedoms are restricted. It is still a prison.

Private Prisons

U.S. taxpayers spend billions of dollars annually on prisons.[20] A good portion of this money goes to providing inmate medical care, feeding the residents, and paying for utilities (electricity, heating oil, water). To accomplish these sorts of tasks, many jurisdictions contract with private companies to furnish food and medical services, educational and vocational training, maintenance, industrial programs, and other services. Although private enterprise has long played a role in U.S. corrections, the scope of services purchased from profit-seeking organizations has expanded greatly in recent decades. In fact, governments now hire corporations to house convicted individuals in privately owned facilities.

There are different forms of private-sector involvement in corrections. Some institutions are both owned and operated by a private enterprise. However, others may be owned by government and operated under contract by a private entity, or owned by a private entity and operated by government on a lease or lease–purchase agreement.

Over the past 30 years, entrepreneurs have made inroads in the corrections arena by building and operating private facilities. Private entrepreneurs argue that they can build and run prisons as effectively, safely, and humanely as any level of government. They also propose that they can do so more efficiently, which saves taxpayers money. Pressured by prison and jail crowding, rising staff costs, and growing public sentiment regarding inefficient government, politicians in the early 1980s found such proposals appealing. In 1986, Kentucky's Marion Adjustment Center became the first privately owned and operated facility for the incarceration of adults with felony convictions who were classified to at least a level of minimum security.

Although a fairly recent development, private management of entire institutions for felony-convicted adults has already become a growth industry. In 1999, 71,208 people were held in private prisons. By the end of 2018, the number had risen to 118,444 people, an increase of about 66 percent.[21] The extent to which individual states use private prisons varies considerably (see Figure 10.4). And it is not a uniquely American phenomenon. At least 11 countries around the world are involved in prison privatization of some sort. For example, Australia and Scotland hold a larger proportion of their incarcerated populations in private facilities than does the United States.[22] The private-prison business in the United States is dominated by CoreCivic (formerly the Corrections Corporation of America), which currently manages 122 correctional centers offering all levels of security.[23]

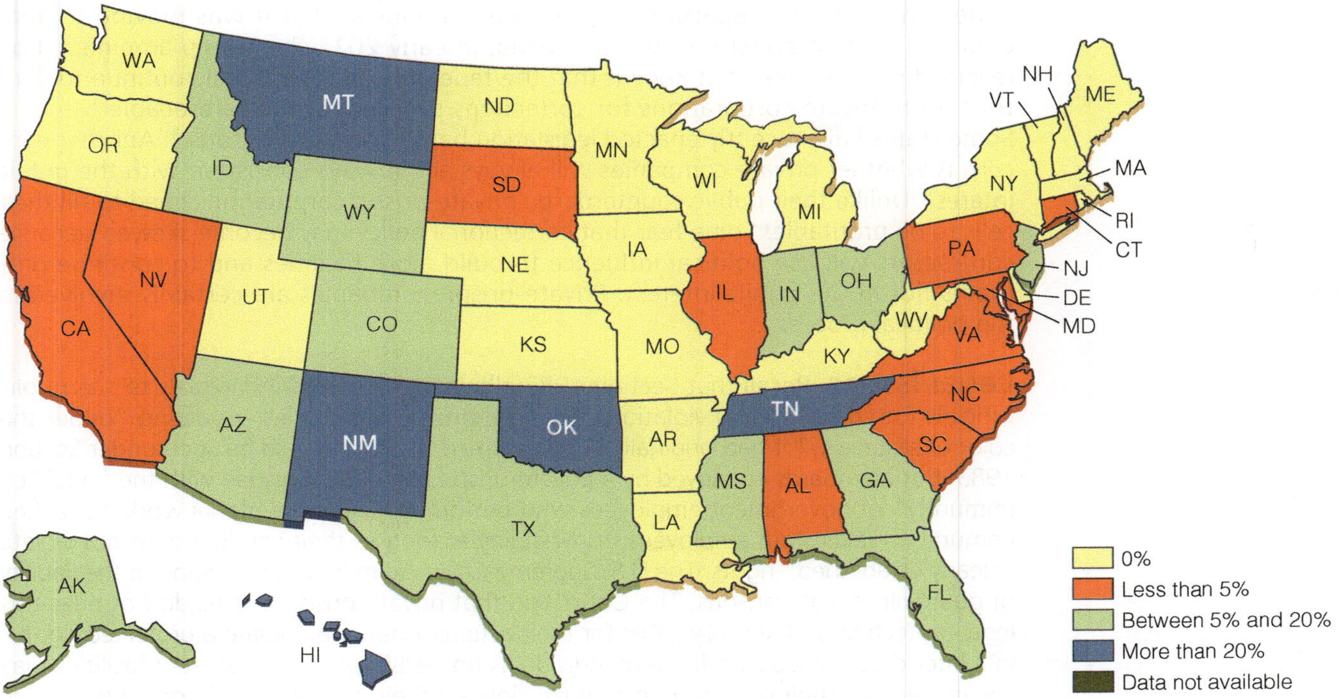

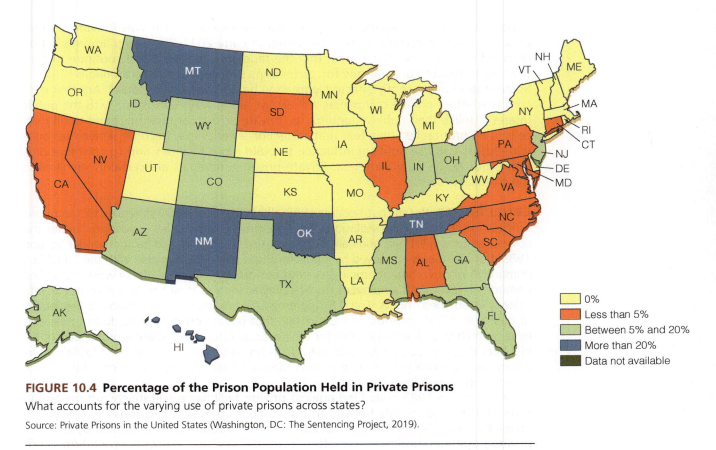

FIGURE 10.4 Percentage of the Prison Population Held in Private Prisons
What accounts for the varying use of private prisons across states?
Source: Private Prisons in the United States (Washington, DC: The Sentencing Project, 2019).

Practical and Ethical Issues Private prisons remain controversial, giving rise to several issues. For example, advocates of privately operated prisons claim that their facilities provide the same level of care as do state-run facilities. But researchers have not yet validated this claim consistently. One study of 48 private and public juvenile correctional facilities concluded that public and private facilities are very similar in terms of environmental quality, including level of freedom, preparation for release, quality of life, and resident danger.[24] The evidence regarding prison programming shows that differences exist between state and private adult institutions: Compared with private prisons, a greater proportion of state and federal correctional facilities provide access to work programs (96.7 versus 55.9 percent), education programs (92.7 versus 59.5 percent), and counseling programs (97.3 versus 74.2 percent).[25] Differences have also been observed when it comes to health-related services, including substance dependency and psychological programs.[26] Do such differences influence recidivism rates? (See "Myths in Corrections.")

Supporters of prison privatization also claim that companies can run prisons more cheaply than the states can. Research on this matter is largely inconclusive. In cases where cost savings can be shown, such savings are fairly modest and result from reductions in staffing, fringe benefits, and other personnel-related costs.[27] For example, research has shown that private prisons pay new officers less and provide employees with nearly 60 fewer preservice training hours than do public prisons.[28] Not surprisingly, correctional officer unions continue to oppose private prisons.

Other issues arise when considering private prisons. Andrea Montes notes that the use of private prisons raises important ethical questions: Do private prisons protect the legal rights of individuals housed in them? Do private prisons unnecessarily expand government social control? Do private prisons use ethical means to achieve correctional goals?[29] Several governments appear to be wrestling with these very

MYTHS in Corrections

Private Versus Public Prisons

THE MYTH: Private prisons are more effective than public prisons in preparing incarcerated individuals for life after prison.

THE REALITY: A study conducted in Minnesota that followed 3,532 individuals released from state prisons found that members of the sample who served their sentence in a private facility were at greater risk of recidivating when compared to people who were incarcerated in public prisons.

Source: Grant Duwe and Valerie Clark, "The Effects of Private Prison Confinement on Offender Recidivism: Evidence from Minnesota," *Criminal Justice Review* 38 (September 2013): 375–94.

issues. In 2016 the Department of Justice announced that it was moving toward ending its use of private prisons. However, in early 2017 the Trump administration reversed course, making it known that the federal government will continue to contract with private corporations for corrections services for the foreseeable future.[30] Some states have recently enacted legislation banning private prisons.[31] Another concern is whether private companies will always act in ways consistent with the public interest. Unlike their public counterparts, private-prison corporations need to fill their cells to be profitable. Some fear that correctional policy may become skewed because contractors will use political influence to build more facilities and to continue programs not in the public interest. Private-prison companies are certainly involved in the political process.

Legal Issues Recall that Section 1983 allows incarcerated individuals to sue public officials for constitutional violations. Because private companies are acting "under the color of state law," it had originally been assumed that they could be sued under Section 1983. But are guards employed by a private-prison company provided with the "qualified immunity" of government employees who perform similar correctional work? Qualified immunity shields state employees from liability as long as their conduct does not violate "clearly established" rights. The U.S. Supreme Court examined the question of the liability of guards in private prisons. The Court said that private-prison guards do not have this legal protection and are fully liable for their actions when they violate a protected right.[32] In a later case the Court ruled that individuals housed in privately operated facilities may sue individual employees alleged to have violated their constitutional rights but cannot sue the corporation itself.[33]

Are Section 1983 suits filed against private facilities qualitatively different than suits filed by individuals housed in public correctional institutions? A study that reviewed a matched sample of Section 1983 suits found that suits filed by those in privately operated facilities more often focused on living and physical conditions, such as religious freedom, harassment, and cruel and unusual punishment. Suits against public facilities more often alleged violations relating to medical treatment and physical security. Interestingly, when evaluating the judicial statements that were issued in response to inmate suits, the authors found that those concerning private facilities "carried greater levels of admonishment" and were "much more stern and corrective in nature."[34]

The idea of privately run correctional facilities has stimulated much interest among the general public and within the criminal justice community. But privatization itself has a long history in criminal justice, dating as far back as the English practice of transporting convicted individuals to North America and Australia. Jeremy Bentham, well known for his panopticon prison design, was himself an entrepreneur who unsuccessfully pursued a contract to construct and operate a prison.[35] In the future there may be further privatization of prison services, or privatization may become only a limited venture initiated at a time of prison crowding, fiscal constraints on governments, and revival of free-enterprise ideology. In any case, the controversy about privatization has forced correctional officials to rethink some strongly held beliefs (see "For Critical Thinking"). In this regard, the possibility of competition from the private sector may have a positive impact.

FOR CRITICAL THINKING

As discussed at the outset of this chapter, the Wyatt Detention Facility is a privately operated correctional facility. The prison holds approximately 500 adult males and females in maximum custody. Assume that you are a high-ranking state official charged with negotiating a contract with a corporation to run a new medium-custody private-prison facility.

1. Would you allow people convicted of violent crimes, such as murder and attempted murder, to be housed in the new prison? Explain your answer.
2. How would you make sure that your state does not experience an escape like the one that happened at Wyatt? Would you write the contract so that the corporation would be fined if an escape occurred? Describe how you would (if at all) hold the corporation accountable for mistakes that put the public at risk.

WHO IS IN PRISON?

LO 5 *Explain who is in prison.*

What are the characteristics of the people in the nation's prisons? Do most convicted individuals have long records of serious offenses, or are many of them first-timers who have committed minor crimes? Do some prison inhabitants have special needs that dictate their place in prison? These questions are crucial to understanding the work of correctional professionals.

Data on the characteristics of incarcerated individuals are limited. The U.S. Bureau of Justice Statistics reports that a majority of state prison residents are men, members of minority groups, and convicted of violent crimes. Approximately 94.2 percent of state prison clients are U.S. citizens (see Figure 10.5). The most common country of origin for foreign individuals in state correctional systems is Mexico, followed by Cuba, El Salvador, Guatemala, and Honduras. Drug offenses were the most common crimes that resulted in the incarceration of foreign nationals.[36]

Four additional factors affect correctional operations: the increased number of elderly individuals in prison, the thousands of prison residents who are mentally ill, the sizable number of incarcerated military veterans, and the increased number of people serving long-term sentences.

The Elderly

Individuals over age 55 serving prison sentences presently make up nearly 12 percent of the prison population.[37] The dramatic increase in the number of older people in prison is explained by two factors: (1) a larger proportion of people serving long-term sentences

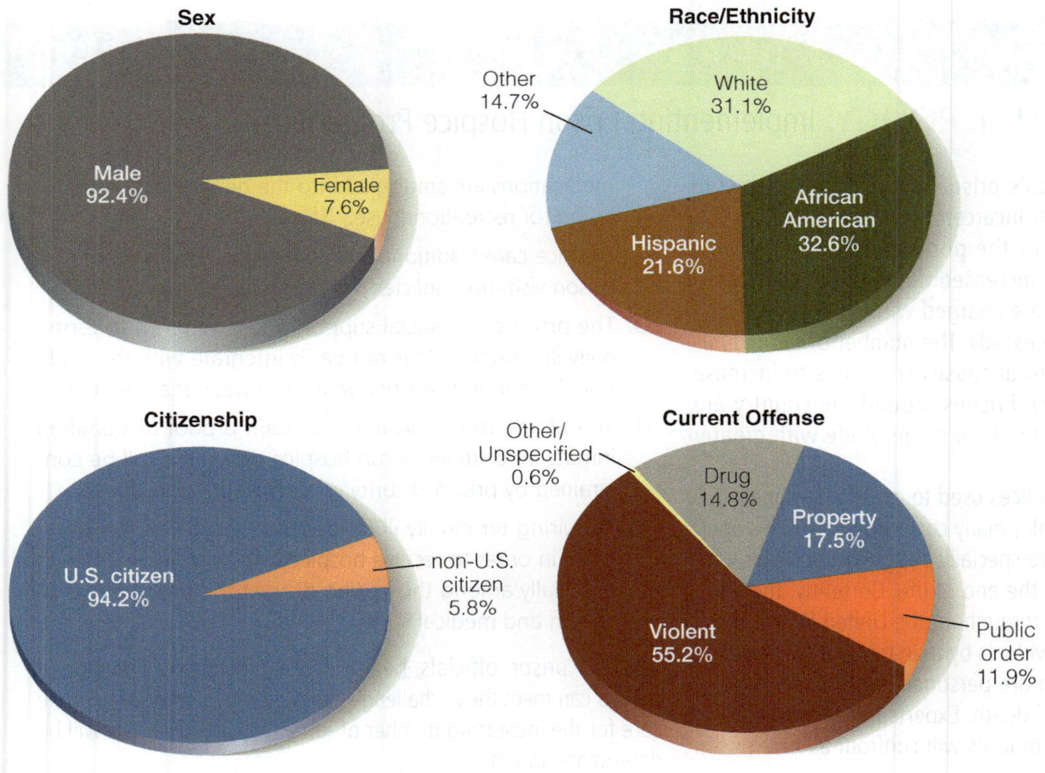

FIGURE 10.5 Who Is in State Prison?
Individuals incarcerated in state prisons tend to be male, racial or ethnic minorities, U.S. citizens, and convicted of violent offenses.

Source: Jennifer Bronson and E. Ann Carson, *Prisoners in 2017* (Washington, DC: U.S. Government Printing Office, 2019).

and (2) increased admissions of older individuals to state prison. Incarcerated elderly individuals have unique service needs regarding housing, medical care, programs, and release.

- *Housing:* Administrators believe that the elderly should usually remain in the general prison population but with special accommodations. These accommodations can range from assigning older individuals to a bottom bunk to housing them in a separate wing with special architectural features, such as grab bars in cells and showers. Some states have specialized facilities for frail people and those with physical or mental disabilities.[38] For example, the Texas Department of Criminal Justice has geriatric units at different prisons to accommodate elderly residents with special needs.[39] Separate facilities and wings also prevent younger, tougher individuals from preying on the elderly. In Oklahoma, people under the age of 40 were transferred out of the state reformatory. Now the institution houses only older individuals. Levels of violence are down considerably. As Warden Tracy McCollum said, "Violence has gone to virtually nothing." McCollum added, "Now it's not a constant state of 'Oh my god, what's going to happen.' "[40]
- *Medical care:* The aging prison population has no doubt contributed to rising health care expenditures.[41] Elderly residents are those most likely to develop chronic illnesses such as heart disease, stroke, and cancer. The cost of maintaining an elderly client is much higher than that of maintaining a younger one. Ironically, while someone is incarcerated, his or her life may be prolonged and the medical care better than if he or she were discharged. To care for dying people in prison, a number of states have created facilities that provide hospice care. (See "Implementing Prison Hospice Programs.")
- *Programs:* Work assignments, recreation, and rehabilitative programs must be tailored to fit the physical and mental abilities of the elderly. For example, older individuals may work part time or engage in greenhouse or craft programs. Exercise designed to keep the elderly resident active

FOCUS ON

CORRECTIONAL POLICY: Implementing Prison Hospice Programs

It is no secret that America's prison population is growing older. Factors such as higher incarceration rates, longer prison sentences, and the aging of the population in free society have all contributed to the increased number of incarcerated elderly individuals. Prisons are charged with caring for all the individuals placed in their custody. The number of individuals who die in prison from natural causes continues to increase (more than 3,000 per year). Prisons around the country are caring for residents during the final stage of life with greater frequency.

Consistent with the practices used to care for terminally ill people outside the prison walls, many correctional facilities operate hospice programs that are specially designed to provide care for people who are nearing the end of life. Currently, there are 69 such programs in prisons throughout the United States. These programs care for dying individuals by managing pain, providing social support to those who are personally isolated, and helping them cope with issues of death. Experts have identified five challenges that correctional officials will confront as new prison hospice programs start up:

1. The use of prescription narcotics to manage the pain of dying individuals could pose security problems if such medications are smuggled into the general prison population for recreational use.
2. Hospice care traditionally entails family involvement that prison visitation policies may not initially accommodate.
3. The provision of social support and care given to terminally ill residents does not easily integrate with the traditional order and security goals of correctional facilities.
4. The ability to recruit and maintain a pool of qualified inmate volunteers to run hospice programs will be constrained by prison security concerns and procedures.
5. Requiring terminally ill residents to forgo medical treatment in order to receive hospice care may prove difficult, especially among those who distrust the prison administration and medical staff.

Whether prison officials, health care workers, and imprisoned people can meet these challenges and effectively provide humane care for the increasing number of terminally ill individuals will be determined in time.

Source: Heath C. Hoffman and George E. Dickinson, "Characteristics of Prison Hospice Programs in the United States," *American Journal of Hospice and Palliative Medicine* 28 (June 2011): 245–52.

contributes to overall health. Work helps increase feelings of self-worth. Even life skills programs for the elderly help these people think ahead toward their release date.

- *Release:* Preparation for release of the elderly to community supervision or to hospice services requires time and special efforts by correctional staff. These include dealing with multiple government and social service agencies to ensure that Social Security and Medicare benefits will be available upon release and that medical care will continue. Staff must see to it that elderly individuals do not remain in prison simply because they have nowhere else to go. Because of the length of their incarceration, many elderly individuals lose contact with their families.

Research indicates that as people get older, they become less dangerous. Only a very small portion of serious crime is committed by people over age 60. But not all elderly people in prison are the same. Some are first-timers who committed their crime after age 50. Others are the so-called "career criminals"; they have been in and out of prison most of their lives. Finally, some received long sentences and aged in prison. Advocates for those in prison argue that not all elderly people who committed crimes should remain incarcerated until they die. Many states are considering community alternatives for low-security elderly incarcerated people. Some programs focus on removing low-risk geriatric clients from overcrowded prisons. The alternative to releasing the elderly seems to be maintaining an ever-larger population of them in prison geriatric wards (see "For Critical Thinking").

FOR CRITICAL THINKING

Advocates of prison privatization argue that profit-seeking corporations, such as the company that runs the Wyatt Detention Facility, can operate facilities more efficiently and more effectively than the government.

1. Given the high cost associated with incarcerating the elderly, do you think that private prisons designed for geriatric people would save the state money? If after such a prison opened it was discovered that the attempt succeeded, would you advocate experimenting further with prison privatization? What if it was discovered that the corporation cut corners, such as withholding medical care, to protect its profit margins?
2. Assume that a new private prison, one which specializes in housing people sentenced to life without parole, has opened in your state. Suppose that the private prison in question boasts that it can rehabilitate these individuals. In fact, it claims that the recidivism risk among people released from its facility will be less than one-half the average among former state prison clients. Would you support allowing the release of such individuals? Explain your answer.

People with Mental Illnesses

Mass closings of public hospitals for people with mental illnesses began in the 1960s. At the time, new psychotropic drugs made treating patients in the community seem a more humane alternative to hospitalization. It also promised to be less expensive. Soon, however, people saw that community treatment works only if patients take their medication. Widespread homelessness was the most public sign that the community treatment approach had its shortcomings. With the expansion of prisons and the greater police emphasis on public-order offenses, many individuals with mental illnesses are now arrested and incarcerated. These people tend to catch a revolving door from homelessness to incarceration and then back to the streets. Currently,

© Timothy Hurst/The Coloradoan

▲ *A mental health counselor talks with an incarcerated individual. Problems associated with mental health are thought to contribute to high recidivism rates.*

14.5 percent of people in prison suffer from serious psychological distress, and 36.9 percent have a history of mental health problems.[42]

The incarceration rate of people with mental illnesses is considerably higher than that of the general population. Incarcerated people with mental illnesses pose particular challenges for correctional professionals. Correctional workers are usually unprepared to deal with them. Further, although some benefit from the regular medication they receive in jail or prison, others suffer as the stress of confinement deepens their depression, intensifies delusions, or leads to mental breakdown. Some commit suicide.

The availability and type of mental health treatment programs in prisons vary. The two most common types involve providing therapy/counseling or dispensing medications.[43] Although medication can help keep these people stable and functioning, some observers fear that prisons tend to overmedicate residents. The cost associated with incarcerating mentally-ill individuals is high. For example, the state of Michigan spends an average of $35,000 annually on incarceration for those without mental health problems. An individual suffering from mental illness costs the state $95,000 each year to imprison.[44]

Military Veterans

It is unfortunate that, after serving in the armed forces, some military veterans are convicted of crimes and sentenced to prison terms. There are approximately 130,000 veterans serving time in America's prisons. The incarceration rate for veterans is actually lower than the rate for nonveterans. In terms of personal characteristics, veterans serving prison sentences are overwhelmingly male (98.9 percent), are between the ages of 35 and 54 years (54.1 percent), are white (50.3 percent), and have at least a high school education (71.7 percent). A majority of imprisoned veterans were adjudicated for violent offenses (64.3 percent) and had been incarcerated previously (73.3 percent).[45] Like all individuals serving prison sentences, imprisoned veterans have certain needs that correctional professionals need to identify and work to meet.

One troubling factor associated with imprisoned veterans is the high rate of mental health problems among this population. Nearly one-half of veterans serving prison sentences suffer from mental health problems. The rate of such problems among incarcerated nonveterans is much lower. The differences between the two groups is more dramatic when looking at post-traumatic stress disorder (PTSD), where the rate among veterans in prison is over twice that of incarcerated nonveterans.[46] To better meet the needs of imprisoned veterans, some states have established special prison units. For example, in Connecticut a special housing unit at the Willard-Cybulski Correctional Institution was opened to assist veterans with two years or less left on their sentence to prepare for the reentry process.[47]

Individuals Serving Long-Term Sentences

The sentencing policies of the last 30 years—three strikes, mandatory minimums, truth-in-sentencing—have increased the number of people serving life sentences. Approximately one-third of such individuals are serving "natural life," which means there is no possibility of parole. Not all of these people serving life sentences were convicted of violent offenses. In fact, about 10,000 lifers were convicted of nonviolent crimes.[48] These long-term residents are often the same people who will eventually become elderly clients, with all the attendant problems.

Individuals serving long-term sentences often suffer from emotional stress, especially earlier in the sentence as they lose contact with their families and come to grips with the bleakness of their future. When compared to veteran lifers, newer residents serving life sentences more easily lose their tempers, often feel angry, and spend more time contemplating revenge. They are also more likely to feel restless, have difficulty sleeping, and experience numbness.[49] Addressing the mental health needs of this special population is critical to preventing sudden suicide attempts.

Long-term residents are generally not seen as control problems. They are charged with disciplinary infractions far less frequently than individuals serving relatively short sentences. Rather, administrators must face the challenge of making the lives of such clients bearable. Many long-term prison residents will eventually be released after spending the best years of their lives behind bars. Will these individuals be able to support themselves when they return to the community?

SUMMARY

1 Explain how today's prisons are linked to the past.

Contemporary prisons are shaped by the past in many ways. For example, many prisons in operation today were built more than a century ago. These prisons were designed to reflect the correctional goals of the time, such as removing people convicted of crimes from the distractions of the city. Many of these prisons are walled structures with large, tiered cell blocks that are located in rural areas. Although the primary goal today is custody, most prisons also provide incarcerated people with programs. This feature of the modern prison can be traced back to the 1960s and 1970s, when the rehabilitation model was dominant. Finally, incarcerated people in today's correctional facilities have various constitutional rights that prison officials must respect. These rights were largely established in the 1960s.

2 Discuss the goals of incarceration.

Three models of incarceration are used, each of which reflects different goals and styles of institutional organization. First, the custodial model emphasizes security, discipline, and order for the purposes of incapacitation, deterrence, or retribution. This model prevailed prior to World War II. The rehabilitation model, which developed during the 1950s, views every aspect of organization as directed toward reforming the person convicted of crime. Toward this end, a variety of treatment programs are used. Finally, the reintegration model emphasizes the maintenance of the person's ties to family and the community. Prisons that employ this model recognize that most imprisoned people will one day return to the community. Accordingly, these individuals are gradually given greater freedom and responsibility as they approach release.

3 Explain the organization of incarceration.

U.S. prisons are operated at the federal and state levels. Many of these prisons are very old and are located in rural areas. State and federal facilities for men operate at different security levels, such as maximum and minimum security, which restrict inmate movement to a greater or lesser degree. Because so few women are imprisoned, most states house them in a single facility. Most prison facilities are owned and operated by governments; however, many states and the federal government contract with private corporations that provide prison services, including housing imprisoned people in privately owned facilities.

4 Discuss the factors that influence the classification of prisons.

State prisons for men are usually classified using three security classifications: maximum, medium, and minimum. A number of states also operate "super-max" prisons, where the most disruptive, violent, and incorrigible men are housed. Maximum-security prisons are designed to prevent escapes and to deter residents from harming one another. Custody is emphasized in these prisons, which are usually run in a military-like fashion. Medium-security prisons are less rigid, and rehabilitation programs are more widely used. Compared with men in maximum-security prisons, those in medium-security facilities have more privileges and contact with the outside world. Finally, minimum-security prisons house the least-violent men, those who are nearing release, and long-termers with clean disciplinary records. Many of these facilities have work release programs. Men in these facilities usually live in dormitories or small private rooms rather than cells.

5 Explain who is in prison.

The overwhelming majority of people in both federal and state prisons are male. A majority of people incarcerated in federal prisons have been convicted of drug offenses, and people in federal prisons tend to come from a higher socioeconomic class than do people in state prisons. The majority of people in federal prisons are white. In state prisons a large number of people are members of racial and ethnic minority groups. A majority are convicted of violent crimes. Correctional officials must increasingly deal with the problems of special populations, including the elderly, people with mental illnesses, military veterans, and individuals serving long-term sentences. The elderly have unique service needs regarding housing, medical care, programs, and release. People with mental illnesses tend to get into fights and break rules more often than do other residents, and treatment varies by institution. Some states have established special units for military veterans to help them successfully reenter free society. Finally, the number of people serving long-term sentences has increased greatly, presenting corrections with the task of making the lives of such individuals bearable.

KEY TERMS

campus style (*p. 272*)
courtyard style (*p. 271*)
custodial model (*p. 266*)
maximum-security prison (*p. 273*)
medium-security prison (*p. 273*)
minimum-security prison (*p. 273*)
radial design (*p. 271*)
rehabilitation model (*p. 266*)
reintegration model (*p. 267*)
telephone-pole design (*p. 271*)

FOR DISCUSSION

1. Is the custodial model most appropriate for organizing prisons that operate at different security levels? What model should be used to organize a minimum-security facility?
2. What are some of the strengths and weaknesses of various prison designs? Are some designs better than others?
3. What questions emerge regarding the practice of contracting with private, for-profit organizations to operate correctional facilities? Should the job of operating prisons be the sole responsibility of the government?
4. Which characteristics of the prison population might present major challenges for the managers of institutions?
5. If you were a warden, how would you handle individuals with long-term sentences?

FOR FURTHER READING

Enns, Peter K. *Incarceration Nation: How the United States Became the Most Punitive Democracy in the World*. Cambridge: Cambridge University Press, 2016. Examines the influence of politics, public attitudes, and the media on the mass incarceration movement in the United States over several decades.

Hallett, Michael A. *Private Prisons in America: A Critical Race Perspective*. Chicago: University of Illinois Press, 2006. Views the prison privatization movement as the latest attempt to oppress and legally discriminate against African American men.

Hallinan, Joseph T. *Going Up the River: Travels in a Prison Nation*. New York: Random House, 2001. From California to North Carolina and from New York to Texas, Hallinan explores one of America's growth industries: its prisons.

Trulson, Chad R., and James W. Marquart. *First Available Cell: Desegregation of the Texas Prison System*. Austin, TX: University of Texas Press, 2009. Charts the desegregation of Texas prisons.

NOTES

1 Melissa Hanson, "James Morales Indicted for Escaping from Wyatt Detention Facility in Rhode Island," *MassLive.com*,www.masslive.com/news/index.ssf/2017/01/fugitive_james_morales_indicte.html, January 17, 2017.

2 Jennifer Bronson and E. Ann Carson, *Prisoners in 2017* (Washington, DC: U.S. Government Printing Office, 2019), 3.

3 Martin Gould, "Dangerous Fugitive Who Escaped a Rhode Island Prison on New Year's Eve Is Captured After Robbing a Bank in Massachusetts," DailyMail.com, www.dailymail.co.uk/news/article-4092578/Dangerous-fugitive-escaped-Rhode-Island-prison-New-Year-s-Eve-prime-suspect-Massachusetts-bank-robbery.html, January 5, 2017.

4 Rick Foster, "Report: Central Falls Prison Where Inmate Escaped Chronically Understaffed," *Sun Chronicle*, www.thesunchronicle.com/news/local_news/report-central-falls-prison-where-inmate-escaped-chronically-understaffed/article_3bb3a910-d297-11e6-9008-07b662c8eb38.html, January 4, 2017.

5 Bronson and Carson, *Prisoners in 2017*, p. 3.

6 James J. Stephan, *Census of State and Federal Correctional Facilities*, 2005 (Washington, DC: U.S. Government Printing Office, 2008).

7 "About Us," www.bop.gov/about, May 1, 2020.

8 "Inmate Citizenship," www.bop.gov/about/statistics/statistics_inmate_citizenship.jsp, March 24, 2017

9 "Treaty Transfers," https://www.bop.gov/inmates/custody_and_care/treaty_transfers.jsp, May 1, 2020.

10 "Inmate Custody & Care," https://www.bop.gov/about/statistics/statistics_inmate_citizenship.jsp, May 1, 2020.

11 Stephan, *Census*, Appendix Table 12.

12 New Jersey Department of Corrections, https://www.state.nj.us/corrections/pages/index.shtml, May 1, 2020.

13 Robert G. Morris and John L. Worrall, "Prison Architecture and Inmate Misconduct: A Multilevel Assessment," *Crime and Delinquency* 60 (October 2014): 1083–109.

14 Randy Martin and David L. Myers, "Public Response to Prison Siting: Perceptions of Impact on Crime and Safety," *Criminal Justice and Behavior* 32 (April 2005): 143–71.

15 Ryan Scott King, Marc Mauer, and Tracy Huling, "An Analysis of the Economics of Prison Siting in Rural Communities," *Criminology & Public Policy 3* (July 2004): 453–80.

16 Daniel P. Mears, Christina Mancini, Kevin M. Beaver, and Marc Gertz, "Housing the 'Worst of the Worst' Inmates," *Crime and Delinquency* 59 (June 2013): 587–615.

17 Stephan, *Census*, Appendix tables 5 and 11.

18 Ibid.

19 Ibid.

20 Tracey Kyckelhahan, *State Corrections Expenditures, FY 1982–2010* (Washington, DC: U.S. Government Printing Office, 2012).

21 E. Ann Carson, *Prisoners in 2018* (Washington, DC: U.S. Government Printing Office, 2020), 27.

22 Cody Mason, *International Growth Trends in Prison Privatization* (Washington, DC: Sentencing Project, 2013).

23 "Find a Facility," www.corecivic.com/facilities, May 4, 2020.

24 Gaylene Styve Armstrong and Doris Layton MacKenzie, "Private Versus Public Juvenile Facilities: Do Differences in Environmental Quality Exist?" *Crime and Delinquency* 49 (October 2003): 554.

25 Stephan, *Census*, Appendix tables 16, 18, and 19.

26 Valerio Baćak and Greg Ridgeway, "Availability of Health-related Programs in Private and Public Prisons," *Journal of Correctional Health Care* 24 (2018): 62–70.

27 James Austin and Garry Coventry, "Emerging Issues on Privatizing Prisons," *Corrections Forum* 10 (December 2001): 11.

28 Curtis Blakely, "Private and State Run U.S. Prisons Compared," *Probation Journal* 51 (2004): 254–56.

29 Andrea N. Montes, "Ethical Concerns about Private (and Public) Corrections: Extending the Focus Beyond Profit-Making and the Delegation of Punishment," *Criminal Justice Policy Review* 31 (May 2020): 609–30.

30 Matt Zapotosky and Chico Harlan, "Justice Department Says It Will End Use of Private Prisons," *Washington Post*, www.washingtonpost.com/news/post-nation/wp/2016/08/18/justice-department-says-it-will-end-use-of-private-prisons/?utm_term=.c5cd257156b3, August 18, 2016; Matt Zapotosky, "Justice Department Will Again Use Private Prisons," *Washington Post*, www.washingtonpost.com/world/national-security/justice-department-will-again-use-private-prisons/2017/02/23/da395d02-fa0e-11e6-be05-1a3817ac21a5_story.html? utm_term=.2430e7de5565, February 23, 2017.

31 Steven Gorman, "California Bans Private Prisons and Immigration Detention Centers," *Reuters*, https://www.reuters.com/article/us-california-prisons/california-bans-private-prisons-and-immigration-detention-centers-idUSKBN1WQ2Q9,October11, 2019; "Nevada Bans Use of Private Prisons," *The Laughlin Times*, www.mohavedailynews.com/laughlin_times/nevada-bans-use-of-private-prisons/article_c17dac7e-8cd7-11e9-929e-333bbacbf4e8.html, June 11, 2019.

32 *Richardson v. McKnight*, 521 U.S. 399 (1997).

33 *Correctional Services Corporation v. Malesko*, 534 U.S. 61 (2001).

34 Curtis R. Blakely and Vic W. Bumphus, "An Analysis of Civil Suits Filed Against Private and Public Prisons: A Comparison of Title 42: Section 1983 Litigation," *Criminal Justice Policy Review* 16 (March 2005): 85.

35 Malcolm M. Feeley, "Entrepreneurs of Punishment: The Legacy of Privatization," *Punishment & Society* 4 (July 2002): 327–33.

36 Editor, "Foreign Inmates: Survey Summary," *Corrections Compendium* 34 (Summer 2013): 18–31.

37 Bronson and Carson, *Prisoner in 2017,* p. 17.

38 Anthony A. Sterns, Greta Lax, Chad Sed, et al., "The Growing Wave of Older Prisoners: A National Survey of Older Prisoner Health, Mental Health and Programming," *Corrections Today 70* (August 2008): 70–76.

39 Human Rights Watch, *Old Behind Bars: The Aging Prison Population in the United State*s (New York: Human Rights Watch, 2012), 50.

40 Graham Lee Brewer, "Older Inmate Population at Oklahoma State Reformatory Means Lower Violence, Higher Medical Needs," *Oklahoman*, http://newsok.com/older-inmate-population-at-oklahoma-state-reformatory-means-lower-violence-higher-medical-needs/article/3905621, November 17, 2013.

41 The Pew Charitable Trusts and the John D. and Catherine T. MacArthur Foundation, *State Prison Health Care Spending: An Examination* (New York: Pew Charitable Trusts, 2014).

42 Jennifer Bronson and Marcus Berzofsky, *Indicators of Mental Health Problems Reported by Prisoners and Jail Inmates, 2011-12* (Washington, DC: U.S. Government Printing Office, 2017), 3.

43 Kenneth Adams and Joseph Ferrandino, "Managing Mentally Ill Inmates in Prisons," *Criminal Justice and Behavior 35* (August 2008): 913–27.

44 Edward Lyon, "Imprisoning America's Mentally Ill," Prison Legal News, www.prisonlegalnews.org/news/2019/feb/4/imprisoning-americas-mentally-ill/, February 4, 2019.

45 Jennifer Bronson and Marcus Berzofsky, *Veterans in Prison and Jail, 2011–2012* (Washington, DC: U.S. Government Printing Office, 2015).

46 Ibid.

47 Mikaela Porter, "New Connecticut Prison Unit Dedicated Monday Helps Veterans Re-enter Civilian Life," *Hartford Courant*, www.courant.com/community/enfield/hc-enfield-prison-dedication-veterans-willard-cybulski-1110-20151109-story.html, November 9, 2015.

48 The Sentencing Project, *Life Goes On: The Historic Rise in LifeSentences in America* (Washington, DC: Author, 2013).

49 American Civil Liberties Union, *A Living Death: Life Without Parole for Nonviolent Offense*s (New York: Author, 2013): 184–86; Margaret E. Leigey, "For the Longest Time: The Adjustment of Inmates to a Sentence of Life Without Parole," *Prison Journal 90* (September 2010): 247–68.

CHAPTER 11

The Prison Experience

©Briana Sanchez/Argus Leader

Lynette Johnson sits next to a photo of her late husband R. J. Johnson who was killed while working as a correctional officer. Prisons can be violent places for those who live there and for those who work there.

IT WAS ANOTHER DAY AT THE STILLWATER FACILITY IN MINNESOTA, A HIGHER-CUSTODY INSTITUTION THAT INCARCERATES ABOUT 1,600 MEN.

The shop foreman was going about his business when he was approached by an individual who told him that an officer was being violently attacked in a nearby area. Upon arrival, the foreman reportedly witnessed Edward Muhammad Johnson repeatedly striking a correctional officer in the face with a hammer, an assault that resulted in the officer's death. Johnson, 42, was serving a 29-year sentence for second-degree murder and second-degree assault after being convicted of killing his girlfriend back in 2002. Johnson had been exposed to violence early in life, witnessing his father murder his mother by shooting her six times when he was 12-years old. According to prison officials, Johnson had difficulty adjusting to prison life. For example, he had spent about 1,700 days (or 4.5 years) in segregation at the time of the attack. Johnson lost his right eye in 2004 when another prison resident stabbed him.

Johnson's victim, Corrections Officer Joseph Gomm, was a 16-year veteran. He is remembered by his friends and family for his quick wit, and his enjoyment of video games, cooking, and animals. During his funeral procession, hundreds of people gathered along streets to pay their respects. If convicted of killing Gomm, Johnson could be imprisoned an additional 47 years.[1]

It is no secret that prisons can be violent places. After all, prisons house individuals convicted of violent offenses, often under crowded conditions. But questions in the case involving Officer Gomm require answers. Why was Gomm's attacker who had a record of violence given access to a hammer? Why was Officer Gomm attacked so viciously? We can better understand the causes of prison violence and the patterns of victimization by examining the social and personal dimensions of life behind the prison walls.

Is Johnson the "typical" type of person who is incarcerated in U.S. prisons? Can we assume that violence is rampant throughout the corrections system? If you were entering prison for the first time, what should you expect?

LEARNING OBJECTIVES

After reading this chapter, you should be able to . . .

1. Discuss the "inmate code" and explain where the values of the prison subculture come from.
2. Analyze the prison economy.
3. Explain the different types of prison violence.
4. Discuss what can be done about prison violence.

FOCUS ON

CORRECTIONAL PRACTICE: Going In: The Chain

MICHAEL SANTOS

Rick Cruz-USA TODAY NETWORK

Michael Santos, whom we have followed through the years while he served a 45-year sentence in federal prison, became known for his prison writings and then was released from prison. You can find his story in Chapter 6.

Have you ever had a time in your life when you just wanted to die, when you thought death would be easier than facing the problems that you know are waiting for you? That was the feeling I had when I was 23 years old, just after a federal judge in Seattle sentenced me to serve 45 years in prison for a nonviolent drug crime.

I remember my thoughts and experiences clearly as I was beginning that term. I had already been detained for about a year—awaiting my trial—before the judge sentenced me. A few weeks after conviction and the imposition of sentence, I knew I'd soon be on my way to prison. It would be a new experience, and one I wasn't looking forward to beginning.

My journey began when one of the guards from the jail came by my cell door early on a Saturday morning to wake me. "Roll up!" he hollered. "Roll up" is jail vernacular ordering a prisoner to pack all belongings and prepare for movement. The moment he said it, I felt it. His words were hanging in the air, like a threat, letting me know I was on my way to a place from where some don't return. "Okay, let's go," I said to myself as I tried to pump up my heart.

I didn't have much, as the jail really limits the amount of personal property a prisoner can keep. The guard marched me to a smoke-filled room where my ankles were shackled together and my wrists were cuffed to a chain wrapped around my waist. There were several other prisoners in the room. We were all chained together, because we were to ride the bus that would deliver us to prison.

I didn't know where I was going, not for several hours anyway. Then I found out. I was off to the U.S. Penitentiary in Atlanta. "Damn," I thought, "why would they be sending me to Atlanta? I'm from Seattle."

It didn't much matter what I thought. I was beginning to realize my thoughts didn't matter to anyone but me. When I was arrested, I pretty much lost my identity and became chattel, property of the U.S. government. Prison guards regulated everything in my life: the clothes I wore, the food I ate, the time I slept, the mail I sent or received. Lawyers even spoke for me. All I did was go through the motions of being human; someone else was always directing me. That is what it means to lose freedom.

What I did begin to think about was my own mortality. What was I going to be after release? I was a young man then, but I wouldn't walk the streets again until I was well over 50 years old. I'd been an adult for only a few years before I got locked up; now prison was going to be my life. Who would I be after release? An old man with nothing: no home, no automobile, no assets. A couple of friends might buy me a doughnut and a cup of coffee, but I'd have nowhere to go. I'd have to start life from nothing—at over 50—and that was a chilling feeling.

The month-long bus ride was hell. We left Seattle, but rather than going directly to Atlanta, we worked our way across the West picking up and dropping off prisoners. I was restrained during the whole time, and the people sitting around me were, for the most part, guys who seemed like they'd been doing time forever. Most were covered with tattoos. I guess the tattoos were supposed to be frightening or something, like they were going to make the prisoner scarier and somehow meaner; they worked. I was learning everyone had their own way of dealing with time. Yet I had enough experience after my year in the county jail to know that I'd do my time alone.

When the bus finally approached the huge penitentiary in Atlanta, I was awestruck by the enormous wall that enveloped the entire prison. It stood 40 feet high, clearly separating the prisoners inside from the community. And the heavily armed guards standing outside the bus made clear there was nothing nice behind that wall.

I was scared, but I was determined to do whatever it took to make it through. I told myself repeatedly I was ready, but now, in retrospect, I realize I could never be ready. There was no room for fear, but fear was everywhere. I could smell it on the bus, on the men. We all waited, looking outside the windows in silence. I knew the only way I was going to make it was to stand up and face it, to go through it; it was with this absolute resolve that I was determined to return to the world.

Finally, the guards began calling us off by last name and prison number. It is not easy walking with a 12-inch chain connected to each ankle, and wrists bound to a chain that runs around the waist, but when my name was called, I managed to wobble through the bus's aisle, hopped down the steps, then began the long march up the stairs leading to the fortress. As I was moving to the prison's doors, I remember glancing over my shoulder, knowing it would be the last time I'd see the world from the outside of prison walls for a long time.

Once I was inside, the plain concrete walls reminded me my time was not going to be easy. As I was getting settled inside the walls, walking through the crowded halls, staring at the desperate faces, I felt the pressure. It was like I was on the road with a million drunk drivers all at once! They were angry with no apparent reason, as if they woke up in the morning and didn't even know themselves why they were mad.

Standing in line to eat breakfast is like going through a busy intersection when the traffic lights don't work; it's easy to crash, to get into a wreck without warning. Bam! That was how fast things happen in the penitentiary. I learned that killers stand 5 feet 6 to 5 feet 8. People who appear harmless are frequently the most dangerous men in the penitentiary. And there is no such thing as a fair fight in prison. You see guys over 6 feet tall, 220 pounds, hitting 5 feet 8, 150-pound guys with a piece of pipe when the smaller guy isn't looking. Fighters get respect from the other prisoners for this kind of thing, that is, recognition for doing "the right thing." I've seen people stabbed and piped in the showers, [the] chow hall, the yard, the theater. People wore phone books taped to their bodies to protect themselves as they walked to the yard. Shanks [knives] were planted everywhere. Prison is really a gladiator school, a battle zone full of desperate men—a place where no one wants to be.

I remember reading somewhere that there are no atheists in foxholes, as every soldier placed in that situation is praying to God. Similarly, there really are no pacifists in prison, as even the most docile-seeming prisoner is capable of extreme violence, and often for no apparent reason. All prisoners feel the tension [that] no matter where a man walks behind the walls, the threat of death is ever present. Seasoned prisoners want newcomers to either run with them or run away from them. They want to mold the way a prisoner behaves, who his friends are, and what he does. I refused to let the others dictate the kind of person I would be, so I pursued my own goals and decided to keep to myself while inside.

Serving a prison term is a consuming experience. Since I didn't want to be consumed, and didn't want to become like many of the people around me, I committed myself to building a better life and focusing on the future, on life outside of prison walls. I knew my road in prison would be long. I was certain the prisoners around me could make the road longer, and none of them could make it shorter. And that's why I've always structured my time to help me avoid them.

Source: Michael Santos was released from federal prison in 2012 after serving 25 years of a 45-year sentence for drug trafficking. Reprinted by permission.

(continued from p. 288)

Even the most hardened person must be tense on entering (or reentering) prison. For the "fish," the newcomer, the first few hours and days engender tremendous worry and anxiety: "What will it be like? How should I act? Will I be able to protect myself?" Like an immigrant starting out in a new country, new residents have trouble with the language, finding strange customs and unfamiliar rules. Unlike the immigrant, however, the newly imprisoned person does not have the freedom to choose where and with whom to live. (See "Going In: The Chain.")

What does being incarcerated mean to residents, guards, and administrators? How do prisons function? Are the officers really in charge, or do the clients "run the joint"? As we examine the different dimensions of prison life, imagine that you are visiting a foreign land and trying to learn about its culture and daily activities. Although the prison may be located in the United States, the traditions, language, and relationships appear foreign to most visitors.

PRISON SOCIETY

LO 1

Discuss the "inmate code" and explain where the values of the prison subculture come from.

The 1934 publication of Joseph Fishman's *Sex in Prison* marked the beginning of the social scientific study of subcultures in maximum-security institutions.[2] Since then, researchers have studied the prison as a functioning community with its own values, roles, language, and customs. In other words, maximum-security prison residents do not serve their time in isolation. Rather, they form a society with traditions, norms, and a leadership structure. Some may choose to associate with only a few close friends; others form cliques along racial or "professional" lines.[3] Still others may be the politicians of the convict society; they attempt to represent convict interests and distribute valued goods in return for support. Just as a social culture exists in the free world, a prisoner subculture exists on the "inside." Membership in a group provides mutual protection from theft and physical assault, the basis of wheeling-and-dealing activities, and a source of cultural identity. The subculture concept helps us understand prison society. Like members of other groups who interact primarily among themselves and are physically separated from the larger world (groups such as soldiers, medical patients, or monks), the incarcerated develop their own myths, slang, customs, rewards, and sanctions. However, the notion that the subculture inside prison is isolated, separate, and opposed to the dominant culture may now be misleading because contemporary prisons are less isolated from the larger society than were big-house prisons. Although prisons do create special conditions that compel residents to adapt to their environment, the culture of the outside world penetrates prison walls through television, magazines, newspapers, and contact with visitors and family. In short, the prison is very much a product of institutional and political relationships between the prison and the larger society.

Norms and Values

inmate code A set of rules of conduct that reflects the values and norms of the prison social system and helps define for inmates the image of the model prisoner.

As in any society, the convict world has certain distinctive norms and values. Often described as the **inmate code**, these norms and values develop within the prison social system and help define the inmate's image of the model prisoner. As Robert Johnson notes, "The public culture of the prison has norms that dictate behavior 'on the yard' and in other public areas of the prison such as mess halls, gyms, and the larger program and work sites."[4] Prison is an ultramasculine world. The culture breathes masculine toughness and insensitivity, impugns softness, and emphasizes the use of hostility and manipulation in one's relations with peers and staff. It makes caring and friendly behavior, especially with respect to the staff, look servile and silly.[5]

Men in prison must project an image of fearlessness and must never show emotion about pain; such feeling is seen as weakness. Humor is one of the ways some people cope. It is used to bridge the gap between a normal and a convict identity.[6]

The code also emphasizes the solidarity of all prison residents against the staff. The two primary rules of the inmate code are "do your own time" and "don't inform on another convict." Following his classic New Jersey study, Gresham Sykes refined the rules embodied in the code as follows:

1. *Don't interfere with inmate interests.* Never inform on another man, don't be nosy, don't have a loose lip, and don't put a guy on the spot.
2. *Don't quarrel with fellow inmates.* Play it cool, don't lose your head, and do your own time.
3. *Don't exploit inmates.* Don't break your word, don't steal, don't sell favors, and honor your debts.
4. *Maintain yourself.* Don't weaken, don't whine, don't cop out, be tough, and be a man.
5. *Don't trust the guards or the things they stand for.* Don't be a sucker, guards are hacks and screws, the officials are wrong and the prisoners are right.[7]

prisonization The process by which an incarcerated person absorbs the customs of prison society and learns to adapt to the environment.

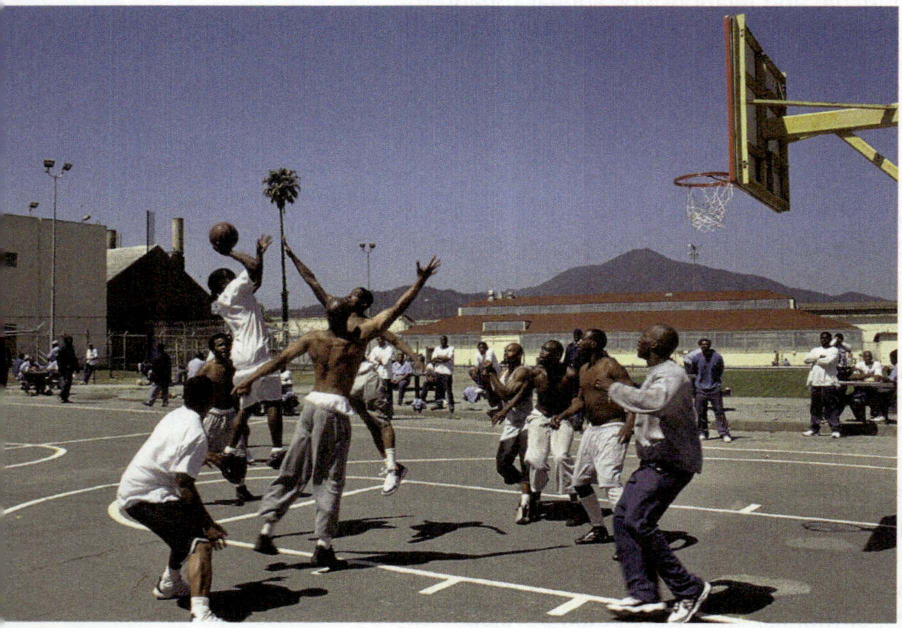
Adam Tanner/The Image Works

▲ *Contemporary prison society is divided along racial, ethnic, and age subgroups—there is no inmate code to which all prisoners subscribe.*

How does the "fish," the newcomer, learn the norms and values of the prison society? In jail awaiting transfer to the prison, the fish hears exaggerated descriptions of what lies ahead. The bus ride to prison and the processing through the prison reception center further initiate the novice. The actions of the staff at the reception center, the folktales passed on by experienced residents, and the derisive shouts of those on the inside all serve as elements of a degradation ceremony that shocks the newcomer into readiness to begin the **prisonization** process. But not all prison residents complete this process. In his pioneering work, Donald Clemmer suggests that such factors as a short sentence, continuation of contacts with the outside, a stable personality, and refusal to become part of the group may weaken prisonization.[8]

The prisoner subculture designates people according to the roles that they play in their society and the extent to which they conform to the code. Among the roles described in the literature are "right guy" or "real man" (an upholder of prisoner values and interests), "square John" (someone with a noncriminal self-concept), "punk" (a passive homosexual), "rat" (someone who squeals or sells out to the authorities), and "gorilla" or "wolf" (an aggressive individual who pursues his own self-interest at others' expense).[9]

A single, overriding inmate code probably does not exist in present-day institutions. Instead, convict society is organized along racial, ethnic, and age lines. Adherence to the inmate code also differs among institutions, with greater modifications to local situations found in maximum-security prisons. Still, the core commandments as described by Sykes many years ago remain.

Reflecting tensions in U.S. society, many prisons are marked today by racially motivated violence, organizations based on race, and voluntary segregation by prison residents by race whenever possible, such as in recreation areas and dining halls.

Do incarcerated people reject the views of conventional society? Research has shown that a vast majority of them hold views on law and justice similar to those held by the general public. But as individuals they also view themselves as exceptions; it is the "other ones" whose norms are contrary to those of society. The research suggests that while incarcerated, the individual must live and survive in an environment "where his movements and options are constrained, his person is insecure, and personal control is highly limited."[10] Thus, many incarcerated people conform to the subculture even though their own values run contrary to the inmate code.

Interviews with former prison residents in California paint a picture of prison society that is in greater turmoil than it was in the past. The presence of gangs, changes in the type of person now incarcerated, and changes in prison policy have all contributed to this turmoil. As the researchers found, "All these elements coalesced to create an increasingly unpredictable world in which prior loyalties, allegiances, and friendships were disrupted."[11]

Given a dynamic prison society without a single code of behavior accepted by the entire population, administrators face a much more difficult range of tasks. They must be aware of the different groups, recognize the norms and rules that members hold, and deal with the leaders of many cliques rather than with a few individuals who have risen to top positions in the inmate society.

Prison Subculture: Deprivation or Importation?

Where do the values of the prison subculture come from? How do they become integrated into a code? Sykes argues that the subculture arises within the prison in response to the pains of imprisonment.[12] These pains include the deprivation of liberty, autonomy, security, goods and services, and heterosexual relationships. Only through full integration into prison society can individuals adapt to and compensate for these deprivations.

An alternative theory holds that the values of the incarcerated community are primarily imported into prison from the outside world. John Irwin and Donald Cressey suggest that the prisoner subculture really combines three subcultures: convict, thief, and "straight."[13] They believe that the system of values, roles, and norms that exists in the adult prison results from the convergence of the convict and the thief subcultures. The convict subculture is found particularly among state-raised youths who have been in and out of foster homes, detention centers, reform schools, and correctional institutions since puberty. These individuals are used to living in a single-sex society, know the ways of institutional life, and in a sense make prison their home. People who belong to the thief subculture consider crime a career and are always preparing for the "big score." Irwin and Cressey note that thieves must exude a sense of "rightness" or "solidness" to be considered "right guys" by their peers. Finally, the "square Johns" or the "straights" bring the culture of conventional society with them to the prison. They are often "one-timers" who identify more with the staff than with the others serving prison sentences. They want to avoid trouble and get through their terms as quietly as possible. In sum, the convict subculture results from deprivations; the thief and straight subcultures are imported.

Unconvinced by these perspectives, Edward Zamble and Frank Porporino believe that the behavior of incarcerated people results from how they cope with and adapt to the prison environment.[14] They note that people come to prison with their own set of preincarceration experiences and values. Entering the institution is stressful for the seasoned resident and the newcomer alike. Each person will adapt the best he or she knows how. Suppose that two individuals are facing long terms. Both will experience the same environment, restrictions, and deprivations of prison. Events in prison are often beyond their control. However, as a result of his background and attributes, one person "will interpret the lack of control as the result of his own inadequacy. In contrast, the second individual interprets the situation as one where others have used and abused him and are continuing to do so." In dealing with their long sentences, the first will likely immerse himself in the inmate social network and take on the behavior and values of other prisoners.... The second inmate will probably ... have weaker ties to the inmate subculture. These behaviors will in turn affect the ways the two men are seen by both staff and other prisoners, and their subsequent treatment will differ.[15]

Thus, whether the subculture inside prison develops because of the deprivations of incarceration or is imported, each person adapts to the institution in his or her own way (see "For Critical Thinking").

Adaptive Roles

On entering prison, a newcomer is confronted by the question "How am I going to do my time?" Some decide to withdraw and isolate. Others decide to become full participants in the convict social system. The choice, influenced by prisoners' values and experiences, helps determine strategies for survival and success. See "How Are You Going to Do Your Time?" to see how four people at a low-security federal prison do their time.

Most males in prison use one of four basic role orientations to adapt to prison: "doing time," "gleaning," "jailing," and functioning as a "disorganized criminal." John Irwin believes that we can classify the great majority of people imprisoned for felonies according to these orientations.[16]

Doing Time Men "doing time" view their prison term as a brief, inevitable break in their criminal careers, a cost of doing business. They try to serve their terms with the least amount of suffering and the greatest amount of comfort. They live by the inmate code in order to avoid trouble, and they find activities to fill their days, form friendships with a few other residents, and generally do what they think is necessary to survive and get out as soon as possible.

Gleaning Individuals who are "gleaning" try to take advantage of prison programs to better themselves and improve their prospects for success after release. They use the resources at hand: libraries, correspondence courses, vocational training, and schools. Some make a radical conversion away from a life of crime.

Jailing "Jailing" is the choice of those who cut themselves off from the outside and try to construct a life within the prison. These are often state-raised youths who have spent much of their lives in institutional settings and who identify little with the values of free society. These individuals seek positions of power and influence in the prison society, often becoming key figures in its politics and economy.

Disorganized Criminal A fourth role orientation—the "disorganized criminal"—describes people who cannot develop any of the other three role orientations. They may be of low intelligence or afflicted with mental or physical disabilities and have difficulty functioning within prison society. They are "human putty" to be manipulated by others. These are also the people who adjust poorly to prison life, develop emotional disorders, attempt suicide, and violate prison rules. As these roles suggest, incarcerated people are not members of an undifferentiated mass. Individuals choose to play specific roles in the prison society. The roles that they adopt reflect the physical and social environment and contribute to their relationships and interactions in prison. How do most people serve their time? Although the media generally portray prisons as violent, chaotic places, research shows that most people want to get through their sentences without trouble.[17]

FOR CRITICAL THINKING

The case discussed at the beginning of the chapter involved a man who murdered a correctional officer. As was noted, Edward Muhammad Johnson had a violent past before the incident occurred.

1. Which theory of prison subculture—deprivation or importation—best explains Johnson's violent attack? Did Johnson bring his attitudes toward correctional officers with him to prison? Did Johnson learn to resolve conflict by using violent means after he arrived in prison? Can both perspectives be used to form an integrated explanation of his violence?
2. Consider Irwin's four role orientations: doing time, gleaning, jailing, and disorganized. After reading the next few pages, what role would you say that Edward Muhammad Johnson played?

FOCUS ON

PEOPLE IN CORRECTIONS: How Are You Going to Do Your Time?

The Federal Correctional Institution at Fort Dix, New Jersey, is a low-security prison holding 3,800 men. Michael Santos, a long-term resident, interviewed some of his peers about their prison experience and future goals. How would you classify the adaptive roles of these men?

LOU

Lou has been in three federal prisons since 1994 and expects to be released soon. He takes each day as it comes. He's not involved in any prison hustles and passes his time lifting weights, playing chess, cheering for the Yankees, and supporting all Puerto Rican events.

Lou says he'll worry about the outside when he's released. While he's inside he wants to focus on "gettin' my body big, 'cause nothin' else matters anyway." He sees nothing to gain by participating in programs, and with no chance of advancing his release date, he also sees nothing to lose by participating in a prison disturbance.

"All I'm trying to do is get through my bid," he says. "I like doin' time my own way. And I ain't changin'......However, if I gotta get down with my peoples I'm ready for whatever. I don't care 'bout the hole or gettin' transferred or none of these super cops runnin' round here. The time keeps tickin' and when I'm out these doors are gonna open. Until then, I'm just gonna do my time. I ain't botherin' nobody. But if someone messes with one of my homies, I don't care if I got one year left or one day left. Some of these muthafuckas ain't got no respect. They break in lockers, cut in line, shit like that. If any of 'em disrespect me or anyone I know though, they're gonna have problems. I'm gonna be there. And I'm comin' wit' everythin' I got. That's just who I am. And people know it."

JERRY

Those perceived to have Mafia connections are given respect within the fences. Although many men try to impress others with their "close" ties to the Mafia, there are in fact few actual leaders. One of the leaders is Jerry.

Jerry has been incarcerated for 16 years and is less than 2 years away from release. Eager to leave prison as soon as possible, he passes his time rather easily and is an expert at avoiding problems inside the joint.

Jerry has a reputation as a stand-up guy who is beyond suspicion of being an informant or doing anything contrary to the rules by which guys "from the neighborhood" live. Like a diplomat, Jerry frequently intervenes to help a friend or acquaintance find a good job or overcome a misunderstanding with others. Jerry is respected for standing by his principles.

PEOPLE IN CORRECTIONS: How Are You Going to Do Your Time? (*continued*)

Jerry spends several hours every day playing gin with others who are equally respected, or he may walk around the track with one or two close friends for exercise; he's never able to make a full circle without being stopped for the requisite handshakes with associates and impostors alike. Always neatly dressed in freshly ironed clothing, Jerry strolls around the compound with the confidence and assurance of a leader who is comfortable in his domain.

During the evening, Jerry's room becomes a gathering place where friends join him to eat, discuss old times, and share news from "the neighborhood." A topic that finds its way into every meal is the concept of honor, the code by which every guy from "the neighborhood" professes to live. This code requires each individual to accept complete responsibility for his actions and for keeping one's mouth shut about one's business. More important, as an honorable man, one would never cooperate with law enforcement. A neighborhood guy will never be a witness to a crime, be it a stolen car, robbery, or even a murder. Society relies on the police to handle its problems; neighborhood guys take care of disputes themselves.

BARRY

Barry is in his fourth year of a 10-year sentence for a nonviolent drug conviction. Although many residents seek jobs that will give them a maximum amount of freedom while in prison, others look for structure in their life.

One place they can find structure is through a job at the UNICOR factory, which sells its products to other federal agencies. Barry originally sought employment in UNICOR because it offered higher pay than any other inmate work assignment. After his first year, he worked his way up to a base pay of $150 per month and with overtime can earn over $200.

Besides the pay, Barry says his job as a clerk for one of the factory managers provides him with a degree of responsibility that he appreciates. His duties are similar to those of a middle-level manager of any large factory. He uses sophisticated computer software applications and recognizes that those skills will prove valuable upon release. As he says, "I do all the work. My supervisor is really just around to make sure I'm not doing anything unauthorized. The factory wouldn't skip a beat without him."

Each morning, Barry reports to work at 7:30 when his supervisor calls roll. He says that he works pretty consistently until the 45-minute lunch break. He's not allowed to use the computers for personal work. If caught, even typing a letter home could result in his being fired and receiving an incident report. Barry says he doesn't break the rules, because he appreciates the job. Not only does it provide the money he needs to live in prison, but it also keeps him current with the technological skills he will need on the outside. As he says, "Most guys in here are completely illiterate when it comes to computers. When they get out, they're going to find out that nearly every job in society requires some knowledge of computers. I'm expecting my computer experience will help overcome my felony conviction."

Source: Adapted with permission from *About Prison*. © 2004 Wadsworth, a part of Cengage Learning, Inc.

LO 2

Analyze the prison economy.

THE PRISON ECONOMY

In prison, as outside, people want goods and services. Although the state feeds, clothes, and houses everyone, amenities are usually scarce. A life of extreme simplicity is part of the punishment, and correctional administrators believe that to maintain discipline and security, rules must be enforced and everybody must be treated alike so none can gain higher position, status, or comfort levels because of wealth or access to goods. Prison residents are deprived of nearly everything but bare necessities. Their diet and routine are monotonous, and their recreational opportunities are limited. They experience a loss of identity (because of uniformity of treatment) and a lack of responsibility.

The number of items that a resident may purchase or receive through legitimate channels differs from state to state and from facility to facility. For example, people in some prisons have televisions, civilian clothing, and hot plates. Not everyone enjoys these luxuries, nor do they satisfy lingering desires for a variety of other goods. Some state legislatures have passed laws further limiting the amenities that residents can enjoy.

Recognizing that these people do have some needs that are not met, prisons have a commissary or "store" from which residents may periodically purchase a limited number of items— coffee, toothpaste, snack foods, and other items—in exchange for credits drawn on their "bank accounts." The size of a bank account depends on the amount of money deposited on the individual's entrance, gifts sent by relatives, and amounts earned in the low-paying prison industries. For a list of items available inside one state prison system, see "Prison Commissary Items."

FOCUS ON

CORRECTIONAL PRACTICE: Prison Commissary Items

Provided here is a list of items that the Mississippi Department of Corrections makes available to individuals housed in minimum- and medium-security facilities.

Item	Price	Item	Price
Coffee, Grains	$4.33	Mustard	$1.20
Soft Drinks	$1.63	Ketchup	$1.20
Water	$0.95	Grape Jelly	$3.47
Men's Boxers	$3.27	AA Batteries	$4.33
Men's T-Shirt	$3.61	Clear Wrist Watch	$4.71
Shower Shoes	$1.93	Candy Bar	$1.34
Tennis Shoes	$23.10	Cinnamon Roll	$0.95
Laundry Bag	$2.66	Salted Peanuts	$0.95
Security Razor	$0.43	Chocolate Chip Cookies	$1.53
Soap Bar	$2.17	Mac & Cheese Packet	$1.40
Security Toothbrush	$0.76	Granola Bar	$0.87
Q-Tips	$1.73	Light Tuna Packet	$2.40
Deodorant	$3.09	Antibiotic Ointment	$2.88
Petroleum Jelly	$1.83	Muscle Rub	$1.53
Comb	$0.24	Laxative	$1.93
Shampoo	$0.76	Playing Cards	$2.41
Dandruff Shampoo	$0.86	Reading Glasses	$0.47

Source: www.mdoc.ms.gov/Inmate-Info/Documents/PriceList_2015_.pdf.

However, the snack foods, health and dental products, and personal supplies (e.g., batteries and envelopes) of the typical prison store in no way satisfy the consumer needs and desires of most residents. Consequently, an informal underground economy is a major element in prison society. Many items taken for granted on the outside are highly valued on the inside. For example, deodorant takes on added importance because of the limited bathing facilities. Goods and services unique to prison can take on exaggerated importance. For example, unable to get alcohol, some people may seek a similar effect by sniffing glue. Or, to distinguish themselves from others, some may pay laundry workers to iron a shirt in a particular way, a modest version of conspicuous consumption.

Research shows that informal "stores" run by the incarcerated are quite common in most cell blocks. Such stores provide the goods (contraband) and services not available or allowed by prison authorities. The prison economy, like a market on the outside, responds to the forces of supply and demand; the risk of discovery replaces some of the risk associated with business in the free world.[18] (See a description of the prison economy in "Carnalito.")

As a principal feature of prison culture, this informal economy reinforces the norms and roles of the social system and influences the nature of interpersonal relationships. The extent of the economy and its ability to produce desired goods and services—food, drugs, alcohol, sex, preferred living conditions—vary according to the extent of official surveillance, the demands of the consumers, and the opportunities for entrepreneurship. Their success as "hustlers" determines the luxuries and power that prison residents can enjoy.

FOCUS ON

PEOPLE IN CORRECTIONS: Carnalito

Carnalito, from Mexico, was convicted in Texas at age 15 for a drug offense and was sentenced to 5 years. He arrived at Fort Dix, a low-security federal prison, when he was 18. He makes his living as a hustler within the prison economy.

At five each morning Carnalito begins his day by taking his customers' dirty clothes to the prison laundry, where he washes, dries, and neatly folds them before returning them. For this service he receives three dollars' worth of commissary goods (such as canned tuna and postage stamps) from each customer. By using Carnalito, his clients are able to avoid the frustration of waiting in line to use the machines and watching over their clothes to avoid theft.

While the clothes are washing, Carnalito performs his assigned duties as a unit orderly, cleaning the first-floor bathrooms of his housing unit. For this work the administration credits 10 dollars each month to his commissary account as "inmate performance pay." Carnalito also does the cleaning duties of three other inmate orderlies who each pay him 15 dollars a month; thus he earns another 45 dollars' worth of commissary items.

By noon each day, having finished his assigned duties, Carnalito begins to gather the ingredients to prepare dinner for a group of five residents. This group does not want to suffer the frustrations of eating in the dining hall among hundreds of other people where fights often break out. Instead, they pay Carnalito a total of $200 per month for cooking their dinner six nights a week. For this fee, Carnalito procures vegetables from kitchen hustlers. He pays them with commissary items and assumes the risk of hiding the vegetables from the guards. The vegetables are combined with commissary items, provided by the dinner group, to complete the meal. The group sends the fee to Carnalito's mother in Mexico.

After providing for his own needs, Carnalito still has about $200 worth of commissary items each month from his earnings. He distributes these excess items by "running a store," allowing others to buy bags of coffee at any time on credit. For every two bags of coffee, however, Carnalito requires that his customers pay three bags back.

Not counting the $200 that his clients send outside for his cooking services, Carnalito earns approximately $400 through his cleaning services and the store. Whenever he accumulates too many commissary items, he makes a deal with other residents who buy these goods at 80 cents on the dollar; the purchasers send the money to Carnalito's address in Mexico.

Carnalito works hard within the prison economy and accumulates at least $500 each month that is deposited in his Mexican bank account. If all continues to move according to plan, he expects to be released from prison in a few years. He will be 21, with nearly $20,000 in U.S. currency in his bank account. He plans to open a business in Mexico upon release.

Source: Written especially for this text by Michael Santos.

Because real money is prohibited and a barter system is somewhat restrictive, the traditional standard currency in the prison economy for many years was cigarettes. They were not contraband, were easily transferable, had a stable and well-known standard of value, and came in "denominations" of singles, packs, and cartons. Furthermore, they were in demand by smokers. Even those who did not smoke kept cigarettes for prison currency. However, many prisons across the country have adopted nonsmoking policies, which has largely brought about an end to the use of cigarettes as prison currency. Today, nonperishable food items, such as ramen noodles, and postage stamps have emerged as the standard forms of currency.[19]

Certain positions in the prison society enhance opportunities for entrepreneurs. For example, residents assigned to work in the kitchen, warehouse, and administrative office steal food, clothing, building materials, and even information to sell or trade to others. The goods may then become part of other market transactions. Thus, exchanging a dozen eggs for a pack of postage stamps may result in reselling the eggs as egg sandwiches, made on a hot plate, for five stamps each. Meanwhile, the kitchen worker who stole the eggs may use the income to get a laundry worker to starch his shirts, a hospital orderly to provide drugs, or a "punk" to give him sexual favors. "Sales" in the economy are one to one and are also interrelated with other underground market transactions.

Economic transactions may lead to violence when goods are stolen, debts remain unpaid, or agreements are violated. Disruptions of the economy may occur when officials conduct periodic "lockdowns" and inspections. Confiscation of contraband may result in temporary shortages and price readjustments, but gradually business returns. The prison economy, like that of the outside world, allocates goods and services, provides rewards and sanctions, and is closely linked to the society it serves.

VIOLENCE IN PRISON

Prisons offer a perfect recipe for violence. They confine large numbers of men in cramped quarters, some of whom have histories of violent behavior. While incarcerated, these men are not allowed contact with women and live under highly restrictive conditions. Sometimes these conditions, coupled with the inability of administrators to respond to the needs of the incarcerated population, spark collective violence, as in the riots at Attica, New York (1971); Santa Fe, New Mexico (1980); Atlanta, Georgia (1987); Lucasville, Ohio (1993); and Chino, California (2009). In Chapter 13 we examine collective violence from a management perspective.

Although prison riots are widely reported in the news media, few people are aware of the level of everyday interpersonal violence in U.S. prisons. For example, each year 34,000 prison residents are physically attacked by other residents.[20] Even so, some evidence suggests that prisons are becoming less violent. The homicide rate among people in state prisons is now approximately 8 per 100,000, which is substantially lower than it was in 1980 (54 per 100,000 people in state prisons). Similarly, the suicide rate in state prisons is now around 21 per 100,000, which is also lower than the rate reported in 1980 (34 suicides per 100,000 people in prison).[21] However, scholars have pointed out that studies tend to focus on only the types of violence that are officially recorded, not the full range of prisoner victimization. Further, great numbers of prison residents live in a state of constant uneasiness, always looking out for people who might demand sex, steal their possessions, or otherwise harm them. In any case, research suggests that the level of violence varies by offender age, institutional security designation, and administrative effectiveness.

Violence and Inmate Characteristics

LO 3

Explain the different types of prison violence.

For the person entering prison for the first time, anxiety and fear of violence are especially high. Individuals who are victimized in prison are significantly more likely than others to be depressed and experience symptoms associated with post-traumatic stress such as nightmares.[22] Even if one is never assaulted, the potential for violence permeates the environment of many prisons, adding to the stress and pains of incarceration. Assaults in our correctional institutions raise serious questions for administrators, criminal justice specialists, and the general public. What causes prison violence, and what can be done about it? We consider these questions when we examine the three main categories of prison violence: prisoner–prisoner, prisoner–officer, and officer–prisoner. But first we discuss three characteristics that underlie these behavioral factors: age, attitudes, and race.

Age Studies have shown that young men between the ages of 16 and 24, both inside and outside prison, are more prone to violence than are older men. Not surprisingly, 92.4 percent of adults in state prison are men, 55.2 percent of whom were convicted of a violent offense, and many of whom are under age 25.[23] Studies also show that young residents face a greater risk of being victimized relative to their older counterparts.[24]

Besides having greater physical strength than older individuals, young residents also lack the commitments to career and family that inhibit antisocial behavior. In addition, many have difficulty defining their position in society. Thus, they interpret many interactions as challenges to their status.

Machismo, the concept of male honor and the sacredness of one's reputation as a man, requires physical retaliation against those who offer an insult. Observers have argued that many homosexual rapes are not sexual but political—attempts to impress on the victim the aggressor's male power and to define the target as passive or "feminine." Some men in prison adopt a preventive strategy, trying to impress others with their bravado, which may result in counterchallenges and violence. Young individuals may seek to establish a reputation by retaliating for slurs on their honor, sexual prowess, and manliness. The potential for violence among such men is obvious.

Attitudes Some sociologists posit that a subculture of violence exists among certain socioeconomic, racial, and ethnic groups. This subculture is found in the lower class; in its value system, violence is condoned in certain situations to resolve interpersonal conflict.[25] Arguments are settled and decisions are made by the fist rather than by verbal persuasion. Many people bring these attitudes into prison with them. Some support for this theory exists. For example, Daniel Mears and his colleagues found that men who adhere to a belief system (or street code) prior to incarceration that promotes, endorses, or otherwise necessitates violence in response to perceived provocations are much more likely to behave violently when serving time in prison.[26]

Race Race is a major divisive factor in today's prisons. Racist attitudes have become part of the inmate code. Forced association—having to live with people one would not likely associate with on the outside— exaggerates and amplifies racial conflict. Violence against members of another race may be how some people deal with the frustrations of their lives. The presence of gangs organized along racial lines contributes to violence in prison.

Prisoner–Prisoner Violence

Although prison folklore may attribute violence to sadistic guards, most prison violence occurs between prison residents. Hans Toch observed that incarcerated individuals are "terrorized by other inmates, and spend years in fear of harm. Some inmates request segregation, others lock themselves in, and some are hermits by choice."[27] The U.S. Bureau of Justice Statistics reports that the rate of prisoner–prisoner assault in U.S. prisons is 28 attacks per 1,000 prison population.[28] But official statistics likely do not reflect the true amount of prisoner–prisoner violence because for various reasons, many people who are assaulted do not make their victimization known to prison officials (see "Do the Right Thing").

Prison Gangs Racial or ethnic gangs (also referred to as "security threat groups," or STGs) are now linked to acts of violence in most prison systems. Gangs make it difficult for wardens to maintain control. By continuing their street wars inside prison, gangs make some prisons more dangerous than any U.S. neighborhood. Gangs are organized primarily to control an institution's drug, gambling, loan-sharking, prostitution, extortion, and debt-collection rackets. In addition, gangs protect their members from other gangs and instill a sense of macho camaraderie.

Contributing to prison violence is the "blood in, blood out" basis for gang membership: A would-be member must stab a gang's enemy to be admitted, and once in, he cannot drop out without endangering his own life. Given the racial and ethnic foundation of gangs, violence between them can easily spill into the general prison

DO THE RIGHT THING

While routinely walking the tier one day, Officer Rodriguez is stopped by Victor Sanchez, a long-term resident whom Rodriguez knows well. Sanchez tells Rodriguez that some other men in the cell block are going to assault his cell mate, Matt Koscki, in the very near future. Koscki is widely regarded by both residents and staff as a loudmouth, thief, and all-around troublemaker. In fact, Rodriguez is of the opinion that most people on the tier, including some of the officers, probably believe that Koscki has earned a beating.

Later that day, while back at his desk, Rodriguez thinks about the information he received from Sanchez. He is confident that the information is good. But Rodriguez has second thoughts about passing it on to his supervisor. Doing so could result in Koscki's potential attackers being transferred to a different unit, but it could also result in Koscki's transfer. How will these men react if their planned assault is stopped? Will someone else step in and assault Koscki? Is the assault inevitable?

"You wanted to see me, Rodriguez?"

Rodriguez looks up from his paperwork to see Lieutenant Jackson. "Hey, Lieutenant. Thanks for dropping by."

WRITING ASSIGNMENT: How would you handle the Koscki situation if you were in Officer Rodriguez's shoes? First, describe the benefits to the social climate of the cell block if you do not report the impending assault. Next, discuss your ethical obligation to protect Koscki and everyone else in your charge from danger. Finally, explain how you would act, and discuss the factors that influenced your decision.

population. Some institutions have programs that offer members a way out of gang life. Referred to as "deganging," these programs educate members and eventually encourage them to renounce their gang membership.

Prison gangs exist to a greater or lesser degree in the institutions of most states and the federal system. One survey found that Montana's prison population has the lowest percentage of known gang members (less than 1 percent) and Oklahoma has the highest (an estimated 70 percent).[29]

Prison gangs are tightly organized and have even arranged the killing of opposition gang leaders housed in other institutions. Research has shown that prisons infested with gangs tend to experience the greatest number of homicides.[30] Administrators say that prison gangs tend to pursue their "business" interests, yet they also contribute greatly to inmate–inmate violence as they discipline members, enforce orders, and retaliate against other gangs. Research shows that gang-affiliated individuals are more likely to be involved in violent misconduct and to be the victims of violence than are nongang individuals.[31]

The National Gang Intelligence Center estimates that there are approximately 230,000 gang members in state and federal prison.[32] The racial and ethnic basis of gang membership has been well documented. Nationwide, reports show that about 36 percent of known prison gang members are black, 28 percent are white, 18 percent are Hispanic, 2 percent are Asian, and 5 percent represent other ethnic groups.[33] Not surprisingly, a lot of prison gang conflict is interracial. In California in the late 1960s, a Hispanic gang—the Mexican Mafia (La EME), whose members had known one another in Los Angeles—took over the rackets in San Quentin. In reaction, other gangs were formed, including a rival Mexican gang, La Nuestra Familia (NF); CRIPS (Common Revolution in Progress); the Texas Syndicate; the Black Guerrilla Family (BGF); and the Aryan Brotherhood (see Table 11.1).[34]

TABLE 11.1 Characteristics of Major Prison Gangs

These gangs were founded in the California prison system from the late 1950s through the 1970s. They have now spread across the nation and are viewed as the major security threat groups in most corrections systems.

Name		Racial Makeup	Origin	Characteristics	Enemies
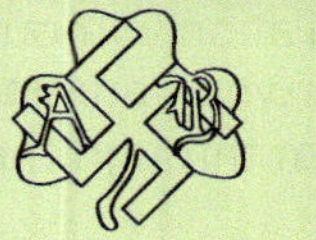	Aryan Brotherhood	White	San Quentin, 1967	Apolitical. Most in custody for crimes such as robbery.	CRIPS, Bloods, BGF
	Black Guerrilla Family (BGF)	African American	San Quentin, 1966	Most politically oriented. Antigovernment.	Aryan Brotherhood, EME
	Mexican Mafia (EME)	Mexican American/ Hispanic	Deuel Vocational Center, Los Angeles, late 1950s	Ethnic solidarity, control of drug trafficking.	BGF, NF
	La Nuestra Familia (NF)	Mexican American/ Hispanic	Soledad, 1965	Protect young, rural Mexican Americans.	EME
	Texas Syndicate	Mexican American/ Hispanic	Folsom, early 1970s	Protect Texan inmates in California.	Aryan Brotherhood, EME, NF

Source: "Major Prison Gangs," www.dc.state.fl.us/pub/gangs/prison.html, March 29, 2017.

Gang conflict in California prisons became a very serious problem in the 1970s. Even today, the size of some of these gangs is staggering.

Administrators use a variety of strategies to weaken gang influence and to reduce violence. These strategies include identifying members, segregating housing and work assignments, restricting possession or display of gang symbols, conducting strip searches, monitoring mail and telephone communications, and providing only no-contact visits.[35] Some correctional departments transfer key gang members to other states in the hope of slowing or stopping a prison gang's activity. Correctional officials believe that segregation, specialized housing units, and restricting visits are the most effective ways of dealing with prison gangs.[36]

Administrators have also set up intelligence units to gather information on gangs. The Florida Department of Corrections Security Threat Intelligence Unit monitors the thousands of gang members incarcerated in Florida prisons. The information that the unit collects is regularly provided to federal, state, and local law enforcement agencies upon request. The unit provides law enforcement officials with valuable information, such as the address where former prison residents will be living, gang affiliation, a list of nicknames and aliases, criminal history, description of tattoos, and a photograph of the individual.[37]

Protective Custody For many victims of prison violence, protective custody is the only way to escape further abuse. Most prison systems have such a unit, along with units for disciplinary and administrative segregation. Individuals who seek protective custody may have been physically abused, have received sexual threats, have reputations as snitches, or fear assault by someone they crossed on the outside who is now a fellow resident. Referred to as the "special management inmates," they pose particular problems for prison administrators, who must provide them with programs and services.

Life is not pleasant for these individuals. Often their physical condition, programs, and recreational opportunities are little better than those for residents who are in segregation because of misbehavior. Usually they are let out of their cells only briefly to exercise and shower. Their only stimulation is from books, radio, and television. Those who ask to "lock up" have little chance of returning to the general prison population without being viewed as a weakling—a snitch or a punk—to be preyed on. Even when administrators transfer them to another institution, their reputations follow them through the grapevine.

Sexual Victimization Given how regularly violent sexual assaults are portrayed in the media, the public's belief that prison rape is common in most U.S. correctional facilities is not too surprising (see "Myths in Corrections"). But in reality, how common is it? The Bureau of Justice Statistics reports that both perpetrators and victims of inmate–inmate sexual victimization tend to be male and between the ages of 25 and 39. While victims tend to be white, the perpetrators tend to be either white or black.[38] In terms of their criminal histories, men who threaten, attempt, or achieve sexual violence in prison tend to have convictions for juvenile robbery and adult sexual assault, and they have also been imprisoned for a longer period than those who do not perpetrate sexual assault.[39] Studies have found that victims of prison sexual assault tend to have one or more of the following characteristics:

- First-time, nonviolent prison residents
- Incarcerated individuals who were convicted of a crime against a minor
- Prison residents who are physically weak
- Individuals who are viewed as effeminate by other prison residents
- Individuals who are not affiliated with a prison gang
- Prison residents who are believed to have "snitched" on others[40]

Also, the Bureau of Justice Statistics reports that most acts of prisoner–prisoner sexual victimization involve a single victim (96 percent) and one assailant (91 percent). Incidents involving two or more perpetrators make up only 9 percent of known incidents of inmateinmate sexual violence.[41]

A study consisting of nearly 7,000 randomly selected people in state prisons found that about 2 percent of males in prison reported that they were sexually assaulted over the six-month study period. The study found that sexual assaults most commonly involved attempted, coerced, or forced oral or anal sex. Assaults such as these most frequently took place during evening hours (38.5 percent between 6:00 P.M. and midnight) and were usually carried out in the victim's cell (46.5 percent). In over half of the sexual assaults (52 percent), a weapon was used by the perpetrator (most commonly a homemade knife, or "shank"). In terms of physical harm, two-thirds of victims reported injuries, but only 5 percent were sent to a hospital outside the prison. Finally, many victims reported that they changed their behavior to avoid future victimization. Such behavioral alterations included avoiding certain areas (40 percent), avoiding certain people (40 percent), keeping more to themselves (43 percent), and spending more time in their cell (43 percent).[42] Results such as these that are able to contextualize sexual victimization are crucial to developing strategies that could help prevent such assaults in the future.

Prison administrators confront various challenges in their attempts to combat sexual violence. For example, many individuals serving prison sentences have reservations about reporting sexual victimization. Some victims fear that prison officials will not protect them from retaliation if they report the incident. Others believe that officials will not take their allegation seriously.[43] Another problem is that many sexual assaults are not reported in a timely manner. One study conducted in the Texas prison system found that only 30 percent of allegations of sexual assault were reported on the day in which the event reportedly occurred. Time lapse is one of the primary reasons why prison officials used rape kits and forensic exams in only 20 percent of all alleged sexual assaults.[44] When incidents of rape are reported, prison wardens overwhelmingly agree that a criminal investigation should take place and, if warranted, charges pressed.[45]

MYTHS in Corrections

Sexual Victimization in State and Federal Prisons

THE MYTH: Because prisons are filled with predatory, violent men who are deprived of heterosexual relationships, abusive sexual contact happens with great regularity.

THE REALITY: Using data from the Survey of Sexual Victimization, the U.S. Bureau of Justice Statistics estimates that 295 nonconsensual sexual acts were reported in state and federal prisons in 2015. At the time, the total prison population was about 1.53 million. Put differently, less than 1 percent of the prison population experienced this type of sexual victimization.

Source: Ramona R. Rantala, *Sexual Victimization Reported by Adult Correctional Authorities, 2012-15* (Washington, DC: U.S. Government Printing Office, 2018), 10

Prisoner–Officer Violence

Yearly, prison residents assault approximately 18,000 prison staff members.[46] Correctional officers do not carry weapons within the institution because they could be seized and used against them. However, prisoners do manage to get lethal weapons and can use the element of surprise to injure an officer. In the course of a workday, an officer may encounter situations that require the use of physical force—for instance, breaking up a fight or moving someone to segregation. Because such situations are especially dangerous, officers may enlist others to help minimize the risk of violence. The correctional officer's greatest fear is unexpected attacks. These may take the form of a missile thrown from an upper tier, verbal threats and taunts, or an officer's "accidental" fall down a flight of stairs. The need to remain constantly watchful against personal attacks adds stress and keeps many officers at a distance from individuals they supervise.

Descriptive research on serious staff assaults reveals some commonalities across incidents. For example, nearly 90 percent of such attacks involved a single assailant and a lone victim. This does not square with the image sometimes portrayed in the movies of a gang of predatory individuals assaulting an unsuspecting guard. Over half of the assaults against staff involved a weapon, such as a homemade knife, blunt object, or liquid mixture (urine). But nearly as often, the assailant relied only on his fists, feet, and teeth. Staff members who were assaulted were not new and inexperienced, nor were they long-term veterans of the cell blocks: The average prison staff victim was 35 years old with 7 years on the job. Most injuries (94.6 percent) suffered

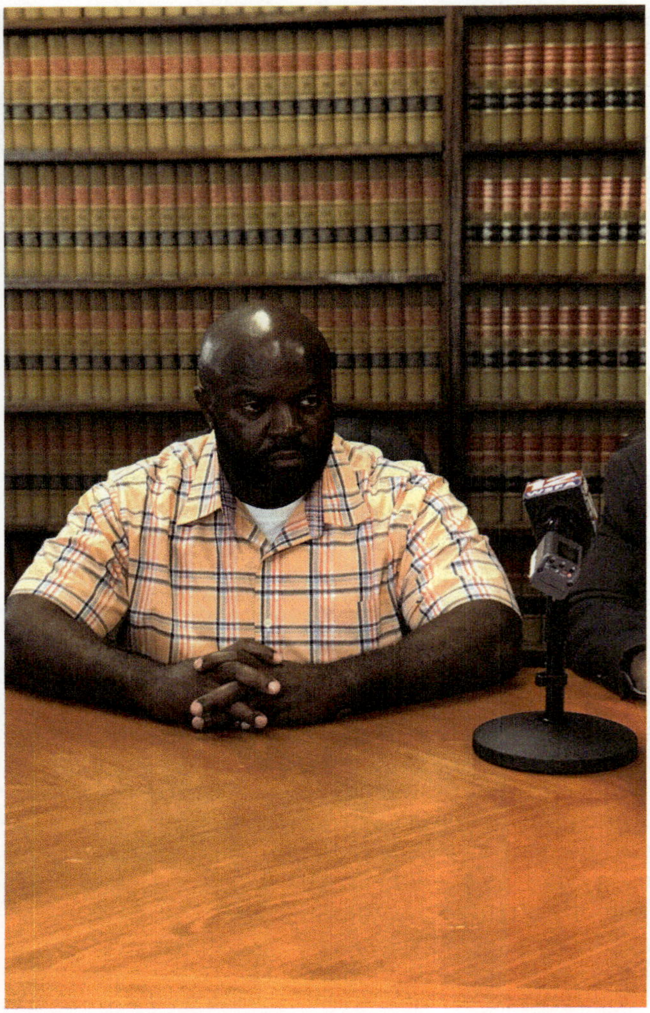

▲ *Former corrections officer Willie Burks was indicted by a grand jury for allegedly failing to stop another officer from assaulting two handcuffed incarcerated individuals.*

by staff were characterized as minor or moderate, not requiring hospitalization. Finally, those who assaulted prison staff tended to be younger and black individuals who were members of prison gangs. Most of these men had been convicted of violent offenses (86.7 percent) and were serving relatively long prison sentences (averaging 34 years).[47]

Despite the fact that violence against officers typically occurs in specific situations and against certain individuals, the news media tend to report on incidents in which guards are taken hostage, injured, and killed. While these rare events may make more interesting news stories, they also underscore the real dangers of prison work.

Officer–Prisoner Violence

A fact of life in many institutions is unauthorized physical violence by officers against prison residents. Stories abound of guards giving individuals "the treatment" when supervisors are not looking. Many guards view physical force as an everyday, legitimate procedure. In some institutions, authorized "goon squads" comprising physically powerful officers use their muscle to maintain order.

From time to time, the media present incidents of the excessive and illegal use of force by prison officials. One widely publicized case of officer–prisoner violence occurred at the California State Prison at Corcoran. Between 1989 and 1995, 43 individuals were wounded and 7 killed by officers firing assault weapons—the most killings in any prison. Guards even instigated fights between rival gang members. During these "gladiator days," tower guards often shot the gang members after they had been ordered to stop fighting. Each shooting was justified by state-appointed reviewers. Eight prison guards were subsequently charged with federal civil rights abuses. The officers were acquitted at trial.[48]

How do we tell when prison officers are using force legitimately and when they are using it to punish individual residents? Correctional officers are expected to follow departmental rules, but supervisors rarely observe staff–prisoner confrontations. Further, prisoner complaints about officer brutality are often not believed until the officer involved gains a reputation for harshness. Still, wardens may feel they must support their officers to retain, in turn, their officers' support. Levels of violence by officers against residents are undoubtedly lower today than in years past. Nevertheless, officers are expected to enforce prison rules and may use force to uphold discipline and prevent escapes. Further, definitions of appropriate force for the handling of particular situations are typically vague (see Chapter 13).

LO 4

Discuss what can be done about prison violence.

Ways to Decrease Prison Violence

Experts point to five factors that contribute to prison violence: inadequate supervision by staff members, architectural design that promotes rather than inhibits victimization, the easy availability of deadly weapons, the housing of violence-prone individuals near relatively defenseless people, and an overall high level of tension produced by close quarters.[49] The physical size and condition of the prison and the relations between clients and staff also affect violence.

The Effect of Architecture and Size Prison architectural design is thought to influence the amount of violence in an institution. Many prisons are not only large but also contain areas where people can avoid supervision. The new-generation prisons—with their small housing units, clear sight lines, and security corridors linking housing units—are largely designed to limit these opportunities and thus prevent violence.

The fortress-like prison certainly does not create an atmosphere for normal interpersonal relationships, and the size of the largest institutions can create management problems. The massive scale of the megaprison, which may hold up to 3,000 people, provides opportunities for aggressive individuals to hide weapons, dispense private "justice," and engage more or less freely in other illicit activities. Size may also result in some people "falling through the cracks" by being misclassified and forced to live among more-violent men.

The relationship between prison crowding and violence is unclear. Some studies have shown that as personal space shrinks, the number of violent incidents rises. Benjamin Steiner and John Wooldredge argue that the inconsistent research findings may be partially explained by the fact that crowding is measured in several different ways (for example, number of people per area, amount of space per person, amount of unshared space per person).[50] Clearly, increasing the size of an institution's population strains the limits of dining halls, athletic areas, educational and treatment programs, medical care, and so forth. To maintain quality of life, prisons need increased resources to offset such strains. In some institutions the population has more than doubled without increases in violence. Good management seems to be a major factor in keeping conditions from deteriorating.

The Role of Management The degree to which inmate leaders are allowed to take matters into their own hands can affect the level of violence inside prison. When administrators run a tight ship, security measures prevent sexual attacks in dark corners, the making of "shivs" and "shanks" in the metal shop, and open conflict among inmate groups. A prison must afford each person defensible space, and administrators need to ensure that every individual remains secure and free from physical attack.

Effective prison management may decrease the level of violence by limiting opportunities for attacks. Wardens and correctional officers must therefore recognize the types of people under guard, the role of prison gangs, and the structure of institutions. John Dilulio argues that no group of prison residents is "unmanageable [and] no combination of political, social, budgetary, architectural, or other factors makes good management impossible."[51] Good management practices have resulted in prisons where people can "do time" without fearing for their personal safety. Wardens exert leadership and manage their prisons effectively so that problems do not fester and erupt into violent confrontations.

Measures suggested to reduce violence are not always clear-cut or applicable to all situations. The following steps have been proposed:

1. Improve classification so that violence-prone men are separated from the general population.
2. For residents who are fearful of being victimized, create opportunities to seek assistance from staff.
3. Increase the size, racial diversity, and training of the custody force.
4. Redesign facilities so that all areas can be put under surveillance; there should be no "blind spots." Use smaller institutions.

5. Install grievance mechanisms or an ombudsperson to help resolve interpersonal or institutional problems.
6. Augment the reward system to reduce the pains of imprisonment.

unit management Tactic for reducing prison violence by dividing facilities into small, self-contained, semiautonomous "institutions."

One administrative strategy that has helped bring order to violence-marked institutions is **unit management**. This approach divides a prison into many small, self-contained "institutions" operating in semiautonomous fashion within the confines of a larger facility. Each of the units houses between 50 and 100 individuals, who remain together as long as release dates allow and who are supervised by a team of correctional officers, counselors, and treatment specialists. The assumption is that by keeping the units small, staff will get to know the residents better and recognize problems early on, and group cohesion will emerge. Further, because the unit manager has both authority and accountability, policies will presumably be enforced consistently and fairly. The unit-management approach has been credited with reducing violence in several state and federal institutions.

In sum, prisons must be made safe. Because the state puts people there, it has a responsibility to prevent violence and maintain order. To eliminate violence from prisons, officials may have to limit movement within the institution, contacts with the outside, and the right to choose one's associates (see "For Critical Thinking"). Yet these measures may run counter to the goal of producing men and women who will be responsible citizens when they return to society.

FOR CRITICAL THINKING

One of the questions surrounding the murder case of Officer Joseph Gomm at the Minnesota Correctional Facility—Stillwater (discussed at the beginning of the chapter) is that the assailant, Edward Muhammad Johnson, had a long history of disciplinary problems.

1. As a warden, how would you ensure that high-risk people do not assault staff? Would you develop a classification system? Would you separate certain individuals? Explain your strategy.
2. Should individuals with disciplinary problems, such as Johnson, be housed in a cell block that uses unit management? How many staff members per resident do you think would be necessary to prevent escapes? Does the fact that the cell block would house a very different type of client, those who may act of violently, make unit management a less appealing administrative strategy?

SUMMARY

1 Discuss the "inmate code" and explain where the values of the prison subculture come from.
The inmate code is a set of norms and values that develops in the prison social system. It defines the model prisoner in the eyes of inmates and provides a code of conduct for living in prison. A man who projects toughness, keeps his distance from the staff, and does his "own time" is held in high regard. One who is emotionally weak, snitches on fellow residents to the staff, and gets involved in other people's business does not enjoy high status. Some scholars argue that the inmate code develops as a response to the prison environment; adaptive roles reflect ways to relieve the pains of imprisonment. Others argue that the prison subculture is primarily imported from the world outside the prison walls.

2 Analyze the prison economy.
Prisons feed, clothe, and house their charges. In some states residents are allowed comforts, such as televisions, that are provided by friends and family members. Clients can also purchase certain goods from the prison commissary (or store). However, an informal economy exists in most prisons to satisfy inmates' consumer demands. Some take advantage of their job assignments to steal goods and provide services in the prison economy. Because real money is prohibited, the traditional standard currency in the prison economy was once cigarettes. However, many states have adopted nonsmoking policies, so nonperishable food goods and postage stamps are now used as a form of currency in many prisons.

3 Explain the different types of prison violence.
The most common type of prison violence involves one prison resident attacking another. However, the true extent of this type of violence is unknown because many incidents do not come to the attention of prison officials. In comparison, prisoner–officer violence is less common. Examples of this type of violence include physical assaults, thrown objects, and verbal threats. Officer–prisoner violence is tightly regulated. However, officers are allowed to use physical force in certain situations, such as attempting to break up a fight. Instances of inmate abuse by officers sometimes come to the attention of the general public, but such occurrences are undoubtedly less frequent today than in years past.

4 Discuss what can be done about prison violence.
The architectural design and size of prison facilities are thought to contribute to prison violence. Many older prisons contain areas where clients can avoid supervision. New-generation prisons are designed to provide staff with clear sight lines and security corridors linking housing units. These features limit opportunities for violence. Older prisons are frequently much larger than newly constructed facilities. Managing large numbers of residents increases the chances that some will be misclassified and forced to live among violent men. Thus, reducing the size of the inmate population is thought to be another way of preventing violence. Finally, effective prison management can reduce prison violence. When administrators run a tight ship, security measures prevent attacks, the making of weapons, and conflict among inmate groups. To succeed, prison managers must recognize the types of people under their guard, the role of prison gangs, and the structure of their institutions.

KEY TERMS

inmate code (*p. 290*)
prisonization (*p. 290*)
unit management (*p. 304*)

FOR DISCUSSION

1. Imagine that you are entering prison for the first time. What are your immediate concerns? How will you deal with them? What problems do you expect to face?
2. Do the values of the prison culture result from the deprivations of prison, or do individuals bring them from the outside? What was the case 50 years ago?
3. If you were the warden of a maximum-security prison for men, what policies would you adopt to prevent violence in the institution?

FOR FURTHER READING

Fleisher, Mark S., and Jessie L. Krienert. *The Myth of Prison Rape: Sexual Culture in American Prisons.* Lanham, MD: Rowan and Littlefield, 2009. Drawing on data from one of the largest studies of inmate sexuality and sexual violence, the authors discuss the dynamics of sexual life behind prison walls.

Presser, Lois. *Been a Heavy Life: Stories of Violent Men.* Urbana: University of Illinois Press, 2008. Presents interview data from men convicted of violent crime, such as murder, rape, robbery, and assault, and evaluates their stories.

Pyrooz, David C., and Scott H. Decker. *Competing for Control: Gangs and the Social Order of Prisons.* London: Cambridge University Press, 2019. A study that reveals how gangs in two Texas prisons fight for control.

Santos, Michael G. *Inside: Life Behind Bars in America.* New York: St. Martin's, 2006. Capturing the voices of his fellow prison residents, Santos makes the tragic and inspiring stories of men—from the toughest gang leaders to the richest Wall Street executives—come alive.

Skarbek, David. *The Social Order of the Underworld: How Prison Gangs Govern the American Penal System.* London: Oxford University Press, 2014. Explains how prions gangs form and the role they play in prison society.

NOTES

1 Mary Divine and Sarah Horner, "The Violent Life of Edward Muhammad Johnson, the Suspect in a Stillwater Prison Guard's Death," Pioneer Press, www.twincities.com/2018/07/19/about-edward-muhammad-johnson-inmate-linked-to-stillwater-prison-guard-joseph-gomms-death/, July 19, 2018; Mary Divine, "Stillwater Prison Inmate Charged with Murder in Bludgeoning Death of Corrections Officer," Pioneer Press, www.twincities.com/2018/08/02/stillwater-prison-inmate-charged-with-murder-in-bludgeoning-death-of-corrections-officer/, August 2, 2018.

2 Joseph Fulling Fishman, *Sex in Prison* (New York: National Liberty Press, 1934).

3 Leo Carroll, *Hacks, Blacks, and Cons: Race Relations in a Maximum Security Prison* (Lexington, MA: Lexington, 1974).

4 Robert Johnson, *Hard Time*, 3rd ed. (Belmont, CA: Wadsworth, 2002), 100.

5 Don Sabo, Terry A. Kupers, and Willie London, "Gender and the Politics of Punishment," in *Prison Masculinities,* edited by Sabo, Kupers, and London (Philadelphia: Temple University Press, 2001), 3, 7.

6 Charles M. Terry, "The Function of Humor for Prison Inmates," *Journal of Contemporary Criminal Justice* 13 (February 1997): 26.

7 Gresham M. Sykes, *The Society of Captives* (Princeton, NJ: *Princeton University Press*, 1958), 63–108.

8 Donald Clemmer, *The Prison Community* (New York: Holt, Rinehart & Winston, 1940), 299–304.

9 Sykes, *Society of Captives*, pp. 84–108.

10 Lucia Benaquisto and Peter J. Freed, "The Myth of Inmate Lawlessness: The Perceived Contradiction Between Self and Other in Inmates' Support for Criminal Justice Sanctioning Norms," *Law and Society Review* 30 (1996): 508.

11 Geoffrey Hunt, Stephanie Riegal, Tomas Morales, and Dan Waldorf, "Changes in Prison Culture: Prison Gangs and the Case of the Pepsi Generation," in *Criminal Justice: Politics and Policies*, 7th ed., edited by George F. Cole and Marc G. Gertz (Belmont, CA: Wadsworth, 1998), 435–47.

12 Sykes, *Society of Captives*, p. 107.

13 John Irwin and Donald R. Cressey, "Thieves, Convicts, and the Inmate Culture," *Social Problems* 10 (1962): 142–55.

14 Edward Zamble and Frank J. Porporino, *Coping, Behavior, and Adaptation in Prison Inmates* (New York: Springer-Verlag, 1988).

15 Ibid., p. 13.

16 Irwin, *Prisons in Turmoil*, p. 67.

17 Pete Earley, *The Hot House: Life Inside Leavenworth* (New York: Bantam, 1992), 44.

18 Mark S. Fleisher, *Warehousing Violence* (Newbury Park, CA: Sage, 1989), 151–52.

19 Aimee Picchi, "Forget Cigarettes—There's a New Prison Currency," *CBS News*, www.cbsnews.com/news/forget-cigarettes-theres-a-new-prison-currency/, August 23, 2016.

20 James J. Stephan and Jennifer C. Karberg, *Census of State and Federal Correctional Facilities, 2000* (Washington, DC: U.S. Government Printing Office, 2003), 8–10.

21 E. Ann Carson and Mary P. Cowhig, *Mortality in State and Federal Prisons, 2001–2016— Statistical Tables* (Washington, DC: U.S. Bureau of Justice Statistics, 2020), 6.

22 Andy Hochstetler, Daniel S. Murphy, and Ronald L. Simons, "Damaged Goods: Exploring Predictors of Distress in Prison Inmates," *Crime and Delinquency* 50 (July 2004): 436–57.

23 Jennifer Bronson and E. Ann Carson, *Prisoners in 2017* (Washington, DC: U.S. Government Printing Office, 2019).

24 Benjamin Steiner, Jared M. Ellison, H. Daniel Butler, and Calli M. Cain, "The Impact of Inmate and Prison Characteristics on Prisoner Victimization," *Trauma, Violence, & Abuse 18* (January 2017): 22.

25 Elijah Anderson, *Code of the Street: Decency, Violence, and the Moral Life of the Inner City* (New York: Norton, 1999).

26 Daniel P. Mears, Eric A. Stewart, Sonja E. Siennick, and Ronald L. Simons, "The Code of the Street and Inmate Violence: Investigating the Salience of Imported Belief Systems," *Criminology* 51 (August 2013): 695–728.

27 Hans Toch, *Peacekeeping: Police, Prisons, and Violence* (Lexington, MA: Lexington, 1976), 47–48.

28 Stephan and Karberg, *Census of State and Federal Correctional Facilities, 2000*, p. 10.

29 Editor, "Gangs/Security Threat Groups," *Corrections Compendium* 34 (Spring 2009): 23–37.

30 Michael D. Reisig, "Administrative Control and Inmate Homicide," *Homicide Studies* 6 (February 2002): 84–103.

31 Katrina A. Rufino, Kathleen A. Fox, and Glen A. Kercher, "Gang Membership and Crime Victimization Among Prison Inmates," *American Journal of Criminal Justice* 37 (2012): 321–37.

32 National Gang Intelligence Center, *National Gang Threat Assessment 2011: Emerging Trends* (Washington, DC: Author, 2011), 30.

33 Editor, "Gangs/Security Threat Groups," p. 23.

34 Alfonso J. Valdez, "Prison Gangs 101," *Corrections Today* 71 (February 2009): 40–43.

35 Gary Hill, "Gangs Inside Prison Walls Around the World," *Corrections Compendium* 29 (January–February 2004): 26; Chad Trulson, James W. Marquart, and Soraya K. Kawucha, "Gang Suppression and Institutional Control," *Corrections Today* 68 (April 2006): 26–31.

36 John Winterdyk and Rick Ruddell, "Managing Prison Gangs: Results from a Survey of U.S. Prison Systems," *Journal of Criminal Justice* (July–August 2010): 730–36.

[37] Office of the Inspector General, *Florida Department of Corrections: Annual Report, 2014-15* (Tallahassee, FL, 2015), 12–14.

[38] Paul Guerino and Allen J. Beck, *Sexual Victimization Reported by Adult Correctional Authorities, 2007–08* (Washington, DC: U.S. Government Printing Office, 2011), 13.

[39] Merry Morash, Seok Jin Jeong, and Nancy L. Zang, "An Exploratory Study of the Characteristics of Men Known to Commit Prisoner-on-Prisoner Sexual Violence," *Prison Journal* 90 (June 2010): 161–78.

[40] Kim English and Peggy Heil, "Prison Rape: What We Know Today," *Corrections Compendium* 30 (September–October 2005): 2.

[41] Guerino and Beck, *Sexual Victimization, 2007–08,* p. 13.

[42] Nancy Wolff and Jing Shi, "Contextualization of Physical and Sexual Assault in Male Prisons: Incidents and Their Aftermath," *Journal of Correctional Health Care* 15 (January 2009): 58–77.

[43] Janine M. Zweig and John Blackmore, *Strategies to Prevent Prison Rape by Changing the Correctional Culture* (Washington, DC: U.S. Department of Justice, 2008).

[44] James Austin, Tony Fabelo, Angela Gunter, and Ken McGinnis, *Sexual Violence in the Texas Prison System* (Washington, DC: JFA Institute, 2006).

[45] Aviva N. Moster and Elizabeth L. Jeglic, "Prison Warden Attitudes Toward Prison Rape and Sexual Assault: Findings Since the Prison Rape Elimination Act (PREA)," *Prison Journal* 89 (March 2009): 65–78.

[46] Stephan and Karberg, *Census of State and Federal Correctional Facilities, 2000,* p. 10.

[47] Jon R. Sorensen, Mark D. Cunningham, Mark P. Vigen, and S. O. Woods, "Serious Assaults on Prison Staff: A Descriptive Analysis," *Journal of Criminal Justice* 39 (March–April 2011): 143–50.

[48] Mark Arax, "8 Prison Guards Are Acquitted in Corcoran Battles," *Los Angeles Times,* http://articles.latimes.com/2000/jun/10/news/mn-39555, June 10, 2000.

[49] Lee H. Bowker, "Victimizers and Victims in American Correctional Institutions," in *Pains of Imprisonment,* edited by Robert Johnson and Hans Toch (Beverly Hills, CA: Sage, 1982), 64.

[50] Benjamin Steiner and John Wooldredge, "Rethinking the Link Between Institutional Crowding and Inmate Misconduct," *Prison Journal* 89 (June 2009): 205–33.

[51] John J. DiIulio, *No Escape: The Future of American Prisons* (New York: Basic, 1990), 12.

CHAPTER 12

The Incarceration of Women

Fred Squillante-USA TODAY NETWORK

Gabrielle Drake holds her newborn daughter in their room at Hope House, a new children's nursery for incarcerated mothers at the Ohio Reformatory for Women.

TWO WOMEN WAITING IN A ROOM FILLED WITH TOYS ENGAGE IN FRIENDLY CONVERSATION.

Both women are holding infants, tending to their needs, showering them with love and affection. Are these women employed at a nursery school? Perhaps they are at their pediatrician's office? Not in this case. The two women in question are both residents of the Ohio Reformatory for Women. They are new mothers and are living with their babies in Hope House, part of the Achieving Baby Care Success program.[1]

This particular program represents just one attempt to assist the estimated 809,800 individuals in state and federal facilities who are parents of children under age 18. Most of these incarcerated individuals are fathers. But a small percentage are mothers. Nationwide, the number of mothers incarcerated in federal and state prisons has increased dramatically over the past 25 years. These women are more likely than men to have lived with their children prior to incarceration.[2] They experience difficulty staying in touch with their children because most states have only one or two prisons for women. Transportation is difficult, visits are short and (at best) infrequent, and phone calls are expensive and irregular.

Advocates of prison parenting programs, such as Achieving Baby Care Success, believe they help strengthen the bond between mother and child. Not only is this beneficial to the kids, but it is also helpful to mothers who will one day parent their children outside the prison walls. The warden of the Ohio Reformatory for Women, Teri Baldauf, noted that "[m]y hope is that the bonding starts, and then they're learning new skills that they can take home to their children." To be eligible for the program, women must be nonviolent offenders, convicted of crimes that did not involve children, and serving a sentence of three years or less.[3]

Because women make up such a small proportion of the prison population, a far larger portion of correctional budgets goes to institutions for men. Yet incarcerated women usually have greater health and program needs than do their male counterparts. In this chapter we review the history of women's incarceration and examine the life of women behind bars.

LEARNING OBJECTIVES

After reading this chapter, you should be able to . . .

1. Explain why women in prison are called the "forgotten offenders."
2. Discuss the history of the incarceration of women.
3. Explain how interpersonal relationships in women's prisons differ from those in men's prisons.
4. Analyze the special issues that incarcerated women face.
5. Discuss the problems that women face when they are released to the community.

LO 1
Explain why women in prison are called the "forgotten offenders."

WOMEN: THE FORGOTTEN OFFENDERS

Often referred to as the "forgotten offenders," women have traditionally received discriminatory treatment from judges, few program resources from prison administrators, and little attention from criminal justice scholars. This neglect may stem from several facts: Women make up a small proportion of the correctional population, their criminality is generally not serious, and their place in the criminal justice system merely reflects the traditional societal attitude that puts all women in a subservient position.

Compared with prisons for men, those for women are fewer and smaller. Joanne Belknap argues that this has resulted in a three-pronged form of institutionalized sexism:

1. Women's prisons are generally located farther from friends and families, making visits from children, other family members, and friends more difficult, particularly for the poor.
2. The relatively small number of women in prison and jail is used to "justify" the lack of diverse educational, vocational, and other programs available to incarcerated women.
3. The relatively small number of women in prison and jail is used to "justify" low levels of specialization in treatment and the failure to segregate women convicted of more-serious crimes and women with mental illnesses from others (as is done in male prisons and jails).[4]

Since the women's movement, scholars have more actively sought to understand women's criminality, the nature of the subculture of women's institutions, and the special problems of this segment of the prison population. In a period when equal opportunity has become public policy, paternalistic and discriminatory decisions by judges, probation officers, wardens, and parole boards concerning incarcerated women have been both criticized and litigated in court. Although women in prison have brought fewer legal cases contesting the conditions of confinement than have men, the right to equal protection under law has prompted state and federal judges to intervene in several disputes.

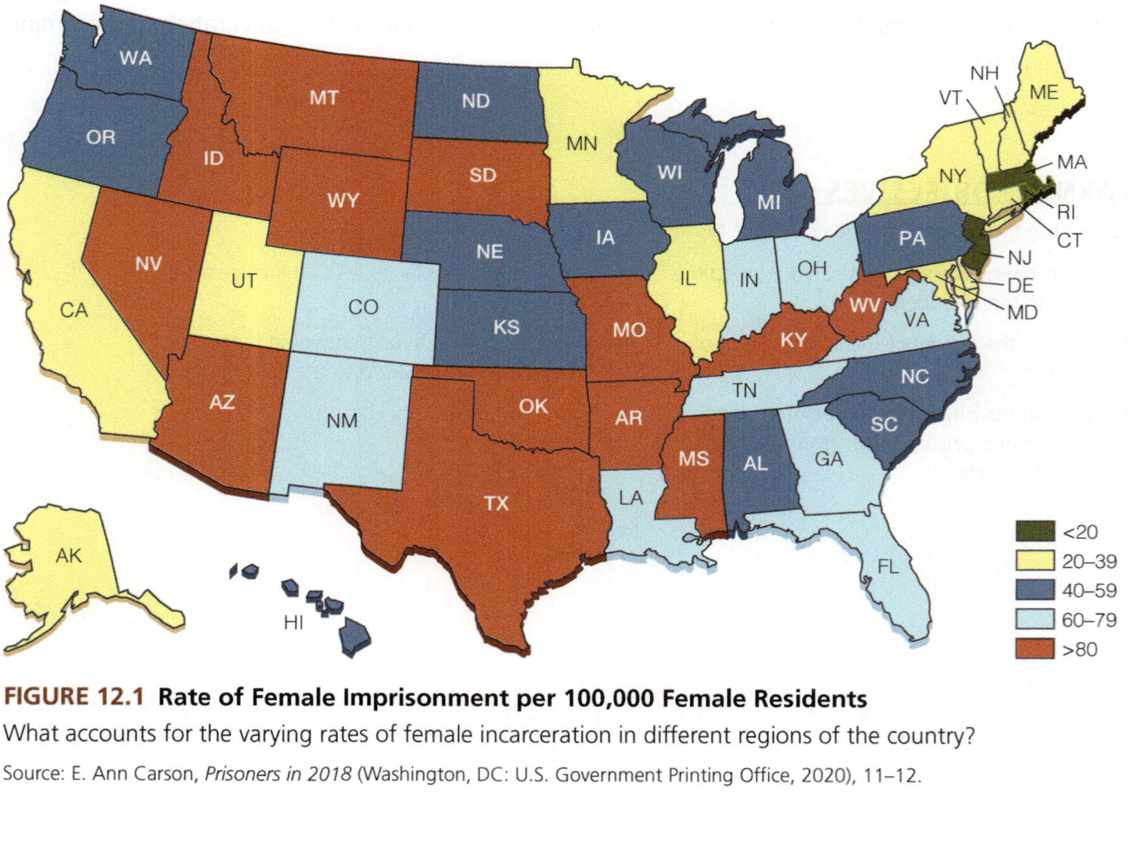

FIGURE 12.1 Rate of Female Imprisonment per 100,000 Female Residents

What accounts for the varying rates of female incarceration in different regions of the country?

Source: E. Ann Carson, *Prisoners in 2018* (Washington, DC: U.S. Government Printing Office, 2020), 11–12.

Women make up only about 7.6 percent of the federal and state prison population.[5] However, the growth rate in the number of incarcerated women has exceeded that of men since 1995. From 1995 to 2018, the male population in state and federal correctional facilities increased by 28.1 percent, whereas that of women increased by 61.9 percent.[6] The number of women now incarcerated in prisons is approximately 110,845. Critics argue that the increased number of women in prison has significantly affected program delivery, housing conditions, medical care, staffing, and security. Figure 12.1 shows the incarceration rate for women in each state.

Some researchers have postulated that as women advance toward a position of equality with men in society, their behavior will become increasingly similar to men's, so criminality among women will increase. Others argue that differences in socializing women and men make it unlikely that the criminality of women will approach that of men, especially in terms of violent crimes.

Women typically account for less than a third of the serious crimes tabulated by the Uniform Crime Reports (see Figure 12.2), but women represent about 64.3 percent of people arrested for prostitution and commercialized vice, 49.7 percent for embezzlement, 36.2 percent for fraud, and 33.8 percent for forgery and counterfeiting.[7] Given that there are far fewer women involved in crime and that their crimes are generally less serious than men's, many observers argue that it is rational for correctional public policy to focus on men.

Showing direct links between women's status and their criminality is impossible, but as women have moved into jobs from which they were formerly excluded, they may have gained the opportunities and skills to commit criminal acts. As Freda Adler remarked many years ago, "When we did not permit women to swim at the beaches, the female drowning rate was quite low. When women were not permitted to work as bank tellers or

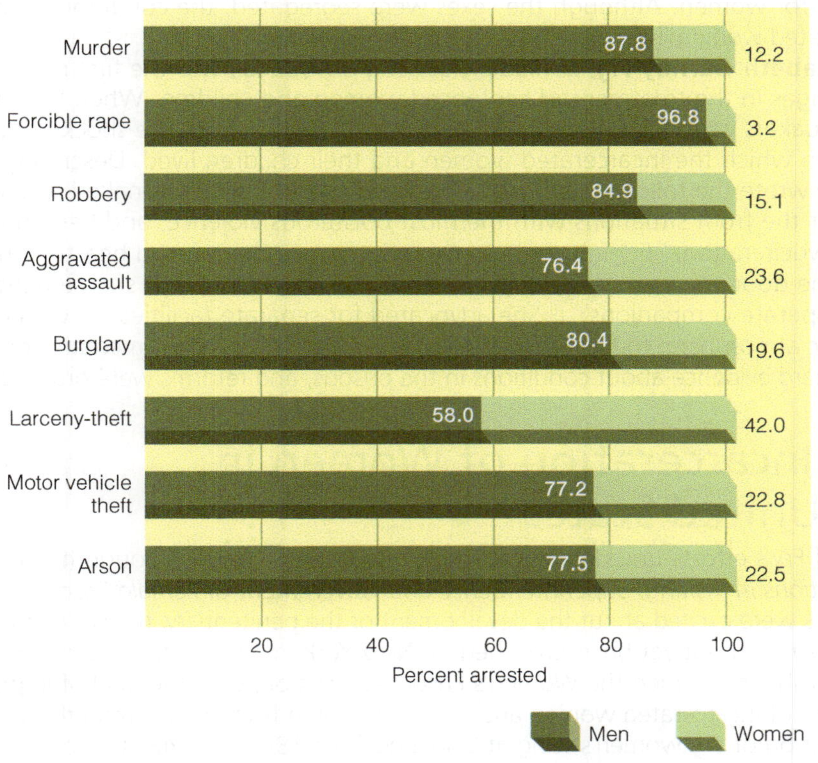

FIGURE 12.2 Percentage of Arrests for Serious Crimes, by Gender
Although many more men than women are arrested, the proportion of arrests of women is highest for larceny-theft. What might account for these data?

Source: Federal Bureau of Investigation, *Crime in the United States, 2018,* https://ucr.fbi.gov/crime-in-the-u.s/2018/crime-in-the-u.s.-2018/topic-pages/tables/table-42

presidents, the female embezzlement rate was low."[8] Critics who challenge this position point out that most property offenses committed by women consist of petty fraud and shoplifting, crimes unrelated to occupation. Others say that the increased incarceration of women is primarily a result of the war on drugs. Still others point to the feminization of poverty since 1960. Women and children are disproportionately affected by poverty in the United States. According to this view, the poverty of young, female, single heads of households, and the way society treats them, have contributed to the increase in women's crime, particularly property offenses.[9]

Women have traditionally received lighter sentences than men for similar offenses. Judges have stated that when they sentence women, they feel compelled to treat them differently from men, and not only because children are often involved. Researchers believe that this differential treatment arises from the fact that most jurists are men and hold typically male attitudes: Women are the weaker sex and require gentle treatment. Other scholars believe that women are now being sentenced harshly whether they have been convicted of first-time drug offenses or have been convicted of assaults against their intimate partners.

LO 2

Discuss the history of the incarceration of women.

HISTORICAL PERSPECTIVE

In the early 1800s reformers began to press for separate correctional facilities and programs for women. Prior to that time, all incarcerated individuals—men, women, children—in Europe and in the United States were housed together in jails and prisons. Historical records indicate that women were punished the same as men: lashed, transported, imprisoned, and hanged. After John Howard's exposé of prison conditions in England in 1777 and the development of the penitentiary in Philadelphia, people began to address the issue of corrections for women. Although the sexes were segregated, the conditions under which incarcerated women lived were atrocious.

Elizabeth Gurney Fry, a middle-class English Quaker, was the first person to press for changes in the treatment of sentenced women and children. When Fry and several other Quakers visited London's Newgate Prison in 1813, they were shocked by the conditions in which the incarcerated women and their children lived. Describing that first visit, Fry wrote the following: "The railing was crowded with half-naked women, struggling for the front situations with the most boisterous violence, and begging with the utmost vociferation." Fry felt she was venturing into a den of wild beasts, "shuddering when the door was closed upon her and she was locked in with such a herd of novel and desperate companions."[10] She advocated for separate facilities for women, with a domestic atmosphere, to be staffed by women. As a result, a parliamentary committee in 1818 heard evidence about conditions in the prisons, and reforms were ordered.

The Incarceration of Women in the United States

News of Fry's efforts quickly reached the United States, partly through her 1827 book, *Observations in Visiting, Superintendence and Government of Female Prisons*.[11] Although reformers were excited about the development of the penitentiary, the issue of corrections for women had not yet been broached. In New York in 1844, Sarah Doremus and Abby Hopper Gibbons formed the Women's Prison Association, with the goal of improving the treatment of incarcerated women and separating them from men. Elizabeth Farnham, the head matron of the women's wing at Sing Sing from 1844 to 1848, sought to implement Fry's ideas but was thwarted by the male overseers and legislators and was forced to resign.

Few women were incarcerated in the United States in the nineteenth century. Unlike their European counterparts, American judges were unwilling to find women guilty unless they were habitually involved in crime.[12] The women who were convicted, as inspectors at Sing Sing noted in 1844, were "the most abandoned representatives of their sex." At this time, prison was "the end of the road for women too far lost to virtue to offer much hope for redemption." Because only men were believed to have the ability to reason and women were supposedly motivated solely by emotions, women who committed crimes posed a much more serious threat to order: As they had gone against their "nature" and were not amenable to reason, how could they be reformed? According to W. Davis Lewis, "It seems to have been regarded as a sufficient performance of the object of punishment, to turn them loose within the pen of the prison and there leave them to feed upon and destroy each other."[13]

Until 1870, most women were housed in the same prisons and treated essentially the same as men.[14] Separate quarters were gradually established for women in prisons intended primarily for men. Most incarcerated women were convicted for crimes against public order, especially prostitution, alcoholism, and vagrancy. The few women sentenced for more-serious offenses were in out-of-the-way quarters without exercise yards, visitors' rooms, or even fresh air and sunlight. At Auburn in 1820, for example, "together, unattended, in a one-room attic, the windows sealed to prevent communication with men, the female prisoners were overcrowded, immobilized, and neglected."[15] Conditions of women imprisoned in other eastern and midwestern states before the Civil War have been similarly documented. All such reports indicate that these women were disregarded, sexually exploited, forced to do chores to maintain the prison, and kept in unsanitary facilities.

BIOGRAPHY

ELIZABETH GURNEY FRY (1780–1845)

Born in Norwich, England, Elizabeth Fry was second only to John Howard as a nineteenth-century advocate of prison reform in Europe. In 1817 she helped organize the Association for the Improvement of Female Prisoners in Newgate, then the main prison in London. This group, made up of wives of Quaker businessmen, worked to establish prison discipline, separation of the sexes, classification of prison inhabitants, female supervision for incarcerated women, adequate religious and secular instruction, and useful employment. Largely through her efforts, such reforms rapidly moved to other prisons in England and abroad.

The Reformatory Movement

As we note in Chapter 3, the 1870 meeting of the National Prison Association in Cincinnati marked a turning point in U.S. corrections. Although the Declaration of Principles did not address the problems of women in any detail, it endorsed separate, treatment-oriented prisons. Right after the Civil War, the House of Shelter, a reformatory for women, opened in Detroit. Run by Zebulon Brockway, it became the model for reformatory treatment. The first independent female-run prison was established in Indiana in 1873, followed by the Massachusetts Reformatory-Prison for Women in 1877 and the Western House of Refuge at Albion (Michigan) in 1893.[16]

The Quakers continued to pursue prison reform. In 1869 Sarah Smith and Rhoda M. Coffin were appointed to inspect correctional facilities for women. They found "the state of morals in our southern prisons in such a deplorable condition that they felt constrained to seek some relief for the unfortunate women confined there."[17] Women volunteers in corrections, following the example of Elizabeth Fry, became quite active in serving others, acting out their religious convictions. Maud Booth, a leader of the Salvation Army, expressed this zeal: "We must work for regeneration, the cleansing of the evil mind, the quickening of the dead heart, the building up of fine ideals. In short, we must bring the poor sin-stained soul to feel the touch of the Divine hand."[18]

Three principles guided female prison reform during this period: (1) separation of incarcerated women from men, (2) provision of differential care, and (3) management of women's prisons by female staff. Nichole Rafter summarizes these principles: "Operated by and for women, female reformatories were decidedly 'feminine' institutions, different from both custodial institutions for women and state prisons and reformatories for men."[19]

Like the penitentiary movement, advocates of women's reformatories favored rural correctional institutions in areas away from the unwholesome conditions of the city. However, the reformatory for women did not emulate the fortress-like penitentiary but instead resembled cottages around an administration building. Many states adopted this plan, expecting that such housing for 20–50 women at a time would create a homelike atmosphere. For example, at the Massachusetts Reformatory-Prison for Women in Framingham, which opened in 1877, the women lived in private rooms rather than cells, had iron bedsteads and bed linens, and, if they behaved well, "could decorate their quarters, enjoy unbarred windows, and have wood slats instead of grating on their doors."[20] Women had opportunities to learn domestic skills suitable to their "true" female nature. The expectation was that upon release they would apply these skills in domestic service or in their own homes.

BIOGRAPHY

MARY BELLE HARRIS (1874–1957)

Born in Pennsylvania, Mary Belle Harris is chiefly known as the first warden of the Federal Institution for Women. She began her work in corrections in 1914 when she became the superintendent of the Women's Workhouse on Blackwell's Island, New York City. She worked to create classification systems, developed educational programs, and pushed for intermediate sentences and parole. These aims were incorporated into the programs at Alderson, which soon became a national model.

The women in these reformatories were primarily convicted of petty larceny, prostitution, or "being in danger of falling into vice." They tended to be viewed as errant or misguided women who needed help and protection within a female environment, rather than being seen as dangerous individuals who had to be isolated to safeguard society. The upper-middle-class Protestant women active in prison reform may have removed the stigma of "fallen women," but they developed programs that treated the women as children. As Rafter points out, the women who lobbied state administrations for reformatories believed they were being helpful, "but in the course of doing good ... [they] perpetuated the double standard that required women to conform to more difficult moral rules than men and punished them if they failed to do so."[21]

Strongest in the East and Midwest, the reformatory movement gradually spread to parts of the South and West. In the South, corrections was tied to the lease system of farm labor. When African American women and children began to appear in large numbers before the criminal courts after the Civil War, officials had difficulty persuading farm leaseholders to accept these "dead hands," so the states created separate asylum farms for them.[22]

As time passed, the original ideals of the reformers faltered, overcome by societal change, administrative orthodoxy, and legislative objections. In 1927 the first federal prison for women opened in Alderson, West Virginia, with **Mary Belle Harris** as warden. She believed that much criminality among women resulted from dependency on men and wanted them to acquire skills to break this bondage and give them self-respect. These aims were incorporated into the programs at Alderson, which soon became a national model.

By the 1930s, as the country moved away from rural and domestic values, increases in the incarcerated population and greater emphasis on custodial care made reformatories seem out of touch with reality. Thus, by 1935 the women's reformatory movement had "run its course, having largely achieved its objective [establishment of separate prisons run by women] in those regions of the country most involved with Progressive reforms in general."[23]

The Post–World War II Years

No distinctive correctional model for women has arisen since the 1940s, perhaps because recent theories about the causes and treatment of criminal behavior do not discriminate between the sexes. As women increasingly have been arrested for more-serious crimes and more drug law violators have been incarcerated, custody has become a larger goal than reformation. Rehabilitative programs, many based on psychological or sociological premises, were implemented in women's institutions in the 1940s and 1950s, as they were in men's facilities. However, some scholars have argued that attention and resources were devoted mainly to men's institutions and that in women's prisons, those individuals convicted of less serious offenses received lower priority than did those convicted of serious crimes. Further, educational and vocational programs for women have been geared toward traditionally "feminine" occupations—hairdressing, food preparation, secretarial skills—that perpetuate gender stereotypes. With less emphasis on rehabilitation, along with the rise in prison populations during the 1970s and 1980s, corrections for women was forced to defer to the rising concern about criminally involved men. Today, demands that women be treated the same as men have increased. However, equal treatment does not mean ignoring important gender differences (see "For Critical Thinking").[24]

FOR CRITICAL THINKING

As discussed at the beginning of the chapter, a significant number of incarcerated women are mothers. Historically speaking, we know that at one time many children accompanied their mothers during their terms of imprisonment. However, contemporary programs designed to strengthen the mother–child bond, such as the Achieving Baby Care Success program in Ohio, are much more humane.

1. Do you agree with supporters of the Achieving Baby Care Success program that newborn children should be with their mothers, regardless of whether their mother is locked up in a correctional facility? Should certain women be excluded from the program? Explain your answer.
2. In the distant past, children who were unfortunate enough to be at their mother's side during her imprisonment were subjected to inhumane and unsanitary conditions. What kinds of adverse reactions might we expect from children today who participate in programs that allow them to stay with their mothers in prison? What types of dangers (if any) do these children face? What kinds of safeguards should be put in place to ensure their safety?

WOMEN IN PRISON

Life in women's prisons both resembles and differs from that in institutions for men. Women's facilities are smaller, with looser security and less-structured relationships with staff members; the underground economy is not as well developed; and incarcerated women seem less committed to the inmate code. Women also serve shorter sentences than do men, so women's prison society is more fluid as new members join and others leave.

Most women's prisons have the outward appearance of a college campus, often seen as a cluster of "cottages" around a central administration/dining/program building. Generally, those facilities lack the high walls, guard towers, and cyclone fences found at most prisons for men. However, recent years have seen a trend to upgrade security for women's prisons by adding razor wire, higher fences, and other devices to prevent escapes.

These characteristics of correctional facilities for women are offset by geographic remoteness and the heterogeneity of the prison population. Few states operate more than one institution for women, so incarcerated women generally live far from children, families, friends, and attorneys (see "Excerpts from a Prison Journal").

There is less pressure to design effective treatment programs for women than for men. Critics argue that correctional programming for women has traditionally been based on assumptions about male criminality and that programs need to be developed that are gender sensitive, recognizing that women are often victimized by family members and intimate partners.[25] Gender-based research highlights the importance of relationships. Criminal involvement often comes through relationships with family members, significant others, or friends. Successful programs relate to the social realities from which the women come and to which they will return.

FOCUS ON

PEOPLE IN CORRECTIONS: Excerpts from a Prison Journal

"THE ROSE"

This is an interview with myself. I've decided to write a book on things happening to me.... Maybe someone else will read it and learn. I'm sitting in jail.

"Jail?" you say.

Sure. Haven't you ever seen one? That's the place you always believed, and were told, the bad people go. It's not true. They send good people there too. Look at me. I'm in a 12-by-20-foot cell with two other "criminally oriented" females. They're OK. One is here for not returning a car to the dealer she borrowed it from—known by some as grand theft auto. The other is in here for writing too many checks on an account with no money.

The bunks are always too high, the mattresses are flimsy, and the pillows are falling apart. The window's got no glass in it; the cold north breeze blows in and freezes your ass off. So, if you ever plan on going to jail, hope it's in the summer.

The wind blows in, sending shivering chills up your spine. Oh! what you'd give to stand outside, with the sunshine beaming down, the birds singing, a tree to touch, a decent glass to drink out of, a proper plate to have your food on, a fork to eat with, a room without names all over the walls.... Hanging your towels over the heater to dry so you'll have a dry towel the next time you take a shower. The heater is a little portable thing that looks like someone took their frustration out on it. And you have to put everything up so it doesn't get wet, because the shower leaks and splatters all over everywhere.... Days of dripping shower, which is the worst sound in the world.

It's a sixty-eight-year-old building with steam heaters that whistle, jailers walking around with keys jingling, the elevator up and down all the time. They never come to get you. The phone rings from sunup to sundown. No calls for you. Calls only yours to be made when it's your turn. Knowing down inside no call will help you out of this mess.

The guys still flirt, no matter where—even through a little window in the door.... One of the girls is sitting under the sink having an obscene pipe conversation with Gary next door. He says it'll make him feel good, going down in history as an obscene pipe caller.

You'll never believe this. They're not trying to break out, just "escape to rape"—each other. I can hear the spoons digging now. Maybe they'll make it—by next year! The "escape to rape" fell through. We all knew it would, but it gave us something to do last night. We must've laughed for four hours straight. We got to do something. You can't just sit around and cry and find someone else to blame things on. A year is a long time when you live it in a box.

PEOPLE IN CORRECTIONS: Excerpts from a Prison Journal (*continued*)

I made the news. Not like most of the people I went to school with. I'm going to write what it says so I'll never forget what Clovis, New Mexico, is really like.

[They spelled my name right!], convicted of issuing a worthless check and distribution of a controlled substance, is charged with being a habitual offender. District Judge gave Ms. a two-year state penitentiary sentence with one year suspended and to be served on parole probation.

Ms. was originally given a suspended one-year sentence for issuing a worthless check. She was also previously given a five-year deferred penitentiary sentence for distribution of a controlled substance and was placed on probation.

Maybe someday I'll understand all this.

The worst feeling in the world was walking away and hearing my son scream for his mom. Knowing that I had to come back upstairs and be locked up. That's the hell in this hole—knowing people are close at hand and you can't touch or feel them.

I think what makes this so hard is that it's Christmastime. I'm almost crazy thinking I'm going to miss Santa Claus, Christmas carols, and my boys' smiling faces Christmas morning.

It's getting close to the time of my departure from a town I grew up in, learned to love. I feel a great loss as I'm going away knowing that returning may be a long ways away. Every passing moment brings thoughts I never conceived of having. I've never felt so alone. I've never felt so lost. I've never had so much taken from me in such a short time.

The strain of waiting for tomorrow has made me nervous, nauseous, and nuts. The three *N*'s. Sounds like a bad disease. I go to a fate that I have no concept of, praying and hoping that I can handle it.

Later, from the State Penitentiary)

I came through the gate knowing very well that it will be many months before I will be able to leave. The Annex (for women) is a building separate from the Big House (for men). I've only been here thirty minutes and I'm already talking like a convict. They gave me a number and issued me two blankets, dark green; two sheets, white; two towels, white; soap; toothbrush and toothpaste. They gave me some books, paper, pen, and envelopes, brought me to this square box half the size of the county jail cell. It has one of the hardest beds I've ever seen, a toilet, a sink, a footlocker, two small bookcases, and a window. You can look out and see desert.

So far the women and matrons here seem very adaptable and willing to help. I've already had cookies, two glasses of milk, and two cups of hot chocolate brought to me before I sleep in my new box, sweet box. Don't get me wrong. I'll take all my days of working, bill collectors, children crying—and headaches, worries, and woes. I'll take my problems just not to hear that steel door slam shut and the key turn in the lock, a matron walk down the hall leaving me with an empty feeling, and a sound of clanking, jangling keys falling off in the distance.

Source: The 24-year-old author of this journal chose the pen name "The Rose." Her identity has been disguised to protect her and her family, including two sons, ages two and six. These excerpts were written in the first five days following her conviction, while she was awaiting transfer from county jail to state prison, and then after her transfer. She served nine months in both maximum- and minimum-security facilities. Edited by Sue Mahan, from her interview notes.

Effective programming begins with effective classification in terms of housing assignments, therapeutic approaches, and educational and vocational opportunities. In many institutions the small number of clients limits the extent to which the needs of individual can be recognized and treated. Housing classifications are often so broad that those who are dangerous or mentally ill are mixed with women who have committed minor offenses and have no psychological problems. Similarly, available rehabilitative approaches may be limited, especially if correctional departments fail to recognize women's problems and needs because of the relatively small population of incarcerated females.

Joanne Belknap points out that the regimen of women's prisons has been described as "discipline, infantilize, feminize, medicalize, and domesticize."[26] The tendency to treat women like children and the emphasis on "domesticating" them have been well documented. However, Belknap also notes that discipline for incarcerated women is generally overly harsh compared with that for men. Drugs are extensively used to "calm" women in prison, and vaginal searches are frequently used to discover contraband.

Characteristics of Women in Prison

What are the characteristics of women in America's prisons? The U.S. Bureau of Justice Statistics reports that 63.2 percent of them are under 40 years old, 53 percent are racial or ethnic minorities, and over 65.1 percent were convicted of a nonviolent offense (see Figure 12.3).[27] The main factors distinguishing incarcerated women from men are the nature of offenses, sentence lengths, patterns of drug use, and correctional history.

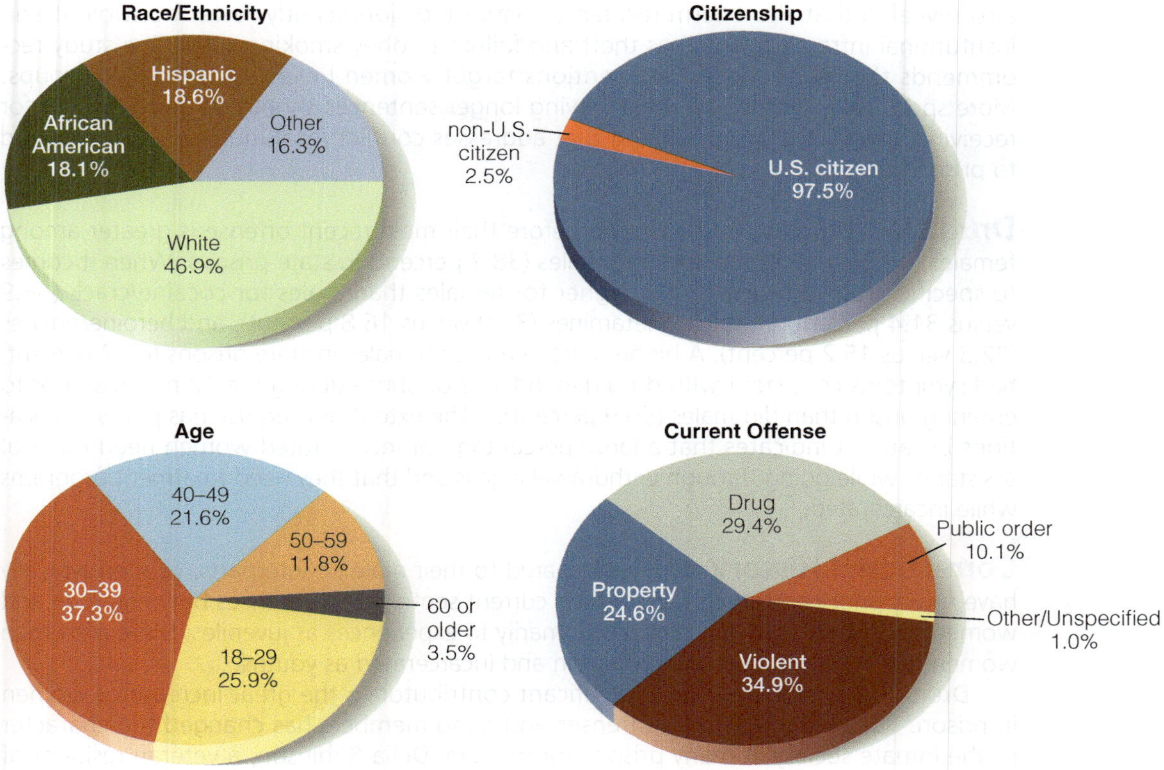

FIGURE 12.3 Characteristics of Women in Prison

Women who are in prison tend to be under the age of 40, convicted of a nonviolent offense, and U.S. citizens.

Source: E. Ann Carson, *Prisoners in 2018* (Washington, DC: U.S. Government Printing Office, 2020).

Offense Although the public commonly believes that most women are incarcerated for minor offenses such as prostitution, sentences for such crimes are usually served in jails; prisons hold people convicted of more-serious offenses, both male and female. According to the Bureau of Justice Statistics, approximately 34.9 percent of women in state and federal prisons are serving sentences for violent offenses (compared with 51.4 percent of men in state and federal prisons), 24.6 percent for property offenses (versus 14.9 percent of men), 29.4 percent for drug-related offenses (versus 17.3 percent of men), and 10.1 percent for public-order offenses (versus 15.7 percent of men).[28] The most striking difference between the sexes concerns violent offenses.

Sentence For all types of crimes, women receive shorter maximum sentences than do men. For example, the average prison sentence for murder is 212 months for women and 256 months for men. Differences between men and women are also present for property offenses (48 months for men, 40 months for women), drug offenses (51 months for men, 41 months for women), and weapons offenses (48 months for men, 41 months for women).[29] Shorter sentences are quite frequently a result of women's less serious criminal background, especially regarding the use of violence, when compared with their male counterparts. Nevertheless, women also serve long sentences in prison.

In their study of adjustment patterns among women incarcerated in Virginia who were serving long-term (more than 10 years), medium-term (2 to 10 years), and short-term (fewer than 2 years) sentences, Caitlin Thompson and Ann Loper found that women serving long- and medium-term sentences reported higher levels of conflict, such as feeling anger, when compared with their short-term counterparts. The study also revealed that short-term residents committed significantly fewer nonviolent and institutional infractions, such as theft and failure to obey smoking rules. The study recommends that correctional interventions target women in specific sentence groups. More specifically, women who are serving longer sentences should be given priority for receiving specialized programming that addresses conflict resolution and stress related to prison life.[30]

Drug Use Drug use in the month before their most recent offense is greater among females (46.8 percent) than among males (38.2 percent) in state prisons. When it comes to specific drugs, involvement is higher for females than males for cocaine/crack (48.9 versus 31.4 percent), methamphetamines (31.0 versus 16.8 percent), and heroine/opiates (22.3 versus 15.2 percent). A higher percentage of females in state prisons (69.2 percent) had symptoms consistent with drug dependence or abuse during the 12 months prior to entering prison than did males (56.9 percent).[31] The extent of drug use has policy implications because it indicates that a large percentage of incarcerated women need medical assistance while going through withdrawal in jails and that they need treatment programs while incarcerated.

Correctional History When compared to their male counterparts, women typically have fewer prior convictions before their current sentence. Differences between men and women on this variable seem related primarily to experiences as juveniles: More men than women report having been on probation and incarcerated as youths.

Drug offenses seem to be a significant contributor to the great increase of women in prison. The upsurge in drug offenses and gang members has changed the character of the inmate society in many prisons for women. Delia Robinson, a veteran resident of Connecticut prisons, told Andi Rierden that she especially disdains the young troublemakers who

> come in off the streets looking like zombies, bone thin and strung out on crack cocaine. "You can tell them by the abscesses on their bodies from shooting liquid dope cut with meat tenderizer. Before long these inmates fatten up on the prison's starchy food and the junk they order from commissary, smuggle in their drugs, and sleep around with women, even though they likely have a boyfriend or husband on the outside. Once released, they'll return to the streets, get arrested and then return to the Farm [prison]. Once settled in they'll unite with old flames and 'just chill.' "[32]

The Subculture of Women's Prisons

Much of the early research on women's prisons focused on types of relationships between incarcerated women. Same-sex relationships were observed, but unlike those in male prisons, where such relationships are sometimes coerced, sexual relationships between women appeared more voluntary. Interestingly, researchers reported that women tended to form pseudofamilies in which they adopted various roles—father, mother, daughter, sister—and interacted as a unit, rather than identifying with the larger prison subculture.[33] Such cooperative relationships help relieve the tensions of prison life, assist the socialization of new arrivals, and permit individuals to act according to clearly defined roles and rules.

When David Ward and Gene Kassebaum studied sexual and family bonding at the California Institute for Women in Frontera in the early 1960s, they found homosexual roles but not familial roles. The women at Frontera seemed to adapt less well to prison, and they did not develop the solidarity with one another that Donald Clemmer and Gresham Sykes found in male institutions. Yet societal expectations for gender and the social roles of women were important in the prisoner subculture.[34]

We need to consider recent shifts in prison life when examining the existing research on women in prison. Just as the subculture of male prisons has changed since the pioneering research of Clemmer and Sykes, the climate of prisons for women has undoubtedly changed. Through interviews with a small group of incarcerated women, Kimberly Greer found support for the idea that prisons for women are less violent, involve less gang activity, and do not have the racial tensions found in men's prisons. However, Greer also observed that women's interpersonal relationships were less stable and less familial than in the past. The women reported higher levels of mistrust and greater economic manipulation.[35] Thus, we must approach past research with caution.

© Erin Bormett/Argus Leader

Women at the South Dakota Women's Prison enjoy a musical performance at an anti-meth rally.

A more explicit attempt to compare the subculture of women's prisons with that of men's was made by Rose Giallombardo. Like John Irwin and Donald Cressey, Giallombardo hypothesized that many subcultural features of the institution are imported from the larger society. For example, she found that women express and fulfill social needs through prison homosexual marriage and kinship. Giallombardo suggests that in many ways, the prison subcultures of men and women are similar, with one major exception: The informal social structure of the female prison is somewhat collectivist. It is characterized by warmth and mutual aid extended to family and kinship members; men adapt by self-sufficiency, a convict code, and solidarity with others who are incarcerated.[36]

The debate over whether the prisoner subculture is caused by deprivation or importation has led to some interesting findings in women's institutions. When Esther Heffernan began her study in a women's institution, she expected to find a unitary inmate social structure arising from within the institution, as Clemmer and Sykes had. But Heffernan found no "clear-cut pattern of acceptance or rejection of the inmate social system, nor any relatively uniform perception of deprivations." Unlike male maximum-security prisons, the prison Heffernan studied—like most other women's prisons—had a diverse population with the whole spectrum of offenses. Heffernan shows what Irwin and Cressey only suggest: Incarcerated individuals with similar orientations developed "distinctive norms and values, a pattern of interrelationships and certain roles that served their own prison needs."[37] The typical convicted woman brings these orientations with her to the prison.

In a more recent study of prison culture, Barbara Owen found that the residents at the Central California Women's Facility have developed various styles of doing time.[38] Based on the in-prison experience, these styles correspond to the day-to-day business of developing a program of activities and settling into a routine. Owen discovered that one's style of doing time stems from one's commitment to a deviant identity and the stage of one's criminal and prison career. These elements influence the extent to which a female prison resident is committed to the "convict code" and participating in "the mix."

The vast majority of women, according to Owen, want to avoid "the mix": "behavior that can bring trouble and conflict with staff and other prisoners." A primary feature of "the mix" is anything for which one can lose good time or be sent to administrative segregation. Being in "the mix" involves "homosecting," fighting, using drugs, and being involved in conflict and trouble. Owen found that most women want to do their time and go home, but some "are more at home in prison and do not seem to care if they 'lose time.'"[39] The culture of being "in the mix" is not imported from the outside but is internal to the prison, as some women prefer the pursuit of drugs, girlfriends, and fighting.

LO 3

Explain how interpersonal relationships in women's prisons differ from those in men's prisons.

Male Versus Female Subcultures

Comparisons of male and female prisons are difficult because most studies have been conducted in either male or female institutions, and most follow theories and concepts first developed in male prisons. However, the following helps clarify subcultural differences:

- Over half of men in prison, but only a third of women, are serving time for violent offenses.
- Women's prisons are less violent than prisons for men.
- Women are more responsive than men to prison programs.
- Men's prison populations are divided by security levels, but most women serve time in facilities where the entire population is mixed.
- Men tend to segregate themselves by race; this is less true for women.
- Men rarely form intimate relationships with prison staff, but many women share personal information with their keepers.

FOR CRITICAL THINKING

Prisons for women differ from male facilities in many ways. They are less violent, women maintain closer ties with staff, and their facilities are not infested with gangs. It is also the case that women are more receptive to correctional programming.

1. Should the fact that women are more amenable to correctional programming influence the allocation of correctional resources? Should we invest more heavily in programming for incarcerated women, such as the Achieving Baby Care Success program?
2. How so (if at all) does the inmate code found in male prisons influence parental roles? Is providing love and support to one's children viewed as weak and soft to those who closely follow the code? What explains the difference in parental roles between men and women who are in prison?

Some critics say that, despite these differences, the current practice of imprisoning women is based on assumptions about violent men.

A major difference between male and female prisons relates to interpersonal relationships. In male prisons, individuals act for themselves and are evaluated by others according to how they adhere to the inmate code. Men believe they must demonstrate physical strength and avoid mannerisms that may imply homosexuality. Male norms emphasize autonomy, self-sufficiency, and the ability to cope with one's own problems, and men are expected to "do their own time." Women place less emphasis on achieving status or recognition and place fewer restrictions on sexual and emotional conduct. In women's prisons, close ties seem to exist among small groups that are similar to families (see "For Critical Thinking").

Although it is true that female prisons are less violent than male facilities, violence still takes place in female institutions. A study of more than 7,000 men and women in state prisons found that certain types of violence, such as slapping, hitting, kicking, and biting, were more common among the women than the men. However, the types of violence used by incarcerated men were typically more serious. For example, men were much more likely to threaten or harm another individual with a shank (knife).[40] The little research that has been conducted indicates that women are less likely than men to engage in violent acts against others.

The differences between male and female prison subcultures have been attributed to the nurturing, maternal qualities of women. Some critics argue that such a conclusion stereotypes female behavior and assigns a biological basis to personality where no basis exists.

MYTHS in Corrections

Sexual Victimization in Prisons for Women

THE MYTH: The likelihood of sexual victimization in prison for women is much lower than in male facilities.

THE REALITY: Using data from the National Inmate Survey, the U.S. Bureau of Justice Statistics reports that inmate-on-inmate sexual victimization was higher among incarcerated women (6.9 percent) than men (1.7 percent).

Source: Allen J. Beck, Marcus Berzofsky, Rachel Caspar, and Christopher Krebs, *Sexual Victimization in Prisons and Jails Reported by Inmates, 2011–12* (Washington, DC: U.S. Department of Justice, 2013), 17.

ISSUES IN THE INCARCERATION OF WOMEN

As noted, the number of incarcerated women has increased immensely over the past two decades. Although departments of corrections have been playing "catch-up" to meet the challenge of crowded facilities, problems persist. These include sexual misconduct by officers, lack of educational and training programs, demands for medical services, and the needs of mothers and their children. We examine each of these issues and the policy implications that they pose for the future.

Sexual Misconduct

LO 4

Analyze the special issues that incarcerated women face.

As the number of women incarcerated has increased, cases of sexual misconduct by male correctional officers have escalated. Staff-on-inmate sexual victimization includes any behavior that is sexual in nature that is directed toward an incarcerated individual by an employee, official visitor, volunteer, or agency representative (see "Myths in Corrections"). Such acts include (1) forms of sexual misconduct (touching genitalia, breasts, or buttocks in a way that is intended to arouse, abuse, or gratify sexual desire); and (2) sexual harassment (sexually suggestive comments, profane language, or obscene gestures).[41] One government study found that 2.3 percent of the female prison population were victims of staff sexual misconduct during the year prior to the survey.[42] A separate study found that 5.4 percent of women reported affirmatively when asked whether prison staff had "touched [their] genitals or sex organs." More than 5 percent reported that they had been grabbed or touched by staff in a sexually threatening manner.[43] Sexual misconduct is harmful in that it jeopardizes facility security, creates stress and trauma for those involved, exposes the agency and staff to potential lawsuits, creates a hostile work environment, and victimizes the vulnerable.[44]

Monetary civil judgments awarded to women for mistreatment while in prison can be costly. For example, officials in Virginia reportedly reached a $10 million out-of-court settlement in class-action suits brought by nine women who said they were sexually abused by a half-dozen correctional officers and an instructor. One of the residents, who had been convicted of murder, was impregnated by a correctional officer.[45] To deal with the problem of sexual abuse in prison, states have enacted statutes prohibiting sexual relations with correctional clients. Despite these laws, better sexual harassment policies, training for officers, and recruit screening are also needed. Some correctional administrators say that part of the problem is the large number of men guarding women (see "Do the Right Thing").

DO THE RIGHT THING

Officer Drew Hanson has worked at the Southwestern Correctional Facility for Women for nearly five years. He was assigned to the prison immediately after graduation from the academy. Hanson works with Officer Jim Clofus. Both of them graduated from the academy in the same class. One day, nearing shift change, Clofus approached Hanson and said that he had something important that he wanted to talk to him about. Hanson agreed to meet him at the Bridge-bender Tavern after work so that they could talk.

At the tavern later that evening, Clofus unloaded what was on his mind. "I've been having sexual relations with Allison Stewart for nearly six months," he said.

"Are you insane, man? She's an inmate. That's sexual misconduct. You could lose your job. You could get locked up. What in hell is going through your mind?" Hanson responded. Clofus continued on, "She told me yesterday that if I didn't start bringing her makeup and other stuff that she's going to tell the brass what we've been doing. I know I screwed up. But I don't want to compound the problem by smuggling contraband into the facility too. What should I do?" Hanson sat quietly shaking his head in disbelief.

WRITING ASSIGNMENT: What would you do if you were in Officer Hanson's shoes? Would you encourage Officer Clofus to turn himself in? Would you turn in Clofus yourself if he refused? How do you think Clofus should be punished? Should Allison Stewart be sanctioned in any way?

Educational and Vocational Programs

A traditional criticism of women's prisons is that they lack the variety of vocational and educational programs usually available in male institutions and that existing programs tend to conform to stereotypes of "feminine" occupations—cosmetology, food service, housekeeping, and sewing. Such training does not correspond to the wider opportunities available to women in today's world. The programs also are less ambitious than those in men's prisons, which offer training for "real-world" jobs.

Many facilities housing men and women offer educational programs. Such programs are designed to help the illiterate learn to read and for others to earn general equivalency diplomas (GEDs). Such programs seem quite important, considering that upon release most women must support themselves and many are financially responsible for children.

To get a good job, workers must have the education necessary to meet the needs of a complex workplace. However, most incarcerated women are undereducated and unskilled, which limits future occupational opportunities. In some institutions, less than half of the incarcerated population have completed high school. Some corrections systems assign these women to classes so they can earn a GED, and others can do college work through correspondence study or courses offered in the institution.

Critics have pointed out that although the female workforce in the broader community has greatly expanded since the 1970s and women now occupy positions formerly reserved for men, incarcerated women are not being prepared for such jobs. Upon release from prison, however, most women have no one to depend on but themselves. They must find a job that will provide income and advancement. Without any means of support, the released individual faces a life dependent on welfare or engaged in illegal activity to fulfill her children's needs and her own. Programs to train incarcerated women for postrelease vocations that can improve their socioeconomic condition are essential if released women are to succeed in the community.[46]

Medical Services

When compared with men, incarcerated women usually have more serious health problems because of their socioeconomic status and limited access to preventive medical care. They also have a higher incidence of serious psychological distress.[47] Many women have gynecological problems as well. Government statistics show that a higher percentage of incarcerated females than males suffer from chronic conditions, such as arthritis, asthma, cancer, heart-related problems, cirrhosis of the liver, and high blood pressure.[48]

©FILE/Jae S. Lee / Tennessean via Imagn Content Services, LLC

▲ *Camille Santos, left, talks to another student, Cyntoia Brown, during a class the Tennessee Prison for Women.*

Pregnant women also need special medical and nutritional resources. Every year about 4.1 percent of women in state prisons are pregnant upon admission. Nearly 95 percent of these women receive an obstetric exam, and about 54 percent receive pregnancy care.[49] Most incarcerated women who are pregnant are older than 35, have histories of drug abuse, have had prior multiple abortions, and carry sexually transmitted diseases. All of these factors indicate the potential for a high-risk pregnancy requiring special medical care.

Pregnancies raise numerous issues for correctional policy, including special diets, abortion rights, access to a delivery room and medical personnel, and length of time that newborns can remain with incarcerated mothers. Another issue is whether expecting mothers should remain shackled during childbirth. Although some states have enacted laws banning the practice, it reportedly still happens. For example, one report investigating reproductive health care in New York state prisons found that 23 of the 27 women interviewed said they were shackled at some point during their childbirth experience.[50] Anti-shackling supporters argue that women in labor do not pose a serious flight risk, especially when a correctional officer is nearby.[51]

Pregnant women must not only cope with the physical aspects of incarceration but also endure psychological stress over whether to have an abortion, who should care for the child after birth, and separation from the child. Many prison systems are allowing nursing infants to stay with their mothers, creating in-prison nurseries, developing special living quarters for pregnant women and new mothers, instituting counseling programs, and improving standards of medical care.

The failure to provide women who are in prison with basic preventive and medical treatments, such as immunizations, breast cancer screening, and management of chronic diseases, will result in more-serious health problems that are more expensive to treat. Poor medical care for the incarcerated merely shifts costs to overburdened community health care systems after the women are released.

Mothers and Their Children

Of great concern to many incarcerated women is the fate of their children. More than half of the women in state prisons are mothers of minors. Few imprisoned mothers see their children during their prison sentence. Many of these women lived with their children prior to being sent to prison, often as a single caretaker. Because of this, many children of incarcerated mothers are cared for by friends and relatives, and some are in state-funded foster care.[52]

Enforced separation of children from their mothers can be devastating. Beth Huebner and Regan Gustafson's research showed that maternal incarceration adversely affects the life chances of imprisoned women's children. Specifically, they found that children of incarcerated women are nearly three times more likely to be convicted of crime as an adult as are individuals whose mother has not been incarcerated.[53] Melinda Tasca and her colleagues found that maternal incarceration also has deleterious effects on children already involved in the juvenile justice system. Indeed, youths whose mothers were incarcerated were 2.41 times more likely to be rearrested within a year after court disposition than were juveniles without an imprisoned mother. In contrast, paternal incarceration did not influence reoffending.[54]

In most states, babies born in prison must be placed with a family member or a social agency within three weeks of birth. Many women fear that neither they nor the children will be able to adjust to each other when they are reunited after their long separation. In some states, innovative programs are now in place to promote the mother–infant bond. Such programs may allow incarcerated women to live with their babies in dorm rooms. Other prisons have developed prison nurseries. Advocates argue that these programs prevent placing the children of incarcerated women in foster care and also allow mothers and children to bond during an important stage in child development.[55] Lorie Goshin and Mary Byrne note that the number of infants involved in prison nursery programs is only a small fraction of the number of children whose mothers are incarcerated. The researchers also point out that nursery programs do not address the large number of older children who are left behind when their mothers are sent to prison.[56]

Imprisoned mothers have difficulty maintaining contact with their children. Because most states have only one or two prisons for women, mothers may be incarcerated 150 or more miles away. Transportation is difficult, visits are short and infrequent, and phone calls are uncertain and irregular. When the children do visit the prison, the surroundings are strange and intimidating. In some institutions, children must conform to the rules

FOCUS ON

CORRECTIONAL PRACTICE: Get on the Bus

A large group of kids, all wearing the same purple T-shirt, scurry about in excitement as they load onto a large bus. Everyone can feel the energy that is in the air. Are these children on their way to an amusement park? Perhaps they are on a school field trip? Not today. Not these kids. It's Mother's Day, and these youngsters are on their way to a California state prison facility to visit their incarcerated mothers. They are taking part in the Get on the Bus program.

The Get on the Bus program is an annual event that transports thousands of children to visit their parents who are serving time in many of California's prisons. Sister Suzanne Jabro, who founded the program, says that the "program exists for the children. They are the hidden victims who are suffering." Jabro believes that the program helps kids stay connected with their mothers. She points out that the children have done nothing wrong and that these kids "just want to be held and loved by their mother, and they need to know that she is safe."

Not only does the program provide children and their caregivers free transportation to the prison facility, which can be hundreds of miles away, but the program also provides participants with meals and snacks for the day and a picture of each child with their parent to take home. After spending four hours visiting with their parent, on the way home on the bus each child receives a letter from their mother.

The program has grown over the years. However, the need is great. Over half of the mothers incarcerated in California prisons report that they have never received a visit from their children. The program is working to address this under the belief that such visitations reduce delinquency rates among the children of incarcerated adults. It also teaches kids the lesson that poor choices have serious consequences. Overall, the program is based on the premise that fostering the parent–child bond helps reduce recidivism among parents.

The Get on the Bus program is funded from donations made by individuals, churches, grants, and other organizations.

Are programs that bring incarcerated parents together with their children under safe conditions worthwhile? If they are shown to be effective at significantly reducing recidivism, should we invest tax dollars in such programs? What other kinds of programs could be used to improve the relationship between incarcerated mothers and their children?

Sources: Center for Restorative Justice Works, "The 17th Annual 'Get on the Bus' Event: Uniting Children with their Mothers and Fathers in Prison," *Market Wired*, April 10, 2017, www.marketwired.com/press-release/17th-annual-get-on-the-bus-event-uniting-children-with-their-mothers-fathers-prison-2208845.htm, April 21, 2017; "Get on the Bus Unites Kids with Moms & Dads," http://www.seecalifornia.com/health/kids-parents-prison.html, August 8, 2020.

governing adult visitation: strict limits and no physical contact. However, other correctional facilities seek ways to help mothers maintain links to their children and nurture their relationships. (See "Get on the Bus" for a discussion of one program that helps children visit their incarcerated mothers.)

Programs to address the needs of imprisoned mothers and their children are being developed and implemented. In some states, children may meet with their mothers at almost any time, for extended periods and in playrooms or nurseries where physical contact is possible. Some states transport children to visit their mothers; some institutions even let children stay overnight with their mothers. Programs are also available so that the mothers can read to their children. For example, 19 percent of female facilities will videorecord mothers reading a book and send the recording to the children. Many more facilities (56 percent) will audiorecord book-reading sessions.[57] But few programs, according to Merry

FOR CRITICAL THINKING

The research clearly shows the negative impact of maternal incarceration on the behavior of children. To many observers, these findings indicate an obvious need to dedicate scarce government resources toward curbing delinquency among the children of the incarcerated. Put simply, doing so is in the interest of public safety.

1. Several general approaches and specific programs have been discussed in this chapter. What type of program designed to strengthen the mother–child bond do you believe is most effective? Should similar programs be put in place so that fathers who are incarcerated can remain bonded with their children?
2. Should parental programming be provided to formerly incarcerated women under correctional supervision in the community? If so, how should such programs differ from those used in prison?

Morash and Pamela Schram, "get beyond the assumption that all that is needed is retraining in parenting skills, or that women's needs are limited to the parenting area."[58]

The emphasis on community corrections as it developed in the 1970s gave rise to programs in which youngsters could live with their mothers in halfway houses. These programs have not expanded as much as expected, however, in part because children upset prison routine. Many states have furlough programs that let women visit relatives and children in their homes during holiday periods and some weekends (see "For Critical Thinking").

RELEASE TO THE COMMUNITY

LO 5

Discuss the problems that women face when they are released to the community.

Women face a variety of problems and challenges upon release from prison: Many of these women are poor, have lost custody of their children and would like it back, have serious health care needs, and have extensive substance abuse histories. Additionally, a large number of women released from incarceration have nowhere to go and must find a place to live. Stable housing is essential for women to regain custody of their children, and it also provides a base from which to hunt for a job, get health care, and receive substance abuse treatment. But obtaining housing is complicated by several factors, including skeptical landlords, who may view women on parole as either financial or security risks, and federal restrictions on subsidized housing.[59]

Despite cutbacks in funding, programs are in place to help women make the transition from prison to the community. The Michigan Prisoner ReEntry Initiative (MPRI) is one such program. The MPRI is made up of different state agencies that work together to assist women at various stages of the reentry process. For example, the program provides returning women with domestic violence services, helps participants find housing, provides assistance with finding a job, and gives women access to other related social services. Researchers Kristy Holtfreter and Katelyn Wattanaporn are very optimistic about the MPRI's potential effectiveness but note that more-extensive evaluation studies are necessary before definitive conclusions can be drawn.[60]

© Sanford Myers / The Tennessean, Nashville Tennessean via Imagn Content Services, LLC

Women who are released from prison often say that reuniting with their children is their highest priority. However, parole officers may have other priorities for their clients, such as staying clean and getting housing and work.

Can programs fully address the needs of women on parole? Overall, the research indicates that a significant majority of women need some assistance to reenter society successfully. Those who do not have friends and family to lean on will need state-funded resources to become self-sufficient, overcome the stigma of having been convicted of a felony, and stay out of prison.[61]

SUMMARY

1 Explain why women in prison are called the "forgotten offenders."

Women make up a small portion of the correctional population. The offenses that women commit are usually less serious than those committed by men. Some observers claim that women's place in the criminal justice system reflects broader societal attitudes that put all women in a subservient position. Unfortunately, the status of "forgotten offender" has several negative consequences, including discriminatory treatment from judges, few prison programs, and little attention from criminal justice scholars.

2 Discuss the history of the incarceration of women.

Until 1870, women were incarcerated in the same prisons as men. Elizabeth Fry helped reform prisons in England by advocating for the separation of the sexes, female supervision of incarcerated women, and useful employment. In the United States, separate quarters were gradually established for women in prisons intended mainly for men. The conditions under which women in prison lived were atrocious. Women were mostly convicted of public-order crimes such as prostitution, alcoholism, and vagrancy. In the 1870s the reformatory movement was under way, advocating (1) separation of women from men, (2) provision of differential care, and (3) management of women's prisons by female staff. In 1927 the first federal prison for women opened in Alderson, West Virginia, with Mary Belle Harris as warden. She believed that much criminality among women resulted from dependence on men. She wanted women to acquire skills and develop self-respect. No distinctive correctional model for women has arisen since the 1940s. Rehabilitative programs were implemented in women's institutions in the 1940s and 1950s, as they were in men's facilities. Educational and vocational programs for women have been geared toward traditionally "feminine" occupations—hairdressing, food preparation, secretarial skills—that perpetuate gender stereotypes. With less emphasis on rehabilitation, along with the rise in prison populations during the 1970s and 1980s, corrections for women was forced to defer to the rising concern about males.

3 Explain how interpersonal relationships in women's prisons differ from those in men's prisons.

Norms in male prisons emphasize autonomy, self-sufficiency, and the ability to cope with one's own problems. Men are expected to "do their own time," and they share very little with one another. In contrast, women develop close ties and form small groups that are similar to families, providing emotional support and sharing resources. Women also place fewer restrictions on sexual and emotional conduct.

4 Analyze the special issues that incarcerated women face.

Four important issues in women's prisons are sexual misconduct, educational and vocational programs, medical services, and mothers and their children. (1) Sexual misconduct, or instances where prison officials sexually exploit women, threatens facility security, creates stress and trauma for those involved, exposes the agency and staff to potential lawsuits, creates a hostile work environment, and victimizes people who are vulnerable. To deal with this problem, states have enacted statutes prohibiting sexual relations with correctional clients. (2) Women's prisons lack the variety of vocational and educational programs usually available in male institutions, and existing programs tend to conform to stereotypes of "feminine" occupations. (3) Women's prisons lack proper medical services, even though women usually have more-serious health problems than do men, as well as gynecological needs. (4) A majority of women in prison were the primary caretakers of children before entering prison, and over half of these women do not see their children while serving their sentence. Some states have implemented visitation programs to address this issue.

5 Discuss the problems that women face when they are released to the community.
Many women who are released from prison have serious health care needs and extensive histories of substance abuse. What is more, many of these women are poor and would like to regain custody of their children. Many of these women have no place to go and must find a place to live, but federal laws restricting subsidized housing and landlords who are reluctant to rent to someone who was in prison can make doing so difficult. Research has demonstrated that women benefit from assistance when reentering society, such as help from friends and family and state-funded resources, to become self-sufficient and stay out of prison.

FOR DISCUSSION

1. How has fragmentation of corrections among federal, state, and local governments affected the quality of services for incarcerated women?
2. If they commit similar crimes, should women receive the same sentences as men do? How might the unequal treatment of incarcerated men and women be rationalized?
3. Imagine that you are the administrator of a women's correctional center. What problems would you expect to encounter? How would you handle these problems?
4. What parental rights should incarcerated individuals have? Should children be allowed to live in correctional facilities with their mothers? What problems would this practice create?
5. How do the social structures of male and female correctional institutions differ? Why do you think they differ in these ways?

FOR FURTHER READING

George, Erin. *A Woman Doing Life: Notes from a Prison for Women*. New York: Oxford University Press, 2010. A vivid description of prison life written by an incarcerated woman.

Kerman, Piper. *Orange Is the New Black: My Year in a Women's Prison*. New York: Spiegel and Grau, 2010. One woman's story of navigating the rules and codes of the prison world.

Morash, Merry. *Women on Probation and Parole: A Feminist Critique of Community Programs and Services.* Hanover: University Press of New England, 2010. Focuses on the challenges that women who are involved with the criminal justice system face and their programming needs.

Sue, Kimberly. *Getting Wrecked: Women, Incarceration, and the Opioid Crisis*. Oakland: University of California Press, 2019. Describes how the opioid crisis has affected women's prisons. The traditional goals of punishment must be balanced with treating women diagnosed with substance use disorder.

Wakefield, Sara, and Christopher Wildeman. *Children of the Prison Boom: Mass Incarceration and the Future of American Inequality*. Oxford: Oxford University Press, 2013. A study showing that the effects of mass imprisonment on children may be greater than on their incarcerated parents.

NOTES

1 Dean Narciso, "New Prison Nursery Brings Moms Coping Skills, Hope," *The Columbus Dispatch,* https://www.dispatch.com/news/20191228/new-prison-nursery-brings-moms-coping-skills-hope, December 28, 2019.

2 Lauren Glaze and Laura M. Maruschak, *Parents in Prison and Their Minor Children* (Washington, DC: U.S. Government Printing Office, 2008).

3 Narciso, "New Nursery Brings Moms Coping Skills, Hope."

4 Joanne Belknap, *The Invisible Woman: Gender, Crime, and Justice,* 3rd ed. (Belmont, CA: Wadsworth, 2007), 189.

5 E. Ann Carson, *Prisoners in 2018* (Washington, DC: U.S. Government Printing Office, 2020).

6 Ibid.; Paige M. Harrison and Allen J. Beck, *Prisoners in 2005* (Washington, DC: U.S. Government Printing Office, 2006), 4.
7 Federal Bureau of Investigation, *Crime in the United States, 2018*, https://ucr.fbi.gov/crime-in-the-u.s/2018/crime-in-the-u.s.-2018/topic-pages/tables/table-42
8 Freda Adler, "Crime, an Equal Opportunity Employer," *Trial,* January 1977, p. 31.
9 Nichole Rafter, *Partial Justice: Women, Prisons and Social Control* (New Brunswick, NJ: Transaction, 1990), 178.
10 E. R. Pitman, *Elizabeth Fry* (New York: Greenwood, [1884] 1969), 55.
11 Lucia Zedner, "Wayward Sisters: The Prison for Women," in *The Oxford History of the Prison,* edited by Norval Morris and David J. Rothman (New York: Oxford University Press, 1995), 333.
12 Feeley and Little point out that for much of the eighteenth century, almost half of those indicted for felony offenses in London were women. The proportion dropped in the nineteenth century as the roles of women changed in the economy, the family, and society. See Malcolm M. Feeley and Deborah L. Little, "The Vanishing Female: The Decline of Women in the Criminal Process, 1687–1912," *Law and Society Review* 25 (1991): 720–57.
13 W. Davis Lewis, *From Newgate to Dannemora: The Rise of the Penitentiary in New York, 1796–1888* (Ithaca, NY: Cornell University Press, 1965), 158–59.
14 Nichole Hahn Rafter, "Equality or Difference?" *Federal Prisons Journal* 3 (Spring 1992): 17.
15 Estelle B. Freedman, *Their Sisters' Keepers* (Ann Arbor: University of Michigan Press, 1981), 15.
16 Zedner, "Wayward Sisters," p. 353.
17 Sara F. Keely, "The Organization and Discipline of the Indiana Women's Prison" (proceedings of the 58th Annual Congress of the National Prison Association, 1898), 275, quoted in Rose Giallombardo, *Society of Women: A Study of a Women's Prison* (New York: Wiley, 1966), 7.
18 Maud Ballington Booth, "The Shadow of Prison" (proceedings of the 58th Annual Congress of the National Prison Association, 1898), 275, quoted in Rose Giallombardo, *Society of Women: A Study of a Women's Prison* (New York: Wiley, 1966), 46.
19 Nichole Hahn Rafter, "Prisons for Women, 1790–1980," in *Crime and Justice,* vol. 5, edited by Michael Tonry and Norval Morris (Chicago: University of Chicago Press, 1983), 147.
20 Freedman, *Their Sisters' Keepers,* p. 69.
21 Rafter, "Prisons for Women," p. 165.
22 Lewis, *From Newgate to Dannemora,* p. 213.
23 Rafter, "Prisons for Women," p. 165.
24 Rafter, "Equality or Difference?" p. 19.
25 Emily M. Wright, Patricia Van Voorhis, Emily J. Salisbury, and Ashley Bauman, "Gender-Responsive Lessons Learned and Policy Implications for Women in Prison," *Criminal Justice and Behavior* 39 (December 2012): 1612–32.
26 Belknap, *The Invisible Woman,* p. 190.
27 Carson, *Prisoners in 2018.*
28 Ibid, pp. 22–24.
29 Sean Rosenmerkel, Matthew Durose, and Donald Farole Jr., *Felony Sentences in State Courts, 2006—Statistical Tables,* Table 3.5, http://bjs.ojp.usdoj.gov/content/pub/pdf/fssc06st.pdf, 2009.
30 Caitlin Thompson and Ann B. Loper, "Adjustment Patterns in Incarcerated Women: An Analysis of Differences Based on Sentence Length," *Criminal Justice and Behavior* 32 (December 2005): 714–32.
31 Jennifer Bronson, Jessica Stroop, Stephanie Zimmer, and Marcus Berzofsky, *Drug Use, Dependence, and Abuse among State Prisoners and Jail Inmates, 2007–2009* (Washington, DC: U.S. Government Printing Office, 2017).
32 Andi Rierden, *The Farm: Life Inside a Women's Prison* (Amherst: University of Massachusetts Press, 1997), 18.
33 Esther Heffernan, *Making It in Prison* (New York: Wiley, 1972).
34 David Ward and Gene G. Kassebaum, *Women's Prisons: Sex and Social Structure* (Hawthorne, NY: Aldine, 1965), 140.
35 Kimberly R. Greer, "The Changing Nature of Interpersonal Relationships in a Women's Prison," *Prison Journal* 80 (December 2000): 442–68.
36 Rose Giallombardo, *Society of Women: A Study of a Women's Prison* (New York: Wiley, 1966).
37 Heffernan, *Making It in Prison,* pp. 16–17.
38 Barbara Owen, *"In the Mix": Struggle and Survival in a Women's Prison* (Albany: State University of New York Press, 1998).
39 Ibid., p. 179.
40 Nancy Wolff and Jing Shi, "Type, Source, and Patterns of Physical Victimization: A Comparison of Male and Female Inmates," *Prison Journal* 89 (June 2009): 172–91.
41 Ramona R. Rantala, *Sexual Victimization Reported by Adult Correctional Authorities, 2012–15* (Washington, DC: U.S. Government Printing Office, 2018), 2.
42 Allen J. Beck, Paige M. Harrison, Marcus Berzofsky, and Christopher Krebs, *Sexual Victimization in Prisons and Jails Reported by Inmates, 2011–12* (Washington, DC: U.S. Department of Justice, 2013), 17.
43 Nancy Wolff and Jing Shi, "Patterns of Victimization and Feelings of Safety Inside Prison: The Experience of Male and Female Inmates," *Crime and Delinquency* 57 (January 2011): 29–55.
44 Susan W. McCampbell and Elizabeth P. Laymen, *Training Curriculum for Investigating Allegations of Staff Sexual Misconduct with Inmates* (Tamarac, FL: Center for Innovative Public Policies, 2000), 3.
45 "$10M Settlement in Prison Sex Abuse Case," CBSNews.com, April 19, 2008, www.cbsnews.com/stories/2008/04/19/national/main4029273.shtml, September 28, 2009.

46 Barbara Bloom, Barbara Owen, and Stephanie Covington, *Gender-Responsive Strategies for Women Offenders* (Washington, DC: U.S. Government Printing Office, 2005), 9.

47 Jennifer Bronson and Marcus Berzofsky, *Indicators of Mental Health Problems Reported by Prisoners and Jail Inmates, 2011–12* (Washington, DC: U.S. Government Printing Office, 2017), 4.

48 Laura M. Maruschak and Marcus Berzofsky, *Medical Problems of State and Federal Prisoners and Jail Inmates, 2011–12* (Washington, DC: U.S. Government Printing Office, 2015), 5.

49 Laura M. Maruschak, *Medical Problems of Prisoners—Statistical Tables,* Table 2, www.ojp.usdoj.gov/bjs/pub/html/mpp/tables/mppt02.htm, revised April 22, 2008, Table 10.

50 Tamar Kraft-Stolar, *Reproductive Injustice: The State of Reproductive Health Care for Women in New York State Prisons* (New York: Correctional Association of New York, 2015).

51 Myrna Raeder, *Pregnancy- and Child-Related Legal and Policy Issues Concerning Justice-Involved Women* (Washington, DC: U.S. Government Printing Office, 2013).

52 Glaze and Maruschak, *Parents in Prison.*

53 Beth M. Huebner and Regan Gustafson, "The Effect of Maternal Incarceration on Adult Offspring Involvement in the Criminal Justice System," *Journal of Criminal Justice* 35 (May–June 2007): 283–96.

54 Melinda Tasca, Nancy Rodriguez, and Marjorie S. Zatz, "Family and Residential Instability in the Context of Paternal and Maternal Incarceration," *Criminal Justice and Behavior* 38 (March 2011): 231–47.

55 Women's Prison Association, *Mothers, Infants and Imprisonment: A National Look at Prison Nurseries and Community-Based Alternatives* (New York: Author, 2009), 5.

56 Lorie Smith Goshin and Mary Woods Byrne, "Converging Streams of Opportunity for Prison Nursery Programs in the United States," *Journal of Offender Rehabilitation* 48 (May 2009): 271–95.

57 Heath C. Hoffman, Amy L. Byrd, and Alex M. Knightlinger, "Prison Programs and Services for Incarcerated Parents and Their Underage Children: Results from a National Survey of Correctional Facilities," *Prison Journal* 90 (December 2010): 397–416.

58 Merry Morash and Pamela J. Schram, *The Prison Experience: Special Issues of Women in Prison* (Prospect Heights, IL: Waveland, 2002), 99.

59 Women's Prison Association, *WPA Focus on Women and Justice: Barriers to Reentry* (New York: Author, 2003).

60 Kristy Holtfreter and Katelyn A. Wattanaporn, "The Transition from Prison to Community Initiative: An Examination of Gender Responsiveness for Female Reentry," *Criminal Justice and Behavior* 41 (January 2014): 41–57.

61 Beth E. Richie, "Challenges Incarcerated Women Face as They Return to Their Communities: Findings from Life History Interviews," *Crime and Delinquency* 47 (July 2001): 368–89.

CHAPTER 13

Institutional Management

This warning sign outside a prison lets everyone know that preventing contraband from entering the prison is one of the highest priorities for prison officials.

STANDING IN FEDERAL COURT, THE DEFENDANT PLEADED GUILTY TO THE CHARGE OF BRIBERY. U.S. District Judge, Kristine Baker, accepted the plea. The defendant in this case was not a high-powered government official who accepted kickbacks for political favors, nor was he a professional sports referee who sold his assistance to ensure victories for specific teams to high stakes gamblers. Josue Duane Garza was a correctional officer at the Federal Correctional Complex in Forrest City, Arkansas. Over the course of 10 months, Garza accepted approximately $40,000 in bribes from individuals incarcerated at the facility to smuggle in cell phones and tobacco.[1]

It is no secret that much of the contraband found in prisons comes in with staff. Researchers have talked about the corruption of prison officer authority for more than 50 years. For example, Gresham Sykes observed that prison officers sometimes tolerated minor rule violations in exchange for cooperation.[2] And, more recently, investigations have focused on identifying and describing different types of relationships between incarcerated individuals and officers that violate departmental policies. Such actions not only jeopardize prison order, constitute an abuse of legal authority, and violate public trust, but also result in criminal prosecutions and civil lawsuits.

The Garza case involved a lot more than an officer buying phones and cigarettes and selling them to facility residents. Indeed, family members of incarcerated individuals mailed Garza contraband and cash to a P.O. Box. Garza was later sentenced to 12 months and one day in federal prison for his role in the smuggling scheme. Following the sentencing, U.S. Attorney Cody Hiland said, "Smuggling illicit cell phones into prison allows convicted felons to continue their criminal activity, even from inside the prison walls. Today's sentence demonstrates that those who seek to profit from these underhanded dealings will soon find themselves among the inmates they formerly enabled." In addition to his prison term, Garza will face one year of supervised release following his incarceration and he will also have to forfeit all proceeds from these crimes.[3]

The prison differs from almost every other institution or organization in modern society. It has unique physical features, and it is the only place where a group of employees manage a group of captives. Imprisoned people must live according to the rules of their keepers and with restricted movements. When reading this chapter, keep in mind that prison managers

1. Cannot select their clients
2. Have little or no control over the release of their clients
3. Must deal with clients who are there against their will
4. Must rely on clients to do most of the work in the daily operation of the institution—work they are forced to do and for which they are not paid
5. Must depend on the maintenance of satisfactory relationships between clients and staff

Given these unique characteristics, how should prisons be run? Further, wardens and other key personnel are asked to perform a difficult job, one that requires skilled and dedicated managers. What rules should guide them?

Remember that a wide range of institutions fall under the heading of "prison." Some are treatment centers serving a relatively small number of clients; others are sprawling agricultural complexes; still others are ranches or forest camps. Although new facilities have opened in recent years, many prisons remain as large, fortress-like institutions with comparable management structures and incarcerated populations.

In this chapter we look at how institutional resources are organized to achieve certain goals. At a minimum, incarcerated individuals must be clothed, fed, kept healthy, provided with recreation, protected from one another, and maintained in custody. In addition, administrators may face the tasks of offering vocational and educational programs and using the prison population as a source of labor in agriculture or industry. To accomplish all this in a community of free individuals would be taxing. To do so when the population consists of some of the most antisocial people in the society is surely a Herculean undertaking, one that depends on organization.

LEARNING OBJECTIVES

After reading this chapter, you should be able to . . .

1. Identify the principles used to organize the functioning of prisons.
2. Discuss the importance of prison governance.
3. Discuss the different job assignments that correctional officers are given.
4. Analyze the negative consequences of boundary violations and job stress among prison staff.

LO 1

Identify the principles used to organize the functioning of prisons.

FORMAL ORGANIZATION

The University of Texas, the General Motors Corporation, and the California State Prison at Folsom are very different organizations, each created to achieve certain goals. Differing organizational structures let managers coordinate the various parts of the university, auto manufacturer, and prison in the interests of scholarship, production, and corrections.

formal organization A structure established for influencing behavior to achieve particular ends.

compliance Obedience to an order or request.

remunerative power The ability to obtain compliance in exchange for material resources.

normative power The ability to obtain compliance by manipulating symbolic rewards.

coercive power The ability to obtain compliance by the application or threat of physical force.

A **formal organization** is deliberately established for particular ends. If accomplishing an objective requires collective effort, people set up an organization to help coordinate activities and to provide incentives for others to join. Thus, in a university, a business, and a correctional institution the goals, rules, and roles that define the relations among the organization's members (the organizational chart) have been formally established.

Amitai Etzioni, an organization theorist, uses the concept of compliance as the basis for comparing types of organizations. **Compliance** is obedience to an order or directive given by another person. In compliance relationships, an order is backed up by one's ability to induce or influence another person to carry out one's directives.[4] People do what others ask because those others have the means—remunerative, normative, or coercive—to get the subjects to comply. **Remunerative power** is based on material resources, such as wages, fringe benefits, or goods, which people exchange for compliance. **Normative power** rests on symbolic rewards that leaders manipulate through ritual, allocation of honors, and social esteem. **Coercive power** depends on applying or threatening physical force to inflict pain, restrict movement, or control other aspects of a person's life.

Etzioni argues that all formal organizations employ all three types of power but that the degree to which they rely on any one of them varies with the desired goal. Thus, although the University of Texas probably relies mainly on normative power in its relationships with students and the public, it relies on remunerative power in relationships with faculty and staff. Although General Motors is organized primarily for manufacturing, it may appeal to "team spirit" or "safety employee of the month" campaigns to meet its goals. And although while managing staff, the warden at

Folsom may rely on remunerative and normative powers to make this facility the best correctional facility in the United States, in working with prison residents he relies primarily on coercive power. The presence in high-custody institutions of "highly alienated lower participants" (the incarcerated), Etzioni says, makes the application or threat of force necessary to ensure compliance.[5]

Coercive power undergirds all prison relationships, but correctional institutions vary in their use of physical force and in the degree to which the incarcerated individuals are alienated. Correctional institutions can be placed on a continuum of custody or treatment goals. At one extreme is the highly authoritarian prison, where the movement of the prison population is greatly restricted, relationships between the supervisors and those who are supervised are formally structured, and the prime emphasis is on custody. In such an institution, treatment goals take a back seat. At the other extreme is the institution that emphasizes the therapeutic aspect of the physical and social environment. Here the staff members help incarcerated individuals overcome problems. Between these ideal types lies the great majority of correctional institutions.

However, this custody–treatment continuum may neglect other aspects of imprisonment. After all, we expect a lot of prisons, including rehabilitating the deviant, punishing the wretched, deterring the motivated, and restraining the habitual. Broadly speaking, the purpose of imprisonment is to fairly and justly punish convicted individuals through periods of confinement that are commensurate with the seriousness of the offense. Thus, the mission with respect to incarcerated individuals has five features:

1. *Keep them in:* The facility must be secure, such that escapes do not happen and contraband cannot be smuggled in.
2. *Keep them safe:* Everybody inside the prison needs to be kept safe, not only from one another but from various environmental hazards as well.
3. *Keep them in line:* Prisons run on rules, and the ability of prison administrators to enforce compliance is central to the quality of confinement.
4. *Keep them healthy:* Individuals serving time in prison are entitled to have care for their medical needs.
5. *Keep them busy:* Constructive activities, such as work, recreation, education, and treatment programs, are antidotes to idleness.[6]

Prison work entails accomplishing this mission in a fair and efficient manner, without causing undue suffering. The state may run correctional institutions with other goals as well, but these are the main ones.

The Organizational Structure

For any organization to be effective, its leaders and staff must know the rules and procedures, the lines of authority, and the channels of communication. Organizations vary in their organizational hierarchy, in their allocation of discretion, in the effort expended on administrative problems, and in the nature of the top leadership.

Concepts of Organization The formal administrative structure of a prison is a hierarchy of staff positions, each with its own duties and responsibilities, each linked to the others in a logical chain of command. As Figure 13.1 shows, the warden is ultimately responsible for the operation of the institution. Deputy wardens oversee the functional divisions of the prison: management, custody, programs, and industry and agriculture. Under each deputy are middle managers and line staff who operate the departments. Functions are subdivided according to prison size and population.

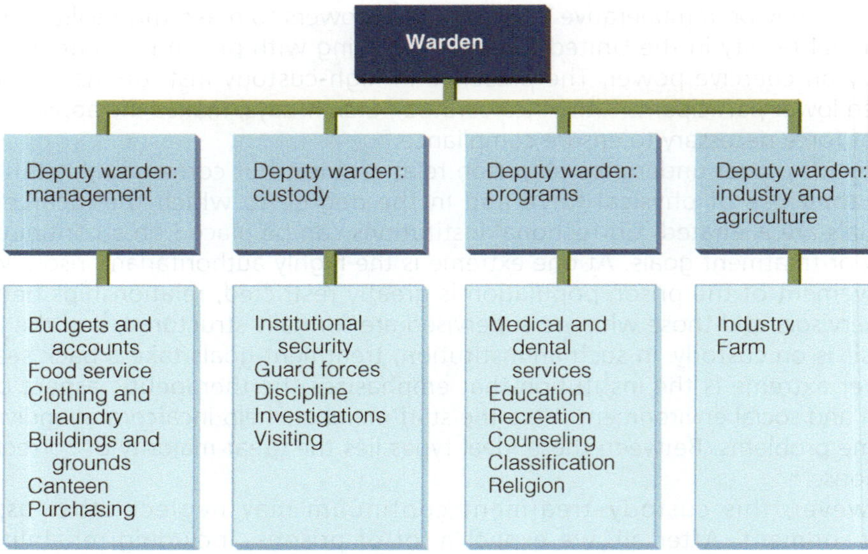

FIGURE 13.1 Formal Organization of a Prison for Adults Convicted of Felonies
The formal organization of an institution may say little about those political and informal relationships among staff members that really govern how the prison operates.

Three principles are commonly used to organize the functioning of hierarchically structured organizations: unity of command, chain of command, and span of control. **Unity of command** is the idea that it is most efficient for a subordinate to report to only one superior. If a worker must respond to orders from two or more superiors, chaos ensues. Unity of command is tied to the second concept, **chain of command**. Because the person at the top of the organization cannot oversee everything, he or she must rely on lower-ranking staff to pass directives down. For example, the warden asks the deputy warden to have custody staff conduct a shakedown; the deputy warden passes the directive to the captain of the guard, who then has the lieutenant in charge of a particular shift carry out the search. The term **span of control** refers to the extent of supervision by one person. If, for example, a correctional institution offers many educational and treatment programs, the deputy warden for programs may not be able to oversee them all effectively. This deputy warden's span of control is stretched so far that a reorganization and further division of responsibilities may be required.

Two other concepts clarify the organization of correctional institutions: line and staff. **Line personnel** are directly concerned with furthering the institution's goals. They have direct contact with the prison residents; such personnel include the custody force, industry and agricultural supervisors, counselors, and medical technicians. **Staff personnel** support line personnel. They usually work under the deputy warden for management, handling accounting, training, purchasing, and so on.

Custodial employees make up the majority of an institution's personnel. They are normally organized along military lines, from deputy warden to captain to correctional officer. The professional staff—such as clinicians, teachers, and industry supervisors—are separate from the custodial staff and have little in common with them. All employees answer to the warden, but the treatment personnel and the civilian supervisors of the workshops have their own titles and salary scales. Their responsibilities do not extend to providing special services to the custodial employees. The top medical and educational personnel may formally report to the warden but in fact look to the central office of the department of corrections for leadership.

The multiple goals and separate employee lines of command often cause ambiguity and conflict in the administration of prisons. For example, the goals imposed on prisons

unity of command
A management principle holding that a subordinate should report to only one supervisor.

chain of command A series of organizational positions in order of authority, with each person receiving orders from the one immediately above and issuing orders to the one(s) immediately below.

span of control
A management principle holding that a supervisor can effectively oversee only a limited number of subordinates.

line personnel Employees who are directly concerned with furthering the institution's goals and who are in direct contact with clients.

staff personnel Employees who provide services in support of line personnel; examples of staff personnel include training officers and accountants.

TABLE 13.1 Primary Duties and Tasks of Prison Wardens

Contemporary prison wardens place great emphasis on maintaining safety and security. They are also responsible for mundane but important duties such as managing the budget and presiding over the physical plant.

Duties			Tasks	
Administer safety and security operations	Approve security and safety policies and procedures	Ensure facility compliance	Assess safety and security systems	Manage intelligence operations
Manage human resources	Promote equal employment opportunities	Manage staff recruitment process	Authorize/recommend hiring staff	Ensure staff development
Manage critical incidents	Review and approve emergency plans	Monitor emergency scenarios	Ensure readiness of emergency response team	Command intelligence team
Manage the budget	Compile budget requests	Establish budget priorities	Submit and justify budget requests	Monitor and control overtime
Foster a healthy institutional environment	Maintain frequent and direct contact with residents	Provide meaningful inmate programs	Provide quality inmate-support services	Provide fair inmate-grievance system
Preside over the physical plant	Administer physical plant maintenance plan	Ensure facility safety, security, and sanitation inspections	Monitor allocation of space	Monitor and allocate resources

Source: Rick Ruddell and Tommy Norris, "The Changing Role of Wardens: A Focus on Safety and Security," *Corrections Today* 70 (October 2008): 39.

are often contradictory or unclear. Conflicts between different groups of personnel (custodial versus treatment staff) and between staff and those who are incarcerated present significant challenges to prison administrators.

The Warden The warden is the chief executive of the institution. The attitude that he or she brings to the job affects the organization. Not long ago the prison warden was an autocrat who ran the institution without direction from departments of corrections or the intrusion of courts, labor unions, or prisoner support groups.[7] Things are quite different today. Contemporary prison wardens need a broad set of skills to manage large groups of employees and to operate facilities in a way that keeps everyone safe. The primary duties and tasks of prison wardens are summarized in Table 13.1.

The prison warden is the institution's main contact with the outside world. Responsible for operating the prison, he or she normally reports to the deputy commissioner for institutions in the central office of the department of corrections. When the warden directs attention and energy outward (to the central office, parole board, or legislature), he or she delegates the daily operation of the prison to a deputy, usually the person in charge of custody. In recent years, wardens in most states have lost much of their autonomy to managers in the central office who handle such matters as budgets, research and program development, public information, and legislative relations. However, the warden's job security still rests on the ability to run the institution effectively and efficiently. At the first sign of trouble, the warden may be forced to look for a new job, and in some states the top management of corrections seems to be in constant flux. In short, today's prison warden must function effectively despite decreased autonomy and increased accountability.

Management Bureaucracies tend to increase the personnel and resources used to maintain and manage the organization. This tendency can especially prevail in public bureaucracies, which strongly emphasize financial accountability and reporting to higher government agencies. Correctional institutions are no exception. Bureaucratic functions often fall to a deputy warden for management, who is responsible for housekeeping

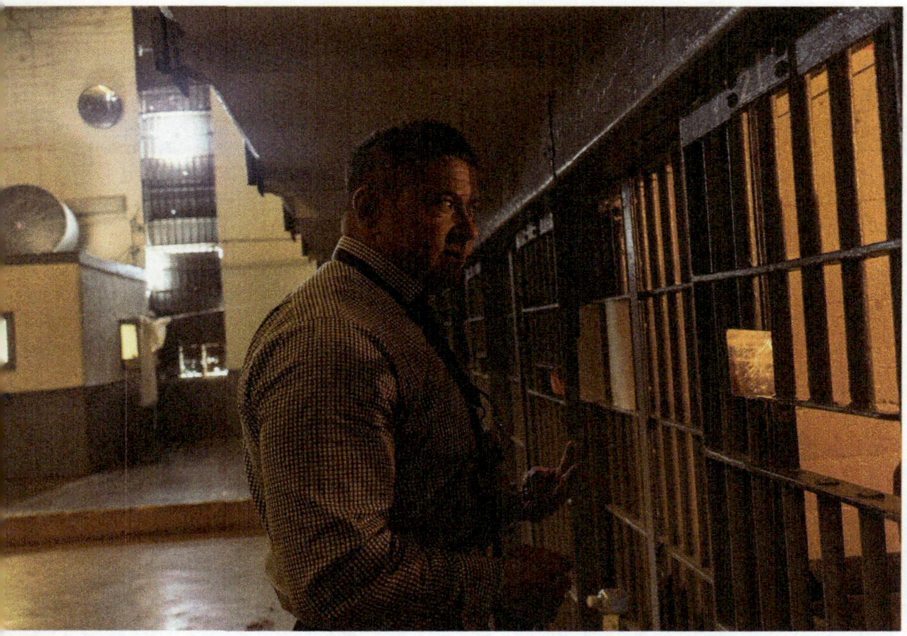

Deputy Warden Jason Monson talks to an individual incarcerated in the Central Unit at the Florence Arizona State Prison Complex.

tasks: buying supplies, keeping up the buildings and grounds, providing food, maintaining financial records, and the like. However, some states centralize many of these tasks in the office of the commissioner to promote accountability and coordination among constituent institutions. For example, buying supplies from one warehouse that serves all state agencies has decreased the discretion of prison management to contract locally for provisions.

Most personnel assigned to manage services for correctional institutions have little contact with the incarcerated; in some facilities they work in buildings separate from the main plant. Only personnel who provide services directly, such as the head of food services, have direct contact with the residents.

Custodial Personnel Later in this chapter we examine in detail the role of the correctional officer. Here, simply note that in most institutions the custodial force has graded ranks (captain, lieutenant, officer) with pay differentials and job titles following the chain of command, as in the military. However, unlike the factory and the military, which have separate groups of supervisors and workers or officers and enlisted personnel, the prison requires its lowest-status employee, the correctional officer, to be both a supervisor (of incarcerated individuals) and a worker (for the warden). This causes role conflict and makes officers vulnerable to corruption by members of the prison population. Officers know the warden is judging their performance by the way they manage their clients, and they can seldom manage without at least some cooperation from these clients. Officers ease up on some rules so residents will more willingly comply with other rules and requests. "Careers in Corrections" offers a view of work as a state correctional officer.

Program Personnel The contemporary correctional institution is concerned not only with punishing but also with encouraging prisoners' participation in educational, vocational, and treatment programs. Such programs have been a part of corrections since the late 1800s, but the enthusiasm for rehabilitation that swept corrections after World War II created a wider variety of programs, as discussed in Chapter 14. Here we need only mention that rehabilitative and educational personnel find it difficult to achieve their goals in institutions whose primary mission is custody.

Industry and Agriculture Personnel Since the invention of the penitentiary, the prison population has provided labor for industry and agriculture. As we show in Chapter 14, the importance of these functions has varied over time and among regions. For instance, in some southern prisons, most residents spend their time tending crops. In the Northeast, prison farms have disappeared because they are uneconomical and ill matched to the urban backgrounds of most prison occupants.

Like other programs, industrial and agricultural production is usually administered outside of the strict custodial hierarchy. But unlike educational or treatment programs, work in a factory or farm requires supervisors. For example, administrators must often mediate disputes over the need for officers in guard towers or housing units and the need for officers in fields or factories.

CAREERS IN CORRECTIONS

Correctional Officer: State

Nature of the Work

State correctional officers work in the great array of reformatories, prisons, prison camps, and penitentiaries that make up American corrections. Regardless of the setting, they maintain order within the institution and enforce rules and regulations. To keep the facility secure, officers must often search incarcerated individuals and their living quarters for contraband, settle disputes, enforce discipline, and communicate prisoner requests to higher levels. Officers may be assigned to housing units, perimeter patrols, or work assignments. Correctional officers usually work an eight-hour day, five days per week, on rotating shifts.

Required Qualifications

Correctional officers must be at least 18–21 years of age, be a U.S. citizen with no felony convictions, and have at least a high school education and some work experience. Most states require qualifying examinations, including personality screenings. Candidates must be in good health and meet fitness, eyesight, and hearing standards. The American Correctional Association sets training guidelines for recruits. Most states have training academies with instruction on legal restrictions, custody procedures, interpersonal relationships, use of firearms, and self-defense. After graduation from the academy, trainees typically receive several weeks or months of training in the job setting under the supervision of an experienced officer.

Earnings and Job Outlook

As states change their criminal laws to be less punitive and deal with budget constraints, the number of correctional officers is expected to decline by 7 percent over the next decade. The median annual salary for state correctional officers is $45,300.

More Information

See the American Correctional Association website.

The Impact of the Structure

The organizational structure of correctional institutions has changed over time. The traditional custodial prison was run as an autocracy, with the warden dominating the guard force and often disciplining employees as strictly as those sentenced to prison. When rehabilitation became a goal and treatment and educational programs were incorporated, a separate structure for programs, often headed by a deputy warden, was added. Its employees were professionals in the social and behavioral sciences, who frequently clashed with autocratic wardens who emphasized custody.

As some institutions began to focus on rehabilitation, correctional planners and scholars frequently contrasted the traditional prison organization with a collaborative model. For example, a 1967 U.S. presidential commission report referred optimistically to the future correctional institution in which a dedicated and professionally trained staff would work with other administrators and with prison residents to identify problems and to strive for rehabilitation.[8] Such an institution would require structural changes to deemphasize the traditionally rigid control function, enlarge the decision-making role of treatment personnel, and allow input from the prison occupants about the operation of the facility. However, by the 1980s it was hard to find either prisons being run this way or correctional leaders advocating that they be so run. Some observers say that no more than a few institutions really followed the collaborative organizational style.

Correctional institutions are more humanely administered today than they were in the past. This change is in part a response to the presence of rehabilitative personnel and programs, the increased training and professionalism of correctional personnel, the intrusion of the courts, and the growth of citizen observer groups that monitor operations. Society will no longer tolerate the harsh conditions once prevalent in prisons.

A formal organizational chart does not convey the whole story of a prison's organization; no chart can show how the people who occupy the positions actually perform. As theorists explain, an informal organization, with its own rules and procedures, chain of command, and channels of communication, exists alongside the formal structure. Every organization has individuals who ignore directives, bypass the chain of command in

FOR CRITICAL THINKING

The case of former correctional officer and convicted contraband smuggler Josue Garza introduced at the outset of this chapter demonstrates the dangers of allowing supervision and related control processes of prison staff to become lax.

1. Which type of power discussed by Amitai Etzioni—remunerative, normative, and coercive—should be exercised in maximum-security prisons to prevent officers from forming contraband smuggling networks with incarcerated individuals? Explain your position.
2. Organizational principles, such as unity of command and span of control, are applied to increase efficiency and effectiveness. Which of these two principles, if not adhered to, is most likely to lead to contraband smuggling by prison staff?
3. What can prison wardens do to help prevent contraband from making its way inside their institutions?

communicating to the top, and negotiate with others who perform parallel or associated functions (see "For Critical Thinking").

How, then, do prisons function? How do residents and staff try to meet their own goals? Although the U.S. prison may not conform to the ideal goals of corrections and the formal organization may little resemble the ongoing reality of the informal relations, order is kept, and a routine is followed.

GOVERNING PRISONS

inmate balance theory A governance theory which posits that for a prison system to operate effectively, officials must tolerate minor infractions, relax security measures, and allow informal leaders to keep order.

Traditionally, prison sociologists have looked at prisons as social systems rather than institutions to be governed. Until fairly recently, our understanding of life inside prison was based on **inmate balance theory**. This perspective was developed in the pioneering works of Donald Clemmer and Gresham Sykes. This theory provides insights on the maintenance of order and the prevention of collective violence.[9] According to this view, for the prison system to operate effectively, officials must tolerate minor infractions, relax security measures, and allow informal leaders to keep order. When officials go too far in asserting their authority by cracking down on privileges, the delicate balance of shared authority is upset, which in turn unleashes collective disorder.

LO 2

Discuss the importance of prison governance.

Criminologists have written about the effects of prison conditions on those who are incarcerated—racial and ethnic cleavages, language and roles, and the informal distribution of authority in prisons. However, as John DiIulio notes, sociological research on prison society does little to help correctional officials manage their facilities. In fact, most of this research implies that administrators can do little to govern because—despite formal rules and regulations—institutions are run mainly through the informal social networks of the keepers and the kept (see Table 13.2 for one set of formal rules

TABLE 13.2 General Rules, Texas Department of Criminal Justice

1.	The possession or use of any tobacco products, paraphernalia, or related products is prohibited.
2.	No loud or boisterous talking, no vulgar or abusive language shall be allowed.
3.	When talking to an employee or official, offenders will stand with arms by their side and call them Mr., Ms., or Officer (Last Name) or use their title. Offenders can identify the officer by the last name on his nameplate that is worn as part of the uniform. Offenders will show respect when talking with employees, officials, visitors and other offenders. Offenders shall answer "yes, sir"; "no, sir"; "yes, ma'am"; or "no, ma'am."
4.	No fighting, scuffling, horseplay, or similar activities will be allowed.
5.	Offenders shall not litter. Trash and garbage will be placed in trash cans.
6.	Offenders shall not alter, disfigure, damage or destroy any state property.
7.	Offenders shall not have playing cards, dice or any other item that can be used for gambling.
8.	Offenders shall not tamper with hand restraints, or any security equipment.
9.	Offenders shall not take posted information from bulletin boards.
10.	Offenders and their living areas may be searched at any time by staff.
11.	Offenders are not allowed in unauthorized areas.
12.	Offenders are not allowed in their work areas except during their work hours, unless approved due to special circumstances.
13.	Offenders shall not traffic and trade postage supplies, or trade any offender's personal property for other commissary items.
14.	Offenders are expected to be dressed and ready when called for work, school, or other turnouts. There shall be no tardiness allowed by offenders.
15.	Offenders shall not wear sunglasses indoors unless medically prescribed.

Source: Texas Department of Criminal Justice, *Offender Orientation Handbook* (Austin: Texas Board of Criminal Justice, 2017), 24–25.

of conduct). DiIulio finds shocking the extent to which correctional officials seem to have accepted sociological explanations for institutional conditions rather than correcting faulty management practices.[10]

DiIulio and others have developed an alternative explanation of prison disorder, which has been dubbed **administrative control theory**.[11] This perspective posits that disorder results from "unstable, divided, or otherwise weak management."[12] Thus, when officials lose control over their institutions, collective disorder and other unruly behaviors within the prison population become more likely. This administrative breakdown has several effects:

administrative control theory A governance theory which posits that prison disorder results from unstable, divided, or otherwise weak management.

1. Incarcerated individuals come to believe their conditions of confinement are not only bad but unjust as well.
2. Officials become indifferent to routine security measures and the day-to-day tasks of prison management.
3. Weak management permits gangs and other illicit groups to flourish. These groups, in turn, may help mobilize disturbances.[13]

What distinguishes a well-run prison from a substandard prison? DiIulio argues that the crucial variable is not the ethnic or racial distribution of the population, the criminal records of those in prison, the size of the institution, the degree of crowding, or the level of funding. What is important is *governance:* sound and firm prison management.

What quality of life should be maintained in a prison? DiIulio states that a good prison "provides as much order, amenity, and service as possible given the human and financial resources."[14] *Order* is defined as the absence of individual or group misconduct threatening the safety of others—for example, assaults, rapes, and other forms of violence or insult. A basic assumption should be that because the state sends people to prison, it is responsible for ensuring their safety there. *Amenity* is anything that enhances the inmates' creature comforts, such as good food, clean bedding, and recreational opportunities. This does not mean that prisons are to function as luxury hotels, but contemporary standards stipulate that correctional facilities should not be deleterious to inmates' mental and physical health. Finally, *service* includes programs designed to improve the life prospects of the incarcerated: vocational training, remedial education, and work opportunities. Here, too, we expect prison residents to be engaged in activities during incarceration that will make them better people and enhance their ability to lead crime-free lives upon release.

If we accept the premise that well-run prisons are important for residents, staff, and society, what are some of the problems that correctional administrators must address? The correctional literature points to four factors that make governing prisons different from administering other public institutions: (1) the defects of total power, (2) the limited rewards and punishments, (3) the co-optation of correctional officers, and (4) the strength of inmate leadership. After we review each of these factors, we will consider the administrative systems and leadership styles that can help make prisons safe and humane and serve inmates' needs.

Correctional officers are heavily outnumbered in prisons, so they have to use their interpersonal skills to maintain authority and keep good order.

The Defects of Total Power

In his classic study of the New Jersey State Prison, Sykes emphasized that although in formal terms correctional officials have the power to induce compliance from those they supervise, in fact that power is limited and in many ways dependent on cooperation.[15] It is from this perspective that the inmate balance theory of management evolved.

Much of the public believes that prisons are run in an authoritarian manner: Correctional officers give orders, and their clients follow them. Strictly enforced rules specify what the captives may and may not do. Staff members have the right to grant rewards and to inflict punishment. In theory, any imprisoned person who does not follow the rules can be placed in solitary confinement. Because the officers have a monopoly on the legal means of enforcing rules and can be backed up by the state police and the National Guard if necessary, many people believe that no question should arise as to how the prison is run.

Certainly, we can imagine a prison society made up of hostile and uncooperative individuals ruled by force. Incarcerated individuals can be legally isolated from one another, physically coerced until they cooperate, and put under continuous surveillance. Although all these things are possible, the public would probably not tolerate such practices for long because people expect correctional institutions to be run humanely.

Also, unlike members of other authoritarian organizations such as the military, incarcerated individuals do not recognize the legitimacy of their keepers and therefore are not always moved to cooperate. No sense of duty propels people living in prison to compliance. This is an important distinction because duty is the backbone of most social organizations. With it, rules are followed—and need not be explained first.

The notion that correctional officers have total power over prison residents has many other flaws. As Sykes points out, "The ability of the officials to physically coerce their captives into the paths of compliance is something of an illusion as far as the day-to-day activities of the prison are concerned and may be of doubtful value in moments of crisis."[16] Forcing people to follow commands is an inefficient way of making them carry out complex tasks; efficiency is further diminished by the ratio of residents to custody staff (10.3 to 1 in federal prisons and 4.9 to 1 in state facilities) and by the potential danger.[17] (See "Myths in Corrections.")

Of course, physical coercion is used to control incarcerated people. Such tactics may violate criminal statutes and administrative procedures, but they have long occurred in prisons throughout the United States—and cannot be considered idiosyncratic or sporadic. For example, a study of a Texas prison found that a small but significant percentage of the officers used physical punishment. Force both controlled the prison population and induced cohesion among officers, maintaining a status differential between officers and residents and helping officers win promotions.[18]

MYTHS in Corrections

Prison Disorder and Mass Incarceration

THE MYTH: America's imprisonment binge of the 1990s, which massively increased the inmate population, resulted in prisons becoming more disorderly.

THE REALITY: Riots, correctional staff murders, inmate homicides, and escapes were rarer in the early 2000s, after adjusting for the size of the inmate population, than in the 1970s and 1980s.

Source: Burt Useem and Anne M. Piehl, "Prison Buildup and Disorder," *Punishment & Society* 8 (2006): 87–115.

Rewards and Punishments

Correctional officers often rely on rewards and punishments to gain cooperation. To maintain security and order among a large population in a confined space, they impose extensive rules of conduct. Instead of using force to ensure obedience, however, they reward compliance and punish rule violations by granting and denying privileges.

Several policies may be followed to promote control. One is to offer cooperative individuals rewards, such as choice job assignments, residence in the honor unit, and favorable parole reports. People who follow the rules receive good time. Informers may also be rewarded, and administrators may ignore conflict among individuals on the assumption that conflict keeps them from uniting against authorities.

The system of rewards and punishments has some deficiencies. One is that the punishments for rule breaking do not represent a great departure from the incarcerated individuals' usual circumstances. Because the residents are already deprived of many freedoms and valued goods—heterosexual relations, money, choice of clothing, and so on—not being allowed, say, to attend a recreational period does not carry much weight as a punishment. In addition, according to the inmate code in a particular prison, the defiant individual may gain standing among the others in the prison. Finally, authorized privileges are given to the client at the start of the sentence and are taken away only if rules are broken, but few further rewards are authorized for progress or exceptional behavior. However, as a resident approaches release, opportunities for furloughs, work release, or transfer to a halfway house can serve as incentives to obey rules.

Gaining Cooperation: Exchange Relationships

One way that correctional officers obtain inmate cooperation is by tolerating minor rule infractions in exchange for compliance with major aspects of the custodial regime. The correctional officer plays the key role in the interpersonal relationships among the incarcerated individuals and serves as the link to the custodial bureaucracy. The correctional officer

> must supervise and control the inmate population in concrete and detailed terms . . . [and] must see to the translation of the custodial regime from blueprint to reality and engage in the specific battles for conformity. Counting prisoners, periodically reporting to the center of communications, signing passes, checking groups of inmates as they come and go, searching for contraband or signs of attempts to escape—these make up the minutiae of [the officer's] eight-hour shift.[19]

Officers are in close association with those they supervise both day and night—in the cell block, workshop, dining hall, recreation area, and so on. Although the formal rules require a social distance between the officers and those who are incarcerated, their physical proximity makes them aware that each depends on the other. To look good to their superiors, the officers need the cooperation of the people they supervise, and the members of the prison population count on the officers to relax the rules or occasionally look the other way.

Even though officers are backed by the state and have the formal authority to punish any individual who does not follow orders, they often discover that the best course of action is to make "deals." As a result, officers buy compliance or obedience in some areas by tolerating rule breaking elsewhere.

Officers are expected to maintain "surface order." They must ensure that the residents conform voluntarily to the most important rules, things run smoothly, and no visible trouble and no cause for alarm emerge. Because officers' job performance is judged on the ability to maintain surface order, both officers and those who are incarcerated have a tacit understanding and bargain accordingly. The assumptions underlying these accommodative relationships can be summarized as follows:

1. Negotiations are central to maintaining control because correctional officers cannot have total control over the prison population.
2. Once an officer defines a set of informal rules with those who are incarcerated, the rules must be respected by all parties.
3. Some rule violations are "normal" and consequently do not merit officers' attention or sanctioning.[20]

Correctional officers must be careful not to pay too high a price for the cooperation of their charges. Under pressure to work effectively, officers may be blackmailed into doing illegitimate favors in return for cooperation. When leadership is thus abdicated, authority passes to the incarcerated.

Informal Leadership

In the traditional prison of the big-house era, administrators asked some members of the prison population to act as informal leaders and help maintain order. As Richard Korn and Lloyd McCorkle observed long ago,

> Far from systematically attempting to undermine the inmate hierarchy, the institution generally gives it covert support and recognition by assigning better jobs and quarters to its high-status members provided they are "good inmates." In this and other ways the institution buys peace with the system by avoiding battle with it.[21]

However, descriptions of the contemporary maximum-security prison raise questions about administrators' ability to run institutions in this way. When the racial, offense, and political characteristics of prison populations began to change in the mid-1960s, the centralized leadership structure was replaced by multiple centers of power. As official authority broke down, some institutions became violent, dangerous places.

Prisons seem to function more effectively now than they did in the recent past. Although prisons are generally more crowded, riots and reports of violence and escapes have declined.[22] In many prisons the inmate social system may have reorganized so that correctional officers again can work through residents respected by their peers. Yet some observers contend that when wardens maintain order in this way, they enhance the positions of some incarcerated individuals at the expense of others. The leaders profit by receiving illicit privileges and favors, and they increase their influence among others who are incarcerated by distributing benefits.

Discipline in Prison

Maintaining order can be burdensome to prison administrators, given the factors just discussed. In an earlier era, people in prison were kept in line with corporal punishment. Today, withholding privileges, erasing good-time credits, and placing individuals in "the hole" (the adjustment center, or administrative segregation) constitute the range of punishments available to discipline the unruly. The U.S. Supreme Court has curbed administrators' discretion in applying these punishments: Procedural fairness must accompany the process by which the disobedient are sent to solitary confinement and by which good-time credit can be lost because of misconduct.

On entering the prison, the newcomer receives a manual, often running up to a hundred pages, specifying the rules that govern almost all aspects of prison life, from permitted clothing to dining-room conduct and standards of personal hygiene. Prominently listed are types of behavior that can result in disciplinary action: rioting, gambling, sexual activity, possession of currency, failure to obey an order, and so on (see "For Critical Thinking"). Prison inhabitants are warned that some rule infractions also violate the state's criminal law and may be handled by the criminal justice system. However, an institutional committee handles most rule violations. This disciplinary committee may commit an individual to punitive segregation for the number of days specified for each class of offense or hand down other sanctions. The manuals vary from state to state; some merely list violations and allow disciplinary committees to exercise their discretion when determining the appropriate punishment.

FOR CRITICAL THINKING

Josue Garza was sentenced to 12 months and one day in federal prison. As was noted, however, Garza's smuggling operation also involved individuals who were incarcerated at the facility.

1. Should the individuals receiving the smuggled goods be punished? If so, what type of punishment should they receive? Transfer to a higher-security prison? Additional years tacked on to their sentences? A period of time served in administrative segregation?
2. Can the threat of punishment be a successful strategy for preventing those who are incarcerated from becoming involved in the distribution of prison contraband, such as cell phones and tobacco? What other steps can be taken to limit opportunities in trafficking prohibited goods?

The Disciplinary Process Custodial officers act like police officers with regard to most prison rules. Minor violations may warrant merely a verbal reprimand or warning, but more-serious violations can result in a "ticket": a report forwarded to higher authority for action. Some corrections systems distinguish between major and minor violations. Major tickets go to the disciplinary committee; minor ones receive summary judgment by a hearing officer, whose decision may be appealed to a supervising captain, whose decision may, in turn, be appealed to the committee. In some systems all disciplinary reports go to a hearing officer, who investigates the charges, conducts the hearing, and determines the punishment. The commissioner of corrections can review hearing officers' decisions and reduce punishments but not increase them.

Such procedures are relatively new. Less than 50 years ago, formal codes of institutional conduct either did not exist or were ignored; the warden had full discretion in punishment, and those who were punished had no opportunity to challenge the charges. In a series of decisions beginning in 1970, the U.S. Supreme Court granted incarcerated individuals certain limited procedural rights: to receive notice of a complaint, to have a fair hearing, to confront witnesses, to have help in preparing for the hearing, and to be given a written statement of the decision (see Chapter 5).[23] However, the Court has also emphasized the need to balance prisoners' rights with state interests. Thus, two years after it guaranteed incarcerated individuals fundamental due process rights, the Court ruled that counsel was not included.[24]

As a result, most prisons developed rules that specify some elements of due process in disciplinary proceedings. In many institutions a disciplinary committee receives charges, conducts hearings, and determines guilt and punishment. Normally, disciplinary committees comprise three to five members of the correctional staff, including representatives of custody, treatment, and classification, with a senior officer acting as chairperson. Sometimes the committees also include a member of the prison population or outside citizens.

As part of the procedure, the incarcerated individual is read the charge and is allowed to present his or her version of the incident and to present witnesses. In some institutions another incarcerated person may help the charged individual. If he or she is found guilty, a sanction is imposed. In such cases an appeal to the warden and ultimately to the commissioner is available. Even with these protections, incarcerated individuals may still feel powerless and fear further punishment if they challenge the disciplinary decisions of the warden too aggressively.

Sanctions Administrative segregation and loss of privileges and good time are the sanctions most often imposed for violating institutional rules. The privileges lost may include visits, mail, access to the commissary, and recreational periods.

The most severe sanction by a disciplinary committee is confinement in administrative segregation. Most institutions limit the amount of time that someone can spend in segregation and regulate conditions with respect to food, medical attention, and personal safety. Twenty days of continuous administrative segregation is the maximum in many prisons, but individuals can be returned to "the hole" after a token period outside.

Maintaining order among individuals who live in close proximity under conditions of deprivation is a challenge. Officers recognize they must walk a narrow line between being too restrictive and overly permissive. They must recognize, too, that their objective is to encourage cooperation and conformity to the rules. But they must also understand that rewards and punishments are limited and that courts now insist that due process be observed in disciplining violators and proceeding against them. This presents a tall order, but with good management practices the objective can be reached. One index of a poorly run institution is a large number of disciplinary violations, showing that staff and their clients cannot prevent disruptive behavior or function with mutual tolerance, let alone respect.

Leadership: The Crucial Element of Governance

As Edwin Sutherland and Donald Cressey observed, any prison is made up of the synchronized actions of hundreds of people, some of whom hate and distrust one another, love one another, fight one another physically and psychologically, think of one another as stupid or mentally disturbed, "manage" and "control" one another, and vie with one another for favors, prestige, power, and money.[25] Still, most prisons do not fall into disarray, although at times certain institutions have approached chaos. Examples include Soledad in California, during a period of racial and political unrest in the 1960s; Walla

Walla in Washington in the 1970s, when an experiment with inmate self-government was attempted; and the Eastham Unit and some other Texas prisons prior to court-ordered reforms in the 1980s. But these are exceptions, and many correctional facilities are well governed. How, then, does management effect a reasonable quality of life in U.S. prisons? Management styles vary, even in bureaucracies. In his study of prison management in California, Michigan, and Texas correctional facilities, John Dilulio argues that prisons should be run in a paramilitary fashion with strict adherence to official rules, regulations, and policies.[26]

Others note the value of alternative approaches. For example, Hans Toch argues that prison administrators should involve staff in problem-solving activities.[27] In his study of higher-custody state prisons, Michael Reisig found that flexible and adaptive managerial approaches are most effective at maintaining low levels of prison disorder.[28] Despite the controversy regarding which management style works best, the consensus among practitioners and researchers is that the quality of prison life is mainly a function of management. ("A Model Prison" describes the unique management practices of Warden Dennis Luther.)

FOCUS ON

CORRECTIONAL POLICY: A Model Prison

Set in the woods outside of Bradford, Pennsylvania, is the Federal Correctional Institution, McKean. Opened in 1989 as a medium-security facility, it houses more than 1,000 men. Until he retired, McKean's warden was Dennis Luther, an administrator who, during his 16 years in prison work, gained a reputation for unorthodox policies.

At a time when politicians were railing against "country club" prisons, Luther ran an institution that earned a 99.3 accreditation rating from the American Correctional Association, the highest in the Bureau of Prisons. Badly overcrowded and with an increasing number of residents convicted of violent offenses, in six years there were no escapes, no murders, no suicides, and only three serious assaults against staff and six recorded against prison residents.

How did he do it? According to Luther, each prison has its own culture, which is often violent and abusive, based on gangs. The staff in such institutions feel they are unable to change it. At McKean, Luther set out to build a different type of culture, based on unconditional respect for the residents as people. As he says, "If you want people to behave responsibly, and treat you with respect, then you treat other people that way." This credo has been translated into "Beliefs About the Treatment of Inmates" which are posted all over the institution to remind both staff and their clients of their responsibilities. They include the following:

- Inmates are sent to prison as punishment and not *for* punishment.
- Correctional workers have a *responsibility* to ensure that inmates are returned to the community no more angry or hostile than when they were committed.
- Inmates are *entitled* to a safe and humane environment while in prison.
- You must believe in man's *capacity* to change his behavior. . . .
- Be *responsive* to inmate requests for action or information. Respond in a timely manner and respond the first time an inmate makes a request. . . .
- It is important for staff to *model* the kind of behavior they expect to see duplicated by inmates. . . .
- There is an *inherent value* in self-improvement programs such as education, whether or not these programs are related to recidivism. . . .
- Staff *cannot,* because of their own insecurities, lack of self-esteem, or concerns about their masculinity, condescend or degrade inmates. . . .
- Inmate discipline must be *consistent* and *fair.*

Luther expects his charges to be responsible, and he holds them to a higher standard than found in most prisons. Those who meet the standards are rewarded. Weekly inspections are held in each cell block, and residents who score high receive additional privileges. Those whose disciplinary records are clean and who excel in the programs can earn their way to the "honor unit." And those who show consistently good behavior are allowed to attend supervised picnics on Family Day.

Dennis Luther is convinced that his methods will work in any prison, even those plagued by violence, overcrowding, and gangs. Many staff members feel the same way. They believe that McKean is a shining example of the difference that good management can make.

Source: Adapted from Robert Worth, "A Model Prison," *Atlantic,* November 1995, pp. 38–44.

Prison systems perform well if leaders can cope with the political and other pressures that contribute to administrative uncertainty and instability. In particular, management is successful when prison directors

1. Are in office long enough to learn the job, make plans, and implement them.
2. Project an appealing image to a wide range of people, both inside and outside of the organization.
3. Are dedicated and loyal to the department, seeing themselves as engaged in a noble and challenging profession.
4. Are highly hands-on and proactive, paying close attention to details and not waiting for problems to arise. They must know what is going on inside yet also recognize the need for outside support. In short, they are strangers neither in the cell blocks nor in the aisles of the state legislature.[29]

From this perspective, making prisons work is a function of administrative leadership and the application of sound management principles. DiIulio's research challenges the traditional assumption of many correctional administrators that "the cons run the joint." Rather, as the success of such legendary administrators as George Beto of Texas, William Fauver of New Jersey, Anna Kross of New York's Rikers Island, and William Leeke of North Carolina demonstrates, prisons can be managed so that residents can serve their time in a safe, healthy, and productive environment.[30]

CORRECTIONAL OFFICERS: THE LINCHPIN OF MANAGEMENT

Over the past 50 years, the correctional officer's role has changed greatly. No longer responsible merely for "guarding," the correctional officer is now considered a crucial professional who has the closest contact with those who are in prison and performs a variety of tasks. Officers are expected to counsel, supervise, protect, and process the individuals under their care. In many jurisdictions, hours are long, pay is low, entry requirements are minimal, and turnover is high. Given these conditions, why would someone want to enter this field?

Who Becomes a Correctional Officer?

The early criminal justice literature either ignored the prison officer or painted a picture of an individual with a "lock psychosis" resulting from the routine of numbering, counting, checking, and locking. Some prison studies gave the impression that officers were incompetent and psychologically inferior, performing the only job they could get. They were viewed as the primary opponents of rehabilitation. Who are the correctional officers? Have they been accurately depicted? What kind of person accepts a job that offers low pay and little hope of advancement?

Studies have shown that a primary incentive for becoming a correctional officer is the security of a civil service job. In addition, because most correctional facilities are located in rural areas, prison work is often better than other available jobs, and overtime or part-time work can often supplement the salary. Until the push of the last 50 years for greater professionalism among correctional workers, many guards joined the ranks because they had few employment opportunities. Today, because of the demand for well-qualified correctional officers, most states have given priority to recruiting quality personnel. Salaries differ from state to state. In addition to their salaries, most officers can earn overtime pay to supplement their base salary.

Over the past 50 years, federal courts, the 1964 Civil Rights Act, and affirmative action programs have dramatically changed the composition of the correctional officer force. How do increases in the number of minority and female officers shape the work environment among correctional officers? One study of more than 4,000 staff members employed in 98 prisons found that men and white employees believe that women and racial and ethnic minorities have better opportunities regarding career advancement. However, the analysis suggests that such opportunities do not actually differ between men and women, nor between whites and members of racial and ethnic minority groups.[31]

Women officers are no longer limited to only working in women's prisons. In state prisons an estimated 73,815 correctional officers (or 25 percent) are women. Many of these women work in adult male correctional facilities. In the Federal Bureau of Prisons, women make up 28.2 percent of the correctional staff.[32] Just as female police officers have often found themselves excluded from certain assignments and from full integration into the force, women who work in corrections have also had to deal with discrimination.

What do men in prison think of the female officers who supervise them? A Texas study examined inmate perceptions of whether female officers performed as well as men. Men serving sentences in minimum custody had a relatively low opinion of the ability of women to perform correctional officers' tasks. However, men in maximum custody had a high opinion of their competency and "felt that such officers would be calm and cool in problem situations."[33] Female officers are thought to exert a "softening" influence on the environment, making it more livable and less violent.

To prepare officers for prison work, most states require cadets to complete a preservice training program. In some states, preservice programs for officers resemble the military's basic training, with a similar emphasis on physical training, discipline, and classroom work. During the typical program, recruits receive training in a variety of topics, including report writing, communicable diseases, manipulation, self-defense, classification, and use of force. In states with large Latino populations, preservice training also includes basic Spanish. The length of preservice training varies from state to state. For example, cadets in Michigan receive 640 hours of training. In contrast, training for new recruits in West Virginia lasts 40 hours.[34]

However, the classroom work often bears little resemblance to problems confronted in the cell block or on the yard. Therefore, on completing the course, the new officer is placed under the supervision of an experienced officer. On the job, the new officer experiences real-life situations and learns the necessary techniques and procedures. Through encounters with the prison population and officers, the recruit becomes socialized to life behind walls and gradually becomes part of that subculture.

For most correctional workers, being a custodial officer is a dead-end job. Although officers who perform well may be promoted to higher ranks such as correctional counselor, few ever move into administration. However, in some states and in the Federal Bureau of Prisons, people with college degrees can move up the career ladder to management positions without having to advance through the ranks of the custodial force.

© Bill Armendariz - Headlight Photo

▲ *After finishing their training, new correctional officers in New Mexico take an oath of office that is administered by a district court judge.*

Role Characteristics

The public has traditionally characterized the correctional officer as a mindless and brutal custodian. This stereotype may be true for some guards, who seek order at any price and use violence to achieve it. The image of toughness "is exalted in the guard subculture, and is the public image (though not the private reality) adopted by most officers."[35] However, officers also have their own, private view of their work, which Robert Johnson defines in terms of human service. That is, officers help those who are incarcerated adapt to and cope with prison life in a mature way. Johnson believes that the human service role makes the officer's job more meaningful, rewarding, and ultimately less stressful.[36]

Correctional officers, then, are human service providers expected to engage in "people-work" within an organizational setting. Human service activities undertaken by officers include (1) providing goods and services, (2) acting as referral agents or advocates, and (3) helping with institutional adjustment problems.[37]

Officers are expected to help incarcerated individuals deal with their personal problems. However, because they work in a bureaucracy, they are also expected to treat clients impersonally and to follow formally prescribed procedures. Fulfilling these contradictory role expectations is difficult, and the long-term physical proximity of officers and members of the prison population heightens this difficulty. "Careers in Corrections" offers a closer view of the work of a federal correctional officer.

Although most prison work is thought to be routine, guarding is not an undifferentiated occupation. Officers supervise the cell blocks, dining areas, and shops; transport individuals to hospitals and courts; take turns serving on the disciplinary board; perch with rifles in guard towers; and protect the prison gates. Unscheduled activities range from offering informal counseling to breaking up fights to escorting incarcerated individuals on family visits in the community.

In most states the custodial staff is organized into ranks of officer, sergeant, lieutenant, and captain. Each sergeant supervises a complement of officers in one area of the prison—housing unit, hospital, and so on. The lieutenants are the main disciplinarians of the institution, conducting shakedowns, breaking up fights, and supervising the removal of individuals to segregation. The few captains on a staff have primarily administrative responsibilities and serve as the link between custodial personnel and the warden and other top management officials.

The military nomenclature and organization extend to the relationships among staff members. Officers are subject to inspections; in some institutions their superiors may give them "tickets" (disciplinary reports). When they are housed in quarters attached to the facility, rules govern their off-duty behavior. To guard against officers' smuggling contraband into the institution, the staff are subject to rigorous discipline. That the rules for and organization of the officers parallel those that govern the prison population is not lost on the correctional staff. "We're all doing time here," they say, "except that we're doing it in eight-hour shifts."

Job Assignments

LO 3

Discuss the different job assignments that correctional officers are given.

Officers may be assigned to one of seven job assignments. These vary according to their location within the institution, the duties required, and the nature of the contact with the incarcerated population. Assignments include (1) block officer, (2) work detail supervisor, (3) industrial shop and school officer, (4) yard officer, (5) administration building assignment, (6) wall post, and (7) relief officer.[38]

Block Officers Compared with other correctional staff, officers in the cell blocks have the closest contact with people serving prison sentences and the greatest potential for inducing behavior change in them. Work in the housing units of some prisons is dangerous because the officers do not carry weapons, are greatly outnumbered, and can be easily overwhelmed by the individuals under supervision.

In units housing 300–400 people, the five to eight block officers are responsible for moving their charges to the dining hall, work sites, infirmaries, and the like. They must oversee unit maintenance, watch for potential breaches of security, help incarcerated individuals with personal problems and answer their questions, enforce rules, ensure the safety of everyone in the prison, and carry out the warden's orders. As such, the cell block officer must have both management and leadership skills.

CAREERS IN CORRECTIONS

Correctional Officer: Federal Bureau of Prisons

Nature of the Work

Making up the largest part of the Federal Bureau of Prisons workforce, correctional officers maintain security and work with incarcerated individuals to prevent disturbances, assaults, and escapes. They monitor and supervise work among the prison population. They also report orally and in writing on inmate conduct and usually maintain a daily log of their activities. Officers are expected to respond to the needs of the incarcerated by directing them to appropriate educational, health, and release planning resources within the institution. About 14,000 officers work in federal correctional institutions.

Required Qualifications

To qualify for an entry-level position as a correctional officer, candidates must meet one of the following criteria required by the Federal Bureau of Prisons:

- A bachelor's degree in any field of study
- At least three years of qualifying work experience such as being a supervisor, teacher, counselor, probation/parole officer, or security guard
- A combination of undergraduate education and qualifying work experience that equals three years

As a condition of employment, new federal correctional officers must undergo 200 hours of formal training within the first year of employment. They must also complete 120 hours of specialized training at the Federal Bureau of Prisons residential training center at Glynco, Georgia, within 60 days after appointment.

Earnings and Job Outlook

The U.S. Department of Labor says that opportunities for correctional officers are expected to decline over the next decade. The annual salary for federal correctional officers ranges from $43,065 to $61,987.

More Information

See the Federal Bureau of Prisons website.

Work Detail Supervisors Prison residents provide labor for feeding, cleaning, and maintaining the institution. A portion of the custodial staff must supervise various work details connected with these tasks. The work area is more relaxed than the cell block. The work groups are small, the officer may engage incarcerated individuals in conversation, and esprit may develop as they work. This is especially true when people work a particular job and shift for an extended time. In the kitchen, laundry, welding shop, or hospital, for example, the inmate– officer relationship is analogous to worker and foreman in a factory.

Industrial Shop and School Officers Officers assigned to the industrial shops and prison school primarily have maintenance and security responsibilities. They work alongside civilians, such as shop supervisors, teachers, and counselors. Here the correctional officers act principally to ensure that members of the prison population who are supposed to be in the shops or school are there at the appointed time. The officers keep attendance, ascertain the whereabouts of absentees, attempt to prevent pilfering, and handle problems and complaints.

Yard Officers The yard is probably the most unstructured environment in the prison. Officers maintain a presence in the area, but they have no specific duties other than "supervising" people serving time in prison. They are expected to preserve order and to be concerned about security.

Administration Building Assignments Officers in the administration building have very little contact with the prison population and interact mainly with administrators, officials from the commissioner's office, and civilians. They provide security at the gates, supervise the visitors' room, and escort outsiders to offices. Because the appearance and behavior of these officers may color the general public's impression of the institution, they are selected carefully.

Wall Posts Officers assigned to the towers or along the walls have almost no contact with the prison population. With nothing but telephone and weapon, the tower guard is solitary and usually bored. Traditionally, these assignments have been reserved for new recruits and partially incapacitated veterans or for officers who do not get along with incarcerated individuals. In more-violent prisons, some correctional officers have sought to flee frustration and trouble by transferring from the cell blocks, dormitories, and yard to the safety of the towers.

Relief Officers Relief officers are assigned to a variety of tasks, depending on vacancies in the staff caused by vacations and sick days. Because they work for only short periods in any particular area of the institution, they do not develop close contacts with members of the prison population. Relief officers are experienced workers who can step into any assignment as needed.

Problems with the Officer's Role

Prison officers must deal with conflicting custodial and treatment goals. They are held responsible for preventing escapes, maintaining order, and ensuring the smooth functioning of the institution, yet they are also expected to counsel the individuals under their supervision and demonstrate an understanding attitude. Beyond the incompatibility of those roles lies the impossible rehabilitative ideal of treating each member of the prison population as an individual in a large people-processing institution. Officers must use discretion yet somehow be both custodial and therapeutic. Thus, if they enforce the rules, they may be considered too rigid, but if their failure to enforce rules threatens security, orderliness, or maintenance, they are not doing their job. They must do all of this in a tense environment where, on average, the ratio is one officer to five residents.[39]

The correctional officer is the key figure in the penal equation, the one on whom the whole system depends. Given the current emphasis on humane custody, the officer must be able to influence those serving time in prison positively.

Job Stress and Burnout

Recruiting and training qualified correctional officers is only half of the equation. Retention is also important. In some states, turnover among correctional officers is more than a third of the entire officer force. In comparison, the national average is about 16.2 percent.[40] High turnover requires correctional departments to allocate scarce resources to recruitment and training. An important part of the correctional administrator's job is to identify and deal with the problems that lead to turnover among prison staff.

Prison work can be stressful. After all, officers are responsible for supervising clients who are there against their will. Research shows that several factors contribute to job stress among correctional officers, including relationships with coworkers, departmental policies, and the length of time on the job.[41]

High stress levels can make managing the prison more difficult and can harm prison staff. For example, one study found that federal correctional officers with higher levels of job stress took more days of sick leave.[42] Stressed-out correctional officers experience more problems at home because they tend to displace their frustration onto their spouse or children. Heart disease, eating disorders, substance abuse, and other health problems are also linked to officers' stress levels.[43] Research shows that high stress levels can also lead to frustration, negative workrelated attitudes, and emotional exhaustion.[44] In short, job stress can lead to burnout.

The research on job burnout shows that prison work affects male and female correctional officers differently. For example, female officers are more likely than their male counterparts to develop a concern for incarcerated individuals' well-being,[45] and they more often express a sense of accomplishment and personal achievement in their work.[46] In the past, female officers experienced higher levels of job stress and burnout, compared with men. These new findings suggest that women are learning to cope better with the stressors associated with prison work. However, this is not to say that women no longer experience problems on the job. Research indicates that female correctional officers still face gender-based harassment. Such harassment contributes to job stress, burnout, and lack of organizational commitment among female officers.[47]

A correctional administrator's ability to reduce job stress and burnout can lead to many positive outcomes. For example, reducing officers' stress levels can result in significant financial savings. Fewer resources are expended in recruiting, hiring, training, and orienting new officers, as well as covering overtime costs to fill the shifts of officers taking stress-related sick time. Retaining experienced officers can also have a positive impact on safety levels; seasoned officers are the ones best equipped to deal with potentially explosive situations involving the prison population. Effectively reducing job stress is good for staff morale, and it demonstrates management's concern for employees. Stress and burnout are among the issues that correctional employees' unions address. Initiatives to address these factors can help foster positive relations between the prison administration and unions.[48] Correctional work is stressful, but prison administrators can reduce the negative effects of stress and burnout by addressing the issue head-on. One line of research that sheds light on ways that prison administrators can reduce job stress and prevent burnout among correctional employees focuses on the concept of organizational justice. More specifically, organizational justice is made up of two important elements. The first, *procedural justice*, relates to the fairness of organizational processes. For example, is the process used to hire new employees fair? How about the ways that supervisors handle promotions and terminations? These and other organizational processes will be judged procedurally just if they are believed to be fair by prison staff members. *Distributive justice*, the second element, focuses on organizational outcomes, such as pay increases, performance evaluations, and job assignments. It is believed that employees compare the work they do with the work of others and judge whether the outputs, such as pay, are fair. If so, then the outputs are judged to be distributively just. Eric Lambert and his colleagues have been able to show that prisons high in organizational justice experience fewer staff-related problems. For example, Lambert and his research team found that both procedural and distributive justice reduced job burnout and turnover intent among employees at a private maximum-security prison.[49]

LO 4

Analyze the negative consequences of boundary violations and job stress among prison staff.

Boundary Violations

When social distance breaks down, officers are more prone to commit **boundary violations**. In their study of a southern state prison system, James Marquart and his colleagues identified three types of violations: "general boundary violations," such as staff–inmate exchanges of material goods or written correspondence; "dual relationships," such as disclosing personal information to incarcerated persons or excessive flirting; and "staff–inmate sexual contact," which includes intercourse and other sexual acts.[50]

boundary violations
Behavior that blurs, minimizes, or disrupts the social distance between prison staff and imprisoned people, resulting in violations of departmental policy.

The situations surrounding prison employees' boundary violations varied. Some violations were characterized as "rescue situations" where prison staff members felt sorry for incarcerated individuals and violated departmental policy in an attempt to help them. Employees involved in these situations seldom expressed remorse for their actions. "Lovesickness situations" frequently involved dual relationship violations where staff members were romantically involved with a member of the prison population. Three-quarters of these situations involved female prison employees who viewed the person in prison as a friend or intimate partner. Although rare, some situations were "predatory," which usually involved male staff members abusing their power to obtain sexual favors from women in prison.[51]

Marquart and his associates found that 80 percent of violations involved dual relationships. These interactions always appeared consensual and were initiated primarily by prison residents. Often, these relationships involved the exchange of deeply personal letters with romantic overtones. In more than half of these cases, the employee was fired. The least common were general boundary violations (8 percent). Many of these cases probably go undetected by prison officials. These violations usually took place in newer prisons, which were staffed with inexperienced employees.

Incidents involving staff–inmate sexual contact (12 percent) are the most serious. Ninety-five percent of these cases resulted in the employee either being terminated or handing in his or her resignation. The following vignette is a typical example:

In a written statement, Officer Adams admitted that she loved inmate D and was involved in a personal relationship with D going on two years. Adams stated that she got to know D through casual conversations, which eventually grew into the present relationship. Adams also stated that she was in love with D and had discussed marriage and life together after he was released. Adams admitted that the two had engaged in acts of sexual intercourse in the chapel. She also admitted that she placed $350 in D's trust fund.[52]

Boundary violations among correctional staff are serious issues that prison managers must confront because such violations contribute to disorder, potentially jeopardize officers' safety, and can result in costly lawsuits. To prevent boundary violations, prison officials seek to recruit well-qualified cadets; they also design preservice training programs that emphasize the need for social distance and that prepare employees to defend themselves against manipulation (see "Do the Right Thing"). The many tasks that prison staff are asked to carry out may seem like an almost impossible mandate.

DO THE RIGHT THING

Shortly after beginning his career as an officer at Pinewood Correctional Complex, Vincent Fernandez was unexpectedly reunited with an old acquaintance, Larry Simpson, who was serving a five- to ten-year sentence. The two hadn't seen each other in years, but they shared many childhood memories from the time when Fernandez's sister babysat both of them. Early on, lessons from the academy stuck with Fernandez, and he tried to keep an appropriate level of social distance between himself and inmate Simpson.

Both men were assigned to the kitchen. As months passed, the personal bond between Fernandez and Simpson strengthened. They frequently reminisced about the "good ol' days," talked sports, and discussed the trials and tribulations of mutual friends. Over time Fernandez became increasingly puzzled about how Simpson could have ended up behind bars. Eventually, Fernandez was transferred to another prison approximately 180 miles away from Pinewood, which meant he would no longer have regular contact with Simpson. A few weeks later, while Fernandez was working at his new facility, a resident approached him and passed him an envelope. It was a letter from Simpson. Simpson explained that his wife had recently filed for divorce and that he was deeply troubled by the situation. He asked Fernandez to write back and advise him on what he should do. Officer Fernandez felt conflicted. On the one hand, he wanted to comfort and support his old friend. On the other, he knew that departmental regulations strictly prohibited written correspondence between staff and the incarcerated.

WRITING ASSIGNMENT: First, explain what you think Fernandez should do in this situation. Next, describe the potential harm of Fernandez corresponding with his childhood friend. Describe what you think would happen if Fernandez's sergeant found out he was communicating with Simpson. Finally, do you think that Fernandez should report Simpson for contacting him?

Use of Force

Although neither corporal punishment nor excessive force is permitted, correctional officers are allowed to use force in many situations. They often confront individuals who challenge their authority or are attacking others who are also incarcerated. Though unarmed and outnumbered, officers must maintain order and uphold institutional rules. Under these conditions, they feel justified in using force.

When may force be used, and how much is allowed? All correctional agencies now have formal policies and procedures with regard to the legitimate use of force. In general, these policies allow only levels of force necessary to achieve legitimate goals. Officers violating these policies may face a lawsuit and dismissal. There are five situations in which it is legally acceptable for officers to use force:

1. *Self-defense:* If officers are threatened with physical attack, they may use a level of force that is reasonable to protect themselves from harm.
2. *Defense of third persons:* As in self-defense, an officer may use force to protect a resident or another officer. Again, only reasonably necessary force may be used.
3. *Upholding prison rules:* If individuals refuse to obey prison rules, officers may need to use force to maintain safety and security. For example, if a person refuses to return to his or her cell, using handcuffs and forcefully transferring the person may be necessary.
4. *Prevention of a crime:* Force may be used to stop a crime, such as theft or destruction of property.

5. *Prevention of escapes:* Officers may use force to prevent escapes because they threaten the well-being of society and order within correctional institutions. Although escape from a prison is a felony, officials may not shoot the fleeing person at will, as in the past. Today, agencies differ in their policies toward escapees: Some limit the use of deadly force to prisoners thought to be dangerous, while others require warning shots. However, officers in Nebraska and Texas may face disciplinary action if they fail to use necessary deadly force. Although the U.S. Supreme Court has limited the ability of police officers to shoot fleeing people who are suspected of felonies, the rule has not been federally applied to correctional officers.[53]

Correctional departments have detailed sets of policies on the use of force. However, correctional officers face many challenges to their self-control and professional decision making. Incarcerated individuals often "push" officers in subtle ways such as moving slowly, or they use verbal abuse to provoke officers. Correctional officers are expected to run a "tight ship" and maintain order, often in situations where they are outnumbered and dealing with troubled people. In confrontational situations, they must defuse hostility yet uphold the rules—a difficult task at best.

Collective Bargaining

Collective bargaining for prison workers is a fairly recent phenomenon. The first prison employee unions with collective-bargaining rights were established in 1956 in Washington, D.C., and New York City. However, the movement did not register major gains until the 1970s, when many states passed laws permitting unionization by public employees.

The unions representing correctional staff include national public employee associations, such as the American Federation of State, County, and Municipal Employees (AFSCME), whose membership includes 85,000 correctional employees, and locally based state organizations, such as the California Correctional Peace Officers Association (CCPOA), with more than 39,750 members. These unions seek to increase wages and benefits, improve working conditions, combat efforts to privatize corrections, and lobby for legislation. Such lobbying efforts have not gone unnoticed among commissioners and other correctional administrators, who often solicit the help of organized labor at budget time.

Because members are public employees, the law prohibits them from striking. But work stoppages and "sickouts" have occurred, and several commissioners have lost their jobs under union pressure. Although previous work stoppages were typically settled within a short time, they made an impact beyond the specific issues in dispute.

The great expansion of the incarcerated population over the past decade has brought a more than 400 percent increase in the number of correctional officers nationwide. In some states this growth has greatly increased union power and resulted in more-formal relationships between employees and administrations: A labor contract stipulates the rights and obligations of each side, and wardens can no longer dictate working conditions. Thus, unionization has brought officers not only better work compensation and job security but also greater control over their work (see "For Critical Thinking"). Seniority now determines work assignments, and officers play a greater role in setting institutional policies. Nonetheless, many people fear that unions and pro-inmate groups may form alliances on certain issues to oppose the administration.

FOR CRITICAL THINKING

As was noted at the beginning of this chapter, much of the contraband inside prisons is brought in by staff. Recall that Josue Garza, a correctional officer, pleaded guilty to bribery for smuggling contraband into the Federal Correctional Complex in Forrest City, Arkansas.

1. Does job assignment have any influence over whether staff smuggle in contraband? Do some assignments that involve more interaction with incarcerated individuals, such as being a block officer, increase the chances that an officer will smuggle in banned goods?
2. What impact did Garza's actions have on the rest of the staff? Did it make their work more stressful? Did Garza's former colleagues become frustrated because the organization failed to detect the smuggling earlier? Did the incident affect how officers felt about the organization in general?
3. How should prison officer unions protect members who are accused of wrongdoing? Should they provide them with legal counsel? If an officer is convicted of a felony, should the union help file an appeal?

SUMMARY

1 Identify the principles used to organize the functioning of prisons.

Prisons are bureaucracies. Accordingly, three organizational principles help explain how they function. Supervision of subordinates follows the principle of unity of command—the idea that each employee reports to only one superior. Following the chain of command principle, each person receives orders from the superior immediately above him or her and issues orders to those immediately below. The span of control principle refers to staff members' ability to supervise only a limited number of subordinates.

2 Discuss the importance of prison governance.

Prison governance refers to the sound and firm management of the prison population and staff. Effective governance is challenging for correctional administrators because the power that officers possess to control incarcerated individuals is limited, officers have few legitimate rewards to provide individuals for good behavior, and available punishments do not represent much of a departure from the daily routines of those who are in prison. Correctional administrators who successfully govern their institutions do not rely on informal leadership to control the population, but rather apply sound management principles to prison operations.

3 Discuss the different job assignments that correctional officers are given.

Officers are assigned different jobs. For example, block officers work in housing units. They do not carry weapons and are greatly outnumbered. They answer questions, enforce rules, and watch for potential security breaches, among other things. Work detail supervisors are officers who oversee small groups of workers who feed the prison population, clean the cell blocks, and maintain the facility. Yard officers are not only expected to maintain a visible presence but also to preserve order and address security threats. The wall-post officer has little contact with anyone. These officers are assigned to the tower or are responsible for patrolling the wall (or fence). This job assignment can be very lonely and boring. Relief officers do not form close ties with incarcerated individuals but can fill in wherever needed.

4 Analyze the negative consequences of boundary violations and job stress among prison staff.

Boundary violations occur when the social distance between prison staff and individuals in prison breaks down and interpersonal relationships form in violation of departmental policy. These relationships can result in higher levels of prison disorder, can jeopardize officer safety, and can result in costly lawsuits. The negative consequences of job stress among prison staff are twofold. First, job stress contributes to turnover. When staff members resign their positions, new employees have to be recruited and trained, which drains resources from correctional budgets. Second, the physical effects of job stress on prison employees are quite serious and include heart disease, eating disorders, and substance abuse. Correctional officers who experience job stress also possess more-negative attitudes toward their work and report higher levels of emotional exhaustion.

KEY TERMS

administrative control theory (*p. 345*)
boundary violations (*p. 356*)
chain of command (*p. 340*)
coercive power (*p. 338*)
compliance (*p. 338*)
formal organization (*p. 338*)
inmate balance theory (*p. 344*)
line personnel (*p. 340*)
normative power (*p. 338*)
remunerative power (*p. 338*)
span of control (*p. 340*)
staff personnel (*p. 340*)
unity of command (*p. 340*)

FOR DISCUSSION

1. How have U.S. prisons changed since the big-house era? What do these changes mean for management?
2. As the superintendent of a prison, what sort of management problems do you face? Which people can help you solve them?
3. How is the idea of total power in the institutional setting defective?
4. As a correctional officer assigned to manage a 40-man housing unit in a maximum-security prison, what problems might you face? How would you handle them?
5. Would you like to be a correctional officer? What aspects of the job make it attractive? What aspects make it unattractive?

FOR FURTHER READING

Bright, Charles. *The Powers That Punish.* Ann Arbor: University of Michigan Press, 1996. An in-depth analysis of the powerful social and political forces that shaped the emergence and operations of one of the world's largest walled prisons—Michigan's Jackson State Prison—in the mid-twentieth century.

Conover, Ted. *New Jack: Guarding Sing Sing.* New York: Random House, 2000. Denied permission to write about the lives of correctional officers, Conover became one himself and served a year at Sing Sing. The book provides an officer's view of a maximum-security institution.

DiIulio, John J., Jr. *Governing Prisons.* New York: Free Press, 1987. Represents a major critique of the sociological view of prisons, arguing that effective governance by correctional officials is the key to maintaining good prisons and jails.

Jacobs, James B. *Stateville.* Chicago: University of Chicago Press, 1977. A classic study of a maximum-security prison that discusses the transformation process of Stateville Penitentiary from a pre-bureaucratic to a bureaucratic organization over a half-century.

Useem, Bert, Camille Graham Camp, and George M. Camp. *Resolution of Prison Riots.* New York: Oxford University Press, 1996. Drawing from the events of eight prison riots, the authors discuss effective strategies and procedures for dealing with collective protests.

NOTES

1 "Former Arkansas Officer Pleads Guilty to Bribery," *Arkansas Democrat-Gazette,* https://www.arkansasonline.com/news/2019/aug/24/former-officer-pleads-guilty-to-bribery/, August 24, 2019.
2 Gresham M. Sykes, *The Society of Captives* (Princeton, NJ: Princeton University Press, 1958).
3 "Former Prison Guard Sentenced to Prison for Smuggling Contraband," U.S. Attorney's Office, Eastern District Court of Arkansas, Department of Justice, https://www.justice.gov/usao-edar/pr/former-prison-guard-sentenced-prison-smuggling-contraband, July 30, 2020.
4 Amitai Etzioni, *A Comparative Analysis of Complex Organizations* (New York: Free Press, 1961), 3.
5 Ibid., pp. 5–7, 27.
6 Charles Logan, "Criminal Justice Performance Measures for Prisons," in *Performance Measures for the Criminal Justice System* (Washington, DC: U.S. Government Printing Office, 1993), 27–28.
7 James B. Jacobs, *Stateville* (Chicago: University of Chicago Press, 1977).
8 U.S. President's Commission on Law Enforcement and Administration of Justice, *Task Force Report: Corrections* (Washington, DC: U.S. Government Printing Office, 1967), 19–57.
9 Donald Clemmer, *The Prison Community* (Boston: Christopher, 1940); Sykes, *Society of Captives.*
10 John J. DiIulio, *Governing Prisons* (New York: Free Press, 1987), 13.
11 Ibid.; Bert Useem and Peter A. Kimball, *States of Siege: U.S. Prison Riots, 1971–1986* (New York: Oxford University Press, 1989).
12 Bert Useem and Michael D. Reisig, "Collective Action in Prisons: Protests, Disturbances, and Riots," *Criminology* 37 (November 1999): 735.
13 Ibid., p. 737.
14 DiIulio, *Governing Prisons,* p. 12.
15 Sykes, *Society of Captives,* p. 41.
16 Ibid., p. 49.
17 James J. Stephan, *Census of State and Federal Correctional Facilities, 2005* (Washington, DC: U.S. Government Printing Office, 2008), 5.

18 James Marquart, "Prison Guards and the Use of Physical Coercion as a Mechanism of Prisoner Control," *Criminology* 24 (1986): 347–66.

19 Sykes, *Society of Captives,* p. 53.

20 Stan Stojkovic, "Accounts of Prison Work: Corrections Officers' Portrayals of Their Work Worlds," *Perspectives on Social Problems* 2 (1990): 223.

21 Richard Korn and Lloyd W. McCorkle, "Resocialization Within Walls," *Annals* 293 (1954): 191.

22 Burt Useem and Ann M. Piehl, "Prison Buildup and Disorder," *Punishment & Society* 8 (2006): 87–115.

23 *Wolff v. McDonnell,* 94 S. Ct. 2963 (1974).

24 *Baxter v. Palmigiano,* 425 U.S. 308 (1976).

25 Edwin H. Sutherland and Donald R. Cressey, *Criminology* (Philadelphia: Lippincott, 1970), 536.

26 Dilulio, *Governing Prisons,* p. 237.

27 Hans Toch, "Trends in Correctional Leadership," *Corrections Compendium* 27 (November 2002): 8–9, 23–25.

28 Michael D. Reisig, "Rates of Disorder in Higher-Custody State Prisons: A Comparative Analysis of Managerial Practices," *Crime and Delinquency* 44 (April 1998): 229–44.

29 Dilulio, *Governing Prisons,* p. 242.

30 John J. Dilulio, *No Escape: The Future of American Corrections* (New York: Basic, 1991), ch. 1.

31 Scott D. Camp and Neal P. Langan, "Perceptions About Minority and Female Opportunities for Job Advancement: Are Beliefs About Equal Opportunities Fixed?" *Prison Journal* 85 (December 2005): 399–419.

32 Stephan, *Census of State and Federal Correctional Facilities, 2005,* Appendix Table 12; Federal Bureau of Prisons, Staff Gender, https://www.bop.gov/about/statistics/statistics_staff_gender.jsp, August 8, 2020.

33 Kelly A. Cheeseman, Janet L. Mullings, and James W. Marquart, "Inmate Perceptions of Security Staff Across Various Custody Levels," *Corrections Management Quarterly* 5 (Spring 2001): 44.

34 Editor, "Correctional Officer Education and Training," *Corrections Compendium* 37 (Fall 2013): 13–25.

35 Robert Johnson, *Hard Times: Understanding and Reforming the Prison* (Belmont, CA: Wadsworth, 2002), 201.

36 Ibid.

37 Lucien X. Lombardo, "Alleviating Inmate Stress: Contributions from Correctional Officers," in *The Pains of Imprisonment,* edited by Robert Johnson and Hans Toch (Prospect Heights, IL: Waveland, 1988), 285–97.

38 Lucien X. Lombardo, *Guards Imprisoned* (New York: Elsevier, 1981), 3.

39 Stephan, *Census of State and Federal Correctional Facilities, 2005,* Appendix Table 14.

40 MTC Institute, *Correctional Officers: Strategies to Improve Retention* (Centerville, UT: Author, 2010), 1.

41 Eugene A. Paoline, Eric G. Lambert, and Nancy Lynne Hogan, "A Calm and Happy Keeper of the Keys: The Impact of ACA Views, Relations with Coworkers, and Policy Views on the Job Stress and Job Satisfaction of Correctional Staff," *Prison Journal* 86 (June 2006): 182–205.

42 Eric G. Lambert, Calvin Edwards, Scott D. Camp, and William G. Saylor, "Here Today, Gone Tomorrow, Back Again the Next Day: Antecedents of Correctional Officer Absenteeism," *Journal of Criminal Justice* 33 (2005): 165–75.

43 Peter Finn, *Addressing Correctional Officer Stress: Programs and Strategies* (Washington, DC: U.S. Government Printing Office, 2000), 11–17.

44 Marie L. Griffin, Nancy L. Hogan, Eric G. Lambert, et al., "Job Involvement, Job Stress, Job Satisfaction, and Organizational Commitment and the Burnout of Correctional Staff," *Criminal Justice and Behavior* 37 (February 2010): 239–55.

45 Robert D. Morgan, Richard A. Van Haveren, and Christy A. Pearson, "Correctional Officer Burnout: Further Analyses," *Criminal Justice and Behavior* 29 (April 2002): 144–60.

46 Joseph R. Carlson, Richard H. Anson, and George Thomas, "Correctional Officer Burnout and Stress: Does Gender Matter?" *Prison Journal* 83 (September 2003): 277–88.

47 Victor Savicki, Eric Cooley, and Jennifer Giesvold, "Harassment as a Predictor of Job Burnout in Correctional Officers," *Criminal Justice and Behavior* 30 (October 2003): 602–19.

48 Finn, *Addressing Correctional Officer Stress,* p. 7.

49 Eric G. Lambert, Nancy L. Hogan, Shanhe Jiang, et al., "The Relationship Among Distributive and Procedure Justice and Correctional Life Satisfaction, Burnout, and Turnover Intent: An Exploratory Study," *Journal of Criminal Justice* 38 (January–February 2010): 7–16.

50 James W. Marquart, Maldine B. Barnhill, and Kathy Balshaw- Biddle, "Fatal Attraction: An Analysis of Employee Boundary Violations in a Southern Prison System, 1995–1998," *Justice Quarterly* 18 (December 2001): 906.

51 Ibid., pp. 900–05.

52 Ibid., p. 899.

53 Christopher R. Smith, *Law and Contemporary Corrections* (Belmont, CA: Wadsworth, 1999), ch. 6.

CHAPTER 14
Institutional Programs

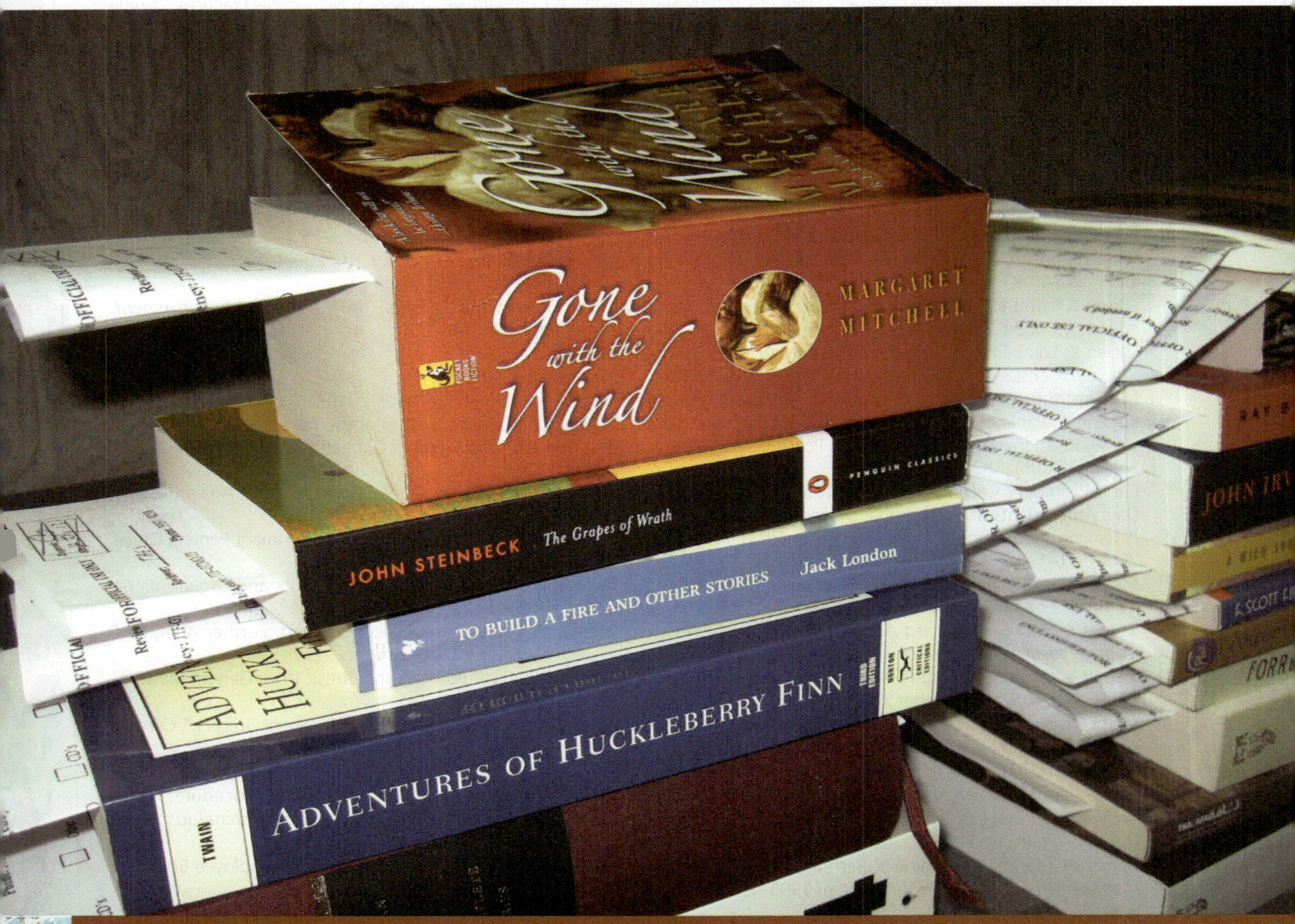

Carol Rosenberg/Miami Herald/MCT/Sipa USA

In a prison, one of the most dominant themes is "doing time." People in prison seek ways of passing time. One of the most common pastimes is reading, and that is why prison libraries are s important. In this prison library, it can be seen that almost every book has someone waiting to check it out.

WOLF BOYS IS A CELEBRATED NONFICTION ACCOUNT OF TWO MEXICAN AMERICAN TEENS FROM LAREDO, TEXAS, WHO GET INVOLVED WITH THE ZETAS DRUG CARTEL FROM MEXICO, ENDING UP AS MURDERERS WHO ARE DESPERATELY PURSUED BY LOCAL DETECTIVE ROBERT GARCIA, HIMSELF AN IMMIGRANT. Written by Dan Slater, the book is a harrowing tale of the chaos at the southern U.S. border, the depraved violence of drug gangs, the way lives get ruined by the drug trade, and—in the end—the apparent futility of the "drug war." Selected as a "Best Book of 2016" by the Chicago Public Library, it is considered by many people a "must read" for anyone who wants to be informed about today's debates on drugs, violence, and the border.

If you are incarcerated in Texas, however, you are not allowed to read it. It has been banned. The Texas Department of Criminal Justice Director's Review Committee put it on the blacklist before it was even published. According to a newspaper report, the Texas authorities were made nervous by a couple of sentences that described some techniques used to smuggle drugs into the United States.[1] So they banned the book, even though the moral of the true story seems unassailable: The two main characters are serving decades in the Texas prison system for their crimes. *Wolf Boys* joins a list of 15,000 books banned for people behind bars in Texas. The authorities have decided that for prison residents to read them is bad for the prison—so by definition it is bad for the people in the prison.

Prison censorship illustrates the paradox of prison programming. Free-world rights do not apply; security trumps everything. The effect can feel arbitrary and even self-defeating. Hidden goals often overcome manifest aims. Limitations in prison programs seem to make sense only as they are refracted through the prism of institutional prerogatives.

And most important, in the end all prison programs boil down to the same set of fundamentals: occupying time. There are other aspects of prison programs that matter, including developing skills, helping the prison run well, and—perhaps most importantly—giving hope. But no prison program can undermine the prison itself.

In this chapter we examine the wide variety of programs in today's prisons. We investigate the role that these programs play in prison life, and we evaluate their effectiveness. We draw conclusions about the value of various kinds of programs and how they fit into the modern prison context.

LEARNING OBJECTIVES

After reading this chapter, you should be able to . . .

1. Describe how correctional programs help address the challenge of managing time in the correctional setting.
2. Describe the ways that security acts as a constraint on correctional programs offered in institutional settings.
3. Explain the meaning of the "principle of least eligibility" and illustrate its importance.
4. Discuss the importance of the classification process and how "objective classification" works.
5. Describe the major kinds of institutional programs that are offered in correctional institutions.
6. Analyze recent developments in the field of correctional rehabilitation.
7. Describe the main types of correctional industries and explain how each works.
8. Explain the current pressures facing correctional programming policies.

LO 1

Describe how correctional programs help address the challenge of managing time in the correctional setting.

MANAGING TIME

The median time served in U.S. prisons is about 23.6 months.[2] Imagine where you were that many months ago and what you were doing. Now imagine that you had spent every day, every hour, since then living behind bars. Think of what you would have missed. Think, too, of how long the prison term would have seemed to have lasted—decades, an eternity.

The theme in prison, the one thread that links all people in prison, is time: "time in the joint," "doing time," "good time," "time left," "straight time." "How much time did you get?" "When do you come up for parole?" "What's your maximum release date?" Many cells prominently display calendars, and some occupants carefully mark the passing of each day. As Adam Gopnik once put it, "The basic reality of American prisons is not that of lock and key but that of lock and clock."[3]

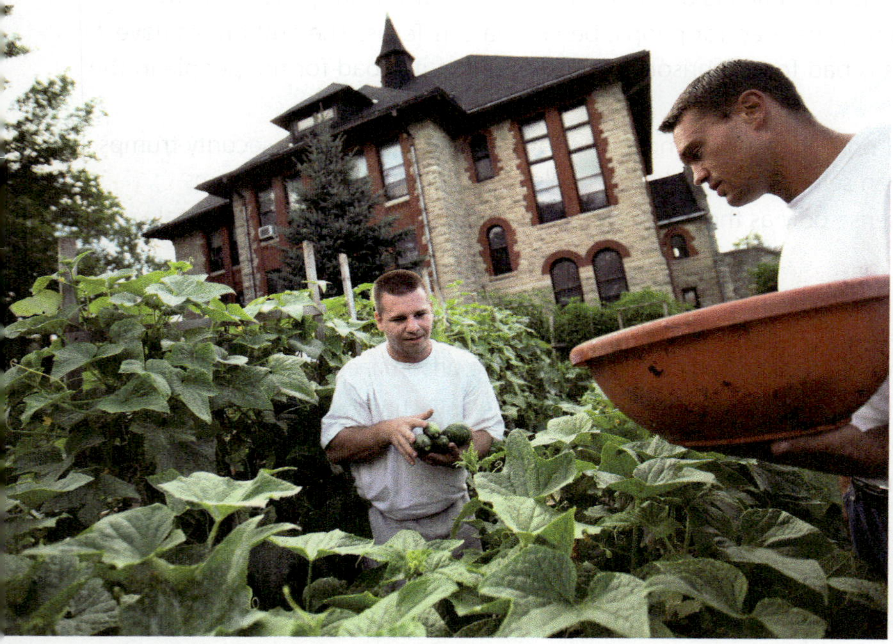

Courtney Perry/Minneapolis Star Tribune/MCT/Sipa USA

▲ *Harvesting cucumbers in the garden at the Minnesota Correctional Facility in Red Wing, Minnesota. Prisons often contain gardens, creating agricultural projects and supplementing the food service.*

Institutional programs mitigate the oppressiveness of time. They also provide opportunities for people in prison to improve their lives, whether the programs involve counseling, education, or merely recreation. When rehabilitation is a dominant correctional goal, the parole board sees participation in a treatment program as an indication of readiness for supervision in the community. Perhaps the main merit of programs is that they keep prison time from becoming dead time. When minutes crawl, the soul grows bitter.

Prison administrators use institutional programs to help manage time. Work assignments occupy the middle hours of the day, treatment and recreational periods are held before and after work assignments, and special programs (Junior Chamber of Commerce meetings, Bible study, Alcoholics Anonymous sessions) take up the remaining hours. Experienced administrators know that the more programs they offer, the less likely that boredom will translate into hostility toward the staff. The less cell time, the fewer tensions. As J. Michael Quinlan, a former director of the Federal Bureau of Prisons, once said, "It is absolutely the most important ingredient in managing a safe and secure institution to keep the inmates productively occupied, in either work or education or drug treatment or structured recreation."[4]

Administrators use prison programs as incentives for good behavior. People in prison know that when they break the rules, they will be denied access to programs, and this will make time go more slowly.

In this chapter we use the broadest possible definition of **prison program**: any formal, structured activity that takes people out of their cells and lets them do something. Programs range from group therapy sessions to chair-making factories, from baseball teams to reading groups. Some programs are designed to rehabilitate; others involve labor; still others deal with spiritual and medical needs. All prison programs serve the fundamental goal of managing time.

prison program Any formal, structured activity that takes people out of their cells and sets them to instrumental tasks.

There are five types of programs. The most debated programs attempt to provide rehabilitation. Many such programs attempt to improve job skills or education; others use psychological, behavioral, or social treatment to try to alter the propensity for criminal behavior. A second type provides medical services. A third type is industrial. Here, people in prison make various products. The fourth type involves daily maintenance of the facility. The fifth comprises recreational programs designed for physical fitness and involvement in positive activities.

Constraints of Security

LO 2

Describe the ways that security acts as a constraint on correctional programs offered in institutional settings.

No matter how beneficial a program is, it must not conflict with security. As the late criminologist Donald J. Newman once joked, even if a thousand evaluations showed that pole-vaulting was a valuable skill, it still would never be taught in prison.

Security requirements impinge on programs in a variety of ways. Whenever a program requires sharp tools or materials that could be fashioned into weapons, heavy security prevails. This is a particular problem for maintenance, but it also affects many industrial programs. Plumbing and electrical operations use knives, pipes, hammers, and wrenches—in other words, weapons. Common prison industries such as woodworking, welding, and auto repair likewise use potentially lethal objects and materials.

Security requires tool counts, searches, and detailed accounting of materials. Often, correctional officers conduct personal searches twice a shift and take inventories three or more times a day. The heavy emphasis on security has two important consequences. First, unceasing surveillance further demoralizes imprisoned people and sharpens their sense of captivity. People in prison are lined up and checked out so often that their consciousness of themselves as security risks is constantly reinforced. The most rudimentary tasks call for a level of control that exacerbates an already dehumanizing environment.

Second, security requirements make maintenance and industrial programs inefficient. Each time a tool is used, it must be signed out and signed in; each time material is obtained, paperwork must be done. Even coffee breaks are circumscribed by security measures. Captives are seldom the most industrious workers, and prison security measures do not improve efficiency.

Despite these negative effects, authorities strenuously support tight control of potentially dangerous items. A handcrafted knife or bludgeon is a potential serious physical risk to everyone in the prison. Yet these stringent security measures may not do much good; even in the most closely monitored prisons, shakedowns uncover hundreds of contrived weapons and other contraband. Many people in prison are ingenious at creating weapons, even out of such items as spoons and ballpoint pens. The only remedy—however weak—is unremitting vigilance. Some institutional programs are simply impractical because the equipment and materials are too easily misused.

Institutional security affects rehabilitative programs in a different way. In classroom work or counseling, everyone knows that all interactions are observed closely for security violations. Even in therapy, a person knows that any remark made to a staff member touching on a possible violation may lead to trouble. Here, too, security makes it difficult to bridge the gap between the keepers and the kept.

The effect of that gap on rehabilitative programs can be quite serious. Treatment success depends on the relationship between the therapist and the client. Many writers have analyzed this matter in some detail; a vivid description by Thomas Harris appears in his groundbreaking book *I'm OK, You're OK.*[5] Harris points out that patients in therapy find it difficult to solve their problems as long as they feel what he calls "not OK": dependent, untrustworthy, incompetent. Yet these are precisely the feelings that security practices in prisons arouse. Prison therapists must therefore fight the environment in which they work: It's not easy to make someone in prison feel OK.

In short, the prison environment adversely affects every program that operates in that setting. People in prison are often coerced into programs or treated as immature or dangerous by staff. Further, whatever people learn inside prison, no matter how sensible, is inevitably distorted by the fact that life inside has little resemblance to life outside, where those lessons are applied and their effectiveness judged. That is why inventive administrators try to make the prison resemble, as much as possible, the outside world into which the released must eventually go. Instead of being treated as docile subjects, people who are incarcerated are enabled to make many decisions about their daily lives and are held accountable for those decisions. For example, the Oregon Department of Corrections promotes an "accountability model" in which people in prison are expected to work, get training, and take responsibility for planning their lives after release.[6] Even in Texas, that bastion of "tough on crime" politics, there is active support for replacing the policies of the past with an emphasis on education and training. This kind of change is new in contemporary corrections, and it is too soon to know how well it will work and how much it will change the basic dynamic between the keepers and the kept.

Still, although the objectives of a prison program—to improve people's sense of themselves or to make them more vocationally competitive—may be laudable, achieving such objectives in a prison is difficult. The need for tight security dilutes the effectiveness of prison programs.

LO 3

Explain the meaning of the "principle of least eligibility" and illustrate its importance.

The Principle of Least Eligibility

Institutional programs are also affected by society's expectation that people in prison will not receive for free any extra services for which law-abiding citizens must pay. According to this **principle of least eligibility**, people in prison, having been convicted of wrongful behavior, should be the least eligible of all citizens for social benefits beyond the bare minimum required by law. Taken to its extreme, the principle would prohibit many institutional benefits for anyone in prison, such as educational courses and cosmetic surgery.

principle of least eligibility
The doctrine that people in prison ought to receive no goods or services in excess of those available to people who have lived within the law.

A good example is provided by what happened to the Pell Grant program in 1994. This program, which provides college loans with beneficial repayment rules, came under attack by Senator Kay Bailey Hutchison, a Texas Republican who argued that paying tuition for prison college courses used $2 million and displaced 100,000 law-abiding students. Even though her facts seemed patently wrong—any student who met Pell eligibility requirements, in prison or in the community, was given funds, and of the four million grants awarded that year only 23,000 went to people in prison—the uproar led Congress to deny eligibility for people in prison. To some it was simply unfair to allow people in prison access to free-world financial benefits. The principle of least eligibility thus outweighed the fact that taking educational programs while incarcerated is one of the surest ways to make a person less likely to return to prison.

Yet policy makers continue to recognize the value of education for rehabilitation: In 2016 the U.S. Department of Education undertook the Second Chance Pell Pilot Program to determine the impact of making Pell Grants available to college students inside prison. The results were widely seen as successful: 64 colleges enrolled over 10,000 incarcerated students and awarded over 600 diplomas in three years of operation.[7] Interest has grown in making students in prison permanently eligible for Pell grants, because postsecondary education is seen as such an economic win-win for the public and the imprisoned alike.[8] (For one college program, see "Education in Prison.")

FOCUS ON

CORRECTIONAL PRACTICE: Education in Prison

Michelle Jones always loved school; she graduated high school and started college before she went to prison. Once in prison, she continued her educational pursuits and enrolled in a college program offered by Ball State University and completed in 2014. Her love: history, which she embraced with a passion characteristic of a true scholar. She started auditing and attending graduate classes at Indiana University. She published academic paper on the history of corrections for women in Indiana, using original documents that people had forgotten existed and she also co-wrote a play on this research.

By 2016, the only step left for her was a PhD. From prison, she applied to the nation's most noted doctoral programs in History, American Studies, and African-American Studies. Based on her leadership in the women's prison, the role model she had become for others incarcerated there and through the advocacy of her faculty and state representatives. her sentence was modified 6 weeks that allowed her to start graduate school on time in 2017. Five of the nine schools she applied to accepted her. She also encountered puzzling resistance from some schools with expansive reputations for political liberalism. She learned that no matter how many awards a person might get—no matter how many achievements and accolades—to some people, the only thing that counts is the label, "felon."

She chose NYU where she is not only finishing a PhD in history, but also serves on the boards of the Lumina Foundation and the Urban Institute and has taken her place as a leading voice for others who face social discrimination and recrimination after leaving prison.

Hers is a truly remarkable story. The telling here glosses over years of heartbreak, hope, hard work, dedication, challenge, pitfalls, relationships, and growth. A woman of accomplishment, her trajectory has taken her to a place anyone would be proud of—but the road to get there is one many might find hard to believe.

She is now a spokesperson for her brothers and sisters behind bars who, as she knows, have unbelievable potential, if only there is an investment. She says, "I knew that I had come from this very dark place. But for 20 years, I was still interested in the world, and I didn't believe my past made me somehow cosmically uneducatable forever."

Education in prison is a door that, when provided in prison, offers a pathway for people whose talents are too often overlooked.

Offering people in prison any services of better quality than those available to law-abiding citizens is difficult for administrators to justify. The general public is often quite hostile to creative programming in prison, and this sentiment affects virtually all programs. The story is told of a miniature golf course in a Connecticut prison, built by prison labor during off hours and using no state funding. It was closed down after a newspaper reporter "exposed" it in a series of stories on the "country-club prison." The principle of least eligibility reflects a strong public ambivalence about correctional programming. Surveys consistently find that citizens support rehabilitation as part of correctional policy. Yet the public also does not want programs that seem to reward criminal conduct, and the public resists paying for programs that seem extravagant. Therefore, prison programs frequently represent only weak versions of free-society programs. If the prison offers job-training programs, they do not prepare people for positions in the most-prestigious or high-paying occupations. If the prison offers psychological services, they frequently take the form of group or individual counseling sessions rather than intensive therapy. Educational classes tend to be basic and barely remedial.

Consider the public reaction to a suit brought by a person incarcerated in an Oregon prison who forced the state to pay $17,000 for a sex-change operation. The surgery is considered a legitimate procedure in free society. This kind of medical care is often justified as crucial to the recipient's psychological or social well-being. However, many observers interpreted its being given free to a member of the least-eligible class as unwarranted exploitation of the public.

Together, the principle of least eligibility and the constraints of security can have a devastating impact on the quality of correctional programming for mental health. No wonder so many correctional programs are understaffed, underfunded, and operate with limited capacity.

LO 4

Discuss the importance of the classification process and how "objective classification" works.

CLASSIFICATION

People who wish to participate in prison programs face still another constraint: the procedures used to classify them with respect to security and programs. At Elmira Reformatory in the 1800s, Zebulon Brockway initiated a process of **classification** to group people in prison according to custody requirements and program needs. During the rehabilitation era, classification was important because treatment was based on a clinical assessment of needs. Although rehabilitation is less emphasized today, prison management still relies on classification, which now focuses on the potential for escape, violence, or victimization.

classification A process by which people in prison are assigned to different types of custody and treatment.

During incarceration, people in prison may be reclassified as they encounter problems or finish treatment programs. Classification also changes upon transfer to another institution or if clients are approaching release to the community.

The Classification Process

In most corrections systems, all those who are prison bound pass through a reception and orientation center where, over three to six weeks, they are evaluated and classified. In some states the center is a separate facility, but often each institution has its own reception center. Social scientists have likened reception and classification to a process of mortification. Much as the army recruit is socialized to military life by basic training, or the college student to a fraternity by pledge week, after sentencing there is a new status of "prison resident" that is shaped by the reception process.

This is a deliberately exaggerated "degradation ceremony" that seeks to depersonalize the inductee. Newcomers are stripped of personal effects and given a uniform, rule book, medical examination, and shower—in part to underscore that they are no longer free citizens.

In prison systems, classification consists mainly of sorting people based on age, seriousness of the offense, prior record, and prior institutional behavior. Such approaches

CAREERS IN CORRECTIONS

Correctional Treatment Specialist

Nature of the Work

Correctional treatment specialists, also known as case managers or correctional counselors, work in both jails and prisons. They may also be found in probation and parole offices, as well as in community correctional centers. In jails and prisons, specialists develop, evaluate, and analyze the program needs as well as individuals' progress. In addition, they plan education and training programs to improve job skills and provide counseling for coping, anger management, and drug or sexual abuse. As the end of the sentence nears, specialists work with parole agencies to develop release plans. Correctional treatment specialists working in parole and probation agencies perform many of the same duties as their counterparts in institutions.

Required Qualifications

In the Federal Bureau of Prisons and most state correctional agencies, entry qualifications for correctional treatment specialists require an undergraduate degree that includes 24 semester hours of social science, plus one year of professional casework experience or two years of graduate education in a social science or two years of a combination of graduate education and professional casework experience. Candidates must be 21 years old, have had no felony convictions, and possess strong writing skills. In some states, correctional treatment specialists are required to complete training sponsored by the department of corrections.

Earnings and Job Outlook

Employment of correctional treatment specialists is projected to grow as fast as the average for all occupations, according to the U.S. Department of Labor. Median annual wages of correctional treatment specialists are $54,290. The bottom 10 percent earn less than $36,370, and the top 10 percent earn $94,860. Higher wages tend to be found in urban areas.

More Information

See the *Occupational Outlook Handbook* website: Probation Officers and Correctional Treatment Specialists.

serve mainly as a management tool to ensure that people are assigned to housing units appropriate to their custody level (low, medium, high, segregation), separated from those who are likely to victimize them (for example, separating the young, slight, and timid from the tougher men), and grouped with members of their work assignment (for example, kitchen duty).

At institutions that emphasize rehabilitation, batteries of tests, psychiatric evaluations, and counseling are administered so that each person can be assessed for treatment as well as custody. Because treatment resources in most prisons are limited, they must be allocated to benefit those who most need them. The diagnostic process serves this purpose.

Different facilities make their classification decisions in different ways. Usually, prison staff present information from presentence reports, police records, and the reception process to a classification committee. The committee then makes program assignments and determines custody status based on procedures prescribed by the department of corrections and the institution's needs. ("Careers in Corrections" offers a closer view of the work of a correctional treatment specialist.) These committees often make their classification decisions primarily on the basis of the institution's needs. For example, enrollment in some treatment and training programs is limited, but demand is great. Thus, the few places in the electricians' course are already filled, and there is a long waiting list. On the other hand, large numbers of people are assigned to housekeeping tasks. See "Do the Right Thing" for more on the issues surrounding such institutional decisions. For years, classification decisions have been heavily criticized because they are based on stereotypes rather than diagnostic criteria to make program and classification assignments. Common stereotypes include members of racial or ethnic gangs, predators who demand everything from sex to cigarettes, weak victim types, and informers seeking protection. By fitting people into a stereotype, the staff routinizes classification, thereby serving staff and organizational needs. Classification results often reflect these stereotypes in ways that may, in the end, have little to do with the person's eventual adjustment to prison.

DO THE RIGHT THING

Members of the classification committee examined the case folders of those who would appear before them. This morning, 10 new admissions to prison were to be classified as to housing and program. Each folder contained basic information about the person's education, prior employment, crime, sentence, and the counselor's evaluation. In the small talk before the first new admission arrived, Ralph MacKinnon, the chief of the classification unit, warned the other members that the computer-programming class was filled and the waiting list was long. However, there was a great need for workers to make mattresses for state institutions.

"But Ralph, some of the guys trying to learn computer programming just can't hack it," said counselor Michael Harris. "I've got a man coming before us who was a math major in college and has already had some computer experience. He would greatly benefit from the extra training."

"That's fine, Mike, but we can't let someone jump ahead, especially when the mattress factory needs workers. I promised Jim Fox we would get him some help."

"But shouldn't we put people into programs that would help them when they get out?" responded Mike.

WRITING ASSIGNMENT: If you were on the classification committee, what would you do? Write a memo to the warden explaining your position.

Objective Classification Systems

Reformers point out that the courts require systems of classification to "be clearly understandable, consistently applied and conceptually complete." This suggests the need for new methods of classification to be implemented, with a means of redress for irregularity.[9]

To meet this need, reformers have developed new predictive and equity-based systems that seek to make classification decisions more objective. *Predictive models* are designed to classify with respect to risk of escape, potential misconduct in the institution, and future criminal behavior. Clinical, socioeconomic, and criminal factors (such as previous prison escapes) are given point values, and the total point score determines the security level. *Equity-based models* use only a few explicitly defined legal variables reflecting current and previous criminal characteristics.

For both types of objective classification systems, a staff member determines an appropriate custody level by entering relevant data, adding up total points for factor scores, and applying numerical criteria to indicate classification. For example, people who score 25 or above might be sent to maximum security, those who score 15 or below to minimum security, and the remainder to medium security. Such variables as race, employment, and education are not used because they are seen as unfair. However, in reality the two models frequently use similar variables for classification, the main difference being that predictive models use statistical techniques to identify the factors that are used and the weights they receive.

Objective systems are more efficient and cheaper than other systems because line staff can be trained to administer and score the instrument without help from clinicians and senior administrators. They also lead to more-consistent classification decisions because the same criteria are applied to every new prison admission.

A problem with all classification systems is that many states "overclassify," placing people in higher custody levels than appears necessary, simply because more high-security space is available. As a result, treatment assignments for which people in maximum-security prisons are not eligible (such as work release) are simply unavailable to the vast majority. This classification policy can have further negative consequences because many privileges are linked to classification level. In Colorado, for example, early release from prison is restricted to people classified as minimum security. In many states the amount of good time that can be earned is tied to security classification. Further, release on parole often depends on a record of successful participation in treatment or educational programs. People often have difficulty explaining to the parole board that they really did want to learn a skill but were given no opportunity to do so because of their high-level security classification.

LO 5

Describe the major kinds of institutional programs that are offered in correctional institutions.

REHABILITATIVE PROGRAMS

Rehabilitative programs aim at reforming a person's behavior. Some people argue that imprisonment is so painful that it is itself reformative: People should want to change their ways to avoid repeating the experience. The reformative power of prison itself is often called a "special deterrence effect." But many scholars contend that imprisonment by itself is not reformative enough, that the person's prison activities must also be reformative. There is much dispute about which rehabilitative programs should be offered and emphasized, whether psychological, behavioral, social, educational and vocational, substance abuse, sex offender, or religious programs.

Psychological Programs

In prison, psychological programs seek to treat the underlying emotional or mental problems that led to criminality. Of course, this assumes that such problems are indeed the primary cause of most criminality—or even that the concept of mental illness makes sense. These assumptions underlie the medical model, discussed in Chapter 3. However, critics have challenged this model repeatedly and vigorously.

In his famous critique, the psychiatrist Thomas Szasz questioned the applicability of the medical model used for physical ailments to the kinds of "problems in living" commonly called mental illness.[10] The notions of diagnosis, prognosis, and treatment are irrelevant to these problems, and they mislead people who try to deal with them. Other critics of mental health treatment in prisons take a much less radical stance: They say that mental illness is an inadequate explanation of criminal behavior. Many additional factors enter a decision to behave criminally: opportunity, rational motivation, skill, acquaintances, anger. No one can demonstrate convincingly that some mental problem underlies all or even most of such decisions. Recent studies of prison and jail populations find rates of mental health problems that are much higher than among the general population; however, those affected still represent only a minority of the correctional population.

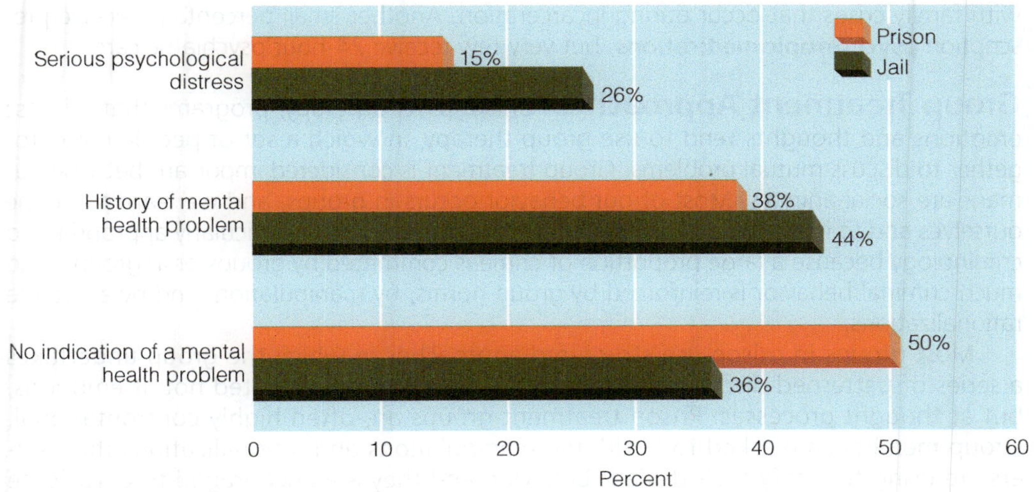

FIGURE 14.1 Mental Health Problems Among the Confined

Not only is mental illness prevalent among those under correctional authority, but people in jail have more mental health problems than people in prison.

Source: Jennifer Bronson and Marcus Berzofsky, *Indicators of Mental Health Problems Reported by Prisoners and Jail Inmates, 2011–2012* (Washington, DC: Bureau of Justice Statistics, June 2017), 1.

The lack of consensus on diagnoses of mental illness indicates some of the drawbacks in the general concept that mental illness underlies much criminal behavior (see Figure 14.1). For example, trained psychiatrists disagree on the diagnosis of patients' mental problems as often as half of the time. If the experts cannot agree on the nature of an "illness," then perhaps the idea of the "illness" itself has no merit. Nevertheless, there is evidence that going to prison makes a person's long-term mental health prospects worse, even though while people are in prison, their mental health can actually improve because of the access to services.[11]

Psychotherapeutic Approaches The unreliability of mental illness diagnosis may be one reason why treatments have been so ineffective. Robert Martinson's groundbreaking review of treatment programs, discussed in Chapter 3, provides perhaps the starkest conclusion: With few exceptions, rehabilitative efforts had no appreciable effect on recidivism.[12] Martinson was referring to a wide variety of programs, but his conclusion applied particularly to programs designed to improve emotional or psychological functioning.

The psychological approach is problematic in prison. Most experts would agree that **psychotherapy**, or "treatment of the mind," has narrow prospects for success even with motivated, voluntary, free patients. Free patients voluntarily enter a financial contract with the therapist for help; either party is free to terminate the agreement at any time. Because the client is the purchaser, it is easy to see why the therapist keeps the client's interest foremost during the treatment process.

psychotherapy In generic terms, all forms of "treatment of the mind"; in the prison setting, this treatment is coercive in nature.

In prison, society purchases the therapist's services. The interests of the purchaser assume more importance to the therapist than do those of the client—in this case, the person in prison. This turns the accepted practices of most therapy upside down. The centerpiece is not the person in prison; instead, it is society's desire that that person develop a crime-free lifestyle. (See "Myths in Corrections.")

Because of the many problems with prison psychotherapy, programs that address emotional health from this frame of reference have become less common in recent years. Today most prison counselors do not practice psychotherapy. While a few incarcerated people receive some sort of counseling, most of this prison treatment tends to focus on concrete problems that people face in adjusting to the prison environment or in dealing

psychotropic medications Drug treatments designed to lessen the severity of symptoms of psychological illness.

MYTHS in Corrections

Prison and Rehabilitation

THE MYTH: Judges should send people to prison to be treated in rehabilitation programs.

THE REALITY: Rehabilitation programs offered in the community for people on probation or parole are twice as effective at reducing recidivism as are those same programs offered in prison.

Source: P. Gendreau, S. A. French, and A. Taylor, *What Works (What Doesn't Work)*, rev. ed., Monograph Series Project (Ottawa, Ontario: International Community Corrections Association, 2002).

with family crises that occur during incarceration. Another small percentage receive prescription **psychotropic medications**, but very few receive 24-hour psychiatric care.

Group Treatment Approaches

Unlike psychotherapy, programs that address emotions and thoughts tend to use group therapy, in which a set of people come together to discuss mutual problems. Group treatment is considered important because humans are social animals. Most of our behavior occurs in groups, and we learn to define ourselves and to interpret our experiences in groups. This fact is particularly appropriate to criminology because a large proportion of crime is committed by groups or in groups, and much criminal behavior is reinforced by group norms, by manipulation, and by elaborate rationalizations.

Most groups in prison use structured approaches in which the group undertakes a series of patterned discussion topics or activities that are targeted not at emotions, but at thought processes. Prison treatment groups are often highly confrontational. Group members are asked to "call" the manipulations and rationalizations that others are using to justify their deviant behavior, and they are encouraged to participate wholeheartedly in the process. Four of the most common group approaches are reality therapy, confrontation therapy, transactional analysis, and cognitive skill building. Group treatment approaches that are based on cognitive skill building have generally proven effective.[13]

Reality therapy has a simple core tenet: People's problems decline when they behave more responsibly. Things get difficult when people fail to behave in ways consistent with life's realities. The therapist's role is to return the client consistently and firmly to the real consequences of his or her behavior, with particular attention to the troubles that follow inappropriate actions. Reality therapy is popular in corrections for three reasons. First, it assumes that the rules which society sets for its members are inescapable. Second, its techniques are easy for staff to learn. Third, the method is short-term and thus highly adaptable to prison.

In **confrontation therapy**, a professional group leader encourages group members to confront one another's rationalizations and manipulations, which are common to criminal thoughts and actions. These sessions can become quite vocal, and people trying to defend themselves can get angry in reaction to aggressive accusations by peers. The therapy aims at pressuring participants to give up their manipulative rationalizations and accept responsibility for the harms their crimes have caused.

Transactional analysis focuses on the roles, or ego states, that people use with others. The aim is to help people realize that their problems commonly result from approaching the world as an angry Parent or weak Child rather than as a responsible Adult. The therapist's role is largely that of teacher; he or she spends much time explaining the concepts of transactional analysis and showing the client how to use them in analyzing his or her own life. Like reality therapy, transactional analysis is considered well suited to corrections because it is simple, straightforward, and short-term.

Cognitive skill building focuses on changing the thought patterns that accompany criminal behavior. Advocates argue that antisocial patterns of reasoning are developed which cause someone to believe that criminal behavior makes sense. To replace these thought patterns, people need to learn new skills and techniques for day-to-day living. The group leader uses a variety of procedures to teach these new skills, including role-playing and "psychodramas," which re-create emotionally stressful past occurrences. The aim of the cognitive approach is to teach people new ways to think about themselves and their actions. Studies show that cognitive programs work when they reflect the gender and culture of the people who are receiving treatment, but they fail if they are not culturally appropriate or are otherwise poorly implemented.[14]

reality therapy Treatment that emphasizes personal responsibility for actions and their consequences.

confrontation therapy A treatment technique, usually done in a group, that vividly brings people face-to-face with their crime's consequences for the victim and society.

transactional analysis Treatment that focuses on patterns of interaction with others, especially patterns that indicate personal problems.

cognitive skill building A form of behavior therapy that focuses on changing the thinking and reasoning patterns that accompany criminal behavior.

behavior therapy Treatment that induces new behaviors through reinforcements (rewards and punishments), role modeling, and other active forms of teaching.

Behavior Therapy

Correctional **behavior therapy** postulates that the differences between people labeled *deviant* and *nondeviant* lie not within the individual but in that person's responses to problems in the environment. According to this idea, what needs reformation is not the thinking or emotions, but behavior. The method seeks to change behavior directly by identifying and altering the environmental conditions that promote problem behavior. The assumption is that behavior is learned and has consequences. It can be unlearned if the consequences are replaced with a more rewarding payoff.

The target of behavior therapy in this case is not criminality per se but the variety of problem behaviors that surround a criminal lifestyle: verbal manipulation and rationalization; deficiency in social skills, such as conversation; inability to control anger and frustration; and so on. Obviously, such behavior can make it difficult to keep jobs, avoid conflict, and handle disappointment. The underlying belief is that criminal behavior is typically related to such crucial personal experiences.

Social Therapy

The broad term **social therapy** is applied to certain programs (often referred to as milieu therapy or positive peer culture) because they seek to develop a prosocial environment within the prison to help develop noncriminal ways of coping outside. They are based on the idea that people learn lawbreaking values and behaviors in social settings from peers to whom they attach importance. To permanently alter these values and behaviors, the peer relationships and interaction patterns must be changed.

social therapy Treatment that attempts to create an institutional environment that supports prosocial attitudes and behaviors.

This approach assumes that true change occurs when a person begins to take responsibility for the social climate within which he or she lives. All actions are directed toward developing a prison culture that promotes a law-abiding lifestyle with appropriate social attitudes. Such a program requires significant shifts in institutional policy to support a prosocial institutional climate. Thus, (1) institutional practices must be democratic rather than bureaucratic, (2) programs must focus on treatment rather than custody, (3) humanitarian concerns have priority over institutional routines, and (4) flexibility is valued over rigidity. The creation of such a **therapeutic community** has found some success in evaluation studies, but they are not guaranteed to work, and some studies have shown less than promising results.[15]

therapeutic community A prison environment where every aspect of the prison is designed to promote prosocial attitudes and behavior.

Clearly, it is exceedingly difficult to turn a prison into a therapeutic community. The approach has been criticized as both inherently impractical and ineffective in reducing crime. How can a prison, intentionally established as a degrading, painful, intrusive setting, be transformed into a caring, supportive environment? How can the keepers, trained to control the kept but vulnerable to their threats, ever give up meaningful institutional authority to people confined in prison without risking their own security and that of the institution?

Educational and Vocational Programs

One of the oldest ideas in prison programming is to teach a skill that can help incarcerated people get a job upon release. Educational and vocational programs provide much to recommend their importance in prison. People in prison constitute one of the most undereducated and underemployed groups in the U.S. population. The formerly incarcerated have limited capability to succeed as wage earners in modern society. Many people believe that criminal behavior stems from this kind of economic incapacity, and they urge the wide use of educational and vocational programs to counter it (see "For Critical Thinking").

FOR CRITICAL THINKING

"Education in Prison" (see p. 361) tells Michelle Jones' story. She is certainly a prison education success story, but she is far from typical; prison education does not send many of its students to places like NYU. Moreover, prison educational programs are not easy to mount and not always successful.

1. Identify characteristics of the prison and its environment that make educational programs more difficult to provide than is the case in the free world. What can be done to overcome these problems? Are there any advantages to the prison setting for providing education? Explain your answer.
2. Some people say the problem with prison educational programs is that the prison is a difficult place to try to educate people. Others say the main problem is the deficits of those who attend the classes. What do you think, and why?
3. A typical person behind bars who needs educational programs also needs vocational training and other forms of treatment, such as drug abuse treatment, to reduce the risk of new criminality. What should the priority be: education, vocational training, or some other risk-reducing treatment? Why?

Educational Programs Nearly two-thirds of people in prison have failed to graduate from high school; two-fifths do not even have a general equivalency diploma (GED). Thus, it is not surprising that programs offering academic courses are among the most popular in today's corrections system. Waiting lists for classes are increasing.

In many systems, everyone who has not completed eighth grade—one person in seven, nationally—is assigned full time to the prison school. Many programs provide remedial help with basic reading, English, and math skills. They also permit people in prison to earn a GED. As we have seen, some institutions offer courses in cooperation with a college or university, although funding for such programs has come under attack. Recall that the Comprehensive Crime Control Act of 1994 bans federal funding in prison for postsecondary education. Some state legislatures have passed similar laws under pressure from people who argue that tax dollars should not be spent on the college tuition of people in prison when law-abiding students must pay for their own education.

Prison educational programs face several practical problems. The ability of many people in prison to learn is often hampered by a lack of basic reading and computational skills. Moreover, research has increasingly shown a link between learning disabilities and delinquency; many have experienced disciplinary as well as academic failure in school. Thus, prison education sometimes must cope with limited academic skills and attitudes poorly suited to learning.

Other factors exacerbate the problems of prison education. The people in the classes are usually well beyond the age associated with their current educational attainment, such as a 29-year-old performing at a sixth-grade level. Few available texts are appropriate for such adults. Imagine a 32-year-old two-time robber with self-inflicted tattoos struggling through a passage in a second-grade reader about Johnnie and Susie learning to bake cookies. The sheer inappropriateness of the material to the age and interests drives many away from remedial schooling.

How successful is prison education as a rehabilitative program? There have been so many studies of education in prison that some researchers have looked at the average affect these studies find. They find that education programs reduce recidivism rates, on the average, by between 28 percent and 43 percent, making this approach among the most effective for any in-prison program.[16] The effects are even greater for participation in college-level programs. The report illustrates some of the largest effects ever found using the meta-analysis method. More recent studies have confirmed that engagement in all levels of education, from GED to college, is associated with lower rates of in-prison disciplinary charges as well as lower rates of recidivism after release from prison.[17]

vocational rehabilitation Prison programming designed to teach cognitive and vocational skills to help people find employment upon release.

Vocational Programs **Vocational rehabilitation** programs attempt to teach a marketable job skill. However, these programs also suffer from the principle of least eligibility: Training often centers on less-desirable jobs in industries that already have large labor pools—barbering, printing, welding, and the like. Other problems also plague prison vocational programs. Often, participants are trained on obsolete or inadequate equipment because prisons generally lack the resources to upgrade. A story is told about a popular print shop apprenticeship program at one large state reformatory that provided training on presses donated by the local newspaper. People who went through the training learned, upon parole, that their "new" skill was unmarketable because the machinery they had learned to operate was so inefficient that the newspaper had junked it (which was why it had been donated).

People in prison also sometimes lack the attitudes necessary to obtain and keep a job—punctuality, accountability, deference to supervisors, cordiality to coworkers. Further, they may lack the ability to locate a job opening and successfully interview. Therefore, most need to learn not only a skill but also how to act in the formal work world. The prison regimen, which tells people what to do and where to be each moment from morning to night, can do little to develop attitudes needed outside the walls.

civil disabilities Legal restrictions that prevent many former prison residents from voting and holding elective office, engaging in certain professions and occupations, and associating with others who are under correctional authority.

Yet another problem is perhaps the most resistant of all. The **civil disabilities** that attach to the formerly incarcerated, discussed in more detail in Chapter 16, severely limit job mobility and flexibility. Occupational restrictions force people into low-paying, menial jobs, which may lead them back to crime. In one state or another, barred occupations include nurse, beautician, barber, real estate salesperson, chauffeur, worker where alcoholic beverages are sold, cashier, stenographer, and insurance salesperson. Unfortunately, some prison vocational programs actually train people for jobs they can never have. Further, the stigma of being formerly incarcerated is either difficult or impossible to overcome.

Despite their detractors, prison vocational programs receive considerable support from many experts because poor job skills seem so closely tied to the problems faced upon release into the community. The additional income and taxes produced by people who have received vocational training in prison may actually offset the cost of the programs and may also reduce recidivism. Even with all these advantages, prison educational and vocational programs are underused. A recent survey of correctional programs in 43 states, sponsored by the Bill and Melinda Gates Foundation, found that only 6 percent of the people who were incarcerated in those states participated in postsecondary educational or vocational training.[18]

Substance Abuse Programs

The link between crime and substance abuse is strong. About half of all people facing charges test positive for drugs at the time of arrest, and most of these arrestees need some form of drug treatment. To serve this large clientele, substance abuse treatment programs have grown rapidly in all parts of the criminal justice system, working with millions of correctional clients on any given day.

For years, people have questioned the effectiveness of drug treatment programs for habituated people in the justice system. Follow-up studies routinely found high rates of rearrest for those leaving these programs, and most participants had instances of relapse as well. The failure of these programs to eradicate drug use among participants led many to believe that drug treatment did not work. However, more-recent research has demonstrated that even though failure rates are high, drug treatment can be a valuable, cost-effective crime-reduction strategy.

One reason for this reinterpretation of drug treatment programs is that different researchers frame the question differently. Instead of asking simply whether there is a relapse, some researchers ask a more complex evaluation question: Do program participants return to drugs and crime at lower rates than do those who were not in the program? The usual answer is yes.

This more complex question stems from recognition of how difficult it is to overcome drug addiction. A small rate of abstinence among program participants may represent a big difference in drug use and crime compared with nonparticipants. Even participants who eventually fail often spend more time drug-free on the streets before relapse, and their new crimes are less serious. These effects can result in significant savings in criminal justice costs and the losses of victims, and long-term reductions in recidivism. Today, the most effective substance abuse treatment programs share several components:

1. The program occurs in phases, with a residential treatment phase lasting between 6 and 12 months.
2. During residential treatment, participants gradually earn privileges in a therapeutic treatment setting.
3. Multiple treatment modalities are used, including individual psychotherapy, group therapy, and vocational rehabilitation.
4. Residential staff and community officials closely coordinate plans for release.
5. Treatment continues after release in the form of therapy groups augmented by drug testing.[19]

Sex Offender Programs

Many correctional officials believe that people convicted of sex crimes represent the most difficult group for correctional treatment. There are several reasons for this. First, there are different types of people convicted of sex crimes: Crimes vary from exhibitionism to rape to child molesting to incest. The treatment needs of one group may not correspond to the needs of another. Yet treatment programs often group all of those who have been convicted of sex crimes together, perhaps because the public and prison officials tend to do so as well.

Second, some people with sex crime histories are far more committed than others, emotionally and personally, to the kind of sexual deviance they practice. Those who are deeply devoted to a version of sexual abnormalcy may find it harder to turn away from their desires and thus may resist treatment more. This may also be why some of these types have high recidivism rates.

Third, providing treatment for this group in prison settings is sometimes problematic. Often, they are targets of harassment, so they are inclined to maintain a low profile. Attending treatment programs can call attention to one's status, leading to trouble with others. The incentives to deny problems with sexual deviance while incarcerated are quite substantial. This is one of the reasons that community-based treatments often do better with this group than prison-based programs.[20] Various kinds of treatments have been tried in prison settings, with varying degrees of success.[21] Relapse-prevention approaches attempt to teach ways to foresee inappropriate arousal before it occurs and how to prevent acting on those feelings. Interpersonal strategies work on social skills, victim awareness, and sexual identity. Other approaches try to break through patterns of denial and rationalization or to build skills in anger control and impulse control. Many treatment programs employ all of these strategies in the hopes that they will reinforce one another and one will eventually work. Treatment programs focus on helping the person to overcome the following:

- Deviant sexual arousal, interests, or preferences
- Sexual preoccupation
- Pervasive anger or hostility
- Emotion management difficulties
- Self-regulation difficulties, or impulsivity
- An antisocial orientation
- Pro-offending attitudes, or cognitive distortions
- Intimacy deficits and conflicts in intimate relationships[22]

A growing body of literature suggests that some treatments for this group reduce recidivism rates. One comprehensive review of treatment programs for people convicted of sex-related crimes concluded that they had a recidivism rate as low as one-half that of people convicted of other types of crimes and that treatment programs can reduce the recidivism rate by about one-fourth, boding well for rehabilitation.[23] Because of the important stake the public has in effective treatment for people convicted of sex crimes, experimentation with new strategies for this group will almost certainly continue.

Religious Programs

Religious programs seem substantially different from the categories discussed thus far. For most of prison history, such programs were a mainstay of prison services but were thought to be an offshoot of prison life rather than a mainstream treatment program. Recently, interest in religious strategies for social problems has grown. People who study crime have noted an emerging literature suggesting that people who are more oriented toward religion are less likely to engage in crime. For some scholars and many activists, religion is seen as an exciting new way to help people change their lives. At least five states—Texas, Kansas, Minnesota, Florida, and Iowa—have opened new prison treatment facilities with a central philosophy of religious teaching. These initiatives have received a lot of attention: Advocates hope that religious programs will reduce recidivism, whereas critics worry about using tax dollars to promote religion. While the courts have ruled that compulsory involvement in religious programs violates the First Amendment,[24] voluntary religious programming stands on solid constitutional ground.[25]

Because the First Amendment guarantees the right to belief and practice, religious programs are available to everyone in prison. The two main religions in prison are Christianity and Islam, but U.S. prisons host the same array of faiths that free society does. Religious programs in prisons also demonstrate regional differences that are similar to those found in free-society religious practices. For instance, in the West and Southwest, Native Americans may fast and sit in sweat lodges, spending up to a day in quiet contemplation. In the Northeast and Southwest, daily Catholic masses are common. In prisons in the southern "Bible Belt," religious programs tend to be evangelical Christian.

Interviews with those who practice religion while incarcerated indicate several reasons why it is helpful in prison. For example, religion often provides a psychological and physical "safe haven" from harsh realities and enables people to maintain ties with their families and with religious volunteers from the outside. Many administrators believe that strong religious groups—even those following nontraditional religions—make a prison easier to run because of a more stabilized prison culture.

Only a few studies of religion in prison have been conducted. The results of these studies are mixed. It appears that religious activity improves adjustment to prison psychologically, helping participants avoid infractions. But there seems to be a pattern that the initial positive impact of religion programs disappears over time, even if people who engage in religion programs in prison receive strong religious support while they are in re-entry.[26] Why religious programs in prison have limiting staying power remains an open question. When religion-based programs operate under proven correctional treatment principles, they can reduce recidivism.[27] However, it is not clear whether the impact comes from the religious aspects of the program or the reliance on proven correctional treatment principles.

The Rediscovery of Correctional Rehabilitation

LO 6

Analyze recent developments in the field of correctional rehabilitation.

After Martinson's 1974 study indicated that prison rehabilitation programs were ineffective, the number of treatment programs began to decrease. According to the new vision, prison was a place that should provide safe and secure custody during punishment. Yet even though some correctional officials willingly abandoned the rehabilitation ideal, many others believed that eradicating rehabilitation from prisons was unwise. In recent years these penologists have become a strong minority voice calling for a renewed emphasis on rehabilitative programs in corrections (see "How to Make Prisons Better").

In their book *Reaffirming Rehabilitation,* Francis Cullen and Karen Gilbert argue that correctional treatment is more humane than mere custody and punishment and that these programs can be effective when appropriately designed and implemented.[28] Following their lead, a team of Canadian researchers analyzed a large number of recent evaluations of correctional treatment and identified six proven principles under which treatment programs will be effective:

1. The programs are directed toward high-risk clients.
2. The programs respond to problems that caused the criminal behavior.
3. The treatments take into account clients' psychological maturity.
4. The treatment providers are allowed professional discretion in how to manage progress in treatment.
5. The programs are fully implemented as intended.
6. There is follow-up support after the treatment programs are completed.

Recent research that looks at a wide array of treatment programs continues to support these ideas, and they have become a core part of what has been called, "Evidence Based Practice" (see Chapter 19).

One of the most important elements of this research on effective treatment programs is the distinction made between criminogenic needs and other kinds of needs.

FOCUS ON

CORRECTIONAL PRACTICE: How to Make Prisons Better

A team of the most respected scholars in corrections has recently suggested seven key reforms for the prison system:

1. *Make prisons less crowded.* Prison crowding makes everything else difficult. It deteriorates the effectiveness of prison programming. It makes security more challenging, creating stress for both staff and people who are incarcerated. The best way to reduce prison crowding is to put fewer people in prison and to have shorter stays for those who are in prison.
2. *Make it possible for people in prison to earn rewards.* There is ample evidence that punishment-oriented systems for managing prisons do not work at maintaining safer prison environments. This is true because threats and sanctions inside the prison do not change the problems that lead to trouble. Offering "carrots, not just sticks" is a much more promising way to make prisons run better.
3. *Use science to improve the conditions of confinement.* Too many prisons are brutal, agonizing places. These conditions are not only inhumane, but they cannot be conducive to achieving the goals of the prison system. Wretched conditions in prisons are not inevitable. Prison lighting, color, and architecture—ideas that are consistent with well-developed theories of situational crime prevention—can be essential to overcoming the stifling prison environment.
4. *Give the public what it wants.* Every recent survey of public opinion confirms that people want the prison system to rehabilitate, not just punish. Programs that enable prisons to accomplish this aim should be central to prison management, not peripheral.
5. *Make wardens accountable for correcting people who go to prison.* Specific prisons should be evaluated on how well the people who go there succeed when they are released. After all, when a person returns to prison for a new crime, it is not only an individual failure—it is also an institutional failure to rehabilitate. These results should be measured. Leaders who are better at getting these results should be rewarded and promoted. Those who cannot should find ways to improve—or find another profession.
6. *Use principles of effective corrections for rehabilitation.* There are now well-established principles of effective correctional programs: focusing on high-risk clients, dealing with criminogenic needs, and employing effective interpersonal strategies. All correctional programs in prisons should be consistent with these principles.
7. *Teach prison officers to be change agents.* Correctional staff should not be merely custodians. If a prison is to be focused on rehabilitation, then every correctional staff member must become a change agent. This requires training about principles of human motivation, what is known about effective correctional strategies, and, most of all, change as the core philosophy of the prison system.

Source: Francis T. Cullen, Daniel P. Mears, Cheryl Leno Jonson, and Angela J. Thielo, "Seven Ways to Make Prisons Work," in *What Is to Be Done About Crime and Punishment? Towards a Public Criminology,* edited by Roger Mathews (London: Palgrave, 2016), 159–96.

criminogenic needs Needs that when successfully addressed by treatment programs result in lower rates of recidivism.

Criminogenic needs are those that, when successfully addressed by treatment programs, result in lower rates of recidivism. The identification of criminogenic needs is an important advance in correctional treatment because it enables program managers to focus their efforts on objectives that are likely to pay off in lower recidivism rates.

Although interest in rehabilitation waned when the philosophy of corrections swung toward crime control, advocates of correctional rehabilitation now point to an increase in consistent evidence that programs meeting the six criteria of success can result in considerable reductions of new criminal activity. Perhaps the time has come for a reformulation of the ethics of correctional rehabilitation: from "nothing works" to "what works, for whom, and why."[29]

To bolster this point of view, several researchers have undertaken systematic reviews of correctional rehabilitation studies in which a broad and careful search for all the studies ever conducted is made, and then the results of those studies are statistically assessed to find patterns of results. Systematic studies are thought to be superior in giving policy makers an understanding of correctional rehabilitation because the use of a large number of studies with a single yardstick for "success" leads to a more reliable conclusion than do other methods.[30]

The most powerful new studies of correctional rehabilitation programs try to express their effectiveness in **cost–benefit ratios**. A cost–benefit study begins with the recognition that crime costs money—victims suffer losses, and the criminal justice system has to use its resources to combat crime. Correctional programs also cost money. Any program that can reduce crime can thus be seen as a potential money saver, at least in the long term, if the savings incurred through the crimes that have been averted outweigh the costs of the program itself. Cost benefits are expressed as ratios: When they are larger than 1, the program saves money; when they are less than 1, the program loses money. Thus, a program with a cost–benefit ratio of 2.25 saves $2.25 for every dollar it costs, while a program with a cost–benefit ratio of 0.50 loses 50 cents per dollar spent on the program.

Recent systematic cost–benefit studies have encouraged advocates for more rehabilitation programs in corrections. Correctional interventions have cost–benefit ratios as high as $7 benefit per $1 cost. This kind of impact has sparked a new interest in rehabilitation. A decade ago, Texas policy advocates estimated that a cut in rehabilitation programs in the state's prison system would be enormously expensive, requiring an additional 12,000 beds at the cost of $600 million, to handle the increased number of people who fail after being released from prison.[31] After Californians passed Proposition 36, mandating treatment programs instead of prison for people convicted of drug crimes, many political leaders took note. Advocates believe that the proposition, despite problems, has been an overall success.[32] This issue has ceased to be seen as primarily liberal, as conservatives have also championed rehabilitation programs for people who have gone to prison.

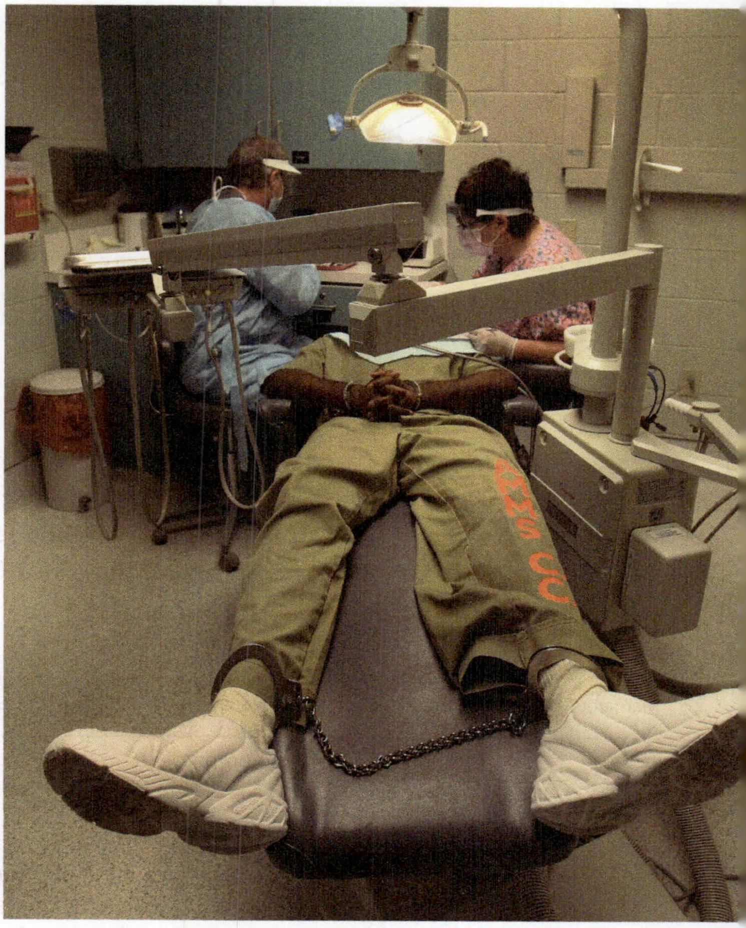
John Smierciak/Chicago Tribune/MCT/Sipa USA

▲ *The larger prisons provide a full range of health care, including health care. IN this Illinois super-max prison, security dictates that dental care is received while handcuffed.*

cost–benefit ratio A summary measure of the value of a correctional program in saving money through preventing new crime.

Prison Medical Services

People who are incarcerated have a well-established right to medical treatment, most effectively defined by the U.S. Supreme Court in *Estelle v. Gamble*.[33] The argument for a right to medical treatment is straightforward and persuasive: Citizens who are confined do not have the capacity to obtain health insurance or sufficient funds to pay for their own health care costs, and to deny necessary treatments would be cruel. Thus, it is only fair to provide basic health care for those who are incarcerated.

This is potentially a very expensive right because of the significant health problems that people bring with them to prison. Some of these problems stem from the high-risk behavior engaged in prior to their incarceration. For example, needle use during drug abuse is the single most frequent cause of HIV transmission and is also the leading cause of **hepatitis C**, a liver disease that kills 5 percent of those infected. Unprotected sex also accounts for high rates of sexually transmitted diseases (STDs). Treatment for most forms of these "lifestyle" diseases (so called because they are typically acquired as a consequence of a high-risk lifestyle) can be complicated and expensive.

hepatitis C A sometimes fatal disease of the liver that reduces the effectiveness of the body's system of removing toxins.

The number of people who require help for these diseases is not small. Much attention has been given to those who are HIV-positive, who number just over 20,000 (see

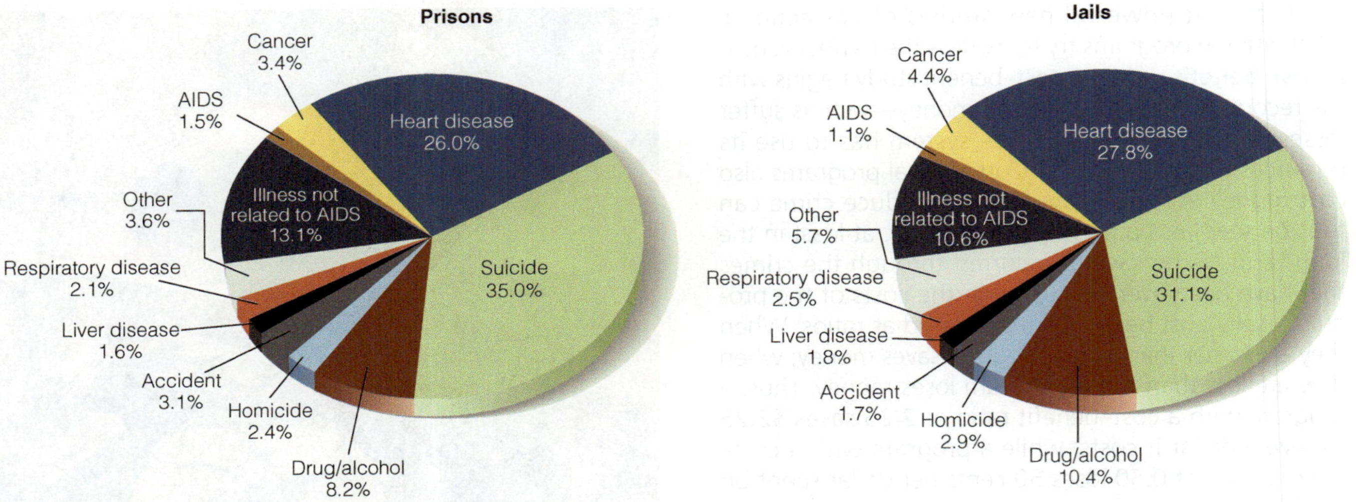

FIGURE 14.2 Leading Causes of Deaths in Prisons and Jails

Despite continuing concern about AIDS in prisons, other health factors are a more common cause of death among people who are incarcerated.

*Primarily cancer and heart, liver, and respiratory diseases.

Sources: E. Anne Carson and Mary P. Cowhig, *Mortality in Local Jails* 2011–2016, *Statistical Tables* (Washington, DC: U.S. Bureau of Justice Statistics, 20203); Margaret E. Noonan, *Mortality in Local Jails and State Prisons, 2000–2011—Statistical Tables* (Washington, DC: U.S. Bureau of Justice Statistics, 2013).

Chapter 6). In 1995 the mortality rate in prison from AIDS was two-thirds the rate of all other causes; by 2010 the medical care for HIV and AIDS was so successful that the rates in prison were similar to those in free society. The number of AIDS-related prison deaths continued to decline (see Figure 14.2).[34] Less attention has been given to those suffering from hepatitis C, whose numbers may exceed 360,000, a stunning 18 percent of the national prison population. However, hepatitis C rates can vary considerably among different regions and are as high as 40 percent in some correctional systems.[35]

The medical treatment regimen for these diseases involves drugs that reduce the negative effects of the diseases and slow bodily deterioration from the infection. But the most important treatment is prevention through a change in lifestyle. Prison programs that seek to halt the spread of disease within the population are educational, showing how the diseases are spread and stressing the value of abstinence from drugs and unsafe sexual contact. To date, needle-exchange programs, which have successfully reduced transmission rates on the streets, have not been tried in U.S. prisons because critics say they indirectly support illicit drug use inside the walls.

In addition to lifestyle diseases, people in prison suffer other maladies found in the general population. The most recent study available found that almost one-third of the state prison population and nearly one-fourth of the federal prison population reported some debility requiring health care (see Figure 14.3). One in five reported suffering a new medical problem subsequent to arriving at the prison, and half of those serving five years or longer reported the onset of a medical problem during incarceration.[36] For these people, the need for availability of "sick call" and regular medical help is no different than that of the population at large, but a person's choice is restricted to whatever options the prison provides.

Most prisons offer medical services through a full-time staff of nurses, augmented by part-time physicians under contract. Nurses can take care of routine health care needs and dispense medicines from a secure, in-prison pharmacy; regularly scheduled visits to the prison by doctors can enable people in prison to obtain checkups and diagnoses. For cases needing a specialist, surgery, or emergency medical care, people must be transported to

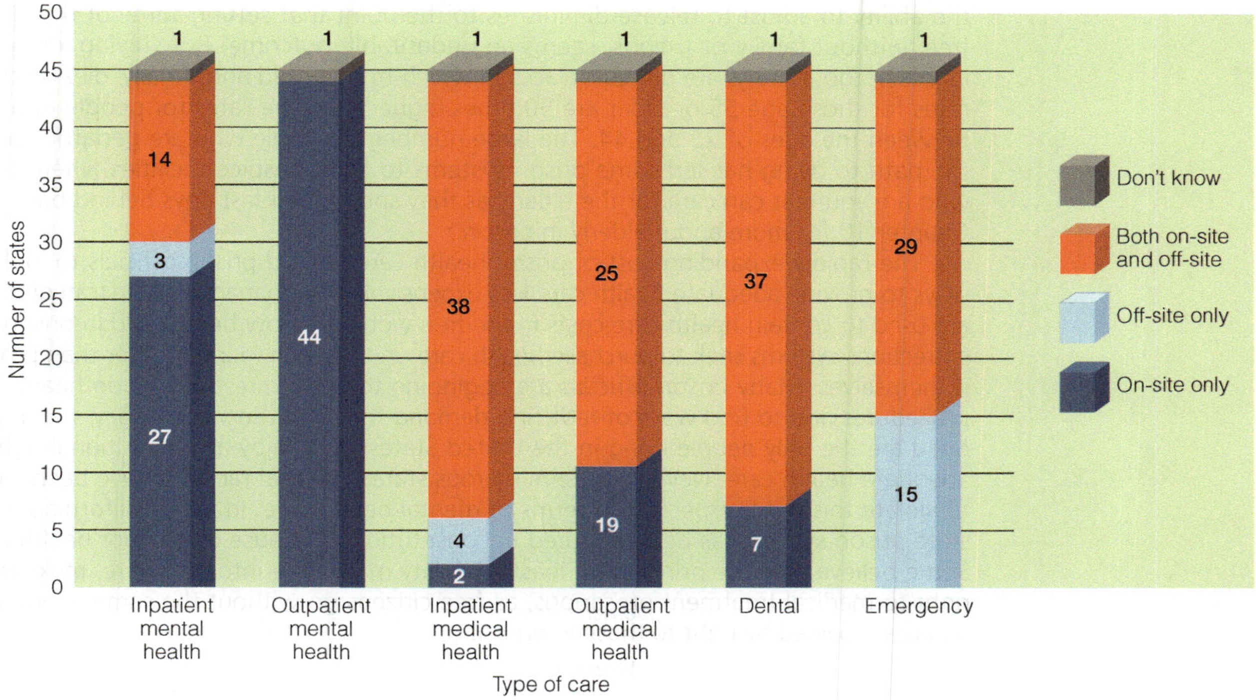

FIGURE 14.3 Health Care Needs of People in Prison

Many types of health care are provided for people in prison; some services are on-site, and others require transfer to receive the service.

Note: Counts are based on responses from 45 participating states only.

Source: Karishma A. Chari, Alan E. Simon, Carol J. DeFrances, and Laura Maruschak, *National Survey of Prison Health Care: Selected Findings* (Washington, DC: National Health Statistics Reports no. 96, 2016).

local hospitals under close security by correctional staff. The aim is for the prison system to provide a range of medical assistance to meet the various needs of the population as a whole. However, because medical care is so expensive, many prison administrators resist providing help until it is absolutely necessary. Complaints among people in prison and observers that prison medical care is "second class" are common, and one study has accused the prison authorities of purposefully abusive health care practices.

Although the needs for health care in prison echo those of the general population, people in prison pose two special needs because of poverty and aging. As a group, people in prison are very poor, so they often bring to the prison years of neglect of their general health. For example, many have neglected their teeth so severely that the resulting unsightly smile makes it hard to get any job requiring contact with business customers. A round of dental repairs can do wonders to alleviate this practical and personal problem, but outsiders might look at such free dental care as a luxury. Other consequences of being poor, such as an inadequate diet and poor hygiene, also affect the general health of the prison population.

By far, the most extraordinary health problem in contemporary corrections is the burgeoning number of elderly people. Penal policies of the 1980s and 1990s have resulted in a dramatic increase in the number of people serving long sentences, and many of them are now beginning to grow old in prison. The number ages 50 and older doubled in the mid-1990s, and this group will likely approach 20 percent of the prison population in coming years. The growing number of geriatric people poses multiple problems for prison authorities. The elderly have more-complicated and more-numerous health problems, overall, and they eventually reach an age where they cannot work productively in prison assignments. As the length of time away from free society increases, the ability to adjust to release diminishes to the point that setting some of the elderly free, without family or friends, seems an undesirable outcome. But staying inside has its costs, too. Prisons are difficult places in which to grow old and, finally, die. Mortality rates for those age 55 or older are 50 times higher than the rates for people in prison between the ages of 25 and 44. The large number of people who are geriatric and on the path to dying has led some prison systems to form hospice facilities where those who are younger can care for the elderly as they spend their last days behind bars. (See Chapter 10 for more about elderly in prison.)

The rapidly expanding cost of prison health care has led prison officials to look for ways to provide adequate health care less expensively. The managed-care strategies that are used to contain health care costs in the free world are now being used in prisons, as corrections systems seek to purchase health care on the open market rather than provide it themselves. Many prison officials are beginning to impose restrictions on health care procedures and to find ways of reducing demand for health services. Today, the imprisoned are the only people living in the United States who enjoy a constitutional right to adequate health care. Nevertheless, numerous state and local facilities have been found to violate this right, especially in terms of mental health care. In fact, California's entire state prison system has been declared unconstitutional because of its poor health care. Some believe that the principle of least eligibility may come into play here, making the right to medical treatment precarious, as free citizens go without the same health care services provided by right to those in prison.

LO 7

Describe the main types of correctional industries and explain how each works.

PRISON INDUSTRY

Historically, hard labor has served as a central part of punishment. It was even a popular belief at one time that a person's labor was legally forfeited as a result of criminality and that the state could expect to profit from the person's incarceration.

Labor was also a way to manage the restlessness and idleness of prison time. Meaningful and productive work came to be seen more recently as one of the best ways to make the long days of prison go faster, and paying for labor could help imprisoned people make hard lives less harsh through the ability to buy daily amenities and goods. Most important, labor was also viewed as part of the reformative process, a belief that continues today.

Some scholars have declared that historians have focused too heavily on the humanitarian and reformist basis for the rise of the penitentiary and reformatory. They argue that this view does not adequately reflect economic motives for the emergence of the prison. In fact, prisons provide a captive labor pool, and restrictions on wages earned by people in prison labor make possible the production of goods at very low cost. In 2012 the U.S. government made roughly $750 million providing prison labor.[37]

The theme of labor for profit is accompanied by a concern about idleness. Much of the history of prison industry revolves around the search for suitable ways to occupy time while also serving the financial interests of forces outside the walls. Four approaches have resulted: (1) the contract labor, piece price, and lease systems; (2) the public account system; (3) the state-use system; and (4) the public works and ways system.

The Contract Labor, Piece Price, and Lease Systems

piece price system A labor system under which a contractor provided raw materials and agreed to a set price to purchase goods made by people in prison.

In the early days of U.S. prisons, people who were incarcerated had their labor contracted out to private employers, who provided the machinery and raw materials for the work. The products made by this contract labor system were then sold on the open market. Alternatively, in the **piece price system** the contractor established a purchase price for goods that were produced with raw materials provided by the contractor. Both arrangements were extremely exploitative. The conditions were like sweatshops, and the fees for labor were paid to the prisons; "free" during the day, the laborers were returned to the prison at night. In the *lease system,* a variation of the piece price system, the contractor maintained the laborers, working them for 12–16 hours at a stretch. These systems enabled many prisons in the later 1800s—even the vaunted Auburn—to operate in the black. The low wages increased the contractors' profit margins. The people in prison, of course, worked for nothing and gained nothing.

Not surprisingly, these arrangements led to extreme corruption as well as exploitation. With sizable contracts at stake, kickbacks and bribes became common practices. Further, wardens took advantage of easy opportunities to line their pockets—and caused predictable public scandals when they were caught.

Soon, organized labor began to attack the prison labor arrangements. Late in the nineteenth century a coalition of humanitarian reformers and labor leaders lobbied successfully for laws prohibiting contract prison labor. States then began to experiment with alternative forms of free-market prison labor.

The Public Account System

When contract labor was outlawed, Oklahoma led the way in instituting the **public account system**. Instead of selling prison labor to private entrepreneurs, in 1909 the state prison itself began to make twine, buying raw materials and using prison labor. Similar twine-making factories existed in Minnesota and Wisconsin prisons. At first, the reform was enormously successful, reducing the costs of twine for Oklahoma farmers and generating profits that defrayed two-thirds of the costs of prison operations, but ultimately the experiment failed. The financial pressure that wardens had felt earlier did not die with the contract labor system, and they often succumbed to it by padding budgets and altering records. In any case, an industry that had such a narrow market could not sustain full prison employment. And when prisons began to turn a profit on goods that the private sector also produced, private industry and labor stopped cooperating.

public account system A labor system under which a prison bought machinery and raw materials with which people inside manufactured a salable product.

The State-Use System

In response to the problems associated with using prison labor to produce goods for the competitive market, many states turned to a **state-use system**, in which people in prison are employed to produce goods and services used only in state institutions and agencies. Many experts consider this arrangement reasonable and beneficial, and many states mandate that their agencies must purchase goods produced by prison labor when they are available. This requirement creates something of a state monopoly on certain products. Today, the state-use system is the most common form of prison industry.

state-use system A labor system under which goods produced by prison industries are purchased exclusively by state institutions and agencies and never enter the free market.

The state-use system has several advantages. Prison labor, which by many accounts is cheaper than outside labor, is not allowed to compete with other labor pools in the open market. At the same time, the state can purchase some goods more cheaply. Under this system, state agencies often buy a great variety of prison-produced items—school chairs and desks, soap and paper towels, milk and eggs, and so on.

This system also has drawbacks. Even when prison products are used only by the government, the system preempts the free-labor market. Moreover, many of the goods produced within the system—license plates, for example—have no close equivalents outside, so skills acquired in prison often do not transfer to outside industries. Even when an analogous outside industry exists, prison industry is so inefficient and its methods so outmoded that people must often shed what they learned there before they can succeed in private industry. For example, farming is a common prison industry, but the enterprise typically teaches few advanced agricultural methods; people usually do manual chores, even though farmhand positions are drying up across the country. The prison farm may be good economics, but it is poor schooling.

The Public Works and Ways System

public works and ways system A labor system under which people in prison work on public construction and maintenance projects.

In a version of the state-use system called the **public works and ways system**, people in prison work on public construction and maintenance projects: filling potholes, constructing or repairing buildings and bridges, and so on. This approach was introduced in the 1920s, when surfaced roads were needed. There has been renewed interest in this approach to prison labor because some state officials believe that the costs of some state goods and services can be vastly reduced if they are provided by people who are incarcerated.

Advocates praise the tremendous economic benefits of this system and point out that people learn new skills while producing goods and services useful to society. However, people in prison do the more arduous jobs on a project, and then outside craftspeople are hired for the skilled work. Some detractors say this is exploitation; the state receives a benefit but does not fairly compensate the workers (see "Thinking Outside the Box").

Prison Industry Historically and Today

Until very recently, the trend in prison industry was shifting away from free-market use of prison labor and toward state monopolies. After 1940, the private use of prison labor, once the most popular form of prison industry, vanished. One reason was that the public had become increasingly aware of the exploitative character of prison industry. Southern prison systems expanded dramatically after the Civil War, and former slaves accounted for much of this growth. The labor of most of them was contracted out in one way or another, leading some critics to argue that industrial capitalists had replaced plantation owners as exploiters of the former slaves.

With the rise of the labor movement, state legislatures passed laws restricting the sale of prison-made goods in order not to compete with free workers. As early as 1819, New York required boots and shoes produced at Auburn to be labeled "State Prison." In another application of the principle of least eligibility, whenever unemployment began to soar, political pressures mounted to prevent prisons from engaging in enterprises that might otherwise be conducted by private business and free labor.

THINKING OUTSIDE THE BOX

PAY PEOPLE IN PRISON MINIMUM WAGE

Prison industry has struggled to succeed for several reasons. The worker has limited incentive to work; the skills involved are often of a low level. The cost of security makes products made in prison more expensive than those same products made outside, even though prison wages are often mere pennies an hour. In that environment, it is not easy to get outside companies to bring production into the prison. On the other hand, outside manufacturers complain that prison labor is so cheap that it gives prison industry a competitive advantage.

What if businesses paid prison labor the federal minimum wage? People working in prison would be able to pay restitution to their victims and provide support for their families. They could be required to reimburse the state for some of the cost of their incarceration and then perhaps leave prison with a little money in a savings account. Advocates say that this would likely reduce recidivism by encouraging prison businesses to be efficient and thus provide better real-life job training for those who are behind bars.

Of course, there are plenty of political problems. With high unemployment rates, seeing people in prison get jobs that others cannot get would be galling for the general public. (It is worth noting, though, that there is nothing to stop an employer from hiring people from the outside to work alongside people who are incarcerated.) While it seems just not quite right that people who have lost their freedom can still earn a living wage, the potential advantages to the state and to industry could make it worth getting used to.

Source: Prison Policy Initiative, www.prisonpolicy.org/prisonindex/prisonlabor.html.

In 1900 the U.S. Industrial Commission endorsed the state-use plan, and in 1929 Congress passed the Hawes–Cooper Act, followed by additional legislation in 1935 and 1940 that banned prison-made goods from interstate commerce. In an excess of zeal, by 1940 every state had passed laws banning imports of prison-made goods from other states. These restrictions crippled production and ended the open-market system of employment. With the outbreak of World War II, however, President Franklin Roosevelt ordered the government to procure goods for the military effort from state and federal prisons. Later, under pressure from organized labor, President Harry Truman revoked the wartime order, and prisons returned to idleness. By 1973, President Nixon's National Advisory Commission on Criminal Justice Standards and Goals found that few people confined in the prison system had productive work. In 1979 Congress lifted restrictions on the interstate sale of products made in state prisons and urged correctional administrators to explore private-sector ways to improve prison industry (for a successful example in Oregon, see "Prison Blues"). In the same year, the free venture program of the Law Enforcement Assistance Administration made funds available to seven states to develop industries. These programs would operate according to six principles: (1) a full workweek, (2) wages based on productivity, (3) private-sector productivity standards, (4) responsibility for hiring or firing workers given to industry staff, (5) self-sufficient or profitable shop operations, and (6) postrelease job placement. Once again, prison labor would compete with free labor. By 1994, 16 states were engaged in free venture prison industry, and 5 states—Nevada, New Hampshire, South Carolina, Tennessee, and Washington—allowed people to earn wages approaching the federal minimum wage.

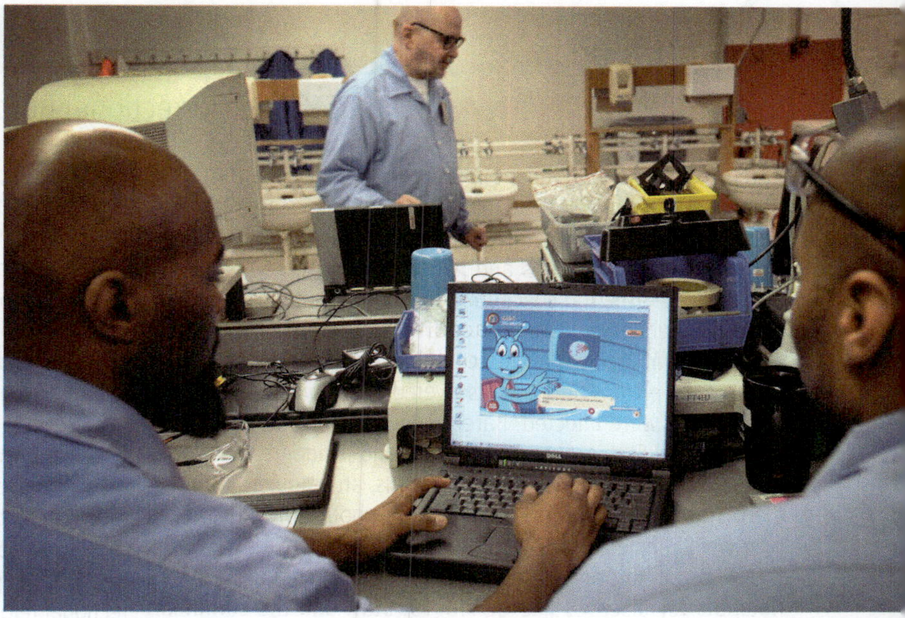
Glen Stubbe/Minneapolis Star Tribune/MCT/Sipa USA

▲ *Educational software is being loaded onto a Dell laptop computer at the Minnesota Correctional Facility in Stillwater, Minnesota. The refurbished computers are provided to public schools as part of the Minnesota Computers for Schools program.*

Since 2000, there has been a renewed interest in channeling prison labor into industrial programs that would relieve idleness, allow wages to be earned and saved for release, and reduce the costs of incarceration. The change in attitude toward prison industries may be related to the fact that many large U.S. firms, in search of cheap labor, have moved operations to the developing countries. The outsourcing of U.S. jobs overseas has become a hot political issue (see "Correctional Industry Competes with the Private Sector"). Because of increased shipping costs and problems of administering plants overseas, some manufacturers may view prison labor as an attractive alternative. Union opposition may weaken if it can be shown that people in prison are not taking jobs away from taxpaying free workers. Indeed, when analysts investigate prison industry, they typically find that goods made in prison are a minuscule portion of the gross domestic product, a small fraction of 1 percent of the total.

At this early date, the supposed efficiencies of private industry in corrections are less dramatic than expected. Prison labor is cheaper than free labor, but recent reforms include higher wages for people in prison than those formerly paid by private contractors, and security requirements drive up costs. However, even if a renewed prison industry is neither efficient nor damaging to free-market labor, it makes sense to have people in prison work. A Federal Bureau of Prisons study shows that those who are employed in prison have fewer disciplinary infractions, get better jobs when released, and stay out of trouble with the law longer than do those who are unemployed while serving their sentences.[38]

FOCUS ON

CORRECTIONAL POLICY: The Correctional Response to COVID-19

In the Spring of 2020, the international pandemic of COVID-19 paralyzed the globe. Within months, the United States led the world in people with confirmed infections and in deaths. Within the United States, prisons and jails quickly became coronavirus hotspots—the top concentration in the country occurred in Trousdale, Tennessee, where in early May, over 1200 people in a correctional facility had tested positive for the virus. Across the country, prisons and jails discovered frightening numbers of people who were infected. Barely 3 months into the epidemic in the United States, over 40,000 staff and residents of prisons and jails had tested positive for the virus, and almost 500 had died. Staff were not spared, comprising about a fifth of those who were infected and 10% of those who died.

It is not surprising that prisons and jails should become hotspots for diseases like COVID-19. Staff and the confined are in close contact. Regular hand washing and the constant disinfecting of cell and congregate areas are not feasible practices—nor is maintaining 6 feet of distance. A high percentage of the population has the kind of underlying conditions that make COVID-19 so fatal. As correctional leaders realized what they were facing, urgent pleas came from professionals and reformers for a response.

What happened was a dramatic and unprecedented set of changes. Many local jails began releasing people who were awaiting trial but could not make bail—especially people who had medical conditions making them vulnerable to the disease. In other places, local law enforcement started to forego bringing minor arrests for jail admissions. In most states, prison administrators looked for ways to accelerate releases of vulnerable members of their prison population. Over 60 official administrative processes were put in place to facilitate releases from jails and prisons. One estimate held that, by mid-May 2020, 43,000 people have been released from jails and almost 25,000 from prisons.

Release practices focused on three groups of those who were confined: those in jail awaiting trial, people over 60 and/or those with compromised health, and people who were within a short period of being released anyway.

Some see the unprecedented response to COVID-19 as an important opportunity to test a larger set of questions about correctional reform. Most people agree that the correctional system is too large, with too many people in prison and jail. What can we learn from the large-scale releases that were untaken in the face of the global pandemic? How did these emergency policies affect the public? Could we think of the COVID-19 response as a field test of the very policies we could implement more broadly to tackle the problem of mass incarceration?

Sources: UCLA COVID-19 Behind Bars Project: https://law.ucla.edu/centers/criminal-justice/criminal-justice-program/related-programs/covid-19-behind-bars-data-project/; Sarah Stillman, "Will Coronavirus Make Us Rethink Mass Incarceration?" *The New Yorker*, May 18, 2020.

PRISON MAINTENANCE PROGRAMS

Running a prison is like running a town. The typical prison must provide every major service available in a community and more: fire department, electrical and plumbing services, janitorial maintenance, mail delivery, restaurant, drugstore, administrative record keeping, and so on. These operations must be coordinated. If only to keep the costs of these services manageable, people in prison do the bulk of the work. The one thing abundant in a prison is human resources, and perhaps the most common types of jobs in any given prison have to do with its day-to-day maintenance.

In most prisons, maintenance jobs constitute an elaborate pecking order of assignments and reveal something about prestige and influence within the facility. The choice jobs involve access to power. For example, a clerical job in the records room (which contains the prison's files) offers a corner on one of the most sought-after commodities in prison: information. Someone in the records room can learn who is doing time for what, who is eligible for privileges (such as reclassification, reassignment, and parole), and what decisions are being made about whom. The contents of prison files are confidential, but it is hard to prevent the records-room clerk from sneaking a look—or from trading the information for goods or favors.

Clerical support jobs are similarly prestigious. Desk assignments permit access to authority figures (and very likely to such favors as flexibility in scheduling, better food, and sometimes information) and make the ones who get them the first contributors to the institutional rumor mill. Often, a person must be trusted and classified as low risk before getting a clerical assignment.

Among the most desirable jobs are those that allow access to goods or services that can be sold within the prison economy. For example, someone who works in the laundry can charge "a fee" as insurance that clothing will be returned neatly folded and without rips or tears.

Also desirable are jobs that provide access to contraband goods. For example, a person on kitchen detail can filch extra food to trade or sell. Library assignments let people make liberal use of law books and other popular reading materials. Assignments to the stockroom or to the dispensary, even with tight security on drugs and other medical items, can pay off in various ways.

Other assignments offer different kinds of benefits. For instance, the electrician's aide and the message runner usually have flexible schedules and relatively varied tasks that make the time go more quickly.

The least desirable jobs are the most plentiful: janitorial services. The newly admitted must often prove themselves for later reassignment by facing mop detail and the like; such assignments are also given as disciplinary measures. Mopping halls and cleaning latrines are not particularly interesting tasks; repeated three or more times a day in the same areas, the work becomes painfully monotonous.

Even so, prison maintenance jobs are essential to managing the prison in two ways. First, they lower the cost of operations by eliminating the need to hire outside labor. Second, the job hierarchy provides rewards and punishments to enforce prison discipline. People who cooperate receive choice assignments; others get the dirty work.

FOCUS ON

CORRECTIONAL PRACTICE: Correctional Industry Competes with the Private Sector

Tennier Industries makes military clothing, and the company's bread and butter is the U.S. military. So in December 2013, losing its $45 million contract with the Defense Department was a tough pill to swallow. It was even tougher when the company had to lay off about 100 workers. Tennier is a major employer in Huntsville, Tennessee, and the economic losses will continue to ripple through the area.

The Defense Department contract went to Unicor, the federal prison industry. This raises a question: How can a prison system take jobs away from the private sector?

Undoubtedly, one of the reasons Unicor was able to submit a winning bid was that its expenses are low. With labor provided by people at a wage of about $1 per hour, Unicor is able to keep its labor costs low. Even so, prison industry operating costs are greater than we might think. If the full costs of the industry are calculated, prison overhead is quite high because of security costs.

But cost is not the only factor. Federal law requires federal agencies to give preferences to Unicor contracts—even when Unicor is not the cheapest proposal—as long as its products are comparable to the private-sector competition. As it turns out, Unicor is usually the cheapest option anyway. Why would the law create advantages for prison labor?

Proponents of this arrangement point out that keeping people who are incarcerated productively employed is good correctional practice. It also means that prison labor is paying some of the costs of running the prison, saving government money. When prison products are state-of-the-art, it is also possible that the prison workers are learning valuable skills that they can put to use when they are released.

Even so, it does not seem fair. Steven Eisen, Tennier's CFO, complained, "Our government screams, howls and yells how the rest of the world is using people in prison or slave labor to manufacture items, and here we take the items right out of the mouths of people who need it."

Some elected officials agree.

"This is a threat to not just established industries; it's a threat to emerging industries," said Representative Bill Huizenga, a Michigan Republican who is the lead sponsor of the proposed overhaul legislation. "If China did this—having their prisoners work at subpar wages in prisons—we would be screaming bloody murder."

But the critics are bumping up against good correctional policy. People who work for Unicor do better on parole than those who do not. And the picture is not as simple as it seems. Unicor itself contracts with the private sector to carry out its projects, thereby creating private-sector jobs. And in the end, the fraction of products purchased by the government that are made in prison is miniscule. What would happen if Unicor were shut down entirely?

Source: Adapted from Diane Cardwell, "Competing with Prison Labor: Companies Say Job Program for Inmates Threatens Jobs on Outside," *The New York Times*, March 15, 2012, B1, B4.

RECREATIONAL PROGRAMS

When people in prison are not at work, in treatment, or in their cells, they are probably engaged in recreation. Organized recreation is a favorite pastime—and often central to the prison experience. Most men's prisons have sports teams—baseball, basketball, even football—and some regularly compete with outside teams. Many prisons also provide such activities as table tennis, weight training, music, drama, and journalism clubs.

Recreational programs have two primary functions in addition to filling time. First, they are integral to prison social life. People in prison vary in intellect and physical capacities; variety in programs enables a community to form, with positive social contacts with others who share their interests and abilities. Second, prison recreational and leisure pursuits can be rehabilitative in several ways. They teach such social skills as cooperation and teamwork, they provide a means for people to grow in experience and enhance their self-image, and they serve as a productive counterpoint to the general alienation of prison.

Recreational programs also present security risks. In a prison, whenever people congregate, they can plan disruptions. Tempers can especially flare in recreation, where there is competition. Although prisons without leisure activities would be torture, recreation requires careful management.

Recently the public has reacted against recreational programming, feeling that free-time programs make prison too easy and even enjoyable. Politicians have thus pressed to shut down recreational programs, especially weight lifting. Administrators point out that people in these programs are often the best behaved; they also argue that trying to run a prison without such activities will cause unrest. Still, the popular sentiment that prison should be unbearable tends to eradicate any programming not directly related to rehabilitation.

LO 8

Explain the current pressures facing correctional programming policies.

PRISON PROGRAMMING RECONSIDERED

Our discussion of prison programs has focused on the types of activities used to occupy time. Underlying this discussion is the question "Is this use of prison time truly useful?" The answer is equivocal (see "The Evidence Base for Prison Programs").

FOCUS ON

CORRECTIONAL PRACTICE: The Evidence Base for Prison Programs

Even though correctional programs have been offered in penal institutions for generations, there is not a very deep body of evidence about how well they work. One reason is that it is hard to carry out good studies in prison settings, especially because it is thought to be unethical to conduct experiments on incarcerated populations. Another reason is that for the last 25 years, prisons have emphasized punishment, and there did not seem to be much reason to study correctional programs. Despite this shortage of good research, a recent summary of the literature on what we know about prison rehabilitation programs concluded that three principles are essential to effective treatment:

1. Employ cognitive–behavioral treatment approaches—that is, work on changing the way people think about and evaluate the behaviors they choose to engage in.
2. Focus on changing criminogenic needs, such as antisocial attitudes and substance abuse.
3. Deliver more-intensive services to those of higher risk and avoid giving services to lower-risk people.

When these three simple principles are followed, prison misconduct rates drop by about one-fourth, and postrelease recidivism rates drop by 20–30 percent. These results suggest substantial costs savings for these treatments, as well as significant benefits in public safety.

Source: Adapted from Paul Gendreau and Paula Smith, "Assessment and Treatment Strategies for Correctional Institutions," in Joel A. Dvoskin, Jennifer L. Skeem, Raymond W. Novaco, and Kevin S. Douglas, eds., *Using Social Science to Reduce Violent Offending* (New York: Oxford University Press, 2011).

People are often sent to prison under the assumption that educational and rehabilitative programs will prepare them to adjust to society when they are released. But most rehabilitative programs have serious shortcomings and limited effectiveness. Further, a large number of people in prison are not even considered to need education, vocational training, or drug/alcohol rehabilitation. Of those who need help in these areas, often less than half actually participate in available programs. Study after study shows that even for programs that are effective, services provided in prison settings are substantially less effective than those same programs offered in the community.

Nonrehabilitative programs—prison industry, prison maintenance, and recreation—pose their own problems for administrators. For example, the need for security severely constrains all prison practices.

Yet a programless prison is unthinkable. People need structured activities so they can fill time with positive pursuits. Moreover, outside workers would not likely perform daily chores, for low wages and at some personal risk, to keep a prison operating.

Some experts have said that prison programs ought to be voluntary. Their philosophical arguments in favor of free choice and against coercion and exploitation certainly sound reasonable. But given the realities of prison life—the need to run the prison, occupy time, and give everyone hope that life will be better after release—it is unlikely that prison programs will change soon in any dramatic way.

SUMMARY

1 Describe how correctional programs help address the challenge of managing time in the correctional setting.

Institutional programs mitigate the oppressiveness of time. They also provide opportunities for people to improve their lives, whether the programs involve counseling, education, or merely recreation. Prison administrators use institutional programs to help manage time. Work assignments occupy the middle hours of the day, treatment and recreational periods are held before and after work assignments, and special programs take up the remaining hours. Experienced administrators know that the more programs they offer, the less likely that boredom will translate into hostility toward the staff.

2 Describe the ways that security acts as a constraint on correctional programs offered in institutional settings.

The heavy emphasis on security has two important consequences. First, unceasing surveillance further demoralizes incarcerated people and sharpens their sense of captivity. Second, security requirements make maintenance and industrial programs inefficient. Treatment success negatively affects the relationship between correctional counselors and clients. In short, the prison environment negatively affects every program which operates in that setting. The need for tight security dilutes the effectiveness of prison programs, except as a means to fill time.

3 Explain the meaning of the "principle of least eligibility" and illustrate its importance.

According to this principle, people in prison, having been convicted of wrongful behavior, should be the least eligible of all citizens for social benefits beyond the bare minimum required by law. Taken to its extreme, the principle would prohibit many institutional benefits, such as educational courses and cosmetic surgery.

4 Discuss the importance of the classification process and how "objective classification" works.

In most corrections systems, the prison bound pass through a reception and orientation center where they are evaluated and classified. Such approaches serve mainly as a management tool to ensure that people are assigned to housing units appropriate to their custody level. At rehabilitative institutions, batteries of tests, psychiatric evaluations, and counseling are administered so that each person can be assessed for treatment as well as custody. New predictive and equity-based systems seek to classify more objectively. Predictive models distinguish with respect to risk of escape, potential misconduct in the institution, and future criminal behavior. Equity-based models use only a few explicitly defined legal variables reflecting current and previous criminal characteristics. Objective systems are more efficient and cheaper than other systems.

5 Describe the major kinds of institutional programs that are offered in correctional institutions.
Rehabilitative programs aim at reforming behavior and help people develop skills so that they can avoid a return to crime. Prison medical services help people behind bars maintain their physical health. Prison industry enables prison residents to work, usually earning a wage for their efforts. Prison maintenance programs are used to keep the prison's physical plant in good running order. Prison recreational programs provide things for people to do in their spare time.

6 Analyze recent developments in the field of correctional rehabilitation.
After Martinson's 1974 study indicated that prison rehabilitation programs were ineffective, the number of treatment programs began to decrease. According to the new vision, prison was a place that should provide safe and secure custody during punishment. Although interest in rehabilitation waned when the philosophy of corrections swung toward crime control, advocates of correctional rehabilitation now point to an increase in consistent evidence that programs can result in considerable reductions of new criminal activity. They argue that the time has come for a reformulation of the ethics of correctional rehabilitation: from "nothing works" to "what works, for whom, and why." Recent systematic cost–benefit studies have encouraged advocates for more rehabilitation programs in corrections.

7 Describe the main types of correctional industries and explain how each works.
Four approaches have been used historically for prison industry: (1) the contract labor system, in which prison labor is sold to private employers who provide the machinery and raw materials for the work and sell the products; (2) the public account system, in which a prison provides machinery and raw materials with which salable products are manufactured; (3) the state-use system, under which goods produced by prison industries are purchased by state institutions and agencies exclusively and never enter the free market; and (4) the public works and ways system, with work on public construction and maintenance projects such as filling potholes and repairing buildings.

8 Explain the current pressures facing correctional programming policies.
Most rehabilitative programs have serious shortcomings and limited effectiveness. Study after study shows that even for programs that are effective, services provided in prison settings are substantially less effective than those same programs offered in the community. Yet a programless prison is unthinkable. People in prison need structured activities so they can fill their time with positive pursuits. Moreover, outside workers would not likely perform daily chores, for low wages and at some personal risk, to keep a prison operating.

KEY TERMS

- behavior therapy (*p. 372*)
- civil disabilities (*p. 374*)
- classification (*p. 368*)
- cognitive skill building (*p. 373*)
- confrontation therapy (*p. 372*)
- cost–benefit ratio (*p. 379*)
- criminogenic needs (*p. 379*)
- hepatitis C (*p. 381*)
- piece price system (*p. 384*)
- principle of least eligibility (*p. 366*)
- prison program (*p. 365*)
- psychotherapy (*p. 372*)
- psychotropic medications (*p. 372*)
- public account system (*p. 384*)
- public works and ways system (*p. 385*)
- reality therapy (*p. 372*)
- social therapy (*p. 373*)
- state-use system (*p. 384*)
- therapeutic community (*p. 373*)
- transactional analysis (*p. 373*)
- vocational rehabilitation (*p. 375*)

FOR DISCUSSION

1. How strictly should the principle of least eligibility be applied? Support your viewpoint.
2. Are some rehabilitative programs more effective or valuable than others? Why or why not?
3. What factors limit the possibility of running prison industries as profit-making ventures? What could be done to improve the profitability of prison industries?
4. Should people in prison be forced to participate in programs? As a correctional officer, what would you do if someone on your cell range did not want to leave his or her cell?
5. Is a programless prison a possibility?

FOR FURTHER READING

Charles Colson Task Force on Federal Corrections. *Transforming Prisons, Restoring Lives: Final Recommendations of the Charles Colson Task Force on Federal Corrections.* Washington, DC: Urban Institute, 2016. A comprehensive review of the problems facing the federal prison system and six major recommendations for reform.

Epperson, Matthew, Nancy Wolff, Robert Morgan, et al. *The Next Generation of Behavioral Health and Criminal Justice.* New Brunswick, NJ: Rutgers University Center for Behavioral Health Services and Criminal Justice Research, 2011. A comprehensive review of the state of mental health treatment in corrections.

Erzen, Tanya, Mary R. Gould, and Jody Lewen, *Equity and Excellence in Practice: A Guide for Higher Education in Prison.* St. Louis: Alliance for Higher Education in Prison, 2019. Guidelines for implementing high quality postsecondary educational programs in prison.

Greifinger, Robert, ed. *Improving Public Health Through Correctional Health Care.* New York: Springer, 2007. Essays on the state of health care in the U.S. prison system, including rehabilitation programming, drug treatment, and medical care.

Human Rights Watch. *Ill Equipped: U.S. Prisons and Offenders with Mental Illness.* New York: Author, 2003. A critical evaluation of the services provided for the mentally ill in U.S. prisons, with a series of proposals for reform.

Karpowitz, Daniel. *College in Prison: Reading in an Age of Mass Incarceration.* New Brunswick, NJ: Rutgers University Press, 2017. Describes the Bard Prison Initiative, which is one of the nation's most successful undergraduate programs for people in prison.

McGuire, James, "What Work with Violent Offenders: A Response to 'Nothing Works'," in J. Stephen Wormith, Leam A. Craig, and Todd E. Hogue (eds.), *The Wiley Handbook of What Works in Violence Risk Management.* New York, NY: Wiley, 2020: pp. 53–79. A summary of the research on how to reduce recidivism among people convicted of violent crimes.

NOTES

1 Stuart Miller, "The Banning of Books in Prisons: 'It's Like Living in the Dark Ages,'" *Guardian*, September 25, 2016.

2 *Federal Justice Statistics 2012—Statistical Tables* (Washington, DC: U.S. Bureau of Justice Statistics, 2015).

3 Adam Gopnik, "The Caging of America," *The New Yorker*, January 30, 2012.

4 *The New York Times*, July 16, 1995, p. 3.

5 Thomas Harris, *I'm OK, You're OK* (New York: Harper & Row, 1969).

6 Oregon Department of Corrections, *Oregon Accountability Model* (Salem: Author, 2013).

7 U.S. Department of Education, *Answering Your Frequently Asked Questions About Second Chance Pell:* https://blog.ed.gov/2019/04/answering-frequently-asked-questions-second-chance-pell/ April 11, 2019.

8 Patrick Oakford, Cora Brumfield, Casey Goldvale, Laura Tatum, Margaret DiZarenga, and Fred Patrick, *Investing in Futures: Economic and Fiscal Benefits of Postsecondary Education in Prison* (New York: Vera Institute of Justice, 2019).

9 *Ramos v. Lamm,* 458 F.Supp. 128 (1979).

10 Thomas S. Szasz, *The Myth of Mental Illness* (New York: Harper & Row, 1969), 30.

11 Lauren C. Porter and Laura DeMarco, "Beyond the Dichotomy: Incarceration Dosage and Mental Health," *Criminology 57* (no. 1, 2019): 136–56.

12 Robert Martinson, "What Works? Questions and Answers About Prison Reform," *Public Interest, Spring* 1974, p. 25.

13 David B. Wilson, "Correctional Programs," in *What Works in Crime Prevention and Rehabilitation: Lessons from Systematic Reviews* , edited by David Weisburd, David P. Farrington, and Charlotte Gill (New York, NY: Springer, 2016).

[14] Grant Duwe and Valerie Clark, "Importance of Program Integrity: Outcome Evaluation of a Gender-Responsive, Cognitive–Behavioral Program for Female Offenders," *Criminology & Public Policy* 14 (no. 2, 2015): 301–28.

[15] Wayne N. Welsh and Gary Zajac, "A Multisite Evaluation of Prison-Based Drug Treatment: 4-Year Follow-up Results," *Prison Journal* 93 (2013): 251–71.

[16] Lois M. Davis, Robert Bozick, Jennifer L. Steele, et al., *Evaluating the Effectiveness of Correctional Education: A Meta-analysis of Programs That Provide Education to Incarcerated Adults* (Santa Monica, CA: RAND, 2013); Robert Boziek, Jennifer Steele, Lois Davis, and Susan Turner, "Does Providing Inmates with Education Improve Postrelease Outcomes? A Meta-analysis of Correctional programs in the United States," *Journal of Experimental Criminology* 14 (2018): 389–428.

[17] Amanda Pompoco, John Wooldridge, Melissa Lugo, Carrie Sullivan, and Edward Latyessa, "Reducing Inmate Misconduct and Prison Returns with Facility Education Programs," *Criminology & Public Policy* 16 (no. 2, 2017).

[18] Kevin Helliker, "In Prison, College Courses Are Few," *Wall Street Journal*, May 4, 2011.

[19] For a summary of evidence on drug abuse treatment, see *Principles of Drug Abuse Treatment for Criminal Justice Populations*, NIH Publication No. 07-5316 (Washington, DC: U.S. Government Printing Office, 2007).

[20] Bruce G. Link, Matthew W. Epperson, Brian E. Perron, et al., "Arrest Outcomes Associated with Outpatient Commitment in New York State," *Psychiatric Services* 62 (no. 5, 2011): 504–08.

[21] Steve Aos and Elizabeth Drake, *Prison, Police, and Programs: Evidence-Based Options That Reduce Crime and Save Money* (Olympia, WA: Washington State Institute for Public Policy, 2013).

[22] Center for Sex Offender Management, *Understanding Treatment for Adults and Juveniles Who Have Committed Sex Offenses* (Washington, DC: U.S. Department of Justice, Office of Justice Programs, 2006).

[23] Karen Terry, *Sexual Offenses and Offenders: Theory, Practice, and Policy,* 2nd ed. (Belmont, CA: Wadsworth, 2012).

[24] *Americans United for Separation of Church and State v. Prison Fellowship Ministries*, 509 F.3d 406 (8th Cir. 2007).

[25] See *Cutter v. Wilkinson*, 544 U.S. 709 (2005), discussed in Lynn S. Branham, "'The Devil Is in the Details': A Continued Dissection of the Constitutionality of Faith-Based Prison Units," *Ave Maria Law Review* 6 (no. 2, 2008): 409.

[26] Richard Stansfield, Thomas J. Mowen, and Thomas O'Connor, "Religious and Spiritual Support, Reentry, and Risk," *Justice Quarterly* 35 (no. 2, 2017): 254–79.

[27] Grant Duwe and Michelle King, "Can Faith-Based Correctional Programs Work? An Outcome Evaluation of the Inner-Change Freedom Initiative in Minnesota," *International Journal of Offender Therapy and Comparative Criminology* 57 (no. 7, 2012): 813–14.

[28] Francis Cullen and Karen Gilbert, *Reaffirming Rehabilitation* (Cincinnati: Anderson, 1982).

[29] To see a list of effective correctional programs—and some that are ineffective—visit CrimeSolutions.gov: https://www.crimesolutions.gov/TopicDetails.aspx?ID=2.

[30] Visit the Campbell Collaboration: https://www.campbell collaboration.org/library.html.

[31] Mike Ward, "Prison Cuts Could Cause Bed Shortage in Two Years," *Austin American-Statesman*, March 1, 2011.

[32] Drug Policy Alliance, *Proposition 36: Improving Lives, Delivering Results* (New York: Author, 2006).

[33] *Estelle v. Gamble,* 95 S. Ct. 285 (1976).

[34] Margaret E. Noonan, *Mortality in Local Jails and State Prisons, 2000–2011—Statistical Tables* (Washington, DC: U.S. Bureau of Justice Statistics, 2013).

[35] Laura B. Strick, *Treatment of Hepatitis C in a Correctional Setting*, www.hepatitisc.uw.edu/go/special-populations-situations/treatment-corrections/core-concept/all, December 11, 2015.

[36] BJS *Bulletin*, January 2001.

[37] *NBC News*, "Inside the Secret Industry of Inmate-Staffed Call Centers," January 12, 2012.

[38] William G. Saylor and Gerald G. Gaes, *PREP Study Links UNICOR Work Experience with Successful Post-release Outcome* (Washington, DC: U.S. Bureau of Prisons, Office of Research and Evaluation, n.d.).

CHAPTER 15

Release from Incarceration

Olivier Douliery/Sipa USA

Former-Trump campaign chairman, Paul Manafort, was released to home confinement from a federal correctional facility after serving approximately one-third of a seven and a half year prison sentence.

MANY OBSERVERS WERE CAUGHT OFF GUARD WHEN IT WAS ANNOUNCED THAT FORMER TRUMP-CAMPAIGN CHAIRMAN, PAUL MANAFORT, WAS BEING TRANSFERRED FROM THE FEDERAL PRISON HOUSING HIM IN WESTERN PENNSYLVANIA. Manafort was serving a seven-and-a-half-year sentence for bank fraud, tax fraud, and other legal violations associated with his political lobbying activities. What many onlookers found surprising was that Manafort had served only about one-third of his prison sentence before being transferred to home confinement. Manafort's release was reportedly part of the Bureau of Prisons attempt to slow the spread of the coronavirus in their facilities. Prisons are hotspots for the virus as social distancing is difficult to maintain. In all, approximately 2,500 individuals in federal prisons were released to home confinement in the effort to combat the virus. It was reported that although Manafort had suffered various medical problems during his incarceration that could increase his vulnerability to the virus, including bouts of the flu and bronchitis, he had yet to serve the minimum amount of time necessary for release.[1]

Nearly 615,000 felony-convicted adults were released in 2018 from state and federal prisons (approximately 1,700 each day).[2] Upon release, most people are not as fortunate as Paul Manafort. Many individuals who are released are physically or mentally impaired. Many individuals return to metropolitan areas, where they will live in poor, crime-ridden neighborhoods. As they leave prison, most people receive a new set of clothes, a small amount of money (referred to as "gate money" or "release allowance"), instructions as to when and where to report to a parole officer, and a bus ticket home. With the great expansion of incarceration since the 1980s, the number of people returning to the community from prison has increased dramatically in the last decade.

Reentry has been described as a "transient state between liberty and recommitment. It is a period of limited duration of supervision whereby an inmate moves to either full liberty in the community or is returned to prison for a new crime or for violating the conditions of release."[3] During the reentry period, many released individuals are on parole. For most of the twentieth century, the term *parole* referred to both a release mechanism and a method of community supervision. It is still used in this general sense, but with changes in sentencing and release policies, the dual usage no longer applies in many states. Now we must distinguish between a releasing mechanism and supervision. Although releasing mechanisms have changed, most formerly incarcerated individuals must still serve a period under supervision.

In this chapter we examine the mechanisms of prison release. Supervision of individuals on parole and their adjustment to the community are discussed in Chapter 16.

LEARNING OBJECTIVES

After reading this chapter, you should be able to . . .

1 Discuss parole and explain how it operates today.

2 Explain the origins and evolution of parole in the United States.

3 Discuss the different mechanisms that are used to release people from correctional facilities.

4 Explain how releasing authorities are organized.

5 List the steps that are taken to ease the individual's reentry into the community.

LO 1

Discuss parole and explain how it operates today.

parole The conditional release of an individual from incarceration, under supervision, after part of the prison sentence has been served.

RELEASE FROM ONE PART OF THE SYSTEM TO ANOTHER

Except for the small percentage of the incarcerated population who will die in prison, all incarcerated individuals are eventually released to live in the community. **Parole** is the conditional release of an individual from incarceration but not from the legal custody of the state. Thus, people who comply with parole conditions and do not further violate the law receive an absolute discharge from supervision at the end of their sentence. If a person on parole breaks a rule, parole may be revoked and the person returned to a correctional facility. Parole, then, rests on three concepts:

1. *Grace or privilege:* The individual could be kept incarcerated, but the government extends the privilege of release.
2. *Contract of consent:* The government enters into an agreement with the incarcerated individual whereby the person promises to abide by certain conditions in exchange for being released.
3. *Custody:* Even though an individual is released from prison, he or she is still the responsibility of the government. Parole is an extension of correctional programs into the community.

Only people convicted of felonies are released on parole; adults convicted of misdemeanors are usually released directly from local institutions on expiration of their sentences. With the rapid growth in the prison population during the past 40 years, it is not surprising that the number of adults on parole has also grown, as shown in Figure 15.1. At year-end 2016, 874,800 individuals were under parole supervision, a nearly 300 percent increase since 1980.[4] With the massive incarcerations of the past decades, the number on parole could possibly reach one million within the next ten years.

State and federal (not local) governments offer parole through a variety of organizational structures. In many states, the parole board (the releasing authority) is part of the department of corrections; in others, it is an autonomous body whose members the governor appoints.

As you read this chapter, keep in mind that, like so many other correctional activities, the decision to release is made in the context of complex and competing goals. Traditionally, parole has been justified in terms of rehabilitation. In theory, parole boards evaluate the person's progress toward rehabilitation and readiness to abide by laws. In practice, they consider other factors as well. Even where determinate sentencing or parole guidelines are in effect, correctional officials can influence release; the decision is not as cut-and-dried as proponents have claimed.

Many questions bear on the release decision no matter what procedures are followed. How will the public react? Who will be blamed if the released individual commits another crime? Is the prison so crowded that an early release is necessary to open up space? How will the person's release affect judges and prosecutors? (*"Kansas v. Hendricks"* considers the U.S. Supreme Court decision that a state can deny release to people who have completed their sentences.)

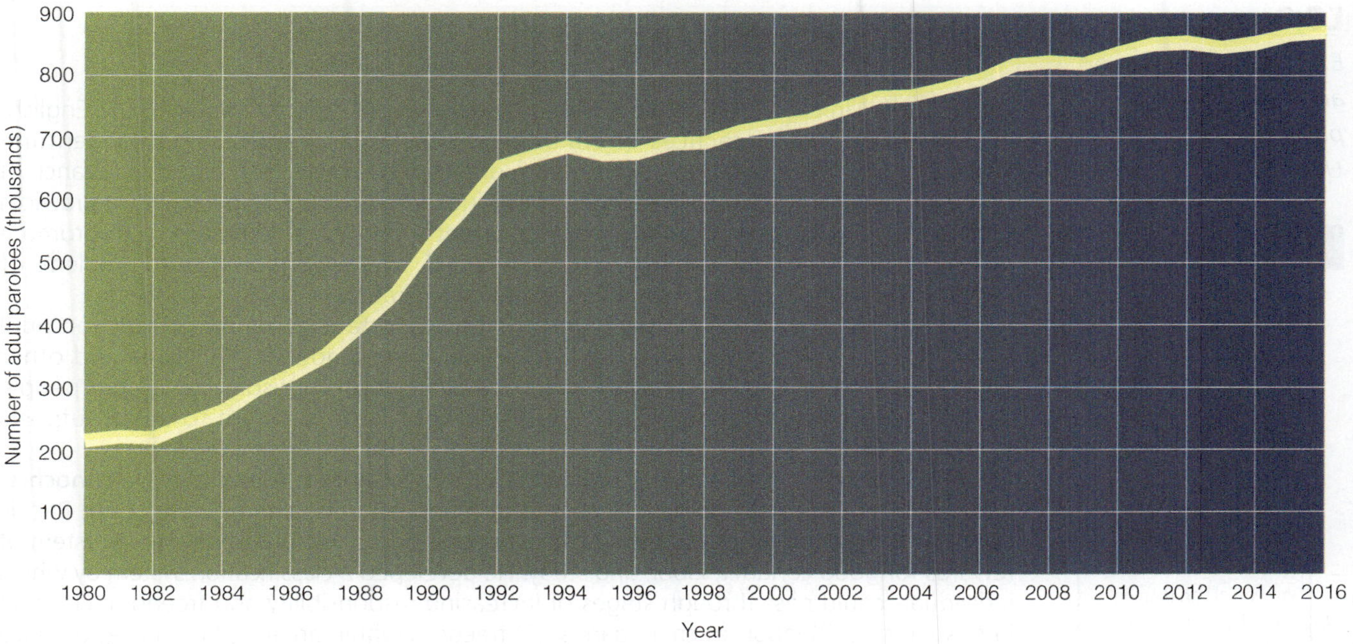

FIGURE 15.1 Numbers of Adults Under Parole Supervision Since 1980
Between 1980 and 2016, the number of adults on parole nearly quadrupled

Source: Ann L. Pastore and Kathleen Maguire, eds., *Sourcebook of Criminal Justice Statistics,* Table 6.1.2010, www.albany.edu/sourcebook/pdf/t612010.pdf, retrieved April 22, 2014; Danielle Kaeble, *Probation and Parole in the United States,* 2016 (Washington, DC: U.S. Government Printing Office, 2018), 3.

FOCUS ON

CORRECTIONAL POLICY: Kansas v. Hendricks

Over a 30-year period, Leroy Hendricks was convicted of six sexual offenses against children and spent much of his adult life in prison. Every time he finished serving a prison sentence or gained parole release, he eventually victimized more children and returned to prison. After serving nearly 10 years in prison for his most recent crime—molesting two teenage boys—he was scheduled to move to a halfway house in the community as the first step toward release.

As Hendricks neared the end of his latest prison sentence, the Kansas legislature passed a new law permitting the state to hold people convicted of sex crimes in mental hospitals *after* they have served their prison sentences. As a result of Kansas's new Sexually Violent Predator Act, Hendricks was transferred from a prison to a mental hospital under a civil-commitment process at the end of his sentence. Hendricks had served the prison sentence imposed for his crime. Yet after serving his full sentence, he did not gain his freedom. The new law permitted Kansas to keep him locked up indefinitely.

Hendricks believed that detaining him after his prison sentence had been served was unfair. He took his case to court, claiming that the law was punishing him a second time for his crime. If that was true, the Kansas law could be violating the constitutional right not to be placed in "double jeopardy"—to be tried or punished twice for the same offense. Hendricks also argued that the law improperly imposed a new punishment on him *after* he committed his crime and served his sentence. Thus, he claimed that the Sexually Violent Predator Act was an "ex post facto law," prohibited by the U.S. Constitution because it applies new rules and punishments that did not exist at the time that an individual violated previously existing laws.

In 1997 the Supreme Court tackled the issues raised by Hendricks, who remained locked up. Four of the nine justices believed Kansas had unfairly created new rules after the fact when it kept Hendricks in custody. The majority of the Supreme Court—only five justices—decided that this was not a second or after-the-fact punishment because Kansas sought to use the law to provide "treatment" rather than to impose "punishment."

Source: *Kansas v. Hendricks,* 521 U.S. 346 (1997).

LO 2

Explain the origins and evolution of parole in the United States.

BIOGRAPHY

CAPTAIN ALEXANDER MACONOCHIE (1787–1860)

Born in Scotland, Maconochie was a naval officer, geographer, and penal reformer. In 1836 he was appointed to a position in the administration of Van Diemen's Land (now Tasmania). Later, he was made superintendent of the Norfolk Island penal colony in the South Pacific. Under his direction, negative marks were initially given to incarcerated individuals but removed from the records of those who performed their tasks well, and they were released when they demonstrated their willingness to accept society's rules.

ORIGINS OF PAROLE

Parole in the United States evolved during the nineteenth century following the English, Australian, and Irish practices of conditional pardon, apprenticeship by indenture, transportation of convicted individuals from one country to another, and the issuance of tickets-of-leave. These were all methods of moving individuals out of prison. Such practices generally did not develop as part of any coherent theory of punishment or to promote any particular goal of the criminal sanction. Instead, they were responses to problems of overcrowding, labor shortages, and the cost of incarceration.

As noted in Chapter 2, England relied on transportation as a major sanction until the mid-1800s. When the United States gained independence, Australia and other Pacific colonies became outlets for England's overcrowded prisons; convicted people were given conditional pardons known as tickets-of-leave and sent to those outposts of the empire.

A key figure in developing parole in the 1800s was **Captain Alexander Maconochie**, who administered British penal colonies in Tasmania and elsewhere in the South Pacific and later in England. Maconochie criticized definite prison terms and devised a system of rewards for good conduct, labor, and study. He developed a classification system by which individuals could pass through stages of increasing responsibility and freedom: (1) strict imprisonment, (2) labor on chain gangs, (3) freedom within an area, (4) a ticket-of-leave or parole with conditional pardon, and (5) full liberty. Like modern correctional practices, this procedure assumed that people should be prepared gradually for release. The roots of the U.S. system of parole can be seen in the transition from imprisonment to conditional release to full freedom.

Maconochie's idea of requiring convicted individuals to earn their early release caught on first in Ireland. There, **Sir Walter Crofton** built on Maconochie's idea that an individual's progress in prison and a ticket-of-leave were linked. After a period of strict imprisonment, people were transferred to an intermediate prison where they could earn marks of commendation based on work, behavior, and education. Those who graduated through Crofton's three successive levels were released on parole, with conditions. Most significant was the requirement that people on parole submit monthly reports to the police. In Dublin a special civilian inspector helped releasees find jobs, visited them periodically, and supervised their activities. Crofton contributed the concepts of the intermediate prison, assistance, and supervision to the modern system of parole.

The English and Irish developments soon traveled across the Atlantic. Conditional pardons and term reductions for good time had been a part of American corrections since the early 1800s, but these individuals were released without supervision. Gaylord Hubbell, the warden of Sing Sing, and Franklin Sanborn, the secretary of the State Board of Charities for Massachusetts, championed the Irish system. In 1870 the National Prison Association incorporated references to the Irish system into the Declaration of Principles, along with such other reforms as the indeterminate sentence and classification based on a mark system.[5]

With New York's passage of an indeterminate sentence law in 1876, Zebulon Brockway, the superintendent of Elmira Reformatory, began to release individuals on parole when he believed they were ready to return to society. Initially, the New York system did not require police supervision, as in Ireland, because people were placed in the care of private reform groups. As the number of individuals on parole increased, however, the state replaced the volunteer supervisors with correctional employees.

Across the United States, as states adopted indeterminate sentencing, parole followed. By 1900, 20 states had parole systems, and by 1925, 46 states did; Mississippi and Virginia finally followed suit in 1942, making them the last of the then 48 states to do so.[6] Beginning in 1910, each federal prison had its own parole board made up of the warden, the medical officer, and the superintendent of prisons of the Department of Justice. The boards made release suggestions to the attorney general. In 1930 Congress created the U.S. Board of Parole, which replaced the separate boards.[7]

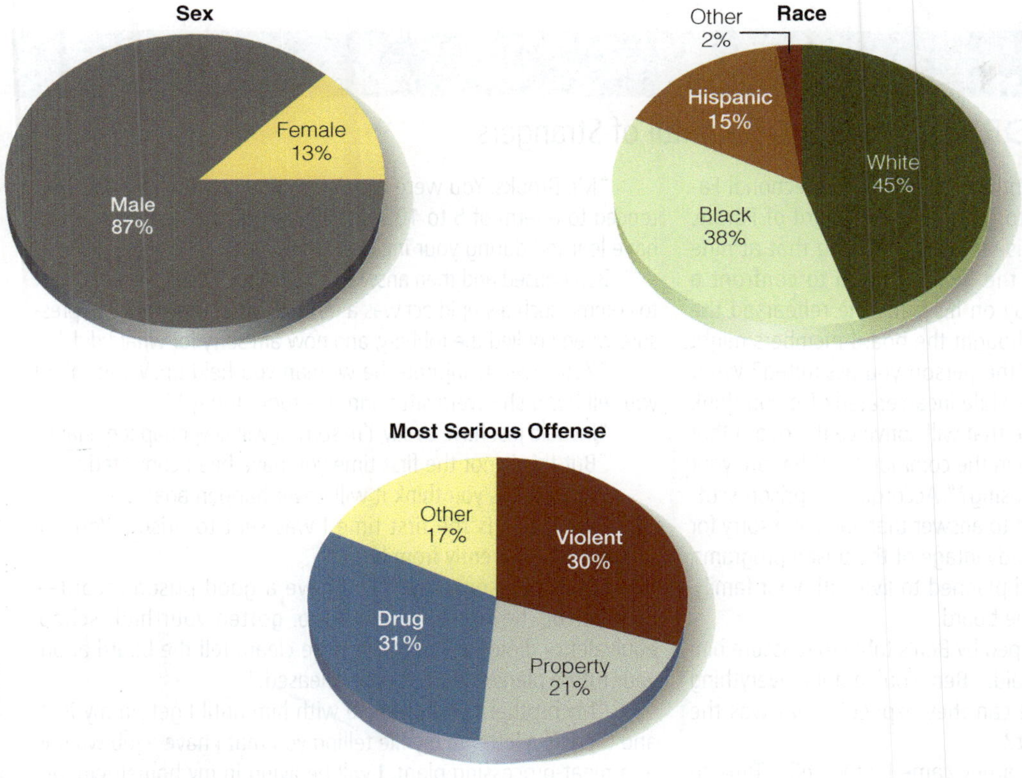

FIGURE 15.2 Characteristics of Adults on Parole

Individuals on parole supervision tend to be male, racial or ethnic minorities, and individuals convicted of nonviolent crimes.

Source: Danielle Kaeble, *Probation and Parole in the United States, 2016* (Washington, DC: U.S. Government Printing Office, April 2018), 24.

BIOGRAPHY

SIR WALTER CROFTON (1815–1897)

Appointed director of the Irish Convict Prisons in 1854, Crofton developed a system for convicted individuals to work toward rehabilitation and early release by moving through three stages of increasing levels of vocational training and privileges. The incarcerated were able to earn "marks" or points for good behavior. This "Irish system" significantly influenced the development of parole in the United States.

Although used in the United States for over a century, parole remains controversial. When someone who has committed a particularly heinous crime becomes eligible for parole or when someone on parole has again raped, robbed, or murdered, the public is outraged. During the 1970s both parole and the indeterminate sentence were criticized on several grounds: Release was tied to treatment success, parole boards were abusing their discretion, and those in prison were being held in "suspended animation." However, remember that although parole may be justified in terms of rehabilitation, deterrence, or protection of society, it has other effects as well. Insofar as it reduces time spent in prison, it affects plea bargaining, the size of prison populations, and the level of discipline in correctional facilities. The characteristics of people on parole are shown in Figure 15.2.

LO 3

Discuss the different mechanisms that are used to release people from correctional facilities.

RELEASE MECHANISMS

From 1920 to 1973 the United States had a nationwide sentencing and release procedure. All states and the federal government used indeterminate sentencing, authorized discretionary release by parole boards, and supervised individuals after release, and they did all of this to rehabilitate people.

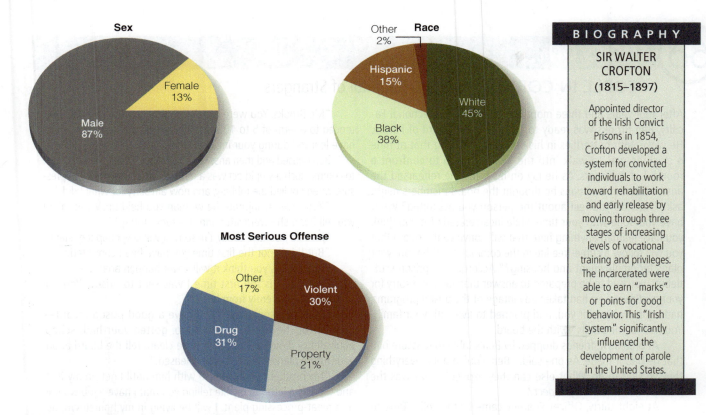

With the 1970s came critiques of rehabilitation, a move to determinate sentencing, and the public's view that the system was "soft" on convicted individuals. Many states and the federal government had abolished discretionary release by parole boards, and

FOCUS ON

PEOPLE IN CORRECTIONS: A Roomful of Strangers

After four years and three months in Stanhope Correctional Facility, Ben Brooks was ready to go before the Board of Parole. He woke with butterflies in his stomach, realizing that at nine o'clock he was to walk into the hearing room to confront a roomful of strangers. As he lay on his bunk, he rehearsed the answers to the questions he thought the board members might ask: "How do you feel about the person you assaulted? What have you done with your time while incarcerated? Do you think you have learned anything here that will convince the board that you will follow a crime-free life in the community? What are your plans for employment and housing?" According to prison scuttlebutt, you had to be prepared to answer that you were sorry for your past mistakes, had taken advantage of the prison programs, had a job waiting for you, and planned to live with your family. You had to "ring bells" with the board.

At breakfast, friends dropped by Ben's table to reassure him that he had it made. As one said, "Ben, you've done everything they've said to do. What else can they expect?" That was the problem: *What did they expect?*

At eight-thirty, Officer Kearney came by the cell. "Time to go, Ben." They walked out of the housing unit and down the long prison corridors to a group of chairs outside the hearing room. Others were already seated there. "Sit here, Ben. They'll call when they're ready. Good luck."

At ten minutes past nine the door opened, and an officer called, "First case, Brooks." Ben got up, walked into the room. "Please take a seat, Mr. Brooks," said the African American seated in the center at the table. Ben knew he was Reverend Perry, a man known as being tough but fair. To his left was a white man, Mr. MacDonald, and to his right a Hispanic woman, Ms. Lopez. The white man led the questioning.

"Mr. Brooks. You were convicted of armed robbery and sentenced to a term of 5 to 10 years. Please tell the board what you have learned during your incarceration."

Ben paused and then answered hesitantly, "Well, I learned that to commit such a stupid act was a mistake. I was under a lot of pressure when I pulled the robbery, and now am sorry for what I did."

"You severely injured the woman you held up. What might you tell her if she were sitting in this room today?"

"I would just have to say, I'm sorry. It will never happen again."

"But this is not the first time you have been convicted. What makes you think it will never happen again?"

"Well, this is the first time I was sent to prison. You see things a lot differently from here."

Ms. Lopez spoke up. "You have a good prison record—member of the Toastmaster's Club, gotten your high school equivalency diploma, kept your nose clean. Tell the board about your future plans should you be released."

"My brother says I can live with him until I get on my feet, and there is a letter in my file telling you that I have a job waiting at a meat-processing plant. I will be living in my hometown, but I don't intend to see my old buddies again. You can be sure that I am now on the straight and narrow."

"But you committed a heinous crime. That woman suffered a lot. Why should the board believe that you won't do it again?"

"All I can say is that I'm different now."

"Thank you, Mr. Brooks," said Reverend Perry. "You will hear from us by this evening." Ben got up and walked out of the room. It had only taken eight minutes, yet it seemed like hours. Eight minutes during which his future was being decided. Would it be back to the cell or out on the street? It would be about ten hours before he would receive word from the board about his fate.

still other states had abolished discretionary release for certain offenses. Further, in some of the states that kept discretionary release, parole boards have been reluctant to grant it. In Colorado, for example, only 26 percent of all cases considered for parole release are approved.[8] Critics charge that eliminating discretionary parole and the widespread reluctance to use grant parole contributed to increases in prison populations over the past four decades.[9]

There are now five basic mechanisms for release from prison: (1) discretionary release, (2) mandatory release, (3) probation release, (4) other conditional release, and (5) expiration release.

discretionary release
The release of an individual from prison to conditional supervision at the discretion of the parole board within the boundaries set by the sentence and the penal law.

Discretionary Release

States retaining indeterminate sentences allow **discretionary release** by the parole board within the boundaries set by the sentence and the penal law. As a conditional release to parole supervision, this approach lets the parole board assess the incarcerated individual's readiness for release within the minimum and maximum terms of the sentence. In reviewing the person's file and asking questions about the individual, the parole board focuses on the nature of the offense, his or her behavior while incarcerated, and participation in rehabilitative programs. This process places great faith in the ability of parole board members to predict accurately the future behavior of people (see "A Roomful of Strangers").

mandatory release The required release of an individual from incarceration to community supervision on the expiration of a certain period, as stipulated by a determinate-sentencing law or parole guidelines.

probation release The release of someone from incarceration to probation supervision, as required by the sentencing judge.

other conditional release A probationary sentence used in some states to get around the rigidity of mandatory release by placing convicted individuals in various community settings under supervision.

expiration release The release of an incarcerated individual into the community without any further correctional supervision; the individual cannot be returned to prison for any remaining portion of the sentence for the current offense.

Mandatory Release

Mandatory release occurs after an individual has served time equal to the total sentence minus "good time," if any, or to a certain percentage of the total sentence as specified by law. Mandatory release is found in federal jurisdictions and states with determinate sentences and good-time provisions (see Chapter 4). Without a parole board to decide if somebody is ready for release and has ties to the community, such as family or a job, mandatory release is a matter of bookkeeping to check the correct amount of good time and to make sure that the sentence has been accurately interpreted. The individual is released conditionally to parole supervision for the rest of the sentence.

Probation Release

Probation release occurs when the sentencing judge requires a period of postcustody supervision in the community. Probation release is often tied to shock incarceration, a practice where a person who is convicted for the first time is sentenced to a short period in jail ("the shock") and then allowed to reenter the community under supervision.

Other Conditional Release

Because of the growth of prison populations, many states have devised ways to get around the rigidity of mandatory release. They place individuals in the community through furlough, home supervision, halfway houses, emergency release, and other programs. These **other conditional releases** also avoid the appearance of the politically sensitive label *discretionary parole*.

Expiration Release

An increasing percentage of incarcerated individuals are given an **expiration release**. These are people who are released from any further correctional supervision and cannot be returned to prison for their current offense. These individuals have served the maximum court sentence, minus good time—they have "maxed out."

In the wake of the "tough on crime" policies of the last four decades,

▲ *Annetta Bryant embraces her son, Calvin, who was released from prison after a campaign highlighted the racial biases that led to his receiving a long sentence.*

FOR CRITICAL THINKING

As noted at the beginning of the chapter, President Trump's former campaign chairman, Paul Manafort, was released from a federal prison where he was incarcerated after being convicted of nonviolent crimes. At the time of his release, he was in his early-70s. Under normal circumstances, Manafort would have been required by law to serve at least 85 percent of his 7.5-year sentence.

1. Some might argue that not requiring Manafort to serve such a large portion of his sentence allowed him to escape justice. Was the potential threat of contracting the virus reason enough to justify Manafort's release? Should Manafort and others who were released return to federal prison after the pandemic ends?
2. Of the different types of release mechanisms used, which one is most appropriate for older individuals, such as Manafort, convicted of nonviolent offenses? What type of release mechanism poses the highest risk of keeping someone imprisoned too long or not long enough? Explain your answers.

the percentage of people released to parole supervision, among all releasees, has dropped. Even when eligible for parole, many individuals have bypassed the board and the controlled, supervised release it provides; instead, they have decided to "stick it out" to the expiration of their sentence and be released to the community without supervision. Critics are concerned that many people who "max out" have spent long terms in prison for serious, violent offenses or have spent extended periods in administrative segregation. They are often hardened, embittered, and likely to return to crime.[10]

Changes in sentencing policies during the 1970s have resulted in shifts in the percentage of individuals released by each of the five mechanisms just described (see "For Critical Thinking"). For example, there has been a major increase in expiration, mandatory, and probation release.[11]

LO 4

Explain how releasing authorities are organized.

THE ORGANIZATION OF RELEASING AUTHORITIES

The structuring of a releasing authority raises certain questions. For example, should it be consolidated with the correctional authority or operate autonomously? How should field services be administered? Should the parole board sit full time or part time? How should board members be appointed? Over the past decade, states have tended to create strong links between the paroling authority and the department of corrections, emphasizing parole board professionalism.

Consolidated Versus Autonomous

Parole boards tend to be organized either inside a department of corrections (consolidated) or as an independent agency of government (autonomous). Some argue that a parole board must be independent to insulate members from the activities and influence of correctional staff. An independent parole board may be less influenced by staff considerations such as reducing the prison population and punishing those who do not follow prison rules. Critics counter that an independent parole board can become unresponsive to correctional needs and programs and is too far removed from prison activities to understand individual cases.

Whether a parole board is independent or a part of a correctional department, it cannot exist in a vacuum. Board members cannot ignore the public's attitudes and fears about crime. If someone on parole commits a crime that arouses public indignation, the board members must make decisions more cautiously in order to avoid public condemnation. Parole boards may also be influenced by departments of corrections and must maintain good relations with them. For example, if an autonomous board conflicts with the department, the department might not provide the board with the information that it needs. Information about particular individuals might become "unavailable," or the state might provide biased information about people whom officials wish to see punished. By contrast, a board closely tied to correctional officials would more likely receive information and cooperation. However, such a board runs the risk of being viewed by prison residents and the general public as merely the rubber stamp of the department.

Field Services

Questions similar to those concerning the organization of the releasing authority surround the organization of field services. For example, should community supervision be administered by an independent paroling authority or by the department of corrections? When the parole board administers field services, proponents say, consistent policies can be developed. The need for programs that address the transition from prison to the community is increasing. Many departments have instituted such pre-parole programs as work release and educational release. Therefore, it is argued, the institutional staff and the parole board must be coordinated—which is easier to do if they are in the same department.

Full Time Versus Part Time

A third set of questions concerns full-time versus part-time boards. Because of the increased complexity of corrections, many people, in both discretionary- and mandatory-release states, hold that administration of parole should be a full-time enterprise. The type of person who serves full time on a parole board differs considerably from the one who serves part time. Membership on a board that meets full time attracts criminal justice professionals, who are usually well paid. However, members of part-time boards, paid by the day, are thought to represent the community better because they have other careers and are independent of the criminal justice system.

Appointment

Members of the paroling authority may be appointed by the governor or by the head of the correctional department. Some people believe that gubernatorial selection insulates the members from the department, provides "better" members, and permits greater responsiveness to public concerns. Others believe that the parole mechanism should be apolitical and operated by people who really know something about corrections.

The selection of members for discretionary parole boards is often based on the assumption that people with training in behavioral sciences can tell which candidates are rehabilitated and ready to return to society. However, in many states, political considerations dictate that members should include representatives of specific racial groups or geographic areas.

THE DECISION TO RELEASE

Eligibility for release to community supervision depends on requirements set by law and the sentence imposed by the court. In states with determinate sentences or parole guidelines, release is mandatory once someone has served the required amount of time. In approximately two-thirds of the states, however, the release decision is discretionary, and the parole board has authority to establish a release date (see Figure 15.3). The date is based on the individual's rehabilitation, behavior while in prison, and plan for reentry into the community.

The Discretionary Release Process

Based on the assumptions of indeterminate sentences and rehabilitative programs, discretionary release is designed to allow the parole board to release individuals to conditional supervision in the community when they are deemed "ready" to live as law-abiding citizens.

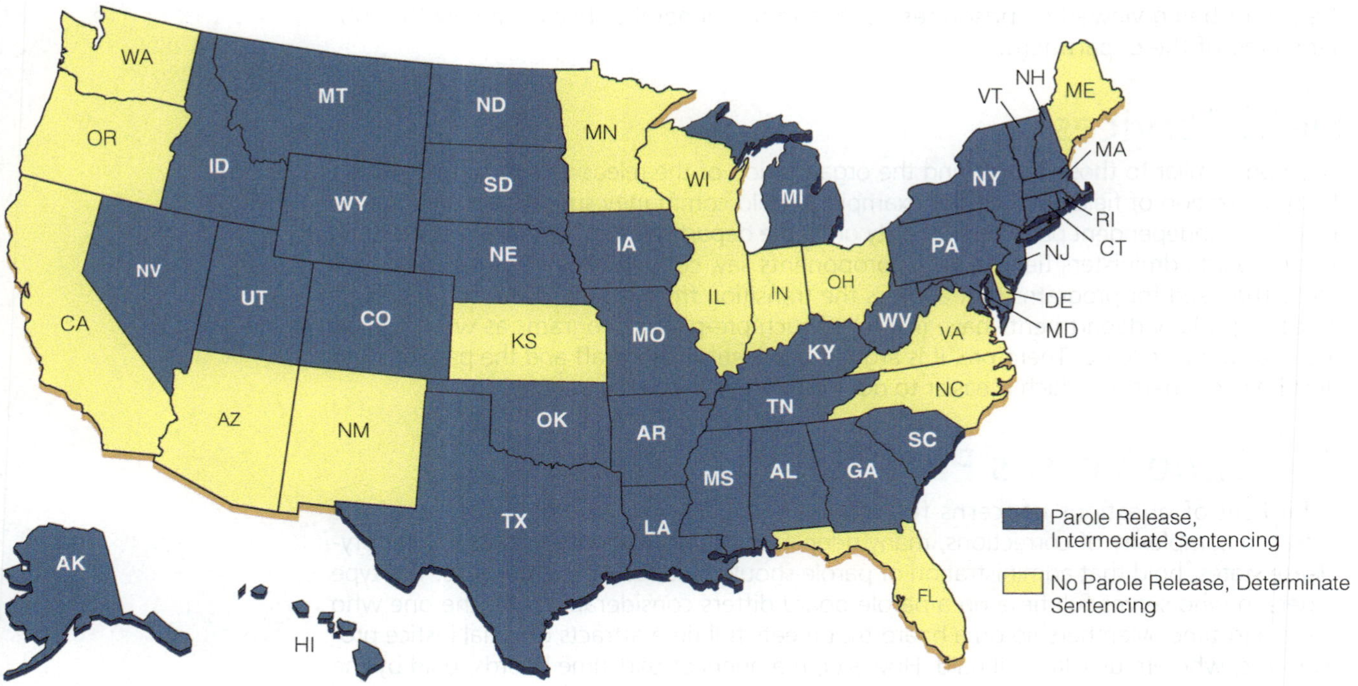

FIGURE 15.3 Parole Boards and Sentencing Structure by State

Source: Edward E. Rhine, Kelly Lyn Mitchell, and Kevin R. Reitz, *Levers of Change in Parole Release and Revocation* (Minneapolis, MN: Regents of the University of Minnesota, 2019), 8.

Procedure Eligibility for a release hearing in discretionary states varies greatly. Appearance before the parole board is a function of the individual sentence, statutory criteria, and the individual's conduct before incarceration. Often, the person is eligible for release at the end of the minimum term of the sentence minus good time. In other states, eligibility is at the discretion of the parole board or is calculated at one-third or one-half of the maximum sentence. However, many states provide a variety of mechanisms for release, as shown in Table 15.1.

Consider the case of Ben Brooks for an example of the computation of parole eligibility (see Figure 15.4). At the time of sentencing, Brooks had been held in jail for 6 months awaiting trial and disposition of his case. He was given a sentence of a minimum of 5 years and a maximum of 10 years for robbery with violence. Brooks did well at the maximum-security prison to which he was sent. He did not get into trouble and was thus able to amass good-time credit at the rate of one day for every four that he spent on good behavior. In addition, he was given meritorious credit of 30 days when he passed his high school diploma equivalency test. After serving 3 years and 4 months of his sentence, he appeared before the board of parole and was granted release into the community.

Release Criteria What factors guide the parole board decision? A parole board gives each person up for release a formal statement of the criteria for making the decision. These standards normally include at least eight factors concerning the individual:

1. Nature and circumstances of offense and current attitude toward it
2. Prior criminal record
3. Attitudes toward family members, victim, and authority in general
4. Institutional adjustment and participation and progress in programs for self-improvement

TABLE 15.1 Ten Release Mechanisms in South Carolina

Until a task force on overcrowding consolidated some of the provisions, South Carolina recognized more than 10 ways to leave a prison (besides escape or death). All the following types of release have been specified in the state statutes or administrative procedures.

Type of Release	Eligibility	Calculation
Discretionary parole	Anyone convicted of a felony	"Life," eligible at 20 years. Less than 10 years, eligible at 1/4 of sentence. 10 years or more, eligible at 1/3 of sentence.
Good time	Anyone convicted of a felony	Lifers earn 15 days off maximum term for every 30 days in prison; others can earn 20 days for every 30 days in prison.
Earned work credits	Anyone convicted of a felony who is on special work assignments	1 day off maximum term for every 2 days in work assignment up to 180 days per year.
Extended work release	Anyone convicted of a felony who has no more than 1 prior conviction	Placed on work release status 2 months before parole eligibility.
Supervised furlough I	Anyone convicted of a felony who has a clean disciplinary record, less than 5-year sentence, less than 2 prior convictions	Released 6 months before parole eligibility.
Supervised furlough II	Anyone convicted of a felony who has 6 months clean record	Released 6 months before parole eligibility.
First-day-of-month rule	Anyone convicted of a felony	Released on first day of month in which eligibility is reached (after other reductions).
Emergency release provision	Anyone convicted of a felony who is within 90 days of eligibility for parole	When prison reaches state of crisis because of crowding, governor may roll back sentences to reduce numbers.
Provisional parole	Anyone convicted of a felony	Released 90 days before eligibility at discretion of parole board.
Christmas parole	Anyone convicted of a felony	If parole eligibility is reached between December 18 and January 30, released on December 18 at discretion of parole board.

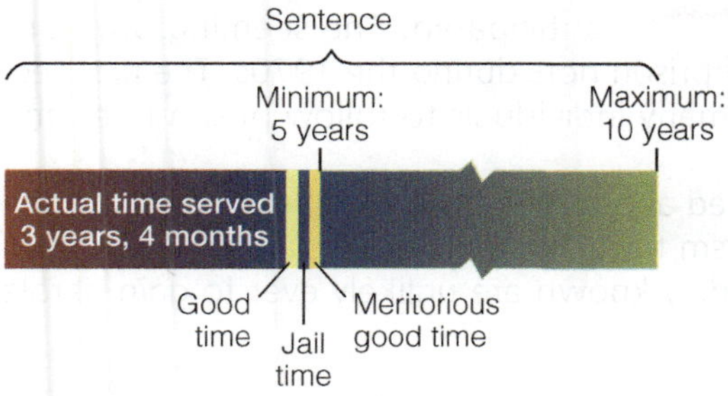

Maximum sentence	3,650	days (10 years)
Minimum sentence	1,825	days (5 years)
"Jail time"	– 180	
	1,645	
Meritorious "good time"	– 30	
	1,615	
"Good time" (1 for 4)	– 404	
Paroled: actual time served	1,211	days (3 years, 4 months)

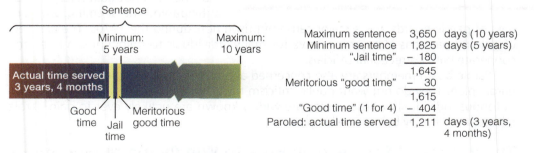

FIGURE 15.4 Computing Parole Eligibility for Ben Brooks

Various good-time reductions to the minimum sentence are allowed in most corrections systems to determine eligibility for parole. Note how a 5- to 10-year sentence can be reduced to a stay of 3 years, 4 months.

DO THE RIGHT THING

The five members of the parole board questioned Jim Allen, an individual with a long history of sex offenses involving teenage boys. Now approaching age 45 and having met the eligibility requirement for a hearing, Allen respectfully answered the board members.

Toward the end of the hearing, Richard Edwards, a dentist who had recently been appointed to the board, spoke up: "Your institutional record is good, you have a parole plan, a job has been promised, and your sister says she will help you. All of that looks good, but I just can't vote for your parole. You haven't attended Dr. Hankin's behavior modification program for persons convicted of sex crimes. I think you're going to repeat your crime. I have a 13-year-old son, and I don't want him or other boys to run the risk of meeting your kind." Allen looked shocked. The other members had seemed ready to grant his release.

"But I'm ready for parole. I won't do that stuff again. I didn't go to that program because electroshock to my private area is not going to help me. I've been here five years of the seven-year max and have stayed out of trouble. The judge didn't say I was to be further punished in prison by therapy."

After Jim Allen left the room, the board discussed his case. "You know, Rich, he has a point. He has behaved himself and has also served a good portion of his sentence," said Brian Lynch, a long-term board member. "Besides, we don't know if Dr. Hankin's program works."

"I know, but can we really let someone like that out on the streets?"

WRITING ASSIGNMENT: Assume that you are a member of the parole board considering whether to release Jim Allen. Write a short essay discussing the following questions: Would you consider the results of the behavior modification program for people convicted of sex crimes relevant when making your decision? Do you think that the purpose of the sentence is to punish Allen for what he did or for what he might do in the future? How would you vote on Allen's parole request?

5. History of community adjustment
6. Physical, mental, and emotional health
7. Insight into causes of past criminal conduct
8. Adequacy of parole plan

Although the published criteria may help familiarize those serving prison sentences with the board's expectations, research shows that the actual decision is typically based on various kinds of information, including institutional behavior, crime severity, and criminal history. Surprisingly, input from victims, whether in support of or in opposition to release, has little effect on the parole decision.[12]

Research suggests that mental health should be carefully considered. One study found not only that released individuals with serious mental illness returned to prison more frequently than healthy individuals but also that the median amount of time they spent free in the community was significantly shorter (385 days versus 743 days).[13] It is frequently said that parole boards release only good risks, but as one parole board member has said, "There are no good-risk men in prison. Parole is really a decision of when to release bad-risk persons."

Other considerations weigh heavily on the parole board members. If parole is not regularly awarded to most individuals who gain eligibility, morale among the incarcerated may suffer as they fear that they will not gain release when anticipated. The seeming arbitrariness of parole boards was a major cause of prison riots during the 1970s. The prospect of gaining parole is a major incentive for many individuals to follow prison rules and cooperate with correctional officials.

Parole board members are also concerned about the public and the adequacy of the parole plan. They do not want public criticism for making controversial decisions. Thus, notorious individuals whose crimes are widely known are unlikely ever to gain parole release, even if they behave well in prison.

The Prisoners' Perspective: How to Win Parole "If you want to get paroled, you've got to be in a program." This statement reflects one of the most controversial aspects of discretionary release: its link to treatment. Although correctional authorities emphasize the voluntary nature of most treatment services and clinicians argue that coercive therapy cannot succeed, many individuals in prison believe they must "play the game." Most parole boards cite an individual's progress in self-improvement programs as one criterion for release.

Although participation in prison programs is technically voluntary, the link between participation and release poses many legal and ethical problems, as illustrated by the case of Jim Allen in "Do the Right Thing." In some states, individuals convicted of drug or sex offenses may be expected to participate in treatment programs. However, the corrections system may not have enough places in these programs to serve all of them. Some incarcerated individuals may wait long periods before gaining admission, or they may be in an institution that does not have the treatment they need. Because they cannot force the prison system to transfer them to the appropriate institution, incarcerated individuals may become frustrated hearing about other people gaining parole while they are not given the opportunity to prove themselves to the board. Moreover, some kinds of treatment programs, especially for those convicted of sex crimes, may involve intrusive counseling therapies or medications that have lingering physical effects and a limited likelihood of success. However, threatened with denial of parole if they refuse to participate, individuals seeking release may not feel able to decline such treatments.

Consequences of Discretionary Parole During a riot at New Jersey's Rahway Prison, rioters held aloft a banner that boldly proclaimed, "Abolish parole!" Why? Individuals serving time in prison often criticize the somewhat capricious actions of some parole boards. They also point out that indeterminate sentences and discretionary release leave them in limbo. The uncertainty is demoralizing.

When release is discretionary, the parole board's power is much like that of the sentencing judge. Detractors emphasize that unlike the judge, the board makes its decisions outside the spotlight of public attention. In addition, they contend that whereas sentencing is done with due process of law, a parole hearing offers few such rights.

Supporters of discretionary release maintain that parole boards can make their decisions without community pressure and can rectify sentencing errors. Arguably, legislatures often respond to public pressure by prescribing unreasonably harsh maximum sentences—30, 50, even 100 years. But most penal codes also prescribe minimum sentences that are closer to the actual time served; thus, the parole board can grant release after a "reasonable" period of incarceration.

Structuring Parole Decisions

In response to the criticism that the release decisions of parole boards are somewhat arbitrary, many states have adopted parole guidelines. Release is usually granted to individuals who have served the amount of time stipulated by the guidelines and who meet the following three criteria:

1. They have substantially observed the rules of the institution in which they have been confined.
2. Their release will not depreciate the seriousness of the offense or promote disrespect for the law.
3. Their release will not jeopardize the public welfare.

As with sentencing guidelines, a severity scale ranks crimes according to their seriousness, and a salient factor score measures both the person's criminal history (drug arrests, prior record, age at first conviction, and so on) and risk factors regarded as relevant to successful completion of parole (see Table 15.2 and Table 15.3).

By placing an individual's salient factor score next to his or her particular offense on the severity scale, the board, the individual serving time, and correctional officials can calculate the **presumptive parole date** soon after the person enters prison. This is the date by which the individual can expect to be released if there are no disciplinary or other

presumptive parole date The presumed release date stipulated by parole guidelines if an individual serves time without disciplinary or other incidents.

TABLE 15.2 Criminal History/Risk Assessment Under the Oregon Guidelines for Adults

The amount of time to be served is related to the severity of the offense and to the criminal history/risk assessment of the individual. The criminal history score is determined by adding the points assigned to each factor in this table.

	Factor	Points	Score
A.	No prior felony convictions as an adult or juvenile:	3	
	One prior felony conviction:	2	
	Two or three prior felony convictions:	1	
	Four or more prior felony convictions:	0	—
B.	No prior felony or misdemeanor incarcerations (that is, executed sentences of 90 days or more) as an adult or juvenile:	2	
	One or two prior incarcerations:	1	
	Three or more prior incarcerations:	0	—
C.	Verified period of three years conviction-free in the community prior to the present commitment:	1	
	Otherwise:	0	—
D.	Age at commencement of behavior leading to this incarceration was _____; D.O.B. was _____		
	26 or older and at least one point received in Items A, B, or C:	2	
	26 or older and no points received in A, B, or C:	1	
	21 to under 26 and at least one point received in A, B, or C:	1	
	21 to under 26 and no points received in A, B, or C:	0	
	Under 21:	0	—
E.	Present commitment does not include parole, probation, failure to appear, release agreement, escape, or custody violation:	2	
	Present commitment involves probation, release agreement, or failure to appear violation:	1	
	Present commitment involves parole, escape, or custody violation:	0	—
F.	Has no admitted or documented substance abuse problem within a three-year period in the community immediately preceding the commission of the crime conviction:	1	
	Otherwise:	0	
	Total History/Risk Assessment		—

Source: Adapted from State of Oregon, Board of Parole, *ORS* Chapter 144, Rule 255-35-015.

problems during incarceration. The presumptive parole date may be modified on a scheduled basis. The date of release may be advanced because of good conduct and superior achievement or postponed if there are disciplinary infractions or if a suitable community supervision plan is not developed.

The Impact of Release Mechanisms

Parole release mechanisms do more than determine the date at which a particular person will be sent back into the community. Parole release also has an enormous impact on other parts of the system, including sentencing, plea bargaining, and the size of prison populations.

One important effect of discretionary release is that an administrative body—the parole board—can shorten a sentence imposed by a judge. Even in states that have

TABLE 15.3 Number of Months to Be Served Before Release Under the Oregon Guidelines

The presumptive release date is determined by finding the intersection of the criminal history score (see Table 15.2) and the category of the offense. Thus, an individual with an assessment score between 8 and 6, convicted of a category 3 offense, could expect to serve between 10 and 14 months.

	Criminal History/Risk Assessment Score			
Offense Severity	11–9 Excellent	8–6 Good	5–3 Fair	2–0 Poor
Category 1: bigamy, criminal mischief I, dogfighting, incest, possession of stolen vehicle	6	6	6–10	12–18
Category 2: abandonment of a child, bribing a witness, criminal homicide, perjury, possession of controlled substance	6	6–10	10–14	16–24
Category 3: assault III, forgery I, sexual abuse, trafficking in stolen Vehicles	6–10	10–14	14–20	22–32
Category 4: aggravated theft, assault II, coercion, criminally negligent homicide, robbery II	10–16	16–22	22–30	32–44
Category 5: burglary I, escape I, manslaughter II, racketeering, rape I	16–24	24–36	40–52	56–72
Category 6: arson I, kidnapping I, rape II, sodomy I	30–40	44–56	60–80	90–130
Category 7: aggravated murder, treason	96–120	120–156	156–192	192–240
Category 8: aggravated murder (stranger–stranger, cruelty to victim, prior murder conviction)	120–168	168–228	228–288	288–life

Source: Adapted from State of Oregon, Board of Parole, *ORS* Chapter 144, Rule 255-75-026 and Rule 255-75-035.

mandatory release, various potential reductions built into the sentence mean that the full sentence is rarely served. For example, good time can reduce punishment even if there is no parole eligibility.

To understand the impact of release mechanisms on criminal punishment, we need to compare the amount of time actually served in prison with the sentence specified by the judge. Eligibility for discretionary release is ordinarily determined by the minimum term of the sentence minus good time and jail time.

The probability of release well before the end of the formal sentence encourages plea bargaining by both prosecutors and the accused. Prosecutors can reap the benefits of quick, cooperative plea bargains that look tough in the eyes of the public. Meanwhile, the accused agrees to plead guilty and accept the sentence because of the high likelihood of early release through parole.

Beyond the benefits to prosecutors, parole discretion may benefit the overall system. Discretionary release mitigates the harshness of the penal code. If the legislature must establish exceptionally strict punishments as a means of conveying a "tough on crime" image to frustrated and angry voters, parole can effectively permit sentence adjustments that make the punishment fit the crime. Everyone convicted of larceny may not have done equivalent harm, yet some legislatively mandated sentencing schemes impose equally strict sentences. Early release on parole can be granted to an individual who is less deserving of strict punishment, such as someone who voluntarily makes restitution, cooperates with the police, or shows genuine regret.

Discretionary release is also an important tool for reducing prison populations in states with overcrowded prisons and budget deficits. Even states that abolished parole boards, instituted mandatory sentences, and adopted truth- in-sentencing laws in the 1980s are now finding loopholes that allow them to release incarcerated individuals early. Governors in a number of states have released or plan to release people from prison because of crowding and costs. Such plans are not always received favorably.

A major criticism of discretionary release is that it has shifted responsibility for many primary criminal justice decisions from a judge, who holds legal procedures uppermost,

FOR CRITICAL THINKING

President Trump's former campaign chair, Paul Manafort, was convicted of nonviolent crimes. This was his first criminal conviction. While incarcerated, he maintained a good relationship with his family and did not cause problems for prison staff. Finally, at the time of his release, he appeared to be in reasonably good physical and mental health.

1. If you were serving on a parole board that was considering a similar case, how would you weigh the above information? What factors would you place more emphasis on? What other issues would you consider when determining whether the person should be released?
2. When parole decisions are made, one of the important factors is whether the individual will jeopardize the public welfare. Gauge the threat to public safety and well-being that Paul Manafort poses. What circumstances would make Manafort a greater threat to public safety?

to an administrative board, where discretion rules (see "For Critical Thinking"). Judges know a great deal about constitutional rights and basic legal protections, but parole board members may not have such knowledge. In most states with discretionary release, parole hearings are secret, with only board members, the individual being considered for release, and correctional officers present. Often, no published criteria guide decisions, and individuals are given no reason for the denial or granting of parole. However, an increasing number of states permit oral or written testimony by victims as well as members of the incarcerated individual's family.

Should society place such power in the hands of parole boards? Because there is so little oversight regarding their decision making and so few constraints on their decisions, some parole board members will make arbitrary or discriminatory decisions inconsistent with the constitutional system and civil rights. Generally, the U.S. legal system seeks to avoid determining people's fates through such methods.

LO 5

List the steps that are taken to ease the individual's reentry into the community.

RELEASE TO THE COMMUNITY

One impact of the explosive growth of the nation's prison population is the huge increase in the number of people serving prison sentences who are being released to the community after serving their terms. As noted at the outset of this chapter, nearly 615,000 felony-convicted individuals— about 1,700 per day—returned home from federal and state prisons in 2018. The problem of "making it" in the community is discussed in Chapter 16; here we describe the ways that people in prison are prepared for release.

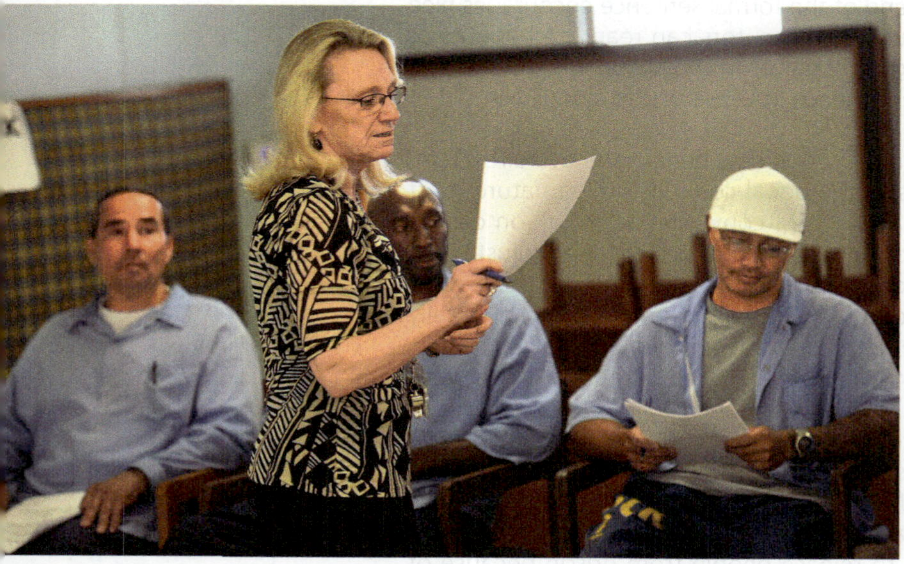

Dan Rosenstrauch/Bay Area News Group/TNS

▲ *Collette Carroll talks to a group of men at San Quentin State Prison who are participating in the California Reentry Institute, a program that supports men through the transition from prison to freedom.*

The great increase in the number of people returning to the community from prison has stimulated action by Congress and the states to provide assistance to people on parole and to reduce the staggering amount of recidivism among them. The Second Chance Act is federal reentry legislation that was signed into law in 2008. It is designed to ensure the safe and successful return of individuals released from prison through grants to states and communities to support reentry initiatives focused on employment, housing, substance abuse and mental health treatment, and children and family services.

From the philosophy of community corrections has come the reintegration model. Here the goal is to prepare people for reentry into society through the gradual allocation of freedoms and responsibilities during incarceration. Where this model has been adopted, individuals are placed at a high level of custody when they enter the prison, and they are periodically evaluated. As they progress, the level of custody is lowered so they can reestablish family ties and begin to heal the harm done by their crime and incarceration. In some states, furloughs can be arranged, and visitations at the institution can increase. Toward the latter part of the sentence, people may be placed on work release, transferred to a halfway house, or given other opportunities to live in the community.

All states have some form of prison program designed to prepare people for release to community supervision. The individual receives prerelease counseling about the conditions of supervision, as well as help in searching for employment and a place to live. In some systems these activities begin as far as two years in advance of the targeted release date; in others they begin only after that date is confirmed.

One innovative prerelease program is Oregon's Parenting Inside Out. This program is rooted in the assumption that improving familial ties and increasing social support are keys to successful reentry. The program teaches those nearing release about the various ways that a person can function as a parent. The program also provides participants with skills in parent–child interactions, such as monitoring and supervision, positive encouragement, appropriate and consistent discipline, and family problem solving. Other topics, such as emotion regulation, healthy adult relationships, and child temperament, are also covered. The program is available to individuals who have been released from prison.[14] Research indicates that programs designed to increase the social support available to individuals released from prison, such as Parenting Inside Out, should prove beneficial in terms of increasing the chances of successful reentry.[15]

FOCUS ON

CORRECTIONAL PRACTICE: Jacksonville Re-Entry Center

It's a Monday evening. A Florida man, Darian Jones, stands on a stage in front of approximately 1,500 people. He tells the crowd about his path, which included 13 years of incarceration. His is a story of redemption that includes gainful employment, owning a car, strengthened family bonds, and a life free of criminal activity. But according to Jones, his story may not have been possible without the assistance he received from the Jacksonville Re-Entry Center (JREC), a program that is designed to help reduce the recidivism rate among formerly incarcerated men and women who are returning to daily life in Duval County.

Upon return from prison, many individuals experience great difficulty seeing to it that their own basic needs are met. Among such needs are food, clothing, employment, shelter, medical care, transportation, banking, and the like. The JREC aims to help those who were recently incarcerated by helping them meet these and other needs. The program not only provides clean clothing and nutritious food, but also provides those in need with bus passes, transitional housing, access to a mental health professional, and the ability to see a nurse practitioner. The program annually serves more than 600 people.

Sheriff Mike Williams, one of the strongest and most visible supporters of the program, says the "concept is a proven one: reintegrating former offenders into our community by providing them with the necessary resources to secure housing, access healthcare providers and participate in work readiness training." The available evidence on the success of the program seems to support Williams's view. Among JREC participants, the recidivism rate was 12.5 percent in the fiscal year 2015–2016. However, because funding is scarce, the program reaches only about 40 percent of people returning to the community each year from prison.

Although the program has helped people such as Darian Jones successfully reintegrate back into society, the program cannot alleviate all the strains that program participants experience. For example, Florida has harsh laws when it comes to prohibiting those convicted of felonies from voting. Jones wishes he were able to vote. "What you're telling me is that, when I'm released from prison, I'm basically a second-class citizen," said Jones.

Source: Ben Conarck, "Fighting Recidivism: Jacksonville's Re-Entry Program Lifts Ex-Offenders," *Florida Times-Union,* http://jacksonville.com/metro/public-safety/news/2017-04-01/fighting-recidivism-jacksonville-s-re-entry-program-lifts-ex, April 1, 2017.

MYTHS in Corrections

Revolving Doors?

THE MYTH: Most people on parole return to prison before they complete supervision.

THE REALITY: Nearly 57 percent of people on parole successfully complete their sentence while under supervision in the community.

Source: Danielle Kaeble, *Probation and Parole in the United States, 2016* (Washington, DC: U.S. Government Printing Office, 2018), 22.

The best prerelease programs provide a multiweek, full-time training program for individuals who are within 60 days of release from prison. These individuals are given training in the attitudes needed to get and keep a job, communication skills, family roles, money management, and community and parole resources (see "Jacksonville Re-Entry Center" for an example). The individuals and their needs are evaluated. Each person is then given a list of five objectives to achieve within 30 days of being paroled, as well as the names and addresses of five public or private agencies that can be contacted for assistance. During the training program, each person participates in at least one mock job interview and acquires a driver's license.

Other programs include transfer of the participating individuals to a housing unit reserved for prereleasees. One week of the four-week period is devoted to family readjustment training. With the emphasis on reintegration and community supervision, incarcerated individuals are no longer confined to one cell in one institution for the duration of their terms. Instead, they move about a great deal from one security level to another and from one institution to another as they prepare for release. However, critics argue that only a small percentage of people receive prerelease planning. (See "Myths in Corrections.") In most states, participating in these programs is voluntary and is available to only a small proportion of the prison population that is nearing release.

SUMMARY

1 Discuss parole and explain how it operates today.

Parole is the conditional release of an individual from incarceration but not from the legal custody of the state. In order to receive an absolute discharge from supervision, people on parole must comply with a specified set of conditions and must not violate the law. If the released individual breaks a rule, then parole may be revoked and the person returned to a correctional facility. Only people convicted of a felony are released on parole. Adults convicted of a misdemeanor are usually released directly from local institutions on expiration of their sentence.

2 Explain the origins and evolution of parole in the United States.

Parole in the United States evolved during the nineteenth century, following the English, Australian, and Irish practices of conditional pardon, apprenticeship by indenture, transportation of convicted individuals, and the issuance of tickets-of-leave. After the passage of an indeterminate sentencing law in 1876, the Elmira Reformatory in New York began to release people on parole. By 1900, 20 states had parole systems, and by 1942, all of the then 48 states operated parole systems. At the federal level, individual federal prisons had their own parole boards beginning in 1910. In 1930 Congress created the U.S. Board of Parole to replace separate boards.

3 Discuss the different mechanisms that are used to release people from correctional facilities.

In states that use indeterminate sentences, parole boards are used to grant discretionary release. When making their decision whether to release an individual, the parole board considers the nature of the offense, the individual's behavior, and participation in rehabilitation programs. In contrast, mandatory release occurs after an individual has served time equal to the total sentence minus good time, or to a certain percentage of the total sentence as specified by law. This form of release does not rely on the judgment of a parole board. A third release mechanism, probation release, occurs when the sentencing judge requires a period of postcustody supervision in the community. This type of release is often tied to shock incarceration and is more

4 Explain how releasing authorities are organized.

Parole boards tend to be organized either inside a department of corrections (consolidated) or as an independent agency of government (autonomous). Some argue that a parole board must be independent to insulate members from the activities and influence of correctional staff. Others believe that an independent parole board can become unresponsive to correctional needs and programs. Some parole boards are full time, while others are part time. Membership on a board that meets full time attracts criminal justice professionals. Members of part-time boards are thought to represent the community better because they have other careers and are independent of the criminal justice system. Members of the paroling authority may be appointed by

common among individuals who were convicted for the first time. Many states also have other conditional release mechanisms, such as placing individuals in the community through furlough, home supervision, halfway houses, or emergency release. Finally, expiration release is used when individuals have "maxed out" their sentence and are released from correctional supervision. These people cannot be returned to prison for their current offense.

5 List the steps that are taken to ease the individual's reentry into the community.

All states have some form of prison program designed to prepare incarcerated individuals for release to community supervision. The individual receives prerelease counseling about the conditions of supervision, as well as help in searching for employment and a place to live. The best prerelease programs provide a multiweek, full-time training program for individuals who are within 60 days of release. Individuals are given training in the attitudes needed to get and keep a job, communication skills, family roles, money management, and community and parole resources. Individuals then receive a list of objectives to achieve after being paroled, as well as the names and addresses of public or private agencies that can be contacted for assistance. Other programs include transfer of the participating individuals to a housing unit reserved for individuals scheduled to be released. With the emphasis on reintegration and community supervision, incarcerated individuals are no longer confined to one cell in one institution for the duration of their terms. Instead, they move about a great deal from one security level to another and from one institution to another as they prepare for release.

the governor or by the head of the correctional department. In many states, political considerations dictate such appointments, and training in the behavioral sciences is not always given highest priority.

KEY TERMS

discretionary release (*p. 400*)
expiration release (*p. 401*)
mandatory release (*p. 401*)
other conditional release (*p. 401*)
parole (*p. 396*)
presumptive parole date (*p. 407*)
probation release (*p. 401*)

FOR DISCUSSION

1. How does mandatory release affect the corrections system? How will corrections adjust to this harnessing of the discretion of parole boards and judges?
2. What factors should a parole board consider when it evaluates an incarcerated individual for release from prison?
3. Suppose, as a parole board member, you are confronted by a man who has served 6 years of a 10- to 20-year sentence for murder. He has a good institutional record, and you do not believe him to be a threat to community safety. Would you release him to parole supervision at this time? Why or why not?

4. Suppose that you have been asked to decide whether the department of corrections or an independent agency should have authority over release decisions. Where would you place that authority? Why?

5. Given the current public attitude toward individuals involved in criminal activity, what do you see as the likely future of parole release?

FOR FURTHER READING

Hardy, Jason. *The Second Chance Club.* New York: Simon & Schuster, 2020. A former parole officer in New Orleans reveals the turbulent life that awaits individuals released from prison in Louisiana.

Morris, Norval. *Maconochie's Gentlemen: The Story of Norfolk Island and the Roots of Modern Prison Reform.* New York: Oxford University Press, 2001. Morris shows how Maconochie's life and efforts on Norfolk Island provide a model for the running of correctional institutions today.

National Research Council. *Parole, Desistance from Crime, and Community Integration.* Washington, DC: National Academies Press, 2008. This study considers a number of important research and policy questions that relate to parole, community supervision, and the future of reentry to the community.

Reamer, Frederic G. *On the Parole Board.* New York: Columbia University Press, 2016. Reamer shares his experiences as a member of Rhode Island parole board for 24 years.

Thompson, Anthony C. *Releasing Prisoners, Redeeming Communities.* New York: NYU Press, 2008. An examination of the role that race plays in the reentry process.

NOTES

1 Eileen Sullivan, "Paul Manafort, Trump's Ex-Campaign Manager, Released to Home Confinement," *The New York Times,* www.nytimes.com/2020/05/13/us/politics/paul-manafort-released-coronavirus.html, May 13, 2020.

2 E. Ann Carson, *Prisoners in 2018* (Washington, DC: U.S. Government Printing Office, 2020), 13.

3 Alfred Blumstein and Allen J. Beck, "Reentry as a Transient State Between Liberty and Recommitment," in *Prisoner Reentry and Crime in America,* edited by Jeremy Travis and Christy Visher (New York: Cambridge University Press, 2005), 3.

4 Ann L. Pastore and Kathleen Maguire, eds., *Sourcebook of Criminal Justice Statistics,* Table 6.1.2009, www.albany.edu/sourcebook/pdf/t612010.pdf, April 22, 2014; Danielle Kaeble, *Probation and Parole in the United States, 2016* (Washington, DC: U.S. Government Printing Office, 2018), 3.

5 Harry Elmer Barnes and Nedgley K. Teeters, *New Horizons in Criminology* (Englewood Cliffs, NJ: Prentice-Hall, 1944), 550, 553.

6 Lawrence M. Friedman, *Crime and Punishment in American History* (New York: Basic, 1993), 304.

7 Peter B. Hoffman, "History of the Federal Parole System: Part I (1910–1972)," *Federal Probation* 61 (September 1997): 23.

8 Jorge Renaud, *Eight Keys to Mercy: How to Shorten Excessive Prison Sentences* (Northampton, MA: Prison Policy Initiative, 2018), 2.

9 Kevin R. Reitz and Edward E. Rhine, "Parole Release and Supervision: Critical Drivers of American Prison Policy," *Annual Review of Criminology* 3 (2020): 285.

10 Katharine Bradley and R. B. Michael Oliver, "The Role of Parole," in *Policy Brief* (Boston: Community Resources for Justice, 2001).

11 E. Ann Carson and Daniela Golinelli, *Prisoners in 2012: Trends in Admissions and Releases, 1991–2012* (Washington, DC: U.S. Government Printing Office, 2013).

12 Joel M. Caplan, "Parole Release Decisions: Impact of Victim Input on a Representative Sample of Inmates," *Journal of Criminal Justice* 38 (May–June 2010): 291–300.

13 Kristin G. Cloves, Bob Wong, Seth Latimer, and Jose Abarca, "Time to Prison Return for Offenders with Serious Mental Illness Released from Prison," *Criminal Justice and Behavior* 37 (February 2010): 175–87.

14 "Parenting Inside Out," www.parentinginsideout.org, May 27, 2019.

15 Andy Hochstetler, Matt DeLisi, and Travis C. Pratt, "Social Support and Feelings of Hostility Among Released Inmates," *Crime & Delinquency* 56 (October 2010): 588–607.

CHAPTER 16

Making It: Supervision in the Community

Homeboy Electronics Recycling, located in a warehouse in downtown Los Angeles, dismantles and shreds discarded electronics. It also refurbishes and sells electronics, like audio equipment and computers. Homeboy Industries hires primarily the formerly incarcerated, and is an example of the kind of innovative programming that creates employment opportunities for people newly released from prison.

HECTOR GUADALUPE WAS 13 WHEN HE STARTED SELLING DRUGS.

That was 2 years before his mother died of cancer. His father had already died. Life in Williamsburg, Brooklyn, for a youngster in his circumstances was not easy. It wasn't that Guadalupe had nothing to offer. He was a good student in school, and an athlete. He had a talent for building and leading teams, a good mind for business, and drive to succeed. But he was poor, and the neighborhood he grew up in was tough and unforgiving.

When you come from the streets, success can come from adapting to the world you live in. Guadalupe started by selling on the streets, but he did not want to stop there. He had a knack for business, and an eye for sales. By the time he was 18, he was boss to a string of local dealers up and down the East Coast, running an operation that brought in tens of thousands of dollars a day.

Until the Feds caught up with him. In 2003, at the age of 23, he pleaded guilty to intrastate drug distribution, and was sentenced to Federal prison. For almost three of those years, he would be in solitary confinement, where in a 6×9 cell, he adopted spiritual and physical disciplines that changed his life: meditation, yoga, and conditioning. He lost 90 pounds and grew stronger in mind and body.

Eventually back in the yard, he started teaching the disciplines to a hungry group of men looking for a way to create strength from the weakness of their situations. He organized a group of men who began giving lessons on fitness. They were successful inside—prison lore is that they were making good money, working with people inside the prison and out. Again, Guadalupe's business acumen and entrepreneurial spirit paid off.

After serving 10 years, he was released in 2012. Despite his skills and record of business successes, he started to confront the same barriers that face everyone leaving prison. Even though he gained certified as a personal trainer, he spent a frustrating six months looking for work. "I filled out applications to every corporate health club in Manhattan," said Hector Guadalupe. "Nobody wanted to hire me. Couldn't get second interviews. As soon as people were figuring out that I had a past, I couldn't get hired anywhere."

Finally, one gym decided to take a chance on him. He immediately stated to build a clientele, becoming one of the most popular trainers in the gym.

But that is not the end of the story. Hector Guadalupe is driven by his dreams and bolstered by his talent for building things. He soon opened up his own training business, with enough clients to start adding partners. This start-up became the Second U Foundation, whose motto is "Build a Better U." The Foundation works with the formerly incarcerated to prepare them for careers after release from prison, offering a six-week intensive program for people fresh out of prison. Most of the more than 200 graduates of the program end up with careers as personal trainers. Some go on to other businesses.[1]

Guadalupe's story is a heart-warming example of what is true about many people leaving prison: untapped talents, incredible challenges, and astonishing possibilities. Too many go without the support they need to show what they can do, to realize their potential. And so there is also heartbreak—too many people in reentry fail.

In this chapter we focus on how people try to "make it"—the struggles of formerly incarcerated people to stay out of prison. Because the experience of reentry is so intensely personal, in this chapter we listen to people involved in the postrelease business—people who have been incarcerated and the parole officers who supervise them—talk about their experiences. Many people who are released from incarceration fail; about half of them return to prison within six years. Most are under the scrutiny of agents of the state; all face significant legal, familial, and social strains. How many of us would not be vulnerable to misconduct under such pressures? People in reentry play against a stacked deck, and the fact that so many succeed is testimony to their perseverance.

LEARNING OBJECTIVES

After reading this chapter, you should be able to . . .

1. Describe the major characteristics of the postrelease function of the corrections system.
2. Define community supervision and revocation of community supervision.
3. Explain how community supervision is structured.
4. Analyze the constraints on community supervision.
5. Describe residential programs and how they help people on parole.
6. Identify the major problems that people on parole confront.
7. Explain why some people on parole are viewed as dangerous and how society handles this problem.
8. Describe the effectiveness of postrelease supervision.

LO 1

Describe the major characteristics of the postrelease function of the corrections system.

OVERVIEW OF THE POSTRELEASE FUNCTION

The popular notion is that once people have completed their prison sentences, they have paid their "debt" and are ready to start life anew. The reality is that the vast majority of people released from prison remain subject to correctional authority for some time. For many, the parole officer represents this authority; for others, the staff of a halfway house or work release center does. The "freedom" of release is constrained: The person's whereabouts are monitored, and his or her associations and daily activities are checked.

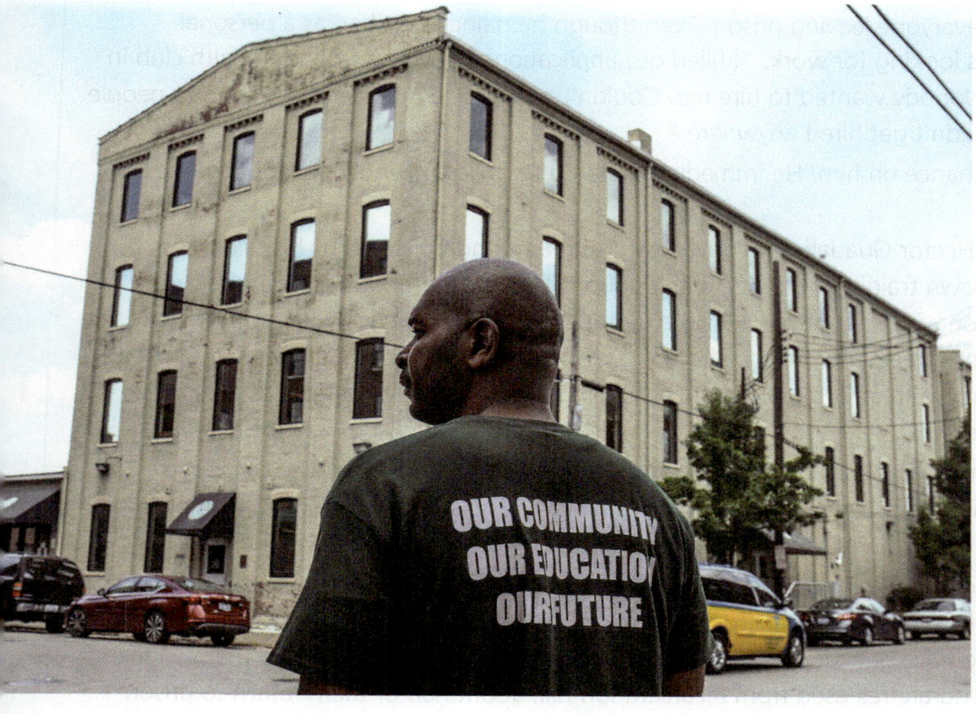

© Michael Clevenger/Courier Journal via Imagn Content Services, LLC

▲ *Brandon Weathers' shirt says it all. He lives in the pictured halfway house while he attends technical college to build his skills for a long-term career after prison.*

People on parole are released from prison on condition that they abide by laws and follow rules designed both to aid their readjustment to society and to control their movement. People on parole may be required to abstain from alcohol, keep away from undesirable associates, maintain good work habits, and not leave the community without permission. These requirements, called **conditions of release**, regulate conduct that is not criminal but that is thought to be linked to the possibility of future criminality. Figure 16.1 shows specific conditions of release in a New Jersey parole contract.

At the same time, the way people are released from prison into the community has changed.

State of New Jersey
STATE PAROLE BOARD

Certificate of Parole

Page 1 of 4

The State Parole Board, by virtue of the authority conferred upon it by the provisions of P.L. 1979, c.441 (C.30:4-123.45, et seq.) and under the rules and regulations promulgated pursuant thereto, does hereby grant a parole to XXXX XXXXXX, SP#XXXXXX, who was convicted of the crime(s) and sentenced as indicated below:

Date of Sentence and Offense	County and Term	Relation and Assessment(s)
XXX XX, XXXX XXXXXXX XXXXXXXX	XXXXXX XXX	XX.XX

TOTAL TERM: XXX

Said inmate is now confined in the **XXXXXX XXXXXXX XXXX** by virtue of the sentence(s) imposed for the said conviction of the crime(s) aforesaid. This parole is applicable solely to said aforesaid sentence(s) and to no other, limited by and subject to the conditions annexed hereto and made a part hereof, and is effective on XXXXXXX XXXXXX or as soon thereafter as a suitable parole plan has been approved by the State Parole Board, and upon the further condition that the said inmate accepts the conditions contained herein and annexed hereto, as evidenced by his/her signature affixed hereto and to a copy hereof retained as a part of the record of the parolee.

This parole is subject to revocation for violation of the conditions annexed hereto and forming a part hereof.

IN TESTIMONY WHEREOF, I have hereunto set my hand, and caused our Seal to be affixed this **XXXXXX** day of **XXX** in the year of our Lord one thousand nine hundred and NINETY-THREE.

STATE PAROLE BOARD

Certifying Member(s): XXXXXXXXXX XXXXXXX   XXXXXX XXXXXX

GENERAL CONDITIONS OF PAROLE:

From the date of your release on parole until the expiration of your maximum sentence(s) or until you are discharged from parole, you shall continue to be under the supervision of the Bureau of Parole. A warrant for your arrest may be filed and this parole may be revoked for serious or persistent violations of the conditions of parole. You shall not be credited for time served on parole from the date a parole warrant is issued for your arrest if you are in violation of parole to the date that you are arrested and placed in confinement for violation of parole.

1. You are required to obey all laws and ordinances.
2. You are not to act as an informer for any agency which requires you to violate any conditions of your parole.
3. You are to report in person to your District Parole Supervisor or his/her designated representative immediately after you are released on parole from the institution, unless you have been given other written instructions by the institutional parole office, and you are to report thereafter as instructed by the District Parole Supervisor or his or her designated representative.
4. You are to notify your Parole Officer immediately after any arrest and after accepting any pre-trial release, including bail.
5. You are to obtain approval of your Parole Officer:
   a. For any change in your residence or employment location.

Witness ______________ Dated ______________ 19 ____

______________ Signature

SPB-130

State of New Jersey
STATE PAROLE BOARD
XXXXXX XXXXXXX, SP#XXXXXX

Certificate of Parole

Page 2 of 4

   b. Before leaving the state of your approved residence for longer than 24 hours, except as otherwise directed for good cause by the Parole Officer.
6. You are required not to own or possess any firearm, as defined in N.J.S.2C:39-1f, for any purpose.
7. You are required not to own or possess any weapon enumerated in N.J.S.2C:39-1r.
8. You are required to refrain from the use, possession or distribution of a controlled dangerous substance, controlled substance analog or imitation controlled dangerous substance as defined In N.J.S.2C:35-2 and N.J.S.2C:35-11.
9. You are required to make payment to the Bureau of Parole of any assessment, fine, restitution, D.E.D.R. penalty and Lab Fee imposed by the sentencing court and/or the New Jersey State Parole Board.

Total Fine(s)/Penalty(s):
Total VCCB Assessment(s):
Total Restitution:

SPECIAL CONDITION(S):

You will be paroled to any outstanding detainer(s) only initially; thence upon resolution of said detainer(s), you will be released to a parole plan acceptable to the New Jersey Bureau of Parole with the following Special Conditions:

You are to participate in random urine monitoring acceptable to the District Parole Office until discharge is approved by the District Parole Supervisor. You are to refrain from the use of any controlled dangerous substance.

You are to participate in and comply with the regulations of an out-patient drug counseling program acceptable to the District Parole Office until discharge is approved by the District Parole Supervisor. You are to refrain from the use of any controlled dangerous substance.

You are to participate in a Narcotics Anonymous Program with a community sponsor acceptable to the District Parole Office until discharge is approved by the District Parole Supervisor. You are to refrain from the use of any controlled dangerous substance.

You are to participate in and comply with the regulations of an out-patient alcohol counseling program acceptable to the District Parole Office until discharge from such is approved by the District Parole Supervisor. You are to refrain from alcohol usage.

You are to participate In an Alcoholics Anonymous Program with a community sponsor acceptable to the District Parole Office until discharge is approved by the District Parole Supervisor. You are to refrain from alcohol usage.

You are to participate in mental health counseling acceptable to the District Parole Office.

I HEREBY ACKNOWLEDGE THE IMPOSITION OF THE SPECIAL CONDITION OF PAROLE THAT I ENROLL AND PARTICIPATE IN A MENTAL HEALTH COUNSELING PROGRAM. I ACKNOWLEDGE MY NEED TO PARTICIPATE IN A MENTAL HEALTH COUNSELING PROGRAM AND ACKNOWLEDGE THAT I MUST FULLY COOPERATE WITH THE TREATMENT STAFF OF THE DESIGNATED PROGRAM. I HEREBY AUTHORIZE THE DESIGNATED REPRESENTATIVES OF THE DEPARTMENT OF CORRECTIONS AND THE STATE PAROLE BOARD TO RELEASE EITHER VERBALLY OR IN WRITING ALL DIAGNOSTIC PROGNOSTIC AND TREATMENT RECORDS PERTAINING TO MY MEDICAL AND MENTAL HEALTH TO THE STAFF OF ANY MENTAL HEALTH AGENCY REQUESTED TO PROVIDE OR PROVIDING SERVICES TO ME. I ACKNOWLEDGE THAT I UNDERSTAND THAT THIS AUTHORIZATION TO RELEASE INFORMATION MAY NOT BE

Witness ______________ Dated ______________ 19 ____

______________ Signature

SPB-130

FIGURE 16.1 New Jersey Conditions of Release

The newly released must comply with specific conditions in order to remain in good standing on parole.

In the 1970s, the vast majority of people were released from prison by a parole board. Yet only those released by parole would be accountable to a parole officer. Today, however, most people are released from completing their sentences, but for nearly all of these, a term on parole supervision awaits anyway. For many who have completed their sentences, the role of the parole board in determining whether there is support from family or friends is neglected. Too many people released from prison are not fully prepared for their entrance into the community.

conditions of release
Restrictions on conduct that people on parole must obey as a legally binding requirement of being released.

The freedom of those who are released outright—either because they have completed their maximum term (the maximum sentence minus good time) or, as in the state of Maine, because there is no parole supervision—is also less complete than it may seem. The person leaving prison still has many serious obstacles to overcome: long absence from family and friends, legal and practical limitations on employment possibilities, the suspicion and uneasiness of the community, even the strangeness of everyday living. The outside world can seem alien and unpredictable after even a short time in the artificial environment of prison. Old friends and old ways can be a temptation—and studies show that this can often spell trouble.[2]

No truly "clean" start is possible. The "former convict" status is nearly as stigmatizing as the "convict" status, and in many ways more frustrating. Most people look at a person on parole askance, which is an embittering experience for many trying to start over.

LO 2

Define community supervision and revocation of community supervision.

Community Supervision

Restrictions on people on parole are rationalized on the grounds that people who have been incarcerated must readjust to the community gradually so they will not simply fall back into preconviction habits and associations. Some people hold that trying to impose standards of conduct on people on parole that are not imposed on others is both wrong and likely to fail. Moreover, the newly paroled people find themselves in such daunting circumstances that they may have great difficulty living according to the rules.

When releasees first come out of prison, their personal and material problems are staggering. In most states they are given only clothes, a token amount of money, a copy of the rules governing their release, and the name and address of the parole officer to whom they must report within 24 hours. Although a promised job is often a condition of release, an actual job may be another matter. Most releasees are unskilled or semiskilled, and parole stipulations may prevent them from moving to areas where they could find work. If they are African American and under age 30, they join the largest group of unemployed in the country, with the added handicap of the "former convict" status.

Reentry problems help explain why most parole failures occur relatively soon after release—nearly one-quarter during the first six months. With little preparation, people move from the highly structured, authoritarian prison life into the complex, temptation-filled free world. They are expected to summon up extraordinary coping abilities; not surprisingly, the social, psychological, and material overload sends many of them back. Figure 16.2 summarizes some key characteristics of people released from prison.

Revocation

When people fail on parole, their parole is revoked, and they are returned to prison to continue serving their sentences. Parole can be revoked for two reasons: (1) committing a new crime or (2) violating conditions of parole (a "technical violation"). Technical violations are controversial because they involve noncriminal conduct, such as failure to report an address change to the parole officer.

Critics of parole argue that it is improper to re-imprison someone for minor infractions. In practice, revocations seldom result from a single rules violation—prisons are far too crowded. To be returned to prison on a technical violation, someone usually must show persistent noncompliance or give the parole officer reason to believe that he or she has returned to crime. Most revocations occur only when the person on parole is arrested on a serious charge or cannot be located by the officer.

Perspectives on parole status in the community have changed over the years. Early reformers saw parole decisions as grace dispensed by the correctional authority. Such parole could be revoked at any time and for any reason. Later reformers viewed parole as a privilege, earned by good behavior in prison and retained by adherence to parole conditions. More recently, some commentators have begun to describe parole as a right of people who have served enough time in prison, and they urge that technical violations be eliminated as a basis for return to prison. The "rights" view does not now prevail officially in any parole system, although the state of Washington strictly limits the penalties that may be imposed on technical violators.

If parole is a privilege, then its revocation is not subject to due process or rules of evidence. In some states, liberal release policies have been justified on the grounds that parole can be swiftly revoked whenever the parole rules are violated. Under the New York statute, for example, if a parole officer has reason to believe that someone has lapsed or is about to lapse into criminal conduct or into criminal company, or has violated any important condition of parole, the officer may make an arrest. The officer's power to recommend revocation hangs over the person on parole like the proverbial sword of Damocles, suspended by a hair.

When the parole officer alleges a technical violation of parole, the U.S. Supreme Court requires a two-stage revocation proceeding. Although the Court has exempted revocation proceedings from the normal requirements of a criminal trial, many due process rights must be followed.[3] In the first stage the parole board determines whether there is probable cause that a violation has occurred. (Probable cause is the criterion for deciding whether evidence is strong enough to uphold an arrest or to suggest issuing an arrest or warrant.) The person on parole then has the right to be notified of charges, be informed of evidence,

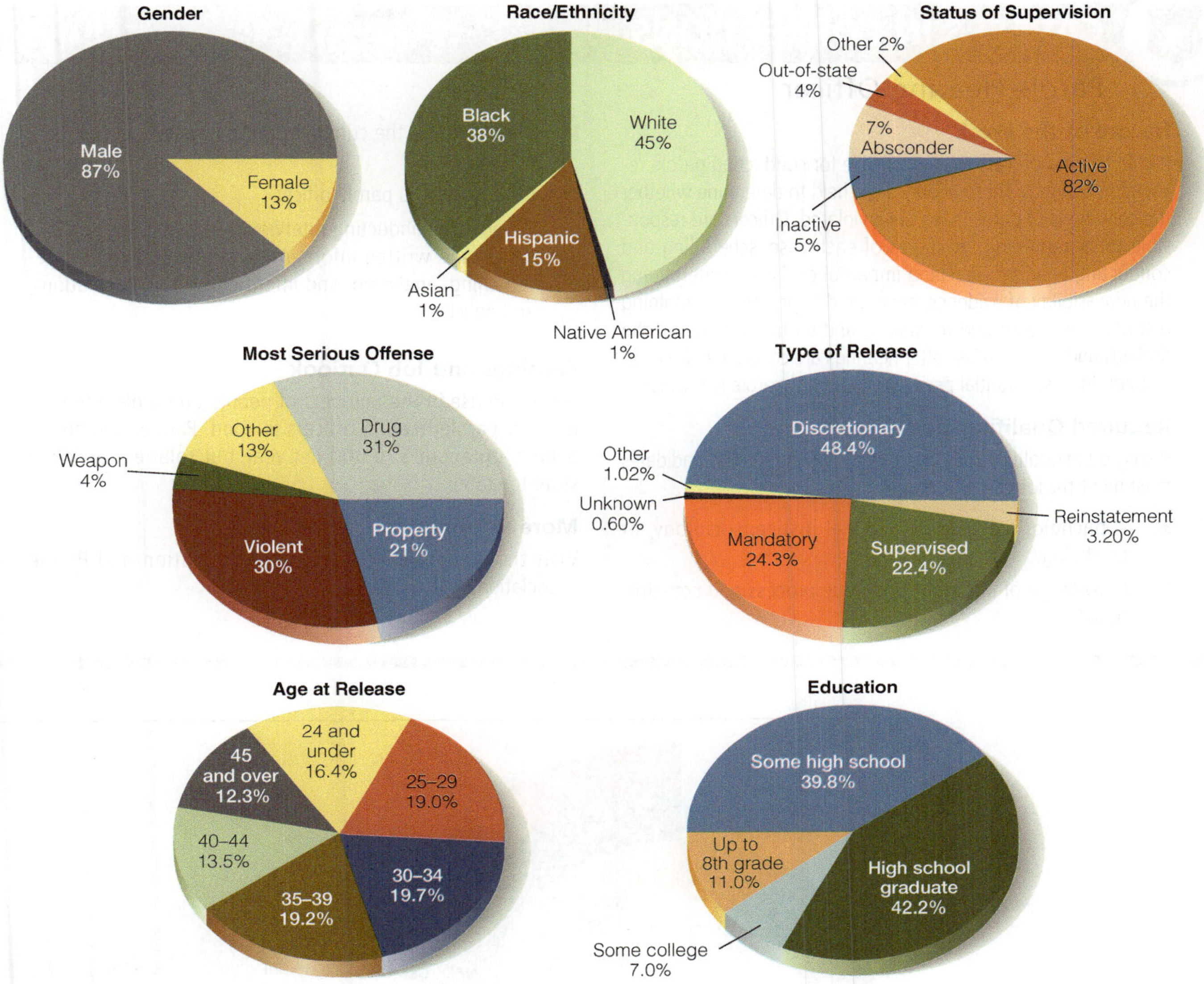

FIGURE 16.2 Personal Characteristics of People Released from Prison

Prison releasees tend to be men in their thirties who have an inadequate education and were incarcerated for nonviolent offenses.

*Non-Hispanic

Source: Danielle Kaeble and Mariel Alper, Parole and Probation in the United States, 2018-2018 (Washington, DC: U.S. Bureau of Justice Statistics, 2020)

be heard, present witnesses, and confront the parole board's witnesses (providing that no witness would be endangered by such a confrontation). In the second stage the parole board decides if the violation is severe enough to warrant return to prison. See "Careers in Corrections" for information on the career of a parole hearing officer.

The total number of parole revocations is difficult to determine. A combined revocation and recommitment rate of approximately 25 percent within three years of release has been reported for years, but newer results show a more complicated situation.

First, parole is only a part of the picture. As we showed in Chapter 15, even though a growing portion of people released from prison are not sent home by the parole board, most of them still face some supervision authority. The odds aren't good. Within three years, 68 percent of people released from prison are arrested for a new crime, and 44 percent are arrested during the first year after their release. Within five years, almost 21 percent have an arrest for a violent crime. By the fifth year, 55 percent have been returned to prison at least once for a new crime or a technical violation of the conditions of release.[4] (See Figure 16.3.)

CAREERS IN CORRECTIONS

Parole Hearing Officer

Nature of the Work

Parole hearing officers are responsible for conducting parole revocation hearings. These hearings are held to determine whether the conditions of parole have been violated. Officers are responsible for determining the issues of each case, scheduling and conducting hearings, reaching impartial decisions, determining the admissibility of evidence, ensuring due process, maintaining records of evidence and testimony, and writing reports on the findings and actions taken after hearings are conducted. Reincarceration for a substantial period may result if parole is revoked.

Required Qualifications

Background qualifications vary by state, but generally candidates must meet the following criteria:

- A bachelor's degree in criminal justice, sociology, or psychology
- Knowledge of laws regarding due process and constitutional rights
- Knowledge of the criminal justice system, especially the parole system
- Experience as a parole officer
- Experience conducting interviews, verifying documented verbal and written information, report writing, and researching, analyzing, and interpreting laws, regulations, and policies

Earnings and Job Outlook

Given the rise in the numbers of people on parole, the outlook for parole hearing officers is good. Parole hearing officers earn about $70,000 per year, but salaries vary from state to state.

More Information

Visit the website of the American Probation and Parole Association.

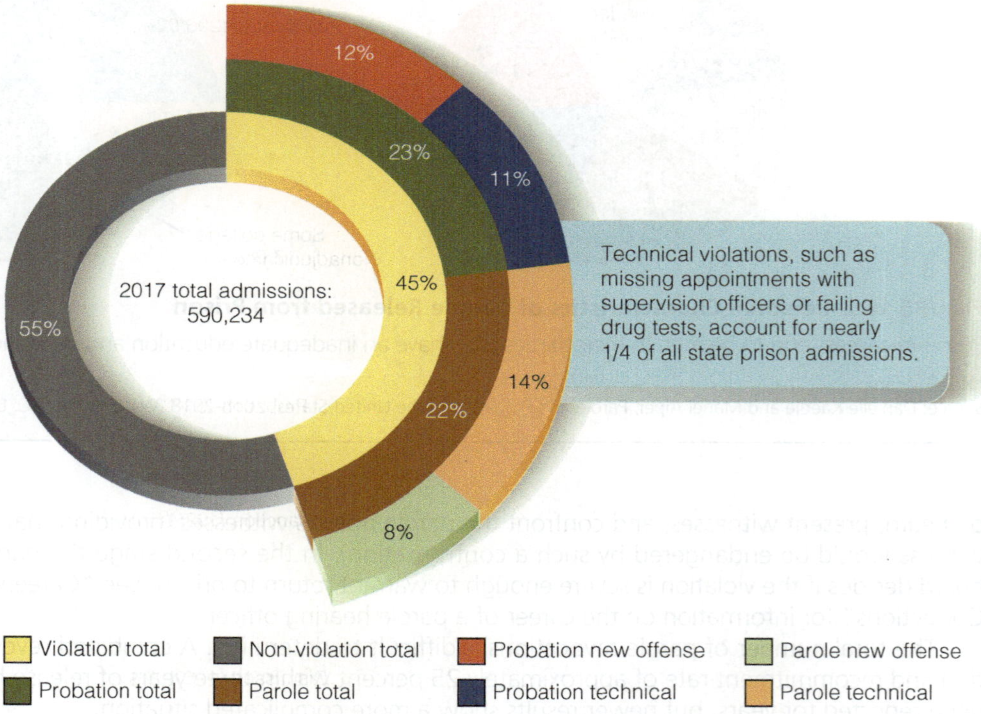

FIGURE 16.3 Rates and Types of Failure for People Released from Prison, 2005–2011

The percentage who successfully complete their parole term and are discharged from supervision varies by time and time frame. What factors might account for these shifts?

Sources: Mariel Alper, Matthew R. Durose, and Joshua Markman *2018 Update on Prisoner Recidivism: A 9-Year Follow-up (2005-2014)* (Washington, DC: U.S. Bureau of Justice Statistics, 2018); Matthew R. Durose, Alexia D. Cooper, and Howard Snyder, *Recidivism of Prisoners Released in 30 States in 2005: Patterns from 2005–2010* (Washington, DC: U.S. Bureau of Justice Statistics, 2014).

Technical rules violation rates vary dramatically by state. These vast differences have little to do with the way clients behave and a great deal to do with the way the system enforces its rules. When someone is determined to have violated a condition of parole, the parole agency has several options: (1) return the person to prison, (2) note the violation but strengthen supervision rather than revoke parole, or (3) note the violation but take no action at that time. Differences in failure rates among the states may reflect agency supervision policies, prison crowding, or political pressures to remove people from the community.

Nationally, as many as one-third of all new prison admissions are violators of conditional release; of this group, nearly two-thirds are returned to prison for technical violations (see Figure 16.4). Most parole violations occur in the initial months following release—the highest rate of failure is in the first year—but people can fail even after long periods of successful adjustment. (See "Should People Serving Long Sentences Be Released Early?")

The typical length of reconfinement for a technical parole violation varies by original charge. Specifically, those whose original charges are the most serious can expect to serve the most time for their violation, as much as a year or more, before being

FOCUS ON

CORRECTIONAL POLICY: Should People Serving Long Sentences Be Released Early?

William Taylor III looked around his new apartment. He said, with wonderment in his voice, "My window has blinds, and I can open and close them!"

Taylor was looking around his apartment with a certain measure of unexpected joy. He had been in prison for 18 years on a life sentence for two robbery convictions, looking at a hard minimum of 25 years under California three-strikes law. But when Californians voted to amend the law in 2012, Taylor was one of 3,000 people whose nonviolent crimes made him eligible for a resentencing hearing. He made such a good impression—his conduct in prison had been stellar—that the judge released him to a drug treatment facility. After he completed seven months of therapy at the facility, the officials decided it was time for him to move out into his own place.

Taylor's case is an example of what experts say should be happening more often—reconsidering life sentences for people who are sufficiently rehabilitated that their incarceration can no longer be justified by concerns for public safety. According to the Sentencing Project, there are 160,000 people serving life sentences, and 50,000 of them are not eligible for parole. Those eligible for parole will often serve 25 years or more before they are released—an amount of time that is more than double what people on life sentences served before the "get tough" movement began in the 1980s.

But it turns out that there is growing evidence for the wisdom of releasing people who have served long terms in prison, rather than making them stay incarcerated into old age. In California, people like William Taylor III—released after three-strikes sentencing reform—have less than a 5 percent return-to-prison rate. In Michigan, less than 1 in 100 of the 5,000 people released after serving time for murder, manslaughter, or sex crimes were back in prison after three years.

These low recidivism rates derive from two factors. First, many people who get life sentences committed very serious crimes that do not represent a pattern but were rather an extreme reaction to an extreme situation—often involving drugs or alcohol. Second, after years in prison, by far most of those in prison for life terms have "aged out" of their criminal risk. Many scholars have observed that age is the most dominant factor in determining a person's risk, and people who are released after these sentences tend to be in their fifties or sixties.

Of course, there are other reasons for keeping people in prison on long sentences. Their crimes are often extremely serious—murders, typically. Family members of their victims often argue that release will denigrate the seriousness of the crime. And there is the issue of stakes—if somebody released on a life sentence does commit a crime, the political consequences are severe.

Still, for people who want to reduce the prison population without endangering public safety, there are more than 300,000 people age 50 or older in U.S. prisons. Most of these people have outlived their risk level and are an appealing target.

Sources: Erik Eckholm, "Out of Prison and Staying Out, After 3rd Strike in California," *The New York Times*, February 27, 2015, pp. A1, A16; Nazgol Ghandnoosh, *Delaying a Second Chance: The Declining Prospects for Parole on Life Sentences* (Washington, DC: Sentencing Project, 2017); Barbara Levine and Elsie Kettenun, *Paroling People Who Committed Serious Crimes: What Is the Actual Risk?* (Lansing, MI: Citizens Alliance on Prisons & Public Spending, 2014).

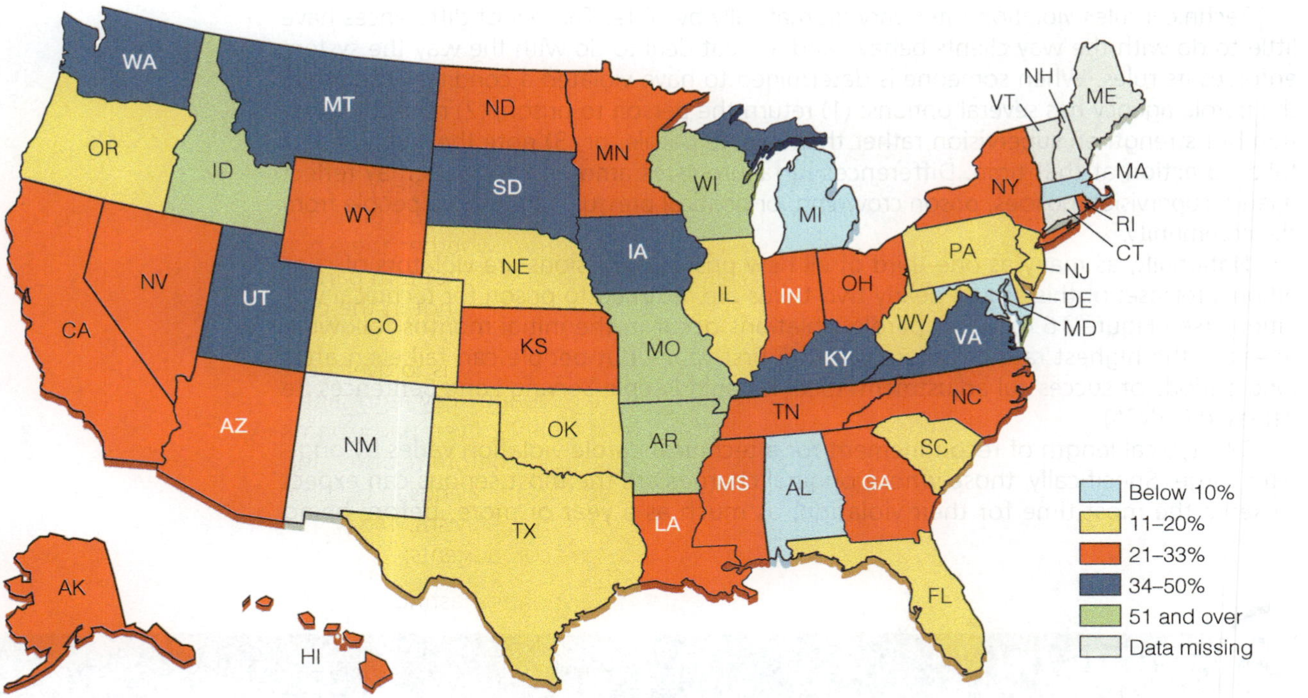

FIGURE 16.4 Percentage of Prison Population Who Are Probation and Parole Violators

Source: Council of State Governments, *Confined and Costly: How Supervision Violations are Filling Prisons and Burdening Budgets* (NY: Council of State Governments, 2019), https://csgjusticecenter.org/publications/confined-costly/

released a second time. The guidelines of the Federal Parole Commission recommend up to 8 months for people who do not have a history of violations and 4–12 months for persistent violators, for those whose violations occur less than 8 months after release, and for those found to have a negative employment or school record during supervision. Most states do not have such guidelines. The person whose parole is revoked may be required to serve the remainder of the unexpired sentence. Figure 16.5 shows the different rates of success of people released from prison under parole supervision.

LO 3

Explain how community supervision is structured.

THE STRUCTURE OF COMMUNITY SUPERVISION

Three forces influence a newly released person's adjustment to free society: the parole officer, the parole bureaucracy, and the experiences of the person in reentry. Carl Klockars notes that the structure of these relationships can determine the results of supervision. Klockars describes supervision as a series of phases of changing attachments, as shown in Figure 16.6. In the initial stages of supervision, the strongest attachment is between the officer and the bureaucracy, as the officer seeks to make sure the parolee is following the rules. There is a minor attachment between the client and the officer, while the client maintains a suspicion of the bureaucracy's rules, denoted by a negative attachment which does not change. As the client and officer get to know each other better, however, the officer's strongest attachment gradually shifts from the bureaucracy to the person on parole. Finally, the two develop rapport, the ability to communicate positively and with mutual trust.[5]

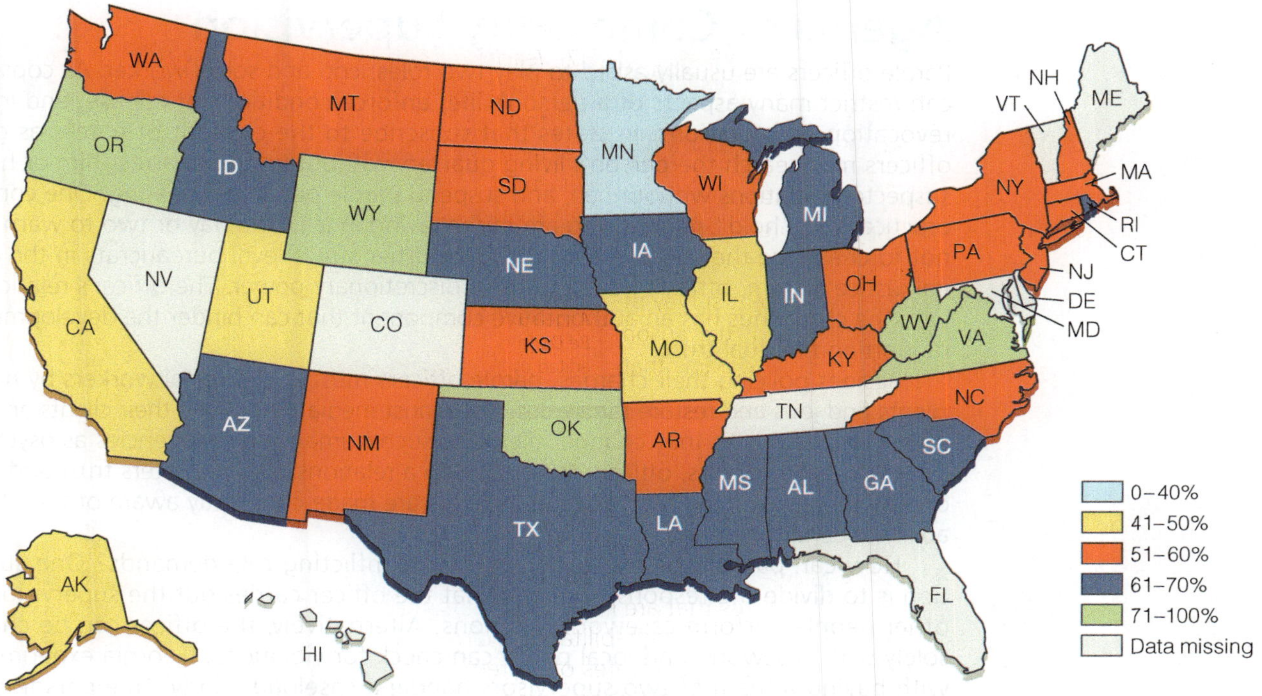

FIGURE 16.5 Percentage of Success after Release from State Prison to Parole Supervision

Why do some states seem to do a better job at helping people make it after prison?

Source: Thomas P. Bonczar and Laura M. Maruschak, *Probation and Parole in the United States, 2012* (Washington, DC: U.S. Bureau of Justice Statistics, 2013).

This model explains why minor rule violations can be overlooked: Over time, the parole officer identifies more closely with the person in reentry than with the bureaucracy. But the process does not always follow that pattern. Often, rapport never develops, and the attachment even sours. When strain develops between the client and both the officer and the bureaucracy, success is very difficult to achieve.

What determines the outcome of the supervision process? The answer lies in a complex web of attitudes, situations, policies, and random events. First, consider in detail two major forces: the parole officer and the bureaucracy.

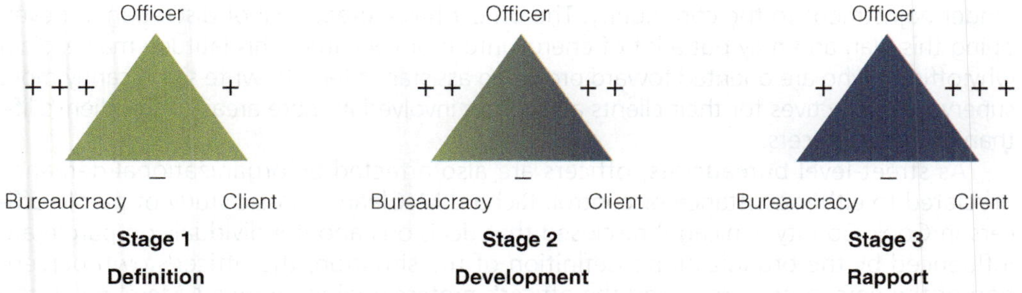

FIGURE 16.6 Positive and Negative Attachments at Three Stages of the Supervision Process

Clients and their parole officers tend to develop a positive attachment as supervision proceeds.

Source: Carl B. Klockars, "A Theory of Probation Supervision," *Journal of Criminal Law, Criminology, and Police Science* 63 (1972): 550–57.

Agents of Community Supervision

Parole officers are usually asked to play two roles: cop and social worker. As cops, they can restrict many aspects of a person's life, enforce conditions of release, and initiate revocation for violations. In states that subscribe to the concept of parole as grace, officers may search the person's living quarters without warning, arrest him or her for suspected violations without bail, and suspend parole pending a hearing. One common practice is to "hold" people who are misbehaving in jail for a day or two to warn them not to challenge the officer's authority. Like other street-level bureaucrats in the criminal justice system, officers have extensive discretionary power. The officer's relationship with the client thus has an authoritative component that can hinder the development of rapport and mutual trust.

Besides policing their charges, parole officers must act as social workers by helping clients find jobs and restore family ties. They must mediate between their clients and various organizations as they channel clients to such human service agencies as psychiatric clinics. As caseworkers, officers must develop a relationship that fosters trust and confidence, which is not likely to develop if clients are made constantly aware of the officers' ability to send them back to prison.[6]

How can parole officers reconcile these conflicting role demands? One suggestion is to divide the responsibilities so that the officer carries out the supervision and other people perform casework functions. Alternatively, the officer can be charged solely with casework, and local police can check for violations. Georgia experimented with having a team of two supervisors handle a caseload jointly. One person (often a former police officer) was the surveillance officer, and the other was the probation officer, providing assistance. However, the distinction often became vague: People on parole often looked to surveillance officers for help and saw probation officers as enforcing the conditions of supervision. Despite the conflict, it seems that any person having supervisory contact with a person reentering society from prison must perform both roles.

The parole officer's style has been referred to as one of two "hidden conditions" of supervision. Officers have certain expectations about how clients will behave and therefore how to treat them. Some officers take a parental approach; welfare workers approach the job as professional caseworkers; punitive officers see themselves as community protection agents; passive agents are bureaucrats. Each approach leads to a style of interaction with people on parole—gruff, distant, or friendly—that informally determines the supervision process. In fact, style can overwhelm other aspects of the work. For instance, Elliot Studt's famous study of parole officers in California revealed that their individual styles were so varied that each could almost be thought of as a separate agency.[7]

The second hidden condition of supervision is the supervision plan. In most agencies there is a supervision (or treatment) plan that states what the person on parole is going to do about the problems (unemployment, drug abuse, marital conflict, and so on) that hinder adjustment to the community. The officer has a great deal of discretion in developing this plan and may put a lot of energy into it or very little. This latitude may explain why officers who are oriented toward providing assistance tend to write significantly more supervision objectives for their clients and to get involved in more areas of the client's life than do other officers.

As street-level bureaucrats, officers are also affected by organizational demands unrelated to either assistance or control. Richard McCleary's classic study of parole officers in Cook County (Chicago) disclosed that decisions about individuals on parole are influenced by the organization's definition of the situation, the officer's own perception of the person on parole, and the officer's professional reputation.[8] Members of the parole bureaucracy strive to maintain desirable professional conditions: a good working atmosphere, independence from supervisory oversight, and the use of discretion. Certain people on parole are viewed as threatening to the status quo because they make trouble for their officers and for the officers' superiors; therefore, they elicit special responses from their officers.

McCleary believes that by typing each person on parole from the start, the officer neutralizes potential trouble. On the basis of parole files, initial interviews, and home visits, the officer categorizes clients as sincere, criminally inclined, or dangerous. "Dangerous" refers not to people who are potentially violent, but rather to those few who may act irrationally or unpredictably, who do not respond to warnings, and who go out of their way to make trouble. The "dangerous" ones are the most worrisome, for an officer has the most difficulty maintaining control over them. McCleary found that, surprisingly, one way to control them is to bargain with them:

> All right, Johnny, this is how it is. I've got you on paper for the next seven years, but I'll make a deal with you. You give me two years of good behavior and I'll recommend you for early discharge. When I say "good behavior," though, I mean cooperation. When I tell you to do something, you do it. You don't argue with me about whether I'm right or wrong or whether it's fair or not, or even whether I have the right to tell you to do it. You just do it. If you give me two years of cooperation like that, I'll give you an early discharge.[9]

Thus, parole officers represent one set of forces that affect a person's chance of making it. Officers can support or hinder adjustment. They "read" people on parole and then decide how they will treat them. Apart from their formal power to revoke parole on the basis of violations, they have even greater informal power—to make life difficult or easy, depending on the way they approach their jobs. "Careers in Corrections" offers a closer view of the work of a parole officer.

The Community Supervision Bureaucracy

Parole officers do not work in a vacuum. Although the job often attracts people who like flexible schedules and substantial latitude, every officer works in an organizational context, usually in close contact with other officers. Parole officers therefore face limits in their approaches to cases. The limits derive from both the specific need to manage a

CAREERS IN CORRECTIONS

Parole Officer

Nature of the Work

Like their probation counterparts, parole officers supervise people reentering the community from prison through personal contact with their clients and their clients' families. Unlike probation officers, who are generally employed by the county, parole officers are employed by the state.

In most jurisdictions they are armed peace officers with the power of arrest. As an essential ingredient in the reentry process, parole officers help their clients readjust to the community and find housing and employment. They monitor behavior to ensure that parole requirements are met. If the conditions are not met or there is another crime, the officer may recommend revocation of the parole. Fieldwork may take the officer to high-crime areas where there is a risk of violence.

Required Qualifications

Background qualifications for parole officers vary by state, but a bachelor's degree in social work, criminal justice, or a related field is usually required. Some agencies require previous experience or graduate work. Candidates must be 21 years of age, have no felony convictions, have a valid driving license, and have no restrictions on carrying a firearm. Most parole officers receive formal training and typically work as a trainee for up to one year.

Earnings and Job Outlook

The number of parole officers is expected to grow as the number of people leaving prison increases during the next decade. Starting salaries for parole officers vary by region, but the national median salary is $53,020.

More Information

Visit the website of the American Probation and Parole Association. You can also obtain career information from your state's parole office.

TABLE 16.1 The Varying Levels of Parole Supervision in New York State

Most parole systems vary the amount of supervision according to the risk of recidivism, the length of time on parole, and the response to the supervision.

	Supervision Level		
Type of Contact	Intensive	Active	Reduced
Reporting to parole office	Weekly or semimonthly	Monthly or up to but not exceeding every 2 months	Quarterly or less frequently up to and including annually
Employment check	Monthly	Every 2 months	Same as reporting
Employment visit	Every 3 months	Every 3 months	At least as frequently as reporting
Home visit	Every 3 months	Monthly	Not mentioned
Other and collateral visits	More frequently than active or reduced	Not mentioned	Not mentioned

Source: Adapted from David T. Stanley, *Prisoners Among Us* (Washington, DC: Brookings Institution, 1976), 96.

heavier workload than is feasible in the available time and the general need to respond to organizational philosophies and policies.

Workload In his award-winning study of human services, Michael Lipsky points out that the difficulties faced by many clients of human services are so complex that "the job … is in a sense impossible to do in ideal terms."[10] One tool that parole organizations find useful in the face of this reality is a classification system that structures the parole supervision relationship. The system lets the parole bureaucracy prescribe rules for allocating officers' time, with priority given to those clients most in need. The system in New York is typical (see Table 16.1). In general, officers spend more time with the new releases than with those who have been out for some time. The level of supervision is later adjusted to "active" or "reduced" surveillance, depending on how the releasee functions in the community. As the officer gains confidence in the person on parole, only periodic check-ins may be required. Finally, at the end of the maximum length of the sentence or at the time specified by the parole board, the client is discharged from supervision.

Reformers have long held that parole caseloads should include no more than 36 cases per officer. In reality, caseloads vary dramatically but average about 80 cases per officer. This is smaller than the average probation caseload, but the services required by people on parole are greater. Some recent studies suggest that smaller caseloads might work better, as long as the officer in charge of the caseload follows evidence-based supervision principles.[11]

The caseload affects how often an officer can have contact with cases and how much help can be given. Some states structure low, specialized caseloads for officers who supervise certain types of cases, but even with specialized caseloads, time available for each case can be minimal, often less than an hour per month. One reason for the small contact time is that officers must spend time on bureaucratic duties such as paperwork and being out in the field helping people on parole deal with other service agencies—medical, employment, educational. Parole officers spend as much as 80 percent of their time doing nonsupervisory work.

Philosophy and Policy Originally, parole officers worked directly for parole boards, and some boards still favor this arrangement because it means that the parole officer's strategies more closely follow their philosophy. In recent decades, however, parole field staffs have increasingly become part of correctional departments. With the growing emphasis on parole's links to other aspects of community corrections and on the use of prerelease programs, halfway houses, and other community-based services, the rationale is that institutional and field activities need to be coordinated months before a person is released on parole.

Many states combine probation and parole staffs because they perform similar functions. As pointed out, however, probation officers have ties to judges, whereas parole is seen as part of corrections. Parole has a greater law enforcement orientation: Parole agents in some states carry guns, and all are sworn officers. Agents with social work orientations thus seem more likely to gravitate toward probation.

Field service operations vary in their overall philosophy of supervision. Traditionally, cases are assigned to their officers on the basis of where they live so that reporting and field supervision are easier for both parties. (If an area has an unusually large number of people to be supervised, agencies can adjust boundaries in order to keep parole officers' caseloads roughly equal in size.) In theory, this geographic assignment helps parole officers work more closely with community service agencies in providing services. In practice, however, officers in such agencies can become isolated from their peers, their supervisors, and social services. Such officers ordinarily draw little attention to their efforts unless a client creates a problem (perhaps by a new arrest), so there is an incentive to monitor cases closely to avoid unpleasant surprises. The traditional field services agency gives its officers much latitude, and it is understood that they will be left alone until a client's behavior draws a superior's attention. They are often merely told, "Cover your bases." In recent years this traditional model of parole field services has come under criticism.

There has never been much evidence that an isolated caseload under the complete discretion of a parole officer is a particularly effective way to organize the work. Moreover, a renewed emphasis on rehabilitation has led some administrators to conclude that specialization can improve services by allowing parole officers to concentrate on particular problems. Thus, one officer may handle drug users, another may supervise the unemployed, and so on. The argument for specialization is that homogeneous workloads make better use of staff expertise and that officers can better understand and respond to clients who have similar characteristics. Yet this strategy breeds discontent among officers because the specialties often conflict. For one thing, it is difficult to equalize workloads. For instance, who can tell whether it takes more or less effort to supervise 30 drug addicts than to supervise 40 people on parole for sex crimes? Moreover, because officers want to think that their jobs are important, they often clash over whose work (and special clientele) is the most central to the agency's mission.

Because of these problems, a premium is sometimes placed on brokering services from other agencies—referring people to social services that specialize in certain areas, such as employment training or drug treatment. The officer's main role then is to determine the client's most serious problems, locate agencies that handle such problems, and help the client make use of the agencies' services. Although brokering helps involve clients with established community services, the small amount of direct contact between officers and the people they supervise may lead to a lack of accountability and insufficient control over the case.

In the end, this emphasis on control is what matters most in the philosophy of an agency. A parole officer can handle cases in whatever way he or she sees fit as long as the caseload is "under control." But no matter what a parole officer might believe—and no matter how skilled he or she may be—the officer must know where the clients are and how well they are doing. Clients who are recently released from prison will always be plagued with recurring difficulties; however, without a sense that the officer is "in charge," problems can quickly arise that cause the public to question the capacity of parole to serve the community's need for safety.

LO 4

Analyze the constraints on community supervision.

Constraints on Officers' Authority Parole officers are often portrayed as having absolute authority over their clients, as being able to manage people in any way they see fit. It is more accurate to say that in using discretion, officers balance many constraints.

The bureaucratic context pressures parole officers to "go along with the system," just as police officers are pressured to cover for their partners. In this respect, parole resembles other correctional functions: Line workers are isolated from administration and depend on one another for support. They feel constrained to behave supportively and to let well enough alone. As one parole supervisor said,

> I won't stand for one of my parole officers (POs) second-guessing another. If I tolerated that, I'd have grudges going on here. Pretty soon I'd have an office full of snitches. A few years ago, I had a PO who couldn't keep his nose out of the other caseloads. I spoke to him about it but that didn't do any good. He thought he was the conscience of the Department of Corrections. I finally got fed up with his meddling and I gave him a taste of his own medicine. I went over to his files and found unfinished work for him to do.[12]

Parole officers perform their jobs in ways that maintain office norms without threatening their coworkers. However, office norms reduce their discretion because the unwritten rules often force them to take actions in regard to problems that they might otherwise have handled differently. In recent times, for example, jails and prisons have become so overcrowded that officers feel informal (but very clear) pressures not to crowd the institutions further with revocations for "nonserious" violations.

The parole bureaucracy, then, affects the postrelease experience in several ways. First, it provides rules and policies for managing workloads that would otherwise be unbearable. Second, it structures the activities of parole officers according to traditional philosophical orientations. Finally, it provides a context of unwritten and informal norms that define appropriate and inappropriate officer conduct.

LO 5

Describe residential programs and how they help people on parole.

RESIDENTIAL PROGRAMS

Residential programs are used when people are first released from prison. Most house between 10 and 25 people at any one time from medium- or minimum-security facilities. Placing heavy emphasis on involvement in regular community functions, treatment staff help residents work out plans to address their problems.

community correctional center A small-group living facility, especially for those who have been recently released from prison.

Residential programs are often referred to as **community correctional centers**. Most require living on the premises while working in the community. They usually provide counseling and drug treatment and impose strict curfews on residents when they are not working. Many of these facilities are renovated private homes or small hotels. Individual rooms, coupled with group dining and recreation areas, help these facilities achieve a homelike ambience. By obeying the rules and maintaining good behavior in the facility, residents gradually earn a reduction in restrictions—for instance, the ability to spend some free time in the community. The idea is to provide treatment support while promoting the step-by-step adjustment to community life.

Residential centers face problems, however. With high staff–resident ratios, they are relatively expensive to operate; they represent a real savings in costs only when they enable a jurisdiction to avoid construction of a new prison. Some centers have high failure rates—one-third or more of the residents may be rearrested in a year—but the main problems with these centers are political. Misbehavior by residents makes them unpopular with the local community. Just one serious offense can result in a strong public backlash. Citizens typically do not want groups of releasees living in their midst (as noted earlier, NIMBY stands for "Not in My Back Yard!").

work release center A facility that allows residents to work in the community during the day while residing in the center during nonworking hours.

The most common type of community correctional center is the halfway house, or **work release center**. This idea originated in Wisconsin in 1913 with the passage of the Huber law, which let people in prison work in gainful occupations outside the prison as long as they returned to their cells at night.

Two kinds of work release programs are available today. In the more secure of the two, people in prison work during the day (often in groups) and then return at night to a group housing unit. In the other version, sometimes called *work furlough*, people work and live at home during the week and return to the prison for the weekend.

The idea underlying the halfway house is straightforward: Returning to the community after institutionalization requires an adjustment, and a relatively controlled environment improves adjustment. Because studies indicate that the highest failure rates occur in the early months of parole, this idea seems plausible. Recently, halfway houses have become more than mere stopping points for people released from custody; they now employ direct treatment methods (such as therapeutic community techniques). By these standards, how have the release programs fared? The earliest studies of people in residential release programs tended to find that they performed slightly worse on parole and had higher rates of return to prison than did those given regular parole supervision. Later studies have uncovered more-positive results, and today most experts agree that work release can play a role in the successful adjustment of those released from a state prison. Although there is still no incontestable scientific evidence that these centers "work," the research certainly indicates that work release is preferable to remaining in prison.

One basic problem is the schizophrenic environment within which the programs operate. On the one hand, without these programs many corrections systems would be unable to manage their ballooning populations. On the other, relying on release programs makes leaders of corrections systems vulnerable to highly publicized failures, especially when someone commits a heinous crime.

Certainly, release programs do not inevitably lead to successful reintegration. Moreover, there is some evidence that halfway houses increase crime in the immediate vicinity where they operate.[13] Perhaps the timing is faulty: People do not necessarily benefit from such assistance at the release stage. Or, more likely, the simple mechanism of graduated release may just not be up to the task of eradicating the negative impact of prison. In any case, the only thing we know for sure is that the effectiveness of programs for people who are being released from incarceration has been disappointing.

THE EXPERIENCE OF POSTRELEASE LIFE

LO 6

Identify the major problems that people on parole confront.

The new releasee faces three harsh realities: the strangeness of reentry, unmet personal needs, and barriers to success. Each must be dealt with separately; each poses a challenge to the newly released.

The Strangeness of Reentry

Although release from prison can be euphoric, it can also be a letdown, particularly for someone who reenters the community after two, three, or more years away. The images in their minds of friends and loved ones represent snapshots frozen in time, but in reality everyone has changed (as has the person reentering the community): moved away, taken a new job, grown up, or, perhaps most disturbing, become almost a stranger. Initial attempts to restore old ties thus can be threatening and deeply disappointing. How many relationships—with spouses, children, and old friends—can survive unscarred the strain of long separation?

Moreover, freedom is now an unfamiliar environment. In prison, every decision about daily life is made by others, so routine decision-making skills atrophy. There are plenty of sad/funny stories about the newly released person looking at a menu for the first time in years and panicking at the prospect of choosing a meal and ordering it. Compare this simple task with the more important tasks of getting a job, finding housing, and so on. Returning to the streets after years behind bars is a shock; the most normal, unremarkable events take on overwhelming significance. Max described his postrelease experience to a team of researchers:

> Basically, everything had been changed. You can go in for six months and come back out and see a great change in society itself. But the main thing was trying to adjust to, say, stuff like the phone system, try to adjust to the ways people are acting and what is going on in your community ... and um, they put you out with no money and they say go make it. And that is kind of hard, it is real hard, if you are not strong you usually fall back into the things you used to do in order to get you right back into, caught back up in the same old circle. If you had a strong family support, a strong background, someone who would look out for you as far as giving you a job, giving you some money, then you might be able to survive a while. But, if not, more than likely you will go back.[14]

In time the strangeness of the free world can become a source of discomfort and pressure. To deal with this strangeness, people are tempted to reach out to the familiar—old friends and old pastimes—and this can lead to trouble. Said one young person on parole,

> I wasn't tempted when I first got out because I wanted to do right, I didn't want to go back. I didn't want to be—I didn't want to have someone else controlling my life anymore. I wanted to be, you know, my own decision-maker, so therefore it was—I know not to hang out with them, you know, but it's still like pressure, you know, still pressure, do you want to come around? It's like the devil, you know, really.
>
> You know you're trying to do right, he's still going to do whatever he can to bring you back out there with him. Peer pressure is a major thing in dealing with this.[15]

Recent research on recidivism suggests that there is a process of desistance from crime that begins at the moment a person is released from prison. Some people are "spontaneous desisters" who, once they leave, will never return to crime. For others the process of desisting is long term and may continue for a decade.[16] For the parole supervision process, it may be crucial to distinguish the people who are immediately going to be successes from people who will take longer to do so.

Supervision and Surveillance

Most of those released from prison are far from free. They must report to a parole officer and undergo community supervision until their full sentence has been completed. The people who provide the supervision tend to define their work as "support," but the person released might not agree.

One underlying message of supervision, no matter how supportive, is that the person under supervision is not really free. There are rules to be obeyed and authorities to heed. The promise of release, with its aura of freedom, soon dissipates into a hard reality: People released from prison may think they have paid their debt to society, but they cannot yet rejoin their fellow citizens. There is always the chance of running afoul of the authorities and being faced with return:

> Stay out two years, wipe the slate clean, flunk a piss test, they put me back in prison again. I ain't done nothing wrong. And that is what my parole officer saying, "Wow, you ain't committed no crime." I didn't commit one then but they say I did. I couldn't afford a lawyer at the time. I work for the city of Tallahassee, I couldn't afford a lawyer. And that is another thing about being in the project, we can't afford a good attorney to represent us in the right proper way to get us off. A lot of those cases that go on down there, they would throw them out. Because you don't have an attorney, you don't know the law, they get you .... It's bad on us. It is really bad.[17]

Supervision is not a uniformly adverse experience. For many on parole, the officer will serve as an important source of tangible help with problems that might otherwise never be overcome. And it seems that supervision may help, overall (see "Making It: One Person's Story"). In both Canada and the United States, people released under supervision have fewer returns to prison for new crimes than do those who leave without supervision.[18]

FOCUS ON

PEOPLE IN CORRECTIONS: Making It: One Person's Story

In 1987 federal officers arrested me for my role in drug trafficking. Despite being guilty, I was in my early 20s and not ready to accept responsibility for the bad decisions of my youth. I proceeded through trial. A jury convicted me. I faced a lengthy sentence that would keep me confined for decades.

Locked in Tacoma's Pierce County Jail, I waited for sentencing. I remember lying on the concrete rack. The walls and ceiling felt as if they were closing in, suffocating my spirit. I prayed for guidance. I found that guidance in a philosophy book that was crammed into one of the jail's book carts.

By reading about Socrates, I learned to question the status quo. From other people in jail, I heard guidance on how to serve time. Many suggested that the best way to serve time would be to forget about the world outside. From staff members, I heard "You've got nothin' comin'."

I rejected those ideas. Instead, I began to think about the best possible outcome. I stared at the ceiling of my solitary cell and asked questions.

How can I influence others to see me as something more than a cocaine dealer?

What do taxpaying citizens expect from me?

How can I earn my way back in to society when I get out?

Those types of questions led to an adjustment strategy. The strategy would guide me through prison. I would focus on educating myself. I would focus on contributing to society in some type of meaningful, measurable way. And I would focus on building a support network.

My judge sentenced me to 45 years in federal prison. As long as I avoided disciplinary infractions, I could earn credit for good behavior. With credit for good behavior, I could conclude my sentence in 26 years. As the weeks turned into months, and the months turned into years, and the years turned into decades, I prepared for my eventual return to society.

While in federal prison, I wrote letters to universities. I explained that I didn't have any financial resources and that I had been a poor student in high school. But I wanted to do better. In time, I found schools to admit me. They allowed me to study through correspondence. Later, professors from Mercer University began offering courses inside the penitentiary. In 1992, Mercer awarded my undergraduate degree. Then I began studying toward a graduate degree through correspondence. In 1995, Hofstra University awarded my master's degree.

Wanting to contribute to improved outcomes of our nation's prison system, I studied and wrote about prisons, the people they held, and strategies for growing through confinement. That disciplined plan gave me strength. It gave me a reason to think critically. I had to weigh how every decision in prison could lead me closer to success, as I defined success.

I wanted to emerge from prison with my dignity intact and with opportunities to contribute.

With a clear vision of how I wanted to get out, I had a solid reason to avoid complications inside. I focused on my studies, on my writing, on my fitness, and on proving worthy of the strong support network that I was building. Through that disciplined approach, opportunities opened. I began to write for publication. As I wrote more, mentors came into my life. They visited me in federal prison, inspiring me to work harder. In 2003 I married the love of my life inside of a federal prison's visiting room. Through the final decade of my imprisonment, I built a quasi-life with my wife. We visited whenever possible. We prepared for my return to society.

In 2013 I concluded my obligation to the Bureau of Prisons. I had 29 years of postrelease supervision ahead with a federal probation officer. Yet the decisions I made in prison put me on a course for success. I had a strong support network. Within three weeks of concluding my prison term, San Francisco State University hired me to teach as an adjunct professor. I taught "The Architecture of Incarceration," sharing with students the influences that led to our nation's commitment to mass incarceration. We discussed how this movement led to the greatest social injustice of our time, and intergenerational cycles of recidivism. We discussed what we could do better.

Besides teaching university students, I launched Earning Freedom. Through this company, I create programs and services for people in prison. I want them to learn strategies that others taught me. I also create bridges to help formerly incarcerated people transition into the job market. And through conference presentations, I spread awareness on steps we can take to improve outcomes of our nation's prison system.

In February of 2017, less than four years after concluding my prison term, authorities released me from supervision.

Free at last!

Source: Written especially for this text by Michael Santos.

The Problem of Unmet Personal Needs

People on parole are aware that they must deal with critical needs to make it on the streets.[19] Education, money, and a job tend to top the list.[20] Yet they are not always realistic about how to meet their needs. Participation in vocational and educational programs

THINKING OUTSIDE THE BOX

VOUCHERS FOR PAROLE

People on parole have many needs, as we have seen. But it is often difficult for them to obtain the services that would help them with their problems. Some agencies do not want to work with criminal justice clients, and other agencies employ a coercive style that makes people reluctant to seek their help. Sometimes, as well, a parole officer will require someone to go to an agency that is not very effective, and participation in the service is not optional.

It is questionable whether this is the best way to provide services. Experts have long observed that when a client is resistant to a service agency—for whatever reason—the services are often less effective.

One solution is to let the person on parole select which services are wanted and which agencies will be selected to provide them. This is done through a voucher system. Each year, people on parole are given vouchers that they can use to purchase services directly: drug treatment, job training, and the like. Such a strategy means that the best agencies have the most business. It also means that if someone is not getting what is really needed, a different service provider can be hired.

Do you think that such a system would help people "make it" in the community after prison? What kinds of problems might it create?

in prisons has been declining over the past decade, and only a minority of people in prison who need drug treatment receive it while incarcerated. Many who face release cannot identify the specific things they must avoid doing in order to stay out of trouble (see "Thinking Outside the Box").

Some people on parole face even more-serious needs as they reenter the community: a history of drug or alcohol abuse, serious mental disorders requiring psychiatric services, and the possibility of homelessness.[21] In fact, leaving prison increases the chances a person will be homeless, with the risk of homelessness growing in severity during the first 18 months after release. Frequently, community supervision addresses these needs, but far too often it does not, with severe results:

> I really tried to stay out of trouble, but it's very difficult, you know. Like once you're into a routine and the people you're hanging about with and everything, and plus you're always getting hassled by the police…. It was about this time that I left home … and I was on the streets for a very long time … because I was homeless, I couldn't get a … job … but I still had… fines that I had to pay… So I am stuck in this rut. I've got to pay these fines or go to jail, and I've got to live as well. So I was committing more crimes, going back to court and getting more fines, and it was just a vicious circle. So the next thing I ended up back in prison again.[22]

Going to prison also has a negative impact on one's intimate relationships. People may face the problem of trying to reestablish relationships with their children, who have been raised by someone else while they were behind bars. Or they may find it harder to establish strong marital relationships. Going to prison often results in marital breakup. The importance of trying to maintain strong intimate relationships is underscored by the fact that if social bonds improve during reentry, the chances of recidivism go down.

Barriers to Success

Soon after release, people in reentry learn that they have achieved an in-between status: They are back in society but not totally free. They face restrictions beyond the close monitoring of the parole officer. Indeed, the practice in the United States is to impose a range of restrictions and prohibitions on people who have been convicted of a felony, especially those who have gone to prison, more so than any other Western nation. Many restrictions

FOCUS ON

POLICY: Former Felons Get the Vote in Florida...or Do They?

On November 6, 2018, Floridians who entered the voting booth were offered the option of approving the following amendment:

> *No. 4 Constitutional Amendment Article VI, Section 4. Voting Restoration Amendment This amendment restores the voting rights of Floridians with felony convictions after they complete all terms of their sentence including parole or probation. The amendment would not apply to those convicted of murder or sexual offenses, who would continue to be permanently barred from voting unless the Governor and Cabinet vote to restore their voting rights on a case by case basis.*

The voters overwhelmingly approved it, assuming that they had restored voting rights to most people who had completed their sentences after having been convicted of a felony. The measure, supported by nearly two-thirds of the voters, was scheduled to take effect on January 8, 2018, invalidating the state's previous practice of a lifetime ban on former felon's ability to vote.

It looked like it would enfranchise up to 1.4 million people in a state whose elections were often decided by vary narrow margins. But the legislature acted quickly to put reigns on the law, when it voted to require all fines and fees be paid by anybody with a felony conviction, before they would be allowed to vote—even when corrections said their sentence had expired. The reasoning was that anybody with leftover fines or fees had not really finished the sentence, no matter what the corrections system said.

Reformers cried, "Foul!" They pointed out the legislature passed the voter restriction law on entirely partisan lines—Republicans voting in favor, Democrats opposed. The partisanship exposed the true intent, which was to subvert the will of Floridians who voted to restore voting rights. They said that people with felony convictions—overwhelmingly African American and poor—tend to vote for Democrats, and so the Republican-dominated legislature wanted to keep them out of the voting booth.

The new law was disputed on the basis that it violated federal voting rights, going to the federal courts. In May 2020, Judge Robert L. Hinkle of the United States District Court in Tallahassee, Florida, ruled in favor of the plaintiffs, finding that the law passed by the legislature was unconstitutional—akin to the poll-tax systems made prohibited by the 24th Amendment to the Constitution.

The story does not end here. Florida will appeal the decision of the lower Federal District Court, and whoever loses at the appellate level will most assuredly appeal that decision. The room that must be made for former felons to vote is an issue that may be decided by The Supreme Court.

Sources: Rachel Kaufman, "Confusion, Potential Delays, as Florida Prepares to Restore Voting Rights to Felons," *Next City*, December 7, 2018: https://nextcity.org/daily/entry/confusion-as-florida-prepares-to-restore-voting-rights-to felons?gclid=CjwKCAjw_LL2BRAkEiwAv2Y3SeF4Ep400XQoTtlt19pZU0JJr6ZCK1Aio9UTnVa8kGjSpvLMOC5KQBoCY2YQAvD_BwE; Patricia Mazzei, "Florida Law Restricting Felon Voting Is Unconstitutional, Judge Says," *The New York Times*, May 24, 2020.

are statutory, stemming from a common-law tradition that people who are incarcerated are "civilly dead" and have lost all civil rights. Compounding their adjustment problems are myriad impediments to employment.

Civil Disabilities The right to vote and the right to hold public office are two civil rights that are generally limited on conviction of a felony. Sixteen states return the right to vote after release from prison; 21 states return it after the sentence is completed and the person is no longer in prison, on parole, or on probation; but 11 states disenfranchise people for life for some or all felony convictions (see Figure 16.7).[23] Only through a pardon is full citizenship restored. Twenty states return the right to hold public office to people following discharge from probation, parole, or prison; 19 states permanently restrict that right except for people who have been pardoned. Many states deny other civil rights upon a felony conviction, such as serving on juries, holding public office, and holding positions of public trust (which include most government jobs).

An estimated 6.1 million voting-age Americans, including 1 out of every 13 African Americans, cannot vote because of their felony convictions.[24] Thus, in Alabama and

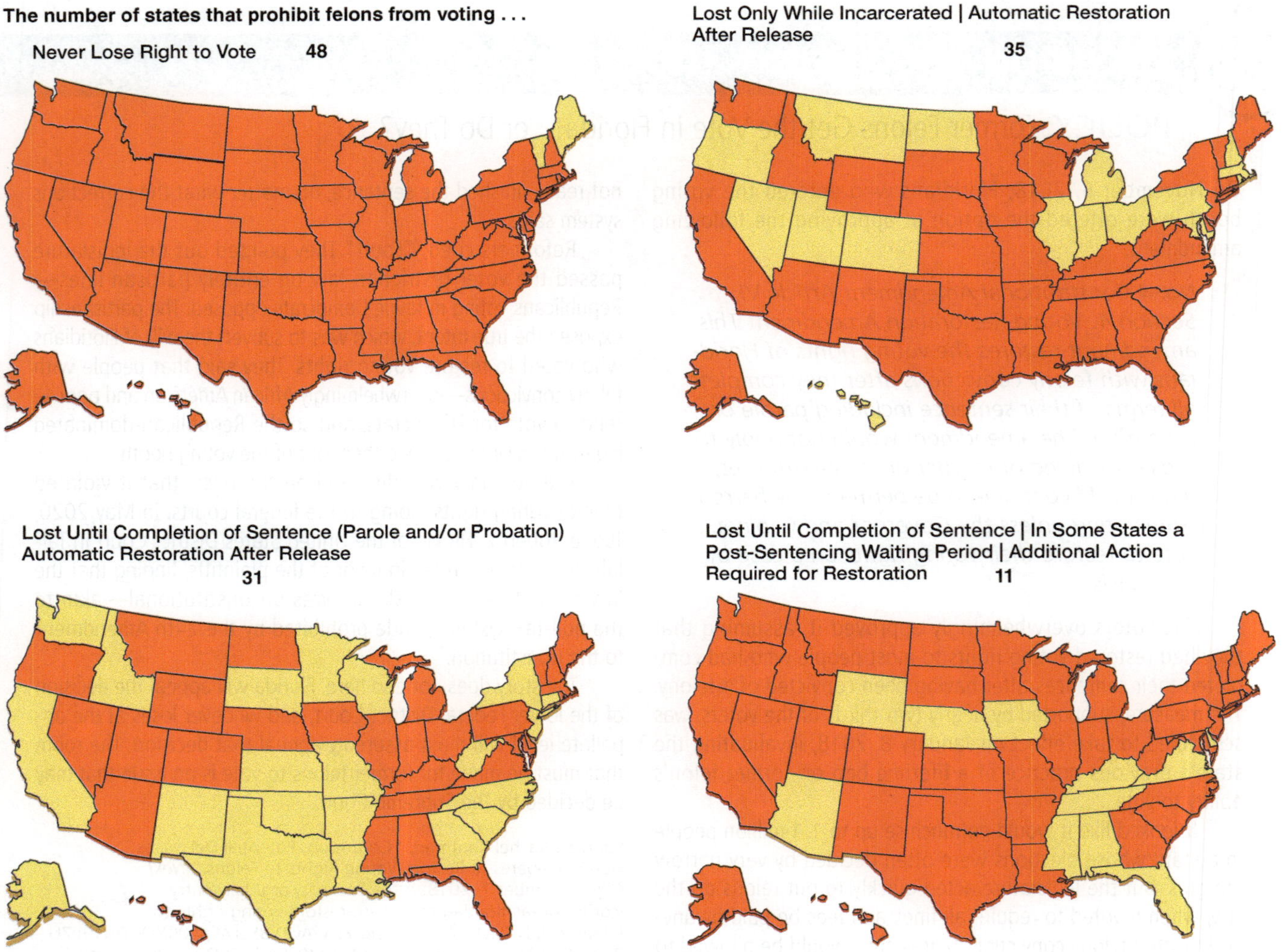

FIGURE 16.7 Voting Rights for People Convicted of Felonies

Florida is the largest of 11 states that can permanently strip some or all felony-convicted people of their right to vote. States have clemency processes to restore voting rights in some cases.

Source: National Conference of State Legislatures, *Felon Voting Rights, 2020*, https://www.ncsl.org/research/elections-and-campaigns/felon-voting-rights.aspx

---

Florida, one-third of African American men are permanently ineligible to vote, and in Iowa, Mississippi, New Mexico, Virginia, and Wyoming, one-fourth of this group is thus affected.

The political implications of voter disfranchisement are remarkable. That is one of the reasons that the Democratic governor of Virginia, Terry McAuliffe, restored the voting rights of 200,000 Virginians in 2016—most people assumed that they would vote overwhelmingly Democratic. Under the same assumption, researchers have shown that Al Gore would have won the presidency in 2000 if felony-convicted people had been allowed to vote.

Voting may be the most notable civil disability of people who have been in prison, but other legal barriers also directly affect those trying to make it after serving their time. Many of the more-recent obstructions to reentry have come about through federal legislation. The Legal Action Center published a state-by-state analysis of legal barriers in reentry,[25] including the following:

1. *Public assistance and food stamps:* Changes in federal welfare laws that were enacted in 1996 put in place a lifetime eligibility ban for food stamps and Temporary

Assistance to Needy Families (TANF: child welfare) for anyone convicted of a drug-related felony. States had the option of dropping out of some aspects of the federal ban. Only 12 states did so, leaving 38 states refusing food stamps, TANF, or both.

2. *Public housing:* Federal regulations allow any public housing authority (subsidized housing provider) to evict any person (or the person's family) when the person is arrested for a drug-related crime, and any returning felony-convicted person may also be refused housing.
3. *Driver's licenses:* A 1992 federal law withheld some highway funds unless the states suspended the licenses of people convicted of a drug crime. Twenty-seven states now suspend licenses automatically.
4. *Adoptions and foster care:* Fifteen states bar those with criminal records from adopting children or serving as foster parents.
5. *Student loans:* The Higher Education Act of 1998 makes students convicted of drug-related crimes ineligible for grants, loans, or work assistance.

Employment Barriers to employment are both formal and informal. Employers hesitate to hire people on parole because they view a conviction as evidence of untrustworthiness. Thus, to the cumulative effect of statutory and informal discrimination we must add sometimes unrealistic expectations for employment. As one person on parole explains,

> Contrary to my prison expectations, finding employment was not an easy task. In fact, it took me over six weeks to find my first job, even though, at least for the first month, I made a conscientious and continuing effort to find employment. I quickly found that I had no marketable skills. My three years' experience working for a railroad before I was imprisoned provided me with no work skills transferable to other forms of employment. Nor did my prison assignments in the tag shop (making license plates and street signs), in the soap shop (making soap), or as a cellhouse worker prove to be of any assistance. The only job openings available to me were nonskilled factory work and employment in service-oriented businesses. Finally, after six weeks, I found employment mixing chemicals in vats for placement later in spray cans. After two weeks the personnel manager told me that he had to discharge me because I had lied about my criminal history (I had). Even though my foreman spoke up for me, supposedly company policy had to be followed.[26]

The legal barriers to employment are perhaps the most frustrating because they constitute an insurmountable wall blocking job opportunities. In many states, several occupations require licenses that are denied to any releasee. The courts have upheld these bans when the work has a connection to the person's past criminal conduct. For example, it is constitutional for a state to prohibit the employment in day-care centers of people convicted of child molestation. Other statutes bar from specified jobs any person who "gave evidence of moral turpitude or a lack of good moral character"—characteristics that many people attribute to the formerly imprisoned. Over the last 20 years, some employment prohibitions have been eliminated, but others have been imposed. Some of the changes are dramatic, so in many states some people have now entered professions closed to them for centuries, yet public reaction to specific cases has resulted in new prohibitions in some locations (see "For Critical Thinking").

Making matters worse, such statutes bar some of the jobs that people were trained to do, either before they were incarcerated or while they were in prison. For instance, all states bar employment as barbers (even though many prisons provide training programs in barbering), beauticians, and nurses. Further, well-paying jobs tend to be reserved for people with no criminal record. Indeed, the newly released

FOR CRITICAL THINKING

Some people say that those who commit crimes should be ineligible for special work programs. They think that the fact of a prior conviction makes a person a risk to the community, and even if the risk is minimal, the past crime should exclude the person from extra help in getting a job. These people worry that making work available to someone with a serious criminal record could mislead youngsters into thinking they can break the law without consequence and unintentionally punish the people who did not break the law by giving a community job to someone who did.

Others feel exactly the opposite. They say that giving people who have made mistakes a second chance provides an incentive for people to straighten out their lives. Work programs also help the person transition back to regular life and therefore prevent crime.

1. What do you think? Should people with criminal records be a priority for work programs? Should they be allowed to take jobs even though someone else without a criminal record might want the same job?
2. If you think that there should be some restrictions on work program status, how long should someone who has been to prison be barred from this status, and why?
3. What are the social consequences of your point of view, both positive and negative?

may find themselves legally barred from jobs that they held before they were incarcerated. In most states, civil service regulations or special statutes bar or restrict governmental employment. Even a prior arrest for a felony without a conviction can lead to rejection. Sometimes, a prior arrest as a juvenile is an absolute bar to employment in a criminal justice occupation in many states, despite the fact that criminal justice agencies that have hired releasees rate their job performance equal to or better than that of the average employee.

People with criminal records report that potential employers (and landlords, as well) find it hard to overlook these records when they are disclosed in an interview.[27] This appears to be particularly true when the crime was considered violent.[28] That is why so many people looking for work after they leave prison try to hide their criminal history. This approach is not advisable, though. When employers are required to run a background check and find the history, they almost never hire the person. Conversely, many employers

FOCUS ON

CORRECTIONAL PRACTICE: What should be done to make reentry more effective?

Everyone agrees that the first year after prison is the toughest. Many people fail during that year—some studies find that almost half get rearrested and a fourth end up back in prison. There has been limited systematic attention paid to the experiences that make that year so difficult. That is why sociologist Bruce Western set out to learn more about what transpires in that first year after prison. Selecting a sample of about 130 people released from prison in Massachusetts, Western's study interviewed them repeatedly, providing an understanding not just of the issues their subjects faced, but also an opportunity to get a better grasp of those problems as they were being encountered. In a method that provided what Western calls a "granular look" at life after prison.

What emerges is a portrait of a group of people who face interlocking sets of problems that make the high rates of failure seem inevitable. Most people who leave prison struggle to find a stable place to live; jobs are hard to get and hard to keep; there is no money; healthcare is unavailable; intimate relationships are difficult to sustain. When you add to these contextual problems the fact that many people in reentry from prison struggle with drug and alcohol addiction, as well as a variety of moderate and serious mental health issues, the resilience of many in this population is what comes through. It is easy to wonder why the failure rates aren't even higher.

Some of the facts that come out are disturbing. Over 40 percent of the subjects had seen someone being killed. Half had been victims of physical or sexual abuse. Most came from homes where instability was the rule rather than the exception. One of the points Western stresses is that hard distinction that is so commonly made between victims and perpetrators becomes much more fuzzy from his analysis. Many of those in his study committed awful, disturbing crimes. Just as many had been victims of such crimes—not infrequently, the same person was both a former victim and a former perpetrator. It is easy to see why trauma is such a big factor in the first year after prison—trauma from incarceration and trauma from life.

Western sees reentry reform as a matter of basic social justice. He calls for a host of changes in the way we deal with people freshly out of prison. There should be less emphasis on enforcing tough rules and more intentional assistance provided. Making it after prison would be easier if those in their first year after prison had access to guaranteed housing and health care, drug treatment, and transitional employment. The problems people returning homeward are not insurmountable—as demonstrated by how many people do succeed. But it is not in society's interest to make the year after prison so hard.

Source: Bruce Western, *Homeward: Life in the Year After Prison* (NY: Russell Sage, 2018).

who run a background check when one is not legally required decide to hire the person anyway—so again, hiding the background seems to have little advantage.[29] Without question, however, getting the job is important to the person released from prison. One study found that people coming out of prison who were cleared to work in the health care industry after a background check were significantly less likely to be arrested again, and they earned an average of $16,000 more per year in wages.[30]

The options for most people after prison remain severely limited. The quandary is real: Should applicants tell prospective employers about their criminal records and risk being denied a chance to prove themselves? Or should they lie and risk being fired if their criminal records come to light? These questions are highlighted when employers are reluctant to hire people who have been in prison, especially when their crimes involved violence (see "Should We 'Ban the Box?'"). As one person said,

> It took me a month to get a job. I filled out applications and did all the things that he said.

FOCUS ON

CORRECTIONAL POLICY: Should We "Ban the Box"?

One of President Barack Obama's most significant criminal justice initiatives was to expand "ban the box" requirements for hundreds of federal jobs and to entice dozens of large U.S. corporations to do the same—including General Motors and Coca-Cola. His lead gave an enormous boost to the national "Ban the Box" movement.

"Ban the Box" is shorthand for eliminating from initial screening job applications the requirement that a person disclose any previous convictions for felonies. This allows people with felony convictions to present their job qualifications in the best manner possible, just like anyone else. If they get to the job interview, then they are expected to disclose their conviction and what they have done to overcome it. Experience shows that if people who have felony records can get to the interview stage, they have a good chance of being hired.

Many Americans subscribe to the philosophy that once a person has paid his or her debt to society by serving time in prison, a new page should be turned in that person's life. So the fact that the consequences of a criminal conviction are permanent for almost everyone who has a felony record runs contrary to common public opinion. Lifetime effects of a felony record on earnings, employment, and access to welfare and education are almost too numerous to list. Nationally, there are more than 30,000 laws that restrict access to employment and other basic rights that the rest of us enjoy.

Many of these laws reflect the values of a bygone time—a "get-tough-on-crime" era in which almost anything that could make the lives of releasees harder was conceived of as a way to deter people from crime. We now know that these laws were largely counterproductive, making it harder for people to transition into law-abiding lifestyles. Seen in the bright light of today's interest in improved reentry, laws such as these are increasingly being targeted for change.

People believe that "Ban the Box" is good policy for two reasons. First, after a few years, an old felony record is no longer relevant to a person's likelihood of a new crime. And because about one man in four has a felony record, we would be creating a permanent class of underemployed if we did not provide for a way that the record can be overcome by current accomplishments, such as education and training. "Ban the Box" is not without its critics. Conservatives worry that previous criminal history is something employers deserve to know when they are choosing applicants to interview. Progressives worry that employers will be less likely to hire African Americans because they will assume that information about previous criminal justice involvement is being withheld.

This movement is just one of the ways that the collateral consequences of criminal convictions can be addressed. If it makes sense in the job market, then similar strategies with voting, housing, education, and financial support may also make sense.

Sources: Maxwell Strachan, "Target to Drop Criminal Background Questions in Job Applications," *Huffington Post,* November 29, 2013; Pew Center on the States, *Collateral Costs: Incarceration's Effect on Economic Mobility* (Washington, DC: Author, 2010); National Employment Law Project, *State Reforms Promoting Employment of People with Criminal Records: 2010–11 Legislative Round-up* (Washington, DC: Author, 2011); Mike Vuolu, Sarah Lageson, and Christopher Uggen, "Criminal Record Questions in an Era of 'Ban the Box,'" *Criminology & Public Policy* 16 (no. 1, 2017): 139–66.

> I tried to practice honesty and I didn't get no contact back, nobody called me. So I kept waiting and kept praying, and I didn't even fill out an application for the job that I have now.
>
> A friend I knew before I went in, he told me to wait, you know, one day before I go to this place and sign up, he was going to talk to the man for me, and he talked to him and I got the job.[31]

Studies have shown that prison terms damage job prospects, in part because they detach people from the support systems that might help them find jobs, reducing the possibility of meaningful employment from a group already facing poor job possibilities. People who go to prison did not have good job prospects to begin with, and poor employment histories continue after incarceration. A one-year follow-up study of 300 men released from prison to live in Cleveland confirmed the difficult prospects they face. Both employment and earning levels were quite low for this group. Only 37 percent had full-time jobs, and more than half were unemployed.[32] A similar study in Chicago found that only 30 percent were employed about six months after release from prison, and less than a quarter were employed full time.[33] There is evidence that going to prison leads to a short-term increase in the likelihood of holding a job because of parole supervision, an effect that quickly erodes after time. But going to prison also has a long-term and permanent effect on wages, reducing what a person will earn over the course of his or her work life. Yet even with all these problems, getting a job really matters—studies confirm that people released from prison who are able to find work they feel good about doing have lower recidivism rates.[34]

One important study shows how much impact the stigma of a criminal conviction has on employment prospects. The sociologist Devah Pager sent out student actors who posed as job applicants to respond to want ads. The applicants were matched in four ways. Two said they had criminal convictions; two said they did not. Two were African American; two were white. The actors who said they had a criminal conviction were less than half as likely as the others to be invited back for a second interview. The African American actors, regardless of what they said about their *criminal* records, were the least likely to be invited back for a second interview. That means that the noncriminal African American actor was less likely to get called back than the *criminal* white actor. This research suggests that young male African Americans who have been to prison suffer a double stigma of race *and* criminal record.[35]

Clearly, people returning from prison face bleak employment prospects. Overcoming the barriers is not easy, but one recent effort has shown promise. The Ready4Work Reentry Initiative uses a multifaceted approach by combining several social services—drug/alcohol abuse counseling, family services, job training, and job placement—and having clients follow the guidance of a trained community mentor. The initiative has resulted in higher rates of employment and lower rates of recidivism.[36] Moreover, studies of the Center for Employment Opportunities (CEO), a New York City nonprofit organization, also show that poor employment prospects can be overcome. CEO initially places people recently released from prison in transitional employment work teams for minimum-wage service jobs. This starts the paychecks coming. CEO then provides job readiness and placement training during this initial phase of employment. Eventually the clients are moved into long-term, permanent jobs. CEO's clients have higher rates of employment and lower rates of recidivism than do those released from prison who are not in the program—and only about 1 in 20 of their clients ends up back in prison during the first year of employment.[37]

Employment initiatives are more difficult to implement when the overall economy is struggling. When jobs are scarce, people reentering from prison find it harder to get them, like everyone else. The consequences are pretty serious—violent recidivism appears to rise when economic conditions are weak,[38] and all crime committed by people in reentry declines under good economic conditions.[39]

Expungement and Pardon

One long-term solution is expungement of criminal records. In theory, **expungement** means the removal of a conviction from state records. In practice, although people whose records have been expunged may legally say they have never been convicted, the records are kept and can be made available on inquiry. Moreover, the legal procedures for expungement are generally both cumbersome and inadequate. Expungement provides little true relief.

expungement A legal process that results in the removal of a conviction from official records.

The same is true of a **pardon**, an executive act of clemency that effectively excuses the person from suffering all the consequences of conviction for a criminal act. Contemporary pardons serve three main purposes: (1) to remedy a miscarriage of justice, (2) to remove the stigma of a conviction, and (3) to mitigate a penalty. Full pardons for miscarriages of justice are rare but do occur. For example, you may have read of individuals released from prison and pardoned after the discovery that the crime had been committed by someone else (see "Coming Back After Being Wrongfully Convicted"). Pardons are most commonly given to expunge the criminal records of people convicted for the first time, but overall they are given infrequently.

pardon An action of the executive branch of the state or federal government excusing an offense and absolving a person of the consequences of his or her crime.

There is good reason to increase the use of expungements and pardons for people who have been able to keep their records clean for a certain amount of time. Recent research has revealed a "redemption" point that occurs after a period of maintaining a clean record. At this point, people who have been to prison no longer represent a greater risk of new criminality than do others of a similar age, even those who have never been arrested.[40] Policy makers have argued that to speed along the postrelease return to normal life, those who show good adjustment in parole should be able to earn an earlier discharge. These proposals all recognize that having a prison record is a difficult status and that the sooner we can ameliorate it, the better things will be for the person with a record and for society as well.

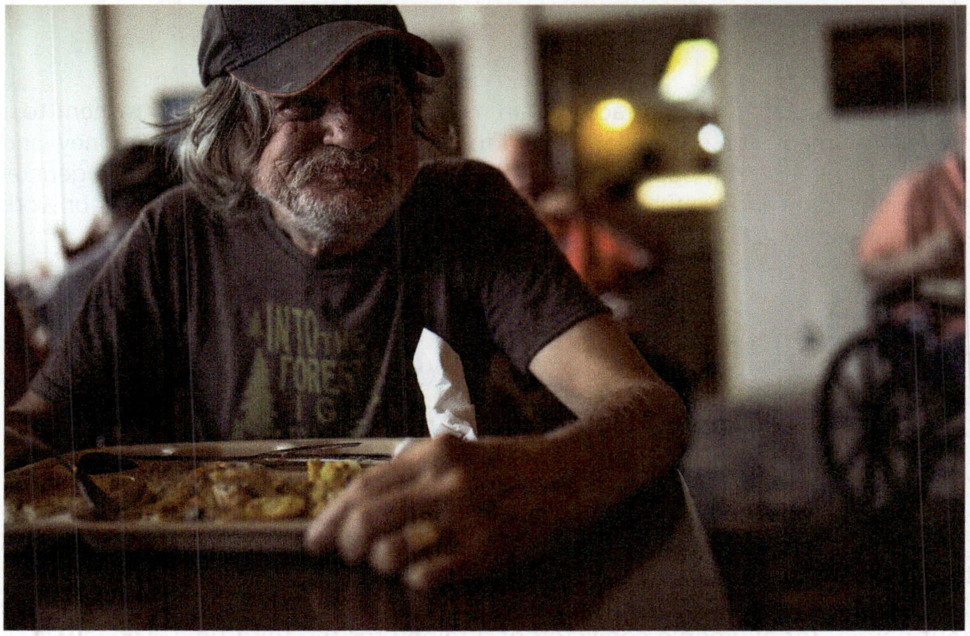

When a person leaves prison without ay community prospects, homelessness is the common result. This is particularly true for the elderly, such as Gordon Nickert, here having a meal at St. Bernard's Friendship Room, a soup kitchen in Alpena, Michigan.

FOCUS ON

PEOPLE IN CORRECTIONS: Coming Back after Being Wrongfully Convicted

Some of the people who are incarcerated were wrongfully convicted—either the state violated the constitution in the procedures used to convict them, or they simply did not commit the crimes for which they are serving time. While these are different kinds of exoneration, they both have the same legal and practical effect: The person who is in prison should not have been there and so is released back to the community. Nobody knows how many people in prison were wrongfully convicted, but estimates are that at least 1 in 400 fits this category, totaling at least 3,000 people (many estimates run much higher).

What is it like to reenter society after spending years behind bars for a wrongful conviction? How is it different from the more typical reentry?

There are complicated emotions. Imagine: day after day in prison, knowing that you should not be there. Feeling voiceless, maybe even hopeless. There is the slow, grinding process of the legal system reviewing your case. Almost always there are disappointments. Then one day you are out. You are elated, hungry to get your life back. But are you also bitter? Do you feel cheated?

What if your time in prison had been spent on death row?

Sociologists Saundra D. Westervelt and Kimberly J. Cook conducted a detailed study of 18 people who had been sentenced to death row before their convictions were overturned. They spent an average of 13 years in prison, most of the time on death row.

What the researchers learned was that people who are exonerated face all the same transitional issues that others face. That is, it is hard to adjust to freedom after the structure of prison life. Getting set up again is not easy—finding a job, getting housing, reconnecting to family, becoming reacquainted with the everyday nature of free life.

But there is a twist. An exoneree can never really forget the fact that an unfathomable unfairness has happened. The damaged relationships seem to be unwarranted losses that must be grieved. It is hard to reconcile the time that was lost. There is a special urgency to reclaiming the public and private status of innocence, even though it seems such a difficult thing to do. There are no obvious ways to go about it, and nobody seems to be able to understand.

Ironically, people who are exonerated face all the same practical impediments of the usual person coming home from prison, but with an additional burden of how to deal with being a victim of injustice.

Source: Saundra D. Westervelt and Kimberly J. Cook, *Life After Death Row: Exonerees' Search for Community and Identity* (New Brunswick, NJ: Rutgers University Press, 2012).

People released from prison face certain misgivings about reentry: adjustment to a strange environment; the unavoidable need for job training, employment, money, and support; and limitations on opportunities. The stigma of conviction remains. The general social condemnation adds to the pressures of being monitored by a parole officer or work release counselor.

LO 7

Explain why some people on parole are viewed as dangerous and how society handles this problem.

THE PERSON ON PAROLE AS "DANGEROUS"

Few images are more disturbing than that of a person, just released from prison, arrested for committing a new violent or sexual crime, especially when that crime is against a stranger. The most heinous of these incidents make national news and captivate the nation's attention. In response to the murder of 12-year-old Polly Klaas in 1993, California passed a three-strikes law mandating long prison terms, up to life without parole, for all people convicted of a felony for the third time. The law is so broad that it even applied to a man who recently strong-armed a pizza from a vendor along a boardwalk. After Dominic Cinelli, serving time for murder, was paroled in Massachusetts, he shot and killed police officer John Maguire. The public uproar led to a complete overhaul of the parole system. The rape and murder of four-year-old Megan Kanka in New Jersey by a person who had been paroled on a previous sex crime led to a series of "sex offender notification laws," called "Megan's Law" after the victim. More than two-thirds of the states and the federal government have passed such laws, and many other states are considering laws extended to cover an even wider range of violent crimes.[41] Figure 16.8 shows an example of a notification bulletin from Washington State.

The fact of repeat violence fuels a public perception that people on parole represent an ongoing threat to the public welfare. It also contributes to a belief that the criminal justice system is too lenient and therefore allows communities to be unsafe. For many parole officers, notification laws or their lack present an ethical dilemma (see "Do the Right Thing").

But how accurate are the public perceptions, and how necessary are the laws? Notification laws are thought to make the public feel more "in control" by letting residents know if a person with a violent criminal past is going to live nearby. However, research finds that notification laws seem to have heightened public discomfort about all people who have been to prison by calling more attention to the problem. Further, people reentering society from prison report numerous problems as a consequence of public notification: threats or ostracism from a neighbor, eviction, losing a job, and/or being pressured by authorities. Pressures that result from notification lead large numbers of people on parole simply to ignore the requirement. One study of these laws in New York found that housing restrictions tended to force people away from areas in which they could receive services and be adequately supervised, leading the author to conclude that the laws aided neither rehabilitation nor public protection.[42] A similar study in California found that these laws tended to force people convicted of sex crimes to live in more socially disadvantaged areas.[43]

DO THE RIGHT THING

The state had not adopted its own version of Megan's Law requiring police and neighborhood notification of the presence of a person who had been convicted of a sex offense.

As parole officer Todd Whetzel sat in his office looking over the record of his newest client, John Paterson, the word *pedophile* leaped from the paper.

Paterson had been convicted of molesting an 11-year-old boy and had served 7 years of a 10-year term before his release on parole. The 37-year-old Paterson was to live with his mother in Mansfield, the community of 50,000 where he grew up.

Examining the record, Whetzel noted that the molestation had occurred in the capital city, some 200 miles from Mansfield. He didn't remember a news story in the *Mansfield Chronicle* about the crime or the sentence imposed. For all he knew, only Paterson, his mother, and he knew of the conviction.

Whetzel thought about the alternatives. On the one hand, the law did not require notification, and releasing the information would violate Paterson's privacy. Certainly, it would be almost impossible to help Paterson find a job if his secret were known. On the other hand, what if Paterson ended up molesting a child in Mansfield?

WRITING ASSIGNMENT: What would you do in Whetzel's place? Write two editorials for the local newspaper, one in favor of disclosure and one against it.

Certainly, people who are released from prison represent a greater risk to community safety than do other citizens. But isolated tragedies can exaggerate the actual danger to the public, especially considering that people on parole are such a tiny proportion of the citizens on the streets. Nevertheless, this small proportion can have a large impact. A California study showed that having more people released from prison into a given neighborhood was associated with an increase in crime there.[44] Nonetheless, the consistent increase in the number of people released from incarceration—from 180,000 in 1980 to more than 641,000 today—has not been accompanied by an increase in crime nationally (see Figure 16.9).[45]

Some people worry that the public preoccupation with potential repeat criminality makes it harder for people on parole to succeed. Certainly, new notification laws open up the possibility that some citizens will want to harass people on parole and refuse to let them live in their neighborhoods. Most of the laws expressly forbid such harassment by private citizens, and a New Jersey man was arrested after he fired five bullets into the home of a man paroled after a rape conviction; the man had lived quietly in the neighborhood for 16 years.

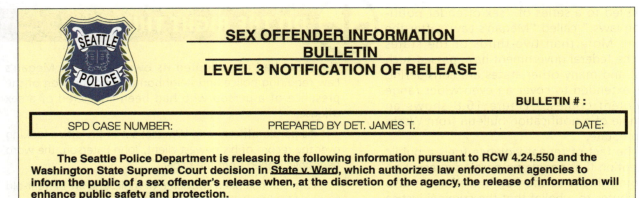

SEX OFFENDER INFORMATION BULLETIN
LEVEL 3 NOTIFICATION OF RELEASE

BULLETIN # :

SPD CASE NUMBER:	PREPARED BY DET. JAMES T.	DATE:

The Seattle Police Department is releasing the following information pursuant to RCW 4.24.550 and the Washington State Supreme Court decision in State v. Ward, which authorizes law enforcement agencies to inform the public of a sex offender's release when, at the discretion of the agency, the release of information will enhance public safety and protection.

The individual who appears on this notification has been convicted of a sex offense that requires registration with the sheriff's office in the county of their residence. Further, their previous criminal history places them in a classification level which reflects the potential to reoffend.

This sex offender has served the sentence imposed on him by the courts and has advised the King County Department of Public Safety that he will be living in the location below. HE IS NOT WANTED BY THE POLICE AT THIS TIME. THIS NOTIFICATION IS NOT INTENDED TO INCREASE FEAR; RATHER, IT IS OUR BELIEF THAT AN INFORMED PUBLIC IS A SAFER PUBLIC.

The Seattle Police Department has no legal authority to direct where a sex offender may or may not live. Unless court ordered restrictions exist, this offender is constitutionally free to live wherever he chooses.

Sex offenders have always lived in our communities; but it wasn't until passage of the Community Protection Act of 1990 (which mandates sex offender registration) that law enforcement even knew where they were living. In many cases, law enforcement is now able to share that information with you. Citizen abuse of this information to threaten, intimidate or harass registered sex offenders will not be tolerated. Further, such abuse could potentially end law enforcement's ability to do community notifications. We believe the only person who wins if community notification ends is the sex offender, since sex offenders derive their power through secrecy.

The Seattle Police Department Crime Prevention Division is available to help you set up block watches and to provide you with useful information on personal safety. Crime Prevention may be reached at 684-7555. If you have information regarding current criminal activity of this or any other offender, please call 9-1-1.

Ogden, Willard W M 3/30/68
Age 27

5'7" 155 lbs., Brown hair, Blue eyes,

Scars on right hand and right forearm.

Willard Ogden was released from the Washington State Penitentiary at Walla Walla after serving 5 years and 8 months for a conviction of Statutory Rape in the first degree and Indecent Liberties. These crimes were committed in Richmond, Washington during June and July of 1988. The victim was a 3-year-old female who resided in the same apartment complex as Ogden. The crimes were accomplished by leading the child into some woods near the apartment complex and behind a nearby school gymnasium. Ogden was often seen at the complex only in the company of small children. He sometimes offered them cookies. Ogden is an untreated sex offender who has refused deviancy treatment. He is at a high risk to reoffend. Odgen is on Post Release Supervision with the Department of Corrections. He has registered as a sex offender as required by law and has recently moved to the 800 block of Casparus St. in downtown Seattle.

Additional sex offender information:
As of the date of this bulletin, there are 8,703 sex offenders who have registered as required (since 2/28/90) and are living in Washington State. 1,900 of these are registered to King County addresses. 863 are registered to addresses within the city limits of Seattle. State-wide there are an additional 2,132 sex offenders who are required to register and have not and are actively being pursued by law enforcement.

FIGURE 16.8 Sex Offender Notification Bulletin, State of Washington

Is it fair to tell a person's neighbors that he or she has been in prison for a sex offense? How should it be done?

Source: Carl Poole and Roxanne Leib, *Community Notification in Washington State: Decision-Making and Costs* (Olympia: Washington State Institute for Public Policy, 1995), 24.

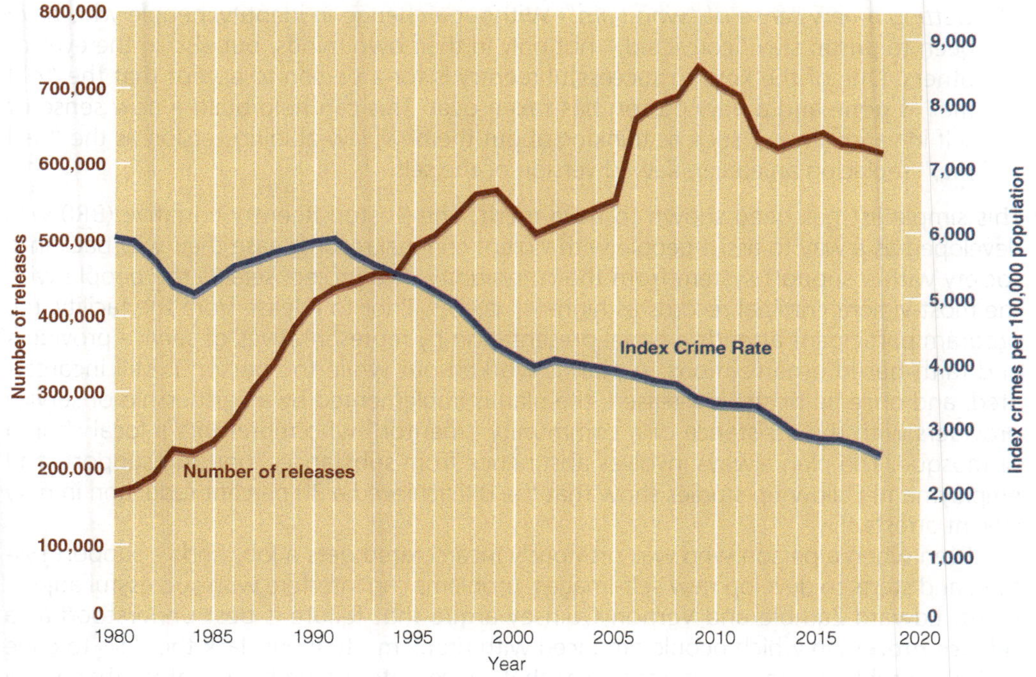

FIGURE 16.9 Crime Rate and Releases from State and Federal Prisons, 1980–2009
Even though the number of people released into the community has increased steadily for almost three decades, crime has not increased during that time.

Sources: James P. Lynch and William J. Sabol, *Prisoner Reentry in Perspective, Crime Policy Report*, vol. 3 (Washington, DC: Urban Institute, 2001), 7, reprinted by permission; U.S. Bureau of Justice Statistics, *Prisoners* data series, 2001-2018; Federal Bureau of Investigation, *Crime in the United States*, data series, 2001-2018.

THE ELEMENTS OF SUCCESSFUL REENTRY

Prison is such a harsh experience that it would seem unlikely that most who are allowed to leave would eventually return. But the problems just discussed make it easier to see why so many people fail. Adjustment to the community is neither simple nor easy. It can be thought of as comprising two different paths: finding supports for adjustment and avoiding relapse.

Shadd Maruna, who has interviewed a large number of men who are trying to make it after serving time in prison, has identified several adjustment supports that are necessary for successful reentry.[46] Four of the most important are these:

1. *Getting substance abuse under control:* No long-term adjustment is possible unless drug and alcohol abuse are curtailed. For many newly released people, this means drug treatment reinforced by drug testing. It also means cutting ties to drug-using friends.
2. *Getting a job:* For most people fresh out of prison, success starts with a job good enough to provide the money to pay the bills and settle debts. The job is important, not just for the money but also for the way it redirects a person's time and energy from the negative to the positive.
3. *Getting a community support system:* Family and friends are quite important for supporting adjustment, but so are community institutions such as churches and organized athletics. Establishing good, strong contacts with these sources of support is a key to staying out of trouble, partly because a person cannot keep those supports when returning to the old way of life.

4. *Getting a new sense of "who I am":* Without a change in identity, people who have been to prison stay "convicted," not only in their own minds, but also in the eyes of others. One of the keys to successful reentry is for a person to accept that the "old me" is gone and a new person has taken over. This can help build a new sense of self in various ways, such as thinking about the new, law-abiding version as the "real me," replacing an earlier, flawed version of the self.

This simple list has been shown to have merit. The Boston Reentry Initiative (BRI) was developed as a way to assist people with violent criminal records ease their way back into society with a support system from the community. The project selects the people with the most-violent criminal records as high-risk clients. Prior to release from the facility, the program participant attends a panel presentation by representatives of service providers and faith-based organizations. A plan is worked out while the person is still incarcerated, and once he or she is released, the plan is implemented by a partnership of service providers with the assistance of a community "mentor" who represents a local church or mosque. The plan always involves abstinence from substances, housing support, and employment. Follow-up studies show that the BRI achieved a 30 percent reduction in new violent arrests.[47]

Even when a person who was previously incarcerated gets a job, finds a support system, and starts to develop new self-images, problems can interfere with successful adjustment. Edward Zamble and Vernon Quinsey argue that failure is best understood as a **relapse process** in which people are faced with problem situations, lack the skills to cope with the problems, and select responses that exacerbate the problems rather than solve them.[48] An example of this occurs when a newly released person disagrees with his or her boss. Rather than "go with the flow," the person may feel that the only way to save face is to refuse to follow the boss's instructions. When this happens a few times, the person is fired, and the poor job history that results makes getting and keeping a job even harder than before. Until the person learns how to deal effectively with the kinds of problems that set up failure, recidivism remains the likely result. Postrelease supervision is thought to be one of the main ways to teach better coping skills. But does it?

relapse process The scenario that occurs when poor decision making makes adjustment problems worse, leading eventually to recidivism.

POSTRELEASE SUPERVISION

As we have seen, postrelease supervision can be viewed as a game of three "players"—the officer, the client, and the administration. But how effective is that game? How do we determine its effectiveness? Further, what might the game be like in the future? Will its rules change?

LO 8

Describe the effectiveness of postrelease supervision.

How Effective Is Postrelease Supervision?

The effectiveness of corrections is usually measured by rates of recidivism—the percentage of people who return to criminal behavior after release. However, because the concept of recidivism means different things to different people, the measures of recidivism also represent different things. The rates reported vary from 5 to 50 percent, depending on how one counts three things: (1) the event (arrest, conviction, parole revocation), (2) the duration of the period over which the measurement is made, and (3) the seriousness of the behavior. Typically, an analysis of recidivism is based on rearrest or reimprisonment for either another felony conviction or for a parole violation for up to three years after release. National figures show that less than half of those who are released from prison remain arrest-free for three years. Yet a three-year follow-up can be misleading—a recent nine-year follow-up of a large sample of people released from prison in 2005 found that of those who had no new arrest in the first three years after release, 42 percent were rearrested in years 4 through 9.[49]

Because many postrelease arrests are minor, almost half of those arrested successfully complete their supervision terms. A recent study by the Pew Center on the States found that 43.3 percent of people released in 2004 were reincarcerated within the next three years. That is a high rate, but the same study found indications that the reincarceration rate has been dropping in many locations, probably because of improvements in supervision strategies.[50]

But it is hard to know how much of this success results from parole work and how much reflects sheer determination. A recent report by the Urban Institute found almost no differences in arrest rates between people who were supervised on parole after release from prison and those who were not. This study shows that parole boards are able to select good-risk cases for early release but that when the differences in risk were taken into account, people who were paroled did not do much better than people released outright from prison. The study concluded that "the public safety impact of supervision is minimal and ... does not appear to improve recidivism outcomes for violent offenders or property offender[s] released to mandatory parole [supervision]."[51] Mandatory release seems to work only for people convicted of property crimes who have been granted early parole. A New Jersey study found that parole prevents new crimes, but at the cost of high rates of technical revocations that cancel out the advantage.[52]

Of course, parole supervision is not the only factor affecting the rates of success. Community characteristics are also important. When jobs are plentiful and housing is adequate, people on parole have a chance to do better.[53] It has also been shown that access to nearby services and other positive neighborhood factors can help people on parole to succeed at higher rates.[54]

People who look at results such as these argue that an important strategy for improving supervision effectiveness is case management. One element of case management is to impose on the supervision effort a structure of established approaches that will likely succeed, rather than leaving the supervision style to the officer's discretion. It is hoped that people on parole will fare better, both in their criminal behavior and social adjustment, under these approaches. This kind of case management is based on tangible services such as job training and money for transportation to work, with close monitoring of progress—we know that job-related services reduce recidivism and increase earnings.[55]

Jill Toyoshiba/Kansas City Star/TNS

▲ *Journey House opened in Kansas City, Mo., as a place for women released from prison to have a place to live. Nuns also live in the house and help the women get on their feet and stay out of trouble.*

In short, the effectiveness of parole supervision has earned, at best, mixed reviews. Yet because people on parole who remain crime-free for two years often succeed thereafter, correctional administrators continue to revise parole practices in ways that will help people make it. A review of the literature on parole supervision offers this list of evidence-based priorities for policy changes:

- Develop and use valid risk-assessment instruments.
- Target supervision strategies to deal with the critical needs of high-risk cases.
- Create incentives for people in reentry to succeed.
- Support those in reentry with problem-solving approaches that help them comply with parole conditions.
- Be sensible about revoking parole.[56]

The limited impact of supervision has led scholars to search for new methods to deal with people who are returning to the community from prison. Some now argue that reentry needs to be bolstered by the authority of the court system, through **reentry courts**. These courts specialize in handling the problems faced by the recently released.

reentry courts Courts that supervise a person's return to the community and adjustment to his or her new life.

...e adjustment by getting the judge involved in the case with gradu- ...s and positive reinforcement for change. Some critics argue that if all ...ts do is increase the amount of pressure on people returning from prison, ...ll fail as most similar programs have failed. But if they focus on getting the ...sees involved in their communities and contributing to the welfare of their envi- ...onments, they will transform the way the formerly incarcerated are seen by other citizens—and they will ultimately succeed where traditional methods have not. While reentry courts are still being evaluated, one high-quality study suggests that this approach is promising— reentry court participants were almost half as likely to be revoked. What is surprising about this, however, is that they were not less likely to be rearrested or reconvicted. This indicates that a main value of re-entry courts is the way they work creatively with people who are struggling to make it.[57]

What Are Postrelease Supervision's Prospects?

Although many changes have been made in the way people are released from prison, supervision practices do not always reflect these changes, as is noted in Chapter 15. Even states that have altered their release laws or policies seem to recognize that people need some help or control in the months after release, and research suggests that parole does help them stay crime-free, at least during the early months on the outside. Therefore, most people in prison will eventually experience some form of postrelease supervision, whether in the form of parole, work release, or some other program.

Nonetheless, the nature of supervision will likely change significantly over the next few years. Evidence increasingly suggests that supervision is not appropriate for everyone but should be oriented toward those who are most likely to fail and who require close supervision. The broad discretionary power of the parole officer is disappearing. In its place, a much more restrictive effort is becoming popular, one in which limited special conditions are imposed and stringently enforced. The helping role of the officer—as counselor, referral agent, and so forth—is being freed from the coercive role, and the help offered is increasingly seen as an opportunity that a person may choose not to take. Postrelease supervision is likely to be streamlined in years to come as the courts continue to review officers' decisions and their agencies' policies.

What is not likely to change is the situation of the person who has been released. Poor training and poor education lead to poor job prospects; public distrust leads to discrimination. People who have been released from prison will need to hone their strategies if they are to succeed in the community.

SUMMARY

1 Describe the major characteristics of the postrelease function of the corrections system.

The vast majority of people released from prison remain subject to correctional authority for some time. For many, the parole officer represents this authority; for others, the staff of a halfway house or work release center does so. The "freedom" of release is constrained: The person's whereabouts are monitored, and associations and daily activities are checked. The person reentering society has many serious obstacles to overcome: long absence from family and friends, legal and practical limitations on

2 Define community supervision and revocation of community supervision.

People on parole are released from prison on condition that they abide by laws and follow rules designed both to aid their readjustment to society and to control their movement. The person may be required to abstain from alcohol, keep away from undesirable associates, maintain good work habits, and not leave the community without permission. These requirements, called conditions of release, regulate conduct that is not criminal but that is thought to be linked to the possibility of future

employment possibilities, the suspicion and uneasiness of the community, even the strangeness of everyday living. The outside world can seem alien and unpredictable after even a short time in the artificial environment of prison. No truly "clean" start is possible. The "former convict" status is nearly as stigmatizing as the convict status, and in many ways it is more frustrating. Most people look askance at someone who has just been released from prison—an embittering experience for many trying to start over.

3 Explain how community supervision is structured.

Three forces influence the newly released person's adjustment to free society: the parole officer, the parole bureaucracy, and the experiences of the person in reentry. The structure of these relationships can determine the results of supervision. The attachments among the three change over time. Initially, the officer is most attached to the bureaucracy, but over time the officer's strongest attachment gradually shifts from the bureaucracy to the client as rapport is established. The client never loses suspicion of the bureaucracy. Parole officers are usually asked to play two conflicting roles: cop and social worker. As street-level bureaucrats, officers are influenced by the organization's definition of the situation, the officer's own perception of the client, and the officer's professional reputation. Moreover, parole officers do not work in a vacuum. They face limits that derive from both the specific need to manage a heavier workload than is feasible in the available time and the general need to respond to organizational philosophies and policies.

5 Describe residential programs and how they help people on parole.

Residential programs serve people when they are first released from prison. Most house between 10 and 25 people at any one time from medium- or minimum-security facilities. Placing heavy emphasis on involving the people in regular community functions, treatment staff help work out plans to address their problems. Residential programs usually provide counseling and drug treatment, and impose strict curfews on residents when they are not working. By obeying the rules and maintaining good behavior in the facility, residents gradually earn a reduction in restrictions—for instance, the ability to spend some free time in the community. The idea is to provide treatment support while promoting the step-by-step adjustment to community life.

criminality. When people fail on parole, their parole is revoked, and they are returned to prison to continue serving their sentences. Parole can be revoked for two reasons: (1) committing a new crime or (2) violating conditions of parole (a "technical violation"). Technical violations are controversial because they involve noncriminal conduct, such as failure to report an address change to the parole officer.

4 Analyze the constraints on community supervision.

The bureaucratic context pressures parole officers to "go along with the system," just as police officers are pressured to cover for their partners. Parole officers perform their jobs in ways that maintain office norms without threatening their coworkers. However, office norms reduce their discretion because the unwritten rules often force them to take actions in regard to problems that they might otherwise have handled differently.

6 Identify the major problems that people on parole confront.

Although release from prison can be euphoric, it can also be a letdown, particularly for people who return after two, three, or more years away. The images in their minds of friends and loved ones represent snapshots frozen in time, but in reality everyone has changed. Moreover, returning to the streets after years behind bars is a shock; the most normal, unremarkable events take on overwhelming significance. But the most salient fact is that most people released from prison are far from free. People on parole must report to a parole officer and undergo community supervision until their full sentence has been completed. They are also aware that they must meet critical needs to make it on the streets. Education, money, and a job tend to top the list, but health care is also a high priority. People also learn that they have achieved an in-between status: They are back in society but not totally free. They face restrictions on opportunities, including many impediments to employment.

7 Explain why some people on parole are viewed as dangerous and how society handles this problem.

Few images are more disturbing than that of a person recently released from prison who is arrested for committing a new violent or sexual crime, especially when that crime is against a stranger. Certainly, people who are released from prison represent a greater risk to community safety than do other citizens. But isolated tragedies can exaggerate the actual danger to the public, especially considering that people on parole are such a tiny proportion of the citizens on the streets. Moreover, the consistent increase in people released from prison—from 180,000 in 1980 to over 641,000 today—has not been accompanied by an increase in crime nationally.

8 Describe the effectiveness of postrelease supervision.

The effectiveness of corrections is usually measured by rates of recidivism, the percentage of people who return to criminal behavior after release. Nationally, less than half of those who are released from prison remain arrest-free for three years. Because many of these arrests are minor, almost half of those arrested successfully complete their supervision terms. Further, 60 percent complete their parole terms without being returned to prison. But the effectiveness of parole supervision has earned, at best, mixed reviews. The nature of supervision will likely change significantly over the next few years as interest in the problem of reentry has reawakened.

KEY TERMS

community correctional center (*p. 430*)
conditions of release (*p. 419*)
expungement (*p. 441*)
pardon (*p. 441*)
reentry courts (*p. 448*)
relapse process (*p. 446*)
work release center (*p. 431*)

FOR DISCUSSION

1. Imagine that you have just been released from prison after a five-year term. What are the first things you will do? What problems do you expect to face?
2. It is said that probation officers tend to take a social work approach and parole officers tend to take a law enforcement approach. How might these differences in approach be explained?
3. Why are some parole officers reluctant to ask that a client's parole be revoked for technical violations? What organizational pressures may be involved?
4. Why are so many occupations closed to people convicted of felonies?
5. Do you think that neighborhood notification laws for people released from prison who were convicted of sex crimes increase public safety? Do these laws merely make it harder for these people to succeed? Why?

FOR FURTHER READING

Bushway, Shawn, Michael A. Stoll, and David F. Weiman, eds. *Barriers to Reentry? The Labor Market for Released Prisoners in Postindustrial America.* New York: Russell Sage Foundation, 2007. A series of studies of employment-related issues facing people who are returning from prison.

Delgado, Melvin. *Prisoner Reentry at Work: Adding Business to the Mix.* Boulder, CO: Lynne Rienner, 2012. An argument for the creation of "social enterprises," small businesses that incorporate social services, to aid in the reentry process.

Jonson, Cheryl Lero, and Francis T. Cullen. "Prisoner Reentry Programs." In Michael Tonry, ed., *Crime and Justice: A Review of Research.* Chicago: University of Chicago Press, 2015. A comprehensive review of theory and practice in reentry programs, with an emphasis on evidence-based policies.

Maruna, Shadd. *Making Good: How Ex-convicts Reform and Rebuild Their Lives.* Washington, DC: American Psychological Association, 2001. Classic, award-winning analysis of how formerly incarcerated individuals develop new personal identities and stay away from crime.

Nixon, Vivian and Daryl Atkinson, *What We Know: Solutions from our Experiences in the Justice System*. NY: NYU Press, 2020. Essays by formerly incarcerated scholars and advocates about the kinds of changes that are needed in the justice system.

Price-Spratlen, Townsand, and William Goldsby. *Reconstructing Rage: Transformative Reentry in the Era of Mass Incarceration*. New York: Lang, 2012. A curriculum for people in reentry and their families to understand how to transform reentry experiences into community empowerment.

Tosteson, Heather and Charles D. Brokett, *Sharing the Burden of Repair: Reentry after Mass Incarceration*. Decatur, GA: Wising Up Press, 2020. An anthology of inspiring stories about the struggles and successes of re-entry form prison.

Western, Bruce *Homeward: Life in the Year After Prison*. NY: Russell Sage. 2018. A study of the reentry experiences of people during their first year after release from prison, with recommendation for reform.

NOTES

1 See Katherine Rosman, "Feel Like You're in Prison? These Trainers Actually Were," *The New York Times,* April 14, 2020; Christian Bonavides, " Second U Foundation Gives the Formerly Incarcerated a Second Chance," *PIX 11,* November 4, 2019; Second Chance Foundation: https://asecondufoundation.org

2 John H. Bowman IV and Thomas Mowen, "Building the Ties that Bind, Breaking the Ties that Don't," *Criminology & Public Policy* 16 (no. 3, 2017): 753–74.

3 *Morrissey v. Brewer,* 408 U.S. 471 (1972).

4 Mariel Alper, Matthew R. Durose, and Joshua Markman *2018 Update on Prisoner Recidivism: A 9-Year Follow-up (2005-2014)* (Washington, DC: U.S. Bureau of Justice Statistics, 2018).

5 Adapted from Carl B. Klockars, "A Theory of Probation Supervision," *Journal of Criminal Law, Criminology, and Police Science* 63 (1972): 550–57.

6 Rosemary Ricciardelli, "Parolee Perceptions of Case Management Practices During Reintegration," *Victims & Offenders* 13 (no. 6, 2018): 777–97.

7 Elliot Studt, *Surveillance and Service in Parole* (Washington, DC: U.S. Government Printing Office, 1973).

8 Richard McCleary, *Dangerous Men: The Sociology of Parole,* 2nd ed. (Albany, NY: Harrow & Heston, 1992).

9 Ibid., p. 113.

10 Michael Lipsky, *Street-Level Bureaucracy* (New York: Russell Sage Foundation, 1980), 82.

11 Sarah Kuck Jalbert, William Rhodes, Michael Kane, et al., *A Multisite Evaluation of Reduced Probation Caseload Size in an E vidence-Based Practice Setting* (Washington, DC: U.S. Department of Justice, National Institute of Justice, 2011).

12 McCleary, *Dangerous Men,* p. 63.

13 Jordon M. Hyatt and SeungHoon Han, "Expanding the Focus of Correctional Evaluations Beyond Recidivism, "The Impact of Halfway Houses on Public Safety," *Journal of Experimental Criminology* 14 (no. 1, 2018): 187–211.

14 Dina R. Rose, Todd R. Clear, and Judith A. Ryder, *Drugs, Incarceration, and Neighborhood Life: The Impact of Reintegrating Offenders into the Community,* final report to the National Institute of Justice (New York: John Jay College of Criminal Justice, 2001), 88.

15 Ibid., p. 80.

16 Megan Kurlycheck, Shawn D. Bushway, and Robert Brame, "Long-term Crime Desistance and Recidivism Patterns—Evidence from the Essex County Convicted Felon Study," *Criminology* 50 (no. 1, 2012): 71–104.

17 Ibid., p. 92.

18 Amy L. Solomon, Vera Kachnowski, and Avinash Bhati, *Does Parole Work? Analyzing the Impact of Postprison Supervision on Rearrest Outcomes* (Washington, DC: Urban Institute, 2005), 15.

19 Julia Moschion and Guy Johnson, "Homelessness and Incarceration: A Reciprocal Relationship?" *Journal of Quantitative Criminology* 35 (no. 4, 2019): 855–87,

20 David J. Harding, Jessica J. B. Wyse, Cheyney Dobson, and Jeffrey D. Morenoff, *Making Ends Meet After Prison: How Former Prisoners Use Employment, Social Support, Public Benefits, and Crime to Meet Their Basic Material Needs* (Ann Arbor: University of Michigan Institute for Social Research, Population Studies Center Research Report 11-748, 2013).

21 Bruce Western *Homeward: Life in the Year After Prison* (NY: Russell Sage, 2018).

22 Shadd Maruna, *Making Good: How Ex-convicts Reform and Rebuild Their Lives* (Washington, DC: American Psychological Association, 2001), 96.

23 National Conference of State Legislatures, *Felon Voting Rights, 2020*, https://www.ncsl.org/research/elections-and-campaigns/felon-voting-rights.aspx

24 Christopher Uggen and Sarah Shannon, *State-Level Estimates of Felon Disenfranchisement in the United States, 2010* (Washington, DC: Sentencing Project, 2012); see also Jean Chung, *Felony Disenfranchisement: A Primer* (Washington, DC: Sentencing Project, 2016).

25 Legal Action Center, *After Prison: Roadblocks to Reentry* (New York: Author, 2004); see also Sentencing Project, *A Lifetime of Punishment: The Impact of the Felony Drug Ban on Welfare Benefits* (Washington, DC: Author, 2013).

26 Robert M. Grooms, "Recidivist," *Crime and Delinquency* 28 (October 1982): 542–43.

27 Simone Ispa-Landa and Charles Loeffler, "Indefinite Punishment and the Criminal Record: Stigma Reports Among Expungement Seekers in Illinois," *Criminology* 54 (no. 3, 2016): 387–412.

[28] Megan Denver, Justin T. Pickett, and Shawn D. Bushway, "The Language of Stigmatization and the Mark of Violence: Experimental Evidence on the Social Construction and Use of Criminal Record Stigma," *Criminology* 55 (no. 3, 2017): 664–90.

[29] Michael Stoll and Shawn Bushway, "The Effect of Criminal Background Checks on Hiring Ex-offenders," *Criminology & Public Policy* 7 (no. 3, 2008): 371–404.

[30] Megan Denver, Garima Siwach, and Shawn Bushway, "A New Look at the Employment and Recidivism Relationship Through the Lens of a Criminal Background Check," *Criminology* 55 (no. 1, 2017): 174–204.

[31] Rose, Clear, and Ryder, *Drugs, Incarceration, and Neighborhood Life,* p. 104.

[32] Christy A. Visher and Shannon M. E. Courtney, *One Year Out: Experiences of Prisoners Returning to Cleveland* (Washington, DC: Urban Institute, 2007).

[33] Christy A. Visher and Vera Kachnowski, "Finding Work on the Outside: Results of the 'Returning Home' Project in Chicago," in *Barriers to Reentry? The Labor Market for Released Prisoners in Postindustrial America,* edited by Shawn Bushway, Michael A. Stoll, and David F. Weiman (New York: Russell Sage Foundation, 2007), 80–114.

[34] Robert Apel and Julie Horney, "How and Why Does Work Matter? Employment Conditions, Routine Activities, and Crime Among Adult Male Offenders," *Criminology* 55 (no. 2, 2017): 307–43.

[35] Devah Pager, "Two Strikes and You're Out: The Intensification of Racial and Criminal Stigma," in *Barriers to Reentry?,* pp. 151–73.

[36] Shawn Bauldry, Danijela Korom-Djakovic, Wendy S. McClanahan, et al., *Mentoring Formerly Incarcerated Adults: Insights for the Ready4Work Reentry Initiative* (Philadelphia: Public/Private Ventures, 2009).

[37] Joseph Broadus, Sara Muller-Ravett, Arielle Sherman, and Cindy Redcross, *A Successful Prisoner Reentry Program Expands: Lessons from the Replication of the Center for Employment Opportunities,* www.mdrc.org/publication/successful-prisoner-reentry-program-expands, January 2016.

[38] Daniel P. Mears, Xia Wang, and William D. Bales, "Does a Rising Tide Lift All Boats? Labor Market Changes and Their Effects on the Recidivism of Released Prisoners," *Justice Quarterly* 31 (no. 5, 2014): 822–51.

[39] Lance Hannon and Robert DeFina, "The State of the Economy and the Relationship Between Prisoner Reentry and Crime," *Social Problems* 57 (2010): 611–29.

[40] Alfred Blumstein and Kiminori Nakamura, "Redemption in the Presence of Widespread Criminal Background Checks," *Criminology* 47 (no. 2, 2009): 327–59.

[41] Erica Goode, "States Seeking New Registries for Criminals," *The New York Times,* May 21, 2011, pp. 1, 16.

[42] Kelly M. Scotia, "The Policy Implications of Residence Restrictions on Sex Offender Housing in Upstate NY," *Criminology & Public Policy* 10 (no. 2, 2011): 349–90.

[43] John R. Hipp, Susan Turner, and Jesse Jannetta, "Are Sex Offenders Moving into Social Disorganization? Analyzing the Residential Mobility of California Parolees," *Journal of Research in Crime and Delinquency* 47 (no. 4, 2010): 558–90.

[44] John R. Hipp and Daniel K. Yates, "Do Returning Parolees Affect Neighborhood Crime? A Case Study of Sacramento," *Criminology* 47 (no. 4, 2009): 619–56.

[45] E. Ann Carson and Elizabeth Anderson, *Prisoners in 2015* (Washington, DC: U.S. Bureau of Justice Statistics, 2016).

[46] Maruna, *Making Good,* p. 83.

[47] Anthony A. Braga, Anne M. Piehl, and David Hureau, "Controlling Violent Offenders Released to the Community: An Evaluation of the Boston Reentry Initiative," *Journal of Research in Crime and Delinquency* 46 (no. 4, 2009): 411–36.

[48] Edward Zamble and Vernon Quinsey, *The Criminal Recidivism Process* (Cambridge, England: Cambridge University Press, 1997).

[49] Alper, DuRose and Markman, *2018 Update on Prisoner Recidivism,* p. 1.

[50] Pew Center on the States, *State of Recidivism: The Revolving Door of America's Prisons* (Washington, DC: Pew Charitable Trusts, 2011).

[51] Solomon, Kachnowski, and Bhati, *Does Parole Work?,* p. 15.

[52] Pew Charitable Trusts, *The Impact of Parole in New Jersey* (Philadelphia: Author, 2013).

[53] Xia Wang, Daniel P. Meares, and William D. Bales, "Race Specific Employment Contexts and Recidivism," *Criminology* 48 (no. 4, 2010): 1171–211.

[54] John R. Hipp, Joan Petersilia, and Susan Turner, "Parolee Recidivism in California: The Effect of Neighborhood Context and Social Service Agency Characteristics," *Criminology* 48 (no. 4, 2010): 947–80.

[55] Bruce Western, *From Prison to Work: A Proposal for a National Reentry Program* (Washington, DC: Brookings Institute Hamilton Project, 2008).

[56] Peggy Burke and Michael Tonry, *Successful Transition and Reentry for Safer Communities* (Silver Spring, MD: Center for Effective Public Policy, 2006).

[57] Lama Hassoun Ayoub, "The Impact of Reentry Court on Recidivism: A Randomized Controlled Trial in Harlem, New York," *Journal of Experimental Criminology* 16 (no. 1, 2020): 101–17.

CHAPTER 17

Corrections for Juveniles

While the juvenile corrections system has important differences from the adult corrections system, it also has many similarities. This juvenile detention facility in Pendleton, Indiana, looks and operates a lot like the adult prison next door.

THE STATE OF CONNECTICUT IS CONSIDERING CHANGES TO ITS JUVENILE JUSTICE LAWS that just a few years ago would have been unthinkable. Reformers have proposed modifying the state's laws so that the "age of majority" is 21, not 18. This would mean that up to the age of 21, a person arrested in Connecticut would be treated as a juvenile by the state's legal system.[1]

This change would be remarkable for two reasons. First, no other state sets such a threshold. The norm in the United States is to use 18 as the juvenile court cutoff age—41 states and the District of Columbia use that standard. States that use a different standard go *younger*, not older. Eight states use the age of 17 as the determination of who is a juvenile, and one—North Carolina—sets 16 as the age.[2] Raising the age of juvenile court jurisdiction to 21 would place Connecticut alone among the states.

The second reason is the motivation for making this change: science, not politics. There is growing scientific evidence that the pattern of development of the human brain means that people under the age of about 21—in fact, maybe even all the way up to 24 or so—find it biologically more difficult to control their behavior. Studies now show that the adolescent brain, especially during puberty, operates differently from the adult brain. Chemicals produced in the adolescent brain make it harder for people of this age to resist peer pressure and the temptations of intense pleasure; they find it more difficult to evaluate the potential negative consequences of choices.[3] The resulting penchant for poor judgment and inept decision making means that holding youths accountable in the same way as we do adults makes little sense. Politically, it may seem that public opinion sides with treating young people who commit violent criminal acts as though they are adults, but from the standpoint of science and moral philosophy, young people are not responsible for their conduct in the same way that adults are.

After years of juvenile justice reform in the other direction—lowering the age of eligibility for adult court in order to make it easier to punish young people—it seems that the more appropriate move is in the other direction. Today, most states that treat 17-year-olds as adults are looking at changing their laws. Doing so seems to make sense. States that have changed the maximum age of juvenile jurisdiction from 16 to 18, allowing the juvenile court to handle cases that used to go to adult court, have both saved money and experienced less recidivism.[4]

In this chapter we explore the juvenile corrections system, constructed to handle the juveniles whose conduct is serious enough for corrections to be involved. This is about half of the 744,500 who were arrested and ended up going to court in 2018—the vast majority of them the "usual" cases involving juvenile misconduct and crime.[5]

Although separate from adult corrections, the juvenile system is linked to it at many points. What sets the juvenile corrections system apart is differences in philosophy, procedures, and programmatic emphasis. The philosophy of juvenile corrections places a higher premium on rehabilitation and prevention, as opposed to punishment, than does its adult counterpart. Less dominated by firm due process rules, the procedures of juvenile corrections support a degree of informality and discretionary decision making. This informality is in part intended to enable program administrators to develop innovative strategies that promise to keep juveniles from returning to crime as adults.

LEARNING OBJECTIVES

After reading this chapter, you should be able to . . .

1. Describe the nature and extent of youth crime today.
2. Analyze the history of the development of juvenile corrections in the United States.
3. Describe the new "evidence-based" movement in juvenile corrections, and explain how it has affected juvenile justice.
4. Present the rationale for dealing differently with juveniles and adults.
5. Explain how serious juvenile delinquency differs from most delinquency and what this implies for the juvenile justice system.
6. List the ways that juveniles are sanctioned.
7. Describe the special problems that youth gangs pose.
8. Assess the future of juvenile corrections.

LO 1

Describe the nature and extent of youth crime today.

THE PROBLEM OF YOUTH CRIME

It disturbs us to think of a child as "dangerous" or "sinister," but the daily news forces us to consider the unpleasant truth that some young people commit serious crimes. In 2018, about 1,100 youths were arrested for homicide, 8,000 for rape, and a troubling 26,100 for aggravated assault.[6] Some of these cases became national news stories. The incidents remind us that some juveniles are capable of deeply distressing behavior. Because these cases alarm and frighten us, the need for greater confidence in the juvenile justice system has become a major issue for correctional professionals and policy makers.

Even so, extremely serious juvenile crime incidents are rare. In a nation with 73.4 million people under 18 years of age, only 54,400 were arrested for a violent crime in 2018—about .07 percent of the population. After rising between 1988 and 1994, the juvenile violent crime rate has dropped by 40 percent since 2005; it is now the lowest it has been since at least 1980. Property crime by juveniles has decreased by three-fourths since its peak in 1992.[7] Yet when Americans are asked to identify the most serious problems facing children, they often cite drugs and crime.

This pattern of reducing juvenile involvement in the corrections system is paralleled by dramatic reductions in youth victimization by crime. The National Crime Victimization Survey (NCVS) is an annual, national survey carried out by the U.S. Census Bureau and the U.S. Department of Justice. The NCVS obtains a sample of U.S. households and asks the residents questions about the crimes they have experienced during the previous 12 months. When the survey results are analyzed by the age of the victim, a startling trend emerges. In 1994 about 12 percent of youths ages 12–17 reported being a victim of an assault, and about half of them were victims of violent crime. That number has been falling ever since. In 2015, the most recent year for which we have data, only 1.64 percent of the same age group said they had been assaulted, with again about half reporting a serious violent crime.[8]

Despite this good news, most Americans are unsettled by juvenile crime for reasons beyond the numbers. Young people represent the future. We expect them to be busy growing up—learning how to become productive citizens and developing skills for a satisfying life. We do not expect them to be committing crimes that damage the quality of the community.

Because they are starting criminal behavior so young, we worry about the future—how long before a young person's criminal career fades? How much damage will be left in its wake?

LO 2

Analyze the history of the development of juvenile corrections in the United States.

THE HISTORY OF JUVENILE CORRECTIONS

Throughout history, children who have gotten in trouble have faced dire circumstances. During the Middle Ages, children were seen as property of the male head of the household, and the patriarch could deal with his possessions however he wished. Brutality was not uncommon. When a parent lacked resources, the children went without food. When parents ran afoul of the law, children lost their protectors and were left to fend for themselves. When children themselves broke the law, they faced the same kinds of punishments faced by adults. The plight of children was a factor in the reform of laws dealing with them in England during the 1600s and 1700s.

Juvenile Corrections: English Antecedents

During the early 1600s in England, governments began to consider the plight of the child. In much the same way that the crown claimed property rights throughout the realm, children were seen as falling under the protection of the king or queen. Under the doctrine of ***parens patriae***—literally, "parent of the nation"—the crown could act as guardian of any child, especially one with rights to inherited property.

parens patriae The "parent of the nation"—the role of the state as guardian and protector of all people (particularly juveniles) who are unable to protect themselves.

The Elizabethan Poor Laws (1601) established the basis for officials to take charge of vagrant and delinquent children, placing them under the authority of church wardens and other overseers. Most ended up in poorhouses or workhouses, working under oppressive conditions akin to slavery. The same fate befell the children of widows who lacked means of support. When children broke the law, the same authorities who handled adults processed them, exposing the children to adult punishments.

In the 1800s, when reformers such as John Howard visited the gaols and poorhouses in England, the decrepit conditions and the treatment of women and children in these dark, disease-filled facilities appalled them. As we saw in Chapter 2, reformers called for a new approach to imprisonment. The plight of children in the system helped galvanize public sentiment for change.

Juvenile Corrections in the United States

Table 17.1 outlines five periods of American juvenile justice. Each period was characterized by changes that reflected the social, intellectual, and political currents of the time. During the past 200 years, population shifts from rural to urban areas, immigration, developments in the social sciences, political reform movements, and the continuing problem of youth crime have all influenced the treatment of juveniles in the United States.

The Puritan Period (1646–1824) The English procedures were maintained in the American colonies and continued into the 1800s. The earliest attempt by a colony to deal with problem children was the passage of the Massachusetts Stubborn Child Law in 1646. With this law the Puritans of the Massachusetts Bay Colony conveyed their view that the child was evil and that families needed to discipline youths. Those who would not obey their parents were to be dealt with by the law.

The Refuge Period (1824–1899) During the early 1800s, reformers urged the creation of institutions where delinquent, abused, and neglected children could learn good work and study habits, live in a disciplined and healthy environment, and develop "character." The first such institution was the House of Refuge in New York, which opened in 1825. By 1850, almost every large city had such an institution operated by private charities.

According to the reformers, residents were to be trained in job skills, provided with religious instruction, and held accountable with strict but sympathetic discipline. In practice, these ideals were difficult to attain. Most refuge houses came to resemble the adult prisons of the day, with cruelty by staff, hostilities among the residents, and an overriding sense of harshness and alienation in daily life. Although reformers felt they were bringing a kind of "social love" into the lives of wayward youths, what in fact occurred was at best an indifferent institutionalization and at worst a kind of social oppression. Historians have pointed out that the reformers were well intentioned but that the actual impact of these reforms differed greatly from their aims.

TABLE 17.1 Juvenile Justice Developments in the United States

Period	Major Developments	Causes and Influences	Juvenile Justice System
Puritan 1646–1824	Massachusetts Stubborn Child Law (1646)	Puritan view of child as evil; economically marginal agrarian society	Law provides Symbolic standard of maturity Support for family as economic unit
Refuge 1824–1899	Institutionalization of deviants; House of Refuge in New York established (1825) for delinquent and dependent children	Enlightenment; immigration and industrialization	Child seen as helpless, in need of state intervention
Juvenile Court 1899–1960	Establishment of separate legal system for juveniles; Illinois Juvenile Court Act (1899)	Reformism and rehabilitative ideology; increased immigration, urbanization, large-scale industrialization	Juvenile court institutionalized legal irresponsibility of child
Juvenile Rights 1960–1980	Increased "legalization" of juvenile law; *Gault* decision (1967); Juvenile Justice and Delinquency Prevention Act (1974) calls for deinstitutionalization of juveniles adjudicated for status offenses	Criticism of juvenile justice system on humane grounds; civil rights movement by disadvantaged groups	Movement to define and protect rights as well as to provide services to children
Crime Control 1980–2005	Concern for victims, punishment for serious crimes, transfer to adult court for serious crimes, protection of children from physical and sexual abuse	More-conservative public attitudes and policies; focus on serious crimes by repeaters	System more formal, restrictive, punitive; increased percentage of police referrals to court; incarcerated youths stay longer periods
Evidence-Based 2005–present	Evaluating programs and policies; doing "what works"	Focus on programs and reducing system costs; evidence about youth brain development	Reduced use of confinement; focus on prevention

Sources: Adapted from Barry Krisberg, Ira M. Schwartz, Paul Litsky, and James Austin, "The Watershed of Juvenile Justice Reform," *Crime & Delinquency* 32 (January 1986): 5–38; U.S. Department of Justice, *A Preliminary National Assessment of the Status Offender and the Juvenile Justice System* (Washington, DC: U.S. Government Printing Office, 1980), 29.

BIOGRAPHY

JULIAN W. MACK (1866–1943)

One of the foremost innovators in juvenile justice, Mack presided over Chicago's juvenile court from 1904 to 1907. He believed that the proper work of the court depended on the judge, supported by probation officers, caseworkers, and psychologists. He sought as much as possible to avoid using reformatories and tried to bring the expertise of social service professionals to the courts.

Some have described the refuge-house movement as an aspect of the conflict between the native-born upper classes and the burgeoning inner-city immigrant poor, commonly referred to in those days as the "dangerous classes." The teeming cities alarmed the elite, who saw them as cauldrons of social problems that threatened the core of contemporary civic life.

In the mid-1800s, when frontier settlements were crying out for labor, delinquent and neglected urban children were often removed from their homes and "placed out" to these faraway places to work on farms or in small businesses. These arrangements resembled those made for the indentured servants of the previous century.

Eventually, critics began to complain about the growing abuses of the refuge-house strategy. It had become apparent that the adult court system was not a satisfactory way to deal with juveniles. These courts often treated juveniles more harshly than adults who had committed the same crimes. It had also become obvious that the problems of urban youths had not been solved.

During the Progressive era, at the end of the 1800s, reformers called the "child savers" worked for new ways to deal with children in trouble. A reform group in Chicago ushered in the modern juvenile justice system.

The Juvenile Court Period (1899–1960)

The first juvenile court was established by a legislative act in Cook County (Chicago), Illinois, in 1899. The impetus for the reforms came from the Chicago Women's Club, which had asked the Chicago Bar Association to conduct a study of the problems of handling juveniles and to recommend a model code for a new system. The thrust of the resulting legislation was to give judges broad discretion in handling juvenile cases. Judge **Julian W. Mack** presided over Chicago's juvenile court and made it a model for the nation.

Based on *parens patriae*, the new juvenile court took the role of guardian, the substitute parent of the child. Decisions about a juvenile's fate were linked less to guilt or innocence and more to the "best interests" of the child. The main tenets of the juvenile court can be summarized as informality, individualization, and intervention.

Informality was intended to move juvenile corrections away from the formality and due process requirements of the adult courtroom. Instead of rules of evidence and cross-examination, judges would run the sessions as conversations in which interested people such as parents, teachers, and social workers could comment on the case. The court was encouraged to establish a relaxed, informal atmosphere so that the needs of the child could be understood. Formal rules were thought to hinder the exploratory conversation and unnecessarily limit the potential solutions.

Individualization was based on the idea that each child ought to be treated as a unique person with unique circumstances. It was considered mistaken to handle a case solely on the basis of misbehavior type. Two children, each of whom had broken into a home, might have different needs that led to the misconduct. Criminality was thus seen as a "symptom" of trouble, only one of the problems facing the child. By treating each child as different, better solutions to children's problems could be crafted.

Intervention was the method of the juvenile court. The final aim of all juvenile processing was "adjustment"—to help the child develop a law-abiding lifestyle. Thus, the court was not to punish children but to identify and solve the problems that led them astray and to provide treatment that would avert a life of crime.

To implement this approach, the juvenile court developed its own language, procedures, and rules. In place of standard adult processing practices, the juvenile system established a new version to achieve its new aims. Table 17.2 compares the terminology of the adult and juvenile systems. There was widespread enthusiasm for the new juvenile court model. Following the Chicago example, within a few years every state revised its penal code and established a separate juvenile court. The age of jurisdiction often varied—some states took juveniles as old as 18 or 19, whereas others allowed anyone over age 16 to be handled as an adult. The courts were given jurisdiction over delinquent, neglected, and dependent children. A **delinquent** child is one who has committed an act that if committed by an adult would be criminal. A **neglected** child is one who is not receiving proper care because of some action or inaction of his or her parents. This includes not being sent to school, not receiving medical care, being abandoned, or not receiving some other care necessary for the child's well-being. A **dependent** child either has no parent or guardian or, because of the physical or mental disability of a parent or guardian, is not receiving proper care.

delinquent A child who has committed an act that if committed by an adult would be criminal.

neglected A child who is not receiving proper care because of some action or inaction of his or her parents.

dependent A child who has no parent or guardian or whose parents are unable to give proper care.

TABLE 17.2 Comparison of Terminology in the Adult and Juvenile Justice Systems

Function	Adult System	Juvenile System
Taking into custody	Arrested	Detained (police contact)
Legal basis for holding	Charged	Referred to court
Formal charges	Indicted	Held on petition
Person charged	Defendant	Respondent
Determination of guilt	Trial	Hearing
Outcome of court case	Verdict	Finding
Term for "guilty"	Convicted	Adjudicated (as responsible)
Sanction	Sentence	Disposition
Custodial sentence	Incarcerated	Placed or committed
Incarceration facility	Prison	Training school
Release supervision	Parole	Aftercare

Despite the enthusiasm, problems arose with the informal approach. Sometimes, judges and attorneys ran roughshod over rights, imposing the law in ways that seemed opposed to the youngsters' true interests. Judges were allowed to tailor dispositions, but many people suspected that lower-class children and ethnic minorities received harsher, less sympathetic treatment. Finally, the failure of intervention to stem recidivism led the community to distrust the effectiveness of juvenile court.

The Juvenile Rights Period (1960–1980) The Juvenile Rights Period was a reaction to what was widely perceived as the shortcomings of the juvenile court. The informality so valued by the reformers sometimes meant that evidence regarding guilt was allowed when it would have been excluded for an adult. Permission to individualize dispositions sometimes allowed judges to ignore the facts of the case and allow their biases to inform decisions that may have been wildly inequitable. Interventions were too frequently more severe for youths than those that adults would have received for the same crime. In short, all too often the best interests of the child were not always served by the limited legal protections the juvenile court provided.

This line of reasoning resonated with many critics of the juvenile court movement, and it certainly gained traction with the U.S. Supreme Court. By the 1960s, liberal reform groups such as the American Civil Liberties Union rallied to protect the rights of juveniles. In a series of decisions, the U.S. Supreme Court extended to juveniles many of the due process rights accorded adults (see Table 17.3). By 1990, most of the

TABLE 17.3 Major Decisions by the U.S. Supreme Court Regarding the Rights of Juveniles

Since the mid-1960s, the Supreme Court has gradually expanded the rights of juveniles but has continued to recognize that the logic of a separate system for juveniles justifies differences from some adult rights.

Case	Significance for Juveniles
Kent v. United States (1966)	"Essentials of due process" are required for juveniles.
In Re Gault (1967)	The "essentials" of due process required by *Kent*—notice, hearing, counsel, cross-examination—are specified.
In Re Winship (1970)	A standard of "beyond a doubt" is required for delinquency matters.
McKeiver v. Pennsylvania (1971)	Jury trials are not required for juvenile court hearings.
Breed v. Jones (1975)	Waiver to adult court following adjudication in juvenile court violates the constitutional guarantee against double jeopardy.
Smith v. Daily Mail Publishing Co. (1979)	The press may report certain aspects of juvenile court cases and matters.
Eddings v. Oklahoma (1982)	The age of an accused person must be considered as a mitigating factor in capital crimes.
Schall v. Martin (1984)	Preventive pretrial definition is allowed for juvenile respondents who are found to be "dangerous."
Stanford v. Kentucky (1989)	Minimum age for capital punishment is 16.
Roper v. Simmons (2005)	To impose the death penalty on someone for a crime committed before the age of 18 violates the Eighth Amendment prohibition of "cruel and unusual punishments."
Graham v. Florida (2010)	Extends *Roper v. Simmons* to prohibit life without parole sentences for juveniles who do not commit homicide.
Miller v. Alabama (2012)	The Eighth Amendment forbids a sentencing scheme that mandates life in prison without possibility of parole for juveniles convicted of homicide.
Montgomery v. Louisiana (2016)	Holds that *Miller v. Alabama* is retroactive and applies to all juveniles.

criminal justice rights enjoyed by adults also applied to youths. But along with adult rights soon came a public reaction to treat young, serious criminal activity the same way as for adults.

The Crime Control Period (1980–2005) The public alarm over crime that dominated crime policy starting in the 1970s and fueled a get-tough movement with adults spilled over to affect juvenile justice policy, beginning in the 1980s. Conservative critics argued that juvenile authorities treated young people far too leniently. Stories were told about crimes that would have landed an adult in jail but for which a juvenile received nothing more than probation. Alarm over serious and violent juvenile offenses, particularly those committed by urban youths, resulted in a broad public movement for increasing the use of waiver to adult court (before adjudication in juvenile court), increasing the sanctions for those remaining in juvenile court, or both. This pressure to treat juveniles as adults and to mete out stern punishment for serious crimes eroded much of the enthusiasm for the juvenile court reforms that had dominated the conversation a century earlier (see "Myths in Corrections").

Even though the reforms of recent decades changed the procedures and, to a lesser extent, the practices of the juvenile justice system, in many respects the underlying philosophy of the juvenile court had remained very much as the original reformers intended. The justice system treats juveniles differently from adults by placing less emphasis on punishment and more on individualized treatment. The rationale for this difference is that juveniles differ in important ways from adults, ways that ought to be considered in the way the law works.

MYTHS in Corrections

The Age of Delinquency

THE MYTH: Young people who are over the age of 18 should be handled in adult court because adult court will better prevent criminality.

THE REALITY: People between the ages of 18 and 24 who are processed by adult courts are more likely to recidivate than similar youths who end up avoiding adult court. Most people who engage in delinquency stop their criminality in their twenties. But when youths under the age of 24 are handled in adult court, they do not fare as well as those who are diverted from the court system, and they experience a myriad of other problems as well. This suggests that interventions that focus on services rather than punishment for this age group may be called for.

Source: Human Impact Partners, *Juvenile Injustice: Charging Youth as Adults Is Ineffective, Biased, and Harmful* (Oakland, CA: Human Impact Partners, 2017).

The Evidence-Based Period (2005–Present) Policy makers around the country are rethinking the get-tough approach, and a new policy ethic is beginning to surface: evidence. Both legislators and juvenile justice administrators are asking "What do we know about reducing juvenile crime, and how can we design the juvenile justice system to take better advantage of that knowledge?" The answer to this question includes not only studies of juvenile correctional programs but also developmental studies of juveniles themselves—including the physiology of the adolescent brain and the sociology of peer behavior.

LO 3

Describe the new "evidence-based" movement in juvenile corrections, and explain how it has affected juvenile justice.

Asking this question has led to the emergence of a new generation of community-based strategies to reduce juvenile crime *before* the justice system is invoked. Rather than a heightened policy of crime control that emphasizes surveillance, arrest, and incarceration, this new era tends to look to a host of studies that have provided added clarity to our understanding of what works and what does not. They suggest three principles:

1. *Limited use of detention and incarceration*. It has become clear that putting youths in correctional facilities often exacerbates the problems that lead to criminality while too infrequently preparing the youths for adjustment to society after release. Instead, current policy emphasizes diverting as many youths as possible from juvenile justice, especially confinement, and using a variety of community-based options (described later in this chapter). As confirmation of this new thinking, the number of juveniles incarcerated in the United States fell by 26 percent between 1985 and 2013.[9] According to the FBI, arrest rates for juveniles are dropping significantly (see Figure 17.1).
2. *A focus on prevention in the community*. Juvenile justice interventions with youths convicted of serious crimes are often seen as coming too late. If the crimes could have been prevented, everyone would benefit—the victim, the youths, and the society at large. Several studies have shown that earlier intervention into the lives of **at-risk youths** leads to better outcomes in terms of juvenile delinquency and also saves money. Indeed, when the juvenile court gets involved in a youth's life, the chances of that youth later entering the adult system increase. As a result, the newest programs for juveniles try to focus on at-risk youths early in their lives and

at-risk youths Young people who demonstrate characteristics of being more likely than others at their age to end up as juvenile delinquents in their teen years.

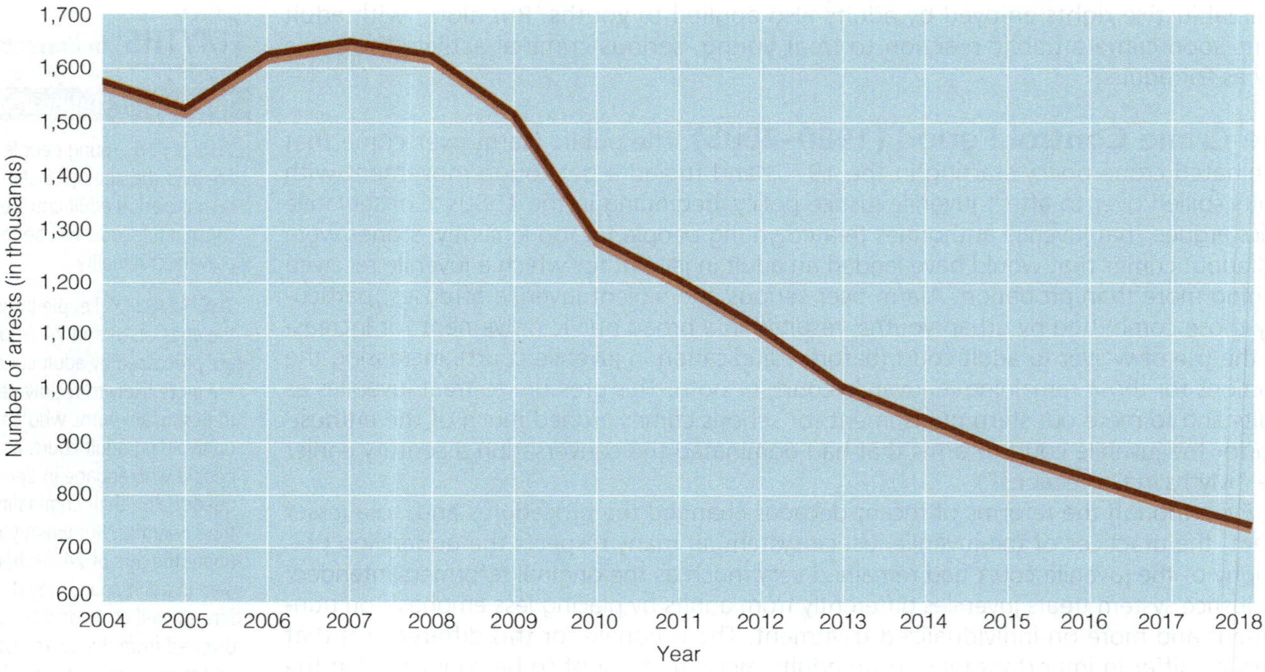

FIGURE 17.1 Juvenile Arrests, 2004–2015

Arrests of juveniles have declined by more than half from 2009 to 2018.

Source: Office of Juvenile Justice and Delinquency Prevention: https://www.ojjdp.gov/ojstatbb/ezajcs/asp/process.asp.

provide noncorrectional support and services devoted to diverting them from serious crime in later years.

3. *Designing programs based on proven strategies*. Today, policy makers have access to hundreds of studies of juvenile justice programs and their outcomes. It is possible to rethink current juvenile justice policies in light of a growing foundation of evidence about what works and what does not. Juvenile justice activists have partnered with leading reformers in legislatures and in the justice system to strip juvenile justice of old programs that have not worked and replace them with empirically proven strategies.

LO 4

Present the rationale for dealing differently with juveniles and adults.

WHY TREAT JUVENILES AND ADULTS DIFFERENTLY?

Evan Miller was 14 when he and a friend spent a long evening using drugs and drinking alcohol. Somewhere in the middle of their carousing, they ended up beating up the neighbor who originally sold them the drugs, leaving him in his trailer and setting fire to it. The neighbor died. Miller was originally charged as a juvenile but was soon sent to adult court to be tried there because the charges were so serious. A jury found him guilty of murder in the course of arson, and he was sentenced to life without parole, as provided by the statutes of Alabama. Miller appealed this sentence, and the appeal was eventually heard by the U.S. Supreme Court.

In recent years the Court has been restricting severe sentences for juveniles (see Table 17.3). In 2005 the Court ruled that the death penalty was unconstitutional for juveniles.[10] Five years later the Court determined that life without parole could not be imposed in juvenile cases where there was no homicide.[11] The question raised by the Miller case was whether *any* crime committed by a juvenile was serious enough to justify a sentence of life in prison without parole.

The Court said "no." In an opinion written by Justice Elena Kagan, the court argued that juveniles, because of their age, must be treated differently from adults:

> Youth matters in determining the appropriateness of a lifetime of incarceration without the possibility of parole. The mandatory penalty schemes . . . prevent the sentencer from considering youth and from assessing whether the law's harshest term of imprisonment proportionately punishes a juvenile. [But] imposition of a State's most severe penalties on juveniles cannot proceed as though they were not children.[12]

Four years later, the Supreme Court made the Miller case retroactive, requiring a new hearing for every person serving a life without parole sentence that was imposed for a crime committed as a juvenile.[13]

What is it about juveniles that means they should be treated differently? (See "Thinking Outside the Box.") What justifies a separate justice system? Five reasons are generally given.

Juveniles Are Young and May Easily Change Most correctional professionals believe that juveniles are more susceptible than adults to the influence of treatment programs. The young are not as entrenched in negative peer associations, nor do they penetrate as deeply into criminal activity. Because the habits of the young are less well formed, they may be more easily altered (see "For Critical Thinking").

But the youthfulness of juveniles is a double- edged sword. Age is a predictor of recidivism: The younger the juvenile is when arrested—and the more serious the misconduct—the more likely that person will be arrested again. As a consequence, correctional workers must deal with the fact that although younger people are more malleable, many will find it hard to stay out of trouble.

Juveniles Have a High Rate of "Desistence" All else being equal, age is the best predictor of recidivism: The younger the person is, the more likely that he or she will fail under community supervision. But this statistic can be misleading because juveniles, as a group, have lower failure rates than do adults. Most juveniles who get in trouble with the law once never get arrested again. Despite the high success rate of

THINKING OUTSIDE THE BOX

INCREASING THE AGE OF ADULT RESPONSIBILITY

Many people believe that young people are maturing at an earlier age. There is anecdotal evidence that this is true. But specialists in youth development disagree. They argue that important dimensions of youth—amenability to treatment, capacity for moral reasoning, and ability to make changes—suggest that the juvenile justice system, with its special way of treating youths, should be extended into the early twenties. (As we saw at the beginning of this chapter, Connecticut is considering using 21 as the cutoff age.)

Experts now say that young men in their early twenties who break the law resemble youths in their attitudes and responses much more than they do true adults. They may be physically "men," but in their thinking and their experiences they are still immature. This means that their culpability is more like that of traditional juveniles and that their responsiveness to programs is more likely to be good if the programs are built for young adults rather than older ones.

Psychodynamically, does it actually make sense to think of three groups: juveniles up until about 18, young adults until about 25, and adults? How would this classification translate to criminal justice and corrections?

FOR CRITICAL THINKING

In 2003 Terrance Graham was sentenced to life without parole at the age of 17. His appeal of that sentence went all the way to the U.S. Supreme Court, which overturned the sentence and barred the imposition of life without parole sentences for juveniles convicted of nonhomicide offenses (*Graham v. Florida*). As Justice Stevens said, "Society changes. Knowledge accumulates. We learn, sometimes from our mistakes. Punishments that did not seem cruel and unusual at one time, may, in the light of reason and experience, be found to be cruel and unusual at a later time."

But what about youths who commit homicide?

The Sentencing Project, a penal reform organization, has argued that life without parole ought never be imposed on juveniles because of their reduced culpability and their unique capacity for reform.

They point to the case of Anthony, who is in prison for life after being convicted of a homicide when he was 16. Despite being offered a plea of 40 years, his court-appointed attorney, who had never tried a murder case before, suggested that Anthony go to trial. He ended up with a sentence of life without parole, while his two companions, both older, received substantially shorter sentences.

Anthony has been described by many as a model resident, with only one minor infraction since arriving in prison 14 years ago. Since Anthony came to prison, he has earned three associate's degrees and is currently working toward his bachelor's degree. He has developed and organized holiday plays and regularly serves as a tutor in prison. Says the Sentencing Project, "He is more than worthy of release and our collective acceptance."

1. Do you agree? Should Anthony's sentence to life without parole be overturned? Why or why not?
2. Are there some kinds of juveniles who ought to be taken off the streets forever?
3. Explain how your views fit in with important values of our country. What potential problems might arise from adopting your views?

Source: Adapted from Marc Mauer, Ashley Nellis, and Kerry Myers, *The Meaning of Life: The Case for Abolishing Life Sentences* (New York: New Press, 2018).

juveniles, a look at those who do fail will turn up large numbers whose criminality began at a very early age, simply because so many youths are arrested in the first place. Even studies of the most serious juvenile delinquents, though, find evidence of high rates of success: Less than one-fourth of youths who end up in custodial placements are returned to incarceration because of new offenses,[14] and even the most serious juvenile delinquents who have been labeled "chronic" by the courts are, for the most part, free of crime by the time they reach their mid-twenties.[15] A long-term study of 1,314 juveniles who had committed serious crimes found that most of them greatly reduce their offending over time and that juvenile institutions do not reduce recidivism, while community-based supervision and drug treatment do reduce it.[16]

Juveniles' Families Are an Important Part of Their Lives For juveniles the role of family is critical to the success of correctional efforts. The juvenile is, by virtue of age, deeply connected to his or her immediate family (parents, siblings, and extended family) in ways that do not characterize adult relationships. Under the laws of most states, for example, the juvenile actually becomes a ward of the state, and the court (usually through probation officers) accepts joint responsibility for the young person. Under the law, then, the court system is a partner with the family in the supervision effort. Many think that this approach is reasonable because the child's delinquency is taken as evidence that the parents are not capable of effective supervision without support from the court.

Juveniles Are Easily Influenced by Their Peers With isolated exceptions, juvenile crime is a group phenomenon. Young people gather to socialize, and a common part of their behavior is testing boundaries and challenging one another to try new things. We often associate the criminal behavior of young people with gangs, but all studies find that group criminality can arise without gangs. Especially during the preadolescent and teen years, peer relationships are the most important influences on most youths.[17] It is not easy for youths to resist the pressure to engage in delinquent acts while in a group.

Juveniles Have Little Responsibility for Others For an adult, successful adjustment to the community involves taking on productive adult roles: parent, worker, citizen. By contrast, juveniles are typically responsible only for their own behavior. Juvenile self-responsibility typically concerns school performance and behavior, compliance with a curfew, and developing interpersonal skills, among other things.

Differences Between Adults and Juveniles, in Perspective

The differences just listed underscore some of the reasons why a separate juvenile justice system makes sense to most correctional professionals. Young people differ from older ones in sufficiently important ways to justify different strategies carried out by separate correctional authorities.

However, these differences do not always work out as juvenile correctional workers might intend. For example, family dynamics often contribute to delinquent behavior. Inadequate parental supervision may leave the child free enough to get into trouble. Conflicts between the child and adults may promote delinquency as the child's way of "getting back" or even unintentionally calling attention to the conflict. Abuse by parents, as well as alcoholism, drug addiction, or mental illness in parents, may contribute to problems that end in delinquency. Such adults often resist taking a positive role in the supervision effort. They may be hostile to the efforts of the correctional worker or may excuse or condone the child's misbehavior.

Peer groups can also cause problems. Minor delinquents can drift from the everyday rule-breaking of truancy, fighting, and drinking into far more serious crime. This can happen especially when the group encourages ever-greater risk taking. Although we might all remember instances of violating curfews, drinking alcohol, and other delinquent acts that seemed merely "fun," many of the most serious forms of delinquency begin with just this sort of misbehavior.

Finally, keeping a juvenile in the ordinary environment of most young people—schools and neighborhoods—may not be easy. When a child disrupts the school setting through aggressive or threatening behavior, the school authorities usually want that youngster removed. When neighbors fear the open violence of a gang member, the judge will face strong pressure to send that person to a juvenile institution. When a juvenile fails in the school and on the streets, few options are available to keep him or her from sinking further into the corrections system.

THE PROBLEM OF SERIOUS DELINQUENCY

LO 5

Explain how serious juvenile delinquency differs from most delinquency and what this implies for the juvenile justice system.

The juvenile justice system is predicated on what we might call "normal" delinquency. This idea may seem contradictory but emphasizes that delinquent behavior is common in teenage years. There is no legal or textbook definition of *normal*; rather, the term represents a set of assumptions about kinds of misbehaviors that are associated with growing up. Because some level of delinquency is, in this sense, normal, people may react to it with less alarm than to similar misbehavior by adults. People may believe that juveniles require not a punitive correctional response but a developmental one; their behavior is a part of a common adolescent pattern.

It would be naive to think that the juvenile justice paradigm applies equally to every young person who breaks the law. As noted, for each difference between adults and juveniles, there are well-known cases where the distinction does not apply. Some juveniles are already hardened and are unlikely to change; some will continue criminal behavior well into adulthood; some lack families who will provide meaningful supervision; some are loners, unaffected by peer influences; some are already in adult roles, with jobs, spouses, and children. About three-quarters of juveniles who engage in serious crime recidivate within 7 years.[18] What should we do when a young person does not act as we would expect a typical juvenile to act?

status offenses Misbehaviors that are not against the law but are troubling when done by juveniles because they are so young.

Status offenses are misbehaviors that are not against the law but are troubling because the person is so young: running away, being truant, and being ungovernable. Society does not expect children to act this way; when they do, the juvenile court may get involved and provide a bit of structure that the parent has not. In 2018 a total of 97,800 youths were found to have committed status offenses; the most common causes were being truant (62 percent), drinking under age (9 percent), being "ungovernable" (9 percent) and missing curfew (4 percent). These sorts of status offense findings are rare, applied to less than one-half of 1 percent of the youth population.[19] Even so, some critics think the status offense system is not good for children because as matters of judgment, status offenses depend on social expectations for how children "should" act. This may be one of the reasons why girls are so much more likely to be involved in this kind of case than in other forms of delinquency (see Table 17.4).

One of the most important considerations is whether the behavior of the juvenile is age appropriate. What people find "normal" for different ages can vary greatly. For example, when a 14-year-old becomes angry and engages in hostile, irrational behavior, most people would think of him or her as merely "troubled." However, the same behavior by a 17-year-old would be seen as immature. In the same way, when a very young juvenile—for example, a preteen—engages in an extremely violent act, we are alarmed by the antisocial behavior of a young person who should be learning to live by society's norms. Clearly, assumptions about the "normalcy" of delinquency depend on how the misbehavior fits the juvenile's age and level of development.

Similarly, people expect misbehavior to take place in a social context. It does not surprise or unduly alarm people when youths occasionally resort to delinquency as a way of becoming a member of their group. Of course, gangs are an extreme example, but most people find even gangs understandable to a point. The lone child who commits crime for personal pleasure rather than social acceptance is comparatively rare, and people do not perceive such behavior as "normal" in a young person's development. The public also finds it hard to understand when a youngster engages in gratuitous violence. Some youths commit petty property offenses, stealing things they want or vandalizing places they resent. A few get into schoolyard fights. But children who kill one another or plot to hurt someone are deeply unsettling. The label "delinquent" seems far too weak for these acts.

Unusual juvenile criminality has been one reason why some question the wisdom of having a separate juvenile justice system. They say society ought to treat all criminal acts with the seriousness they deserve, regardless of age. To the extent that age contributed to the gravity of the act, it could be taken as an aggravating or mitigating factor in sentencing. Certainly, age would also be a consideration in designing and managing correctional programs. Young people could be assigned to programs based partly on age and maturity. But critics of juvenile justice argue for ending the separate system of justice because there are so many exceptions to the "norms" on which the juvenile justice system is based.

In spite of the many proposals to reform juvenile justice, so far no nationwide movement has sought to abolish juvenile court. Thus, today's most common approaches are applied within the separate system of justice for juveniles, described in the next sections.

TABLE 17.4 Percentage of Petitioned Status Offense Cases Involving Females, 2013

When girls misbehave, the juvenile justice system often treats them as having committed status offenses rather than as delinquents.

Status Offense	Percentage of All Cases
Runaway	54%
Truancy	45%
Ungovernability/Disorderly conduct	42%
Liquor law violations	42%
Curfew	30%

Source: Office of Juvenile Justice and Delinquency Prevention, *Petitioned Status Offenses*: https://www.ojjdp.gov/OJSTATBB/court/qa06601.asp.

SANCTIONING JUVENILES

Originally, separating juvenile justice from adult justice was intended to enable justice workers to give the highest priority to preventing crime by rehabilitating delinquents. Juvenile correctional agencies provide a range of services, from diversion to probation, detention, and aftercare. Although rehabilitation does indeed figure prominently in their practices, that ethic is quite fragile in reality.

Overview of the Juvenile Justice System

Juvenile corrections suffers from the same type of fragmentation as its adult counterpart does, with agencies sometimes operated under the courts, sometimes under the executive branch; sometimes housed with the institutional function, sometimes separated from it; sometimes run by counties, sometimes run by the state. Such fragmentation makes generalizing about juvenile correctional policies difficult. Nearly any policy arrangement a person can imagine exists somewhere, and what is true of one jurisdiction may not be true of the next.

In 2018 almost 728,280 juveniles were arrested, representing seven percent of all arrests made by the police.[20] As Figure 17.2 shows, juveniles are involved in a much smaller proportion of violent crime arrests than property crime arrests.

Less than a third of juveniles were arrested for serious (UCR Part I) crimes: murder, sexual assault, aggravated assault, robbery, burglary, larceny-theft, arson, and motor vehicle theft. Of juvenile arrestees, 74 percent were male, and 27 percent were age 15

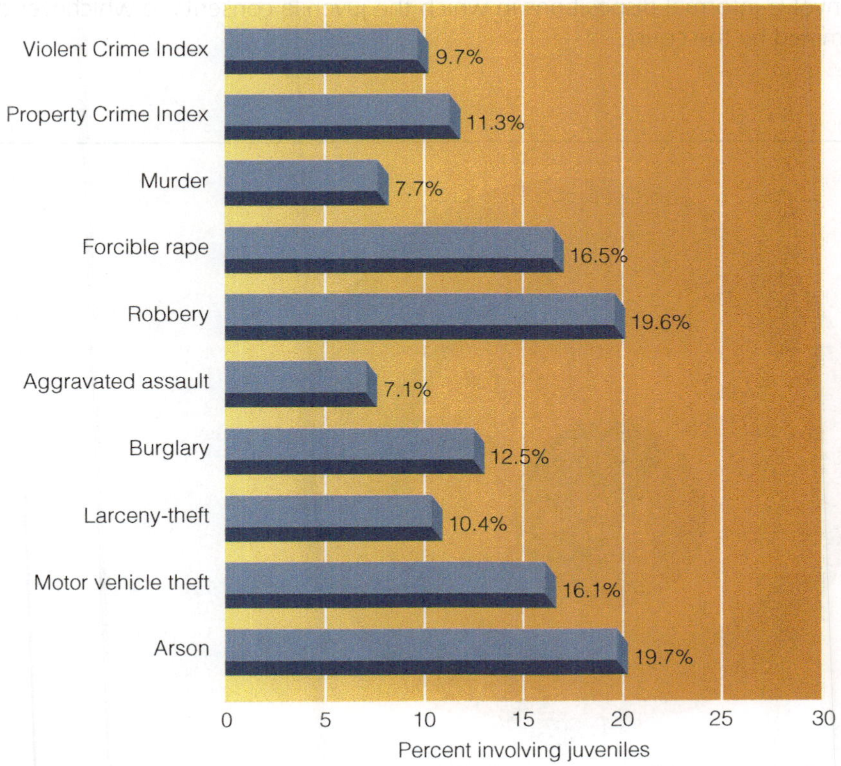

FIGURE 17.2 Percentage of All Arrests That Are Juveniles, 2018

Juveniles are involved in a much smaller proportion of violent crime arrests than property arrests.

Source: Federal Bureau of Investigation, *Crime in the United States, 2018*, "Arrests by Age" (Table 38).

or younger. People of color made up 30.7 percent of the juvenile population but were arrested out of proportion to their numbers. Especially troubling is the fact that of those arrested for violent offenses, 38 percent were African American.[21] A juvenile arrest solves proportionately fewer crimes than does an adult arrest. This is true because juveniles tend to commit crimes in groups and are more likely to be arrested for their crimes, thus solving fewer crimes with more arrests.

Such numbers are alarming: 21,225 juveniles were arrested for aggravated assault, a serious, violent personal crime. Further, arrest rates are increasing faster for girls than for boys. Yet we must take these numbers in their proper context. In all, barely 0.01 percent of all Americans ages 10–17 were arrested for a violent offense in 2018. Violent crime among young people is alarming, but it is not common. And the juvenile portion of all crime is dropping as well. In fact, some analysts argue that a major part of the overall crime drop is a result of lower rates of criminal activity by juveniles.[22]

In fact, juveniles who have committed felonies are not all violent, nor are all of them chronic. People who commit violent crimes have threatened others with physical harm. People whose criminal activity is considered "chronic" break the law in a continuing, repetitive pattern. Figure 17.3 shows the overlap of these types of juveniles—some juveniles engage in all three patterns, but most only engage in one. Youths who commit violent crimes generally commit the fewest crimes overall.

LO 6

List the ways that juveniles are sanctioned.

Disposition of Juveniles

About 943,000 juveniles were referred to juvenile court in 2018.[23] The first decision made in a juvenile court is whether or not to file a petition of juvenile jurisdiction. If the petition is granted, there is a hearing on the merits of the charges, with the intention of making the juvenile a ward of the court if the charges are sustained. Cases that are not petitioned involve informal dispositions in which the juvenile consents to whichever outcome is determined by the court.

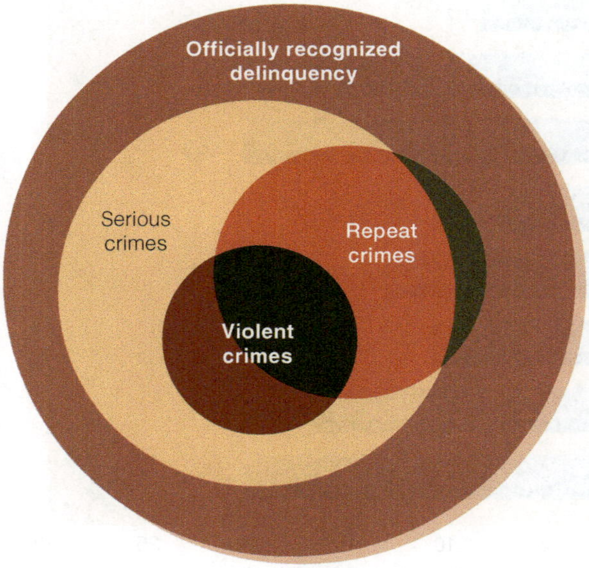

FIGURE 17.3 The Overlap of Violent, Serious, and Repeat Juvenile Crime

Juveniles who most concern us have important differences in their patterns of offense.

Source: Office of Juvenile Justice and Delinquency Prevention, *Juveniles and Victims: 1997 Update on Violence* (Washington, DC: U.S. Government Printing Office, 1997), 25.

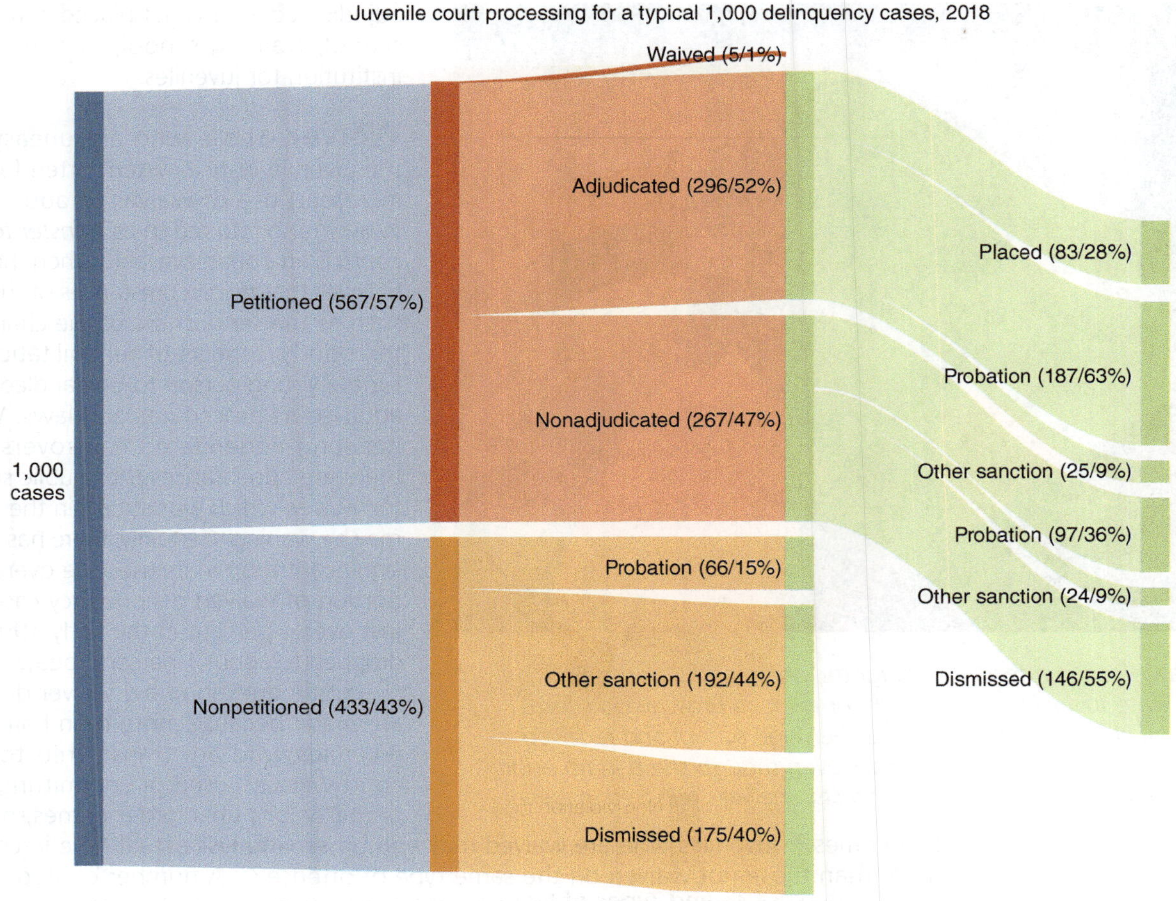

FIGURE 17.4 Juvenile Court Processing of Delinquency Cases, 2018

Source: Office of Juvenile Justice and Delinquency Prevention, *Detailed Offenses: https://www.ojjdp.gov/ojstatbb/ezajcs/asp/detail.asp.*

As Figure 17.4 shows, nearly half of the referrals to juvenile court do not result in a petition. Of these cases, 40 percent have their charges dismissed, and another 15 percent are assigned to informal probation. On rare occasions, nonpetitioned juveniles receive placements, typically in mental health facilities; more commonly, some alternative sanction results. The petition decision is largely invisible, but it has major implications. Recent studies have shown that African American youths who are arrested by the police are one-fourth more likely to be petitioned to the juvenile court than are white youths.[24]

When a petition is filed, the court must consider whether it will take jurisdiction in the case. In about 1 percent of cases, jurisdiction is waived to adult court. In the usual case, the juvenile must decide whether or not to contest the charges—if so, an adjudication hearing follows, in which the accuracy of the charges are considered. Almost half of the time, the charges are sufficiently minor, the facts are in so little dispute, or the likely disposition is sufficiently acceptable that the juvenile waives this hearing, and the court proceeds directly to disposition of the charges. Without an adjudication hearing, charges are usually dismissed. It is also common for the juvenile to accept a probation term or some other moderate penalty.

The juvenile usually contests the charges in the petition if they are serious or the disposition is potentially severe. While original charges against juveniles end up being dismissed more than 30 percent of the time, once adjudication starts, dismissal is rare. Further, even though the usual disposition is a term of probation, more than one-fourth of

Creola Cotton comforts her daughter, Shaquanda, at the Ron Jackson State Juvenile Correctional Complex, in Brownwood Texas. Cotton, 14, shoved a hall monitor at her high school and received a sentence of up to 7 years in prison, even though she had no prior record. After widespread public protests, she was released in a year.

adjudicated youths get placed in a reform school, training school, or some other institution for juveniles.

Waiver Those who are uneasy with the juvenile justice system often favor an increased use of waiver to adult court. *Waiver* (also referred to as *transfer to adult court*) is an option available when the court believes that the circumstances of the case, such as the seriousness of the charges or the poor prospects of rehabilitation, call for the young person to be handled under adult-court procedures and laws. Waiver has long engendered controversy, and there are appearances that public support for waiver, which was strong in the 1990s, may be waning. Certainly, there has been a significant drop in its use. The overall proportion of waived delinquency cases was just over 4 percent in the early 1990s but dropped to about 1 percent today.[25]

Some question how waiver decisions are made because more than half of the juveniles who are transferred to adult court were accused of committing drug, property, or public order crimes, not violent crimes.[26] Juveniles who are waived may end up serving less actual time in confinement than those not waived on the same type of offense.[27] A number of studies now suggest that sending juveniles to adult court leads to higher recidivism rates, suggesting that adult punishments may actually exacerbate crimes rather than deter them.[28] Finally, African American youths are vastly overrepresented among those cases waived to criminal court.[29] Concerns about the fairness of waiver laws and practices have grown, and in recent years at least 21 states have made changes that restrict the practice of juvenile waiver (see Figure 17.5).[30]

Because the number of juveniles waived to adult court is so small, the number of juveniles serving time in adult facilities is also small. Recent data suggest that less than 2 percent of the adult prison population is under the age of 17 and that around 3,400 juveniles are held in local jails (three-quarters serving sentences from adult courts)—less than 1 percent of the jail population.[31] The young person in an adult facility is a management problem because of special needs, not because of large numbers.

Diversion The conceptual opposite of waiver is diversion. Although waiver attempts to avoid the lenient treatment of the juvenile justice system, diversion seeks to avoid the burdensome consequences of formal processing. It is based on the recognition that often, the best way to avoid a juvenile getting involved more deeply in the juvenile justice system is to avoid placing them in the system in the first place.[32] This informal adjustment to a case can occur at any stage of the juvenile justice process, but it is most often chosen prior to filing formal charges in a petition to the court. If juveniles feel fairly treated at the earliest stages of contact with the juvenile justice system, they are less likely to become involved in the system subsequently.[33]

Diversion can take two forms. The most direct form is simply to stop processing the case in the expectation that the main objectives of the justice process have been achieved—the juvenile has realized the wrongness of the conduct and has shown a convincing willingness to refrain from it in the future. This form of diversion is seldom final—if the young person returns to court on a new referral, the old charge may be considered again with the new one.

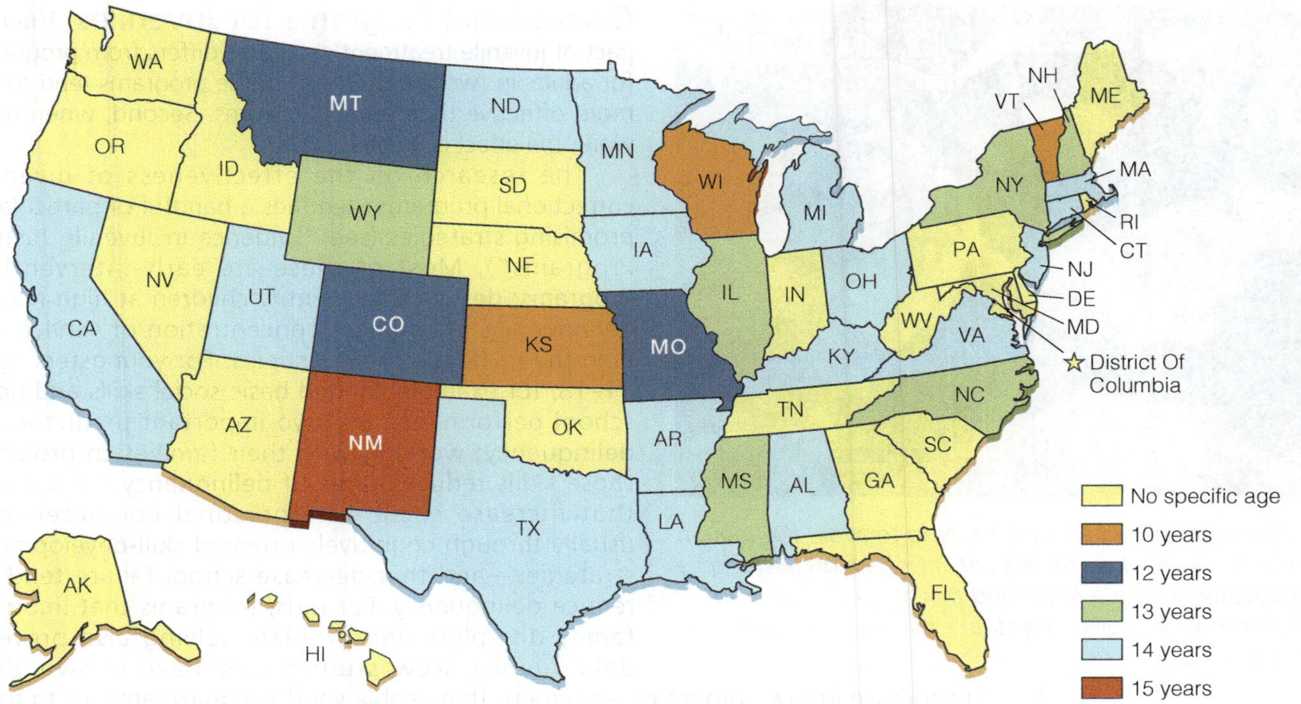

FIGURE 17.5 The Youngest Ages at Which Juveniles May Be Transferred to Adult Criminal Court

Source: Office of Juvenile Justice Delinquency Prevention, *Statistical Briefing Book*, https://www.ojjdp.gov/ojstatbb/structure_process/qa04105.asp?qaDate=2011, accessed April 15, 2017.

In the second form, juveniles are diverted to specific programs. This option may be selected when the court determines that the young person's delinquency is a result of certain problems in the child's life that may best be addressed by a program designed to help. These diversion programs often deal with developmental issues such as the child's social skills or response to frustration in school performance. Diversion to mental health treatment for emotionally disturbed youths is also commonly preferred to formal processing.

The logic of diversion is based on the developmental pattern of delinquency. It is thought that most juveniles drift into delinquent behavior gradually, as a part of growing up. As their misconduct becomes more serious, they "signal" a need for help to get off the pathway to delinquency. The diversion strategy tries to provide that help as early as possible. For example, misbehaviors such as stubbornness, resistance to authority, and interpersonal aggressiveness, when exhibited in preadolescence, indicate a risk of later delinquency. This is why diversion programs which help disruptive children learn to cope and those which retain children in school are considered important aspects of delinquency prevention that do not require formal juvenile processing. Whatever the logic and wisdom of diversion, it used to be the most frequent strategy for addressing complaints against juveniles.

There are so many different types of diversion programs for juveniles, as well as mechanisms for getting youths diverted into these programs, that a simple summary of their overall effectiveness is not possible. One recent review of the many different kinds of diversion concluded that these programs sometimes help youths but sometimes hurt them—depending on the strategy that each program entails.[34] There is an inherent risk of "widening the net," and juveniles can sometimes be labeled delinquent when their misconduct is not very serious or unusual for young people. This suggests that the question about diversion effectiveness lies in knowing who is being diverted, how, and to what kind of intervention.

Heather Stone/Chicago Tribune/MCT/Sipa USA

▲ *Some juvenile facilities work hard to avoid the feel of a prison, even when the security level is high. Here, girls sit outside next to a fence and talk at the Illinois Youth Center at Warrenville, the state's maximum-security prison for girls.*

Correctional Programs for Juveniles The impact of juvenile treatment programs differs from programs for adults in two ways. First, juvenile programs tend to be more effective than adult programs. Second, when they work, the effect is greater.

The research on the effectiveness of juvenile correctional programs identifies a handful of particularly promising strategies (see "Evidence in Juvenile Justice Programs"). Most of these are early-intervention programs, designed to identify children at high risk of delinquency, providing a concentration of services to help them change their destinies. For youngsters ages 11–18, for example, limited basic social skills and poor school performance are two important predictors of delinquency; working with their families to promote those skills reduces rates of delinquency.[35] Programs that increase social interpersonal competence—usually through cognitively oriented skill-development strategies—and that decrease school failure tend to reduce delinquency. For girls, programs that improve family discipline and problem solving also prevent delinquency. New studies also have shown that "restorative justice" programs—programs that enable youths to make amends to their victims for the harms they have caused—have significant value.[36]

In short, evidence increasingly suggests that the systematic support of all aspects of family life for families in which at-risk youths are being raised reduces delinquency and antisocial behavior over the long run and saves money as well, and the earlier such programs are used in the child's life, the better.[37]

FOCUS ON

CORRECTIONAL PRACTICE: Evidence in Juvenile Justice Programs

Recent reports have tried to summarize what we know about juvenile justice, with a special emphasis on juvenile correctional programs. They base much of what we know on *meta-analyses* of more than 600 studies, published and unpublished. Systematic reviews support certain strategies as most likely to be effective:

1. *Interventions with a "therapeutic" philosophy*. Programs that attempt to rehabilitate young people by working on their behavioral problems and thinking patterns reduce recidivism rates by as much as 25 percent. Programs that attempt to build job and classroom skills reduce recidivism rates by 10 percent or more. In contrast, programs that try to change behavior through imposing discipline or emphasizing punitive deterrence actually *increase* recidivism rates by nearly 10 percent.
2. *Working with high-risk youths*. Programs that target services to high-risk youths are more likely to be effective than programs designed to work with moderate- or low-risk youths, and this is especially true when youths have a history of violence. Programs that provide intensive services for first-time delinquents often result in *higher* failure rates than if those services had not been provided.
3. *Program quality*. Programs that provide a broader array of services, provide greater intensity of services, and are implemented more completely have a better chance of being effective. Programs that are badly managed or have weak administrators are more likely not to work.

The implication of these reviews is that programs for juveniles can be purposefully designed to be effective. They can also be designed in such ways as to make failure much more likely. In order to help policy makers develop more-effective programs, sociologist Mark Lipsey has designed a program-assessment system that can be used to build programs that reflect the evidence about what we know is effective.

Sources: Mark W. Lipsey, James C. Howell, Marion R. Kelly, et al., *Improving the Effectiveness of Juvenile Justice Programs: A New Perspective on Evidence-Based Practice* (Washington, DC: Center for Juvenile Justice Reform, 2010); Mark W. Lipsey, "The Primary Factors That Characterize Effective Interventions with Juveniles: A Meta-analytic Overview," *Victims & Offenders* 4 (2009): 124–47.

Although evidence for the value of early intervention for at-risk youths has been strong for quite a few years, political support has been slower to develop. Until recently, a public that has been willing to invest billions in bricks and mortar for more prison cells tended to see intervention programs as "soft" social welfare. Today, that seems to be changing. In many jurisdictions around the country, new political energy has been developing for expanded intervention programs, which may be charting a new future for juvenile justice.

Detention Approximately 24 percent of juvenile arrestees are detained.[38] Most juvenile detention is brief—the median stay is just over two weeks; for serious charges of violent crime, the median stay is 26 days—until an initial appearance before a juvenile court judge (or judicial referee, who represents the court in detention hearings).[39] After a petition decision is made, most juveniles are released to their families. But about one out of five, found to endanger others or be at risk of flight, is kept in detention for days or weeks until an adjudication hearing can be scheduled.

Federal law requires that juveniles housed in adult jails be segregated from adult residents and be taken before a magistrate for an initial appearance within 24 hours of arrival in the facility. As minors under special protection of the court, these juveniles also have legal rights to education and basic services, yet most juveniles receive little special programming.

Such programming clearly should be a priority. Many juveniles in detention have special needs that make treatment appropriate. Juvenile delinquents disproportionately suffer from learning disabilities that make them lag in school performance, and time in detention only makes matters worse after release. Still other juveniles are members of gangs, which places them at risk of assault by other members detained in the same facilities. Studies show that detention experiences significantly worsen later subsequent behavior and increase the chance of continued delinquency.[40] In general, detention centers for juveniles are places where great strides could be made in preventing delinquency by dealing with youths in crisis, but far too little is being done.

Adjudication When the juvenile court receives a case, the facts of the case are heard, and the court determines if the facts justify the determination that the youth did commit the alleged offense and therefore is "delinquent." Nationally, in 2018, 422,100 cases brought to juvenile court were adjudicated delinquent.[41] After an adjudication of delinquency, the court imposes a *disposition*, called a "placement." The typical dispositions available to the court are probation, school-based programs, intermediate sanctions, community programs, and out-of-home placement: confinement.

Juvenile Probation Almost two-thirds of the time, youth who have been adjudicated delinquent are placed on probation and released to the custody of a parent or guardian—roughly 260,200 cases in 2018.[42] Although probation has been the most common disposition for many years, the number of probation placements nationally has declined by more than 50 percent since a peak in 1997, corresponding to a similar drop in the number of cases found delinquent.[43] Often, the judge orders the delinquent to undergo some form of education or counseling. The delinquent may also have to pay a fine or make restitution while on probation—though recent studies have pointed out that the imposition of fees and fines on juveniles is self-defeating, keeping impoverished youths entangled in the system.[44]

The differences between adult probation and juvenile probation are subtle and stem from the differences between adults and juveniles, described earlier. Juvenile probation officers often try to develop personal relationships with their clients, a move discouraged for adult probation officers. To achieve this bond, juvenile probation officers often engage in recreation with their clients or accompany them to social activities. Through this bond, officers seek a youngster's trust, which they hope will form the basis for long-lasting behavioral change. Sometimes officers will mix the child on probation with other young people who are not under court supervision to further his or her reintegration into more socially acceptable peer relationships. Often, adult mentors are called in to give children effective role models; mentoring programs reduce antisocial activities and school misbehavior by as much as one-third.

In carrying out supervision, the probation officer must work closely with community social service agencies that are involved with the juvenile and the family. Probation officers spend time in the schools, talk to teachers and guidance counselors, and learn about programs for troubled youths, such as recreational programs and youth counseling programs. Probation officers also establish close contact with family service agencies, welfare providers, and programs that support young mothers and provide substitutes for missing fathers. In some respects the probation officer serves as a linchpin for the array of community services that might help a young person stay out of trouble. "Careers in Corrections" offers a closer view of the work of a juvenile probation officer.

Working in the Schools Most juveniles spend a significant portion of their day in school; up to age 16, they are required by law to be in school. Recent studies have criticized schools for "zero-tolerance" approaches to classroom discipline. Rapid expulsion of students who misbehave (or get involved in the juvenile court) leads many of these youths to drop out of school, a precursor of a life of crime. The propensity of school to reject youths who are struggling with behavioral problems has been called the **school-to-prison pipeline** because so many of these youths who fail in school end up in prison.[45] Juvenile justice agencies—probation in particular—typically develop school-based programs to increase overall effectiveness with youths under the supervision of the juvenile court.

school-to-prison pipeline
The situation in which many youths who fail in school end up in prison.

School-based programs typically have three objectives: keep potential truants in school, reduce school violence, and improve the academic performance of at-risk youths. Studies have shown that school programs specially designed to get services for at-risk youths can reduce the rate of serious juvenile misconduct while also improving performance.[46] Although some school-based delinquency-prevention programs have shown promise, experts believe they need to be adopted with caution. When the courts get involved in schools, there is always a danger that they will deepen the

CAREERS IN CORRECTIONS

Probation Officer—Juveniles

Nature of the Work

Juvenile probation officers are responsible for the supervision and guidance of youths under age 18 who have been referred to them by the court, police, or social service agencies. Through the development of close ties with juveniles' families, school authorities, and health agencies, probation officers help juveniles meet their educational and treatment needs. They also monitor their behavior to ensure that court-ordered requirements are met. Caseload size varies by agency, by the needs of the juveniles, and by the risks that they pose. Caseloads for juveniles tend to be lower than those for adults on probation. Officers may be on call 24 hours per day to provide supervision and assistance.

Required Qualifications

Background qualifications for juvenile probation officers vary by state, but a bachelor's degree in social work, criminal justice, or a related field from a four-year college or university is usually required. Some agencies require previous experience with youths or graduate work. Candidates must be 21 years of age and have no felony convictions. Most juvenile probation officers receive both formal and on-the-job training.

Earnings and Job Outlook

The number of probation officers for juveniles is expected to grow about as fast as other occupations during the next decade. Probation officers handling a juvenile caseload report a high level of personal satisfaction in their work. Juvenile probation officers earn about $53,020 per year.

More Information

Visit the website of the American Probation and Parole Association. Career information can also be obtained from your state, juvenile court, or probation office.

involvement of pre-delinquent youths in the juvenile justice system rather than prevent it. And because research shows that officials are more likely to involve minority youths in the justice process than white youths, even when their misbehavior is the same, the problem of racial disparities arises.[47] Moreover, because the consequences of a juvenile record are so broad and onerous, many experts oppose school programs that may lead to higher rates of formal processing of juveniles who get in trouble in school.

This is in fact how the "school-to-prison pipeline" gets going—it starts out with an arrest for relative innocuous problem behavior, one that many juveniles engage in but few get arrested for. The arrest creates a juvenile record, and the prior record becomes the justification for an ever-accelerating level of intrusion into the youngster's life. That explains the secret behind one of the more successful school programs: Do not arrest in the first place.[48]

Effective school-based programs have been developed to accomplish various objectives. Successful school-safety programs focus on reducing bullying behavior and eliminating weapons and drugs on school grounds. School dropout programs create networks of services within the community; this concentration of efforts seeks to increase an at-risk youth's academic self-confidence and personal commitment to staying in school, while also reducing problem behaviors.[49] With so many juveniles processed by the juvenile justice system later returning to public schools, there is a need to find effective programs for these youths who have been identified as at risk.

Intermediate Sanctions for Juveniles The complaint that few sanctioning options exist between traditional probation and custodial dispositions is perhaps even more true in juvenile justice than in criminal justice. Only about 9 percent of delinquents receive an intermediate sanction. One reason for slowness in developing juvenile intermediate sanctions is that traditional juvenile corrections already resembles intermediate sanctions. Adult probation is interested in intensive supervision as an intermediate sanction, but adult intensive supervision probation (ISP) caseloads are often about the same size as many traditional juvenile caseloads—in the twenties or thirties. The adult system develops electronic monitored home detention; the juvenile system has routinely used curfews that restrict youths to home except during school hours. Community service and restitution have been standard juvenile court dispositions for many years.

Some juvenile probation agencies have begun to develop intensive supervision approaches that are far more intensive than adult ISPs. A juvenile ISP officer may carry 15 cases or fewer and may well see each client almost every day—more than once a day if necessary. Police–probation partnerships intensify juvenile intensive supervision even further because the police add surveillance to the probation services. Juvenile corrections systems have also developed work-based community service, restitution centers where young people work to pay victims back, and after-school assignments that minimize free time. Under intermediate sanctioning approaches, juveniles may be required to complete programs to increase their awareness of the impact of crimes on victims, and they may be sent to summer camps that require community service in the form of cleaning parks and other public places.

One of the most widespread new intermediate sanctions for juveniles is the boot camp. Results have not been promising, with most studies showing that boot camp graduates do no better than do youths placed in other programs; in fact, some boot camp graduates actually do worse than those placed in other alternatives. (See Chapter 9.) This situation has led to the development of specialized aftercare caseloads of boot camp graduates to try to reduce their failure rate.

Juvenile Community Corrections Despite the lukewarm evaluations of juvenile community corrections (see Chapter 22), interest has continued in this approach for two main reasons. First, most people realize that removing a young person from the community is an extreme solution, reserved for extreme cases. Disrupting community

© Stan Carroll, The Commercial Appeal, Memphis Commercial Appeal via Imagn Content Services, LLC

▲ *School resource officers, such as Leatha Clark, spent time with HLHS students, getting to know them and helping them stay out of the criminal justice system.*

and family relationships can interfere with long-term prospects for successful adjustment by damaging these already fragile supports. Second, and just as compelling, for most youths the institutional stay will be short— six months to a year in custody is common. Eventually, the youth returns to the community, and the real work of successfully adjusting to community life occurs there. Advocates of community corrections ask, "Why wait?"

Community corrections offers additional advantages for juveniles. The cost of custody in a juvenile training school is usually at least double that for an adult in prison, which means there is more money to work with in creating incentives to keep young people out of trouble and in designing and implementing effective alternatives in the community. Moreover, public opinion toward the young, even when there is a criminal conviction, is not as harsh as that toward adults, so it is easier to obtain public support for juvenile community corrections. Finally, because youth incarceration numbers are smaller than adult numbers, it is easier to show success in saving money by diverting juveniles to local programs.

A program in Ohio, gaining national acclaim, seeks to return funds to communities that retain juveniles rather than sending them to state-run schools. RECLAIM Ohio, described in Chapter 9, provides a significant payback to county leaders who can show that juveniles who might have been sent to training schools paid by state taxes are instead being kept in local, innovative programs designed especially for local needs. The program has proved popular because it appeals to conservative ideals of cost-effective public policy and local control, while appealing to liberal beliefs about the rehabilitation of juveniles.

Juvenile Incarceration In 2018 about 37,500 youths were held in some sort of residential placement—a juvenile institution. Just more than half of the 1,510 juvenile institutions in the United States are public institutions, and they hold about 71 percent of all placed youths. The national incarceration rate (including detention) is just over 100 per 100,000 juveniles ages 10–18, almost three-quarters of whom have been committed following adjudication. As with the adult incarceration rate, there is a wide range among the states, with the highest rate in Wyoming (302) and the lowest in Connecticut (27). But juvenile placements have been dropping nationally, with an overall drop of nearly two-thirds since 1997 (see "Reducing Incarceration for Juveniles").[50] Recently, reformers have expressed a concern that the large drop in juvenile incarceration may be accompanied by an increase in the amount of time they spend in custody.[51]

There is a growing consensus among political leaders and policy makers alike that the large reductions in the number of youths placed in residential facilities is a very good development. For one thing, U.S. juvenile incarceration rates are two to ten times as large as those of other nations around the world. Just as important, youth incarceration is extremely expensive, up sevenfold since 1995 and costing in some places as much as a quarter of a million dollars per child per year.[52] Finally, youths who are exposed to incarceration as juveniles have higher rearrest rates and lower rates of participation in the labor market than do their peers who, having similar records of misconduct, do not get exposed to incarceration.[53]

Policy makers are also concerned about the overrepresentation of incarcerated African American juveniles. The Juvenile Justice and Delinquency Prevention Act of 1988 requires states to determine whether the proportion of minorities in confinement exceeds their pro portion in the population. If such overrepresentation is found, states must demonstrate efforts to reduce it. *Disparity* means that the probability of receiving a particular outcome (for example, being detained in a short-term facility rather than not being

FOCUS ON

CORRECTIONAL POLICY: Reducing Incarceration for Juveniles

In the United States, incarceration rates for juveniles have been dropping for more than two decades, and today they are the lowest that they have been since 1975. In the last 10 years, 43 states saw a decline in their rates of juvenile placement; nearly all of them saw a drop of more than 10 percent.

What is the reason for this change?

For one thing, the dropping juvenile crime rate has meant that fewer juveniles are being brought into the system. But this explanation, by itself, is not sufficient—after all, crime has been dropping for almost 20 years, but adult prisons continued to grow throughout most of that period. What is it about juvenile corrections?

Three key factors seem to be the most important sources of this change.

First, policy makers became concerned about racial injustice. Statistics showed a vast disparity in rates of confinement for nonwhite youths, as compared to whites, even for similar delinquency charges. A belief that the system was racially unjust led private reform groups such as the Annie E. Casey Foundation to take on the issue.

Second, the conditions of juvenile confinement, with poor or nonexistent treatment programs, did not promote rehabilitation. In fact, in many systems the treatment of juveniles behind bars was thought to be deplorable, with the result of high rates of recidivism. Civil litigation against several states' juvenile justice systems of confinement made it convenient for policy makers to begin to experiment with alternative strategies for handling juveniles who broke the law. Third, when those new strategies were studied, they proved to be effective at reducing return to crime. And just as important, they were far less expensive to operate than traditional confinement.

Reducing confinement for youths is quickly becoming the preferred policy: cheaper, more effective, and more humane.

Sources: Justice Policy Institute, *Measuring Reform: Focus on Juvenile Confinement* (Washington, DC: Author, 2013); Amanda Paulson, "Juvenile Incarceration Reached Its Lowest Rate in 38 Years," *Christian Science Monitor*, February 27, 2013.

detained) differs among different groups. If more African Americans are detained than others, this, in turn, may lead to more of them being adjudicated in juvenile court and may lead to a larger proportion being placed in residential facilities. Table 17.5 shows the rate of African American overrepresentation (as a proportion of the population) at each major decision point of the juvenile corrections system.

TABLE 17.5 Overrepresentation of African Americans in the Juvenile Corrections System

African American youths are almost twice as likely to be arrested as are whites. At subsequent stages the overrepresentation, while still a problem, is less pronounced.

	Rates per 100		
Type of Ratio[a]	White	African American	Overrepresentation of African Americans
Juvenile arrests to population[b]	6.1	11.5	1.9
Cases referred to juvenile arrests	68.9	75.6	1.1
Cases detained to cases referred	18.4	25.1	1.4
Cases petitioned to cases referred	54.9	64.7	1.2
Cases waived to cases petitioned	0.7	0.8	1.1
Cases adjudicated to cases petitioned	70.6	58.5	0.8
Placements to cases adjudicated	21.5	26.5	1.2

[a] For example, 6.1 white youths were arrested per 100 youths in the general population, 68.9 white youths out of 100 white youths who were arrested were also referred, and so forth.
[b] Population ages 10–17 equals 25,994,400 (white) and 5,431,300 (African American).

Source: Howard N. Snyder and Melissa Sickmund, *Juveniles and Victims: 2006 National Report* (Pittsburgh: National Center for Juvenile Justice, 2006), 189.

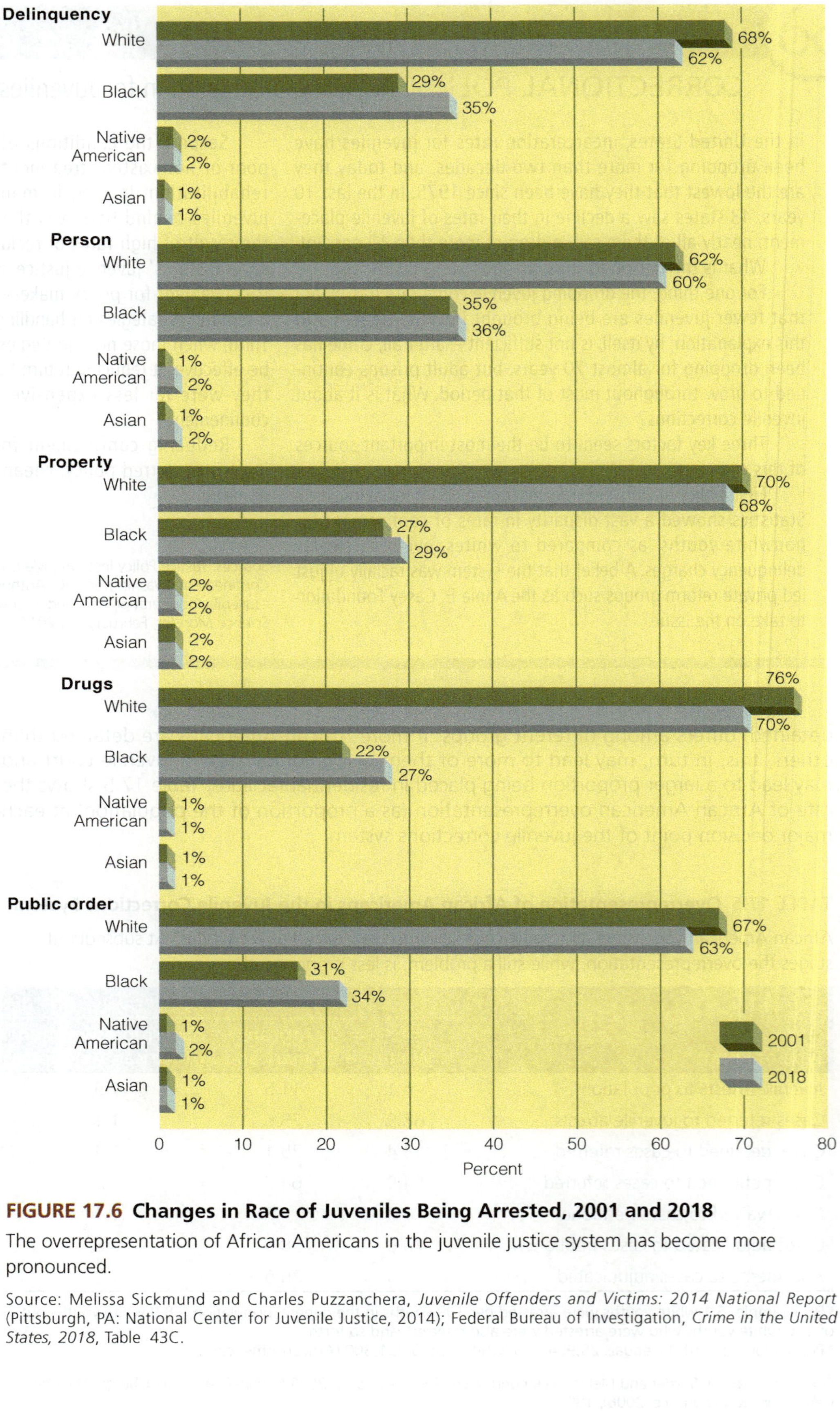

FIGURE 17.6 Changes in Race of Juveniles Being Arrested, 2001 and 2018

The overrepresentation of African Americans in the juvenile justice system has become more pronounced.

Source: Melissa Sickmund and Charles Puzzanchera, *Juvenile Offenders and Victims: 2014 National Report* (Pittsburgh, PA: National Center for Juvenile Justice, 2014); Federal Bureau of Investigation, *Crime in the United States, 2018*, Table 43C.

The disproportionate confinement of minority juveniles often stems from disparity in the early stages of case processing (see Figure 17.6). Racial disparities in juvenile dispositions are troubling in their own right, but they are made even more problematic by the consequences that often follow juvenile incarceration. Recent research finds that placing a juvenile in an institution dramatically reduces the chances that he or she will finish high school while significantly increasing the chances of later incarceration as an adult.[54] The impact of this trend on racial disparity can be seen in the disproportionately large numbers of uneducated African American adults in prison.

Institutions for juveniles include foster homes, residential centers, reform schools, and training schools. In recent years more juveniles are also being sent to adult prisons. These institutions vary in the degree of security and the amount of programming available. Figure 17.7 displays the types of juvenile custodial facilities. We now describe them in order of least to greatest amount of custody supervision.

Foster homes and residential centers typically take small numbers of delinquents. These locations are not considered punitive—judges use foster homes and residential centers when the juvenile's family cannot provide an adequate setting for the child's development. Foster homes are often run by a married couple, and the juveniles live in them, sometimes as cohabitants with the adults' biological children. The court pays the couple a per diem for each foster child, usually not enough to cover all the expenses involved, and the adults in the home provide supervision in cooperation with probation officers. Foster children attend the local school system and operate under whatever restrictions the foster parents and the probation officer deem suitable—curfews, associations, leisure activities, and the like. Residential centers operate much like foster homes, with residents attending local schools and living under certain restrictions. The main difference is that residential centers are run by professional staff, not adult volunteers. It may also be the case that a small amount of treatment programming occurs in residential centers, usually as group counseling

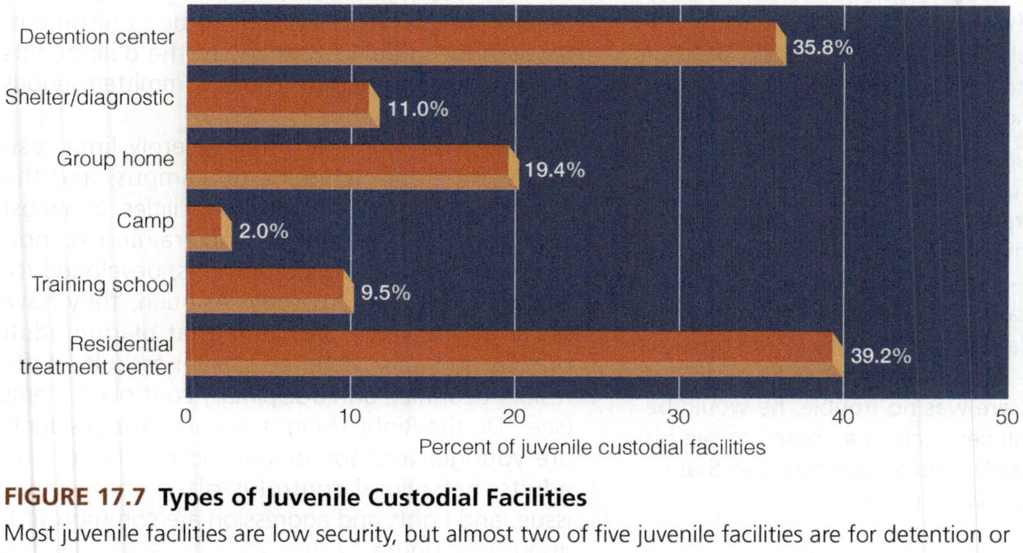

FIGURE 17.7 Types of Juvenile Custodial Facilities

Most juvenile facilities are low security, but almost two of five juvenile facilities are for detention or long-term placement.

Note: Details may not add to 100% because some places have more than one type of facility.

Source: Sarah Hockenberry, Melissa Sickmund, and Anthony Sladky, *Juvenile Residential Facility Census, 2014* (Washington, DC: Office of Juvenile Justice and Delinquency Prevention, 2016), 3.

CAREERS IN CORRECTIONS

Juvenile Group-Home Counselor

Nature of the Work

Juvenile group-home counselors are responsible for supervising and guiding youths under age 18 who have been placed in a group home by a juvenile court. They spend their days with youths who reside in the home, provide one-on-one counseling, and implement treatment programs dealing with the special problems of youths. Typically, they work with 8–12 youths at a time in a residential setting.

Required Qualifications

Background qualifications for juvenile group-home counselors vary by state, but a bachelor's degree in social work, criminal justice, or a related field from a four-year college or university is usually required. Some agencies require previous experience with youths or graduate work. Candidates must be at least 21 years old and have no felony convictions. Most juvenile group-home counselors receive both formal and on-the-job training.

Earnings and Job Outlook

The number of juvenile group-home counselors is expected to be stable during the next decade. Juvenile group-home counselors report a high level of personal satisfaction in their work. They earn about $40,000 per year, with entry-level salaries under $25,000 in many regions.

More Information

Visit the website of the American Probation and Parole Association. Career information can also be obtained from your state, juvenile court, or probation office.

DO THE RIGHT THING

Residents of the Lovelock Home had been committed by the juvenile court because they were either delinquent or neglected. All 25 boys, ages 7–15, were streetwise, tough, and interested only in getting out. The institution had a staff of social services professionals who tried to deal with the educational and psychological needs of the residents. Because state funding was short, these services looked better in the annual report than to an observer visiting Lovelock. Most of the time, the residents watched television, played basketball in the backyard, or just hung out in one another's rooms.

Joe Klegg, the night supervisor, was tired from the eight-hour shift that he had just completed on his "second job" as a daytime convenience-store manager. The boys were watching television when he arrived at seven. Everything seemed calm. It should have been—Joe had placed a tough 15-year-old, Randy Marshall, in charge. Joe had told Randy to keep the younger boys in line. Randy used his muscle and physical presence to intimidate the other residents. He knew that if the home was quiet and there was no trouble, he would be rewarded with special privileges such as a "pass" to see his girlfriend. Joe wanted no hassles and a quiet house so that he could doze off when the boys went to sleep.

WRITING ASSIGNMENT: Does the situation at Lovelock Home raise ethical questions, or does it merely raise questions of poor management practices? What are the potential consequences for the residents? For Joe Klegg? What is the state's responsibility? Write an essay that addresses each of these questions.

sessions. See "Careers in Corrections" for more on being a juvenile group-home counselor. Studies show that the quality of s residential placement's treatment programs is an important factor in its ability to prevent recidivism.[55]

Compared with group homes, reform schools and training schools offer far less freedom for the child placed within them. They do not hesitate to impose a strict regime, and they regard one of their functions to be punishment. As seen in Figure 17.8, many of the delinquents assigned to these facilities have committed serious offenses.

These 24-hour facilities severely limit residents' freedom. School is on campus, and the residents work to maintain the facilities. In almost every way, reform schools and training schools are the equivalent of adult prisons, developed for adolescents under custody. As such, they have some of the same problems that plague adult prisons and jails: violence, sexual assault, staff–resident conflict, and disciplinary control problems (see "Do the Right Thing"). Because the residents are younger and somewhat more volatile than adults, behavioral control is often an everyday issue, and fights and aggression are common situations (see Figure 17.9).

Juvenile Aftercare The term **aftercare** refers to services provided to juveniles after they have been *placed*—that is, removed from their home and put under some form of custodial care. Aftercare operates in a way similar to adult parole.

aftercare Services provided to juveniles after they have been removed from their home and put under some form of custodial care.

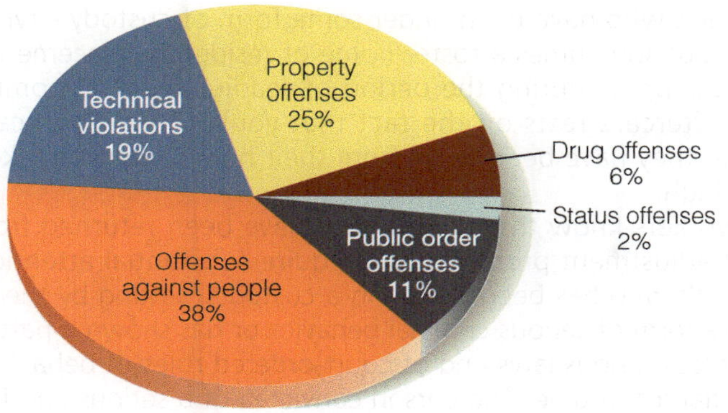

FIGURE 17.8 Juvenile Delinquents in Public Custodial Facilities: Types of Offenses
Some youths in confinement are there for violent crimes, but the majority are confined for other, less serious offenses.

Note: Percentages do not add up to 100 due to rounding.

Source: Office of Juvenile Justice and Delinquency Prevention, *Juvenile Crime: https://www.ojjdp.gov/ojstatbb/crime/jar.asp*

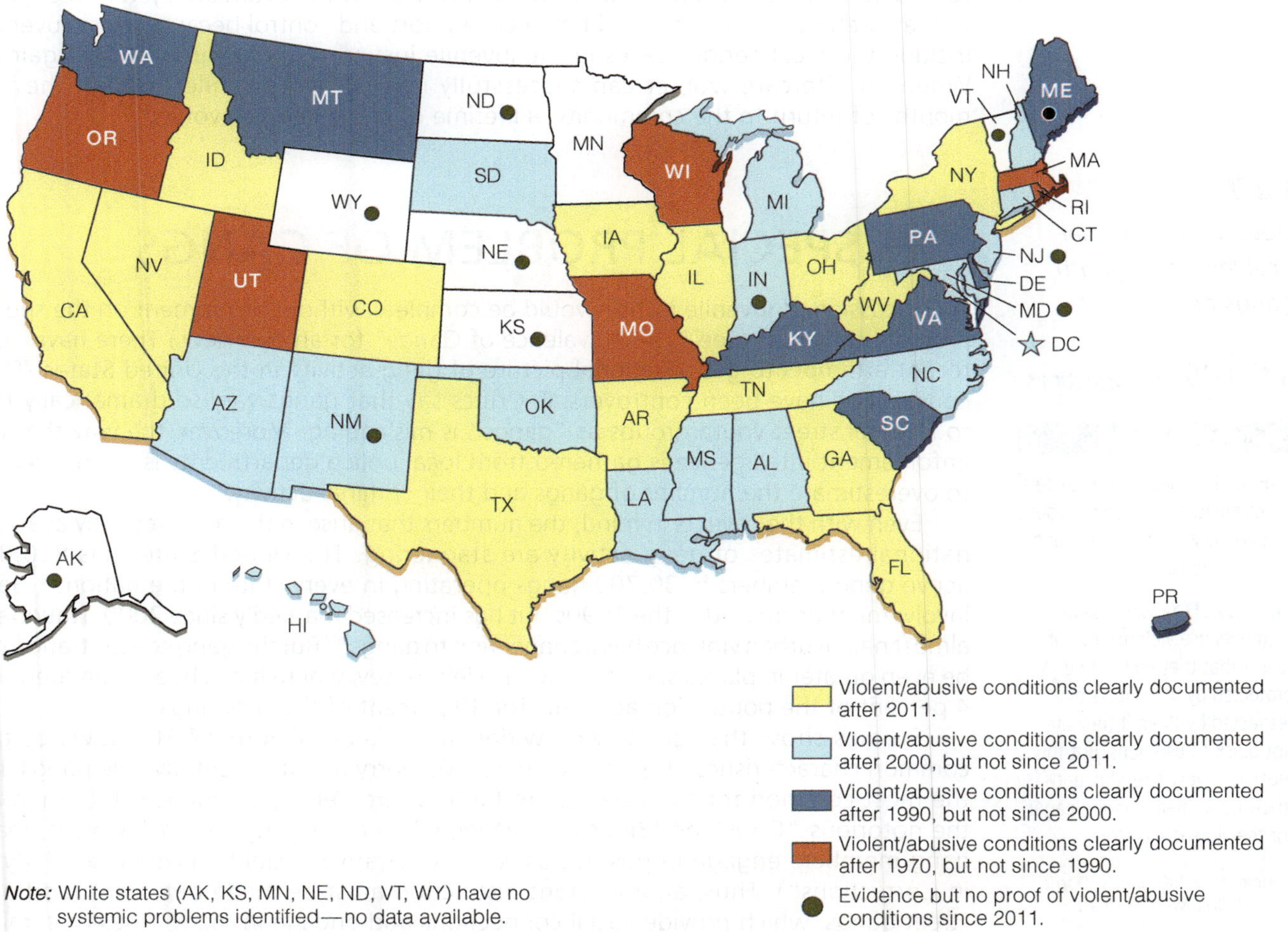

FIGURE 17.9 Map of Mistreatment of Juveniles in Correctional Facilities
Most U.S. states have recently documented evidence of mistreatment of the juveniles who are locked up in the state's correctional facilities.

Note: White states (AK, KS, MN, NE, ND, VT, WY) have no systemic problems identified—no data available.

Source: Richard A. Mendel, *Maltreatment of Youth in U.S. Juvenile Corrections Facilities: An Update* (Baltimore: Annie E. Casey Foundation, 2015).

It receives juveniles who have been under some form of custody—typically the state's training school, but sometimes a foster home or residential placement—and provides supervision and support during the period of readjustment to community life. The importance of aftercare rests on the fact that youths face significant obstacles of adjustment after they have been away from their homes, which makes their chances of failure quite high.

Aftercare workers know that youths who have been returned from confinement face significant adjustment problems and require substantial attention and support. First of all, a youth who has been placed in a custodial setting by the court has either engaged in some form of serious criminal behavior or has shown a pattern of persistent disobedience of less serious laws and of court-ordered rules of behavior. In either case, there is a potential for trouble. The person convicted of a serious and frightening crime faces a fearful community, a family who may not welcome his or her return, and a school system that doubts the juvenile's readiness to behave. The persistent delinquent has been a source of trouble to family, neighbors, school officials, and others, and he or she will not be received with open arms. The aftercare worker negotiates the return to the community by helping the juvenile understand the community's apprehension while showing the community evidence that the juvenile deserves a second chance.

The aftercare worker must also closely follow the juvenile's adjustment, even while serving as advocate. The risk of recidivism is high enough that the community feels a stake in the aftercare scrutiny. All involved in the aftercare system recognize that a careful balance is needed between support and control because these juveniles include the most-serious cases in the juvenile justice system. Much is to be gained. When an aftercare worker can successfully negotiate a juvenile through the first months of return to the community, a lifetime of crime can be avoided.

LO 7

Describe the special problems that youth gangs pose.

THE SPECIAL PROBLEM OF GANGS

No discussion of juvenile justice would be complete without a comment on the special problem of gangs. (See "The Prevalence of Gangs" for an overview.) There have been recent attempts to get a national picture of gang activity in the United States. Their conclusions have been controversial. Critics say that gangs vary so dramatically that to label all street youth groups as "gangs" is misleading. Moreover, the way that law enforcement intelligence is gathered from local police departments is almost certain to overestimate the number of gangs and their criminal activity.

Even with the caveats in mind, the numbers that arise in the most recently available national estimates of gang activity are staggering. The United States has 850,000 active gang members in 30,700 gangs operating in every state in the nation.[56] Gang involvement decreased in the 1990s but has increased markedly since 2000. Nationally, almost half of urban violence has a connection to gangs.[57] But the gang concentration can be even greater in places such as Newark, New Jersey, where it has been estimated that 4 percent of the population accounts for 40 percent of the shootings.[58]

Studies show that gangs vary widely in makeup. Figure 17.10 shows certain common characteristics of gang members. We worry about violent juvenile gangs, but the most common forms of gangs are far less threatening to public safety than are the notorious "Crips" or "Bloods." Further, while most gangs are not violent, many gang members engage in positive as well as negative social behaviors (see "Myths in Corrections"). Thus, an important distinction must be made between traditional street gangs, which provide social connections and engage in many types of criminal conduct, and drug gangs, which are organized into cohesive business structures and often use violence as a business method.

MYTHS in Corrections

Juvenile Gangs

THE MYTH: Most gang members are committed to violence because they like their violent lifestyle and are not scared of being hurt.

THE REALITY: Many gang members use violence out of fear—that they will not be protected by their peers or respected by them if they are not quick to use guns. But this lifestyle is very stressful, and many gang members are eager for the violence to stop.

Source: David Kennedy, *Don't Shoot! One Man, a Street Fellowship, and the End of Violence in Inner-city America* (New York: Bloomsbury, 2012).

FOCUS ON

CORRECTIONAL POLICY: The Prevalence of Gangs

In 2012, the National Gang Center conducted a survey of 3,500 U.S. law enforcement jurisdictions to determine the nature and extent of youth gangs. The most recent survey estimated that there were 30,700 gangs with 850,000 members actively operating in the United States.

Slightly less than 30 percent of all responding jurisdictions had gang activity taking place in them—a figure that is at its lowest point in almost 10 years. As might be expected, gang activity is more concentrated in larger cities, where 85 percent report active gang presence. By contrast, only 15 percent of rural police departments report gang activity.

Although much gang violence is drug related, the center had previously concluded from studies of gangs that "most youth gangs lack the necessary organizational structure and capacity to effectively manage drug distribution operations; however, [an individual's] drug use and drug sales have been shown to increase after joining a gang, and then decrease after a period of incarceration." Two other factors that influence the level of gang violence are intergang conflict over "turf" and young men returning from prison who—quite often—provoke violence when they reconnect with their old gang relationships.

Sources: Arlen Egley Jr., James C. Howell, and Meena Harris, *Highlights of the 2012 National Youth Gang Survey* (Washington, DC: Office of Juvenile Justice and Delinquency Prevention, 2014); Arlen Egley Jr. and James C. Howell, *Highlights of the 2009 National Youth Gang Survey* (Washington, DC: Office of Juvenile Justice and Delinquency Prevention, 2011).

Gangs permeate the work of correctional officials. In custodial facilities, they create a profound challenge in terms of controlling the population and managing the potential for intergang conflict. In community settings, gangs provide hostile competition to the prosocial programs developed by correctional leaders. For the community, gangs are a primary source of fear and peril. Especially when gang members are armed, the presence of a gang can destabilize neighborhood life.

Recent initiatives have shown some success with gangs. For example, Functional Family Therapy—an approach that engages gang members in the context of their families—can prevent gang involvement for high-risk youth.[59] There is also evidence that becoming a parent can be a turning point for gang members, leading them away from gang involvement.[60]

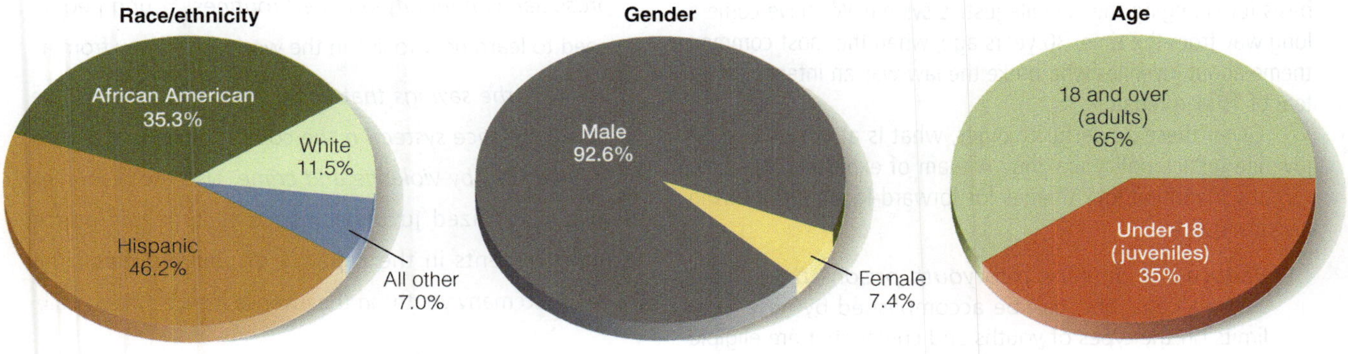

FIGURE 17.10 Characteristics of Youths Who Belong to a Gang

Source: National Gang Center, *National Youth Gang Survey Analysis*, https://www.nationalgangcenter.gov/Survey-Analysis/Demographics#anchorage.

LO 8

Assess the future of juvenile corrections.

THE FUTURE OF JUVENILE JUSTICE

High-profile gang criminality and the recent spate of school shootings have ended the anonymity of juvenile correctional work. Public policy makers are turning their attention to the juvenile justice system. In the 1990s this meant that many of the themes of reform in adult corrections since the 1970s were replayed in the juvenile justice arena. This led to public calls for get-tough measures that pressured the increase of waiver of serious juveniles to the adult court, with longer and harsher punishments. We should not have been surprised to see the familiar echoes of changes in the adult system arising in respect to juveniles, once the public spotlight landed there.

However, reform efforts for juveniles seem today to be turning away from the pattern exhibited by the adult process. Some of this reflects facts about youths who commit crimes. No matter how the media portray extreme cases, the everyday juvenile remains unsophisticated and susceptible to change under appropriate programs. Most juvenile crime is still minor misbehavior, not at all like the highly charged cases of serious violence that dominate the news. To paint all juveniles with a broad brush would not only be unwise but also inaccurate.

Some of this shift also reflects a growing respect for evidence about effective policy for young people who commit crimes. While it is clear that the relative anonymity once enjoyed by the juvenile justice system is now past, it is also clear that the new attention being paid to juvenile justice policy should not and will not result in a simple replay of the stricter adult system. Some of this has to do with widespread dissatisfaction with the adult model, but just as important has been a new respect for evidence that suggests a different strategy will work out better (see "The Four Rs of Juvenile Justice Reform").

FOCUS ON

CORRECTIONAL PRACTICE: The Four Rs of Juvenile Justice Reform

There have been momentous shifts in juvenile corrections during the last 20 years. Juvenile arrest rates are down by two-thirds; incarceration rates are down by 60 percent. The number of youths housed in adult prisons is down by more than 80 percent. At the same time, the explosive implications of research on adolescent development—especially research on the maturation of the chemistry of the brain—have created a powerful scientific basis for changing the juvenile justice system. We have come a long way from the time, 30 years ago, when the most common theme about juveniles who broke the law was an intense public fear of "superpredators."

Given these powerful changes, what is at the horizon of juvenile justice policy making? A team of experts in the field recently identified four themes for forward-looking reforms in juvenile justice:

1. *Reduce the pipeline into youth prisons by at least 50 per- cent.* This can be accomplished by new legal limits on the types of youths and crimes that are eligible for juvenile placement.
2. *Reform the culture of the juvenile corrections profession.* There is too much emphasis on the imposition of punitive controls on juveniles in the system and not enough emphasis on achieving positive outcomes in a youth's life in the family, the school, and the community.
3. *Replace youth prisons with homelike residential facilities that enable youths to learn leadership skills and develop prosocial, community-oriented routines.* Young people need to learn how to live in the world, not away from it.
4. *Reinvest the savings that come from a more effective juvenile justice system in the communities that are so traumatized by violence and crime.* Use the resources of a downsized juvenile justice system to finance improvements in the capacity of communities from which so many youths in the juvenile justice system hail.

Source: Patrick McCarthy, Vincent Schiraldi, and Miriam Shark, *The Future of Youth Justice: A Community-Based Alternative to the Youth Prison Model* (Washington, DC: National Institute of Justice, 2016).

SUMMARY

1 Describe the nature and extent of youth crime today.

In a nation with 74 million people 18 years of age or younger, only 40,272 (about .005 percent of the population) were arrested for violent crime in 2015. After rising between 1988 and 1994, the juvenile violent crime rate has dropped by 60 percent since 2005; it is now the lowest it has been since at least 1980. Property crime by juveniles has decreased by about half since the peak in 1991. Yet when Americans are asked to identify the most serious problems facing children, they cite drugs and crime.

2 Analyze the history of the development of juvenile corrections in the United States.

American juvenile justice has gone through several historical periods. During the Puritan period (1646–1824), the leaders of the Massachusetts Bay Colony viewed the child as evil and believed that the family needed to discipline youths. In the refuge period (1824–1899), reformers urged the creation of institutions where delinquent, abused, and neglected children could learn good work and study habits, live in a disciplined and healthy environment, and develop character. The juvenile court period (1899–1960) focused on the idea of *parens patriae*, in that the new juvenile court took the role of guardian, the substitute parent to the child. By the 1960s, liberal reform groups rallied to protect the rights of juveniles during the juvenile rights period (1960–1980). In a series of decisions, the U.S. Supreme Court extended to juveniles many of the due process rights accorded adults. In the crime control period (1980–2005), a broad public movement favored increasing the use of waiver to adult court (before adjudication in juvenile court), increasing the sanctions for those remaining in juvenile court, or both, effectively treating juveniles much more stringently.

3 Describe the new "evidence-based" movement in juvenile corrections, and explain how it has affected juvenile justice.

Policy makers around the country are rethinking the get-tough approach to juvenile justice, and a new policy ethic is beginning to surface: evidence. The movement has three principles: (1) limited use of detention and incarceration, (2) a focus on prevention in the community, and (3) designing programs based on proven strategies.

4 Present the rationale for dealing differently with juveniles and adults.

Five differences between juveniles and adults are used to justify separate justice systems: (1) juveniles are young and may easily change, (2) juveniles have a high rate of "desistence," (3) juveniles' families are an important part of their lives, (4) juveniles are easily influenced by their peers, and (5) juveniles have little responsibility for others.

5 Explain how serious juvenile delinquency differs from most delinquency and what this implies for the juvenile justice system.

The juvenile justice system is predicated on what we might call "normal" delinquency, or misbehaviors that people expect juveniles to do, given their age. Serious delinquency involves status offenses, which are misbehaviors that are not against the law but are troubling because the person is so young: running away, being truant, and being ungovernable. It would be naive to think that the juvenile justice paradigm applies equally to every young person who breaks the law. Some juveniles are already hardened, some will continue criminal behavior into adulthood, some lack families, some are loners, and some are already in adult roles. Unusual

6 List the ways that juveniles are sanctioned.

Juveniles are sanctioned by detention, probation, school programs, intermediate sanctions, community corrections, incarceration, and aftercare. Approximately 21 percent of juvenile arrestees are briefly detained until an initial appearance before a juvenile court judge or judicial referee. About one out of five is found to endanger others or be at risk of flight, so he or she is kept in detention for days or weeks until an adjudication hearing can be scheduled. In one-half of cases, the juvenile delinquent is placed on probation and released to the custody of a parent or guardian. Often, the delinquent must undergo some form of education or counseling; he or she may also have to pay a fine or make restitution while on probation. Only about

juvenile criminality has been one reason why some question the wisdom of having a separate juvenile justice system. They say that society ought to treat all criminal acts with the seriousness they deserve, regardless of age, because there are so many exceptions to the "norms" on which the juvenile justice system is based.

7 Describe the special problems that youth gangs pose.

The United States has 850,000 gang members in 30,700 gangs, which are involved in perhaps half of urban violent crimes. Studies show that gangs vary widely in makeup. Most gangs are not violent, and many gang members engage in positive as well as negative social behaviors. Traditional street gangs provide social connections and engage in many types of criminal conduct, whereas drug gangs are organized into cohesive business structures and often use violence as a method of business. Gangs permeate the work of correctional officials. In custodial facilities, they create a profound challenge in terms of controlling the population and managing the potential for intergang conflict. In community settings, gangs provide hostile competition to the prosocial programs developed by correctional leaders. For the community, gangs are a primary source of fear and peril. Especially where gang members are armed, the presence of the gang can destabilize neighborhood life.

15 percent of delinquents receive an intermediate sanction: ISP and boot camps are the most common. Despite the lukewarm evaluations of juvenile community corrections, interest has continued in this approach. For most youths the institutional stay will be short—usually six months to a year. Aftercare refers to services provided to juveniles after they have been placed—removed from their home and put under some form of custodial care. Aftercare operates in a way similar to adult parole.

8 Assess the future of juvenile corrections.

The public today calls for get-tough measures. There is more pressure to increase waiver of serious juveniles to the adult court, where their sentences may be longer and their punishments harsher. Few are surprised to see these familiar echoes of changes in the adult system arising in respect to juveniles, now that the public spotlight has landed there. However, it is unlikely that reform for juveniles will exactly reproduce the adult process. No matter how the media portray extreme cases, the everyday juvenile remains unsophisticated and susceptible to change under appropriate programs. Most juvenile crime is still minor misbehavior, not at all like the highly charged cases of violence that dominate the news. Some middle ground will be found.

KEY TERMS

aftercare (*p. 481*)
at-risk youths (*p. 463*)
delinquent (*p. 459*)
dependent (*p. 460*)
neglected (*p. 459*)
parens patriae (*p. 457*)
school-to-prison pipeline (*p. 474*)
status offenses (*p. 466*)

FOR DISCUSSION

1. How has the experience of growing up changed over the last few centuries? Why are these changes important for juvenile justice?
2. How do the differences between adults and juveniles affect policies in juvenile justice? How are adults and juveniles similar under the law?
3. Are the many differences in terminology between the adult and juvenile systems important? Why or why not?
4. In what ways do juvenile institutions differ from adult institutions? How does this affect institutional management? What does this difference mean for juveniles who are housed in adult facilities?
5. Should we have a separate juvenile justice system? Why or why not?

FOR FURTHER READING

Bernstein, Nell. *Burning Down the House: The End of Juvenile Prison*. New York: NYU Press, 2014. A history of the development of juvenile custodial facilities and attempts to reform them.

Bonnie, Richard J., Robert L. Johnson, Betty M. Chemers, and Julie A. Schuck, eds. *Reforming Juvenile Justice: A Developmental Approach*. Washington, DC: National Academies Press, 2013. An authoritative review of research on juvenile development, juvenile justice policy, and juvenile justice practice.

Brotherton, David C. *Youth Street Gangs: A Critical Appraisal*. London and New York: Routledge, 2015. A review of research about street gangs, with a perspective that youth peer groups are normal social activities and that much of the "gang literature" takes a biased view of this activity.

Fader, Jamie. *Falling Back: Incarceration and Transitions to Adulthood for Urban Youth*. New Brunswick, NJ: Rutgers University Press, 2015. An ethnographic study of young men of color returning to their communities after incarceration in juvenile institutions.

Kennedy, David M. *Don't Shoot: One Man, a Street Fellowship, and the End of Violence in Inner-city America*. New York: Bloomsbury, 2012. A detailed description of the development of a proven strategy for dealing with violent gangs.

Kim, Catherine Y., Daniel J. Larsen, and Damon T. Hewitt. *The School-to-Prison Pipeline: Structuring Legal Reform*. New York: NYU Press, 2010. A discussion of the problem of at-risk youths leaving school early and becoming involved in the juvenile justice system, and how legal reforms could reduce the problem.

Lauger, Timothy R. *Real Ganstas: Legitimacy, Reputation, and Violence in the Intergang Environment*. New Brunswick, NJ: Rutgers University Press, 2012. A study of the relationships between members of rival gangs in Indianapolis.

Loeber, Rolfa, and David P. Farrington. *From Delinquency to Adult Crime: Criminal Careers, Justice Policy, and Prevention*. New York: Oxford University Press, 2012. A series of papers by prominent criminologists exploring the way that juvenile delinquency relates to later adult crime.

Nellis, Ashley. *Return to Justice: Rethinking our Approach to Juveniles in the System*. New York: Rowman & Littlefield, 2015. A comprehensive review of programs and policies in the juvenile justice system, with recommendations for reform.

Rosenfeld, Richard, Mark Edberg, Xiangming Fang, and Curtis S. Florence. *Economics and Youth Violence: Crime, Disadvantage, and Community*. New York: NYU Press, 2013. A series of studies that explore the relationship between urban poverty and youth crime.

Youth Violence: What We Need to Know. Report of the Subcommittee on Youth Violence of the Advisory Committee to the Social, Behavioral, and Economic Science Directorate, National Science Foundation. Washington, DC: National Science Foundation, 2013. A critical examination of knowledge about the nature and control of youth violence.

NOTES

1. Kelan Lyons, "Juvenile Justice Advocates: Let's 'Raise the Age' Again," *The Connecticut Mirror*, February 20, 2020: https://ctmirror.org/2020/02/10/juvenile-justice-advocates-lets-raise-the-age-again/.
2. Office of Juvenile Justice and Delinquency Prevention, *Statistical Briefing Book: Jurisdictional Boundaries:* https://www.ojjdp.gov/ojstatbb/structure_process/qa04101.asp?qaDate=2018.
3. Laurence Steinberg, *Age of Opportunity: Lessons from the New Science of Adolescence* (New York: Eamon Dolan, 2015); Richard J. Bonnie, Robert L. Johnson, Betty M. Chemers, and Julie A. Schuck, eds., *Reforming Juvenile Justice: A Developmental Approach* (Washington, DC: National Academies Press, 2013).
4. Justice Policy Institute, *Raising the Age: Shifting to a Safer and More Effective Juvenile Justice System* (Washington, DC: Author, 2017); Charles E. Loeffler and Aaron Chalfin, "Estimating the Crime Effects of Raising the Age of Majority," *Criminology & Public Policy* 16(no. 1, 2017): 45–71.
5. Office of Juvenile Justice and Delinquency Prevention, *Case Processing Statistics*: https://www.ojjdp.gov/ojstatbb/ezajcs/asp/process.asp.
6. Office of Juvenile Justice and Delinquency Prevention, *Detailed Offenses*: https://www.ojjdp.gov/ojstatbb/ezajcs/asp/detail.asp.
7. Ibid., https://www.ojjdp.gov/ojstatbb/ezajcs/asp/detail.asp.
8. Nicole White and Janet Lauritsen, *Violent Crime Against Youth, 1994–2010* (Washington, DC: U.S. Bureau of Justice Statistics, 2012); Jennifer L. Truman and Rachel E. Morgan, *Criminal Victimization* (Washington, DC: U.S. Bureau of Justice Statistics, 2015).
9. Hockenberry and Puzzanchera, *Juvenile Court Statistics 2013*, p. 46.

10 *Roper v. Simmons*, 543 U.S. 551 (2005).
11 *Graham v. Florida*, 560 U.S. 48 (2010).
12 *Miller v. Alabama*, 567 U.S. 460 (2012).
13 *Montgomery v. Louisiana*, 577 U.S. (2016).
14 Howard N. Snyder and Melissa Sickmund, *Juveniles and Victims: 2006 National Report* (Pittsburgh: National Center for Juvenile Justice, 2006), 234.
15 Michael E. Ezell and Lawrence E. Cohen, *Outgrowing Serious Crime: Continuity and Change in the Criminal Offending Patterns of Chronic Offenders* (New York: Oxford University Press, 2005).
16 E. P. Mulvey, L. Steinberg, A. R. Piquero, et al., "Trajectories of Desistance and Continuity in Antisocial Behavior Following Court Adjudication Among Serious Adolescent Offenders," *Development and Psychopathology* 22 (2010): 453–75.
17 E.M. Hoeben and K. J Thomas, "Peers and Offender Decision-making," *Criminology & Public Policy* 18 (no. 4, 2019): 759–84.
18 Robert Brame, Edward P. Mulvey, Carol A. Schubert, and Alex R. Piquero, "Recidivism in a Sample of Serious Adolescent Offenders," *Journal of Quantitative Criminology* 34 (no. 2, 2018): 167–87.
19 Office of Juvenile Justice and Delinquency Prevention, *Petitioned Status Offenses*: https://www.ojjdp.gov/ojstatbb/court/qa06603.asp
20 Federal Bureau of Investigation, Crime in the United States, 2018, Table 38.
21 Office of Juvenile Justice and Delinquency Prevention, *Demographics*: https://www.ojjdp.gov/ojstatbb/ezajcs/asp/demo.asp.
22 Graham Farrell, Gloria Laycock, and Nick Tilley, "Debuts and Legacies: The Crime Drop and the Role of Adolescent-Limited and Persistent Offending," *Crime Science 4* (no. 16, 2015).
23 Office of Juvenile Justice and Delinquency Prevention, *Case Processing Statistics*: https://www.ojjdp.gov/ojstatbb/ezajcs/asp/process.asp.
24 George E. Higgins, Melissa L. Ricketts, James D. Griffith, and Stephanie A. Jirard, "Race and Juvenile Incarceration: A Propensity Score Matching Examination," *American Journal of Criminal Justice* 38 (no. 1, 2013): 1–12.
25 Office of Juvenile Justice and Delinquency Prevention, *Detailed Offenses*: https://www.ojjdp.gov/ojstatbb/ezajcs/asp/detail.asp.
26 Sentencing Project, *How Tough on Crime Became Tough on Kids: Prosecuting Teenage Drug Charges in Adult Courts* (Washington, DC: Author, 2016).
27 Richard L. Redding, "Juvenile Transfer Laws: An Effective Deterrent to Delinquency?" *OJJDP Bulletin*, June 2010.
28 Steven N. Zane, Brandon C. Welsh, and Daniel P. Mears, "Juvenile Transfer and the Specific Deterrence Hypothesis: Systematic Review and Meta-analysis," *Criminology & Public Policy*, 15 (no. 3, 2016): 901–26.
29 Benjamin Adams and Sean Addie, *Delinquency Cases Waived to Criminal Court 2007* (Washington, DC: Office of Juvenile Justice and Delinquency Prevention, 2010). See also Joe M. Brown and John R. Sorenson, "Race, Ethnicity, Gender and Waiver to Adult Court," *Journal of Ethnicity in Criminal Justice* 11 (no. 3, 2013): 282–95.
30 Neelum Arya, *State Trends: Legislative Changes from 2005 to 2010 Removing Youth from the Adult Criminal Justice System* (Washington, DC: Campaign for Youth Justice, 2011).
31 Office of Juvenile Justice and Delinquency Prevention, *Juveniles in Adult Jails*: https://www.ojjdp.gov/OJSTATBB/corrections/qa08700.asp?qaDate=2018.
32 Ryan T. Motz, J. C. Barnes, Avshalom Caspi, Louise Arsenault, Francis T. Cullen, Renate Houts, Jasmin Wertz, and Terrie Moffit, "Does Contact with the Justice System Deter or Promote Future Delinquency? Results from a Longitudinal Study of British Adolescent Twins," *Criminology* 58 (no. 2, 2020): 307–35.
33 Lee Ann Slocum and Stephanie Ann Wiley, "'Experience of the Expected?' Race and Ethnicity in the Effects of Police Contact with Youth," *Criminology* 56 (no. 2, 2018): 412–32.
34 Daniel P. Mears, Joshua J. Kuch, Andrea M. Linsdey, et al., "Juvenile Court and Contemporary Diversion: Helpful, Harmful or Both?" *Criminology & Public Policy 15* (no. 3, 2016): 953–82.
35 Paul Boxer, Meagan Docherty, Michael Ostermann, et al., "Effectiveness of Multisystemic Therapy for Gang-Involved Youth Offenders: One Year Follow-up Analysis of Recidivism Outcomes," *Children and Youth Services Review* 73 (2017): 107–12.
36 Jennifer S. Wong, Jessica Bouchard, Jason Gravel, et al., "Can At-Risk Youth Be Diverted from Crime? A Meta-analysis of Restorative Justice Diversion Programs," *Criminal Justice and Behavior* 43 (no. 10, 2016): 1293–309.
37 Howard A. Liddle, Gayle A. Dakoff, Cynthia L. Rowe, Craig Henderson, Paul Greenbaum, Wei Wang, and Linda Alberga, "Multidimensional Family Therapy as a Community-Based Alternative to Residential Treatment for Adolescents with Substance Abuse and Co-occurring Mental Health Disorders," *Journal of Substance Abuse Treatment* 90 (2018): 47–56.
38 Office of Juvenile Justice and Delinquency Prevention, *Delinquency Cases:* https://www.ojjdp.gov/OJSTATBB/court/qa06301.asp?qaDate=2018.
39 Snyder and Sickmund, *Juveniles and Victims: 2014*, p. 198.
40 Uberto Gatti, Richard E. Tremblay, and Frank Vitaro, "Iatrogenic Effect of Juvenile Justice," *Child Psychology and Psychiatry* 50 (no. 8, 2009): 991–98.
41 Office of Juvenile Justice and Delinquency Prevention, *Delinquency Cases:* https://www.ojjdp.gov/OJSTATBB/court/qa06401.asp?qaDate=2018.
42 Ibid.
43 Ibid.

44 Jessica Feierman, *Debtors' Prison for Kids? The High Cost of Fines and Fees in the Juvenile Justice System* (Washington, DC: Juvenile Law Center, 2016).

45 Kerrin C. Wolf and Aaron Kupchik, "School Suspensions and Adverse Experiences in Adulthood," *Justice Quarterly* 34 (no. 3, 2016): 407–30.

46 John Paul Wright, Pamela A. McMahon, Claire Daley, and J. Paul Haney, "Getting the Law Involved: A Quasi-experiment in Early Intervention Involving Collaborations Between Schools and the District Attorney's Office," *Criminology & Public Policy* 11 (no. 2, May 2012): 227–50.

47 Higgins, Ricketts, Griffith, and Jirard, "Race and Juvenile Incarceration."

48 Semantha Melemed, "How a Philly Cop Broke the School-to-Prison Pipeline," *Philadelphia Inquirer*, September 26, 2016.

49 Wright, McMahon, Daley, and Haney, "Getting the Law Involved."

50 Ibid.

51 Nate Balis, "State of the Initiative," address to the Juvenile Detention Alternatives Initiative National Inter-site Conference, April 18, 2017, Orlando, Florida.

52 Patrick McCarthy, Vincent Schiraldi, and Miriam Shark, *The Future of Youth Justice: A Community-Based Alternative to the Youth Prison Model* (Washington, DC: National Institute of Justice, 2016).

53 Holly Nguyen, Thomas A. Loughren, Ray Paternoster, et al., "Institutional Placement and Illegal Earnings: Examining the Crime School Hypothesis," *Journal of Quantitative Criminology* 33 (no. 2, 2017): 207–35.

54 Anna Aizer and Joseph J. Doyle Jr., "Juvenile Incarceration, Human Capital and Future Crime: Evidence from Randomly- Assigned Judges," NBER Working Paper No. 19102, www.nber.org/papers/w19102, June 2013.

55 Michael T. Baglivio, Kevin T. Wolff, Katherine Jackowski, Gabrielle Chapman, Mark A. Greenwald, and Katherine Gomez, "Does Treatment Quality Matter?" *Criminology & Public Policy* 17 (no. 1, 2017): 147–80.

56 Arlen Egley, James C. Howell, and Meena Harris, *Highlights of the 2012 National Youth Gang Survey* (Washington, DC: Office of Juvenile Justice and Delinquency Prevention, 2014).

57 Ibid.

58 Andrew V. Papachristos, Anthony A. Braga, Eric Piza, and Leigh S. Grossman, "The Company You Keep? The Spillover Effects of Gang Membership on Individual Gunshot Victimization in a Co-offending Network," *Criminology* 53 (2015): 624–49.

59 Terence P. Thornberry, Brook Kearly, Denise C. Gottfredson, Molly P. Slothower, Deanna N. Devlin, and Jamie J. Fader, "Reducing Crime Among Youth at Risk for Gang Involvement," *Criminology & Public Policy* 17 (no. 4, 2018): 953–89.

60 David C. Pyrooz, Jean Marie McGloin, and Scott H. Decker, "Parenthood as a Turning Point in the Life Course for Male and Female Gang Members: A Study of Within-Individual Changes in Gang Membership and Criminal Behavior," *Criminology* 55 (no. 4, 2017): 869–99.

PART THREE

Correctional Issues and Perspectives

In Part 3—"Correctional Issues and Perspectives"—we turn our attention to important issues and debates now taking place in the corrections system. Some of these, such as the death penalty, have been going on for some time. Others, such as community justice, reflect new ideas under development. Dynamics surrounding race and ethnicity influence almost every policy and practice that the corrections system uses. A new chapter on immigration reflects an important current policy debate. In this concluding part of our book, we consider some of the most interesting and challenging issues facing the corrections system today.

GUEST PERSPECTIVE

The Role of Correctional Leadership in the Shifting Paradigm

MARCUS O. HICKS, ESQ

Marcus O. Hicks

The era of "lock 'em up and throw away the key" is over. Day after day, correctional systems across the United States are realizing that the antiquated philosophy leads to increased recidivism, burgeoning corrections budgets, and broken families. Those of us who are responsible for developing, operating, and modifying correctional systems must have courage in the face of apathy to adapt and to respond to issues posed by modern day correctional management. Appropriate leadership in the ever-shifting correctional paradigm is more important now than ever before.

As the Commissioner of the New Jersey Department of Corrections (NJDOC), my approach to leading the second largest agency is to progressively develop solutions to modern day correctional challenges, with a focus on the rehabilitation of offenders and safety for all.

What does it mean to balance progressive initiatives with firmly established safety and security protocol? In New Jersey, where 35 percent of offenders in prison suffer from substance use disorders, it means establishing a comprehensive, multi-faceted Medication Assisted Treatment (MAT) program. Coupling Food and

Drug Administration (FDA)-approved medications with behavioral therapy in a correctional setting is unconventional. We spend significant resources on keeping correctional facilities free from illegal drugs. Understanding the effectiveness of a particular strategy while balancing the very real safety needs of everyone in our custody requires nuanced leadership that simply was not considered in past administrations.

Among the most basic responsibilities of any correctional system is ensuring the safety of those in our custody while protecting their human dignity. These principles should not be mutually exclusive. It is the reason why we have taken aggressive action to ensure compliance with the Prison Rape Elimination Act (PREA). For our female population, gender-specific programming and services have become the norm and for the first time, NJDOC houses inmates based on their gender identity.

It has long been discussed the importance of education in recidivism-reduction. We know that education leads to increased job opportunities, which is a critical component that helps to break the cycle of incarceration. Incentivizing educational attainment was important for the NJDOC. We implemented a program in which offenders who enroll and complete academic and vocational programming will earn time remission off of their sentence. The idea is that those individuals who exemplify the initiative to create and complete their educational goals are likely to succeed. These individuals, upon release, are less likely to recidivate, which helps to ensure public safety.

Despite one's best efforts, there will be times in which issues in the community will become issues in a correctional system. This microcosmic view mandates that practitioners must be adept at evolving and responding to unexpected crises. COVID-19 is an example of a global phenomenon that shook the world, and had devastating impacts in New Jersey. As such, COVID-19 required us to quickly adapt to an unprecedented and unseen challenge. We became one of the first correctional systems in the nation to employ universal testing for our staff and offenders to support our operations management and most importantly, support staff and inmate safety.

The future of corrections in the State of New Jersey is bright. We are on the precipice of criminal justice reform, boast lower than average recidivism rates, and enjoy the lowest prison population in the history of the Garden State. We have been able to focus on officer and staff resiliency to ensure that those who are responsible for caring for others are themselves cared for. Modern-day correctional leadership must encompass an ability to balance all of these initiatives. Practitioners, students, and the community at large are depending on our ability to maintain this balance. It is the only true way of ensuring rehabilitation and public safety goals are not mutually exclusive.

CHAPTER 18

Incarceration Trends

Aerial Archives/Alamy Stock Photo

Modern prisons are enormous complexes with numerous buildings serving a host of functions, including housing, treatment, and industry.

AFTER DECADES OF EXPANDED USE OF INCARCERATION IN THE UNITED STATES, RATES HAVE LEVELED OFF.

In fact, if incarceration were an Olympic sport, the United States would not win a medal (431 per 100,000 population). The gold medal would go to El Salvador (604 per 100,000 population). Turkmenistan would win the silver medal (552 per 100,000 population). And the bronze medalist would be Thailand (526 per 100,000 population). By comparison, the incarceration rate (per 100,000 population) of England and Wales is 140; Australia, 172; China, 118; Canada, 114; France, 100; Ireland, 78; Germany, 75; Netherlands, 61; and Japan, 41. The incarceration rate worldwide is 145 per 100,000 population.[1] The incarceration rate in the United States increased dramatically between 1980 and 2010. Following the three-decade expansion of the prison population in the United States, the Pew Charitable Trusts commented that "you'd think the nation would finally have run out of lawbreakers to put behind bars."[2]

Recent estimates suggest that the growth in the incarceration rate may have peaked and that imprisonment is now on the decline. But the recent dip in the incarceration rate is not being attributed to a lack of available convicted individuals to incarcerate. Rather, economic concerns explain part of the decline. Prisons are expensive. States spend nearly $50 billion each year on corrections, three-quarters of which goes toward operating correctional institutions.[3] States around the country have employed a variety of strategies to reduce correctional budgets. There are two ways to substantially reduce the cost of incarceration: send fewer people to prison and have people who are sent to prison stay for shorter periods. Many states are closing or consolidating prisons. The state of Texas recently closed two state facilities. Doing so will save the state an estimated $20 million per year. Over the past decade, Texas has now shuttered 10 prisons.[4]

It is far too soon to tell whether incarceration rates will return to pre-1990 levels or whether rates are simply in a temporary holding pattern and will once again increase in the future. In this chapter we explore explanations for the rise in incarceration since 1980.

We also consider ways of dealing with prison crowding and examine its impact on the system. Finally, we evaluate the argument that incarceration is cost-effective for society.

LEARNING OBJECTIVES

After reading this chapter, you should be able to . . .

1. Discuss the explanations for the dramatic increase in the incarceration rate.
2. Explain what can be done to deal with the prison population crisis.
3. Analyze the impact of prison crowding.
4. Discuss whether incarceration pays.

LO 1

Discuss the explanations for the dramatic increase in the incarceration rate.

EXPLAINING PRISON POPULATION TRENDS

From 1930 through 1980, the incarceration rate in the United States remained fairly stable. During this period the rate of sentenced individuals in federal and state facilities fluctuated from a low of 93 per 100,000 population in 1972 to a high of 139 in 1980. However, the average rate of incarceration increased dramatically in the 1980s (200 per 100,000) and 1990s (389 per 100,000). This growth trend continued into the twenty-first century. The average incarceration rate in the early 2000s was nearly 490 per 100,000. More recently, the average has dipped slightly to 467 per 100,000 between 2010 and 2018 (see Figure 18.1).[5] At the current rate of decline, the prison population will be cut by 50 percent in 2091.[6]

This tremendous growth has dramatically changed the demographic and offense composition of the prison population. African Americans and Hispanics now make up a large percentage of residents in U.S. correctional facilities. These individuals are also

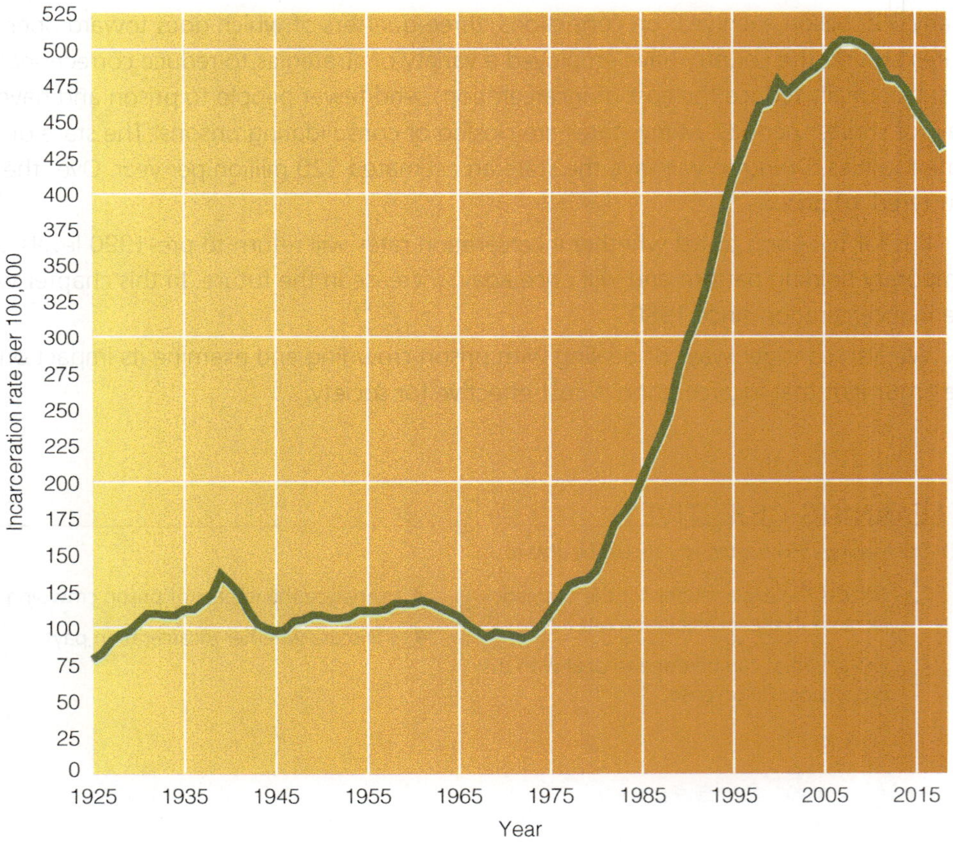

FIGURE 18.1 Incarceration Rate per 100,000 Population

Between 1940 and 1974, the incarceration rate held steady. Only since 1975 has a continuing increase occurred. The rate today is nearly double what it was in 1986.

Source: E. Ann Carson, *Prisoners in 2018* (Washington, DC: U.S. Government Printing Office, 2020), 9.

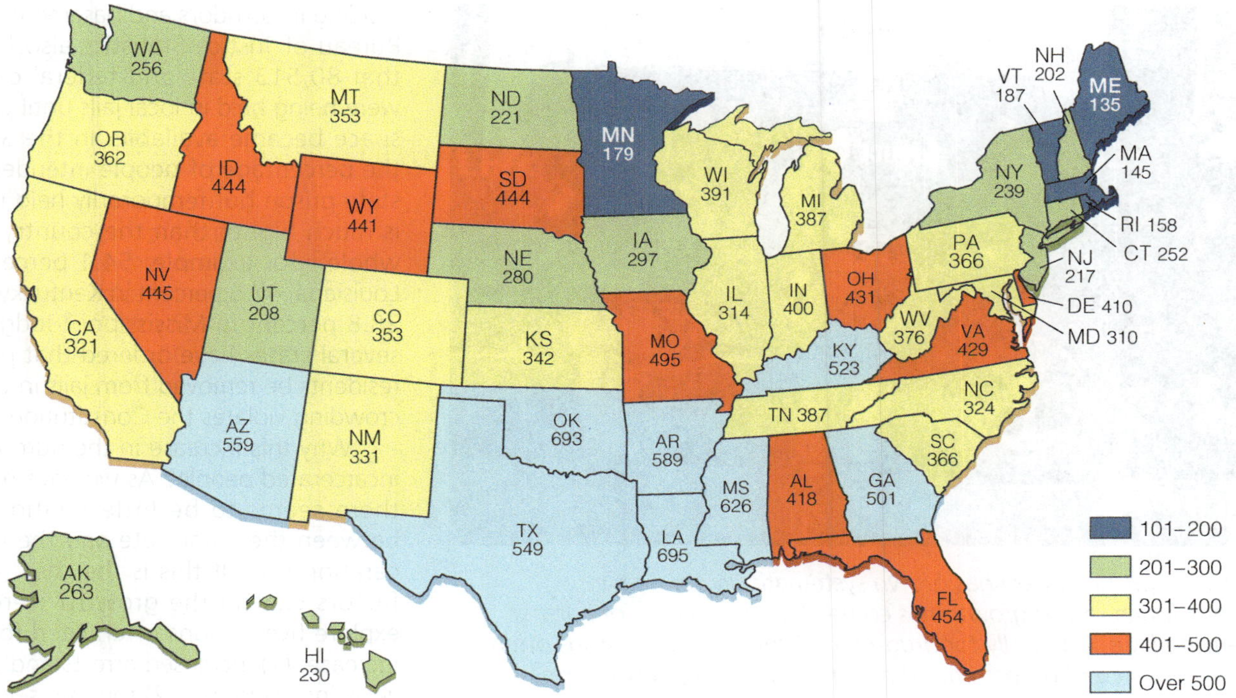

FIGURE 18.2 Incarceration Rate per 100,000 Population by State

What can be said about the differences in incarceration rates among the states? There are not only regional differences but also differences among neighboring states that seem to have similar demographics and crime characteristics.

Source: E. Ann Carson, *Prisoners in 2018* (Washington, DC: U.S. Government Printing Office, 2020), 11–12.

more likely to be middle-aged, and more women are being incarcerated. Since 1980, the percentage of people serving time for violent offenses has declined, and the number incarcerated for drug violations has increased.

The size of the prison population differs between states. As Figure 18.2 shows, the four states with the highest incarceration rates (Louisiana, Oklahoma, Arkansas, and Mississippi) are in the South. Many argue that southern attitudes toward crime and punishment account for that region's high prison population. The penal codes in many southern states provide for long sentences, and people incarcerated there spend extended periods in institutions. It is also the region with the highest African American population, which is incarcerated in numbers far greater than its proportion to the overall population.

The skyrocketing prison population has resulted in crowding in some prisons. The U.S. Bureau of Justice Statistics has reported that the federal prison system and prisons in 22 states are operating above capacity.[7] In many states new prison residents have been crowded into already bulging institutions, with some

▲ *Mass incarceration has changed the demographic and offense composition of the prison population. There are now more African Americans, Hispanics, women, and middle-aged prisoners than there were in the 1970s.*

© Sam Upshaw Jr./Courier Journal

The U.S. prison system has grown systematically for nearly 40 years. Much of this growth has come about as a result of harsher sentencing laws, especially for drug-related crime. Routine stops often turn up evidence of drug crimes that can lead to long prison terms.

residing in corridors and basements. The Bureau of Justice Statistics also found that 80,513 state and federal clients were being held in local jails until prison space became available. In the South the percentage of people intended for state prison but temporarily held in jail is much higher than the country as a whole—for example, 54.1 percent in Louisiana, 47.5 percent in Kentucky, and 28.8 percent in Mississippi.[8] Judges in several states have ordered that prison residents be removed from jails in which crowding violates the Constitution.

Why this increase in the number of incarcerated people? As we have noted, there seems to be little relationship between the crime rate and the incarceration rate. If this is the case, what factors explain the growth? Here we explore five reasons often cited for the increase: (1) increased arrests and more likely incarceration, (2) tougher sentencing, (3) prison construction, (4) the war on drugs, and (5) state and local politics. None of these reasons should be viewed as a single explanation. Rather, each contributes to the equation, with some having a greater impact than others.

Increased Arrests and More Likely Incarceration

Some analysts argue that the billions of dollars spent by federal, state, and local governments on the crime problem are paying off. When the crime rate began to rise dramatically in the mid-1960s, the incarceration rate was proportionally low. Crime rates for serious offenses have now declined, but the estimated number of arrests for some offenses has increased dramatically. For example, in 1970 an estimated 322,300 adults were arrested for drug violations. The number of arrests in this category exceeded to 1.5 million by 2000.[9] Over the past two decades, drug arrests have remained relatively steady.[10]

A large portion of the prison population is made up of individuals who are being returned to prison for new crimes or parole violations (see Chapter 16). About 67 percent of those entering state prisons do so directly as a result of a new court commitment, and nearly 30 percent of admissions are people who returned to prison for violating the conditions of their parole.[11] Prison admissions because of parole violations are a bigger problem in some states than in others. For example, parole violators make up a large percentage of individuals admitted to prison in Washington (74.9 percent) but a relatively small percentage in Virginia (0.4 percent).[12] Overall, the percentage of new court commitments has flattened while the number of people on parole returned to prison has increased greatly.

Tougher Sentencing

Some observers think that a hardening of public attitudes toward those convicted of crimes is reflected in longer sentences, in a smaller proportion of those convicted being granted probation, and in fewer people being released at the time of their first parole hearing.

As discussed in Chapter 4, in the past three decades the states and the federal government have passed laws that increase sentences for most crimes. Those convicted of violent offenses serve the longest sentences. In comparison, individuals convicted of property and drug offenses serve less time.[13]

Mandatory-sentencing laws greatly limit the discretion of judges with regard to the length of sentences for certain crimes. The shift to determinate sentences, truth-in-sentencing laws, and a drop in release rates have contributed to the higher prison population. However, recall the difference between the sentence given by the judge and the actual time served in prison. In the past, with indeterminate sentences, most incarcerated individuals went before the parole board when they had served the minimum sentence minus jail time and good time, and most were released on their first attempt to gain parole.

Prison Construction

The increased rate of incarceration may be related to the creation of additional space in the nation's prisons and the economic impact of the construction boom. Public attitudes in favor of more-punitive sentencing policies have influenced legislators to approve building more prisons. Between 1990 and 2005, more than 500 prisons were built across the country, increasing the number of facilities nationwide by 42 percent.[14] A study by the Urban Institute found that Texas, the state with the greatest number of prisons (137), increased the number of its facilities by more than 700 percent between 1979 and 2000.[15] Even with the decline in the crime rate during the past decade and tougher economic times in many states, new prison construction continues.

According to organizational theorists, available public resources such as hospitals and schools are used to their fullest capacity. Prisons are no exception. When prison space is limited, judges reserve incarceration for only the most violent individuals. However, additional prisons may present a variation of the "Field of Dreams" scenario—build them and they will come. Research supports this view. William Spelman analyzed state prison populations from 1977 to 2005. He found that state spending on prison construction was a salient predictor of subsequent prison population size.[16] Creation of additional prison space may thus increase the incarceration rate.

For health and safety reasons, crowded conditions in existing facilities cannot be tolerated. Many states attempted to build their way out of this problem because the public seemed to favor harsher sentencing policies, which would require more prison space. With many states holding large budget surpluses during the booming economy of the 1990s, legislatures were willing to advance the huge sums required for prison expansion. Pressures from contractors, building-material providers, and correctional officer unions also spurred the expansion. Yet many states that tried to build their way out of their crowded facilities found that as soon as a new prison came on line, it was quickly filled.

The War on Drugs

Crusades against the use of drugs have recurred in U.S. politics since the late 1800s. The latest manifestation began in 1982, when President Ronald Reagan declared another "war on drugs" and asked Congress to set aside more money for drug enforcement personnel and for prison space. This came at a time when the country was scared by the advent of crack cocaine, which ravaged many communities and resulted in an increased murder rate. In 1987 Congress imposed stiff mandatory minimum sentences for federal drug law violations, laws that many states copied. The "war" continued during succeeding administrations, with each president urging Congress to appropriate billions for an all-out law enforcement campaign against drugs.

The war on drugs has succeeded on one front by packing the nation's prisons with those convicted of drug offenses. The number of people sentenced to prison for drug crimes has increased steadily. In 1980 only 6 percent of individuals in state prison had been convicted of a drug offense; today, the percentage is higher in both state prisons

TABLE 18.1 Incarceration Rates and Violent Crime Rates per 100,000 in Selected Neighboring States

Politics and community values seem to vary in the amount of emphasis that they place on imprisonment as a solution to crime.

	Incarceration Rate	Violent Crime Rate
Pennsylvania	366	306
New York	239	351
Idaho	444	227
Utah	208	233
Oregon	362	286
Washington	256	312

Sources: E. Ann Carson, *Prisoners in 2018* (Washington, DC: U.S. Government Printing Office, April 2020), 11–12; Federal Bureau of Investigation, *Crime in the United States, 2018*, https://ucr.fbi.gov/crime-in-the-u.s/2018/crime-in-the-u.s.-2018/topic-pages/tables/table-5, retrieved May 7, 2020.

(14.8 percent) and federal prisons (47.3 percent).[17] Some scholars believe that the war on drugs has accomplished very little. Illegal drug markets are resilient to the mass incarceration of drug users and dealers. As one group of drug dealers is shipped off to prison, another group stands ready to replace them. This constant supply of eager replacements frustrates the intended deterrent and incapacitation effects of longer prison sentences for those convicted of drug crimes.[18]

State and Local Politics

Incarceration rates vary among the regions and states, but why do states with similar characteristics differ in their use of prisons? Can it be that local political factors influence correctional policies?

One might think that there would be an association among the states between crime rates and incarceration rates—the more crime, the more people in prison. Yet as discussed earlier, some states with high crime rates do not have correspondingly high incarceration rates. Even when states have similar socioeconomic and demographic characteristics—poverty, unemployment, racial composition, drug arrests—variations in incarceration rates often exist and remain difficult to explain. For example, Utah and Idaho have similar social characteristics and crime rates, yet the incarceration rate in Idaho (444 per 100,000 population) is more than double the rate found in Utah (208 per 100,000 population).[19] One can find other examples where neighboring states have similar violent crime rates and very different incarceration rates (see Table 18.1).

In recent years scholars have shown that the location of prisons makes a significant economic and political impact in some states. A good example of this relationship is found in the state of New York, which in the 1970s enacted tough sentencing laws such as 15 years to life for some nonviolent, first-time drug offenses. Over the next 20 years, the state's prison population increased dramatically. Most of the incarcerated individuals ended up in new prisons located in the northern, rural, economically impoverished region of the state. One study notes that two-thirds of these prison residents are from New York City, while 91 percent of the imprisoned individuals are held in upstate counties.[20]

The U.S. Bureau of the Census counts incarcerated individuals as "residents" of the community where the facility is located. Because state and federal aid, such as Medicaid, foster care, and social service block grants, is distributed on the basis of population, this has meant that aid for the distressed inner cities from which the people come is diverted to the sparsely populated counties where their former residents are incarcerated.

Probably the most extensive research on the link between politics and incarceration has been done by David Greenberg and Valerie West. They analyzed variations in the levels of incarceration among the 50 states over a 20-year period. A basic assumption of their study was that incarceration is a response to the volume of crime, but only in part. They expected that a state's responses to crime would also be influenced by its ability to finance incarceration, by its political culture, and by levels of public anxiety and fear. Here are the main findings of this research:

1. States with high violent crime rates have higher levels of imprisonment.
2. States with higher revenues have higher prison populations.
3. States with higher unemployment and where there is a higher percentage of African Americans in the population have higher prison populations.
4. States with more-generous welfare benefits have lower prison populations.
5. States with more political conservatives have not only higher incarceration rates, but their rates also grew more rapidly than did the rates of states with fewer conservatives.
6. Political incentives for an expansive prison policy transcended Democratic and Republican affiliations.[21]

Examining states' criminal justice policies makes us aware of the role that politics plays in the incarceration formula. As we have seen, many factors, not just the crime rate, have influenced the incarceration experiment.

Public Policy Trends

It is difficult to point to one factor as the main cause of the rapid increase in the incarceration rate during the past several decades. As we have seen, several plausible hypotheses exist. But researchers recognize that the size of the prison population is not driven by the amount of crime; it is driven by public policy. Public policies are forged in the political arena. Politicians are aware that the public is concerned about crime; the public also has little sympathy for people who break the law. In a democracy, political leaders respond to public demands to deal with problems such as crime. The public has supported greater use of incarceration. Appeasing demand for increased punishments may not effectively reduce crime rates, but it can alleviate political pressure to "do something" (see "Do the Right Thing").

For decades now, lawmakers have passed legislation designed to incarcerate a greater number of adjudicated individuals for longer periods. This objective has been accomplished. Increased law enforcement and prosecution spending, mandatory-sentencing laws, truth-in-sentencing requirements, enhanced drug law enforcement, and tough parole policies have provided the two necessary conditions for sustained prison population growth—an increase in the number of prison admissions and an increase in the average length of stay. Have these policies succeeded? Proponents

DO THE RIGHT THING

While sitting at his desk, Representative Leon Donohue taps his fountain pen on a stack of papers. Staring out the window, he contemplates an upcoming vote on House Bill 65. If enacted into law, the bill would require adults who possessed 50 grams of cocaine to serve at least 10 years in prison. The most recent opinion poll showed that 52 percent of the public supports the bill.

Donohue has remained undecided and has said very little in the press about the matter. The congressman believes that cocaine is a threat to public health and is associated with many social problems, such as gun violence, family disruption, and addiction. But he is also concerned about whether the state can afford to implement a new mandatory-minimum sentencing law. The Department of Corrections has already sustained a substantial budget reduction during the last legislative session, and more cuts are expected in the near future. This new law will likely contribute to an already large prison population that is unaffordable.

Donohue considered voting in support of the bill if it lacked the governor's support. However, the governor has yet to indicate whether she would sign the bill into law or veto it.

There is quick succession of knocks at the door as it opens and the congressman's chief of staff enters. "OK, Congressman, we need to get you to the floor. Voting on Bill 65 has started."

"I'm ready, Sam. Let's do it."

WRITING ASSIGNMENT: First, how you would vote on House Bill 65 if you were in Donohue's position? Next, discuss whether the representative should let the results from the recent public opinion poll influence his decision. Should concerns about the state's budget take precedence over "tough on crime" laws? Finally, if the bill becomes law, where should the state look for additional money to fund its prisons?

FOCUS ON

CORRECTIONAL POLICY: Decarceration Strategies

Since 2009, the incarceration rate in the United States has started to slowly decline. Reductions have been observed in 42 states. One study that focused on decarceration in five states—Connecticut, Michigan, Mississippi, Rhode Island, and South Carolina—found that the following strategies were used to reduce prison populations:

1. Taking steps to initiate reforms and to maintain momentum, which often entailed bipartisan political leadership.
2. Reducing prison admissions by decreasing the number of new prison commitments, which frequently involved adjusting criminal penalties.
3. Decreasing the number of individuals sent back to prison for violating conditions of community supervision, which sometimes involved reducing terms of community supervision.
4. Increasing prison releases by enhancing the efficiency and feasibility of release, which included the use of risk/needs assessment.
5. Reducing the amount of time served to qualify for release, which sometimes involved reducing penalties for aggravating circumstances.

Source: Dennis Schrantz, Stephen T. DeBor, and Marc Mauer. *Decarceration Strategies: How 5 States Achieved Substantial Prison Population Reductions* (Washington, DC: The Sentencing Project, 2018).

argue that the decline in crime has come about because large numbers of convicted individuals are in prison. But critics argue that mass imprisonment has had little impact on the crime rate, is extremely expensive, and has harmed society.

In the aftermath of the fiscal crisis of the late-2000s, many states have done an about-face in terms of correctional policy and have either proposed or enacted various cost-cutting reforms. Many lawmakers who formerly advocated get-tough laws have come to the realization that mass imprisonment is something that their state simply can no longer afford. Along with others, these officials have begun looking for ways to reduce the size of the prison population in a way that will not jeopardize public safety. In addition to greater use of intermediate sanctions and nonprison alternatives to help curb the number of new prison admissions, states have enacted reforms to shorten the average length of stay in prison. "Earned time" policies are one type of reform that has some momentum. These policies reduce the amount of time that people spend in prison when they participate in specific programs. This reform is different from "good time" credits that award individuals for rule-compliant behavior. Earned time is most frequently tied to educational programs but is also associated with work assignments, rehabilitative programs, and meritorious service. Supporters of earned time policies argue that this approach creates an incentive structure that encourages those who are incarcerated to work, participate in programming, and prepare for their eventual release. In many states, however, violent individuals with long sentences are not eligible for earned time credits.[22] See "Decarceration Strategies" for information on other strategies that could reduce the size of prison populations and help relieve budgetary pressures.

Although the falling crime rate, state budget deficits, and economy turmoil may result in fewer incarcerated Americans, the U.S. prison population is very large when compared to the rest of the developed world. Further, not all state corrections systems are taking measures to lower incarceration, so growth still continues in some states (see "For Critical Thinking").

FOR CRITICAL THINKING

As was noted at the beginning of the chapter, officials around the country are looking for ways to reduce the size of their state's prison population. Among the approaches that have been tried thus far include closing or consolidating prison facilities and restructuring existing laws to give judges more discretion when dealing with people on parole.

1. What types of reforms do you believe would be most effective at (a) reducing the number of new prison admissions and (b) reducing the amount of time that people stay in prison? What challenges would you foresee in implementing these policies? Describe the type of convicted individual that these reforms would and would not apply to.
2. How can politicians who are working to balance budgets convince the general public that it is possible to reduce the size of the prison population without jeopardizing public safety?

DEALING WITH OVERCROWDED PRISONS

LO 2

Explain what can be done to deal with the prison population crisis.

Currently, 22 state prison systems operate above capacity. The federal system operates at about 12 percent above capacity.[23] Crowded prisons may violate constitutional standards, decrease access to programs and services, create major administrative problems, and perhaps even increase violence.

Departments of corrections are usually unable to control the flow of people sent to them by the courts. When the number of individuals exceeds prison capacity, administrators face an immediate need for space. To deal with their overcrowded prisons, states adopt a variety of strategies. A mixture of these strategies may best suit the needs of a particular corrections system.

There are four possible approaches that states may take to address overcrowding.[24] Each approach has economic, social, and political costs, and each entails a different amount of time for implementation and impact. For example, the null strategy could be implemented immediately, whereas intermediate sanctions would require several years of development to begin to reduce prison crowding. New construction would take the longest, often seven or eight years.

The Null Strategy

Proponents of the **null strategy** say that nothing should be done, that prisons should be allowed to become increasingly congested. Of course, this may be the most politically acceptable approach in the short run; taxpayers need not pay for new construction. In the long run, however, the resulting crowding may cause prisons to become more disorderly as staff members become demoralized and incarcerated individuals take control. Ultimately, the courts may declare conditions in the facilities unconstitutional and take over their administration.

null strategy The strategy of doing nothing to relieve crowding in prisons, under the assumption that the problem is temporary and will disappear in time.

Opponents of incarceration may support this approach on philosophical grounds because they fear that other strategies will only result in greater numbers being imprisoned. They may reason as well that with the prisons filled, those convicted of nonviolent offenses will be placed on probation or diverted from the system.

The Construction Strategy

The approach that usually comes to mind when legislators or correctional officials confront prison crowding is to expand the size and number of facilities. But given contemporary state budgets and the recent unwillingness of voters in some states to authorize bond issues for new prisons, the **construction strategy** may not be always as feasible as it seems.

construction strategy The strategy of building new facilities to meet the demand for prison space.

Lawmakers in Alabama proposed the construction of three new prison facilities that is estimated to cost a combined $900 million. Supporters argue that the new prisons are necessary to deal with crowding. Additionally, replacing old and dilapidated facilities will result in cost savings estimated to be nearly $80 million annually.[25]

As noted previously, opponents of new construction believe that given the nature of bureaucratic organizations, prison cells will always be filled. Many states that have adopted the construction strategy have found this to be true.

Intermediate Sanctions

Prisons are a costly and scarce resource. Some observers argue that rather than merely building more institutions, corrections should reserve prison space for those convicted

New Jersey's Cooper's Point Park, outside of Camden, used to be a prison. It was repurposed as a public park after the state closed the prison.

of violent offenses who have not been deterred by prior punishments. As discussed in Chapter 9, intermediate sanctions have been advocated as one way to punish in the community those individuals who require some kind of punishment and supervision short of incarceration. Recall that intermediate sanctions include community service, restitution, fines, boot camp, home confinement, and intensive probation supervision. Judges can fashion sentences using combinations of these punishments to fit the needs of the client and the severity of the offense. When applied to individuals convicted of nonserious offenses, intermediate sanctions enjoy a high level of public support.[26]

Some critics contend that even if such alternatives were fully incorporated, they would affect only people convicted of first-time, marginal offenses; they are not appropriate for recidivists if crime control is a goal. They also assert that the availability of intermediate sanctions merely widens the net of social control, with the result that more citizens come under correctional supervision.

Prison Population Reduction

Correctional officials normally have little or no control over the intake of newly convicted individuals. Few state legislatures require that sentencing-guideline framers consider prison capacity when stipulating incarceration lengths. The main ways that correctional officials can reduce prison populations include various "backdoor strategies," such as parole, work release, and good time, to get people out of prison before the end of their term in order to free up space for newcomers. The utility of such strategies is reduced if legislatures mandate that higher portions of sentences be served and reduce good-time allocations.

LO 3

Analyze the impact of prison crowding.

THE IMPACT OF PRISON CROWDING

Prison crowding directly affects the ability of correctional officials to do their work because it decreases the proportion of incarcerated individuals in programs, increases the potential for violence, and greatly strains staff morale. The makeup of the prison population in terms of age, race, and criminal record also affects how institutions are operated. Because prison space is an expensive resource, we can expect—in the absence of expansion—that corrections will be working increasingly with the most-serious individuals, as those convicted of less-violent crimes are placed on probation for lack of cells.

A large percentage of the admissions to prison each year are parole violators—individuals released from prison who have violated the conditions of their parole. Alfred Blumstein and Allen Beck studied court recommitment to prison for new offenses among individuals released in four states: California, New York, Illinois, and

Florida. The percentage returned to prison for new offenses varied greatly. California had a recommitment rate of 67 percent, New York and Illinois each had a rate of 52 percent, and Florida had a rate of 47 percent. The researchers found that 80 percent of California's recommitments stemmed from technical violations, compared with 56 percent in New York, 21 percent in Florida, and 18 percent in Illinois. The four states had similar percentages of people on parole recommitted for new crimes. Some would argue that California's extensive use of technical violations is justified as a crime-prevention measure. However, the researchers argue that compared with the other states, nothing clearly indicates that this strategy makes a meaningful difference in the criminal activity of released individuals.[27]

As a direct consequence of the higher incarceration rate, courts have cited several states for maintaining prisons so crowded that they violate the Eighth Amendment's prohibition against cruel and unusual punishments. Courts have imposed population ceilings, specified the number of individuals per cell, set the minimum floor space per person, and ordered the removal of individuals from overcrowded prisons and jails.

Does crowding cause ill health, misconduct, violent behavior, and recidivism among incarcerated individuals? In measuring the influence of crowding, we must look further than the number of individuals housed in a prison designed for a certain capacity. The architecture of the building, the use of either cells or dormitories, inmate characteristics, management practices, and the past experiences of prison residents with regard to social density all impinge on the problem. At the least, most researchers would agree on the following points. First, individuals housed in large, open-bay dormitories are more likely to visit clinics and to have high blood pressure than are individuals in other housing arrangements (single-bunked cells, double-bunked cells, small dormitories, or large, partitioned dormitories). Second, prisons that contain dormitories have somewhat higher assault rates than do other prisons. Finally, prisons with populations that allow less than 60 square feet per person tend to have high assault rates.[28]

DOES INCARCERATION PAY?

LO 4

Discuss whether incarceration pays.

As noted at the outset of this chapter, the United States ranks very high in the developed world for incarcerating its citizens. Many critics argue that individuals whose crimes do not warrant the severe deprivation of liberty are being sent to prison. They also argue that the policy debate does not consider many of the unintended consequences of imprisonment such as disrupted families and disintegrated communities.

Supporters of incarceration believe that current policies have succeeded in lowering the crime rate. They say that most incarcerated individuals have committed serious crimes, often with violence, and that they are recidivists. Not to incarcerate recidivists, they claim, is costly to society.

Is incarceration misused in the United States? One explanation of why we incarcerate more people is simply that we have more crime than other countries. Studies generally indicate that the United States, on average, experiences higher rates of violent crime.[29]

A major debate among researchers and policy makers concerns the cost-effectiveness of imprisonment. A study published by the Obama administration reported that a $10 billion investment in incarceration would result in a 1 to 4 percent reduction in crime rates (or 55,000 to 340,000 crimes) per year. The same report demonstrated that the same level of investment in hiring police officers would result in a 5 to 16 percent reduction in crime.[30] Discussions of the merits of incarceration must take into account other available strategies for reducing crime.

In light of the reduction in crime over the past decade, are current incarceration policies effective? Some have suggested that the United States has reached a tipping point of "diminishing returns" from its investment in prisons. Others argue that while the increase in imprisonment in the 1980s and 1990s may have prevented crime, a further increase over today's levels is unlikely to do the same. As a Pew Charitable Trusts study notes, "Increasing the proportion of convicted criminals sent to prison, like lengthening time served beyond some point, has produced diminishing marginal returns in crime reduction." This does not mean that incarceration will have no impact—"just that the benefits to public safety of each additional prisoner consistently decreases."[31]

Is the incarceration of *all* convicted individuals cost-effective? Studies in various states raise questions about the social costs of incarcerating "drug-only offenders." These are individuals whose only adult crimes have been drug crimes. Each of these states imprisons a substantial portion of people in this category, but studies have shown that for each one incarcerated, a replacement enters the market. Critics argue that the incarceration of large numbers of such people is not an efficient use of valuable prison space. Some of the cells could be better reserved for high-risk individuals convicted of property and violent offenses.[32]

Again, many people point to the decline in the crime rate since the mid-1990s as an indication that mass incarceration has worked. Is this true? As with other social policy questions, we have no clear-cut answer. Researchers point to many social and economic factors as contributing to the drop in crime, such as shifts in law enforcement, economic expansion, decline in the use of crack cocaine, and demographic changes, in addition to expanded use of incarceration.[33] Bruce Western's analysis of the effects of imprisonment on crime rates shows that mass incarceration helped reduce crime and violence but that the contribution was not large. He estimates that the increase in state prison populations from 725,000 to 1.2 million individuals reduced the rate of serious crime 2 to 5 percent. This decline was purchased for $53 billion in incarceration costs.[34] (See "Careers in Corrections" for more on the job of a research analyst.)

Another question comes out of this debate: Should incarceration policies be judged solely by comparing prison costs with crime reduction? Critics point to the hidden costs to society that incarceration brings. These include families being left without a wage earner and caretaker, the loss of young men to their communities, the redirection of government resources from societal needs such as health care and education, and the damage done to children by the absence of a parent.

Some have also argued that removing young men from their families and friends weakens the networks of informal social control in their communities. Dina Rose and Todd Clear note that incarceration rates are highest in high-crime neighborhoods. Unfortunately, these are the very places where single-parent families live, children are left unsupervised, and property is devoid of guardianship. Mass incarceration may have the unintended consequence of further disrupting informal social controls that help curb crime, especially in socially disorganized areas.[35] Research by Jillian Turanovic and her colleagues, which involved interviewing the caregivers of children whose parents were incarcerated, found support for Rose and Clear's argument. Specifically, the researchers found that a majority of their sample reported that they had experienced financial problems, increased emotional turmoil, strained interpersonal relationships, and difficulty controlling children whose parents were incarcerated. Interestingly, however, Turanovic and associates also found that a not-insignificant portion of their sample reported that parental incarceration had either been positive or resulted in no change at all. For example, some caregivers noted that incarcerating the parents resulted in a more stable and less stressful environment that was more conducive to consistent care and supervision.[36]

CAREERS IN CORRECTIONS

Research Analyst, State Department of Corrections

Nature of the Work

Research analysts conduct research and operate offender-management databases. They also design and maintain department reporting systems, distribute monthly and quarterly reports, and provide data support to management teams. Analysts also provide data support when partnering with universities and other state agencies on research projects.

Required Qualifications

Background qualifications vary by state, but generally candidates must meet the following criteria:

- A master's degree or higher, including multiple college-level classes in statistics
- Ability to operate statistical software programs
- Familiarity with the research methods and statistical techniques commonly used in correctional and evaluation research
- Ability to analyze and interpret data, write clearly, and prepare research reports

Earnings and Job Outlook

In general, government employment is projected to grow. Applicants for such positions, including those in the state department of corrections, may face competition, but individuals with higher educational attainment will prove more competitive. The median annual salary for research analysts was $84,810 in 2019.

More Information

See the Justice Research and Statistics Association website.

Does incarceration pay? Until a host of crucial methodological problems are solved, no definitive answer will emerge. In particular, we need a more accurate estimate of the number of crimes that each felony-convicted individual commits, a better method of calculating the social costs of crime and incarceration, and a way of determining costs that includes correctional capital, operating costs, and indirect costs. Even if we were to refine the method and obtain a more accurate view of the cost–benefit differential, certain political and moral issues would have to be addressed before a rational incarceration policy could be designed (see "For Critical Thinking").

FOR CRITICAL THINKING

Many states have considered releasing nonviolent individuals from prison in an attempt to save money.

1. Releasing individuals from prison will undoubtedly save states money. What other types of benefits might result from planned prison releases? Will the families of those who are incarcerated benefit? Will the business community benefit?
2. Should politicians cut correctional budgets to deal with budgetary shortfalls? Should other items in state budgets, such as health, social services, higher education, elementary education, and secondary education, be cut as well? Where should the majority of cuts come from?

SUMMARY

1 Discuss the explanations for the dramatic increase in the incarceration rate.

Five factors have been put forward to explain the growing incarceration rate. First, there has been a nationwide trend for the police to make more arrests and for the courts to impose incarceration on those convicted of committing crimes. This has led not only to higher numbers of new prison admissions but also to a high number of formerly incarcerated individuals returning to prison.

2 Explain what can be done to deal with the prison population crisis.

Four primary strategies have been identified for dealing with prison crowding. The null strategy is to "do nothing." Another approach is simply to build more prisons. However, many people oppose this strategy because of the financial cost involved. Another strategy is to use intermediate sanctions for people convicted of less-serious, nonviolent offenses and to reserve prison space for violent individuals. Intermediate sanctions

Second, tougher sentencing laws have resulted in people spending more time, on average, in prison. Third, a large number of new prisons have been built in recent decades, greatly expanding society's ability to incarcerate people. Fourth, the war on drugs has resulted in the imprisonment of large numbers of people convicted of drug offenses. Fifth, state and local political factors,such as the proportion of the population who are political conservatives, are also related to higher state incarceration rates.

3 Analyze the impact of prison crowding.

The problem of prison crowding has become more pressing as greater numbers of individuals are sentenced to prison. Correctional officials are responsible for providing humane treatment and living conditions for the individuals in their facilities. The federal courts sometimes intervene when correctional officials fail to meet their responsibilities. Measuring the effects of crowding involves more than looking at capacity; researchers also need to consider the architecture of the building, the use of either cells or dormitories, inmate characteristics, management practices, and the past experiences of people who are in prison.

are an attractive approach because they allow the individual to maintain ties to the community, and the sentencing judge can combine these sanctions to address the needs of the client and the severity of the offense. Critics of the intermediate sanctions approach argue that increasing the availability of such sanctions also serves to widen the net of social control, thus increasing the number of citizens under correctional supervision. Finally, some advocate the reduction of the prison population through various "backdoor strategies," such as parole, work release, and good time.

4 Discuss whether incarceration pays.

Supporters of incarceration believe that incarceration lowers the crime rate. They argue that most incarcerated individuals have committed serious crimes, and many of them are recidivists. If we do not incarcerate these individuals, society pays the price. Opponents of current penal policies note that the United States now incarcerates more of its citizens than does any other developed country in the world. These individuals also believe that many people in correctional facilities do not require imprisonment and that there are many unintended consequences associated with incarceration, such as disrupted families and disintegrated communities. Unfortunately, a host of crucial methodological problems in social science research make it difficult to answer whether incarceration pays.

KEY TERMS

construction strategy (*p. 501*)

null strategy (*p. 501*)

FOR DISCUSSION

1. Which of the many hypotheses advanced to explain the rise in the incarceration rate seems most plausible to you? What other reasons might be added?
2. Which of the strategies for dealing with crowded prisons seems most viable to you? What other strategy might be considered?
3. Imagine that you are incarcerated in a prison that is over capacity. What are some of the factors that will influence the way that you serve your time?
4. How would you respond to the argument that the American prison is becoming a place where the urban poor receive better housing, health care, education, and job training than they do on the outside?
5. The incarceration rate has become a political issue. How would you summarize the two sides?

FOR FURTHER READING

Austin, James, and John Irwin. *It's About Time: America's Imprisonment Binge*. 4th ed. Belmont, CA: Wadsworth, 2012. The authors argue that the "grand imprisonment experiment" that has dominated recent U.S. crime-reduction policy has failed miserably and should be abandoned.

Barker, Vanessa. *The Politics of Imprisonment: How the Democratic Process Shapes the Way America Punishes Offenders*. New York: Oxford University Press, 2009. A skillful analysis showing how New York, California, and Washington developed different punishment regimens as a result of variations in political institutions, democratic traditions, and social trust.

Dagan, David, and Steven Teles. *Prison Break: Why Conservatives Turned Against Mass Incarceration*. New York and Oxford: Oxford University Press, 2016. Discusses recent policy changes away from mass incarceration in conservative states such as Texas and Georgia.

Jacobson, Michael. *Downsizing Prisons*. New York: NYU Press, 2005. Examines specific ways that states have begun to transform their prison systems. Offers policy solutions and strategies that can increase public safety as well as save money.

Wakefield, Sara, and Christopher Wildeman. *Children of the Prison Boom: Mass Incarceration and the Future of American Inequality*. New York and Oxford: Oxford University Press, 2014. Documents the deleterious effects of paternal incarceration on the lives of children, including behavioral disorders, mental health problems, infant mortality, and homelessness.

Western, Bruce. *Punishment and Inequality in America*. New York: Russell Sage Foundation, 2006. Argues that mass incarceration contributed a little to the decline in the crime rate but that the gain in public safety was purchased at a cost to the economic well-being and family life of poor minority communities.

NOTES

1 E. Ann Carson, *Prisoners in 2018* (Washington, DC: U.S. Government Printing Office, 2020), 9; Roy Walmsley, *World Prison Population List*, 12th ed. (London: King's College, International Centre for Prison Studies, 2018).

2 Pew Charitable Trusts, *Public Safety, Public Spending: Forecasting America's Prison Population 2007–2011* (Washington, DC: Author, 2007), ii.

3 Tracey Kyckelhahn, *State Corrections Expenditures, 1982–2010* (Washington, DC: U.S. Government Printing Office, 2012).

4 Jolie McCullough, "As the Texas Prison Population Shrinks, the State is Closing Two more Lockups," *The Texas Tribune*, www.texastribune.org/2020/02/20/texas-closing-two-prisons/, February 20, 2020.

5 Carson, *Prisoners in 2018*, p. 9.

6 Nazgol Ghandnoosh, *U.S. Prison Population Trends: Massive Buildup and Modest Decline* (Washington, DC: The Sentencing Project, 2019), 3.

7 Ibid., pp. 25–26.

8 Ibid., pp. 27–28.

9 Federal Bureau of Investigation, *Crime in the United States 2000*, 216, https://ucr.fbi.gov/crime-in-the-u.s/2000, retrieved May 12, 2020.

10 Federal Bureau of Investigation, *Crime in the United States 2018*, Table 29, https://ucr.fbi.gov/crime-in-the-u.s/2018/crime-in-the-u.s.-2018/tables/table-29, retrieved May 12, 2020.

11 Carson, *Prisoners in 2018*, p. 13.

12 Ibid., p. 14.

13 Brian Reaves, *Felony Defendants in Large Urban Counties, 2009—Statistical Tables* (Washington, DC: U.S. Government Printing Office, 2013), 30.

14 James J. Stephan, *Census of State and Federal Correctional Facilities, 1995* (Washington, DC: U.S. Government Printing Office, 1997), iv; James J. Stephan, *Census of State and Federal Correctional Facilities, 2005* (Washington, DC: U.S. Government Printing Office, 2008), 1.

15 Sarah Lawrence and Jeremy Travis, *The New Landscape of Imprisonment: Mapping America's Prison Expansion* (Washington, DC: Urban Institute, 2004), 10.

16 William Spelman, "Crime, Cash, and Limited Options: Explaining the Prison Boom," *Criminology & Public Policy 8* (February 2009): 29–77.

17 Jennifer Bronson and E. Ann Carson, *Prisoners in 2017* (Washington, DC: U.S. Government Printing Office, 2019), 21 and 23.

18 Alfred Blumstein, "Bringing Down the U.S. Prison Population," *Prison Journal* 91 (2011): 12S–26S.

19 Carson, *Prisoners in 2018*, pp. 11–12.

20 Peter Wagner, *Detaining for Dollars: Federal Aid Follows Inner-city Prisoners to Rural Town Coffers* (Springfield, MA: Prison Policy Initiative, 2002), 4.

21 David F. Greenberg and Valerie West, "State Prison Populations and Their Growth, 1971–1991," *Criminology 39* (August 2001): 615–54.

22 Alison Lawrence, *Cutting Corrections Costs: Earned Time Policies for State Prisoners* (Washington, DC: National Conference of State Legislatures, 2009).

23 Carson, *Prisoners in 2018*, p. 25.

24 Alfred Blumstein, "Prisons," in *Crime*, edited by James Q. Wilson and Joan Petersilia (San Francisco: Institute for Contemporary Studies, 1995), 402.

25 Mike Cason, "Alabama Will Build 3 Prisons for Men, Ivey Announces," *AL.com*, www.al.com/news/2019/02/alabama-will-build-3-prisons-for-men-ivey-announces-do-not-publish.html, February 12, 2019.

26 Christopher Hartney and Susan Marchionna, *Attitudes of U.S. Voters Toward Nonserious Offenders and Alternatives to Incarceration* (Oakland, CA: National Council on Crime and Delinquency, 2009), 6.

27 Alfred Blumstein and Allen J. Beck, "Reentry as a Transient State between Liberty and Recommitment," in *Prisoner Reentry and Crime in America*, edited by Jeremy Travis and Christy Visher (New York: Cambridge University Press, 2005), 76.

28 Gerald G. Gaes, "The Effects of Overcrowding in Prison," in *Crime and Justice: A Review of Research*, vol. 6, edited by Michael Tonry and Norval Morris (Chicago: University of Chicago Press, 1985), 95.

29 Philip Cook and Mataliya Khmilevska, "Cross-national Patterns in Crime Rates," *in Crime and Justice: A Review of Research*, vol. 33, edited by Michael Tonry (Chicago: University of Chicago Press, 2005), 331–46.

30 Executive Office of the President, *Economic Perspectives on Incarceration and the Criminal Justice System* (Washington, DC: President's Council of Economic Advisors, 2016), 6.

31 Pew Charitable Trusts, *Public Safety*, p. 24.

32 Anne M. Piehl, Bert Useem, and John J. DiIulio Jr., *Right-Sizing Justice: A Cost–Benefit Analysis of Imprisonment in Three States* (New York: Center for Civic Innovation at the Manhattan Institute, 1999).

33 Jenni Gainsborough and Marc Mauer, *Diminishing Returns: Crime and Incarceration in the 1990s* (Washington, DC: The Sentencing Project, 2000).

34 Bruce Western, *Punishment and Inequality in America* (New York: Russell Sage Foundation, 2006), 187.

35 Dina R. Rose and Todd R. Clear, "Incarceration, Social Capital, and Crime: Implications for Social Disorganization Theory," *Criminology* 36 (August 1998): 441–80.

36 Jillian J. Turanovic, Nancy Rodriguez, and Travis C. Pratt, "The Collateral Consequences of Incarceration Revisited: A Qualitative Analysis of the Effects on Caregivers of Children of Incarcerated Parents," *Criminology* 50 (2012): 913–59.

CHAPTER 19

Race, Ethnicity, and Corrections

© Danielle Parhizkaran/NorthJersey.com via Imagn Content Services, LLC

Black Lives Matter protests drew large crowds across the nation condemning the death of George Floyd at the hands of Minneapolis police

DURING THE SUMMER OF 2020, IN THE MIDST OF AN INTERNATIONAL COVID-19 PANDEMIC IN WHICH MORE THAN 100,000 PEOPLE HAD ALREADY DIED, HUNDREDS OF THOUSANDS OF AMERICANS TOOK TO STREETS TO PROTEST RACISM. The immediate spark for these demonstrations was the killing of George Floyd, when a Minneapolis policeman kneeled on his neck for almost nine minutes, strangling him to death while a crowd watched, begging him to stop. But the simmering coals of injustice spread well beyond police brutality to include inequities in health care, housing, education—every realm of public life. On every list of grievances was the problem of racial disparities in mass incarceration.

Indeed, racial disparity in the correctional system is a daunting problem. African American men born in the 1960s are more likely to go to prison than to finish a four-year degree or serve in the military.[1] About one-fifth of African Americans in prison are serving a life sentence.[2] Some have argued that the U.S. prison system is designed as a way to imprison African American men,[3] though not everyone agrees. Yet nobody can dispute the disparate impact that the prison system has had on young men of color. The social consequences of this disparity must trouble us all.

With all this, incarceration rates for African Americans are dropping faster than rates for Whites or Hispanics. Between the years 2008 and 2018, the decline in the rate of black adults in prison was twice that of white adults.[4] This change is particularly true for black women in prison, who are now outnumbered by white women. Not that there is imprisonment equality: African Americans are still locked up at rates much higher than other racial groups. Black women are almost two times more likely to end up in prison than white women; black men are almost six times more likely to be in prison than white men. But the trends cited above mean that the size of the discrepancy is declining: The gap in the rate of imprisonment shrank by 35 percent for black men and more than 50 percent for black women. What is going on?

It is hard to know for sure. Nationally, as we said in Chapter 1, the generation-long growth in imprisonment seems to be waning. To the extent that this reduction in the use of prison reflects changes in policies of enforcing drug laws, it may mean fewer African Americans in prison because so much of the "drug war" was waged in predominantly black neighborhoods and affected those residents most significantly.[5] In fact, the much larger reduction in imprisonment for black women is consistent with the idea of a slowdown in the war on drugs because so many women go to prison for drug-related crimes. For most of the 40-year expansion of the prison system, race was one of the core issues in the size of the growth, but since 2010, that does not seem to be the case.[6]

Does this mean the penal system has become racially fair? That conclusion is not warranted. As we shall see in this chapter, there are many ways in which race remains an important issue in the corrections system. If we are to have a justice system without racial bias, a lot of work must still be done.

In this chapter we explore how issues about race and ethnicity affect the corrections system. The implications are often complex. Further, strong feelings abound concerning race, class, crime, and punishment; often, the debate produces more heat than light. We begin by discussing the concepts of race and ethnicity. We then focus on the indisputable fact that African Americans and Hispanics are subjected to the criminal justice system at considerably higher rates than are other ethnic and racial groups. Two questions arise: What are the causes of this disparity? What are its main effects?

LEARNING OBJECTIVES

After reading this chapter, you should be able to . . .

1. Analyze the meaning of race and ethnicity.
2. Explain how varying visions of race and punishment influence our thinking on this issue.
3. Describe the significance of race and punishment.

RACE IN THE CORRECTIONAL CONTEXT

Race and ethnicity are pervasive themes in contemporary U.S. culture. In no area are these concepts more significant than in punishment. For one thing, people of color are far more likely than whites to be caught up in the criminal justice system. Today, African American adults are incarcerated in U.S. prisons and jails at a rate of 1,501 per 100,000 and Hispanic adults at a rate of 797—compared to white adults at a rate of 268.[7] African Americans make up almost 33 percent of the prison population but only about 13 percent of all U.S. residents. African Americans are seven times more likely than whites to have been incarcerated at some time in a state or federal prison. When all punishments—probation, intermediate sanctions, incarceration, and parole—are taken into account, more than one in three African American men in their twenties are currently under correctional supervision.

These patterns begin early. Among African Americans below age 18, rates of referrals to juvenile court are 50 percent higher than rate for whites.[8] People under 18 who are sentenced to confinement are 20 percent more likely to be African American than white.[9] In America's inner cities, the figures that emerge are astounding. In cities such as Washington, D.C., and Baltimore, Maryland, more than half of all African American adults under 40 are under some form of correctional control.

Figures such as these have alarming implications. For many Americans—especially young men of color and their families—the penal system is not an abstraction but a reality of everyday life (this issue is discussed at greater length in Chapter 22). Those who do not report to correctional authorities probably have a brother, an uncle, or a father who does. Under these circumstances, the law represents a continuum of state presence, from the police on the streets to the courthouse and jail downtown to the prison out in the countryside.

This pervasiveness of corrections in the lives of people of color has evolved gradually, fueled by the 1980s war on drugs and the enormous growth of our penal system. Since 1973, the overall correctional population has increased by more than 600 percent and has disproportionately affected Americans of color and their families. But sheer numbers do not tell the full story. In the everyday thinking of many Americans, crime—particularly violent crime—is a racial phenomenon. When white Americans imagine burglars, robbers, or rapists, they often think of African American men, and they think fearfully of African American men in general. When George Zimmerman shot and killed Trayvon Martin in Florida in 2012, he claimed self-defense—even though Martin was unarmed. Likewise, when Ahmaud Arbery was shot and killed by Gregory and Thomas McMichael when he was out taking a jog, the killers claimed they were chasing a potential felon. To some, the mere presence of a black man wearing a hoodie, walking in a white neighborhood at night, or running through a white neighborhood during the day, is ground for suspicion.

As we will see, people have differing views about where these images come from and how accurate they are. Certainly, that so many white Americans feel this way is itself an important social fact. It means that ordinary African American or Hispanic men walking down the street, minding their own business, will frequently find themselves confronted with suspicious looks or fearful, even hostile, glares from fellow citizens. This kind of racism, as well as the multiple instances of police brutality and murders of black Americans, has been a major impetus for the Black Lives Matter movement.[10] How many whites have ever crossed the street in order to avoid walking near a group of young men of color who somehow seemed menacing? Where did the notion to fear young men of color come from?

THE CONCEPTS OF RACE AND ETHNICITY

LO 1

Analyze the meaning of race and ethnicity.

The United States is a multiracial, multiethnic society. From colonial times, through the period of slave trade, and then through the mass migrations from all over the world, ours has been one of the most diverse societies ever to exist. By culture and by law, we are all Americans, but we are not a melting pot. Rather, we are a mosaic, with each new immigrant group seeking its place in the broader community. Where once immigrants felt great pressure to become assimilated into the dominant Euro-American society and to sacrifice their own cultural identity, the trend since the end of World War II has been to honor the many cultures that the nation comprises.

Although we can point to many immigrant groups who have successfully moved up the socioeconomic ladder and into the middle class, we know that many members of both old and new groups have not. Native Americans, who lived here long before the arrival of Europeans, were decimated by disease and war, and then finally herded to reservations, where many have lived precariously. African Americans, most of whose ancestors were brought to this country as slaves, have been held back by racial discrimination and economic exploitation. Newer groups such as Hispanics and Asians have also faced discrimination, have had to work at low-wage jobs, and have been otherwise restricted in their efforts to achieve.

Race and ethnicity are complex concepts. **Race** is usually assumed to be a biological concept that divides humankind into categories related to skin color and other physical features. However, social scientists also look at the ways in which groups define themselves and are defined by others. Today, the concept of race is controversial: That so many Americans have interracial backgrounds makes accepting a purely biological approach difficult. As the American Association of Physical Anthropologists has put it, "Pure races, in the sense of genetically homogenous populations, do not exist in the human species today, nor is there any evidence that they have ever existed in the past."[11] Scientists agree that whatever biological differences there may be between the races, they do not generate differences in behavior that have criminal justice implications.

race Traditionally, a biological concept used to distinguish groups of people by their skin color and other physical features.

Therefore, race is controversial to the extent that it has political and social implications. For example, many transfers of funds from the federal government to the states for social programs are calculated according to race-based formulas.

Ethnicity is a concept used to classify people according to their cultural characteristics—language, religion, and group traditions. Ethnicity is usually reported by subjects themselves, rather than stemming from an outside observer making a visual identification, as in the case of race. Ethnic groups exist among white Americans—for example, Irish, Italians, Poles—as well as among the black, Asian, and Hispanic communities.

ethnicity A concept used to distinguish people according to their cultural characteristics—language, religion, and group traditions.

In the Northeast and in Florida, sizable black communities are made up of immigrants from Africa and the West Indies whose culture differs from that of the larger group of African Americans who migrated to the northern cities from the agricultural South. Asians have immigrated from many countries and are multiethnic, multilingual, and multiracial. Hispanics are also multiethnic and multiracial. We use the category "Hispanic" to distinguish Spanish-speaking Americans, yet this group is made up of people, some of whom are black and some white, from Puerto Rico, Mexico, Cuba, and many other countries.

In this chapter we focus primarily on correctional issues that relate to African Americans. Members of this group are under correctional supervision out of proportion to their numbers in the general population, so issues of racial and ethnic disparities are most apparent with regard to these Americans.

LO 2

Explain how varying visions of race and punishment influence our thinking on this issue.

VISIONS OF RACE AND PUNISHMENT

disparity The unequal treatment of one group by the criminal justice system, compared with the treatment accorded other groups.

discrimination Differential treatment of an individual or group without reference to its behavior or qualifications.

African Americans and Hispanics are subjected to the criminal justice system at much higher rates than is the white majority. A central question is whether these racial and ethnic disparities result from discrimination. A **disparity** is a difference between groups that can be explained by legitimate factors. For example, the fact that 18-to 24-year-old men are arrested out of proportion to their numbers in the general population is a disparity explained by the legal factor that they commit more crime. It is not thought to be the result of a public policy of singling out young men for arrest. **Discrimination** occurs when groups are differentially treated without regard to their behavior or qualifications. For example, discrimination occurs if people of color are routinely sentenced to prison regardless of their criminal history.

Explanations for the cause of racial disparities in the criminal justice system can be roughly grouped according to three themes. Some observers argue that these disparities result from the system operating as a giant sieve to differentiate people who have contact with the criminal justice system so that more men of color end up under correctional authority because they commit more crimes. Others claim that the sieve is racist and that the system treats men of color more harshly than it does white men. And still others argue that the criminal justice system operates within the broader context of our society's racism and merely represents a vehicle for its expression. We will consider each of these views in turn.

Differential Criminality

Nobody denies the disparity concerning people of color in the criminal justice system. However, there is controversy over whether the disparity results from discrimination. In their informative book *The Color of Justice,* Samuel Walker, Cassia Spohn, and Miriam DeLone point out that the criminal justice system is supposed to take into account differences between people who have committed serious crimes and those whose crimes have been petty, and such considerations might result in disparity.[12] Logically, then, more people of color will end up in corrections if they commit worse crimes and have more-serious prior records than do whites.

This general view covers a range of perspectives. The most extreme versions contend that some people are, by nature, more predisposed to commit crimes.[13] This position implies the existence of something akin to a "criminal class" of people who constitute an ongoing danger to society. When this view incorporates a conclusion that one of the predisposing factors toward criminality is having dark skin, we can see why the view is vulnerable to charges of racism.[14] In fact, recent studies have shown that when black children get in trouble in school, those with darker skin tone have a greater chance of being expelled—and this relationship is particularly strong for girls.[15] It is hard to reconcile findings such as these with the view that sociobiological factors are what result in large numbers of Hispanics and African Americans being processed by the criminal justice system.

self-report study An investigation of behavior (such as criminal activity) based on subjects' responses to questions concerning activities in which they have engaged.

In fact, the evidence to support a view that people of color are inherently more likely to be involved in crime is paltry at best and nonexistent at worst. **Self-report studies,** in which individuals are asked to report on their own criminal behavior, have shown that nearly everyone admits to having committed a crime during his or her lifetime, although most people are never caught. Table 19.1 shows the results of the first self-report study, conducted with a cross-section of citizens in 1947, in which an astonishing 99 percent of respondents admitted to at least one criminal offense since turning 16.[16] A more-recent study of 4,000 public school students—now considered a classic and one of the most heavily cited studies in criminology—found that 49 percent of African American youths and 44 percent of white youths reported having committed a delinquent act during the preceding year.[17] Some self-report studies of illicit drug use have found that whites are slightly more likely than African Americans to admit to using illegal substances, and it has been estimated that there are five times more

TABLE 19.1 Percentage of Men and Women Who Admitted Committing Offenses, by Type of Crime, 1947

Most adults have committed an offense in their lifetime.

Type of Crime	Men	Women
Petty theft	89%	83%
Disorderly conduct	85	76
Malicious mischief	84	81
Assault	49	5
Tax evasion	57	40
Robbery	11	1
Falsification and fraud	46	34
Criminal libel	36	29
Concealed weapons	35	3
Auto theft	26	8
Other grand theft	13	11
Burglary	17	4

Source: Adapted from James Wallerstein and Clement J. Wyle, "Our Law-Abiding Law-Breakers," *Probation* 35 (April 1947): 112.

white drug users than African American ones. Yet the number of whites in prison for drugs is only less than 20 percent higher than African Americans, roughly the same number of whites, blacks, and Hispanics are sentenced to more than one year in state prison for drug offenses.[18] Almost half of black (25 percent) and three-fifths Hispanic (59 percent) people in federal prisons in 2018 were convicted of drug offenses.[19] Once again, the argument that African Americans are more criminal than whites by nature is not sustained by the evidence.

Less-stringent versions of this argument rest on the fact that criminality is related to socio-economic disadvantage and that many people of color suffer that to a great degree. Figure 19.1 shows the percentage of children of whites, African Americans, and Hispanics who live in poverty; Figure 19.2 compares the family incomes of various racial groups.

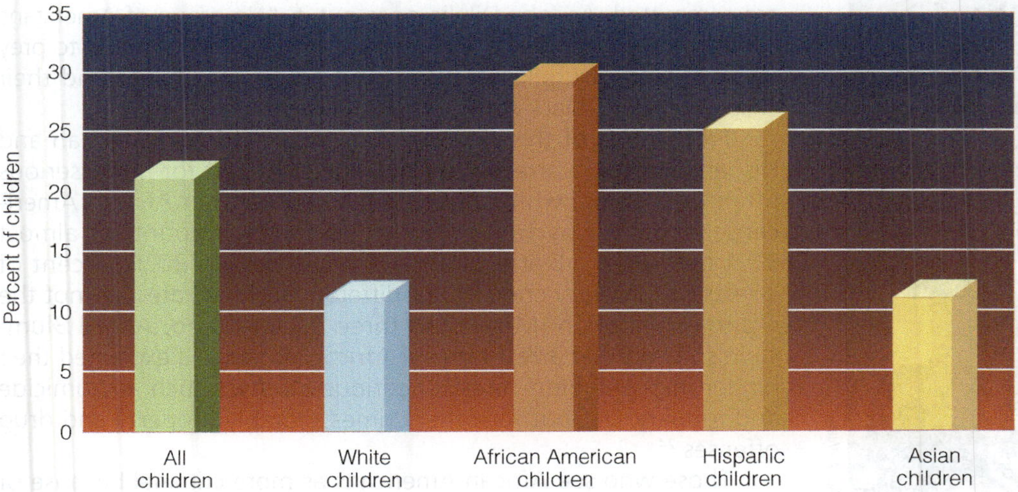

FIGURE 19.1 Children in Poverty, by Race and Ethnicity, 2018

One of the most disturbing aspects of contemporary U.S. society is the increasing proportion of children who live in poverty.

Source: Chil Trends, *Children in Poverty,* https://www.childtrends.org/indicators/children-in-poverty, 2020.

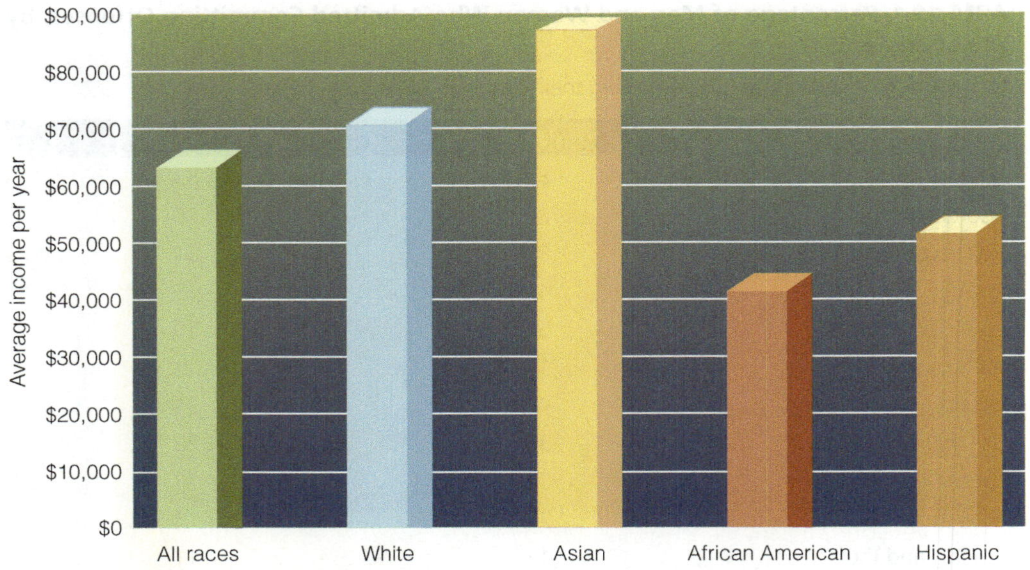

FIGURE 19.2 Mean Annual Household Income by Race, 2018

Disparity of income continues to be a basic characteristic of U.S. society.

Source: U.S. Census Bureau, Current Population Survey, 2018 and 2019 Annual Social and Economic Supplements.

Rafael Ben-Ari/Alamy Stock Photo

▲ *Aggressive policing practices, especially the routine use of "stop and frisk," can put a strain on relationships between the police and the community.*

These figures show the vast racial disparity in wealth in the United States, and studies show that this disparity is increasing.[20] Young people who live in poverty and disadvantage may develop what has been called the "code of the street," which includes a greater willingness to use violence.[21]

Social problems such as poverty, single-parent families, and unemployment contribute to higher crime rates. It is logical, then, to expect Hispanic and African American men to engage in more crimes than do whites. Not only do these higher criminality rates result from disadvantage; they also reproduce it—the victims are most often other people of color who live in the communities where the crimes are committed. As John Dilulio once put it, "No group of Americans suffers more when violent and repeat criminals are permitted to prey upon decent, struggling, law-abiding inner-city citizens and their children than ... black America's silent majority."[22]

Proponents of this view point out that African American and Hispanic men are arrested more frequently and for more-serious offenses than are white men. The FBI reports that African Americans—about 13 percent of the population—account for almost 37.4 percent of all arrests for violent crime and 30.1 percent of arrests for property crime.[23] But differential arrest rates are not the entire explanation. More than three decades ago, Alfred Blumstein showed that arrest rates of African Americans explained their higher imprisonment rates for serious offenses such as homicide and robbery, but not for other crimes, notably property and drug offenses.[24]

Those who see African Americans as more criminal because of social factors differ in their solution to the problem. Some, such as Dilulio, think we can do little other than impose long prison sentences, especially for repeaters, and "let 'em rot."[25] They say we need to focus our resources on today's youths in order to prevent their getting into serious crime in the first place. Others argue that we need new crime control policies that work to reduce the social problems contributing to the higher crime rates of African Americans and Hispanics. Still others contend that the social disadvantage under which people have to live should be taken into account when they are sentenced.

A Racist Criminal Justice System

Racial discrimination occurs if people who are otherwise similar in their criminality are treated differently by the criminal justice system because of their race. African Americans account for just over one-fourth of all arrests while making up only 13 percent of the population,[26] but the fact that people of color are arrested more often than whites does not mean they are more prone to crime. For example, African Americans are arrested for drug offenses at more than twice their rate in the population.[27] Yet studies show that African American youths "have substantially lower rates of use of most licit and illicit drugs,"[28] and 1 out of 11 poor white youths say that they sold illegal drugs in the previous years, compared to only 1 in 20 poor African American youths.[29] Sentencing for drug crimes also contributes to the high rates of incarceration of African Americans. At one time, federal sentences for the possession of crack cocaine were 100 times more severe than for the powder version, and similar disparities apply in many states.[30] Yet scientists have shown that the pharmacology of cocaine is the same for both its powder and crystal forms, and the physiological effects are identical.[31] The only difference between these possession crimes is that whites tend to use cocaine in its powder form, whereas people of color tend to use crack cocaine.

In 2009 President Barack Obama declared that "the disparity between sentencing crack and powder-based cocaine is wrong and should be completely eliminated."[32] A year later, he signed the Fair Sentencing Act of 2010, eliminating mandatory minimum sentencing for simple possession of crack and vastly reducing the other sentencing disparities between crack and powder cocaine. But this was hardly a rousing victory for reformers: The penalty for crack is now 18 times more severe than for powder, and state systems frequently mirror the federal system. Much of the nation's racial disparity in rates of incarceration has resulted from drug policies that select and punish African Americans at far higher rates than whites.

These discrepancies do not center on drugs alone. Poor male whites ages 15–18 are one-third more likely to report they have attacked someone or stolen something and almost half again as likely to have used drugs and alcohol (except marijuana) as their African American counterparts. Nonetheless, African American youths are more likely to be arrested for *all* these crimes.[33] As we showed in Chapter 14, rates of confinement for juvenile crime have been dropping dramatically for more than a decade. But here the disparities are as striking as those for adults: The institutional commitment rate for blacks is more than four times higher than that for whites, even though their arrest rate is just twice as high.[34] In fact, poor white youths end up incarcerated less often than rich black youths.[35]

Such facts raise questions about bias in the criminal justice system (see "Do the Right Thing"). Do police, prosecutors, and judges

DO THE RIGHT THING

You are the chief judge of a criminal court that serves Elm Hill, an inner-city, 90 percent minority area. You are very proud of your probation department, which has been a beacon of quality for over two decades. The long-term chief probation officer, who is largely successful for building such an excellent department, has announced her retirement after 39 years of service.

You have to appoint her successor. There are two outstanding assistant chief probation officers. Both have had very strong careers, they enjoy the confidence of the peers in the office, and you are certain that both would do a very good job. One, Michael Frank, is black, has 17 years of experience on the job, and scores well on the civil service exam. He grew up in Elm Hill and still lives there. The other, Jeffrey Baker, is white, has 20 years of experience, and scores at near the top of the civil service exam. He lives in a nearby suburb.

The other judges in the courthouse assume that you will follow the civil service scores. Several probation officers have said to you privately that it will hurt morale not to take seniority into account. Yet the retiring chief has advised you to appoint Mr. Frank. As she said, "While both Frank and Baker can do this job ably, nothing will inspire the confidence of the community more than to have the next chief be a person who shares their background."

WRITING ASSIGNMENT: Discuss what you would do if you were in a position to appoint the new chief probation officer. Give reasons for your decision.

treat whites and people of color equally? A great deal of research has been conducted on race and criminal justice processing, but no simple conclusions can be drawn. Some believe that evidence of overt discrimination is weak, at best showing only small amounts of bias in the decisions of police officers and judges. In fact, there is some evidence that police are less likely to use lethal force against blacks than whites.[36] Nonetheless, evidence mounts that small decision-making biases at each stage of the justice system add up to a much larger total effect on punishments.[37]

The disparity between crime rates and punishment patterns is key to the claim by some scholars that the criminal justice system is biased against minority groups. The rate of incarceration of lower-class and minority citizens is indeed greater than even their higher rates of offending would justify. In every U.S. state, African American incarceration rates are at least twice as high as those for whites.[38]

Recent writers have pointed out an irony regarding these disparities. They were not the simple result of a call from white political leaders to police black communities more aggressively. Many of the sentencing reforms that have produced such profound racial differences in punishment came about, in part, from voices of outrage about violent crime from leaders of the African American community. There was a call for policy makers to take black victimization seriously and to use focused law enforcement to help these communities fight crime and drugs.[39]

Whatever the public opinion has been, there can be no doubt that people of color are more likely to be processed in the criminal justice system. Figure 19.3 compares the race of people who committed a crime, as identified by victims, to the race of arrestees and shows that the odds of African Americans being arrested are slightly higher than those of whites. It seems reasonable to conclude that small, seemingly insignificant disparities at each stage of the criminal justice process may add up to significant overall disparities. One national study concluded that racial differences in crimes and arrests explained the racial disparity in incarceration rates for serious and violent crimes, but not for drug crimes, weapon crimes, and aggravated assault.[40]

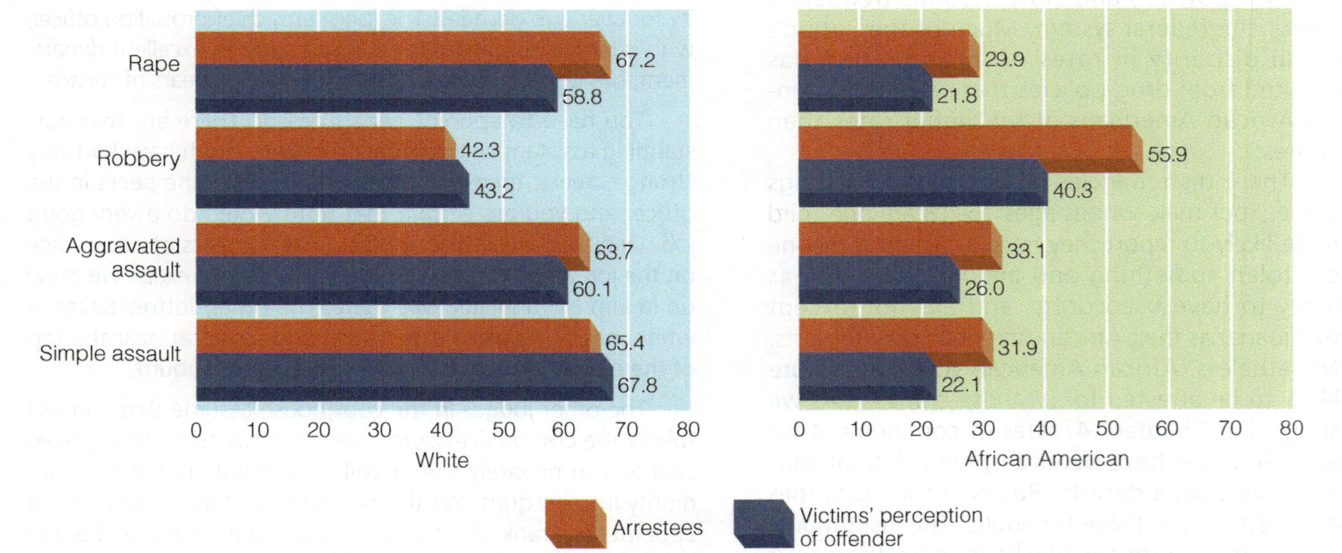

FIGURE 19.3 Comparison of Uniform Crime Reports and National Crime Victimization Survey Data on Race

The victim's perception of the race of the person who committed the crime often differs from the race of the person who was arrested.

Source: Samuel Walker, Cassia Spohn, and Miriam DeLone, *The Color of Justice: Race, Ethnicity, and Crime in America*, 6th ed. (Belmont, CA: Wadsworth, 2018), 71.

Criminal justice officials need not act in overtly racist ways in order to produce this kind of gap between arrest rates and punishment rates. At each stage of the process, the criminal justice system operates according to principles that, although not overtly discriminatory to men of color, may tend to disadvantage them. The number of minority arrests may be greater because police patrols are more heavily concentrated in residential areas where nonwhites live, areas where drug use may be more open and more likely to be observed by police. Police are more likely to be proactive in stopping and searching black men than whites.[41] This kind of aggressive policing of poor neighborhoods leads many minority citizens to develop negative attitudes toward the law. Because pretrial-release practices take into account factors such as employment status, living arrangements, and prior criminal record, the underemployed and unemployed tend to be unable to make bail and thus languish in jail awaiting trial. Prosecutors may also be less likely to dismiss charges against poor, unemployed, single men—many of whom are African American— especially if they have a prior record. And poor people are less likely to have a private attorney. Research has shown that all these factors are related to sentence severity.

These step-by-step decisions of the system mean that African Americans, the unemployed, and the poor often appear at sentencing hearings with more-extensive prior records and fewer prospects for reform. Thus, what appears discriminatory may simply represent the functioning of an impersonal bureaucratic system. After all, evidence of discrimination in sentencing is disputable and ambiguous."[42]

Perhaps criminal justice system officials, acting under the daily pressures and routines of bureaucratic decision making, use filtering criteria to move cases along. (See "Do Evidence-Based Decision-Making Systems Reinforce Racial Disparities in the Criminal Justice System?")
The criteria they use would be difficult to dispute: When a crime is not serious, when the person who is arrested appears contrite and unlikely to repeat the offense, when the evidence is weak or contradictory, or when the accused person has a respectable prior history, then the system chooses to dismiss the case or downgrade the punishment. Is this truly racism? Perhaps it depends on how one defines the term. But there is no denying that people of color receive harsher outcomes at important stages of the justice system, from arrest[43] to juvenile waiver[44] to charging for crimes[45] to plea bargaining[46] to adult sentencing.[47] That is, criminal justice operates as a system, and any one of the many decisions in the system can contribute to racial disparity.

Some reformers have considered ways to eliminate racism from the criminal justice system. The solution depends on how the problem is defined. If racism exists because individuals within the system are themselves racist, then the solution is plain: These people need to adjust their attitudes or else be removed from their jobs. The problem is a bit more complicated if the problem is not racist people but disadvantageous rules and practices, such as treating the unemployed less leniently than those who have jobs. Here the solution would lie in revamping the decision-making criteria to exclude biased factors and in finding ways to control the discretion of officials to use the new criteria.

A Racist Society

Some people claim that eliminating racism from the criminal justice system is not likely to occur because the system is embedded in a larger racist society. In fact, the strongest voices claim that the system operates as an instrument of such racism.

There is indeed evidence of broader racism in the way society asks the criminal justice system to operate. For example, some have claimed that prison is used as a place to confine people who cannot find jobs when the economy falters—and many of these unemployed are African American men. Michael Tonry argued that the 1990s war on drugs was "foreordained to affect disadvantaged black youths

FOCUS ON

CORRECTIONAL POLICY: Do Evidence-Based Decision-Making Systems Reinforce Racial Disparities in the Criminal Justice System?

In the era of "evidence-based policies," system decision makers increasingly rely upon "structured decision-making tools" to guide their decisions. These tools provide lists of factors that, by policy, should be used to make discretionary decisions, such as prior record, and they oblige the decision maker to consider those factors with prespecified weights in arriving at a decision. Most often, these tools, called "instruments," provide an empirical and objective assessment of a person's "risk to the community," and this assessment then shapes the eventual decision. Objective decision-making instruments have become common at all stages of justice decisions, from sentencing to prison classification, from parole release to community supervision.

Advocates say that the use of "instruments" improves decisions. It makes decision makers less likely to be idiosyncratic because they all work from the same set of written policy factors. It makes them more accurate, too, because the assessments of risk are based on science rather than instinct. But critics wonder if instruments also tend to reinforce the underlying racial disparities in the system. The most important factors in these instruments are always measures of prior record—including arrests that never resulted in a conviction. These critics point out that law enforcement policies, especially regarding drug law enforcement, make poor people, especially those of color, more likely to get arrested by the police. Once the record is there, it places the person under ever more strict correctional control, in prison or in the community. The strictness of control, in turn, puts a person under greater surveillance and therefore more susceptibleto new arrests and violations. It becomes a vicious cycle—instruments point to risk, leading to greater correctional intrusion, longer sentences, and more risk of exposure to law enforcement.

Other issues associated with race can also become factors in an instrument: educational attainment, economic stability, familial criminality, employment history, and the like. It is at least worrisome that the factors in an instrument could legitimate the consequences of underlying social inequality. In fact, recent scholars have started thinking of incarceration as "contagious" in that young people who are exposed to it through parents and family are much more likely to experience it as adults. Perhaps people in this circumstance are more "at risk," but much of this is not of their own doing.

No less an authority than former U.S. Attorney General Eric Holder has questioned the use of instruments, speculating that "they inadvertently undermine our efforts to ensure individualized and equal justice."

This is a new debate in the "evidence-based" justice movement. Until the advocates can demonstrate that these instruments are not only free of bias but also do not tend to exacerbate existing bias, critics will doubt their value.

Sources: Kristian Lum, Samarth Swarup, Stephen Eubank, and James Hawdon, "The Contagious Nature of Imprisonment: An Agent-Based Model to Explain Racial Disparities in Incarceration Rates," *Journal of the Royal Society Interface* 11 (no. 98, 2014); Julia Angwin, Jeff Larson, Surya Mattu, and Lauren Kirchner, "Machine Bias," *ProPublica,* May 23, 2016; Jennifer Skeem and Christopher T. Lowenkamp, "Risk, Race, and Recidivism: Predictive Bias and Disparate Impact," *Criminology* 54 (no. 4, 2016): 680–712.

disproportionately [and was based on] the willingness of the drug war's planners to sacrifice young black Americans."[48]

Many observers further believe that the relationship between racism and the criminal justice system is reciprocal. Devah Pager's groundbreaking studies of employment discrimination make the point that young African American men who have *no* criminal record are less likely to get entry-level jobs than are young white men *with* prison records. In this way, incarceration and racism mutually reinforce each other. The presence of a criminal record further damages the job prospects of young African American men, but the social stigma of being a young African American man is already a barrier to employment.[49] It becomes a catch-22. When an African American with a criminal record fails to disclose it at a job interview, he faces disciplinary action if it is discovered in a routine background check. But if he has no record, and no background check is required, the potential employer may assume he has a record anyway.[50] Ironically, evidence suggests that performing a background check is advantageous to African American men applying for a job, even when they have a record.[51] Whatever issues there are in the employability of African American men, especially those who are undereducated, the large number of them who go to prison reinforces the stereotype (see "Incarceration

FOCUS ON

CORRECTIONAL POLICY: Incarceration and Inequality

The rate of incarceration in the United States varies dramatically by race. Blacks are locked up at a rate of 1,745 per 100,000—by comparison, the Hispanic rate is 820 and the white rate is 478. In other words, while Hispanics are almost twice as likely as whites to be in prison, blacks are almost four times as likely. In five states—New Jersey, Wisconsin, Iowa, Minnesota, and Vermont—blacks are *ten times* more likely than whites to be in prison.

There is a debate about why this disparity exists, and the degree to which the cause is some form of policy or structural factors. But there is growing consensus that the disparity is not just a result of inequality but that it is also an engine of it, in a sort of malignant spiral of cause and effect.

Some scholars now argue that mass incarceration has been a cause of the large and growing racial disparities in the United States. They use sophisticated statistical methods and new types of data to show how going to prison leads to substantial differences in life experiences. Almost one-third of all African American college dropouts are in prison, a rate almost five times that of whites. White men are almost 10 times more likely to graduate from college than to go to prison, while African American men are two times more likely to go to prison than to finish college.

The implications of these facts ripple their way through the lives of people who are affected by these men who cycle through the prison system. When the large numbers of men who are behind bars are included in the unemployment rate, the gap between unemployment rates for African American men and every other group in society grows. Going to prison reduces expected hourly wages and dramatically reduces the chance of employment after release—for African Americans, but not for whites. Likewise, going to prison reduces the likelihood of ever getting married for African American men, but not for whites or Hispanics, even after a child is born and even though incarcerated men are just as likely to produce children as are nonincarcerated men. Marriages of all those who have been to prison are more likely to end in divorce.

In short, the growth in the use of incarceration has had devastating effects on African American men, the labor markets of their communities, and their families and children. These undesirable social effects of incarceration ought to be a matter of significant discussion regarding incarceration policy. For the most part, however, when new legislation about prison sentences is proposed, these matters never arise. Is that a sign of a racist society?

Sources: Ashley Nellis, *The Color of Justice: Racial and Ethnic Disparities in State Prisons* (Washington, DC: Sentencing Project, 2016); Bruce Western, *Punishment and Inequality in America* (New York: Russell Sage Foundation, 2006), 11.

and Inequality"). Thus, employers who hire young African American men tend to do so only after completing a criminal history background check, something that is not usually done at the entry level.

Thus, confronted with the reality of crime committed by people of color, the criminal justice system reacts in a way that reflects public horror and revulsion by removing large numbers of people of color from their communities. Racist institutions, it is argued, help produce the higher crime rate among minorities, and then racist fears of people of color help justify treating them more harshly when they are caught.

A significant idea underlying this point of view is the **racial threat hypothesis**, which holds that white fear of and antagonism toward African Americans will be greatest in areas where the proportion of African Americans approaches that of whites because in these areas, African Americans constitute a greater perceived threat to whites. In areas that are mostly white or mostly African American, whites will feel less threatened. Studies of racial disparities in imprisonment support the racial threat hypothesis because the rates of incarceration disparity are lowest in places where African Americans are either a very small minority or a very large minority of the larger population.[52] Studies of policing also find that patterns of drug arrests of African Americans are consistent with the racial threat hypothesis.[53]

racial threat hypothesis The belief that white fear of African Americans is least when whites are the majority but greatest when African Americans are a substantial minority.

Throughout history and even today, the image of the "black criminal" has been a common scapegoat and tool manipulated by white people for various purposes. In the South after the Civil War and into the mid-twentieth century, fear of African American rapists of white women was an excuse to lynch some young men and keep the rest in perpetual fear of summary execution. In 1988 the image of Willie Horton, an African American who was convicted of a felony and then released under Massachusetts

Melanie Stetson Freeman/Christian Science Monitor/The Image Works

▲ *For too many young men in impoverished minority communities, encounters with the criminal justice system are a fact of life.*

Governor Michael Dukakis's administration, was purposefully used to fuel white fears of crime and help portray George Bush as "tough on crime." Bush was eventually elected president, with strong support from voters fearful of street crime. The dirty taste of the race-baiting nature of that aspect of the campaign stays with us, even decades later. And in the 1990s, when Susan Smith, who is white, wanted to cover up her murder of her two young sons, she invented an African American assailant—and the general public believed her without batting an eye. At the same time, critics have pointed out that harsh new sentencing laws are almost always the product of crimes against white victims, and never follow crimes against black victims.[54]

The overrepresentation of African Americans in the justice system has also led to an ominous consequence—disenfranchisement. All but two states (Vermont and Maine) forbid voting by felony-convicted people while they are incarcerated, but over half the states deny the right to vote to anyone under correctional supervision (whether in custody or in the community), and seven states deny the vote to anyone ever convicted of a felony. One study estimated that 13 percent of African American men—1.4 million—are *permanently* banned from voting in the states where they live.[55] (When Floridians voted overwhelmingly to return the vote to people who had completed their criminal sentences, the state legislature, fearing a tide of Democratic voters, imposed new restrictions, making it harder for them to vote.)

The loss of the vote has, for these Americans, denied access to political participation in a way that has racially disparate effects. Critics of this policy point out that a high percentage of African American men are, as a consequence, prevented from influencing political policies that affect their lives. The problem is not small. In Florida, for example, where nearly half a million men are denied the vote as a consequence of their felony record, if *two-tenths of a percent* of that group had voted in the 2000 election, Al Gore almost certainly would have been elected president because he was overwhelmingly supported by African Americans who did vote. The policy is seen as so indefensible that some experts feel we should allow felony-convicted people to vote, even if they are still under sentence.

If people of color are overrepresented in the justice system because the larger society is racist, the solution seems a bit daunting. Nobody knows a way to rapidly rid our society of policies, practices, and, perhaps most importantly, attitudes of racism (see "For Critical Thinking"). Even an optimist would think that a generation or more of vigilance to eradicate racism might be necessary.

FOR CRITICAL THINKING

Recently, a panel of reformers was assembled by the Aspen Institute, a think tank in Washington, D.C., and Colorado, to consider the problem of racism in the justice system and how to confront it. Among the recommendations coming from this group is a call for "racial impact statements" before laws are passed. Such statements would require those proposing any legislation to demonstrate that the new law will not adversely affect racial or ethnic equality. For example, this would mean that drug law sentencing reform would have to show that it will not exacerbate disparities in racial equality.

1. What do you think about the idea of racial impact statements?
2. Do you think that racial impact statements are likely to accomplish their goals of improved racial justice? Will there be unintended consequences? If so, how could they be overcome?
3. What else could be done to improve racial equality throughout the justice system?

Source: Marc Mauer, "Advocacy for Racial Justice: Prospects for Criminal Justice Reform," in *Race, Crime, and Punishment: Breaking the Connection in America*, edited by Keith O. Lawrence (Washington, DC: Aspen Institute, 2011), 163–74.

WHICH IS IT: RACE OR RACISM?

We can illustrate the complications of the racism issue with a hypothetical case. Suppose that Wilson, who is white, and Edwards, who is African American, were each convicted of burglary. If Wilson received probation with a $5,000 fine and 200 hours of community service while Edwards received six months in jail, would you think that the verdict was racist?

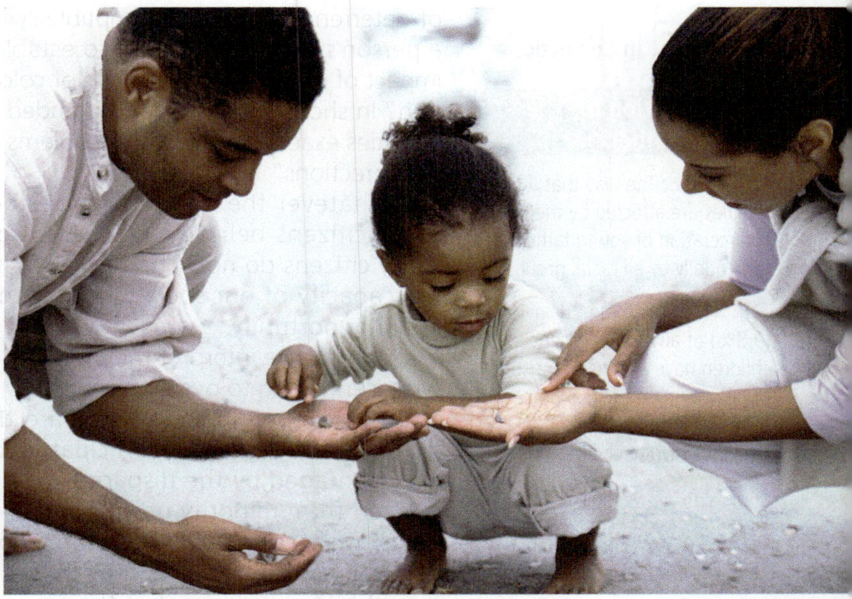
Purestock/Getty Images

▲ *The concept of social justice means that society is a place where all kinds of families can flourish. Does the way the criminal justice system works promote social justice?*

Would it change your opinion to learn that, at sentencing, Wilson's attorney argued that a jail term would cost Wilson his job as a construction worker and would leave his unemployed wife and two children without a source of financial support? Or to learn that Edwards had no job and that his two children had already been living without his income as he sat in jail, awaiting trial? When the law tries to take into account these sorts of concerns, however reasonable they seem, it runs the risk of inadvertently penalizing those who have fewer resources.

The situation becomes even more complicated if we learn that this is Wilson's first offense but Edwards's second. The jail term makes a bit more sense for a repeater. But we have to keep in mind that young African American men often experience arrests that result in charges being dropped, for whatever reason. To consider such arrests at sentencing may be unfair and indirectly biased.

What if the reason that Wilson received a fine is that he had a job in the first place and could afford to pay? Edwards might claim that he went to jail because he was unemployed but that if the system would help him get a job, he could pay a fine.

All these scenarios raise the question of whether the system is reasonable, biased, or simply part of a larger set of social inequities. There is no obvious answer.

LO 3

Describe the significance of race and punishment.

THE SIGNIFICANCE OF RACE AND PUNISHMENT

In some respects, it does not matter which of the competing views is most accurate. The real repercussions of racial disparities in the criminal justice system have already become a force that criminal justice policy makers must face.

The fact that such a high percentage of young African American men are behind bars must be understood in terms of what these young men cannot be doing. They cannot be earning a living, attending school, parenting their children, or supporting their partners; they cannot be voting or otherwise partaking of free society. We can only speculate about the implications of the fact that so many of this generation's young men of color have passed through the criminal justice system. But we also must wonder whether this experience might not further alienate this group and prevent them from identifying with the society that sent them there. Does growing up with fathers, uncles, and brothers absent from home because of the system breed respect for the law, or revulsion and enmity, in the many children affected this way? Does the prison stand as a fearful symbol

MYTHS in Corrections

Incarceration of Young Fathers

THE MYTH: The way that families are affected by the incarceration of young fathers is felt equally by all racial groups.

THE REALITY: Almost 1 in 10 (9.3%) of all African American children have a father in prison or jail, compared to 3.5 percent of Hispanic children and 1.2 percent of white children.

Source: Bruce Western, *Punishment and Inequality in America* (New York: Russell Sage Foundation, 2006).

of deterrence or as a contemptible symbol of the inevitable power of the state to disrupt a person's life? In the effort to establish and preserve order, does the disproportionate impact of corrections on people of color instead produce suspicion and even social disruption? In short, does the heavy-handed use of the criminal justice system in minority communities exacerbate the very problems of social disorder it is trying to correct? See "Myths in Corrections" for more.

Whatever the real reason behind the disparities in the criminal justice system, many citizens believe that such disparities exist because of racism, and at least as many citizens do not. The result is a polarization of attitudes about race that discolors the capacity of our society to remember its traditional values of fairness, equity, and equal opportunity.

How do we interpret the problems of race that we see in our corrections system? And what can we do to overcome them?

Most people believe there are three solutions. First, we must open the corrections system to greater participation by people who come from the groups historically disadvantaged by the disparate treatment. Special efforts to employ young men and women from minority groups will in the long run reduce the predominance of white policy makers in this area. Studies of African American police officers, judges, and correctional officers find that their decisions about cases are very similar to those of their white coworkers, but their greater presence in criminal justice roles of authority benefits everyone.

Second, we must ferret out and refuse to tolerate incidents of blatant racism in justice practices or policy. This is easier said than done, of course, because there is so much disagreement about what exactly a racist policy is. For example, should people who do not have jobs be as eligible for bail as those who have stakes in the community? Should police spend as much time aggressively combating white-collar crime as they do street crime? Ensuring that criminal justice policies are free of racial and ethnic bias is nonetheless a high priority for tomorrow's correctional leaders. Scaling back punishments, as California did with Proposition 47, reducing the number of people in prison for low-level crimes, has reduced racial disparity in imprisonment in that state.[56]

Finally, we must recognize that as long as racism is a force in the larger society, any attempts to eradicate it from the criminal justice system will have only marginal prospects for success. As long as some groups are unfairly excluded from society's opportunities, they will have less motivation to obey its laws. And the corrections system will be their adversary.

SUMMARY

1 Analyze the meaning of race and ethnicity.

Race and ethnicity are complex concepts. Race is usually assumed to be a biological concept that divides humankind into categories related to skin color and other physical features. However, social scientists also look at the ways in which groups define themselves and are defined by others. Today the concept of race is controversial: That so many Americans have interracial backgrounds makes accepting a purely biological approach difficult. Race is also controversial to the extent that it has political and social implications. For example, many transfers of funds from the federal government to the states for social programs are calculated according to race-based formulas. Ethnicity is a concept used to divide people according to their cultural

2 Explain how varying visions of race and punishment influence our thinking on this issue.

There are three main viewpoints about the disproportionate involvement of people of color in the criminal justice system. (1) People argue that the proportions stem from differential criminality. More people of color end up in corrections because they commit worse crimes and have more-serious prior records than do whites. Some people believe that sociobiological factors result in large numbers of Hispanics and African Americans being processed by the criminal justice system, but there is little evidence to support this view. A less-extreme version of this argument rests on the fact that criminality is related to socioeconomic disadvantage, which many people of color suffer. (2) Some argue that the criminal justice system is racist. Racial

characteristics—language, religion, and group traditions. Ethnicity is usually reported by subjects themselves, rather than stemming from an outside observer making a visual identification, as in the case of race. Ethnic groups exist among white Americans—for example, Irish, Italians, Poles—as well as within the black, Asian, and Hispanic communities.

disparities become racial discrimination if people who are otherwise similar in their criminality are treated differently by the criminal justice system because of their race. For example, African Americans are arrested for drug offenses at more than twice the rate of whites, even though African American youths have substantially lower rates of use of most legal and illegal drugs. Reforming the system depends on how we define the problem—in terms of racist attitudes or in terms of social disparities related to race. (3) Finally, some claim that society itself is racist. They argue that eliminating racism from the criminal justice system is not likely to occur because the system is embedded in a larger racist society. Many observers further believe that the relationship between racism and the criminal justice system is reciprocal. Racist institutions, it is argued, help produce the higher crime rate among minorities, and then racist fears of people of color help justify treating them more harshly when they are caught.

3 Describe the significance of race and punishment. The repercussions of racial disparities in the criminal justice system remain a problem that criminal justice policy makers must face. The fact that such a high percentage of young African American men are behind bars must be understood in terms of what these young men cannot be doing. They cannot be earning a living, attending school, parenting their children, or supporting their partners; they cannot be voting or otherwise partaking of free society. We can only speculate about the implications of the fact that so many of this generation's young men of color have passed through the criminal justice system. As long as some groups are unfairly excluded from society's opportunities, they will have less motivation to obey its laws.

KEY TERMS

discrimination (*p. 514*)
disparity (*p. 514*)
ethnicity (*p. 513*)
race (*p. 513*)
racial threat hypothesis (*p. 521*)
self-report study (*p. 514*)

FOR DISCUSSION

1. What are five main reasons that people of color are overrepresented in the criminal justice system? Does overrepresentation represent a problem? What, if anything, can be done to change the pattern?
2. What impact does a high incarceration rate have on minority communities? What implications does this impact have for the effectiveness of the criminal justice system?
3. How does the close relationship between politics and criminal justice policy reflect issues of race and punishment?
4. If you were writing a sentencing code, would you give people lighter sentences if they came from disadvantaged backgrounds? Why or why not?
5. What are the most important steps to take to reduce racial differences in punishments? Why?

FOR FURTHER READING

Forman, James Jr. *Locking Up Our Own: Crime and Punishment in Black America*. New York: Farrar, Straus & Giroux, 2017. A former prosecutor describes the community-based movement in black communities that led to a round of more-severe sentences for drug crime and violence.

Johnson, Devon, Patricia Y. Warren, and Amy Farrell, eds. *Deadly Injustice: Trayvon Martin, Race, and the Criminal Justice System*. New York: NYU Press, 2015. Essays on race in the criminal justice system, including discussions of police, community policies, punishment, and public perceptions of crime.

McCorckle, Jill A. *Breaking Women: Gender, Race, and the New Politics of Incarceration*. New York: NYU Press, 2013. A study of the way that tougher drug policies have affected the experience of incarceration by women.

Muhammad, Khalil Gibran. *The Condemnation of Blackness: Race, Crime and the Making of Modern Urban America*. Cambridge, MA: Harvard University Press, 2010. Historical study of the way that society came to define black people as "dangerous."

Pager, Devah. *Marked: Race, Crime, and Finding Work in an Era of Mass Incarceration*. Chicago: University of Chicago Press, 2007. A series of studies that demonstrate how the growth of incarceration is the foundation for the way that African American men are discriminated against in the job market.

Tonry, Michael. *Punishing Race: A Continuing American Dilemma*. New York: Oxford University Press, 2011. Describes the historical, sociological, and political foundations for racial disparity in the criminal justice system.

Walker, Samuel, Cassia Spohn, and Miriam DeLone. *The Color of Justice: Race, Ethnicity, and Crime in America*. 6th ed. Belmont, CA: Wadsworth, 2018. Gives an up-to-date review of studies of race, crime, and justice at all stages of the criminal justice system, from arrest to punishment.

Western, Bruce. *Punishment and Inequality in America*. New York: Russell Sage Foundation, 2006. An exhaustive empirical analysis of the way that prison growth has affected young African American men and contributed to racial inequality.

NOTES

1 Bruce Western, *Punishment and Inequality in America* (New York: Russell Sage Foundation, 2006).

2 Ashley Nellis, *Still Life: America's Increasing Use of Life and Long-Term Sentences* (Washington, DC: Sentencing Project, 2017).

3 Michele Alexander, *The New Jim Crow: Mass Incarceration in the Age of Colorblindness*, 2nd ed. (New York: New Press, 2012).

4 E. Ann Carson, *Prisoners in 2018* (Washington, DC: U.S. Department of Justice, Bureau of Justice Assistance, 2020).

5 Walter Enders, Paul Pecorino, and Ann-Charlotte Souto, "Racial Disparity in US Imprisonment Across States and Over Time," *Journal of Quantitative Criminology* 35 (no. 2, 2019): 265–392.

6 Michael C. Campbell, Matt Vogel, and Joshua Williams, "Historical Contingencies and the Evolving Importance of Race, Violent Crime, and Region in Examining Mass Incarceration in the United States," *Criminology 53* (no. 2, 2015): 180–203.

7 E. Ann Carson and Elizabeth Anderson, *Prisoners in 2015* (Washington, DC: U.S. Bureau of Justice Statistics, 2016), 10.

8 Office of Juvenile Justice and Delinquency Prevention, *Racial and Ethnic Fairness*, https://www.ojjdp.gov/ojstatbb/special_topics/qa11603.asp?qaDate=2018, 2020.

9 Office of Juvenile Justice and Delinquency Prevention, *Age on Census Date by Race and Ethnicity in the United States*, 2017, https://www.ojjdp.gov/ojstatbb/ezacjrp/asp/Age_Race.asp., 2020

10 To learn more, go to http://blacklivesmatter.com.

11 "AAPA Statement on Biological Aspects of Race," *American Journal of Physical Anthropology* 101 (1996): 569–70.

12 Samuel Walker, Cassia Spohn, and Miriam DeLone, *The Color of Justice: Race, Ethnicity, and Crime in America*, 6th ed. (Belmont, CA: Wadsworth, 2018).

13 Two classic examples are offered by James Q. Wilson and Richard J. Herrnstein, *Crime and Human Nature* (New York: Simon & Schuster, 1985), and Richard J. Herrnstein and Charles Murray, *The Bell Curve: Intelligence and Class Structure in American Life* (New York: Free Press, 1994).

14 Brian D. Johnson and Ryan D. King, "Facial Profiling: Race, Physical Appearance, and Punishment," *Criminology* 55 (no. 3, 2017): 520–47.

15 Lance Hannon, Robert DeFina, and Sarah Bruch, "The Relationships Between Skin Tone and School Suspension for African Americans," *Race and Social Problems 5* (no. 4, 2013): 281–95.

16 James F. Wallerstein and Clement J. Wyle, "Our Law-Abiding Law-Breakers," *Probation* 35 (April 1947): 107–19.

17 Travis Hirschi, *Causes of Delinquency* (Berkeley: University of California Press, 1969).

18 Carson and Anderson, *Prisoners in 2015*.

19 Carson, *Prisoners in 2018*, p. 23.

20 Walker, Spohn, and DeLone, *The Color of Justice*, ch. 3.

21 Eric A. Stewart and Ronald L. Simmons, *The Code of the Street and African-American Adolescent Violence* (Washington, DC:U.S. Department of Justice, 2009).

22 John J. DiIulio Jr., "The Question of Black Crime," *Public Interest*, Fall 1994, p. 3.

23 Federal Bureau of Investigation, *Crime in the United States, 2018* (Washington, DC: Author, 2016), Table 43A.

24 Alfred Blumstein, "On the Racial Disproportionality of the United States' Prison Population," *Journal of Criminal Law and Criminology* 73 (1982): 1259–81.

25 John DiIulio, "Let 'em Rot," *Wall Street Journal*, January 26, 1995.

26 Sentencing Project, *Report of the Sentencing Project to the United Nations Human Rights Committee Regarding Racial Disparities in the United States Criminal Justice System* (Washington, DC: Author, 2013).

27 Federal Bureau of Investigation, *Crime in the United States 2018*, Table 43A.

28 Lloyd D. Johnston, Patrick M. O'Malley, Jerald G. Bachman, and John E. Schulenberg, *Monitoring the Future: National Results on Drug Use, 1975–2005* (Washington, DC: National Institute on Drug Abuse, 2006).

29 Western, *Punishment and Inequality*, p. 41.

30 Nicole D. Porter and Valerie Wright, *Cracked Justice* (Washington, DC: Sentencing Project, 2011).

31 Joseph J. Palamar, Shelby Davies, Danielle C. Ompad, et al., "Powder Cocaine and Crack Use in the United States: An Examination of Risk for Arrest and Socioeconomic Disparities in Use," *Drug and Alcohol Dependence* 149 (2015): 108–16.

32 Quoted in Tavis Smily (with Stephanie Robinson), Accountable: Making America as Good as Its Promise (New York: Atria, 2013), 225.

33 Melissa Sickmund and Charles Puzzanchera, *Juvenile Offenders and Victims: 2014 National Report* (Pittsburgh: National Center for Juvenile Justice, 2014).

34 Joshua Rovner, *Racial Disparities in Youth Commitments and Arrests* (Washington, DC: Sentencing Project, 2016).

35 Khaing Zaw, Darrick Hamilton, and William Darity Jr., "Race, Wealth and Incarceration: Results from the National Longitudinal Survey of Youth," *Race and Social Problems* 8 (no. 1, 2016): 103–15.

36 Lois James, Stephen M. James, and Bryan J. Vila, "The Reverse Racism Effect: Are Cops More Hesitant to Shoot Black Than White Suspects?" *Criminology & Public Policy* 15 (no. 2, 2016): 457–79.

37 Besiki Luka Kutateladze, "Tracing Charge Trajectories: A Study of the Influence of Race in Charge Changes at Case Screening, Arraignment, and Disposition," Criminology 56 (no. 1, 2017): 123–53.

38 Ashley Nellis, *The Color of Justice* (Washington, DC: The Sentencing Project, 2016).

39 James Forman, Jr., *Locking Up Our Own: Crime and Punishment in Black America* (New York: Farrar, Straus & Giroux, 2017).

40 Allen J. Beck and Alfred Blumstein, "Racial Disproportionality in US State Prisons: Accounting for the Effects of Racial and Ethnic Differences in Criminal Involvement, Arrests, and Time Served," *Journal of Quantitative Criminology* 34 (no. 4, 2017): 853–83.

41 Shytierra Gaston, "Producing Race Disparities: A Study of Drug Arrests Across Place and Race," *Criminology* 57 (no. 3, 2019): 424–51.

42 Walker, Spohn, and DeLone, *The Color of Justice*.

43 Sentencing Project, *Report of the Sentencing Project.*

44 Joe M. Brown and John R. Sorenson, "Race, Ethnicity, Gender and Waiver to Adult Court," *Journal of Ethnicity in Criminal Justice* 11 (no. 3, 2013): 181–95.

45 Sonja B. Starr and M. Marit Rehavi, "Mandatory Sentencing and Racial Disparity: Assessing the Role of Prosecutors and the Effects *of Booker," Yale Law Journal* 123 (no. 1, 2013): 2–80.

46 Christi Metcalfe and Ted Chiricos, "Race, Lease, and Charge Reduction: Assessment of Racial Disparities in the Plea Process," *Justice Quarterly* 35 (no. 2, 2018): 223–53.

47 Jeffrey T. Ulmer, Michael T. Light, and John Kramer, "Racial Disparity in the Wake of the *Booker/Fanfan* Decision: An Alternative Analysis to the USSC's 2010 Report," *Criminology & Public Policy* 10 (no. 4, 2011): 1077–118. See also William D. Bales and Alex R. Piquero, "Racial/Ethnic Differentials in Sentencing to Incarceration," Justice Quarterly (February 13, 2012).

48 Michael Tonry, *Malign Neglect: Race, Crime, and Punishment in America* (New York: Oxford University Press, 1995), 123.

49 Devah Pager, *Marked: Race, Crime, and Finding Work in an Era of Mass Incarceration* (Chicago: University of Chicago Press, 2007).

50 Maurice Emsellem and Beth Avery, *Racial Profiling in Hiring: A Critique of "Ban the Box Studies"* (Washington, DC: National Employment Law Project Policy Brief, 2016).

51 Michael A. Stoll, "Ex-offenders, Criminal Background Checks, and Racial Consequences in the Labor Market," *University of Chicago Legal Forum 2009* (no. 1, 2009).

52 Bradley Keen and David Jenkins, "Racial Threat, Partisan Politics and Racial Disparities in Prison Admissions: A Panel Analysis," *Criminology* 47 (no. 1, 2009): 209–38.

53 David Eitle and Susanne Monahan, "Revisiting the Racial Threat Thesis: The Role of Police Organizational Characteristics in Predicting Race-Specific Drug Arrest Rates," *Justice Quarterly* 26 (no. 3, 2009): 528–61.

54 Teresa C. Kulig and Francis T. Cullen, "Where is Latisha's Law? Black Invisibility in the Social Construction of Victimhood," *Justice Quarterly* 33 (no. 4, 2016): 973–1013.

55 Jeff Manza and Christopher Uggen, *Locked Out: Felon Disenfranchisement and American Democracy* (New York: Oxford University Press, 2007).

56 John MacDonald and Steven Raphael, "Effect of Scaling Back Punishment on Racial and Ethnic Disparities in Criminal Case Outcomes," *Criminology & Public Policy,* https://onlinelibrary.wiley.com/doi/abs/10.1111/1745-9133.12495, 2020.

CHAPTER 20

The Death Penalty

AP Images/Alabama Department of Corrections

Chuck Berman/Chicago Tribune/TNS/Sipa USA

When a person is executed, selected members of the public are allowed to be witnesses.

A 61-YEAR-OLD MAN LIES STRAPPED TO A GURNEY. He is waiting to die. Members of the death team busily work to locate a usable vein from which to administer a lethal drug cocktail. Doyle Lee Hamm has been on Alabama's death row for 30 years. He was sentenced to death for killing a man during a robbery. But the team is having difficulty finding a vein to use. Hamm is a former intravenous drug user and many of his veins are badly damaged. He has other medical problems too, including advanced lymphatic cancer and Hepatitis C. After poking Hamm several times with a needle and not finding a vein, the execution is called off just before the death warrant expires. Hamm becomes one of the few people sentenced to death in American history to exit an execution chamber alive. When asked to comment on the evening's events, Corrections Commissioner Jeff Dunn said, "I wouldn't necessarily characterize what we had tonight as a problem." Weeks later, it was announced that the Alabama Attorney General's office and Hamm's legal team had reached a settlement. Although details associated with the agreement were not announced, the state agreed to abandon efforts to execute Hamm.[1]

A three-drug procedure was developed in the late 1970s as a fail-safe execution method. Three poisonous chemicals are injected, in succession, into the bloodstream of the condemned. The first, a barbiturate, is designed to sedate the condemned individual and suppress respiration. The second, a neuromuscular paralytic, halts breathing and body convulsions. The third, a potassium electrolyte, stops the heart. Usually a medical examiner can confirm the death within minutes—but not always.

Over the past decade, virtually every state with an active death penalty has seen legal challenges to the use of lethal injection. Courts in some states have ruled that a doctor must be present during the execution to monitor the condemned person for signs of pain. The American Medical Association states that physicians who take part in executions violate medical ethics. In other cases the type of drugs, their amount, and their combination have also been attacked as inducing suffering, thus violating the cruel and unusual punishments clause of the Eighth Amendment.

In 2015 the U.S. Supreme Court addressed the constitutionality of lethal injection. By a 5–4 ruling in *Glossip v. Gross,* the Court ruled against the plaintiffs who claimed that Oklahoma's three-drug protocol, especially the drug midazolam, caused excruciating pain. The Court stated that the condemned men "failed to establish a likelihood of success on the merits of their claim that the use of midazolam violates the Eighth Amendment." In the dissenting opinion, justices once again questioned the constitutionality of the death penalty.[2] Regardless, the majority ruling allows states who use midazolam to resume their execution schedule.

Lethal injection is the latest attempt to impose capital punishment in a way that is legal and fair and will not offend modern cultural sensibilities. Over the past hundred years, capital punishment changed from the noose to the firing squad to the gas chamber to the electric chair. Each change in technique stemmed from the idea that the new method would be more civilized and less gruesome. However, each method has had its drawbacks, resulting in bodies twitching, burning, and gagging—often for extended periods. Lethal injection was supposed to avoid at least the appearance of cruel and unusual punishment. The assumption was that the condemned person would merely lie down on a gurney, receive an injection, fall asleep, and die.

There seems to be a new uncertainty about capital punishment. The challenges to the use of lethal injection represent only one of several trends, including fewer executions, fewer individuals being sent to death row, increased numbers of death row inhabitants cleared by DNA, and gubernatorial moratoria suspending the use of capital punishment in Oregon (2011), Colorado (2013), Washington (2014), Pennsylvania (2015), and California (2019). Yet as a nationwide public opinion poll found, about 56 percent of people in this country still support capital punishment for murderers.[3] Why is there such ambivalence toward the death penalty?

In this chapter we focus on the moral, political, and legal issues of the death penalty debate. In addition, we examine the factors associated with death row, including the death row population, which contains a disproportionate number of poor, undereducated minority men.

LEARNING OBJECTIVES

After reading this chapter, you should be able to . . .

1. Compare and contrast the issues in the debate over capital punishment.
2. Explain the history of the death penalty in America.
3. Discuss the legal issues that surround the death penalty.
4. Characterize the individuals on death row.
5. Speculate about the future of capital punishment.

LO 1

Compare and contrast the issues in the debate over capital punishment.

THE DEBATE OVER CAPITAL PUNISHMENT

Retribution, deterrence, and incapacitation are usually cited as the reasons for keeping the death penalty. Retribution reflects the belief that one who takes another's life deserves a punishment equal to the victim's fate, deterrence reflects the hope that the execution will deter others from crime, and incapacitation reflects the desire to keep the person from committing future crimes.

Photo by Sarah J. Glover/Philadelphia Inquirer/MCT/Sipa USA

Ernest van den Haag, a supporter of capital punishment, notes that arguments about the death penalty are either moral or utilitarian. He has summarized his moral argument supporting retribution as follows: "Anyone who takes another's life should not be encouraged to expect that he will outlive his victim at public expense. Murder must forfeit the murderer's life, if there is to be justice."[4] Opponents of the death penalty argue that only God has the right to take a life; the state does not. Opponents also emphasize that mistakes can and have been made, resulting in innocent people being executed. Further, they claim that the death penalty discriminates against poor people and racial minorities because they disproportionately receive this sentence. Van den Haag counters by claiming that abolitionists would continue to oppose capital punishment even if they could be certain that "none but the guilty are executed, and without discrimination or capriciousness."[5]

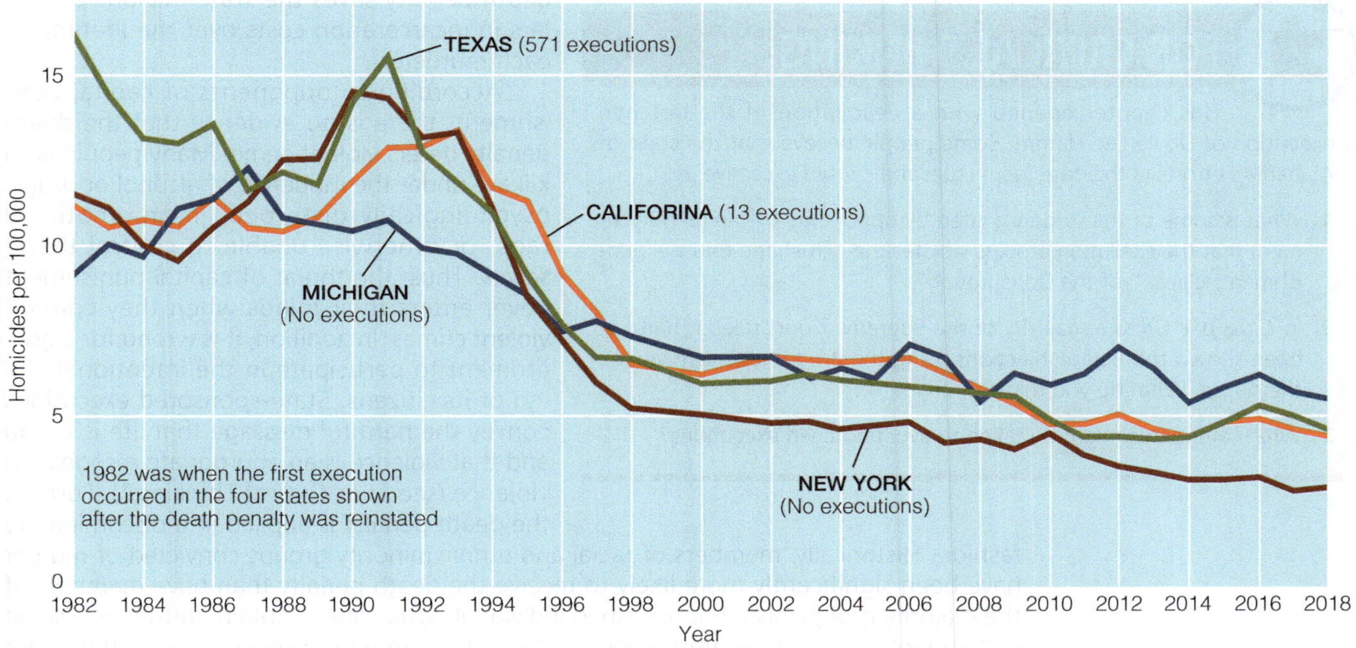

FIGURE 20.1 Comparing Homicide Rates and Executions in Four States

The homicide rates in four states with different approaches to the death penalty follow a similar trend. Texas has the highest number of executions. California has the largest death row population but few executions. New York abolished the death penalty in 2004 and has had no executions, and Michigan has no death penalty.

Sources: Death Penalty Information Center, www.deathpenaltyinfo.org, May 16, 2020; Crime in the U.S., https://ucr.fbi.gov/crime-in-the-u.s, May 16, 2020.

The utilitarian argument for capital punishment is based on the belief that executions of wrongdoers deter others from committing the crime. The general deterrence position sounds reasonable to most people, yet there is no effective means to prove it scientifically. It is incredibly difficult to demonstrate that someone was actually deterred from an action because he or she recognized the consequences.

Many studies have looked closely at murder rates, comparing states that have the death penalty with those that do not. Most of these studies have found no deterrent effect of the penalty. For example, Ruth Peterson and William Bailey examined homicide rates in adjacent states over a 12-year period. They found that the murder rate in states *with* the death penalty was higher than in those *without* it.[6] As shown by Figure 20.1, four states with differing capital punishment policies—California, Michigan, New York, and Texas—have not differed in their homicide rates over the last 30 years. Studies showing that executions deter potential murderers have been challenged on methodological grounds.[7] A comprehensive review conducted by the National Research Council concluded that "research to date on the effect of capital punishment on homicide is not informative about whether capital punishment decreases, increases, or has no effect on homicide rates."[8]

The public argument runs along the same lines as the academic debate. According to supporters, the death penalty indeed deters individuals from committing violent acts—individuals will be less likely to kill if they know that they face execution for doing so. In addition, the death penalty serves justice by paying killers back for their horrible crimes. Society exacts an appropriate measure of revenge ("an eye for an eye"), and victims' families can be reassured that the murderer received a just punishment and will not kill others. By executing murderers, society emphasizes the high value placed on life. The death penalty also prevents murderers from doing further harm. Finally, the

FOR CRITICAL THINKING

This chapter opened with a description of the botched execution of Doyle Lee Hamm. Some people believe that the state of Alabama's efforts in this case were cruel and caused excessive pain.

1. What is some of the evidence cited by opponents of capital punishment that the execution process violates the "cruel and unusual punishments clause" of the Constitution?
2. In *Glossip v. Gross* a majority of the Supreme Court ruled it had not been shown that lethal injections using the drug midazolam violate the clause. What do you think?
3. What safeguards might be taken to avoid botched executions?

death penalty saves the state millions of dollars in incarceration costs over the lifetime of each murderer.

According to opponents of capital punishment, there is no evidence that the death penalty deters violent crime. Many people who kill are under the influence of alcohol or drugs, psychologically disturbed, in an emotional rage, or otherwise unable to control themselves. Thus, the threat of capital punishment never enters their minds when they commit violent crimes. In addition, it is wrong for a government to participate in the intentional killing of its citizens. State-sponsored executions convey the harmful message that life is cheap and that violence is an appropriate response to violence (see "For Critical Thinking"). Further, the death penalty is applied in a discriminatory fashion. Historically, members of racial and ethnic minority groups convicted of murder have been significantly more likely to receive the death penalty than have members of the majority group. Also, impoverished individuals who cannot obtain pretrial release on bail and who are represented by public defenders are more likely to receive the death penalty than are other people convicted of murder. Finally, innocent people have been executed.

LO 2

Explain the history of the death penalty in America.

THE DEATH PENALTY IN AMERICA

The death penalty has generated controversy ever since colonial times. As discussed in Chapter 2, until the middle of the 1700s punishment in Europe and the American colonies focused on the body of the individual. Along with mutilation, whipping, and dismemberment, death was a common punishment for a range of felonies—from premeditated murder, to striking one's mother or father (New York), to witchcraft and adultery (Massachusetts). Executions were carried out in public until the 1830s, when most were withdrawn behind prison walls.[9] In some regions, however, particularly in the West and South, public executions continued into the twentieth century. The last public execution in the United States took place on August 14, 1936, when an estimated 20,000 spectators converged on the small town of Owensboro, Kentucky. The death penalty has strong historical roots in American culture. Yet even though capital punishment was common, as far back as the 1600s critics argued that the death penalty was immoral and an ineffective deterrent.

Death Row Population

Between 1930 and 1967, 3,859 men and women were executed by state and federal authorities (see Figure 20.2). In 1935, 199 people were put to death; after that, the number of executions began to fall steadily. An average of 128 individuals per year were executed during the 1940s, 72 during the 1950s, and 19 during the 1960s until 1967, when the U.S. Supreme Court ordered a stay of executions pending a hearing on the issue. This decline led some observers to believe that the United States, like the countries of Europe, would ultimately cease applying the death penalty either by law or de facto through lack of use. But this was not the case. After the Supreme Court reaffirmed the constitutionality of the death penalty in 1976, state legislatures quickly enacted new laws providing for the execution of convicted murderers under some circumstances, and

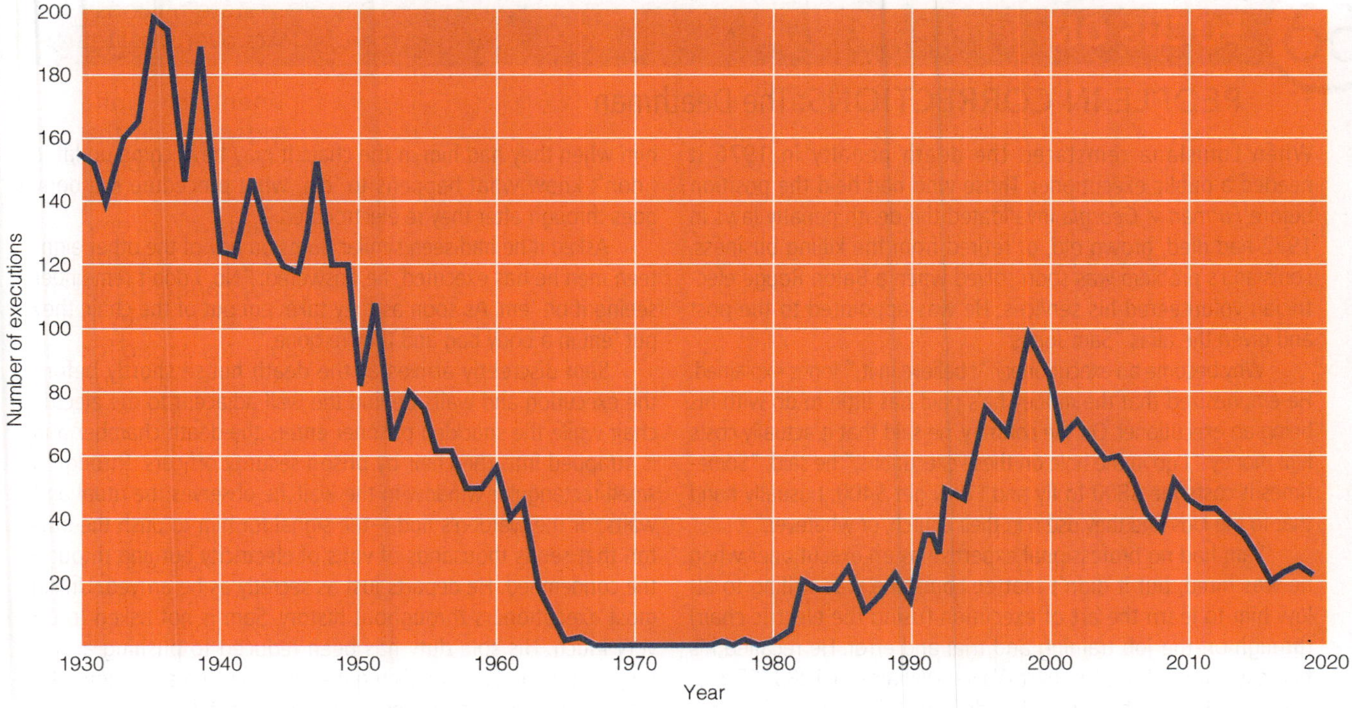

FIGURE 20.2 People Executed in the United States

The steady decline in executions after 1940 gave abolitionists the impression that, as in Europe, the death penalty would eventually become a thing of the past. That belief was shattered when states resumed executions in 1977.

Source: Death Penalty Information Center, www.deathpenaltyinfo.org, May 16, 2020.

executions resumed. (See "The Deathman.") From 1977 to March 2020, 1,516 people have been executed.

The number of people facing the death penalty has increased dramatically since 1976. Only during the past several years has the number of people on death row begun to fall. On January 1, 2020, 2,620 people were awaiting execution.[10] Death penalty opponents argue that the smaller death row population reflects a public wary of executions, concern about whether capital punishment is carried out fairly, and media coverage of individuals who were wrongly convicted.

Public Opinion

In a democracy, public opinion usually has an important impact on public policy. Since 1936, the Gallup organization has been asking the public, "Are you in favor of the death penalty for a person convicted of murder?" Responses to this question have shifted greatly over the past 80 years. Most Americans favored capital punishment until 1960, when public support gradually declined, reaching a low of 42 percent in 1966. However, with the rise in crime in the late 1960s, opinion shifted to a tougher stance. Legislators, always ready to respond to public concerns, began to press for changes in sentencing laws and urged that the death penalty be reinstated. By 1994, 80 percent of Americans supported the death penalty. Since that high point, the percentage has gradually dropped; by 2019, it was 56 percent.[11] Figure 20.3 traces these shifts in public support for the death penalty.

However, support for capital punishment plunges when life imprisonment without the possibility of parole (LWOP) is presented as an alternative. Public opinion data collected by Gallup shows that when given LWOP as an explicit alternative to the death

FOCUS ON

PEOPLE IN CORRECTIONS: The Deathman

When Louisiana reinstated the death penalty in 1976 it needed a public executioner. Those who had held the position before *Furman v. Georgia* invalidated the death penalty laws in 1972 had died, grown old, or retired from the killing business. Louisiana's problem was soon solved when a Baton Rouge electrician volunteered his services. He was appointed to the post and given the alias "Sam Jones."

Why become an executioner? "I believe in it," Jones explained. He emphasized that the money he's paid has little to do with his being an executioner. On the contrary, he said that it actually costs him money. "I go in the hole on these executions," he said, "Sometimes it costs me $800 to fly and I only get $400. I usually hand that to the kids and they use it in their church, or whatever."...

Sam had no professional expertise as an executioner when he was hired, but it didn't matter. Louisiana was willing to allow him to learn the art of execution (using the electric chair) through on-the-job training and trial and error. He recalled his first execution, that of Robert Wayne Williams in 1983. "Everybody has their doubts when they do something for the first time and, sure, I had mine. The first time I was nervous because it was the first time. I didn't doubt I could do it, but I didn't know what to expect. I had no previous experience, and I'd never seen one [an execution] before."

Sam was shown color post-execution photographs of Robert Wayne Williams, and asked if he had seen the burns on Williams's body before. There was a long pause while he studied the pictures. "No, I've never seen that," he said, shaking his head. "That's the first time I've seen that. I didn't see that on him when they had him in the chair. It may have come up later. I don't know what happens to 'em, what procedure the body goes through after they're electrocuted."

Asked if he had seen similar burns on any of the other eighteen men he has executed, he answered: "No, I don't remember seeing it on 'em. As soon as they take 'em out of the chair, they put 'em in a body bag and they're gone."

Sam discreetly arrives at the death house shortly before the execution and waits behind the wall adjacent to the electric chair while the shackled prisoner enters the death chamber and is strapped into the chair by prison security officers. Through a small rectangular window in the wall, he observes the ritual and waits for the warden's nod—the signal for him to push the button that sends thousands of volts of electricity burning through the condemned. He departs just as secretly as he arrived. Unlike most executioners throughout history, Sam is not asked to do very much. His sole duty has been reduced to pushing a button, ... though Louisiana's requirement that the executioner be a certified electrician implies a larger responsibility.

Sam Jones performed his last execution in Louisiana on July 22, 1991. Corrections authorities said that regardless of how executions are conducted in the future, the services of "Sam Jones" would no longer be needed, bringing his tenure as official state executioner to an end.

Source: This interview with Sam Jones was conducted by the editors of the *Angolite,* the newspaper of the Louisiana State Penitentiary. Excerpted from Wilbert Rideau and Ron Wikberg, *Life Sentences: Rage and Survival Behind Bars* (New York: Times Books, 1992), 311–18.

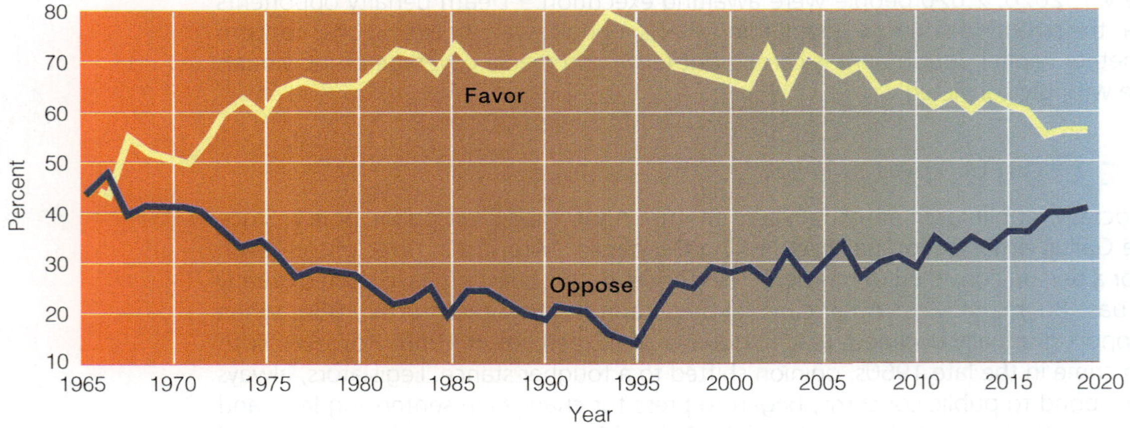

FIGURE 20.3 Attitudes Toward the Death Penalty for People Convicted of Murder

After 1965, public opinion in favor of the death penalty increased greatly for decades. However, after climbing to a high of 80 percent in 1994, support for capital punishment for convicted murderers has generally declined. What factors may have brought about this change?

Note: Respondents were asked, "Are you in favor of the death penalty for a person convicted of murder?" Percentages do not add up to 100 because 2–7 percent of the respondents each year reported "no opinion."

Source: Gallup.com, www.gallup.com/poll/1606/death-penalty.aspx, May 16, 2020.

penalty, the percentage of Americans favoring the death penalty drops to 36 percent. Sixty percent of Americans prefer LWOP to the death penalty.[12]

With 28 states and the federal government now authorizing capital punishment, 34 death sentences were pronounced in 2019.[13] Again, during that same year 2,620 people were on death row. However, as of this writing, the number of executions since 1976 has never exceeded 98 (in 1999) in any one year. Capital punishment remains a controversial issue, one that the courts, correctional professionals, scholars, and the public seem unable to resolve.

As has been noted previously, a number of countries around the world do not use capital punishment. Included among the countries that have abolished the death penalty are Australia, Canada, France, Germany, Mexico, and the United Kingdom. Of the countries that use capital punishment for ordinary crimes, such as murder, it is estimated that China had the highest number of executions (estimated to be more than 1,000) in 2018, followed by Iran (253), Saudi Arabia (149), Vietnam (85), and Iraq (52).[14] How does the U.S. level of support for the death penalty compare to support in other countries? As Figure 20.4 shows, support is higher in a number of countries and lower in others.

LO 3

Discuss the legal issues that surround the death penalty.

THE DEATH PENALTY AND THE CONSTITUTION

Death obviously differs from other punishments in that it is final and irreversible. As a result, the U.S. Supreme Court has examined the decision-making process in capital cases to ensure that the Constitution's requirements regarding due process, equal protection, and cruel and unusual punishments are fulfilled. Because life is in the balance, capital cases must be conducted according to higher standards of fairness and more-careful procedures than are other kinds of cases. Several important Supreme Court cases illustrate this imperative.

Key U.S. Supreme Court Decisions

In *Furman v. Georgia* (1972), the Supreme Court ruled that the death penalty was itself not unconstitutional, but the way it was administered constituted cruel and unusual punishment. The justices pointed to the ambiguity of the wording in the statutes of some states and the lack of systematic administration of the sentence. Although a majority of justices objected to the way in which the death penalty was applied, they could not agree on reasons why it was unconstitutional. Two justices argued that the death penalty always violates the Eighth Amendment's prohibition on cruel and unusual punishments, but other members emphasized that the procedures used to impose death sentences were arbitrary and unfair. The decision invalidated the death penalty laws of 39 states and the District of Columbia.[15]

Over the next several years, 35 states enacted new capital punishment statutes that provided for more-careful decision making and more-modern methods of execution, such as lethal injection. The new laws were tested before the Supreme Court in 1976 in the case of *Gregg v. Georgia*.[16] The Court upheld those laws that required the sentencing judge or jury to take into account specific aggravating and mitigating factors in deciding which convicted murderers should be sentenced to death. Instead of deciding guilt and imposing the death sentence in the same proceeding, states created "bifurcated" proceedings in which a trial determines guilt or innocence, and then a separate hearing focuses exclusively on the issues of punishment. Under the *Gregg* decision, the prosecution uses the punishment-phase hearing to focus attention on the existence of "aggravating factors," such as excessive cruelty displayed in the murder or a prior record of violent crimes. The decision makers must also focus on "mitigating factors," such as the person's youthfulness, developmental disabilities, or lack of a criminal record. The aggravating and mitigating factors must be

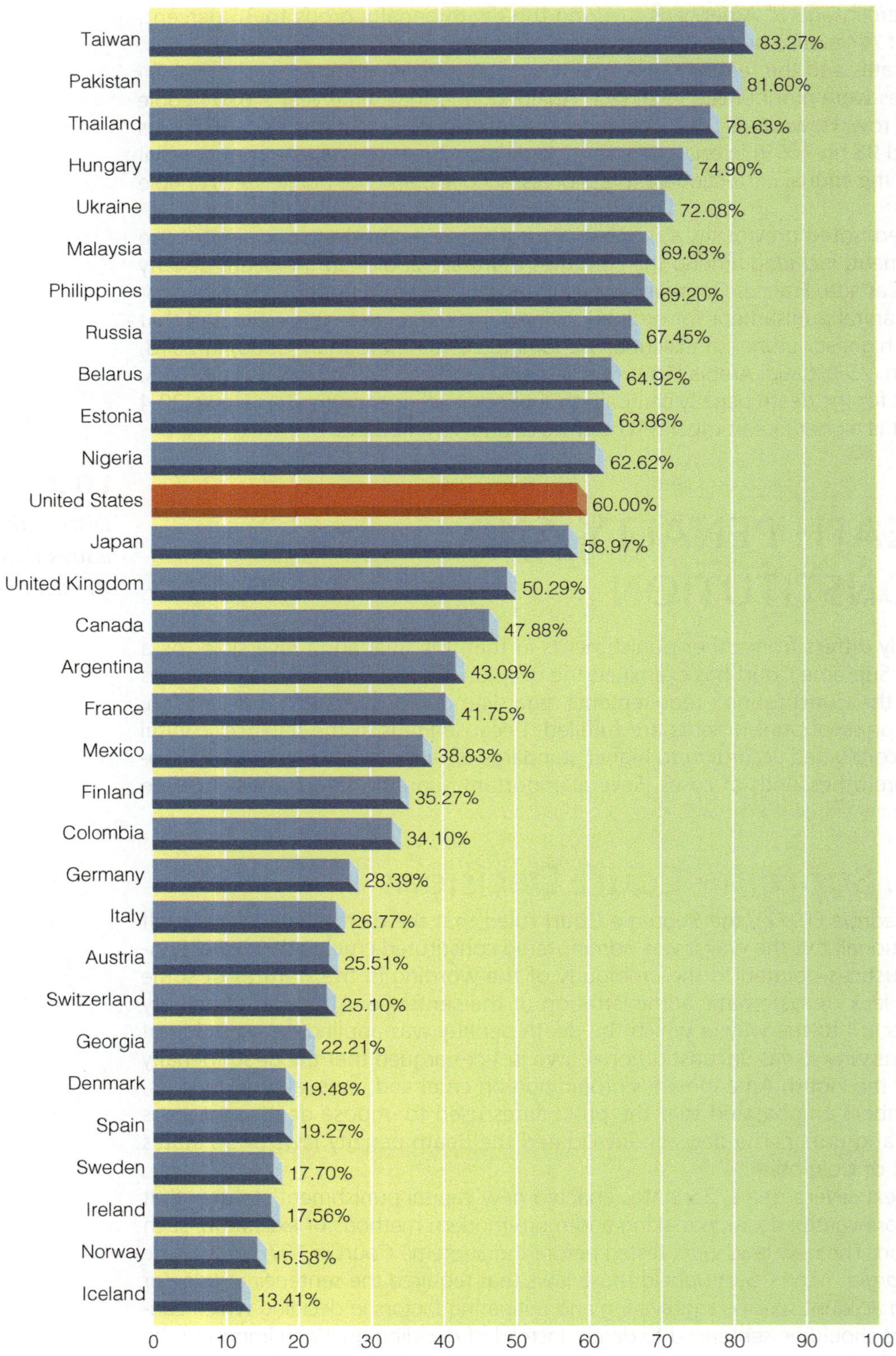

FIGURE 20.4 Support for the Death Penalty around the World

In the United States, polls show that approximately 60 percent of the adult population supports the use of the death penalty. As this figure shows, support for the death penalty is higher in some countries and lower in others. What factors explain these differences?

Source: James Unnever, "Global Support for the Death Penalty," *Punishment & Society* 12 (2010): 463–84.

weighed together before the judge or jury can make a decision about whether to impose a death sentence. The purpose of the two-stage decision-making process is to ensure thorough deliberation before someone is given the ultimate punishment. The Court also endorsed "proportionality review," in which a higher appellate court reviews each death sentence to see if the death penalty was also imposed in similar cases.[17]

In *McCleskey v. Kemp* (1987), opponents of the death penalty believed that the U.S. Supreme Court severely limited their movement. In this case the Court rejected a challenge on the grounds of racial discrimination to Georgia's death penalty law.[18] Warren McCleskey, an African American, was sentenced to death for killing a white police officer during a furniture store robbery. Before the Supreme Court, McCleskey's attorney cited research showing a disparity in the imposition of the death penalty in Georgia, based on the race of the victim and, to a lesser extent, the race of the accused person. Researchers had examined more than 2,000 Georgia murder cases and found that people charged with killing whites had received the death penalty 11 times more often than had those convicted of killing African Americans. Even after compensating for 230 factors, such as the viciousness of the crime and the quality of the evidence, the study showed that the death sentence was four times more likely to be imposed when the victim was white. Although 60 percent of Georgia homicide victims are African Americans, all seven people put to death in that state since 1976 had been convicted of killing white people, and six of the seven murderers were African Americans.[19]

By a 5–4 vote, the Court rejected McCleskey's assertion that Georgia's capital-sentencing practices violated the equal protection clause of the Constitution by producing racial discrimination. The slim majority declared that McCleskey would have to prove that the decision makers acted with a discriminatory purpose in deciding his case. The Court also concluded that statistical evidence showing discrimination throughout the Georgia courts did not provide adequate proof. McCleskey was executed in 1991.

In June 2002 the Supreme Court broke new ground, heartening opponents of the death penalty. First, in *Atkins v. Virginia* it ruled that execution of the developmentally disabled was unconstitutional.[20] Daryl Atkins, who has an IQ of 59, was sentenced to death for killing Eric Nesbitt in a 7-Eleven store's parking lot. Justice John Paul Stevens, writing for the *Atkins* majority, noted that since 1989 a national consensus had emerged rejecting execution of the developmentally disabled. He pointed out that the number of states prohibiting such executions had gone from 2 to 18. The decision also noted that the characteristics of the developmentally disabled "undermine the strength of procedural protections" guaranteed in the Constitution. This point is in keeping with the argument of experts who say developmentally disabled people's suggestibility and willingness to please lead them to confess. At trial they often have problems remembering details, locating witnesses, and testifying credibly on their own behalf. However, the Court gave little guidance to the states as to what criteria should be used to determine whether someone is developmentally disabled.

Second, in *Ring v. Arizona* (2002) the Supreme Court ruled that juries, rather than judges, must make the crucial factual decisions about whether a convicted murderer should receive the death penalty.[21] *Ring v. Arizona* overturned the law of that state and four others—Colorado, Idaho, Montana, and Nebraska—where judges alone decided whether there were aggravating factors that warrant capital punishment. The decision also raised questions about the procedure in four other states—Alabama, Delaware, Florida, and Indiana—where the judge decided life imprisonment or death after hearing a jury's recommendation. The *Ring* opinion also says that any aggravating factors must be stated in the indictment, thus also requiring a change in federal death penalty laws.

In 2005 the Supreme Court reduced the scope of capital punishment even further. In *Roper v. Simmons* a majority of the justices decided that convicted individuals cannot be sentenced to death for crimes they committed before they reached the age of 18.[22] Prior to that decision, the United States was among only a half-dozen countries in the entire world with laws that permitted death sentences for juveniles. Because the Court was divided on the issue, some observers wonder if further changes in the Court's composition could lead to a reversal of this decision.

▲ *When the Nebraska legislature repealed the death penalty in 2015, some citizens mobilized to get it back on the books. In 2016, under intense public pressure, the legislature reinstated the death penalty.*

Continuing Legal Issues

The case law since *Furman* indicates that capital punishment is legal as long as it is imposed fairly. However, opponents continue to raise several issues in litigation. Now that the developmentally disabled and juveniles have been excluded from eligibility for the death penalty, some people argue that convicted individuals who are mentally ill should also be excluded. Issues have also arisen about the effectiveness of representation provided by defense attorneys. Many critics are concerned about the impact of using death-qualified juries. Questions have also been raised about the use of capital punishment for crimes other than murder. Other cases continue to raise concerns about the lengthy periods that condemned individuals spend on death row because of appeals. Finally, issues have arisen concerning the requirements of international law as they apply to the administration of capital punishment in the United States.

Execution of the Mentally Ill Insanity is a recognized defense for commission of a crime because mens rea (criminal intent) is not present. But should people who become mentally ill after they are sentenced to death be executed? The Supreme Court responded to this question in 1985 in *Ford v. Wainwright*.[23] In 1974 Alvin Ford was convicted of murder and sentenced to death. There was no suggestion at his trial or sentencing that he was mentally incompetent. Only after he was incarcerated did he begin to exhibit delusional behavior, claiming that the Ku Klux Klan was part of an elaborate conspiracy to force him to commit suicide and that his female relatives were being tortured and sexually abused somewhere in the prison.

With evidence of these delusions, Ford's counsel invoked the procedures of the Florida law governing the determination of competency of a condemned individual. Three psychiatrists examined Ford for 30 minutes in the presence of witnesses, including counsel and correctional officials. Each psychiatrist filed a separate and conflicting report with the governor, who subsequently signed a death warrant. Ford then appealed to the U.S. Supreme Court.

Justice Thurgood Marshall, writing for the majority, concluded that the Eighth Amendment prohibited the state from executing the insane—the convicted person must comprehend both the fact that he or she had been sentenced to death and the reason for it. Marshall cited the common-law precedent that questioned the retributive and deterrent value of executing a mentally ill person. In addition, he argued, the idea is offensive to humanity. The justices also found the Florida procedures defective because they did not provide for a full and fair hearing on the competence of the individual.

Although the Supreme Court has ruled that the insane should not be executed, the issue arose again in Arkansas in 1991. Rickey Ray Rector killed two men, one of whom was a police officer. He then shot himself in the temple, lifting three inches off the front of his brain, leaving him with the mental capabilities of a small child. He was convicted at trial and given the death sentence. In prison he howled day and night, jumped around, exhibited other aspects of abnormal behavior, and seemed to have no idea that he was to be executed.

The U.S. Supreme Court rejected his appeal. The Arkansas Parole and Community Rehabilitation Board unanimously turned down a recommendation that Governor Bill Clinton commute the death sentence to life imprisonment without parole. Clinton declined to halt the execution, and Rector was given a lethal injection on January 24, 1991.

Although the Supreme Court has ruled that the insane should not be executed, how competence should be determined remains an issue. A second issue concerns the morality of treating an individual's mental illness so that he or she *can* be executed, a policy opposed by the American Medical Association. In 2003 the U.S. Eighth Circuit Court of Appeals held that Arkansas could force Charles Singleton, who was on death row, to take antipsychotic drugs to make him sane enough to execute. Singleton was executed on January 6, 2004.[24]

After the ruling in *Atkins,* Michael Bies appealed his death sentence, arguing that his mental illness was a mitigating factor in his crimes. The state claimed that he was not mentally ill. Bies claimed double jeopardy, which would bar the state from relitigating his mental illness. In a unanimous opinion the Supreme Court wrote that state courts do not violate the double jeopardy clause if they rehear mental illness claims.

Effective Counsel In *Strickland v. Washington* (1984) the Supreme Court ruled that people accused in capital cases have the right to representation that meets an "objective standard of reasonableness."[25] As noted by Justice Sandra Day O'Connor, the appellant must show "that there is a reasonable probability that, but for counsel's unprofessional errors, the result of the proceeding would have been different."[26]

David Washington was charged with three counts of capital murder, robbery, kidnapping, and other felonies, and an experienced criminal lawyer was appointed as counsel. Against his attorney's advice, Washington confessed to two murders, waived a jury trial, pleaded guilty to all charges, and chose to be sentenced by the trial judge. Believing the situation was hopeless, his counsel did not adequately prepare for the sentencing hearing. On being sentenced to death, Washington appealed. The Supreme Court rejected Washington's claim that his attorney was ineffective because he did not call witnesses, seek a presentence investigation report, or cross-examine medical experts on the client's behalf.

An extensive investigation into Illinois defense attorneys' competence conducted by the *Chicago Tribune* found that 33 people sentenced to death since 1977 were represented by an attorney who had been, or was later, disbarred or suspended for conduct that was "incompetent, unethical or even criminal." These attorneys included David Landau, who was disbarred one year after representing a Will County person sentenced to death, and Robert McDonnell, convicted of a felony and the only lawyer in Illinois history to be disbarred twice. McDonnell had represented four men who landed on death row.[27]

In March 2000 a federal judge in Texas ordered the release of Calvin Jerold Burdine after 16 years on death row. At his 1984 trial, Burdine's counsel slept through long portions of the proceedings. As the judge said, "Sleeping counsel is equivalent to no counsel at all."[28]

Most people in capital cases are indigent and are provided counsel by the state. Critics argue that defense in capital cases is a highly specialized area of the law and that inexperienced attorneys should not be assigned to indigent cases. In most jurisdictions, counsel appointed to represent these clients receive only modest fees.

The right to effective counsel was reaffirmed by the Supreme Court in June 2003, when it overturned the death sentence of Kevin Wiggins. The seven-member majority declared that Wiggins's inexperienced lawyer had failed to provide adequate representation. During the sentencing phase, lawyers had failed to present mitigating evidence to the jury of the horrendous abuse that Wiggins had endured throughout his childhood. In a similar situation an inexperienced attorney was appointed by an Alabama judge to assist two more-seasoned lawyers to defend Holly Wood, a man charged with murdering his girlfriend. At the sentencing hearing the young attorney failed to present evidence to the jury that his client was developmentally disabled and that his life should be spared. The jury, by a vote of 10–2, the minimum allowed under Alabama law, recommended death.[29] Whether the justices of the U.S. Supreme Court will create clearer or stricter standards for defense attorneys remains to be seen.

Death-Qualified Juries Should people who are opposed to the death penalty be excluded from juries in capital cases? (See "Do the Right Thing.") In *Witherspoon v. Illinois* (1968), the Supreme Court held that potential jurors who

DO THE RIGHT THING

You have been called for jury duty for a trial in which the prosecutor will seek the death penalty. You are opposed to capital punishment but conflicted about how you will answer the prosecutor's question regarding your stance. If you are true to your beliefs, the prosecutor is likely to bar you from serving on the jury. If you are not forthcoming about your opposition, you might land on the jury and vote against a sentence that would result in execution.

WRITING ASSIGNMENT: Develop a scenario in which you are asked by the prosecutor your position on capital punishment. In this scenario, answer the question and give reasons for your position.

have general objections to the death penalty or whose religious convictions oppose its use cannot be automatically excluded from jury service in capital cases. However, it upheld the practice of removing, during voir dire (preliminary examination), those people whose opposition is so strong as to "prevent or substantially impair the performance of their duties." Such jurors have become known as "Witherspoon excludables." The decision was later reaffirmed in *Lockhart v. McCree* (1986).[30]

In *Uttecht v. Brown* (2007) the Supreme Court appears to have enhanced the state's ability to remove potential jurors with doubts about the death penalty. In a 5–4 decision the Court upheld the trial court judge who excused from the jury a person who had merely expressed doubts, not uniform opposition, to the death penalty.[31]

Because society is divided on capital punishment, opponents argue that death-qualified juries, those deemed able to judge a capital case fairly and impartially, do not represent a cross-section of the community. Researchers have also found that "juries are likely to be nudged toward believing the defendant is guilty and toward an imposition of the death sentence by the very process of undergoing death qualification."[32] Another impact is "a major bleaching of juries," according to Samuel Gross, a professor at the University of Michigan Law School: "Many more African Americans are excluded than whites." The biggest demographic predictor of attitudes toward the death penalty is race.[33]

Mark Costanzo points to research indicating that death qualification has several impacts. First, those who are selected for jury duty are more conviction prone and more receptive to aggravating factors presented during the penalty phase. A second, subtler impact is that jurors answering the questions about their willingness to vote for a death sentence often conclude that both defenders and prosecutors anticipate a conviction and a death sentence.[34]

Execution for Child Rape Because of the heinous nature of the crime, several states have sought to enact laws permitting use of the death penalty for adults who rape children, even when the children have not been murdered. Patrick Kennedy was convicted and sentenced to death in 2004 by Louisiana for the rape of his eight-year-old stepdaughter. The sentence was upheld by the Louisiana Supreme Court. In *Kennedy v. Louisiana* (2008) the U.S. Supreme Court, in a 5–4 decision, held that a capital sentence where the crime did not involve murder was in violation of the Eighth and Fourteenth amendments.[35] The justices cited their decision in *Coker v. Georgia* (1977), which ruled that the use of the death penalty for rape of an adult was unconstitutional. Since that decision, it had generally been assumed that the death penalty could be imposed only for murder.[36] The narrow division of the Court in the *Kennedy* decision has led observers to believe that a shift in the composition of the Court could reverse the decision.

Appeals Many argue that the appellate process for death sentences takes too long, traumatizes victims' families, and burdens states with millions in extra costs for defense attorneys and for housing convicted killers. Others point out that an appellate process that thoroughly examines each case is necessary because during the 1990s, 26 percent of state death sentences were overturned during the first level of the appeals process.

A study of 1,676 cases resolved between 1992 and 2002 in 14 states found that the time from the date of the death sentence to the completion of a direct appeal was a median 966 days. Petitioning the U.S. Supreme Court added 188 days if certiorari (judicial review) was denied and a median 250 days where certiorari was granted and the issues decided on the merits.[37] The 60 people executed in 2005 had been under sentence of death an average of 12 years and 3 months, 15 months longer than those executed in 2004. During this time, sentences were reviewed by the state courts and, through the writ of habeas corpus, by the federal courts.

The writ of habeas corpus (see Chapter 5) is the only means by which the federal courts can hear legal challenges by individuals incarcerated in state facilities. A long time is required to exhaust state appeals before filing a habeas corpus petition in the federal courts. Intervening court decisions have frequently reinterpreted the law to help the individual's case. Yet in two 1990 decisions the Court limited the ability of condemned individuals to base appeals on new favorable rulings issued after their convictions.

In a major ruling affecting death penalty appeals, the Court sharply curtailed the ability of condemned individuals to file multiple challenges to the constitutionality of their sentences. In *McCleskey v. Zant* (1991) the Court ruled that, except in exceptional circumstances, the lower federal courts must dismiss a person's second and subsequent habeas corpus petitions. Observers believe that this ruling will result in states' carrying out death sentences more quickly.[38]

In 1993 the Supreme Court further restricted appeals to the federal courts when it ruled that an individual who presents belated evidence of innocence is not ordinarily entitled to a new hearing in a federal court before execution. This ruling centered on the case of Leonel Herrera, who was convicted in Texas and sentenced to death for the 1982 murder of two police officers. Ten years later, Herrera's nephew asserted in an affidavit that before he died in 1984, his father, Raul, had confessed to the crime, asserting that Leonel had not shot the officers. Statements from three other people who had previously named Raul Herrera as the murderer were presented to the court. Texas law provides only 30 days for filing a motion for a new trial based on newly discovered evidence. The Supreme Court rejected Leonel Herrera's argument that his case should be reopened because of the new evidence. The chief justice, writing for the majority, observed that only in "truly persuasive" cases should a hearing be held.[39] Herrera was executed on May 12, 1993. His last words were "I am innocent; I am innocent. God bless you all."

The late William Rehnquist, who served as chief justice from 1986 to 2005, actively sought to reduce the opportunities for people awaiting capital punishment to have their appeals heard by multiple courts. In 1996 President Clinton signed the Anti-Terrorism and Effective Death Penalty Act, which requires individuals on death row to file habeas appeals within one year and requires that federal judges issue their decisions within strict time limits.

Appellate review is a time-consuming and expensive process, but it also makes an impact. A major study of death penalty appeals found that two out of three convictions were overturned on appeal, mostly because of serious errors by incompetent defense lawyers or overzealous police officers and prosecutors. From 1973 through 2013, a total of 8,466 people entered prison under sentence of death. During that time, 1,359 (16.1 percent) prisoners were executed, 3,586 (42.4 percent) had their death sentence removed by appellate court decisions and reviews or by commutations, 509 (6 percent) died while awaiting execution, and the remainder were awaiting execution.[40]

Michael Radelet, William Lofquist, and Hugo Bedau examined the cases of 68 individuals on death row who were later released because of doubts about their guilt.[41] These cases account for one of every five individuals executed during the period 1970–1996. Correction of the miscarriage of justice for about one-third of these people took four years or less, but it took nine years or longer for another third of them. Had the expedited appeals process and limitations on habeas corpus been in effect, would these death sentences have been overturned?

International Law The last decade has seen a huge increase in the number of foreign nationals entering the United States, legally or illegally. Not surprisingly, many of these foreigners are convicted of crimes unrelated to their immigration status. Since 2014, 127 foreign nationals from 32 countries have been sent to death row. As of April 2014, 127 foreign nationals from 32 countries were on death row.[42] The rights of foreign nationals in the criminal justice system have added a new dimension to legal issues surrounding the death penalty.

The United States is a signatory of the Vienna Convention on Consular Relations, which requires notification of consular officials when a foreign national is arrested. This aspect of international law benefits Americans who face punishment in foreign countries. However, individual prosecutors and police throughout the United States are apparently unaware of the law because several dozen foreign nationals have been convicted and sentenced to death in the United States without their consular officials being informed.

Mexico, Germany, and Paraguay have filed complaints against the United States for violating the Vienna Convention in death penalty cases. In April 2004 the International Court of Justice in The Hague, Netherlands, ruled that international law had been violated and ordered the United States to review the death sentences of Mexicans held on U.S. death rows. The International Court has no power to force the United States to take action, but President George W. Bush announced in February 2005 that the United States would comply with the Vienna Convention. In light of this announcement, the Supreme Court decided not to rule on a pending case brought by a Mexican citizen on death row in Texas (*Medellin v. Dretke*).[43] Instead, the majority of justices decided to wait and see how the Texas courts would handle the cases of 12 Mexican nationals on death row. In November 2006 the Texas Court of Criminal Appeals, in a long and complex ruling, said that the president did not have the power to direct such a review. Writing for the nine-member court, Judge Michael Keasler said, "We hold that the president has exceeded his constitutional authority by intruding into the independent powers of the judiciary."[44]

The issue returned to the U.S. Supreme Court in May 2007, when the justices accepted an appeal from Jose E. Medellin. In a brief filed on behalf of Medellin, U.S. Solicitor General Paul Clement urged that the Supreme Court overturn the Texas court's decision, arguing that to let that court's ruling stand would place the United States at odds with international law and the World Court. However, the justices felt differently and held in *Medellin v. Texas* (2008) that the president did not have the power to order the states to follow the Vienna Convention.[45]

Whether international law will spur additional issues and arguments concerning the death penalty remains to be seen. For example, in 2002 the Supreme Court declined to rule in a death row case that asserted a violation of the cruel and unusual punishments clause because the petitioner had spent 27 years in solitary confinement on death row under exceptionally restrictive conditions.[46] The condemned man cited judicial decisions by foreign courts, such as the Privy Council of Great Britain and the European Court of Human Rights, that stated a delay of 15 years between trial and execution can render a capital punishment conviction "degrading, shocking or cruel." Several justices of the Supreme Court have made it clear that they do not believe that international law has any application to the American criminal justice system, but other justices have cited foreign cases to support specific decisions.

LO 4

Characterize the individuals on death row.

INDIVIDUALS ON DEATH ROW

Nearly 12,000 arrests for murder and non-negligent manslaughter were made in 2018, yet fewer than 50 individuals received the death penalty during that same year.[47] The Supreme Court has ruled that juries must weigh aggravating and mitigating factors before recommending the sentence in capital cases. What other factors might contribute to the selection of only a few for execution? Does who they are, where the crime was committed, or who the prosecutor was make any difference? Is race a factor?

Who Is on Death Row?

Individuals on death row tend to be poorly educated men. Further, the number of minority group members on death row is far out of proportion to their numbers in the general population (see Figure 20.5). Approximately two-thirds (or 67.3 percent) of people on death row have a prior felony conviction, 9.0 percent have a prior homicide conviction, and 27.9 percent were on probation or parole or in prison at the time of the capital offense.[48] (See "Myths in Corrections" for more.)

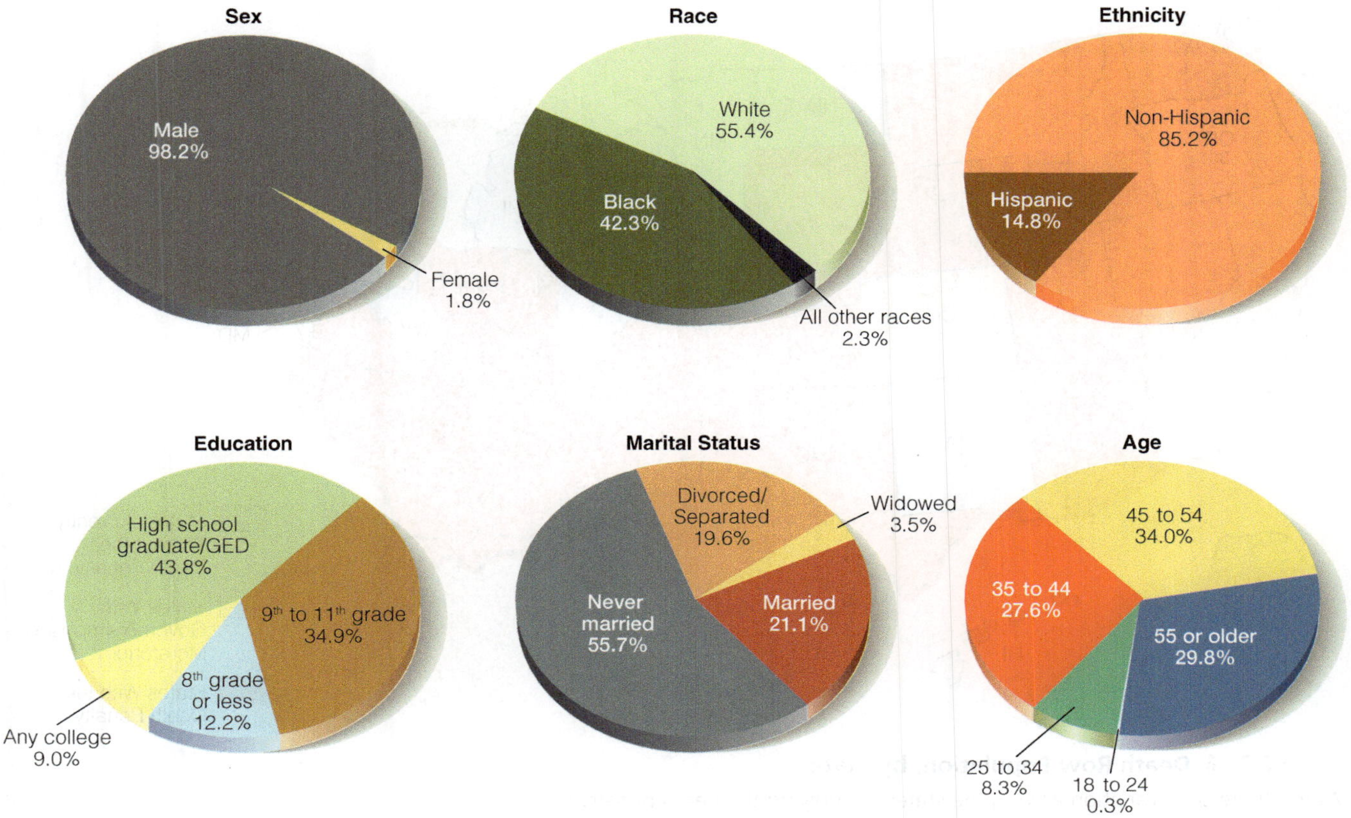

FIGURE 20.5 Characteristics of People on Death Row

Like other incarcerated people, individuals on death row tend to be male and racial minorities.

Note: Pie charts may not total 100% due to rounding.

Source: Elizabeth Davis and Tracy L. Snell, *Capital Punishment, 2016* (Washington, DC: U.S. Government Printing Office, 2018), 7.

As of 2016, only 55 women were on death row. Since 1976, only 16 women have been executed.[49] Although 13 percent of arrestees for murder are women, judges and jurors seem reluctant to sentence women to death.[50] However, what some view as a double standard may end as public attitudes toward women change.

Where Was the Crime Committed?

Of particular interest is the distribution of individuals on death row among the states, as shown in Figure 20.6. About 50 percent of those under sentence of death are in the South, 37 percent in the West, and 7 percent in the Midwest. Approximately 6 percent are in the northeastern states. Also revealing is the fact that of the executions from 1977 to March 2020, about 65 percent have been carried out in five states: Texas (569), Virginia (113), Oklahoma (112), Florida (99), and Missouri (89).[51] (See Figure 20.7.)

Who Was the Prosecutor?

A study on death penalty cases since 1976 revealed that the ultimate sanction is not distributed evenly across geographic areas in the United States. Indeed, it tends to be handed down as a sanction in specific counties. More specifically, the analysis revealed that 15 counties were responsible for a majority of executions.[52] Although Harris County (Houston) has been known as the "death penalty capital" among critics of capital punishment, that "honor" was eclipsed in 2006 by Maricopa County (Phoenix).[53]

MYTHS in Corrections

They May Kill Again

THE MYTH: Public safety is often a reason given in support of the death penalty. There is concern among many that a murderer will kill again.

THE REALITY: A study of the 589 individuals on death row whose sentences were converted to life imprisonment because of Furman v. Georgia (1972) found that of the 322 eventually paroled, 75 were returned to prison for a technical parole violation or a nonviolent crime, 32 returned to prison because of a violent crime, and 5 killed again.

Source: Joan M. Cheever, *Back from the Dead* (West Sussex, England: Wiley, 2006), 56.

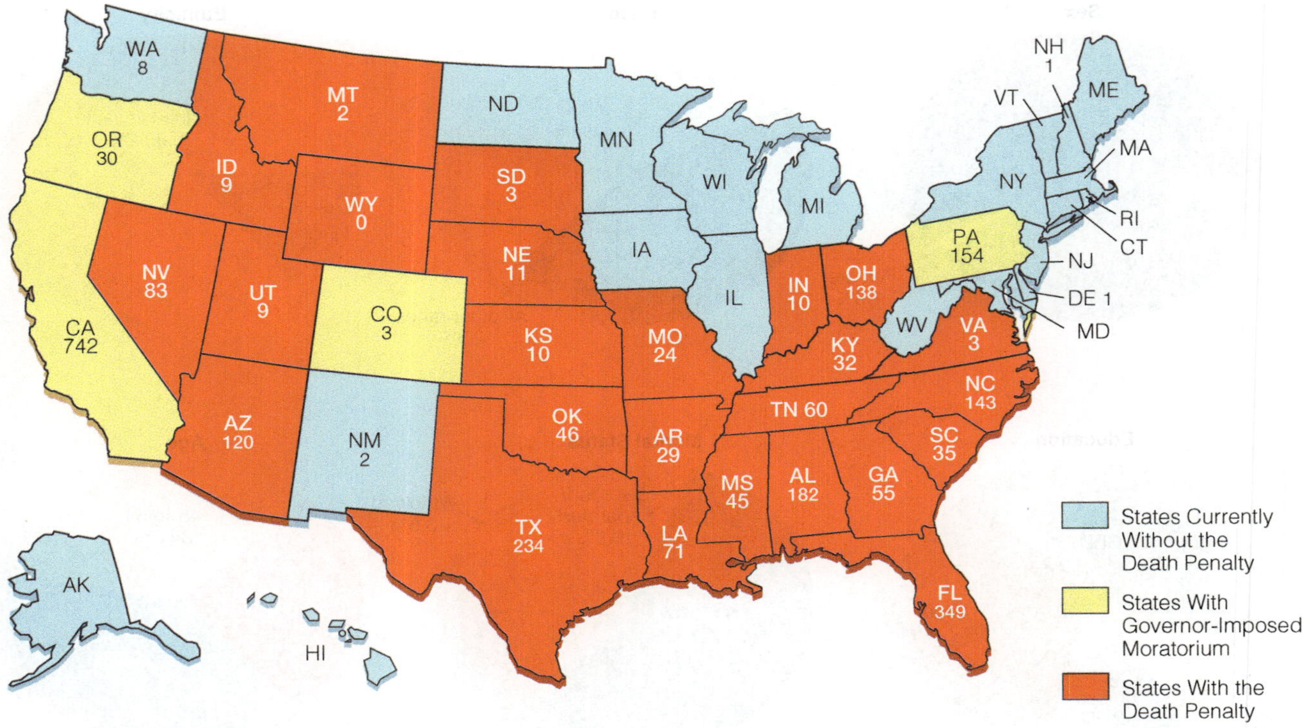

FIGURE 20.6 Death Row Population, by State

Why is there such variation among the states in applying the death penalty?

Source: Tracy L. Snell, *Capital Punishment, 2017: Selected Findings* (Washington, DC: U.S. Government Printing Office, 2019), 3.

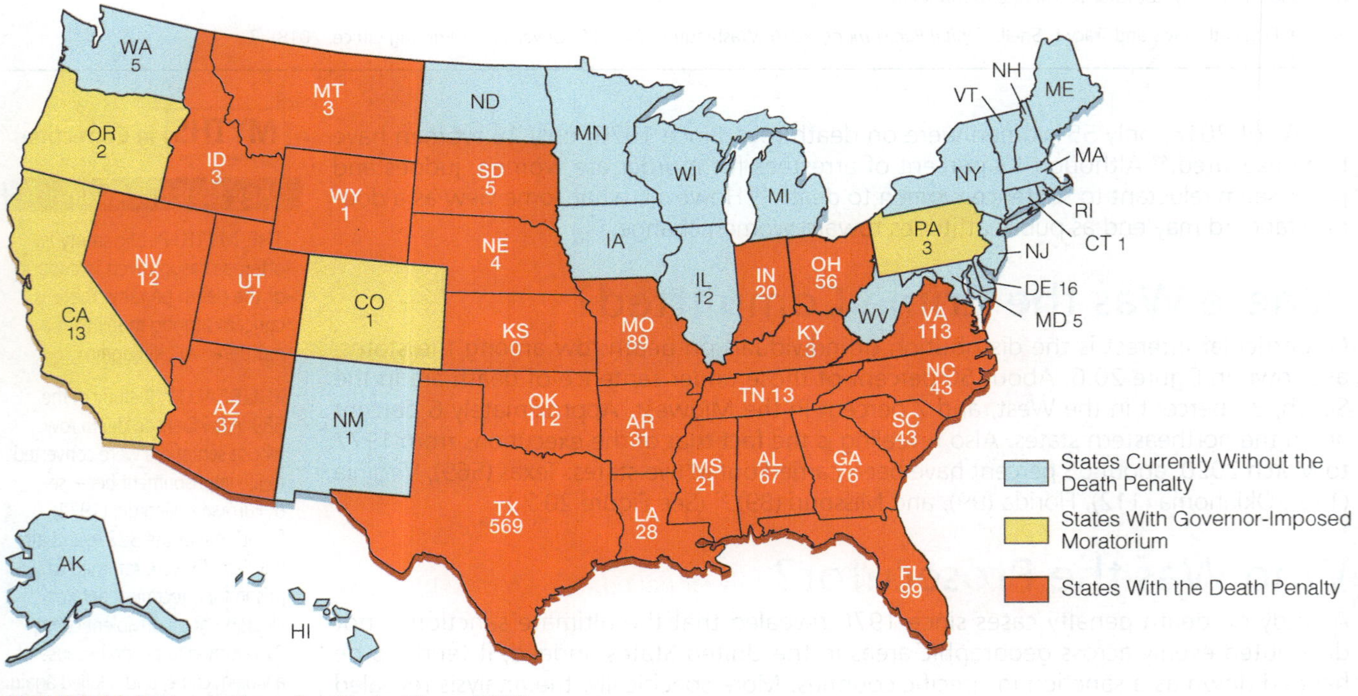

FIGURE 20.7 Executions by State Since 1976

What might explain the wide variation in the use of the death penalty across states?

Source: Death Penalty Information Center, *Facts About the Death Penalty* (Washington, DC: Author, March 2020), 3.

Even within states, the probability that a prosecutor will ask for the death penalty differs. For example, of the 289 people executed in Texas from 1977 to 2002, 67 were from the Houston area (5.3 executions per 1,000 murders), where the district attorney was a vocal advocate of the death penalty. In contrast, the district attorney in the Dallas area was more circumspect; only 26 people from that area have been executed (3.1 executions per 1,000 murders). But the real surprise is the Corpus Christi area, where 10 were executed—a whopping 13 executions per 1,000 murders.[54] The discretionary power of prosecutors explains many of these differences. Political factors may be at work in some areas to the extent that prosecuting attorneys and judges expect to be reelected if they campaign on their death penalty record.

Was Race a Factor?

Many assume that African American men are overrepresented on death row because they make up about 42 percent of the people living on death row yet compose a much smaller portion of the U.S. population. However, research has shown that African Americans commit about 50 percent of all murders nationally in states with the death penalty and those without it. Researchers found that juries are least likely to impose a death sentence in black-on-black murders (which make up the majority of murder cases involving African Americans). A death sentence is more likely in white-on-white cases and most likely when the perpetrator is African American and the victim is white.[55]

Research by David Baldus, George Woodworth, and Charles Pulaski Jr. found that imposition of the death penalty in Georgia was influenced by the race of the murder victim and, to a lesser extent, the race of the condemned.[56] Recall our earlier discussion of the Supreme Court's ruling that this did not constitute a breach of equal protection in *McCleskey v. Kemp*.

Is Georgia unique, or is the victim's race a determinative factor in other states? Samuel Gross and Robert Mauro examined the death penalty in Arkansas, Florida, Georgia, Illinois, Mississippi, North Carolina, Oklahoma, and Virginia. In each state they found that the death sentence was more likely to be imposed if the victim was white rather than African American. The ratios varied from 10:1 in Georgia and Mississippi to 5:1 in Virginia.[57] A study of the death penalty in North Carolina found that cases in which victims were white were 3.5 times more likely to result in a death sentence than were those in which the victims were people of color.[58]

Does the evidence from these states indicate racism, or do other factors play a role? Robert Bohm examined racial disparity and discrimination in two Georgia judicial circuits and suggested that institutional racism, such as the few African American prosecutors, defense attorneys, and judges in the system, is what influences capital punishment decisions. He believes that one result of the Supreme Court's decision in *McCleskey v. Kemp* is that it will be almost impossible to show racism in individual cases. Bohm quotes Georgia State Senator Gary Parker as saying, "The Supreme Court's decision in *McCleskey v. Kemp* has been interpreted by prosecutors and judges in the South as a clear message that they are not to be held accountable in the courts for racial discrimination that occurs in capital trials."[59]

A CONTINUING DEBATE

LO 5

Speculate about the future of capital punishment.

In recent years, courts, governors, and legislatures in many of the death penalty states have acted to abolish or limit executions. Since 1973, the exoneration of 167 individuals on death row has added to the concern that innocent people may be executed.[60] New Jersey abolished the death penalty in 2007. Several other states followed suit, including New Mexico (2009), Connecticut (2012), Maryland (2013), and Delaware (2016). Most recently, the legislature in New Hampshire abolished the death penalty by overriding a gubernatorial veto.[61]

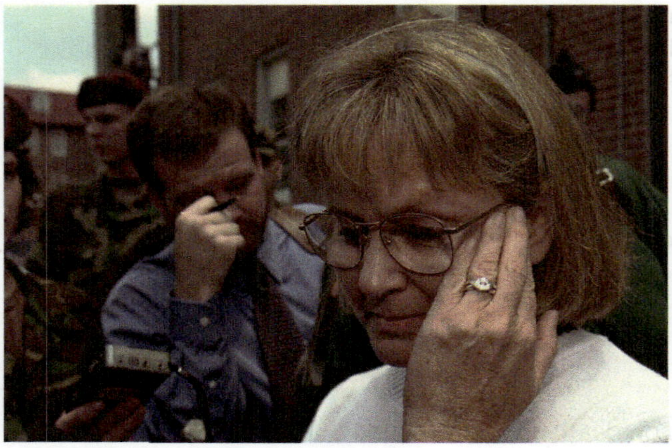

▲ *Kathy Branson, mother of murder victim Kianna Jackson, and Jackson's grandmother, Diane Menzies, talk about their heartbreak at the sentencing hearing for Steven Dean Gordon, who was convicted of the kidnapping, sexual assault, and murder of Kianna.*

Use of the death penalty has dropped in recent years. The number of death sentences has declined by more than half since the 1990s, and the number of executions has also decreased. Do these actions signify a shift in U.S. policy and opinion regarding the death penalty? Although debate on this important public policy issue has gone on for more than 200 years, no consensus has formed.

Individuals who oppose the death penalty argue that poor people and members of minority groups receive a disproportionate number of death sentences. Opponents also cite the finality of death, in light of the number of acknowledged mistakes that have been made in the past, as sufficient reason to oppose capital punishment. Nationally, people have been released each year because of such factors as perjured testimony, withheld evidence, or mistakes of identification; some of these exonerated individuals are released directly from death row.

Opponents further note that to try, convict, and execute someone accused of murder costs much more than trying that individual in a noncapital case and keeping him or her in prison for 20 years. A study in Oregon found that the average cost for a death penalty case was nearly double what was spent on a non-capital murder case. The researchers concluded that "maintaining the death penalty incurs a significant financial burden on Oregon taxpayers."[62]

Proponents of the death penalty claim that it deters people from committing violent acts and that justice demands that murderers suffer retribution, regardless of cost. They further argue that, given the high levels of violent crimes in the United States, we must retain the severest penalties. To give someone a life sentence of incarceration for murder diminishes the worth of the victim, is costly to society, and does not lessen the possibility that the individual will do further harm either while incarcerated or on parole. In answer to the charge that the death penalty is administered in an arbitrary and capricious manner, observers argue that the system in place today ensures that the death penalty is reserved for only those convicted of the most heinous crimes.

Will the United States increase the pace of executions, allow the number of individuals with death sentences in prison to grow, or provide some alternatives such as life imprisonment without parole for those convicted of murder? Might the United States follow the European pattern of de facto abolition before de jure abolition? These questions remain unanswered.

SUMMARY

1 Compare and contrast the issues in the debate over capital punishment.

Arguments for the death penalty include the following: The death penalty deters people from committing violent acts; it achieves justice by paying killers back for their horrible crimes; it prevents people from committing future acts while on parole; it is less expensive than holding individuals in prison for life. Arguments against the death penalty include the following: No hard evidence proves that the death penalty is a deterrent; it is wrong for the government to participate in the intentional killing of its citizens; the death penalty is applied in a discriminatory fashion; innocent people have been sentenced to death.

2 Explain the history of the death penalty in America.

The death penalty was common for a range of offenses during the early settlement of America. Public executions were common until the 1830s, when most of them were moved inside prison walls. The number of states without the death penalty has increased in recent years. In some states the law is still on the books, yet there have been few or no executions in the last 40 years.

3 Discuss the legal issues that surround the death penalty.
The Eighth and Fourteenth amendments to the Constitution prohibit cruel and unusual punishments and require equal protection under the law, respectively. The U.S. Supreme Court has held that the death penalty is not unconstitutional unless it is administered in a cruel and unusual fashion (*Furman v. Georgia,* 1972). This position was upheld in *Gregg v. Georgia* (1976), as long as the penalty is administered fairly and the judge and jury consider mitigating and aggravating circumstances. This position has been extended to prohibit execution of the developmentally disabled or juveniles and to prohibit it in cases where the offense is not murder. Legal issues concerning execution of the mentally ill, effective counsel, death-qualified juries, the appeals process, and the impact of international law continue to appear before the Court.

4 Characterize the individuals on death row.
Individuals on death row tend to be poorly educated men from low-income backgrounds. The number of minority group members is far out of proportion to their numbers in the general population. Other factors influencing who is on death row include the location of the crime, the prosecutor, and the race of the accused person and the victim.

5 Speculate about the future of capital punishment.
Although the public supports the death penalty, some argue that this support is shallow. The increased number of individuals on death row shown to be innocent seems to have caused a decrease in the number who receive capital punishment and the number who are executed. Several states have recently abolished capital punishment, despite public support for it.

FOR DISCUSSION

1. What are the main arguments supporting and opposing capital punishment? Which one seems to you the most important?
2. Which of the continuing legal issues should the Supreme Court scrutinize as being in violation of the Eighth Amendment?
3. Given that the death penalty has been abolished in other Western democracies, why do people in the United States still support it?
4. What alternatives to death might achieve the retributive, deterrent, and incapacitative goals of capital punishment?
5. What does the future hold for the death penalty?

FOR FURTHER READING

Banner, Stuart. *The Death Penalty.* Cambridge, MA: Harvard University Press, 2002. A history of the death penalty in America from the early colonial period to the execution of Timothy McVeigh in 2001.

Beck, Elizabeth, Sarah Britto, and Arlene Andrews. *In the Shadow of Death: Restorative Justice and Death Row Families.* New York: Oxford University Press, 2006. The personal stories of families victimized by murder who seek restorative justice with the person who killed their loved one.

Cheever, Joan M. *Back from the Dead.* West Sussex, England: Wiley, 2006. Follows those 589 people released from death row as a result of *Furman v. Georgia*. Of the "Class of '72," 322 have been paroled, 32 have been reincarcerated for a violent crime, and 5 have killed again.

Galliher, John F., Larry W. Koch, David Patrick Keys, and Teresa J. Guess. *America Without the Death Penalty.* Boston: Northeastern University Press, 2002. Case studies of nine states without the death penalty. Examines the relationship between death penalty abolition and such factors as economic conditions, public opinion, murder rates, and population diversity.

National Research Council. *Deterrence and the Death Penalty*. Washington, DC: National Academies Press, 2012. A comprehensive effort to review the research on the deterrent effect of capital punishment. The report finds little evidence to support the contention that the death penalty reduces homicides.

Zimring, Franklin E. *The Contradictions of American Capital Punishment.* New York: Oxford University Press, 2003. A study that wonders why the United States has not followed other developed countries in abolishing the death penalty.

NOTES

[1] Roger Cohen, "Death Penalty Madness in Alabama," *The New York Times*, www.nytimes.com/2018/02/27/opinion/death-penalty-alabama-doyle-lee-hamm.html, February 27, 2018; Melissa Brown, "Alabama, Death Row Inmate Reach Settlement after Botched Execution,," *Montgomery Advertiser*, www.montgomeryadvertiser.com/story/news/crime/2018/03/27/https-montgomeryadvertiser-story-news-local-solutions-journalism-2018-03-20-can-alabama-try/461862002, March 27, 2018.

[2] *Glossip v. Gross*, 576 U.S. ___ (2015); Adam Liptak, "Supreme Court Allows Use of Execution Drug," *The New York Times*, www.nytimes.com/2015/06/30/us/supreme-court-execution-drug.html?_r=0, June 29, 2015.

[3] Gallup.com, www.news.gallup.com/poll/1606/death-penalty.aspx, May 19, 2020.

[4] Ernest van den Haag, "For the Death Penalty," *The New York Times*, October 17, 1983. See also van den Haag, "Justice, Deterrence and the Death Penalty," in *America's Experiment with Capital Punishment*, edited by James R. Acker, Robert M. Bohm, and Charles S. Lanier (Durham, NC: Carolina Academic Press, 1998), 139–56.

[5] Ibid.

[6] Ruth D. Peterson and William C. Bailey, "Murder and Capital Punishment in the Evolving Context of the Post-*Furman* Era," *Social Forces* 66 (1988): 774–807.

[7] See Isaac Ehrlich, "The Deterrent Effect of Capital Punishment: A Question of Life and Death," *American Economic* Review 65 (1975): 397–417; also see William J. Bowers and Glenn L. Pierce, "The Illusion of Deterrence in Isaac Ehrlich's Research on Capital Punishment," *Yale Law Journa*l 85 (1975): 187–208; Lawrence R. Klein, Brian E. Forst, and Victor Filatov, "The Deterrent Effect of Capital Punishment: An Assessment of the Estimates," in *Deterrence and Incapacitation*, edited by A. Blumstein, J. Cohen, and D. Nagin (Washington, DC: National Academy of Sciences, 1978).

[8] National Research Council, *Deterrence and the Death Penalty*, edited by Daniel S. Nagin and John V. Pepper (Washington, DC: The National Academies Press, 2012), 2.

[9] Louis P. Masur, *Rites of Execution: Capital Punishment and the Transformation of American Culture, 1776–1865* (New York: Oxford University Press, 1989).

[10] "Facts About the Death Penalty," *Death Penalty Information Center*, https://files.deathpenaltyinfo.org/documents/pdf/FactSheet. f1585003454.pdf, May 19, 2020.

[11] Gallup.com, www.news.gallup.com/poll/1606/death-penalty. aspx, May 19, 2020.

[12] Jeffrey M. Jones, "Americans Now Support Life in Prison Over the Death Penalty," *Gallup.com*, https://news.gallup.com/poll/ 268514/americans-support-life-prison-death-penalty.aspx, November 25, 2019.

[13] Death Penalty Information Center, *The Death Penalty in 2019: Year End Report,* www.deathpenaltyinfo.org/facts-and-research/dpic-reports/dpic-year-end-reports/the-death-penalty-in-2019-year-end-report, May 19, 2020.

[14] Amnesty International, *Death Sentences and Executions 2018* (London: Amnesty International Publications, 2019), 4–5.

[15] *Furman v. Georgia*, 408 U.S. 238 (1972).

[16] *Gregg v. Georgia,* 428 U.S. 153 (1976).

[17] Leigh B. Bienen, "The Proportionality Review of Capital Cases by State High Courts After *Gregg*: Only 'The Appearance of Justice?' " *Journal of Criminal Law and Criminology* 87 (Fall 1996): 130–285.

[18] *McCleskey v. Kemp,* 478 U.S. 1019 (1987).

[19] David C. Baldus, George F. Woodworth, and Charles A. Pulaski Jr., *Equal Justice and the Death Penalty: A Legal and Empirical Analysis* (Boston: Northeastern University Press, 1990).

[20] *Atkins v. Virginia,* 122 S. Ct. 2242 (2002).

[21] *Ring v. Arizona,* 122 S. Ct. 2428 (2002).

[22] *Roper v. Simmons,* 125 S. Ct. 1183 (2005).

[23] *Ford v. Wainwright,* 477 U.S. 399 (1985).

[24] www.deathpenaltyinfo.org, February 18, 2007.

[25] Welsh S. White, "Effective Assistance of Counsel in Capital Cases: The Evolving Standard of Care," *University of Illinois Law Review* (1993): 323.

[26] *Strickland v. Washington,* 466 U.S. 668 (1984).

[27] Ken Armstrong and Steve Mills, "82 Death Sentences Tossed Out," *Chicago Tribune,* November 14, 1999, p. 1, and November 15, 1999, p. 1.

[28] *The New York Times,* March 2, 2000, p. A19.

[29] *Wiggins v. Smith*, 539 U.S. 510 (2003); Adam Liptak, "Death Penalty Case Reveals Failing," *The New York Times*, June 9, 2009, p. A14.

[30] *Witherspoon v. Illinois,* 391 U.S. 510 (1968); *Lockhart v. McCree,* 4776 U.S. 162 (1986).

[31] *Uttecht v. Brown,* No. 06-413 (June 4, 2007).

[32] J. Luginbuhl and M. Burkhead, "Sources of Bias and Arbitrariness in the Capital Trial," *Journal of Social Issues* 7 (1994): 103–12.

[33] Adam Liptak, "Facing a Jury of (Some of) One's Peers," *The New York Times,* July 20, 2003.

[34] Costanzo, *Just Revenge*, pp. 24–25.

[35] *Kennedy v. Louisiana*, No. 07-343 (2008).

[36] *Coker v. Georgia*, 453 U.S. 584 (1977).

[37] Barry Latzer and James N. G. Cauthen, *Justice Delayed? Time Consumption in Capital Appeals: A Multi-state Study* (Washington, DC: National Institute of Justice, 2007).
[38] *McCleskey v. Zant,* 111 S. Ct. 1454 (1991).
[39] *New York Times,* January 26, 1993, p. 1.
[40] Tracy L. Snell, *Capital Punishment, 2013—Statistical Tables* (Washington, DC: U.S. Department of Justice, 2014), 19.
[41] Michael L. Radelet, William S. Lofquist, and Hugo Adam Bedau, "Prisoners Released from Death Rows Since 1970 Because of Doubts About Their Guilt," *Thomas M. Cooley Law Review* 13 (1996): 907.
[42] Death Penalty Information Center, *Foreign Nationals*, www.deathpenaltyinfo.org/death-row/foreign-nationals, May 19, 2020.
[43] *Medellin v. Dretke,* 125 S. Ct. 2088 (2005).
[44] Marco Robbins, "Court in Texas Says Bush Wrong on Mexican Cases," *San Antonio Express News,* November 15, 2006.
[45] *Medellin v. Texas,* 552 U.S. 491 (2008).
[46] *Foster v. Florida,* 527 U.S. 990 (2002).
[47] Federal Bureau of Investigation, *Crime in the United States 2018,* https://ucr.fbi.gov/crime-in-the-u.s/2018/crime-in-the-u.s.-2018/topic-pages/tables/table-29, May 19, 2020; Death Penalty Information Center, *Death Sentences in the United States since 1977*, https://deathpenaltyinfo.org/facts-and-research/sentencing-data/death-sentences-in-the-united-states-from-1977-by-state-and-by-year, May 19, 2020.
[48] Snell, *Capital Punishment,* 2013, p. 12.
[49] Death Penalty Information Center, www.deathpenaltyinfo.org/women-and-death-penalty, May 10, 2017.
[50] Federal Bureau of Investigation, https://ucr.fbi.gov/crime-in-the-u.s/2015/crime-in-the-u.s.-2015/tables/table-37, May 10, 2017.
[51] Death Penalty Information Center, *Executions by State and Region Since 1976,* https://deathpenaltyinfo.org/executions/executions-overview/number-of-executions-by-state-and-region-since-1976, May 19, 2020.
[52] Richard C. Dieter, The *2% Death Penalty: How a Minority of Counties Produce Most Death Cases at Enormous Costs to All* (Washington, DC: Death Penalty Information Center, 2013).
[53] Jahna Berry, "Death-Penalty Backlog Strains Justice System," *Arizona Republic,* February 22, 2007.
[54] "The Nation in Numbers: Mortal Justice," *Atlantic,* March 2003, pp. 40, 41.
[55] Blume, Eisenberg, and Wells, "Explaining Death Row."
[56] David Baldus, Charles Pulaski, and George Woodworth, "Comparative Review of Death Sentences: An Empirical Study of the Georgia Experience," *Journal of Criminal Law and Criminology* 74 (1983): 661–85. Victim-based discrimination has been found in several southern states. See, for example, Alan Widmayer and James Marquart, "Capital Punishment and Structured Discretion: Arbitrariness and Discrimination After Furman," in *Correctional Theory and Practice,* edited by Clayton A. Hartjen and Edward E. Rhine (Chicago: Nelson-Hall, 1992), 178–96.
[57] Samuel R. Gross and Robert Mauro, *Death and Discrimination: Racial Disparities in Capital Sentencing* (Boston: Northeastern University Press, 1990), 109–10.
[58] Common Sense Foundation, *Landmark North Carolina Death Penalty Study Finds Dramatic Racial Bias* (Raleigh, NC: 2001).
[59] Robert M. Bohm, "Capital Punishment in Two Judicial Circuits in Georgia," *Law and Human Behavior* 18 (1994): 335.
[60] Death Penalty Information Center, "Innocence Database," www.deathpenaltyinfo.org/policyissues/innocence-database, May 20, 2020.
[61] Ibid., "State by State," www.deathpenaltyinfo.org/states-and-federal-info/state-by-state, May 20, 2020.
[62] Death Penalty Information Center, *Costs of the Death Penalty,* https://deathpenaltyinfo.org/costs-death-penalty#financialfacts, May 11, 2017.

CHAPTER 21

Immigration and Justice

Lucy Nicholson/REUTERS

Detention facilities for undocumented immigrants often hold young children awaiting deportation decisions.

IN 2005, *NEWSWEEK* MAGAZINE CALLED THE THEN OBSCURE MS-13 "THE MOST DANGEROUS GANG IN AMERICA."[1] News accounts of the gang had been scary, indeed: cold-blooded revenge killings, brutal enforcement of gang discipline, menacing recruitment methods, drug and gun markets, and unnerving membership rituals have all been attributed to the gang. Even so, MS-13 remained unfamiliar to most Americans until the last few years.

What brought MS-13 into public awareness was the way the Trump Administration used them as explicit proof of failures in immigration policy. At his 2018 State of the Union Address, President Trump introduced the parents of Kayla Cuevas and Nisa Mickens, two 16-year-olds who were murdered by MS-13 gang members in the Brentwood community on Long Island, New York. He pointed to the murders as the consequence of current immigration policies and called on Congress to "close the deadly loopholes that have allowed MS-13, and other criminals, to break into our country."[2]

MS-13 gang violence is certainly a problem. But like many other aspects of immigration in America, a closer look reveals a more complex situation. Many Americans have the impression that MS-13 is populated by illegal entries by "unaccompanied minors" who cross the southern border of the United States and ask for asylum. There are cases of this happening, including some of those responsible for murders on Long Island. But experts say that by far, most MS-13 gang members came to the United States to escape problems at home and were recruited by MS-13 once they got here. Nevertheless, the gang didn't increase in size—it has had the same estimated 10,000 members for more than a decade. In fact, the gang does not originate outside the United States, but rather was formed in Los Angeles in the 1980s and was later exported to Central America. Of the hundreds of thousands of unaccompanied minors intercepted by border patrol agents since 2012, only 56 were suspected of MS-13 ties.[3] Researchers have found that police often make an assumption that certain youth from some neighborhoods are MS-13 members—just because they are immigrants from El Salvador—they are wrong.[4] The gang is indeed a problem, but it is homegrown not imported.

Illegal immigration is a conundrum. It has grown as a national concern in recent years, with no obvious solutions and difficult trade-offs. We are, after all, a nation largely made up of immigrants, but at the same time what makes us a nation is having borders that enable us to call ourselves a nation. The corrections system has increasingly been called upon to address the problem of illegal border crossings. In this chapter we investigate the issue of immigration generally, and the role of corrections in addressing it. In doing so we explore some of today's most pressing public policy problems, as well as some of our most contentious political debates.

LEARNING OBJECTIVES

After reading this chapter, you should be able to . . .

1. Define the nature of illegal immigration and describe the extent of the problem.
2. Summarize the history of immigration in the United States.
3. Define the different types of immigration under the law.
4. Describe the immigration justice system.
5. Identify key issues in immigration justice.

LO 1

Define the nature of illegal immigration and describe the extent of the problem.

undocumented resident (undocumented immigrant) A foreigner who resides in the United States illegally, whether by crossing illegally, overstaying a visa, or other means.

ILLEGAL IMMIGRATION

It is against the law to be in the United States without some legal basis or documentation—that is, citizenship, green card, or visa. People who are here without such documentation are "illegal aliens," more properly referred to as **undocumented residents** or **undocumented immigrants**. To address the problem of undocumented immigrants, the United States operates a large justice system that interacts continuously with the regular justice system, functioning partly outside that system and partly within it—an immigration justice system. For many years the immigration justice system functioned mostly invisibly. Recently, however, the problem of people living in the United States without citizenship or other lawful residency has become a hotly debated public problem.

The immigration justice system, as we shall see, has its own specialized police, courts, and correctional agencies. The agencies do not operate in isolation from the larger justice apparatus, but often rely upon it for support in carrying out their functions. Yet creating a separate immigration justice system, with a function that both overlaps with and is distinct from the U.S. justice system, prompts a number of questions about how the immigration system should function and whether it is operating as it should.

Current immigration practices in the United States are informed by the history of immigration. The separate immigration justice system intersects with correctional practice at multiple points. The politics of immigration offer crucial feedback to correctional leadership about how immigration issues are handled. What has resulted is a broad immigration public policy that has decisive implications for correctional practice today.

The numbers illustrate how important immigration has become as a public policy issue. There are 10.6 million people living in the United States who do not have legal status—about 3.2 percent of the U.S. population as a whole—a number that has declined almost 10 percent since 2010.[5] Approximately 60,000 undocumented were under Department of Justice custody, 40,000 in immigration detention facilities, at least 3,600 of whom are unaccompanied children.[6] Among the regular prison population, about 105,000 are not citizens—just over 7 percent of all people in prison.[7] Figure 21.1 shows the recent undocumented immigration patterns across the country.

Aside from the sheer size of the system, immigration enforcement has become a polarizing political issue for other reasons. In the presidential election of 2016, the U.S.–Mexico border and the nation's policies regarding people illegally living in America were prevailing issues. Donald J. Trump made strict immigration enforcement a core part of his campaign, saying of Mexicans who had illegally come to America that "They are, in many cases, criminals, drug dealers, rapists, etc." and linking terrorism to foreign nationals.[8] One of his first executive actions as president was to try to prohibit the entry of people from certain nations. The public reaction included public rallies and protest marches in the streets.

In the discussion that follows, we first consider the immigration justice system as a part of the larger U.S. approach to justice. We touch on the law enforcement and adjudication functions because doing so is necessary to fully understand the immigration system. However, our focus is on the corrections-related functions: detention and confinement. As they are carried out, these functions bear a resemblance to the custody functions of jails and prisons—in fact, jails and prisons are where immigrants who are under the authority of the immigration justice system tend to be confined. But as we will see, the immigration versions of confinement do not have many of the characteristics of confinement in the regular justice system. For example, immigration confinement does not ordinarily place a high priority on rehabilitation. Due process of law often takes a backseat to law enforcement and public safety. Sometimes entire families are confined. Conditions are problematic. Legal rights seem to lose emphasis. In all, the immigration justice system operates often like a poor relative of the larger justice system, with fewer resources, less public scrutiny, and a greater history of problems. The increasing strain on correctional resources operates under the radar of many public officials.

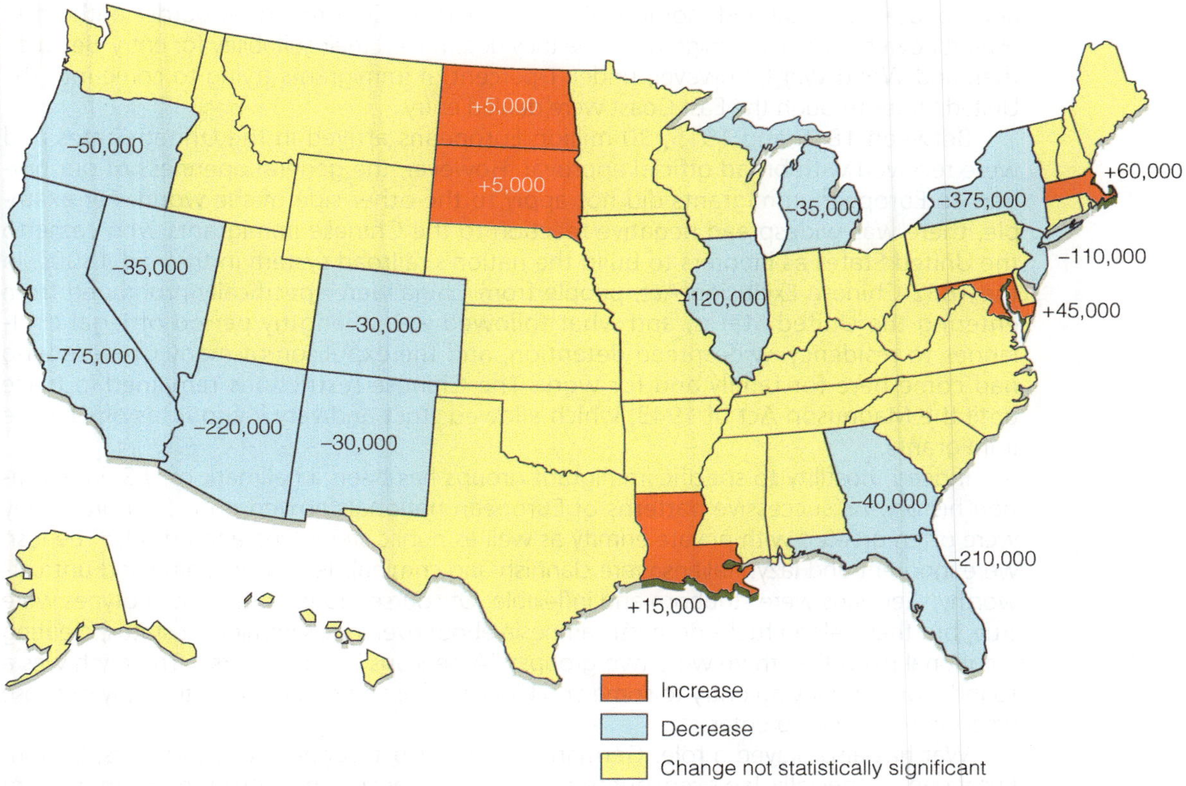

Note: All numbers are rounded. Significant changes based on 90% confidence interval.

FIGURE 21.1 States' Changes in the Number of Undocumented Immigrants, 2007–2017

Some states have seen increases in the number of undocumented immigrants while others have seen decreases. What explains these differences?

Source: Jens Manuel Krogstad, Jeffrey S. Passel, and D'Vera Cohn, *5 Facts About Illegal Immigration in the U.S.* (Washington, DC: Pew Research Center, 2019).

Immigration History

LO 2

Summarize the history of immigration in the United States.

About 1 percent of the U.S. population is Native American. The remaining 99 percent—almost everyone reading this book—is made up of immigrants. By far, of course, most of today's immigrant population comprises U.S. citizens, having been born on U.S. soil or else descended from someone born here. But it is worthwhile to recognize that the United States is a nation of immigrants and that immigration to this continent has a long history.

In fact, for the first century of the nation's existence, there were no formal legal controls on immigration.[9] Agents of the individual states working at ports of entry exercised broad but unofficial discretion to deny entry for people who were ill or otherwise undesirable, but the general practice was to maintain an open border—especially to bring in new laborers to help a growing nation thrive. Until the late 1880s, when public concern arose about some immigrants who were seen as integrating poorly into the country or were otherwise unwelcome, most people entered the United States without any problem.

The national regulation of immigration began with the Immigration Act of 1882, which established federal authority over who was allowed to cross any of the U.S. borders. The law was intended to enable federal border authorities to refuse entry to anyone who lacked appropriate "physical and moral qualities."[10] In 1883 Congress gave border authorities explicit power to detain immigrants while they determined their suitability for entry. Between then and World War I, however, under 1 percent of immigrants trying to come into the United States through the East Coast were denied entry.

Between 1815 and 1915, 30 million Europeans arrived in the United States and were received with broad official approval. However, the general openness of our borders to European immigrants did not apply to the other side of the world. For example, there was widespread negative reaction to the Chinese immigrants who came to the United States as laborers to build the nation's railroad system in the mid-1800s. In the 1882 Chinese Exclusion Act, people from China were specifically prohibited from entering the United States, and what followed was a lengthy period of legal challenges to residency, widespread detention, and the expulsion of many Chinese who had come here for family and for work. The Chinese restrictions remained in place until the Magnuson Act of 1943, which allowed strict and very low quotas of Chinese immigrants.

Indeed, hostility to specific immigrant groups has been a hallmark of U.S. immigration history. As successive patterns of European nationals arrived on U.S. shores, they were often greeted with private enmity as well as public stereotype and ridicule: The Irish were ignorant and lazy; Italians were clannish and criminal; Jews were shifty and untrustworthy; Germans were stubborn and inflexible. Of course, none of these stereotypes were true, but they helped fuel a domestic amnesia about everyone's immigrant status, creating a national myth that there were two groups: "Americans" and "others." The myth was a foundation for denying entry to some and blocking full and equal access to many of those who were allowed to enter.

War has also played a role. Germans faced distrust during the world wars; Eastern Europeans, especially Jews, encountered suspicion because of anticommunism; and, of course, the Japanese were infamously subjected to a national policy of concentration camp detention during World War II. Earlier in our history, Mexicans living in America were readily attacked during the Mexican-American War, and peaceful Native Americans were slaughtered during the westward expansion.

Even with this deeply troubling history, it is fair to say that no nation on Earth can match the U.S. record of openness to newcomers and "melting pot" attitude. Our nation proudly (and rightly) echoes the famous line by Emma Lazarus, written in 1883: "Give us your tired, your poor."[11] But there has always been ambivalence—perhaps it is not too much to add this: please, not too tired, nor too poor nor too "different."

LO 3

Define the different types of immigration under the law.

Types of Immigrants Under the Law

After World War I, with the passage of the Emergency Quota Act, immigration policy was linked to the U.S. census, setting nation-specific quotas that capped rates of admission based on population patterns within the country. While this approach has a certain logic, critics rightfully pointed out that it made immigration impervious to changes taking place in the world, and—because of the historical patterns of immigration to date—privileged Europeans over Africans, South/Central Americans, and Asians, people who were from places that had large waiting lists of individuals wanting to come to America.

Immigration and Nationality Act of 1965 Act that abolished an earlier quota system based on national origin and established a new immigration policy based on reuniting immigrant families and attracting skilled labor to the United States.

In response to this critique, the **Immigration and Nationality Act of 1965** altered the policy by creating preferred immigration categories for relatives of current residents, those with important skills, and refugees of violence or unrest. Each preferential category was given an immigration cap, revised regularly, to give a kind of rationality to the nation's immigration policy and to allow for informed debate about the nation's priorities.

These preferred immigration categories, even though they are often disputed, are still used today (see Figure 21.2). To understand how they work, it is important not to conflate different types of immigration statuses. When it comes to the immigrant justice system, noncitizen immigrants may have one of four main statuses.[12]

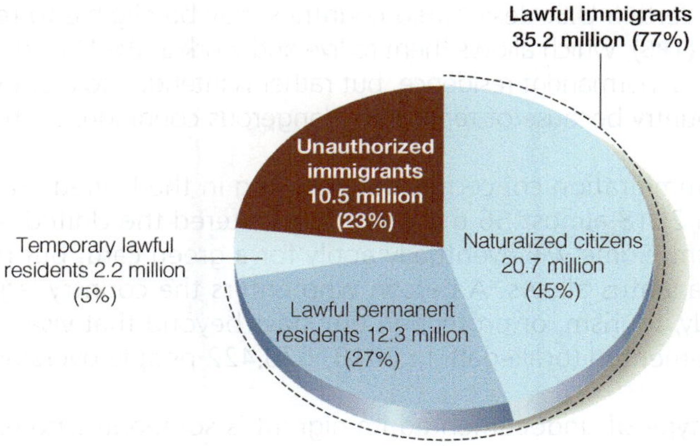

FIGURE 21.2 Types of Legal and Illegal Immigrants in the United States

About one-fourth of immigrants in the United States lack legal documentation—almost the same as the number who have permanent legal status.

Source: Jynnah Radford, *Key Findings about U.S. Immigrants* (Washington, DC: Pew Research Center, 2019).

green card A permit allowing a foreign national to live and work permanently in the United States.

refugee A person who has been forced to leave his or her country in order to escape war, persecution, or natural disaster.

asylee A person allowed to reside in the United States after leaving a troubled and/or dangerous country.

People residing in the country on regular visas may be eligible to receive a **green card** that allows them permanent residency in the United States. There are three main ways to obtain a green card: through a family member, through employment, or by having refugee/asylee status. The family green card program permits permanent U.S. residency for legal spouses, unmarried children under the age of 21, and parents of U.S. citizens and green card holders, as long as they meet the standard eligibility criteria. There is a cap of 480,000 on the number of family green cards made available each year, with a minimum of 226,000. The employment green card program enables up to 140,000 people to obtain permanent residency if they meet one of several categories of employment skill priorities (such as being scientists or technicians). The refugee or asylee green card program allows people who were admitted to the country as refugees or qualifying family members of asylees, as well as those who were granted asylum, to apply for a green card one year after their entry into the country. While both refugees and asylees have been persecuted or fear persecution in their home country, **refugees** by definition reside outside the United States, while **aslyees** reside within the country. In 2018, 22,405 people entered the United States as refugees, and 13,248 were granted asylum.[13]

There are other ways to receive a green card. The Immigration Act of 1990 created the diversity immigrant visa program, sometimes referred to as the green card lottery, in which 50,000 visa applicants are chosen at random from countries that send fewer than 50,000 people annually to the United States. Those whose applications are randomly selected and who also meet education and employment criteria are granted green card residency.

Daviad Ryder/REUTERS

▲ *Taking the Oath of Allegiance is the solemn moment when immigrants finally achieve their dream of becoming U.S. citizens.*

temporary protected status (TPS) A status given to foreign nationals from designated countries with temporary adverse conditions, such as armed conflict or environmental disaster.

People from certain U.S.-designated countries may be eligible to receive **temporary protected status (TPS)**, which allows them to live and work in the United States temporarily. TPS is not a route to permanent residence, but rather is intended to assist those who cannot return to their country because of temporary dangerous conditions such as war or natural disaster.

One major immigration concern is people living in the United States without legal authorization. In 2018 almost 56 million people entered the United States on a visa—mostly for tourism. Some will eventually apply for a green card, but many stay only as long as their visa status allows. A person who enters the country legally on a temporary visa for study, tourism, or protection but stays beyond that visa's termination date becomes undocumented (or illegal). In 2018, 676,422 people overstayed their visa termination date.[14]

The second type of undocumented immigrant is someone who enters the country illegally, with no valid visa for entry. Because the unlawful entries are surreptitious, it is not possible to get a firm count of how many there are, but current estimates put the number at under 200,000 per year, and falling.[15] What this means is that most of the people who are in the United States without legal authorization entered legally but did not leave after their legal authorization expired. The public stereotype of illicit border crossings is one way that undocumented immigrants come to live in the United States, but it is not the most common way.

LO 4

Describe the immigration justice system.

THE IMMIGRATION JUSTICE SYSTEM

The task of enforcing immigration laws falls partly on the federal government and partly on state and local governments. The role of the federal government is established by its constitutional authority to defend and protect the nation's borders, an authority carried out through the various immigration statutes enacted by the U.S. Congress. Immigration law is federal law. State and local authority derives from two factors: First, local justice officials have the most contact with citizens and are more likely to directly encounter violations of immigration law. Second, local and state correctional agencies provide basics such as housing and transportation, so they are more likely to encounter violations when dealing with residents in those forums as well.

To carry out its role, the federal government has established specialist agencies whose sole responsibility is enforcement of immigration law. The immigration justice system (IJS) operates as a specialized criminal justice system devoted to issues arising from immigration law. For the federal criminal justice system, immigration cases have become a major part of the workload (see Figure 21.3).

Policing

The police function of the IJS is performed by two agencies, U.S. Immigration and Customs Enforcement (ICE) and U.S. Customs and Border Protection (CBP), each of which operates as a division of the Department of Homeland Security (DHS).[16] Created in 2003 after the 9/11 attacks, ICE is responsible for investigating illegal cross-border activity such as human trafficking and cybercrime, terrorism, and immigration violations, including identifying and apprehending undocumented immigrants. The CBP has major responsibility for enforcing laws at the border—keeping terrorists and their weapons from entering the United States, thwarting drug trade, and preventing entry by people who do not have a legal right to be in the United States. One way to distinguish the two functions is that CBP protects the integrity of the borders while ICE deals with internal problems that arise from breaches of that integrity. Together, these police agencies employ more than 80,000 people in a broad range of tasks including customs, investigation, crime-scene work, and enforcement actions.

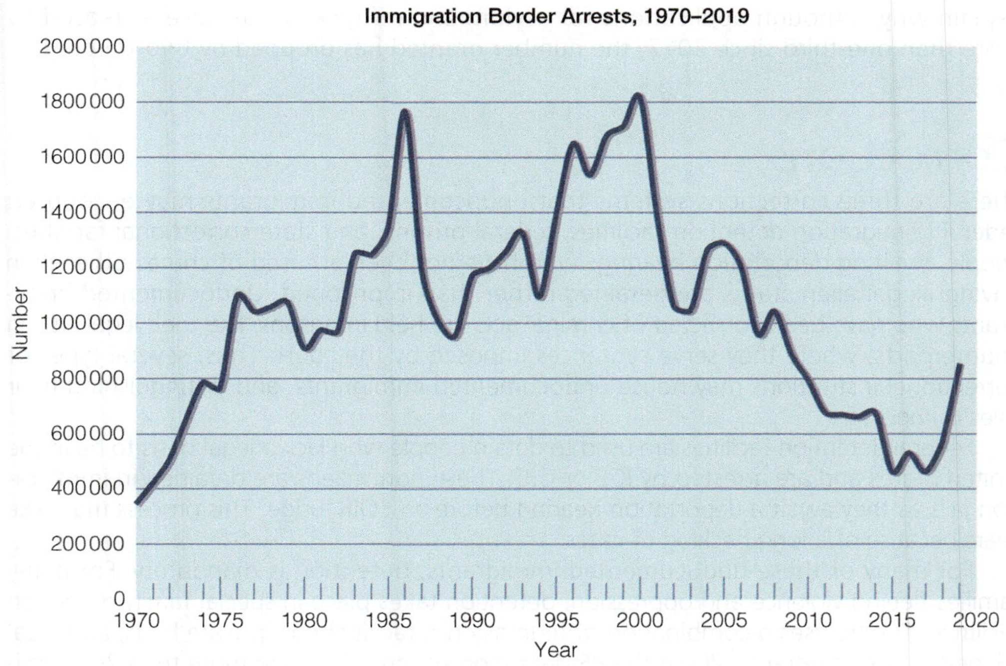

FIGURE 21.3 Immigration Border Arrests, 1970–2019

After 30 years of very high levels of border arrests by immigration police, the number of arrests fell for a decade. Are they starting to go back up?

Source: Department of Homeland Security, *2018 Yearbook of Immigration Statistics* (Washington, DC: Department of Homeland Security, 2020), https://www.dhs.gov/immigration-statistics/yearbook/2018/table33.

Neither ICE nor CBP works in isolation. These police agencies must cooperate with each other and with other federal police agencies (such as the Federal Bureau of Investigation, the Drug Enforcement Agency, and the Bureau of Alcohol, Tobacco, Firearms, and Explosives) to carry out their functions effectively. Federal-level partnerships are only part of the story, however, as all the DHS policing agencies must coordinate their work with local and state police as well. The local police are often the ones who have first contact with undocumented immigrants. Without a communication channel to the federal agencies, that contact will not result in an immigration arrest.

Courts

Criminal cases filed against undocumented immigrants are handled by the criminal courts holding jurisdiction for the alleged crime: State courts hear state criminal cases, and federal courts hear federal criminal cases. People found guilty in those courts are sanctioned according to the applicable law.

Located within the U.S. Department of Justice (DOJ) is the Executive Office for Immigration Review (EOIR). The EOIR was created in 1983 through an internal DOJ reorganization that combined the Board of Immigration Appeals (BIA) with the immigration-judge function previously performed by the former Immigration and Naturalization Service (INS), now part of DHS. The EOIR adjudicates immigration cases under the authority of the U.S. attorney general, including immigration court proceedings, appellate reviews, and administrative hearings. There are currently 58 EOIR courts in the United States, and the backlog of cases is growing. By being part of the DOJ, the work of the courts is effectively located within the political machinery of the White House rather than in the court system. The political sensitivity of the decisions may explain why, although applications for asylum and refugee status have increased by more than one-third since 2012, the number granted has dropped by two-thirds.[17]

Corrections

There are three corrections systems that undocumented immigrants may encounter: federal immigration detention facilities, federal prisons, and state correctional facilities. People awaiting deportation hearings who have not been accused of crimes other than having illegal alien status are detained rather than imprisoned. Undocumented immigrants who have been convicted of criminal acts are held in prisons, like their legal citizen counterparts, where they serve sentences imposed by the court. Thus, several types of correctional institutions may house undocumented immigrants, and distinguishing their roles is important.

Federal detention facilities are used to detain people who lack a legal basis to be in the United States and are arrested by ICE or CBP. These noncitizens are detained in immigration jails as they await a deportation hearing before an EOIR judge. This process may take years because of a long backlog of cases.

For many of these undocumented immigrants, detention is mandatory. For many families fleeing violence and oppression, detention takes place in special family detention facilities. The IJS uses a combination of federally run facility beds, private beds, and local jail beds under contract. Within the IJS detention system, there are more than 200 facilities and almost 35,000 beds. In 2018, there were 39,000 people in these facilities, and the number has risen since then with no official count.[18]

Nearly two-thirds of the immigration beds used for detention are in privately owned facilities that operate under contract with DHS. Two concerns have been raised about these private facilities. First, the contracts call for a certain minimum number of cells to be occupied. This creates a financial incentive for federal authorities to arrest enough undocumented immigrants to meet the terms of the contracts. A more pressing concern is that, too often, IJS detention facilities are crowded, with entire families sometimes detained there. The facilities operate like jails (see "For Critical Thinking"). All the problems of private correctional facilities operating in other settings (see Chapter 10) apply to IJS facilities for federal detainees.[19] Critics complain that basic services are subpar.[20] In one such facility, conditions were so bad that a class action suit was filed claiming a violation of basic federal rights, including a charge that detainees were required to work for $1 per day.[21] Another location has faced allegations of sexual assaults carried out by staff against female detainees.[22] In locations where neither federal detention facilities nor private facilities are available, detainees are held in local jails, with costs reimbursed by the federal government.

The justice system's state and federal prisons hold convicted illegal immigrants. Those who have been convicted of federal crimes are incarcerated by the Federal Bureau of Prisons (FBOP). About 6 percent of people serving a sentence in FBOP were convicted of immigration offenses, and about 18 percent of people

FOR CRITICAL THINKING

People being held in immigration lockup often experience chillingly brutal conditions. Health care is often inadequate; food is substandard. Facilities are crowded, and many are unsafe—sexual assaults and physical abuse have been documented far too frequently. In many of these private facilities, children are victims of routine mistreatment in ways that might make a parent lose custody of a child under different circumstances. What makes the situation even more troubling is that private facilities try to make a profit, and these conditions are used to minimize the costs of detention and therefore maximize profits.

People who run facilities for profit have always been financially accountable for the conditions of their facilities. Taking away the profits of these operations is thought to be enough of a deterrent to make those who run them pay attention to the quality of care. But complaints have remained high, and the pressure to keep profits flowing can distort decision making and make it hard for administrators to do the right thing, in the face of stockholders who want returns.

1. Holding the administrators and their companies criminally liable might add an extra level of deterrence for those who might be tempted to cut corners. Would this be a good idea?
2. What could be some of the unanticipated consequences of holding these administrators criminally liable?

Source: Ben 'Norton, "Privatized For-Profit Immigrant Detention Centers Are a 'Living Nightmare,' Investigation Shows," *Salon*, May 16, 2017.

in federal prisons are not U.S. citizens.[23] State correctional facilities hold at least 70,000 undocumented immigrants who have been convicted of state crimes.[24] Undocumented immigrants who are convicted of state or federal crimes and who serve their sentences for those crimes in correctional facilities do not go free after "doing their time." Except in unusual cases, these people are released from correctional facilities directly to federal detention facilities, where they are scheduled for deportation hearings—with expulsion the usual outcome. Accurate figures for the number of undocumented immigrants in jails and prisons do not exist, and estimates vary. On the high end, it is estimated that nearly $2 billion is spent annually to incarcerate undocumented immigrants in state and federal facilities.[25] This includes more than 25,000 people who are locked up in local facilities and paid for by the federal government. The number of people in state prisons who will eventually be scheduled for deportation is much larger. Difficulties in counting undocumented immigrants housed in correctional facilities are far outweighed by the lack of information on probation and parole. No definitive counts of undocumented immigrants on probation and parole have ever been conducted. One national survey found estimates that varied from 1 percent of a caseload to 85 percent of some caseloads.[26] Coordination policies between probation and parole and the federal enforcement agencies are currently in flux. Some agencies closely coordinate their efforts with ICE, and people on probation who do not do well are transferred to detention facilities. Other agencies remain at arm's length with federal authorities because they think that strong, positive connections to the immigrant community are important to their own overall success in working with local cases.

ISSUES IN IMMIGRATION JUSTICE

LO 5

Identify key issues in immigration justice.

For the health of the nation, it is important to get our immigration policy right. Politically, immigration is a heated topic. Our shared historical identity is as a nation that not only welcomes immigrants but is also a place where they can thrive—this is a central feature of the American Dream. But this idea conflicts with the prevailing need for national security, which begins—in many people's thinking—with border security. Then, of course, alongside our pride in the American Dream, there has always been uneasiness with the cultural fit between newcomers and those who already live here, and many people worry about assimilation of new arrivals into the U.S. way of life.

In fact, every dispute about immigration seems to have two sides. Economists tell us that immigration is an economic engine, boosting labor and making the nation youthful. However, the flip side is that immigrant labor depresses wages and takes jobs from people who already live here. Progressive thought holds that the nation's cultural diversity is a strength that sets the United States apart from other nations; however, critics wonder if too much diversity makes for a kind of cultural chaos, where what it means to be an American loses its content.

Yes, it is important to get immigration policies right, but there is no broad consensus about what that means. However, evidence is growing that addresses the most pressing issues of immigration. For example, it now seems that programs requiring employers to e-verify the immigration status of their employees may not only reduce illegal immigration, but also reduce crime.[27] Over the coming years, as issues related to immigration continue to come to the forefront, the best way to address many of these controversies may become clearer. In the discussion that follows, we identify important justice-related problems in immigration and summarize their current state.

Immigration and Crime

In March 2017, President Donald J. Trump signed an executive order creating the Office of Victims of Immigration Crime Engagement (VOICE), which would serve victims of violent crimes committed by "removable aliens"—that is, undocumented immigrants. This office is new, but it was created to publicize crimes committed by immigrants and upgrade services for the victims of those crimes. Trump signed this order to keep a campaign pledge to focus on immigration as a public safety issue.

What is the connection between immigration and crime? The answer depends upon the way the question is approached. Broadly speaking, there is plentiful research evidence to suggest that immigrants engage in crime at a lower rate than nonimmigrants. Foreign-born residents of America are arrested at lower rates than those born here.[28] Neighborhoods that have higher concentrations of people born outside the United States have lower crime rates, after controlling for other social and economic variables.[29] They also have lower rates of recidivism.[30] For these reasons, the American Society of Criminology has taken the position that there is no need for VOICE and that policies should instead recognize that immigration tends to improve public safety rather than detract from it.

Officials who point to a connection between immigration and crime say they are not referring to the overall level of criminality of foreign-born U.S. residents. Instead, they are calling attention to the way that some criminal groups—especially in the Southwest—are involved in drug markets and routinely engage in violence. They also point to the notorious problem of powerful drug-related gangs in South and Central America, suggesting a potential for spillover to the United States, especially along the border.[31] This way of looking at the immigration problem parallels historical concerns about other foreign-born groups and organized crime—for example, Irish, Greeks, Jews, and, perhaps most notably, Italians (and "the Mafia").

Undocumented immigrants, it could be argued, are outside the law and so face no incentive to obey the law. That may be true in some cases, but the countervailing argument—that people who lack documentation are loath to call the authorities' attention to themselves and therefore are less likely to engage in risky behavior—is just as logical, and evidence suggests it is a more prevalent reaction. Many—perhaps most—undocumented immigrants come to attention of the authorities through inconsequential events such as motor vehicle stops or medical problems, and high-profile criminal events are, in fact, quite rare. In 2018, U.S. Border Patrol reported there were a total of 5,149 convictions of undocumented immigrants, of which 541 were crimes against the person (and only 2 were homicides).[32] This is remarkable, since they intercepted over 800,000 people that year.

As the debate about immigration and crime continues, some current conclusions seem reasonable. In the broadest sense, immigration itself does not pose a hazard for public safety—on the contrary, immigration seems to have contributed to safer, more viable community life.[33] Yet immigration provokes fears of "the other" and especially fears of transported criminal activity from the homeland to the United States. Although this can be a legitimate concern, it is not clear how much this is a problem of the integrity of the borders as opposed to the effectiveness of domestic law enforcement. Most importantly, immigration is a galvanizing political issue that seems to be guided as much by emotion as by reflection upon the facts.

Immigration and Terrorism

Because of continuing threats of international terrorism, the relationship between immigration and terrorism is a potent public safety issue. During the presidential campaign of 2016, it seemed that every couple of weeks saw a violent terrorist attack of some sort. One of the most galvanizing events was a mass attack that occurred in December 2015 in San Bernardino, California, carried out by a married Muslim couple, Syed Farook and Tashfeen Malik. Farook was a U.S.-born citizen, and Malik was a legal permanent resident. Although the FBI determined that they were "homegrown terrorists," there were urgent public questions about border security. A national debate ensued about whether U.S. immigration policies contributed to a greater risk of terrorism.

Fueling this debate, the Senate Subcommittee on Immigration and the National Interest (led by two Republican presidential candidates) announced the results of its analysis of the immigration histories of 580 people "implicated in terrorism" since 2014. The subcommittee had determined that 380 of the individuals on this list were foreign born, and wrote to President Obama to urge him to drastically alter the administration's immigration policies.[34] Then-candidate Donald J. Trump proposed "a total and complete shutdown of Muslims entering the United States."[35] After taking office, President Trump signed executive orders temporarily suspending immigration from seven predominantly Muslim countries.

Critics of these restrictive immigration policies point to abundant evidence that Muslim immigration does not have a strong connection to terrorism. Analyzing the data reported by the Senate subcommittee, NYU School of Law's Brennan Center for Justice pointed out that only a tiny minority of the cases actually involved violence against U.S. citizens—most of the charges involved immigration fraud or obstruction of justice, and many of the cases concerned non-Muslim terrorism, especially terroristic acts by the far right.[36] Independent analyses of terrorist attacks against U.S. citizens on U.S. soil determined that people born in Muslim-majority countries account for a very small fraction of the acts—indeed, the odds of an American dying at the hands of a foreign-born terrorist are a miniscule 0.00003 percent.[37]

In response to the ratcheting up of immigration enforcement by the DHS, some cities with a large number of undocumented residents have designated themselves **sanctuary cities**. This means that they have enacted local ordinances and/or implemented local policies that specify noncooperation with federal immigration authorities in searching for and arresting undocumented residents living there. Sanctuary-city policies vary, but they all have the purpose of protecting undocumented residents from aggressive law enforcement actions by ICE. Sanctuary-city police do not cooperate with ICE in detaining undocumented residents, questioning people to determine the lawfulness of their presence in the United States, or providing intelligence about noncriminal residents (see "Sanctuary Cities").

sanctuary city A city that limits its cooperation with the national government effort to enforce immigration law.

Children and Families of Undocumented Immigrants

Deferred Action for Childhood Arrivals (DACA) A law that allows certain undocumented immigrants who entered the country as minors to receive a renewable two-year period of deferred action from deportation.

Some of the saddest stories about immigration involve families that have been broken apart by the enforcement of immigration policies. Many of these families include parents who arrived in the United States as infants themselves. They have no memory of any other place they call home. About two-thirds of adult undocumented immigrants have lived in the United States for a decade or more.[38] That means they have been here long enough to form families of their own, to have their children enter the school system, and to become part of their communities. Indeed, any children these adults have who are born here are, by law, themselves U.S. citizens, regardless of their parents' status. Many—most—of these families comprise parents who are active in the workforce and children who are in school preparing to enter the workforce; these are families abiding by the law, paying taxes, and contributing to community life (see "Myths in Corrections").

Many people have questioned the reasonableness of an immigration policy that would break up families such as these by deporting adults back to their countries of origin. In 2012 the White House started a program named **Deferred Action for Childhood Arrivals (DACA)**, which enables children who have been mostly raised in the United States, but lack documentation, to receive a renewable two-year exemption that defers deportation on condition of study or work and no legal infractions. These children are referred to as "Dreamers" because they were brought here seeking the American Dream. Within four years of DACA's creation, almost 750,000 people of the estimated 1.7 million who were eligible had applied for and been granted

Eleven-year-old Ronyde Christina Ponthieux is a US citizen, but her father, Rony Ponthieux, is not. As the Trump administration phased out the Temporary Protected Status (TPS) program, Rony, a registered nurse who had been a legal resident under the TPS program for nearly a decade, must return to his native Haiti by July 22, 2019, or risk becoming an undocumented immigrant at risk of deportation.

FOCUS ON

CORRECTIONAL PRACTICE: Sanctuary Cities

Sanctuary city is not a formal legal designation; it is an intentional political practice. Cities that designate themselves "sanctuaries" do so because they want to support undocumented residents who live there productively and peacefully. In these cities, such residents are seen as assets: members of the work- force, students in the school system, and contributing members of the community. If a person without legal residency is arrested for a serious crime, he or she is processed by the criminal justice system just like anyone else. In non–sanctuary cities, upon conviction city officials will generally inform immigration officials. But in sanctuary cities, leaders resent the federal government's intrusion into immigrant communities, which provokes fear and reduces cooperation with city authorities. Some of the nation's largest cities, including New York City, Los Angeles, and Chicago, have declared themselves sanctuaries. This kind of sentiment is so strong in some places that many people consider the entire state of California to be a "sanctuary."

That local officials could openly resist the law enforcement initiatives of the federal government is controversial. Officials in Washington see these acts as provocative, reminiscent of the civil rights era, when many cities in the South resisted the federally mandated integration of schools and other public facilities. These officials have argued that state and local governments are not at liberty to defy federal law enforcement, and the response by federal authorities has included threats to block federal funding for local services and to hold local officials in contempt of federal law.

Some places have experienced state–local conflict on this issue. Cities such as Austin, Texas, have widespread public support and local law enforcement backing for being sanctuaries. However, state legislators have passed laws requiring local authorities to check for legal residency when they make routine stops—failure of a police officer to do so is now a criminal offense.

Corrections is affected by the "sanctuary" designation in two ways. First, in cities where there is strong support for sanctuary status, jails get caught in the middle. Strict cooperation with the federal authorities would mean that any person booked into a jail for any crime would be checked for immigration status and turned over to federal authorities by local correctional officials if legal documentation is lacking. But jail administrators in sanctuary settings try to determine the seriousness of the booking charges and the extent of prior contact with the justice system. When they think the charges are not serious or the person is not a threat to the community, they do not inform ICE.

The second effect comes from federal reaction to sanctuary-city practices. The U.S. Department of Justice has threatened to withhold grant funds from justice agencies operating in such cities, and this could significantly affect jail funding. Because Federal Appeals Courts have differed on whether DOJ can withhold funds, the issue may have to be settled by the U.S. Supreme Court.

People on both sides of the issue believe that they are advancing fundamental values. Proponents of sanctuary cities see themselves as keeping a commitment to inclusion, diversity, and openness to others. Opponents see themselves as simply maintaining the integrity of the nation's borders and immigration laws. The issue has become heavily contested, and the full story of U.S. sanctuary cities is only starting.

Sources: United States Conference of Catholic Bishops, *Sanctuary Cities* (Washington, DC: Author, 2017); Alex Kotlowitz, "The Limits of Sanctuary Cities," *The New Yorker*, November 23, 2016.

Deferred Action for Parents of Americans and Lawful Permanent Residents (DAPA) A law that allows certain parents of Americans or lawful permanent residents (green card holders) to obtain permission to work and to stay in the United States for three years.

DACA status.[39] On the other hand, **Deferred Action for Parents of Americans and Lawful Permanent Residents (DAPA)** is a law that allows certain parents of Americans or lawful permanent residents (green card holders) to obtain permission to work and to stay in the United States for three years (see "DACA and DAPA"). The DACA program was an initiative of the Obama administration, and it has not received wholesale support. Some states have opposed the initiative, implementing state policies that make DACA status problematic and prohibit eligibility for state benefits. Early signs are that the Trump administration is ready to subject Dreamers to arrest and deportation, even when they have complied with the DACA requirements. During the Trump administration's first 100 days, immigration arrests were up by more than one-third. Most of the increase involved arrests of people without any criminal record, including Dreamers.[40] In *Department of Homeland Security v. California Board of Regents*,[41] the U.S. Supreme Court rejected the Trump Administration's attempt to administratively end the DACA program, saying they had failed to meet the procedural criteria to justify such an administrative action.

Americans believe in and celebrate family life. There is a sense of uneasiness with the way that current policy affects families, often tearing them apart, often punishing children for what their parents did. At the same time, there is strong sentiment that something needs to be done about the 10.6 million people living in the United States without legal documentation. The lack of a political consensus about such actions has left millions of people in limbo, vulnerable to the law, still participating in their communities, and anxious about their circumstances (see Figures 21.4 and 21.5).

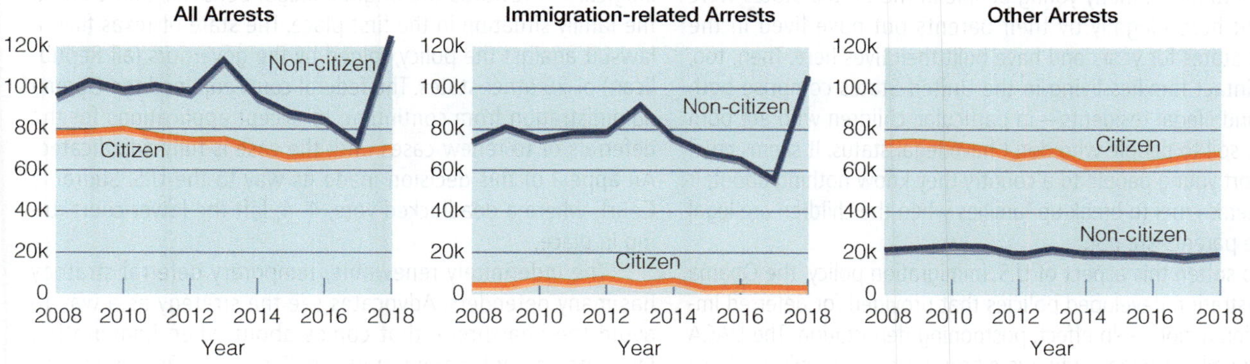

FIGURE 21.4 Federal Law Enforcement—Arrests of Citizens and Non-citizens

Most arrests by federal agents are of non-citizens, and that pattern is increasing. However, arrests of non-citizens tend to be for immigration offenses, and not offenses against a person or against property.

Source: The Marshall Project, "Why Are Feds Arresting More Non-Citizens? https://www.themarshallproject.org/2019/08/23/why-are-the-feds-arresting-more-non-citizens.

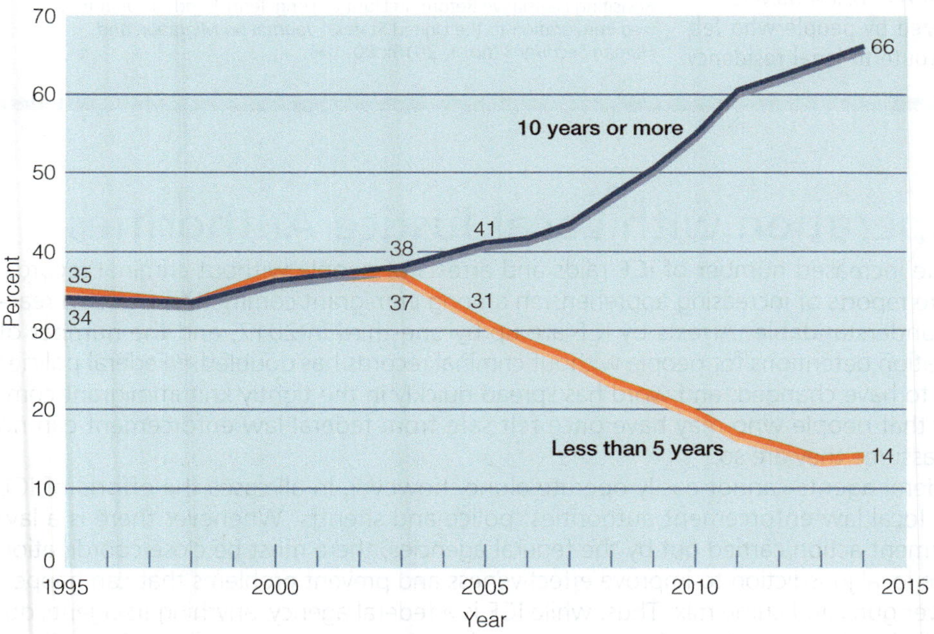

FIGURE 21.5 Percent of Adult Undocumented Immigrants Who Have Been Living in the United States for 10 or More Years Versus 5 Years or Less

In the 1990s the percentage of short-term and long-term undocumented adults living in the United States was about the same, but today long-termers outnumber short-termers by almost five to one.

Source: Jeffrey S. Passell and D'Vera Cohn, *Overall Number of U.S. Unauthorized Immigrants Holds Steady Since 2009* (Washington, DC: Pew Research Center, 2019).

MYTHS in Corrections

Illegal Mexican Immigration

THE MYTH: There has been a vast increase in the number of people who illegally enter the United States from Mexico.

THE REALITY: The number of people illegally entering the United States from Mexico grew steadily from 1990 to 2006. Between 2007 and 2017, the number declined by about 2 million. Mexicans are no longer the largest group entering the United States illegally.

Source: Jynnah Radford, *Key Findings about U.S. Immigrants* (Washington, DC: Pew Research Center, 2019).

FOCUS ON

CORRECTIONAL POLICY: DACA and DAPA

The enforcement of immigration law is complicated by two knotty situations. Many young people in the United States were brought here illegally by their parents but have lived in the United States for years and have built their lives here. Then, too, many intact families living in the United States comprise both legal and illegal residents—in particular, children who are born on U.S. soil to people who don't have legal status. It seems cruel to deport young people to a country they know nothing about; it also seems cruel to break up families when the children are legal but the parents are not.

To soften this aspect of U.S. immigration policy, the Obama administration developed policies that provided for deferred immigration actions—in effect, postponing deportation. The DACA program allows people who were brought here as children, have lived here for at least five years, and have no significant criminal justice history to defer deportation indefinitely as long as the young person registers with authorities every two years. The companion program, DAPA, was developed for the parents of a legal permanent resident and is renewable every three years, after registration with authorities.

It was estimated that there were 4.4 million people eligible for these two deferral programs. By 2016, more than 2 million people had applied for and received DACA or DAPA waivers.

The program was heavily criticized by people who felt that the deferral strategy creates a route to legal residency that has no basis in law. More important, they say, it is illogical—it rewards the original illegal behavior that created the family situation in the first place. The state of Texas filed a lawsuit against the policy, joined by the governors (all Republican) of 25 other states. The federal court enjoined the Obama administration from continuing to accept applications for the deferrals or to renew cases until the case is fully adjudicated. An appeal of this decision made its way to the U.S. Supreme Court, where a deadlocked vote, 4–4, left the lower-court ruling in place.

The indefinitely renewable, temporary deferral strategy has many defenders. Advocates see the strategy as a way to avoid the heartbreak that comes about when immigration law enforcement actions split families apart. Opponents say this approach undermines the integrity of our borders. Until the issue is resolved as a matter of law, people who live in this vulnerable status, no matter how law-abiding or community involved, will remain one police contact away from being deported. And those who signed up for the program have now identified themselves to authorities as being here illegally.

Source: Robert Warren and Donald Kerwin, "Beyond DAPA and DACA: Revisiting Legislative Reform in Light of Long-Term Trends in Unauthorized Immigration to the United States," *Journal on Migration and Human Security* 3 (no. 1, 2015): 80–108.

Cooperation with Local Justice Authorities

With the increased number of ICE raids and arrests of people without criminal records, there are reports of increasing apprehension among immigrant communities. Such a reaction is understandable. Arrests by ICE are up by one-third in 2017, and the number of immigration detentions for people without criminal records has doubled.[42] Federal policies appear to have changed, and word has spread quickly in the tightly knit immigrant community that people who may have once felt safe from federal law enforcement can no longer assume they are so.

Federal agents cannot easily operate alone, however. In all cases the efforts of ICE require local law enforcement authorities: police and sheriffs. Whenever there is a law enforcement action carried out by the federal agencies, there must be close coordination with the local jurisdiction to improve effectiveness and prevent problems that can happen whenever guns and crime mix. Thus, while ICE is a federal agency, anything its agents do, especially in cities with dense immigrant populations, requires the participation of local police. In fact, the U.S. Department of Justice has asked local law enforcement officials to help identify the undocumented residents of their cities so they can be arrested (see "Do the Right Thing").

Local justice authorities have responded to the more aggressive policy with ambivalence. In some places, law enforcement officials have been eager to expand their efforts to enforce the law, find undocumented residents, and arrest them to be deported. They have embraced the new ICE posture and vowed to work closely with ICE leadership in searching out people who are in the United States illegally.

Other law enforcement leaders see the new federal aggressiveness as counterproductive. These local police officials say that their strategy is based on close ties with the local community, and they have built a philosophy of "community policing" that is incompatible with police practices that the community perceives as harassment. They add that immigrants are a primary source of information they use to devise effective policing strategies at the local level, and if this information dries up, communities will become less safe.

Another issue is that down through the years, immigrants have been made scapegoats for social problems. At different times in history, stereotypes have dominated the way we thought about Chinese, Irish, Italians, Jews, and Japanese. So it should not surprise us that stereotypes dominate the way we tend to think about Muslims and Mexicans.

But justice policy should be based on evidence, not stereotypes.[43] Evidence tells us that many of the policies we have enacted in recent years to deal with immigration as a criminal justice issue are either shortsighted, self-defeating, or misdirected (see "Thinking Outside the Box"). Yet the American story about immigration has not been totally negative. It has also been a story of the triumph of progressive thought and tolerance over fear and distrust. We will be well served if that pattern continues.

DO THE RIGHT THING

Juvenile Probation Officer Vincent O'Leary works in an urban department in a branch that serves a community that is home to many Central American immigrants. The city's mayor has declared the city a sanctuary city, a decision that has provoked a great deal of negative reaction in the local press. O'Leary's boss, the chief probation officer, came to the job as a former member of ICE, and he has said privately that he strongly supports law enforcement actions against people on probation who lack a legal basis to be in the United States. Publicly, he has said nothing because he reports to the chief judge, who is close to the mayor.

In other words, the politics are pretty intense.

One of O'Leary's recent cases, Juan Emeriste, is 15 years old. He has requested and been denied DACA status because of his juvenile delinquency record—a minor charge for shoplifting. His delinquency seems like an aberration because he is a well-liked high school sophomore who has an A–average in his courses. When O'Leary first interviewed him, he admitted the charges but said that he was trying to take a toy for his baby brother because he had nothing else to give him for his birthday. The chief probation officer has said privately that he wants all undocumented clients reported to ICE because the conviction makes them eligible for deportation. But given his own boss's position, he does not force the issue. O'Leary is certain Juan is a good kid and believes that if he reports him to ICE, Juan will be deported.

WRITING ASSIGNMENT: If you were O'Leary, what would you do? What action would be most likely to promote the ideals of justice? Why?

THINKING OUTSIDE THE BOX

A PATH TO CITIZENSHIP FOR THE LAW-ABIDING

One of the most vexing complications of immigration law involves families where one of two things is true: They have been living successfully and productively in the United States for years, despite the lack of documentation, or some family members are documented while others are not. Although it is true that every person living in the United States without legal authorization is violating the law, it is also true that we have a deep interest in family integrity and productive citizenship. Two criteria for people who want to become naturalized citizens is that they be law-abiding and self-supporting. What if we made these criteria the most important conditions of permanent residency? What if how you behave in the United States became a more important standard than how you got here? How would that idea work? Would it solve problems or make more problems? How would border security have to work if these were our criteria for permanent residency?

SUMMARY

1 Define the nature of illegal immigration and describe the extent of the problem.

It is against the law to be in the United States without some legal basis or documentation: citizenship, green card, or visa. People who are here without such documentation are "illegal aliens," more properly referred to as undocumented immigrants. There are 11.3 million people living in the United States who do not have legal status allowing them to be here—about 3.5 percent of the U.S. population as a whole.

2 Summarize the history of immigration in the United States.

The United States is a nation of immigrants, and there is a long history of immigration to this country. For the first century of the nation's existence, there were no formal legal controls on immigration. A national regulation of immigration began with the Immigration Act of 1882, which established the federal authority over who was allowed to cross any of the U.S. borders. Between 1815 and 1915, 30 million Europeans arrived in the United States and were received with broad official approval. But hostility to specific immigrant groups has been a hallmark of U.S. immigration history. With the 1882 Chinese Exclusion Act, people from China were specifically excluded from entry into the United States. Eastern Europeans, especially Jews, encountered suspicion because of anticommunism, and the Japanese were subjected to a national policy of concentration camp detention during World War II. After World War I, immigration policy was linked to the U.S. census, setting nation-specific quotas that capped rates of admission based on population patterns within the country.

3 Define the different types of immigration under the law.

There are four main kinds of noncitizen immigrants. People residing in the country on regular visas may be eligible to receive a green card allowing them permanent residency in the United States by one of three ways: through a family member, through employment, or by having refugee/asylee status. People from certain U.S.-designated countries may be eligible to receive temporary protected status (TPS), which allows them to live and work in the United States temporarily. A person who enters the country legally on a temporary visa for study, tourism, or protection but stays beyond that visa's expiration date becomes illegal (or undocumented). And people who enter the country with no valid visa are also considered undocumented.

4 Describe the immigration justice system.

The Immigration Justice System—the IJS—operates as a separate criminal justice system devoted to issues arising from immigration law. The police function of the IJS is performed by two agencies, U.S. Immigration and Customs Enforcement (ICE) and U.S. Customs and Border Protection (CBP), each of which operates as a division of the Department of Homeland Security (DHS). Located within the U.S. Department of Justice is the Executive Office for Immigration Review (EOIR), which adjudicates immigration cases, including immigration court proceedings, appellate reviews, and administrative hearings. While awaiting an EOIR hearing, noncitizens are detained in immigration jails. To carry out the detention, the IJS uses a combination of federally run facility beds, private beds, and local jail beds under contract.

5 Identify key issues in immigration justice.

(1) What is the connection between immigration and crime? (2) What is the connection between immigration and terrorism? (3) What is the relationship between refugees/asylum seekers and crime, including terrorism? (4) How has U.S. immigration policy, especially Deferred Action for Childhood Arrivals (DACA), affected children and families? (5) How should the immigration justice system cooperate with local justice system authorities, especially those in sanctuary cities?

KEY TERMS

asylee (*p. 555*)
Deferred Action for Childhood Arrivals (*DACA*) (*p. 561*)
Deferred Action for Parents of Americans and Lawful Permanent Residents (*DAPA*) (*p. 562*)
green card (*p. 555*)
Immigration and Nationality Act of 1965 (*p. 554*)
refugee (*p. 555*)
sanctuary city (*p. 561*)
temporary protected status (*p. 556*)
undocumented resident (undocumented immigrant) (*p. 552*)

FOR DISCUSSION

1. The United States prides itself on being an "immigration nation." Yet throughout history, a succession of different immigrant groups has faced antagonism: Chinese, Irish, Italians, Japanese, Germans, and Jews. Now Mexicans and Muslims face hostility. Why does this happen? What can be done about it?
2. There are different routes to illegal immigration. What are the main ways that people get into the United States illegally? How do these routes represent different challenges to enforcement agencies? What can be done to stem them?
3. How are immigration and crime related? What would an evidence-based crime policy look like, with regard to immigrants?

FOR FURTHER READING

Bagelman, Jennifer J. *Sanctuary City: A Suspended State*. New York: Palgrave, 2015. A critical assessment of sanctuary cities throughout history and in today's political environment.

LaFree, Gary, and Joshua D. Freilich, eds. *Handbook on the Criminology of Terrorism*. Hoboken, NJ: Wiley-Blackwell, 2016. A collection of essays on the nature of and prevention of terrorism.

Miller, Holly Ventura, and Anthony Peguero, *Routledge Handbook on Immigration and Crime*. New York: Routledge, 2018. Scholarly essays on a crime and gangs throughout history and in the current context.

Owens, Emily G., Francis Fasani, and Giovanni Mastrobuoni. *Does Immigration Increase Crime? Migration Policy and the Creation of the Criminal Immigrant.* New York: Cambridge, 2019. An authoritative review of the history of public alarm about immigrants and crime, as well as the voluminous social science on the problem.

Takei, Carl, Michael Tan, and Joanne Lin. *Shutting Down the Profiteers: Why and How the Department of Homeland Security Should Stop Using Private Prisons*. New York: American Civil Liberties Union, 2016. A critical assessment of U.S. correctional policies for the detention of people suspected of immigration crimes.

NOTES

1 Andrew Romano, "The Most Dangerous Gang in America," *Newsweek*, March 27, 2005: https://www.newsweek.com/most-dangerous-gang-america-114579.

2 Nicole Einbinder, "Why Trump Talked About MS-13 Gang Violence in His State of the Union," *PBS Frontline*, January 31, 2018.

3 Hannah Dreier, "I've Been Reporting on MS-13 for a Year. Here Are the 5 Things Trump Gets Most Wrong," *ProPublica*, June 25, 2018: https://www.propublica.org/article/ms-13-immigration-facts-what-trump-administration-gets-wrong.

4 Maya P. Barak, Kenneth Sebastian Leon, and Edward R. Maquire, "Conceptual and Empirical Obstacles in Defining MS-13," *Criminology & Public Policy* 19 (no. 2, 2020): 563–89.

5 Robert Warren, "Reverse Migration to Mexico led to US Undocumented Population Decline, 2010–2018," *Journal on Migration and Human Security* 8 (no. 1, 2020): 32–41.

6 Department of Homeland Security, *2018 Yearbook of Immigration Statistics* (Washington, DC: Department of Homeland Security, 2020): https://www.dhs.gov/immigration-statistics/yearbook/2018/table33.

7 E. Ann Carson, *Prisoners in 2018* (Washington, DC: U.S. Bureau of Justice Statistics, 2020).

8 Donald J. Trump, quoted by Hunter Walker, "Donald Trump Just Released an Epic Statement Raging Against Mexican Immigrants and 'Disease,'" *Business Insider,* July 6, 2015.

9 Daniel Wilsher, *Immigration Detention: Law, History, Politics* (New York: Cambridge University Press, 2012).
10 Ibid., p. 12.
11 Emma Lazarus, "The New Colossus," in *Selected Poems* (New York: Library of America, 2005).
12 American Immigration Council, "Fact Sheet: How the United States Immigration System Works," https://www.americanimmigrationcouncil.org/research/how-united-states-immigration-system-works, August 12, 2016.
13 Nadwa Mossaad, *Refugees and Asylees, 2018* (Washington, DC: Department of Homeland Security, 2019).
14 U.S. Department of Homeland Security, *Entry/Exit Overstay Report, FY 2019* (Washington, DC: Author, 2020).
15 Robert Warren and Donald Kerwin, "The 2,000 Mile Wall in Search of a Purpose: Since 2007 Visa Overstays Have Outnumbered Undocumented Border Crossers by a Half Million," *Journal on Migration and Human Security* 5 (no. 1, 2017): 124–36.
16 U.S. Citizenship and Immigration Services (USCIS) is a non-police agency within DHS that handles asylum requests, refugee cases, and all other applications for visas.
17 Nadwa Mossaad, *Refugees and Asylees,* 2018,
18 Wendy Sawyer and Peter Wagner, *The Whole Pie* (Northampton MA: Prison Policy Initiative, 2020).
19 Carl Takei, Michael Tan, and Joanne Lin, *Shutting Down the Profiteers: Why and How the Department of Homeland Security Should Stop Using Private Prisons* (New York: American Civil Liberties Union, 2016).
20 Human Rights Watch, *Systemic Indifference: Dangerous and Substandard Medical Care in U.S. Immigration Detention* (Washington, DC: Author, 2017).
21 Kirk Mitchell, "Class Action Suit: Immigrants Held in Aurora Required to Work for $1 a Day, Threatened with Solitary if Refused," *Denver Post,* March 2, 2017.
22 Joseph Goldstein, "Brooklyn Prison Supervisors Charged with Sexually Assaulting Inmates," *The New York Times,* May 25, 2017.
23 Federal Bureau of Prisons. "US Prison Population Citizenship," June, 2020: https://www.bop.gov/about/statistics/statistics_inmate_citizenship.jsp.
24 Carson and Anderson, *Prisoners in 2015.*
25 Joel Gehrke, "Report: U.S. Spent $1.87 Billion to Incarcerate Illegal-Immigrant Criminals in 2014," *National Review,* July 28, 2015.
26 Dianne Kincaid, "Community Supervision of Undocumented Immigrants in the United States: Probation and Parole's Role in the Debate," *Journal of Offender Rehabilitation* 46 (no. 4, 2008): 91–100.
27 Aaron Chalfin and Monica Deza, "Immigration, Enforcement, Crime, and Demography: Evidence from the Legal Arizona Workers Act," *Criminology & Public Policy* 19 (no. 2, 2020): 515–62.
28 Marjorie S. Zatz and Hilary Smith, "Immigration, Crime, and Victimization: Rhetoric and Reality," *Annual Review of Law and Social Science* 8 (2014): 141–59; Min Xie and Eric P. Baumer, "Reassessing the Breadth of the Protective Benefit of Immigrant Neighborhoods: A Multilevel Analysis of Violence Risk by Race, Ethnicity, and Labor Market Stratification," *Criminology* 56 (no. 2, 2018): 302–32.
29 Christopher J. Lyons, Maria B. Vélez, and Wayne A. Santoro, "Neighborhood Immigration, Violence, and City-Level Immigrant Political Opportunities," *American Sociological Review* 78 (2013): 604–32.
30 Javier Ramos and Marin R. Wenger, "Immigration and Recidivism: What is the Link?" *Justice Quarterly* 37 (no. 3, 2020): 346–460.
31 See Dan Slater, *Wolf Boys: Two American Teenagers and Mexico's Most Dangerous Drug Cartel* (New York: Simon & Schuster, 2016).
32 U.S. Customs and Border Protection. *Criminal Alien Statistics, 2020* (Washington, DC: U.S. Department of Homeland Security, 2020): https://www.cbp.gov/newsroom/stats/cbp-enforcement-statistics/criminal-alien-statistics.
33 Michael T. Light and Ty Miller, "Does Undocumented Immigration Increase Violent Crime?" *Criminology* 56 (no. 2, 2018): 370–401.
34 "Sessions: 65% of All Terror Convicts Were Foreign Born, Half from Muslim Nations," Washington Examiner, www.washingtonexaminer.com/sessions-65-of-all-terror-convicts-were-foreign-born-half-from-muslim-nations/article/2594658, June 22, 2016.
35 Jenna Johnson, "Trump Calls for 'Total and Complete Shut- down of Muslims Entering the United States,'" *The Washington Post,* December 17, 2015.
36 Andrew Lindsay, *What the Data Tells Us About Immigration and Terrorism* (New York: Brennan Center for Justice, 2017).
37 AJ Willingham, Paul Martucci, and Natalie Leung, "The Chances of a Refugee Killing You—and Other Surprising Immigration Stats," CNN Politics, www.cnn.com/2017/01/30/politics/immigration-stats-by-the-numbers-trnd, January 30, 2017
38 Jens Manuel Krogstad, Jeffrey S. Passel, and D'Vera Cohn, *5 Facts About Illegal Immigration in the U.S.* (Washington, DC: Pew Research Center, 2017).
39 Angela Adams and Kerry S. Boyne, "Access to Higher Education for Undocumented and 'Dacamented' Students: The Current State of Affairs," *Indiana International & Comparative Law Review* 25 (no. 1, 2015).
40 Laura Meckler, "Immigration Arrests Rise Under Trump," *Wall Street Journal,* May 18, 2017, p. A3.
41 No. 18–587. Argued November 12, 2019—Decided June 18, 2020.
42 Maria Sacchetti, "ICE Immigration Arrests of Noncriminals Double Under Trump," *The Washington Post,* April 16, 2017.
43 See "Statement of the American Society of Criminology Executive Board Concerning the Trump Administration's Policies Relevant to Crime and Justice," https://www.asc41.com/policies/ASC_Executive_Board_Statement_on_Trump_Administration_Crime_and_Justice_Policies.pdf, May 12, 2017.

CHAPTER 22

Community Justice

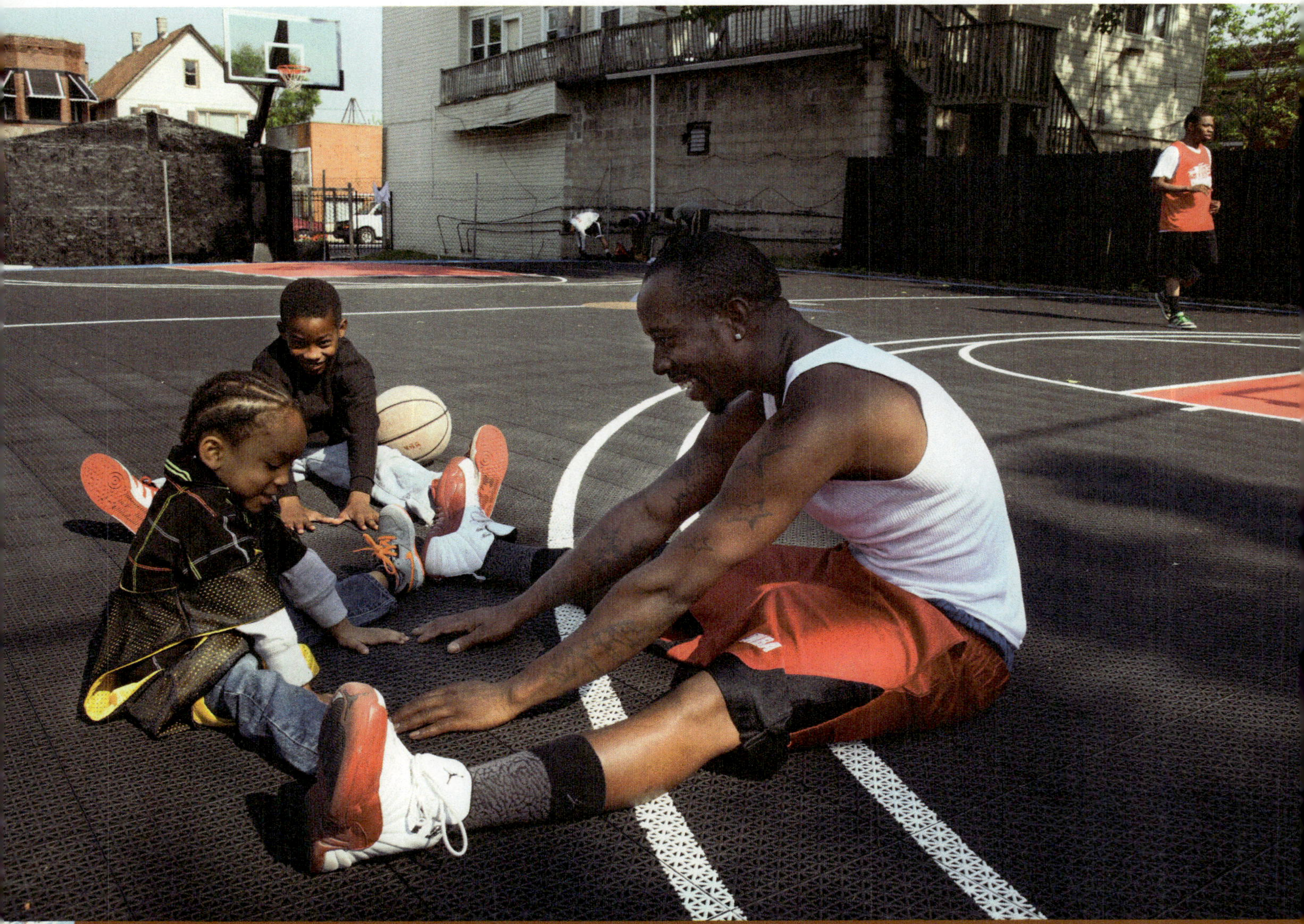

Melanie Stetson Freeman/Christian Science Monitor/The Image Works

Community justice is concerned about how the justice system affects children, families, and neighborhoods.

WRITING IN *NATION*, JOURNALIST KATY RECKDAHL TELLS THE STORY OF STEVEN ALEXANDER, who was a sixth grader in New Orleans when his mother, Carmen Demourelle, was sentenced to 12 years in prison for pickpocketing.[1] By all accounts, Demourelle was always a good, loving mother to Steven and his three siblings—she supported them financially, was strict about their schoolwork, enforced an early bedtime on school nights, and kept them away from peers who were troublemakers. But she supplemented her sporadic work as a beautician by occasionally picking pockets and selling small amounts of drugs. It eventually caught up with her.

The prison she went to was only an hour away, but contact between Demourelle and her children dwindled to once a year or so. The rest of the story is all too familiar. The four Demourelle children moved in with their grandmother, who worked nights. Supervision waned, schoolwork went unfinished, and the kids began hanging out at night with "bad influences." Steven never finished the seventh grade, and soon enough all his siblings had dropped out of school and were pregnant, addicted to drugs, or both.

Eventually, Demourelle got out of prison—her prison record was exemplary, and she was released early. But for the children, a lot had already happened—in Steven's case, his functional illiteracy made it hard to keep a job and almost impossible to get into a job training program.

With the enormous growth in imprisonment since the 1970s, these family experiences have become more common. More than five million minors have had a parent in prison during their childhood years; up to two million have a parent currently incarcerated at the time of this writing (2020).[2] An estimated 113 million adults have an immediate family member who has been to prison or jail.[3] For children, the consequences of parental incarceration are substantial: Having a parent go to prison increases a child's chances of dropping out of school, developing learning disabilities, acting out in school, and suffering medical and emotional illness.[4] Given all of this, it is not surprising that having a parent go to prison also increases a child's odds of getting in trouble with the law.[5] These effects are particularly concentrated among the urban poor, and while 1 out of 28 children has a parent in jail, black children are six times more likely to have a parent in prison than are white children.

The consequences for these largely impoverished communities that send people to prison are not much better than the consequences for children. For one thing, incarceration is a highly concentrated experience, based on location. Some urban neighborhoods have as many as one-fourth of their adult males in prison at any given time, while in other places incarceration is rare. High-incarceration neighborhoods are more economically disadvantaged, struggle with greater deficits in housing and other human services, find it difficult to support effective public schools, and have fewer institutions that promote physical health.[6] In fact, social scientists have shown that the advent of mass incarceration in the United States has degraded the nation's overall public health.[7]

Because of this concentration of social problems, there is a tightly coupled cycle in which the problems associated with impoverished urban areas tend to reproduce themselves over time: Poverty leads to disadvantage, which leads to criminality, which leads to prison, which leads to poverty.[8]

This situation is worsened by the extensive exposure to violence that occurs for children and adults in high-incarceration places, leading to a kind of debilitating trauma that also continues through the generations. The way that people cycle in and out of prison in these places aggravates symptoms of poor mental health, as people struggle with dual forces of trauma and hopelessness.[9] It is now well accepted that high rates of incarceration concentrated in the poorest neighborhoods of our cities have exacerbated economic inequality, and without addressing mass incarceration it will be very difficult to overcome the extreme level of social inequality in the United States.[10] Something needs to be done.

LEARNING OBJECTIVES

After reading this chapter, you should be able to . . .

1. Define community justice and show how it differs from criminal justice.
2. Identify the arguments in favor of community justice.
3. Describe the problems that community justice faces.
4. Explore the future prospects of community justice.

THE NEED FOR A NEW APPROACH

It is impossible to understand the U.S. penal system without also recognizing that it is the largest in the world. As shown in Chapter 1, it incarcerates more people per capita than does any other nation, and several times more people than some other democracies incarcerate. When we factor in the people under community supervision, the U.S. system is currently punishing 1 out of every 37 adults—2.7 percent of all adults.[11] Nowhere else in the world, and at no other time in history, has an equivalent of this massive system of punishment existed.

The growth of the penal system is not random. It has been concentrated among four groups, according to the following characteristics:

- *Age:* Most people in the penal system are ages 20–45.
- *Race/ethnicity:* Two-thirds of those under correctional control are minority group members.
- *Gender:* Nearly nine-tenths of correction's clients are men.
- *Socioeconomic status:* The penal population is dominated by poor people, the frequently unemployed, and those who have little education and few skills.

These four characteristics of the penal population result in an important spatial dynamic in the corrections system: Most of the people who cycle through probation, prisons, and parole come from a limited number of impoverished communities. Not every correctional client hails from our nation's poorest places, of course; people who get convicted of crimes come from every neighborhood.

As we have seen, in some places the concentration of residents who have experienced the corrections system is astoundingly high. This neighborhood effect is referred to as the **spatial concentration** of criminal justice. In these neighborhoods, arrests are common, especially for drugs, and going to prison is a common problem, alongside others such as poverty, broken families, joblessness—and crime.

spatial concentration A phenomenon of criminal justice in which certain neighborhoods have very high numbers of arrests and of people going to prison.

Why does this happen? We have spatial concentration because U.S. neighborhoods are segregated along racial/ethnic and income lines, and these are two of the ways that corrections is also concentrated. Our prisons and probation offices deal frequently with poor people of color, and the neighborhoods where they live become places where the business of corrections is a dominant theme.

In these places the criminal justice system traditionally works, one case at a time, to help clean things up. People who have committed crimes are arrested, prosecuted, and punished. Increasingly, they are removed from the streets for a term of incarceration. Almost all return after a period behind bars. At times it seems that the police, courts, and corrections systems work at odds with one another and with these troubled places. Police arrest "bad guys"; courts put them in prison, where they get no better and often get worse; and corrections watches them closely once they are back on the streets, waiting to start the process all over again. For these communities, many people are "missing" on any given day, behind bars somewhere, but because they cycle through the justice system, the actual ones who are missing change from one day to the next, and almost every young man gets his turn. What is to be done? The people being processed through the justice system have committed crimes and cannot be ignored. But more of the same kind of response seems to be counterproductive. In the face of this conundrum, a growing group of reformers has argued that in these communities, community justice is a better approach. Community justice seeks not just to apprehend lawbreakers and punish them; it also seeks to improve and strengthen the communities from which they come.

In this chapter we explore the developing idea of community justice. We discuss it as a philosophy of justice and a strategy of corrections. We ultimately investigate its strengths and weaknesses as an emerging strategy for troubled communities that are hit hard not just by crime but also by criminal justice.

DEFINITION OF COMMUNITY JUSTICE

LO 1

Define community justice and show how it differs from criminal justice.

Community justice is a new idea that has gathered considerable support among practitioners and policy makers across the country. A large number of municipalities have recently undertaken community justice initiatives of one sort or another. The particulars of these initiatives vary because different places tailor strategies to the particulars of their own crime problems. However, all pursue similar goals.

The rapid growth in new and innovative community justice projects is remarkable for two reasons. First, these projects have arisen as a result of local desires to develop more-proactive responses to crime. Second, they receive funding not from large federal grants but rather from local resources that are redirected from traditional approaches to community justice strategies.

As you may have gathered, community justice is not a simple idea that can be explained in a single sentence. It can be thought of as a *philosophy* of justice, a *strategy* of justice, and a series of justice *programs*.

A Philosophy of Justice

As a philosophy, community justice is based on a pursuit of justice that goes beyond the traditional three tasks of criminal justice—apprehension, conviction, and punishment. Community justice recognizes that crime and the problems that result from it greatly impede the quality of community life. Thus, the community justice approach not only seeks to respond to criminal events through traditional means; it also sets as a goal the improvement of quality of community life, especially for communities afflicted by high levels of crime. Robert Sampson and his col leagues have coined the term **collective efficacy** to denote the type of life that communities need in order to reduce crime.[12]

collective efficacy Mutual trust among neighbors, combined with willingness to intervene on behalf of the common good, especially to supervise children and maintain public order.

A Strategy of Justice

The strategy of the community justice approach combines three contemporary justice innovations: community policing, environmental crime prevention, and restorative justice.

Each of these innovations holds promise as a way of preventing crime and reviving community safety.

Community Policing The community policing approach to law enforcement employs problem-solving strategies to identify ways to prevent crimes by getting to root causes instead of relying on arrests as a way to respond to criminal events. Rather than reacting to 911 calls for service, community policing attempts to identify crime "hot spots" and change the dynamics of those places that seem to make crime possible. Rather than keeping citizens at arm's length, police officers actively seek partnerships with residents and citizen groups in pursuit of safer streets. Rather than a hierarchical paramilitary structure, community policing seeks to decentralize decision making to officers at the local areas; it also seeks to design area-specific strategies for overcoming crime.

By the end of the 1990s, the community policing movement had become enormously successful. Over 80 percent of police departments said they practiced some form of community policing, and most observers credited the approach as being partly responsible for the drop in crime in the latter half of the decade.

Environmental Crime Prevention In some cities, 70 percent of crimes occur in 20 percent of the city's locations. What produces such high concentrations of crime? And what can be done about those places?

The environmental crime-prevention approach begins with an analysis of why crime tends to concentrate in certain locations and certain times. Next, environmental crime-prevention specialists try to change the places that crimes tend to occur—to change them in ways that reduce crime. They bring light to darkened street corners that otherwise attract gangs as hangouts, establish procedures to keep elevators in repair so that people need not use isolated stairways to get to their apartments, change the traffic flow in streets that used to serve as drug markets, and restore open areas so that they serve as playgrounds rather than vacant lots.

Restorative Justice The restorative justice approach to sanctioning seeks to restore the victim, the lawbreaker, and the community to a level of functioning that existed prior to the criminal event. The restorative justice approach calls for an admission of what was done and affirmative steps to make restitution. There are four basic types of restorative justice strategies: mediation, community reparative boards, family group conferencing, and circle sentencing. In all of these strategies, the parties to the criminal event are brought together to decide what steps must be taken to help victims recover from the crime. Then the person who caused the harm takes responsibility by becoming involved in programs designed to help reduce the chances of new criminal behavior.

With growing support from studies, restorative justice programs are becoming increasingly popular (see "Common Justice"). Research has shown that when compared with traditional criminal justice, restorative justice programs result in greater satisfaction for all parties affected by a crime. Some studies also suggest that recidivism rates may be lower for some restorative justice strategies, even for people convicted of very serious offenses.[13] Critics point out that the rhetoric of restorative justice is not always matched by the activities of corresponding programs because coercive methods are sometimes employed to enforce participation in "restorative" strategies.

Justice Programs

Programs of community justice include a varied package of methods. Listing just some of them illustrates the range and innovative nature of community justice:

- Crime mapping identifies where the problem of crime is most concentrated.
- Citizen advisory groups help identify and prioritize local crime problems.
- Citizen partnerships between justice agencies and citizen groups improve the legitimacy of justice programs and help justice officials tailor the programs to address community needs.

FOCUS ON

CORRECTIONAL PRACTICE: Common Justice

On the subway in Brooklyn, New York, a group made up mostly of Christian youths attacked a group of youths who were wishing fellow passengers "Happy Hanukkah." A number of participants were involved in the attack, and a number of people were harmed. One of the assailants, a young female, attacked and beat one of the Hanukkah celebrants, pulling out her hair and causing her injury. The district attorney referred the case to a restorative justice program called Common Justice.

Common Justice brings people who have been harmed by violent crime together with the person who harmed them, offering to work with both parties to develop solutions for each person's situation that will produce better results for everyone affected by the crime. Rather than prison, people engaged in violent crime get a chance to make true amends for what they have done and to change their lives; those who are injured by the crime get a chance to confront the person who hurt them, explain why the crime was so very hurtful, and get a different kind of closure as the person who hurt them comes to grips with what was done in a way that the regular criminal justice system rarely seems to promote.

The victim (whom Common Justice calls the "harmed party") agreed to participate in the Common Justice program. The defense counsel was contacted, and the defendant (whom Common Justice calls the "responsible party") was screened. The responsible party then entered a plea of guilty to assault in the third degree as a hate crime, and sentencing was suspended so she could participate in the program.

Common Justice provides an important opportunity for healing to those harmed by a range of crimes, including assault, burglary, and robbery. The project involves those harmed by younger adults (ages 16 to 24) facing felony charges. If—and only if—the harmed parties welcome the opportunity, these cases are diverted into a conferencing process designed to recognize the harm done, identify the needs and interests of those harmed, and determine a range of appropriate actions to hold the responsible party accountable. Common Justice's staff closely monitors responsible parties' compliance with the resultant agreements—which may include extensive community service, rehabilitative and educational programming, violence-intervention classes, and restitution, among other sanctions—and connects those harmed by crime with appropriate services. The project serves as an alternative to incarceration for those responsible and an avenue to healing for those harmed.

Common Justice cases proceed through four stages: *engagement*, in which the parties are enrolled in the program; *preparation,* in which the parties and their support people (who may be family, friends, neighbors, and so forth) are prepared for the conference and those harmed are connected with urgently needed services; *circle or dialogue*, in which the parties and their support people come together to address the harm and reach agreements that the responsible party can fulfill to make things as right as possible; and supervision and *follow-up*, in which harmed parties are supported and referred to uniquely tailored services, and responsible parties are rigorously supervised as they complete their agreements.

In the case between the Christian and Jewish youths, after the conclusion of the preparatory period, Common Justice staff started a dialogue between the two people who had only had one terrible connection before this. The program convened first one and then a second and final conference in the case. Together, the parties reached a robust and powerful set of agreements. Once they had done so, in the final go-round the moderator asked each person to say just a couple of words about how they were feeling. The responsible party's mother said this to the harmed party:

> If someone did to me what my daughter did to you, I don't know if I would have anything but hate in my heart for them. You have to be the most generous, kind, compassionate person I have ever met. Your family must be very proud of you, and they must be beautiful people to have raised someone like you. My family is indebted to you forever for what you've given us, and while I know I'll never know how you suffered, and I can't imagine what you've been through, I pray that what my daughter does in this program brings you a little bit of the peace you deserve. Thank you.

The harmed party was next to speak. She had suffered from post-traumatic stress since the incident, and her life had been profoundly changed by what happened. After she became involved in Common Justice, those symptoms began to relent. She paused before speaking, smiled, and said, "I feel relieved. I feel excited and grateful about what happened here. This is an amazing experience. I don't know what to say. . . . I feel joyful. Just joyful."

The responsible party, who had agreed to everything asked of her and was therefore faced with a demanding set of agreements to complete, said through tears to the harmed party in a solemn and unwavering voice, "I know you've said apologies don't mean a lot to you, so instead let me just say: thank you. From the bottom of my heart, thank you. I owe you everything I have, and I won't let you down." When the participants finished going around the circle, they all broke bread together, and after the harmed party agreed, the harmed party and the responsible party hugged. They had touched only once before in their lives—during the violent incident that initiated this process.

When this case occurred, the newspapers cited it as an example of monstrosity and hate. When the case came to Common Justice, the harmed party was understandably furious. Because of the nature of the crime, Common Justice screened the case with extraordinary care and a degree of skepticism. There was a point

(continued)

CORRECTIONAL PRACTICE: Common Justice (*continued*)

in the conference where it seemed uncertain whether the group would reach agreements, or to what extent the agreements they could reach would satisfy the harmed party's needs. With the hard work of everyone in the circle, they moved to a better place than any of the participants, including the program staff, had dared to anticipate. The result stands as a testimony to what is possible between people when a process makes space for their full humanity and the best parts of themselves to emerge.

- Local organizations of police, prosecutors, judges, and correctional officials develop local strategies of crime prevention.
- Citizens and victims are involved in sentencing decisions to increase their confidence in the wisdom of the sanctions.
- Community service sanctions people who committed a crime and restores victims and their communities.
- Restorative justice is used as a means of strengthening a person's integration into the community.

Most of all, community justice is concerned with taking seriously the problems faced by people who live with high levels of crime, some of whom are themselves involved in crime. When Walter Harrison, a Boston probation officer working on a community justice project, goes to work, he practices community justice in a way that reflects all of these particular programs, not just one or two in isolation. He is not out to arrest young people but is there to help keep them safe. He is not saying, "I am a probation officer, not a policeman"; rather, he is trying to practice probation in a way that is relevant to the particular needs of the people on probation, their families, and their neighbors, each of whom is concerned about being safe.

HOW COMMUNITY JUSTICE DIFFERS FROM CRIMINAL JUSTICE

Community justice differs from traditional criminal justice in four important ways: It is based on the neighborhood rather than on the legal jurisdiction, it uses problem-solving strategies rather than adversarial strategies, it is restorative rather than retributive, and it strives to improve the community through a strategy called "justice reinvestment."

Neighborhoods

Neighborhoods are typically quite different from legal jurisdictions. For most important crimes, the state or federal government has legal jurisdiction within politically determined boundaries. But crime problems vary greatly within those jurisdictions. We see this when we compare cities such as Miami with towns such as Lake City; both lie within Florida, but each has unique crime and justice problems. Even within a city, crime problems vary with the income levels, racial composition, and economic status of each neighborhood. The Miami neighborhoods of Liberty City and Coconut Grove show stark contrasts in their socioeconomic and crime characteristics. Chicago is said to have 343 discrete neighborhoods, each with a different social profile and crime problem, as well as different justice concerns. Would we want to apply standardized criminal justice policies to these different neighborhoods in Miami and in Chicago? It follows that these local areas have different needs for justice services and priorities.

Traditional justice attempts to develop standardized approaches to crime problems that are applied uniformly across the entire legal jurisdiction. By contrast, community justice attempts to tailor strategies to fit important differences across neighborhoods within the same legal jurisdiction.

Problem Solving

Problem solving in the context of community justice differs from that of adversarial justice in its fundamental aims. The adversarial process is thought to have succeeded when the innocent citizen is found not guilty and the guilty citizen is fairly punished. In contrast, the problem-solving approach succeeds when the problem behind a crime is resolved. That is why the traditional criminal justice system is concerned almost exclusively with the person who was convicted of the crime and ends this concern once the punishment has concluded. Community justice extends its sights to solving the underlying problems faced by everyone affected by the crime, even including others in the neighborhood.

Problem solving as a core aspect of criminal justice is gaining support through a variety of means—from police decisions to correctional policy. A recent report by the National Institute of Justice found that crime fighting has evolved away from isolated arrest and prosecution strategies toward coordinated efforts that cut across agencies and levels of government. The idea is to continue to fight crime in the traditional way—by arresting and prosecuting people—but to try as well to identify the problems that produce the crime and address them systematically.

Restoration

Restoration is the solution sought in the problem-solving philosophy of community justice. This means that the losses suffered by the victim as a result of the crime are restored, the threat to local safety is removed, and eventually the person returns to being a fully participating member of the community. When the crime is so serious that full restoration is not possible, community justice seeks as much restoration as can be provided (see "For Critical Thinking").

Justice Reinvestment

The most elaborate vision of community justice is expressed as **justice reinvestment**.[14] The idea of justice reinvestment begins with two related realizations. First, more than $80 billion is spent annually on prisons in the United States,[15] often incarcerating people with little or no hope of access to rehabilitation services. The vast majority of people convicted of drug crimes come from disadvantaged communities where schools are poor, family life is pummeled by poverty and disruption, and chances for good jobs are minimal. We are used to thinking of this as a problem of urban neighborhoods, but new research shows that satellite cities and suburbs are also affected.[16]

justice reinvestment A strategy to redirect funds currently spent on prisons to community public safety projects.

That means that our crime policy requires people convicted of crimes to spend a year or two in prison yet eventually return to the same disadvantages as before, with no improvement in their life prospects and no changes in the places they are returning to.[17] In the long run the $80 billion accomplishes little more than interrupting and disrupting the lives of community residents.

The community justice ideal is to improve the quality of community life. Justice reinvestment is a strategy that seeks to funnel the vast resources of the criminal justice system into activities and projects that improve community life (see "Do the Right Thing"). In place of prison sentences, justice

FOR CRITICAL THINKING

Danielle Sered, who wrote *Accounting for Violence* (see "Community Justice and Violence—Common Justice"), envisions a new kind of response to violence. This response is based on two main ideas: (1) victims need a chance to speak about how the crime has affected them, and often this means directly engaging the person who committed the crime; and (2) outcomes of the case can be found that are much more productive for everyone concerned. This entails a kind of restorative justice for violent crime. People might argue that people accused of violent crimes should be ineligible for restorative justice processes, but this claim is based on the idea that the main beneficiary of restorative justice is the person who is accused of the crime.

1. What about the victim? If a person who has suffered a crime—even a serious one—would rather go through a restorative justice process than the traditional justice system, should he or she be allowed to do so?
2. Is this a good idea or a distortion of the criminal law? Explain your answer.

DO THE RIGHT THING

You are the governor of a state that has recently engaged in an aggressive "justice reinvestment" agenda. You have been able to close three prisons, saving over $100 million in the correctional budget. Originally, the plan was to reinvest the savings in high-crime areas to help make those places safer. But your state's fiscal crisis has meant layoffs of teachers and health care workers, and people are alarmed about their loss of services.

The legislature is proposing to divert half the savings to use as a general tax rebate, distributed to all the state's residents. Your advisors caution you that if you don't reinvest these funds in the neighborhoods where people return from prison, those who return will find it harder to make it and may well end up right back in prison.

WRITING ASSIGNMENT: How should you spend the money, and why? Write an essay explaining your decision.

reinvestment advocates envision (1) work programs in which people who have been convicted of crimes help renovate neighborhood spaces, both public and private; (2) family programs that increase support to improve children's school performance; (3) housing strategies that provide low-cost places to live; and (4) health care support for people without health insurance. Through reallocating criminal justice funding toward education, housing, health care, and jobs, the long-term aim is to improve community life in ways that can specifically decrease crime rates and promote further improvement of the community's quality of life.

Justice reinvestment strategies rest on the idea that improving communities will not only reduce crime; it will also strengthen those communities.[18] For a long time, the evidence on the effectiveness of community investments was seen as mixed. In particular, most programs based on the idea of "weed-and-seed" (arrest people who are criminally active first, then build social programs) have had disappointing records in preventing crime.[19] More-recent studies have shown that financial support for local community infrastructure in high-crime areas has a direct effect on reducing violent crime.[20] In fact, one project in Richmond, California, found that paying gang members a stipend of only $1,000 per month to stop the violence results in very substantial reductions in gun and other violence.[21] In the summer of 2020, demonstrators who said "defund the police" were not calling for an end to policing. They wanted to reallocate some of the police budget to pay for community priorities.[22]

The justice reinvestment movement has had significant governmental support from the U.S. Department of Justice, which gave $6 million in 2008 to test run the Justice Reinvestment Initiative. The work in more than half the U.S. states has succeeded in some places but not in others.[23] Overall, officials believe the results have been promising enough that $27.5 million is now committed to this work each year.[24]

Overview of Differences

These four differences—concerning neighborhoods, problem solving, restorative justice, and justice reinvestment—show how the community justice approach strikes a different path from that of traditional criminal justice. Community justice does not replace the need for criminal justice, but it fills in where the justice system fails to meet community needs.

Table 22.1 compares these differences between community justice and traditional criminal justice. The latter operates as a centralized bureaucracy staffed by

TABLE 22.1 Community Justice and Criminal Justice—Some Comparisons

Community justice differs from criminal justice in the key strategies employed by each.

Community Justice	Criminal Justice
Based in a neighborhood.	Based in a state or local jurisdiction.
Focused on solving crime problems.	Focused on processing cases.
Uses partnerships with citizens and social service agencies.	Uses professionals who operate in isolation from citizens and other agencies.
Goal is improved community safety.	Goal is apprehension, conviction, and punishment.

FOCUS ON

CORRECTIONAL PRACTICE: Community Justice and Violence—Common Justice

As we have pointed out, "community justice" has many meanings, with system-wide manifestations involving police, courts, and corrections. Recently, the Vera Institute of Justice published a report by Common Justice that outlined one organization's point of view on the principles that undergird community justice. The report begins with the observation that the greatest challenge for justice lies with violent crime. Most contemporary proposals for reform are expressly directed at low-risk people convicted for the first time and/or convicted of nonviolent crimes. But with over half of the prison population serving time for violent crimes, and with the way violent crime cycles through the generations and affects people with such debilitating trauma, they call for a new approach in responses to violence that employs four overarching principles:

1. *Responses should be survivor-centered.* Too many people who survive violence do not believe the justice will be reasonable in its response—either to them or to the person who committed the violence—so they do not report the crime. When violence survivors describe what they need, they often emphasize the need to fully heal from the violence more than to severely punish the person who hurt them. They want answers about what happened to them, to have their voices heard in the response to the violence, to be assured that it will not happen again—but most of all, they want the support necessary to fully heal.
2. *Responses should be accountability-based.* Central to the idea of being survivor-focused is the accountability of the person who engaged in violence. This is a more demanding expectation than mere punishment; to be punished is to be passive, but for a person to accept responsibility for violence—to become accountable for it—requires active work: fully taking responsibility for the actions, feeling remorse for the harm, and doing whatever is possible to repair that harm. A basic requirement of justice is for the system to make this kind of accountability possible.
3. *Responses should be safety-driven.* Too often, the justice system's responses to violence serve to encourage more violence. Too often, the context in which violence occurs is ignored and the response to violence is indifferent to the call for an end to the cycle of violence. A profound concern for the continuing safety of the people affected by violence, including the people who committed acts of violence, is the most basic foundation of a just system of responses to violence.
4. *Responses should be racially equitable.* Racial injustice sits at the core of too much of the violence that people experience in America. Violent crime disproportionately affects people of color, as does the punitive justice system. Adding one disproportional problem onto another does not promote social equity. The way we respond to violence must have racial equity as a core aim.

If these four principles are applied in the way we respond to violence, Common Justice argues that this experience confirms a new possibility for justice in which prisons and punishment are not the core of the justice system, but healing and community quality of life become the key.

Sources: Danielle Sered, *Accounting for Violence: How to Increase Safety and Break Our Failed Reliance on Mass Incarceration* (New York: Vera Institute of Justice, 2017); Danielle Sered, *Until We Reckon: Violence, Mass Incarceration, and the Road to Repair* (New York: The New Press, 2019).

professional workers whose job is to process criminal cases. Community justice strives to be a localized, community presence of specialists who develop partnerships with various agencies and citizen groups in order to deal with the problems that result from crime. Of course, community justice is not the opposite of criminal justice. All agents of justice operate under the same penal code, use the same legal authority, and face the same constitutional constraints.

Community justice is not as concerned with the individuals and their criminality as much as it is with the general issue of community safety. Because of this variation, community justice work tends to use the tools of justice in different ways and sets different priorities for taking action. For example, community-policing officers make arrests just as traditional law enforcement officials do. But criminal justice often sees the arrest as "closing" a case, especially when it is followed by a conviction. Community justice workers see the arrest as a first step in the problem-solving process involving the impact of the crime and the future of the person who has been arrested. In cases where crimes do not result in arrest, community justice workers see just as much a need for problem solving and restoration of community safety as in those cases with arrests. Community justice concerns itself with the life of the community, and the community includes the crime victims, the convicted person, and others alike.

LO 2

Identify the arguments in favor of community justice.

ARGUMENTS FOR COMMUNITY JUSTICE

Community justice has gained public support because although crime damages community life, traditional criminal justice does not address that damage. Citizens' groups and justice system leaders are coming together to develop ways to use criminal justice resources to address the damage that results from crime and crime fighting in high-crime localities. The arguments for community justice can be illustrated by three common assertions of the community justice movement.

Crime and Crime Problems Are Local

Community justice concerns itself with the quality of life in a community. Two deficits prevent a reasonable quality of life: lack of resources and lack of safety. In communities that have high concentrations of crime, these impediments to quality of life go hand in hand.

Ever since the landmark work of Clifford Shaw and Henry McKay,[25] criminologists have known that crimes tend to concentrate in certain areas. These high-crime areas are also the areas with other social problems: poverty, broken families, unemployment, and other maladies that criminologists refer to as "social disorganization." The concentration of social problems, the most troublesome of which is crime, makes these areas the least desirable places to live. People who live there tend to do so because they have few other choices. For people stuck in socially disorganized areas, life is dominated by problems of safety. Troublemakers rule the public spaces, making the streets unsafe.

Lacking financial and personal resources to create safety, residents of high-crime areas live under a permanent risk of harm. Problems of violence stem directly from problems of social disorganization. These neighborhoods also tend to become the places where those who were incarcerated live after release from prison or jail or while under community supervision. Figure 22.1 is a map of Brooklyn, New York, showing the number of prison and jail admissions in 2004, considered a classic "million-dollar block" map. This extraordinary concentration in some neighborhoods of residents involved in the criminal justice system represents but one year's involvement. Stretched across the three to five years that a typical person is under correctional control, a picture emerges of a neighborhood of residents who are quite frequently under supervision. Part of what makes high-crime residential areas different from other places is the high concentration of justice system clients who live there.

© Ryan Garza

▲ *Jae Bass poses for a photo with his daughter Daria Bass in front of an abandoned house on Collingwood Street in Detroit. He calls upon the leaders in Detroit to make investments into neighborhoods to make them better places for families, rather than investing in the prison system.*

Community justice is particularly concerned with these locations. Taking into account the families, associates, employers, and neighbors of people who have committed crimes, the distinction begins to fade between those formally under control of the state and those with whom their lives are directly intertwined. By focusing on quality of life in neighborhoods, community justice accepts responsibility for services to those who are not targets of state coercive penal control. The rationale is that because so much of community life is affected by the large number of justice-involved people living in these locations, corrections must focus not only on those actually under correctional authority but also on the many people whose lives they affect. These place-based strategies are most effective when they are focused on quite small unit targets, such as individual neighborhood blocks.

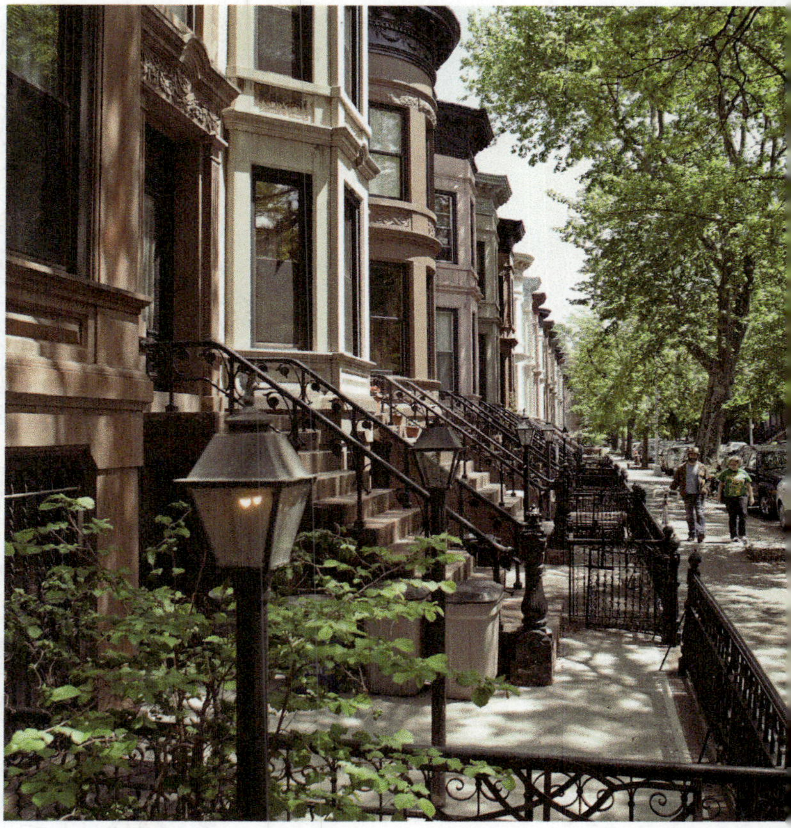

Paul Matzner/Alamy Stock Photo

▲ *Is community justice only for problem places, or does it make sense everywhere, even for places that do not lack for resources?*

Crime Fighting Too Often Damages the Quality of Life

What can be done in high-crime communities? The "trail 'em and nail 'em" approach of many criminal justice agencies seems to work poorly for the justice-involved people and their families living in these areas. The criminal justice system is designed as an adversarial attack on crime, implemented by identifying and accusing people of crimes, then removing them from the community upon conviction. Nationally, over 600,000 people are released back into the community each year, having served an average of just over two years in prison. The usual correctional thinking about them calls for individualized case management: assessing each person's risk and needs, then developing a supervision plan for reentry.

Recently, some researchers have begun to consider the impact of high incarceration rates on community life.[26] They point out that removing people from the community often disrupts families and, when it becomes pervasive in a neighborhood, leads to a sense of alienation from the law. Imagine, they say, living in a neighborhood where just about everyone has been arrested and almost every man has been to prison or jail. Under those conditions the legitimacy of the legal system itself comes into question, and the impact of the threat of punishment erodes. (See "Myths in Corrections.")

Problem communities in our cities may have reached critical levels of justice system involvement in residents' lives. Rather than coming from a response to violent crime, this involvement has stemmed from drug policy, one of the main reasons that some neighborhoods have high rates of arrest and incarceration.[27] In several of our major cities, as noted earlier, one-fourth or more of all African American men are under some form of justice system control. In particularly hard-hit sections of some cities, as many as one-fourth of that group is behind bars. This problem does not belong just to the ghettos of large cities. A study of a medium-sized southern city found one neighborhood in which 2 percent of all residents had been removed and placed in prison in one year alone, and one of the results may have been increases in crime.[28] If the community justice advocates are correct, such neighborhoods suffer repeated challenges— absorbing the losses incurred as these residents are removed while at the same time dealing with those who have returned from prison or jail.[29]

By pursuing restorative justice, community justice seeks to ameliorate some costs of crime for these residents. By using a problem-solving, crime-prevention approach, community justice seeks to break the cycle of criminal behavior that has a grip on these communities. The federally funded "weed-and-seed" projects, which sought to work in high-crime communities and build the capacity for residents to deal more effectively with the problems that cause crime, showed that where communities mobilize well in partnership with criminal justice and other social services, crime goes down. Although most weed-and-seed projects failed to mobilize communities effectively—and thus failed to reduce crime—the few that did had good results.

MYTHS in Corrections

What Do They Want?

THE MYTH: People in poor communities want "bad guys" to be taken off their streets and sent to prison.

THE REALITY: People in poor communities tell researchers that they want to be safe but that they also want their family members, even the ones involved in crime, not to have to go to prison.

Source: Dina R. Rose, Todd R. Clear, and Judith Ryder, "Drugs, Incarceration, and Neighborhood Life: The Impact of Reintegrating Offenders into the Community" (final report to the National Institute of Justice, October 2001).

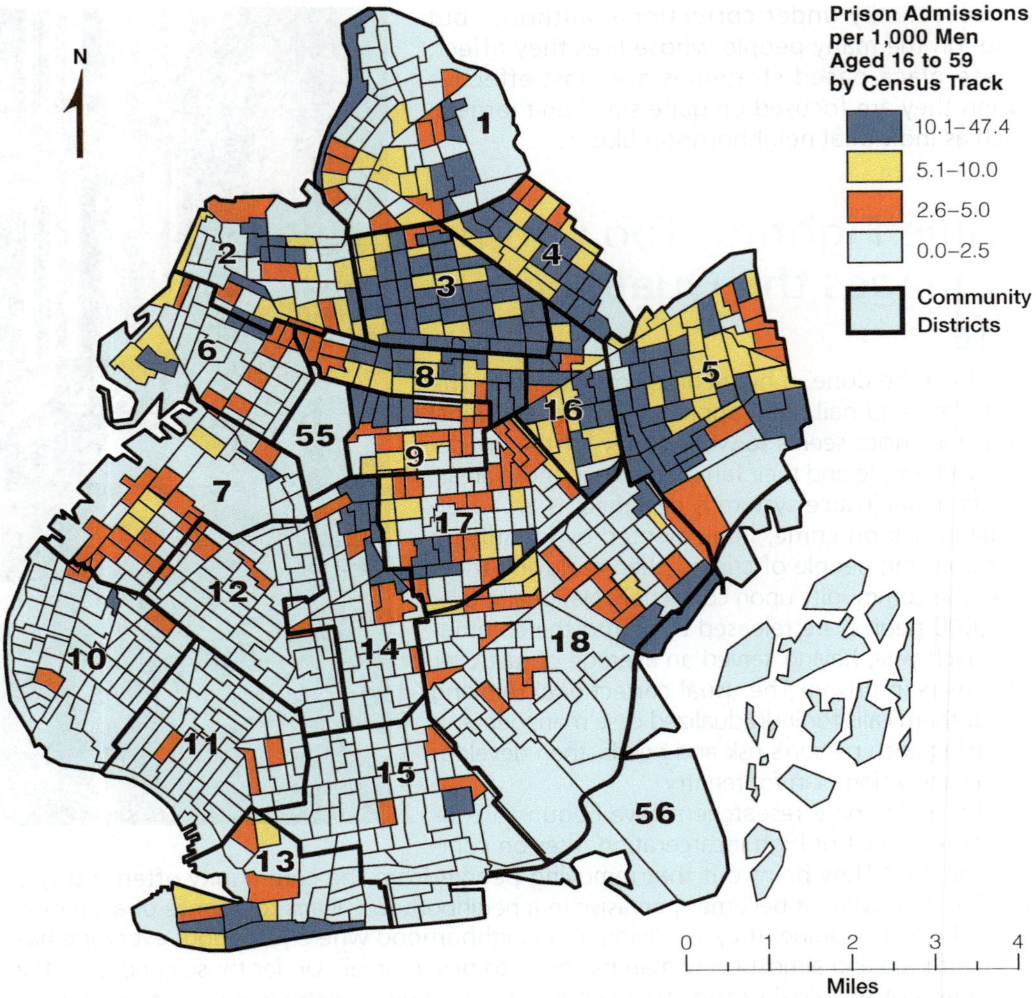

FIGURE 22.1 Male Residents of Brooklyn, New York, City Council Districts Admitted to Prison or Jail, 2004

The data show the residence of men admitted to prison or jail in one year. What is the impact of such a high concentration of formerly incarcerated people living in a neighborhood?

Source: Eric Cadora and Charles Swartz, *Justice Mapping Project* (New York: Columbia University, 2007).

Proactive Rather Than Reactive Strategies Are Needed

Restorative justice and problem-solving strategies illustrate one of the essential differences between the philosophies of traditional criminal justice and community justice: The former is reactive, whereas the latter is proactive. Reactive approaches begin only after a crime has occurred—and only after victims and communities have suffered the costs of crime. Proactive approaches seek to prevent crimes from occurring in the first place.

The proactive approach is based on the assumption that preventing crimes is the most efficient aim of justice. Crime prevention not only saves money because of fewer people being processed, but it also avoids costs to the victim and the community.

Advocates of traditional criminal justice often point out that one way to prevent crimes is to incapacitate through incarceration. Proponents of community justice respond that because most of those who go to prison eventually return to society, and because

THINKING OUTSIDE THE BOX

SOCIAL IMPACT BONDS

Correctional agencies are inherently conservative organizations—averse to taking risks—and for good reason. When a correctional agency takes a risk and fails, the consequences are often dire. There can be new victims of crime, and the public can become very critical of the corrections system. But organizational conservatism makes it hard for correctional agencies to innovate because innovation always has risks. Moreover, it is not easy for the corrections system to find the kinds of resources needed to mount new and innovative services when it can barely afford business as usual.

This same dynamic does not apply to the private sector. Creative thinking is how the private sector thrives, and innovation is rewarded. Following this model, reformers have begun writing about the potential value of social impact bonds (SIBs) as a way of getting private investors involved in correctional innovation.

Under the social impact bond model, a government contracts with a financier from the private sector, such as an investment firm, to provide the up-front capital needed to offer innovative correctional services. The government repays the private investor based upon rates of recidivism, or whether a former correctional client returns to criminal behavior. The repayment calculations are based on the amount of money the government saves when people in correctional services do not return to prison. If the recidivism rate is 60 percent, the investor will get half the original investment back; 50 percent recidivism means a 75 percent return; 40 percent brings 100 percent repayment; and after that, the investor makes a profit. A 20 percent recidivism rate might even mean a doubling of return on the original investment.

There are plenty of technical issues in setting up SIBs, from measuring recidivism to estimating cost savings. But the idea has become intriguing to people who think the private sector ought to be involved in improving the quality of public life.

The New York City Department of Corrections carried out an experiment with an SIB approach to treat young men imprisoned in Rikers Island, the New York City jail. Goldman Sachs put up nearly $10 million to fund a new approach for treatment, Adolescent Behavioral Learning Experience, for more than 3,000 adolescent males. The recidivism rate that it had to beat was about 50 percent.

The results demonstrated both the promise and the challenge of the approach. People who were exposed to the treatment in fact had a lower recidivism rate. But the total amount of jail time averted by the lower recidivism rate did not generate enough actual savings in jail time to enable the investor to be paid back in "profits." SIBs are promising, but they require a substantial amount of planning if they are to succeed.

Sources: Jeffrey B. Liebman, *Social Impact Bonds: A Promising New Financing Model to Accelerate Social Innovation and Improve Government Performance* (Washington, DC: Center for American Progress, 2011); Vera Institute of Justice, *Impact Evaluation of the Adolescent Behavioral Learning Experience (ABLE) Program* (New York: Author, 2016).

many of these are less capable of making it after having been to prison than before, the effects of incapacitation on the crime rate are overstated. They also present evidence that strategies based on arrest and incarceration do not work in the long run.[30]

Proactive strategies for environmental crime prevention are becoming increasingly popular. These approaches seek to identify and overcome the problems in a community that lead to crimes: Vacant lots that attract idle youth groups are turned into appealing playgrounds that attract children and their parents; corner liquor stores are turned into corner grocery stores; dark alleyways are cordoned off and made available to residents as backyards; drug thoroughfares have their traffic patterns rerouted to enable residents to feel safer.

Individual problem-solving strategies can also be proactive. After incarceration, people who have trouble finding a job may work instead on community reclamation projects for pay, and children who have limited adult supervision are encouraged to attend fun after-school programs that strengthen skills and provide adult contact outside of school settings.

David Kennedy, director of the Center for Crime Prevention and Control at John Jay College of Criminal Justice, is developing a new form of proactive strategy. In this effort he works with community leaders to present the community's norms to gangs and others involved in crime. The crime-prone members often feel connections to their families and neighbors; the work aims at using this sense of connection as a force for change.

Examples of this work have yielded remarkable results in cities as diverse as Washington, D.C.; High Point, North Carolina; and Indianapolis, Indiana.[31]

The common thread in all this is to move away from an individual-based, reactive, retributive criminal justice system toward a community-based, proactive, restorative justice strategy (see "Thinking Outside the Box"). Community justice seeks to build a greater experience of justice for those communities hardest hit by crime.

LO 3

Describe the problems that community justice faces.

PROBLEMS OF COMMUNITY JUSTICE

The image of community justice presented by its advocates is attractive. This is one reason why the concept of community justice has become more popular in recent years. Yet community justice is a new idea, and observers have raised several important questions about its prospects. In particular, three central questions have been raised concerning individual rights, social inequality, and increased costs. Any attempt to embrace community justice will inevitably face these issues.

Impingement on Individual Rights

In a community justice model, different communities vary in the ways they pursue public safety and improved quality of life. For example, if localities determine justice (and crime) priorities, then services such as policing and prosecution may differ in the ways they allocate resources or take practical actions, even though they operate under identical criminal codes. How far can these differences go before they violate our belief in equality under the law? To what extent can a locality exert its unique vision of social control without infringing on freedoms of "deviant" members who are in the minority? Will a neighborhood justice movement take on characteristics of vigilantism? If so, what will stop that trend?

As citizens become more active in various aspects of the justice process, they undercut the state's role in presiding over that process. The adversarial ideal assumes that the state accuses a citizen and brings to bear evidence that supports the accusation. The dispute is between the state and the accused person. Inserting neighbors and residents into that arrangement muddies the water by creating a third party to the dispute. It is unclear what the precise role of the third party ought to be—observational, participatory, advisory, or even advocative? Whichever, the presence of that third party means that the state and its adversary can no longer be concerned only about each other. The concern for rights' protections extends beyond those of the accused person to the rights of victims and, indirectly, to affected community members. The question is this: What does the growth of interest in the community mean for the rights of a person suspected of a crime? Communities are important, but because individual characteristics promote serious delinquency more than community characteristics do, some people wonder if a focus on communities will lead us to ignore individuals' problems that need to be addressed.

We must be uneasy about the implications of any developments that undermine the protection of rights. Perhaps the finest contribution of Western civilization to modern life is the idea of the sanctity and dignity of the individual. This idea is given life in the form of legal rights, in which citizens stand equal to one another as well as to the state. Any movement toward community justice taken at the expense of this priceless heritage would impose a cultural cost of profound dimensions. Community justice ideals *will* alter established practices of substantive and procedural criminal law. The test will be to devise changes that protect precious civil liberties.

Social Inequality

Neighborhoods differ not only in their crime control priorities but also in their capacities, resources, and resilience in meeting crime problems. The same inequalities that individuals face in the United States play out as a community dynamic. The justice system really operates as two different systems, one for those with financial resources and another for those without them. Is there any assurance that the same kind of inequality will not come to characterize community justice?

This is not a small concern. The higher victimization rates of African Americans and Latinos are caused, almost completely, by the fact that they live in disadvantaged places where violence persists. Further, poor communities, particularly those hit hard by crime, also tend to lack resources to regulate neighborhood problems and pursue social control.[32] These communities do not come together to solve problems, and they have low rates of citizen participation in civic life. One lesson of community policing has been that in troubled neighborhoods, getting citizens to take responsible action in regard to their crime problems is often difficult.

The more-prosperous localities will also have disproportionate political influence in many city and county governments. They will be better at organizing to influence the crime priorities, directing the funding decisions, and protecting their residents from negative effects of change. A community justice model that enables localities to pursue interests and preferences will inevitably raise the potential for these more-successful communities to strengthen their position in relation to other localities. Community justice cannot treat all communities as having equal importance or as being independent from one another. The most effective community organizations tend to be "neighborhood associations" that advance the needs of identifiable sections of a city, but the poorest communities tend to lack them. Therefore, we must recognize that communities exist within larger social and political systems and that local problems and the public policies created to address them must be understood within this broader context.

Inequality breeds crime. It would be a dismal irony if community justice, advanced to help places deal more effectively with their crime problems, instead contributed to the very dynamics that make those problems worse. If the problem of inequality is to be avoided, some local areas will likely require more help than others to take advantage of the promise of community justice.

Increasing Criminal Justice Costs

We spend nearly $100 billion on the criminal justice system every year. The cost of justice is increasing, and the burden it places on local areas through taxes interferes with the capacity to fund schools, provide health care, and maintain basic services. A community justice model calls for criminal justice organizations to augment current services. How will this arrangement be paid for?

The disparity between community resources and crime rates means that local revenues cannot provide the basis for funding community justice. As indicated, the very communities that most suffer from crime are the least able to pay to combat it. Some mechanism for shifting financial resources from affluent communities to impoverished ones will be needed. This will obviously raise sensitive political issues because taxpayers are leery of spending for services that do not directly benefit them. In addition, some way of shifting costs *within* the existing justice budget will be needed.

Money for new programs is scarce, and a proposal to greatly increase the funding of justice work will be met with skepticism. Community justice programs that shift the onus for crime fighting to the community without providing resources to do it are doomed to fail.

Community justice therefore depends on a shifting of resources within existing justice functions. The overall dollar costs of justice cannot be expected to rise too much; what can occur is a change in the allocation of justice dollars to provide support for new activities in place of previous functions. Community justice calls for collaboration between criminal justice agencies and other government and community social welfare agencies and services. Coordinated efforts will enhance effectiveness by combining the resources of different agencies that are using similar strategies to obtain different ends. For example, while one agency's objective may be increasing employment within a neighborhood, doing so may also reduce criminal activity.

LO 4

Explore the future prospects of community justice.

THE FUTURE OF COMMUNITY JUSTICE

Community justice is a new idea. It has proved very popular, but the important question of any new idea in correctional work is whether it has staying power. We might wonder whether the community justice movement will be a brief aspect of today's justice politics or, as its advocates intend, a long-term force in the reform of the justice system.

The popularity of community justice derives in part from deep dissatisfactions with contemporary justice politics. Many have become alarmed by the trends described in earlier chapters, such as the increased use of surveillance and the ever-growing size of correctional populations. Because it embraces community safety without the emphasis on "toughness" or surveillance, community justice provides an attractive alternative for many who are disillusioned with existing strategies.

In some ways community justice is a throwback. Those who promote local, informal, and citizen-supported responses to crime seem to have an image of the way that communities traditionally dealt with misbehavior in the past—by collective effort to overcome it. If community justice is desirable because it calls us to a nostalgic past, it is likely to be short-lived. Modern problems call for modern solutions, not fuzzy history.

Ironically, the past has also been marked by a harsh and dehumanizing approach to dealing with deviance. If the community justice movement successfully develops and demonstrates a true alternative to traditional criminal justice—with local, problem-solving, restorative, and proactive solutions to crime problems—then traditional bureaucratic justice will itself someday be a thing of the past.

SUMMARY

1 Define community justice and show how it differs from criminal justice.

As a philosophy, community justice is based on a pursuit of justice that goes beyond the traditional three tasks of criminal justice—apprehension, conviction, and punishment. As a strategy, community justice combines three contemporary justice innovations: community policing, environmental crime prevention, and restorative justice. As a series of programs, community justice includes a varied package of methods. Most of all, community justice is concerned with taking seriously the problems faced by people who live with high levels of crime, some of whom are themselves involved in crime. Community justice differs from traditional criminal justice in four important ways: It is based on the neighborhood rather than on the legal jurisdiction, it uses problem-solving strategies rather than adversarial strategies, it is restorative rather than retributive, and it strives to improve the community through a strategy called justice reinvestment.

2 Identify the arguments in favor of community justice.

Community justice has gained public support because although crime damages community life, traditional criminal justice does not address that damage. Citizens' groups and justice system leaders are together developing ways to use criminal justice resources to address the damage that results from crime and crime fighting in high-crime localities. The arguments for community justice can be illustrated by three common assertions of the community justice movement: (1) Crime and crime problems are local; thus, local strategies and solutions are needed. (2) Crime fighting too often damages the quality of life, so strategies directed toward improving the quality of life are needed. (3) Proactive rather than reactive strategies are needed because reaction never solves the original problems that lead to crime.

3 Describe the problems that community justice faces. Three central concerns have been raised about the prospects of community justice: (1) Impingement on human rights may occur if a focus on community well-being undermines the rights of individuals accused of a crime. (2) Social inequality may result because impoverished neighborhoods lack the human and capital resources to tackle their own problems. (3) Criminal justice costs may increase to cover the new programs and augmented services demanded by the community justice model.

4 Explore the future prospects of community justice. We might wonder whether the community justice movement will be a brief aspect of today's justice politics or, as its advocates intend, a long-term force in the reform of the justice system. The popularity of community justice derives in part from deep dissatisfactions with contemporary justice politics. Those who promote local, informal, and citizen-supported responses to crime seem to have an image of the way that communities traditionally dealt with misbehavior in the past—by collective effort to overcome it. If the call for community justice is not much more than a call for a return to the past, it will not last long. But if the community justice movement successfully develops and demonstrates a true alternative to traditional criminal justice—with local, problem-solving, restorative, and proactive solutions to crime problems—then traditional bureaucratic justice will someday be a thing of the past.

KEY TERMS

collective efficacy *(p. 573)*
justice reinvestment *(p. 577)*
spatial concentration *(p. 572)*

FOR DISCUSSION

1. Would you rather live in a neighborhood where the effects of traditional criminal justice or those of community justice were most strongly felt?
2. Why do you think that the community justice movement is so popular? Will it last, or will it soon be over? Why?
3. What impediments block greater cooperation among correctional agencies, such as probation, and other government services, such as the police or social welfare? How can these impediments be overcome?
4. Do you think that citizens want to get involved in their own crime-prevention problems? Why or why not?

FOR FURTHER READING

Brown, David, Chris Cuneen, Melanie Schwartz, et al. *Justice Reinvestment: Winding Back Imprisonment.* Basingstoke, UK: Palgrave MacMillan, 2016. Describes justice reinvestment as a way to reduce over-incarceration of aboriginal Australians.

Byrne, James, ed. *Special Issue on Restorative Justice: Victims & Offenders* 11 (no. 1, 2016). Eleven papers on the application of restorative justice to various justice system stages.

Harvell, Samantha, Jeremy Welsh-Loveman, and Hanna Love. *Reforming Sentencing and Corrections Policy.* Washington, DC: Urban Institute, 2016. An evaluation of the federal government's Justice Reinvestment Initiative, carried out in 26 states.

Sered, Danielle. *Accounting for Violence: How to Increase Safety and Break Our Failed Reliance on Mass Incarceration.* New York: Vera Institute of Justice, 2017. A study calling for four new community justice principles in responding to violence.

Sered, Danielle. *Until We Reckon: Violence, Mass Incarceration, and the Road to Repair*. New York: The New Press, 2019. Comprehensive, empirically based argument for restorative justice as a way to deal with injustice and violence.

Sharkey, Patrick. *Stuck in Place: Urban Neighborhoods and the End of Progress Toward Racial Equality.* Chicago: University of Chicago Press, 2013. Explains how urban segregation and concentrated disadvantage made racial equality less attainable.

Vitale, Alex S. *The End of Policing*. New York: Verso, 2017. The argument for divesting in traditional policing and investing in community quality of life.

Weisburd, David, Wim Bernasco, and Gerben J. N. Bruinsma, eds. *Putting Crime in Its Place*. New York: Springer, 2009. A series of papers assessing crime-prevention strategies based on street-level projects.

NOTES

1 Katy Reckdahl, "Mass Incarceration's Collateral Damage: The Children Left Behind," *Nation*, January 5, 2015.

2 Annie E. Casey Foundation, *A Shared Sentence: The Devastating Toll of Parental Incarceration on Kids, Families, and Communities* (Baltimore, MD: Author, 2016).

3 Brian Elderbroom, Laura Bennett, Shanna Gong, Felicity Rose,, and Zoë Towns, *Every Second: The Impact of America's Incarceration Crisis on Families* (Washington, DC: Public Welfare Foundation, 2018): https://www.publicwelfare.org/wp-content/uploads/2019/04/CJ-EverySecond.FWD_.us_-December-Report-on-family-incarceration.pdf.

4 Leila Moresy and Richard Rothstein, *Mass Incarceration and Children's Outcomes* (Washington, DC: Economic Policy Institute, 2016); Christopher Wildeman and Signe Hald Andersen, "Paternal Incarceration and Children's Risk of Being Charged by Early Adulthood: Evidence from a Danish Policy Shock," *Criminology* 55 (no. 1, 2017): 32–58; Peggy C. Giordano, Jennifer E. Copp, Wendy D. Manning, and Monica A. Longmire, "Linking Parental Incarceration and Family Dynamics Associated with Intergenerational Transmission: A Life-course Perspective," *Criminology* 57 (no. 3, 2019): 395–423.

5 David P. Farrington, Maria M. Ttifi, and Rebecca V. Crago, "Intergenerational Transmission of Convictions for Different Kinds of Offenses," *Victims & Offenders* 12 (no. 1, 2017): 1–20; Michael E. Roettger and Raymond R. Swisher, "Associations of Fathers' History of Incarceration with Sons' Delinquency and Arrest Among Black, White, and Hispanic Males in the United States," *Criminology* 49 (no. 4, 2011): 1109–48; Joseph Murray, Rolf Loeber, and Dustin Pardini, "Parental Involvement in the Criminal Justice System and the Development of Youth Theft, Marijuana Use, Depression, and Academic Performance," *Criminology* 50 (no. 1, 2012): 255–302; Christopher Wildeman, "Parental Incarceration, Child Homelessness, and the Invisible Consequences of Mass Imprisonment," *Annals of the American Academy of Political and Social Science* 651 (no. 1, 2014): 74–96.

6 Saneta de Vuono-powell, Chris Schweidler, Alicia Walters, and Azedah Zohrabi, *Who Pays? The True Cost of Incarceration on Families* (Oakland, CA: Ella Baker Center, 2015).

7 Christopher Wildeman, "Incarceration and Population Health in Wealthy Democracies," *Criminology* 54 (no. 2, 2016): 360–82.

8 Patrick Starkey, Stuck in Place: *Urban Neighborhoods and the End of Progress Toward Racial Equality* (Chicago: University of Chicago Press, 2013).

9 David Cloud, *On Life Support: Public Health in the Age of Mass Incarceration* (New York: Vera Institute of Justice, 2014).

10 Michelle S. Phelps and Devah Pager, "Inequality and Punishment: A Turning Point for Mass Incarceration?" *Annals of the American Academy of Political and Social Science* 633 (January, 2016): 185–203.

11 Lauren E. Glaze and Danielle Kaeble, *Correctional Populations in the United States, 2015* (Washington, DC: U.S. Bureau of Justice Statistics, 2016).

12 Robert J. Sampson, Stephen W. Raudenbush, and Felton Earles, "Neighborhoods and Violent Crime: A Multilevel Study of Collective Efficacy," *Science* 277 (August 15, 1997): 1–7.

13 USAID, *What Works in Reducing Community Violence: A Meta-review and Field Study for the Northern Triangle* (Washington, DC: Author, 2016); Grant Duwe, "Can Circles of Support and Accountability (CoSA) Significantly Reduce Sexual Recidivism? Results from a Randomly Controlled Trial in Minnesota," *Journal of Experimental Criminology* 14 (no. 2, 2018): 463–84.

14 Susan Tucker and Eric Cadora, *Ideas for an Open Society: Justice Reinvestment* (New York: Open Society Institute, 2003), 1.

15 Michael McLaughlin, Carrie Pettus-Davis, Derek Brown, et al., "The Economic Burden of Incarceration in the U.S." Working Paper #CI072016, Concordance Institute for Advancing Social Justice, Washington University, Saint Louis, MO, 2016.

16 Jessica T. Simes, "Place and Punishment: The Spatial Concentration of Mass Incarceration," *Journal of Quantitative Criminology* 34 (no. 3, 2018): 513–33.

17 David J. Harding, Jeffrey D. Morenoff, and Claire W. Herbert, "Home Is Hard to Find: Neighborhoods, Institutions, and the Residential Trajectories of Returning Prisoners," *Annals of the American Academy of Political and Social Sciences* 647 (no. 1, 2013): 214–36.

18 Marshall Clement, Matthew Schwarzfeld, and Michael Thompson, *The National Summit on Justice Reinvestment and Public Safety: Addressing Recidivism, Crime, and Corrections Spending* (New York: Justice Center of the Council of State Governments, 2011).

19 Maria B. Velez and Christopher J. Lyons, "Making or Breaking Neighborhoods: Public Social Control and the Political Economy of Urban Crime," *Criminology & Public Policy* 13 (no. 2, 2014): 225–35.

20 David M. Ramey and Emily A. Shrides, "New Parochialism, Sources of Community Investment, and the Control of Street Crime," *Criminology & Public Policy* 13 (no. 2, 2014): 193–216; Rob Allen, *Rehabilitation Devolution—How Localising Justice Can Reduce Crime and Imprisonment* (London: Transform Justice, 2015).

21 A. M. Wolf, A. Del Prado Lippman, C. Glesmann, and E. Castro, *Process Evaluation for the Office of Neighborhood Safety* (Oakland, CA: National Council on Crime and Delinquency, 2015).

22 Alex S. Vitale, *The End of Policing* (New York: Verso, 2017).

23 Samantha Harvell, Jeremy Welsh-Loveman, and Hanna Love, *Reforming Sentencing and Corrections Policy* (Washington, DC: Urban Institute, 2016).

24 Council of State Governments, *Justice Reinvestment Initiative*, www.pccd.pa.gov/Documents/Justice%20Reinvestment/JRI%202016_TwoPager.pdf, April 24, 2017.

25 Clifford R. Shaw and Henry D. McKay, *Juvenile Delinquency and Urban Areas* (Chicago: University of Chicago Press, 1942).

26 For a review, see Todd R. Clear, *Imprisoning Communities: How Mass Incarceration Makes Disadvantaged Places Worse* (New York: Oxford University Press, 2007), ch. 5.

27 Ryan S. King, *Disparity by Geography: The War on Drugs in American Cities* (Washington, DC: Sentencing Project, 2008); see also Scott Duffield Levy, "The Collateral Consequences of Seeking Order Through Disorder: New York's Narcotics Eviction Program," *Harvard Civil Rights–Civil Liberties Law Review* 43 (no. 2, 2008): 539–80.

28 Todd R. Clear, Dina R. Rose, Elin Waring, and Kristen Scully, "Coercive Mobility and Crime: A Preliminary Examination of Concentrated Incarceration and Social Disorganization," *Justice Quarterly* 20 (no. 1, 2003): 33–64.

29 Robert DeFina and Lance Hannon, "The Impact of Mass Incarceration on Poverty," *Crime & Delinquency* 59 (no. 4, 2013): 562–86.

30 Bernard E. Harcourt, *Illusion of Order: The False Promise of Broken Windows Policing* (Cambridge, MA: Harvard University Press, 2001); see also Ralph B. Taylor, Philip W. Harris, Peter R. Jones, and Doris Weiland, "Short-Term Changes in Arrest Rates Influence Later Short-Term Changes in Serious Male Delinquency Prevalence: A Time-Dependent Relationship," *Criminology* 47 (no. 2, 2009): 657–797.

31 National Network for Safe Communities, *Results*: https://nnscommunities.org/impact/results/.

32 Robert J. Sampson, Jeffrey D. Morenoff, and Stephen Raudenbush, "Social Anatomy of Racial and Ethnic Disparities in Violence," *American Journal of Public Health* 95 (no. 2, February 2005): 224–32.

CHAPTER 23

American Corrections: Looking Forward

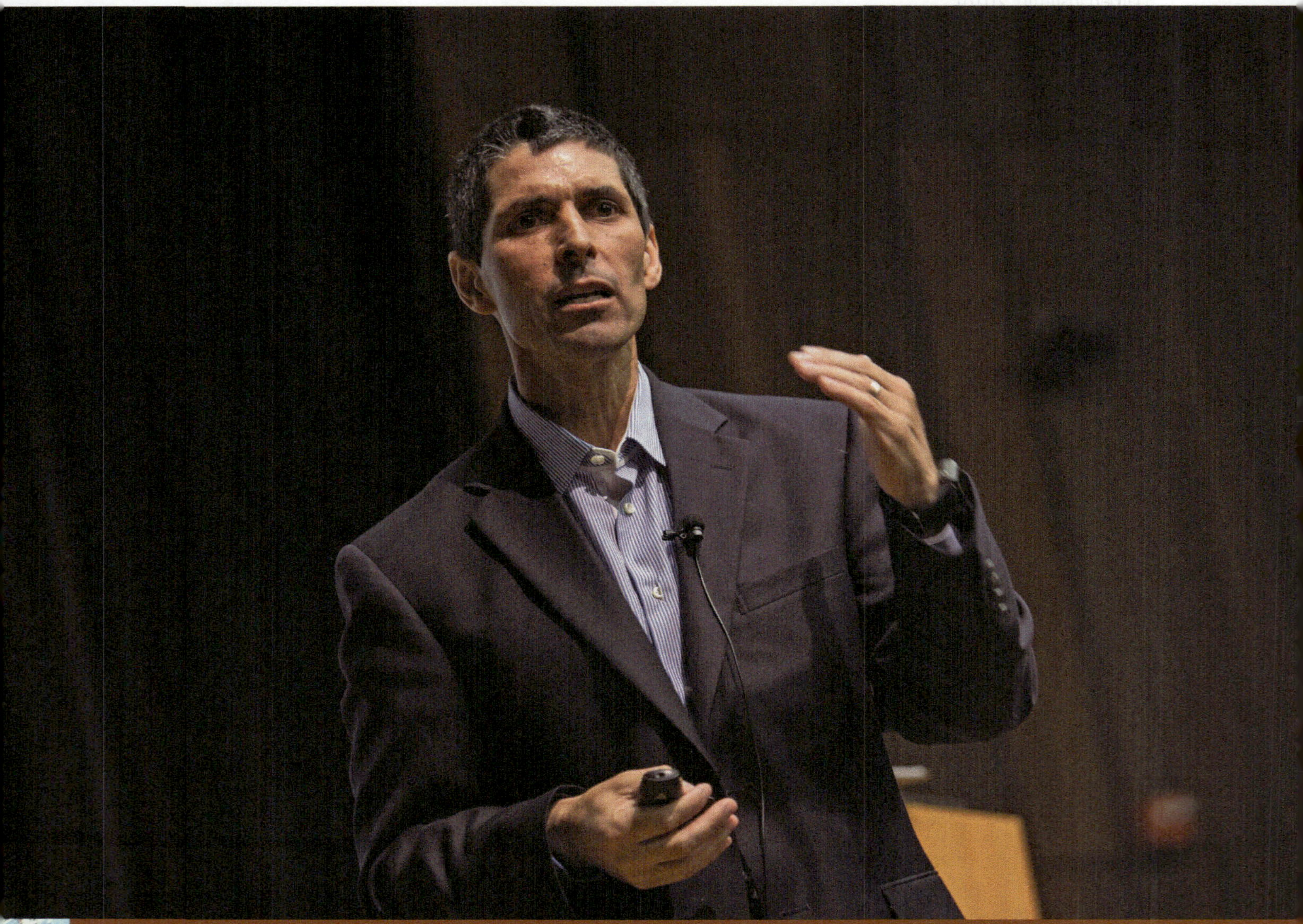

Michael Santos

Michael Santos spent more than two decades in federal prisons on a conviction for drug distribution. Out since 2013, he is an inspiring public speaker and helps advise others on how to survive prison and succeed in reentry.

AT VARIOUS POINTS IN THIS BOOK, WE HAVE HEARD FROM MICHAEL G. SANTOS, WHO STARTED WRITING FOR US WHEN HE WAS IN FEDERAL PRISON. Santos was convicted in 1988 of violating a serious federal drug statute: continuing criminal enterprise for interstate trafficking and distribution. This is also known as the "kingpin" law, designed to take down the top people in a drug ring. Despite the fact that Santos had neither weapons nor a violent background, and even though there was no history of imprisonment, the judge imposed a 45-year sentence. With good time and parole, he was released on August 12, 2013. He spent 26 years behind bars. (See his narrative in Chapter 6, p. 159, and Chapter 11, p. 288-289.)

Santos's situation encapsulates the correctional story of the last three decades. He committed a crime that involved some of what America has most feared over the last 25 years: marketing serious drugs. He was sentenced at a time when penalties had been recently expanded to allow for truly long terms for certain people convicted of drug crimes. As a result, most of his life—nearly all of his adult life—was spent behind bars. While incarcerated he obtained a master's degree, wrote books and articles, developed a passion for penal code reform, and, a few years ago, married Carol, a person he calls "the love of my life." Now, Santos documents his journey of returning to society on his website, which includes a daily journal, a YouTube video channel, and his course notes as a lecturer at San Francisco State University. His time behind bars was not wasted, but so much of his potential to contribute to society went by the wayside, with the years stretching on and on.

By all accounts, Santos ceased being a danger to the community many, many years ago. He became a person who served out his term, with little hope for clemency or pardon, despite many attempts to change his sentence.

Now he is out, working successfully, making contributions to society, and giving back to those who faced obstacles much like those he faced. Looking back, it is hard to justify the decades of his time behind bars. Within a few years of his sentencing, he had become a changed man. But there was little that he—or we—could do about it.

The rationale under which he was sentenced—drugs are a social scourge that justifies a lifetime behind bars—had complete sway over our nation, and he was just one of thousands caught up in the clutches of a system gone extreme. His story is very much a paradigm of what American corrections has been about for the last 30 years.

LEARNING OBJECTIVES

After reading this chapter, you should be able to . . .

1. Analyze how the philosophy of the U.S. corrections system has changed over the years and what effects such changes have had.
2. Explain the major dilemmas facing the corrections system and how they might be resolved.
3. Identify four substantial trends that face corrections and describe their importance.
4. Explain what "good leadership" means in the context of the current corrections system of the United States, and list what it will take for leaders to more widely implement "what works" in corrections.
5. Describe the aspirations for the U.S. corrections system and how those aspirations might be achieved.

LO 1

Analyze how the philosophy of the U.S. corrections system has changed over the years and what effects such changes have had.

AMERICAN CORRECTIONS TODAY

As we pause to think about the future of corrections, we might begin by asking what the American corrections system is best known for, today, across the world.

There was a time when the U.S. corrections system was the most progressive in the world. When the modern prison was invented after the American Revolution, it was envied internationally (see Chapter 3). When the nation's penologists met in Cincinnati in 1870, they affirmed a mission of rehabilitation that became a model for corrections systems around the globe. At the start of the twentieth century, modern probation was invented here—another innovation to be copied worldwide. For most of the nineteenth and twentieth centuries, the U.S. corrections system remained at the forefront of thinking about the best ways to deal with people who break the law, and U.S. methods were widely celebrated and emulated.

Today, the U.S. corrections system no longer serves as a progressive beacon for the world's systems of punishment. If a panel of experts were asked to characterize the U.S. system, they would likely say little about forward-thinking programs or leading innovations of thought. Instead, they would say that what sets the U.S. corrections system apart from all others is that it is so *big*.

Since the mid-1970s, by every measure the American corrections system has grown by unprecedented amounts (see Chapters 1 and 18). Since 1973, the U.S. rate of imprisonment has increased from under 100 per 100,000 to almost 500 per 100,000. Including probation, parole, and jails, the number of people under correctional control has also hugely increased in that time, from under a million to almost seven million.

This growth has disproportionately affected minority group members (see Chapters 4 and 19). For example, recall that more than one in three African American men in their twenties is currently under correctional control—more African American men are behind bars than attend colleges and universities. Some observers estimate that in Los Angeles about one in three African American youths will be arrested each year. It is not hard to see why many residents in these communities believe that the criminal justice system is designed to oppress them and that the corrections system is intended to remove men from their neighborhoods.

It is also hard to believe that over the past 40 years we have deliberately created the corrections system we really want. To the contrary, most of those in charge of today's corrections system would argue that what we are doing is self-destructive and that an overhaul of the corrections system is long overdue. But there is little agreement about the best aims of reform (see Chapter 4).

This lack of agreement is one reason why it is not really accurate to refer to the unprecedented growth in corrections since the early 1970s as an "experiment." Experiments must be planned, and some hypotheses about how and why they might work must be advanced. The surge in correctional populations has resulted from disjointed, incremental policy shifts in sentencing and law enforcement practices. For example, the number of people serving time in U.S. prisons for drug crimes has increased by over 700 percent since 1980, more than five times the rate of increase of people in prison for other crimes; this was largely the result of the war on drugs of the 1980s and 1990s. Two decades later, almost nobody would say we have "won" that war. Indeed, as we saw in Chapter 1, liberals and conservatives alike agree that the corrections system—especially the prison system—is too big and too expensive. Indeed, it is now starting to contract. Now what?

As we have suggested elsewhere in this book, there are signs that this story is changing. For consecutive years, the prison population has dropped—the first time this has happened in 40 years. In almost every state in the nation, policy makers are looking for ways to increase the effectiveness of correctional programs, reduce the size of the prison population, and make the collateral consequences of a felony conviction less onerous. In the 2010s, something of a national consensus seemed to emerge that what we refer to as the Great Punishment Experiment is at least waning, if not ending (see "What Does the Public Want?").

FOCUS ON

CORRECTIONAL PRACTICE: What Does the Public Want?

We are used to a belief that the American public has punitive attitudes toward crime. This has been a notable political "truth," starting with Richard Nixon's 1968 campaign for president, which focused on "crime in the streets," and continuing with Ronald Reagan in 1980, who called for "law 'n' order" as a centerpiece of his justice policy. In 1994, Bill Clinton signed into law a federal grant program to support "truth in sentencing," which created some of the harshest sentencing reforms of the last 40 years. In the presidential campaign of 1988, George H. W. Bush made a core political issue out of Willie Horton, who, while serving a life sentence for murder, was given a weekend furlough and used his freedom to commit assault, armed robbery, and sexual assault. These and many other stories from U.S. electoral politics give the impression of a public hungry for severe punishments of those who break the law.

But are American attitudes punitive today, or are they changing?

There is reason to think that support for "get-tough" policies that dominated the 1970s through the 1990s is waning. A recent national survey found that 62 percent of Americans support "rehabilitating or treating the person" as opposed to "punishing the person" or "keeping the person off the street." Less than one-fifth think that the purpose of corrections should be to punish, and one-third say that the corrections system should prevent future crimes through treatment and rehabilitation.

Even in very conservative places, attitudes seem to be shifting. For example, a survey of citizens in Texas found more support for treatment than punishment as the primary aim of the corrections system. Indeed, respondents in the Texas survey supported treatment over punishment by a more than two-to-one margin, even for people who were convicted for repeat crimes. Almost four-fifths supported diverting people convicted of drug crimes from prison into drug treatment programs.

Critics caution not to make too much of surveys such as this. After all, they say, Donald Trump ran on a "get tough" platform, and voters put him into the White House. But across the country, there is a growing sense that voters have a more nuanced attitude about crime than the hardline stance that dominated political discourse for decades.

Sources: Angela J. Thielo, Frances T. Cullen, Derek M. Cohen, and Cecilia Chouhy, "Rehabilitation in a Red State: Public Support for Correctional Reform in Texas," *Criminology & Public Policy* 15 (no. 1, 2016): 137–70; Zogby Analytics, "Public Opinion Poll Findings on Jails and Local Justice Systems," www.safetyandjusticechallenge.org/wp-content/uploads/2016/04/SJC-Zogby-Analytics-Polling-Memo-1.pdf.

In this closing chapter, we step back to look at the big picture of corrections. What can we make of the corrections system we have described in this book? Where is it headed, and what issues does it face? We explore these questions with a critical eye because even though nobody can truly foresee the future, the way we ask ourselves about the future tells us a great deal about how we feel about the present. We begin with a discussion of five dilemmas that corrections faces—indeed, has always faced throughout history—and follow this with an examination of current trends in corrections. We then consider three key pressing challenges that anyone interested in corrections must face.

FIVE CORRECTIONAL DILEMMAS

LO 2

Explain the major dilemmas facing the corrections system and how they might be resolved.

A *dilemma* is a situation that forces one to choose between two unsatisfactory alternatives. Corrections faces many dilemmas—any worker in the field will attest to this. We have selected five dilemmas as particularly important because they are what we consider "orienting" dilemmas for corrections. That is, not only must each corrections system confront them as it moves further into the twenty-first century, but the way it confronts them will profoundly affect the resolution of most other issues—from daily problems in management to larger considerations.

Indeed, today's difficulties and tomorrow's potential solutions are quite bound up in how these five dilemmas were faced in the past. Unlike much of the material in this book, our description of the dilemmas is not an objective restatement of facts and studies; rather, it is a subjective interpretation of many facts, studies, and observations. We return to the systems perspective as we identify five core concerns: mission, methods, structure, personnel, and costs.

Mission

Corrections lacks a clear mission. One reason for this is that it has so many different clients—people under correctional authority (in one way or another), the general public, other government agencies—each of which has its own expectations of corrections. In simple terms, we recognize that people under correctional supervision want fairness, leniency, and assistance; the public wants protection from and punishment of criminally involved people; government agencies want cooperation and coordination. Obviously, these expectations often come into conflict. Thus, one goal of corrections must be to ultimately disentangle the expectations and establish a set of priorities for handling them.

At the same time, none of these competing expectations can be ignored. How do courts respond when corrections fails to provide rehabilitative services? How does the public respond to instances of brutal recidivism? How do government agencies manage balky correctional officials and growing correctional costs?

One common solution in corrections is to attempt to meet all expectations: provide the services that are requested, take actions to protect citizens when public safety becomes an issue, cooperate with agencies when asked to do so. The advantage of this approach is that corrections can avoid the strains that accompany goal conflict, such as making hard choices about priorities. Of course, this supposed advantage can never be fully realized. The conflicts between serving clients and protecting the community, or between coordinating government practices and providing assistance or protection, are real. When corrections tries to meet all these competing expectations equally, correctional workers must resolve the conflicts informally.

Corrections must confront the problems created by ambiguity of mission. Doing so requires that choices be made. In the early 1960s most people agreed that the primary mission of corrections was rehabilitation, but the devaluation of treatment and the movement toward harsh, mandatory sentences left a void in this area. Some observers have suggested that corrections must take on the role of client management; others have argued that the role of corrections is risk control; still others have suggested punishment as its mission. Today, community justice has worked its way into many correctional mission statements.

Whatever the choice, correctional leaders must articulate their philosophy of corrections and establish a clearer policy to guide its implementation. Both staff members and people outside the system must be aware of what corrections does and what they can expect from its efforts.

Methods

Obviously, if the correctional mission is unclear, the best correctional strategies and techniques will be ambiguous as well. When goals are in conflict, staff members have difficulty choosing among competing methods to perform their work: surveillance or service, custody or treatment. But this is not the only problem with correctional methods; much more significantly, correctional techniques often do not seem to work.

A debilitating lack of confidence results when apparently promising strategies, upon evaluation, turn out to lack merit. The list of failed correctional methods includes smaller caseloads, general counseling, family therapy, group treatment, boot camps, and being "scared straight." These and many other methods have been promoted as "the answers" to various pressing problems. Each time another correctional strategy proves ineffective, the failure feeds an already pervasive feeling among workers and the public that corrections is incapable of performing its basic functions well.

This is one reason why the short-term history of corrections seems dominated by fads. As each "innovative" technique or program is implemented, corrections is confronted by the method's limited ability to immediately solve the technical problems that it was intended to solve. Consequently, it is replaced by something newer still.

The effects of these frequent changes in approach are largely negative. No firm, central technical process is allowed to develop and mature. Because corrections works with people, its central technologies should involve interpersonal communication and influence; however, the parade of new programs subtly shifts the emphasis from process to procedures. The dynamic work of corrections is stalled by the static and routinized activities that ebb and flow with each new program. Bureaucratic approaches to management, such as warehousing people, come to dominate the technical approach to the job. Workers become cynical about changes and about the potential of the work itself. Who can blame them? The most experienced correctional workers have seen many highly praised programs come and go, having failed to produce the expected results.

EDOVO

▲ *Technology has been slow to come into the prison system, but prison administrators now realize that people need to know how to use new technologies as preparation for their lives after reentry.*

Another issue associated with correctional methods is fairness. In recent years the concept of just deserts has become popular, and much effort has been devoted to ways to achieve it. Although the just deserts model of criminal justice is quite elaborate, it boils down to a single generalization: People should be punished equally in accordance with the severity of their offenses. This seems to be a straightforward assignment.

Yet something is wanting in the doctrine of just deserts. The fact is that the most stringent correctional methods are applied in practice almost exclusively to the poor and predominantly to minorities. One is left with the feeling that merely to be "equal" in our application of state power under these circumstances is not really to be fair in the broadest sense of the term. Genuine fairness must enhance the lives and the potential of those we bring under correctional control. But if the history of corrections has taught us anything, it is that we often injure the people we try to help. We know little about how to provide effective assistance to people in the corrections system, but it is certainly not enough just to punish them equally. The dilemma of methods is complex. Can we overcome the tradition of faddism in corrections without becoming stodgily bureaucratic in method? Can we improve the life chances of correctional clients without injuring them further despite good intentions? Do we really want to "lock people up and throw away the key?" (See "Myths in Corrections.")

Structure

Corrections is simply not in a position to significantly influence its own fate. Much of this inability has to do with its structure—internal and external. Internally, corrections is a process divided against itself. Jails, prisons, probation, and parole all struggle with one another; the practices of each become contingencies for the others. Externally, corrections represents the culmination of the criminal justice process, and it has little formal capacity to control the demand for its services. Thus, correctional leaders face two structural dilemmas.

First, their colleagues are often the ones who put the most immediate obstacles in the way of their attempts to manage their operations effectively. Second, the corrections system depends on significant factors outside of its control. The practical consequences of these structural dilemmas are sometimes quite startling.

In many jurisdictions, for example, large amounts of money have been spent renovating old jails or building new ones because the existing facilities are substandard, overcrowded, or both. Too often, the new version is soon just as overcrowded as the old one was, or else it is deemed legally substandard. The fault rests with the inability of corrections to coordinate architectural planning with the programmatic needs of such nonjail agencies as the courts and probation.

MYTHS in Corrections

Is Recidivism Inevitable?

THE MYTH: Once a person commits a crime, he or she will always pose a higher risk to the community than people who have never committed a crime.

THE REALITY: After the passage of sufficient time, people who have a criminal conviction have no more risk of a new arrest than those who have never been arrested. For people convicted of robbery, the time period needed is about eight years; for people convicted of burglary, the span is about four years.

Source: Alfred Blumstein and Kiminori Nakamura, "Redemption in the Presence of Widespread Criminal Background Checks," *Criminology* 47 (no. 2, 2009):327–59.

What initially seemed to be a problem of how much space is available really reflects a problem of how available space is used, which, in turn, is influenced by people other than jail administrators. The courts (through sentencing and pretrial release), law enforcement (through arrest), and probation and parole (through revocation) all use jail space for their own purposes. The lack of agencies to ameliorate the effects of population growth on corrections can eliminate the benefits of opening a new prison. This is only one of the deficiencies that repeatedly occur in correctional planning.

Formally, the problem of structure in corrections is one of interdependence and coordination. In some ways the ability of corrections to function effectively depends on external processes that it must respond to, influence, or at least understand. To do so, its own processes must be better coordinated with those of the external agencies that produce the dependence—and the dissension.

The problem is that there is really no easy way to coordinate these processes. Separation of powers is both a constitutional and a traditional bulwark of our government. Each agency is protective of its own power and reluctant to reduce it by coordination or planning. Thus, when a new jail is being designed, the approval of the municipal engineering bureau is seen as a hurdle to be cleared rather than a potential resource to be tapped. Each time an interagency control is put into place, it becomes an obstacle rather than a coordinating mechanism.

Most correctional administrators find that their greatest frustrations lie in getting other agencies to avoid actions that severely constrain their ability to function. A recent trend has been the formation of "partnerships" meant to improve coordination, whether high-level commissions composed of heads of correctional, justice system, judicial, and executive-branch agencies or task forces of line-level personnel. This is a promising step, but a small one.

Personnel

Because corrections is a people-processing operation, its personnel are its main resource. The two essential goals in regard to staff are (1) attracting the right kinds of people to work in corrections and (2) motivating them to remain once they are employed. Corrections traditionally has not done well in either area.

The initial recruitment problem frequently stems from the low starting salaries. Although salaries vary widely from place to place, correctional employees often earn less than workers in comparable positions elsewhere. For example, correctional officers frequently begin at wages lower than those of local law enforcement officers. Likewise, the starting salaries of probation and parole officers, who are normally required to have a college degree, often are not competitive with those offered to social workers and teachers.

For this reason, correctional positions may be regarded as a good entry to the work world. A person new to the job market can obtain stable employment for a year or two while seeking alternative employment. The most-qualified individuals find it relatively easy to move on to other occupations; less-qualified people often stay longer, some for their entire careers (see "Do the Right Thing").

DO THE RIGHT THING

You are the director of a small, nonprofit agency that provides services to people who are in reentry from prison. You employ some people with criminal records because you have found that they can be very effective with the kinds of clients your agency deals with. Before you hire people with a record, however, you check their background very carefully, and you keep careful track of their work, especially in the early months of their career.

One of your employees, Hidalgo Vegas, has been especially successful for the last three years. He has a 10-year-old felony conviction for drug sales, and during that period of his life, when he used drugs regularly, he had several misdemeanor arrests and convictions, mostly low-level misdemeanor crime—never involving violence. But yesterday Vegas came into your office to tell you he has been arrested in a domestic dispute, and the charge is assault. He says he and his wife were fighting, and things got out of control. Your investigation indicates that he shoved her around a bit but did not hit her. The prosecutor says that the victim will not press charges. But his counseling job in your agency often requires Vegas to work with people who have domestic violence in their background.

What do you do? Fire him? Let him keep working? Take a different action?

WRITING ASSIGNMENT: Write an essay discussing the ethical issues involved in this situation, and also indicate the choice you would make about retaining Vegas as your employee.

Further, as a result of collective bargaining, most correctional employees receive equal pay raises regardless of performance. Inevitably, a system of equality becomes a disincentive to employees whose work efforts surpass those of others. Too frequently, significant personnel decisions such as promotions, raises, and increased responsibilities are completely out of the hands of correctional administrators.

In times of fiscal abundance, salary is not as great a problem, but decades of salary crunches in government employment, combined with a constricted job market, can embitter many correctional employees. The organizational culture of many correctional operations is dominated by animosity toward management and cynicism toward the job. Too often, correctional employees feel unappreciated, manipulated, and alienated. Under these conditions, it is exceedingly difficult for a corrections system to perform its "peoplework" function effectively because its most valuable resource—the staff—is demoralized.

On the surface, the solution to the personnel problem seems simple: Measure the performance of staff, reward those who are productive, and get rid of those who are not. Unfortunately, this approach does not work easily in government employment (and may not always work so well in the private sector, either). For one thing, correctional performance is exceedingly difficult to assess. Although the general yardsticks of recidivism, institutional security, and so forth provide useful measures of correctional performance, they are inadequate indicators of an individual's performance. Who can say that when a person on parole fails, it was the parole officer's fault? Indeed, it might represent an officer's successful surveillance.

Secondary performance measures, such as contacts with clients, paperwork, and training, are therefore often substituted for primary measures of job success. These secondary measures tend to be fairer because they fall within the staff 's control. But for a secondary measure of performance to be useful, it must be clearly related to organizational success. In this respect, most secondary measures in corrections are inadequate. In another vein, government employment is often sought because of its purported job security; altering the personnel picture to overcome lethargy is likely to cause extreme strain among the staff.

Unfortunately, the correctional leader's choices regarding personnel issues involve no short-term solutions. The answer, if there is one, lies in long-term staff development. A sound staff is built by innovative methods of selection and promotion; professional growth on the job is encouraged by incentives for education and training. "Human resource" management approaches are taken to involve staff in the operations of the organization. However, turnover at the top of the correctional hierarchy may be so great that the administrator who tries to address personnel issues may not be around to reap the rewards of his or her efforts.

Costs

One of the most notable aspects of corrections is that it is expensive. The cost of building a prison exceeds $100,000 per cell (not including financing). Each personnel position represents expenditures equal to twice his or her annual salary when fringe benefits, retirement costs, and office supplies are included. The processing of a convicted person through the corrections system usually reaches at least $25,000 in direct costs and nearly half that much again in indirect costs (such as defaulted debts, welfare to families, and lost wages and taxes). The decision to punish someone is a decision to allocate precious public resources, often irretrievably. Correctional administrators understand all this now more than ever. Allocating correctional resources wisely is a huge challenge. The economic consequences of these decisions reach far into society, affecting communities, public priorities, and even the nation's future fiscal health.

States facing the need to pay for a variety of public policy priorities, such as education and health care, today have an unprecedented concern about correctional costs. The public is beginning to question the advisability of correctional growth. The desire to punish criminally involved people is not always backed up by a willingness to pay for the punishment.

The ambivalence about punishment and funding has left correctional leaders in a bind. The arguments for expansion of large, secure facilities must be weighed against equally strong arguments for increased emphasis on community-based corrections. These arguments are in some ways easy to understand. The public continues to care deeply about controlling crime, but there is also a growing public sentiment to do something about "mass incarceration."

Most correctional officials recognize that focusing on prisons is a regressive rather than a progressive approach. Many of our existing secure facilities are decrepit and need to be replaced, but the evidence is quite strong that (1) prison construction does not alleviate crowding and (2) the incapacitation strategy for crime control is both imperfect and highly prone to error. Officials also know that once a prison is built, it represents a continuing management focus for as long as it is used—in contrast to field services, which are much more responsive to change and innovation. To this must be added a growing empirical literature that a number of nonprison strategies for controlling crime exist that are far cheaper than prison.

As we have seen, however, the nation may be on the verge of a change. One of America's worst economic recessions started in 2008, forcing virtually every state to reduce spending. One area receiving great scrutiny was corrections—especially budgets for prisons. After a generation of ever-growing correctional costs, state legislators started looking for equally effective but less expensive ways to deal with people convicted of serious crimes. Some states have had significant success reducing their prison populations without increasing crime, and as these experiences become more widely known, policy makers will look for ways to repeat this work. By the time of this writing, at least two-thirds of the states have passed legislation with an eye to reducing prison populations. (See "How Much Does Corrections Cost Our Society?") The economic crisis that accompanied the COVID-19 pandemic will pose similar fiscal challenges, as state and local governments face daunting losses in tax revenues.

FOCUS ON

CORRECTIONAL PRACTICE: How Much Does Corrections Cost Our Society?

It is well-known that prisons are expensive. The average annual cost of keeping an adult in prison ranges from \$30,000 to \$50,000 per year, depending on which state's corrections system is being measured. Building a prison can cost \$100,000 or more per prison cell. For juveniles, the cost figure can be as much as five times that amount. Probation and parole also have costs. Researchers tell us that state and local governments spend \$80 billion annually on their corrections systems.

But these are only the direct "cash" costs of the corrections system each year. There are many so-called "hidden costs" in a system of punishment. These include costs that are borne by families and children when a wage-earning relative goes to prison—estimated to be \$70 billion. The income support that families forgo while a person is incarcerated is augmented by the lifelong deficit in income that occurs because of a prison record—another \$230 billion. Health costs associated with a prison stay amount to over \$90 billion. The disruption that families and children experience in divorce, loss of housing, and interruptions in education costs almost \$70 billion. The way going to prison translates into intergenerational patterns of incarceration adds a whopping \$400 billion in costs.

In fact, economists estimate that the total direct and indirect costs of our prison system reach \$1 trillion in lost and diverted revenue experienced by individuals, families, and governments. This kind of calculation makes reform of the justice system a fiscal priority. If the size and scope of the corrections system can be reined in, the economic benefits might be substantial.

Of course, crime itself imposes a very large fiscal burden on families, communities, and the government. So while we can create a more fiscally healthy society by reducing the size of our corrections system, it needs to be done in a way that does not increase the amount of crime, or the economic benefits will be washed away by those increases in crime.

Source: Michael McLaughlin, Carrie Pettus-Davis, Derek Brown, et al., *The Economic Burden of Incarceration in the U.S.* (St. Louis: Concordance Institute for Advancing Social Science, Washington University, 2016).

To this puzzle must be added the recent trend toward privatization of corrections. For a while, privatization seemed like the wave of the future. But with problems in private prison performance (see Chapter 10), combined with the desire to reduce imprisonment, the momentum for private prisons has waned. Only time will reveal the long-term impact of privatization; meanwhile, it is a potential threat to administrators' ability to manage the system. Most privatization plans call for skimming off the best of the worst—those convicted of nonserious crimes who can be efficiently processed. Thus, the government-run part of the corrections system faces the possibility of having to manage only the most costly, most intractable clients on a reduced budget.

FOUR CURRENT TRENDS IN THE U.S. CORRECTIONS SYSTEM

LO 3

Identify four substantial trends that face corrections and describe their importance.

The future is produced by the way the forces of the present play out over time. But foretelling the future is not so easy. It is possible to know the major forces buffeting the corrections system, but it is not so easy to know exactly how those forces will change it. In 1972, when most experts were talking about how the prison system had failed and how community corrections was the future for corrections, who would have thought that we were about to embark on almost four decades of growth in prison populations? In the early 1990s, looking back at a decade of rising crime, who would have thought that we were about to experience more than two decades of dropping crime rates?

So if we want to foresee the future of corrections, we must begin with two facts. The forces that will produce the future of corrections lie right in front of us. Yet we do not know, with certainty, how those forces will play out to produce the future.

With that caveat in mind, we here identify four forces that are at work today and will create the corrections of the future. We will describe the forces themselves because we are confident that they will prove to be very important. In our thinking about how these forces will affect corrections over the coming years, we will be more tentative.

Evidence-Based Practice

In recent years a premium has been placed on "evidence" about corrections that derives from studies of correctional policy. Of course, different kinds of studies produce different kinds of evidence. For example, if a person wants to know about prison culture, the best way is to spend time in a prison watching how people interact with one another and then documenting it. If a person wants to know what people think about a correctional policy problem, the best way to find out is an opinion survey. Typically, however, when a person thinks about evidence regarding corrections, the outcome is an answer to the question "What works?" We want to know which correctional programs have the greatest effect on reducing recidivism rates so that we can make them more widely available. The desire to increase the evidence base for correctional practice has grown to the point that it is now referred to in shorthand: EBP (evidence-based practice). The scientific method for determining "what works" is to conduct an evaluation, and the best kind of evaluation is called a "random field trial." Borrowed from the field of medicine, the **random field trial** creates an experiment in which some people are given the treatment and an identical group is not, so whatever the difference in how the two groups turn out—recidivism rates, for example— it is believed that the difference is caused by the treatment.

random field trial Evaluating the effectiveness of a program by randomly assigning some people to the program and others to no program, and seeing which group does better.

EBP has come to stand for a strategy of correctional development. In this strategy the professional field becomes increasingly cognizant of new studies of correctional effectiveness, and increasingly, over time, the field will be providing proven programs that reduce recidivism. It is an appealing image of an ever-smarter, ever-more-effective corrections system, learning continually from the results of its programs, jettisoning the failures and embracing the successes.

There is reason to think that EBP will fundamentally improve the effectiveness of correctional work. EBP is one of those rare ideas getting wide acceptance from many different correctional constituents: conservatives and liberals alike, old-timers and new-generation leaders, practitioners and academics who study corrections. As new studies come in, the hunger for an increasingly strong evidentiary base for correctional practice grows.

But there are also doubters. Critics point out that the transitory political problems with which correctional leaders grapple are often far more important influences on correctional programs than scientific studies, no matter how well done. By the same token, designing and carrying out random field trials are expensive, and most such experiments yield equivocal results. Ironically, EBP has an inherently conservative strategy because it does not easily avail itself of new ideas that, while unproven, may promise extraordinary benefits.

Techno-Corrections

Just as the role of technology is expanding in every aspect throughout the contemporary world, technology will grow in importance in the field of corrections.[1] Indeed, it is already happening. We can easily visualize the importance of technology for the corrections system of the future by a brief look at its impact over just the last few years.

A good example of this is provided by electronic monitoring (EM). When they first came on the market a quarter-century ago, EM devices seemed like some sort of space-age gimmick, alien to most correctional professionals. The promise of EM was simple: know the whereabouts of people under community supervision at times when they are not reporting to their community supervision officer. But many—perhaps most—community correctional leaders were dubious. Some thought the idea silly because simply knowing where a person was at any given time said almost nothing about what the person was doing there. If the idea is to change behavior, critics said, then how does a monitor contribute to that aim?

There were also significant technical problems. Some EM systems were beset with technical failures; some places had trouble implementing the managerial controls necessary to make the technology work. For example, what probation officer wants to get up in the middle of the night to check on a person on probation who is AWOL? The early studies were not very promising. EM systems seemed not to save money and not to reduce rates of failure.

techno-corrections
Achieving correctional goals through the use of new technologies.

But the appeal of technology is strong. This is the essence of **techno-corrections**. The idea that the community corrections agency can have a constant awareness of where its clients were at any given time was too attractive to die easily. Imaginative administrators experimented with targeted use of the EM device on high-risk clients or clients who might otherwise go to prison. A new generation of community correctional workers felt more comfortable with the emphasis placed on technology. And studies began to find that EM could enhance the effectiveness of corrections. Eventually, EM systems became more common, and judges have gotten used to them as an option in their sentencing decisions in most jurisdictions.

We are in the early stages of a similar story about tablets. In a handful of jurisdictions—both prisons and jails—administrators have experimented with providing tablets to people incarcerated there. The tablets have censured access to the internet, allowing reading texting and email communication. Some people think these experiments have been wildly successful, reducing internal conflicts, providing access to resources, and helping people prepare for release. Time will tell if this sort of technological access will become standard policy rather than just an experiment.

Perhaps this is the life story of many correctional technologies: appealing imagery, problematic initial implementation, revision and improvement, and then customary practice. If this scenario is true, then today's technologies will be tomorrow's basic strategies.

As we have demonstrated throughout the book, there are many new ideas about applying technology to corrections. Most of these have to do with ways of increasing the surveillance capacity of the corrections system: drug testing, eye-recognition systems, spatial monitoring systems, and computer-aided decision making. Institutions try to prevent possible disturbances with cameras placed in important locations. There is no question that the surveillance and control functions of corrections will be increasingly influenced by developments in technology.

But there have also been important technical developments in the human aspects of correction work. Risk assessment systems are nearly ubiquitous, and ways of improving them are constantly being tested. Mapping technologies have also made it easier to identify where services need to be located so that clients in reentry can access them more readily. Treatment regimens are being developed and standardized as strategies for supervision. As described in Chapter 8, *motivational interviewing*—proven ways of communicating with people and motivating them—is now being used widely with people who are on probation or parole. A future question will be whether the human technologies will stay strong in the face of the strong appeal of the control technologies.

Falling Crime Rates

After hitting its peak in 1991, the violent crime rate started to drop. Between that peak year and 2018, the violent crime rate fell by over 50 percent.[2] Crime continues to fall. There can be no question that this long-term reduction in violent crime has been one of the most important external dynamics affecting the corrections system. The pattern for nonviolent crime has been similar, with multiple decades of dropping rates. As the rate of serious crime dropped, the "get-tough" era also waned.[3]

The problem is that the way changes in crime rates affect the corrections system is not very straightforward. Earlier in this book, we made the point that today's crime rates are similar to crime rates in the 1970s but that the corrections system handles about five times more people now than it did then. During the decades that crime was dropping, most states' corrections systems grew anyway. It was not until 2010, in fact, that the first nationwide drop in the number of people in prison was recorded. Simply because the crime rate falls does not mean that the corrections system will shrink (see "The Size of the Prison Population").

Yet as concern about crime abates, the pressure on the corrections system is reduced. Some people see this as an enormous opportunity for innovation and improvement in correctional strategies. When crime was a pressing public issue, the corrections system seemed always to be playing catch-up, trying to deal with its clients under ever-changing rules; for instance, laws affecting repeat crimes, sex crimes, drunk driving, and others have been in almost constant flux for a quarter of a century. But with crime rates dropping, those pressures have declined, creating a window of opportunity for correctional reform on its own terms rather than in reaction to legislative initiatives.

But even small spikes upward in crime are cause for alarm. A jump in violent crime in 2014, for example, was worrisome for correctional reformers at the time, until it proved to be short-lived. Yet while crime rates remain the lowest they have been in more than a generation, if crime rates continue to increase, all bets are off.

LO 4

Explain what "good leadership" means in the context of the current corrections system of the United States, and list what it will take for leaders to more widely implement "what works" in corrections.

Professionalization

The number of correctional employees grew as the correctional population was growing. They have also developed as a far more professional employee pool than they ever were before.

The signs of this new professionalization are widespread. In the last 40 years a new national discipline of "criminal justice" has grown from a fledgling major with a weak reputation to a nationally respected field of study. New journals have been developed presenting the best research available on crime, justice, and corrections. Professional

FOCUS ON

CORRECTIONAL POLICY: The Size of the Prison Population

There is a great deal of policy interest these days in saving money on prisons. Because it is impossible to save much money on the running of a prison—costs of meals and recreation are a small portion of the overall cost of confinement— the desire to save prison dollars translates into a desire to close prisons. But how is that to be done?

There is, of course, the obvious point about scale. If the goal is to close a prison, then diverting a few people from prison cannot achieve it. Prisons house hundreds of people, and hundreds need to be diverted before a prison becomes empty. This is why a small initiative designed as an alternative to incarceration is not enough—especially if a lot of the people who are placed in the alternative option end up in prison anyway when they fail to abide by the program's rules. Experience shows that opening a few new programs almost never results in the ability to close a prison.

What is the answer? At one level, the answer is very simple. Recently, two criminologists coined the phrase "Iron Law of Prison Populations" to refer to a very simple idea: The size of a prison population is determined by (1) the number of people who are sent to prison and (2) how long they stay. The implication is clear: To reduce the size of a prison population enough to allow the closing of a prison, the flow into prison and the stay in prison must be changed.

From a policy perspective, the flow into prison comes from two routes. Judges sentence people to prison, and people on probation or parole are revoked and sent to prison. In states such as California, where about half of prison intake comes from probation and parole revocations, reducing the rate of community supervision failure—especially by reducing technical revocation—can have a substantial impact on the prison population. Other states, such as Florida, have low rates of technical revocation. For these states, any policy designed to reduce the flow into prison will have to address judicial sentences in the first place by increasing the use of probation for people convicted of felonies.

Length of stay is an entirely different issue. Nationally, prison length of stay has nearly tripled in the last 30 years. If prison sentences were to revert back to the level used in 1980, length of stay would be cut almost in half.

This analysis suggests that the solution to large prison populations is not more prison programs. It is sentencing reform. The policy problem is not only one of numbers; it also has an important political dimension. Policy makers need to find a way to stem the flow into prison and the unnecessarily long stays there, and they also need to find the political wherewithal to get the public to support them in this endeavor. No politician wants to be branded as "soft on crime." So how does a responsible public leader reduce the prison system and stay in office?

Sources: Todd R. Clear and James Austin, "Reducing Mass Incarceration: Implications of the Iron Law of Prison Populations," *Harvard Review of Law and Policy* 3 (no. 1, 2010): 308–24; James F. Austin, "Reducing America's Correctional Populations: A Strategic Plan," *Justice Research and Policy* 12 (no. 3, 2010).

associations such as the American Probation and Parole Association and the American Corrections Association now offer professional certification programs for people who will become probation or parole officers; the National Institute of Corrections also offers training.

The emergence of a profession has had two important consequences for corrections. The first consequence is that the field is "smarter," and performance meets a higher standard. With a large number of people who have advanced degrees in their areas of specialty, and with a host of employees who have special certification in areas such as substance abuse treatment and mental health, the standard of work for the field has improved. This augurs well for the future, as new methods and new knowledge provide a stronger foundation of training and abilities for those who do the work of the field.

But the creation of a strong professional core for the field has also added a new dynamic to it. Correctional employees are no longer content to merely follow the leadership of the administration of their agencies. With professional skills and knowledge of their own, the new correctional professional expects to have a say in the strategies undertaken by corrections systems and the programmatic priorities that correctional policy makers set. They have become a distinct voice in the milieu of correctional action, advocating policy and arguing for action in a way that reflects professional interests, not just narrow personnel matters. In many places, correctional staff have organized into unions, as well, and this has created its own pressure on the corrections systems for pay and other workplace considerations.

It is these various aspects of professionalization that will pose some of the more interesting dynamics as the field moves forward in the coming years. Will the profession be a force for new and exciting ideas, or will it resist change? Will the new correctional professional adapt to the new techno-corrections changes of the field, or will there be conflict? Whatever answers to these questions the future holds, it is clear that the advance of professionalism in corrections has been one of the most important forces in the field today.

THREE CHALLENGES FOR THE FUTURE OF CORRECTIONS

LO 5

Describe the aspirations for the U.S. corrections system and how those aspirations might be achieved.

After nearly 40 years of correctional growth, there are still many questions to be answered. If this had been a deliberate experiment, we would have a much clearer picture by now. The crime rate today is about what it was in 1973, the year that prison populations first began to grow.

Indeed, during most of those years we saw crime rates that were much higher than those of today. Some claim that the crime rates would have been even higher had we not expanded the corrections system. However, to have the same crime rates but *seven times* the number of people under correctional supervision suggests that correctional expansion has not been an efficient crime-prevention method, to say the least.

Further, state correctional budgets have more than doubled in the past decade. At the same time, public investments in education, transportation, and the like have declined in many places. Some argue that the fiscal consequences of a bigger corrections system have taken a toll that should be considered in evaluating this trend.

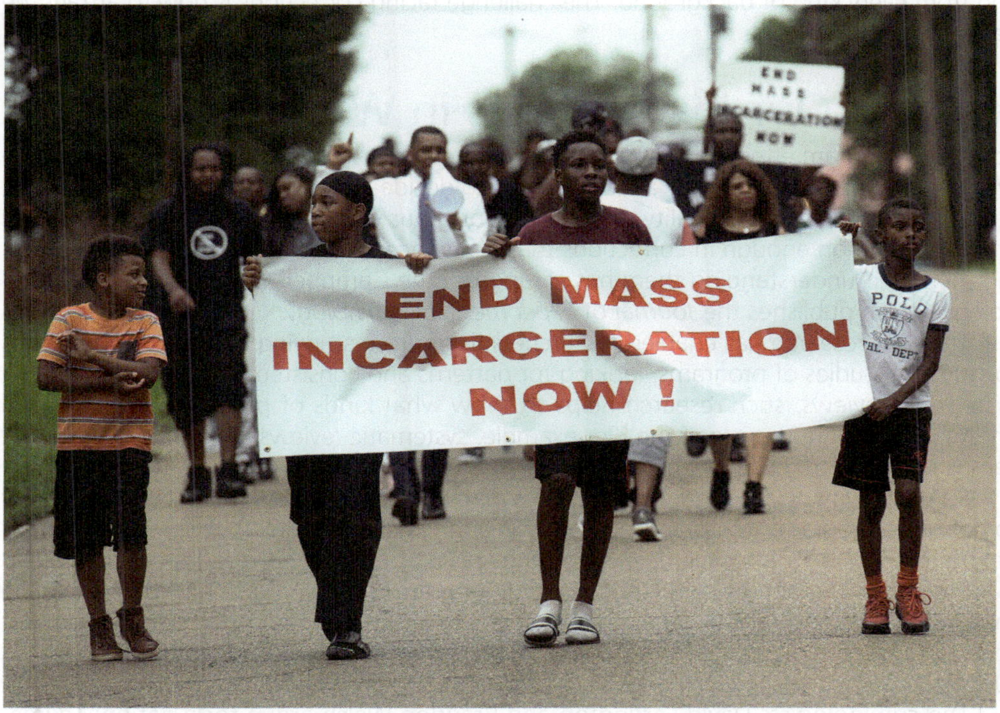

© Barbara Gauntt/Clarion Ledger

After almost 40 years of correctional growth in the US, sentiment has changed and many people think the time has come to reduce the size of the prison system.

If we could go back to the early 1970s and begin again to build a corrections system with an eye toward the year 2018, would we aim for the costly, cumbersome behemoth we have today? Most people would say no.

But what are we to do? Of course, we cannot re-create history. However, we can examine today's corrections system in light of what we want it to become. Here are three challenges for re-creating corrections with an eye to the future.

Reinvigorate a New Correctional Leadership

The field of corrections will get nowhere without effective leadership. It is from its leaders that corrections will receive the vision for a new future; it is from its leaders that corrections will find the capacity to embark on the difficult road of change.

Great leaders are not so easy to come by. Many studies of leadership suggest an important idea about "fit"—how the skills of a leader need to "fit" the problems being confronted. In other words, different situations call for different kinds of leaders because the skills needed for solving one kind of problem are not the same as those needed for a different kind. For example, historians tell us that Winston Churchill's tenacity and tirelessness were perfect for England during wartime, but his lack of interest in give-and-take did not work well after peace was restored. When a leader's skills fit the situation, effective leadership follows.

What are the characteristics of the situation that corrections now faces? The key consideration that the new generation of correctional leaders will face is how to redirect an enormous enterprise in need of a new vision. Numerous pressures—political, economic, and social—have created the corrections system in its current form. Leaders will have to balance these pressures effectively while promoting a new correctional agenda.

At the same time, correctional leadership will never be *solely* about a vision for the future. The problem of leadership is subtle. Good leaders have strong vision for their work, but they also have an on-the-ground ability to motivate people working in the system to do their best. While education and experience are known to be important qualities in effective leadership, history also tells us that good leaders come from all walks of life and from every kind of background. The challenge facing corrections is how to attract the best leaders to the field.

Refocus Our Investments in What Works

Studies of program effectiveness have grown dramatically in recent years. Where once we would have been lucky to have a study or two to decide a course of action, we now have literally hundreds of high-quality studies to inform our work in corrections. Such studies are now common enough in corrections that a new academic society devoted to promoting them and understanding them has sprung up: the Campbell Collaboration on Criminology, which publishes the *Journal of Experimental Criminology*.

The new research has enabled researchers to go from studying correctional programs to studying studies of programs, looking for patterns and consistencies in findings. Called *systematic reviews,* such research helps to show what kinds of programs are powerful and what kinds are not promising. For example, systematic reviews have shown that boot camps do not work but that therapeutic communities often do.

So while we know a great deal about "what works," we know much less about how to get good programs into practice (see "Thinking Outside the Box"). Programs that have been proven to be ineffective have surprising staying power, while programs with a solid track record are sometimes difficult to mount. Programs that work often involve providing the kind of support that the general public tends to reject. Programs that fail often present appealing goals, such as "scaring kids straight," and therefore engender unwarranted support.

The criminologists David Farrington and Brandon Welsh argue for a national crime-fighting strategy that focuses not just on people who have been convicted of crimes, but also on children. They say we need the following:

THINKING OUTSIDE THE BOX

SUCCESS FUNDING

One of the most troubling aspects of the growth of the penal system has been its costs. The growth of the corrections system has cost multiple billions of dollars, diverting to the corrections system precious resources that are needed for other public priorities such as health care, education, and infrastructure. One of the ironies is that the funding practices of the justice system often reward growth. Sheriffs are reimbursed for the size of the jail population; private facilities get a per diem for every person they house. Judges can send a person to state prison for technical failures on probation, thereby making the state pay for the incarceration while reducing the workload of local probation officers. Police get grants that are evaluated on the basis of the number of arrests they make rather than the crime rate; they also get to keep some of the proceeds of civil forfeitures. Prosecutors get evaluated on the basis of the length of sentences they win in their cases.

Recently, the Brennan Center for Justice began a project that argued for "success" funding. One example is social impact bonds that link profits to lower recidivism rates. Another possibility could be police performance indicators that link to crime rates rather than arrest rates. Federal grant money could be tied to evidence-based strategies that have a cost-effectiveness criterion. Prosecutors could be evaluated, not by convictions or sentences, but by program completion rates and recidivism rates. Drug initiatives could be evaluated on drug use rates, not cases processed. The idea is to identify (a) what works and (b) what shrinks the system, and then organize the funding to reward accomplishments on those measures.

Source: Inimai Chettiar, Lauren Brooke-Eisen, and Nicole Fortier (with Timothy Ross), *Reforming Funding to Reduce Mass Incarceration* (New York: Brennan Center for Justice, 2013).

- *Early prevention measures* implemented in the early years of a child's life from (or sometimes prior to) birth through early adolescence, with a focus on reaching children and youths before they engage in delinquency in the first place.
- *Risk-focused, evidence-based programs* that identify the key risk factors for offending and implement prevention methods designed to counteract them, methods that systematic research has proven to be successful.
- *A National Council on Early Prevention*, modeled after successful nationwide approaches used in Europe, that seeks to support the early crime-prevention strategy.
- *Local-level prevention* that collaborates with other government departments, develops local problem-solving partnerships, and involves citizens.
- *Communities That Care,* a strategy of comprehensive, locally driven approaches that use promising individual, family, school, and community programs.[4]

There is no dearth of crime-prevention or crime-control strategies that work. A decade ago, 30 leading criminologists wrote short essays in *Criminology & Public Policy* describing policies that deserved widespread adoption because of the extent of research supporting them.[5] Most of their suggestions were not "new" ideas but well-documented ones, ranging from the elimination of past felony screening for employment to earned release from parole supervision. The fact that 30 such essays could be written testifies to our ample knowledge base for effective crime policy. The fact that they *needed* to be written is testimony to how far our policies now stray from what we already know makes sense. The challenge that we face is bringing our practice more into line with our knowledge. This is not just a challenge of knowledge. It is also a challenge of leadership.

Reclaim the Moral and Ethical High Road

There is something disturbing about the new American punitiveness. All of us would agree that people who break the law should be punished, so the mere fact of punishment is not disturbing. Plainly, however, the U.S. corrections system is far more punitive today

FOR CRITICAL THINKING

The United States hands out some of the longest sentences in the free world. The median (rough average) time served in the United States is about three years, but those who serve more than the average time are often behind bars for a decade or longer. Michael G. Santos provided the example that opened this chapter, but there are many more. Often, long sentences are for violent crimes, and the longest sentences are typically reserved for people who have repeated their criminality.

1. Do sentences like this make sense? What is their main objective—to protect society or to punish serious crime? In either case, do they work?
2. If you think that they work, what about all of the collateral consequences that go with a large prison system? If you think that they do not work, what should be done instead?

than it has been for a long time, maybe ever. Comparing the 1970s with today, people who are convicted of crimes are more than twice as likely to go to prison, and those who go to prison serve sentences that are at least twice as long as before (see "For Critical Thinking"). Further, people on probation or parole face a larger set of requirements, which means they are more likely to fail and be sent to prison. But even *that* is not the heart of the matter because people can reasonably disagree about whether U.S. prison sentences are too likely or too long, or whether supervision methods are too stringent.

What is disturbing about the U.S. corrections system is the way it has been so much harsher than the other systems of free societies. Here are some of the practices that have been used in the U.S. corrections system at some point in the last decade:

- Chain gangs cleaning roads and wearing black-striped shirts
- Men in jail made to wear pink underwear
- Signs in yards and on cars saying the owner has been convicted of a crime
- Children serving time in adult prisons
- Eviction of people from their homes because of convictions for drug crimes
- Refusals of college loans because of convictions for drug crimes
- Life sentences for stealing candy or pizza as repeat criminality

Other worrisome practices plague the U.S. corrections system. Health care in some prison systems is appallingly bad, especially for the mentally ill. In California, for example, the shockingly deficient health care was so bad that the federal courts acknowledged that the entire prison system was unconstitutional.[6] Many correctional programs emphasize being tough and providing close surveillance as more important than providing support and promoting positive change. A nationwide spate of laws demonize people designated as "sex offenders" irrationally and contribute to fear and retributive actions that are counterproductive in terms of correctional aims and democratic values. The growth of surveillance alone is cause for concern.

The social costs of the growth of the penal system have been borne most substantially by minority communities that already struggle with poverty and other forms of disadvantage. Among them are broken families, deteriorated health, teenage pregnancies, weakened labor markets, juvenile delinquency, and even more crime. As a nation committed to basic ideas of social justice, these consequences of a burgeoning corrections system must concern us (see Chapters 19 and 22).

The corrections system we have built does not highlight what is best about our American heritage: optimism, entrepreneurial spirit, and a belief in the possibilities that arise when people are allowed to pursue their dreams. There are good reasons why so many of the Western democracies around the world look elsewhere for new horizons in correctional practice.

The next generation of correctional leaders can aim the sights of the American corrections system toward higher aspirations. Part of this can be accomplished by molding a smarter corrections system, emphasizing the kinds of strategies that good studies tell us will bear fruit and turning away from approaches that do not. But part of this will just as surely be about basic values. The challenge facing us all is how to articulate those values in a compelling way—how to clarify what corrections is all about in language and imagery that make us, once again, a beacon of freedom and justice for the world to see.

MYTHS in Corrections

Can Corrections Change?

THE MYTH: The corrections system is too buffeted by political and social forces to be able to change.

THE REALITY: The corrections system changes when people with new vision devote themselves to improving it.

Sources: Three hundred years of history and the present realities described in this book.

CHANGING CORRECTIONS: A FINAL VIEW

Throughout this book we have portrayed corrections as a system buffeted by its environment, changing yet unchanging. External pressures arise to move correctional leadership in one direction, only to be replaced by counterpressures. One state abolishes parole release; another reinstates early-release mechanisms. One prison reduces its treatment programs; another adds professional counseling staff. The image is one of an unplanned, reactive management style rather than a planned, proactive attempt to lead corrections down a path of gradual improvement (see "Myths in Corrections").

Although this image is largely accurate, it is also changing, partly because corrections continues to develop. Several forces contribute to this change—predominantly, professional associations and government agencies.

Perhaps the greatest influence is exercised by the National Institute of Corrections (NIC), a division of the Federal Bureau of Prisons in the Department of Justice. The NIC has served as (1) a national clearinghouse of information about correctional practices, (2) a source of technical assistance to local and state correctional agencies that wish to upgrade their practices, and (3) a training operation, both basic and advanced, open to any correctional employee. The NIC has become to corrections what the FBI is to law enforcement: a strong force for professional standards, policy and procedural improvement, and general development of the field.

Similarly, the American Correctional Association (ACA) has become an active lobbyist for the field. A quarter-century ago, it promulgated a set of national standards for correctional practices in jails, prisons, and field services. Correctional agencies that meet these standards may be accredited, much as universities are accredited by outside agencies. Although the ACA has faced its share of criticism, its work indicates the kind of ground-level upgrading going on in corrections today.

The American Probation and Parole Association (APPA) serves a function similar to that of the ACA but is focused on field services. It has only recently begun a highly visible national campaign to organize the profession and to develop an improved professional consciousness of the importance of field services in probation and parole.

As important as these forces for change are, a new force for steady correctional growth and development is likely to outstrip them all. That force is represented by the person who is reading this book: you, the student of corrections. For most of its history, the field has been the domain of amateurs—part-time reformers who were moved by zeal to help people in prison and local workers who took the jobs because nothing else was available. In recent years, corrections has become a field of study for people interested in long-term professional careers, perhaps *people like you*. This is a dramatic change because it represents a group of potential correctional employees who can sustain the field's growth and development. This, more than any other influence, may be a stabilizing force for corrections in the years to come.

SUMMARY

1 Analyze how the philosophy of the U.S. corrections system has changed over the years and what effects such changes have had.

There was a time when the U.S. corrections system was the most progressive in the world. For most of the nineteenth and twentieth centuries, the U.S. corrections system was at the forefront of thinking about the best ways to deal with people who break the law, and U.S. methods were widely celebrated and emulated. Instead, what now sets the U.S. corrections system apart from those elsewhere in the world is that it is so *big*. Since the mid-1970s, by every measure the American corrections system has grown by unprecedented amounts. Including probation, parole, and jails, the number of people under correctional control has also hugely increased in that same time, from under a million to more than seven million. It is hard to believe that over the past 40 years we have deliberately created the corrections system that we really want. To the contrary, most of those in charge of today's corrections system would argue that what we are doing is self-destructive and that an overhaul of the corrections system is long overdue.

2 Explain the major dilemmas facing the corrections system and how they might be resolved.

Corrections faces five core dilemmas: (1) Mission: corrections lacks a clear mission, and it operates in an environment of competing expectations that cannot be ignored. Correctional leaders must articulate their philosophy of corrections and establish a clearer policy to guide its implementation. (2) Methods: when goals are in conflict, staff members have difficulty choosing among competing methods to perform their work: surveillance or service, custody or treatment. We must overcome the tradition of faddism in corrections and embrace the methods that improve the life chances of correctional clients. (3) Structure: correctional leaders' colleagues are often the ones who put the most immediate obstacles in their way, and the corrections system depends on significant factors outside of its control. Through the formation of "partnerships," the impact of structural problems can be reduced. (4) Personnel: two essential goals are attracting the right kinds of people to work in corrections and motivating them to remain once they are employed. A sound staff is built by innovative methods of selection and promotion; professional growth on the job is encouraged by incentives for education and training. (5) Costs: corrections is expensive. The public desire to punish criminally involved people is not backed up by a willingness to pay for the punishment. Making the costs of correctional policies clear is an essential step in making such policies effective.

3 Identify four substantial trends that face corrections and describe their importance.

Four important forces now shaping corrections are (1) evidence-based practice, which seeks to base correctional programs on solid evidence about "what works"; (2) techno-corrections, which alters the strategies of the corrections system by using new technologies such as electronic monitoring; (3) falling crime rates, which open the door for a reduction in the number of people processed by the corrections system; and (4) professionalization, which has resulted in an improvement in the skill set of those who work in the field.

4 Explain what "good leadership" means in the context of the current corrections system of the United States, and list what it will take for leaders to more widely implement "what works" in corrections.

There have been many studies of leadership, and they suggest an important idea about "fit"—how the skills of a leader need to be the right ones for the problems being confronted. Good leaders have strong vision for their work, but they also have an on-the-ground ability to motivate people working in the system to do their best. While education and experience are known to be important qualities in effective leadership, we also know from history that good leaders come from all walks of life and from every kind of background. The challenge facing corrections is how to attract the best leaders to the field.

5 Describe the aspirations for the U.S. corrections system and how those aspirations might be achieved. There are three challenges for re-creating corrections:
(1) Reinvigorate a new correctional leadership. It is from its leaders that corrections will get the vision for a new future; it is from its leaders that corrections will find the capacity to embark on the difficult road of change. The skills of a leader need to be the right ones for the problems being confronted. Further, good leaders have a strong vision and the ability to motivate people in the system to do their best. The challenge facing corrections is how to attract the best leaders to the field. (2) Refocus our investments in what works. Studies of program effectiveness have grown dramatically in recent years. While we know a great deal about "what works," we know much less about how to get effective programs into practice. Some argue for a national crime-fighting strategy that focuses not just on people who have been convicted of crimes, but also on children. Whatever strategies we employ, we need to focus on bringing our practice more into line with our knowledge. (3) Reclaim the moral and ethical high road. The corrections system we have built does not highlight what is best about our American heritage: optimism, entrepreneurial spirit, and a belief in the possibilities that arise when people are allowed to pursue their dreams. The challenge facing us all is how to articulate those values in a compelling way—how to clarify what corrections is all about in language and imagery that make us, once again, a beacon of freedom and justice for the world to see.

KEY TERMS

random field trial (*p. 599*) **techno-corrections** (*p. 600*)

FOR DISCUSSION

1. Why has the corrections system in the United States grown so much? What are the pros and cons of this growth?
2. What are the most important goals for correctional leadership? Is having a powerful vision for the system more important than managerial ability? Why or why not?
3. What are the alternative philosophies to the punitive philosophy currently in vogue in the U.S. corrections system? Are these alternatives feasible? Preferable?
4. Do you see yourself in a correctional career? What might you do to improve the corrections system?

FOR FURTHER READING

Clear, Todd R., and Natasha Frost. *The Punishment Imperative: The Rise and Failure of the Great Punishment Experiment*. New York: NYU Press, 2013. An assessment of the reasons for the get-tough movement and its failures.

Dolovich, Susan, and Alexandra Natapoff. *The New Criminal Justice Thinking*. New York: NYU Press, 2017. A critical assessment of the national opportunity for criminal justice reform in America.

Pfaff, John. *Locked In: The True Causes of Mass Incarceration— and How to Achieve Real Reform*. New York: Basic Books, 2017. An empirical analysis of the causes of the growth of the prison system and how to overcome them.

Simon, Jonathon. *Governing Through Crime*. New York: Oxford University Press, 2007. An examination of the politics of correctional reform.

Smart on Crime Coalition. *Smart on Crime: Recommendations for Congress*. Washington, DC: Author, 2010. A series of recommendations based on democratic principles and social science evidence dealing with all aspects of the criminal justice system, including corrections.

Stuntz, William J. *The Collapse of American Criminal Justice*. Boston: Belknap Press of Harvard University Press, 2012. A far-reaching critique of the current status of American criminal justice and a call for reform.

Whitman, James Q. *Harsh Justice: Criminal Punishment and the Widening Divide Between America and Europe*. New York: Oxford University Press, 2003. Compares the history of the development of penology in the United States with that of Europe.

NOTES

1 Tony Fabelo, "*Technocorrections*": *The Promises, the Uncertain Threats* (National Institute of Justice Research in Brief, 2000).

2 Statista Research Department, Reported *Violent Crime Rate in the U.S. 1990–2019*, https://www.statista.com /statistics/191219/reported-violent-crime-rate-in-the-usa-since-1990/, 2020.

3 Pew Center on the States, *Key Findings from a National Survey of 1,200 Registered Voters Conducted March 7–14, 2010*, www.pewtrusts.org/~/media/assets/2010/webinarnationalresearch publicattitudescrimepunishment2010.pdf?la=en, 2010.

4 David P. Farrington and Brandon C. Welsh, *Saving Children from a Life of Crime: Early Risk Factors and Effective Interventions* (New York: Oxford University Press, 2007).

5 *Criminology & Public Policy* 6 (no. 4, 2007).

6 *Coleman et al. v. Schwarzenegger*, U.S. District Court for California, No. C01-1351, February 10, 2009.

GLOSSARY

absconders People who fail to appear for a court date for no legitimate reason.

administrative control theory A governance theory which posits that prison disorder results from unstable, divided, or otherwise weak management.

aftercare Services provided to juveniles after they have been removed from their home and put under some form of custodial care.

alcohol abuse The disruption of normal living patterns caused by high levels of alcohol use, frequently leading to violations of the law while under the influence of alcohol or in attempting to secure it. Chronic alcohol abusers are generally referred to as alcoholics.

Antabuse A drug that when combined with alcohol causes violent nausea; it is used to control a person's drinking.

asylee A person allowed to reside in the United States after leaving a troubled and/or dangerous country.

at-risk youths Young people who demonstrate characteristics of being more likely than others at their age to end up as juvenile delinquents in their teen years.

authority The ability to influence a person's actions in a desired direction without resorting to force.

bail An amount of money, specified by a judge, to be posted as a condition for pretrial release to ensure appearance of the accused individual at trial.

behavior therapy Treatment that induces new behaviors through reinforcements (rewards and punishments), role modeling, and other active forms of teaching.

benefit of clergy The right to be tried in an ecclesiastical court, where punishments were less severe than those meted out by civil courts, given the religious focus on penance and salvation.

boot camp A physically rigorous, disciplined, and demanding regimen emphasizing conditioning, education, and job training, designed primarily for the young.

boundary violations Behavior that blurs, minimizes, or disrupts the social distance between prison staff and imprisoned people, resulting in violations of departmental policy.

campus style An architectural design by which the functional units of a prison are individually housed in a complex of buildings surrounded by a fence.

career criminal A person who sees crime as a way of earning a living, who has numerous contacts with the criminal justice system over time, and who may view the criminal sanction as a normal part of life.

case law Legal rules produced by judges' decisions.

chain of command A series of organizational positions in order of authority, with each person receiving orders from the one immediately above and issuing orders to the one(s) immediately below.

civil disabilities Legal restrictions that prevent many former prison residents from voting and holding elective office, engaging in certain professions and occupations, and associating with others who are under correctional authority.

civil liability Responsibility for the provision of monetary or other compensation awarded to a plaintiff in a civil action.

classical criminology A school of criminology that views behavior as stemming from free will, that demands responsibility and accountability of all perpetrators, and that stresses the need for punishments severe enough to deter others.

classification A process by which people in prison are assigned to different types of custody and treatment.

classification systems Specific sets of objective criteria, such as offense histories, previous experiences in the justice system, problems in life circumstances, and substance abuse patterns, applied to all clients to determine the best correctional programs.

clear and present danger Any threat to security or to the safety of individuals that is so obvious and compelling that the need to counter it overrides the guarantees of the First Amendment.

client-specific planning Process by which private investigative firms contract with the person who was convicted to conduct comprehensive background checks and suggest to judges creative sentencing options as alternatives to incarceration.

coercive power The ability to obtain compliance by the application or threat of physical force.

cognitive skill building A form of behavior therapy that focuses on changing the thinking and reasoning patterns that accompany criminal behavior.

collective efficacy Mutual trust among neighbors, combined with willingness to intervene on behalf of the common good, especially to supervise children and maintain public order.

community correctional center A small-group living facility, especially for those who have been recently released from prison.

community corrections A model of corrections based on the assumption that reintegrating the convicted individual into the community should be the goal of the criminal justice system.

community justice A model of justice that emphasizes reparation to the victim and the community, approaching crime from a problem-solving perspective, and citizen involvement in crime prevention.

community model for jails An innovative model for jail administration that promotes a sense of community across the board, while using community to promote rehabilitation.

community service Compensation for injury to society by the performance of service in the community.

compelling state interest An interest of the state that must take precedence over rights guaranteed by the First Amendment.

compliance Obedience to an order or request.

conditions of release Restrictions on conduct that people on parole must obey as a legally binding requirement of being released.

confrontation therapy A treatment technique, usually done in a group, that vividly brings people face-to-face with their crime's consequences for the victim and society.

congregate system A penitentiary system developed in Auburn, New York, in which prison inhabitants were held in isolation at night but worked with others during the day under a rule of silence.

constitution Fundamental law contained in a state or federal document that provides a design of government and lists basic rights for individuals.

construction strategy The strategy of building new facilities to meet the demand for prison space.

continuum of sanctions A graded range of correctional management strategies based on the degree of intrusiveness and control, along which a client is moved based on his or her response to those correctional programs.

contract labor system A system under which the labor of convicted individuals was sold on a contractual basis to private employers that provided the machinery and raw materials with which prison residents made salable products in the institution.

corporal punishment Punishment inflicted on the convicted person's body with whips or other devices that cause pain.

corrections The variety of programs, services, facilities, and organizations responsible for the management of individuals who have been accused or convicted of criminal offenses.

cost–benefit ratio A summary measure of the value of a correctional program in saving money through preventing new crime.

courtyard style An architectural design by which the functional units of a prison are housed in separate buildings constructed on four sides of an open square.

crime control model of corrections A model of corrections based on the assumption that criminal behavior can be controlled by more use of incarceration and other forms of strict supervision.

criminogenic needs Needs that when successfully addressed by treatment programs result in lower rates of recidivism.

custodial model A model of correctional institutions that emphasizes security, discipline, and order.

day fine A criminal penalty based on the amount of income a person earns in a day's work.

day reporting center A facility where people under pretrial release or with probation violations can attend daylong intervention and treatment sessions.

Deferred Action for Childhood Arrivals (DACA) A law that allows certain undocumented immigrants who entered the country as minors to receive a renewable two-year period of deferred action from deportation.

Deferred Action for Parents of Americans and Lawful Permanent Residents (DAPA) A law that allows certain parents of Americans or lawful permanent residents (green card holders) to obtain permission to work and to stay in the United States for three years.

deinstitutionalization The release of a mental patient from a mental hospital and his or her return to the community.

delinquent A child who has committed an act that if committed by an adult would be criminal.

dependent A child who has no parent or guardian or whose parents are unable to give proper care.

determinate sentence A fixed period of incarceration imposed by a court; it is associated with the concept of retribution or deserved punishment.

developmental disability The inability to learn or develop skills at the same rate as most other people because of a problem with the brain.

direct supervision A method of correctional supervision in which staff members have direct, continual physical interaction with people confined in the jail.

discretionary release The release of an individual from prison to conditional supervision at the discretion of the parole board within the boundaries set by the sentence and the penal law.

discrimination Differential treatment of an individual or group without reference to its behavior or qualifications.

disparity The unequal treatment of one group by the criminal justice system, compared with the treatment accorded other groups.

drug abuse The disruption of normal living patterns by the use of illegal chemical substances to the extent that social problems develop, often leading to criminal behavior.

drug court A special court for people convicted of drug-abuse-related crimes.

electronic monitoring Community supervision technique, ordinarily combined with home confinement, that uses electronic devices to maintain surveillance.

equal protection The constitutional guarantee that the law will be applied equally to all people, without regard for such individual characteristics as gender, race, and religion.

the Enlightenment, or the Age of Reason A cultural movement in England and France during the 1700s, when concepts of liberalism, rationality, equality, and individualism dominated social and political thinking.

ethnicity A concept used to distinguish people according to their cultural characteristics—language, religion, and group traditions.

evidence-based practice Using correctional methods that have been shown to be effective by well-designed research studies.

exchange A mutual transfer of resources based on decisions regarding the costs and benefits of alternative actions.

expiration release The release of an incarcerated individual into the community without any further correctional supervision; the individual cannot be returned to prison for any remaining portion of the sentence for the current offense.

expungement A legal process that results in the removal of a conviction from official records.

federalism A system of government in which power and responsibilities are divided between a national government and state governments.

fee system A system by which jail operations are funded by a set amount paid each day per person held.

felon disenfranchisement A term used to describe laws that either temporarily or permanently restrict the voting rights of individuals convicted of felony offenses.

Fentanyl A powerful, synthetic opioid.

forfeiture Government seizure of property and other assets derived from or used in criminal activity.

formal organization A structure established for influencing behavior to achieve particular ends.

galley slavery Forced rowing of large ships or galleys.

general deterrence Punishment that is intended to be an example to the general public and to discourage the commission of offenses by others.

good time A reduction of a person's prison sentence, at the discretion of the prison administrator, for good behavior or for participation in vocational, educational, and treatment programs.

green card A permit allowing a foreign national to live and work permanently in the United States.

habeas corpus A writ (judicial order) asking a person holding another person to produce this person and to give reasons to justify continued confinement.

hands-off policy A judicial policy of noninterference concerning the internal administration of prisons.

hepatitis C A sometimes fatal disease of the liver that reduces the effectiveness of the body's system of removing toxins.

home confinement Sentence whereby people serve a term of incarceration in their own home.

house of correction Detention facility that combined the major elements of a workhouse, poorhouse, and penal industry by both disciplining individuals who were housed in the facility and setting them to work.

hulks Abandoned ships that the English converted to hold convicted people during a period of prison crowding between 1776 and 1790.

Immigration and Nationality Act of 1965 Act that abolished an earlier quota system based on national origin and established a new immigration policy based on reuniting immigrant families and attracting skilled labor to the United States.

incapacitation Depriving a person of the ability to commit crimes against society, usually by detaining the person in prison.

indeterminate sentence A period of incarceration with minimum and maximum terms stipulated so that parole eligibility depends on the time necessary for treatment; it is closely associated with the rehabilitation concept.

inmate balance theory A governance theory which posits that for a prison system to operate effectively, officials must tolerate minor infractions, relax security measures, and allow informal leaders to keep order.

inmate code A set of rules of conduct that reflects the values and norms of the prison social system and helps define for inmates the image of the model prisoner.

intensive supervision probation (ISP) Probation granted with conditions of strict reporting to a probation officer who has a limited caseload.

intermediate sanctions A variety of punishments that are more restrictive than traditional probation but less severe and costly than incarceration.

jail A facility authorized to hold pretrial detainees and sentenced misdemeanants for periods longer than 48 hours. Most jails are administered by county governments; sometimes they are part of the state government.

judicial reprieve A practice under English common law whereby a judge could suspend the imposition or execution of a sentence on condition of good behavior.

justice reinvestment A strategy to redirect funds currently spent on prisons to community public safety projects.

lease system A system under which people who were convicted of crimes were leased to contractors who provided these individuals with food and clothing in exchange for their labor. In southern states they worked in mines, lumber camps, and factories, and on farms as field laborers.

least restrictive methods Means of ensuring a legitimate state interest (such as security) that impose fewer limits to prisoners' rights than do alternative means of securing that end.

lex talionis Law of retaliation—the principle that punishment should correspond in degree and kind to the offense ("an eye for an eye and a tooth for a tooth").

line personnel Employees who are directly concerned with furthering the institution's goals and who are in direct contact with clients.

lockup A facility authorized to hold people before court appearances for up to 48 hours. Most lockups (also called drunk tanks or holding tanks) are administered by local police agencies.

long-termer A person who serves a lengthy period in prison, such as 10 years or more, before his or her first release.

mandatory release The required release of an individual from incarceration to community supervision on the expiration of a certain period, as stipulated by a determinate-sentencing law or parole guidelines.

mandatory sentence A sentence stipulating that some minimum period of incarceration must be served by people convicted of selected crimes, regardless of background or circumstances.

mark system A system in which prison residents are assessed a certain number of marks, based on the severity of their crime, at the time of sentencing. Individuals could reduce their term and gain release by reducing marks through labor, good behavior, and educational achievement.

maximum-security prison A prison designed and organized to minimize the possibility of escapes and violence; to that end, it imposes strict limitations on the freedom of residents and visitors.

mediation Intervention in a dispute by a third party to whom the parties in conflict submit their differences for resolution and whose decision (in the correctional setting) is binding on both parties.

medical model A model of corrections based on the assumption that criminal behavior is caused by social, psychological, or biological deficiencies that require treatment.

medium-security prison A prison designed and organized to prevent escapes and violence, but in which restrictions on residents and visitors are less rigid than in maximum-security facilities.

mental illness A health condition involving changes in thinking, emotion, and/or behavior that can cause problems in social, work, or family activities.

methadone A drug that reduces the craving for heroin; it is used to spare addicts from painful withdrawal symptoms.

Methamphetamine Highly addictive stimulant that is made from amphetamine.

minimum-security prison A prison designed and organized to permit residents and visitors as much freedom as is consistent with the concept of incarceration.

motivational interviewing A method for increasing the effectiveness of correctional treatment by having the probation officer interact with the client in ways that promote the client's stake in the change process.

neglected A child who is not receiving proper care because of some action or inaction of his or her parents.

new-generation jail A facility with a podular architectural design and management policies that emphasize interactions with staff and provision of services.

normative power The ability to obtain compliance by manipulating symbolic rewards.

null strategy The strategy of doing nothing to relieve crowding in prisons, under the assumption that the problem is temporary and will disappear in time.

ombudsman A public official who investigates complaints against government officials and recommends corrective measures.

Opioid Any of a range of prescription pain killers.

other conditional release A probationary sentence used in some states to get around the rigidity of mandatory release by placing convicted individuals in various community settings under supervision.

pardon An action of the executive branch of the state or federal government excusing an offense and absolving a person of the consequences of his or her crime.

parens patriae The "parent of the nation"—the role of the state as guardian and protector of all people (particularly juveniles) who are unable to protect themselves.

parole The conditional release of an individual from incarceration, under supervision, after part of the prison sentence has been served.

penitentiary An institution intended to isolate individuals convicted of a crime from society and from one another so that they could reflect on their past misdeeds, repent, and thus undergo reformation.

performance-based supervision An approach to probation that establishes goals for supervision and evaluates the effectiveness of meeting those goals.

piece price system A labor system under which a contractor provided raw materials and agreed to a set price to purchase goods made by people in prison.

podular unit Self-contained living areas designed to hold 12–25 people, composed of individual cells for privacy and open areas for social interaction. New-generation jails are made up of two or more pods.

positivist school An approach to criminology and other social sciences based on the assumptions that human behavior is a product of biological, economic, psychological, and social factors and that the scientific method can be applied to ascertain the causes of individual behavior.

power The ability to force a person to do something he or she does not want to do.

precedent Legal rules created in judges' decisions that serve to guide the decisions of other judges in subsequent similar cases.

presentence investigation (PSI) An investigation and summary report of a convicted person's background that helps the judge decide on an appropriate sentence. Also known as a presentence report.

presentence report Report prepared by a probation officer, who investigates a convicted person's background to help the judge select an appropriate sentence.

presumptive parole date The presumed release date stipulated by parole guidelines if an individual serves time without disciplinary or other incidents.

presumptive sentence A sentence for which the legislature or a commission sets a minimum and maximum range of months or years. Judges are to fix the length of the sentence within that range, allowing for special circumstances.

pretrial diversion An alternative to adjudication in which the accused person agrees to conditions set by the prosecutor (for example, counseling or rehabilitation) in exchange for withdrawal of charges.

preventive detention Detention of an accused person in jail to protect the community from crimes that he or she is considered likely to commit if set free pending trial.

principle of interchangeability The idea that different forms of intermediate sanctions can be calibrated to make them equivalent as punishments despite their differences in approach.

principle of least eligibility The doctrine that people in prison ought to receive no goods or services in excess of those available to people who have lived within the law.

prison An institution for the incarceration of people convicted of crimes, usually felonies.

prison program Any formal, structured activity that takes people out of their cells and sets them to instrumental tasks.

prisonization The process by which an incarcerated person absorbs the customs of prison society and learns to adapt to the environment.

probation A sentence allowing the convicted individual to serve the sanctions imposed by the court while he or she lives in the community under supervision.

probation center Residential facility where persistent probation violators are sent for short periods of time.

probation release The release of someone from incarceration to probation supervision, as required by the sentencing judge.

procedural due process The constitutional guarantee that no agent or instrumentality of government will use any procedures other than those procedures prescribed by law to arrest, prosecute, try, or punish any person.

psychotherapy In generic terms, all forms of "treatment of the mind"; in the prison setting, this treatment is coercive in nature.

psychotropic medications Drug treatments designed to lessen the severity of symptoms of psychological illness.

public account system A labor system under which a prison bought machinery and raw materials with which people inside manufactured a salable product.

Public Safety Assessment A check-off system that provides an objective rating of a person's likelihood to fail to show up for court hearings and the likelihood that the person will be rearrested before those court hearings.

public works and ways system A labor system under which people in prison work on public construction and maintenance projects.

punitive conditions Constraints imposed on some probation clients to increase the restrictiveness or painfulness of probation, including fines, community service, and restitution.

race Traditionally, a biological concept used to distinguish groups of people by their skin color and other physical features.

racial threat hypothesis The belief that white fear of African Americans is least when whites are the majority but greatest when African Americans are a substantial minority.

radial design An architectural plan by which a prison is constructed in the form of a wheel, with "spokes" radiating from a central core.

random field trial Evaluating the effectiveness of a program by randomly assigning some people to the program and others to no program, and seeing which group does better.

rational basis test Requires that a regulation provide a reasonable, rational method of advancing a legitimate institutional goal.

reality therapy Treatment that emphasizes personal responsibility for actions and their consequences.

recidivism The return of a former correctional client to criminal behavior, as measured by new arrests or other problems with the law.

recognizance A formally recorded obligation to perform some act (such as keep the peace, pay a debt, or appear in court when called) entered by a judge to permit a person who has been charged with or convicted of a crime to live in the community, often on posting a sum of money as surety, which is forfeited by nonperformance.

reentry courts Courts that supervise a person's return to the community and adjustment to his or her new life.

reformatory An institution for young individuals convicted of crimes that emphasized training, a mark system of classification, indeterminate sentences, and parole.

refugee A person who has been forced to leave his or her country in order to escape war, persecution, or natural disaster.

regional jail A facility operated under a joint agreement between two or more government units, with a jail board drawn from representatives of the participating jurisdictions and having varying authority over policy, budget, operations, and personnel.

regulations Legal rules, usually set by an agency of the executive branch, designed to implement in detail the policies of that agency.

rehabilitation The goal of restoring a convicted person to a constructive place in society through some form of vocational or educational training or therapy.

rehabilitation model A model of correctional institutions that emphasizes the provision of treatment programs designed to reform the individual.

reintegration model A model of correctional institutions that emphasizes maintenance of the individual's ties to family and the community as a method of reform, in recognition of the fact that the individual will be returning to the community.

relapse process The scenario that occurs when poor decision making makes adjustment problems worse, leading eventually to recidivism.

release on recognizance (ROR) Pretrial release option used when the judge believes the person's ties in the community are sufficient to guarantee his or her appearance in court.

remunerative power The ability to obtain compliance in exchange for material resources.

restitution Compensation for financial, physical, or emotional loss caused by the crime, in the form of either payment of money to the victim or to a public fund for crime victims, as stipulated by the court.

restitution center Facility where people who fall behind in restitution are sent to make payments on their debt.

restoration Punishment designed to repair the damage done to the victim and community by a person's criminal act.

retribution Punishment inflicted on a person who has infringed on the rights of others and so deserves to be penalized. The severity of the sanction should fit the seriousness of the crime.

sanctuary city A city that limits its cooperation with the national government effort to enforce immigration law.

school-to-prison pipeline The situation in which many youths who fail in school end up in prison.

secular law The law of the civil society, as distinguished from church law.

selective incapacitation Making the best use of expensive and limited prison space by targeting for incarceration those people whose incapacity will do the most to reduce crime in society.

self-report study An investigation of behavior (such as criminal activity) based on subjects' responses to questions concerning activities in which they have engaged.

sentencing disparity Divergence in the lengths and types of sentences imposed for the same crime or for crimes of comparable seriousness when no reasonable justification can be discerned.

sentencing guidelines An instrument developed for judges that indicates the usual sanctions given previously for particular offenses.

separate confinement A penitentiary system developed in Pennsylvania in which each convicted individual was held in isolation from other people, with all activities, including craft work, carried on in the cells.

sex crimes Sexual acts prohibited by law, such as rape, child molestation, or prostitution, motivated by economic, psychological, or situational reasons.

sex offender registry A public website that lists the names, addresses, and crimes of people who have convicted of specified sex crimes; sometimes neighbors are notified when a person living nearby is on such a website.

shock incarceration A short period of incarceration (the "shock"), followed by a sentence reduction.

shock probation A sentence by which an individual is released after a short incarceration and resentenced to probation.

situational client A person who in a particular set of circumstances has violated the law but who is not given to criminal behavior under normal circumstances and is unlikely to repeat the offense.

social control Actions and practices, of individuals and institutions, designed to induce conformity with the rules and norms of society.

social therapy Treatment that attempts to create an institutional environment that supports prosocial attitudes and behaviors.

span of control A management principle holding that a supervisor can effectively oversee only a limited number of subordinates.

spatial concentration A phenomenon of criminal justice in which certain neighborhoods have very high numbers of arrests and of people going to prison.

specific deterrence (special or **individual deterrence)** Punishment inflicted on convicted individuals to discourage them from committing future crimes.

staff personnel Employees who provide services in support of line personnel; examples of staff personnel include training officers and accountants.

stakes The potential losses to victims and to the system when someone recidivates; stakes include injury from violent crimes and public pressure resulting from negative publicity.

standard conditions Constraints imposed on all probation clients, including reporting to the probation office, reporting any change of address, remaining employed, and not leaving the jurisdiction without permission.

state-use system A labor system under which goods produced by prison industries are purchased exclusively by state institutions and agencies and never enter the free market.

status offenses Misbehaviors that are not against the law but are troubling when done by juveniles because they are so young.

statute Law created by the people's elected representatives in legislatures.

street-level bureaucrats Public service workers who interact directly with citizens in the course of their work, granting access to government programs and providing services within them.

system A complex whole consisting of interdependent parts whose operations are directed toward common goals and are influenced by the environment in which they function.

technical violation The failure to abide by the rules and conditions of probation (specified by the judge), resulting in revocation of probation.

techno-corrections Achieving correctional goals through the use of new technologies.

technology A method of applying scientific knowledge to practical purposes in a particular field.

telephone-pole design An architectural plan for a prison calling for a long central corridor crossed at regular intervals by structures containing the prison's functional areas.

temporary protected status (TPS) A status given to foreign nationals from designated countries with temporary adverse conditions, such as armed conflict or environmental disaster.

therapeutic community A prison environment where every aspect of the prison is designed to promote prosocial attitudes and behavior.

therapeutic justice A philosophy of reorienting the jail experience from being mostly punitive to being mostly rehabilitative.

totality of conditions The aggregate of circumstances in a correctional facility that, when considered as a whole, may violate the protections guaranteed by the Eighth Amendment, even though such guarantees are not violated by any single condition in the institution.

transactional analysis Treatment that focuses on patterns of interaction with others, especially patterns that indicate personal problems.

transportation The practice of transplanting individuals convicted of crimes from the community to another region or land, often a penal colony.

treatment conditions Constraints imposed on some probation clients to force them to deal with a significant problem or need, such as substance abuse.

undocumented resident (undocumented immigrant) A foreigner who resides in the United States illegally, whether by crossing illegally, overstaying a visa, or other means.

unit management Tactic for reducing prison violence by dividing facilities into small, self-contained, semiautonomous "institutions."

unity of command A management principle holding that a subordinate should report to only one supervisor.

urinalysis Technique used to determine whether someone is using drugs.

utilitarianism The doctrine that the aim of all action should be the greatest possible balance of pleasure over pain, hence the belief that a punishment inflicted on a person convicted of committing a crime must achieve enough good to outweigh the pain inflicted.

victim impact statement A description in a PSI of the costs of the crime for the victim, including emotional and financial losses.

vocational rehabilitation Prison programming designed to teach cognitive and vocational skills to help people find employment upon release.

wergild "Man money"—money paid to relatives of a murdered person or to the victim of a crime to compensate them and to prevent a blood feud.

widening the net Increasing the scope of corrections by applying a diversion program to people charged with offenses less serious than those of the people the program was originally intended to serve.

work release center A facility that allows residents to work in the community during the day while residing in the center during nonworking hours.

wrongful conviction A conviction that occurs when an innocent person is found guilty by either plea or verdict.

INDEX

Boldface numbers refer to the page on which the term is defined.

1950 1960 1970 1980

1916 Thomas Mott Osborne, *Society and Prisons*

1924 Congressional authorization of Federal Bureau of Prisons

1925 Federal Probation Act

1929 National Commission on Law Observance and Enforcement (Wickersham Commission)

1930 Federal Bureau of Prisons established

1939 George Rushe, *Punishment and Social Structure*

1948 U.N. creates special section on prevention of crime and treatment of offenders

1954 National Prison Association becomes American Correctional Association

1958 Gresham Sykes, *The Society of Captives*

1964 *Cooper v. Pate:* State prisoners may sue officials in federal courts

1965 California Probation Subsidy Act

1967 *In re Gault* requires counsel for juvenile offenders

1967 President's Commission on Law Enforcement and Administration of Justice

1968 Crime and Safe Streets Act

1970 *Holt v. Sarver* declares Arkansas prison system unconstitutional

1971 American Friends Service Committee, *Struggle for Justice*

1971 David Rothman, *The Discovery of the Asylum*

1972 *Furman v. Georgia* declares death penalty as currently administered unconstitutional

1973 National Advisory Commission on Criminal Justice Standards and Goals

1973 Minnesota Community Corrections Act

1974 Robert Martinson, *What Works?*

1976 *Gregg v. Georgia* upholds death penalty law

1977 James B. Jacobs, *Stateville*

1980 John Irwin, *Prisons in Turmoil*

1980 *Ruiz v. Estelle* declares Texas prison system unconstitutional

1925 Prison at Stateville, Illinois, based on Bentham's panopticon design

1927 Warden Mary Belle Harris opens federal institution for women in Alderson, West Virginia

1930 Thirty states and federal government use probation

1934 Alcatraz opens

1935 Execution of 199 offenders in United States: highest rate in 20th century

1936 Last public execution, Owensboro, Kentucky

1971 Prison riot in Attica, New York

1977 California, Illinois, and Michigan first states to use determinate sentencing

1950 1960 1970 1980